MENTAL HEALTH REVIEW TRIBUNALS

LAW AND PRACTICE

To F

an

James Cooke a

AUST
LBC Inform:
Sy

CANAD/
The Carsw(
Tor

NEW ZI
Bro
Auc

SINGAPORE a
Thompson Infor
Sing

MENTAL HEALTH REVIEW TRIBUNALS

LAW AND PRACTICE

by

Anselm Eldergill

*Solicitor, Alexander Maxwell Scholar, Mental Health Act Commissioner
(Chairman, Legal and Ethical Committee), Mental Health Review Tribunal
Panel of Solicitors (Member, Interviewer and Assessor)*

LONDON, DUBLIN, HONG KONG
SWEET & MAXWELL
1997

Published in 1998 by Sweet & Maxwell Ltd of
100 Avenue Road, Swiss Cottage, London NW3 3PF
Printed by Bath Press,
Bath

A Catalogue record for
this book is available
from the British Library

ISBN: 0421 48330X

The information in this publication was supplied by Anselm Eldergill.

© Anselm Eldergill/Sweet & Maxwell Ltd
1998

Acknowledgments

Most of all, I wish to thank my wife, Helen, for her wholehearted support and the sacrifices which she has made throughout this lengthy project. Without her help the book could not have been completed. I also received tremendous support from James Cooke, formerly the Chairman of the South East and South West Thames Mental Health Review Tribunals, and from David Evans, formerly the Chairman of Sweet & Maxwell. Sadly, both of them died before the book they encouraged was published and it is also dedicated to them. I should, in addition, particularly like to thank the following: the trustees of the Alexander Maxwell Law Scholarship Trust; my parents; and William Bingley, the Chief Executive of the Mental Health Act Commission, and Dr. Elizabeth Parker, then one of the medical Commissioners, who respectively read the legal and medical chapters. Their many useful comments have necessarily improved the quality of the text. I also wish to thank my family for acting as readers; Joanne Dickson and Lynne Knapman of the Crown Office, for kindly allowing me access to records held there; my editors, Julian Dady, Robert Rule and Paul Wright; my colleagues in chambers, David Gollancz and Anton Alexander; Mrs. Marion Hobson, the Secretary to the Mental Health Review Tribunal for Northern Ireland; Nick Jordan and Nigel Shackleford of the Home Office's Mental Health Unit; Jan Farenden of the Department of Health; Ian Bynoe, formerly Legal Director of MIND; Michael Christie, Regional Chairman of the North Thames MHRT; Professor John Gunn of the Institute of Psychiatry, for allowing me access to its library; my colleagues at the Mental Health Act Commission; Emma Robinson of Trace Wordflow, London EC2, for providing a Lexmark Optra printer; and the staff at the Law Society's Library.

Anselm Eldergill
November 1997

The Alexander Maxwell Law Scholarship Trust

v

The Publishers and Author wish to thank the following for permission to reprint material from publications to which they have copyright:

BRADLEY: *Disease, Diagnosis and Decisions* (1993), pp. x–xi, p.27, p.39. Copyright John Wiley & Sons Limited. Reproduced with permission.

BUTTERWORTHS: *All England Law Reports and Butterworths Medico Legal Reports*. Extracts reproduced by permission

CARSON, D (Ed.): *Risk-taking in Mental Disorder; Analyses, Policies and Practical Strategies* (1990). Extracts reproduced by permission of SLE Publications Ltd.:

— GUNN "Clinical approaches to the assessment of risk", pp 15–16
— PICKERSGILL "Balancing the public and private interests"
— PRINS "Social factors affecting the assessment of risk; with special reference to offender patients"

GELDER, *et al.: Oxford Textbook of Psychiatry* (3rd ed., 1996), p.283. Reproduced by permission of Oxford University Press.

GOSTIN and RASSABY; *Representing the Mentally Ill and Handicapped. A Guide to Mental Health Review Tribunals* (1980), pp.170–174. Reproduced by permission of Quartermaine House Publishers.

HAWTON and CATALAN: Attempted suicide: a practical guide to its nature and management (2nd ed., 1987). Reproduced by permission of Oxford University Press.

LEWIS: "Psychopathic disorder. A most elusive category" 4 *Psychological Medicine* 133. Reproduced by permission of Cambridge University Press.

SIMS and OWEN: *Psychiatry* (6th ed., 1993), pp. 28 and 34. Reproduced by permission of the publisher W B Saunders Company Limited London.

THE INCORPORATED COUNCIL OF LAW REPORTING FOR ENGLAND & WALES: *The Law Reports* and *Weekly Law Reports*. Extracts reproduced by permission.

THE ROYAL PHARMACEUTICAL SOCIETY OF GREAT BRITAIN and the BRITISH MEDICAL ASSOCIATION: *British National Formulary*, 33, March 1997); p.159, Tables 4.2.1–4.2.3, 4.3.1–4.3.3, 4.8, 4.9.2. Reproduced by permission. Published by Pharmaceutical Press.

Preface

The primary aim of this book is to provide professionals of all disciplines with the materials which they need in order properly to prepare, present and determine mental health review tribunal cases. Because hearings do not take place at a court venue, those attending them have no immediate access to a law library. Furthermore, many practitioners have difficulty obtaining copies of reported and unreported decisions concerning tribunals' powers. I have tried to help them by including case summaries which are sufficiently detailed to both ensure their accuracy and to enable the decisions to be distinguished if the facts are materially different. Similar problems are often encountered when it comes to keeping abreast of health and social services developments about matters such as risk assessments, discharge planning, and the provision of services following discharge. The book therefore summarises and distinguishes the most important legislation and circulars. Further difficulties arise when the medical reports are only available shortly before the hearing or instructions are received late in the day. There is often then an urgent need for information which helps the practitioner to analyse the medical evidence. The medical chapers in Part III contain a glossary of medical terms, international diagnostic guidelines for the major forms of mental disorder, information about treatment and prognosis, details of drugs prescribed to treat mental disorder, medical abbreviations in common usage, and other material of this kind. All of this information will, of course, be far too much for an individual to assimilate in a single evening. The introduction and overview, together with the questions listed on pages 932–941, are designed to help lawyers, in particular barristers, who only have a few hours within which to come to terms with the subject. I have throughout made extensive use of tables and flow-charts, because it seemed to me that there was a need for a book in this area which presents some of the material in this, more digestible, form. The legal contents necessarily extend beyond tribunal law and procedure. The patient's representative, and to a lesser extent the tribunal members, require a working knowledge of associated areas of mental health law and practice. They need to know how a patient's detention is authorised, renewed and terminated; when judicial review and habeas corpus proceedings may be more appropriate remedies; when compulsory treatment may be given; what are the functions of bodies such as the Mental Health Act Commission and the Secretary of State; and so forth. Richard Jones' *Mental Health Act Manual* already contains extensive notes on the 1983 Act and I have therefore concentrated on explaining first principles, both in relation to the law and medicine. A recurring theme is that it is essential to try to analyse, expose and understand the underlying logic of the various subjects covered in the book. The importance of always going back to first principles cannot be over-emphasised and, on its own, the rote learning of definitions does not take matters very far. Some people, of course, object to any detailed exposition of the law on the ground that such an approach is "legalistic." On closer examination, the word usually means nothing more than "legal", so that the objection is merely to the burden of learning and applying the law. Where the liberty of the individual is involved, the overriding consideration must always be to ensure that the law is correctly applied and rigorously observed, albeit in as informal a setting, and as informal a manner, as possible. I should lastly add that I have received out-patient treatment for depression in the past. It is important that practitioners acknowledge that mental health is relative, and that they are not ashamed of any problems which they themselves have experienced, if the burden experienced by people who have been detained and cannot hide their histories is to be reduced.

Anselm Eldergill
September 1997

Table of chapters

PART III — MEDICAL ISSUES

Table of contents

xxiii

TABLE OF CASES

Conventions

Where a page number below appears in bold, this indicates that a summary of the facts of the case and the judgment are to be found there. Entries which are not highlighted indicate a reference to the case in the text.

Abbreviations

For the benefit of readers who are not lawyers, only decisions which are considered to determine important points of law are reported in the two main series of law reports. These series are The Law Reports and the All England Reports [abbreviated "All E.R."]. The former should be cited where a case is reported in both. Most of the reported mental health case law will be found in the Queen's Bench volumes of The Law Reports [abbreviated "Q.B."] or in the Weekly Law Reports [abbreviated "W.L.R."]. However, cases considered on appeal will be located in the Appeal Cases volumes for the relevant year [abbreviated "A.C."]. A number of interesting judgments not reported in either series have been summarised in the daily law reports of *The Times* or *The Independent*. Old case law may be found in law reports dating back to the sixteenth century and beyond. Some of these series predate the commencement of the modern reports and are named after a private compiler [*e.g.* Vesey's Reports]. The following are examples of the standard citations used throughout the book to denote the source of a case report.

Citation	*Where the judgment will be found*
[1982] A.C. 546	Commencing on page 546 of the volume of reported Appeal Cases judgments for the year 1982 [The Law Reports series].
[1981] 3 All E.R. 878	Commencing on page 878 of the third volume of the All England Reports for the year 1981.
(1762) 3 Burr. 1362	Commencing on page 1362 of the third volume of the series of private law reports compiled by Burroughs.

TABLE OF STATUTES

TABLE OF STATUTORY INSTRUMENTS

PART I — INTRODUCTION AND OVERVIEW

1. Introduction and overview

The Constitution of the United Nations Educational, Scientific and Cultural Organisation, written in 1946, begins with the words, "Since wars begin in the minds of men, it is in the minds of men that the defences of peace must be constructed." Every war and act of cruelty that ever took place, and every work of art or act of love and devotion, was conceived within, and executed at the instigation of, a small object weighing about three pounds — the brain. Although a person's conduct is the external expression of internal processes taking place within his brain, it would not be practical to see every harmful act as the product of faulty thought processes which necessitate medical intervention and excuse the individual of legal responsibility. All functional systems of morality assume that individual actions reflect deliberate choices. The law, as the social expression of the common moral code, presumes that individuals possess reason and foresight (sufficient capacity to understand the nature and possible consequences of their acts); self-control (sufficient capacity to refrain from unlawful or harmful acts); and so, also, free will (the individual could have omitted to act as he did). By liberty we can only mean a power of acting or not acting according to the determination of the will. This hypothetical liberty is universally allowed to belong to everyone who is not a prisoner and in chains.[1] Those capable of acting are responsible for their actions and omissions, and, being responsible for them, accountable to others for their behaviour. The counterpart of freedom and autonomy is accountability for acts freely and autonomously done. While it is difficult to see how a society could function on any other basis, because social existence depends upon co-ordination and co-operation, which in turn requires restraint in individual action,[2] these principles have required qualification in cases where an incapacitated adult is unable to assume this burden of legal responsibility. Such incapacity, and the ways of dealing with it, may take many forms. In terms of the criminal law, a fair trial is only possible if the defendant has sufficient understanding to participate in the trial process and "if punishment is to be justified at all, the criminal's act must be that of a responsible agent: that is, it must be the act of one who could have kept the law which he has broken."[3] Alternatively, it may consist of a lack of capacity to understand the nature of some act or transaction of sufficient importance that an individual may only legally undertake it if he understands the consequences of committing himself and freely consents to that. For example, the act of marriage, the making of a gift, will or contract, the conduct of litigation, the election of a legislative body, and the giving of consent to intrusive medical treatment. The purpose of the restrictions here is generally to protect the individual from exploitation, to protect others, or to ensure the proper performance, for the benefit of all, of public duties. Not surprisingly, the law has responded to the problem that some citizens lack capacity to act by curtailing their freedom of action, sometimes in conjunction with giving others the responsibility of making important decisions for

---

[1]   D. Hume, *An Enquiry concerning Human Understanding* (ed. Sir L.A. Selby-Bigge, Oxford University Press, 1893), p.95.

[2]   R.W.M. Dias, *Jurisprudence* (Butterworths, 5th ed., 1985), p.112.

[3]   H.L.A. Hart, *Punishment and the Elimination of Responsibility* (The Athlone Press, 1962), p.5.

them. Ultimately, whether individuals "should be allowed certain liberties at all depends on the priority given by society to different values and the crucial point is the criterion by which it has to be decided that a particular liberty should or should not be allowed, or that its exercise is in need of restraint."[4] In extreme cases, where an individual lacks sufficient capacity to appreciate that his actions are seriously jeopardising his own welfare or that of others, the law countenances his detention and treatment without consent. As will be seen, it is with this issue, and the circumstances which justify or necessitate such deprivation of liberty, that mental health review tribunals are concerned.

INFORMAL TREATMENT AND COMPULSION

The law concerning persons who suffer from mental disorder is a vast subject and practically every area of law makes some special provision for persons whose capacity or responsibility for their acts is impaired. For the sake of convenience, the law concerning mentally disordered persons may be said to fall into five broad categories: detention and restraint; the administration of medicine and other treatments; the management of property and legal affairs; legal capacity and responsibility under criminal and civil law; constitutional rights and obligations. The main statute which deals with the subject of mental disorder, the Mental Health Act 1983, includes provisions relating to the first three of these areas but this book is concerned only with the first of them: detention and restraint and the legal process by which patients compelled to receive treatment or care may have the necessity or justification for that reviewed by mental health review tribunals. It is important at the outset to distinguish these independent judicial bodies from another statutory body called the Mental Health Act Commission. The latter is a non-judicial, quasi-independent, body which arranges visits to detained patients and the investigation of certain complaints made by or in respect of them. Thus, tribunals are inferior courts which review whether a particular patient should remain subject to compulsion whilst the Commission, which is part of the National Health Service, is concerned with ensuring that patients who are detained are treated humanely and according to the law.

TREATMENT ON AN INFORMAL BASIS

The vast majority of people who receive in-patient psychiatric treatment are treated without resort to compulsory powers and they are known as "informal patients." Although informal patients are sometimes still referred to as "voluntary patients," the terms are not synonymous. A significant number of informal patients lack sufficient capacity to consent to their admission, are mentally incapable of organising their own discharge, or remain in hospital informally only because compulsory powers will be invoked if they refuse treatment or attempt to leave. Informal admission may be particularly disadvantageous for people who are mentally incapacitated in that the necessity for their being in hospital, and the treatment and care which they receive there, are not susceptible to periodic external review by the Mental Health Act Commission or a mental health review tribunal. Whilst the use of compulsory powers deprives the person affected of certain legal rights, it also confers other rights in substitution. Since these are framed as duties exercisable by

---

[4]   R.W.M. Dias, *Jurisprudence* (Butterworths, 5th ed., 1985), p.109.

4

third parties on the patient's behalf, they may in practice more than compensate the patient for the loss of rights the existence of which he is unaware or, if aware of them, incapable of exercising. Although most formal patients understandably wish to be informal, there are nevertheless a number of patients who are incapable of understanding or exercising the legal rights which constitute the practical benefits of being an informal patient.

COMPULSORY TREATMENT AND CARE

In 1954, a Royal Commission was appointed to review the existing law concerning mental illness and mental deficiency. It reported in 1957[5] and many of its recommendations were adopted in the Mental Health Act 1959. This statute was later amended by the Mental Health (Amendment) Act 1982 but the basic legal framework remained unchanged. The present statute is largely a consolidating Act but it has itself recently been amended by the Mental Health (Patients in the Community) Act 1995 and the Crime (Sentences) Act 1997.

Repeal of certification procedures

Under the Lunacy Act 1890 and related legislation, the order of a justice of the peace, or some other judicial authority, was generally necessary before a person could be compulsorily admitted to hospital or received into guardianship. The Royal Commission of 1954–57 advocated the repeal of these certification procedures. In their place, it recommended that a person's detention or reception into guardianship should be legally authorised upon an application for that being accepted by the hospital to which admission was sought or, in the case of guardianship, accepted by the social services authority concerned. The Royal Commission's opinion was that,

> .".. a sufficient consensus of medical and non-medical opinion on the need to compel a patient to accept hospital or community care would normally be provided through [1] an application for the patient's admission made by a relative or mental welfare officer, ... [2] two supporting medical recommendations, [3] the acceptance of the patient as suitable for the form of care recommended, and [4] the continuing power of discharge vested in the nearest relative, the hospital or local authority medical staff, the members of the hospital management committee or local authority, and the Minister of Health. To refer the application and medical recommendations to a justice of the peace before the patient's admission would not in our view provide a significant additional safeguard for the patient ..."[6]

Creation of mental health review tribunals

The most distinctive feature of the post–1959 application procedures is that the individual is deprived of his liberty following an application for his detention being made not to a court but to the managers of a hospital. Similarly, reception into guardianship, and the imposition of supervision following a patient's discharge from hospital, respectively involve the acceptance of an application by the relevant local social services authority and Health Authority. The procedures cannot properly be described as administrative because, in constitutional terms, they involve the detention or restraint of one of the Queen's subjects. But, equally, it would be inaccurate

[5] *Report of the Royal Commission on the Law relating to Mental Illness and Mental Deficiency 1954–57*, Chairman—Lord Percy, Cmnd. 169 (1957).
[6] *Ibid*, p.148.

to describe them as a judicial process for no judicial authority, such as a magistrate, is involved. Because the proposed new procedures did not involve any judicial body, the Royal Commission recommended that where, *after the event*, a patient desired a formal review of the justification for his detention or guardianship this need should be met by the establishment of new independent review bodies.[7] Their establishment would give those patients who desired it opportunities to have the justification for the use of compulsion investigated by a strong independent body consisting of both medical and non-medical members.[8] In the Royal Commission's view, the functions of such a tribunal would be confined to reviewing the continuing need for compulsion:

> "We should make it clear that these review tribunals would not be acting as an appellate court of law to consider whether the patient's mental condition at the time when the compulsory powers were first used had been accurately diagnosed by the doctors signing the recommendations, or whether there had been sufficient justification for the use of compulsory powers at that time, nor to consider whether there was some technical flaw in the documents purporting to authorise the patient's admission ... The review tribunal's function would be to consider the patient's mental condition at the time when it considers his application, and to decide whether the type of care which has been provided by the use of compulsory powers is the most appropriate to his present needs, or whether any alternative form of care might now be more appropriate, or whether he could now be discharged from care altogether."[9]

When compulsion is justifiable — guiding principles

The Royal Commission of 1954–57 also spelt out the circumstances in which it considered that the use of compulsory powers was justified. Paragraph 317 of its report states:

> "We consider that the use of special compulsory powers on grounds of the patient's mental disorder is justifiable when:
>
> a. there is reasonable certainty that the patient is suffering from a pathological mental disorder and requires hospital or community care; and
>
> b. suitable care cannot be provided without the use of compulsory powers; and
>
> c. if the patient himself is unwilling to receive the form of care which is considered necessary, there is at least a strong likelihood that his unwillingness is due to a lack of appreciation of his own condition deriving from the mental disorder itself; and
>
> d. there is also either—
>
>> i. good prospect of benefit to the patient from the treatment proposed — an expectation that it will either cure or alleviate his mental disorder or strengthen his ability to regulate his social behaviour in spite of the underlying disorder, or bring him substantial benefit in the form of protection from neglect or exploitation by others;
>>
>> ii. a strong need to protect others from anti-social behaviour by the patient."

---

[7]   *Report of the Royal Commission on the Law relating to Mental Illness and Mental Deficiency*, Cmnd. 169 (1957), pp.148–149.

[8]   *Ibid*, p.12.

[9]   *Ibid*, pp.150–151.

The terms of the subsequent Mental Health Act 1959 gave expression to the Commission's views about when compulsion is necessary or justified and, during the Parliamentary debate of 5 May 1959, the Minister of Health explained the Government's aims in relation to the new civil procedures in the following terms:

> "We had in mind all the time to try and assemble a structure which would reflect the balance of the considerations we must have in mind. They are, firstly, the liberty of the subject, secondly, the necessity of bringing treatment to bear where treatment is required and can be beneficial to the individual and, thirdly, the consideration of the protection of the public. All through I have tried steadily to keep in mind that what we are trying to do is to erect as balanced a structure as we may which can give effect to all those things in harmony with each other."[10]

Applications founded on diagnosis and risk

The present statute by and large adopts the same approach. The criteria for making an application for a person's detention or guardianship, and the criteria to be applied by a tribunal when determining whether any patient must be discharged, always comprise at least two grounds. The first of these grounds (the diagnostic ground) requires considering whether the patient is suffering from a mental disorder the nature or degree of which makes in-patient treatment appropriate or, as the case may be, warrants his reception into guardianship or detention for assessment. The second ground (the risk ground) requires considering whether the individual's detention, restraint or treatment is "necessary" or "justified" on his own account (specifically for his health, safety or welfare) or that of others (in order to protect them). The criteria which comprise the second ground are therefore directed towards the issue of risk — specifically, the likelihood of undesirable consequences if the individual is allowed a citizen's usual freedom to decide how to act and what medical treatment or social care to accept. The risks involved in restoring a patient's liberty to him may consist of a likelihood of significant deterioration in his health, a risk to his physical safety, or a risk to others. In some cases, others may be at risk from the individual quite independently of whether or not he is mentally disordered at a given moment in time. There may be a general risk of domestic violence and an offender cured of his mental disorder may still be disposed to commit crime. Hence, the need for both statutory grounds and, unless psychopathy is an issue, the duty to release a person who though a threat to others is not mentally disordered or, if he is, the danger does not arise from this fact. Assessing risk in the context of mental disorder (the second question) therefore also requires forming a judgement about the extent to which any identified risks are a feature or consequence of mental disorder (the first question). Whether a patient's detention is justified or necessary in a particular case will often partly depend upon what arrangements have been, or can be, made for his treatment outside hospital. The patient's willingness to accept appropriate treatment as an informal in-patient, and his capacity to adhere to any agreed treatment programme and discharge plan, will also be highly relevant. But, to summarise, the circumstances in which an individual's liberty may be interfered with under the 1983 Act are that he has a serious mental disorder and, in consequence of this, is either at significant risk or others are at significant risk from him.

---

[10]   *Hansard*, H.C. Vol. 605, col. 276.

It can be seen that the assessment of risk is an integral part of any decision to invoke or to rescind compulsory powers and tribunals must assess the likely risk to the patient's health and safety and the risk to others if he is discharged. Risk cannot be avoided and all decisions to discharge or not to discharge involve the assumption of a risk. In the case of a decision to discharge, the risk is that the individual will use his greater freedom in a way which is injurious to himself or others. The risks involved in not discharging may similarly include an increased likelihood of harm to the patient or others but, more often, consist of the possibility that a citizen is detained who could safely be discharged. In other words, there is a risk of injustice, and a lawyer ought to be as concerned to eradicate injustice as a doctor is to eradicate disease. A tribunal which declines to discharge cannot be faulted insofar as no one will ever know whether its assessment of the patient's case was right or wrong. The person who is not released is thereby prevented from demonstrating that if released he would have resettled safely in the community. However, the converse is not also true. A tribunal which discharges risks catastrophe and, if the patient then either attempts or commits suicide, or some serious offence against a third party, public criticism. Yet, however careful the assessment of the nature and extent of the risks involved in discharge, it is inevitable that some patients will later take their own lives or, more rarely, commit a serious offence outside hospital. These events also happen in hospitals, and in respect of patients granted leave or discharged by their consultants. The occurrence of such tragedies does not *per se* demonstrate any error of judgement on the part of those who discharged or supervised the patient. The public cannot be made entirely safe from the risk of offending and, arguably, cannot properly expect any higher measure of protection before persons committed to hospital are released compared with those sent to prison. It must also be borne in mind that all in-patients are themselves members of the public and at increased risk of being victims of violence for as long as they are detained on a psychiatric ward. Thus, the tribunal system aims to ensure both that members of the public are not unnecessarily detained and also that members of the public are protected from people who must necessarily be detained. Balancing these different considerations is a formidable task.

Persons unable to appreciate or avoid obvious risk

While the public must be realistic about the problems involved in assessing risk and deciding what is an acceptable risk, it is equally important that tribunal members do not add to their burden in cases involving non-offenders by balancing risks which are constitutionally matters for the citizen to weigh in his own mind. The purpose of invoking compulsory powers is not to eliminate that element of risk in human life which is simply part of being free to act and to make choices and decisions. Rather, their purpose is to protect the individual and others from a particular and somewhat limited kind of risk — that which arises when a citizen is of unsound mind and his judgement of risk, or his capacity to control behaviour he knows puts himself or others at risk, is in consequence of this markedly impaired. The key issue is the patient's judgement and appreciation of his situation, the way in which he will use his liberty if it is restored to him and he is again free to make decisions for himself. It cannot be over-emphasised that a citizen who has not offended against society is generally entitled to place a high premium on his liberty, even to value it more highly than his health. Within certain limits, he is as entitled as the next man to make what others may regard as errors of judgement and, in particular, to behave in a way which a doctor regards as irrational in the sense that it does not best promote his health. Thus, a person may chain-smoke cigarettes even though the risks involved in this activity, both to the individual and others, are significant and potentially life-threatening. Although the individual's judgement is partially impaired by his addiction, nevertheless he is able to fully comprehend the medical advice and so, in this sense, is able to rationally assess and assume, or not, the risks involved in exercising his freedom to follow or ignore that advice. Likewise, a patient who has been receiving treatment for mental disorder is not to be compelled to follow medical advice simply because he disagrees with all or part of that advice, provided the choices he proposes making if set at liberty are not manifestly irrational. Accordingly, if the medical opinion is that a patient needs to continue taking medication and this should be given in depot form, it is not irrational *per se* for the patient to prefer to take prophylactic medication orally simply because from a medical viewpoint this is the treatment of second choice. If the patient can rationally explain that for him the slightly increased risk of relapse is outweighed by the disadvantages for him of injections, and other persons are not at risk, such a way forward represents a reasoned balance of the risks involved.

MENTAL HEALTH ACT 1983

Several powers exercisable under the 1983 Act authorise a person's detention while others permit only some restriction of liberty short of this, such as the appointment of a guardian or the imposition of supervision in the community. The statutory framework is such that a person may not be detained for more than 72 hours unless the managers of a hospital have accepted an application for his admission to hospital (under Part II of the Act) or his detention there has been authorised by a criminal court or by the Home Secretary (under Part III of the Act). The Act does not define what is meant by detention but, in an Australian case, it was said that the word "refers to the case of a person lawfully held against his will, one who is not free to depart when he pleases."[11] Nor are the powers of the patient's detainers specified in any detail. However, a power to detain implies a power to physically restrain if need be (otherwise the patient could leave when he wished) and protecting others, including other patients, implies a power to segregate the patient from them. The better view is therefore that, if the occasion requires it, using reasonable force to restrain a detained patient, or to remove him to a separate seclusion room, represents a lawful exercise of the *statutory* power of detention. On this point, the House of Lords has held that a statutory power to detain and treat a patient implies a power to use reasonable force on occasion in order to ensure that control is exercised over him.[12] The circumstances in which the common law permits the restraint or treatment without consent of a person not lawfully detained under the Act are limited. His detention may be justified if immediately necessary to prevent a breach of the peace[13] and it is similarly lawful to restrain, and if need be detain, a "furious" or

---

[11]   *Paul v. Paul* (1954) V.L.R. 331.
[12]   Dicta of Widgery C.J. adopted by the House of Lords in *R. v. Bracknell JJ. ex p. Griffiths* [1976] A.C. 314 at 318.
[13]   *R. v. Howell* [1982] Q.B. 416; *Albert v. Lavin* [1982] A.C. 546; *McConnell v. Chief Constable of Greater Manchester Police* [1990] 1 W.L.R. 364.

"dangerous" "lunatic" whose state of mind is such that he is a danger to himself and others.[14] Furthermore, a doctor may administer to a patient who lacks the capacity to give or to communicate consent to that treatment whatever treatment is judged in his best interests as being necessary to preserve his life, health or well-being or to ensure improvement or prevent deterioration in his physical or mental health.[15]

WHERE TO FIND THE LAW AND GUIDANCE

The legislation concerning the detention, restraint and release of persons detained under the 1983 Act is set out in the table below.

1983 ACT — MAIN LEGAL MATERIALS AND PRACTICE GUIDELINES

Primary legislation

- Mental Health Act 1983, *as amended by*

- Mental Health (Patients in the Community) Act 1995

- Crime (Sentences) Act 1997

Secondary legislation

- Mental Health (Hospital, Guardianship and Consent to Treatment) Regulations 1983 (S.I. 1983 No. 893), *as amended by*

- The Mental Health (After-care under Supervision) Regulations 1996 (S.I. 1996 No. 294)

- The Mental Health (Hospital, Guardianship and Consent to Treatment) (Amendment) Regulations 1996 (S.I. 1996 No. 540)

- The Mental Health (Hospital, Guardianship and Consent to Treatment) Amendment Regulations 1997 (S.I. 1997 No. 801)

Secondary legislation on mental health review tribunals

- Mental Health Review Tribunal Rules 1983 (S.I. 1983 No. 942), *as amended by*

- The Mental Health Review Tribunal (Amendment) Rules 1996 (S.I. 1996 No. 314)

- The Mental Health Review Tribunals (Regions) Order 1996 (S.I. 1996 No. 510)

Guidance on the legislation

- Mental Health Act 1983: Memorandum on Parts I to VI, VIII and X (D.H.S.S., 1987).

- Mental Health Act 1983: The Code of Practice published pursuant to section 118 of the Act (Department of Health and Welsh Office, 2nd ed., 1993).

---

[14] *Brookshaw v. Hopkins* (1772) Lofft. 240 at 243; *Anderton v. Burrows* (1830) 4 Car. & P. 210 at 213; *Re Greenwood* (1855) 24 L.J.Q.B. 148; *Fletcher v. Fletcher* (1859) 1 El. & El. 420; *Scott v. Wakem* (1862) 3 F. & F. 328 at 333; *Symm v. Fraser* (1863) 3 F. & F. 859 at 882–883; *Re Shuttleworth* (1846) 9 Q.B. 651; *Re Gregory* (1901) A.C. 128; *Black v. Forsey and others*, 1987 S.L.T. 681.

[15] See *Re F* [1990] 2 A.C. 1; [1989] 2 W.L.R. 1025; [1989] 2 F.L.R. 376.

Jones' comprehensively annotated *Mental Health Act Manual* (Sweet & Maxwell, 5th ed., 1996) contains all of the relevant legislation to September 1996.[16] Guidance on the correct interpretation and implementation of the statutory provisions may be obtained from various sources: case law; the Department of Health's Memorandum on the 1983 Act; the Code of Practice prepared by the Mental Health Act Commission and published by the Department of Health; the Commission's biennial reports; legal textbooks and articles; professional legal advice.

DEFINING MENTAL DISORDER (CHAP. 2)

The legal purpose served by defining mental disorder and its various forms is to define as far as practicable the group of citizens to whom the different statutory provisions apply, and the circumstances in which resort may be made to compulsory powers. According to section 1 of the 1983 Act, the term "mental disorder" means "mental illness, arrested or incomplete development of mind, psychopathic disorder and any other disorder or disability of mind." Provided that the other statutory conditions are satisfied, a person who suffers from "mental disorder" generally may be detained for assessment for up to 28 days. For certain purposes, the Act then distinguishes four particular "forms" or classes of mental disorder: mental illness, psychopathic disorder, severe mental impairment, and mental impairment. In particular, a person must suffer from a condition which falls within at least one of the four specific statutory classes before he can be detained for prolonged treatment, received into guardianship, or placed under statutory supervision following discharge. The reader should refer to chapter 2 for a precise definition of these various terms but the following diagram describes their essential features.

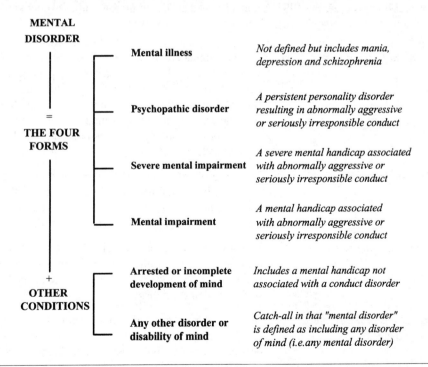

MENTAL DISORDER

= **THE FOUR FORMS**

- **Mental illness** — *Not defined but includes mania, depression and schizophrenia*
- **Psychopathic disorder** — *A persistent personality disorder resulting in abnormally aggressive or seriously irresponsible conduct*
- **Severe mental impairment** — *A severe mental handicap associated with abnormally aggressive or seriously irresponsible conduct*
- **Mental impairment** — *A mental handicap associated with abnormally aggressive or seriously irresponsible conduct*

+ **OTHER CONDITIONS**

- **Arrested or incomplete development of mind** — *Includes a mental handicap not associated with a conduct disorder*
- **Any other disorder or disability of mind** — *Catch-all in that "mental disorder" is defined as including any disorder of mind (i.e. any mental disorder)*

---

[16] It is also helpful to be familiar with the main statutes concerning the provision of health and social services: the National Health Service Act 1977, Medical Act 1983, Registered Homes Act 1984, National Health Service & Community Care Act 1990, Health Authorities Act 1995.

During the year ending 31 March 1996, 8670 — or 98.2 per cent. — of the 8826 patients admitted to NHS hospitals for treatment under Part II of the Act were classified as suffering from mental illness. Of the remainder, 85 were classified as mentally impaired (1 per cent.), 55 as having a psychopathic disorder (0.6 per cent.), and only 16 as suffering from severe mental impairment (0.2 per cent.). Of those admitted under Part III of the Act, 1225 were classified as mentally ill (92.3 per cent.), 57 as mentally impaired (4.3 per cent.), 44 as having a psychopathic disorder (3.3 per cent.), and only one patient as suffering from severe mental impairment (0.1 per cent.). Looked at overall, this means that about 14 of every thousand persons compulsorily admitted to hospital suffered from mental impairment, 10 from a psychopathic disorder, and less than two from severe mental impairment.[17]

RELEVANT PERSONS AND BODIES (CHAP. 3)

It is useful to have some understanding of the legal functions of those people and bodies involved in the detention and compulsory treatment of patients. However, at this stage, it is really only necessary to know two things. Firstly, that important statutory powers are vested in a person's nearest relative and who is a person's nearest relative is most often determined by referring to a list of relatives set out in section 26. Secondly, several statutory powers may only be exercised by an approved social worker (or ASW), that is by a social worker approved to exercise them after completing special training.

FOUR KINDS OF LEGAL AUTHORITY FOR COMPULSION

For present purposes, the 1983 Act can be seen as providing four quite distinct kinds of authority for a person's compulsory detention or restraint—

Civil applications	As recommended by the Royal Commission of 1954–57, it is lawful to detain a person in hospital, or to subject him to guardianship or supervision in the community, following the acceptance of an application made by his nearest relative or an approved social worker and founded on medical evidence.
Short-term powers	The purpose of certain short-term powers is to detain an individual for up to 72 hours so that the need to make an application can be assessed or the necessary application procedures completed.
Criminal court orders	Various orders set out in Part III of the Act are exercisable by a criminal court in respect of a defendant who suffers from, or who appears to suffer from, mental disorder.
Directions of the Home Secretary	The Home Secretary, who has responsibility for the Prison Medical Service, may direct that a person in custody be transferred to hospital for psychiatric treatment.

---

[17]   Statistical Bulletin 1997/4, Department of Health (1997).

CIVIL APPLICATIONS UNDER PART II (CHAP. 4 & CHAP. 6)

Part II of the Act provides for five different kinds of application. With the possible exception of persons detained in an emergency, under section 4, the acceptance of any such application gives the person affected an immediate right to apply to a mental health review tribunal.

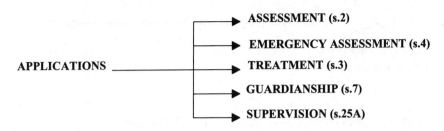

APPLICATIONS

- ASSESSMENT (s.2)
- EMERGENCY ASSESSMENT (s.4)
- TREATMENT (s.3)
- GUARDIANSHIP (s.7)
- SUPERVISION (s.25A)

A person's nearest relative or an approved social worker may apply under section 2 for that person to be detained in hospital for up to 28 days so that his mental state can be assessed and any treatment given which is assessed to be necessary. Such an application must be founded on two medical recommendations but practice shows that, in urgent cases, fulfilling this requirement may occasionally lead to undesirable delay in effecting the admission. Section 4 therefore sets out an emergency procedure whereby a person may be admitted for assessment on the basis of a single medical recommendation. If this procedure is adopted, the authority to detain the patient ceases after 72 hours unless the second section 2 recommendation has by then been received. Provided a further recommendation is received within that time, the individual's detention may continue for the remainder of the 28-day section 2 period. Subject to a single caveat which need not be referred to here, detention beyond 28 days is only permissible if a fresh application, one made under section 3, has been accepted by the managers of the hospital. Their acceptance of an application under this section authorises them to detain the person concerned for a further six months. Where necessary, that authority to detain the patient may be renewed for a second period of six months, and thereafter for one year at a time. When a patient is detained in hospital for treatment, section 25A now provides that an application may be made for him to be supervised in the community when he leaves hospital. Finally, and quite separately, an application may be made under section 7 for a person to be placed under the guardianship of a local social services authority or a private individual for up to six months. As with section 3 applications, a supervisor's authority and a guardian's authority lapse after six months unless renewed for a further six months and thereafter at yearly intervals. It should be noted that some patients are admitted to hospital under section 3, there being no legal requirement to first assess under section 2 before deciding that prolonged treatment is necessary. It is also important to realise that the powers conferred by the five different types of application are not mutually exclusive. In the first place, a person detained in hospital may be transferred into guardianship, and vice-versa. Secondly, it is common for one application to be replaced by another. For example, section 4 might be used to admit a person to hospital in an emergency. If the second medical recommendation required by section 2 is then received on the following day, within the permitted 72 hour period, the patient may be detained for the remainder of the 28 day period which commenced with his admission to hospital. A section 3 application will follow if, before the 28 days expires, it becomes clear that a more prolonged period of detention and compulsory treatment is necessary. If it then becomes apparent that the patient will require statutory supervision after he ceases to be detained under section 3 and leaves hospital, a supervision application may at that point be made.

Section 4 ⟶ Section 2 ⟶ Section 3 ⟶ Section 25A

Emergency admission for assessment/treatment *Continued for up to 28 days* *Detention for treatment* *Supervision following discharge*

SHORT-TERM POWERS NOT EXCEEDING 72 HOURS

The application procedures just described require both the presence of the individual whose mental health is in issue, so that he may be assessed and examined, and sufficient time to arrange the attendance of those persons who must interview and examine him. Problems will occur where access cannot be obtained to a person's home in order to conduct an assessment of his need for admission; where the seriousness of a person's mental condition only becomes apparent at a time when no doctor or approved social worker is immediately available; or where an informal patient attempts to leave hospital in circumstances which suggest that it is necessary to make an application for him to be detained there. The Act therefore makes provision for a number of short-term powers of detention, which enable a person to be detained so that his mental state and situation may be assessed and/or any necessary application made. The person's detention not having been authorised in any of these cases by the acceptance of a formal application, the Act does not authorise his treatment without consent. That being so, any medication administered without the consent of an individual detained under one of these powers is only lawful if justifiable under the common law. Because of the short-term nature of the powers, persons so detained have no right to apply to a mental health review tribunal. Consequently, apart from the following brief remarks and occasional references in the text, the powers are not considered further.

Detention of in-patients under section 5(2)

If it appears to the doctor in charge of an informal in-patient's treatment that an application ought to be made under section 2 or 3 of the Act, he may furnish a written report to that effect to the managers of the hospital. Upon furnishing such a report, the patient may be detained in the hospital for a period of 72 hours. The doctor in charge of the patient's treatment may nominate one other registered medical practitioner on the hospital staff to deputise for him in his absence, that is to exercise this power as and when necessary.

Detention of in-patients under section 5(4)

It is not uncommonly the case that neither the doctor in charge of an informal patient's treatment or his nominated deputy is present on the ward when some event occurs which seems to make it clear that the patient needs to be detained. Section 5(4) therefore empowers nurses of appropriate seniority to authorise an informal patient's detention for up to six hours. More particularly, if it appears to such a nurse, *firstly,* that a patient is suffering from mental disorder to such a degree that it is necessary for his health or safety, or for the protection of others, to immediately restrain him from leaving the hospital, and, *secondly,* that it is not practicable to secure the immediate attendance of a doctor for the purpose of furnishing a report under section 5(2), the nurse may record that fact in writing. The patient may then be detained in the hospital until the doctor in charge of the patient's treatment or his nominated deputy arrives, subject to a maximum period of detention of six hours. If the doctor who attends then authorises the patient's detention under section 5(2), the 72-hour detention period under that section is treated as having commenced at the time when the nurse made his record under section 5(4).

Removal from private premises to a place of safety under section 135

Section 135 empowers a magistrate to authorise a police constable to remove a person from private premises to a place of safety. A warrant may be issued if, having heard oral evidence from an approved social worker, it appears to the magistrate that there is reasonable cause to suspect that that a person believed to be suffering from mental disorder is *either* living alone and unable to care for himself *or* is being ill-treated, neglected, or kept otherwise than under proper control, in the premises specified. The constable who removes the patient must be accompanied by an approved social worker and by a registered medical practitioner. Once removed, the individual may be detained at a place of safety — usually a hospital or police station — for a period not exceeding 72 hours.

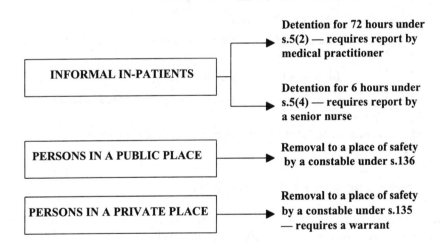

Removal from a public place to a place of safety under section 136

If a police constable finds in a place to which the public have access a person who appears to him to be suffering from mental disorder and to be in immediate need of care or control, the constable may remove him to a place of safety if he thinks it necessary to do so in that person's interests or to protect others. The individual may be detained there for a period not exceeding 72 hours, for the dual purpose of, *firstly,* enabling him to be examined by a registered medical practitioner and to be interviewed by an approved social worker and, *secondly*, of making any necessary arrangements for his treatment or care. These arrangements not uncommonly involve making an application under Part II for the person's admission to hospital.

PART III OF THE ACT (CHAP. 5)

Part III of the Mental Health Act 1983 comprises various provisions relating to "patients concerned in criminal proceedings or under sentence," and they are briefly summarised in the following table. The orders and directions made under these sections do not involve the nearest relative or an approved social worker making an application to the court. Rather, the magistrates court, Crown Court, or Home Secretary, makes the order if satisfied both as to the medical evidence and the propriety of doing so.

PART III OF THE MENTAL HEALTH ACT

Section	Purpose
	Court orders made during the course of the criminal proceedings
35	Remand to hospital for a report on the accused's mental condition.
36	Remand of accused to hospital for treatment.
38	Admission to hospital to determine whether a hospital order is an appropriate disposal.
	Court orders which bring criminal proceedings to an end
37	1. Guardianship order; 2. Hospital order
41	Restriction order — imposed where necessary to protect the public from serious harm.
	Directions by warrant of the Secretary of State
47	Transfer to hospital of a person serving a term of imprisonment who is in need of treatment.
48	Transfer to hospital of a non-prisoner in urgent need of treatment.

ORDERS MADE BY A CRIMINAL COURT

As can be seen from the table above, the orders which a criminal court may make during the course of criminal proceedings are of two kinds.

Orders which do not dispose of the case before the court

In the first group are those orders which do not dispose of the case before the court. For example, a criminal court may remand a defendant to hospital for a report on his mental condition, in order to assist it in deciding how most appropriately to deal with him. In each instance, the matter not having been disposed of, the case will come back before the court and, because it retains jurisdiction over the defendant, his detention in hospital remains a matter for that court. Consequently, the patient has no right to apply to a tribunal for his release.

Orders which do dispose of the case before the court

In the second group are those orders which dispose of the case before the court and are alternatives to the normal sentencing options. As to these, section 37 provides that a court may direct that an offender be admitted to hospital for treatment or be received into guardianship. With minor exceptions, these orders have the same consequences as do applications for admission for treatment and guardianship under Part II of the Act. That is, they authorise the patient's detention or guardianship for up to six months, after which the continuance of the compulsory powers requires periodic renewal. The making of a guardianship order or a hospital order being a final order which brings the criminal court proceedings to an end, the defendant may not go back to the court which imposed the order to seek its termination. They are, however, orders of potentially indefinite duration and the patient is therefore given a right to periodically apply to a tribunal for his discharge.

Restriction orders

What is most noteworthy about Part III of the Act is the power of the Crown Court under section 41 to restrict the operation of the normal statutory provisions concerning the return to the community of a patient whom it sends to hospital under section 37. The court may do this by attaching to the hospital order what is known as a restriction order. Such an order may only be made if it appears to be necessary in order to protect the public from serious harm. As has been noted, the purpose of these restrictions is to restrict the circumstances and ways in which the patient may be allowed outside hospital. This objective is achieved in several ways. In the first place, the Home Secretary is involved in the management, but not the treatment, of a restricted patient. Such a patient may not be permitted to be absent from the hospital, or transferred to a less secure hospital, without the Home Secretary's consent. Nor, in effect, may he be discharged from hospital otherwise than by the Home Secretary or a mental health review tribunal. Furthermore, conditions may be attached to any discharge and a patient who fails to comply with these conditions, or whose mental health deteriorates, may be recalled to hospital by the Home Secretary. No fresh order is necessary.

DIRECTIONS OF THE HOME SECRETARY

The next situation that must be catered for is that of persons in prison whose mental health deteriorates to such an extent that they require treatment in a psychiatric hospital. The Home Secretary is responsible for the prisons, including the Prison Medical Service, and he has long had a power to transfer to hospital prisoners whose cases fulfil certain criteria.

Transfer directions and restriction directions

Under section 48, the Home Secretary may transfer a person awaiting trial before a criminal court — known as a "transfer direction" — but, if he does so, he must also direct under section 49 that the defendant shall be subject to the restrictions just described — called a "restriction direction." Under section 47, he may similarly transfer a person serving a sentence of imprisonment. Whether a restriction direction is also given under section 49 is in this case a matter for his discretion. Patients who are transferred from custody to hospital by direction of the Secretary of State may be detained for a potentially indefinite period and arrangements must be made for their detention to be independently reviewed. The Act therefore again provides that they may apply to a tribunal for a review of the justification for their detention.

Effect of the directions

The general position is that, unless restrictions were also imposed (see below), a transferred patient is treated as if a hospital order had been made by a criminal court, which, in turn, means that his position is similar to that of a section 3 patient. A tribunal which considers his case may, and sometimes must, discharge him in exactly the same circumstances as any other person detained for treatment on this basis. If restrictions were imposed — and their imposition is mandatory in the case of persons awaiting trial — then the powers of a tribunal which considers the patient's case are further restricted. This limitation recognises that there are two authorities for the patient's detention: a court has authorised his detention in prison and the Home Secretary has authorised his detention in hospital. The basic position is that a tribunal may with the Home Secretary's consent discharge a serving prisoner into the community but persons awaiting trial must, unless granted bail, remain detained, either in hospital or in prison. In the latter case therefore, the tribunal's function is essentially limited to advising on the issue of whether the person still needs to be detained in hospital rather than in prison.

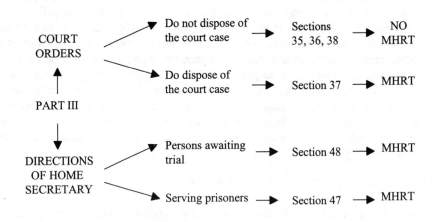

THE USE MADE OF POWERS OF DETENTION

As can be seen from the following table, most patients admitted to hospital for psychiatric treatment are admitted there informally — that is, without any formal application, order or direction being made authorising their detention there. Thus, during the year to 31 March 1996, only 26,215 (that is 9.7 per cent.) of the 271,000 patients admitted to NHS psychiatric hospitals were admitted under the 1983 Act. This compares with about 27 per cent. in 1955. However, those bare statistics do not tell the whole story. Many more of the patients compulsorily admitted in 1955 remained detained for a considerable period of time. On 31 December 1955, only 42,900 (that is 28 per cent.) of 153,100 hospital in-patients were persons who today would be regarded as informal patients. Although the Department of Health no longer keeps records of how many in-patients are detained at the end of each statistical year, probably some 85 per cent. of in-patients are nowadays in hospital informally.

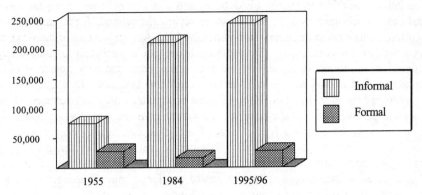

Number of formal and informal admissions to hospital during 1955, 1984 and 1995/96

Sources: Statistical reports published by Department of Health and predecessor bodies.

Use of Part II and III

In terms of the usage made of the various powers, the vast majority of patients are detained under section 2 or 3. During the year 1995/96, 12,833 of the 27,453 patients admitted to hospital were detained under section 2 (46 per cent.) and a further 9,538 under section 3 (35 per cent.).[18]

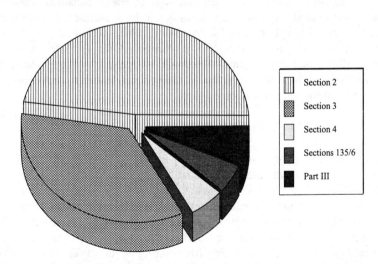

Formal admissions to hospital under the Mental Health Act 1983 during 1995–96

Source: Statistical Bulletin 1997/4, Department of Health, March 1997

---

18   It should be noted that the Department of Health's statistics do not include the use made of section 5.

MENTAL HEALTH REVIEW TRIBUNALS

Any power given to one person over another is capable of being abused, the more so if the latter is not free to escape his detainer and if his word is not given the same weight as that of other men. Tribunals which review the grounds for an individual's detention, guardianship or supervision under the 1983 Act are but one of the ways in which the law seeks to ensure that individuals are not unjustifiably or unlawfully detained or otherwise ill-treated. In the first place, each statutory power is only exercisable, that is only available, if certain conditions laid down by Parliament in the statute appear to be satisfied. Secondly, the powers may only be exercised by an authorised person, such as the patient's consultant or nearest relative, a court, an approved social worker, or a senior nurse. Thirdly, no person may be detained for more than 72 hours except on the basis of written or oral medical evidence and only then if some application has been accepted or an order or direction made. Fourthly, those involved in depriving a fellow citizen of his liberty must exercise reasonable care, certify their opinion that the statutory conditions are satisfied, and, in most instances, specify the circumstances and reasons justifying those opinions. Fifthly, those detaining an individual may only use reasonable force and it is a criminal offence to ill-treat or to wilfully neglect a patient: an unqualified power to control, restrain or discipline a person receiving hospital treatment would be unacceptable and the law does not permit the arbitrary use of power. Sixthly, if the conditions of detention are so poor as to amount to a breach of the hospital's duty of care to the patient, damages will be recoverable for any injury resulting from that negligence. Seventhly, patients who are unnecessarily or unjustifiably detained have access to a tribunal, whilst those unlawfully detained have available to them the remedies of habeas corpus and judicial review, and possibly the prospect also of release by a tribunal. Eighthly, complaints about the way in which a patient was or is being detained or treated are potentially investigable by a number of complaints bodies including the Mental Health Act Commission, which periodically visits psychiatric hospitals. Finally, patients have the protection of the European Convention on Human Rights and Fundamental Freedoms, as applied by the European Court of Human Rights, which protection has in recent times tended to prove more effective than the domestic remedies afforded them.

MHRTs — LAW AND PROCEDURE

With the possible exception of section 4 patients, all patients detained in pursuance of an application made under Part II may apply to a tribunal for their discharge. Similarly, unless the court which made the order has not yet disposed of the patient's case, all patients detained for treatment under Part III may make an application. The cases of patients detained for treatment are also periodically referred to a tribunal if no application has been made for a certain period of time. At its simplest, tribunal proceedings consist of a beginning (the making of an application or reference), a middle (the procedure for dealing with it), and an end (the determination of the application or reference).

Jurisdiction and powers

Being a creature of statute, a mental health review tribunal has no inherent jurisdiction. As is normal, the 1983 Act defines when a person may apply, when his case must be referred, and the powers of such a tribunal. More particularly, the law is to be found in Part V of the Act — which comprises sections 65–79 — and the basic framework is quite simple. Sections 66–71 determine when a person may apply and when his case must, or may, be referred. A tribunal's powers in unrestricted cases are then set out in section 72 and their powers in restricted cases are found in sections 73 (patients subject to restriction orders), 74 (patients subject to restriction directions), and 75 (conditionally discharged restricted patients).

Procedural rules

The procedure adopted by tribunals — matters such as the preparation of reports and the conduct of the hearing — is governed by rules made under the Act, the purpose of which is to ensure that each case is dealt with fairly and in a uniform manner. Although there are many different routes whereby a person may come to be detained or subject to guardianship under the Act, it would be unnecessarily complicated and serve no obvious purpose to draft separate procedural rules for dealing with each case just because this is so. All patients who are subject to guardianship or who are detained otherwise than under section 2 are detained either for an indefinite period or for renewable periods of like duration, that is for six or twelve months at a time. That being so, the Mental Health Review Tribunal Rules 1983 are drafted so as to be generally applicable to all cases other than those involving patients detained for assessment. For the sake of convenience, the rules are divided into seven parts, followed by two schedules. Of these—

- Part I of the rules defines the meaning of terms used in the rules.

- Part II deals with preliminary matters such as the form of the application, the preparation of reports, and the appointment of a tribunal.

- Part III contains various general provisions such as the disclosure of documents, the directions which a tribunal may make, the transfer of proceedings from one tribunal to another.

- Part IV deals with the way in which a hearing shall be conducted.

- Part V regulates the procedure following the hearing (the making, recording and communication of a tribunal's decision, the giving of reasons for that decision) and also includes miscellaneous provisions concerning time limits, the service of notices, and irregularities.

- Schedule 1 sets out in detail the contents of the reports required under Part II.

Proceedings involving patients detained for assessment

In the case of patients detained for assessment, the authority for their detention will in the normal course of events expire after 28 days and the Act therefore provides that a tribunal shall hear any application made by or in respect of such a patient within seven days of its receipt. This requirement necessarily means that the usual procedures for dealing with tribunal applications, for instance the content of the reports which must be prepared, need to be somewhat abbreviated. Part VI of the rules therefore includes various provisions which apply only to tribunal proceedings involving patients detained for assessment and it also provides that certain rules applicable in all other cases shall not apply or only in a modified form.

MHRTs — WHERE TO FIND THE LEGAL PROVISIONS

	Class of patient	Power of discharge	Applications and references	Tribunal procedure
Unrestricted patients	*Patients detained for assessment*	Section 72(1)(a)	Sections 66–69(1)	Part VI of MHRT Rules 1983
	Patients detained for treatment	Section 72(1)(b)		MHRT Rules 1983
	Patients subject to guardianship	Section 72(4)		
Restricted patients	*Patients subject or liable to supervision*	Section 72(4A)		
	Patients liable to be detained under a restriction order	Section 73	Sections 69(2)-71	
	Patients liable to be detained under a restriction direction	Section 74		
	Conditionally discharged restricted patients	Section 75		

A TRIBUNAL'S POWERS (CHAP. 7 & CHAP. 8)

The decisions by which a tribunal may determine an application or reference — its powers — are limited by statute. Although it is common to leave their consideration until last they should as with any form of legal proceedings be addressed first. Before advising a patient whether to apply to a tribunal it is necessary to first consider if it has power to grant the form of relief sought. And, if an application is then made, the case strategy and preparation should focus on persuading the tribunal to exercise some power which it may lawfully exercise. Although there are several different routes by which a person may come to be liable to detention, guardianship or supervision under the Act, the purposes for which compulsory powers may be invoked and the reasons which justify their continuance are rather fewer. That being so, the Act divides the cases which a tribunal may consider into seven main categories for the purpose of defining its decision-making powers.

Patients detained in hospital for assessment

A tribunal's powers when dealing with the case of a patient admitted to hospital under section 2 are set out in section 72. A tribunal must discharge a patient whom it considers satisfies the statutory criteria for being discharged set out in section 72(1)(a) — "mandatory discharge." Where the mandatory discharge criteria are not satisfied, it may still discharge the patient at its discretion if it considers that is appropriate having regard to all the circumstances of the case — "discretionary discharge." A tribunal which discharges a patient may direct that the discharge take effect on a specified future date, rather than forthwith, regardless of whether discharge is mandatory or discretionary. A tribunal which does not discharge may, with a view to facilitating a patient's discharge on some future date, recommend that he be granted leave of absence, transferred to another hospital, or transferred into guardianship. In the event that its recommendation is not complied with, the tribunal may further consider the case. In summary, a tribunal is obliged to discharge if the relevant statutory criteria are satisfied, may in other cases discharge at its discretion and, where it does not discharge, may make certain statutory recommendations with a view to facilitating discharge in the future.

Unrestricted patients liable to be detained for treatment

The majority of patients who are detained in hospital for treatment are not subject to special restrictions. Whatever the original authority for such a patient's detention, the Act provides that tribunals shall apply the same discharge criteria and have the same powers in all cases involving unrestricted patients detained for treatment. A tribunal's powers are similar to those in respect of patients detained for assessment, so that the cases of all unrestricted patients are dealt with in a comparable way. In particular, a tribunal is required to discharge a patient who satisfies the statutory criteria for being discharged set out in section 72(1)(b), may at its discretion discharge a patient where this is not so and, if it does not discharge, may make the same kinds of recommendations as in a section 2 case. Discharge may, as before, either be forthwith or on a specific future date. There are, however, three important differences. When deciding whether to exercise its discretionary power of discharge, a tribunal must have regard to certain statutory matters set out in section 72(2). Furthermore, a tribunal which does not discharge may recommend that a supervision application be made; and it may also direct that the form of mental disorder from

23

which the patient is recorded as suffering on the authority for his detention be amended, so as to show that he is suffering from some other form. A similar power of reclassification would be superfluous in section 2 cases because all patients detained for assessment are classified as suffering from "mental disorder" generally rather than from one or more of its particular forms.

Patients subject to guardianship

Somewhat different statutory criteria and powers are required where a tribunal reviews the case of a patient who is subject to guardianship. Section 72(4) provides that a tribunal shall discharge a patient from guardianship if the criteria set out there are satisfied. As before, a tribunal also possesses a discretionary power to discharge a patient whom it does not consider satisfies the criteria for mandatory discharge. Because a guardianship application or order specifies the form of disorder from which the patient has been found to suffer, a tribunal has the same power to reclassify a patient whom it does not discharge from guardianship as it does an unrestricted patient detained for treatment. There the similarities end. A tribunal has no power to direct a patient's discharge from guardianship on a specified future date so that any discharge must take effect forthwith. Moreover, a tribunal which does not discharge a patient from guardianship has no power to make statutory recommendations with a view to facilitating his future discharge from guardianship. In part, this is because the recommendations which a tribunal may make when reviewing a patient's liability to detention would be irrelevant or inappropriate in guardianship cases. Recommending leave of absence would be otiose because a guardianship patient cannot be granted leave of absence. Similarly, recommending transfer to hospital would contravene the original statutory premise that a tribunal's functions in unrestricted cases are limited to discharging patients or facilitating their discharge. Except in so far as recently provided for by the 1995 Act, a tribunal has no power to further restrict a person's freedom.

Patients subject to after-care under supervision

The powers of a tribunal dealing with the case of a patient who is subject to after-care under supervision, or who is to be so subject when he leaves hospital, are the same as in guardianship cases. The tribunal must direct that the patient shall cease to be so subject if it is satisfied that the statutory criteria set out in section 72(4A) are not complied with. If this is not the case, the tribunal may still at its discretion direct that the patient shall cease to be subject to supervision. Where a tribunal does not direct that a patient shall cease to be subject or liable to supervision, it may reclassify the form of disorder from which he is recorded as suffering. As with guardianship, it has no power to make any statutory recommendations with a view to facilitating a patient's discharge from statutory supervision at a later date.

Patients admitted to hospital for treatment under a restriction order

The essence of a restriction order is that the usual powers by which a patient detained for treatment in pursuance of a hospital order may be discharged or granted greater freedom are restricted. This principle extends to tribunals so that its usual powers either do not apply or only in a restricted way. The single superficial similarity is that a tribunal must discharge a patient who satisfies the same statutory criteria as apply to unrestricted patients who have been detained for treatment. Because a tribunal has no discretionary power of discharge in restricted cases, it must discharge a patient whom it is satisfied meets the criteria for being discharged and not discharge a patient unless it is satisfied that is the case. Where a restriction order patient satisfies the mandatory discharge criteria, the discharge may be absolute or subject to conditions. The effect of conditional discharge is that the orders remain in force and the patient may be recalled to hospital for further treatment, for example if he relapses or fails to comply with the conditions of his discharge. Absolute discharge is mandatory where a tribunal is satisfied that it is not appropriate for a patient whom it must discharge to be liable to recall in this way and its effect is to bring both the hospital and restriction order to an end. Where a patient is conditionally discharged, it may be impossible for the conditions imposed on his discharge to be satisfied immediately. For example, where it is a condition of discharge that he resides at a supervised hostel but no suitable place is available. The Act therefore provides that a tribunal may defer a direction for a patient's conditional discharge until such time as it is satisfied that suitable arrangements have been made which meet the conditions imposed — "deferred conditional discharge." If it later transpires that arrangements cannot be made which allow the conditions attached to the patient's discharge to be satisfied, the tribunal's direction for the patient's discharge will eventually be deemed never to have been made. A tribunal's power in restriction order cases to defer the coming into force of a conditional discharge direction should not be confused with its power to direct the discharge of an unrestricted patient on a specified future date. In the latter case, the tribunal's direction discharging the patient is effective and complete the moment it is made; it is not provisional upon future events. A tribunal which does not discharge a restriction order patient from hospital has no power to make recommendations of the kind it may make in unrestricted cases and probably no power to reclassify. In summary, a tribunal may only discharge a restriction order patient who satisfies the statutory criteria for being discharged. Where that is not the case, and the patient is therefore not discharged, the tribunal has no power to make statutory recommendations nor, probably, to reclassify him.

TRIBUNALS' POWERS

Powers and duties	Unrestricted patients			Restricted patients
	Detained for assessment	Detained for treatment	Subject to supervision or guardianship	Detained for treatment under a restriction order
Mandatory discharge	•	•	•	•
Discretionary discharge	•	•	•	
Discharge on specified future date	•	•		
Statutory recommendations to facilitate discharge	•	•		
Recommendations re making supervision application		•		
Power to reclassify		•	•	?

Patients removed to hospital for treatment under a restriction direction

Section 47 provides that the Secretary of State may by warrant direct the transfer to hospital of a patient who is serving a sentence of imprisonment. Section 48 similarly provides that the Secretary of State may remove to hospital certain other categories of detained persons, such as defendants remanded in custody pending trial. In each case, the Secretary of State may, and in some cases must, also make a restriction direction under section 49. A tribunal's powers are further restricted where it considers the case of a patient who is liable to be detained for treatment and subject to a restriction direction. In essence, it must approach the case as if the patient were subject to a restriction order rather than a restriction direction. It must therefore apply the discharge criteria applicable in such cases and reach a finding as to whether, if that were the case, it would be obliged to direct the patient's absolute or conditional discharge. It must notify the Home Secretary of its finding. What then happens depends upon whether the patient is liable to be detained under section 47 or 48.

RESTRICTION DIRECTION CASES

Tribunal's findings, etc.	Section 47 patients	Section 48 patients
• *Patient does not satisfy the discharge criteria.*	Patient remains in hospital.	
• *Patient satisfies criteria for conditional discharge — MHRT recommends that patient not be remitted to custody as a result of its finding.*	Tribunal directs patient's conditional discharge if Secretary of State gives notice within 90 days that it may do so; otherwise patient remains in hospital.	Patient remains in hospital.
• *Patient satisfies criteria for conditional discharge — MHRT makes no recommendation about remission to custody.*	Tribunal directs patient's conditional discharge if Secretary of State gives notice within 90 days that it may do so; otherwise patient transferred to prison.	Patient remitted to custody — 90 day rule does not apply.
• *Patient satisfies criteria for absolute discharge.*	Tribunal directs patient's absolute discharge if Secretary of State gives notice within 90 days that it may do so. Otherwise patient transferred to prison.	

Restriction direction patients detained under section 48

Where a tribunal notifies the Home Secretary that a restricted patient detained under section 48 satisfies the criteria for absolute discharge, the Secretary of State must direct that the patient be remitted to prison or such other institution in which he might have been detained had he not been removed to hospital. Where a tribunal instead notifies the Home Secretary that the patient satisfies the criteria for conditional discharge then, similarly, the Secretary of State shall remit him to custody under section 74 unless the tribunal also "recommended" that the patient should continue to be detained in hospital.

Restriction direction patients detained under section 47

Section 47 patients are in a somewhat more favourable position. Where a tribunal notifies the Secretary of State that the patient satisfies the criteria for absolute discharge, the tribunal shall so discharge the patient if, within the following 90 days, the Secretary of State serves notice on the tribunal that the patient may be absolutely discharged. Otherwise, at the expiration of that period, the managers of the hospital must transfer the patient to prison or to such other institution in which he might have been detained had he not been removed to hospital. Where a tribunal notifies the Secretary of State that a patient satisfies the criteria for conditional discharge, it may also "recommend" that he continue to be detained in hospital if the Secretary of State does not give notice that he may be conditionally discharged by the tribunal. If the Secretary of State serves notice on the tribunal within 90 days that the patient may be so discharged, the tribunal shall direct his conditional discharge, failing which the managers must transfer the patient to prison at the expiration of that period unless the tribunal "recommended" otherwise.

Conditionally discharged restricted patients

Where a tribunal considers the case of a restriction order or restriction direction patient who is not liable to be detained because he has been conditionally discharged, its ordinary power of discharge is self-evidently irrelevant — the patient has already been discharged. Section 75 therefore provides that a tribunal may do one of four things when dealing with such a case: make no direction at all, in which case the patient remains discharged on the same conditions as before; vary an existing condition of his discharge; impose a new condition of discharge; or direct that the restriction order or direction shall cease to have effect.

The limits of a tribunal's powers (Chap. 9)

Chapter 9 deals with three issues which are mainly of interest to lawyers. These are the burden and standard of proof in tribunal cases; whether a tribunal may have regard to irregularities in the authority for the patient's detention, guardianship or supervision; and the extent to which tribunal directions are binding.

TRIBUNAL PROCEDURE

The procedure to be adopted by tribunals when dealing with cases is that set out in the Mental Health Review Tribunal Rules 1983 although, as with all tribunals, the rules must be applied in accordance with the principles of fairness known as the rules of natural justice.

Commencing the proceedings (Chap. 10)

Where authorised by the Act, an application may be made by a patient, his nearest relative or by the person presently exercising the nearest relative's statutory functions. Rights of application vary according to the authority for the patient's detention, guardianship or supervision. Patients' cases may also be referred to a tribunal. Part V requires the hospital managers and the Secretary of State to do this if the patient has not had a tribunal for a certain period of time. It also gives the Secretary of State a discretion to refer cases at other times. Where an application is received from a section 2 patient, the tribunal must hear it within seven days. In other cases, there are no similar time limits. The tribunal will give notice that the proceedings have been commenced and decide whether it has power to postpone considering the case. If a prior application or reference is outstanding in respect of the same patient, the tribunal may join the proceedings. If the patient moves to the area of another tribunal during the proceedings, his case may be transferred to that tribunal. In certain circumstances, an application or reference may be withdrawn or deemed to be withdrawn.

Obtaining reports on the patient (Chap. 11)

In cases involving detained patients, the managers of the relevant hospital are what is known as "the responsible authority." The rules impose on the responsible authority and, in cases involving restricted patients, the Home Secretary, a duty to furnish a statement about the patient to the tribunal. The extent of this obligation, and the information and reports which the statement must include, are set out in the rules but, broadly speaking, a medical and a social work report is required in all cases. The grounds upon which part of a statement may be withheld from a patient, or a nearest relative applicant, are that the material's disclosure would adversely affect the patient's health or welfare or that of others. Rule 12(1) provides that the parties may submit written comments on the statement to the tribunal. Chapter 11 includes consideration of various matters relevant to the preparation of medical and social circumstances reports, including the legislation relating to the provision of social services; patients' finances; the preparation of independent reports and their disclosure.

Risk assessment and discharge planning (Chap. 12)

As has already been noted, the statutory criteria to be applied by a tribunal when determining whether a patient must be discharged always comprise at least two grounds, the second of which is directed towards the issue of risk. In particular, the likelihood of undesirable consequences if the individual is allowed a citizen's usual freedom to decide how to act and what medical treatment or social care to accept. Chapter 12 sets out the general principles of risk assessment and, in particular, assessments of the risk of suicide, homicide or serious violence. The remainder of the chapter is concerned with discharge planning, the aim of which is essentially to minimise acceptable risks. In relation to unrestricted patients, this involves considering the relationship between the plethora of enactments, directions, guidelines and codes concerning the discharge of patients and their after-care, following which the guidelines concerning the discharge and supervision of restricted patients are summarised.

Directions and other pre-hearing matters (Chap. 13)

Following the receipt and disclosure of the responsible authority's statement or that of the Secretary of State, the other formal stages in the proceedings prior to the hearing are giving notice of the proceedings; directing that further information or reports be furnished where appropriate; giving any other directions necessary to ensure the speedy and just determination of the application; appointing the tribunal members; conducting the pre-hearing medical examination; and giving notice of the hearing. Each tribunal has a legal chairman whose most important functions are to exercise the tribunal's powers under the rules in relation to such preliminary or incidental matters.

The hearing (Chap. 14)

Hearings take place at the hospital where the patient is liable to be detained, most often in the board-room or a committee room. Rules 21 and 22 set out the basic hearing procedure. From a legal viewpoint, the issues to be considered are whether the hearing should or must be held in private or public; who is entitled, or may be required, to attend or appear; who may be excluded; the pre-hearing deliberations; the hearing itself and taking the evidence; the effect of irregularities in the conduct of the proceedings, including any failure to comply with the rules; the power to adjourn; and sanctions.

The tribunal's decision and appeals (Chap. 15)

The manner in which a tribunal reaches its decision, the recording of that decision and the reasons for it, and their communication to the parties, are subject to various procedural requirements set out in the rules. A decision may be set aside if the tribunal had no power to make it, it was founded on an error of law, it was reached in an unfair manner, it was irrational, or the reasons given for it were inadequate or unintelligible. If a tribunal's decision is legally flawed, it may be challenged by asking the tribunal to state a point of law for the High Court's determination or by way of judicial review. Habeas corpus is also considered in this chapter.

LEGAL REPRESENTATION (CHAP. 16)

Representation before tribunals is the norm and some 90 per cent. of patients in Wales are now legally represented. Rule 10 of the 1983 rules is concerned with representation, and it provides that an authorised representative may take all steps which his client is required by the rules to take and do all such things as his client is authorised by them to do. The other chapters of this book are in the form of a textbook, aiming to give a balanced and impartial account of the legal and medical considerations relevant to all practitioners, including tribunal members. The representative's role is not at all neutral, since it is to present a case for discharge in accordance with the client's instructions, and this one chapter therefore departs from that approach. Its aim is simply to assist lawyers in the preparation and presentation of tribunal cases, and the chapter commences with a detailed outline of the material covered. It is, however, worth emphasising two subjects here, for the benefit of those instructed to undertake their first case late in the day.

Formality and manner

Practitioners new to the field are often anxious about how they should approach and deal with people who have a serious mental health problem. In terms of professional conduct, the principles are the same as for any client attending the office — to serve the client without compromising the solicitor's integrity or his overriding duty to the court and the judicial process. On a personal level, being able to take proper instructions, helping the client to formulate what it is he wants, and then pursuing those objectives in a constructive way, may require more empathy than is usually necessary in most other legal fields. It should be borne in mind that detained patients often feel uncomfortable and disadvantaged in a formal situation such as a interview. They may have low self-esteem, since much mental ill-health takes root in such ground, and, in other cases, a poor self-image is a necessary fertiliser of disease. The individual's false belief that his opinions are of no significance is potentially reinforced by being detained and so compelled to accept the views of others; by his subordinate status as a layman in discussion with a professional adviser; and by his status as an ill and irrational patient receiving a rational, sane, visitor. The client may be perplexed by the recent turn of events or by the ward routine. Containment on an acute psychiatric ward is a frightening, and in itself largely untherapeutic, experience at the best of times, the more so if the person is unfamiliar with the environment. Helping the client to relax and gaining his trust, by appreciating his predicament and treating him at all times respectfully and as an equal, are therefore prerequisites to making progress. The ways of responding to the individual's sense of humiliation at being categorised as mentally abnormal depend very much on how he himself has reacted to this slight. In some cases it helps to acknowledge that mental health is, like physical health, a relative term and that we are all at some level both well and ill, normal and abnormal, at any one time. With people who are seriously depressed, their feelings are often best understood as a bereavement — in some cases, a result of the death of another important person but more often their own death or the loss of something important within them. In cases involving mania, it is similarly valuable to appreciate that grandiosity cloaks feelings of inadequacy or depression — time and again, people in a manic phase say that they are not truly careless or content whatever their behaviour may superficially suggest. Whatever social approach is adopted, the use of medical adjectives to define the person rather than the condition affecting him is insulting, and akin to describing a person with leprosy as a "leper." To refer to someone as a "schizophrenic" or as a "paranoid schizophrenic" is to imply that his personality has been so distorted by the illness that the latter is now the feature which most tellingly defines him as a person. By implication, it is more accurate to describe him in this way than to say that he is a person who has an illness called schizophrenia. From there, it is quite easy for a lawyer to drift into seeing his contribution, and legal presumptions about human liberty, as having only a marginal relevance. To summarise, the usual principles governing the solicitor-client relationship apply and few problems will arise provided the solicitor is courteous and avoids being patronising.

Taking instructions

It is generally possible to take detailed instructions and a detailed interview avoids unpleasant surprises later. Where time permits, it is useful to maintain a reasonably comprehensive case summary. By observing and listening to the client and others, the representative can be aware of the strengths and weaknesses of his case, the likely content of the reports and oral evidence, and any inconsistencies between the client's account and objectives and what is observed. Except in wholly exceptional circumstances, the usual rules governing the solicitor-client relationship apply. The

Guide to the Professional Conduct of Solicitors states that a solicitor is under a duty to keep confidential a client's affairs, but a solicitor also owes a duty to act in the best interests of the client. Whether departing from a solicitor's duty of confidentiality towards his client may ever be justified on this ground is disputed. Because many clients are willing to discuss their mental experiences more freely with their solicitor, partly because of the cloak of privacy, it is often the case that the solicitor is aware of mental phenomena not recorded in the case notes as being present and not aired at the hearing. The general view is, however, that a solicitor remains bound in all situations by the normal duty of confidentiality. If the solicitor knows that the patient is experiencing certain symptoms of mental disorder, he may not positively assert that that is not the case, even if this is the responsible medical officer's evidence. That would amount to misleading the tribunal. Accordingly, the position is analogous to that where a solicitor knows that a defendant in criminal proceedings has previous convictions. He may not describe him as being of good character simply because the court knows of none. The qualified view is that in wholly exceptional circumstances a solicitor would be justified in disclosing something told to him in confidence. For example, if a tribunal was clearly proceeding on the erroneous basis that there was no immediate significant risk of suicide or homicide. Finally, on the matter of professional conduct, the tendency of a few solicitors to practise their clients must be deplored. This form of contempt consists of telling the client which answers to questions invariably asked by tribunals are commonly interpreted as pointers towards discharge.

MEDICAL ISSUES

Because tribunal proceedings are a mixture of law and medicine, a purely legal approach to the work is unproductive, even for lawyers; it is not sufficient to understand only the legal part of what is a medico-legal subject. The rote-learning of definitions is, however, unhelpful. It is more useful to develop an appreciation of the concepts embraced by the terms; otherwise, what the individual propounds is not always clear even to himself. Furthermore, the tendency to regard legal and medical terms as having value-free fixed meanings, rather than as expressing concepts, is misplaced and merely reflects a failure to appreciate the problems which all professions experience in reaching agreement about ideas. In dealing with medical terms and concepts, priority has generally been given in the text to the views of leading British medical practitioners, such as Robert Kendell and Graham Bradley, and to definitions contained in internationally recognised medical publications such as the *International Classification of Diseases*.

MENTAL HEALTH AND MENTAL DISORDER (CHAP. 17)

Medical science approaches mental disorders as diseases which can be studied objectively in terms of abnormal cell structures and chemical imbalances. The practice of medicine consists of the application of knowledge concerning human biology to the prevention and treatment of illness. This is often referred to as the biomedical approach to mental disorder. Psychiatry is that branch of medicine concerned with the study, diagnosis, treatment and prevention of mental disorder.

Personality

Personality, as it is commonly understood, is what makes one individual different from another. It is the ingrained patterns of thought, feeling, and behaviour characterizing an individual's unique lifestyle and mode of adaptation, which result from constitutional factors, development, and social experience. An individual's personality both determines and reflects his unique adjustment to his environment, including the unique way in which he becomes mentally ill. Not all conditions characterised by abnormal mental functioning are, however, conceived of as an illness. Certain forms of mental disorder are categorised simply as being disorders of the personality. Here, the individual's abnormal mental state is considered to be the manifestation of his normal — if compared to other people abnormal — personality rather than the product of an illness overlying and distorting that personality.

The brain and the mind

The brain is the organ of the body within which thoughts, feelings, emotions, perceptions, sensations and moods are generated, experienced and memorised in response to stimuli received from the world outside it (the body and the environment). What we call mental states are functional states resulting from the complex interaction of our brain with the world outside it. By analogy, breathing is the interaction of air and the lungs. Although the concept of a mind is fundamental to the law, it is simply a term used either to describe either the brain's present functioning (synonymous in this sense with the individual's "mental state") or to describe its tendency to function and respond to events outside it in certain habitual ways (the individual's mind in this sense being synonymous with his personality). Ryle has observed that it is a striking feature of the brain that it does not have unlimited access to its own workings, so that the brain may submit itself to analysis and other forms of treatment over a lengthy period in an attempt to discover the cause or aims of its own processes.

THE BRAIN, MIND AND PERSONALITY

- *Brain* — The organ of the body within which thoughts, feelings, emotions, perceptions, sensations and moods are generated, experienced and memorised in response to stimuli received from the world outside it (the body and the environment).

- *Mind* — The way in which the brain functions, both in the present (an individual's mental state) and its tendency to function and respond to events outside it in certain habitual ways (the individual's personality — his tendency to certain mental states).

- *Mental state* — An individual's contemporaneous thoughts, feelings, emotions, perceptions, sensations, and mood.

- *Personality* — The whole system of relatively permanent abilities and tendencies distinctive of a given individual's brain.

Normal and abnormal health

A diagnosis of mental disorder implies a departure from a state of health and any consideration of what constitutes an individual's personality or mind necessarily leads on to the question of what constitutes an unhealthy or abnormal personality or mind. In practical terms, mental health may be described as that standard of mental functioning necessary for a person to perform the activities which are expected of him, according to the norms of the society in which he lives. Disability or handicap arising from disease, illness, or injury must be absent. For the scientist, the problem of defining what is abnormal is particularly acute when considering mental phenomena and, in such cases, distinctions between normal and abnormal states are ultimately arbitrary and prescriptive. However one defines what is normal, most individuals will be found to conform to the norm in relation to some but not all of their mental characteristics so that, when taken in aggregate, most of us fail to escape some departure from the norm. What we regard as illness or disorder appears to shade insensibly into normality so that abnormality may be the result of disease in some cases and in others the expression of variability.

Disorders

The term "disorder" is not an exact term but simply implies the existence of a clinically recognisable set of symptoms or behaviour associated in most cases with distress and with interference with personal functions. In practice, the classification of certain disorders as mental or psychiatric is largely determined by the historical fact that these conditions have generally been treated by psychiatrists.

Illnesses

An "illness" may be seen as the difference between a person's current state of being and functioning and his state of health immediately prior to the onset of a decline in his health, whether subjectively or objectively apparent. It represents an interference with the individual's ability to discharge those functions and obligations that are expected of him. In conventional usage, "mental illness" is more specific than "mental disorder" because the latter term includes abnormal behaviour associated with or resulting from an individual's personality or limited intelligence.

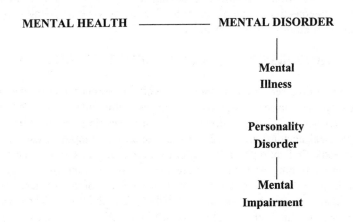

MENTAL HEALTH ———————— MENTAL DISORDER

Mental
Illness

Personality
Disorder

Mental
Impairment

Diseases and the disease model

The term "disease" may be taken to refer to a deterioration of health which results from disordered biological processes. More specifically, disease is a process involving undesired and unwilled changes either in the anatomy of the body or in the way a part of the body functions. A disease may also be described as an illness but not all illnesses are diseases — that is, not all illnesses are attributable to changes in the structure of the body, such as the brain, or to the way in which those structures function. The medical model of illness is dominated by the concept of disease, which may be depicted symbolically as a sequence —

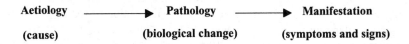

Aetiology	Pathology	Manifestation
(cause)	(biological change)	(symptoms and signs)

Viewing this sequence in reverse, the patient's disease comprises symptoms and signs which are the manifestations of certain pathological changes in the structure or functioning of his body, changes initiated by a particular cause or causes (the aetiology). Many diseases are caused by exposure of the individual to environmental influences and social deprivation, and the characteristics of each individual, and each disease, are the results of the interplay of two basic factors: inherited genetic constitution and environment.

Aetiology

Aetiology is literally the study of causes and the aetiology of a disease consists of the postulated causes that initiate the disease process, control of which may lead to its prevention. Because the disease model holds that pathological bodily changes are the direct cause of the patient's symptoms and signs, the aetiology is therefore a step removed from this stage and refers to the causes of that pathology (disease process). Ideas about what causes mental disorder depend on how mental health and, by elimination, mental disorder are defined. Cause is inferred and involves a retrospective interpretation of the likelihood of an association between events. Failure to realise that what is regarded as having caused a person to become unwell depends on the perspective of the onlooker has led to many sterile debates about the causes of different kinds of mental disorder.

ASSESSING THE PRESENCE OF MENTAL DISORDER (CHAP. 18)

A person may be diseased but symptom-free, which is another way of saying that, following the onset of disease, pathological changes within the body may or may not make themselves evident. When they do, they are described as "manifestations" which, by medical custom, are usually distinguished as "symptoms and signs." A sign is an objective indication of a disease or disorder that is observed or detected by a doctor upon examining and interviewing the patient, in contrast to a symptom which is noticed or reported by the patient. However, in common usage, the term "symptoms" also includes objective signs of pathological conditions. The severity of a symptom can be rated on a number of different criteria, such as frequency, intensity, duration, tolerability or degree of incapacitation. The mental state examination is equivalent to the detailed physical examination in general medicine and assessment is the process of collecting information relevant to the diagnosis, management, and treatment of a patient's clinical condition. It includes distinguishing or recognising the presence of a disease or disorder from its manifestations. The recording of a patient's symptoms, and the conduct of any special investigations, is initially undertaken to identify the type of disorder from which he suffers — symptoms being pointers towards the underlying pathology, and, following on from this, pointers both to the most appropriate form of treatment and the likely response to that treatment.

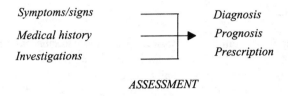

ASSESSMENT

CLASSIFYING AND DIAGNOSING MENTAL DISORDER (CHAP. 19)

Diagnosis forms part of the assessment process and, in general usage, the term refers to the process of identifying the specific mental disorder from which the patient suffers. A diagnosis is a short-hand way of describing what is wrong with a patient and it involves assigning the patient's case to a particular known class, such as schizophrenia, by reference to an accepted classification of mental disorders. Classification is the grouping of things according to a logical scheme for organising and classifying them. Phenomena are assigned to designated classes on the basis of perceived common characteristics and particular diagnostic classes should be associated with particular prognoses and outcomes. The way in which the classification tree is constructed affects the results produced so that a person may meet the criteria for a diagnosis of schizophrenia set out in one classification but not another. Although acknowledged not to be particularly satisfactory, the symptomological approach to classification is by default used in psychiatry. Clusters of symptoms may be observed to occur in conjunction and to develop or remit according to a broadly identifiable pattern, persisting for a characteristic length of time. These clusters of symptoms therefore occur together as identifiable constellations or syndromes — "syndrome" being a Greek word meaning "running together." The syndrome can be named and classified, *e.g.* schizophrenia. Whether certain recognised syndromes do in reality represent distinct disease processes depends upon the correctness of the observations and inferences made about the way certain symptoms coalesce, as well as on the validity of this kind of disease reasoning. As matters presently stand, conditions such as schizophrenia are ultimately concepts the validity of which has yet to be demonstrated. The diagnostic methods used by different clinicians are not always comparable so that a patient's diagnosis but not his condition may change over time. This is because diagnoses are subject to therapeutic fashions and innovations and depend upon the classification and operational criteria being used. Providing a classification is used appropriately, it must ultimately be conceded that it embraces a different population of patients than do other competing operational criteria. Most studies suggest that agreement about the presence or absence of physical signs is not very good, much of the agreement being due simply to chance.

TREATMENT AND OUTCOME (CHAP. 20)

A prognosis is a medical assessment of the probable course and outcome of a patient's condition. It is assumed that each disease has a certain natural course although this can sometimes be interfered with by treatment. Consequently, the diagnosis of a particular disease enables the clinician to make an assessment of the likely outcome —a prognosis— and also to choose an appropriate form of treatment. While a diagnosis should provide therapeutic and prognostic indicators, in psychiatry these are often relatively weak and the actual outcome may differ from that prognosed.

Onset and course

The onset, course and duration of a disorder are often described as either acute or chronic. The term "acute" describes a disorder or symptom that comes on suddenly, may or may not be severe, and is usually of short duration. "Chronic" describes a disorder or set of symptoms that has persisted for a long time, rather than being of sudden onset and short duration; there is little discernible change in the symptomology from day to day.

Outcome

The outcome may be recovery; a complete or partial remission of the symptoms, sometimes followed by relapse; or characterised by chronicity, with little or no change in the presence or intensity of the patient's symptoms. Recovery (or "cure" where recovery follows treatment) describes the elimination of the disease or disorder producing the patient's symptoms. Remission denotes a temporary disappearance or reduction in the severity or symptomology of a disease or a period during which this occurs. A proportion of patients recover, or their symptoms remit, naturally for reasons other than any treatment administered to them. The residual phase of an illness is the phase that occurs after remission of the florid symptoms of the full syndrome. Relapse describes the recurrence of a disorder after an apparent recovery or a return of the symptoms after their remission. Sequelae are the complications of a disorder. For example, the sequelae of a cold may include bronchitis.

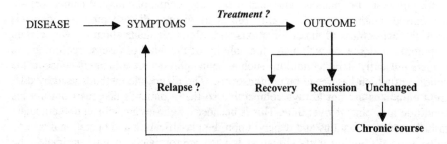

DESCRIBING THE OUTCOME

Describing the consequences for the individual

The *International Classification of Impairments, Disabilities and Handicaps* uses the terms impairment, disability and handicap to describe the consequences for the individual concerned of a disease or injury. All three concepts depend on deviations from norms. The sequence underlying illness-related phenomena is presented as follows:

$$\text{DISEASE or INJURY} \longrightarrow \text{IMPAIRMENT} \longrightarrow \text{DISABILITY} \longrightarrow \text{HANDICAP}$$

An impairment is a permanent or temporary loss or abnormality of bodily structure or function. The fact that part of the body is impaired may or may not affect the individual's ability to perform different activities, but, if so, the impairment has a disabling effect. A disability is a restriction or lack of ability to perform *an activity* in the manner or within the range considered normal for a human being as a result of impairment. As in horse racing, the state of being handicapped is relative to others, so that a handicap is any disadvantage resulting from an impairment or disability which limits or prevents fulfilling *a role* that is normal for that person.

The treatment of mental disorder

The alleviation of suffering and the cure of the underlying condition causing the patient to suffer are the main goals of medicine. The treatment of mental disorder can be divided into five broad categories: surgical (psychosurgery); physical (ECT); chemical (psychotropic drugs); psychological (nursing, psychological and social therapy); and complementary ("alternative" remedies). Procedures such as seclusion and continuous observation are not generally regarded as forms of treatment, merely ways of isolating or protecting a patient who requires treatment. To treat a person suffering from disease or disorder is not the same thing as to cure him. Most drugs prescribed to treat psychiatric disorders are equivalent to the chemical sprays used by gardeners to control the more extreme, unwanted, external manifestations of a diseased or poorly nourished plant. There are few if any specific treatments in psychiatry. Depressive, schizophrenic and manic illnesses may all respond to ECT; schizophrenic and manic illnesses both respond to neuroleptics; depressive and anxiety states both respond to cognitive psychotherapy; and so on. Likewise, a seemingly common disorder may respond to a number of different treatments.

Psychosurgery

Psychosurgery is little used and largely reserved for the management of patients with chronic obsessional and depressive disorders which have not responded to prolonged treatment with more usual therapies.

Electro-convulsive therapy

Electro-convulsive therapy is generally considered to be the first line of treatment where a depressive illness is associated with life-threatening complications, such as failure to eat and drink or a high risk of suicide, or the patient is unable to tolerate antidepressant medication in high doses.

AETIOLOGY

The interplay of genes and environment, being the causes of

PATHOLOGY/DISEASE

Disordered biological processes which manifest themselves as the

SYMPTOMS AND SIGNS OF DISEASE

Some of which may over time be observed to occur in conjunction or according to a broad pattern, thus allowing for the development of

A CLASSIFICATION OF DISEASES

To which a medical practitioner can refer when making an

ASSESSMENT OF A PATIENT'S MENTAL CONDITION

And, in particular, the symptoms and signs,thus allowing him to make a

DIAGNOSIS OF A KNOWN CLASS (TYPE) OF DISORDER

associated with a known

PROGNOSIS

being the likely course and outcome, and a known plan of

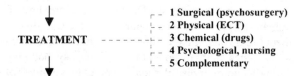

TREATMENT - - - - - - - -
1 Surgical (psychosurgery)
2 Physical (ECT)
3 Chemical (drugs)
4 Psychological, nursing
5 Complementary

Thus allowing treatment to be prescribed, which may or may not be effective, but leads eventually to the

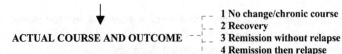

ACTUAL COURSE AND OUTCOME
1 No change/chronic course
2 Recovery
3 Remission without relapse
4 Remission then relapse

which may leave the patient with some degree of

| **Impairment** | **Disability** | **Handicap** |
| *abnormality of bodily structure or function* | *reduced ability to perform certain activities* | *disadvantage which limits fulfilling a role normal for that person* |

REVISED BIOMEDICAL MODEL

Medication

The traditional division of psychotherapeutic drugs according to their actions is as follows: (1) antipsychotics, (2) antidepressants, (3) antimanics, (4) antiepileptics, (5) anxiolytics, and (6) hypnotics. Optimizing the results of drug therapy involves applying the five Ds : diagnosis, drug selection, dose, duration and dialogue. A prescribed drug may bring about a satisfactory response, have inadequate effect, or have intolerable side effects. Treatment failure is determined by treatment aims and expectations. In the case of compliant patients, the two most important causes of treatment failure involving psychotropic drugs are underdosing and an inadequate therapeutic trial of a drug. Different patients require different amounts of a drug for optimal therapeutic effect. No standard dose exists and the correct dose must be determined empirically. The British National Formulary contains recommended guideline maximum doses for most drugs, with separate guidance for special categories of patients such as the elderly, children and pregnant women. Although virtually all available drugs are equivalent in overall efficacy, they differ immensely in how well they are tolerated and how lethal they are in overdose. Accordingly, the most important reasons to choose a drug are often its relative side-effect profile and safety. Ways of dealing with adverse effects include withdrawing the medication causing the undesired effects and (if necessary) substituting an alternative drug for the target condition; reducing the dosage; and treating the unwanted symptoms.

SUMMARY OF BASIC CONCEPTS

The final chapters consider those medical conditions most commonly encountered in tribunal proceedings: personality (psychopathic) disorders; mood disorders; schizophrenia; and a range of organic disorders. Some compromises are inevitable. The approach adopted here is to consider in detail those conditions most commonly encountered in tribunal practice, rather than to consider, in correspondingly less detail, all those conditions which may sometimes be encountered. Before moving on, it is, however, helpful to draw together the main concepts, and a flowchart showing the various sequences of the biomedical model appears on the previous page. When an individual has been denied his liberty, clarity of thought is essential and the medical evidence said to warrant such an interference may be systematically scrutinised with this flowchart in mind. Sometimes, of course, the patient's behaviour is so grossly disturbed that the predominant issue is straightforward, being whether his behaviour can be managed outside a hospital setting or without resort to compulsion. However, in many cases, the issues are more subtle. They revolve around questions such as the prognosis and the likelihood of any improvement made being maintained; the causes of the current episode of illness and whether relapse is likely because those causes remain unaddressed; whether the symptoms justify the diagnosis and, if not, whether an alternative diagnosis is associated with a more favourable prognosis; whether the patient is disabled or handicapped and the required level of support outside hospital. While tribunals sometimes assert that they are not concerned with the diagnosis, because there is no dispute about the fact that the legal form of mental disorder from which the patient suffers is mental illness, it can be seen that this is not correct. If the medical evidence has any weight as medical evidence, rather than as a mere record of observed behaviour, this additional weight can only stem from an acceptance of the validity of the biomedical model. This is the structure supporting the doctor's inferences and opinions about the likely medical and social consequences of not accepting his opinion, and the foundation of his claim to expertise. If a medical practitioner's opinion deserves this expert status, but it is then established that a particular patient's condition has been misdiagnosed, the grounds upon which the patient's detention and compulsory treatment have been justified at best require reformulation. For the biomedical model dictates that a certain diagnosis is associated with a particular treatment plan and prognosis, that is a particular mode of proceeding. Materially different facts necessitate materially different conclusions.

PERSONALITY DISORDERS (CHAP. 21)

The concept of personality implies a certain cohesion and consistency of the personality as a backdrop upon which the vicissitudes of illness and other circumstances may make transitory patterns, but the underlying features remain constant. The terms "personality disorder" and "behaviour disorder" are often used interchangeably, mainly because the nature of an individual's personality is frequently inferred from his behaviour. However, any particular kind of profoundly disturbed behaviour can be exhibited by more than one personality group with different mechanisms pertaining to each. Moreover, whether or not an abnormality of personality actually manifests itself in the form of disordered behaviour, and is defined as a personality disorder, depends to a considerable extent on social circumstances. Definitions of personality disorder are usually value-based. A person is considered to have an abnormal personality if he has to an excessive extent a personality trait which is considered to be undesirable (*e.g.* aggression) or possesses insufficiently a trait considered necessary for a person to be normal (*e.g.* empathy). The section of the International Classification of Mental and Behavioural Disorders (ICD–10) which deals with "disorders of adult personality and behaviour" subdivides them into various types according to clusters of traits that correspond to the most frequent or conspicuous behavioural manifestations. These sub-types are considered to be widely recognised as major forms of personality deviation.

Paranoid personality disorder

A paranoid personality disorder is characterized by excessive sensitivity to setbacks and rebuffs; a tendency to bear grudges; suspiciousness and a pervasive tendency to misconstrue the neutral or friendly actions of others as hostile or contemptuous.

Dissocial personality disorder

A dissocial personality disorder is a personality disorder which usually comes to attention because of a gross disparity between behaviour and the prevailing social norms and is characterized by callous unconcern for the feelings of others; gross and persistent attitude of irresponsibility and disregard for social norms, rules and obligations; incapacity to maintain enduring relationships, though having no difficulty in establishing them; very low tolerance to frustration and a low threshold for discharge of aggression, including violence; incapacity to experience guilt and to profit from experience, particularly punishment; marked proneness to blame others, or to offer plausible rationalizations, for the behaviour that has brought the patient into conflict with society. From a medical viewpoint, the term "dissocial personality disorder" is synonymous with psychopathic disorder. There has never been any consensus about whether psychopathic disorder is an illness with social consequences which can be treated medically or a social condition which needs to be managed or addressed in a non-medical environment. These differences of opinion are linked to different ideas about responsibility and free will and the extent to which the personalities of some people do not enable them to resist or to refrain from anti-social conduct. Various treatment strategies have been suggested although none of them has been shown to be effective in a controlled evaluation. The options include psychotherapy and treatment in a therapeutic community.

MOOD DISORDERS (CHAP. 22)

In mood disorders, the fundamental disturbance is a change of mood to elation or depression (with or without associated anxiety). This mood change is normally accompanied by a change in the overall level of activity and most other symptoms are either secondary to, or easily understood in the context of, such changes. Most of these disorders tend to be recurrent and the onset of individual episodes is often related to stressful events or situations. Mood disorders tend to be cyclic in nature, with stable seasonal fluctuations in the incidence of suicide, and many depressed people experience diurnal variation of mood.

Mood and affect

A distinction is often drawn between an individual's mood and his affect. A person's affect is how he appears to be emotionally affected by a particular idea or mental representation; for example, he is happy, sad or indifferent upon being given certain news. Mood is the pervasive and sustained emotion which colours an individual's whole personality and perception of events.

Unipolar and bipolar disorder

Depression and mania may be viewed as lying at two opposite poles and classifications of mental disorder generally distinguish between unipolar and bipolar mood disorders. According to the classical model, the disturbed mood of some people will be confined to either depression or mania — unipolar disorder. The mood of other individuals is more variable, sometimes located at one pole (depression), sometimes at the other (mania). Mood disorders characterised by fluctuations of this kind are referred to as bipolar disorders and the patient's history characteristically includes one or more episodes of both depression and mania. However, it now seems to be the case that some 80–90 per cent of patients experiencing mania will eventually experience a full depressive episode, although the converse is not also true — only 10 per cent of patients suffering from depression will later have a manic episode. It is therefore relatively rare for patients to suffer only from repeated episodes of mania and even these patients resemble those who have at least occasional episodes of depression in terms of their family history, premorbid personality, age of onset, and long-term prognosis. Because this is so, patients who experience a second manic episode are, according to the ICD–10 classification, reclassified as suffering from a "bipolar affective disorder" rather than from recurrent manic episodes, despite the absence of any history of intervening depression.

Depressive episodes

The classification of depressive episodes specifies three levels of severity — mild, moderate, and severe. Severe depressive episodes are of two kinds — severe depressive episode without psychotic symptoms and and severe depressive episode with psychotic symptoms The management of severe depressive episodes may necessitate hospital admission and, if there is a significant risk of suicide, continuous observation. In-patient treatment almost invariably includes medication or ECT. Cognitive therapy or some other kind of psychological treatment may be indicated and several trials suggest that the relapse rate following cognitive therapy is lower than after drug treatment alone. In rare, intractable, cases psychosurgery is occasionally offered. The outcome for mood disorders is generally more favourable than for schizophrenia.

Manic episodes

Manic episodes are characterised by elevated mood and an increase in the quantity and speed of physical and mental activity. They usually begin abruptly and last for between two weeks and four of five months, with a median duration about four months. The risk of recurrence is high, particularly if the first episode occurs before the age of 30 years, although recovery is usually complete between episodes. Three degrees of severity of manic episode are specified in the ICD classification, all of which share the common underlying characteristics of elevated mood and an increase in the quantity and speed of physical and mental activity: hypomania; mania without psychotic symptoms; and mania with psychotic symptoms. Treatment may require hospitalisation and three different drugs are widely used — chlorpromazine, haloperidol and lithium. The first line of treatment in an acute manic episode is antipsychotic medication (*i.e.* chlorpromazine or haloperidol), often in conjunction with an anti-manic or mood-stabilising drug, such as lithium.

SCHIZOPHRENIA AND RELATED PSYCHOSES (CHAP. 23)

The majority of people detained under the Mental Health Act 1983 are diagnosed as suffering from a form of mental illness known as schizophrenia. Schizophrenia is commonly thought of as a psychiatric term for a range of experiences which the majority of the population describe as "madness." Beyond the public perception, what schizophrenia is is difficult to define and it is impossible to point to any single defining pathology, symptom or cluster of symptoms, common to all people so diagnosed. It is therefore important to realise at the outset that schizophrenia is a model the validity of which has yet to be demonstrated. For introductory purposes, the description of schizophrenia in the International Classification of Diseases gives an idea of the broad range of experiences associated with the diagnosis:

> "The schizophrenic disorders are characterised in general by fundamental and characteristic distortions of thinking and perception, and by inappropriate or blunted affect ... The most intimate thoughts, feelings, and acts are often felt to be known to or shared by others, and explanatory delusions may develop, to the effect that natural or supernatural forces are at work to influence the afflicted individual's thoughts and actions in ways that are often bizarre. The individual may see himself or herself as the pivot of all that happens. Hallucinations, especially auditory, are common and may comment on the individual's behaviour or thoughts ... Perplexity is also common early on and frequently leads to a belief that everyday situations possess a special, usually sinister, meaning intended uniquely for the individual. In the characteristic schizophrenic disturbance of thinking ... thinking becomes vague, elliptical, and obscure, and its expression in speech sometimes incomprehensible. Breaks and interpolations in the train of thought are frequent, and thoughts may seem to be withdrawn by some outside agency. Mood is characteristically shallow, capricious, or incongruous. Ambivalence and disturbance of volition may appear as inertia, negativism, or stupor. Catatonia may be present."

Paranoid, hebephrenic and catatonic schizophrenia

Three sub-types of schizophrenia have classically been recognised: paranoid, hebephrenic and catatonic. However, the persons assigned to each of the three categories show a marked variability both in terms of their symptoms and outcomes. Paranoid schizophrenia is dominated by relatively stable, often paranoid delusions, usually accompanied by hallucinations, particularly of the auditory variety, and perceptual disturbances. Disturbances of affect, volition and speech, and catatonic symptoms, are absent or relatively inconspicuous. Hebephrenic schizophrenia is a form of schizophrenia in which affective changes are prominent, delusions and hallucinations fleeting and fragmentary, behaviour irresponsible and unpredictable, and mannerisms common. The mood is shallow and inappropriate, thought is disorganised, and speech is incoherent. There is a tendency to social isolation. Catatonic schizophrenia is dominated by prominent psychomotor disturbances that may alternate between extremes such as hyperactivity and stupor, or automatic obedience and negativism. Constrained attitudes and postures may be maintained for long periods. Episodes of violent excitement may be a striking feature.

Course, outcome and treatment

Historically, schizophrenia was believed to run a progressive downhill course while affective disorders relapsed repeatedly but recovered fully each time. However, the outcome varies between prolonged recovery, an intermittent course, and prolonged psychosis of severe or mild degrees. Approximately one-third of patients diagnosed as suffering from schizophrenia completely recover from their illnesses, one-third show an intermediate outcome, and in one-third of cases the illness takes the traditional deteriorating course. It is not possible to predict which patients will respond to antipsychotic medication, or to distinguish those patients who will make a natural recovery from those who will require medication in order to improve. It appears that the number of patients receiving medication who relapse within a given period is about half that of patients taking a placebo. Nevertheless, medication probably only postpones rather than prevents relapse. Medication and social intervention appear to produce the best outcome and psychotherapy adds little. The major therapeutic effects of antipsychotic drugs are seen when used to treat acute psychoses. Their effects include a reduction of positive symptoms such as hallucinations, delusions and thought disorder. There is also a normalisation of psychomotor disturbance (excitement or retardation) and information processing. Antipsychotics are also used in the long-term treatment of patients in remission (maintenance therapy).

ORGANIC DISORDERS (CHAP. 24)

Chapter 24 describes the brain and nervous system and deals with organic disorders commonly arising in old age, such as dementia; epilepsy; endocrine disorders; and toxic disorders.

Disorders commonly affecting older people

Older people experience the same range of mental disorders and mood disorders contribute up to half the workload of a comprehensive psychogeriatric service. Compulsory admission is used for about five per cent of people aged 65 or over who come into psychiatric wards. Delirium is a state of acute mental confusion characterized by impairment of consciousness which manifests itself as reduced clarity of awareness of the environment. It is quite common among older people, particularly those with concurrent physical illness. Dementia is not a single disease but a generic term covering numerous conditions that have certain clinical features in common. More particularly, it is a syndrome associated with a variety of diseases in which there is degeneration and atrophy of the brain. The characteristics of a dementing illness are global intellectual impairment (impairment of several aspects of cognition at the same time) and preservation of clear consciousness. Memory impairment and loss of intellectual capacities are severe enough to interfere with social or occupational functioning. In the majority of cases, the type of dementia is established as Alzheimer's disease, which is found at post-mortem in 60 per cent of deceased hospitalized patients previously diagnosed as having dementia. Cerebro-vascular disease including strokes is established as the cause in a further 20 per cent of cases and a combination of the two in another 10 per cent. Both diagnoses are presumptive and must await confirmation after death.

Epilepsy

About 4–6 persons per thousand suffer from epilepsy and patients are said to have epilepsy if they have a chronic condition characterised by recurrent seizures. Seizures are characterised by abnormal electrical activity in the brain. Anti-convulsive drugs form the mainstay of treatment.

Endocrine disorders

The endocrine system consists of a collection of glands that produce hormones, secreting them directly into the bloodstream. A hormone is a chemical messenger which, having been formed in one organ or gland, is carried in the blood to a target organ or tissue where it influences activity. Endocrine disorder can be accompanied by prominent mental irregularity and epochs of life marked by endocrine change, such as pregnancy and the menopause, appear to be associated with special liability to mental disturbance. With some endocrine disorders, such as myxoedema and Addison's disease, the psychiatric abnormalities are regularly intrusive to such a degree that there is a constant risk of mistaken diagnoses.

Toxic psychoses

The taking of certain drugs and the abuse of alcohol may adversely affect the user's mental state. It may initially be unclear whether the ingestion of illegal drugs has triggered an episode of mental illness, which may then be prolonged, or whether the symptoms will begin to subside once the drug exits the body. Prolonged high doses of amphetamines may lead to a mental state indistinguishable from paranoid schizophrenia. Some studies suggest that excessive use of cannabis over long periods of time can cause psychiatric disturbance but the evidence is inconclusive. The effects of cocaine are similar to those of amphetamines and it blocks the re-uptake of dopamine. Euphoria is usually the predominant change of mood associated with LSD but this may be followed later by sudden swings to depression, panic or a profound state of desolation. The psychoses which follow are usually of schizophrenic type. Wernicke's Encephalopathy is an *acute* organic reaction to severe thiamine deficiency, often resulting from alcoholism combined with an inadequate food intake. Wernicke's Encephalopathy may progress to the *chronic* condition known as Korsakoff's psychosis, from which only about 20 per cent. of patients recover. Here, there is profound impairment of recent memory.

FINAL REMARKS

A free man is he that is not hindered from doing that which he has the will to do. By liberty we mean a power of acting or not acting according to the determination of the will and this hypothetical liberty is universally allowed to belong to everyone who is not a prisoner and in chains.[19] Mere incapacity to attain a goal is not lack of freedom, it being nonsense to say that a person is not free to do that which he is in any case incapable of doing. Liberty is therefore the area within which an individual can act unobstructed by others and coercion implies the deliberate interference of other human beings within the area in which they would otherwise act.[20] The words freedom and liberty are interchangeable and to coerce a man is to deprive him of freedom.[21] The wider the area of non-interference the wider a person's freedom and the disagreement historically has been about how wide this area should be. The goal is equality of liberty insofar as circumstances permit. Complete liberty, that is anarchy, where the individual free from any control or restriction is free to do or not to do according as he chooses, leads but to boundless interference with others, the suppression of the weak by the strong, injustice, inequality. The fulfilment of some of our ideals (such as justice) makes the fulfilment of others (such as liberty) impossible, such that the notion of total human fulfilment is a formal contradiction. No one can be absolutely free and all must give up some of their liberty to preserve the rest, but total self-surrender is self-defeating. Furthermore, the liberty of some at times depends on the restraint of others in that the freedom of some must at times be curtailed to secure the freedom of others. Where there is no law there is no freedom or justice and certain actions are worse for us than the amount of restraint needed to repress them. The "extent of a man's, or a people's, liberty to choose to live as they desire must be weighed against the claims of many other values, of which equality, or justice, or happiness, or security, or public order are perhaps the most obvious examples."[22] Whether individuals "should be allowed certain liberties at all depends on the priority given by society to different values and the crucial point is the criterion by which it has to be decided that a particular liberty should or should not be allowed, or that its exercise is in need of restraint."[23] In the context of legislation concerning mental health, the importance to members of society of individual liberty, of protecting them from harm arising from laws which permit considerable freedom of action, of protecting incapacitated persons from exploitation or self-harm, of alleviating suffering and illness, and of restoring to health those members of society whose health has declined, are all legitimate aims, in that they reflect values embraced by virtually all members of society. But "we are faced with

---

19 D. Hume, *An Enquiry concerning Human Understanding* (ed. Sir L.A. Selby-Bigge, Oxford University Press, 1893), p.95.

20 John Stuart Mill, *On Liberty* (Wm. Collins Sons & Co. Ltd., 1962, first publ. 1859), p.135. Mill was of the opinion that the "only purpose for which power can rightfully be exercised over any member of a civilized community, against his will, is to prevent harm to others. His own good, either physical or moral, is not a sufficient warrant ... Over himself, over his own body and mind, the individual is sovereign." This passage, often quoted in articles on mental health legislation, seems to have most often been read from a secondary source, because no reference is ever made to the important qualification which forms the first sentence of the very next paragraph: "It is, perhaps, hardly necessary to say that this doctrine is meant to apply only to human beings in the maturity of their faculties ... Those who are still in a state to require being taken care of by others, must be protected against their own actions as well as against external injury."

21 Sir Isaiah Berlin, *Four Essays on Liberty* (Oxford University Press, 1969). The summary here is largely based on the essay, "Two Concepts of Liberty," first published in 1958.

22 *Ibid.,* p.170.

23 R.W.M. Dias, *Jurisprudence* (Butterworths, 5th ed., 1985), p.109.

choices between ends equally ultimate, and claims equally absolute, the realisation of some of which must inevitably involve the sacrifice of others. Indeed, it is because this is their situation that men place such immense value upon the freedom to choose."[24] The temper of our own times is such that the current emphasis in mental health practice is very much on public safety, rather than individual liberty, and recent mental health legislation is to be construed with regard to this fact. Nevertheless, the enduring impression left after spending many years visiting psychiatric wards is not one of fear or dangerousness, but of suffering and an often disarming kindness on the part of those who have lost their liberty. Although compelled to submit to the will of others, and forced to accept medication which, if mentally beneficial, often produces severe physical discomfort, and may physically disable for life, most patients remain dignified and courteous, and retain the compassion to respond to the plight of others in a similarly unfortunate situation. Equally remarkable is their striving to be free members of society after many years outside society, even when many other higher faculties are profoundly impaired. A hospital is not a prison but for the individual concerned both involve detention and a complete loss of that right most important to him, so that Byron's words — "Eternal spirit of the chainless Mind ! / Brightest in dungeons, Liberty ! thou art" — are often an apt description of the individual's predicament. This desire for autonomy, and many people cannot conceive of a life which is worthwhile and fulfilling without such self-determination, is not to be confused with any desire to abuse liberty, and so not to be caught up in the contemporary controversies about how the law should respond to those who show a disregard for the law and for civic responsibility. On the one hand stands liberty, a right which the law should always favour and guard, on the other licence, a use of liberty to contravene the law, which the law must of necessity always punish. While it is not infrequently necessary to deprive an individual of his liberty on the ground of mental disorder, and one must have the courage to do that where necessary, one must always be appreciative of the enormity of the act — of the fact that the right enjoyed by those others present, and denied to this individual, is the most important right known to English law. While there is broad agreement that tribunals have carried out their functions conscientiously, the conduct of an independent review months after the commencement of a person's detention can never adequately compensate him for the loss of the right to judicial hearing before the event. Nor, when a person has been detained under an administrative procedure, can it be just to provide that he is not entitled to be released unless he can satisfy a court of law that there are no grounds in law for detaining him — if his detainers cannot show the existence of grounds for his detention then it is objectionable to continue to detain him merely because he cannot demonstrate their absence.

---

[24]   Sir Isaiah Berlin, *Four Essays on Liberty* (Oxford University Press, 1969), p.168.

PART II — THE LAW

Detention, guardianship and supervision

2. Legal definitions of mental disorder

INTRODUCTION

"Mental disorder" is defined in section 1 and means "mental illness, arrested or incomplete development of mind, psychopathic disorder and any other disorder or disability of mind."[1] The Act distinguishes four particular "forms" or "classes" of mental disorder: mental illness (**060**), psychopathic disorder (**082**), severe mental impairment (**070**) and mental impairment (**070**).[2] No one may be dealt with under the Act as suffering from mental disorder, or from any form of mental disorder, by reason only of promiscuity or other immoral conduct, sexual deviancy or dependence on alcohol or drugs.[3]

THE FOUR FORMS OF MENTAL DISORDER

"Mental illness" is not statutorily defined. Unless the context otherwise requires, the other forms of disorder have the meanings given to them in section 1(2) of the Act—

- "Severe mental impairment" means a state of arrested or incomplete development of mind which includes severe impairment of intelligence and social functioning and is associated with abnormally aggressive or seriously irresponsible conduct on the part of the person concerned and "severely mentally impaired" shall be construed accordingly;

- "Mental impairment" means a state of arrested or incomplete development of mind (not amounting to severe mental impairment) which includes significant impairment of intelligence and social functioning and is associated with abnormally aggressive or seriously irresponsible conduct on the part of the person concerned and "mentally impaired" shall be construed accordingly;

- "Psychopathic disorder" means a persistent disorder or disability of mind (whether or not including significant impairment of intelligence) which results in abnormally aggressive or seriously irresponsible conduct on the part of the person concerned.

---

[1]   Mental Health Act 1983, s.1(2).
[2]   *Ibid.*, s.1(2).
[3]   *Ibid.*, s.1(3).

Significance of the classification

A patient who suffers from one or more of the four specific forms of mental disorder will necessarily come within the general definition of "mental disorder." The converse is not also true. The definition of "mental disorder" includes individuals with a mental handicap not amounting to mental impairment or severe mental impairment and a rather disparate group of people who suffer from some "disorder or disability of mind" not amounting to mental illness or psychopathic disorder.

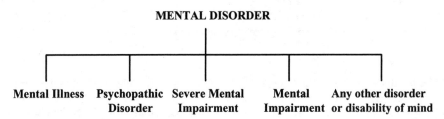

MENTAL DISORDER

Mental Illness	**Psychopathic Disorder**	**Severe Mental Impairment**	**Mental Impairment**	**Any other disorder or disability of mind**

The need for a true mental disorder

The European Convention on Human Rights permits the "lawful detention... of persons of unsound mind" in accordance with a procedure prescribed by law.[4] A "person of unsound mind" means a person who "by definition ... cannot be held fully responsible for his actions."[5] Lawful detention requires "the existence of a specific condition of mental ill-health."[6] Except in emergency cases, the individual concerned must be reliably shown to be of unsound mind, that is to say, a true mental disorder must be established before a competent authority "on the basis of objective medical expertise."[7] This implies that a finding of mental disorder must be consistent with a recognised diagnostic system, such as the International Classification of Diseases (ICD–10, **1117**). For continued confinement to be lawful the disorder must persist.

Previous legal classifications

The legal classification of mental disorders dates back to medieval times and the present scheme should be considered within its historical context. Several terms now in use have their origins in earlier legislation. Where the statutory terminology has been amended, these changes have been partly substantive and partly euphemistic. The authority for the detention or guardianship of some patients whose cases are reviewed by tribunals dates back to these earlier provisions and will originally have been founded upon the grounds of "subnormality," "mental deficiency," or an obsolete definition of "psychopathic disorder." In practice, care needs to be taken to ensure that such patients are "mentally disordered" as now defined by the law.

---

[4]   European Convention on Human Rights, Art. 5(1)(e). The term "person of unsound mind" was also used in the Mental Treatment Act 1930 but replaced by the term "mental illness" in 1959.

[5]   *X. v. United Kingdom* (1981) 4 E.H.R.R. 181, at para. 82. However, the term is "not one that can be given a definitive interpretation ... it is a term whose meaning is continually evolving as research in psychiatry progresses, an increasing flexibility in treatment is developing and society's attitudes to mental illness change, in particular so that a greater understanding of the problems of mental patients is becoming more widespread." *Winterwerp v. The Netherlands* (1979) 2 E.H.R.R. 387.

[6]   *X. v. United Kingdom* (1981) 4 E.H.R.R. 181, at para. 79.

[7]   *Winterwerp v. The Netherlands* (1979) 2 E.H.R.R. 387.

Admission trends

During the year ending 31 March 1996, 8670 (or 98.2 per cent.) of the 8,826 patients admitted to NHS hospitals for treatment under Part II of the Act were classified as suffering from mental illness. Of the remainder, 85 were classified as mentally impaired (1 per cent.), 55 as having a psychopathic disorder (0.6 per cent.), and 16 as suffering from severe mental impairment (0.2 per cent.). Of those admitted to NHS hospitals under Part III, 1225 were classified as mentally ill (92.3 per cent.), 57 as mentally impaired (4.3 per cent.), 44 as having a psychopathic disorder (3.3 per cent.), and only one patient as suffering from severe mental impairment (0.1 per cent.). Overall, this means that about 14 of every thousand persons compulsorily admitted to hospital suffered from mental impairment, 10 from a psychopathic disorder, and less than two from severe mental impairment.[8]

THE PURPOSE OF CLASSIFICATION

To a significant extent, the statutory terms are terms of art and have no fixed or static meaning. They are "generic terms,"[9] "administrative groupings,"[10] adopted for the purpose of legal categorisation. Their ambit will fluctuate over time as the meaning of "mental illness" and the words used to define the other terms fluctuate in response to changes in medical knowledge and social attitudes. However, legally defining "mental disorder" and sub-dividing disorders into different classes does serve the useful purpose of defining, as far as practicable, the group of citizens to whom the various statutory provisions apply and the circumstances in which resort may be made to compulsory powers.[11] Although the classes are defined in very general terms, and so permit a medical practitioner or a tribunal a broad discretion, the prohibitions in section 1(3), and the fact that the classes exist and are defined at all, demonstrates that the terms are not infinitely elastic or meaningless. While each is capable of sustaining a wide interpretation, each ultimately has a boundary.

THE CONSEQUENCES OF CLASSIFICATION

The way in which a person's mental state is legally classified has important consequences. Provided that the other statutory conditions are satisfied, a person who suffers from "mental disorder" generally may be admitted to hospital for assessment.[12] However, a person must suffer from a condition which falls within one or more of the four specific statutory classes before he can be detained for treatment, received into guardianship, or subjected to statutory supervision following discharge.[13] For some purposes, the statutory procedures further distinguish between what have come to be known as the "major" (mental illness and severe mental impairment) and "minor" (psychopathic disorder and mental impairment) forms of mental disorder.[14]

---

[8]   *Statistical Bulletin 1997/4* (Department of Health, 1997).

[9]   The phrase used in the *Report of the Committee on Mentally Abnormal Offenders*, Cmnd. 6244 (1975).

[10]   The phrase used in the *Report of the Royal Commission on the Law Relating to Mental Illness and Mental Deficiency*, Cmnd. 169 (1957).

[11]   See paragraph 60 of the *Report of the Royal Commission on the Law Relating to Mental Illness and Mental Deficiency*, Cmnd. 169 (1957): "More general terms will however also be needed to describe the ... main groups which need to be differentiated for broad administrative or legal purposes ... because there are differing considerations in connection with the use of compulsory powers."

[12]   See Mental Health Act 1983, s.2(2)(a).

[13]   See *ibid.*, ss.3, 7, 25A, 36, 37, 38, 43, 44, 47 and 48.

[14]   The terms were coined by Bridge J. in *Re V.E. (Mental Patient)* [1972] 3 W.L.R. 669, at 677–678.

Classification of mental impairment or psychopathic disorder

A person who suffers only from a minor form of mental disorder may not be remanded or removed to hospital for treatment under sections 36 or 48 of the Act. Interim orders apart,[15] no application, order or direction may be made authorising such a person's admission to hospital for treatment unless in-patient treatment is likely to alleviate or prevent a deterioration of his condition.[16] Nor may the authority for an unrestricted patient's detention be renewed for a further period unless it appears that further in-patient treatment is likely to confer such a benefit.[17] A tribunal is not, however, required to discharge a patient who is liable to be detained on account of such a form of mental disorder merely because it is of the opinion that his condition is untreatable in this sense.[18]

Classification of "mental illness" or "severe mental impairment"

Where the conditions specified in the Act are satisfied, a person who suffers from mental illness or severe mental impairment may be detained or received into guardianship under any of the provisions in the Act. It is not a prerequisite of admission or renewal that in-patient treatment is likely to alleviate or prevent a deterioration of his condition.

RECLASSIFICATION

When a person is received into guardianship, admitted to hospital for treatment or placed under statutory supervision, the application, order or direction which authorises that will specify the form or forms of mental disorder from which he has been found to suffer.[19] Sections 16, 20, 21B, 25F and 72 of the Act allow the application, order or direction to be amended if it later appears that the patient is suffering from a form of disorder other than that specified. The reclassification of an unrestricted patient who is detained for treatment may necessitate his immediate discharge.

Reclassification at the time of renewal

A restriction order or restriction direction once made remains in force until discharged. In all other cases, the authority for a patient's detention, guardianship or supervision will lapse unless periodically renewed for periods of six or twelve months at a time in accordance with the provisions of sections 20 or 25G. The authority is renewed upon the medical officer in charge of his treatment furnishing a report stating that in his opinion the statutory conditions for renewal are satisfied. In order to form an opinion as to this, the doctor is required to examine the patient during the final two months of the period of detention, guardianship or supervision which is drawing to a close.[20]

---

[15] See Mental Health Act 1983, s.38.

[16] A person who suffers from or is suspected to suffer from such a form of disorder may, irrespective of the condition's treatability, be received into guardianship, detained for assessment under Part II, remanded to hospital for the preparation of a report under section 35, or detained in pursuance of an interim hospital order under section 38.

[17] See Mental Health Act 1983, s.20(4).

[18] See *R. v. Canons Park Mental Health Review Tribunal, ex p. A* [1994] 3 W.L.R. 630, C.A.

[19] There are two exceptions. No form of mental disorder is recorded in the case of a patient who is admitted to hospital under section 5 of the Criminal Procedure (Insanity) Act 1964, nor where a section 2 patient is transferred into guardianship under section 19(1)(a) of the 1983 Act.

[20] Mental Health Act 1983, ss.20(3), 20(6).

Section	To whom it applies	When it applies
▪ Section 16		Reclassification other than when furnishing a report renewing the authority for the patient's detention or guardianship.
▪ Section 20	*Unrestricted detained patients and patients subject to guardianship*	Reclassification in the course of furnishing such a renewal report.
▪ Section 21B(8)		Reclassification of a patient who has returned to the place where he is required to be after more than 28 days absence from there without leave.
▪ Section 25F	*Unrestricted patients subject to after-care under supervision*	Reclassification other than when furnishing a report renewing the authority for the patient's supervision.
▪ Section 25G		Reclassification in the course of furnishing such a renewal report.
▪ Section 72(5)	*All unrestricted patients*	Reclassification by a tribunal which does not direct that the patient shall cease to be liable to be detention or subject to guardianship or statutory supervision.

The renewal criteria

In cases involving patients who are detained for treatment, the form or forms of mental disorder which the responsible medical officers finds the patient is suffering from at the time of his examination determine the conditions which must be satisfied before he may complete a report renewing the patient's detention.[21] If the responsible medical officer's opinion is that a patient suffers only from psychopathic disorder or mental impairment, the authority for his detention may only be renewed if it appears that medical treatment in a hospital is likely to alleviate or prevent a deterioration of the patient's condition ("the treatability test").[22] Where, however, his opinion is that the patient suffers from mental illness or severe mental impairment, renewal is permissible on the alternative ground that he would, if discharged, be unlikely to be able to care for himself, to obtain the care which he needs, or to guard himself against serious exploitation ("the vulnerability test"). The grounds for renewing the detention of a patient who suffers from mental illness or severe mental impairment are therefore somewhat broader.

---

[21] Where a patient is subject to guardianship or after-care under supervision, the same renewal criteria apply irrespective of the particular form of mental disorder from which the patient suffers. See *ibid.*, ss.20(7) and 25G(4).

[22] Mental Health Act 1983, s.20(4).

Reclassification upon the furnishing of a renewal report

It may be the case that the form of mental disorder specified in a renewal report differs from the form(s) previously specified. Where this happens, the Act provides that the application, order or direction shall have effect as if the form of disorder specified in the renewal report were specified in the original document, and in any such case the medical practitioner need not also furnish a report under section 16 or 25F (see below). No additional right of application to a Mental Health Review Tribunal arises where reclassification is effected through the furnishing of a renewal report, nor need the patient or his nearest relative be informed that reclassification has taken place.

Reclassification other than at the time of renewal

Sections 16 and 25F enable an unrestricted patient's condition to be reclassified by the registered medical practitioner in charge of his treatment at a time other than when furnishing a renewal report.[23] More specifically, if it appears to that doctor that the patient is suffering from a form of disorder other than the form or forms specified in the application, order or direction, he may furnish a report to that effect. Upon doing so, the application, order or direction takes effect as if the form of mental disorder recorded in the report were specified in it. The hospital managers, guardian or responsible after-care bodies, as the case may be, must ensure that the patient and his nearest relative are informed of the report. They may then apply to a tribunal during the following 28 days, unless the report relates to a detained patient and has the effect of terminating the authority for his detention (see below).[24]

Patients who are liable to be detained

If the effect of a report furnished under section 16 is that an unrestricted patient detained for treatment is suffering from psychopathic disorder or mental impairment, but not from mental illness or severe mental impairment, the report must also state the responsible medical officer's opinion as to whether further medical treatment in hospital is likely to alleviate or prevent a deterioration of the patient's condition. Where his opinion is that such treatment is not likely to have that effect, section 16(2) provides that the hospital managers' authority to detain the patient shall cease. In all other cases, the right to apply to a tribunal referred to above arises.

Reclassification under section 72(5)

Section 72(5) provides that a tribunal which does not terminate the authority for an unrestricted patient's detention, guardianship or supervision may direct that the form of disorder from which he is recorded as suffering shall be amended. It has been noted that the form of disorder from which a patient suffers has no legal significance in guardianship and supervision application cases — the grounds for renewal are the

---

[23]   In the case of a patient subject to after-care under supervision it is his community responsible medical officer (**148**) who furnishes such a report. Where a patient subject to guardianship has a private guardian it is his nominated medical attendant (**148**). In all other cases, the report is furnished by the patient's responsible medical officer (**147**).

[24]   There is one exception to this. Where a patient subject to after-care under supervision is reclassified in this way, he may request that the responsible after-care bodies do not inform his nearest relative. See page 452.

same in all cases. In the case of detained patients, the renewal criteria do vary according to the form of disorder from which the patient suffers. Nevertheless, where a tribunal directs reclassification from a major to a minor disorder, or vice-versa, its direction does not thereby determine the renewal criteria to be applied by the patient's responsible medical officer when he examines the patient at the close of that particular period of detention. Those criteria are determined by the form(s) of disorder from which that medical officer, or his successor, finds the patient to be suffering at the time of his examination.[25]

Patients absent without leave for more than 28 days

As to the new provisions concerning the reclassification of unrestricted patients who are returned to the place where they are required to be after more than 28 days absence without leave, see pages 294 and 628. The effect is similar to that just described. If a report furnished under section 21B in respect of a returned patient has the effect of renewing the authority for his detention or guardianship then no additional right to apply to a tribunal arises if it also has the secondary effect of reclassifying him. However, if a report furnished under section 21B merely has the effect of reclassifying him, because it does not also have effect as a renewal report, a right to apply to a tribunal does arise by virtue of the patient's reclassification.

DUAL CLASSIFICATION

A patient may suffer from more than one psychiatric condition at the same time. For example, a person who suffers from a psychopathic disorder or mental impairment may later develop a mental illness. The Act recognises this fact and provides that a person may be legally classified, or reclassified, as suffering from more than one form of mental disorder at the same time.[26]

Whether the classes overlap

The case of *W. v. L.*[27] is sometimes taken as authority for the proposition that a single psychiatric condition may be classified under two legal classes at the same time. The reported facts were that there was a consensus of medical opinion to the effect that the patient suffered from a psychopathic disorder as statutorily defined; he had a persistent disorder which resulted in seriously irresponsible conduct. However, a "distinguished consultant" who later examined him concluded that the conduct which other doctors had previously ascribed to a disordered personality was in fact the result of an organic condition, that is a mental illness. Lord Denning M.R. concluded that there was evidence upon which the county court judge was entitled to

---

[25]   See the wording of section 20. Given that the medical officer is not bound by the classification made by the Crown Court or the Court of Appeal in cases where either of those courts makes a hospital or guardianship order, there can be no reason for believing that he is bound by any previous classification made by a tribunal. More generally, see the judgment of Laws J. in *R. v. South Western Hospital Managers, ex p. M.* [1993] Q.B. 683 as to the extent to which directions made by a tribunal are binding.

[26]   See paragraph 188 of the *Report of the Royal Commission on the Law Relating to Mental Illness and Mental Deficiency*, Cmnd. 169 (1957): "From the medical point of view ... there is no clear-cut distinction between our ... groups ... One patient may exhibit symptoms of more than one type of disorder, simultaneously or at different times, and at one time may, for administrative or legal purposes, be regarded as falling into a different group from that in which he has previously been classified."

[27]   *W. v. L.* [1974] Q.B. 711, 719, C.A.

be satisfied that the patient had a mental illness and "not merely ... a psychopathic disorder" and Lawton L.J. observed that "although the case may fall within the definition of 'psychopathic disorder' ... it also falls within the classification of 'mental illness.'"

Chronic mental illness

The proposition which has been derived from that decision certainly has significant legal and practical consequences. Because mental illness is undefined and psychopathic disorder is so generally defined, the conditions of many mentally ill patients will necessarily be classifiable within both classes unless some account is taken of the historical development of the terms and the clinical and lay associations which they bear — associations which Parliament would have had in mind when it gave the classes their names. Specifically, all patients with a chronic mental illness have a persistent disorder or disability of mind and, consequently, any chronic mental illness which results in abnormally aggressive or seriously irresponsible conduct will constitute a psychopathic disorder. Thus, if section 1(2) is literally interpreted, chronic paranoid schizophrenia will often also come within the definition of a psychopathic disorder as will any chronic mental illness which is severely socially disabling or results in self-injurious conduct.

"Persistent disorder of personality"

Insofar as there is a problem, it stems in part from the fact that the original definition of psychopathic disorder in the 1959 Bill, which referred to a "persistent disorder of personality," was amended during the Parliamentary debates in an attempt to emphasise that something more than a disorder of personality was required; the phrase "a disorder or disability of mind" was therefore substituted for it. However, this evidently had the unintended consequence of leading the doctors in *W. v. L.*, and arguably the court also, to classify as psychopathically disordered a patient whose conduct was not attributable to a persistent disorder of personality. In doing so, the historical distinction between mental illness and psychopathic disorder was eradicated to such an extent that it may reasonably be doubted whether Parliament intended this when it conceived of two broad groups of psychiatric disorders sufficiently distinct to warrant delineation as separate legal classes.

The limitations of W. v. L.

Although some writers have referred to the proposition as if part of the *ratio decidendi*, the point in issue was whether there was evidence of mental illness, which clearly there was. No detailed consideration was therefore given to whether there was evidence of a personality disorder existing independently of the organic illness or the relationship between the two; that issue was academic in terms of the decision which had to be made. The decision is arguably peculiar to a statutory framework which no longer exists following the abolition of the age-limits relating to the civil admissions.

Illnesses, disorders and disabilities

"Mental illness" is undefined except by its own name, which is meant to convey without more a kind of disorder different to "psychopathic disorder" — a term which literally means a disorder of the soul. Mental illness is an "illness," that is something which affects a person's previous ("premorbid") state of health and well-being. It is literally and specifically "an illness of the mind" and not merely a "disorder or disability of mind." In psychopathic disorder, the patient's mind is persistently disordered or disabled but not through illness. To this extent the concept of personality is incorporated within the definition. Unless one preserves this distinction, "mental illness" becomes synonymous with "disorder or disability of mind" so that as many detained patients are likely to fall within both classes as in either of them.

Summary

The law has historically distinguished between lunacy, idiocy and moral insanity. Although the terminology has changed, the present legal classification is essentially a reworking of the same framework and the distinction is worth preserving. A classification of mental illness only is appropriate where a patient's symptoms, including his conduct, are the manifestations of an illness. Psychopathic disorder will be the appropriate classification where a person's conduct is neither the result of a mind affected by illness nor associated with a significant mental handicap. If there is evidence of a disorder of disability of mind which has persisted prior to the onset of illness then a dual classification is permissible but not otherwise.

WHETHER THE CLASSES ARE COMPREHENSIVE

In the fourth edition of Halsbury's Laws, it was said that in ordinary usage the term "mental illness" in the 1959 Act "apparently covers ... all persons who suffer from mental disorder but are not within the categories of severe subnormality, subnormality or psychopathic disorder as defined."[28] As a statement of the law, this was and is a simplification. Section 1(2) makes it clear that persons who suffer only from a condition of arrested or incomplete development of mind are not to be dealt with under the longer-term powers, from which it may be inferred that it would be unlawful to classify them as mentally ill in an attempt to circumvent the prohibition. The presence of the words "any other disorder or disability of mind" in the general definition of "mental disorder" also indicates that not all mental disorders are reducible to one of its four forms. Although not characterised by mental handicap, these "other disorders or disabilities of mind" do not amount to mental illness or a psychopathic disorder. They are essentially psychiatric conditions which are capable of being sufficiently serious to warrant compulsory assessment and treatment for a limited, defined period but not the use of compulsory powers of a potentially unlimited duration.

Mental disorders requiring the use of long-term powers

A stronger view would therefore be that the four forms of mental disorder are comprehensive insofar as Parliament intended, if the medical opinion is that a patient's mental condition is sufficiently disordered that compulsion under one of the longer-term powers is necessary, that condition will *per se* be classifiable within one of the four statutory classes. Specifically, it may be categorised for legal purposes as a "mental illness" if it does not fall within the statutory definitions of the other three forms. In support of the proposition, it may be contended that the term "mental illness" as used in the Act is a legal rather than a clinical concept. Consequently, its

---

[28]   *Halsbury's Laws of England* (Butterworths, 4th ed., 1980), Vol. 30, p.563.

interpretation is ultimately not restricted by any clinical sense in which it is used. Section 1(3) provides that no person may be legally classified as suffering from mental illness solely on account of the matters set out there. Had Parliament intended that the term's interpretation should be further restricted, those prohibitions would have been specified, either by extending the exceptions in section 1(3) or by defining mental illness.

The need for an illness

The view does not seem wholly satisfactory even when expressed in this way. Although the concept of "mental illness" was conceded to be undefinable, there is ample evidence that Parliament considered that the words sufficiently defined themselves as to warrant their use to denote a class of mental disorders fundamentally different from the others; these conditions were illnesses with all that connotes. The concept of an illness embodied within the term was one well understood by the doctors who would bear the responsibility of recommending the use of compulsory powers of an indefinite duration to prospective applicants. It cannot have been Parliament's intention been that the fourth class was to be seen as nothing more than an infinitely elastic administrative category capable of encompassing all other disorders requiring indefinite treatment. Had that been the case, the longer-term powers would be exercisable in respect of persons suffering from one of the three defined forms of disorder or from *"any other disorder or disability of mind"* of the requisite nature or degree. It is therefore preferable to say that the classes are virtually comprehensive as concerns persons who require indefinite treatment or guardianship because of a mental disorder which is associated with or leads to abnormally aggressive or seriously irresponsible conduct on their part; regard being had to the fact that, where no illness or mental handicap can be discerned which accounts for their behaviour, the disorder or disability of mind causing it must be shown to have existed over a considerable period of time. The classes are not, however, in any way comprehensive as regards mental disorders which do not affect a person's conduct in either of these ways. Such a person may only be placed under a guardian or compelled to accept indefinite treatment if there is medical evidence of an illness, that is some condition affecting the individual's ordinary, pre-existing state of mental health. The formulation is clumsy but attempting to simplify it further risks blurring the basic premise that there are some disorders which warrant the use of compulsory powers of a defined duration but not powers capable of existing indefinitely.

MENTAL ILLNESS

A significant proportion of patients detained on the legal ground of mental illness are diagnosed as suffering from schizophrenia (**1227**) or a mood disorder (**1193**). These conditions are universally accepted as constituting mental illness in law. Although "mental illness" is not statutorily defined, the Act does provide that no person may be dealt with as suffering from mental illness by reason only of promiscuity or other immoral conduct, sexual deviancy or dependence on alcohol or drugs.

HISTORICAL DEVELOPMENTS IN TERMINOLOGY

Since early on in English legal history a distinction has generally been drawn between lunatics, whose incapacity was or might be temporary and intermittent, and idiots or natural fools, who lacked capacity from birth and who were incurable.[29] The statutes of the eighteenth and nineteenth centuries variously provided for the apprehension or certification of "lunatics," the "insane," and persons "of insane mind" or "of unsound mind."[30] The terminology of the nineteenth-century statutes was, however, inconsistent. Under the Idiots Act 1886 the terms "idiot" and "imbecile" did not include "lunatics" but the Lunacy Acts of 1845 and 1890, and the Lunatic Asylums Act 1853, provided that the term "lunatic" did include "idiots" as well as "persons of unsound mind."

Mental Treatment Act 1930

The Mental Treatment Act 1930 required that the use of the word "lunatic" cease and substituted for it the term "person of unsound mind."[31] In *Buxton v. Jayne*,[32] Devlin L.J. said that the alteration did not suggest an intent to alter the sense of the Lunacy Act 1890, but rather to substitute a word with less disagreeable associations. The 1930 Act also provided for the voluntary or temporary treatment of persons suffering from "mental illness," whether certifiable under the Lunacy Act as being of "unsound mind" or not.[33] "Mental illness" was not defined and nor has it been in subsequent statutes.

Percy Report (1957)[34]

The Percy Commission of 1954–57 reviewed the statutory terminology. It recognised that the division of mental disorders into legal classes was based on administrative rather than clinical considerations.[35] The Commission considered that the public attitude towards mental disorder had outgrown the term "person of unsound mind." It noted that the term "mentally ill" was by then in general usage in respect of persons dealt with under both the 1890 and 1930 Acts.[36] A new terminology was needed to "mark a step forward from ancient prejudices and fears and to be an outward sign of a real advance in public sympathy."[37] Accordingly, the Percy Report recommended the use in any new statute of the phrase "mental illness," which would be used in the same sense as before and therefore include those who became mentally infirm in old age.[38]

---

[29] See *e.g.* the statutes Praerogativa Regis, Attainder and Forfeiture for Treason (1541), Fines and Recoveries (1580–81); *Beverley's Case* (1603) 4 Co. Rep. 123b; Co. Lit. 247a and 1 Hale P.C. 34; and *ex p. Cranmer* (1806) 12 Ves. 445, *per* Lord Erskine.

[30] For a description of the statutes, see chapters 3, 4 and 9 of the *Report of the Royal Commission on the Law Relating to Mental Illness and Mental Deficiency*, Cmnd. 169 (1957).

[31] Mental Treatment Act 1930, s.20(5). The phrase "criminal lunatic" continued, however, until 1948 when it was replaced by the term "Broadmoor patient."

[32] *Buxton v. Jayne* [1960] 2 All E.R. 688 at 697, C.A.

[33] Mental Treatment Act 1930, ss.1–5.

[34] *Report of the Royal Commission on the Law Relating to Mental Illness and Mental Deficiency*, Cmnd. 169 (1957).

[35] *Ibid.*, para. 185.

[36] *Ibid.*, para. 182.

[37] *Ibid.*, para. 184.

[38] *Ibid.*, para. 189.

Mental Health Act 1959

In accordance with the Commission's recommendation, the use of the phrase "mental illness" was adopted in the Mental Health Act 1959 in preference to "person of unsound mind." Its meaning was left undefined,[39] the Ministry of Health's opinion being that its interpretation was matter for clinical judgment.[40] Subsequently, the absence of any statutory definition has occasionally led to problems in practice.[41]

Butler Report (1975)[42]

The Butler Report considered that the expression denoted "a disorder which has not always existed in the patient but has developed as a condition overlying the sufferer's usual personality."[43] No comprehensive short definition was possible, because the term covered a large group of dissimilar disorders.[44] The Committee proposed that a special verdict, "Not guilty on evidence of mental disorder," should be returnable in criminal proceedings where at the time of the act or omission charged a defendant was suffering from "severe mental illness,"[45] which it defined as follows—[46]

"A mental illness is severe when it has one or more of the following characteristics:—

a. lasting impairment of intellectual functions shown by failure of memory, orientation, comprehension and learning capacity;

b. lasting alteration of mood of such degree as to give rise to a delusional appraisal of the patient's situation, his past or his future, or that of others, or to lack of any appraisal ;

c. delusional beliefs, persecutory, jealous or grandiose;

d. abnormal perceptions associated with delusional misinterpretation of events;

a. thinking so disordered as to prevent reasonable appraisal of the patient's situation or reasonable communication with others."

A Review of the Mental Health Act 1959 (1978)

In 1975, the Government established an interdepartmental committee to review the Act. The Committee's initial suggestions were set out in a consultative document

---

[39]   The Minister of Health referred to the two forms of subnormality and psychopathic disorder as the three "definable forms of mental disorder" (*Hansard*, H.C. Vol. 598, col. 709). In the House of Lords, the Lord Chancellor referred to them by saying that "unlike 'mental illness' these terms are not in general use at present, and we have thought it desirable to define them for the guidance of those applying the compulsory powers" (*Hansard*, H.L. Vol. 216, col. 607).

[40]   *Mental Health Act 1959: Memorandum on Parts I, IV to VII and IX* (D.H.S.S., 1960), para. 40.

[41]   "The view seems to have been taken that doctors and others ... would not in practice have much difficulty in fitting any particular case into its appropriate classification. The facts of this case show how difficult the fitting of particular instances into the statutory classification can be," *per* Lawton L.J. in *W. v. L.* [1974] 1 Q.B. 711 at 719, C.A.

[42]   *Report of the Committee on Mentally Abnormal Offenders*, Cmnd. 6244 (1975).

[43]   *Ibid.*, p.5 and glossary, p.xiv.

[44]   *Ibid.*, para. 5.24.

[45]   *Ibid.*, paras. 18.20 and 18.30.

[46]   *Ibid.*, para. 18.35. Appendix 10 to the Report sets out the conditions which the Committee envisaged would constitute severe mental illness.

published in August 1976.[47] This included a definition of "mental illness" which was virtually identical to the definition of "severe mental illness" in the Butler Report, except that the word "lasting" in paragraphs (a) and (b) of the latter was replaced by the words, "more than temporary." However, when the Government set out its proposals for an amending Bill in a White Paper published in September 1978,[48] it proposed that "mental illness" should remain undefined. Although a few suggestions had been made as to how mental illness might be defined, those comments had underlined the difficulties of producing a definition which would be likely to stand the test of time. Nor, it was said, had there been much evidence that the lack of a definition had led to particular problems.[49]

Mental Health (Amendment) Act 1982

The D.H.S.S.'s notes on the 1982 Bill stated that the expression "mental illness" covered "a wide range of illnesses which may require treatment in hospital and for which the term is in general medical use."[50] The lack of a statutory definition had not caused "any" difficulties in practice.

MENTAL HEALTH ACT 1983

The 1983 Act was a consolidating statute and it repeats the position introduced by the Mental Health (Amendment) Act 1982. The Department of Health's view, expressed in its memorandum on the Act, remains that the term's "operational definition and usage is a matter for clinical judgment in each case."[51] The present legal meaning of mental illness differs from that in the 1959 Act in that section 1(3) states that no person shall be dealt with under the Act as suffering from mental illness by reason only of sexual deviancy or dependence on alcohol or drugs. The 1959 Act had provided simply that such a classification could not be made by reason only of promiscuity or other immoral conduct. The meaning of the phrase "sexual deviancy" is considered below (089). Dependence on alcohol or drugs does not preclude the detention of persons who develop organic psychoses, such as Korsakoff's psychosis, as a result of alcohol or drug abuse.[52]

A form of mental disorder*

The term "disorder" is used in the International Classification of Diseases "to imply the existence of a clinically recognisable set of symptoms or behaviour associated in most cases with distress and with interference with personal functions."[53] Mental illness is one form of mental disorder. It is not defined except by its own name, which is meant to convey without more a form of disorder different to psychopathic

---

[47] *A Review of the Mental Health Act 1959* (H.M.S.O., 1976).
[48] *Review of the Mental Health Act 1959*, Cmnd. 7320 (1978), p.11.
[49] *Ibid.*, para. 1.17.
[50] *Mental Health (Amendment) Bill: Notes on Clauses, House of Commons* (D.H.S.S., 1982).
[51] *Mental Health Act 1983: Memorandum on Parts I to VI, VIII and X* (D.H.S.S., 1987), para. 10.
[52] According to the *Memorandum*, ".. there are no grounds for detaining a person in hospital because of alcohol or drug abuse alone, but it is recognized that alcohol or drug abuse may be accompanied by or associated with mental disorder. It is therefore possible to detain a person who is dependent on alcohol or drugs if he or she is suffering from a mental disorder arising from or suspected to arise from alcohol or drug dependence or from the withdrawal of alcohol or a drug, if all the other relevant conditions are met." *Ibid.*, para. 16.
[53] *ICD–10 Classification of Mental and Behavioural Disorders: Clinical Descriptions and Diagnostic Guidelines* (World Health Organisation, 1992), p.5.

disorder and mental impairment. An illness may be seen as the difference between a person's current state of being and functioning and his state of health immediately prior to the onset of a decline in his health, whether subjectively or objectively apparent. Thus, a disease may also be described as an illness but not all illnesses will be diseases, that is attributable to a change in the body's structure. Mental illness is literally and specifically "an illness of the mind" and not simply, as with psychopathic disorder, a "disorder or disability of mind." In psychopathic disorder, the patient's mind is persistently disordered or disabled but not through illness; to this extent the concept of personality is incorporated within its definition. Unless one preserves this distinction, "mental illness" becomes synonymous with "disorder or disability of mind" and as many detained patients are likely to fall within both classes than in either of them.

JUDICIAL GUIDANCE

The courts have historically been reluctant to attempt to define the term "mental illness" and, prior to that, the term "of unsound mind."[54] The only recent judicial guidance is to be found in the case of *W v. L.*

W. v. L.

[1974] Q.B. 711   *C.A. (Lord Denning M.R., Lawton and Orr L.JJ.)*

The facts of the case were that the patient had placed a cat in an oven; cut the throat of another, having first got it to inhale ammonia; hung a dog and a puppy, using wire on one occasion; and used a knife to threaten his spouse, who was seven months pregnant. There was concern for the future safety of the baby. Notwithstanding all this, the patient's wife refused to consent to an application for his admission to hospital for treatment. County court proceedings were commenced to have the patient's wife displaced as the statutory nearest relative, so that an application could then be made. Although medical opinion was united that the patient suffered from a psychopathic disorder, the 1959 Act provided that no application could be made for his detention for treatment if this was the only form of mental disorder from which he suffered. That was the main problem faced by the county court. The county court judge found the patient to be suffering from mental illness and, having done so, held that his wife's refusal to consent to an application was unreasonable.

Court of Appeal

The appeal against the county court's order was unanimously dismissed by the Court of Appeal. Lord Denning M.R.'s reasons for dismissing the appeal were based solely on the fact that the medical evidence before the county court judge "convinced him that this was mental illness. In particular, a "distinguished consultant" had examined the patient during the 28–day observation period. He had concluded that the acts of cruelty occurred in a state of altered consciousness and were the product of an organic condition, rather than a sadistic, disordered, personality. Since the organic illness resulted in behaviour from which others needed to be protected, the admission criteria were satisfied and the consultant had therefore completed the necessary medical recommendation. On his evidence, the husband "was not suffering merely from a psychopathic disorder." Orr L.J. concurred with Lord Denning M.R.

---

[54] See *e.g. Whysall v. Whysall* [1960] P. 54 at 62–4 and *Buxton v. Jayne* [1960] 2 All E.R. 688 at 697, *per* Lord Devlin : "I am not going to attempt a definition of just what is meant by unsound mind, an expression which the Act itself leaves undefined, nor am I going to search for equivalent language."

The third opinion was given by Lawton L.J., who was troubled by the "large gap" in the legislation in respect of adults diagnosed as suffering from psychopathic disorders "of a kind which were likely, if uncontrolled, to cause harm to others." He expressed concern that a doctor anticipating such harm could only wait "in a state of agonised expectation" to see if it materialised. He concluded that this was "a clear case of the law shutting the stable door after the horse has bolted" and the county court judge had been correct to "safeguard this little baby from the possibility of harm." Within this context, His Lordship said that the words "mental illness" are—

> "ordinary words of the English language. They have no particular medical significance. They have no particular legal significance. How should the courts construe them? ... in the way that ordinary sensible people would construe them. That being in my judgment the right test, then I ask myself, what would the ordinary sensible person have said about the patient's condition in this case if he had been informed of his behaviour ...? In my judgment such a person would have said: 'Well, the fellow is obviously mentally ill.'[55] ... If that be right, then, although the case may fall within the definition of 'psychopathic disorder' ... it also falls within the classification of 'mental illness'; ... it is that application of the sensible person's assessment of the condition, plus the medical indication [of an EEG test] which in my judgment brought the case within the classification of mental illness."

Commentary on W. v. L.

Notwithstanding the reference to "a sensible person's assessment" and the results of an EEG test, the above passage has subsequently been sharply criticised by two eminent writers on mental health law, Gostin[56] and Hoggett,[57] and it may conceivably be faulted on a number of other grounds:

- The words "mental illness" are fairly evidently not ordinary words of the English language. Not only Parliament and the courts but also psychiatrists, philosophers and lexicographers have all failed to agree a simple working definition that adequately encompasses such complex phenomena. It is therefore improbable that ordinary people, however sensible, could do so.

---

[55] The point somewhat ignores the possibility that an ordinary sensible man in *W. v. L.* might have shared the view of the majority of doctors involved in the case and have replied, "Well, the man is obviously a psychopath" since that observation would equally well fit the lay view. The remark attributed to the bystander really says nothing about what constitutes mental illness *per se*. If it has any legal relevance, it is more to do with what constitutes florid mental illness, what used to be called "lunacy" or "unsoundness of mind" (the nature or degree of mental illness required to warrant detention). As Hoggett implies (see Footnote 58), it is an observation about madness.

[56] According to Gostin, "Lord Justice Lawton's view must be unacceptable — mental illness was envisaged as a serious form of mental disorder and it could not be dependant upon any common person's misinformed view of behaviour which is perhaps only eccentric, non-conforming or anti-social. In the absence of any statutory definition of mental illness much will depend on medical opinion, which should be well founded upon behavioural evidence and adequate clinical assessment." L. Gostin, *Mental Health Services — Law and Practice* (Shaw & Sons), para. 9.02.

[57] "It is impossible not to think of this as the 'man must be mad' test. It simply adds fuel to the fire of those who accuse the mental hygiene laws of being a sophisticated machine for the oppression of unusual, eccentric or inconvenient behaviour... It pays scant regard to the painstaking efforts of psychiatrists to distinguish mental health from mental illness by means of carefully described deficiencies, not in behaviour, but in mental functioning." B. Hoggett, *Mental Health Law* (Sweet & Maxwell, 4th ed., 1996), pp.32–33.

- The notion that the words "mental illness" have no particular legal significance is untenable in the context of an Act which provides that different admission, renewal and discharge criteria shall be applied according to the form of disorder from which a patient is found to suffer, and which makes provision for reclassifying patients. Indeed, since the effect of Lawton L.J.'s opinion that the patient was mentally ill had the very significant legal consequence that the patient thereby lost his liberty, the opinion would appear to contradict the proposition used to sustain it.

- If, however, it is correct that the words "mental illness" have no legal significance, their inclusion in the statute would appear to be superfluous.

- The contention that the words have no particular medical significance is difficult to reconcile with a statute which requires that admissions on the ground of mental illness must be founded upon the recommendations of two medical practitioners, one of whom has special experience in the diagnosis or treatment of mental disorder, and both must agree that the patient suffers from mental illness.

- While most people could diagnose mental illness in someone floridly ill, some cases such as that in *W. v. L.* are diagnostically difficult; few ordinary sensible people would be able to recognise an insidious mental illness from the results of a CT scan, EEG or psychometric testing.[58]

- The test would not appear to satisfy the requirement imposed by the European Convention that detention on the ground of unsoundness of mind requires that a "true" mental disorder be established according to objective medical evidence and expertise.

- Insofar as tribunals are concerned, the formulation is really a statement of the lay member's role, which is to provide balance, as a representative of the community outside the legal and medical professions, and to give the responsible lay person's view.[59]

Subsequent case law

The validity of the "Lawton test" was raised as an issue in the case of *ex p. Hayes,* in the context of an appeal against a Mental Health Review Tribunal's finding.

R. v. Mental Health Review Tribunal, ex p. Hayes

9 May 1985 (unreported)   *C.A. (Ackner, Griffiths, Browne-Wilkinson L.JJ.)*

The patient was a restricted patient who was not discharged by the tribunal which reviewed his detention. The tribunal's reasons for its decision included the passage, "It was the 'lay' opinion of the tribunal that the patient is 'not totally sane', that is applying the standard test of mental illness he suffers from a

---

[58]   Although most of the doctors who examined the patient in *W. v. L.* were not of the opinion that he was mentally ill, and the case was diagnostically difficult, it is notable that Lawton L.J. said that the fact that he was mentally ill would nevertheless have been "obvious" to an ordinary lay person.

[59]   *Mental Health Review Tribunals for England and Wales, Annual Report 1994* (Department of Health, May 1995), Appendix 13.

disorder." In the Court of Appeal, it was argued that the tribunal was not entitled to rely "wholly" upon what was expressed to be the lay opinion of the tribunal. Ackner L.J. observed that the so-called "lay opinion" was in fact the test mentioned by Lawton L.J. in *W. v. L.* In the event, the point of law being argued was not determined because the court decided, on the facts, that the tribunal had not relied purely on the Lawton test: their decision had gone on to deal with the medical criteria and issues in the manner which the patient's counsel said was the right approach, that is ignoring the lay opinion.

Commentary

Detention on the ground of mental illness requires evidence of the presence of such an illness from two fully registered medical practitioners, one of whom must be approved by the Secretary of State as having special experience in the diagnosis or treatment of mental disorder. No application, order or direction authorising treatment may be made unless those two doctors agree that the condition constitutes a mental illness. No court may require them to describe as mental illness a condition which they do not regard as constituting such a form of mental disorder. Likewise, the fact that a prospective applicant may think a person is mentally ill is immaterial. When assessing the presence of mental illness and signing medical recommendations, the doctors owe a duty of care to the patient. However, a medical opinion is no more than that. Authority to detain a person requires an application, order or direction. The medical opinion must therefore be satisfactory from the point of view of the person to whom the recommendation is given. It will not be satisfactory, and the grounds for detention will not be made out, if the doctors' opinion is based on an interpretation of the term which is inconsistent with the statutory framework, does not accord with an established body of medical opinion, or is significantly at variance with what ordinary, sensible people understand the term to mean. If this is correct, the reference made by Lawton L.J. to the ordinary, sensible person is an important part of any formal finding that a person is mentally ill. It is, however, arguably the last stage of any such finding. A testing of medical opinion against ordinary standards of commonsense rather than the use of lay opinion to define what constitutes mental illness — if an ordinary, sensible person met the patient in the street would he *also* think that the patient was mentally ill?

OTHER CONTEMPORARY GUIDANCE

Several international bodies have attempted to define the term and definitions are to be found in various foreign statutes. Mental illness is statutorily defined in the Northern Irish but not the Scottish legislation.

United Nations Principles, Guidelines & Guarantees

Mental illness is defined in the United Nations' *"Principles, Guidelines and Guarantees for the Protection of Persons Detained on Grounds of Mental Ill-Health or Suffering from Mental Disorder"*[60] as "any psychiatric or other illness which substantially impairs mental health." The expression "a mentally ill person" is taken to mean, "a person who, because of mental illness, requires care, treatment or control for his own protection, the protection of others or the protection of the community, and for the time being is incapable of managing himself or his affairs."

---

[60]   *Principles, Guidelines and Guarantees for the Protection of Persons Detained on Grounds of Mental Ill-Health or Suffering from Mental Disorder* (United Nations, 1986).

Mental Health (Northern Ireland) Order 1986

Mental illness is defined in the 1986 Order — the Northern Irish equivalent to the 1983 Act — as meaning "a state of mind which affects a person's thinking, perceiving, emotion or judgment to the extent that he requires care or medical treatment in his own interests or the interests of other persons."[61]

THE AMBIT OF THE TERM

The breadth of the term — how many different kinds of disorder or disability of mind the term encompasses when used in a legal context — has already been considered (059). The second factor which determines the term's ambit is, for want of a better word, the depth of the term — if a particular condition, such as depression, is potentially classifiable as a mental illness, how serious must that condition be before it constitutes a "mental illness" for the purposes of the Act? Everyone experiences feelings of depression at some time during their lives but, for most people, their depression is mild and ephemeral and not generally regarded as abnormal. For others, the disturbance of mood is more pervasive and seemingly not related to any specific event. Physical symptoms associated with depression may also be apparent, such as poor appetite and weight loss. Although the pattern of symptoms and signs may be regarded by a doctor as "a depressive disorder," the majority of people who are clinically depressed in this sense are able to continue their ordinary daily activities, and their acquaintances may not realise they are clinically depressed or receiving treatment for depression. For the purposes of the Act, are these people to be regarded as mentally ill and also therefore as mentally disordered? The issue is important for patients and tribunals alike. A supervision application may only be made if a detained patient who has leave to be absent from hospital is presently mentally ill. Likewise, a patient's case may only be referred to a tribunal under section 86 if he suffers from mental illness. Furthermore, in guardianship and supervision application cases, a tribunal is only obliged to discharge the patient on medical grounds if satisfied that he is not suffering from mental illness. Providing their decision is not irrational, it would be lawful for a tribunal not to discharge such a patient on this ground if it was not satisfied that he was not mentally ill; even though it was satisfied that any mental illness which might be present was not of a nature or degree warranting supervision or guardianship. That situation could arise where the health of a patient who had previously been moderately or severely depressed was now coping in the community by making occasional visits to his family doctor and obtaining repeat prescriptions, in which case his present level of mentally functioning would, when compared to that of the population at large, be wholly unremarkable.

The nature or degree of mental illness and unsoundness of mind

In *Buxton v. Jayne*,[62] Devlin L.J. said that "the unsoundness of mind, whose presence is essential to justify a compulsory order, manifestly means more than mental illness which qualifies a person to be a voluntary patient ... in ordinary language "certifiable" is perhaps more likely to be used to express the same idea." By the time that case was disposed of, the Percy Commission had already recommended that the term "person of unsound mind" be replaced by "mental illness," commenting that:

---

[61] Mental Health (Northern Ireland) Order 1986, Art. 3(1).
[62] *Buxton v. Jayne* [1960] 2 All E.R. 688 at 697.

"Our first administrative group of patients consists of those suffering from mental illness. We use this term in its usual present sense, including those who become mentally infirm in old age. This group includes:—

    a.   a very large group of patients who need medical and social services in the community or in hospital who are not at present subject to compulsory powers, and

    b.   a smaller number who need similar services and who are at present subject to compulsory admission to hospital or community care, in certain circumstances, as "persons of unsound mind."[63]

The Commission went on to say that the medical and social conditions in which it was justifiable to use compulsory powers could be identified in future without retaining the term "person of unsound mind," which would fall into disuse.[64] In essence, this was achieved by requiring that any mental illness present must be of the requisite "nature or degree." The use of these qualifying words was therefore consequential upon the abandonment of the old terms "lunatic," "person of unsound mind" and "certifiable" and the need for some phrase indicating that not everyone suffering from mental illness could be subjected to compulsion. The sense in which the words "mental illness" were used by the Percy Commission was repeated in the D.H.S.S.'s *Memorandum* on the 1959 Act[65]—

"The term 'mental illness' is not defined. Its interpretation is a matter for medical judgment, but it is expected that when it is qualified by the words 'of a nature or degree which warrants the detention of the patient in hospital for medical treatment' ... it will be taken as equivalent to the phrase 'a person of unsound mind' which has been in use hitherto in connection with compulsory detention ... When it is not qualified by these limiting words, however, the term ... carries its normal (much wider) meaning."

Commentary

Having regard to the above, a person must suffer from a mental illness of the requisite nature or degree before he may be subjected to compulsory powers. However, once compulsory powers have been invoked, because a patient's condition is of this nature or degree, the legal position of a tribunal in relation to a patient subject to supervision in the community — whether under guardianship, conditional discharge, or after-care under supervision — would appear to be as follows. It is not obliged to terminate the use of compulsory powers in relation to a patient whom it considers may still be suffering from mental illness unless it is satisfied that he is entitled to be discharged on one of the other statutory grounds.[66] In this context, these are essentially that guardianship is not necessary for the patient's health or safety or to protect others; that a failure to receive after-care services will not give rise to a substantial risk of serious harm; that it is inappropriate for a conditionally discharged patient to remain subject to restrictions. Whether the patient has recovered or is simply in remission, the nature and severity of his symptoms, the

---

[63]   *Report of the Royal Commission on the Law Relating to Mental Illness and Mental Deficiency*, Cmnd. 169 (1957), para. 189.

[64]   *Ibid.*, para. 189.

[65]   *Mental Health Act 1959: Memorandum on Parts I, IV to VII and IX*, (D.H.S.S., 1960), para. 40.

[66]   The statutory criteria for detention or guardianship under Part II and the criteria to be applied when determining whether any patient must be discharged always comprise at least two grounds. The first of them addresses the "diagnostic question" while the criteria which comprise the second ground are directed towards the issue of risk. See p.723.

likelihood of relapse, the likely consequences of relapse, and so forth, will necessarily affect a tribunal's thinking about these other grounds for discharge. Nevertheless, where the degree of compulsion being exercised stops short of deprivation of liberty, and relates instead to some form of control in the community, the unifying thread is that a tribunal's decision does not turn on the nature or degree of any illness which may presently exist. This reflects the fact that, short of actual recovery, continued treatment under supervision in the community may be necessary or appropriate because of the consequences which may follow its discontinuance.

MENTAL IMPAIRMENT AND SEVERE MENTAL IMPAIRMENT

The Mental Health Act 1983 provides that a person may be detained for treatment or received into guardianship on the ground that he is suffering from some kind of mental impairment or severe mental impairment of the requisite nature or degree. These legal classes indicate the presence of a mental handicap associated with some form of conduct disorder.

HISTORICAL DEVELOPMENTS IN TERMINOLOGY

The legal use of the word "idiot" can be traced back to the twelfth century statute Praerogativa Regis. Medieval idiocy examinations involved visual inspection together with questions on orientation, memory, intellect and judgement. "Idiocy" and "simplicity" were distinguished, the former requiring, as with the Court of Protection criteria today, incapacity to manage one's land, goods and general affairs. The terminology of the nineteenth-century statutes was inconsistent. The Lunacy Acts of 1845 and 1890, and the Lunatic Asylums Act 1853, provided that the term "lunatic" included "idiots" as well as "persons of unsound mind." Under the Idiots Act 1886, however, the terms "idiot" and "imbecile" did not include "lunatics." The use of the word "imbeciles" in the 1886 Act marked a change in nomenclature and denoted a degree of mental handicap not amounting to "idiocy."

Radnor Report (1908)[67]

In 1904 the Radnor Commission was appointed to consider the needs of "feeble-minded" and other mentally disordered people who were not considered certifiable under the Lunacy Acts, and the need for special forms of treatment for them and for "idiots." The Commission's report, published in 1908, was followed by the enactment of the Mental Deficiency Act 1913.

Mental Deficiency Acts of 1913 and 1927

The Mental Deficiency Act 1913 distinguished four classes of "mental defectives," namely "idiots," "imbeciles," the "feeble-minded" and "moral defectives."[68] The 1927 Act substituted the term "moral imbecile" for "moral defective" and amended the statutory definitions of all the classes.[69] The classificatory system adopted in the

---

[67]   *Report of the Royal Commission on the Care and Control of the Feeble-Minded*, Cd. 4202 (1908).
[68]   The statutory classification thus closely followed Morel's 1839 classification of such states of mind.
[69]   Under the 1959 Act, persons previously classified as "moral defectives" or as "moral imbeciles" generally fell within the new class of "psychopathic disorder."

statutes resembles in some respects that in use today. All persons who suffered from an "arrested or incomplete development of mind existing before the age of eighteen" were "mental defectives" but the sub-class within which an individual was placed depended on the degree of mental handicap present and the resulting social consequences. The statutory definitions of the terms "idiot," "imbecile" and "feeble-minded" are set out in table on the following page.

"Idiot"

The term "idiot" was usually interpreted as applying to patients whose mental abilities and living skills never developed beyond those of a baby or a young child of up to about four years of age. Some never learnt to walk, others were able to develop the use of their hands and rudimentary speech but, in all cases, constant care was required throughout life.[70]

"Imbecile"

"Imbecile" generally denoted a patient who when fully grown had a mental age equivalent to that of a child between three and six or seven years old; the majority of individuals so categorised could be taught to walk and to wash and to feed themselves, and some were able to develop a high degree of manual dexterity.[71]

"Feeble-minded"

"Feeble-minded" covered a disparate group of patients. At one extreme were those who needed much the same help as "imbeciles" but who were not so classified in order to avoid distress to their families. At the other extreme were patients whose intelligence was little if at all below average but who were "emotionally unstable." Because of "pathological defects or abnormalities of personality," many people who were feeble-minded behaved in a way which made it necessary in certain circumstances to subject them to special forms of control.[72]

Percy Report (1957)[73]

The Percy Commission considered that patients who suffered from "mental illness" and "severe subnormality" might require in-patient care even though their condition was not responsive to treatment and their prognosis was poor. In contrast, the "higher-grade feebleminded and moral defectives and other psychopathic patients" formed a second distinctive group, detainable if treatable but whose conditions were not of a type which rendered them incapable of independent living or at risk of serious exploitation.[74] The legislation which followed reflected this distinction to the extent that the definitions of mental subnormality and psychopathic disorder in the 1959 Act included a treatability component. The distinction is still drawn in the present Act, but to a lesser extent: see, as can be seen from the conditions which must be satisfied before compulsory admission may take place or a patient's detention may be renewed.

---

[70] *Report of the Royal Commission on the Law Relating to Mental Illness and Mental Deficiency*, Cmnd. 169 (1957), para. 163.

[71] *Ibid.*, para. 164.

[72] *Ibid.*, para. 166.

[73] *Report of the Royal Commission on the Law Relating to Mental Illness and Mental Deficiency*, 1954-1957, Chairman—Lord Percy, Cmnd. 169 (1957).

[74] *Ibid.*, para. 187.

LEGAL CLASSIFICATIONS OF MENTAL IMPAIRMENT

Mental Deficiency Act 1927	Mental Health Act 1959	Mental Health Act 1983
"IDIOTS"	**"SEVERE SUBNORMALITY"**	**"SEVERE MENTAL IMPAIRMENT"**
"Persons in whose case there exists mental defectiveness of such a degree that they are unable to guard themselves against common physical dangers" (s.1(1)(a)).	"A state of arrested or incomplete development of mind which includes subnormality of intelligence and is of such a nature or degree that the patient is incapable of living an independent life or of guarding himself against serious exploitation or will be so incapable when of age to do so" (s.4(2)).	"A state of arrested or incomplete development of mind which includes severe impairment of intelligence and social functioning and is associated with abnormally aggressive or seriously irresponsible conduct on the part of the person concerned" (s.1(2)).
"IMBECILES"		*If treatment is unlikely to alleviate or prevent a deterioration of the patient's condition, his detention may nonetheless be renewed if he would otherwise be unlikely to be able to care for himself, to obtain the care which he needs or to guard himself against serious exploitation (see s.20).*
"Persons in whose case there exists mental defectiveness which, though not amounting to idiocy, is yet so pronounced that they are incapable of managing themselves or their affairs or, in the case of children, of being taught to do so" (s.1(1)(b)).		
"FEEBLE-MINDED PERSONS"	**"SUBNORMALITY"**	**"MENTAL IMPAIRMENT"**
"Persons in whose case there exists mental defectiveness which, though not amounting to imbecility, is yet so pronounced that they require care, supervision and control for their own protection or for the protection of others or, in the case of children, that they appear to be permanently incapable by reason of such defectiveness of receiving proper benefit from the instruction in ordinary schools" (s.1(1)(c)).	"A state of arrested or incomplete development of mind (not amounting to severe subnormality) which includes subnormality of intelligence and is of a nature or degree which requires or is susceptible to medical treatment or other special care or training of the patient" (s.4(3))	"A state of arrested or incomplete development of mind (not amounting to severe mental impairment) which includes significant impairment of intelligence and social functioning and is associated with abnormally aggressive or seriously irresponsible conduct on the part of the person concerned" (s.1(2)).
"For the purposes of this section, 'mental defectiveness' means a condition of arrested or incomplete development of mind existing before the age of eighteen years, whether arising from inherent causes or induced by disease or injury" (s.1(2)).		*In general, a person who suffers from mental impairment may not be admitted to hospital for treatment unless such treatment is likely to alleviate or prevent a deterioration of his condition (see ss. 3, 37 and 47).*

INTERNATIONAL CLASSIFICATION OF DISEASES (10th REVISION) : MENTAL RETARDATION

Diagnosis	Synonyms	Usual I.Q. range	Intellectual and social functioning
F73 Profound Mental Retardation	*Idiocy, profound mental subnormality*	Under 20	Comprehension and use of language is limited to, at best, understanding basic commands and making simple requests. The most basic and simple visuo-spatial skills of sorting and matching may be acquired, and the affected person may be able with appropriate supervision and guidance to take a small part in domestic and practical tasks. Most are immobile or severely restricted in mobility, incontinent, and capable at most of only very rudimentary forms of nonverbal communication. They possess little or no ability to care for their own basic needs, and require constant help and supervision.
F72 Severe Mental Retardation	*Severe mental subnormality*	20 to 34	The category is broadly similar to that of moderate mental retardation in terms of the clinical picture. Most people in this category suffer from a marked degree of motor impairment.
F71 Moderate Mental Retardation	*Imbecility; moderate mental subnormality.*	35 to 49	Individuals are slow in developing comprehension and use of language, and their eventual achievement in this area is limited. The level of development of language is variable: some of those affected can take part in simple conversations while others never learn to use language, though they may understand simple instructions and learn to use manual signs. Discrepant profiles of abilities are common, with some individuals achieving higher levels in visuo-spatial skills than in tasks dependent on language, while others are markedly clumsy but enjoy social interaction and simple conversation. Achievement of self-care and motor skills is also retarded, and some need supervision throughout life. A proportion learn the basic skills needed for reading, writing, and counting. They are usually able to do simple practical work, if the tasks are carefully structured and skilled supervision is provided. Completely independent living is rarely achieved. The majority show evidence of social development in their ability to establish contact and to communicate with others.
F70 Mild Mental Retardation	*Feeble-mindedness, mild mental subnormality, moron.*	50 to 69	Individuals acquire language with some delay but most achieve the ability to use speech for everyday purposes. Many have particular problems in reading and writing. Most of those in the higher ranges of mild mental retardation are potentially capable of work demanding practical abilities, including unskilled or semi-skilled manual labour. Most achieve full independence in self-care (eating, washing, dressing, bowel and bladder control) and in practical and domestic skills, even if the rate of development is considerably slower than normal. In general, the behavioural, emotional, and social difficulties, and the need for treatment and support arising from them, are more closely akin to those found in people of normal intelligence than to the specific problems of the moderately and severely retarded.

Mental Health Act 1959

The 1959 Act repealed the Mental Deficiency Acts and removed the terms "mental deficiency," "mental defectiveness" and "defective" from the other Acts in which they occurred. Persons suffering from mental impairment were sub-divided into two main classes, the "subnormal" and the "severely subnormal."

"Severe subnormality"

The opinion of the Percy Commission was that all patients previously certified as "idiots" or "imbeciles" would be reclassified as suffering from "severe subnormality,"[75] as would some half to two-thirds of the "feeble-minded" patients then in mental deficiency hospitals.[76] More generally, an I.Q. of below 50 to 60 (equivalent to a child aged 7½ to 9 years) would be a strong pointer towards the existence of "severe subnormality."[77]

"Subnormality"

As to "subnormality," the *Memorandum* on the Act, published by the D.H.S.S., stated that the patients who would in future be classed as subnormal, rather than severely subnormal, "are intellectually dull, but their main problem is one of emotional instability. Many of them need psychiatric treatment as well as training."[78]

MENTAL HEALTH ACT 1983

Section 145(1) provides that, unless the context otherwise requires, "mental impairment" and "severe mental impairment" have the meanings given to them in section 1(2) of the Act—

- "severe mental impairment" means a state of arrested or incomplete development of mind which includes severe impairment of intelligence and social functioning and is associated with abnormally aggressive or seriously irresponsible conduct on the part of the person concerned and "severely mentally impaired" shall be construed accordingly;

- "mental impairment" means a state of arrested or incomplete development of mind (not amounting to severe mental impairment) which includes significant impairment of intelligence and social functioning and is associated with abnormally aggressive or seriously irresponsible conduct on the part of the person concerned and "mentally impaired" shall be construed accordingly.

Reasons for the amendments

The terminology and definitions presently in force date back to the Mental Health (Amendment) Act 1982, the present statute being a consolidating Act. The Government's proposals for an amending Act were set out in a White Paper, "*Review*

---

[75]   *Report of the Royal Commission on the Law Relating to Mental Illness and Mental Deficiency*, Cmnd. 169 (1957), para. 191.

[76]   *Ibid.*, para. 193. Essentially those "imbeciles" who had previously been classified as "feeble-minded" in order to spare their parents distress.

[77]   *Ibid.*

[78]   *Mental Health Act 1959: Memorandum on Parts I, IV to VII and IX* (D.H.S.S., 1960), para. 7.

of the Mental Health Act 1959,"[79] which acknowledged that the terms "subnormality" and "severe subnormality" caused "offence and distress."[80] The 1982 Act replaced them with the phrases "mental impairment" and "severe mental impairment" and amended the statutory definitions of the classes—

- No mentally handicapped person could henceforth be classified as mental impaired or severely mentally impaired unless his handicap was associated with abnormally aggressive or seriously irresponsible conduct on his part[81] and both his intelligence *and* social functioning were impaired. Previously, subnormality of intelligence only sufficed.

- The definition of mental impairment was relaxed in that it was no longer a condition of such a classification that the patient's condition required or was susceptible to treatment.[82]

- Under the 1959 Act as drafted, "severely subnormality" had required that a patient's mind was arrested or incompletely developed to such a nature or degree that he was incapable of living an independent life or guarding himself against serious exploitation. This criterion was removed and, under the present classification, severe mental impairment instead requires that a mentally handicapped patient's level of social functioning is severely impaired. The reference to living an independent life was no longer thought appropriate.

"ARRESTED OR INCOMPLETE DEVELOPMENT OF MIND"

The phrase was first used in the 1913 Act — to define "mental defectiveness" — and its use has been continued in subsequent statutes. It indicates a failure to attain developmental milestones because of innate limitations rather than immaturity of personality, lack of education or poor parenting. An organic aetiology is identifiable in a minority of persons who are mildly retarded, in the majority of those moderately or severely retarded, and in almost all cases of profound retardation.[83]

The ICD–10 Classification

The statutory terminology has tended to reflect changes in the terms used in psychiatric classificatory systems and the definition of "mental retardation" in the 10th Revision of the International Classification of Diseases commences with the same words[84]—

---

[79]   *Review of the Mental Health Act 1959*, Cmnd. 7320 (1978).

[80]   *Ibid.*, para. 1.21.

[81]   The change aimed to ensure that mentally handicapped people were not subjected to compulsory powers unless the behaviour associated with their state justified their use. A point repeated in paragraph 10 of the *Memorandum* on the 1983 Act.

[82]   Although a person suffering from mental impairment cannot be detained for treatment unless such treatment is likely to alleviate or prevent a deterioration of his condition, and treatability became in all cases a precondition of renewal, the definition of medical treatment was broadened to include habilitation and rehabilitation under medical supervision. A further consequence of the amendment was that tribunals are not bound to discharge a person whose condition is untreatable, because that fact does not preclude him from being classified as mentally impaired. Furthermore, the age limits relating to the detention for treatment of persons suffering from subnormality were removed.

[83]   *ICD–10 Classification of Mental and Behavioural Disorders: Clinical Descriptions and Diagnostic Guidelines* (World Health Organisation, 1992).

[84]   *Ibid.*, p.226.

"A condition of arrested or incomplete development of mind, which is especially characterized by impairment of skills manifested during the developmental period, skills which contribute to the overall level of intelligence, *i.e.* cognitive, language, motor, and social abilities. Retardation can occur with or without any other mental or physical condition."

The classification sub-divides conditions of mental retardation into four main categories: mild (F70), moderate (F71), severe (F72) and profound (F73).

Mental infirmity in old age, etc.

Where a mind which has fully developed subsequently becomes impaired, for example through old age or as the result of organic injury resulting from an accident, that condition will not constitute mental impairment. That remains the case however severe the effects on the individual's intellect and social functioning, and however abnormally aggressive or seriously irresponsible the conduct which results.

"IMPAIRMENT"

In its White Paper, "*Review of the Mental Health Act 1959*," the Government proposed substituting for "subnormality" and "severe subnormality" the phrases "mental handicap" and "severe mental handicap." However, the word "impairment" was substituted for "handicap" at the committee stage in the House of Lords because it—

- "distinguishes the small minority of mentally handicapped people who need to be detained in hospital or received into guardianship from the great majority who do not."[85]

- "reflects developments in the understanding of mental handicap and indicates that a person's potential intelligence and social functioning have suffered 'injurious lessening or weakening' [Oxford English Dictionary]; it is preferred to 'subnormal' which compares him to a notional norm."[86]

- "is already in very appropriate usage, as it is used by the World Health Organisation to describe any loss or abnormality of psychological, physical or anatomical structure or function."[87]

Impairment of intelligence

A person may not be classified as suffering from mental impairment unless his intelligence is significantly impaired, nor classified as being severely mentally impaired unless it is severely impaired.

---

[85] *Mental Health (Amendment) Bill: Notes on Clauses, House of Commons, (D.H.S.S., 1982), p.11. A point repeated in paragraph 10 of the Memorandum on the 1983 Act.*

[86] *Mental Health (Amendment) Bill: Notes on Clauses, supra,* p.14. According to the White Paper of September 1978, the definition of "subnormality" in the 1959 Act, which referred only to "subnormality of intelligence," was felt not to adequately reflect the behavioural aspects of mental handicap and it was therefore proposed to include in the definition of mental handicap the words "significant impairment of intelligence and social functioning." *Review of the Mental Health Act 1959,* Cmnd. 7320 (1978), para. 1.21.

[87] *Hansard,* H.L. Vol. 426, col. 532.

Significant impairment of intelligence

An individual's level of intellectual functioning is normally determined by assess-ment with a general intelligence test. The ICD–10 classification provides that, if proper standardised tests are used, an I.Q. range of 50 to 69 is indicative of mild retardation. Similarly, the diagnostic criteria for mental retardation in the DSM–IV classification include an I.Q. of 70 or below. As to what constitutes *severe impair-ment* of intelligence, both classifications distinguish four levels of mental retardation (profound, severe, moderate and mild) and include guidelines as to the I.Q. range which is in general indicative of each class—

GUIDELINE I.Q. LEVELS

	ICD–10	*DSM–IV*	*%. of the mentally retarded population*
Profound	Below 20	Below 20 to 25	1–2%
Severe	20 to 34	20–25 to 35–40	3–4%
Moderate	35 to 49	35–40 to 50–55	10%
Mild	50–69	50–55 to approx. 70	85%

Impairment of social functioning

The inclusion of this criterion in the legal definitions "emphasises the importance of social functioning — this includes the ability to eat, control one's bodily functions, communicate, wash, dress, learn new skills, recognise hazards and display reason-able judgement and foresight. The lack of these abilities is as much a part of mental handicap as low intelligence."[88] A person may not be classified as suffering from mental impairment unless his level of social functioning is significantly impaired nor may he be classified as severely mental impaired unless it is severely impaired. In general, there is a positive association between intelligence, as measured by I.Q. score, and social functioning at lower I.Q. levels but this association declines at the mild and moderate levels of mental retardation.

The ICD–10 and DSM–IV classifications

The ICD–10 and DSM–IV classifications both emphasise that a diagnosis of mental retardation requires not only significantly sub-average intellectual functioning but also significant deficits in social or "adaptive" functioning. A definite diagnosis requires a reduced level of intellectual functioning resulting in diminished ability to adapt to the daily demands of the normal social environment. The table on page 73 summarises the main impairments in social functioning associated with mental retardation. Various methods are commonly used to assess a patient's level of social functioning, based on behaviour observed by professionals and carers and social assessment testing.

---

[88]   See Footnote 86.

Both the 1983 Act and the ICD–10 classification recognise that mentally retarded individuals are at greater risk of exploitation and physical or sexual abuse. Under the 1959 Act, a classification of severe subnormality required that the patient's handicap be of such a nature or degree that he was incapable of living an independent life or of guarding himself against serious exploitation. The references in the definition to independent living and serious exploitation were omitted from the definition of severe mental impairment in the present statute. The reason given was that "many mentally handicapped people would be unable to live completely alone without support from family or the social services, but that in itself would not justify the use of compulsory powers."[89] The logic is faulty since that constitutes a reason for retaining rather than discarding the qualification. Removing incapacity to live an independent life, or to guard oneself against serious exploitation, from the definition has the opposite effect to that intended: it allows all people so handicapped to be classified as severely mentally impaired and, since those disabilities are no longer a prerequisite of such a finding, persons with higher social skills also.

ABNORMALLY AGGRESSIVE OR SERIOUSLY IRRESPONSIBLE

The meanings of these words are considered below, in relation to psychopathic disorder (**088**). In this context, it may be noted that the International Classification of Diseases (ICD–10) sub-divides conditions of mental retardation into four main categories (**077**) and provides that clinicians may use a fourth character to specify the extent of any behavioural impairment which is not due to an associated disorder such as epilepsy:

- 0   no, or minimal, impairment of behaviour.

- 1   significant impairment of behaviour requiring attention or treatment.

- 8   other impairments of behaviour.

- 9   is used without mention of impairment of behaviour.

So, for example, a classification of F72.1 denotes a person who suffers from severe mental retardation associated with significant impairment of behaviour requiring attention or treatment.

"AND IS ASSOCIATED WITH"

With psychopathic disorder, the patient's persistent disorder or disability of mind must "result" in abnormally aggressive or seriously irresponsible conduct rather than "be associated" with it. In cases of mental impairment, it suffices that the arrested or incomplete development of mind and the conduct disorder are associated in some way. This is because it may be difficult in practice to establish any clear causal relationship between the two, on account of the fact that both features developed in parallel. However, where a patient's conduct disorder arises from a co-existent mental illness, a classification of mental impairment will not be appropriate.

---

[89]   *Mental Health (Amendment) Bill: Notes on Clauses, House of Commons* (D.H.S.S., 1982), p.15.

Mental impairment and mental illness

Mentally impaired individuals can experience the full range of mental disorders and, indeed, the prevalence of other mental disorders is at least three to four times greater than in the general population.[90] However, the diagnosis of other psychiatric conditions in persons with more than mild retardation may be difficult because of limited language development. epilepsy, and neurological and physical disabilities, are common in the moderately and severely retarded. Severe neurological or other physical disabilities affecting mobility are common, as are epilepsy and visual and hearing impairments, in the profoundly retarded.

Mental impairment and psychopathic disorder

The definitions of mental impairment and severe mental impairment to some extent overlap with that of a "psychopathic disorder" in section 1(2). A psychopathic disorder is "a persistent disorder or disability of mind (whether or not including significant impairment of intelligence) which results in abnormally aggressive or seriously irresponsible conduct on the part of the person concerned." Where the I.Q. of a person with a serious conduct disorder is reported as being slightly above or below 70, a tribunal may not be satisfied that the patient is mentally impaired but nevertheless not discharge him on the basis that he has, or may have, a psychopathic disorder of the requisite nature or degree.

SEVERE MENTAL IMPAIRMENT AND MENTAL IMPAIRMENT

A classification of "severe mental impairment" requires that both a patient's intelligence and his social functioning are severely impaired. Likewise, a classification of "mental impairment" requires significant impairment of both intelligence and social functioning.[91] The concepts underlying the legislation have remained more constant than the frequent changes in terminology may initially suggest. In particular, the provisions concerning "idiocy," "imbecility," "severe subnormality" and "severe mental impairment" have all tended to focus not on the condition's treatability but on the individual's vulnerability due to profound retardation — incapacity to live an independent life, severe impairment of social functioning, inability to care for himself or to obtain such care, the risk of serious exploitation. Conversely, the provisions relating to "feeble-mindedness," "subnormality" and "mental impairment" have tended to be directed towards the role of medical treatment, care or training, rather than a need to protectively care for the individual concerned (072).

The importance of the distinction

Whether a person is mentally impaired or severely mentally impaired has important legal consequences. In the case of a person who is severely mentally impaired, it is not a condition of admission that treatment is likely to alleviate or prevent a deterioration of his condition. Similarly, the fact that a patient's condition is unlikely to be treatable in this sense does not preclude a renewal of detention if, in the event of release, he would be unlikely to be able to care for himself, to obtain the care he

---

[90]   *ICD–10 Classification of Mental and Behavioural Disorders: Clinical Descriptions and Diagnostic Guidelines* (World Health Organisation, 1992).

[91]   The current *Memorandum* emphasises that in order for a person to have a mental impairment for the purposes of the 1983 Act, the impairment must be either severe or significant, rather than "slight." *Mental Health Act 1983: Memorandum on Parts I to VI, VIII and X* (D.H.S.S., 1987), para. 12.

needs or to guard himself against serious exploitation (the "vulnerability test").[92] Where a tribunal considers the case of a severely mentally impaired patient who does not satisfy the criteria for being discharged, that tribunal must have regard to the vulnerability test before exercising any discretionary power of discharge.

Admission under Part III

A person suffering from severe mental impairment who is involved in criminal proceedings may be remanded to hospital for treatment by the Crown Court or transferred there for treatment by the Secretary of State. In magistrates courts proceedings, the court may make a hospital or guardianship order without first convicting him of an imprisonable offence provided the court is satisfied he did the act or omission charged. The underlying premise behind these provisions is that a mentally impaired person per se does not suffer from such a serious impairment of intelligence and social functioning as to render him unfit for custody pending trial or unfit for trial.

Sexual offences legislation

It is an offence for a person to have unlawful sexual intercourse with a woman who is "a defective"[93]; to procure a "defective" to have unlawful sexual intercourse in any part of the world;[94] to take such a person out of the "possession" of her parent or guardian with the intention that she shall have unlawful sexual intercourse[95]; to induce or knowingly permit a "defective" to use premises for the purpose of having unlawful sexual intercourse[96]; or to cause or encourage the prostitution of such a person in any part of the world.[97] A "defective," whether male or female, cannot give consent to an act which in the absence of a valid consent constitutes an indecent assault.[98] A man who is suffering from "severe mental handicap" cannot in law consent to a homosexual act in private, whether buggery or an act of gross indecency. The terms "defective" and "severe mental handicap" both mean "a person suffering from a state of arrested or incomplete development of mind which includes severe impairment of intelligence and social functioning." In the context of the 1983 Act, this means that it is a legal presumption that a person who is so handicapped as to be severely mentally impaired is incapable of giving a valid consent to sexual relations. However, persons whose level of intelligence and social functioning is such that they are properly classifiable as "mentally impaired" are presumed to be as capable as any other citizen of consenting or not consenting to sexual relations.

Case law

In *R. v. Hall (John Hamilton)*,[99] the defence argued that no sexual offence had taken place because the victim was not a "defective" within the meaning of the Sexual

---

92   "Detention will not be renewed unless there is an expectation of further benefit from treatment, except in the case of the mentally ill and severely mentally handicapped. Here the Bill recognises that the health services have a responsibility to care for mentally ill and severely mentally handicapped people whose disorder may make them unable to care for themselves ...": *Reform of Mental Health Legislation,* Cmnd. 8405 (1981), para. 20.
93   Sexual Offences Act 1956, s. 7.
94   *Ibid.,* s.9.
95   *Ibid.,* s.21.
96   *Ibid.,* s.27.
97   *Ibid.,* s.29.
98   *Ibid.,* ss.14 (indecent assault on a woman) and 15 (indecent assault on a man).
99   *R. v. Hall (John Hamilton)* (1988) 86 Cr.App.R. 159.

Offences Act 1956. The young woman's reading comprehension was that of a child aged 7 years and 5 months and her I.Q. of 53 placed her in the bottom one per cent. of the general population. When she gave evidence, both the judge and counsel had difficulty in "getting any sense out of her." The Court of Appeal was dismissive of the defence case, stating that there was "ample" evidence that she was a "defective"; "it is unnecessary to rehearse it."

Pointers towards the severity of mental impairment

Each case must be assessed on its own facts. However, based on the observations made above, the following pointers towards whether a person is mentally impaired or severely mentally impaired may provide a useful starting point.

Pointers towards mental impairment

- An I.Q. above 60 — even if the patient's level of social functioning is severely impaired, his intelligence cannot generally be said to be more than "significantly impaired."

- A capacity to consent to sexual relations and to protect oneself against serious exploitation.

- A general capacity or potential for self-care and independent living.

- A general level of functioning such that if involved in criminal proceedings it would not be inappropriate for the ordinary bail, custody and trial provisions to apply.

Pointers towards severe mental impairment

- An ICD–10 or DSM–IV classification of moderate, severe or profound mental retardation will almost certainly indicate severe mental impairment.

- A lack of capacity for independent living and an inability to obtain necessary care for oneself will also point towards severe impairment.

- An inability to guard oneself against serious exploitation or to give a valid consent to sexual relations.

- A disability so severe that if involved in criminal proceedings it might be inappropriate on medical grounds for the patient to be kept in custody pending trial.

PSYCHOPATHIC DISORDER

Apart from interim orders made under section 38, a person who suffers only from a psychopathic disorder may only be detained for treatment for a potentially indefinite period if treatment is likely to alleviate or prevent a deterioration of his condition. Approximately 25 per cent. of the population of the three special hospitals are legally classified as suffering from a personality disorder as are just under 10 per cent. of all persons detained in regional secure units.[100]

HISTORICAL DEVELOPMENTS IN LEGAL TERMINOLOGY

The way in which medical usage of the term has developed is reviewed in chapter 21 (**1186**).

The Lunacy Acts

Prior to the coming into force of the Mental Deficiency Act 1913, persons who would today be classified as having a psychopathic disorder were not generally certifiable under the Lunacy Act 1890, except by stretching the terms used in the Lunacy Acts beyond their generally accepted meaning. Their mental disorder did not reflect or result in severe limitation of intellect or loss of reason so that they were neither "idiots" nor "lunatics."[101]

The Radnor Commission (1904–08)[102]

In 1904, the Radnor Commission was appointed to consider the needs of "feebleminded" and other mentally disordered people considered to be certifiable under the Lunacy Acts. The Commission's report, published in 1908, was followed by the enactment of the Mental Deficiency Act 1913. The Radnor Report recommended that "moral imbeciles" should be liable to care and control. When determining whether a person could properly be described as a moral imbecile, the Commission suggested that the issue should be "whether the facts interpreted by the evidence of vicious or criminal propensities and incorrigibility proved that the will and judgment were so abnormal as to amount to mental disorder."[103]

"Moral insanity"

The Radnor Report drew a distinction between "moral imbeciles," whose conduct developed in childhood and was attributable to an arrested or incomplete development of mind,[104] and the "morally insane." Although the characteristics and behaviour of the latter were similar to those of a moral imbecile, their disorder developed in adulthood in a personality which had matured normally. The

---

[100] *Report of the Department of Health and Home Office Working Group on Psychopathic Disorder* (Department of Health and the Home Office, 1994), p.11.

[101] See the *Report of the Royal Commission on the Law Relating to Mental Illness and Mental Deficiency*, Cmnd. 169 (1957), para. 154; *Report of the Royal Commission on the Care and Control of the Feeble-Minded*, Cd. 4202 (1908).

[102] *Report of the Royal Commission on the Care and Control of the Feeble-Minded*, Cd. 4202 (1908).

[103] *Report of the Royal Commission on the Law Relating to Mental Illness and Mental Deficiency*, Cmnd. 169 (1957), para. 156.

[104] Following Pinel, there was a tendency to see moral imbecility as a form of mental deficiency, the result of a degeneration of that part of the brain which dealt with morality and feelings.

Commission considered that the morally insane were persons "of unsound mind" and therefore lunatics certifiable under the 1890 Act. However, in practice, the term "person of unsound mind" was not usually extended to cover the morally insane.

Mental Deficiency Act 1913

In line with the recommendations of the Radnor Report, section 1 of the 1913 Act defined "moral imbeciles" as persons suffering from an arrested or incomplete development of mind existing before the age of eighteen years "who from an early age display some permanent mental defect coupled with strong vicious or criminal propensities on which punishment has had little or no deterrent effect."

Mental Deficiency Act 1927

The 1927 Act amended the statutory definitions in section 1. The term "moral imbeciles" was replaced by "moral defectives," defined as "persons in whose case there exists mental defectiveness coupled with strongly vicious or criminal propensities and who require care, supervision and control for the protection of others."[105]

Percy Report (1957)

The Percy Commission, whose report was followed by the enactment of the Mental Health Act 1959, suggested the use of the term "psychopathic disorder" as a legal category, which would include both "moral imbeciles" and the "morally insane" and, additionally, many persons then classified as feeble-minded.[106]

The feeble-minded, psychopaths and moral defectives

The Commission viewed "feeble-minded people, psychopaths and moral defectives" as essentially a homogenous group: "When a wide meaning is given to the term "psychopath" and to the term "feeble-minded," many persons could equally well be described by either term, and moral defectives ... could also be described by either of the other terms."[107] In the Commission's view, what distinguished such individuals most clearly from "normal people" was their general social behaviour. Although it was not easy to clearly describe these behavioural characteristics, this difficulty was "a difficulty of language rather than diagnosis." The Commission had no doubt that those who interpreted the Mental Deficiency Acts as including, among the feeble-minded and moral defectives, patients whose intelligence was within the normal range but whose mental development was incomplete, were correctly interpreting the intention behind those Acts.[108] In the event, the Government took the view that the Commission's wide use of the term "psychopathic" involved so great a departure from the sense in which it was normally used by the medical profession and the public as to be liable to lead to confusion.[109] The 1959 Bill therefore sub-divided the category of persons to which the Commission applied the term "psychopathic" into two categories, "subnormal" and "psychopathic."

---

[105]   Mental Deficiency Act 1927, s.1(1)(d).
[106]   *Report of the Royal Commission on the Law Relating to Mental Illness and Mental Deficiency,* Cmnd. 169 (1957), para. 190.
[107]   *Ibid.*, para. 170.
[108]   *Ibid.*, para. 162.
[109]   See the Lord Chancellor's (Viscount Kilmuir) speech to the House of Lords on 4 June 1959 (*Hansard,* H.L. Vol. 216, col. 670).

Mental Health Act 1959

The Mental Deficiency Acts were repealed by the 1959 Act, section 4(4) of which introduced the legal classification of "psychopathic disorder," defined as "a persistent disorder or disability of mind (whether or not including subnormality of intelligence) which results in abnormally aggressive or seriously irresponsible conduct on the part of the patient, and requires or is susceptible to treatment." A number of amendments were made to the definition originally drafted.[110] Most of these were carried over to the 1983 Act and they are therefore considered below in relation to the present statutory definition.

Treatability

An attempt was made during the Committee stage in the House of Lords to remove from the definition the words "and requires," so as to ensure that the category would be confined to persons who "will really benefit from medical treatment."[111] The Government's position was explained by the Lord Chancellor, Viscount Kilmuir, who said that the inclusion of the words allowed action to be taken in a case where the doctor hoped that a patient would respond to treatment.[112]

Age limits

The Act prohibited the reception into guardianship or the detention for treatment under what is now section 3 of any person aged 21 or over on the ground of psychopathic disorder. Furthermore, where a person aged under 21 was received into guardianship, the guardianship application ceased to have effect upon his reaching the age of 25. Similarly, an application for treatment ceased to have effect unless, during the two months preceding the patient's 25th birthday, his patient's responsible medical officer furnished a report stating that he would, if released, be likely to act in a manner dangerous to himself or others.[113] Although an "arrested or incomplete development of mind" did not form part of the statutory definition, the Act still viewed psychopathic disorder as essentially a developmental disorder, although detention or guardianship was not precluded if the disorder resulted in offending later in life and there was some prospect that it might still be treated. The inclusion of the words "whether or not including subnormality of intelligence" also suggested a continuing belief that psychopathic disorder ("moral defectiveness") was sometimes associated with "mental deficiency."

Butler Report (1975)

The Butler Report considered that the terms "psychopathic disorder" and "psychopath" were unsatisfactory from both the medical and legal point of view, but recognised that it was not easy to think of short, more appropriate, alternatives. Although the former was a generic term, adopted for the purpose of legal categorisation and capable of covering a number of specific diagnoses, reliable specific diagnoses had yet to be developed.[114] The class of persons to whom the term related

---

[110]   The original definition in the Bill was as follows: "'Psychopathic disorder' means a persistent disorder of personality (whether or not accompanied by sub-normality of intelligence) which results in abnormally aggressive or seriously irresponsible conduct in the part of the patient, and requires or is susceptible to medical treatment."

[111]   *Hansard*, H.L. Vol. 217, cols. 91 and 93.

[112]   *Ibid.*, col. 98.

[113]   Parliament debated the sections of the relating to psychopathic disorder at some length.

[114]   *Report of the Committee on Mentally Abnormal Offenders*, Cmnd. 6244 (1975), paras. 5.2 and 5.13.

did not represent a single class identifiable by any medical, biological or psycho-logical criteria.[115] It was not possible to identify "psychopathic disorder" as defined by the Act with a particular sub-category of the International Classification of Diseases, several of which might include patients who showed "abnormally aggress-ive or seriously irresponsible conduct."[116] It was no longer a useful or meaningful concept and its use as a statutory term should be abandoned and replaced in the Act by the recognised classification of personality disorder, which would not be statutorily defined.[117]

Review of the Mental Health Act 1959 (1978)[118]

In January 1975 the Government announced its intention to review the 1959 Act and an inter-departmental committee of officials was set up to undertake this review. The Committee's initial suggestions were set out in a consultative document published in August 1976. Following the completion of this consultative exercise, the Government's proposals for change were set out in a White Paper, "Review of the Mental Health Act 1959." The Government accepted that "the Act should establish a clear requirement that psychopaths should only be detained under compulsory powers where there is a good prospect of benefit from treatment." However, the Government proposed that the words "and requires or is susceptible to medical treatment" be omitted from the statutory definition of psychopathic disorder since they did not appear appropriate as part of a definition. A "prospect of benefit from treatment" requirement should be incorporated instead into the criteria for compulsory admission and renewal of detention.[119] The White Paper also proposed abolishing the age limits in the 1959 Act.

Reform of Mental Health Legislation (1981)[120]

The object of the White Paper was to explain the changes proposed in the Mental Health (Amendment) Bill which the Government had presented to Parliament.[121] The White Paper indicated that the Government had considered whether psychopathic disorder should be excluded from the Act but had decided against it—

"The weight of current medical thinking is that most psychopaths are not likely to benefit from treatment in hospital and are for the penal system to deal with when they do commit offences but that there are some persons suffering from psychopathic disorder who can be helped by detention in hospital. For this reason, this category is not excluded from the Act."[122]

Mental Health (Amendment) Act 1982

The 1982 Act implemented the proposals in the Government's White Papers of 1978 and 1981, the effect of which is that the statutory definition of psychopathic disorder is now broader than ever before.

---

[115]   *Report of the Committee on Mentally Abnormal Offenders*, Cmnd. 6244 (1975), para. 5.23.
[116]   *Ibid.*, para. 5.18.
[117]   *Ibid.*, para. 5.24.
[118]   *Review of the Mental Health Act 1959*, Cmnd. 7320 (1978).
[119]   *Ibid.*, para. 1.26.
[120]   *Reform of Mental Health Legislation*, Cmnd. 8405 (1981).
[121]   *Ibid.*, para. 1.
[122]   *Ibid.*, para. 12.

MENTAL HEALTH ACT 1983

The 1983 Act was a consolidating provision and simply repeated the amendments set out in the 1982 Act. Section 1(2) states that "psychopathic disorder" means "a persistent disorder or disability of mind (whether or not including significant impairment of intelligence) which results in abnormally aggressive or seriously irresponsible conduct on the part of the person concerned." No person may be dealt with as suffering from psychopathic disorder "by reason only of promiscuity or other immoral conduct, sexual deviancy or dependence on alcohol or drugs."[123]

Working Group on Psychopathic Disorder (1986)

In 1986 an interdepartmental D.H.S.S. and Home Office working group identified, without in any way resolving, the inherent problems flowing from the uncertainties about the concept of psychopathic disorder; its diagnosis, treatability, and relationship with offending; the practical difficulties involved in assessing, particularly in an artificial environment, whether the disorder had ameliorated; and what implications (if any) this had for the patient's likely future behaviour upon discharge.

Reed Working Group on Psychopathic Disorder (1994)[124]

In September 1992, the Department of Health and Home Office set up a working group, under the chairmanship of Dr. John Reed, to review the treatment options for people with personality (psychopathic) disorders, their appropriate location, and the arrangements for placing offenders in need of treatment. The subsequent report noted that the term embraced a range of severe personality disorders, the group of people so labelled being extremely heterogeneous. Because the statutory definition rested on behaviour, "it brackets together a wider range of clinical states. It does not help to provide a clear basis for deciding which offenders should be treated as patients and which should be dealt with in the penal system. Comparable problems do not arise over the other categories of mental disorder in the Act where there is much greater professional consensus on both definition and treatment."[125] Following the lead given in the Butler Report, the working group recommended that the term "psychopathic disorder" be replaced in the 1983 Act by "personality disorder," which should not be defined further.[126] A review of the literature on the outcome of treatment, commissioned by the group, concluded that there was insufficient evidence to determine whether or not persons with psychopathic disorder could be successfully treated and no conclusive evidence of the efficacy of long-term hospitalisation.[127]

---

[123] Mental Health Act 1983, s.1(3). Gibbens observed as far ago as 1961 that some psychiatrists had extended the concept beyond a narrow group of dangerously anti-social individuals to include "those with alcoholism and drug addiction, those with sexual and marital disorders and those with employment disorders." T.C.N. Gibbens, "Treatment of Psychopaths" *Journal of Mental Science* (1961) 107, 181.

[124] *Report of the Department of Health and Home Office Working Group on Psychopathic Disorder* (Department of Health and the Home Office, 1994).

[125] *Ibid.*, p.4.

[126] *Ibid.*, pp. 35 and 39.

[127] B. Dolan and J. Coid, *Psychopathic and Antisocial Personality Disorders — Treatment and Research Issues* (Gaskell, 1993). Dell had previously found that the main determinant of the length of stay in special hospitals was not what happened to the patient in hospital but the nature of the index offence. Violent assaults, particularly sexual assaults or assaults directed against strangers, were associated with longer periods of detention. In contrast, in those patients suffering from mental illness (mostly schizophrenia), the severity and chronicity of the illness, and not the nature of the offence, were associated with longer detention. S. Dell, *et al.*, "Detention in Broadmoor: factors in length of stay" *British Journal of Psychiatry* (1987) 150, 824–827.

TERMS USED IN THE 1983 ACT

The meaning of the various terms used in the statutory definition of a psychopathic disorder is considered here.

"Persistent"

"Persistent" means "that there must be signs that the disorder has existed over a considerable period of time ... before the diagnosis is made."[128] Its use is intended:

> "to ensure that patients are not classified as psychopathic for the purpose of the compulsory detention ... until the personality disorder ... can be shown to have existed for a considerable period of time. It may be possible to deduce this from the symptoms occurring over such a period, but not all these symptoms amount to abnormally aggressive or seriously irresponsible conduct. There may be a pattern of abnormal behaviour culminating in a seriously aggressive act, such as sexual assault. The earlier signs might have been less serious but quite sufficient to show the doctor that the underlying disorder of personality had been there persistently. That should be sufficient to allow the diagnosis to be made without waiting for serious aggression to be repeated several times before the patient can be sent for treatment."[129]

"Disorder or disability of mind"

As drafted, the 1959 Bill referred to a "persistent disorder of personality" rather than a "persistent disorder or disability of mind." During the Committee stage in the House of Lords, Baroness Wootton of Abinger unsuccessfully moved to replace "persistent disorder of personality" with the words "a mental abnormality," on the ground that "a disorder of personality is often understood to mean something which manifests itself only in behaviour ... We are particularly anxious that persons who are going to be labelled as 'psychopaths' should manifest some abnormality of mind other than their persistently anti-social behaviour."[130] Following discussion of this concern in Committee, the Lord Chancellor introduced an amendment replacing the phrase "persistent disorder of personality" with the words "persistent disorder or disability of mind":

> "Very often the patient's behaviour provides the main symptoms on which the diagnosis is based; but anti-social behaviour of the sort described in the later words of the definition is not in itself enough to establish the diagnosis unless the pattern of behaviour shows other abnormal features which indicate that there is an underlying disorder ... the introduction of the term 'mind' helps to make this clear."[131]

Class of persons embraced by the term

In a statute dealing with mental disorder, the words "disorder or disability of mind" could not be broader and, as the Butler Report noted, the class of persons to whom the term relates do not represent a single class identifiable by any medical, biological or psychological criteria.[132]

---

128 *Per* the Lord Chancellor (Viscount Kilmuir), *Hansard,* H.L. Vol. 216, col. 756.
129 *Per* the Lord Chancellor (Viscount Kilmuir), *Hansard,* H.L. Vol. 217, col. 97.
130 *Hansard,* H.L. Vol. 217, cols. 91-92.
131 *Per* the Lord Chancellor (Viscount Kilmuir), *Hansard,* H.L. Vol. 217, col. 951.
132 *Report of the Committee on Mentally Abnormal Offenders*, Cmnd. 6244 (1975), para. 5.23.

"Whether or not including significant impairment of intelligence"

The words "whether or not accompanied by (subnormality of intelligence)" in the 1959 Bill were replaced in the 1959 Act by the phrase "whether or not including," which remains part of the statutory definition. The words maintain the historical notion, dating back to 1839, that "mental deficiency" and "psychopathic disorder" are somehow linked. Significant impairment of intelligence does not suffice but equally its presence will not rule out a classification of psychopathic disorder where there is evidence of a disorder or disability of mind which has persisted over time.

"Which results in"

It has been suggested that the concept of psychopathy is logically defective insofar as it infers mental disorder from anti-social behaviour while purporting to explain anti-social behaviour by mental disorder.[133] That would only be so if the words "associated with" or "including" were used. In fact, the reference to a conduct disorder after the words "results in" does not attempt to explain the disorder or disability of mind, rather its consequences. There must first and foremost be a disorder or disability of mind which has persisted over time. However, where that is established, a person is not to be liable to indefinite compulsory treatment or guardianship unless that disorder or disability can be shown to have seriously affected the person's conduct.

"Abnormally aggressive or seriously irresponsible conduct"

The definition requires that the disorder or disability of mind be persistent, rather than the patient's abnormally aggressive or seriously irresponsible behaviour. During the Committee stage in the House of Lords, Baroness Wootton of Abinger unsuccessfully moved to substitute for the words "which results in abnormally aggressive or seriously irresponsible conduct on the part of the patient" the words "which results in *dangerously and* persistently irresponsible conduct."[134]

Non-clinical considerations

In *ex p. Ryan (1991)*,[135] Nolan L.J. referred to a medical report prepared for the tribunal, in which the responsible medical officer wrote that whether the patient's sexual assault on a child amounted to seriously irresponsible conduct was "more in the realms of ethics and law than of clinical judgment, and I will not express a personal opinion." His Lordship accepted this, saying—

> "No doubt whether the conduct is the result of the disorder is ... a medical question. Whether it amounts to seriously irresponsible or abnormally aggressive behaviour seems to me ... to raise questions other than of a purely clinical nature."

"Abnormally aggressive"

The "word 'abnormally' emphasises that this is not what one might call ordinary aggression ... There is something peculiar about it: it is a symptom of mental disorder."[136] Various follow-up studies of patients discharged from special hospitals have

---

[133]   See the *Report of the Committee on Mentally Abnormal Offenders*, Cmnd. 6244 (1975), para. 5.20.
[134]   *Hansard*, H.L. Vol. 217, cols. 91–92.
[135]   *R. v. Trent Mental Health Review Tribunal, ex p. Ryan* [1992] C.O.D. 157.
[136]   *Per* the Lord Chancellor (Viscount Kilmuir), *Hansard*, H.L. Vol. 217, col. 97.

shown that those with psychopathic disorders are more likely than most other groups to reoffend.[137] Hostility (negative appraisals of other people) is differentiated from aggression (the behavioural tendency to react with verbal or physical aggression) in Blackburn's psychometric scales of hostility and aggression.

"Seriously irresponsible "

The Butler Committee considered it important to note that the statutory definition of psychopathic disorder included under the criterion of serious irresponsibility persons such as compulsive gamblers.[138] Although it is often said that a single relatively minor offence, such as the theft of an item from a supermarket, constitutes seriously irresponsible conduct this must be doubtful.

Application in a tribunal context

The court's finding that the patient was, at the time of sentence, suffering from a psychopathic disorder is taken as proof that the patient had at that time a psychopathic personality; it then becomes very difficult to establish that that is no longer the case. In a study of forty special hospital tribunal cases involving persons classified as having a psychopathic disorder, Peay found that the principal indication of the disorder was usually the nature, context and repetition of offending behaviour, although psychometric testing and examinations of the patient's early history and school work were sometimes mentioned as serving to confirm (or count against) the diagnosis. A major problem for the patient was overcoming the contention that the only reason why no abnormally aggressive or seriously irresponsible conduct had recently manifested itself was because of his detention in a secure environment.[139]

THE PROHIBITIONS IN SECTION 1(3)

Section 1(3) provides that nothing in the statutory definition of a psychopathic disorder shall be construed as implying that a person may be dealt with under the Act as suffering from such a disorder "by reason only of promiscuity or other immoral conduct, sexual deviancy or dependence on alcohol or drugs.[140] It is the interpretation of the phrase "sexual deviancy" which has mainly caused problems in practice, particularly in relation to paedophilia.

Sexual Deviancy

The 1959 Act did not expressly preclude the classification of a person as a "psychopath" by reason only of sexual deviancy. In 1975, the Butler Committee observed that it would be wrong to assume that sexual offenders are necessarily mentally disordered on that count alone. The Committee considered that it was necessary "to distinguish, among the generality of those who commit sexual offences, those who do so as a result of sexual deviancy, a condition recognised by

---

[137]   M. Norris, *Integration of special hospital patients into the community* (Gower, 1984); D.A. Black, "A 5–year follow-up study of male patients discharged from Broadmoor Hospital" in *Abnormal offenders, delinquency and the criminal justice system* (ed. J. Gunn & D.P. Farrinton, Wiley, 1982); G. Tennent and C. Way, "The English special hospital, a 12–17 year follow-up study: a comparison of violent and non-violent re-offenders and non-offenders" *Medicine Science & the Law* (1984) 24 81–91.

[138]   *Report of the Committee on Mentally Abnormal Offenders*, Cmnd. 6244 (1975), para. 5.13.

[139]   J. Peay, *Tribunals on Trial* (Clarendon Press, 1989).

[140]   See Footnote 125.

the International Classification of Diseases as a mental disorder ..."[141] The Mental Health (Amendment) Act 1982 had the effect of taking sexual offenders outside the legal definition of psychopathic disorder unless there was evidence of abnormally aggressive or seriously irresponsible conduct other than sexual deviancy. One effect of the new provisions was that tribunals were required to discharge any patient, restricted or unrestricted, whose detention as a "psychopath" was founded on sexual deviancy alone or who, once that deviancy had been discounted, did not suffer from a psychopathic disorder which was of a nature or degree making detention appropriate. Tribunals have understandably experienced problems implementing the prohibition and a number of tribunal decisions concerning patients admitted to hospital following conviction for a sexual offence have been judicially reviewed.

R. v. Mental Health Review Tribunal, ex p. Clatworthy

[1985] 3 All E.R. 699   *Q.B.D., Mann J.*

The patient had been convicted in 1967 of the indecent assault of two young girls: he had sat next to them in a cinema and placed his hand underneath the dress of one girl and touched the leg of the other outside her clothing. He had previously been convicted of a number of similar offences and also of attempted buggery. The court imposed a restriction order of five years' duration, at the expiration of which the patient remained detained under a notional hospital order. In 1984, his case was considered by a tribunal. The responsible medical officer's evidence, which was supported by a second consultant psychiatrist, was that the diagnosis of a psychopathic disorder appeared to be based on the applicant's sexual offending. There was no other evidence that he was abnormally aggressive or seriously irresponsible. As his main problem was one of sexual deviance, his condition did not constitute a "mental disorder." Notwithstanding this evidence, the tribunal refused to direct the patient's discharge, stating in their reasons that they were satisfied that he continued to suffer from psychopathic disorder, and saw no change in his condition from the time of his admission in 1967.

Mann J.

Quashing the tribunal's decision,

"It may be at once observed that the effect of sub-s. (3) is apparently to prevent there being a condition of psychopathic disorder when the abnormally aggressive or seriously irresponsible conduct consequent on the persistent disorder or disability of mind is conduct which is a manifestation of sexual deviancy. It may also be observed that it can be contended that sexual deviancy does not mean tendency to deviation but means indulgence in deviation. That contention would achieve support from its context, the context being promiscuity or other immoral conduct and dependence on alcohol or drugs." ...

The grounds for the reasons invite immediately the question: what are the features of psychopathic disorder as defined by the 1983 Act apart from sexual deviancy? The evidence as I read it is that there is no other feature and sexual deviancy is to be discounted under the Act ... It is, I think, appropriate to observe that the definition of psychopathic disorder with which I am now concerned is a definition first introduced into the law by the 1983 Act."

---

[141]   *Report of the Committee on Mentally Abnormal Offenders*, Cmnd. 6244 (1975), para. 3.25.

R. v. MHRT (Mersey Region) ex p. Davies

CO/1723/85, 21 April 1986.   *Q.B.D., Russell J.*

The patient, who had two previous convictions for indecent assault, was convicted in 1967 of indecently assaulting a young girl whom he enticed to a lonely spot. He was made the subject of a restriction without limit of time. He was granted home leave at the end of December 1982. In March 1983, he approached some young children in the street, mainly girls, and showed them a pornographic magazine. As a result, he was recalled from leave to a special hospital, where he was detained when his case was reviewed by a tribunal in July of that year. Two medical reports before the tribunal concluded that the patient did not suffer from a psychopathic disorder as defined by the Act. The Secretary of State opposed discharge and noted that a medical report from the special hospital had, with reference to the recent incident, described the patient "as a danger to others by reason of his inability to control his deviant sexual impulses and his total lack of insight." The Home Secretary was "conscious also that the incident ... in April 1983 was not thought by those then responsible for his care to be a spontaneous act of foolishness but a serious, sinister, premeditated attempt to lure the girls away." The Home Secretary considered that the patient's rehabilitation should take place with extreme caution and, preferably, via transfer to a local hospital where "his sexual attitudes may be closely monitored." The patient was described as having a bland, superficial attitude to his offences against children.

The tribunal's decision

The tribunal was of the opinion that the tribunal was suffering from a psychopathic disorder and it did not direct the patient's discharge:

> " We are not satisfied that the Applicant could at present overcome the enormous problems with which he will be faced if released into the community without giving way to the uncontrollable impulses which resulted in the offence which occasioned the order in 1967 ... The Applicant's conduct whilst on leave in 1983 which resulted in his return to [the special hospital], and in recent months when he has become sullen and morose and been disruptive is consistent in the view of the Tribunal of one suffering from psychopathic disorder. The incident in March 1983 demonstrates an inability to learn from past events. ... In the light of the Applicant's conduct as recently as March 1983 it is necessary for the protection of other persons that the Applicant should receive medical treatment in Hospital. "

The application for judicial review

The subsequent application for judicial review, which was based on the reasons given for the tribunal's decision, was dismissed. Section 1(3) was not referred to in the judgment and the court decided that the reasons given by the tribunal were adequate, and that there was no unfairness.

R. v. Mersey Mental Health Review Tribunal, ex p. D

The Times, 13 April 1987   *Q.B.D., Russell L.J. and Otton J.*

Having been found guilty but insane to a charge of murder in 1939, the patient had subsequently been detained in a special hospital and was subject to restrictions. In 1969, he was reported to have engaged in sexual behaviour with men of "infantile mentality," during which he twice placed his hands around the throat of a fellow patient, in one case rendering his partner unconscious. He had at various times admitted an attraction to young boys, and psychological testing had disclosed "to varying degrees" his "sexual deviation." In March 1984, he was found to have in his possession a photograph of a boy wearing swimming trunks. His case was considered by a tribunal in August 1986. The responsible medical officer, and the psychologist treating him, gave evidence that he no longer suffered from a psychopathic disorder.

The tribunal's decision

The tribunal did not accept this evidence and decided not to discharge. Its reasons included the following passage:

> "We are not persuaded in the light of the history of the applicant and his behaviour between January 1969 and July 1971 when he behaved in a dangerous manner towards young persons and the discovery of a photograph of a young boy in his possession as recently as 1984 that his condition can be described as one suffering only from a *tendency* towards sexual deviation."

The application for judicial review

The patient applied for judicial review of the tribunal's decision, on an unrelated ground. The court observed that his counsel had "realistically" accepted that the tribunal's finding was open to it and did not attack it.

R. v. Mental Health Act Commission, ex p. X

(1988) 9 B.M.L.R. 77   *Q.B.D., Stuart-Smith L.J., Farquharson J.*

The patient was described as a compulsive paedophile and he had been convicted of 16 offences of indecency or indecent assault on young boys under the age of 16 during the previous decade. He had served custodial sentences on three occasions. One of the arguments advanced before the court was that the treatment which it was proposed to give him — a drug which reduced the testosterone to castration levels — was not treatment for mental disorder but treatment for sexual deviancy, and so did not require authorisation under section 57 of the Act.

Stuart-Smith L.J.

Stuart-Smith L.J. observed that it had become clear during the hearing that responsible medical officer considered that the treatment was for the patient's mental disorder as well as for his sexual deviancy, and the point was therefore not pursued. His Lordship added that "in practice ... it seems likely that the sexual problem will be inextricably linked with the mental disorder, so that the treatment for the one is treatment for the other, as in this case."

R. v. Secretary of State for the Home Department, ex p. K.

[1990] 1 All E.R. 703   *Q.B.D., McCullough J.*

In January 1971, the patient was convicted of the manslaughter of a neighbour's 12-year-old daughter. Her condition when found indicated that she had been raped, asphyxiated, cut with a sharp instrument and bitten. The patient had previous convictions for rape, indecently assaulting a girl aged seven, and having sexual intercourse with a girl aged between 13 and 16. He had only been out of prison for some six weeks before committing the index offence. The court was satisfied that he was suffering from a psychopathic disorder and it directed his admission to a special hospital, in pursuance of a hospital order and a restriction order made without limit of time.

The first tribunal

In March 1985, a tribunal reviewed his case. A special hospital consultant gave evidence that in his opinion the patient was not a danger to himself or others and the chief psychologist there said that he was now functioning at a normal level. Given the unanimous medical evidence that the patient was not presently suffering from any form of mental disorder, but taking the view that it was appropriate for him to remain liable to recall, the tribunal conditionally discharged him from hospital.

The Crown Court proceedings

In October 1985, the patient made an unprovoked attack on a girl of 16 whom he saw walking along a road in the afternoon. The next night, he attacked a young woman of 21. After speaking to her, he held her neck in an arm lock and put his hand over her mouth, pulling her into an entry and then pushing her to a crouching position. When interviewed, the patient said only that he did not know why he had done it. A sexual motive for each assault was suspected but could not be proved. Subsequently, the patient pleading guilty in each case to assault occasioning actual bodily harm. He was described in court by his leading counsel as "so disturbed mentally that he cannot control the impulses from which he suffers." However, a special hospital medical report concluded that he had a severe personality disorder, probably with some psycho-sexual involvement, and an alcohol problem. This could not be equated with a psychopathic disorder and, in the doctor's opinion, he was not suffering from a mental disorder as defined by section 1. The judge imposed a sentence of six years imprisonment, describing the patient as "a very dangerous man ... in particular to young girls and young women."

The second tribunal

In 1986, the patient reapplied to the tribunal, once more seeking his absolute discharge from the hospital and restriction orders. The medical evidence before the tribunal was again unanimously of the view that the patient was not suffering from any form of mental disorder. The tribunal accepted this evidence but, as before, also considered it appropriate for him to remain liable to be recalled.

The application for judicial review

The subsequent judicial review proceedings turned on issues unrelated to section 1(3). However, it is noteworthy in this context that, notwithstanding the serious sexual offending, two tribunals were satisfied that the patient's condition and behaviour did not constitute a psychopathic disorder.

R. v. Trent Mental Health Review Tribunal, ex p. Ryan

[1992] C.O.D. 157   *Q.B.D., Nolan L.J.*

Having been convicted of three serious indecent assaults on young girls in 1972, the patient was subject to a restriction order. In 1986, whilst conditionally discharged from hospital, he was convicted of a further offence of sexual assault on a young girl and sentenced to imprisonment. On completing his sentence he was recalled to hospital. In December 1990, his case was considered by a tribunal. The psychologist's report for the tribunal stated that "one must assume that his paedophilic interests remain essentially untreated." The patient was not discharged and its reasons included the following passage:

> "The tribunal reminded itself of section (1) subsection (2) ... and concluded that it could not be satisfied that the patient was not suffering from psychopathic disorder. His conduct towards young females has been 'seriously irresponsible' resulting from psychopathic disorder."

Nolan L.J.

Nolan L.J. observed that the tribunal was entitled to say that it was not satisfied "in so far as they went on to conclude that his conduct towards young females had been seriously irresponsible resulting from psychopathic disorder." Neither the tribunal's decision, nor that of the High Court, made reference to sub-section 1(3) or to the judgment in *ex p. Clatworthy.*

Commentary

In some of the summarised cases, reference was made by the tribunals to features other than sexual deviancy that were considered to be indicative of a psychopathic disorder: uncontrollable impulses; lack of insight; lack of remorse; a bland, superficial attitude; sullen, morose and disruptive behaviour; an inability to learn from past events; and so forth. Even when generous account is taken of any other features which might be evidence of a psychopathic disorder, not all of the cases heard after *ex p. Clatworthy* are reconcilable with the approach set out there. An honest assessment of the case law virtually dictates a concession that tribunals have at times been disinclined to apply the prohibition in section 1(3), as interpreted in *ex p. Clatworthy,* and the courts have been reluctant to interfere. In the absence of a provision for transferring such offenders to prison, tribunals have often been faced with the prospect of discharging into the community persons whose tendency to sexually deviant behaviour remains uncurbed. The question arises whether the approach set out in *ex p. Clatworthy* represents an exhaustive statement of the law. Probably the only issue genuinely in doubt is whether the phrase "sexual deviancy" was intended by Parliament to take outside the Act persons whose abnormally aggressive or seriously irresponsible conduct consists only of serious sexual offending. Certainly, a major concern at the time the amendment was made was to put a stop to the practice of dealing with homosexuals, sexually active women, alcoholics and drug users on the basis that their behaviour was a form of mental disorder requiring medical treatment. The reference in section 1(3) to "immoral conduct" would no doubt include prostitution; the reference to "promiscuity" consensual sexual relations with multiple partners; the reference to "sexual deviancy" homosexuality, since, statistically, it represents a deviation from biological and social norms. As to sexual offending, an isolated sexual offence is not always the manifestation of an innate, uncontrollable, impulsive tendency towards sexually deviant behaviour. Any element of impulsivity or lack of control may be the consequence of taking alcohol or drugs. In other cases, the offence may simply be a way of exerting control over a partner or humiliating the victim: first and foremost a serious form of assault, rather than the product of innate sexual tendencies which deviate from the norm.[142] It is possible therefore that the prohibition concerning sexual behaviour

---

[142] The analysis here ignores the view that all unlawful violence is per se a symptom of mental disorder and, unless an individual's own health or safety is significantly at risk, this should be the main or sole criterion according to which decisions about detention and compulsory treatment are made. Although the view has much to commend it, it is very much a minority view.

which deviates from the norm was solely intended to exclude persons who engage in lawful sexual activity, or conduct which, although unlawful, is not explicable in terms of an uncontrollable, constitutional, tendency towards that behaviour. This kind of behaviour is quite different from behaviour which arises out of repetitive, obsessional and irresistible thoughts about sexual contact with children and the compulsive acts which result from such obsessions. The inability to mentally control such habitual thoughts and behaviour, despite its criminal nature and the strong social taboos against acting on such thoughts, is arguably a form of obsessional disorder — no less than in a man who cannot resist the thought that the door he has just closed did not make the right sound and that he must keep closing it until it does. It is therefore the obsessive-compulsive aspect of the behaviour which represents the persistent disorder or disability of mind, and brings the person within the Act, rather than the behaviour itself — which may be indulged in by persons without those ingrained traits in their personality. By analogy, if a man rapes a woman in response to some voice telling him to do so, it is not the rape which constitutes mental disorder — other men commit rape for quite different reasons — but the mental thought which gave rise to the act of sexual deviancy. Yet no one would say that the individual is not mentally disordered because the thought manifested itself as a sexually deviant act. If this is correct, there is a clear distinction between sexually deviant behaviour which does not result from a persistent disorder or disability of mind — that is a persistent mental disposition towards such behaviour — and sexually deviant behaviour which results from a persistent disability of mind in the form of a persistent mental disposition towards it. A finding that a person in the first category is mentally disordered would be a finding based on sexual deviant conduct alone, and so unlawful. A finding that a person in the second category is mentally disordered would not, however, be a finding based solely on sexual deviant conduct. It is not a finding based solely on "indulgence in deviation," being founded also on the existence of a persistent disability of mind in the form of an irresistible tendency towards such sexually deviancy. If so, the dicta in ex p. Clatworthy may be extended along the following lines:

> "The effect of subsection (2) is to prevent a person from being classified as having a psychopathic disorder unless his aggressive or seriously irresponsible conduct results from a persistent disorder or disability of mind. Furthermore, by subsection (3), he may not be dealt with as suffering from such a disorder by reason *only* of sexual deviancy. Sexual deviancy means indulgence in behaviour which deviates from sexual norms. That conclusion achieves support from its context, the context being promiscuity or other immoral conduct and dependence on alcohol or drugs. The combined effect of the two subsections is therefore that indulgence in conduct which deviates from sexual norms cannot on that ground alone be categorised as seriously irresponsible or abnormally aggressive conduct which is the result of a disorder or disability of mind. One is not entitled to conclude solely from the fact that the individual's behaviour deviates from sexual norms that he therefore has a disordered or disabled mind. If, however, there is evidence that his sexually deviant conduct is the product of a persistent disorder or disability of mind then any finding that such a person is mentally disordered is not one founded *only* on sexual deviancy. It is one founded on sexual deviancy and the existence of a persistent disorder or disability of mind."

3. Relevant terms and parties

INTRODUCTION

Many different individuals and bodies may be involved in the detention, treatment or care of an individual and in any subsequent tribunal proceedings. It is important to have some understanding of their functions and any statutory definitions relating to them. Where a term is defined in section 145(1) of the Mental Health Act 1983, the meaning given there applies "unless the context otherwise requires."

- The patient (**098**) is the focus of the tribunal proceedings and the other private individual with a statutory role is the patient's nearest relative (**100**). Special considerations may apply if the patient is a child (**115**).

- Unless he has been received into guardianship, or is subject to supervision, the patient will be liable to detention in a hospital (**131**). It is the managers of that hospital (**141**) who have authority to detain him there in accordance with the provisions of the 1983 Act.

- Unless the hospital is a private establishment, it will form part of the National Health Service for which the Secretary of State for Health (**126**) is accountable to Parliament. NHS hospitals are managed by NHS trusts (**131**). Health Authorities (**130**) purchase in-patient and other medical services from these trusts.

- Various health service professionals will then be involved in the patient's treatment. In addition to their clinical duties, medical practitioners (**146**) and nurses (**149**) have a number of statutory functions to perform.

- Patients who leave hospital or who are subject to guardianship will require support from local social services authorities (**151**), including community care (**154**). Many statutory functions under the 1983 Act may only be exercised by approved social workers (**160**), that is by social workers who have undergone special training in the statutory procedures.

- A number of executive or judicial bodies may be involved. The Home Secretary (**162**) has responsibility for some patients whose discharge from hospital may place the public at risk of serious harm. The Mental Health Act Commission (**169**) is a quasi-independent body which visits detained patients and investigates certain complaints made by or in respect of them. Mental Health Review Tribunals (**190**) are independent judicial bodies which review whether a patient should be subject to compulsory powers at all.

THE PATIENT

The Mental Health Act 1983 provides that, unless the context otherwise requires, and except in relation to matters concerning the Court of Protection, the word "patient" means "a person suffering or appearing to suffer from mental disorder.[1] By section 1(1), the provisions of the Act have effect with respect to the reception, care and treatment of mentally disordered patients, the management of their property and other related matters. In the context of tribunal proceedings, the "patient" is simply the person whose case is under review. During the year ending on 31 March 1996, 271,000 people were admitted to hospital for in-patient psychiatric treatment, of whom some 26,000 were detained under the 1983 Act.

RESTRICTED PATIENTS

A "restricted patient" is a patient who is subject to a restriction order or a restriction direction, or an order having like effect.[2] Where the Crown Court orders the admission of a defendant to hospital at the conclusion of criminal proceedings, it may also make what is known as a restriction order. Similarly, where the Home Secretary directs the transfer of a person from prison to hospital, he may further direct that the patient shall be subject to a "restriction direction." If such restrictions are in force, their effect is that the patient cannot be transferred to another hospital, or granted leave to be absent from the hospital grounds, without the Home Secretary's consent. Furthermore, the patient's discharge from hospital requires either the Home Secretary's consent or a direction made by him or by a Mental Health Review Tribunal. A restricted patient's discharge may initially only be conditional, in which case he can be recalled to hospital for further treatment if his mental state or behaviour deteriorates or he breaches one of the condition of his discharge. Notwithstanding the wording of section 1(1), a restricted patient remains a "patient" for the purposes of the Act until such time as he is absolutely discharged from the restrictions — that is, regardless of whether or not he appears to be suffering from mental disorder at a particular moment in time.[3]

The restricted population

There are approximately 100,000 in-patients in psychiatric units in England and Wales of whom 1,900 or so are restricted patients. About 1,200 of them are detained in special hospitals, the remainder being in regional secure units and local hospitals. The great majority have been convicted of serious offences of violence — 530 of homicide, 700 of other violent offences, 230 of a sexual offence, and 250 of arson. In addition to the in-patient population, there are about 1,000 conditionally discharged restricted patients living in the community.

INFORMAL PATIENTS

The vast majority of people undergoing in-patient psychiatric treatment are not liable to be detained and of those who are detained only a small minority are subject to special restrictions. Patients who are treated without resort to formal compulsory

---

[1]   Mental Health Act 1983, s.145(1).
[2]   *Ibid.*, s.79(1).
[3]   *R. v. Merseyside Mental Health Review Tribunal, ex p. K* [1990] 1 All E.R. 694, *per* Butler-Sloss L.J. at 699.

powers are known as "informal patients." Section 131(1) of the Mental Health Act 1983 provides that nothing in the statute "shall be construed as preventing a patient who requires treatment for mental disorder from being admitted to any hospital or mental nursing home in pursuance of arrangements made in that behalf and without any application, order or direction rendering him liable to be detained under this Act."

Voluntary patients

Not all "informal patients" are "voluntary patients" and the terms are not synonymous. A significant number of informal patients lack the capacity to consent to their admission, are mentally incapable of organising and arranging their own discharge, or remain in hospital informally only because compulsory powers will be invoked if they refuse treatment or attempt to leave. The 1983 Act provides three mechanisms for protecting these citizens. Firstly, it is an offence to ill-treat or to wilfully neglect them.[4] Secondly, certain invasive treatments such as psychosurgery must be independently authorised and may only be administered to an informal patient who is able to give a valid consent to the treatment.[5] Thirdly, the statute empowers the Secretary of State to extend the Mental Health Act Commission's remit so that it includes keeping under review the care and treatment of informal patients.[6] However, no such direction has yet been given. Informal admission may be particularly disadvantageous for people who are mentally incapacitated in that the necessity for their being in hospital, and the treatment and care which they receive there, are not susceptible to periodic external review by the Mental Health Act Commission or a Mental Health Review Tribunal. Whilst the use of compulsory powers deprives the person affected of certain legal rights, it also confers other rights in substitution. Since these are framed as duties exercisable by third parties on the patient's behalf, they may in practice more than compensate the patient for the loss of rights the existence of which he is unaware or, if aware of them, incapable of exercising. Although most formal patients understandably wish to be informal, there are nevertheless a number of patients who are incapable of understanding or exercising the legal rights which constitute the practical benefits of being an informal patient.

OTHER ASPECTS OF A PATIENT'S LEGAL STATUS

Having regard to the above, a patient's legal status under the 1983 Act may be that he is an informal patient, a person who is liable to be detained in a hospital, or someone subject to guardianship or statutory supervision in the community. If a child, he may also be subject to some order made under the Children Act 1989. His legal status in other respects is relative and depends on his relationship to the individual involved in his detention, treatment or care, and the activity being undertaken. He is his doctor's patient, and his solicitor's or social worker's client, so these professionals owe him a duty of care and are bound by certain professional rules of conduct. In other contexts he may be a complainant, a plaintiff, a testator, a resident of a local authority, a Member of Parliament's constituent, a patient of the Court of Protection, and so forth. In constitutional terms, he is a subject of the reigning sovereign in proceedings before English and Welsh courts but, in essence, a

---

4   Mental Health Act 1983, s.127.
5   *Ibid.*, s.57.
6   *Ibid.*, subss. 121(4) and (5).

citizen for the purpose of proceedings before the European Court of Human Rights. Hence, interventions justified domestically as the lawful exercise of the sovereign's historical powers over subjects of the realm have not infrequently later been reinterpreted as abuses by the executive of a citizen's rights. To summarise, a patient's legal status is defined with a particular purpose in mind and his status determines his legal rights and duties, the powers and duties exercisable by others in respect of him, and the legal procedures to be followed.[7]

THE NEAREST RELATIVE

The patient's nearest relative has several important functions under the Act. These include—

- power to apply for the patient's admission to hospital or reception into guardianship;

- power to require that an approved social worker (an ASW) assesses the patient, with a view to that person making an application under the Act;

- power to object to the making of a guardianship application or a section 3 application by an approved social worker;

- power to discharge the patient from detention or guardianship under Part II of the Act;

- power in some cases to apply to a tribunal for the patient's discharge.

A patient's other relatives may apply to the county court for the appointment of an acting nearest relative (111) and an approved social worker must have regard any wishes expressed by them before deciding whether to make an application for the patient's admission to hospital or reception into guardianship. Subject to these exceptions, they have no powers or rights under the Act.

THE STATUTORY FRAMEWORK

Section 145(1) provides that, unless the context otherwise requires, the term "nearest relative" in relation to a patient has the meaning given in Part II of the Act.[8]

---

[7] Conventionally, the statutory term "legal functions" means powers and duties. A person's "rights" may be said to consist of his lawful expectation that (1) other people will not exercise power over him which they do not lawfully possess; (2) that they will exercise duties legally owed by them to him; and (3) that they will not impede the exercise by him of legal powers or duties vested in him and exercisable over or owed to others. For every right there must always exist a corresponding duty so that, at any given time, the volume of rights and duties in a society is always equal and precisely balanced.

[8] Note, however, that in those rare cases where a patient is removed to England and Wales from Scotland under Part VII of the Mental Health (Scotland) Act 1984, the nearest relative under Scottish law at the time of his removal is to be treated as his nearest relative under the 1983 Act: Mental Health (Scotland) Act 1984, ss.77(1) and 128. The main difference relates to the priority given to carers over persons with whom the patient resides.

Within Part II of the Act—

- Sections 26–28 define who are a patient's relatives for the purposes of the Act and which of them is to be regarded as the "nearest relative";

- Sections 29–31 provide that the county court may in certain circumstances by order direct that some other person or authority exercises a patient's nearest relative's functions under the Act;

- Section 32 states that a nearest relative may, in the circumstances prescribed by regulations, appoint some other person to exercise his statutory functions on his behalf.

When these provisions are considered together, the basic framework for determining who is entitled to exercise the nearest relative's powers and duties is that set out in the table immediately below.

NEAREST RELATIVE PROVISIONS — THE BASIC FRAMEWORK

- If a section 29 order is in force, statutory references to the nearest relative are to be construed as referring to the person authorised by the order and one need go no further. However, such orders are rare in practice.   **111**

- In the case of patients aged under 18, the usual rules set out in section 26 for determining who is the nearest relative apply unless he is in care, subject to a residence order, or has a guardian appointed under children's legislation, in which case sections 27 and 28 apply.   **106**

- *In all other cases*, the nearest relative is determined according to the provisions of section 26. That being so, where the patient ordinarily resides with, or is cared for, by a relative (whether his spouse or someone else) then that person will generally be the nearest relative.   **103**

- If more than one relative ordinarily resides with or cares for the patient, priority is given to the person who ranks highest on the statutory list of relatives and, as between persons of equal rank (*e.g.* children), to the eldest of them.   **104**

- The person who qualifies as the nearest relative may authorise some other person to exercise on his behalf his statutory functions.   **109**

"RELATIVE"

Before it is possible to ascertain who is a patient's nearest relative, it is necessary to know the group of people who are his relatives. Section 26 lists the categories of people who constitute a patient's relatives for the purpose of the Act. A relationship of the half-blood is to be treated as a relationship of the whole blood and an illegitimate child treated as the legitimate child of his mother and, if his father has parental responsibility for him, of his father also.[9] The table immediately below sets out the "statutory list" of persons who constitute a patient's "relatives."

---

[9]   Mental Health Act 1983, s.26(2)(b).

• "husband or wife," which includes a person who has been living with the patient as her/his husband or wife for a period of not less than six months or, in the case of in-patients, had been so living with the patient before the patient was admitted to hospital;	s.26(1)(a)
• children, including adopted children but excluding step-children;	s.26(2)(b)
• parents, including the parents of an adopted child;	s.26(2)(c)
• brothers and sisters;	s.26(2)(d)
• grandparents;	s.26(2)(e)
• grandchildren;	s.26(2)(f)
• uncles and aunts;	s.26(2)(g)
• nephews and nieces;	s.26(2)(h)
• any other persons with whom the patient has ordinarily resided for a period of not less than five years or who, in the case of in-patients, had so resided with him for such a period prior to admission.	s.26(7)

Priority of relatives

Although all of the above persons are relatives of the patient, the order of the statutory list is significant. When determining who is a patient's "nearest relative," the Act may give priority to first living person on the list, so that a child of the patient, being a person coming within the second category, takes priority over a parent of the patient, being a person in a category further down the list.

Children born to unmarried parents

Because an illegitimate child is treated as the legitimate child of his mother so any of the listed persons related to that child through his mother will necessarily also be relatives under the Act. Likewise, any children of that illegitimate child will be regarded as the legitimate grandchildren of their unmarried grandmother and related to her for statutory purposes. Conversely, if the father of an illegitimate child is not a relative of that child under the Act, because he does not have parental responsibility, then so too are all the father's blood-relatives disqualified from being relatives under the Act.

Unmarried fathers and parental responsibility

The unmarried father of a child will acquire parental responsibility for the child, *inter alia*, by entering into a parental responsibility agreement with the child's mother[10] or by virtue of a court order that he shall have parental responsibility.[11]

---

[10]   Children Act 1989, s.2(2)(b).
[11]   *Ibid.*, s.4(1)(b).

Persons ordinarily residing with the patient for 5 years

The provision that persons "with whom" a patient has ordinarily resided for five years are deemed to be relatives of his under the Act has given rise to considerable comment. In *Shah v. Barnet London Borough Council*,[12] it was said that, unless the statutory framework or the legal context require a different meaning, "ordinarily" resident refers to a man's abode in a particular place which he has adopted *voluntarily* and for settled purposes for the time being, as part of the regular order of his life. Some writers have suggested that persons living with a patient for five years in a residential or nursing home, long-stay ward, special hospital, prison or monastery may therefore be relatives of his under the Act. Consequently, in the absence of any known spouse or blood-relative with a prior entitlement, the eldest of them will be his "nearest relative" and have power to apply for his admission to hospital, to discharge him from detention under Part II, and so forth. It is, however, submitted that Parliament cannot have intended that the phrase should be construed in so indiscriminate a way, and the precise wording of section 26(7) is against such a view. Ordinarily residing at the same address as the patient does not suffice; the person must be someone "with whom" he ordinarily resides. A person cannot be said to reside "with" the tenants of another flat or bedsit in the same building nor, in the case of student or other residential accomodation, to reside with persons who occupy different rooms in the same building, even if they share a common place of residence and certain communal facilities.[13] To ordinarily reside with someone indicates a voluntary agreement to live with a particular person rather than an involuntary or institutional requirement that a prison cell or a ward bedroom is shared with him. There must be some element of choice before a person may be said to "ordinarily" reside "with" another such that, as matters stand, if one of them moves the other, being a person who ordinarily resides with him, would be likely to also move with him, either immediately or as soon as circumstances permit. Conversely, the fact that one of the occupants of a house or flat is temporarily absent from that place, for example as a result of being admitted to hospital, does not of itself alter the fact that they ordinarily reside together. The question whether a person resides "with" another is one of fact in each case.[14]

"NEAREST RELATIVE"

It is convenient to summarise the effect of sections 26–28 by dealing separately with three different situations commonly encountered in practice (and it may be noted that in the first two situations described it is legally impossible for more than one person to be the "nearest relative") —

- cases where there is a relative who ordinarily resides with or cares for the patient, whether that person is his spouse or some other person;

- cases where that is not so;

- cases involving patients aged under 18 who are in care, or in respect of whom a residence order has been made or a guardian appointed under children's legislation.

---

[12]   *Shah v. Barnet London Borough Council* [1983] 1 All E.R. 226, H.L., *per* Lord Scarman at 235.
[13]   See *e.g. Evans v. Evans* [1948] L.J.R. 276; *Wheatley v. Wheatley* [1950] K.B. 39; *Curtin v. Curtin* [1952] 2 Q.B. 552. In these cases on maintenance, a wife was held not to be "residing with" her husband if they occupied different parts of a house.
[14]   *Middleton v. Bull* [1951] W.N. 517.

It should be noted that a person's nearest relative may change during the period of his detention, for example because a relative attains the age of 18 or because the patient and his spouse separate.[15] Furthermore, the Act does not expressly provide that a nearest relative who makes a tribunal application, but ceases to qualify as the nearest relative prior to the hearing, shall be deemed to remain the patient's nearest relative for the remainder of the proceedings.[16] Rather, it is for the new nearest relative to decide whether to continue them or to request that the application be withdrawn.[17]

Patients who ordinarily reside with or are cared for by a relative

The general rule is that where a patient ordinarily resides with or is cared for by a relative, that relative is his "nearest relative" unless s/he is a person other than the patient's husband or wife[18] who is less than 18 years old.[19]

Hospital in-patients

In the case of in-patients, the relative who ordinarily resided with, or cared for, the patient immediately prior to admission will be the nearest relative *unless* s/he is the patient's husband or wife and the couple have since separated either by agreement or under a court order, or one of them has deserted the other for a period which has not come to an end, *or* (in the case of other relatives) is a person aged under 18.[20]

Patients residing with or cared for by more than one relative

Where more than one relative is, or has been, ordinarily residing with or caring for the patient, preference is given to the one who ranks highest in the statutory list (**102**) and, if two or more of them are still equally entitled, to the eldest relative within that class — subject to the caveat that relatives of the whole blood, even if younger, are preferred to those of the half-blood within the same class.[21]

---

[15]   See *e.g.* the wording of s.26(5)(c) ("is a person ... for the time being under 18 years of age" *c.f.* "at the time of admission"), s.30(6) ("notwithstanding that the person who was the patient's nearest relative when the order was made is no longer his nearest relative"), and s.30(1)(b).

[16]   There is no provision equivalent to that in Mental Health Act 1983, Sched. 5, para. 11, which provided that "Where at any time before 30th September 1983 an application to a Mental Health Review Tribunal has been made by a person who at that time was the patient's nearest relative and the application has not then been determined and by reason of the coming into force of section 26 of this Act that person ceased to be the patient's nearest relative on that date, that person shall nevertheless be treated for the purposes of the application as continuing to be his nearest relative."

[17]   Allied to this point, the wording of section 25(1)(b) suggests that the new nearest relative may immediately give notice of his intention to discharge the patient notwithstanding that his predecessor was barred from doing for a period of six months, which period has not yet expired.

[18]   As defined in the table of relatives (**102**).

[19]   For the avoidance of doubt, a person who ordinarily lives with the patient, but who is not a blood relative or the patient's husband or wife, is not a "relative" (and therefore cannot possibly be the "nearest relative" under this rule) unless s/he has ordinarily resided with the patient for five years.

[20]   A person who qualifies as the nearest relative because, prior to the patient's admission, he ordinarily resided with him or cared for him in the United Kingdom, the Channel Islands or the Isle of Man, must also be discounted if he later takes up residence outside those territorial boundaries. The fact that priority may be given to the relative who ordinarily resided with or cared for the patient prior to his admission is unsatisfactory in the case of some long-stay patients. That person may no longer ordinarily care for, or reside with, the patient. The better view may therefore be that the effect of s.26(4) is limited to ensuring that a relative who does ordinarily reside with or care for the patient does not lose his priority by virtue only of the fact that the latter is in hospital. If, following admission, that relative ceases to ordinarily reside with or care for the patient then his priority ceases also.

[21]   Where a patient ordinarily resides with two relatives, only one of whom ordinarily cares for him, the carer is not thereby preferred to the other. For example, where a patient and his adult brother ordinarily reside with an aunt who cares for the patient, the brother is the nearest relative.

An unrealistically complicated example illustrates the principles. Immediately prior to admission, a male patient ordinarily resided with his wife, widowed mother aged 55, two sisters aged 19 and 17, and a half-brother aged 30. There are no other relatives. His spouse will therefore be the nearest relative since of the various persons in the household she ranks first in the list of relatives above. If, following admission, the patient and his spouse separate or one of them deserts the other, the patient's mother will at that point become his nearest relative. If the patient's mother then dies, the sister aged 19 will be the nearest relative. If she in turn dies, the patient's half-brother will assume the title until such time as the youngest sister assumes the age of 18, at which point she (being a relative of the whole blood) will have a prior entitlement.

Married patients

The Act provides that where a married patient has lived with someone else as that person's man or wife for at least six months, the cohabitee shall not be treated as the nearest relative unless the parties to the marriage are permanently separated, either by agreement or by order of a court, or one of them has deserted the other for a period which has not yet come to an end.[22] In practice, it will be rare for a patient to have lived with someone else as that person's man or wife for such a period and yet not be in desertion. The Act similarly provides that unless the parties to a marriage are separated or one of them is in desertion, a person who is deemed to be a relative because he has been ordinarily residing with the patient for five years is not to be treated as the patient's nearest relative in preference to the legal spouse.[23] Again, the qualification is generally of only academic interest: a husband or wife, ranking highest in the list of relatives, will automatically have a prior entitlement unless s/he ordinarily resides at a different address from the patient, in which case one of them has usually deserted the other or they are separated by agreement.

Patients who have not resided with or been cared for by a relative

The second situation concerns patients who have no relatives who ordinarily reside with or care for them or who, prior to admission, were not ordinarily residing with or being cared for by a relative on such a basis. In the case of married patients, this will generally be because the parties have separated or one of them has deserted the other, in which case, unless the separation or desertion has proved not to be permanent, the spouse must be discounted; if there has been a reconciliation, the spouse is the nearest relative. Subject to this, the Act provides that the nearest relative is the person ranking highest in the statutory list of relatives who is not disqualified from acting as such under either of the following grounds[24]—

---

[22] Mental Health Act 1983, s.26(6).

[23] *Ibid.*, s.26(7)(b).

[24] The 1983 Act originally included a third ground. Section 38 of the Sexual Offences Act 1956 provided that, where a person was convicted of incest under section 10 or 11 of that Act, the court could divest that person of all authority over the girl or boy. Section 26(5)(d) of the Mental Health Act 1983, since repealed by the Children Act 1989, in turn disqualified a person against whom a divesting order was in force from being the victim's nearest relative. The effect of the repeal is that, unless the court appointed a guardian for the victim when making the divesting order, and that guardianship remains in force, the fact that a divesting order was made is irrelevant when determining a person's nearest relative.

- that he is for the time being under the age of 18;

- in the case of a patient ordinarily resident in the United Kingdom, the Channel Islands or the Isle of Man, that he is a person who ordinarily resides outside those countries.[25]

As before, preference is given as between two or more persons within a particular class to relatives of the whole blood and, if more than one, to the eldest of them.

Example

A patient who is detained under section 3 lived alone prior to admission and was not cared for by any of his relatives. His wife deserted him some years previously. He has three other relatives, being a brother aged 40 who lives in Wales; a daughter aged 24 who lives and works in the Republic of Ireland; and a son aged 17 who lives in England. The nearest relative is the patient's brother as both children are to be discounted in determining the issue. However, the patient's son will assume the function on his eighteenth birthday.

No nearest relative

One effect of the statutory scheme is that a patient may have no nearest relative. Where this is so, or it is not reasonably practicable to ascertain whether he has such a relative, an application may be made to the county court for an order appointing an individual or a local social services authority to exercise the functions of a nearest relative (**111**).

Nearest relative mentally or physically incapacitated

Where the nearest relative is incapable of acting as such by reason of mental disorder or other illness, he nevertheless remains the patient's nearest relative until such time (if any) as the County Court directs that his statutory functions shall be exercisable by some other person or by a local social services authority (**111**).

Patients aged under 18

In the case of patients aged under 18, the usual rules for determining who is the nearest relative apply unless a residence order[26] is in force, or the patient is in the

---

[25] Where a patient is himself ordinarily resident outside the United Kingdom, the Channel Islands or the Isle of Man, the ordinary place of residence of his relatives is immaterial when determining which of them is the nearest relative for the purposes of the Act. See Mental Health Act 1983, s.26(5)(a); *Mental Health Act 1983: Memorandum on Parts I to VI, VIII and X*, (D.H.S.S., 1987), para. 68. The point most commonly arises in respect of patients who are citizens of the Republic of Ireland or who are detained whilst visiting England or Wales on holiday.

[26] A "residence order" means an order settling the arrangements to be made as to the person with whom a child is to live (Children Act 1989, s.8(1)). An order ceases to have effect when the child reaches the age of 16 unless the court making the order directed that it should continue beyond that date (Children Act 1989, s.91(10)), in which case it will cease when the child reaches 18 (*ibid.*, s.91(11)). Except in exceptional circumstances, a court shall not make an order in respect of a child aged 16 or over (Children Act, s.9(7)). A residence order may be made in favour of two or more persons (*Ibid.*, s.11(4)). The making of a residence order with respect to a child discharges any existing care order (*ibid.*, s.91(1)).

care of a local authority,[27] or a guardian has been appointed under children's legislation.[28] The fact that a patient is a ward of court has no bearing on who is his nearest relative.[29]

Care order in force

Where a care order is in force, the local authority in whose care the patient is "shall be deemed to be the nearest relative of the patient in preference to any person except the patient's husband or wife (if any)."[30] In this context, the reference to a patient's "husband or wife" excludes relationships outside marriage.[31]

Residence order in force

Where a residence order is in force, the Act provides that "the person named in the residence order shall, to the exclusion of any other person, be deemed to be his nearest relative."[32] In fact, more than one person may be named in a residence order, in which case both (or all) of them are probably deemed to be the nearest relative (see below).

Guardian appointed under children's legislation

Where a guardian has been appointed for a patient under children's legislation, "the guardian (or guardians, where there is more than one) ... shall, to the exclusion of any other person, be deemed to be his nearest relative."[33] Where a patient has a guardian and is also the subject of a residence order, it is probably the case that the guardian(s) and the person(s) named have an equal entitlement.

Joint nearest relative(s)

In the case of a patient aged under 18, it is possible for more than two individuals to be the nearest relative. This will occur where more than one guardian has been appointed, where a residence order names more than one person, or where, for example, a patient who has a guardian is also the subject of a residence order. The fact that more than one person might be named in a residence order seems not to

---

27 Section 31 of the Children Act 1989 provides that a court may make an order placing a child who has not reached the age of 17 in the care of a designated local authority (ss.31(1) and (3)). The court must be satisfied that the child is suffering, or is likely to suffer, significant harm which is attributable to the care given to the child, or likely to be given to him if the care order is not made, not being care which it is reasonable to expect a parent to give to him (s.31(2)). A care order continues in force until the child reaches the age of 18 unless discharged earlier (Children Act 1989, s.91(12)). The making of a care order with respect to a child who is a ward of court brings that wardship to an end (s.91(3)).

28 Mental Health Act 1983, s.28(3), as substituted by the Children Act 1989, s.108(5), Sched. 13, para. 48, provides that the term "guardian" in this context does not include a guardian appointed under the Mental Health Act. Section 5(13) of the Children Act 1989 provides that a guardian may only be appointed in accordance with the provisions of that section. Guardianship ends when the child reaches the age of 18, unless brought to an end earlier (ibid., s.91(7)(8)).

29 It does, however, affect the exercise by the nearest relative of his functions under the Act.

30 Mental Health Act 1983, s.27(a), as substituted by the Children Act 1989, s.108(5), Sched. 13, para. 48(1). In normal circumstances, an approved social worker considering whether to make an application for admission for treatment must therefore consult the local authority before applying.

31 The definition of a husband or wife in section 26(6) commences with the words, "In this section ..."

32 Mental Health Act 1983, s.28(1)(b), as substituted by the Children Act 1989, s.108(5), Sched. 13, para. 48. Section 26(5) applies if relevant.

33 Mental Health Act 1983, s.28(1)(a), as substituted by the Children Act 1989, s.108(5), Sched. 13, para. 48. Section 26(5) applies if relevant. Where a patient who has a guardian is in care, the local authority will be the nearest relative.

have been foreseen. In the case of guardians, the wording of section 28(1) is ambiguous. The intention may be that there is only ever one statutory nearest relative, albeit that more than one person may be involved in fulfilling the statutory functions of "the" nearest relative.[34] Alternatively, the wording allows the alternative interpretation that a patient has two or more nearest relatives in such circumstances.[35] Clearly, disputes could arise between two or more persons equally entitled. For example, one may object to a section 3 application being made by an approved social worker but not the other. Similarly, one guardian might apply for the patient's admission without the other's consent and against his wishes. Conversely, one them might make an order for the patient's discharge but the other not join in the making of that order. Although it is possible to devise ways of dealing with such problems in the medium term, for example by making an application under the Children Act 1989,[36] this does not resolve the issue of whether any power exercised by one of the persons entitled is valid, nor is of much assistance to a social worker or the managers of a hospital faced with such predicaments.

Mental Health Act 1959

Section 28 derives from section 51 of the Mental Health Act 1959 which provided that "the person or persons having the guardianship or custody of the patient shall, to the exclusion of any other person, be deemed to be his nearest relative." The Guardianship of Infants Act 1925 was in force at the time and it provided that the widowed mother of an infant "shall be guardian of the infant, either alone or jointly with any guardian appointed by the father";[37] that a guardian appointed by deed or will "shall act jointly" with the surviving parent;[38] and that "where two or more persons act as joint guardians ... and they are unable to agree on any question affecting the welfare of the infant, any of them may apply to the court for its direction, and the court may make such order regarding the matters in difference as it may think proper."[39] Parliament's intention would therefore appear to be that if two people are jointly the nearest relative, the exercise of any statutory power vested in the nearest relative — for example, to apply for a patient's admission, to object to his admission, or to discharge him — is only valid if it constitutes a joint decision. That this is so is supported by the following passage in the *Report of the Royal Commission on the Law Relating to Mental Illness and Mental Deficiency*[40]—

> "426. If the patient's nearest relatives are two or more relatives equal in kinship to the patient, and one of them wishes the patient to be discharged and another wishes the patient to remain for further treatment, neither should have absolute authority to override the other. It should be left to the discretion of the hospital authorities whether to discharge the patient or not. We should expect the hospital normally to discharge if any one of the patient's nearest relatives seems able to make reasonable arrangements for the patient's care."

---

[34]   In the same way that the office of "The Secretary of State" is one in law.

[35]   Because the 1959 Act allowed emergency applications under section 29 to be made by any relative of the patient, it might be argued that Parliament did not balk at the idea that there could be more than one person qualified to exercise a statutory power. Likewise, it might have envisaged that disputes between guardians could be dealt with under children's legislation.

[36]   Or, arguably, by making an application under section 29 of the Mental Health Act 1983.

[37]   Guardianship of Infants Act 1925, s.4(1).

[38]   *Ibid.*, s.5(3).

[39]   *Ibid.*, s.6.

[40]   *Report of the Royal Commission on the Law Relating to Mental Illness and Mental Deficiency*, Cmnd. 169 (1957), para. 426.

DELEGATION OF THE NEAREST RELATIVE'S FUNCTIONS

The Act expressly provides that the Secretary of State may make regulations enabling the functions of a nearest relative under Part II of the Act to be performed by any person authorised by the nearest relative.[41] The regulations provide that any authority, and any notice revoking such an authority, shall be made in writing[42] and shall take effect on receipt of that written authority or revocation by the person authorised.[43] A nearest relative may not authorise to act on his behalf a person who is disqualified from acting as a patient's nearest relative by virtue of section 26(5) of the Act.[44] Where at the time any authority or revocation is made, the patient to whom it relates is liable to be detained under the Act, a copy must also be given forthwith to the managers of the hospital where the patient is liable to be detained.[45] Similarly, where a patient is at the time subject to guardianship, a copy shall be given forthwith to the responsible local social services authority and, if a private guardian is acting, to the guardian also.[46]

Revocation of the authority

While the nearest relative may revoke an authority previously given to another person, the regulations do not expressly provide that the person authorised may later refuse to act further on the nearest relative's behalf. Although it has been suggested that the authority continues until such time (if ever) as the nearest relative revokes it, this seems unlikely. As drafted, the regulations do not make it an express condition of delegating authority that the person named consents to exercise the functions at time the authority is given. However, this must be presumed[47] as therefore may the right of the person authorised to later withdraw any consent to act which he originally gave. Section 32(1)(e) is specifically an "enabling" provision and its purpose is limited and confined to displacing the statutory presumption that a function given to a particular person by statute cannot be delegated to, or performed by, another (*delegatus non potest delegare*). In the absence of such a provision, any exercise of those functions by another person would, even if done with the nearest relative's consent, be *ultra vires*. It is submitted therefore that an authority validly given under section 32 and regulation 14 ceases to have effect if —

- The nearest relative who gave it dies or by notice revokes the authority.

- The person authorised becomes a person to whom section 26(5) applies, *e.g.* he takes up ordinary residence outside England and Wales, the Channel Islands or the Isle of Man.

- The person authorised renounces the authority.

- A person other than the person who gave the authority becomes the nearest relative, *e.g.* a child of the patient upon attaining the age of 18.[48]

---

[41]   Mental Health Act 1983, s.32(2)(e).
[42]   Mental Health (Hospital, Guardianship and Consent to Treatment) Regulations 1983, regs. 14(1), 14(2)(a).
[43]   *Ibid.*, reg.14(3).
[44]   *Ibid.*, reg. 14(1).
[45]   *Ibid.*, reg. 14(2)(b).
[46]   *Ibid.*, reg. 14(2)(c).
[47]   Unless one presumes this, it would be lawful to authorise a third party (even a stranger) to exercise the functions without obtaining his prior consent.
[48]   One could alternatively argue that the authority continues until such time as it is revoked by the person who has subsequently, by process of law, become the nearest relative.

The effect of an authority given under section 32

A person duly authorised under regulation 14 does not thereby become the patient's statutory nearest relative. Rather, he has authority to exercise the nearest relative's functions under Part II of the Act on the latter's behalf. Section 32(1)(e) provides that regulations may in particular make provision for enabling the functions of the nearest relative "under this Part of this Act" to be performed by any person authorised by that relative, in such circumstances and subject to such conditions as the regulations may prescribe. Regulation 14(1) of the 1983 Regulations then states that the nearest relative may authorise another person to perform the "functions conferred upon the nearest relative by or under Part II of the Act." In contrast to the wording used in section 29(1) and (6), in relation to county court appointments, a person authorised under section 32 is therefore authorised only to exercise the nearest relative's functions under Part II. Moreover, section 32(1) does not provide, as section 29(6) does, that references to the nearest relative elsewhere in the Act shall be read as referring to the person having the functions of that relative.

Whether authorised person can exercise rights under Part V

The question arises whether any authority given under regulation 14 also enables the person authorised to fulfil the nearest relative's functions under the other Parts of the Act, in particular his rights of application to a tribunal, and other functions, under Part V. There appears to be no obvious justification for enabling a nearest relative to authorise another individual to exercise his functions under Part II but not those exercisable under Part V. Indeed, such a construction gives rise to the anomalous position that the person authorised is thereby empowered to discharge the patient but not to apply to a tribunal for the patient's discharge, for example if the responsible medical officer bars the patient's discharge under section 25. Similarly, although a notice of reclassification under section 16 would be served on the person authorised under section 32, it would nevertheless be for the nearest relative to decide whether to apply to a tribunal following the reclassification.

Mental Health Act 1959

Section 32(1)(e) of the 1983 Act derives from, and is identical to, section 56(2)(f) of the 1959 Act. Under the 1959 Act, patients' and nearest relatives' rights to apply to a tribunal were also set out in the same Part of the Act as section 56. Consequently, the reference in section 56 to the person appointed being authorised to exercise the nearest relative's functions "under this Part of this Act" included exercising his tribunal rights of application. However, when the new Act was drafted, the various references to tribunal rights of application were removed from that Part of the Act and placed in a separate Part dealing with Mental Health Review Tribunals (Part V). Unfortunately, the draftsman clearly overlooked the need consequentially to amend section 32 so as to take account of the fact that the nearest relative's powers were no longer concentrated in one Part of the Act.

Summary

The reference to Part II of the Act in section 32 appears to be a drafting error rather than to reflect any intention on Parliament's part to draw a fine distinction between the various powers. In other words, the intention remained that the person appointed was thereby authorised to exercise any tribunal rights of application.

ORDERS APPOINTING AN ACTING NEAREST RELATIVE

The county court may by order direct that a local social services authority, or a person whom it considers to be a proper person to act as a patient's nearest relative, shall exercise the functions of a patient's nearest relative under the Act. An order may not be made unless the proposed authority or individual consents to act in that capacity. A person or authority appointed by the court under section 29 is referred to below as the "acting nearest relative."

The application

An application may be made by an approved social worker, by a relative of the patient, or by any person with whom the patient is residing (or last resided before he was admitted to hospital).[49]

The grounds of the application

An order may be made on one or more of the following grounds —

The no fault grounds

a   that the patient has no nearest relative within the meaning of the Act, or that it is not reasonably practicable to ascertain whether he has such a relative, or who that relative is (s.26(3(a));

b   that the nearest relative of the patient is incapable of acting as such by reason of mental disorder or other illness (s.26(3(b));

The fault grounds

c   that the nearest relative of the patient unreasonably objects to the making of a guardianship application or a section 3 application in respect of the patient (s.26(3(c));

d   that the nearest relative of the patient has exercised without due regard to the welfare of the patient or the interests of the public his power under Part II to discharge the patient from hospital or guardianship, or is likely to do so (s.26(3(d)).

It should be emphasised that the first ground refers to an individual who is unable to exercise his functions, rather than to a person who is capable of acting but acting in a wholly irrational way.[50] As concerns the last ground, where the nearest relative gives notice of his intention to discharge the patient and the grounds for issuing an order barring discharge exist (**612**), the responsible medical officer will exercise this power and it is unusual for the local authority to then apply to the county court for the nearest relative's displacement.

---

[49]   Mere residence at the material time suffices and it is not necessary that the applicant ordinarily resides with the patient.

[50]   See *e.g.* Mental Health Act 1983, s.29(4), which links ground (b) to ground (a) rather than to grounds (c) or (d), from which it may be inferred that if ground (b) exists this will not give rise to any need to extend the duration of the section 2 period. This is because the nearest relative will be incapable of making any objection to a proposed section 3 application.

The significance of the grounds of an application or order

Applications and orders made under ground (c) and (d) relate to the way in which the nearest relative has exercised, or is likely to exercise, his statutory powers. In contrast, applications and orders made upon grounds (a) and (b) involve no assertion or finding of inappropriate or unreasonable conduct. The ground upon which an order is made affects its duration and who may later apply for its discharge. Likewise, the precise effect of lodging an application under section 29 turns on the grounds upon which it is sought.

The effect of a pending application

A section 2 application generally authorises the patient's detention for up to 28 days only. However, where a county court application made under one or both of the fault grounds is pending at the expiration of that period, the period for which the patient may be detained under section 2 is extended until the court application is finally disposed of; and, if an order appointing an acting nearest relative is made, for a further seven days. However, this extension of the section 2 period does not prevent the patient from being discharged under section 23 before the county court case is disposed of, including by the nearest relative whose displacement is being sought.[51] It should be emphasised that a county court application based *solely* on one or both of the no-fault grounds does not have this effect of extending the section 2 period.

The effect of an order under section 29

The general position is that, while an order under section 29 is in force, the nearest relative's functions under the Act are exercisable by the acting nearest relative and references in the Act to a nearest relative's functions are to be construed accordingly. In particular, it is the acting nearest relative who may make an application under Part II, discharge the patient in the circumstances specified in sections 23–25, and exercise the ordinary rights of a nearest relative to apply to a tribunal under sections 66 and 69. Where a local social services authority is appointed and the patient is detained in hospital, that authority is required to arrange for visits to be made to the patient on behalf of the authority and to take such other steps in relation to the patient as would be expected to be taken by his parents.[52] By way of compensation, the displaced nearest relative may make one application to a tribunal for the patient's discharge during each year the order remains in force.[53]

Duration of orders

An order made under one of the no-fault grounds may be made for a specified period in which case the order, unless previously discharged, ceases to have effect on that date. In the case of a county court order made for an unspecified period, the date on which it expires depends upon the patient's legal status on the day the order was made —

---

[51] See *e.g. Mental Health Act 1959: Memorandum on Parts I, IV to VII and IX*, (D.H.S.S., 1960), para. 131. The nearest relative's power of discharge is, however, qualified by the power to bar discharge under section 25, except in cases involving guardianship.

[52] Mental Health Act 1983, s.116(2)(c). The duty applies whatever the age of the patient.

[53] Mental Health Act 1983, s.66(1)(h). There is a difference between being displaced and replaced. The patient's nearest relative remains unchanged by the county court order but the court appointee is authorised to exercise his functions.

• Patients who at the time when the county court order was made were subject to guardianship or liable to be detained under section 3, 37, 47 or 48	The county court order will expire on the date the application, order or direction authorising the patient's detention or guardianship comes to an end (transfers under section 19 are to be disregarded).
• Patients who at the time the county court order was made were informal patients or detained under sections 2, 4, 5, 35, 36, 38, 135 or 136 of the Act.	The county court order will expire if the patient is not received into guardianship or detained under section 3, 37, 47 or 48 within the period of three months beginning with the date of the county court's order. If the patient is so detained or received within that period, the county court order expires on the day that application, order or direction comes to an end.

The fact that the authority conferred by a section 29 order expires upon the patient ceasing to be liable to be detained for treatment or subject to guardianship is commonly not appreciated by social workers, who often believe that the order remains in force until such time as it is discharged by the court. As a result, further section 3 applications may be made in the mistaken belief that the nearest relative's power to object to the patient's admission is still exercisable by the court appointee.

Discharging county court orders

While a county court order remains in force, an application for its discharge may be made to the court by the "acting nearest relative" or, where the order was made on one of the no-fault grounds, by the patient's nearest relative.[54] However, if the court order was instead made on one of the fault grounds, the displaced nearest relative may not apply to the court for its discharge. This prohibition takes account of the fact that s/he previously exercised the powers in a way which caused the court to appoint someone else to exercise them.[55]

Variation of county court orders

During the period the court's order remains in force, the "acting nearest relative" or an approved social worker may apply to the county court for the order to be varied, by substituting for the authority or person previously appointed any other local social services authority or individual who, in the opinion of the court, is a proper person to act in that capacity and is willing to do so.[56]

---

[54] For example, a nearest relative who was previously incapacitated but who has since recovered may apply for the order's discharge. Similarly, where the order was made because the patient had no known nearest relative at the time, if a nearest relative is later identified or located, he may apply for the order's discharge. Mental Health Act 1983, s.30(1)(b).

[55] If the displaced person later ceases to be the patient's nearest relative, because some other relative subsequently acquires a prior entitlement, his successor may apply for the order's discharge. This reflects the fact that the newly entitled individual was not the person whose unreasonable conduct led to the court order being sought and then made. Mental Health Act 1983, s.30(1)(b).

[56] Mental Health Act 1983, s.30(2).

Procedure concerning section 29 applications

The court procedure is set out in Order 49, Rule 12 of the County Court Rules 1981. The application is made by originating application, supported by an affidavit. A fee is payable. The application, together with any supporting documents, is filed in the court for the district in which the patient's place of residence is situated. If the patient is receiving in-patient treatment at the time, his place of residence is deemed to be the hospital. The nearest relative must be made a respondent to the application, unless it is being made because the patient has no identifiable nearest relative, and the patient must not made a respondent.

Evidence

The judge may interview the patient in the presence of or separately from the parties, either at court or elsewhere. Alternatively, the judge may direct the district judge to interview the patient and to report to him in writing. The hearing is held in chambers unless the court orders otherwise. The publication of information relating to the proceedings is a contempt of court.[57] The court may accept any report made by a doctor as *prima facie* evidence of the facts stated in that report, and may similarly accept any report by a social worker or officer of the hospital where the patient is receiving in-patient treatment. The nearest relative must be told the substance of any part of the report bearing on his fitness or conduct which the judge considers to be material to the fair determination of the application. In *B. v. B. (mental health patient)* [1980] 1 W.L.R. 116, the Court of Appeal held that it was sufficient that the medical reports were handed to the nearest relative's legal adviser in circumstances where the adviser could give advice and take instructions.

Case law

The leading case is *W. v. L* [1974] Q.B. 711 (**064**).[58] The issue in that case was how the county court should approach the question of whether a nearest relative's objection to a section 3 application being made was unreasonable. The following passage is taken from Lord Denning M.R.'s judgment (at 717H–718D) —

> "This brings me to the final question: is the wife unreasonable in objecting to the making of an application for the husband's detention? This is a difficult question ... No doubt she feels that she can cope. She says that she knows her husband better than anyone else does; she will see that he takes his tablets; she is quite satisfied that neither she nor the baby will be in danger. So if you look at it from her own point of view, she may not be unreasonable. But I do not think it correct to look at it from her own point of view. The proper test is to ask what a reasonable woman in her place would do in all the circumstances of the case ... So we come to this: looking at it objectively, what would a reasonable woman in her place do when faced with this wife's problem? It seems to me that a reasonable woman would say: my husband ought to go in for treatment and he ought to be detained until he is cured. It is too great a risk to have him at home whilst the baby is so small. Her objection is therefore unreasonable."

---

[57] Administration of Justice Act 1960, s.12.
[58] Although not legally binding, various county court judgments are also referred to in the textbooks: *N. v. S.*, Croydon County Court, 1 January 1983; *Re B*, Liverpool County Court, 29 November 1985; *S. v. G.*, Sheffield County Court [1981] J.S.W.L. 174.

CHILDREN

The law concerning the psychiatric assessment and treatment of children can be considered under four main headings: (1) the statutory provisions in the Mental Health Act 1983; (2) the statutory provisions in the Children Act 1989 and related legislation; (3) wardship and the High Court's inherent jurisdiction; (4) the common law. Some of the provisions of the Children Act supplement the powers available under the 1983 Act, whilst others may provide an alternative, and sometimes less restrictive, method of managing the child's case. In appropriate cases, the High Court's inherent jurisdiction may be invoked, so as to enable a child to be detained and given compulsory treatment otherwise than under the 1983 Act.

MENTAL HEALTH ACT 1983

Where a child is in care, a guardian has been appointed for him under children's legislation, or a residence order is in force, special rules apply when determining who is the child's nearest relative (**106**). Subject to a few exceptions, most of the powers exercisable under the 1983 Act apply to children as they apply to adults. Under Part II of the Act, neither a guardianship application nor a supervision application may be made unless the person concerned is 16 or older. Similarly, under Part III, a guardianship order may only be made if the accused has attained the age of 16 years, and nor may a child be committed to the Crown Court under section 43. However, for the purposes of Part III, the term "child" means a person under the age of 14 years, while a "young person" is someone who is aged 14 or over but not yet 18.[59] Unless subject to restrictions, the cases of detained children aged under 16 must be referred to a tribunal at yearly intervals (**631**).

CHILDREN ACT 1989

For the purposes of the Children Act 1989, a child is a person under the age of 18.[60] The main orders of relevance to the mental health of children are summarised in the table on the following pages. A child who is in hospital informally, or who is subject to guardianship under the Mental Health Act 1983, may not be kept in secure accommodation for more than 72 hours during any consecutive 28-day period without the authority of a family proceedings court (**121**). Various provisions in the 1989 Act enable a court to authorise the psychiatric examination or assessment of a child, but a child of sufficient understanding to make an informed decision has a statutory right to refuse to be examined or assessed. If it is necessary to have in place some statutory framework for supervising a child in the community, only the Children Act orders are available if the child is aged 15 or younger. Conversely, if the child is aged 17, the available orders are a guardianship application or a supervision application under the Mental Health Act 1983. It is only in the case of 16 year-olds that a local authority contemplating an unsupervised child's case may choose between the two frameworks. The definition a "hospital" in the Children Act 1989 excludes a High Security Hospital, but is otherwise the same as that found in section 145(1) of the Mental Health Act 1983.

---

[59] Mental Health Act 1983, s.55(1); Children and Young Persons Act 1933, s.107(1). Section 99 of the 1933 Act (which relates to the presumption and determination of age) applies for the purposes of Part III of the 1983 Act: see Mental Health Act 1983, s.55(7).

[60] Children Act 1989, s.105(1).

CHILDREN ACT 1989 ORDERS

Order or authority	Sect.	Power	Statutory criteria
Police protection	s.46	Where a constable has reasonable cause to believe that a child would otherwise be likely to suffer significant harm, he may remove the child to suitable accommodation and keep him there or take such steps as are reasonable to ensure that the child's removal from any hospital in which he is being accommodated is prevented. Maximum duration of 72 hours.	46.—(1) Where a constable has reasonable cause to believe that a child would otherwise be likely to suffer significant harm he may— (a) remove the child to suitable accommodation and keep him there; or (b) take such steps as are reasonable to ensure that the child's removal from any hospital, or other place, in which he is then being accommodated is prevented.
Emergency protection order	s.44	An order directing the production of a child and authorising either his removal to accommodation provided by or on behalf of the applicant or the prevention of the child's removal from hospital — a court making such an order may give directions with respect to the psychiatric examination or assessment of the child (s.44(6)). Maximum initial duration of 8 days, but may be extended for a further 7 days.	Unless there have been problems gaining access to a child, the court may make the order if, but only if, it is satisfied that— (a) there is reasonable cause to believe that the child is likely to suffer significant harm if— (i) he is not removed to accommodation provided by or on behalf of the applicant; or (ii) he does not remain in the place in which he is then being accommodated.
Local authority enquiries	s.47	A local authority may be under a duty to make enquiries to enable them to decide whether they should take any action to safeguard or promote a child's welfare.	47.—(1) Where a local authority— (a) are informed that a child who lives, or is found, in their area— (i) is the subject of an emergency protection order; or (ii) is in police protection; or (b) have reasonable cause to suspect that a child who lives, or is found, in their area is suffering, or is likely to suffer, significant harm, the authority shall make, or cause to be made, such enquiries as they consider necessary to enable them to decide whether they should take any action to safeguard or promote the child's welfare.
Child assessment order	s.43	An order authorising a child's assessment, e.g. a psychiatric examination or assessment. A court may treat the application as an application for a child protection order and no court shall make a child assessment order if satisfied that there are grounds for making an emergency protection order and that it ought to make such an order. Maximum duration of 7 days.	The court may make the order if, but only if, it is satisfied that— (a) the applicant has reasonable cause to suspect that the child is suffering, or is likely to suffer, significant harm; (b) an assessment of the state of the child's health or development ... is required to enable the applicant to determine whether or not the child is suffering, or is likely to suffer, significant harm; and (c) it is unlikely that such an assessment will be made, or be satisfactory, in the absence of an order made under this section.

116

Interim care order	s.38	An order made upon adjourning an application for a care order or supervision order — the court may give directions with regard to a psychiatric examination or assessment (s.38(6)). Maximum initial duration of 8 weeks with renewals of 4 weeks at a time.
		38.—(2) A court shall not make an interim care order or interim supervision order under this section unless it is satisfied that there are reasonable grounds for believing that the circumstances with respect to the child are as mentioned in section 31(2) (see below)
Interim supervision order	s.38	An order made upon adjourning an application for a care order or supervision order — the court may direct that the child should undergo a psychiatric examination or assessment (s.38(6)). Maximum initial duration of 8 weeks with renewals of 4 weeks at a time.
Care order	s.31	An order placing the child in the care of the designated local authority, which authority becomes the child's nearest relative under the 1983 Act. No care order or supervision order may be made with respect to a child who has reached the age of 17 (or 16, in the case of a child who is married).
		"31.—(2) A court may only make a care order or supervision order if it is satisfied— (a) that the child concerned is suffering, or is likely to suffer, significant harm; and (b) that the harm, or likelihood of harm, is attributable to— (i) the care given to the child, or likely to be given to him if the order were not made, not being what it would be reasonable to expect a parent to give to him; or (ii) the child's being beyond parental control.
Supervision order	s.31	An order putting a child under the supervision of a designated local authority — the order may require the child to live at a specified place; to present himself to specified persons at specified times; to participate in specified activities; to submit to a medical or psychiatric examination; to undergo out-patient or in-patient psychiatric treatment. Lasts one year but may be extended to maximum period of 3 years.
Secure accommodation order	s.25	Section 25 applies to children who are not detained under the 1983 Act. A child to whom section 25 applies may not be kept in secure accommodation for more than 72 hours in any period of 28 consecutive days without the authority of a family proceedings court.
		A child may not be placed or kept in accommodation provided for the purpose of restricting liberty ("secure accommodation") unless he is likely to injure himself or other persons if kept in any other description of accommodation or he has a history of absconding, is likely to abscond from any other description of accommodation, and, if he absconds, is likely to suffer significant harm (s.25(1)(a)). See s.31(9) and (10).

Statutory definitions: "harm" means ill-treatment or the impairment of health or development; "development" means physical, intellectual, emotional, social or behavioural development; "health" means physical or mental health; "ill-treatment" includes forms of ill-treatment which are not physical. Where the question of whether harm suffered by a child is significant turns on the child's health or development, his health or development shall be compared with that which could reasonably be expected of a similar child. See s.31(9) and (10).

CHILD ASSESSMENT ORDERS

A child assessment order is an order authorising the assessment of a child, *e.g.* a psychiatric examination or assessment. Such an order must specify the date by which the assessment is to begin and shall have effect for such period, not exceeding seven days beginning with that date, as may be specified in the order.[61] It is the duty of any person who is in a position to produce the child to produce him to such person as may be named in the order and to comply with any directions made by the court.[62] The child may only be kept away from home if it is necessary for the purposes of the assessment and insofar as specified in the order.[63]

The statutory grounds

A court hearing an application for a child assessment order may make the order if, but only if, it is satisfied that[64]—

    a.   the applicant has reasonable cause to suspect that the child is suffering, or is likely to suffer, significant harm;

    b.   the assessment of the state of the child's health or development, or of the way in which he has been treated, is required to enable the applicant to determine whether or not the child is suffering, or is likely to suffer, significant harm;

    c.   it is unlikely that such an assessment will be made, or be satisfactory, in the absence of an order under this section; *and it is not satisfied that*

    d.   there are grounds for making an emergency protection order and that it ought to make such an order instead.

Psychiatric examinations and assessments

A child assessment order authorises any person carrying out the assessment to do so in accordance with the terms of the order.[65] However, regardless of this, if the child is of sufficient understanding to make an informed decision, he may refuse to submit to a medical or psychiatric examination or other assessment.[66]

Related law

Notwithstanding a child's statutory right to refuse to submit to a psychiatric examination or assessment specified in a child assessment order, all children, including those over 16, can be treated without their consent if a person with parental responsibility, or the High Court exercising its inherent jurisdiction, gives consent **(124)**.

---

[61]   Children Act 1989, s.43(5).
[62]   *Ibid.*, s.43(6).
[63]   *Ibid.*, s.43(9).
[64]   *Ibid.*, s.43(1).
[65]   *Ibid.*, s.43(7).
[66]   *Ibid.*, s.43(8).

CARE ORDERS AND SUPERVISION ORDERS[67]

On an application by a local authority, or the NSPCC., a court may make an order placing the child in the care of a local authority, or putting him under the supervision of such an authority or of a probation officer.[68] In the case of an application for a care order, the court may instead make a supervision order, and vice-versa.[69] Where an application for a care or supervision order is adjourned, the court may make an interim care order or an interim supervision order with respect to the child.[70] No care order or supervision order (or interim order of such a kind) may be made with respect to a child who has reached the age of 17 (or 16, in the case of a child who is married). Such orders cease to have effect when the child reaches 18.

The statutory grounds

A court may only make a care order or supervision order if it is satisfied[71]—

- a. that the child concerned is suffering, or is likely to suffer, significant harm; *and*

- b. that the harm, or likelihood of harm, is attributable to—

  - i the care given to the child, or likely to be given to him if the order were not made, not being what it would be reasonable to expect a parent to give to him; or

  - i the child's being beyond parental control.

Deciding whether any harm is significant

"Harm" in this context means the impairment of health or development or ill-treatment (including sexual abuse and non-physical ill-treatment). Where the question of whether harm suffered by a child is significant turns on the child's physical or mental health, or his physical, intellectual, emotional, social or behavioural development, his health or development shall be compared with that which could reasonably be expected of a similar child.[72]

Effect of a care order

While a care order is in force, the designated local authority has parental responsibility for the child and has the power to determine the extent to which a parent or guardian may meet his parental responsibility for him.[73] However, the local authority shall not limit the extent of their involvement unless they are satisfied that it is necessary to do so in order to safeguard or promote the child's welfare.[74]

---

[67] Children Act 1989 s.31; Sched. 3, Pts. I and II.
[68] *Ibid.*, s.31(1). The local authority designated in the order must be the authority within whose area the child is ordinarily resident or, if applicable, the authority within whose area any circumstances arose in consequence of which the order is being made: see s.31(8). Such an application may be made on its own or in any other family proceedings. *Ibid*, s.31(4).
[69] *Ibid.*, s.31(5).
[70] *Ibid.*, s.38(1).
[71] *Ibid.*, s.31(2).
[72] *Ibid.*, s.31(10).
[73] *Ibid.*, s.33(3).
[74] *Ibid.*, s.33(4).

Effect of a supervision order

While a supervision order is in force, it is the duty of the supervisor to advise, assist and befriend the supervised child; to take such steps as are reasonably necessary to give effect to the order; and, if the order is not complied with, or the supervisor considers that the order may no longer be necessary, to consider whether or not to apply to the court for its variation or discharge.[75] The relevant law concerning supervision orders and medical treatment is set out in Schedule 3 to the Children Act 1989, although paragraphs 3 and 4 of that Schedule (which concern medical examinations and treatment) do not apply to interim supervision orders. The effect of the provisions in the Schedule is similar to that of a guardianship order made under the 1983 Act combined with a supervision and treatment order, or a psychiatric probation order, made under criminal legislation. For example, a supervised child may be required to comply with directions given by the supervisor which require him to live at a specified place; to present himself at specified places on specified days; and to participate in specified activities. The order may also require the supervised child to undergo a psychiatric examination or to submit to a specified period of psychiatric treatment, including in both cases as a resident patient. However, if the child has sufficient understanding to make an informed decision, such medical requirements may not be included in the order unless the court is satisfied that the child consents to their inclusion.

Interim orders and psychiatric assessments

A court may not make an interim care order or an interim supervision order unless it is satisfied that there are reasonable grounds for believing that the child's circumstances are such that the statutory grounds for making a full order exist.[76] Where the court makes an interim order, "it may give such directions (if any) as it considers appropriate with regard to the medical or psychiatric examination or other assessment of the child; but if the child is of sufficient understanding to make an informed decision he may refuse to submit to the examination or other assessment."[77] The court may alternatively direct that there is to be no such examination or assessment, or no such examination or assessment unless the court directs otherwise.[78] Any of the directions just referred to may be given at the time the interim order is made or at any time it is in force, and provision is made for persons involved in the case to apply for the variation of directions previously given.[79]

Supervision orders and the inherent jurisdiction

A child's refusal to submit to an examination or assessment may be overridden by the High Court in the exercise of its inherent jurisdiction. In *South Glamorgan County Council v. W. and B.* [1993] 1 F.L.R. 574, the court made an interim care order and directed that the 15-year old child in that case should receive a psychiatric examination and assessment, if necessary at an assessment unit. She exercised her statutory right of veto, under section 38(6), and refused to be examined. The local authority next applied for leave to invoke the inherent jurisdiction of the High Court,

---

[75] Children Act 1989, s.35(1).
[76] *Ibid.*, s.38(2).
[77] *Ibid.*, s.38(6).
[78] *Ibid.*, s.38(7).
[79] *Ibid.*, s.38(8).

so as to overrule her wishes. The High Court granted leave and made an order that she be examined against her wishes, using force if necessary.[80]

SECURE ACCOMMODATION[81]

Secure accommodation orders are made under section 25 of the 1989 Act. That section, and the associated regulations, do not apply to any child who is detained under the 1983 Act.[82] They do apply to children subject to guardianship under that 1983 Act, and to those admitted to hospital as informal patients by a parent or (if in care) by the local authority. A child to whom section 25 applies may not be kept in secure accommodation for more than 72 hours (whether or not consecutive) during any period of 28 consecutive days without the authority of a family proceedings court.[83] Secure accommodation is accommodation provided for the purpose of restricting liberty and includes a behaviour modification unit at a hospital where the regime is intended to restrict liberty.[84] Whether or not a hospital unit, mental nursing home or clinic is provided for that purpose is a matter of fact. Where a secure accommodation order has been made, it permits, but does not require, the child to be kept in secure accommodation. It is therefore for the applicant to decide whether it is in the child's best interests to seek the order and whether or not to give effect to any order then made.

The statutory grounds

Criminal proceedings aside, the criteria for making a secure accommodation order are the same in all cases, that is regardless of whether the child is being accommodated in a community home or in secure hospital accommodation. A child who is in care or who is being accommodated by a local authority, Health Authority or NHS trust, or being provided with accommodation in a mental nursing home—

> "may not be placed or kept in accommodation provided for the purpose of restricting liberty ("secure accommodation") unless he is likely to injure himself or other persons if kept in any other description of accommodation[85] or he has a history of absconding, is likely to abscond from any other description of accommodation, and, if he absconds, is likely to suffer significant harm.[86]

The application and evidence

Any necessary court application should be made by the relevant NHS trust or Health Authority unless the child is in care or is provided with accommodation by a local authority, in which case the local authority must make the application. The court must appoint a guardian ad litem unless it is satisfied that this is not necessary in

---

80 See also *Re J (A Minor) (Medical Treatment)* [1992] 2 F.L.R. 165, which involved a child subject to supervision who was suffering from anorexia nervosa.

81 See Children Act 1989, s.25; The Children (Secure Accommodation) Regulations 1991 (S.I. 1991 No. 1505); The Children (Secure Accommodation) (No. 2) Regulations 1991 (S.I. 1991 No. 2034); The Children Act 1989 Guidance and Regulations, Vol. 4, Residential Care (Department of Health, 1991). The regulations do not apply to children detained under the Mental Health Act 1983.

82 Children (Secure Accommodation) Regulations 1991 (S.I. 1991 No. 1505), reg. 5(1).

83 Children (Secure Accommodation) Regulations 1991, reg. 10(1).

84 *R. v. Northampton Juvenile Court, ex p. London Borough of Hammersmith* [1985] Family Law 25.

85 Children Act 1989, s.25(1)(b).

86 *Ibid.*, s.25(1)(a). The welfare of the child is a relevant but not paramount consideration and the principles of section 1 do not apply: *Re M (a Minor) (Secure accommodation order) The Times, 10 November 1994.*

order to safeguard the child's interests.[87] It is desirable to have a psychiatric report available as evidence[88] and hearsay evidence is admissible.[89] A court which adjourns an application may make an interim order permitting the child to be kept in secure accommodation during the adjournment period.[90] In the case of interim orders, there is no maximum period of detention but the proceedings should be heard without delay and take note of the serious nature of restrictions of liberty.[91]

The decision and appeals

The family proceedings court must determine whether the statutory grounds set out in section 25 are satisfied.[92] It is obliged to make the order if satisfied as to the statutory grounds, but has a discretion as to the length of the order.[93] An order should be for no longer than is necessary and unavoidable.[94] Thus, while the maximum period for which a court may authorise a child to be kept in secure accommodation is three months,[95] the court should not automatically make an order of that length but consider what is necessary in the particular circumstances.[96] Unless the child has been remanded to secure accommodation by a criminal court, the court may further renew the authority for periods not exceeding six months at a time.[97] The magistrates must give full reasons for their decision.[98] Appeals against the granting or refusal of applications are heard in the High Court.[99] They should be listed for an early hearing because the matter involves deprivation of liberty.[100]

CHILDREN ACCOMMODATED BY NHS BODIES

Where a child is provided with accommodation by a Health Authority or NHS trust for a consecutive period of at least three months, or with the intention of accommodating him for such a period, the authority or trust must notify the local authority within whose area the child appears to be ordinarily resident.[101] The local authority must take such steps as are reasonably practicable to determine whether the child's welfare is adequately safeguarded and promoted while he is so accommodated. They must further consider the extent to which (if at all) they should exercise any of their functions under the Children Act with respect to the child.[102] The departmental guidance states that authorities should find out whether contact between the child and his parents is adequate; obtain written assurances from the authority or trust that proper parental contact is being established or maintained; if appropriate, contact the parents; and arrange to visit the child within 14 days if contact has ceased, or there are other matters which suggest that the child's welfare

---

[87] Children Act 1989, s.41(1).
[88] *R.(J.) v. Oxfordshire County Council* [1992] 3 All E.R. 660.
[89] Hearsay Evidence Order (S.I. 1991 No. 1115).
[90] Children Act 1989, s.25(5).
[91] *Oxfordshire C.C. v. R.* [1992] 1 F.L.R. 648.
[92] Children Act 1989, s.25(3).
[93] *Ibid.*, s.25(4).
[94] *W v. North Yorkshire County Council* [1993] 1 F.C.R. 693
[95] Children (Secure Accommodation) Regulations 1991, reg.11.
[96] *Re W (A Minor) (Secure Accommodation Order)* [1993] 1 F.L.R. 692.
[97] Children (Secure Accommodation) Regulations 1991, reg.12.
[98] Family Proceedings Court (Children Act 1989) Rules 1991, r.21; *Oxfordshire C.C. v. R.* [1992] 1 F.L.R. 648.
[99] Children Act 1989, s.94.
[100] *Oxfordshire CC v. R.* [1992] 1 F.L.R. 648.
[101] Children Act 1989, s.85(1) and (3).
[102] *Ibid.*, s.85(4).

is not being safeguarded.[103] The Health Authority or trust must also notify the local authority when they cease to accommodate the child.[104]

Mental nursing homes

Similar provisions apply in the case of mental nursing homes, the obligation to give notice being placed on the person carrying on the home.[105] In this case, it is an offence to fail, without reasonable excuse, to give such notice.[106]

Mental Health Act 1983

Where a child or young person in care who appears to be suffering from mental disorder is admitted to a hospital or nursing home, the authority must arrange for visits to be made to him on behalf of it, and take such other steps as would be expected to be taken by his parents.[107]

PROVIDING SERVICES FOR CHILDREN IN NEED

The general legislative provisions concerning the provision of community care services (154) do not apply to children or only in a qualified way. For example, sections 21 and 29 of the National Assistance Act 1948 apply only to persons aged over 18. Similarly, section 21 of, and Schedule 8 to, the National Health Service Act 1977 do not apply to children. However, under the Children Act 1989, every local authority has a "general duty" to safeguard and promote the welfare of children in need within their area by providing a range and level of services appropriate to those children's needs.[108]

Children in need

A child is, *inter alia*, to be taken to be in need if he is disabled or if, without the provision for him of such services, he is either unlikely to achieve or maintain a reasonable standard of mental health or development or his mental health or development is likely to be significantly impaired.[109] Development in this context includes intellectual, emotional, social or behavioural development.[110]

Services provided

The services provided may include giving assistance in kind or, in exceptional circumstances, in cash.[111] Furthermore, a service may be provided for the family of a child in need, or for any member of his family, if it is provided with a view to safeguarding or promoting the child's welfare.[112] Services provided under the section are means-assessed but cannot be imposed unless a care or supervision order is in force. Being a general duty, the duty to provide services under section 17 does not give rise to any right enforceable by an action for damages.

---

103   *Guidance*, Vol. 4, para. 1.99.
104   Children Act, s.85(2).
105   *Ibid.*, s.86(1).
106   *Ibid.*, s.86(4).
107   Mental Health Act 1983, s.116.
108   Children Act 1989, s.17(1)(a). For the purpose principally of facilitating the discharge of this general duty, each local authority has the specific powers and duties set out in Part 1 of Schedule 2 to the Act. *Ibid.*, s.17(2).
109   *Ibid.*, s.17(10).
110   *Ibid.*, s.17(11).
111   *Ibid.*, s.17(6).
112   *Ibid.*, s.17(3).

Section 8 of the Family Law Reform Act 1969 provides that a child aged 16 or 17 who is capable of expressing his own wishes can give valid consent to medical treatment.[113] More particularly, section 131(2) of the Mental Health Act 1983 provides that nothing in that Act shall prevent a child aged 16 or 17 who is capable of expressing his own wishes from arranging his own informal admission to hospital, or from remaining in hospital after he has ceased to be detained.[114] The position of children aged under 16 was considered in *Gillick v. West Norfolk and Wisbech Area Health Authority* [1986] A.C. 112. It was held that a child aged 15 or under may be capable of giving a valid consent to medical treatment including medical examination and, if so, that consent cannot be overridden by his parents. Whether a particular child of such an age can give a valid consent to proposed treatment depends on the circumstances, including his intellectual capacity to understand advice.[115]

Overriding children who do not consent

Section 8 of the Family Law Reform Act 1969 does not explicitly address the situation of a competent 16 or 17-year old child who refuses to consent to treatment. The position here is that the child's parents may override his decision to refuse treatment. The effect of section 8 is limited to enabling a competent minor aged 16 or over to consent to treatment: it does not remove the parents' co-existing right to give consent on the child's behalf. Likewise, if a "Gillick-competent" child aged 15 or under refuses treatment, but someone with parental responsibility consents, the treatment can be given notwithstanding the child's refusal.[116] Accordingly, in *Re K, W. and H. (Minors: Medical Treatment)* [1993] 1 F.L.R. 854, a High Court application for a specific issue order, declaring that it was permissible to treat three adolescent girls whose behaviour was highly disturbed, was dismissed as unnecessary because the hospital had for each of them the consent of a person with parental responsibility. Where a care order is in force, the local authority has parental responsibility and may therefore give any necessary consent.[117] The case of

---

[113]   "8.–(1)The consent of a minor who has attained the age of sixteen years to any surgical, medical or dental treatment which, in the absence of consent, would constitute a trespass to his person, shall be as effective as it would be if he were of full age; and where a minor has by virtue of this section given an effective consent to any treatment it shall not be necessary to obtain any consent for it from his parent or guardian ...(3) Nothing in this section shall be construed as making ineffective any consent which would have been ineffective if this section had not been enacted."

[114]   "131.–(1) Nothing in this Act shall be construed as preventing a patient who requires treatment for mental disorder from being admitted to any hospital or mental nursing home in pursuance of arrangements made in that behalf and without any application, order or direction rendering him liable to be detained under this Act, or from remaining in any hospital or mental nursing home in pursuance of such arrangements after he has ceased to be so liable to be detained. (2) In the case of a minor who has attained the age of 16 years and is capable of expressing his own wishes, any such arrangements as are mentioned in subsection (1) above may be made, carried out and determined [even though there are one or more persons who have parental responsibility for him (within the meaning of the Children Act 1989)]."

[115]   Speaking of medical treatment generally, Lord Scarman said: "It will be a question of fact whether a child seeking advice has sufficient understanding of what is involved to give a valid consent in law. Until the child achieves the capacity to consent, the parental right to make the decision continues save only in exceptional circumstances. Emergency, parental neglect, abandonment of the child, or inability to find the parents, are examples of exceptional situations in which it will be reasonable for a doctor to proceed without the parent's consent."

[116]   *Re R (A Minor) (Wardship: Medical Treatment)* [1991] 4 All E.R. 177; *Re W* [1992] 3 W.L.R. 758.

[117]   In the absence of any parental responsibility, the local authority could seek a court direction, under s.8 of the Children Act 1989, or through the exercise of the inherent jurisdiction of the court.

R. v. Kirklees Metropolitan Borough Council, ex p. C [1993] 2 F.L.R. 187 concerned a 12-year old child in care who was admitted by the local authority to hospital for assessment. The court held that she was not "Gillick-competent" to accept or reject treatment and, furthermore, the council acting *in loco parentis* was competent to assent on her behalf.

Overriding the parent

A decision by a parent to consent, or to refuse to consent, to an operation may in turn be overridden by the court. In *Re C (A Minor) (Wardship: Medical Treatment)* [1990] Fam. 26, the ward of court was terminally ill and it was held that the court could and would authorise treatment to relieve the ward's suffering. In *Re E (A Minor) (Wardship: Medical Treatment)* [1993] 1 F.L.R. 386, a 15-year old Jehovah's Witness suffering from leukaemia was made a ward of court. Leave to perform a blood transfusion was given on the basis that the boy's welfare "should be looked at objectively."

Obtaining court approval

Section 8 of the Children Act 1989 makes provision for specific issue orders, which are orders giving directions for the purpose of determining a specific question which has arisen, or which may arise, in connection with any aspect of parental responsibility for a child. However, no court may make such an order with respect to a child who is in the care of a local authority.[118] This means that the local authority can only obtain court approval for some step involving a child in care by invoking the court's inherent jurisdiction, under section 100 of the Children Act 1989.

The inherent jurisdiction

Section 100 of the Children Act 1983 limits the circumstances in which the High Court's inherent jurisdiction may be exercised.[119] However, the jurisdiction is sometimes invoked in relation to difficult questions about medical treatment. In *Re W (A Minor) (Medical Treatment)* [1993] Fam. 64, the child was a 16-year old girl in care who was suffering from anorexia nervosa. The local authority decided that treatment without her consent might be necessary. It therefore applied for the High Court to exercise its inherent jurisdiction so that the local authority could move the child to a treatment unit and give her medical treatment without her consent. Lord Donaldson M.R. held that there was "now ample authority for the proposition that the inherent powers of the court under its *parens patriae* jurisdiction are theoretically limitless and they certainly extend beyond the powers of the natural parent. The court does have the power to override the refusal of a minor, whether over or under 16, and even if 'Gillick-competent.'"

Detention under the inherent jurisdiction

In *Re C (Medical treatment: court's jurisdiction) The Times,* 21 March 1997, the 16 year old child had a history of absconding from a clinic which was treating her for

---

118   Children Act 1989, s.9(1).
119   "100.–(2) No court shall exercise the High Court's inherent jurisdiction with respect to children—
      (a) so as to require a child to be placed in the care, or put under the supervision, of a local authority;
      (b) so as to require a child to be accommodated by or on behalf of a local authority; (c) so as to make a child who is the subject of a care order a ward of court; or (d) for the purpose of conferring on any local authority power to determine any question which has arisen, or which may arise, in connection with any aspect of parental responsibility for a child."

anorexia nervosa. The clinic would not take her back without a court order or a care order. The local authority did not wish to apply for a care order and so asked the court, under its inherent jurisdiction, to make an order detaining her for treatment, using reasonable force if necessary. The court held, firstly, that the clinic did not constitute secure accommodation and, secondly, that it had such an inherent power to direct that a minor should be detained in a specified institution for treatment using reasonable force if necessary. Such an order should be of limited duration and subject to early review.

THE NATIONAL HEALTH SERVICE

The structure of the National Health Service (NHS) was reorganised on 1 April 1996. The previous structure and the new structure are shown in the diagrams on the following pages.

SECRETARY OF STATE FOR HEALTH

The Secretary of State for Health is accountable to Parliament for the Department of Health and the National Health Service in England.[120] The Department's health strategy for England is set out in the 1992 White Paper *The Health of the Nation*.[121] It is the Secretary of State's duty to continue to promote a comprehensive health service designed to secure improvement in the mental health of the people of England and Wales and, for that purpose, to provide or secure the effective provision of services in accordance with the National Health Service Act 1977. More specifically, the Secretary of State has a duty to provide hospital accommodation and such facilities for the prevention of illness, the care of persons suffering from illness and the after-care of persons who have suffered from illness as he considers are appropriate as part of the health service, and to such extent as he considers necessary to meet all reasonable requirements. The Department's funding is negotiated annually with the Treasury, through the public expenditure survey.

NHS Policy Board

The Secretary of State sets the Department of Health's strategy and objectives and approves the allocation of resources to meet those objectives. In relation to the objectives and performance of the NHS, the Secretary of State is supported by the NHS Policy Board which he chairs.

NHS Executive

The Secretary of State is not normally involved in the day-to-day management of the National Health Service although he is consulted on the handling of matters that give rise to Parliamentary or public concern. The NHS Executive, the headquarters of which is based in Leeds, provides the central management of the NHS, dealing with all operational matters in accordance with the overall strategy set by the Policy Board. The body is responsible for assessing health needs, research and development, formulating operational policy, securing and allocating resources, developing and regulating the internal market, and supporting Ministers.

---

[120]   The Secretary of State for Wales is mainly responsible for health and social services in the principality.

[121]   The Health of the Nation, Cm. 1986 (1992).

NHS STRUCTURE PRIOR TO 1 APRIL 1996

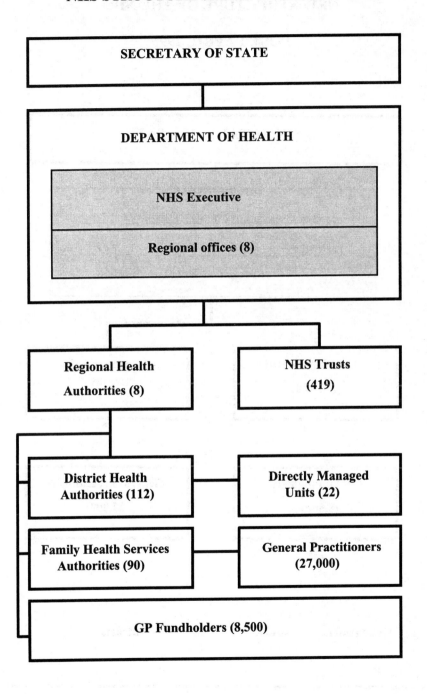

NEW STRUCTURE OF THE NHS

POST 1 APRIL 1996

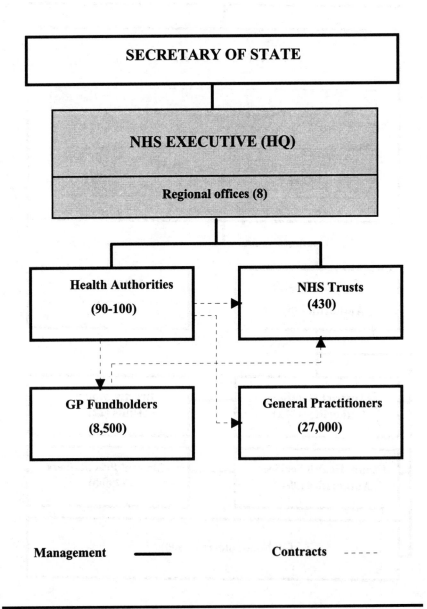

NHS Executive regional offices

The size and complexity of the NHS means that its central management must operate through a regional structure. Eight NHS Executive regional offices were established in April 1994 so as to be able to take over the responsibilities of the Regional Health Authorities on 1 April 1996, upon their abolition. The regional offices monitor the NHS trusts but do not become involved in detailed operational matters, which are the responsibility of local health authorities and the trusts themselves.

The regions

The regions covered by the eight regional offices are as follows: East Anglia and Oxford (Area 1), North Thames (2), South Thames (3), South West England (4), West Midlands (5), North West England (6), North East England and Yorkshire (7), and Trent (8). There is one Mental Health Review Tribunal for each region.

HEALTH AUTHORITY STRUCTURE PRIOR TO APRIL 1996

The Health Authorities Act 1995 came into force on 1 April 1996. Previously, three different kinds of health authority had been responsible for NHS functions at a regional or local level—

- District Health Authorities assessed the local population's need for health care and purchased hospital and community health services for the people in their area. Some DHAs merged to form larger purchasing units or collaborated together in "purchasing consortia."

- Family Health Services Authorities regulated and managed services provided by General Practitioners, dentists, pharmacists and opticians. They paid GPs in accordance with previously agreed contracts and investigated complaints relating to such services.

- In many parts of the country, DHAs and FHSAs established joint management arrangements but the law required them to maintain separate existences.

- Eight Regional Health Authorities allocated resources to the DHAs and FHSAs, directed them to perform certain functions, and themselves provided a range of region-wide services.

- The Secretary of State, in turn, gave directions to the RHAs about the performance of their functions.

HEALTH AUTHORITIES ACT 1995

The main purpose of the Health Authorities Act 1995 was to streamline central management and to encourage the integrated purchasing of primary and secondary care. The main changes effected by the Act were two-fold—

- Firstly, the abolition of the Regional Health Authorities and their replacement by regional NHS Executive offices (see above). The regional offices are responsible for monitoring NHS trusts and developing the purchasing function within the health service; providing a link between central management and the NHS trusts, and so ensuring that agreed national policies are implemented; approving applications for GP fundholder status and setting GP fundholder budgets (see below); arbitrating in the event of disputes.

- Secondly, the merger of District Health Authorities (DHAs) and Family Health Services Authorities (FHSAs) to form new unitary Health Authorities; in effect, joint purchasing bodies. The new authorities are expected to work with local authority social services departments in the commissioning of social care, so as to ensure a more integrated strategy for local services.

HEALTH AUTHORITIES

The establishment of the new health authorities meant the creation of a single authority at local level with responsibility for implementing national health policy. The core functions taken over from the old DHAs and FHSAs included the following —

- evaluating the health and healthcare needs of the local population.

- establishing a local health strategy to implement national priorities and meet local health needs in collaboration with local people and the providers of health services.

- implementing that local health strategy by purchasing health services for patients through contracts with NHS and other providers, and working with GPs, NHS trusts and non-NHS providers to shape the delivery of services and improve the effectiveness of health care.

- monitoring the delivery of health services to ensure that objectives are achieved including regulating and managing services provided through GPs, dentists, opticians and pharmacists ("Family Health Services Contractors").

- bringing pressure to bear on providers to raise the quality of care and efficiency by setting standards, monitoring performance, and exercising choice between competing providers.

- working with and influencing other statutory and voluntary organisations to improve people's health.

SPECIAL HEALTH AUTHORITIES

Under the National Health Service Act 1997, the Secretary of State may establish Special Health Authorities for the purpose of performing any functions which he may direct the body to perform on his behalf. The Mental Health Act Commission is a Special Health Authority.

NHS TRUSTS

Individual hospitals are managed by NHS trusts, which therefore provide hospital and community services on behalf of the Secretary of State. Prior to their establishment, hospitals were directly managed by the local District Health Authority. The core function of an NHS trust is to deliver health services according to the purchasing Health Authority's specifications. NHS trusts are responsible to their purchasers for meeting standards of service and "cost and volume targets." They are required to break even financially, to earn a six per cent. return on their capital, and to comply with financial targets set by the Secretary of States. The NHS regional offices are responsible for monitoring their performance and for approving their "business plans." The Secretary of State may by order made by statutory instrument dissolve an NHS trust if he considers it appropriate in the interests of the health service.

Constitution and functions

Every NHS trust is a body corporate having a board of directors consisting of a chairman appointed by the Secretary of State and executive and non-executive directors (that is to say, directors who respectively are and are not employees of the trust). All of the trust's directors are full and equal members of the Board and jointly responsible for carrying out the functions of the trust. Orders establishing an NHS trust must be made by statutory instrument and specify the functions of the trust. Those functions will include any statutory functions under the Mental Health Act 1983. The trust is required to carry out these functions "effectively, efficiently and economically" and to comply with any directions given to it by the Secretary of State. A trust may enter into contracts for the carrying out of any of its functions jointly with any Health Authority, with another NHS trust or with any other body or individual. trusts should appoint a committee to undertake the duties of managers under the 1983 Act and it should comprise "informed members of the trust and appointed outsiders, suitably informed."[122]

GP FUNDHOLDERS

All General Practitioners provide medical services and some of them may also purchase hospital services. GP fundholders may purchase a defined range of services for their patients, including out-patient services and drugs. Other services are purchased for the patients of GP fundholders by health authorities. As the number of fundholders increases, they will share with such authorities joint responsibility for purchasing services for their patients.

HOSPITALS

Various provisions in the Mental Health Act 1983 provide for a person's admission to or detention in a hospital. Although it may seem obvious what a hospital is, the legal position is in fact far from clear.

This section is arranged as follows—

---

[122]   *Mental Health Act 1983: Code of Practice*, (2nd ed., 1993), para. 24.4.

"HOSPITAL"

Section 145(1) provides that, unless the context otherwise requires, "hospital" means any of the following —

   a.   any accommodation provided by a local authority and used as a hospital by or on behalf of the Secretary of State under the National Health Service Act 1977.

   b.   any of the following homes or institutions which is vested in an NHS trust (**131**) or in the Secretary of State (**126**) for the purpose of his functions under the National Health Service Act 1977, including clinics, dispensaries and out-patient departments maintained in connection with them—

- a maternity home

- an institution for the reception and treatment of persons suffering from illness (including persons suffering from mental disorder)

- an institution for the reception and treatment during convalescence of persons requiring medical rehabilitation.

"HOSPITAL WITHIN THE MEANING OF PART II OF THE ACT"

The Act refers in places to a "hospital within the meaning of Part II of the Act." For the purposes of that Part of the Act, section 34(2) provides that references to a hospital are to be construed as including a mental nursing home which is registered to receive patients who are liable to be detained under the 1983 Act.[123] Perhaps confusingly, most of the references to "a hospital" in Parts III, V and VI of the Act are also to be construed as referring to "a hospital within the meaning of Part II of the Act," rather than to a hospital as defined in section 145(1), and so include mental nursing homes registered in this way.

---

[123]   "Registered" here means registered under section 23(5)(b) of the Registered Homes Act 1984. "Reception" means "taking people into a building and receiving them there." *Re Couchman, Couchman v. Eales* [1952] 1 Ch. 391, *per* Dankwerts J. at 396.

Mental nursing homes which are registered to receive detained patients are sometimes referred to in practice as "private hospitals." A mental nursing home which is not registered to receive detained patients is not a hospital for the purposes of Part II of the Act, and so cannot admit patients in pursuance of an application made under sections 2,3 or 4. Nor can its residents be detained there under section 5(2) or (4).[124] With the exception of NHS hospitals (**132**), any premises used for the reception of one or more mentally disordered patients, which provide nursing or other medical treatment (including care, habilitation and rehabilitation under medical supervision), constitute a mental nursing home,[125] and must be registered as such.[126] Where a mental nursing home is registered to receive detained patients, the particulars of the registration must be entered by the Secretary of State in a separate part of the register maintained by him,[127] and that fact specified in the certificate of registration.[128] The certificate must be kept affixed in a conspicuous place in the home.[129] It will specify the maximum number of patients who may be kept there at any one time[130] and may include conditions as to the category of persons who may be received there.[131] In certain circumstances, the Secretary of State may cancel a person's registration.[132] Where this occurs, or a person solely registered in respect of a home dies, special provisions apply if one or more residents are liable to be detained there. Notwithstanding the cancellation, the registration continues in force for a period of two months or until every patient has ceased to be liable to be detained, whichever occurs first.[133] Experience demonstrates that it cannot be assumed that even large "private hospitals" which treat detained patients are registered to receive them. The establishment's status as a hospital should always be verified, by examining the displayed certificate of registration, and an application for habeas corpus made in appropriate cases.

PARTS III , V AND VI OF THE ACT

Except where otherwise expressly provided, or where the context requires a different meaning, references to a "hospital" in Parts III (mentally disordered offenders), V (mental health review tribunals) and VI (removal and return of patients within the United Kingdom) of the Act are to be construed as referring to "a hospital within the meaning of Part II," and therefore as including mental nursing homes registered to receive detained patients. There is in fact now only one express exception. This is that the Secretary of State may not remove a person to a mental nursing home under

---

[124] A restricted patient may, however, be conditionally discharged to an unregistered mental nursing home. Even though he is liable to be detained under the hospital order originally imposed by the court, he is not liable to be detained at the home. Similarly, section 17 leave may be granted to a patient (whether restricted or not) so as to enable him to reside at an unregistered mental nursing home. Again, he is not liable to be detained at that home, being liable to detention only at the hospital from which he has leave to be absent.

[125] Registered Homes Act 1984, s.22.

[126] *Ibid.*, s.23(1).

[127] *Ibid.*, s.23(5)(b). In practice, the Health Authority for the area keeps and maintains the register on the Secretary of State's behalf.

[128] *Ibid.*, s.23(5)(a).

[129] *Ibid.*, s.23(6). Normally the certificate will be found affixed to the wall in the reception area.

[130] *Ibid.*, s.29(1).

[131] *Ibid.*, s.29(2). For example, that the facility is registered to receive detained patients suffering from a psychopathic disorder.

[132] As to the circumstances in which a person's registration may be cancelled, see *ibid.*, s.28.

[133] *Ibid.*, s.36(2).

section 46. Prior to 1 October 1997, it was also unlawful for him to transfer prisoners and other persons in custody to a mental nursing home under section 47 or 48, although he commonly did so **(381)**.[134]

"HOSPITAL" FOR THE PURPOSES OF PART IV

A wider meaning still is given to the term "hospital" for the purposes of Part IV of the Act (the consent to treatment provisions). Here, any reference to a hospital "includes a mental nursing home," including therefore homes not registered to receive detained patients.[135] The wider definition is necessary because the section 57 consent procedures apply to informal patients who require psychosurgery or other forms of section 57 treatment. Some of these patients might in theory be receiving informal treatment at an unregistered mental nursing home. Such a home may also have residents who are liable to be detained for treatment but have been sent there on leave, in which case medication and ECT may only be administered if authorised under section 58.

DEFINITIONS OF A HOSPITAL

Part of the Act	Section	Definition of a hospital
General definition	145(1)	"In this Act, unless the context otherwise requires— ... 'hospital' means— (a) any health service hospital within the meaning of the National Health Service Act 1977; and (b) any accommodation provided by a local authority and used as a hospital by or on behalf of the Secretary of State under that Act; and 'hospital within the meaning of Part II of this Act' has the meaning given in section 34."
Hospital within the meaning of Part II	34(2)	"Except where otherwise expressly provided, this Part of this Act applies in relation to a mental nursing home, being a home in respect of which the particulars of registration are for the time being entered in the separate part of the register kept for the purposes of section 23(5)(b) of the Registered Homes Act 1984 as it applies in relation to a hospital, and any reference in this Act to a hospital to which this Part of this Act applies, shall be construed accordingly."
Part III	55(5)	"Section 34(2) above shall apply for the purposes of this Part of this Act as it applies for the purposes of Part II of this Act."
Part IV	64(1)	"In this Part of this Act ... 'hospital' includes a mental nursing home."
Part V	79(6)	"In this Part of this Act, unless the context otherwise requires, 'hospital' means a hospital within the meaning of Part II of this Act."

---

[134]   Mental Health Act 1983, s.47(1), as amended by Crime (Sentences) Act 1997, ss.49(3) and 56(2), Sched. 6.

[135]   Mental Health Act 1983, s.64(1).

SECURE NHS HOSPITALS

A number of patients whose cases tribunals review are detained in high secure or medium secure hospital units. There are presently three special hospitals (High Security Hospitals) in England and Wales: Ashworth Hospital in Lancashire, Broadmoor Hospital in Berkshire, and Rampton Hospital in Nottinghamshire. Unless the context otherwise requires, section 145(1) provides that the term "special hospital" has the same meaning as in the National Health Service Act 1977, section 128 of which provides in turn that the term has the meaning given to it in section 4. That section imposes a duty on the Secretary of State for Health to—

> "provide and maintain establishments (in this Act referred to as 'special hospitals') for persons subject to detention under the Mental Health Act 1983 who in his opinion require treatment under conditions of special security on account of their dangerous, violent or criminal propensities."

Informal patients and those not requiring special security

Somewhat at variance with section 4, there are at any one time a handful of special hospital patients who are not detained there under the 1983 Act. It has also been the case that some detained special hospital patients considered suitable for transfer on clinical grounds have nevertheless remained there for a number of years for want of a less secure placement. The lawfulness of such continued detention is questionable if the delay is substantial and it is not disputed that the patient does not require detention in conditions of special security, on account of his propensities. The patient may therefore consider applying for judicial review — specifically, an order of mandamus requiring the Home Secretary to direct his transfer under section 123 — preparatory to making an application to the European Court of Human Rights.

Regional Secure Units

Although not a statutory concept, the reader should be aware that there are in excess of twenty regional secure units for the assessment, treatment and care of patients who require conditions of medium rather than high security. Special hospital patients are often referred to RSUs with a view to transfer, as the first formal stage along the pre-discharge process.

TRANSFERS AND REMOVALS BETWEEN HOSPITALS

The statutory framework concerning the movement of patients between different wards and different hospitals is as follows—

a. Applications for admission must be addressed to the managers of "the" hospital to which admission is sought.

b. A patient detained under section 5(2) may be detained in "the" hospital for 72 hours.

c. No legal formalities have to be observed before a patient may be moved from one ward to another ward within the same hospital. The patient continues to be detained in "the" hospital and movement within "the" hospital is not inconsistent with the existing authority for his detention.

d. Section 19(3) authorises the removal of a patient who is detained in a hospital in pursuance of an application, order or direction to another hospital for which the same managers are responsible. Because this involves no transfer of legal responsibility for the patient's detention to different managers, and the managers are already authorised to detain him, no formal transfer document is necessary. The patient is simply deemed to have been detained from the outset at the hospital to which he is removed.[136]

e. Moving a detained patient to a differently managed hospital can be achieved in one of two ways. Firstly, by granting him leave to be absent from the hospital where he is liable to be detained and imposing a condition of leave that he resides at the second hospital.[137] However, if section 17 is used in this way, the managers of the second hospital have no authority to detain him, since the application or order only authorises his detention at the hospital specified in it. If the aim is *both* to move the patient to a different hospital, and to transfer the authority to detain him to the managers of that hospital, this can only be achieved by means of a formal transfer under section 19(1).

f. The word "transfer" in section 19 therefore denotes a transfer of the authority, and responsibility, for the patient's detention to different managers and section 19 distinguishes between the "transfer" of a patient under section 19(1) and the "removal" of a patient under section 19(3).

g. The authority to detain a patient under section 5(2) cannot be transferred to different managers under section 19, because they are not liable to be detained by virtue of an application. However, they may be removed from one hospital to another hospital for which the same managers are responsible.[138] The original reason for this limitation was that all hospitals within the same district had the same managers — the local District Health Authority — and each district had its own psychiatric facility. Consequently, the limitation caused no practical problems and ensured that the application procedures were not disrupted by the patient being moved to a different district before the section 2 or 3 application had been completed.

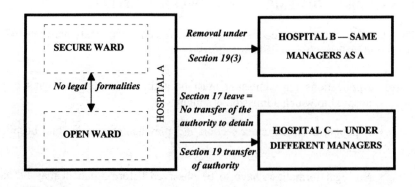

---

136   Mental Health Act 1983, s.19(2) and (3).
137   See *ibid.*, ss.17(1) and (3), 18(2).
138   See the precise wording of Mental Health Act 1983, subss. 19(1) and (3).

DEVELOPMENT OF SATELLITE UNITS

The way in which a hospital is defined in section 145 has important practical consequences. Many hospitals now have "rehabilitation wards" or "hospital hostels" situated in the community a number of miles from the main hospital. These are often converted guest houses with 24-hour nursing cover and a dozen or so "residents." Unless the context otherwise requires, such establishments come within the statutory definition of a hospital and so constitute in-patient facilities. Accordingly, patients seemingly discharged from hospital to local "hostels" of this kind remain in-patients. The statutory criteria for renewing their liability to detention may be satisfied and, if so, compulsory treatment continue during their residence there. It may be argued that such arrangements contravene the statutory framework because they amount to the creation of community treatment orders otherwise than by legislation. However, had such a facility not been available the patient would probably have continued to be detained on a long-stay ward at the main hospital. Either way, he continues to require continuous nursing care reinforced by some element of compulsion and his legal position is neither better nor worse. Furthermore, the more natural setting of a small satellite ward set away from the main hospital is, for rehabilitative purposes, usually more therapeutic.

Detained patients subject to restrictions

A further practical consequence of the development of hospital hostels concerns tribunal proceedings involving restricted patients. Because "discharge" in this context means discharge from hospital, and not merely discharge from liability to detention, a patient who requires further treatment in an in-patient setting cannot be discharged (**515**). If the patient's condition has improved, so that he is ready to leave the main hospital, and take up residence at a highly staffed local hostel, he can be discharged if it is managed by the local authority but not if it is managed by the local NHS trust, and so constitutes hospital premises. In the latter case, although the patient may appear to an outsider to receiving care in the community his legal status remains unchanged — it is as if he had moved wards within the main hospital. He may then live "in the community" for a number of years before eventually being conditionally discharged. While there is sometimes a meaningful distinction between "hospital hostels" and local authority hostels, if the former provide intensive nursing cover but the latter do not, the distinction is not always easy to make because of increasing co-operation between health and social services. If the trend continues and purely residential arrangements, such as group homes, constitute hospital premises then what constitutes being an in-patient is likely to become increasingly artificial.[139] Although a restricted patient who moves to a hostel may feel aggrieved that he has not been formally discharged, the Home Secretary may be equally concerned if the legal position is that his consent is not required before a restricted patient is moved from the main hospital "into the community." For, if the patient's legal status as an in-patient remains unchanged, taking up residence requires no prior discharge or transfer and, at least superficially, no leave to be absent from hospital under section 17 — in which case, nor does the move require the prior consent of the Home Secretary (**336 et seq.**). As to this, the courts may be inclined to hold—

---

[139] As to this, the better argument is that group homes are not institutions which receive and treat patients and so, even if vested in an NHS trust, they are not hospitals for the purposes of the Act.

a.   that the community ward is part of the same hospital as that within which the patient is presently detained;

b.   in consequence, section 19 does not apply because the patient is not being transferred or removed a different hospital;

c.   similarly, the discharge provisions in sections 23, 42 and 73 do not apply because the patient is not being discharged from hospital;

d.   nevertheless, moving the patient from the main hospital to the community ward involves him being absent from hospital for the time it takes to complete the journey between the two sites;

e.   consequently, it is necessary to obtain the Secretary of State's consent to the patient being absent from hospital during the journey;

f.   by refusing his consent to such leave of absence, the Home Secretary can prevent the patient from being moved "into the community" without his approval in this way.[140]

Commentary

The development of community-based resources since 1983 has introduced a certain tension into the statutory definition of a hospital and its practical application in the context of the detention and discharge provisions. It may be argued that arrangements of the kind outlined, involving removal to a community ward, are consistent with the way in which Parliament defined a hospital, which definition includes convalescent homes and any institution providing medical treatment. Alternatively, it may be contended that the statutory context, in relation to the detention and discharge of patients, suggests that only NHS premises at which there is always a medical practitioner on the site are hospitals — the notion of a hospital without a

---

[140]   The main objection to this argument is simply that it is contrived. No one would argue that the hospital managers' power to move an unrestricted patient to a community ward, or to remove him to a different hospital managed by them, is conditional on the responsible medical officer granting section 17 leave. At any rate, the problem will slowly be alleviated as more and more use is made of section 47 of the Crime (Sentences) Act 1997. This section came into force on 1 October 1997. It provides that a hospital order, hospital direction, or section 47 transfer direction may, if restrictions are attached, specify the hospital unit within which the patient is to be detained, *e.g.* secure unit *x* at the specified hospital. Where this power is used, any reference in the 1983 Act to a hospital (*e.g.* in sections 17(1) and 19(3)) is to be construed accordingly. The effect will be that the Home Secretary's consent is required before such a patient can lawfully have escorted leave to attend the hospital shop or be moved to an open ward on the same site, let alone moved to a community ward. At least initially, most restricted in-patients will not, of course, be detained in pursuance of an order or direction which specifies a particular unit. Consequently, the 1997 Act also provides that the managers no longer have power to remove a restricted patient to a *different* hospital under their management without the Home Secretary's consent: Mental Health Act 1983, s.19(3), as amended by Crime (Sentences) Act 1997, s.49(2), and Sched. 1, Pt. II, para. 5(c), as inserted by *ibid.*, s.49(4). The amendment does not, however, prevent the managers from moving patients whose orders do not specify a unit between wards within the *same* hospital (including therefore moving such patients to a community ward, unless the journey requires the Home Secretary's consent under section 17 or the community facility constitutes a separate hospital for these purposes). The fact that the statutory definition of a hospital — what constitutes a hospital and what constitutes a separate hospital — is not clarified in the 1997 Act necessarily does nothing to clarify the position of unrestricted patients, in particular whether small community residential units vested in an NHS trust are wards of the main hospital, etc.

doctor on site being too broad. That it is too broad can arguably be inferred from the discharge framework for restricted patients, although many mental nursing homes which are hospitals for the purposes of the Act do not routinely have a medical practitioner on the premises. A further interpretation is simply that "community wards" and NHS hostels are separate hospitals for the purposes of the Act — in the same way that one body of managers (the District Health Authority) managed a number of hospitals at the time the statute was enacted. With the creation of NHS trusts to manage hospitals, such a trust may similarly manage a number of hospitals, the main hospital being one and a satellite hostel (not being in the same physical location) another for the purposes of the 1983 Act.

EFFECT OF THE CREATION OF NHS TRUSTS

The simple framework set out in the 1983 Act for detaining, removing and transferring patients was undermined when the National Health Service & Community Care Act 1990 created NHS trusts to manage hospitals, without in any way amending the definition of a hospital in section 145(1). Previously, all hospitals within a district had the same hospital managers, the local District Health Authority. If it was necessary to move a patient from the psychiatric ward of the local District General Hospital to a surgical ward, following a suicide attempt, the patient remained detained in the same hospital by the same managers. Consequently, no legal formalities had to be observed. Likewise, if a secure psychiatric unit was on the same site, but set apart from the District General Hospital, permitting the patients to wander the hospital grounds, or taking them to the general hospital for dental treatment, involved no legal formalities. The patient had not left the hospital where he was liable to be detained so no formal leave of absence was required. The position now is that different floors of a General Hospital may be managed by different NHS trusts. For example, the local General Hospital NHS trust may manage the first and second floors, and also those wards on the third floor which admit patients for physical conditions. The local Mental Health NHS trust may manage the open psychiatric ward on the third floor, the secure unit set apart in the General Hospital grounds, and a number of wards left on the site of the old asylum, situated some miles away. Worse still, some psychiatric wards may be shared by two Mental Health NHS trusts, both having beds on the ward. As will be seen, trying to apply the legal framework devised in 1983 for the detention, removal and transfer of patients to this new managerial system has proved difficult.

Assumptions on which the Act is based

Before analysing the problems, it is helpful to refer to a number of statutory provisions which demonstrate that the Act was drafted on the assumption that all of the wards on a single site would form a single hospital managed by a single group of managers. The Act provides that an application for admission shall be addressed to the managers of "the" hospital to which admission is sought.[141] Following admission, the application authorises "the" managers to detain the patient in accordance with the provisions of the Act. Section 37 provides that a court may authorise an offender's admission to and detention in "such" hospital as may be specified in the order.[142] Evidence must first be received, *inter alia*, from the managers of "the" hospital" that a bed is available.[143] Sections 47 and 48 similarly provide that the Secretary of State

---

[141]   Mental Health Act 1983, s.11(2).
[142]   *Ibid.*, s.37(1).
[143]   *Ibid.*, s.37(4).

may by warrant direct that certain categories of person in custody shall be removed to and detained in "such" hospital as may be specified in the direction."[144]

Moving patients between differently managed wards

The issue that arises from reading these sections is what legal formalities must be completed (if any) before a detained patient may be moved from one ward to another in the same hospital building if those wards are separately managed? Providing the patient in each case remains detained in "the" hospital, can he be moved between differently managed wards or units within that hospital without any formal transfer of the authority for his detention or the grant of leave? If a literal interpretation of sections 17–19 is taken, such a variation involves neither the patient leaving the hospital or being "transferred to another hospital." Certainly, when each hospital was managed by the same District Health Authority, no legal formalities were necessary because such a move did not involve a change of hospital or a change of managers. Section 5(2) provides another example of the problem. The original statutory principles underlying this provision were that patients so detained need not be detained throughout the 72–hour period at the same hospital but must, if moved, continue to be detained by the same managers. However, these principles were based on the assumption that moving patients between wards or units on the same hospital site never involved a change of managers. Following the creation of NHS trusts, any opinion that section 5(2) patients can be informally moved to a ward managed by another NHS trust is consistent with the statutory premise that such patients may be informally moved between wards within the same hospital. However, it contradicts the statutory principle that authority to detain such a patient cannot be transferred to different hospital managers, informal movement between wards being permitted because of the presumption that the patient's management would remain unchanged. Conversely, the opinion that section 5(2) patients cannot be informally moved between differently managed units avoids the above inconsistency but is inconsistent with the original statutory assumption, expressed in section 145(1), that one institution equals one hospital.

The respective arguments

It can be argued that section 19 is only concerned with the transfer or removal of a patient from one institution to another. Section 19(3) provides that a patient may be removed to "any other such hospital" managed by the same trust while the transfer provisions in section 19 only apply if a patient is moved from "a hospital" to "another hospital." It was always intended that moves between wards within a single institution would be internal, informal, arrangements not subject to any legal formalities. The authority conferred by section 5(2) is that the patient may be detained for 72 hours in "the" hospital and moving him from a general to a psychiatric ward does not infringe this; he remains detained in the hospital. Against this, it must be acknowledged that Parliament foresaw none of this. The essential distinction between a transfer and a removal is that removal involves no change in the managers responsible for the patient's detention. Where it is proposed to transfer the authority to detain him from one set of people to another this must be done formally by way of a section 19 transfer entered into by both sets of managers. Furthermore, it is clear from the transfer-removal distinction that Parliament did not

---

[144]   Mental Health Act 1983, ss.47(1) & 48(1).

intend that responsibility for patients detained under section 5(2) should be transferred between managers. Arguing that general hospitals remain one hospital for the purposes of the Act means that even patients detained in pursuance of an application or order can be moved about at random, without any need for section 17 leave or a formal transfer of responsibility. Although the idea that one institution can comprise two hospitals seems odd at first glance, it is no different from a block of flats within which each floor has a different legal owner. The idea only seems strange because for historical reasons such institutions are known by a single name. The context now requires that the term "hospital" in section 145 means *that part* of an institution which is vested in an NHS trust.

Summary

It is submitted that—

- Where two or more NHS trusts manage different parts of an institution which is a hospital for the purposes of the National Health Service Act 1977, each separately managed part is a hospital for the purposes of the admission, detention and discharge provisions in the Mental Health Act 1983.

- Accordingly, where it is proposed to move a patient from one ward or unit within the hospital grounds to another under different management, this requires the grant of leave of absence under section 17 or a formal transfer of the authority to detain the patient under section 19. In cases involving restricted patients, such a move therefore requires the consent of the Secretary of State.

- Patients detained on a general ward under section 5(2) may not be removed to a psychiatric ward under section 19(3) if that ward is separately managed. Nor can the authority to detain them be transferred to another NHS trust under section 19(1). Nor can they be granted leave of absence under section 17(1) subject to a condition that they reside on the psychiatric ward, since they have no responsible medical officer who can grant such leave. In extreme cases, their removal may be justified under common law and recourse may probably be had to section 4.

THE HOSPITAL MANAGERS

Formal responsibility for ensuring that detained patients are dealt with in accordance with the provisions of the Mental Health Act 1983 rests with the managers of the hospital or mental nursing home concerned, as defined by section 145(1). Section 118(1)(a) expressly provides that the Code of Practice prepared by the Mental Health Act Commission on behalf of the Secretary of State may include guidance for managers in relation to the admission of patients to hospitals and mental nursing homes under the Act.

Type of hospital	Managers of the hospital
• Hospitals vested in an NHS trust	The trust
• Accommodation provided by a local authority and used as a hospital by or on behalf of the Secretary of State under the NHS Act 1977	The Health Authority, or Special Health Authority, responsible for the administration of the hospital
• Special hospitals	The Secretary of State
• Mental nursing homes registered under the Registered Homes Act 1984	The person or persons registered in respect of the home

STATUTORY FUNCTIONS OF THE MANAGERS

The managers' statutory functions are as follows —

- To receive applications, medical recommendations and reports furnished under Part II of the Act.[145]

- To scrutinise applications and medical recommendations furnished under Part II, to consent to their amendment, and to give notice that a recommendation appears to be insufficient to warrant the detention of the patient.[146]

- To ensure that each detained patient understands the provision under which he is detained, the effect of that provision, his rights of application to a tribunal, and the effect of the provisions referred to in section 132(2).[147]

- To detain patients in accordance with the provisions of the Act.[148]

- To discharge a patient who is liable to be detained if they deem that appropriate.[149]   •

- To notify the person appearing to be the nearest relative of a patient's impending discharge.[150]

- To give notice to the relevant persons of the furnishing of any report reclassifying the patient,[151] renewing his liability to detention for a further period,[152] or barring his discharge.[153]

- To refer the cases of patients to a mental health review tribunal in the circumstances specified in section 68.

---

[145]   Mental Health Act 1983, ss. 4(4)(a), 5(1)(2) and (5), 11(2), 14, 16(1) and 134(1).
[146]   *Ibid.*, s.15.
[147]   *Ibid.*, s.132.
[148]   *Ibid.*, ss. 6(2), 35(9)(b), 36(8), 40(1)(b), 40(3)(b).
[149]   *Ibid.*, ss.23(2)–(5).
[150]   *Ibid.*, s.133.
[151]   *Ibid.*, s.16(4).
[152]   *Ibid.*, s.20(3).
[153]   *Ibid.*, s.25(2).

- To authorise a person to keep a patient granted leave of absence in his custody,[154] or to take into custody and return to hospital a patient who is absent without leave.[155]

- To remove patients, if they think appropriate, from one hospital to another which is also under their management[156] or make arrangements for a patient's transfer to another hospital or into guardianship under section 19.

- To give evidence to a court that arrangements have been made for a patient's admission under Part III of the Act.[157]

- To fulfil the obligations of the responsible authority in tribunal proceedings involving patients who are liable to be detained in a hospital under their management.

- To return patients to prison in the circumstances specified in section 74(3).

- To receive requests made under section 134 for the withholding of a postal packet made under section 134, and to comply with directions of the Mental Health Act Commission concerning the release of any postal packets previously withheld by them from a patient by them.[158]

- To investigate complaints made by patients.[159]

DELEGATION OF FUNCTIONS TO OFFICERS

By section 32(3), regulations may determine the manner in which the functions of the managers under Part II of the Act are to be exercised and those regulations may specify the circumstances in which, and the conditions subject to which, any functions may be performed by officers of, or other persons acting on behalf of, the managers. The Mental Health (Hospital, Guardianship and Consent to Treatment) Regulations 1983 provide that —

- Where, under the regulations, the managers of a hospital are required to make any record or report, that function may be performed by an officer authorised by those managers to perform that function.[160]

- The managers may authorise in writing any officer or class of officers on their behalf to scrutinise medical recommendations, to consent to the amendment of an application or medical recommendation under section 15(1), and, if necessary, to give the written notice required by section 15(2).[161]

---

[154] Mental Health Act 1983, s.17(3).
[155] *Ibid.*, ss.18(1) and (2).
[156] *Ibid.*, s.19(3).
[157] *Ibid.*, ss.35(4), 36(3), 37(4), 38(4), 54(1).
[158] *Ibid.*, s.121(8).
[159] Where, after such an investigation, the complainant remains dissatisfied, he may then ask the Mental Health Act Commission to conduct a further investigation. *Ibid.*, s.120(1)(b)(i). See p.176.
[160] Mental Health (Hospital, Guardianship and Consent to Treatment) Regulations 1983, reg. 3(6).
[161] Mental Health (Hospital, Guardianship and Consent to Treatment) Regulations 1983, reg. 4(2).

- The managers' functions under regulation 7, in relation to the transfer of patients under section 19, may be performed by an officer authorised by them.[162]

Mental Health Act Administrators

The managers of most hospitals appoint a "Mental Health Act Administrator" to perform those functions which may be delegated to an officer. In some hospitals, the administrator may have other responsibilities and be known as the "Patients Affairs Officer" or the "Patients Services Officer." Admission documents are generally scrutinised twice, once by the administrator and once by a medical scrutineer, being a consultant appointed to undertake the task. The managers will themselves then periodically examine admission documents, often monthly or quarterly, and in that way monitor the performance of the scrutineers.

Functions which may not be delegated

The power to make an order for discharge under section 23 may not be delegated by the managers to officers, that is an employee of theirs.[163]

ORDERS FOR DISCHARGE AND MANAGERS' HEARINGS

In recent years it has become common for patients to "appeal to the managers" against their detention under the Act, sometimes in preference to making an application to a Mental Health Review Tribunal. This is because section 23 provides that an order in writing discharging a patient from detention may be made by the managers. As the managers of an NHS trust are "the trust," which is a body corporate, some mechanism must be devised which allows this power of discharge to be exercised by the trust. Section 23(4) therefore provides that three or more members of the trust, or of a committee or subcommittee of the trust,[164] may be authorised for the purpose. The persons authorised may include the chairman of the trust and non-executive directors but none of them may be employees of the trust. The three managers appointed to hear the "appeal" usually receive medical and social work reports and follow a procedure loosely based on that set out in the Mental Health Review Tribunal Rules 1983. It must, however, be emphasised that the hospital managers' "appeal hearing" does not have a statutory basis. *The Mental Health Act Commission's First Biennial Report* set out the correct position —

> "A detained patient's so-called 'appeal to the Managers' for his discharge has often caused misunderstanding in hospitals which we have visited. The leaflets which were published officially, as samples of the written information required to be given by Managers to detained patients, inform patients that they can request Managers to discharge them. This has often become called 'an appeal to the Managers,' but it is a non-statutory 'appeal' or request, not a set procedure laid down by the Act ... The Act therefore confirms their right to make an 'order' of discharge, but says nothing about the grounds for doing so, and nothing about an 'appeal' by a patient for them to do so ... The 'appeal' to the Managers should not be seen as a substitute for, but as additional to, the formal right of appeal which Parliament has provided."[165]

---

162   *Ibid.*, reg. 7(5).
163   Mental Health Act 1983, ss. 23 and 32(3).
164   Members of a committee or sub-committee of the trust authorised to make orders for discharge are sometimes misleadingly and erroneously referred to as the "independent managers" of the hospital.
165   *Mental Health Act Commission: First Biennial Report, 1983–85* (H.M.S.O., 1985), para. 8.13.

Mental nursing homes

A mental nursing home properly registered under the Registered Homes Act 1984 is treated as a "hospital" for most purposes of the 1983 Act (**132**). Section 145(1) of the 1983 Act provides that, unless the context otherwise requires, the term "the managers" means "the person or persons registered in respect of the home." The managers may discharge a patient from liability to detention but any order is only valid if it has three signatories. However, the "person or persons" registered may be fewer than three individuals. The Royal Commission of 1954–57 appears to have anticipated this and also the fact that a small nursing home might not have a management committee or Board of Governors.[166] That being so, the 1959 Act provided that the registration authority and any health service body financing the patient's placement could discharge him. The purpose of doing so was to ensure that there would always be some management body (and not just some judicial body) which could order the patient's discharge. The Mental Health (Amendment) Act 1982 later extended what is now section 23(4). This subsection provides that the power to make an order of discharge may be exercised (i) by any three or more members of the body of persons having power to discharge, or (ii) by three or more members of an authorised committee or sub-committee of that "body of persons." Whether this was intended to enable a private company or a single registered person to appoint a committee or sub-committee of "independent managers" may be debated.

Disadvantages of managers' hearings

Managers hearings undoubtedly have significant disadvantages compared with the statutory tribunal process. In the first place, a panel comprised solely of lay persons is not well qualified to rigorously examine the legal and medical grounds for a patient's detention. However fair the managers strive to be, their relationship to the hospital staff giving evidence is not entirely independent. In many hospitals, obtaining free legal representation at the hearing is difficult. The hearing procedure itself is not governed by statutory instrument, or elsewhere defined, and there are no statutory discharge criteria to be applied. Consequently, some managers will direct discharge if the patient no longer satisfies the original criteria for admission; others apply the renewal criteria in section 20; others apply the tribunal discharge criteria in section 72; while yet others apply no statutory criteria, treating the issue as a matter for their discretion subject to not acting irrationally. The latter is probably the correct approach. Section 2 patients may find that they are outside the time-limits for lodging a tribunal application if they wait on the outcome of a managers' application, in the belief that they have an unanswerable case for discharge. The proportion of patients discharged by the managers is generally low, considerably lower than the proportion of patients discharged by tribunals. One hospital in England is known not to have discharged any patients during a period of eighteen years holding such appeals. Such a pattern of outcome over many years clearly represents a tremendous input in terms of professional time without any obvious corresponding benefit in terms of protecting citizens from unwarranted detention.

---

[166] *Report of the Royal Commission on the Law Relating to Mental Illness and Mental Deficiency,* Cmnd. 169 (1957), para. 826.

TERMS DEFINING MEDICAL PRACTITIONERS

The 1983 Act uses various terms to describe medical practitioners and certain powers and duties may only be performed by a doctor who has been specially appointed for the purpose or who is responsible for the patient's treatment. Consultant psychiatrists undertake full responsibility for the clinical care of patients requiring specialised psychiatric treatment, heading a team or "firm" of junior doctors. There are several grades of "junior doctors" and the consultant is responsible for ensuring that they only undertake tasks which they are competent to perform.

"REGISTERED MEDICAL PRACTITIONER"

The registrar of the General Medical Council is required by the Medical Act 1983 to keep two registers of medical practitioners. The Act makes provision for three kinds of registration: full registration, limited registration and provisional registration.[167]

Significance of registration

The term "registered medical practitioner" in the Mental Health Act means a fully registered person within the meaning of the Medical Act.[168] Accordingly, only a person who is fully registered may provide a medical recommendation or report or perform the other statutory functions of a medical practitioner under the Mental Health Act.[169] A person who is not fully registered is statutorily barred from holding an appointment as a medical officer in any hospital or other place for the reception of persons suffering from mental disorder.[170]

MEDICAL PRACTITIONERS APPROVED UNDER SECTION 12(2)

The detention or guardianship of any patient whose case a tribunal may review must be founded upon the written recommendations or reports of two fully registered medical practitioners; and one of them must be furnished by a practitioner who has been approved by the Secretary of State as "having special experience in the diagnosis or treatment of mental disorder."[171] Whether or not a doctor has "special experience in the diagnosis or treatment of mental disorder" at the time he applies for accreditation is the sole criterion for approval under the section.[172] In practice, registrars and psychiatrists in higher grades may be section 12 approved, as are a few general practitioners.

---

[167] In certain circumstances, which are specified in the Medical Act 1983, a person who has only been provisionally registered, or who has limited registration, is deemed to be a fully registered medical practitioner.

[168] Interpretation Act 1978, Sched. 1.

[169] Section 48 of the Medical Act 1983 also expressly provides that a certificate required by any enactment from a medical practitioner shall not be valid unless the person signing it is fully registered.

[170] Medical Act 1983, s.47.

[171] Mental Health Act 1983, ss.12 and 54. Guidance on the procedures to be adopted in granting such approval is contained in Department of Health Circular No. HSG (96)3. The granting of approval has been delegated to Health Authorities: National Health Service (Functions of Health Authorities and Administration Arrangements) 1996, reg.3.

[172] See *R. v. Trent Regional Health Authority ex p. Somaratne* (1993) 18 B.M.L.R. 143, C.A.

"RESPONSIBLE MEDICAL OFFICER"

Informal patients and those who are liable to be detained but not liable to compulsory treatment under Part IV of the Act do not have a responsible medical officer.

Patients who are liable to be detained

Where a detained patient is liable to compulsory treatment under Part IV of the Act, the registered medical practitioner in charge of his treatment (who will usually, but not necessarily, be a consultant psychiatrist) is his "responsible medical officer."[173] Certain functions under the Act may only be performed by a patient's responsible medical officer and may not be delegated to a junior doctor on the hospital staff: the power to grant the patient leave of absence and to revoke any leave previously granted; the duty to periodically review a patient's liability to detention and the power to renew it for a further period; the power to discharge a patient under section 23 or to bar his discharge by the nearest relative; the duty to furnish periodic reports on a restricted patient to the Secretary of State; the power to authorise the administration of treatment to a capable and consenting patient under Part IV of the Act.

Patients subject to guardianship cases

In guardianship cases, the responsible medical officer is the medical officer authorised by the local social services authority to act as the patient's responsible medical officer.[174]

"APPROPRIATE MEDICAL OFFICER"

Restricted patients do not have an appropriate medical officer. The power to reclassify the form of mental disorder from which any other detained patient is recorded as suffering is exercisable by his "appropriate medical officer." Similarly, if such a patient is taken into custody after having been absent without leave for more than 28 days, it is his appropriate medical officer who must examine him in order to determine whether he should continue to be detained. However, the distinction is superfluous in practice, and can be ignored, since the Act provides that a detained patient's responsible medical officer will in all cases also be his "appropriate medical officer."

Patients subject to guardianship

Where a patient is subject to guardianship, his appropriate medical officer has other functions in addition to reclassifying the form of mental disorder recorded and reporting on patients who have been absent without leave. It is his duty to periodically determine whether the criteria for renewing the guardianship are satisfied and, where they are, he has the power to authorise the guardianship's continuance for a further period — functions performed in the case of an

---

[173] Mental Health Act 1983, ss.34(1)(a), 55(1), 64(1).
[174] Mental Health Act 1983, s.34(1)(b). The authority may appoint a registered medical practitioner to fulfil the functions of the responsible medical officer for a particular patient or appoint a particular doctor to act as the responsible medical officer in respect of all the patients under its guardianship. It may even appoint medical practitioners on an ad hoc basis to fulfil some particular function of a responsible medical officer under the Act the performance of which is due.

unrestricted detained patient by his responsible medical officer.[175] However, in cases where a local social services authority has been appointed as a patient's guardian, the distinction is as meaningless in practice as before, since the responsible medical officer is again also the appropriate medical officer. The distinction between a responsible and an appropriate medical officer is only of any practical consequence in those rare cases where a private individual, rather than a local authority, has been appointed as the patient's guardian (*see* "nominated medical attendant").

"NOMINATED MEDICAL ATTENDANT"

Where a private guardian is appointed for a patient, that individual is required to nominate a registered medical practitioner to act as the patient's medical attendant.[176] The "nominated medical attendant" is the patient's "appropriate medical officer" but not "his responsible medical officer." As in other guardianship cases, the responsible medical officer is the doctor appointed and authorised to fulfil that role by the local social services authority.[177] As to their respective functions, it is for the appropriate medical officer/nominated medical attendant to reclassify the patient and to renew the guardianship if appropriate but the responsible medical officer who possesses the power to discharge the patient under section 23.

"MEDICAL PRACTITIONER IN CHARGE OF THE TREATMENT OF THE PATIENT"

Informal patients and detained patients who are not liable to compulsory treatment under Part IV of the Act do not have a responsible (or an appropriate) medical officer. The Act cannot therefore provide that the power conferred by section 5(2), to detain an informal patient for 72 hours, is one exercisable by the patient's responsible medical officer. Some other term or phrase is required and the Act instead states that the power may be exercised by "medical practitioner in charge of the treatment of the patient," or by his nominated deputy.

COMMUNITY RESPONSIBLE MEDICAL OFFICER (CRMO)

Where a patient is subject to after-care under supervision, the Health Authority must ensure that there is at all times a registered medical practitioner approved under section 12 in charge of the medical treatment provided for him as part of his section 117 after-care services. This doctor is called the patient's community responsible medical officer.[178] His duties include renewing the patient's liability to statutory supervision for further periods, reclassifying the form of mental disorder from which the patient is recorded as suffering, and directing that the patient shall cease to be subject to after-care under supervision.

---

[175] Mental Health Act 1983, s.20.

[176] Section 9(2) provides that, "Regulations under this section ... shall provide for the appointment, in the case of every person subject to the guardianship of a person other than a local social services authority, of a registered medical practitioner to act as the nominated medical attendant of the patient."

[177] Section 34(1)(b) states that the responsible medical officer is the registered medical practitioner authorised to act by the "local social services authority" (defined in s.145(1)) rather than the "responsible local social services authority" (defined in s.34(3)). However, this appears to be a drafting error and it may be inferred that, if the patient lives within the area of one authority and his private guardian in another, only the latter authority may authorise a doctor to act as the patient's responsible medical officer.

[178] Mental Health Act 1983, s.34(1).

148

SECOND OPINION APPROVED DOCTORS ("SOADS")

Part IV of the Act provides that some forms of treatment for mental disorder may not be given to a detained patient who does not consent to the treatment, or who is incapable of doing so, unless a registered medical practitioner appointed for the purposes of that Part of the Act has certified that the proposed treatment should be given. Section 121(2) provides that the Mental Health Act Commission shall, on the Secretary of State's behalf, appoint registered medical practitioners to provide second opinions and certificates under Part IV and persons so appointed are conventionally known as Second Opinion Approved Doctors ("SOADs").

THE MEDICAL MEMBER OF THE TRIBUNAL

The membership of each regional Mental Health Review Tribunal comprises legal members, medical members and what are customarily known as "lay members." The medical members are registered medical practitioners appointed by the Lord Chancellor after consultation with the Secretary of State for Health.[179] At least one of the members appointed to consider an individual patient's case must be a medical member[180] who has no personal connection with the patient and has not recently treated him in a professional medical capacity.[181] Under the tribunal rules, it is the function of the medical member to examine the patient prior to the hearing and to take such other steps as he thinks necessary to form an opinion of the patient's mental condition.[182] In practice, the medical member will be a consultant psychiatrist.

NURSES AND OTHER HEALTH SERVICE PROFESSIONALS

A member of the ward nursing staff may sometimes prepare a short nursing report on a patient whose case is being reviewed by a tribunal or give oral evidence as part of the responsible authority's case. Such reports are not a formal requirement under the Mental Health Review Tribunal Rules 1983. The statutory functions of a nurse under the 1983 Act are limited.

"REGISTERED NURSE"

The United Kingdom Central Council (U.K.C.C.) maintains a professional register of nursing staff[183] which is arranged by parts, each of which is indicative of the different qualifications and kinds of training which a nurse may receive. Where the term "registered nurse" is used, it means a nurse registered in a part of the professional register.[184] The registered nurse in charge of a ward will generally be referred to in practice as the "charge nurse," "ward sister" or "ward manager."

---

[179]   Mental Health Act 1983, s.65(2), Sched. 2, para. 1(b).
[180]   *Ibid.*, para. 4(b).
[181]   Mental Health Review Tribunal Rules 1983, r.8(2)(c).
[182]   *Ibid.*, r.11.
[183]   See Nurses, Midwives and Health Visitors Act 1979, s.10.
[184]   Interpretation Act 1978, Sched. 1. Nurses who were registered prior to September 1992 may elect to keep their previous title of "registered general nurse" (RGN), "registered mental nurse" (RMN), "registered mental handicap nurse" (RMHN), or registered sick children's nurse (RSCN). Prior to September 1992, a person could undertake a two year training leading to registration on the second part of the registered as an "enrolled nurse" and the term may also be encountered occasionally. Nurses registered after September 1992 are all known by the same title of "registered nurse."

Unregistered nursing staff

The nursing complement on a ward usually includes both registered nurses and unqualified nursing staff. Unregistered persons are often referred to as "nursing assistants," "health care assistants" or "nursing auxiliaries." The term "Project 2000 student" may be used to denote a person training for registration as a nurse.

"NURSES OF THE PRESCRIBED CLASS"

The six-hour power of detention conferred by section 5(4) may only be exercised by "a nurse of the prescribed class," that is a nurse registered in Part 3 of the professional register (first level nurse trained in nursing persons suffering from mental illness); Part 5 (first level nurse trained in the nursing of persons suffering from mental handicap); Part 13 (nurses qualified following a course of preparation in mental health nursing); or Part 14 (nurses qualified following a course of preparation in mental handicap nursing).

STATUTORY FUNCTIONS OF NURSES

The power in section 5(4) aside, nurses have only one other statutory function unique to them under the 1983 Act. Before a medical practitioner appointed by the Secretary of State (a "SOAD") may complete a certificate authorising the administration of treatment under Part IV of the Act, he is required to first consult a "nurse" who has been professionally concerned with the patient's treatment.[185]

PROFESSIONS SUPPLEMENTARY TO MEDICINE

Medical practitioners and nurses apart, no other professionals involved in providing medical treatment have any defined statutory powers or duties towards the patient under the 1983 Act. Their therapeutic role may, of course, be fundamental and they are occasionally called upon to furnish a tribunal with a short report. A multi-disciplinary team normally consists of a nurse, psychiatrist, social worker, occupational therapist and psychologist. The main therapists working in the treatment of mental illness are *occupational therapists* who develop and promote skills necessary for independent living; *art, music, and drama therapists* involved in the psychotherapies; *speech therapists; physiotherapists*, who influence psychological health through physical approaches such as the use of relaxation, exercise and the management of disabilities; and *dieticians* offering dietary advice for anorexia or dietary neglect.

Clinical psychologists

A clinical psychologist can provide detailed assessments of a patient's cognitive functioning. They may assess suitability for an increasing range of behavioural therapies and coping techniques. It is the clinical psychologist who administers psychological tests which assess a patient's intellectual functioning, attitudes and personality traits, and undertakes counselling or behaviour modification techniques.

---

[185] Mental Health Act 1983, ss.57(3)(b) and 58(4).

Occupational therapists

An occupational therapist assesses a patient's occupational, self-care and general living skills. This form of assessment is particularly useful for persons with chronic mental health problems and those recovering from acute illness. Previously, the occupational therapist's skills were aimed at diverting the patient's attention from his inner conflicts by arranging relaxing occupations, such as craft work. The present aim is geared more towards developing relationships within the framework of group occupational activities which will help patients to gain an understanding of their particular patterns of behaviour. For example, group discussions, readings, and psychodrama. Patients with chronic illnesses may require help in pursuits such as cooking, budgeting, and shopping, and the detention of some special hospital patients predates the introduction of decimalisation. In industrial therapy, the aim is to create a situation approximating normal working conditions. The work is often graded with the aim of gradually improving the participant's concentration.[186]

Physiotherapists

The physiotherapist deals with problems unrelated to the patient's psychiatric illness; conditions directly or indirectly caused by the patient's mental state (such as nerve lesions from severed wrists in suicide attempts); and conditions inextricably bound up with the patient's mental state (such as asthma, physical disabilities in a person with brain dysfunction, rehabilitation programmes for persons who have suffered strokes). Persons with physical handicaps will require their assistance. The physiotherapist teaches and supervises the patient through a prescribed exercise programme designed to strengthen weak muscles and prevent deformities.

SOCIAL SERVICES AUTHORITIES

Local social services authorities have responsibility for patients under guardianship, for the after-care of certain patients following their discharge from hospital, and for the appointment of approved social workers. This section is arranged as follows—

---

[186]   See M.J. Sainsbury, *Key to Psychiatry* (John Wiley & Sons, 3rd ed.)

"LOCAL SOCIAL SERVICES AUTHORITY"

Unless the context otherwise requires, the term means a council which is a local authority for the purpose of the Local Authority Social Services Act 1970.[187]

"RESPONSIBLE LOCAL SOCIAL SERVICES AUTHORITY"

The term is defined in section 34(3) and is relevant to cases involving guardianship. Where a local authority is itself acting as the patient's guardian, it is the responsible local social services authority. Where a private guardian has been appointed, the responsible local social services authority is that for the area in which the guardian — not the patient — resides. It is the responsible local social services authority to which guardianship applications and reports renewing the guardianship must be addressed and which has power to discharge the guardianship.[188]

FUNCTIONS OF SOCIAL SERVICES AUTHORITIES

Some of the most important social services functions under the 1983 Act and related legislation are summarised in the table on the following page. Under the Local Authority Social Services Act 1970, every local authority is required to establish a social services committee to deal with matters relating to the discharge by the authority of its statutory "social services functions."

Delegation of functions under Local Government Act 1972

Section 10 provides that, subject to any express provision to the contrary, an authority may discharge any of its functions through a committee or sub-committee; an or officer of the authority; another authority; jointly with one or more local authorities.[189] Under section 101(2), committees have a wide power to sub-delegate to sub-committees and officers and, similarly, sub-committees may authorise officers to fulfil functions on their behalf, *e.g.* to consider and accept guardianship applications.

Delegation of functions under Mental Health Act 1983

Section 32 provides that certain functions may be delegated in the circumstances prescribed by regulations. Where a local social services authority is required under the Mental Health (Hospital, Guardianship and Consent to Treatment) Regulations 1983 to make any record or report, that function may be performed by an officer authorised by that authority.[190] The regulations also permit the authority to authorise an officer or class of officers to consent on its behalf to the rectification of incorrect or defective guardianship applications or recommendations.[191]

---

[187] Mental Health Act 1983, s.145(1).
[188] This fact is often not appreciated by social workers so that applications and renewal reports are furnished to the authority within whose area the patient resides even though the guardian is resident elsewhere. In such cases, any purported acceptance of the application and reception into guardianship is void *ab initio*.
[189] See *The Encyclopaedia of Forms and Precedents* (Butterworths, 5th ed., 1991), Vol. 26 (39).
[190] Mental Health (Hospital, Guardianship and Consent to Treatment) Regulations 1983, reg. 3(6).
[191] *Ibid.,* reg. 5(2). See also Mental Health Act 1983, s.8(4).

National Assistance Act 1948

ss.21–27   • *Provision of residential accommodation for adults suffering from mental disorder*

ss.29–30   • *Promoting the welfare of adults who suffer*

s.48   • *Providing temporary protection of property belonging to persons in hospital or accommodation provided under Part III of the Act.*

Disabled Persons (Employment) Act 1958

s.3   • *Provision of facilities for enabling disabled persons to be employed or work under special conditions.*

Health Services and Public Health Act 1968

s.45   • *Promotion of welfare of old people.*

Chronically Sick and Disabled Persons Act 1970

s.2   • *Provision of certain welfare services.*

National Health Service Act 1977

s.21   • *Prevention, care and after-care.*

Mental Health Act 1983

Pts. II, III and IV   • *Welfare of the mentally disordered; guardianship of persons suffering from mental disorder; exercise of functions of nearest relative*

ss.66, 67, 69(1)   • *Exercise of functions of nearest relative in relation to Mental Health Review Tribunal proceedings*

s.114   • *Appointment of approved social workers*

s.115   • *Entry to and inspection of private premises*

s.116   • *Welfare of certain hospital patients*

s.117   • *After-care of detained patients*

s.130   • *Prosecutions under the 1983 Act*

Registered Homes Act 1984

Pt. I   • *Registration of Residential Care Homes*

National Health Service and Community Care Act 1990

s.46   • *Preparation of plans for community care services.*

s.47   • *Assessments of need for community care services.*

COMMUNITY CARE SERVICES

Community care refers to the policy of providing services and support which people affected by problems of ageing, mental illness, mental handicap, or physical or sensory disability, need in order to be able to live as independently as possible in their own homes, or in "homely" settings, in the community. is concerned with community care. More specifically, "community care services" are defined in Part III of the National Health Service and Community Care Act 1990 as being services which a local authority may provide, or arrange to be provided, under any of the following provisions[192] —

- Part III of the National Assistance Act 1948 (**687**)

- Section 45 of the Health Services and Public Health Act 1968 (**689**)

- Section 21 of and Sched. 8 to the National Health Service Act 1977 (**688**)

- Section 117 of the Mental Health Act 1983 (**413**)

National Assistance Act 1948, Part III

Part III of the National Assistance Act 1948 empowers a local authority to make arrangements for providing residential accommodation and other services for persons suffering from mental disorder.

Accommodation

Section 21 provides that a local authority may with the Secretary of State's approval, and to such extent as he directs shall, arrange the provision of residential accommodation for persons aged 18 or over who ordinarily reside in the authority's area and who, by reason of mental disorder, are in need of care and attention which is not otherwise available to them. Accommodation provided under Part III may be managed by the local authority itself, or by another local authority (with that authority's agreement), or be a nursing or residential care home managed by a voluntary organisation or other body. For the purposes of Part III, an in-patient in a hospital managed by an NHS trust is deemed to be ordinarily resident in the area in which he was ordinarily resident immediately before he was admitted as a patient to the hospital.

Promoting the welfare of persons suffering from mental disorder

Section 29 provides that a local authority may with the Secretary of State's approval, and to such extent as he directs shall, make arrangements for promoting the welfare of persons ordinarily resident in the authority's area who, being aged 18 or over, suffer from mental disorder of any description.[193] Arrangements may in particular be made for: informing persons of the services available for them under section 29; instructing them in ways of overcoming the effects of their disabilities; providing suitable work, including workshops and hostels where persons engaged in workshops may live; providing recreational facilities. By *Circular* 19/74, provision may be made under section 29 for occupational, social, cultural and recreational

---

[192] National Health Service and Community Care Act 1990, s.46(3). For a more detailed description of the services which may be provided under these statutory provisions, see p.687 *et seq.*
[193] National Assistance Act 1948, s.29.

facilities at day centres and similar establishments, and for social worker advice and support.[194] A local authority may employ as their agent any voluntary organisation or person carrying on, professionally or by way of trade or business, activities which consist of or include the provision of services for any person to whom section 29 applies, being an organisation or person appearing to the authority to be capable of providing that service.

Health Services and Public Health Act 1968, s.45

Section 45 provides that a local authority may with the Secretary of State's approval, and to such extent as he directs shall, make arrangements for promoting the welfare of old people. A local authority may employ as their agent any voluntary organisation or person carrying on, professionally or by way of trade or business, activities which consist of or include the provision of services for old people, being an organisation or person appearing to the authority to be capable of promoting the welfare of old people.

National Health Service Act 1977, s.21 and Sched. 8

Schedule 8 provides that a local authority may with the Secretary of State's approval, and to such extent as he directs shall, make arrangements for the purpose of preventing illness, for the care of persons suffering from illness, and for the after-care of persons who have been so suffering. In particular, the authority may, and where directed shall, make arrangements for the provision of centres or other facilities "for training them or keeping them suitably occupied." Section 21 provides that these services in relation to "prevention, care and after-care" are functions exercisable by local social services authorities.[195]

Mental Health Act 1983, s.117

Section 117 imposes a duty on the Health Authority and the local social services authority to provide, in co-operation with relevant voluntary agencies, after-care services for patients who have been detained in hospital for treatment and who then cease to be detained and leave hospital.

Community care plans and charters

Section 46(1) of the National Health Service and Community Care Act requires local authorities to prepare and publish a plan for the provision of community care services in their area.[196] This plan must therefore make provision for section 117 after-care services. Recent Government guidance also requires that local authorities to publish a community care charter, although this requirement does not have the force of statute. Where a social circumstances report appears to make inadequate provision for a patient's after-care, a copy of the authority's community care plan and a copy of the local Community Care Charter may be obtained, in order to establish the facilities available locally, the patient's entitlement to them, and local targets for completing assessments of patients' needs for those services.

---

[194]   Social work and related services to help in the identification, diagnosis, assessment and social treatment of mental disorder and to provide social work support and other domiciliary and care services to people living in their own homes and elsewhere.

[195]   Health authorities have a parallel duty to provide services for this purpose, in so far as these are considered appropriate as part of the health service: National Health Service Act 1977, s.3(2)(a).

[196]   National Health Service and Community Care Act 1990, s.46(1).

CARE MANAGEMENT AND CARE PACKAGES

The National Health Service and Community Care Act 1990 gives local social services authorities primary responsibility for co-ordinating the assessment of community care needs. However, where, during the course of an assessment, it appears to such an authority that the provision of health or housing services may be needed, the authority must invite the relevant agencies to participate in the assessment. Departmental guidance stresses the need to ensure that social services care management for severely mentally ill people is effectively integrated with the care programme approach, the development of which is the responsibility of health authorities.[197]

TERMINOLOGY OF CARE MANAGEMENT

Assessment	The process of defining needs and determining eligibility for assistance against stated policy criteria.
Care package	A combination of services designed to meet the assessed needs of a person requiring care in the community.
Care Planning	The process of negotiation between assessor, applicant, carers and other agencies on the most appropriate ways of meeting assessed needs within available resources and incorporating them into an individual care plan.
Care Management	Any strategy for managing, co-ordinating and reviewing services for the individual in a way that provides for continuity of care and accountability to both the client and the managing agency. Previously referred to as "case management."
Care Manager	Any practitioner who undertakes all, or most, of the "core tasks" of care management. The care manager may carry a budgetary responsibility but is not involved in any direct service provision. Previously known as a "case manager."
Purchaser	The budget holder who contracts to buy a service.

Seven stages of care management

The aim of "care management" is to tailor community care services to individual need.[198] It involves assessing an individual's need for services and then, where necessary, designing and implementing a "care package" agreed with the patient, his carers, and contributing agencies. Care management consists of seven integrated stages[199] —

---

[197] See *Executive Letter* EL(93)119 and CI(93)35, (Department of Health, 23 December 1993), para. A8.

[198] Social Services Inspectorate, *Care Management and Assessment: Summary of Practice Guidance* (Department of Health, 1991), para. 7.

[199] Social Services Inspectorate, *Care Management and Assessment : Practitioners' Guide* (Department of Health, 1991).

- publishing information about the services available.

- determining the level of assessment to be carried out.

- assessing the needs of the client.

- planning a care package in light of the assessment and available resources.

- implementing that care plan

- monitoring the delivery of the care plan.

- reviewing the care plan at specified intervals, to ensure that services remain relevant to the individual's needs.

Care managers

"Care managers" act as brokers for services across the statutory and independent sectors. In theory, they should not be involved in providing services nor have any managerial responsibility for the services which they arrange. Once a person has been assessed to need services, a care plan should be drawn up. This care plan should ensure, as far as possible, that normal living is preserved or restored, primarily by providing the services within the user's home, including (where necessary) day and domiciliary care, respite care, and the provision of disability equipment and adaptations to the home. The problems and difficulties encountered in monitoring these requirements are well known — inadequate collaboration between disciplines, poor documentation, users "slipping through the net," problems associated with users who are unwilling to co-operate, and a lack of an appropriate range of services.

The assessment

Section 47(1) of the National Health Service and Community Care Act 1990 provides that where it appears to a local authority that any person for whom they may provide or arrange community care services may be in need of any such services, that authority shall carry out an assessment of the individual's needs for those services and, having regard to the results of that assessment, shall then decide whether his needs call for the provision by them of any such services.[200]

Assessing the ability of carers

It is now also necessary to assess the ability of unpaid carers to provide care before reaching any decision about whether the patient's needs require the authority to provide community care services. The Carers (Recognition and Services) Act 1995 came into force on 1 April 1996. A carer is defined by the statute as an individual who provides or intends to provide a substantial amount of care on a regular basis for a person whose need for community care services is being assessed under section

---

[200]   Notwithstanding that after-care provided under section 117 of the 1983 Act is a "community care service," it should be emphasised that the duty to provide such after-care for patients to whom that section applies is mandatory (**413**).

47(1)(a) of the National Health Service and Community Care Act 1990.[201] Under the 1995 Act, a carer may "request" that the local authority carries out an assessment of his ability to provide, and to continue to provide, care for the patient before it makes any decision as to whether the patient's needs call for the provision of community care services. The local authority "shall" then carry out such an assessment and shall take the results of that assessment into account before making a decision.[202] Unless the Secretary of State gives directions about the form such an assessment shall take, it shall be carried out "in such manner and take such form as the local authority consider appropriate."[203]

INVOLVEMENT OF THE INDEPENDENT SECTOR

The National Health Service and Community Care Act 1990 made a number of fundamental changes to the provision of health and social care for persons suffering from mental disorder. The underlying philosophy is to separate out the functions of purchasing and providing such care, so as to create an "internal market" in the health service and a "mixed economy of care" in relation to social services. The general position now is that any community care services which may be provided by a local authority may also be provided by an agency from the independent sector; indeed, the Government has made it clear that local authorities are expected to make maximum use of the independent sector. Just as the role of Health Authorities has become one of purchasing health services provided by NHS trusts, so local authorities are being promoted and developed as "enabling authorities" and "commissioning agencies," seeking out and purchasing community care services from a range of public and non-public providers. In some respects, the current legislation marks a return to the situation which previously existed under the Lunacy Act 1890.[204] The enabling and commissioning roles of a local authority involve it identifying the need for care among the population it serves; planning how best to meet those needs; setting an overall strategy in terms of priorities and targets; seeking out, and purchasing, the required services from a range of providers in the voluntary and private sectors, as well as the public sector (that is developing a mixed economy of care); and monitoring the quality of services which it has purchased. Because local authorities· still provide some services themselves, the aim of developing a mixed economy of care is attainable only if the authority separates out its own purchasing and providing functions. Local authority staff involved in assessing an individual's needs and purchasing the required services should not also be involved in providing local authority services. For, if they were, they might not be disposed to purchase alternative, more suitable, services available in the independent sector. A new terminology has developed which reflects the underlying philosophy of the reforms so that, for example, citizens who need community care services are now referred to as "consumers."

201 Carers (Recognition and Services) Act 1995, s.1(1)(b). The person whose need for community care services is being assessed is referred to in the Act as "the relevant person" — see s.1(1)(a) — but is here referred to as the patient.

202 Ibid., s.1(1).

203 Ibid., s.1(4). Where a carer's needs have been assessed in this way, he cannot then have a second assessment carried out under section 8 of the Disabled Persons (Services, Consultation and Representation) Act 1986: see s.1(5). Note also that where an individual provides, or will provide, care either as a volunteer for a voluntary organisation or by virtue of a contractual obligation, he cannot request an assessment under s.1 of his ability to provide care: see s.1(3).

204 See e.g. the Lunacy Act 1890, ss. 169, 243 and 269.

Mixed Economy of Care	The use of independent providers (including the voluntary sector) alongside public services, to increase the available range of care options.
Agency	Any organisation, statutory or private, which provides social care, health care or housing services in the community.

THE INDEPENDENT SECTOR

Individuals, bodies or organisations not wholly maintained or controlled by a Government department or any other authority or body instituted by Special Act of Parliament or incorporated by Royal Charter. The independent sector comprises the voluntary sector and the private sector.

Voluntary sector	Voluntary organisations in which any surpluses are re-invested into the work of the organisation and managed by unpaid management committees, trustees or directors.
Private sector	Non-voluntary agencies in the independent sector.

THE PUBLIC SECTOR

Any facility maintained or controlled by a Government department or local authority or any other authority or body instituted by special Act of Parliament or incorporated by Royal Charter.

Statutory sector	Those bodies required by parliamentary statute to provide a service, principally local authorities and health authorities.

INDIVIDUALS INVOLVED IN PROVIDING SERVICES

Key worker	The practitioner involved in providing services who has most contact with the user: although the key-worker may undertake a co-ordinating function similar to that of a care manager, he remains directly involved in the services being provided.
Carers	A person who is not employed to provide the care in question by any independent or public sector body. Normally, a person who is looking after an adult with mental health problems in the home, where the latter's dependence on the carer "exceeds that implicit in normal relationships between family members.

FINANCING THE COMMUNITY CARE SERVICES

On 1 April 1993, responsibility for providing financial support to individuals entering voluntary and private sector residential and nursing home care was transferred from the Department of Social Security to local social services authorities. The local authorities are to pay for the full cost of care and retrieve from residents any Income Support, Residential Allowance and charges as appropriate. This was accompanied by changes in DSS benefits for new residents of residential care and nursing homes and by the establishment of new assessment procedures.[205] People who enter homes under the new funding structure and who need public financial support no longer have their care costs met by social security. Anyone seeking to enter an independent sector home at public expense must approach the local authority for a care and financial assessment. The local authority will then consider whether it would be appropriate, and cost effective, to keep that person in the community. Residents will be able to claim help from the normal Income Support system of personal allowances and premiums and from Housing Benefit. They will receive assistance on the same basis as that which they could obtain in their own homes.[206] Local authorities make some use of their power to "top up" for residents under pension age. Some Health Authorities also "top up" people with learning disabilities in independent sector homes who have been discharged from long-stay hospitals. The Department of Health's view is that they expect local authorities to use their bargaining power to negotiate reduced fees for residential care. Any potential for reduced fees may, however, only be achievable through "casualisation" of staff — lower wages and more part-time employment particularly in urban areas where a local labour force is more readily available.[207] There is no consensus about whether it is lawful to charge for after-care services which a local authority is under a statutory duty to provide under section 117.

APPROVED SOCIAL WORKERS

The term "approved Social Worker" means an officer of a local social services authority appointed to act as an approved social worker for the purposes of the Act.[208] No person may be so appointed unless he is approved by the authority as having appropriate competence in dealing with persons who are suffering from mental disorder.[209] Before approving a person for appointment, a local social services authority must have regard to such matters as the Secretary of State may direct."[210] Each local social services authority in England and Wales is required to appoint a sufficient number of approved social workers "for the purpose of discharging the functions conferred on them by the Act."[211]

---

[205]   Those people already receiving D.S.S. support for institutional care on 31 March 1993 will continue to do so until their placements end (the "preserved rights" arrangements).

[206]   *Third Report of the House of Commons' Health Committee* (H.M.S.O., 1993), paras. *8.17–8.18.*

[207]   *Ibid.,* Q.40.

[208]   Mental Health Act 1983, s.145(1).

[209]   *Ibid.,* s.114(2).

[210]   *Ibid.,* s.114(3). The Secretary of State's directions are contained in D.H.S.S. Circular No. (86)15. Provided the authority has regard to the various matters which the Secretary of State requires it to give consideration to, there is no breach of statutory duty if it then departs from that guidance. See *e.g. De Falco v. Crawley Borough Council* [1980] 1 All E.R. 913, *per* Bridge L.J. at 925.

[211]   Mental Health Act 1983, s.114(1).

Concept of approved social workers

Under the 1959 Act, mental welfare officers were authorised to apply for a patient's admission to hospital. The White Paper of 1978 recognised doubts in some quarters about their effectiveness in the admission procedures.[212] In particular, widespread concern had been expressed about the lack of specialist knowledge on the part of many social workers engaged in mental health practice.[213] The Government therefore proposed that social workers should be approved by local social services authorities in the same way that medical practitioners are "approved" under what is now section 12(2). Social workers nowadays undergo a 60-day training course prior to approval and undertake refresher training at regular intervals.

Statutory duties of an approved social worker

An approved social worker is under a duty to make an application under Part II in any case were he is satisfied that an application ought to be made in respect of a person within his authority's area and is of the opinion, having regard to any wishes expressed by the patient's relatives and other relevant circumstances, that it is necessary or proper for him to apply.[214] Before making a guardianship application or a section 3 application, he must first consult the patient's nearest relative, unless this is impracticable or would involve unreasonable delay.[215] An approved social worker owes a duty of care to the patient. That duty of care is personal and "it is the business of the duly authorised officer, rather than that of the doctor, to see that the statutory powers are not used unless the circumstances warrant it."[216]

Statutory powers of an approved social worker

The following statutory functions exercisable by social workers are reserved to social workers who are approved under the Act —

- The power to enter and inspect premises under section 115.

- The power to apply for a warrant under section 135(1).

- The conduct of assessments under sections 13 and 136.

- The making of guardianship applications and applications for admission under Part II of the Act.

- The power to take into custody a patient who is absent without leave.

- The making of applications to the county court under the 1983 Act.

- The right of access to a patient under guardianship where access is required by the guardian.

---

[212] *Review of the Mental Health Act 1959*, Cmnd. 7320 (1978).
[213] *Ibid.*, para. 3.9.
[214] Mental Health Act 1983, ss.11(4), 13(1) and (5). An approved social worker may also make an application in respect of a patient outside his local authority area but is not under a duty to do so.
[215] Mental Health Act 1983, s.11(4).
[216] *Buxton v. Jayne* [1960] 1 W.L.R. 783, *per* Devlin L.J. at 784. See also *R. v. Barnsley* (1849) 12 Q.B. 193; *R. v. Wakefield* 48 J.P. 326.

THE SECRETARY OF STATE

Unless the contrary intention appears, the term "'Secretary of State' means one of Her Majesty's Principal Secretaries of State."[217] In practice, the Secretary of State for Health (126) is responsible for the National Health Service and for exercising certain powers which are not specific to restricted patients. The Home Secretary is responsible for overseeing the movement of restricted patients between hospitals and their discharge and supervision in the community.

THE HOME OFFICE

The Home Secretary's responsibilities in relation to restricted patients are discharged on a day to day basis by the Home Office's Mental Health Unit,[218] which is situated at 50 Queen Anne's Gate, London SW1H 9AT. The rationale for the current arrangement was established by the Royal Commission of 1954–1957.[219] The Committee considered that the care of people with mental health problems was a medical issue but, where a mentally disordered offender posed a particular danger to the public, his discharge should be controlled by a central authority who would have special regard to the protection of the public. The Home Secretary was the logical choice as the central authority, bearing in mind his traditional role in the area. The Home Secretary is responsible for protecting the public from unjustifiable risk and his primary concern is to ensure that the public's safety is never made subordinate to the patient's interests. When exercising his powers, the Home Secretary seeks to give precedence to public safety considerations while supporting the objectives of rehabilitation. The risk is generally that of serious harm to the person, covering offences of violence and sexual offending.

Organisation of the Mental Health Unit

Most of the day-to-day casework is dealt with at official level but Ministerial agreement is sought on most proposals for discharge, transfer or recall. It may also be sought in other circumstances, particularly where the case has attracted considerable public interest or presents particular difficulties.[220] The Head of the Division is supported by six Grade 7 officers, nine Higher Executive Officers, 18 Executive Officers, and nine Administrative Officers. Work on the files of restricted patients is divided among these staff members according to the nature of the case and the first letter of the patient's surname. Hence, one of the Grade 7 officers may have day-to-day responsibility for all patients whose surnames begin with the letters A, G, H and I, with routine work on files relating to patients whose surnames begin with the letters Ga–Go being carried out by a particular Executive Officer and/or an Administrative Officer, and so forth. The cases of patients who are subject to a restriction direction, or whose transfer to hospital under sections 47 or 48, is being organised are dealt with within the Mental Health Unit by what is known as the Prison Transfer Group.[221]

---

[217]　Interpretation Act 1978, s.5 and Sched. 1.

[218]　Formerly known as the Home Office's C3 Division.

[219]　*Royal Commission on the Law Relating to Mental Illness and Mental Deficiency*, Cmnd. 169 (1957).

[220]　In some cases, the Home Secretary is assisted by the Advisory Board on restricted patients, which is informally known as the Aarvold Board. This is a non-statutory body which advises him about the discharge, or transfer between hospitals, of restricted patients whose potential risk to public safety is thought to be particularly difficult to assess. The Board is considered further below (165).

[221]　Formerly known as the Incoming Cases Unit.

STATUTORY FUNCTIONS

The Home Secretary's main statutory and non-statutory functions are summarised below.

FUNCTIONS OF THE HOME SECRETARY

Statutory functions

- *directing the discharge of a restricted patient, whether absolutely or subject to conditions, under s.42*

- *consenting to a restricted patient being discharged under s.23 by his responsible medical officer or the hospital managers*

- *consenting to a restricted patient being granted leave of absence under s.17*

- *consenting to the transfer of a restricted patient under s.19*

- *directing the transfer of a special hospital patient under s.123*

- *recalling a conditionally discharged to hospital under s.42*

- *directing a patient's admission to a hospital other than that specified by the court in a hospital order, under s.37(5)*

- *specifying the hospital to which a patient found unfit to plead or not guilty by reason of insanity shall be admitted*

- *directing the removal to hospital for treatment of a person in custody, under ss.46–48*

- *directing the remission to prison of a patient previously removed to hospital for treatment, under ss.50, 51, 53 and 74*

- *referring to a tribunal the case of a restricted patient who has been recalled to hospital or whose case has not been considered by a tribunal for a certain period of time, under s.71*

- *removing "alien patients" under s.86 and referring their cases to a tribunal*

- *providing statements on restricted patients to tribunals*

- *considering periodic, and special oral and written reports, on detained and conditionally discharged patients and deciding or advising on appropriate courses of action*

Non-statutory functions

- *keeping under review the law and practice relating to offender patients*

- *commissioning research and providing statistics in relation to mentally disordered offenders*

- *encouraging the diversion of mentally disordered offenders from the criminal justice system or from prison*

- *servicing the Advisory Board on Restricted Patients (165)*

THE HOME SECRETARY AND TRIBUNAL PROCEEDINGS

Although the Home Secretary is not a party to tribunal proceedings, he has a "vital role"[222] to play by virtue of his responsibility for public safety. The focus of this involvement is to bring to the tribunal's attention relevant information on file about the patient, and to ensure that it is made aware of the Home Secretary's view about the patient's potential dangerousness and his suitability for discharge.

Home Office Statements

Where tribunal proceedings involve a restricted patient, the Home Secretary is required by the Mental Health Review Tribunal Rules 1983 to provide the tribunal with a statement on the patient. If the patient is detained, this statement has to be furnished within three weeks of the Home Office's receipt of the responsible authority's statement. In cases involving conditional discharged patients, the Home Office is responsible for obtaining reports from the supervisors and for providing a statement within six weeks of receipt by him of the notice of application (**663, 700**).

Representation

The Home Secretary may be represented at a tribunal hearing by Counsel in particularly difficult cases, where his view cannot adequately be conveyed in a written statement. This might, for example, occur where a responsible medical officer is arguing strongly for the discharge of a patient whom the Home Office believes is still highly dangerous.

Action following a tribunal's decision

If a tribunal has directed a patient's immediate discharge and he has left hospital, the Mental Health Unit will be notified of the after-care details and the conditions of discharge approved by the tribunal. According to Pickersgill, the Home Office will consider whether the detailed arrangements are satisfactory, consulting as necessary the patient's responsible medical officer or the newly appointed supervisors before reaching a decision. The Home Secretary might then vary the conditions, for example changing the condition of residence or imposing supervision conditions if the tribunal imposed none. The Home Secretary's statutory role, the recall provisions, and the need for reports on the patient to be periodically submitted, are explained to both nominated supervisors in writing. If it is felt that a tribunal has erred in law in reaching its decision, this view is usually communicated to the tribunal expressing this view and clarification sought. The Home Office may challenge the decision by way of judicial review proceedings in the High Court.[223]

Restriction direction cases

Where a tribunal notifies the Home Secretary that a serving prison who has been transferred to hospital under a restriction direction would, if subject to a restriction order, be entitled to be discharged, the Home Secretary has 90 days within which to approve the patient's discharge, if he deems that to be appropriate.

---

[222] The phrase used by Farquharson J. in *R. v. Nottingham Mental Health Review Tribunal, ex p. Secretary of State for the Home Department*, *The Times*, 25 March 1987.

[223] A. Pickersgill, "Balancing the public and private interests" in *Risk–taking in Mental Disorder; Analyses, Policies and Practical Strategies* (ed. D. Carson, S.L.E. Publications, 1990).

Tribunal decision that patient not be discharged

If a tribunal recommends a particular course of action to the Home Office, this is noted, specifically drawn to the responsible medical officer's attention, and considered in the context of the case's overall management.

THE AARVOLD BOARD

In cases where there seems to be a continuing risk of re-offending which is extremely difficult to predict, the Home Secretary seeks the views of the Advisory Board on Restricted Patients. The Board is a non-statutory body and its remit is fundamentally different from that of a Mental Health Review Tribunal. When considering a proposal for allowing a restricted patient greater liberty, the Board's only concern is to offer the Home Secretary advice on whether the proposal is soundly based and acceptable having regard to public safety. It is not concerned with safe-guarding the liberty of the individual.

Establishment and history

The establishment and history of the Aarvold Advisory Board has been well summarised by Egglestone.[224] The Board was established in 1973 in accordance with recommendations of the Aarvold Committee.[225] The Committee found that there was a small proportion of restricted patients in whose cases the risk of serious reoffending was particularly difficult to predict and where special care was therefore required when assessing proposals for their discharge or transfer to a less secure hospital —

> "The patients concerned could not necessarily be identified by reference to the form of their mental disorder nor even to the nature or severity of their offence; rather, in the committee's own words, the 'nature of personality deviance is probably more important than a particular psychiatric label.' Hard and fast rules could not be laid down, but sadists, some sexual offenders and some arsonists were likely to justify special assessment. Detailed selection would depend on a close examination of each individual restricted patient's case, but the common features expected to be present were a clearly unfavourable or an unpredictable psychiatric diagnosis, and an indication that there was a risk of the patient harming other persons."[226]

The Aarvold Report recommended new procedures to identify cases requiring special care in assessment and the creation of an advisory board to assist the Home Secretary in reaching decisions in such cases.

Board membership

The Board is chaired by a member of the judiciary and comprises a senior barrister, two forensic psychiatrists, a chief probation officer, a deputy director of social services and two members with special experience of the criminal justice system. The members are appointed for a three-year term and may be reappointed for a second term.

---

[224] F. Egglestone, "The Home Office: The advisory board on restricted patients" in *Principles and Practice of Forensic Psychiatry* (ed. R. Bluglass and P. Bowden, Churchill Livingstone, 1994).

[225] *Report on the Review of Procedures for the Discharge and Supervision of Psychiatric Patients subject to Special Restrictions*, Cmnd. 5191 (1973).

[226] F. Egglestone, "The Home Office: The advisory board on restricted patients" in *Principles and Practice of Forensic Psychiatry* (ed. R. Bluglass and P. Bowden, Churchill Livingstone, 1994).

Selection of cases for reference to the Board

Approximately 50 cases are referred to the Board each year. The decision whether to refer a case rests with the Minister or a principal in the Home Office's Mental Health Unit. Some of the factors which are commonly influential are summarised below.

FACTORS AFFECTING REFERRAL TO THE AARVOLD BOARD

Type of offence	Offences involving serious violence, sexual offending, poisoning and arson are more likely to justify reference than other offences, particularly if there is a long history of offending.
Circumstances of the offence	Offences committed against strangers, which were random or part of a series of similar offences, may be more likely to justify referral to the Board than those committed in a family setting or where obvious stress factors triggered the offence.
Type of disorder	The Home Office considers that patients suffering from psychopathic disorder are likely to be more difficult to assess than those suffering from mental illness. Accordingly, all cases of patients suffering from psychopathic disorder should be considered for reference to the Board, as should cases where the diagnosis is unclear.
Proposal under consideration	Between 15 and 20 per cent of all transfer and discharge recommendations are put to the Board. The first move from a special hospital to another hospital will generally cause greater concern than will a move from a regional secure unit to a local hospital. Only exceptionally is the conversion of trial leave at a hospital to formal transfer referred to the Board.
Authority for the patient's detention	The cases of restricted patients detained under sections 47 and 49 are not generally considered by the Advisory Board. The risk involved in the transfer or discharge of mandatory life sentence prisoners who are to be released directly from hospital is normally assessed by the Parole Board. Discharge is generally by way of release on life licence.
Public disquiet	Some cases, although not justifying referral on other grounds, are referred to the Board because of the level of public interest in the case or the notoriety of the patient, in order to ensure that public confidence is maintained in the system.
Referrals from other agencies	Occasionally other agencies may recommend that a proposal is referred, *e.g.* the responsible medical officer, the patient's advocate, or the Board itself. However, referrals are ultimately a matter for the Mental Health Unit and the Minister.

Sources: F. Egglestone, "The Home Office: The advisory board on restricted patients" in *Principles and Practice of Forensic Psychiatry* (ed. R. Bluglass and P. Bowden, Churchill Livingstone, 1994).

How references are dealt with

The Board usually meets once a month and deals with four or five cases at each meeting. Its members are provided with dossiers about the cases to be considered. Egglestone lists the contents of the dossiers prepared for monthly meetings. They contain: full details of the index offence; the psychiatric reports prepared at the time of the trial and all subsequent key medical reports, including the responsible medical officer's formal recommendation for leave, transfer or discharge; relevant nursing or psychologists' reports; and, where discharge is recommended, social work reports on the patient's home circumstances or other arrangements for his accommodation and supervision in the community. One member interviews the patient, the responsible medical officer, and other professional staff in advance of the meeting and prepares a post-visit report for that meeting. Following the meeting, the Minister is provided with a copy of the visit report, a note of the Board's discussion of the case and its findings, and a covering submission from Mental Health Unit.

Communication of Board's findings

The Board's findings are not directly conveyed to the responsible medical officer but, if it is unable to support a proposal and the Board's advice is accepted, the reasons for rejecting the proposal are explained to him.

Information about Board recommendations

The issue of access by patients to information about advice tendered by the Board was considered in the case of *ex. p. Powell*. This case predated the Mental Health Act 1983 and some of the reasons given for the decision clearly no longer hold good. In particular, no statutory provisions equivalent to section 76 of the present Act were in force at the time (**614, 711**).

R. v. Secretary of State for the Home Department, ex p. Powell

Unreported, 21 December 1978[227]   *Q.B.D., Goff J.*

In 1967, a restriction order was imposed following the patient's conviction for causing grievous bodily harm and he was detained in a special hospital. In 1975, the responsible medical officer wrote to the Home Office expressing his opinion that the patient's case was one requiring special care in assessment for a number of reasons, including the nature of the index offence, his previous convictions, the severity and persistence of his anti-social behaviour, and his lack of progress following admission. This recommendation was accepted by the Home Office, with the effect that the patient's case would be referred to the Advisory Board if consideration was later given to his discharge. In 1977, the patient's responsible medical officer recommended to the Home Secretary that the patient be conditionally discharged. His recommendation followed a multi-disciplinary case conference which recommended that course. Accordingly, the patient's case was referred to the Advisory Board for its advice. It appeared that the Advisory Board expressed concern about the proposal that the patient be conditionally discharged. The Home Secretary concluded that the element of risk in agreeing to the patient's release was too great to be accepted and notified the responsible medical officer of his decision by letter.

---

[227]   See L. Gostin and E. Rassaby, *Representing the mentally ill and handicapped: A Guide to Mental Health Review Tribunals*, (Quartermaine House Ltd., 1980), pp.170–174.

Application for judicial review

The patient applied for judicial review, arguing that there had been a breach of the rules of natural justice, in that he was not informed of the matters referred to the Board and therefore was deprived of any opportunity to make representations about them to the Home Secretary before he reached his decision. Although an extra-statutory body, the Aarvold Board was as amenable to judicial review as any other body if it failed to observe the rules of natural justice. Alternatively, if it failed to observe such rules, the Home Secretary's decision was susceptible to judicial review, on the basis that the Board was no more than the arm of the Secretary of State.

Goff J.

Held as follows—

a. The Advisory Board was an extra-statutory body which had no power to make any decision in the patient's case, being a purely advisory body from which the Home Secretary took advice before reaching decisions in such cases. It was difficult to see any distinction between the Home Secretary taking advice from the Board and taking similar advice from an officer in his own department. Such a body was not amenable to judicial review.

b. Insofar as the Home Secretary was concerned, the allegation that he had failed to comply with the rules of natural justice, or had acted unfairly, had to be considered with due regard to the statutory context in which the power was found, taking full account of the relevant procedures established by the Act. The Act contemplated that a patient subject to restrictions had the right to a reference to a Mental Health Review Tribunal. The purpose of the tribunal was that the Home Secretary should receive advice from it. However, although the patient was entitled to an interview, it was not contemplated that he should receive any notification from the tribunal or the Home Secretary of any matters which the tribunal then decided to bring to the Home Secretary's attention.

c. It followed that, if the Home Secretary sought advice from some extra-statutory body, such as the Aarvold Board, no criticism could be directed to the Home Secretary for proceeding in a manner similar to that in which he was entitled to proceed when making his decision after receiving advice from a tribunal. It was, moreover, very understandable that the procedure should be so limited in such cases. The Home Secretary would no doubt desire to obtain the fullest advice before reaching a decision in which he had to consider not only the liberty of the subject but also the public good. In the course of receiving the advice, he might receive opinions which, in the patient's own interest, should not be communicated to him. It might well be for that reason that the *statutory* procedure was so designed that it did not contemplate the various matters referred to in the advice being communicated to the patient before the Home Secretary made his decision. *Application dismissed.*

MENTAL HEALTH ACT COMMISSION

The function of a Mental Health Review Tribunal is to determine whether the continued use of compulsory powers is necessary or appropriate. The Mental Health Act Commission's main functions are to protect the rights of persons who are detained and to ensure the proper performance of the various powers and duties exercisable under the Act.

STATUTORY FUNCTIONS

The Mental Health Act Commission's statutory functions are[228]—

- To keep under review the exercise of the powers and the discharge of the duties conferred or imposed by the 1983 Act so far as relating to the detention of patients or to patients liable to be detained under the Act.

- To make arrangements for authorised persons to visit and interview in private patients detained under the Act in hospitals and mental nursing homes.

- To arrange for the investigation of complaints falling within its jurisdiction.

- To publish, and from time to time revise, a Code of Practice—

  a. for the guidance of registered medical practitioners, managers and staff of hospitals and mental nursing homes and approved social workers in relation to the admission of patients to hospitals and mental nursing homes under the Act; and

  b. for the guidance of registered medical practitioners and members of other professions in relation to the medical treatment of patients suffering from mental disorder.

- To publish a biennial report.

- To perform on the Secretary of State's behalf his functions in relation to the consent to treatment provisions in Part IV of the Act (appointing second-opinion doctors, regulating section 57 treatments, deciding whether patients who are incapable of consenting to treatment or who refuse treatment should be given treatment).

- To review any decision to withhold a postal packet under section 134.

Commission's statutory remit relatively narrow

As the table on the following pages illustrates, the Commission's statutory powers and duties are quite limited compared with those exercisable by the respective Commissions in Scotland and Northern Ireland.

---

[228]   See Mental Health Act 1983, ss.118–121.

FUNCTIONS OF THE RESPECTIVE MENTAL HEALTH COMMISSIONS

Function	Whether function possessed by the Commission		
	MHAC	MWC	MHCNI
General duty (i) to exercise protective functions in respect of persons who may, by reason of mental disorder, be incapable of adequately protecting their persons or their interests (Scotland) or (ii) to keep their care and treatment under review (Northern Ireland).	No	s.3(1) MH(S)A 1984	Art. 86(1) MH(NI)O 1986
Duty to make enquiry into any case where it appears to the Commission that there may be ill-treatment, deficiency in care or treatment, or improper detention of any person who may be suffering from mental disorder.			
Duty to make enquiry into any case where it appears to the Commission that the property of any person who may be suffering from mental disorder may be exposed to loss or damage, by reason of that mental disorder.			
Duty to bring to the attention of the hospital managers or any local authority the facts of any case in which, in the Commission's opinion, it is desirable for them to secure the welfare of any patient suffering from mental disorder by— (a) preventing his ill-treatment; (b) remedying any deficiency in his care or treatment; (c) terminating his improper detention; (d) preventing or redressing loss or damage to his property.	No	s.3(2) MH(S)A 1984	Art. 86(2) MH(NI)O 1986
Duty to give advice on any matter arising out of, or under, the relevant mental health statute which is referred to it by the Secretary of State, a Health Authority, Board, local authority or other such body.			
Duty to bring to the attention of any such body any matter concerning the welfare of such persons which the Commission considers ought to be brought to their attention			
Power to co-opt non-Commissioners to undertake, chair or participate in an inquiry into any possible ill-treatment, deficiency in care or treatment, or improper detention of any person who may be suffering from mental disorder.	No	s.3(8) MH(S)A 1984	Art. 86(4) MH(NI)O 1986

Function		MH(S)A 1984	MH(NI)O 1986
Power to require persons to attend such an inquiry.	No	s.4(1) MH(S)A 1984	Art. 86(4) MH(NI)O 1986
Power to administer oaths and examine witnesses on oath at such an enquiry.	No	s.4(4) MH(S)A 1984	
Statutory provision that it is a criminal offence for a person to refuse or wilfully neglect to attend such an inquiry when served with a notice requiring them to do so.	No	s.4(5) MH(S)A 1984	
Jurisdiction over patients subject to guardianship.	No	ss.3(1), 33(3), 50(2) (3) MH(S)A 1984	Art. 86(1)(2) MH(NI)O 1986
Power to discharge patients subject to detention or guardianship, save for restricted patients.	No	s.3(1) MH(S)A 1984	No *See power to refer to MHRT*
Power to refer to a MHRT the case of any patient who is liable to be detained or subject to guardianship.	No	*See power to discharge*	Art. 86(3), MH(NI)O 1986
Power to recommend to the Secretary of State that a restricted patient should be discharged	No	s.3(3), MH(S)A 1984	No
Power to apply for the appointment of a receiver/curator bonis in respect of a patient if the Commission is satisfied the person concerned is incapable, by reason of mental disorder, of managing and administering his property and affairs.	No	s.93 MH(S)A 1984	No
Duty to notify the Court of Protection, or equivalent body, of any person whom it is satisfied is incapable of managing his property and affairs if Commission considers Court should exercise its powers.	No	*See duty to apply for appt of curator bonis*	s.107(3) MH(NI)O 1986
Duty to notify the Commission of a patient's reception into guardianship and to forward with that notification copies of the application and medical recommendations.	No	s.41(1) MH(S)A 1984	*See Art. 20(1)* MH(N)O 1986
Statutory provision that one medical recommendation in support of a guardianship application shall be given by a SOAD or equivalent.	No	No	
Duty to notify the Commission of any patient who has been absent with leave for more than 28 days and of that patient's later return.	No	s.27(5) MH(S)A 1984	Art. 15(4) MH(NI)O 1986
Duty to notify the Commission of a patient's transfer.	No	s.29(2) MH(S)A 1984	Art. 25(5), 28(10) MH(NI)O 1986

Function	Whether function possessed by the Commission		
	MHAC	MWC	MHCNI *Must notify of any change of guardian*
Duty to notify the Commission as soon as practicable of any permanent change of address of a patient subject to guardianship and if such a patient is absent without leave.	No	Regs 6(1)(2), Mental Health Regs 1984	Art. 7(7) MH(NI)O 1986
Duty to notify the Commission of a patient being detained under s.5(2), s.5(4), or equivalent.	No	s.25(4) MH(S)A 1984	
Duty to notify the Commission without delay of a patient being detained under s.4, or equivalent.	No	s.24(5) MH(S)A 1984	Art. 8(2), 9(10) MH(NI)O 1986
Duty to notify the Commission of a patient being detained under s.2, or equivalent.	No	s.26(4) MH(S)A 1984	
Duty to notify the Commission of a patient being detained under s.3, or equivalent.	No	s.22(2) MH(S)A 1984	*See below — Art. 12(1)*
Provision that detention under section 3, or equivalent, requires medical recommendation signed by a SOAD	No	No	Art. 12(1)
Duty to notify the Commission of the renewal of the authority to detain a patient subject to s.3 or equivalent.	No	s.30(3) MH(S)A 1984	Art. 13(6) MH(NI)O 1986
Provision that a second renewal of a s.3 application, or equivalent, requires medical recommendations signed by two SOADs (or equivalent).	No	No	Art. 13(3) MH(NI)O 1986
Duty to send a copy of any Form 38 or 39 to the Commission.	No	s.98(3) MH(S)A 1984	Art. 64(6) MH(NI)O 1986
Duty to notify the Commission of any patient who is given urgent treatment under s.62, or equivalent, and the nature of that treatment.	No	s.102(4) MH(S) A 1984	Art. 68(4) MH(NI)O 1986
Duty on bodies advised to take steps by the Commission to notify the Commission of the steps taken, or to be taken, and to comply with the requirements of any notice served by the Commission.	No	*See enquiry powers*	Art. 86(6) MH(NI)O 1986

THE INVESTIGATION OF COMPLAINTS

The Commission's duty to keep the operation of the Act under review is fulfilled in two main ways. Firstly, by visiting detained patients and, secondly, by investigating complaints made by them or about the way in which the Act is being used in practice. The Commission's jurisdiction to investigate complaints is conferred by section 120(1)(b) of the Act, from which it can be seen that the persons authorised may investigate two different classes of complaint.

THE COMMISSION'S COMPLAINTS JURISDICTION

120.—(1) The Secretary of State shall ... make arrangements for persons authorised by him in that behalf ...(b) to investigate—

i. any complaint made by a person in respect of a matter that occurred while he was detained under this Act in a hospital or mental nursing home and which he considers has not been satisfactorily dealt with by the managers of that hospital or mental nursing home; *and*

Sub-para. (i) complaints

ii. any other complaint as to the exercise of the powers or the discharge of the duties conferred or imposed by this Act in respect of a person who is or has been so detained.

Sub-para. (ii) complaints

The basic investigatory framework

Section 121(2)(b) provides that the Secretary of State shall direct the Commission to perform his functions under section 120[229] and the basic framework for investigating complaints may be summarised as follows —

- Section 121(2)(b) provides that the Secretary of State shall direct the Mental Health Act Commission to perform on his behalf his functions under section 120(1), which include making arrangements for authorised persons to investigate the two different types of complaint.

- The Commission shall perform these functions subject to and in accordance with such directions as the Secretary of State may give it.

- The persons authorised by the Commission to investigate a complaint only have authority to investigate matters which—

    a. fall within the terms of section 120(1)(b); and

---

[229] The directions are set out in the Mental Health Act Commission (Establishment And Constitution) Order 1983 (S.I. 1983 No. 892), which provides that the Commission shall perform these functions "subject to and in accordance with such directions as the Secretary of State may give to the Commission."

b.   are not excluded from investigation *either* by subsection 120(7) (which relates to the powers and duties involving the Court of Protection) *or* under the arrangements for investigating complaints made by, or on behalf of, the Secretary of State;[230]

- where a person has authority to investigate a particular matter, he may not be required to investigate it, or to continue to investigate it, if in his opinion it is inappropriate to do so;[231]

- there is no statutory duty to furnish a report setting out the results of an investigation, unless the complaint is one which has been made by a Member of Parliament under s.120(1)(b)(ii).

An informal process

Section 120 is significant not only because of what it says but because of what it does not say. For example, it does not—

- authorise the investigation of complaints relating to informal patients or patients subject to guardianship or after-care under supervision;

- confer upon the authorised persons any judicial powers to compel persons to give evidence on oath or to produce documents;

- provide that the way in which complaints are investigated shall be subject to formal rules (in the way that a tribunal's procedure is governed by the 1983 Rules) or regulations (the 1983 regulations are silent as to the Commission's complaints functions);

- narrowly restrict the matters which may be investigated by providing time limits for making a complaint, that clinical complaints may not be investigated, or that only complaints made in writing may be investigated;

- impose any statutory duty to prepare a statement of the reasons why a decision has been taken not to investigate a particular complaint or to prepare a report of the results of an investigation (except where the complainant is an Member of Parliament);

- provide the Commission with any formal powers with which to enforce its findings and recommendations.

With regard to these omissions, it should be noted that the establishment of the Commission post-dated the establishment of the office of the Health Service

---

[230]   No specific matters have been excluded from investigation. Section 121(2)(b) provides that the Secretary of State shall direct the MHAC to perform on his behalf his functions under s.120(1). These functions include not the investigation of complaints but *making arrangements* for their investigation, while, by s.120(2), the arrangements made may exclude matters from investigation in specified circumstances. The most natural reading of these provisions is that the Commission itself may exclude matters from investigation in specified circumstances and it is unnecessary to ask the Secretary of State to specify them.

[231]   See Mental Health Act 1983, s.120(2).

Commissioner, who does possess such formal investigative powers. It was envisaged that the Commission would investigate complaints which could be dealt with informally, *i.e.* investigations not requiring the use of formal powers. Paragraph 263 of the *Memorandum* on the Act states that, "The Commission does not replace or duplicate the work of other individuals and bodies who are able to help patients with their problems, for example ... the Health Service Commissioner." Unlike the Health Service Commissioner, or the Mental Welfare Commission for Scotland, the Commission has no formal powers to enforce recommendations following an investigation. The view taken by Parliament was that the expertise of its members, their eminence within their respective fields, and the quality of their investigations, would ensure that reports were given proper and adequate consideration. The Ashworth Report similarly added that the Commission's power lies in the influence it can wield in drawing to the Secretary of State's, and the public's attention, any question of non-compliance with the Act or short-fall in the quality of patient-care and treatment.

The two classes of complaint

What is now sub-paragraph 120(1)(b)(ii) was added at quite a late stage during the 1982 Bill's passage through Parliament. The inter-relationship between the two sub-paragraphs was poorly thought out at the time and their precise meaning has subsequently proved elusive. The general position is that any person, not just a detained patient, may complain that the Act is not being complied with and the Commission, being responsible for policing the statute, may immediately authorise some person to investigate that allegation. A detained patient may also complain to the hospital managers about the standard of his hospital treatment and care, since they are responsible for it. If he is not satisfied with their response, he may then ask the Commission to arrange a further, independent, investigation. But whether to complain is a matter for the person receiving the treatment and care. The complaints procedure depends upon which sub-paragraph the complaint falls within—

- Because sub-paragraph 120(1)(b)(i) commences with the words "Any complaint," and sub-paragraph 120(1)(b)(ii) with the words "Any *other* complaint," rather than vice-versa, this indicates that all complaints made by a person concerning some matter which occurred while he was detained (including those involving statutory powers and duties) must always first be referred to the hospital managers before the Commission may investigate.

- Conversely, sub-paragraph 120(1)(b)(ii) provides that the Commission never needs to refer to the managers complaints made by patients about the way in which some statutory power or duty was exercised during a period when the complainant was not detained by the managers of a hospital.[232]

- As concerns complaints made by third-parties about the way in which some statutory power or duty was exercised, there is also no obligation to refer them to the managers before investigating them.

---

[232] For example, matters which occurred *prior* to a patient's detention in the hospital (complaints about the sectioning process, the person's detention under section 136, or the manner of his conveyance to hospital), while absent from the hospital, or after he ceased to be detained there (complaints about after-care arrangements).

175

Sub-paragraph (i) complaints

These complaints include both complaints about the way in which some power or duty under the Act has been exercised and a whole range of other grievances about which the Act is silent and imposes no statutory duty (for example, complaints about sexual misconduct, the quality of facilities on a ward, staff rudeness). No person has authority under section 120 to investigate a complaint which falls within sub-paragraph (i) unless the managers of the relevant hospital or mental nursing home have first had an opportunity to investigate it to the patient's satisfaction. If the patient should then be dissatisfied with the results of their inquiry, he may at that stage ask the Commission to appoint an investigator.

Sub-paragraph (ii) complaints

The Commission may investigate complaints by third parties concerning the exercise of some power or duty conferred or imposed by the Act in relation to a detained patient. The word "power" is used several times in the Act.[233] Elsewhere, as in section 136, the word "may" is used to confer a power on some person. In other places, as in section 63, the conferment of a power may be phrased as an exemption: "the consent of the patient shall not be required for any medical treatment ..." Part VII aside, the word "duty" is rarely to be found.[234] The word "shall" is used quite often, but almost invariably to specify the procedure to be followed when exercising a power, e.g., an application *shall* be founded on written recommendations. The statute also prohibits certain acts. For example, section 58(3) provides that no treatment shall be given to a patient after three-months unless authorised by statutory certificate. It is, however, more logical to think of these prohibitions as making clear the absence of any power to do a particular act in the specified circumstances, rather than as a statutory duty not to do the act: section 58(3) simply limits the power to give treatment without consent conferred by section 63 to a period of three months. Likewise with the prohibition that no section 3 application shall be made by an approved social worker except after consulting the nearest relative: this seems to be first-and-foremost a statement that there is no power to make an application unless the relative has been consulted, rather than a statutory duty of consultation. This may be playing with words but there is no duty to consult a nearest relative when assessing a patient for admission. It is simply that the particular power is not exercisable unless the precondition has been satisfied.[235]

Complaint "as to" the exercise of a power or duty

There is ultimately no agreement about whether clinical complaints concerning the prescription of high levels of medication, and general allegations of inadequate care, can be said to be complaints "as to" the exercise of some statutory power or duty. The Act uses the phrase "as to" many times, particularly in section headings. The words are less frequently used in the body of the statute, but most often the usage

---

[233] See *e.g.* sections 5(4), 8(1), 10(1)(b), 11(3), 13(5), 24(1), and 29(3)(d). There are also frequent references in Part III to a court's powers when dealing with a mentally disordered offender, and sections 72–5 set out a tribunal's powers under the Act.

[234] See sections 9(1)(b), 13(1), 13(4), 20, 68, 117, 132, 133, 140 and 141.

[235] Where there is a statutory requirement to do some act, a statutory duty may be reinforced by granting to the person with that duty those powers necessary to enable him to fulfil it. However, where the requirement is to do some act before exercising a power, this is simply circumscribing the power, saying that no power exists unless some prior step has been taken. So, in general, it is fair to say that the Act confers many statutory powers, some of which are qualified, but very few statutory duties.

here is identical to that in the section headings, the words "as to" being synonymous with "concerning" or "in respect of", rather than "relating to."[236] Whether section 120(1)(b)(ii) is capable of embracing decisions not to exercise powers, as well as the way in which powers are exercised, may also be disputed. The better view is perhaps that the sub-paragraph is only concerned with the misuse of powers and the failure to discharge duties, not with decisions not to exercise a power. Another area of doubt is whether complaints about the way in which secondary legislation is implemented may be investigated. If a very legalistic approach is adopted, the words used in sub-paragraph (ii) can be contrasted with those in section 139(1),[237] so that a complaint must concern the exercise of a power or duty found in the Act itself, rather than one which arises from regulations or rules made under it. Because the Code of Practice includes general guidance on medical treatments, guardianship and after-care under supervision, it is at any rate clear that not every failure to observe the Code will give rise to a valid concern that some statutory power or duty has been improperly exercised.[238]

Complaints about clinical decisions, etc.

Many complaints made by third parties concern clinical or quasi-clinical decisions. The third-party's complaint may be that, having regard to improvement in the patient's mental state, the responsible medical officer's decision not to discharge him, or to grant him leave of absence, is unreasonable. A relative may alternatively complain about some aspect of the patient's treatment. For example, the number of drugs being prescribed, the dosage, the quality of nursing care, a want of care, or the lack of occupational therapy. In support, it may be said that the complaints are complaints "as to" the exercise of statutory powers, because the managers have power to detain the patient for treatment and the treatment is being provided compulsorily under sections 58 and 63. If section 63 constitutes a power to give medical treatment for mental disorder, and medical treatment (as defined by section 145) extends to cover the entire care regime, there is certainly very little which lies outside the scope of the power to investigate under s.120(b)(ii). However, for the following reasons, it is submitted that such complaints do not fall within the ambit of sub-paragraph (ii)—

- A sub-paragraph (ii) complaint must be one "as to" the exercise of a power or duty granted or imposed by the Mental Health Act 1983. It is therefore pertinent to ask whether, if that statute did not exist, the act could still lawfully be done or there would still be a duty to do it. A medical practitioner owes all of his patients, detained and informal alike, the same duty of care when it comes to examining them, forming a diagnosis, and prescribing medicines and other forms of treatment. That therefore is a common law obligation, not one imposed by the statute. Nor, more specifically, is the

---

[236] See ss.4(4)(b), 73(1)(a) and (2), 78(4) and (5), 105(2)(4) and (5), 107(1), 118(2), and 126(2). Only relatively rarely, as in sections 24 and 76, is the phrase used in the same sentence as the word "exercise." All one can do is to note that when the words "as to" are used they are generally followed by a reference to a specific power or duty *expressly* conferred or imposed by the Act.

[237] "any act purporting to be done in pursuance of this Act, or any regulations or rules made under this Act ..."

[238] Nevertheless, one purpose of served by publishing the Code is to help to develop good practice, and also uniform practice, in the way in which statutory powers and duties are exercised across England and Wales. The Commission's duty to visit patients allows it to monitor this, and its complaints function allows it to investigate allegations that powers and duties conferred or imposed by the Act have not been exercised in the way intended by Parliament.

doctor's power to prescribe medication, in whatever dose he deems necessary in the light of the patient's condition, one conferred by the Act. Section 58 is concerned with the administration, rather than the prescription, of medication, and the responsible medical officer cannot be required to prescribe treatment which he believes to be clinically inappropriate. What would not exist in most cases if it were not for the statute would be a power to administer a course of treatment to a non-consenting, mentally competent, patient. Certainly, if the doctor was asked on what authority this was being done, he would rely on section 58 or section 63. The statutory power being exercised is therefore not the power to prescribe medicines, or medicines at a certain dosage, but the power to administer those medicines to a non-consenting patient in the circumstances set out in sections 58, 62 and 63, using reasonable force where necessary.

- It is therefore necessary to distinguish between the exercise of the power to give compulsory treatment and the exercise of the doctor's clinical judgement about whether a particular treatment should be given at all. A doctor will, or should, approach each patient's case in the same way regardless of his legal status. A mental state examination leads to the recording of symptoms and signs. These give rise to a diagnosis, which is a pointer towards the most appropriate treatment and the prognosis. At this point, no statutory power has been exercised: reaching a clinical decision does not involve exercising a statutory power. The treatment may be declined by a patient entitled to refuse it, given with the patient's consent, or administered without his consent, using reasonable force where necessary. The power granted by the Act is not one of examination, diagnosis and prescription, but one to give, without the patient's consent, that treatment deemed to be clinically appropriate. A complaint that the power to give treatment compulsorily is being exceeded is a complaint "as to" the exercise of the statutory power, *e.g.* a complaint that excessive force was used or that the treatment was not authorised under section 58. However, a complaint that the patient has been misdiagnosed as suffering from schizophrenia, and should not be prescribed antipsychotics, is not a complaint "as to" the statutory power to administer medication without consent. It is a clinical complaint about the diagnosis and prescription decision. The medical (clinical) part of the process is the treatment decision while the legal part (the power) is the administration of that treatment without consent where permitted by law. The power conferred by the Act relates to the second, not the first, process. Unless there is some allegation that the power has been exceeded or otherwise misused, such complaints are merely complaints "as to" the exercise of the doctor's clinical judgement.

- If it is true that all clinical decisions about the prescription of medication and other forms of treatment are acts as to the exercise of a statutory power or duty, it must also be true that any legal proceedings in respect of them require the High Court's leave. However, it difficult to believe that Parliament intended that section 139 should apply to all actions for negligence based on allegedly inadequate medical care and treatment.

- In one sense, every act done in respect of a detained patient is an act done in pursuance of the statute: at some level, it relates to his detention or treatment and would probably not have been done if he had not been detained. However, this is the case with many Acts of Parliament[239] and the proper interpretation of section 120(1)(b) involves establishing the essential difference between the two categories of complaint. If Parliament intended that virtually every aspect of a patient's treatment and care represents an exercise of the statutory power to detain and treat him, there would be no need for two sub-paragraphs differentiating two types of complaint. It must be the case that certain grievances are investigable under sub-paragraph (i) which are not investigable under sub-paragraph (ii). The different, and much narrower, wording of sub-paragraph (ii) suggests an intention to limit the type of complaints which third-parties may make. A natural reading of the subsection suggests that a patient's right to complain was intended to be broader than that of third-parties in one respect and narrower in another. It is wider insofar as a detained patient can clearly complain about anything which has happened during his detention: he is not limited to matters which involve the exercise of some statutory power or duty. It is narrower insofar as complaints about matters which occurred while he was detained in hospital must first be referred to the hospital managers, even if they involve an allegation that some statutory power or duty was improperly exercised.[240]

- A natural reading of the section also suggests that Parliament did not intend the Commission to investigate complaints about a patient's general care and medical treatment concerning which he himself had no grievance. There are good reasons for restricting one person's right to initiate a formal complaint about some other person's diagnosis, treatment and care. A patient who is content with his treatment might otherwise have to submit to being interviewed, and to having his records examined, at the instigation of some interfering relative. Furthermore, it would often be impossible to properly deal with a third-party's complaint that he should be given drug x, or less of drug y, without breaching the confidentiality of the doctor-patient relationship. Either the reasons for not upholding the complaint could not be communicated to the third-party, or their communication would involve disclosing to him confidential information about the patient's symptoms, diagnosis, prognosis, as well as things said by him during patient-doctor interviews.[241]

---

[239] For example, the case of *Burgess v. Northwich* 6 Q.B.D. 264 turned on the phrase "the exercise of any of the powers of the Act" in section 308 of the Public Health Act 1875. Lindley J. recognised that "In one sense, everything the defendants did was in exercise of the powers conferred upon them by the Public Health Act; but, by the expression 'exercise of any of the powers of this Act', in section 308, I understand new powers created by the Act."

[240] Parliament's intention here may have been to restrict the burden on the Commission to investigating complaints which cannot be resolved locally, bearing in mind that it would in any case be the managers whom the Commissioners would have to look to rectify any problems. If they were ready and willing to do so anyway then a independent investigation is unnecessary.

[241] It is sometimes said that a third-party has a personal right to complain under sub-paragraph (ii) about a deceased patient's treatment. However, if this is true, a third-party must also have the same right to complain about the treatment and care being given to a living patient, regardless of whether or not that patient himself has any complaint about it.

- The intention seems to be that everyone, including the patient, has a common interest in ensuring that the various statutory powers and duties are properly exercised. However, it is for the patient himself to decide whether or not he has a complaint about his medical care and treatment. Before it is investigable, a complaint made under section 120(1)(b)(ii) must involve an allegation that a power conferred by the statute has been exercised improperly, that is otherwise than in accordance with the Act. A complaint concerning a clinical decision is not a complaint which is investigable under sub-paragraph (ii), while a complaint that the person in whom Parliament vested a particular power has simply exercised his discretion in the manner envisaged by Parliament (*e.g.* refusing to grant leave or to exercise his power of discharge) seems at best to disclose no case that the power has been exercised otherwise than in accordance with the statutory scheme. If it is contended by a third-party that a patient is not being detained in accordance with the provisions of the Act, that amounts to a complaint about the exercise of the statutory powers. However, if the administration of drug x to patient y has been authorised by the completion of a Form 38 or Form 39 specifying the drug, a complaint by a third-party that the medicine ought not to be prescribed, because the patient does not suffer from schizophrenia, is not a complaint as to the exercise of a statutory power, but a complaint as to the patient's diagnosis and the prescription.[242]

Whether an investigation is appropriate

In deciding whether it is appropriate to investigate a complaint made by a patient, or to continue an investigation in progress, the person authorised will usually have regard to the matters listed below—

Patients' complaints: whether appropriate to investigate

Nature of the complaint	▪ If established, would the matter complained of be likely to give rise to civil or criminal liability, loss of employment or disciplinary proceedings before a professional body?
	▪ Is the complaint really a ward or hospital-based issue, such that it would be better dealt with under the Commission's visitatorial functions?
Complainant's reasons	▪ Why is the complainant asking the Commission to conduct a second investigation?

---

[242] An alternative interpretation of section 120, which relies on the fact that an authorised person cannot be required to investigate a section 120(1)(b)(ii) complaint, may also be suggested. This discretion, it may be said, represents an acknowledgement that many complaints may be said at some remote level to be complaints as to the exercise of a statutory power or duty, in the sense that the act would not have been done had the patient not been detained for treatment. Where any duty to do a particular act is first-and-foremost a common law or professional duty about which the Act is silent, the person authorised may at his discretion decide that it is inappropriate to investigate the matter because it has so little to do with the operation of the statute which it is the Commission's function to keep under review.

- Is the complainant seeking an apology, compensation, disciplinary action against staff, conciliation, or an adjudication of a matter in dispute?

- Is the complainant attempting to use the Commission's complaints machinery in an inappropriate manner, *e.g.* as a way of obviating the usual procedures relating to pre-action discovery or as a way of gaining access to medical records?

Managers'
investigation
- Was the way in which the managers' enquiry was conducted fair and impartial and consistent with established guidelines?

- To what extent were the managers' findings justified in the light of the available evidence? Did the managers obtain all the relevant evidence before arriving at their findings?

- Would a further inquiry simply duplicate what has already been said or, instead, be likely to bring to light new evidence which could materially alter the conclusions which the hospital managers themselves reached?

Alternative
remedies
- Are alternative, more appropriate, courses or remedies available to the complainant (*e.g.* an action for medical negligence, professional disciplinary proceedings, an investigation by the Health Service Commissioner)?

- Would it be more appropriate to refer the case back to the managers for reconsideration (*e.g.* to obtain further evidence or to arrange for the matter to be investigated at a higher level within the hospital management before the Commission itself embarks on an investigation)?

Evidence
- What evidence has been furnished in support of the proposition that some event has taken place which the Commission should arrange to be investigated?

- Is there any evidence of a breach of the Act or of the Code of Practice?

Time factors
- Does the length of time which has elapsed since the events to which the complaint relates took place make an investigation inappropriate?

Prospect of gain
- What purpose would an investigation serve (is there any prospect of "gain" to some person, *e.g.* conciliation, an improvement in practices, or resolution through a clear adjudication of the matters in dispute)?

Resources
- Given the need to use resources carefully, and to investigate serious complaints thoroughly, is the matter sufficiently serious to warrant an external investigation?

CODE OF PRACTICE

The Health of the Nation Key Area Handbook summarises the policies which the Code of Practice recommends that health authorities, local (social services) authorities and the police develop in relation to the treatment and care of persons suffering from mental disorder.[243]

POLICIES REQUIRED UNDER THE CODE OF PRACTICE

Code para.	Policy requirement	Responsibility of —		
		H.A.	L.A.	Police
2.11c	Issue guidance to approved social workers (ASWs) about interpreters.		•	
2.14	Issue practical guidance to ASWs on procedures regarding displacement of nearest relative (s.29).		•	
2.33	Issue guidance to ASWs re request(s) from nearest relative for ASW assessment (s.13(4)).		•	
2.35	Ensure ASWs and doctors receive guidance on use of professional interpreters.	•	•	
10.1	Establish joint policy re. police power to remove person to place of safety (s.136).	•	•	•
10.19	Issue guidance to ASWs on powers of entry (s.135).		•	
11.3	Produce policy with Ambulance Service on conveyance of patients to hospitals (s.6).	•	Take lead	•
13.6	Prepare and publish policy on Guardianship (s.7).		•	
14.6	Hospital Managers' policy on providing information to patients.	•		
16.33	Hospital Managers' "Second Opinion Appointed Doctor" system.	•		
18.13	Policy on the use of restraint.	•		
18.16	Policy on the use of seclusion.	•		
18.27	Policy on the use of locked doors on "open" wards.	•		
18.29	Policy on the use of locked doors and secure areas.	•		
19.2	Policy on behaviour modification programmes.	•		
19.1	Policy on the use of "time-out"	•		
21.2	Policy on procedure re. patients absent without leave	•		
24.15	Special Hospitals policy on withholding mail	SHSA		
25.1	Policy on searching of patients and their belongings	•		
27.3	To produce procedures of aftercare with local voluntary organisations (s.117).	•	•	

---

[243]   *The Health of the Nation Key Area Handbook: Mental Illness*, (Department of Health, 2nd Ed., 1994).

PATIENTS' MAIL

Under section 134 of the Mental Health Act 1983, the Mental Health Act Commission has the function of reviewing certain decisions to withhold mail sent to or by a detained patient.

General law concerning postal services

The relevant features of the statutory scheme under the Post Office Act 1953, and related legislation, may be summarised in the following way—

- subject to exceptions, the Post Office has the exclusive privilege of conveying all letters from one place to another and of performing all the incidental services of receiving, collecting, dispatching and delivering them.[244]

- the following acts expressly authorised by statute do not infringe the exclusive privilege of the Post Office with respect to the conveyance and delivery of letters: (a) the conveyance and delivery of a letter personally by its sender[245]; (b) the sending, conveyance and delivery of a letter by means of a private friend who himself delivers it to the addressee[246]; (c) the sending, conveyance and delivery of a letter concerning the private affairs of the sender or addressee by means of a messenger sent by its sender.[247]

- the term "postal packet" includes letters, postcards, and parcels which might be sent by post, even if in fact delivered or sent by hand.[248]

- the delivery of a postal packet to a postman or to an officer of the Post Office constitutes a delivery to a post office;[249]

- the delivery of a postal packet at the premises to which it is addressed or redirected, or to the addressee's servant, agent or other authorised person, constitutes a delivery to the addressee."[250]

- a postal packet is deemed to be in the course of transmission by post from the time it is delivered to any post office to the time it is delivered to the addressee;[251]

- the Post Office will, on the application of the addressee, redirect postal packets from the original address to another address of the same addressee[252] and a postal packet delivered at the original address may be redirected to the addressee in the United Kingdom.[253]

---

[244] Post Office Act 1953, s.3(1); Post Office Act 1969, s.23(1)(a).
[245] *Ibid.*, s.3(2)(a).
[246] *Ibid.*, s.3(2)(b).
[247] *Ibid.*, s.3(2)(c).
[248] *Mental Health Act 1959: Memorandum on Parts I, IV to VII and IX* (D.H.S.S., 1960), para. 269; *Mental Health (Amendment) Bill: Notes on Clauses, House of Commons* (D.H.S.S., 1982), p.167.
[249] Post Office Act 1953, s.87(2)(b).
[250] *Ibid.*, s.87(2)(c).
[251] *Ibid.*, s.87(2)(a).
[252] Post Office and Post Scheme 1979, Sched. 3, Item 10.
[253] Post Office Act 1953, para. 32(1).

- it is generally an offence for a Post Office employee to open, detain or delay a postal packet, but this offence does not extend to opening, detaining or delaying a postal packet returned by reason that the person to whom it is directed has refused it.[254]

Mental Health Act 1983, s.134

The present law concerning the withholding of patients' post is set out in section 134. In order to appreciate its precise ambit, it is useful to be aware of the way in which the legislation in this area has developed.

Historical developments

Section 41 of the Lunacy Act 1890 required the manager of a hospital to forward unopened certain privileged correspondence, such as letters to a Judge in Lunacy. The manager was given a discretion as to whether or not to forward other letters written by a private patient, for example letters to family and acquaintances. The Commissioners could, and did, direct that every institution having a private patient display a printed notice setting forth the "right of every private patient to have any letter written by him forwarded in pursuance of the last preceding section."[255] These provisions were reviewed by the Royal Commission of 1954–57, which had this to say in its report: [256]

> "As regards the censorship of letters, we recommend that there should be no censorship of out-going letters from patients (whether subject to detention or not) except at the request of individual addressees who ask for letters addressed to themselves to be scrutinised or withheld because they find them distressing."

Mental Health Act 1959

Section 36 provided that a letter addressed to a patient could be withheld from him if the responsible medical officer considered that its receipt was likely to interfere with his treatment or cause him unnecessary distress. Correspondence so withheld was to be returned to the sender by post. A patient's outgoing mail could be withheld from the Post Office in two situations. The first of them was that the addressee had requested in writing that communications addressed to him by the patient should be withheld[257]: this exception was re-enacted in 1983 and forms part of the current law. The second situation was that it appeared to the responsible medical officer that the postal packet would be unreasonably offensive to the addressee or was defamatory of other persons (other than persons on the staff of the hospital) or was likely to prejudice the interests of the patient.[258] The second ground was not to be construed as authorising a responsible medical officer to open or examine a patient's mail unless he considered that the patient was suffering from mental disorder of a kind calculated to lead him to send communications of this kind.[259] Section 36(4), which was also not re-enacted, then went on to provide that, except as provided by the

---

[254]   Post Office Act 1953, s.58.

[255]   Lunacy Act 1890, s.42(1)(a).

[256]   *Report of the Royal Commission on the Law Relating to Mental Illness and Mental Deficiency*, Cmnd. 169 (1957), para. 299.

[257]   Mental Health Act 1959, s.36(2)(a).

[258]   *Ibid.*, s.36(2)(b).

[259]   *Ibid.*, s.36(3).

section, it was unlawful to prevent or impede the delivery of mail to a detained patient, or the delivery to the Post Office of any mail addressed by him and delivered by him for dispatch. According to paragraph 270 of the *Memorandum* on the 1959 Act:

> "270. The right to withhold patients' outgoing correspondence from the post is limited to the circumstances described in paragraphs (a) and (b) of subsection (2) of section 36. The right to open correspondence in order to decide whether a letter should be withheld under paragraph (b) is specifically limited by subsection (3) to cases where the responsible medical officer (or guardian or person authorised by him) believes the patient to be suffering from disorder of a kind which is likely to lead him to send the sort of communications which may be withheld under that paragraph. Other patients' letters may not be opened. The assumption therefore is that no outgoing letters are read by hospital staff unless there are special reasons for doing so, within the terms of subsection (2), in the case of individual patients. In view of this, the Minister considers it no longer suitable that there should be general notices in the wards listing persons to whom letters must be sent unopened; the assumption is that all letters will be sent unopened unless exceptionally it is necessary to use the limited powers conferred by subsection (2)."

Review of the Mental Health Act 1959 (Cmnd. 7320)

The White Paper of 1978 recognised that it was extremely difficult to exercise effective control over distressing incoming communications in an age where patients have easy access to telephones, radios, newspapers and televisions. The Government therefore proposed to remove the power to withhold the in-coming mail of detained patients and of persons under guardianship. The White Paper then considered the situation as regards letters written by patients:

> "8.10 There are similar difficulties over out-going mail. It is not possible to intercept all correspondence which might be offensive since there are alternative methods of sending letters, such as persuading informal patients to post them. Nor is there evidence that detained patients are more likely to write abusive or distressing letters than other patients. There may however be a small number of cases where a patient's letter would be particularly distressing to its intended recipient, for example where a patient who has committed a serious crime writes to his victim or to the victim's relatives; and it seems right to attempt to exercise such control as is practicable in such cases. It is therefore proposed that it should remain possible for the hospital authorities to withhold out-going mail addressed to somebody who has specifically requested that mail addressed to him by a detained patient or a person under guardianship should not be sent to him. Such mail would be returned to the patient who would be entitled to assume that, otherwise, his mail was not being intercepted or interfered with in any way.
>
> 8.11 If detained patients are to have an unhindered right to send letters, with the exception noted in the preceding paragraph, there would no longer seem to be a need for the list in section 36(2)(b) of persons and organisations to whom patients may write without fear of interception ..."

Reform of Mental Health Legislation (Cmnd. 8405)

The White Paper of November 1981, which explained the amendments made to the 1959 Act in the recently published Bill, included the following passage:

41. The Bill also proposes other changes to the law which affect detained patients in hospital. It will considerably curtail the circumstances in which incoming or outgoing mail may be withheld, and will ensure that there is no scrutiny at all of the mail of informal patients. The Bill provides that outgoing mail from a detained patient may be withheld only if the proposed recipient has asked that this should be done with correspondence addressed to him by the patient. Incoming mail will not be opened or withheld at all except in the special hospitals, where exceptional arrangements are needed for security reasons. In the special hospitals, an officer will be authorised to withhold mail if it is necessary in the interests of the patient's safety or to protect others."

The present legislation

The present statute does not authorise interference with the correspondence of an informal in-patient. However, section 134 allows a detained patient's post to be opened, inspected or withheld from the Post Office in certain circumstances. Section 121 provides for an appeal to the Mental Health Act Commission in such cases. Part V of the Mental Health (Hospital, Guardianship and Consent to Treatment) Regulations 1983, the authority for which derives from sections 121(9) an 134(8), regulates the exercise of these powers and the making and determination of applications to the Commission. The functions of the hospital managers under section 134 are discharged on their behalf by a hospital staff member appointed for the purpose — referred to in the regulations as "the person appointed."

STATUTORY GROUNDS FOR WITHHOLDING POSTAL PACKETS

	Incoming post	*Outgoing post*
• *Informal patients*	May not be withheld from the patient.	May not be withheld from Post Office even if addressee has made such a request.
• *Non-special hospital detained patients*	May not be withheld from the patient.	May be withheld from Post Office if addressee has requested this in writing.
• *Special hospital detained patients*	May be withheld from the patient if the managers consider that it is necessary to do so in the interests of his safety or for the protection of other persons	May be withheld from Post Office if (a) addressee has requested this in writing; or (b) the managers consider that it is likely to cause danger to some person, or is likely to cause distress to the addressee or to a person other than a member of staff at that hospital.

Incoming correspondence of detained patients

The Act does not empower the managers to withhold incoming postal packages from a detained patient who is not detained at a special hospital. In practice, some hospitals do not deliver magazines with a sexual content and the authority for this, if any exists, is presumably to be found at common law.

Incoming correspondence of patients detained in a special hospital

A postal packet addressed to a patient detained in a special hospital may be withheld from him if, in the opinion of the hospital managers, it is necessary to do so in the interests of his safety or for the protection of other persons.[260] The managers may open and inspect a postal packet for the purpose of determining whether it is, or it contains, some communication of the such a kind and in order to determine whether the packet should be withheld.[261] If a postal packet, or some item within it, is withheld from the patient, both he and the item's sender (if known) must be notified within seven days. Either, or both of them, may then require the Commission to review the decision.

Outgoing correspondence of detained patients

A postal packet "addressed to any person by a (detained) patient ... and delivered by the patient for dispatch" may be withheld from the Post Office if the addressee has requested that communications addressed to him by the patient should be withheld.[262]

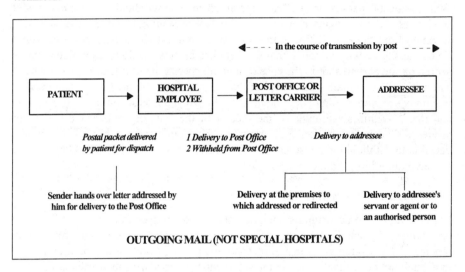

OUTGOING MAIL (NOT SPECIAL HOSPITALS)

Any such request must be made by a notice in writing to the hospital managers, the registered medical practitioner in charge of the treatment of the patient, or the Secretary of State.[263] In relation to this power, the hospital managers may only open a postal packet for the purpose of determining whether there is within it a written communication to a person who has given such a notice.[264] Where a postal packet, or a letter contained in it, is withheld, the hospital managers must record that fact in writing.[265] However, on the assumption that such a notice was given by the addressee, there is no need to give notice to the patient that his letter has been withheld from the Post Office and no appeals procedure.[266] Because the Post Office has a duty to deliver to the addressee mail in the course of transmission by post, the

---

[260]   Mental Health Act 1983, s.134(2).
[261]   *Ibid.*, s.134(4).
[262]   *Ibid.*, s.134(1)(a).
[263]   *Ibid.*, s.134(1).
[264]   *Ibid.*, s.134(4).
[265]   *Ibid.*, s.134(5).
[266]   There is no statutory requirement to notify the patient that a letter has been withheld or that an addressee has given notice under section 134.

1983 Act therefore provides an addressee with the means of avoiding distressing or unwanted communications being delivered to and by the Post Office.

Outgoing correspondence of patients detained in a special hospital

A postal packet delivered by a special hospital patient for dispatch may *also* be withheld from the Post Office if the hospital managers consider that it is likely to cause danger to some person, or is likely to cause distress to the addressee or to a person other than a member of staff at that hospital.[267] The managers may open and inspect any postal packet for the purpose of determining whether there is within it a communication of such a kind and in order to determine whether the packet should be withheld.[268] If a postal packet, or some item within in, is withheld from the Post Office then the patient, but not the intended recipient, must be notified of this within seven days. The patient may then require the Commission to review the decision.

Special hospitals appeals procedure

Where a postal packet or anything contained in it is withheld *(cf. opened)* under section 134, the managers must record that fact in writing.[269] Unless the item was withheld from the Post Office at the addressee's request, the managers must, within seven days, give written notice that the item has been withheld. This notice must be served on the patient and, in the case of incoming post, the sender also (if known).[270] The notice must contain a statement of their right to apply to the Commission and of that body's powers to direct that the item not be withheld, as set out in section 121(7) and (8).[271] Within six months of the receipt of the statutory notice, the patient or sender of the postal packet may apply to the Commission for it to review the decision to withhold the postal packet (or anything contained in it). The Commission is then required to conduct such a review.[272]

Determination of the application

For the purpose of determining such an application, the Commission may direct the production of such documents, information and evidence as it may reasonably require.[273] The Commission may direct that the postal packet, or anything contained in it, shall not be withheld and the managers must comply with such a direction.[274]

---

[267] Mental Health Act 1983, s.134(1)(b). Certain privileged correspondence, whether incoming or outgoing, cannot be withheld from the Post Office or from a special hospital patient. This comprises correspondence passing between a special hospital patient and any of the following persons or bodies: a Minister of the Crown; a Member of either House of Parliament; the Master or any other officer of the Court of Protection; any of the Lord Chancellor's Visitors; the Parliamentary Commissioner for Administration, the Health Service Commissioner for England, the Health Service Commissioner for Wales or a Local Commissioner within the meaning of Part III of the Local Government Act 1974; a Mental Health Review Tribunal; a health authority within the meaning of the National Health Service Act 1977; a local social services authority; a Community Health Council; a probation committee; the managers of the hospital in which the patient is detained; any legally qualified person instructed by the patient to act as his legal adviser; the European Commission of Human Rights or the European Court of Human Rights: MHA 1983, s.134(3).

[268] *Ibid.*, s.134(4).

[269] *Ibid.*, s.134(5).

[270] *Ibid.*, s.135(6).

[271] *Ibid.*, s.134(6).

[272] *Ibid.*, s.121(7).

[273] Mental Health (Hospital, Guardianship and Consent to Treatment) Regulations 1983, reg.18(3).

[274] *Ibid.*, s.121(8).

Redirecting and readdressing mail

It is sometimes claimed that a patient's letter becomes the property of the addressee at the time it is handed to hospital staff, to be disposed of by the addressee as the latter thinks fit. This cannot be so. If a person hands a letter to his spouse to post, it remains the sender's property until it is delivered to the Post Office. So, in the English case of *R. v. Harley* (1843) 1 Car. & Kir. 89, the theft of a bank note from a letter prior to its delivery to the post office was held to be a theft from the sender of the letter, not from the addressee. Furthermore, it may not be possible to deliver some letters. Mailable matter only becomes the property of the person to whom it is addressed when it is deposited in the Post Office although, for other purposes, it may be the property of the Postmaster-General.[275] Because a letter remains the patient's property prior to its delivery to the Post Office, it can only be readdressed, or redirected, by or with the sender's consent. After posting, the Post Office may redirect it in accordance with its statutory scheme and, after delivery to the specified address, any new occupier may readdress it, if the addressee has moved. Although section 134 does not prohibit the redirection of mail, this misses the point, which is that it does not authorise such an interference with the property and rights of another person. A postal packet *"addressed ... by a patient ... and delivered by the patient for dispatch"* may only be withheld from the Post Office if the addressee has requested that communications addressed to him by the patient should be withheld.[276] To this extent, section 134 releases the managers from their general duty to deliver post to the Post Office, but it does not authorise them to readdress or redirect letters not withheld. Furthermore, no addressee has any power to authorise a third party to redirect a person's correspondence prior to its dispatch; only the Post Office may redirect a person's mail in the limited circumstances set out in the post office statutory schemes. As indicated in the White Paper of 1978, mail withheld at an addressee's request (being and remaining the patient's property) should be returned to the patient, who is otherwise entitled to assume that his mail is not being intercepted or interfered with in any way. To summarise, it is for the sender to decide to whom to address his letter and to what address to send it.

INFORMAL PATIENTS

Section 121(4) provides that the Secretary of State may direct the Commission "to keep under review the care and treatment, or any aspect of the care and treatment, in hospitals and mental nursing homes of patients who are not liable to be detained under this Act." No such direction has yet been given and, consequently, the Commission has no power to visit informal patients, or patients subject to guardianship or after-care under supervision. Nor may it investigate complaints made by or in respect of them. It is, however, noteworthy that, when the 1982 Bill was before Parliament, the Minister of Health suggested that the Commission's remit could be extended to informal patients at a particular hospital, rather than extended to all informal patients:[277]

> "The Commission could ask the Secretary of State for permission to look at some in-formal cases and the Secretary of State might give his consent for members of the Commission to exercise, for that hospital, the powers (in section 120(4))"

---

[275] See *R. v. Wendland* (1970) 1 C.C.C. (2d) 382 (Can).

[276] Mental Health Act 1983, s.134(1)(a).

[277] The Minister of Health (Rt. Hon. Kenneth Clarke, M.P.), House of Commons Special Standing Committee, *Hansard*, 17 June 1982, col. 575.

MENTAL HEALTH REVIEW TRIBUNALS

Mental Health Review Tribunals are independent judicial bodies originally established under the Mental Health Act 1959 but now constituted under the Mental Health Act 1983. The hallmarks of a tribunal have been summarised as independence of administration; the capacity to reach a binding decision (which distinguishes them from inquiries); the fact that decisions are reached by a panel of members (often three), rather than by a single judge; a procedure similar to but simpler than that of a court; and permanent existence usually confined to a special type of case.[278] Mental Health Review Tribunals exhibit all these features and their statutory purpose is to review the cases of individuals subject to detention, guardianship or supervision under the Mental Health Act 1983. The proceedings involve "a complex equation of conflicting components all of which tend to give rise to grave public concern, namely the liberty of the subject, the protection of the public and the interests of the patient."[279]

HISTORICAL ORIGINS

The history of Mental Health Review Tribunals can be traced back to two official reports published in 1957.

Franks Report of 1957

The Franks Committee addressed the issue of administrative justice and the work of tribunals. Most statutory tribunals were regarded as specialised courts, the typical statutory tribunal exercising functions essentially judicial in character but of a specialised nature. The cardinal point in all cases was that Parliament has deliberately provided for a decision outside and independent of any Department concerned.[280] Nevertheless, the necessity for administrative justice should not lead to the creation of tribunals for their own sake when the ordinary courts could well take the decisions in question: a "decision should be entrusted to a court rather than to a tribunal in the absence of special considerations which make a tribunal more suitable."[281] It was in the context of this developing tribunal system that the decision was taken to depart from the Lunacy Act principle that decisions affecting individual liberty should be predetermined judicially, and be reviewable instead by a specialised tribunal held after the event.

Percy Report of 1957

The Percy Commission of 1954–57 reviewed the law relating to mental illness and mental deficiency and many of its recommendations were subsequently implemented in the Mental Health Act 1959.[282] Some of these provisions were later revised by the Mental Health (Amendment) Act 1982, although the underlying framework remained unchanged. The present statute is largely a consolidating Act. Prior to 1959, the order of a justice of the peace, or other judicial authority, was

---

[278] J.F. Garner and B.L. Jones, *Administrative Law* (Butterworths, 6th ed., 1985), p.230.
[279] *Mental Health Review Tribunals for England and Wales, Annual Report 1994* (Department of Health, May 1995), Appendix 13.
[280] *Report on Administrative Tribunals and Enquiries*, Cmnd 218 (1957), p.9.
[281] *Ibid.*
[282] *Report of the Royal Commission on the Law relating to Mental Illness and Mental Deficiency*, Cmnd. 169 (1957).

generally necessary before a person could be compulsorily admitted to hospital or received into guardianship. The Royal Commission advocated the repeal of these certification procedures. In their place, it recommended that a person's detention or reception into guardianship should be authorised if an application made by the patient's nearest relative or a specialist mental welfare officer, and supported by two medical recommendations, was accepted by the hospital to which admission was sought or, in the case of guardianship, by the social services authority concerned.[283] Because the proposed procedures did not involve any judicial body, the Commission recommended that if a patient then desired a formal review of the justification for his detention to be formally reviewed, rather than merely to apply to the hospital's own management committee or the local authority for it to exercise its power of discharge, this need should be met by the establishment of a new independent review body.[284] Their establishment would give patients opportunities to have the justification for the use of compulsion investigated by a strong independent body consisting of both medical and non-medical members.[285] The functions of such a tribunal would be to review the continuing need for compulsion.[286]

CONSTITUTION AND ADMINISTRATION

Section 3(1) of the Mental Health Act 1959 established a Mental Health Review Tribunal for each National Health Service region for the purpose of dealing with applications and references made by and in respect of patients under the provisions of that Act. Section 65(1) of the 1983 Act now provides that there shall be one tribunal for each region of England and one tribunal for Wales, the English regions being determined by order of the Secretary of State.[287]

The regions

There are currently eight National Health Service regions in England and The Mental Health Review Tribunals (Regions) Order 1996 provides for eight English tribunals, each of which covers one of these regions.[288]

---

[283] "We consider that a sufficient consensus of medical and non-medical opinion on the need to compel a patient to accept hospital or community care would normally be provided through (an) application for the patient's admission made by a relative or mental welfare officer, ... two supporting medical recommendations, the acceptance of the patient as suitable for the form of care recommended, and the continuing power of discharge vested in the nearest relative, the hospital or local authority medical staff, the members of the hospital management committee or local authority, and the Minister of Health. To refer the application and medical recommendations to a justice of the peace before the patient's admission would not in our view provide a significant additional safeguard for the patient ..." *Ibid.*, p.148.

[284] *Ibid.*, pp.48–149

[285] *Ibid.*, p.12.

[286] "We should make it clear that these review tribunals would not be acting as an appellate court of law to consider whether the patient's mental condition at the time when the compulsory powers were first used had been accurately diagnosed by the doctors signing the recommendations, or whether there had been sufficient justification for the use of compulsory powers at that time, nor to consider whether there was some technical flaw in the documents purporting to authorise the patient's admission ... The review tribunal's function would be to consider the patient's mental condition at the time when it considers his application, and to decide whether the type of care which has been provided by the use of compulsory powers is the most appropriate to his present needs, or whether any alternative form of care might now be more appropriate, or whether he could now be discharged from care altogether." *Ibid.*, pp.150–151.

[287] Mental Health Act 1983, s.65, as amended by Health Authorities Act 1995, s.2 and Sched. 1, Pt. III, para. 107(6).

[288] The Mental Health Review Tribunals (Regions) Order 1996, S.I. 1996 No. 510. The order came into force on 1 April 1996, together with the Health Authorities Act 1995.

THE MENTAL HEALTH REVIEW TRIBUNALS

- **South Thames**

  East Sussex, Kent, Surrey, West Sussex; London boroughs situated south of the River Thames.

  London South Office, Hinchley Wood, Block 3, Crown Offices, Kingston-By-Pass Road, Surbiton, Surrey KT6 5QN. Tel.: 0181 398 4166. Fax 0181 339 0709.

- **South & West**

  Cornwall and the Isles of Scilly, Devon, Dorset, Gloucestershire (including the City of Bristol and the county of South Gloucestershire); Hampshire and the Isle of Wight; Somerset (including the counties of Bath and North-East Somerset and North-West Somerset); Wiltshire.

- **North Thames**

  Essex and Hertfordshire; London boroughs situated north of the River Thames, including the Cities of London and Westminster and the Inner Temple and Middle Temple

  London North Office, Canons Park, Government Buildings, Honeypot Lane, Stanmore, Middlesex HA7 1AY. Tel: 0171 972 2000. Fax 0171 972 3731.

- **Anglia & Oxford**

  Bedfordshire, Berkshire, Buckinghamshire, Cambridgeshire, Norfolk, Northamptonshire, Oxfordshire; Suffolk.

- **Trent**

  The counties of Derbyshire (except those wards in the borough of High Peak within the North West Region), Leicestershire, Lincolnshire, North-East Lincolnshire, North Lincolnshire, Nottinghamshire and South Yorkshire.

  Nottingham Office, Spur A, Block 5, Government Buildings, Chalfont Drive, Western Boulevard, Nottingham NG8 3RZ. Tel: 0115 9294222. Fax 0115 9428308.

- **Northern & Yorkshire**

  Cumbria (except the districts of Barrow-in-Furness and South Lakeland), Durham, East Riding of Yorkshire, Hartlepool, the City of Kingston-upon-Hull, Middlesborough, Northumberland, North Yorkshire, Redcar and Cleveland, Stockton-on-Tees, Tyne and Wear, West Yorkshire, York.

- **North West**

  The counties of Cheshire, Greater Manchester, Lancashire and Merseyside; in the county of Cumbria, the districts of Barrow-in-Furness and South Lakeland; and in the county of Derbyshire, in the borough of High Peak, the wards of All Saints, Gamesley, St. Andrew's, St. Charles, St. Jane's, St. John's, Simmondley and Tintwistle.

  Liverpool Office, Cressington House (3rd Floor), 249 St Mary's Road, Garston, Liverpool, Lancs L19 0NF. Tel: 0151 494 0095. Fax 0151 270133.

- **West Midlands**

  Hereford and Worcester, Shropshire, Staffordshire, Warwickshire, West Midlands.

- **Wales**

  Wales.

  MHRT for Wales, 1st Floor, Crown Buildings, Cathays Park, Cardiff CF1 3NQ. Tel: 01222 825111. Fax 01222 823117.

- **Special hospital cases,**

  Applications and references concerning patients detained at Ashworth Hospital are dealt with by the Liverpool office; those concerning Rampton Hospital patients by the Nottingham office, and those concerning Broadmoor patients by the Hinchley Wood (London South) office.

Administrative support

In the exercise of their statutory functions, tribunals are independent of any government department or Health Authority. However, the 1983 Act places a duty on the Secretary of State for Health to provide each tribunal with officers and servants and such accommodation as they may require.[289] The Secretariat for the eight English tribunals is provided by the Department of Health and there are four regional offices, each of which serves two tribunals. Each office is managed by a Higher Executive Officer — known as the Clerk to the Tribunal — supported by a number of Executive Officers, Administrative Officers and Assistant Administrators. Central management responsibility for the various tribunal offices is held by the Grade 7 Principal of the Department of Health's Health Care (Administration) 5 Branch [HC(A)5]. This principal, who is also responsible for the department's forensic psychiatric services policy, oversees the tribunal budget, co-ordinates the appointment and reappointment of members, and provides executive and administrative support for meetings of the regional chairmen. The Mental Health Review Tribunal for Wales is based in Cardiff and is staffed by Welsh Office officials. Although tribunal clerks are answerable to the regional chairman for the administration of the tribunal, management responsibility for their actions lies with the Department of Health and the Welsh Office.

Financial arrangements

The Act also provides that the Secretary of State (for Health) may defray the expenses of tribunals and pay tribunal members such remuneration and allowances as he, with the consent of the Treasury, determines.[290] Payment is presently made according to daily and half-daily rates together with subsistence allowances. The legal and medical members' fees are broadly equivalent, those of the lay members being approximately 40 per cent. of the rate payable to the other members. Regional chairmen receive an additional retainer. The tribunal budget for 1994/95, excluding a small capital sum of £10,629, is given below.

COSTS OF TRIBUNALS (1994/95)

Type of expense	England (£)	Wales (£)	Combined (£)
Members fees and expenses	4,417,000	210,000	4,627,000
Secretariat staff costs	926,150	102,076	1,028,226
Other running costs	175,054	6,805	181,859
Total costs	5,518,204	318,881	5,837,085

Source : Mental Health Review Tribunals for England and Wales, Annual Report 1994, Department of Health, London, May 1995, p.28.

---

[289] See Mental Health Act 1983, s.65(4).
[290] Section 65(4), which is in identical terms to Mental Health Act 1959, s.3(4).

MEMBERSHIP

The Act states that the provisions of Schedule 2 shall have effect with respect to the constitution of Mental Health Review Tribunals.[291] Paragraph 1 of the schedule provides that each of the regional tribunals shall consist of a number of legally qualified members, a number of medical practitioners, and a number of other persons with suitable experience. Members may be assigned to two or more regional tribunals, in addition to which a member may occasionally sit outside his named region as the need arises.[292] Members hold office under the terms of the instrument under which they are appointed. Appointments are usually for a fixed term of three years, renewable at the discretion of the Lord Chancellor. There is an upper age limit on first appointment of 62 and an upper age limit on reappointment of 70. The duties of the regional chairmen include making recommendations on the appointment and reappointment of all tribunal members while the Council on Tribunals may make "general" recommendations to Ministers about appointments to membership. The Department of Health requests a short curriculum vitae when a member's term of appointment is due to expire. The Lord Chancellor may terminate a member's appointment and members may resign office by notice in writing to the Lord Chancellor. Any member who ceases to hold office is eligible for re-appointment. The membership of the regional tribunals as at 31 December 1994 is given below and the number of legal members includes the regional chairman. There were 432 members in all.

MEMBERSHIP OF MENTAL HEALTH REVIEW TRIBUNALS

Tribunal	Chairman	Legal	Medical	Lay
• *Anglia & Oxford*	Her Honour Judge Norwood	6	12	20
• *North West*	Mr W Greenwood	21	29	31
• *North Thames*	Mr M Christie	14	13	23
• *Northern & Yorkshire*	Mr G Scott	11	18	10
• *South & West*	Miss R Hare QC	15	19	22
• *South Thames*	His Honour Judge H Palmer	20	13	22
• *Trent*	Professor Sir John Wood	8	17	10
• *West Midlands*	Mr P Turner	11	12	12
• *MHRT for Wales*	His Honour Judge G Jones	9	24	10
		115	157	160

---

[291] Mental Health Act 1983, s.65(3).
[292] See Mental Health Act 1983, s.65(2), Sched. 2, para. 5.

LEGAL MEMBERS

The Act provides that each of the regional tribunals shall consist of a number of legal members appointed by the Lord Chancellor and having such legal experience as the Lord Chancellor considers suitable.[293] The Lord Chancellor's Department now advertises for, and formally interviews, prospective legal members to establish their suitability for appointment. In proceedings involving a restricted patient the legal member must be chosen from a panel of legal members approved by the Lord Chancellor to hear such cases.[294]

Administration of judicial appointments

The Lord Chancellor is assisted by the Judicial Appointments Group which has published guidance on appointments to tribunals.[295] The guidance refers to some of the factors taken into account during the recruitment process, such as the candidate's knowledge and experience of the field, his age, health, and character. For each candidate there is a correspondence file and a separate series of notes of the main facts and opinions received about him. Comments from third parties on a candidate's professional and personal suitability for judicial appointment are strictly confidential. To the extent that such information has been computerised, it is exempt from the access provisions in the Data Protection Act 1984. This is because the Lord Chancellor depends "heavily on being given frank and honest opinions about the judicial potential of candidates for office and for this reason it has always been understood that such advice is given in strict confidence."[296] No other part of the system is confidential[297] and the Lord Chancellor's Department accepts that the appointments process should where possible be open to public scrutiny.[298] While the confidentiality of information received from third parties "sometimes gives rise to anxiety that there is an undisclosed black mark against a candidate, ... this is hardly ever the case and a member of the appointments team is always willing to meet a candidate who wishes to know the position and explain it frankly."[299]

Knowledge and experience

According to the guidance, "it is an advantage for candidates to have some knowledge of a tribunal's field of law and procedure but that is not always essential ... candidates are not required to have an extensive knowledge of mental health law although experience is helpful."[300] In practice, it is quite rare for legal members to have a prior knowledge of mental health law or practice and this is perhaps the most frequent criticism of the appointments process.

Candidate's age

The only statutory requirement is that appointees have such legal experience as the Lord Chancellor considers suitable. While legal membership of most statutory tribunals is restricted by statute to solicitors or barristers who have attained a certain

---

[293]   Mental Health Act 1983, s.65(3), Sched. 2, para. 1(a).
[294]   *Ibid.*, s.78(4)(a); Mental Health Review Tribunal Rules 1983, r. 8(3).
[295]   *Judicial Appointments: The Lord Chancellor's Policies and Procedures* (H.M.S.O., 2nd ed., November 1990).
[296]   *Ibid.*, p.2.
[297]   *Ibid.*
[298]   *Ibid.*, p.4.
[299]   *Ibid.*, p.27.
[300]   *Ibid.*, pp.22–23.

minimum age, and have practised professionally for a prescribed number of years, no such formal requirement applies to Mental Health Review Tribunals. However, the Lord Chancellor's policy is that a nominee is "never" considered suitably experienced unless he is aged 35 years or over and has been practising for seven years or more since qualifying.

Candidate's Health

The candidate must satisfy the Lord Chancellor that his health is satisfactory. In some cases a candidate is examined by the Medical Adviser while in others he is asked to arrange for his doctor to submit a report. The guidance does not indicate what view is taken by the Lord Chancellor if a candidate has a history of mental health problems.

Character

Checks are made to confirm that candidates do not have criminal records and further checks are made with the Inland Revenue and HM Customs and Excise to ensure that there have been no past "difficulties" over the payment of tax or VAT.

Functions

The legal member's statutory function is simply to preside at hearings and, as a member of the tribunal, to hear and determine the application or reference in accordance with the law. In more practical terms, the legal member's principal functions, as set out in the job description, are[301] —

- To read the papers received from the tribunal office prior to the hearing and, if necessary, to discuss with the tribunal office the need for any additional reports or information, seeking where necessary a direction from the regional chairman.

- To preside at the hearing and to advise the other members of the tribunal on matters of law, especially with regard to the tribunal's powers and the application of the statutory criteria. As to this, the job description states that presidents "should note that no decisions are reserved to them by the rules and that each member of the tribunal is entitled to an equal voice on matters of law, procedure and substance."[302]

- To meet the other members of the tribunal approximately half an hour before the commencement of the actual hearing in order to discuss and agree preliminary matters.

- At the commencement of the actual hearing, to introduce the members of the tribunal to the patient and to the other persons present and to explain that they are independent; to explain the manner of proceeding which the tribunal proposes to adopt and, in appropriate cases, the tribunal's powers.[303]

---

[301] See "Legal Member's Job Description" in *Mental Health Review Tribunals for England and Wales, Annual Report 1994* (Department of Health, 1995), Appendix 13.

[302] The alternative interpretation is that the president should determine points of law, since he is by definition presiding over the hearing and, inter alia, responsible for ensuring that it is lawfully conducted.

[303] See Mental Health Review Tribunal Rules 1983, r.22(3).

- To ensure that the proceedings are conducted in a fair and impartial manner, avoiding inappropriate formality, excessive length and generally seeing that the tribunal is managed well.

- To take a note of the proceedings.

- At the conclusion of the evidence, to ensure that the tribunal members together deliberate on all relevant matters in addressing the statutory criteria and reaching the tribunal's decision. As to this, the job description states that "once the decision has been agreed the President should draft the reasons therefor, taking into account the contributions of the other members, and should record and sign the decision which has been reached."[304]

- To inform the patient how and when the decision will be communicated to him.[305]

MEDICAL MEMBERS

The Act provides that each of the regional tribunals shall consist of a number of medical members, being registered medical practitioners appointed by the Lord Chancellor after consultation with the Secretary of State for Health or the Secretary of State for Wales.[306] In practice, medical members are invariably consultant psychiatrists or retired consultants. The current practice is for prospective medical members to be interviewed by the appropriate regional chairman and the Clerk to the Tribunal. Their recommendations are then considered by the Department of Health or the Welsh Office before being forwarded to the Lord Chancellor's Department.

Functions

The medical member's principal functions, as set out in the job description, are[307] —

- To conduct a preliminary examination of the patient prior to the hearing and to take such steps as he considers necessary to form an opinion of the patient's mental condition. These steps should include reference to hospital documentation and discussions with hospital staff.[308]

- To inform the tribunal office of any potential problems arising out of the preliminary examination which might affect the hearing procedures, and if necessary refer back to the regional chairman on any matter which he believes requires a preliminary direction.

- To advise the tribunal office, at its request, with regard to the withdrawal of applications, the need for legal representation and similar matters. To inform

---

[304]   See Mental Health Review Tribunal Rules 1983, r.23(2).
[305]   See *ibid.*, r.24(1).
[306]   Mental Health Act 1983, s.65(3), Sched. 2, para. 1(b).
[307]   "Medical Member's Job Description" in *Mental Health Review Tribunals for England and Wales, Annual Report 1994* (Department of Health, 1995), Appendix 13.
[308]   See Mental Health Review Tribunal Rules 1983, r.11.

the tribunal office if he discovers at the preliminary examination that the patient is not legally represented.[309]

- To consider the possibility of any conflict of interest arising from any former contact with the patient and to notify the tribunal office accordingly.[310]

- To report to the other members of the tribunal, when requested, of his preliminary examination and to advise and explain terminology and technicalities as necessary.

- To meet the other members of the tribunal approximately half an hour before the commencement of the actual hearing in order to discuss and agree preliminary matters (**805**).

- To put questions to each of the witnesses who give evidence at the hearing as he considers relevant. As to this, the job description states, "In particular, the medical member may consider it appropriate to question the RMO (responsible medical officer) in relation to the patient's history, progress, treatment, prognosis and future care, although he must bear in mind that the hearing is not a seminar nor a case conference. In appropriate cases he may lead the questioning of the RMO if this has been agreed beforehand with the other members of the tribunal. However, he must appreciate that he performs a dual role at the tribunal as a fact-finder and as a decision-maker and it is therefore essential that his opinion of the patient's mental condition, if it differs significantly from that of the RMO, should be made known to everyone in the course of his questioning. Thus a situation will be avoided where the members of a tribunal are acting on the basis of evidence known only to themselves, which would, of course, be a breach of a fundamental principle of natural justice and likely to invalidate the decision."

- At the conclusion of the evidence, to participate in the members' discussion so as to enable a decision to be reached, and to contribute as appropriate to the drafting of the record of the decision and of the reasons therefor.

LAY MEMBERS

The Act provides that each of the regional tribunals shall consist of a number of persons appointed by the Lord Chancellor, after consultation with the Secretary of State for Health or the Secretary of State for Wales, who have such experience in administration, such knowledge of social services or such other qualifications or experience as the Lord Chancellor considers suitable.[311] These members are known by custom as the tribunal's "lay members." The relevant regional chairman and the clerk to that tribunal interview prospective lay members and their recommendations are then considered by the Department of Health or the Welsh Office before being forwarded to the Lord Chancellor's Department.

---

[309]   See Mental Health Review Tribunal Rules 1983, rr.10 and 19.
[310]   See Mental Health Review Tribunal Rules 1983, r.8(2)(c).
[311]   Mental Health Act 1983, s.65(3), Sched. 2, para. 1(c).

Suitable experience

The general approach as to what constitutes suitable experience is summarised in the most recent annual report on the work of tribunals—

"Lay members need reasonable familiarity with health and social services to enable them to understand why the patient is appealing, what they have experienced in hospital, and what community facilities and social supports might be available to a patient on discharge. Lay members should preferably have some interest in or experience of mental health and/or learning disability. This may have come through membership of a mental health voluntary organisation, being a hospital visitor or befriender, or from life/work experience which brings them into contact with a range of people — for example through being a magistrate, teacher, trade union official, managing a business or being involved in local government or charitable organisations. In practice 'lay' might be thought a misnomer in relation to the present Tribunal lay members who include mental health professionals, hospital administrators, social workers and nurses."[312]

Functions

The lay member's statutory function is simply to act as a member of a tribunal hearing and determining an application or reference by or in respect of a patient. The rationale for including an informed member of the general public in the decision-making process is that any consideration of whether a particular member of society is mentally disordered, and whether his detention is justified or necessary to protect other members of society, is not exclusively a question for lawyers and medical practitioners to determine alone (**1016**). The lay member therefore represents the view of the informed public, the responsible lay person, and his principal functions as set out in the job description are[313] —

- To acquire a basic understanding of the legal framework determining detention, discharge and the powers of the tribunal and some knowledge of health and social services systems.

- To read and consider any papers received from the tribunal office prior to the hearing with a view to ascertaining the main features of the patient's history and the reasons for his detention.

- To consider the possibility of any conflict of interest due to any former contact with the patient and to notify the tribunal office or, as the case may be, the other tribunal members accordingly.

- To meet the other members of the tribunal approximately half an hour before the commencement of the actual hearing in order to discuss and agree preliminary matters (**805**).

- To put such questions to each of the witnesses who give evidence at the hearing as may be relevant and, in appropriate cases, to lead the questioning

---

[312] *Mental Health Review Tribunals for England and Wales, Annual Report 1994* (Department of Health, 1995), p.10.

[313] "Lay Member's Job Description" in *Mental Health Review Tribunals for England and Wales, Annual Report 1994* (Department of Health, 1995), Appendix 13.

of the social worker if this has been agreed beforehand with the other members of the tribunal.

- At the conclusion of the evidence, to participate in the members' discussion so as to enable a decision to be reached, and to contribute as appropriate to the drafting of the record of the decision and of the reasons therefor — "In reaching such a decision the lay member is entitled to an equal voice with the other members of the tribunal on all questions of law, procedure and substance."

REGIONAL CHAIRMEN

The 1983 Act provides that one of the legal members of each regional Mental Health Review Tribunal shall be appointed by the Lord Chancellor as its chairman.[314] The statutory functions of the regional chairmen are to exercise the tribunal's powers as regards the preliminary and incidental matters specified in the rules (777) and to appoint members for particular tribunal hearings. If "for any reason" the chairman is "unable to act" he may appoint another legal member to exercise his functions.[315] The chairmen meet together regularly to consider issues of policy and practice and, perhaps surprisingly given their status as independent judicial bodies, representatives from the Home Office also attend these meetings. The chairmen's various non-statutory duties include the following[316] —

- To be responsible for the administration of the regional tribunal in conjunction with the staff of the tribunal office.

- To preside at a number of hearings so as to acquire a broad experience of members and current issues.

- To provide guidance to members whenever appropriate on preliminary and incidental matters, hearing procedures, including decision making, manner of questioning of witnesses and good practice generally.

- In co-operation with the staff of the tribunal office to organise meetings, conferences and training for members.

- To interview candidates for membership, to assess their suitability and to advise the Department of Health and the Lord Chancellor's Department accordingly.

---

[314] Mental Health Act 1983, s.65(3), Sched. 2, para. 3. Some other tribunals — such as the Social Security, Medical, Vaccine Damage, Disability Appeal and Child Support Appeal Tribunals — have a national President rather than a number of regional chairman. Mental health review tribunals have in the past been criticised, notably by Peay, for inconsistency in their interpretation of their functions, in practice, and in decision-making. At the beginning of the 1990s, the Department of Health Management Consultancy Unit Review of the MHRT Secretariat recommended discussions with the Lord Chancellor's Department concerning the appointment of a national President for MHRTs with a view to ensuring greater consistency in national policy: see His Honour Judge Holden, "Presidential System In Relation To Tribunals" in *Members' Newsheet*, Issue 9 (1992).

[315] Mental Health Act 1983, ss.65(3) and 78(6) and Sched. 2, para. 4; Mental Health Review Tribunal Rules 1983, r.2(1).

[316] "Role of the Regional Chairman" in *Mental Health Review Tribunals for England and Wales, Annual Report 1994* (Department of Health, 1995), Appendix 13.

- To advise the Department of Health and the Lord Chancellor's Department on the suitability of members for re-appointment.

- To monitor the performance and usage of members in his region by, for example, attending tribunal hearings as an observer.

- To meet other regional chairmen regularly in order to devise and agree national policies.

- As necessary to liaise with other agencies, such as health authorities and The Law Society, and provide information on practical and procedural matters.

APPOINTMENT OF MEMBERS IN A PARTICULAR CASE

The members who are to constitute a Mental Health Review Tribunal in a particular case are appointed by the chairman of the tribunal or, if for any reason he is unable to act, by another member of the tribunal appointed for the purpose by the chairman. Of the members so appointed one or more shall be appointed from the legal members; one or more shall be appointed from the medical members; and one or more shall be appointed from the lay members.[317] A member of a Mental Health Review Tribunal for one area may be appointed as one of the persons to constitute a tribunal for another area for the purposes of any proceedings or class or group of proceedings. Where this happens, he is deemed to be a member of that other Tribunal for the purposes of the proceedings for which he was appointed.[318] Where the regional chairman is included among the persons appointed, he is the president of the tribunal; and in any other case the president shall be the legal member or, if more than one of them has been appointed, such one as the chairman may nominate.[319] There is no statutory bar to the same President presiding over successive applications in respect of the same patient.[320] Notwithstanding the above, a tribunal almost invariably consists of three members, one appointed from each category, and it is exceptional for a tribunal to consist of four or more members.

Restricted cases

In any case involving a restricted patient, the president is chosen from a panel of legal members, comprising circuit judges or silk recorders, approved by the Lord Chancellor to hear such cases. For these purposes, the legal members are allocated to one of two regions, North or South. As at 31 December 1994, there were 20 legal members appointed to hear restricted cases in the Southern region, of whom five were Queen's Counsel and 15 Judges (one of whom was also a QC). There were 26 legal members appointed to hear restricted cases in the Northern Region, ten of whom were also QCs.

---

[317] Mental Health Act 1983, s.65(3) and Sched. 2, para. 4; Mental Health Review Tribunal Rules 1983, rr.8 and 31.

[318] Mental Health Act 1983, s.65(3) and Sched. 2, para. 5.

[319] Mental Health Act 1983, s.65(3) and Sched. 2, para. 6.

[320] See *R. v. Oxford Regional Mental Health Review Tribunal, ex p. Mackman, The Times*, 2 June 1986. However, if a tribunal's decision is quashed and a new hearing directed, this will generally be before a differently constituted tribunal.

POWERS AND JURISDICTION

Although a Mental Health Review Tribunal is a court for most purposes, nevertheless its powers are more limited than those of most courts which are not also tribunals. Its powers are those prescribed by or under the statute and it has no inherent jurisdiction. So, for example, it has no jurisdiction to award costs against a party because neither that Act nor the tribunal rules provide for this.

Part V of the Mental Health Act 1983

Part V of the Mental Health Act 1983, which comprises sections 65 to 79, is concerned with Mental Health Review Tribunals, their constitution and powers, and certain related matters of similar importance. It is customary to note that the provisions are to be interpreted in the context of the statutory framework as a whole although this is something of a generalisation because the different Parts of the Act have their own frameworks. For example, the framework in relation to restricted patients admitted by order of the Crown Court — in respect of whom tribunals have no discretionary power of discharge or power to recommend leave or transfer — is manifestly different from that pertaining to persons admitted under Part II without any prior court order or judicial involvement. The general statutory presumption in favour of liberty therefore applies without qualification to the civil procedures, there being no judicial order authorising the citizen's detention. More generally, there is also a presumption that Acts of Parliament are not intended to derogate from the requirements of international law. This presumption has been relied upon to enable courts to have regard to the provisions of the European Convention on Human Rights as a means of restricting the operation of certain statutes.[321] As to the general rules of statutory construction—

- The literal rule states that courts are bound by the words of a statute where those words clearly govern and cover the situation before it and, in such cases, they must be applied with nothing added and nothing taken away. Recourse cannot be had to an earlier statute if the word in the Act in force is clear and unambiguous, and such references cannot be used to suggest or create an ambiguity where none exists.

- The approach to interpreting the fringe meaning of a word used in a statute is something of a legal fiction. The approach in practice tends to be to guess what meaning Parliament would have picked on had it thought of the point, and by reference also to considerations of convenience, social requirements, and accepted principles of fairness.

- The Latin maxim "*noscitur a sociis*" means that "a word may be known by the company it keeps." In construing a statutory provision, courts may look at the section as a whole, even the whole statute, and even at earlier legislation. Exceptionally, a word used twice within a single section has been interpreted as bearing two distinct meanings, *e.g.* the phrase "liable to be detained" in the 1983 Act.

---

[321] See *e.g. ex p. Miah* [1974] 1 W.L.R. 694, *per* Lord Reid; *R. v. Home Secretary, ex p. Bhajan Singh* [1976] 1 Q.B. 207, *per* Lord Denning M.R.; *Ahmad v I.L.E.A.* [1978] Q.B. at p.48, *per* Lord Scarman.

- The "golden rule" (interpretations necessary to avoid absurdity) allows the court to prefer a sensible meaning to an absurd if literally correct meaning, *e.g.* replacing "or" with "and," and the court may read in, ignore or alter a word in the statute being interpreted if not to do so would make the provision unintelligible, absurd, unworkable, totally unreasonable or totally irreconcilable with other provisions within the same Act. The need to apply the rule must, however, be clear-cut.

- The "mischief rule"[322] bids the courts to look at the position before the Act and the mischief that the statute was intended to remedy. The statute is then construed in such a way as to suppress the mischief and advance the remedy.

Mental Health Review Tribunal Rules 1983

The procedure for dealing with authorised applications or references is that set out in the Mental Health Review Tribunal Rules 1983 although, as with all tribunals, the rules must be applied in a way which accords with the basic principles of procedure known as the rules of natural justice or "fairness." Consequently, certain minimum standards of evidence and proof must be observed if justice is to be done.[323] The statutory authority for the rules derives from section 78 of the Act, which provides that the Lord Chancellor may make rules with respect to the making of tribunal applications and references, the proceedings of such tribunals and matters incidental or consequential thereto. Section 78(2) states that the rules may in particular provide for the matters specified in paragraphs (a) to (k) of that subsection. Paragraph (j) is drafted in general terms and empowers conferring on tribunals such ancillary powers as the Lord Chancellor thinks necessary for the purposes of exercising their statutory functions. The rules may be so framed as to apply to all applications or references or instead make different provision for different cases.[324] In particular, they may prescribe the procedure to be adopted in cases concerning restricted patients.[325] The Lord Chancellor's power to make rules is exercisable by statutory instrument[326] and such statutory instruments are subject to annulment in pursuance of a resolution of either House of Parliament.[327] The Council on Tribunals must be consulted before any such rules are made. Subject to these same conditions and limitations, the Lord Chancellor may revoke or amend the rules.[328]

---

[322] The Rule in *Heydon's Case* (1584) 3 Co. Rep. at 7b.

[323] See *e.g. R. v. Deputy Industrial Injuries Commissioner, ex p. Moore* [1965] 1 Q.B. 456.

[324] Mental Health Act 1983, s.78(5).

[325] *Ibid.*, s.78(4).

[326] *Ibid.*, s.143(1).

[327] *Ibid., s.143(2)*. This form of Parliamentary control is known as the "negative procedure." The statutory instrument is laid before the House after it is made and during the following forty days is subject to being made void by a resolution of either the House of Commons or House of Lords. During this period, the document is scrutinised by a committee of both Houses called the Joint Committee on Statutory Insuments. The committee may draw Parliament's attention to certain technical defects, including defects in drafting, but not challenge the merits of or policy behind the instrument. The alternative form of Parliamentary control known as the "affirmative procedure" requires that a draft of the statutory instrument is first approved by a resolution of each House of Parliament. The affirmative procedure applies to orders made under s.68(4) or s.71(3), *i.e.* it does not extend to the tribunal rules made under s.78.

[328] See Interpretation Act 1978, s.14.

Exercise and interpretation of the rules

The tribunal rules are a form of "subordinate legislation."[329] Unless a contrary intention appears, words in a statutory instrument which repeat those used in the Act from which its authority derives should be given a construction identical with that of the statute.[330] The rules are also to be construed (1) so as to be reconciled with the plain terms of the Act under which they are made and, in cases of inconsistency, the subordinate legislation must give way; (2) in accordance with the ordinary meaning of language and, as regards words specially defined, in accordance with the meaning of the definitions similarly construed; and (3) sensibly, in order to give effect to the intention so far as it can be ascertained from the words. Subject to minor exceptions, the provisions in the Interpretation Act 1978 apply "so far as applicable and unless the contrary intention appears."[331] Thus, unless the contrary intention appears, (1) expressions used in the rules have the meaning which they bear in the Act; (2) words importing the masculine gender include the feminine and vice-versa and, similarly, words in the singular include the plural and vice-versa; (3) where a power is conferred or a duty imposed by the rules, it is implied that the power may be exercised or the duty performed from time to time as occasion requires and, if imposed on the regional chairman, that it may be exercised or performed by the present holder of that office. Practice notes provided by the Department of Health for the assistance of officials concerned in the administration of a statute are inadmissible for the purpose of construing a statute and presumably also inadmissible as concerns the construction of statutory instruments.

THE SUPERVISION OF TRIBUNALS

The way in which a tribunal exercises its functions in a particular case is reviewable by the High Court while the way in which they discharge their functions generally is subject to supervision by the regional chairmen, the Council on Tribunals and the Mental Health Act Commission.

Judicial control

A tribunal's decision in any particular case is subject to judicial review by the High Court where it is alleged that its decision was reached unlawfully. Likewise, a tribunal may be required to state a point of law for determination by the High Court if its decision rests on an interpretation of some point of law which is disputed by one of the parties or, in a restricted case, by the Secretary of State.

The Council on Tribunals

Statutory tribunals are subject to supervision by the Council on Tribunals, which was originally established by the Tribunals and Inquiries Act 1958 and is now constituted under the Tribunals and Inquiries Act 1992. The Council is essentially an advisory body and it has no rule-making or decision-making powers. The general functions of the Council, as set out in section 1(1) of the Tribunals and Inquiries Act 1992, and insofar as relevant, are to keep under review the constitution and working of tribunals such as Mental Health Review Tribunals; to report from time to time on their constitution and working; and to consider and report on such particular matters

---

[329] Interpretation Act 1978, s.21.

[330] *Ibid.*, s.11.

[331] *Ibid.*, s.23. Any reference to an "enactment" in the 1978 Act includes an enactment comprised in subordinate legislation.

as may be referred to it by the Lord Chancellor. It may make "general" recommendations about appointments to membership of Mental Health Review Tribunals and the tribunal rules may only be amended by the Lord Chancellor after consultation with the Council.[332] It should be emphasised that, as with the Mental Health Act Commission, the Council's function is not to review a tribunal's decision in a particular case, or the way in which those particular proceedings were conducted or heard. These are matters entirely within the tribunal's discretion unless it is alleged that the flaws were so fundamental that the decision should be set aside, in which case it becomes a matter for the High Court.

Mental Health Act Commission

The Secretary of State for Health is under a statutory duty to keep under review the exercise of the powers and the discharge of the duties conferred or imposed by the Act so far as they relate to patients who liable to be detained under the Act.[333] The Act also provides that the statutory powers and duties which must be kept under review do not include any exercisable by the Court of Protection under Part VII, but no such exception applies to powers and duties exercised by a tribunal under Part V.[334] Thus, they must be kept under review. Moreover, the Secretary of State is further bound by statute to direct the Commission to perform on his behalf this function of keeping under review the way in which the various statutory powers and duties are discharged.[335] Consequently, the Commission has no discretion and must review the workings of tribunals, insofar as they relate to detained patients, although in practice it does so with some reluctance.

STATISTICAL INFORMATION

The number of tribunal applications has steadily increased since the 1983 Act came into force and, since 1988, the number of applications has risen by 10–15 per cent. each year. In 1984, 3558 applications were received, which figure had risen to 12,247 by 1994. The number of applications received by tribunals and the number of cases heard by them in 1994 is set out below.

NUMBER OF TRIBUNAL APPLICATIONS AND HEARINGS IN 1994

	Applications received	Number of hearings	Hearings as % of applications
Section 2 patients	3770	2228	59.1%
Other non-restricted patients	6915	3232	46.7%
Restricted patients	1562	1303	83.4%

Source : Mental Health Review Tribunals for England and Wales, Annual Report 1994, Department of Health, London, May 1995, Appendices 3 and 4.

---

[332] Tribunal and Inquiries Act 1992, ss.5(1) and 8(1).
[333] Mental Health Act 1983, s.120(1).
[334] *Ibid.*, s.120(7).
[335] *Ibid.*, s.121(2)(b).

The number of hearings held is always less than the number of applications and references received. In the case of section 2 applications, which must be heard within one week of receipt, some 40 per cent. of applications did not proceed to a hearing. In almost all of those cases this would have been because the responsible medical officer himself discharged the patient during the intervening period. In other non-restricted cases, over half of the applications did not proceed to a hearing. This partly reflects the fact that there were 11 per cent. more applications in 1994 than in 1993 and applications made towards the end of each year were not be heard until the following year. Some applications would also have been withdrawn although, balancing this, mandatory references cannot be withdrawn. It is therefore likely that about half of all non-restricted patients detained for treatment are discharged by the responsible medical officer prior to any hearing taking place. The fact that fewer cases involving patients detained for treatment proceeded to a hearing reflects the delays which occur in arranging such hearings — the time taken to hear such cases is considerably longer than the time which the average patient spends in hospital. The difference between the number of applications and hearings is significantly less in restricted cases. This reflects the fact that restricted patients continue to be liable to be detained unless discharged by a tribunal or the Secretary of State. It is not possible for the patient's responsible medical officer to unilaterally terminate the patient's liability to detention under the Act.

Number of patients discharged

The proportion of patients discharged by tribunals varies according to the authority for detention. It has been noted that in 1994 tribunals heard 2228 section 2 applications. 18.8 per cent. of patients were discharged, the remaining 81.2 per cent. of patients not being discharged. Because about 41 per cent. of the applications did not proceed to a hearing, this means that some 55–60 per cent. of patients had ceased to be detained under section 2 during the 7–10 period following the making of the application. Of the 3005 hearings involving other non-restricted patients, 15.6 per cent. were discharged while 26.1 per cent. of the 674 hearings involving restricted patients resulted in absolute or conditional discharge. Thus, a higher proportion of restricted patients were discharged than were unrestricted patients detained for treatment and this may reflect the fact that tribunals are more willing to discharge when they can do so subject to conditions.

Regional variations

From the table below it can be seen that there were significant variations between the different tribunals in terms of the proportion of patients discharged. For example, only 8.3 per cent. of section 2 cases and 7.8 per cent. of other non-restricted cases heard by the Northern and Yorkshire Mental Health Review Tribunal resulted in discharge. By contrast, 33.7 per cent. of the section 2 patients whose cases were heard by the Mental Health Review Tribunal for Wales were discharged and 40.5 per cent. of other non-restricted patients. These differences cannot be explained in terms of differences in the number of applications which proceeded to a hearing. Nor can they be explained in terms of a lower, and hence more discriminating, use of compulsory powers in the areas where the discharge rate was relatively low — both the Northern and Yorkshire and the Trent regions have relatively low rates of formal admissions per 100,000 population compared with England as a whole while North Thames has the highest. It would seem therefore that the most likely explanation for the differences lies in the constitution or procedures of the tribunals themselves.

TRIBUNAL DISCHARGES IN 1994 BY REGION

	Section 2 hearings (% apps)	Discharged	Other non-restricted hearings	Discharged
North Thames	426 (59%)	22.3%	519 (38%)	13.1%
Anglia & Oxford	134 (60%)	15.7%	376 (51%)	10.1%
South Thames	352 (58%)	25.9%	383 (41%)	26.6%
South & West	215 (61%)	18.6%	349 (51%)	13.8%
Trent	183 (62%)	12.0%	214 (49%)	13.6%
Northern & Yorkshire	241 (62%)	8.3%	357 (50%)	7.8%
West Midlands	218 (49%)	24.8%	234 (40%)	14.5%
North West	364 (60%)	12.1%	425 (47%)	14.8%
Wales	95 (60%)	33.7%	148 (47%)	40.5%
Total	**2228 (59%)**	**18.8%**	**3005 (45%)**	**15.6%**

Source : Mental Health Review Tribunals for England and Wales, Annual Report 1994, Department of Health, London, May 1995, Appendices 3 and 4.

Special hospital cases

The general pattern that a higher proportion of restricted patients are discharged by tribunals than are unrestricted patients detained for treatment extends to special hospital patients except those at Broadmoor. However, not surprisingly, fewer of them in either category are discharged.

SPECIAL HOSPITAL APPLICATIONS AND HEARINGS IN 1994

	No. of hearings	Discharged MHRT	% discharged
Non-restricted patients	227	7	3.1%
Restricted patients	629	27	4.3%
Total	856	34	4.0%

Source : Mental Health Review Tribunals for England and Wales, Annual Report 1994, Department of Health, London, May 1995, Appendices 3 and 4.

It should, however, be noted that there were different patterns of outcome for the three special hospitals. Five of the seven non-restricted patients discharged by tribunals during by 1994 were detained at Broadmoor, where 61 of the 227 hearings were held. Thus, while 8.2 per cent. of non-restricted Broadmoor patients were discharged, only one of the 74 non-restricted hearings held at Ashworth and one of the 92 hearings held at Rampton resulted in discharge. Proportionately more restricted than unrestricted patients at Rampton and Ashworth were discharged.

SPECIAL HOSPITAL PATIENTS DISCHARGED IN 1994

	% non-restricted	% restricted	% discharged
Broadmoor	8.2%	5.6%	6.4%
Ashworth	1.4%	2.1%	1.9%
Rampton	1.1%	5.5%	4.1%

Source : Mental Health Review Tribunals for England and Wales, Annual Report 1994, Department of Health, London, May 1995, Appendices 3 and 4.

4. Detention and guardianship under Part II

INTRODUCTION

The distinctive feature of compulsory admission under Part II of the Mental Health Act 1983 is that the individual is deprived of his liberty upon an application for his detention being made to the managers of a hospital rather than to a court. Similarly, reception into guardianship involves the acceptance of an application not by a court but by a local social services authority. In each case, the application may be made by the patient's nearest relative (**100**) or an approved social worker (**160**).

THE FIVE TYPES OF APPLICATION

Part II of the Act makes provision for five different kinds of application.

PART II OF THE MENTAL HEALTH ACT

Section	Type of application	Purpose
2	*Admission for assessment*	An application for a person to be detained in hospital for assessment, followed by any necessary treatment, for up to 28 days.
4	*Emergency application*	A section 2 application initially founded upon a single medical recommendation where admission is urgently necessary. Lapses after 72 hours unless the full section 2 procedures have by then been completed.
3	*Admission for treatment*	An application for a person to be detained in hospital for treatment for up to six months. The authority to detain the patient may be renewed for further periods in certain circumstances.
7	*Guardianship application*	An application for a person to be placed under the guardianship of a local social services authority or a private individual for up to six months. The guardian's authority may be renewed for further periods in certain circumstances.
25A	*Supervision application*	An application for a person detained for treatment to be subject to after-care under supervision once he ceases to be liable to be detained.

Part II and Mental Health Review Tribunals

With the possible exception of persons detained under section 4, all patients subject to compulsory powers upon the acceptance of an application may apply to a tribunal for their discharge from detention, guardianship or supervision, as the case may be. Provision is also made for the cases of detained patients to be periodically referred to a tribunal if no application has been made for a certain period of time.

Supervision applications

The provisions in the Mental Health Act 1983 concerning supervision applications were inserted by the Mental Health (Patients in the Community) Act 1995, which came into force on 1 April 1996. The new statutory procedures governing the making of supervision applications differ in many respects from those which apply to the four other kinds of application. Applications which relate to detention in hospital or reception into guardianship all adhere to a similar statutory framework — one which has its origins in the Mental Health Act 1959 and was then readopted in the 1983 statute as originally enacted. A further peculiar feature of the new supervision applications is that they cannot be made unless the patient is already liable to be detained in hospital for treatment. This is because their purpose is to provide a statutory framework for supervising in the community patients who have ceased to be liable to detention for treatment. The pre-existing authority for the patient's detention in hospital for treatment will usually be a previous application made under section 3 but it could equally be a court order or a direction given by the Secretary of State authorising his detention there. These orders and directions, made under Part III of the Act, are considered in the following chapter. Supervision application procedures therefore depart from what may be called the classical model and are initially grafted on to some prior application, order or direction authorising the individual's detention. For these two reasons, and in particular because it is crucial to keep the two different statutory frameworks distinct, they are not further considered in this chapter. They are dealt with later in the context of after-care and what follows in this chapter is exclusively concerned with the four kinds of application contained in the statute as originally enacted.

THE BASIC APPLICATION FRAMEWORK

Subject to a single caveat, the basic framework is the same for all applications authorising detention or guardianship under Part II. Detention or guardianship requires (a) the acceptance by a hospital or local social services authority (b) of an application in the prescribed form (c) made by a qualified person (the patient's nearest relative or an approved social worker) (d) which is founded upon written medical recommendations in the prescribed form (e) of two medical practitioners (f) both of whom have recently examined the patient and have no personal interest (g) and one of whom is approved as having special experience in the diagnosis or treatment of mental disorder. The exception is that in cases of urgent necessity an application for admission for assessment may initially be founded upon a single medical recommendation — this is the emergency application procedure set out in section 4. The medical evidence upon which an application must be founded, and the other legal formalities to be observed, are dealt with later (**253**), following consideration of the grounds of application and the main distinguishing features of each kind of application.

THE GROUNDS OF APPLICATION

Sections 2(2), 3(2), and 7(2) set out the grounds upon which an application may be made for a person's admission to hospital or reception into guardianship. The grounds, while necessarily different, conform to the same basic framework in that two questions must always be addressed. The first of the two grounds has variously been described as the "diagnostic question"[1] and as "the medical question."[2] This requires the existence of a mental disorder the nature or degree of which makes in-patient treatment appropriate or warrants the patient's reception into guardianship or detention for assessment. The second ground requires that detention or guardianship is either "necessary" or "justified" on the patient's own account (specifically his health, safety or welfare) or that of others (in order to protect them). This second ground has been described as a "mixed medical and social question"[3] and as having, like the first, a medical content but also incorporating ethical, social and public policy considerations.[4] An alternative view would be that the first ground requires the existence of a serious mental disorder while the second ground is directed towards the issue of risk — the likelihood of harm resulting if the individual is not subjected to some element of compulsion (**723**).

Cases of psychopathic disorder and mental impairment

A third ground of application must be satisfied in the case of section 3 applications concerning persons suffering from psychopathic disorder or mental impairment, which is that in-patient treatment is likely to alleviate or prevent a deterioration of the patient's condition. This condition has come to be known as the "treatability test" (**222**).

GUIDING PRINCIPLES

The Royal Commission of 1954–57[5] spelt out the circumstances in which it considered that the use of compulsory powers was justified. Paragraph 317 of the Commission's report states—

"We consider that the use of special compulsory powers on grounds of the patient's mental disorder is justifiable when:

a. there is reasonable certainty that the patient is suffering from a pathological mental disorder and requires hospital or community care; and

b. suitable care cannot be provided without the use of compulsory powers; and

c. if the patient himself is unwilling to receive the form of care which is considered necessary, there is at least a strong likelihood that his unwillingness is due to a lack of appreciation of his own condition deriving from the mental disorder itself; and

---

[1]   By Forbes J. in *R. v. Mental Health Review Tribunal, ex p. Pickering* [1986] 1 All E.R. 99.
[2]   By Lawton L.J. in *R. v. Oxford Mental Health Review Tribunal, ex p. Secretary of State for the Home Department; R. v. Yorkshire Mental Health Review Tribunal, ex p. Same* [1986] 1 W.L.R. 1180.
[3]   By Lawton L.J. in *R. v. Oxford Mental Health Review Tribunal, ex p. Secretary of State for the Home Department* (supra).
[4]   By Forbes J. in *R. v. Mental Health Review Tribunal, ex p. Pickering* (supra).
[5]   *Report of the Royal Commission on the Law Relating to Mental Illness and Mental Deficiency,* Cmnd. 169 (1957).

d. there is also either—

    i. good prospect of benefit to the patient from the treatment proposed — an expectation that it will either cure or alleviate his mental disorder or strengthen his ability to regulate his social behaviour in spite of the underlying disorder, or bring him substantial benefit in the form of protection from neglect or exploitation by others;

    ii. a strong need to protect others from anti-social behaviour by the patient."

The statutory framework

The Commission's views found expression in the 1959 Act and the present statute by and large adopts the same approach. The Minister of Health explained the Government's aims in relation to the new civil procedures during the Parliamentary debate of 5th May 1959:

> "We had in mind all the time to try and assemble a structure which would reflect the balance of the considerations we must have in mind. They are, firstly, the liberty of the subject, secondly, the necessity of bringing treatment to bear where treatment is required and can be beneficial to the individual and, thirdly, the consideration of the protection of the public. All though I have tried steadily to keep in mind that what we are trying to do is to erect as balanced a structure as we may which can give effect to all those things in harmony with each other."[6]

MENTAL DISORDER OF THE REQUISITE NATURE OR DEGREE

The first ground of application requires that the patient is suffering from mental disorder, whether generally or from one of its specific forms, and that the nature or degree of this disorder is sufficiently serious to make in-patient treatment appropriate or to warrant his reception into guardianship or detention for assessment. An application in respect of a patient may be made on the grounds that:

• section 2	he is suffering from mental disorder of a nature or degree which warrants the detention of the patient in a hospital for assessment (or for assessment followed by medical treatment) for at least a limited period (s.2(2)(a));
• section 3	he is suffering from mental illness, severe mental impairment, psychopathic disorder or mental impairment and his mental disorder is of a nature or degree which makes it appropriate for him to receive medical treatment in a hospital (s.3(2)(a));
• guardianship	he is suffering from mental disorder, being mental illness, severe mental impairment, psychopathic disorder or mental impairment and his mental disorder is of a nature or degree which warrants his reception into guardianship under this section (s.7(2)(a));

---

[6] The Minister of Health (Mr. Derek Walker-Smith), *Hansard*, H.C. Vol. 605, col. 276.

The presence of a mental disorder

Compulsory admission for assessment requires medical evidence to the effect only that the patient is suffering from mental disorder generally, as defined in section 1(2). However, an application for a person's admission for treatment or for his reception into guardianship requires evidence that the patient suffers from at least one of the four particular forms of mental disorder set out in section 1(2).

"Suffering from"

The term's meaning and relevance was considered during the inquiry into the circumstances surrounding the death of Georgina Robinson, an occupational therapist working at the Edith Morgan Centre at Torbay District General Hospital.[7] *The inquiry team referred to the case of Devon County Council v Hawkins.*[8] Having found that the patient was likely to suffer further epileptic seizures if he ceased taking his medication, the court in that case had held that whether a person "suffers from" epilepsy depends on the prognosis of what will occur if anti-convulsant medication is withdrawn. The Lord Chief Justice observed that it had been said with much force "that so long as it is necessary for a person to be under treatment for a disease or disability, then that person must be held to be suffering from that disease or disability. In my judgment that is in general right." By analogy, whether or not a person who has been receiving psychiatric treatment, but who presently shows no signs of mental disorder, still "suffers from" mental disorder depends on the likely effect of discontinuing treatment. The fact that an illness is asymptomatic does not demonstrate *per se* that he is not suffering from mental disorder or that any disorder from which he does suffer is not of a severe nature.

The nature or degree of the disorder

Where there is evidence of mental disorder, the use of compulsory powers requires that it is of a "nature or degree" which either makes in-patient treatment appropriate or warrants the patient's detention for assessment or reception into guardianship ("the diagnostic question"). Practitioners and tribunals commonly confine their consideration of a patient's mental state to the degree of mental disorder present, seemingly interpreting the words "nature" and "degree" as essentially interchangeable. Accordingly, a patient is considered not to be detainable if his condition has responded to medication and is no longer acute. This approach takes no real account of the nature of the particular disorder and mistakenly equates its "degree" with its "severity." As such, there is a failure to give due weight to the chronicity of the disorder and the prognosis.

"Degree"

The word "degree" focuses attention on the extent to which the person's mental disorder is currently active. If a patient is acutely ill, his condition characterised by obvious and gross abnormalities in his mental state, the degree of mental disorder present will generally be of a level which satisfies the first ground of application. It is noteworthy that the emergency power to detain a patient for six hours under

---

[7]   *The Falling Shadow: One Patient's Mental Health Care 1978–1993* (Duckworth, 1995), pp. 153–169.

[8]   *Devon County Council v Hawkins* [1967] 2 Q.B. 26.

section 5(4) is exercisable by a nurse only if it appears to him that the patient is suffering from mental disorder "to such a degree that it is necessary for his health or safety or for the protection of others for him to be immediately restrained from leaving the hospital." The criteria do not refer to the nature of the patient's disorder. This reflects the fact that the purpose of the power is immediate restraint and reinforces the view that the word "degree" is directed towards the present exacerbations and manifestations of a patient's disorder, rather its nature as revealed by its longer-term consequences.

"Nature"

Many mental disorders wax and wane because they are cyclical in nature, because the patient enjoys periods of remission — for example, during periods of low stress — or because they are intermittently alleviated by a course of treatment. A particular patient may have a long history of readmissions indicative of a severe, chronic condition which is resistant to treatment or a record of poor compliance with informal treatment following previous discharges. Although the degree of disorder may be quite low at any given time, either in absolute terms or relative to his known optimum level of functioning, the serious nature of the disorder is revealed by its historical course. Likewise, with illnesses of recent onset, the prognosis associated with the diagnosis may point strongly towards the probability of a serious, further deterioration of the patient's condition in the near future. In both instances, it may be the nature of the disorder rather than its degree which brings the patient within the first of the grounds for making an application.

Relapsing patients

Where a patient with a chronic condition decides not to continue with medication and his condition is deteriorating, it is often said by those assessing or examining him that he is "not sectionable." By this it is usually meant that the degree of mental disorder falls below what is considered to be the threshold for detention, albeit that the rapidity of the patient's decline suggests that his disorder will soon be of such a degree. In fact, because the nature of the disorder allows such a confident prognosis to be made about its future degree in the absence of any therapeutic intervention, it is not necessary as a matter of law to wait until the condition becomes acute before compelling the patient to receive the treatment which will prevent the otherwise inevitable further decline.

Mental Health Review Tribunals

Within the context of section 3 tribunal proceedings, a patient may have responded to treatment and be in remission by the time the hearing takes place. As such, and given the importance which attaches to a citizen's liberty in English law, the degree of mental disorder which remains may be insufficient to warrant a continuance of his liability to detention. The tribunal is not, however, obliged to discharge unless it is also satisfied that the nature of the patient's disorder, evidenced by his medical history or the outcome usually associated with such conditions, also makes liability to detention inappropriate. Similarly, where the degree of disorder apparent at the time of the hearing is quite low but the patient's recent mental state has been subject to marked fluctuations, the nature of the disorder may mean that the tribunal cannot be satisfied that the first of the grounds for discharge is made out.

"Warrants" and "makes appropriate"

The term "warrants" was used in the 1959 Act in relation to all applications, including those for admission for treatment.[9] The Government considered that the word steered a "reasonably middle course between the words to which objection was taken and the alternatives suggested in Committee — 'essential', 'desirable,' and the like."[10]

Section 3 applications

The grounds for making an application for admission for treatment under the 1959 Act referred to the existence of a form of mental disorder of a nature or degree which "warrants the detention of the patient in a hospital for medical treatment under this section."[11] The 1982 Act amended the provision and a patient's mental disorder need now only be "of a nature or degree which makes it appropriate for him to receive medical treatment in a hospital."[12] The previous reference to "treatment under this section" being warranted remains part of the admission criteria but is now found in section 3(2)(c), that is as part of the "health, safety of protection of others" ground. The purpose of these amendments was to separate out the two questions of whether a patient needs in-patient treatment and whether the use of section 3 is necessary in order to compel him to receive that treatment.[13]

The present distinction

Admission for treatment under section 3 therefore requires instead that the patient's disorder is of a nature or degree which makes it "appropriate" for him to receive medical treatment in a hospital. In the case of section 2 and guardianship applications, it remains the case that the mental disorder from which a patient suffers must be of a nature or degree which "warrants" his detention or reception into guardianship. "Warrants" is therefore used in Part II to denote a condition the nature or degree of which is sufficiently serious to justify the use of compulsory powers, whereas "appropriate" focuses attention on whether the nature or degree of disorder makes in-patient treatment appropriate, without reference to whether compulsory treatment is indicated; if in-patient treatment is appropriate the first of the grounds is made out.

Detention

The term was considered in the Australian case, *Paul v. Paul*,[14] where it was said that, "detention refers to the case of a person lawfully held against his will, one who is not free to depart when he pleases." Detention in hospital must be "warranted" under section 2 whereas the making of a section 3 application requires that the in-

---

[9]   As originally drafted, the Bill referred to a patient's mental disorder, or its particular form, being of a nature or degree "which renders him suitable to be detained in hospital." (See *Hansard*, H.C. Vol. 598, col. 710). The phrase was criticised as "being redolent of the language of the cookery book, and more suited to that than to the language of a Statute" and was therefore replaced by "warrants the detention of the patient." (*Hansard*, H.C. Vol. 605, col. 268.).

[10]   The Minister of Health, *Hansard*, H.C. Vol. 605, col. 268. A more cynical view was provided by the Member of Parliament for Oldham West: "I do not know what 'warrant' means and I doubt whether anyone else does, but, on the whole, I think that the word is not particularly objectionable. We know that anxiety neurosis is an occupational disease of Parliamentary draftsmen and that anything too specific has to be excluded for fear of judicial interpretation." (*Ibid.*, col. 272).

[11]   Mental Health Act 1959, s.26(2)(a).

[12]   Mental Health Act 1983, s.3(2)(a).

[13]   *Mental Health (Amendment) Bill: Notes on Clauses, House of Commons* (D.H.S.S., 1982), p.33.

[14]   *Paul v. Paul* (1954) V.L.R. 331.

patient treatment which the patient needs cannot be provided unless he is detained under that section.[15]

Hospital

The grounds of application under sections 2–4 refer to detention or treatment in a "hospital." As to the statutory meaning of this term, which includes "community wards" and private mental nursing homes which are registered to receive detained patients, see page 131.

Assessment

The meaning of "assessment" is considered below (**231**).

Medical treatment

"Medical treatment" is defined in section 145(1) and, unless the context otherwise requires, it "includes nursing, and also includes care, habilitation and rehabilitation under medical supervision." In *Secretary of State for the Home Department v Mental Health Review Tribunal for Mersey Regional Health Authority,*[16] Mann J. rejected the tribunal's submission that supervision, guidance and rehabilitation which did not necessarily have to be given by nursing or medical staff or under medical supervision, because it could be given in a hostel or other suitable community provision, did not constitute medical treatment within the meaning of section 145(1).[17] However, it is not enough under section 3 that a patient would benefit from treatment in this broad sense. Detention under section 3 requires that in-patient medical treatment is "appropriate", necessary" for the patient's health or safety or for the protection of others, and cannot be provided unless he is detained under that section.

HEALTH, SAFETY, WELFARE AND THE PROTECTION OF OTHERS

The grounds of application include in all cases a second condition that the patient's detention or restraint is "necessary" or "justified" on his own account (specifically his health, safety or welfare) or that of others (in order to protect them from him). The criteria to be satisfied in respect of the patient are that—

• section 2	he ought to be so detained in the interests of his own health or safety or with a view to the protection of other persons (s.2(2)(b)).
• section 3	it is necessary for the health or safety of the patient or for the protection of other persons that he should receive such treatment and it cannot be provided unless he is detained under this section (s.3(2)(c)).
• guardianship	it is necessary in the interests of the welfare of the patient or for the protection of other persons that the patient should be so received (s.7(2)(b)).

---

[15] Mental Health Act 1983, s.3(2)(c).
[16] *Secretary of State for the Home Department v. Mental Health Review Tribunal for Mersey Regional Health Authority* [1986] 1 W.L.R. 1170.
[17] *Ibid.*, at 1173E.

Historical note

During the 1959 Bill's passage through the House of Commons, the words "health or safety" were substituted for the more general phrase "in the interests of the patient",[18] the Government's aim being "to limit compulsory powers to cases in which it is positively necessary to override the wishes of the patient, either in the interests of his own health or safety or for the protection of others."[19]

"Health"

Irrespective of whether a patient's mental disorder has any consequences for his own safety or the well-being of others, he may be detained if such a course of action is necessary for, or in the interests of, his mental or physical health.[20] The term is not statutorily defined in the 1983 Act or the National Health Service Act 1977. The use of the word "health" in relation to the criteria for admission to hospital, but "welfare" in the guardianship criteria, suggests that the perceived risk must be of a kind which necessitates or justifies compulsory medical intervention and not merely social work intervention. In practical terms, health may be described as the standard of physical and mental functioning necessary for a person to perform the activities which are expected of him, according to the norms of the society in which he lives; all *disabling* disease, illness and handicap must be absent (**1031**).

"Welfare"

"Welfare" is also not statutorily defined and nor does the Act contain a check-list of relevant considerations of the kind found in section 1(3) of the Children's Act 1989, which stipulates that the welfare of the child shall be paramount.[21] Although the 1960 regulations obliged a guardian to make arrangements for the patient's general welfare,[22] his welfare was not originally a statutory condition of guardianship under the 1959 Act. Guardianship simply required that it was "necessary in the interests of the patient" that he should be so received.[23] The welfare criterion was inserted later, by sections 7(4) and 12(6) of the Mental Health (Amendment) Act 1982, the Government's reasons for amending the criteria being set out in two White Papers published at the time—

---

[18]   The Lord Chancellor (Lord Kilmuir), *Hansard*, H.L. Vol. 216, col. 754.

[19]   *Ibid.*, col. 671.

[20]   During the Parliamentary debates on the 1959 Bill, the Lord Chancellor rejected a proposal that compulsory admission should be confined to cases where that was necessary for a patient's safety, on the grounds that "many ... who can be cured refuse treatment because their illness itself makes them incapable of appreciating the need for treatment." The Lord Chancellor (Lord Kilmuir), *Hansard*, H.L. Vol. 216, col. 754.

[21]   The Scottish and Northern Irish mental health legislation, which post-dates our Act, also do not include a statutory definition of the term. In the context of children's legislation, the Law Commission considered that, "'Welfare' is an all-encompassing word. It includes material welfare, both in the sense of adequacy of resources to provide a pleasant home and a comfortable standard of living and in the sense of adequacy of care to ensure that good health and due personal pride are maintained. However, while material considerations have their place they are secondary matters. More important are the stability and the security, the loving and understanding care and guidance, the warm and compassionate relationships, that are essential for the full development of the child's own character, personality and talents." Law Commission, *Working Paper No. 96*, para. 6.10.

[22]   Mental (Health Hospital and Guardianship) Regulations 1960, reg. 6.

[23]   Mental Health Act 1959, s.33(2)(b).

"At present an application under section 33 has to be 'necessary in the interests of the patient or for the protection of other persons. This criterion seems unnecessarily wide and the term 'patient's welfare' in place of 'patient' would help to narrow it."[24]

"The Bill proposes that guardianship will be required to be "in the interest of the welfare of the patient or for the protection of other persons" rather than "in the interests of the patient" as at present; this will clarify the purpose of guardianship and ensure that the power is not so wide."[25]

The absence of any statutory definition

As with the decision not to statutorily define "mental illness ,"it may be inferred that Parliament intended that practitioners and tribunals should have a broad discretion when deciding whether certain arrangements are in the interests of the patient's welfare in any given case. The reluctance to define the term probably reflects a recognition that ideas about what promotes a patient's welfare change over time. For example, while it was previously thought that the welfare of most patients was promoted by offering them asylum the underlying principle nowadays is that their welfare is better served by being part of the general community. Nevertheless, although a tribunal has a broad discretion in any particular case, it should be emphasised that any guardianship must be "necessary" in the interests of the patient's welfare (**220**).

"Safety"

During the Parliamentary debates on the 1959 Bill, the Lord Chancellor rejected a submission that compulsory admission procedures should be confined to cases where that was necessary on the ground of "safety," interpreting the word as denoting "persons who were dangerous to themselves or to others, or in danger from others."[26] However, sections 25(1) and 72(1)(b)(iii) distinguish between safety and dangerousness. They provide for the discharge of patients who satisfy the ordinary detention criteria — including in some cases therefore the safety criterion — but who would not, if released, be likely to act in a manner "dangerous" to themselves. The Butler Committee equated "dangerousness with a propensity to cause serious physical injury or lasting psychological harm."[27] Likewise, section 20 differentiates safety from exploitation and lack of care. In particular, section 20(4)(c) prohibits renewing the authority to detain a mentally ill or severely mentally impaired patient whose detention may be necessary for his own safety but whose condition is untreatable unless he would, if discharged, be unlikely to be able to care for himself, to obtain the care which he needs or to guard himself against serious exploitation. The meaning of "safety" must therefore be different in some respect from the meanings which attach to the concepts of dangerousness, exploitation, and neglect.

Risk of physical harm

The concept of a person's safety clearly draws attention to a risk of physical harm to that person rather than mere ill-health, that is a general deterioration of his mental

---

[24]   *Review of the Mental Health Act 1959*, Cmnd. 7320 (1978), para. 4.14.
[25]   Paragraph 44 of *Reform of Mental Health Legislation*, Cmnd. 8405 (1981), explaining the provisions in the 1982 Bill.
[26]   The Lord Chancellor (Lord Kilmuir), *Hansard*, H.L. Vol. 216, col. 754.
[27]   *Report of the Committee on Mentally Abnormal Offenders*, Cmnd. 6244 (1975), para. 4.10.

health and functioning. Where a risk of physical harm exists, this may be because the patient would physically harm himself, seriously neglect himself, or there is a risk that others will harm him. If it is likely that a patient will cause himself *significant* physical harm if he is not detained, he may be said to be likely to act in a manner dangerous to himself. A chronically mentally ill or severely mentally impaired patient who is unable to care for himself, or to obtain the care which he needs, or who is at risk of serious exploitation, will usually require detention for his own safety as well as his health. In the case of other mentally ill patients, however, any risk to their safety if they are discharged may not relate to their ability to care for or protect themselves, for example persons suffering from a paranoid delusional disorder. Having regard to these considerations, it is submitted that the concept of a patient's safety is ultimately concerned with the existence of a risk of physical harm rather than its cause or magnitude. It is immaterial for the purposes of the admission criteria whether the risk arises because of the patient's own acts (dangerous conduct towards himself), his omissions to act (self-neglect), how others act towards him (exploiting or ill-treating him), or omit to act towards him (failing to care for him). If, however, a patient's nearest relative believes that he is fit to be discharged, the nature and magnitude of the risk is relevant to any decision about whether or not his detention may be continued — the issue in this context becomes whether he is then likely to act dangerously towards himself. Likewise, if in-patient treatment is unlikely to even prevent a patient's condition from deteriorating, he must be discharged unless his detention is necessary on account of his vulnerability — the issue in this context becomes whether he would then be neglected or exploited. Perhaps surprisingly, dangerousness is not then a statutory consideration. If this is correct, dangerous conduct and the risks of lack of care or exploitation are all particular ways in which a patient's safety may be at risk.

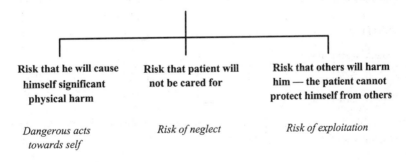

DETENTION NECESSARY OR JUSTIFIED FOR PATIENT'S SAFETY

Risk that he will cause himself significant physical harm	**Risk that patient will not be cared for**	**Risk that others will harm him — the patient cannot protect himself from others**
Dangerous acts towards self	*Risk of neglect*	*Risk of exploitation*

"Protection of other persons"

The Act distinguishes between a necessity to protect others generally and, where a patient's nearest relative is seeking his discharge, the likelihood of the patient then acting dangerously towards others.[28] It has been suggested that statutory references to the "protection of other persons" refer to people and not to their property.[29] This

---

28   See Mental Health Act 1983, ss. 2,3,7, 20, 25 and 72.
29   R. Jones, *Mental Health Act Manual* (Sweet & Maxwell, 5th ed., 1996), p.28.

seems to imply that, when deciding whether the use of compulsory powers is necessary or justified for the protection of third parties, consideration should be confined to the likelihood of the patient causing them bodily or psychological harm — in other words, harming their health or safety. However, there seems no particular reason to restrict the phrase's interpretation in this way, other than that the phrase "or their property" is not expressly added after the statutory words. If Parliament intended such a restriction, it is surprising that the statutory criteria do not simply provide for a patient's detention where this is necessary or justified for his own health or safety or that of others. It would also be strange if a patient who persistently damaged or stole the property of some other person, on account of some delusional belief, could not be detained because there was no risk to that person's physical safety. At any rate, causing damage to a person's property will generally also cause him emotional distress so the two aspects will usually be inextricably linked. It is, however, submitted that the phrase has a more general ambit, indicating a need to protect other persons from the consequences of the patient's actions, including therefore damage to property arising as the result of the patient's mental state. As before, a distinction must be drawn between the need to protect others generally and the likelihood of the patient behaving dangerously towards them, which would appear to imply the existence of a risk of physical harm. Nevertheless, in practice, even if there is no history of physical harm to others the likelihood of such harm being caused in the future may be significant if there is a history of damage to their property. For example, if a person was admitted to hospital after damaging his neighbour's property in the belief that the latter had interfered with his thoughts or conspired against him, there will usually be a risk of future confrontations escalating into violence for as long as those beliefs persist.

NATURE OF RISK NECESSITATING OR JUSTIFYING DETENTION

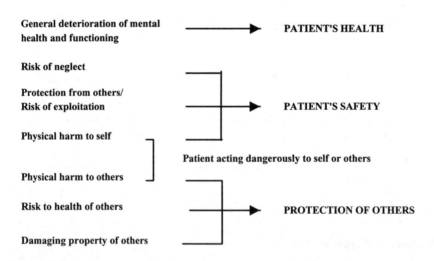

"Ought to be so detained" and "necessary"

A person may not be detained simply because it can be demonstrated that he or other persons have suffered some detriment as a result of his not enjoying sound mental health. The consequences for the patient's health or safety, or for others, if the patient is not detained must be sufficiently serious to justify his detention or to make that necessary. There must be sound evidence to support such a contention since "a man's liberty of movement is regarded so highly by the law of England that it is not to be hindered or prevented except on the surest grounds."[30]

"Ought to be so detained in the interests of" and "with a view to"

The qualifying word originally used in the 1959 Bill was "expedient," which raised the concern that a person might be detained for up to 28 days on grounds of expediency. The condition that the patient "ought to be detained in the interests of" his health and safety or "with a view to" the protection of others was therefore substituted, and these qualifying words are now used in the section 2 admission criteria.[31] Provided that the nature or degree of the patient's disorder warrants his detention for assessment, it does not therefore matter if it is impossible to define the exact manner in which his health or safety or others will suffer if he is not detained. This is logical because the precise nature and extent of any risk to the patient and others if he does not receive treatment is one of the matters to be assessed; and the outcome of the assessment may be that any disorder from which he suffers is, if untreated, unlikely to have significant adverse consequences. The phrase "ought to be detained" means in effect that the patient's detention is "justified"[32] having regard to the possibility of harm to himself or others if he is not. The nature of the risk is necessarily of paramount importance. A significant risk of an insignificant decline in mental functioning would not constitute adequate justification for interfering with an individual's liberty whereas a much smaller risk of a catastrophic outcome, such as suicide, might be.

"Necessary"

In the case of detention under section 3, it must be "necessary" for the health or safety of the patient or for the protection of others that he receives medical treatment in a hospital and that such treatment cannot be provided unless he is detained under section 3. Similarly, guardianship requires that the patient's reception into guardianship is "necessary" in the interests of his welfare or for the protection of others. The fact that any arrangements which may be made by the prospective guardian will generally benefit the patient is therefore insufficient if his welfare can be adequately protected without the use of compulsory powers. "Necessary" is stronger than "makes appropriate" or "justifies" and indicates that the use of compulsory powers is imperative or essential and that no alternative, less restrictive, course of action will meet the needs of the situation.

THE GAF SCALE

The GAF scale devised by the American Psychiatric Association is a useful practical tool for assessing a patient's overall level of functioning and the extent to which his health or safety, or that of others, is at risk at any given time. The patient is rated on a 0–100 scale, with 100 representing superior functioning and 10 "persistent danger of severely hurting self or others."

---

[30] See *Ghani v Jones* [1970] 1 Q.B. 693, *per* Lord Denning M.R.
[31] See *Hansard*, H.C. Vol. 605, cols. 268–69.
[32] The word used in the tribunal discharge criteria in preference to "ought to be detained." See s.72(1)(a)(i).

GLOBAL ASSESSMENT OF FUNCTIONING SCALE (GAF SCALE)

Code	Symptoms
81–90	**Absent or minimal symptoms** (*e.g.*, mild anxiety before an exam), good functioning in all areas, interested and involved in a wide range of activities, socially effective, generally satisfied with life, no more than everyday problems or concerns (*e.g.*, an occasional argument with family members).
71–80	**If symptoms are present, they are transient and expectable reactions to psychosocial stressors** (*e.g.*, difficulty concentrating after family argument); no more than slight impairment in social, occupational, or school functioning (*e.g.*, temporarily falling behind in school work).
61–70	**Some mild symptoms** (*e.g.* depressed mood or mild insomnia) OR some difficulty in social, occupational, or school functioning (*e.g.* occasional truancy, or theft within the household), but generally functioning pretty well, has some meaningful interpersonal relationships.
51–60	**Moderate symptoms** (*e.g.* flat affect and circumstantial speech, occasional panic attacks) OR moderate difficulty in social, occupational, or school functioning (*e.g.*, few friends, conflicts with co–workers).
41–50	**Serious symptoms** (*e.g.*, suicidal ideation, severe obsessional rituals, frequent shoplifting) OR any serious impairment in social, occupational, or school functioning (*e.g.*, no friends, unable to keep a job).
31–40	**Some impairment in reality testing or communication** (*e.g.*, speech is at times illogical, obscure, or irrelevant) OR major impairment in several areas, such as work or school, family relations, judgement, thinking, or mood (*e.g.*, depressed man avoids friends, neglects family, and is unable to work; child frequently beats up younger children, is defiant at home, and is failing at school).
21–30	**Behaviour is considerably influenced by delusions or hallucinations OR serious impairment in communication or judgment** (*e.g.*, sometimes incoherent, acts grossly inappropriately, suicidal preoccupation) **OR inability to function in almost all areas** (*e.g.*, stays in bed all day; no job, home, or friends).
11–20	**Some danger of hurting self or others** (*e.g.*, suicidal attempts without clear expectation of death, frequently violent, manic excitement) **OR occasionally fails to maintain minimal personal hygiene** (*e.g.*, smears faeces) **OR gross impairment in communication** (*e.g.*, largely incoherent or mute).
1–10	**Persistent danger of severely hurting self or others** (*e.g.*, recurrent violence) **OR persistent inability to maintain minimal personal hygiene OR serious suicidal act with clear expectation of death.**

Source: Diagnostic and Statistical Manual of Mental Disorders: DSM-IV (American Psychiatric Association, 4th ed., 1994), p.32.

THE TREATABILITY CONDITION

A third ground of application — commonly referred to as the "treatability test"— must be satisfied in the case of section 3 applications which concern persons suffering from psychopathic disorder or mental impairment. This is that in-patient medical treatment is likely to alleviate or prevent a deterioration of the patient's condition. Alleviation implies that treatment is likely to enable the patient to cope more satisfactorily with his disorder or its symptoms. Medical treatment is defined in section 145(1) and, unless the context otherwise requires, the term includes nursing and also care, habilitation and rehabilitation under medical supervision.

Historical note

Section 4(4) of the Mental Health Act 1959 defined a "psychopathic disorder" as "a persistent disorder or disability of mind ... which results in abnormally aggressive or seriously irresponsible conduct on the part of the patient, *and requires or is susceptible to treatment.*" An attempt was made in the House of Lords to remove the words "requires or" from the definition so as to ensure that the category would be confined to persons who "will really benefit from medical treatment."[33] The Government's position was explained by the Lord Chancellor, Viscount Kilmuir, who said that the inclusion of the words allowed action to be taken in a case where the doctor hoped that a patient would respond to treatment.[34] In 1978, the Government set out in a White Paper its proposals for amending the 1959 Act."[35] It accepted that "the Act should establish a clear requirement that psychopaths should only be detained under compulsory powers where there is a good prospect of benefit from treatment." The Government proposed that the words "and requires or is susceptible to medical treatment" be omitted from the statutory definition of psychopathic disorder, since they did not define the disorder, and a "prospect of benefit from treatment" requirement incorporated instead into the criteria for compulsory admission and renewal.[36] The Mental Health (Amendment) Act 1982 gave effect to these proposals.

Likelihood of initial non-cooperation and deterioration

The question of whether the treatability test is satisfied where the medical evidence indicates that admission is likely to initially bring about a deterioration of the patient's mental state, and the patient is unwilling to cooperate in the only form of treatment likely to be beneficial, was considered in *ex p. A*.

R. v. Canons Park Mental Health Review Tribunal, ex p. A.

[1994] 3 W.L.R. 630   *C.A. (Nourse, Kennedy, Roch L.JJ.)*

The evidence was that group therapy was the only form of treatment likely to alleviate or prevent deterioration of A's condition. However, it required the patient's willing co-operation in order to be likely to have this effect and the patient was unwilling to cooperate. Furthermore, there was evidence that it was likely that detention might result in a temporary deterioration of the patient's condition, due to the patient's dislike of being subjected to a controlled environment.

The submissions

It was submitted by counsel for the tribunal that the treatability test is concerned with the likely effect of treatment if such treatment is given, and is not concerned with the likelihood of the patient refusing such treatment. There was a known treatment which was likely to alleviate or prevent deterioration of the applicant's condition, namely group therapy. Parliament could not have intended

---

[33]   *Hansard*, H.L. Vol. 217, cols. 91 and 93.
[34]   *Ibid.*, col. 98. The Solicitor General (Sir Harry Hylton-Foster) observed that, "though there may be some kind of psychopathic disorder which is not susceptible to medical treatment, it would be a rather tougher thing to say that it is not susceptible to medical treatment in the sense of including 'nursing and ... care and training under medical supervision' which is the definition as it now stands." (*Hansard*, H.C. Vol. 598, col. 833).
[35]   *Review of the Mental Health Act 1959*, Cmnd. 7320 (1978).
[36]   *Ibid.*, para. 1.26.

that a patient should be deemed untreatable simply because the patient withheld co-operation. That would place the key to the patient's being detained in hospital in the patient's own hands and did not accord with medical experience concerning the treatment of those with psychopathic disorders. In such cases, there might be an initial deterioration in the patient's condition. However, detention in a secure environment with nursing care and medical supervision — medical treatment within the Act — could lead to the patient gaining an insight into his condition. One of the skills of nurses and doctors in hospitals for the mentally disordered was to persuade their patients to accept treatment. A period of detention with nursing care and medical supervision was frequently a necessary prelude to treatment by way of therapy. If, during such a period, the patient was likely to gain an insight into his problem or likely to become co-operative then that in itself represented an alleviation of the condition. These submissions were generally accepted by the court.

Roch L.J.

The following "treatability principles" should be applied when deciding whether medical treatment as an in-patient is likely to alleviate or prevent a deterioration of the patient's condition—

a. a patient may not be detained simply to coerce him into participating in group therapy.

b. treatment in hospital will satisfy the treatability test although it is unlikely to alleviate the patient's condition, provided that it is likely to prevent a deterioration.

c. treatment in hospital will satisfy the treatability test although it will not immediately alleviate or prevent deterioration in the patient's condition, provided that alleviation or stabilisation is likely in due course.

d. the treatability test can still be met although initially there may be some deterioration in the patient's condition, due for example to the patient's initial anger at being detained.

e. it must be remembered that medical treatment in hospital covers nursing and also includes care, habilation and rehabilitation under medical supervision.

f. the treatability test is satisfied if nursing care, etc., is likely to lead to an alleviation of the patient's condition in that the patient is likely to gain an insight into his problem or cease to be uncooperative in his attitude towards treatment which would potentially have a lasting benefit.

Kennedy L.J.

In order to satisfy the treatability test, it is not necessary to demonstrate a probability of short term gain. The fact that a patient demonstrates a fixed determination not to co-operate in the administration of psychotherapy in a group setting, which is the only form of therapy known to be beneficial, is not decisive, provided that there is a prospect that that attitude might change. If so, one is entitled to conclude that treatment over a prolonged period — consisting at first of no more than nursing care and gradual persuasion to accept group therapy but followed by group therapy itself — is likely to alleviate or prevent deterioration of the patient's condition, even if at first some deterioration cannot be avoided. Treatability is a matter of clinical judgment.

Summary

It can be seen that the treatability condition is satisfied if medical treatment in its broad statutory sense — which includes nursing care — is eventually likely to bring about some symptomatic relief or prevent the patient's mental health from deteriorating.[37] There are few (if any) conditions which are not treatable in this sense. Accordingly, if the condition was intended by Parliament to further limit the circumstances in which a citizen can be denied his liberty — by requiring a good prospect of benefit from treatment — it must be doubted whether its interpretation by the courts has had any such effect.

APPLICATIONS FOR ADMISSION FOR ASSESSMENT

Under the 1983 Act, and related legislation, a person may be detained in hospital for assessment under section 2 in one of three ways—

- Under Part II of the Act, a person may be admitted to hospital for assessment in pursuance of an application made under section 2 or, in an emergency, under section 4.[38]

- Under Part VI of the Act and under the Mental Health (Scotland) Act 1984, a person who is detained in hospital for assessment in Scotland or Northern Ireland may be removed to a hospital in England or Wales, the effect of which is that the patient is treated as if he had been admitted to that hospital under section 2 on the date of his arrival there.

- Under section 14A of the Criminal Appeal Act 1968.

However, almost all patients detained for assessment are detained following the making of an application under Part II.

Applications under Part II

An application for admission for assessment may be made in respect of a patient on the grounds that —

a. "he is suffering from (**213**) mental disorder (**051**) of a nature or degree (**213**) which warrants (**215**) the detention of the patient in a hospital (**131**) for assessment (or for assessment followed by a medical treatment) (**231**) for at least a limited period (**226**); and

b. he ought to be so detained in the interests of (**221**) his own health (**217**) or safety (**218**) or with a view to (**221**) the protection of other persons (**219**)."[39]

---

[37] *Mental Health Act 1983: Memorandum on Parts I to VI, VIII and X* (D.H.S.S., 1987), para. 19.
[38] Emergency applications under section 4 are considered below (**243**).
[39] Mental Health Act 1983, s.2(2).

The somewhat clumsy phrase "for at least a limited period" is merely intended to emphasise the finite nature of detention under section 2, in contrast to the admission for trea ment provisions which provide for treatment for a potentially unlimited period.[40]

Removal under Part VI

Section 82(1) enables patients who are detained for assessment in Northern Ireland under Article 4 of the Mental Health (Northern Ireland) Order 1986 to be removed to a hospital in England or Wales. Where this occurs, section 82(4A) of the 1983 Act provides that the patient shall be treated as if he had been admitted to hospital in pursuance of a section 2 application made on the date of his admission to hospital in England or Wales.

Removal under the Mental Health (Scotland) Act 1984

The Mental Health (Scotland to England or Wales shall be treated as if they had been detained in pursuance of an application made on the date of their arrival under the corresponding provision in the 1983 Act.[41]

Admission orders under the 1968 Act

Where a person appeals against a verdict that he is not guilty of an offence by reason of insanity and Court of Appeal substitutes a verdict of acquittal, the court may order that he is admitted for assessment under section 2 to such hospital as may be specified by the Secretary of State.[42] The court must be of the opinion, on the written or oral evidence of two registered medical practitioners, one of whom is approved under section 12, that the appellant meets the criteria for being detained under section 2.[43]

THE STATUTORY FRAMEWORK

The detention procedures under section 2 differ from those pertaining to section 3 in a number of significant ways.

The grounds of application

The grounds of application differ in the following respects—

---

[40] "The wording ... points the distinction between the two clauses; that in regard to the one, the treatment required may be of a short-term nature and can be done in the observation period without necessitating the rather more full-scale procedure of Clause 26, in which the application is for admission for treatment, and where there is nothing to suggest that it will be of such a short-term nature ... the words do not appear in Clause 26 because it is without limit of time in the sense that the patient must be suitable for detention." The Minister of Health (Mr. Derek Walker-Smith), *Hansard*, H.C. Vol. 605, col. 275.

[41] Mental Health (Scotland) Act 1984, s.77(2).

[42] Criminal Appeal Act 1968, ss. 12, 13(4)(b) and 14A(2). The 28-day period begins on the date of the "admission order" and the appellant must be admitted within seven days of that date, otherwise there is no authority to detain him in hospital. Pending admission, the appellant may be detained in a place of safety.

[43] Criminal Appeal Act 1968, s.14A(1).

- The grounds of application set out in section 2(2)(a) require only that a patient suffers from mental disorder generally, as defined by section 1(2), rather than from one of the four specific forms of mental disorder. This is logical because a "specific diagnosis of the form of mental disorder ... may not be possible until the assessment has been completed.[44]

- The mental disorder must be of a nature or degree which warrants the patient's detention in a hospital; in section 3 cases, it suffices if the mental disorder is of a nature or degree which makes in-patient treatment appropriate, irrespective of whether detention in hospital is warranted.

- It is a ground of application under section 2 that the patient "ought to be so detained" in the interests of his safety or for the protection of other persons; it is not a condition that admission is "necessary" for those purposes, nor that they cannot be realised unless the patient is detained under section 2. The grounds in section 2(2)(b) are therefore "not quite so stringent"[45] as those set out in section 3(2)(c) for section 3 admissions. The rationale is that assessment under section 2 "may be necessary to see whether the more stringent conditions for longer term admission for treatment are met."[46]

- It is never a condition of admission under section 2 that any treatment which the patient may receive following admission is likely to alleviate or prevent a deterioration of his condition.

Persons assessed not to be mentally disordered

The medical practitioners providing the recommendations in support of the application must be of the opinion that the patient is suffering from mental disorder. The statutory purpose of admission for assessment is therefore not to assess whether the patient is or is not mentally disordered but to assess the mental disorder from which the doctors have certified that in their opinion he suffers. Before forming any such opinion, they must first examine the patient and they owe him a duty to take reasonable care. However, the outcome of a full hospital assessment may occasionally be that the patient does not in fact suffer from mental disorder. Nevertheless, providing the persons involved in the application process acted in good faith and with reasonable care they will be protected by section 139. An alternative way of making essentially the same point is to say that it must appear to the medical practitioners upon carefully examining the patient that he is suffering from mental disorder. Thus, Lloyd L.J. stated, in *R. v. Kirklees Metropolitan Council ex p. C (a Minor)*,[47] that he did not accept the argument that section 2 was "confined to cases where the patient is in fact suffering from mental disorder. Having regard to the definition of a patient in section 145 there is, in my view, power to admit a patient for assessment under section 2, if he appears to be suffering from mental disorder, on the ground that he or she is so suffering, even though it turns out on assessment that [he or] she is not. Any other construction would unnecessarily emasculate the beneficial power under section 2 and confine assessment to choice of treatment."

---

[44] *Mental Health (Amendment) Bill: Notes on Clauses, House of Commons* (D.H.S.S., 1982), p.25. See also *Mental Health Act 1983: Memorandum on Parts I to VI, VIII and X* (D.H.S.S., 1987), para. 23.
[45] *Ibid.*
[46] *Ibid.*
[47] See *R. v. Kirklees Metropolitan Council, ex p. C (A Minor)* [1993] 2 F.L.R. 187.

The application procedures

As with the grounds of application, so the procedures for making an application under section 2 differ from those pertaining to section 3 in several respects—

- An approved social worker is not under a statutory duty to consult the nearest relative prior to making a section 2 application (instead, he must take such steps as are practicable to inform the nearest relative that an application is to be or has been made[48]).

- Although an approved social worker must have regard to any wishes expressed by a patient's relatives, a section 2 application may be made despite the objections of the nearest relative. The Government considered that the stronger provisions applicable in section 3 cases were not appropriate for admission for assessment "which is usually more urgent and lasts for no more than twenty-eight days."[49]

- The medical recommendations upon which a section 2 application is founded need only formally recite that the admission criteria are satisfied; the practitioners completing them are not required to state the grounds or reasons for their opinion, nor to specify whether other methods of dealing with the patient are available and, if so, why they are not appropriate.[50]

The consequences of admission

Here, too, patients detained under section 2 are in a different position from those detained following an application for admission for treatment—

- Admission in pursuance of an application under section 2 does not revoke any pre-existing guardianship application or order, nor does it revoke any outstanding supervision application.

- The authority to detain a patient which is conferred by a section 2 application is, in the normal way, limited to 28 days and may not be renewed for further periods.

- The fact that a section 2 patient is remanded in custody or committed to prison, or is absent without leave during the final week of the 28 day period, does not have the effect of extending the period for which the application remains in force.[51]

- A patient who is detained under section 2 has no statutory right to after-care services under section 117 but, equally therefore, no application may be made for him to be subject to after-care under supervision upon ceasing to be liable to be detained.

---

[48] The Mental Health (Amendment) Act 1982 made a number of important changes to the pre-existing legislation. The requirement, now found in s.11(3), that an approved social worker applicant take steps to inform the person appearing to be the nearest relative that a section 2 application is about to be made, or has been made, and inform him of his discharge powers was introduced.

[49] *Mental Health (Amendment) Bill: Notes on Clauses, House of Commons* (D.H.S.S., 1982), p.26.

[50] Mental Health Act 1983, ss.2(3) and 3(3).

[51] Though see p.239.

Successive section 2 applications

It has been noted that the authority to detain a patient under section 2 expires after 28 days unless a county court application made under section 29 is pending (**112**). In practice, it has not been uncommon for a patient who has recently ceased to be detained under the section to be readmitted to hospital under section 2.

R. v. Wilson, ex p. Williamson

[1996] C.O.D. 42   *Q.B.D., Tucker J.*

The patient was diagnosed as suffering from paranoid schizophrenia and detained in a secure unit. He had convictions for offences against women and had been sentenced to six years imprisonment in 1988 for an offence of attempted rape. During that sentence he was transferred to a secure hospital unit for treatment, before being discharged from there at the end of 1992. Between 22 February and 1 August 1994, he received in-patient treatment as an informal patient. After a short period in the community, he was informally readmitted to hospital but decided to discharge himself on 14 October. He was prevented from doing so by being detained under section 5(2). His father, the statutory nearest relative, did not accept that compulsory admission was appropriate and refused to discuss the matter. On 17 October, the patient was detained under section 2. He applied to a tribunal but was not discharged. A Consultant Forensic Psychiatrist advised that he should remain in hospital for further treatment after the section 2 period expired on 13 November; if he not consent to remaining informally, a section 3 application should be made. Such an application would require the nearest relative's consent and the patient's detention under section 2 could only be continued if a county court application to displace the nearest relative was made before the section 2 period expired on 13 November. In the event, no such application was made. The patient remained in hospital informally but this arrangement was considered to be unsatisfactory, because the doctors believed that he was too dangerous to be allowed to leave hospital. Ms. Wilson, an approved social worker, considered making a section 3 application but the patient's father objected. The local social services authority agreed that the patient could pose a serious risk to others if he left hospital and that prompt action was necessary to prevent this. Because the patient could not be detained under section 3 unless and until a county court order had been made, and because it might take some time to obtain such an order, it was decided that a further section 2 application should be made. Accordingly, on 20 December 1994, Ms. Wilson made such an application and, later that day, the patient was transferred from the open ward where he had been to a locked ward at a different hospital. A section 29 application was eventually made to the county court on 13 January 1995, although it had not been disposed of by the time Tucker J. delivered his judgment on 5 April 1995.

The application for judicial review

The patient applied for judicial review of (i) the approved social worker's decision to make a second section 2 application and (ii) the hospital managers' decision to refuse to release or discharge him once the unlawfulness of the application had been pointed out. It was submitted on his behalf that section 2 provided only for a short-term period of detention for the specified purpose of assessment. The assessment contemplated by section 2 was confined to identifying the core condition. The period limited by the subsection could not be renewed, nor continued, unless a county court application had been made prior to its expiration. Section 2 was a precursor to section 3: once a decision had been taken to proceed under section 3, the need for assessment was over, the condition requiring treatment having been identified. In this case, the decision to apply under section 29, and therefore under section 3 also, had already been

229

taken prior to the decision to make the second section 2 application. The power conferred by section 2 had therefore been misused and the second application was unlawful.

The First Respondent's Case (Ms. Wilson)

Although the patient's medical condition had been diagnosed, there had subsequently been a need to further assess the treatment to be given. Treatment could be provided under section 2 and an "assessment" under that section might include assessing the efficacy of treatment. It had not been necessary to make a section 3 application at the end of the initial section 2 period, nor therefore had it been necessary to apply to the county court for the nearest relative's displacement before that period expired. If the making of a second section 2 application was unlawful in the event that, as here, the patient's behaviour subsequently deteriorated and he became dangerous, there was an hiatus. In fact, that deterioration constituted a new set of circumstances which justified further assessment and a further section 2 application.

The Second Respondent's Case (Hospital Managers)

Counsel for the hospital managers supported the submissions made on the First Respondent's behalf. He queried whether the concluding words of section 2(4) precluded further applications under that section, so as to prevent making a second application during the currency of the first. The matter turned on the meaning of the words used there and the meaning of the term "assessment."

Tucker J.

The final words of subsection 2(4) excluded the possibility of a second section 2 admission being applied for during the currency of the first. They were clear words which did not give rise to any question. Section 2(4) limited the maximum period of detention under that section to 28 days unless a county court application was pending at the expiration of that period. No such county court application had been made before te section expired on 13 November 1994, and that was unfortunate. Having considered the relevant statutory provisions and the *Code of Practice*, the scheme contemplated by the legislature, and laid down in the Act, was clear. A section 2 application was only intended to be of short duration and for a limited purpose — assessment of the patient's condition with a view to ascertaining whether it was a case which would respond to treatment, and whether an application under section 3 would be appropriate. It was intended that the assessment should take place within 28 days, without any extension of time unless it was necessary for the purpose of replacing the nearest relative. Although there was nothing to suggest that section 2 was a once and for all procedure, there was also nothing in the Act which justified successive or back-to-back applications under the section of the kind which occurred here. The section 2 powers could only be used for the limited purpose for which they were intended. They could not be utilised for the purpose of further detaining a patient for assessment beyond the 28-day period or used as a stop-gap procedure. For the reasons given, the decision and the refusal were wrong in law. *Certiorari granted.*[52]

---

[52] The application for mandamus was withdrawn upon counsel for the hospital managers expressing their opinion that section 5(2) would not be available following the court's decision to quash the section 2 authority for the patient's detention. The reason given was that section 5(2) contemplated an in-patient who was not detained: it was "designed for the patient who had been a voluntary patient ... To invoke section 5(2), as a result of a person being an in-patient ... [when following the court's judgment] ... the patient was not a voluntary patient but happened to be [detained] there unlawfully ... would take advantage of unlawful status, and .... the hospital manager[s] would be vulnerable to another judicial review, which would effectively be saying that we were using it for improper purposes."

Commentary

The Scottish courts have adopted a somewhat different approach. In *R. v. Lothian Health Board (No. 2)* [1993] S.L.T. 1021, the patient was detained under the Scottish provision corresponding to section 4 some 24 hours after the 28-day period of detention corresponding to that permitted by section 2 had expired. Section 26(7) of the Mental Health (Scotland) Act 1984 provides that such a patient shall not be "further detained" under the provisions corresponding to sections 2 and 4 "immediately after" the expiry of the 28-day period of detention. The court held that the second period of detention had not commenced "immediately after" the expiry of the first. The question was one of circumstances, having regard to the mischief that the statutory provision corresponding to section 2(4) was enacted to remove.

THE MEANING OF "ASSESSMENT" AND ITS PURPOSE

"Assessment" is not statutorily defined. The need for, and response to, treatment of any patient under medical care is continuously being assessed in a clinical sense. Conversely, from a legal viewpoint, all detained patients are continuously receiving medical treatment because treatment includes nursing care. However, to apply these meanings to the section 2 admission criteria without qualification would be to lose sight of the different purposes of section 2 and section 3 applications. The purpose of both would then be assessment and medical treatment. This is why the Act refers to a section 2 patient's detention for assessment or for assessment *"followed by"* medical treatment.

"Assessment" and "observation"

Section 25 of the 1959 Act provided for the detention for up to 28 days of a person who suffered from a mental disorder which warranted his detention in a hospital "under observation (with or without medical treatment) for at least a limited period."[53]

Mental Health (Amendment) Act 1982

The words "observation (with or without medical treatment)" were then replaced by "assessment (or for assessment followed by medical treatment)" in the 1982 and 1983 statutes. The reason given for this at the time was that the Government preferred the word "assessment," because it implied "more active intervention to help to diagnose a patient's disorder and plan a treatment programme."[54] More particularly,

> "'Observation' is defined in the Oxford English Dictionary as 'the action or an act of observing scientifically; esp the careful watching and noting of a phenomenon in regard to its cause or effect, or of phenomena in regard to their mutual relations, these being observed as they occur in nature (and so opposed to experiment).' 'Assessment' is a wider process ('estimation, evaluation' — OED) of which observation is only a part, and is therefore considered a more appropriate term to reflect current professional practice and to ensure that the patient's needs for treatment are ascertained and met as soon as possible."[55]

---

53   Mental Health Act 1959, s.25(2)(a).
54   *Reform of Mental Health Legislation,* Cmnd. 8405 (1981), para. 17.
55   *Mental Health (Amendment) Bill: Notes on Clauses, House of Commons* (D.H.S.S., 1982), pp.23–24.

The Code of Practice

Chapter 5 of the *Code of Practice* deals with the choice of section when making an application under Part II.[56] Paragraphs 5.2 and 5.3 list a number of section 2 and section 3 "pointers." The Code suggests that section 2 will generally be indicated where the diagnosis and prognosis of a patient's condition is unclear; there is a need to carry out an in-patient assessment in order to formulate a treatment plan; a judgement is needed as to whether the patient will accept treatment on a voluntary basis following admission; a judgement has to be made as to whether a particular treatment proposal, which can only be administered to the patient under Part IV of the Act, is likely to be effective; a patient who has already been assessed, and who has been previously admitted compulsorily under the Act, is judged to have changed since the previous admission and needs further assessment; a patient has not previously been admitted to hospital either compulsorily or informally. Conversely, section 3 will generally be indicated where a patient admitted in the past is considered to need compulsory admission for the treatment of a mental disorder already known to his clinical team, and which has been assessed in the recent past by that team. The Code states that decisions as to which section to invoke should not be influenced by wanting to avoid consulting the nearest relative; the fact that a proposed treatment to be administered under the Act will last less than 28 days; or the fact that a patient detained under section 2 will get quicker access to a tribunal. It is important to realise that the pointers in the Code are not a statement of the law. Rather, they represent practice guidelines as to when the use of one power may be indicated in preference to the other.

Textbook opinion

Gostin states that the term "assessment" *in itself* "may suggest that medical procedures must be limited to those which are necessary to form a diagnosis and to devise a plan of treatment, thus excluding procedures solely for the purpose of treatment (*i.e.* alleviating or curing the patient's condition)."[57] Jones considers that it is unclear whether "assessment" is confined to the process involved in enabling the medical staff to identify the specific statutory form of mental disorder that the patient is suffering from or whether it could also involve the evaluation of the patient's response to treatment.[58]

Judicial opinion

In the case of *ex p. Williamson* (**229**), Tucker J. said that section 2 had the limited purpose of assessing the patient's condition with a with a view to ascertaining, *firstly*, whether it was a case which would respond to treatment and, *secondly*, whether an application under section 3 would be appropriate.

Interpretation in practice

The recent trend amongst practitioners has been to restrict the meaning of "assessment" to something approximating that given by Gostin. This has caused some practitioners to say that, in cases where a patient's medical history and his need

---

[56] *Mental Health Act 1983: Code of Practice* (Department of Health, 2nd ed., 1993).
[57] L. Gostin, *Mental Health Services — Law and Practice* (Shaw & Sons Ltd.), para. 11.05.5.
[58] R. Jones, *Mental Health Act Manual* (Sweet & Maxwell, 4th ed., 1996), p.27.

for treatment is well established, the making or continuation in force of a section 2 application is unlawful. The argument is most commonly encountered in one of three contexts.

"Revolving-door patients" and section 29

The first situation occurs where the nearest relative of a relapsing patient, whose diagnosis and treatment regime is well-established as a result of previous admissions, refuses to consent to an admission to hospital under section 3. The situation quite often arises soon after the expiration of an earlier period of liability to detention, quickly followed by the patient refusing further treatment. A pattern of readmission and discharge develops over the years and it must be acknowledged that, following each readmission, there is generally little in the way of clinical assessment, the diagnosis and the treatment of choice being well-established. The tendency is merely to resume the same plan of treatment as before and to compel the patient to receive as an in-patient the treatment which he would not voluntarily accept as an out-patient. Where this is so, many practitioners take the view that, although detention for treatment is appropriate, the patient cannot be said to warrant detention in a hospital for assessment, and it is unlawful to make a section 2 application. Accordingly, the appropriate course of action is to first apply for the relative's displacement and, if an order is made, to then make an application under section 3.[59]

"Revolving-door patients" and section 72(1)(a)(i)

The second situation arises where, in a situation similar to that just described, the nearest relative is not contactable or does not object to the patient's detention under section 2 but the patient applies to a tribunal following his admission. Under section 72(1)(a)(i), the tribunal is required to discharge him if it is satisfied that he is not, at the time of the hearing, suffering from mental disorder of a nature or degree which warrants his detention for assessment or for assessment "followed" by medical treatment. Relying on the advice in the Code, the patient's solicitor will submit that the patient must, as a matter of law, be discharged forthwith because he is detained only for treatment. His need for treatment is not being assessed.

Tribunals and completed assessments

A similar problem may arise where a tribunal considers the case of a patient who had not previously received psychiatric care prior to being admitted for assessment. Here, there is generally no question about the propriety of using section 2 in preference to section 3 at the time of admission. However, the patient's responsible medical officer may say during his evidence that he has completed his assessment but that the patient requires further treatment before being discharged or granted leave. Based on this concession, the authorised representative will submit that the tribunal is bound to discharge the patient, because it cannot possibly be satisfied that any mental disorder from which he suffers warrants his detention for assessment, or for assessment followed by treatment, irrespective of how serious his condition may be. It is no longer a case of "assessment followed by treatment" but treatment only — specifically, the treatment indicated by the completed assessment and now in progress.

---

[59] The situation here is therefore different from that in *ex p. Williamson* (**229**), where the patient remained in hospital informally after the expiration of an earlier section 2 application, and so was continually receiving in-patient assessment and treatment.

Detention under section 2 following an objection to section 3

The first question which arises from the situations described is whether, when admission under section 3 is openly acknowledged by the professionals involved to be the most appropriate form of application, the patient may nevertheless be detained under section 2 while the reasonableness of the nearest relative's objection is determined by a county court. The 1983 Act does not expressly preclude the use of section 2 as an interim measure in such circumstances. However, Parliament is presumed not to enact legislation which interferes with the liberty of the subject without making it clear that this was its intention. Unless clear statutory authority to the contrary exists, no one is to be detained in hospital without his consent.[60] The present edition of the *Memorandum* on the Act offers no assistance on the question and nor does the *Code of Practice*, although it may fairly be said that such a situation is not listed as a "section 2 pointer" in paragraph 5.2.

The argument against section 2 being available

It may be argued that section 29(3)(c) is intended to deal exhaustively with the situation where the nearest relative objects to a patient's admission for treatment and an approved social worker has only one of only two options: either not to make an application for admission or to apply for the nearest relative's displacement, with a view to making such an application later. Prior to any county court hearing, and a judicial finding that the nearest relative's objection is unreasonable, the patient may not be detained under Part II. Any other view means that a nearest relative who reasonably objects to a patient being again compulsorily admitted for treatment is powerless to prevent his detention. The right to object, on being consulted by an approved social worker, becomes meaningless if the social worker can simply bypass that objection by making an assessment application. The patient may be subjected to compulsory treatment for 28 days, or even longer if county court proceedings are commenced. This, it is said, cannot be correct. Although the Act does not permit the nearest relative to object to the detention for assessment of a person whose condition and need for treatment is not fully understood, its intention is to enable the nearest relative to prevent further compulsory admissions once the diagnosis, prognosis and range of possible treatments are known. At that stage, the nearest relative is presumed to be in a position to make an informed decision about the advantages and disadvantages of further treatment. That being so, any objection to further treatment is binding on the social worker concerned, at least until such time as he can demonstrate to a county court that those objections are unreasonable. Obtaining such a judicial determination need not be a prolonged affair, as was made clear in the case of *B v. B*: "Applications for compulsory admission to and detention in hospital for treatment often have to be made in an emergency. It is not always possible to obtain the opinions of medical practitioners approved by the Secretary of State or a local health authority. Therefore, any doctor can be called on for the purposes of supporting an application to dispense with consent in order to provide the necessary evidence for the county court."[61]

The argument for section 2 being available

The above argument is attractive in many ways but the history and framework of the Act in fact suggests that—

---

60 *R. v. Hallstrom, ex p. W.; R. v. Gardner, ex p. L.* [1986] 1 Q.B. 1090, *per* McCullough J.
61 *B. (A.) v. B. (L.) (Mental Health Patient)* [1980] 1 W.L.R. 116.

- the absence of a section 3 emergency procedure equivalent to section 4 means that the words "for assessment (or for assessment followed by treatment)" are not to be construed in a way which excludes patients whose need for treatment is well-established (**235**).

- the use of section 2 following an objection to detention under section 3 is an option which Parliament intended to be available to professionals, and one of the reasons why it gave the nearest relative no power to object to admission under section 2 (**236**).

- the power conferred by section 11(4) is the right to prevent a patient from being detained for a potentially indefinite period unless a county court order is first obtained; not the power to prevent detention for a finite period (**236**).

- the remedy which the Act gives a nearest relative who objects to a patient's detention under section 2 is the power to discharge the patient unless the responsible medical officer considers that he would then be likely to act in a manner dangerous to himself or others (**237**).

- Parliament intended that, unless a patient clearly requires compulsory treatment for more than 28 days, he should generally be admitted under section 2, even if he is a well-known patient whose need for treatment is well-established (**238**).

The absence of a section 3 emergency procedure

The medical grounds for admission under sections 2 and 4 are the same and an emergency application is a section 2 application initially founded upon a single medical recommendation. Such an application may only be made if it is urgently necessary that the patient is admitted "for assessment (or for assessment followed by treatment)" and compliance with the usual section 2 procedures will involve undesirable delay. If there are some patients who may not be admitted under section 2, because they have previously been fully assessed, then neither may they be admitted under section 4. However, the Act does not include an equivalent emergency procedure by which a person may be detained under section 3 on the basis of a single medical recommendation. It could be that Parliament intended that chronic patients whose conditions have recently been fully assessed (for example, patients with a long history of suicide attempts, where the risk of self-harm is well-established) should not be detainable under section 4 — even if their nearest relative does not object and obtaining a second recommendation would involve undesirable delay. It is more probable, however, that Parliament intended that the single emergency procedure would be available in all cases where admission is urgently necessary. If so, Parliament must have considered that both new patients and chronic, revolving-door, patients alike may warrant detention "for assessment (or for assessment followed by treatment) for at least a limited period." A reading of Hansard confirms this interpretation, as the following paragraph shows.

Mental Health Act 1959, ss. 25 and 29

Section 2 derives from section 25 of the 1959 Act and section 4 from section 29. Clause 25 of the 1959 Mental Health Bill originally provided only for a patient's admission for observation, without any reference to treatment. The Government was initially concerned that if the emergency procedure was also confined to applications for observation, as some Members wished, "there might be cases which ought to be dealt with urgently under the emergency procedure but in which there was no need for observation because the nature of the illness and the need for treatment might already be clear. That was the major difficulty."[62] The phrase "(with or without other medical treatment)" was therefore added after the word "observation" during the Bill's passage through the House of Commons. The Minister of Health, Mr. Derek Walker-Smith, explained that observation was still "an essential object of admission under the Clause, but the Amendment makes it clear that the patient who clearly needs at least a short period of treatment can be admitted under the Clause 25 ..."[63] The Minister continued,

> "The major difficulty which I had in mind is largely met by the new subsection (2) of Clause 25 ... Even in a case where it is clear what treatment will be needed, because the patient comes as an out-patient who is known, or a former in-patient, observation will generally be needed to determine whether the twenty-eight days' compulsory detention is likely to be enough. This revised wording of Clause 25 will enable a patient to be admitted with the primary object of giving the short-term treatment that is needed. The same will apply to emergency applications for observation under Clause 29."[64]

Sections 25 and 29 were re-enacted as sections 2 and 4 of the 1983 Act with only minor modifications, the previous references to observation with or without treatment being replaced by references to assessment or assessment followed by treatment. The reasons for this change of terminology have already been explained. On close examination, it is the significance of the phrase "followed by" rather than "assessment" which has really caused the problems encountered in practice to which reference has been made. There would be no ambiguity if section 2 instead authorised detention for assessment "with or without treatment." Nevertheless, the fact that Parliament did not use the opportunity to introduce a specific section 3 emergency procedure indicates that the original reasons given for a second emergency procedure being unnecessary were still seen as holding good. The existence of an emergency procedure providing only for detention under section 2, and the extracts from Hansard, make it difficult to argue that Parliament intended that chronic well-known patients could no longer be admitted under section 3. Indeed, contrary to what the *Code of Practice* now suggests, Parliament seems to have envisaged that, unless a patient clearly requires compulsory treatment for more than 28 days, the initial admission should be limited to that defined period.

Limits of a nearest relative's power to prevent detention

Paragraph 133 of the *Memorandum* on the 1959 Act, issued by the D.H.S.S., stated that "an application to the county court may be made while the patient is detained for observation after admission under Section 25 or 29 — or he may be so admitted

---

62   The Minister of Health (Mr. Derek Walker-Smith), *Hansard*, H.C. Vol. 605, col. 281.
63   *Ibid.*, col. 269.
64   *Ibid.*, *Hansard*, cols. 281–82.

while an application to the court is pending..."[65] The Government's White Paper of 1978 suggests that this option of admitting a patient under section 25 following an objection to his admission for treatment was intended to remain an option under any new legislation—

"Safeguards in relation to section 25

....2.15 The safeguards for patients detained under section 26 are stronger than those for patients detained under section 25. For example, the Mental Welfare Officer is required to consult the nearest relative where an application is being made for detention under section 26 except where this is not practicable or would cause unreasonable delay. If the nearest relative objects to the application being made, the Mental Welfare Officer cannot proceed. However, on the application of the Mental Welfare Officer or any relative of the patient or any other person with whom the patient is living, a County Court can make an order appointing another person to act as the nearest relative in certain circumstances, for instance where it is established that the nearest relative has unreasonably objected to an application for compulsory admission. In view of the delay which can be involved in this procedure, it is not thought practicable for the patient's nearest relative to have a similar right to veto a section 25 application but it is proposed that the Mental Welfare Officer should be required to take all reasonable steps to inform the nearest relative that a section 25 application has been made and to tell him of his rights of appeal and discharge ... It is considered that the nearest relative should have the same right to discharge a section 25 patient as he does a section 26 patient, but with the same provisos..."[66]

It seems therefore that a reason for not allowing the nearest relative a power to prevent admission under section 2 is precisely to enable the patient to be admitted under a finite, unrenewable, "order" while the reasonableness of that relative's objection to his detention under a potentially indefinite, renewable, "order" is reviewed by the court.[67] It is also arguable that the fact of the nearest relative's objection, ruling out as it does the patient's immediate admission under section 3, may have the effect that detention under section 2 is then "warranted" albeit that it was not warranted prior to the making of the objection.

The nearest relative's power to discharge

The effect of the provisions in sections 23–25 is that where a nearest relative objects to the patient's detention under section 3 and, as a result, he is admitted under section 2, that relative may discharge the patient unless the responsible medical officer considers that the patient would then be likely to act in a manner dangerous to himself or others.[68] This is the remedy given to the nearest relative where a

---

65   *Mental Health Act 1959: Memorandum on Parts I, IV to VII and IX* (Ministry of Health, 1960).

66   *Review of the Mental Health Act 1959*, Cmnd. 7320 (1978), *pp.15–16.*

67   Again, this interpretation is not contradicted by the decision in *ex p. Williamson* (**229**). The patient in that case was admitted under section 2, in the knowledge that his nearest relative objected to a section 3 application being made. The objection there was that the patient was further detained under section 2, for a second period of 28 days, because of the local authority's failure during the first period to apply to the county court for the reasonableness of the objection to be determined.

68   The making of a county court application does not prevent the patient from being discharged under section 23 before the court case is disposed of, including by the nearest relative whose displacement is being sought. See *e.g. Mental Health Act 1959: Memorandum on Parts I, IV to VII and IX* (Ministry of Health, 1960), para. 131. The effect of section 29(4) is to extend beyond 28 days the period for which the managers have authority to detain the patient, not to suspend the operation of section 23. However, except in cases involving guardianship, the nearest relative's power of discharge is ineffective if the patient would, if released, be likely to act dangerously.

section 2 application is made in the circumstances described. The overall effect of the Part II provisions is therefore as follows—

- where the nearest relative objects to a patient's detention under both sections 2 and 3, and there is no likelihood that the patient would act dangerously if not detained, it will often be difficult for the approved social worker to be satisfied that a section 2 application ought to be made, and is necessary or proper.[69] This is because the patient's admission is likely merely to result in him being immediately discharged by the objecting nearest relative. The approved social worker may therefore decide to apply for the nearest relative's displacement and make no application for the patient's admission for the time being.

- where the nearest relative objects to a patient's detention under both sections 2 and 3, and there is evidence that the patient would act dangerously if not detained, there can be no legal or practical objection to the patient being detained under section 2 or 4 (dangerous conduct or the likelihood of it often being a reason for invoking the emergency application procedure). Any attempt to discharge the patient may be barred and he may, if necessary, be detained under section 2 until the reasonableness of the nearest relative's objection to his indefinite detention for treatment is determined by the county court.

Failure to apply promptly for displacement

In practice, a lot of disquiet arises because approved social workers who make a section 2 application following an objection to detention under section 3 do not then promptly apply to the county court for a determination of the reasonableness of the objection. Commonly, a "wait and see" strategy is adopted and a county court application is only made when the 28-day section 2 period is about to expire and further compulsory treatment proves to be unavoidable. Although this may have the benefit of avoiding unnecessary litigation and saving professional time, it also results in the section 2 period being unduly protracted, during which extended period neither the patient nor his nearest relative has any right of application to a tribunal.

The statutory purpose of section 2

The *Code of Practice* states that decisions about whether to make an application under section 2 or section 3 should not be influenced by the fact that a proposed treatment to be administered under the Act will last less than 28 days.[70] This reflects the current fashion of saying that section 3 applications are not more restrictive of individual liberty than section 2 applications, because the authority conferred by the former is not detention for six months, merely detention for up to six months. It is submitted, however, that such a view is wrong. The authority to detain and compulsorily treat a patient which is conferred by an assessment application is finite and non-renewable; that conferred by section 3 renewable and potentially indefinite. Because this is so, the Act provides stronger safeguards in relation to such applications, including prohibiting them if the nearest relative objects unless a

---

69 See Mental Health Act 1983, s.13(1).
70 *Mental Health Act 1983: Code of Practice* (2nd ed., 1993), para. 5.4b.

county court order is first obtained. In providing these stronger safeguards, Parliament clearly did recognise that the power of detention conferred by section 3 represents a greater infringement of personal liberty. Accordingly, it also provided that a person shall not be detained under section 3 unless the in-patient treatment which he requires "cannot be provided unless he is detained under this section." In other words, section 2 should be used if the in-patient treatment can be provided under that section because no more than 28 days' compulsory treatment may be necessary. As such, a principle purpose of section 2 is to ensure that citizens are not liable to indefinite detention and compulsory treatment unless a thorough assessment indicates that there is no viable alternative. It provides an opportunity to explore less restrictive alternatives and to assess, in the light of them and the patient's response to treatment during the 28 day period, the necessity for indefinite compulsory treatment. If medical opinion is then that a prolonged and potentially indefinite period of detention is necessary, no application may be made unless the patient's nearest relative or an approved social worker concurs with this assessment of the situation and, if the former objects, unless a county court order is first obtained.

The meaning of assessment

Having regard to the above, the word "assessment" is something of a statutory term of art. The assessment involves assessing from a clinical viewpoint the patient's need for prolonged treatment and assessing from a legal viewpoint the necessity of prolonged and potentially indefinite compulsory treatment. In reaching a decision about whether any treatment which a patient requires can only be given if he is detained under section 3, it will often be necessary for an assessment to include —

- assessing whether the patient is suffering from mental disorder and, if he is, the statutory form of mental disorder from which he is suffering.

- assessing the cause of any mental disorder and identifying, where relevant, the events which triggered any recent relapse.

- assessing, that is monitoring, the patient's response to any treatment given and forming a prognosis, in order to determine whether any in-patient treatment indicated may be completed within 28 days or a prolonged period of treatment is necessary.

- identifying and assessing what other methods of treating the patient are available and, if so, whether they are appropriate.

- if a prolonged period of in-patient treatment is indicated, assessing whether it can be provided without the patient being detained under section 3.

- assessing whether detention in hospital is actually "necessary" for the patient's health or safety or for the protection of others, rather than merely justifiable with those purposes in mind.

239

- assessing whether, in the case of a patient found to suffer from mental impairment or psychopathic disorder, further treatment is likely to alleviate or prevent a deterioration of his condition.

- consulting the nearest relative and ascertaining his views on the use of further compulsory powers in the context of the patient's response to treatment during the section 2 period.

It must be emphasised that because a person has previously been detained under section 3, it does not follow that prolonged liability to detention in hospital is again necessary. The relapse may be at an early stage and there may be alternative treatments or community facilities which were not previously available. The patient may historically make a good response to in-treatment and a full assessment within a hospital setting may allow effective short-term treatment to be given. In any case, the statutory issue is not whether a patient is a well known but whether he presently satisfies the more stringent criteria for detention under section 3. In particular, whether the in-patient treatment which he needs cannot be provided unless resort is had to section 3.

The tribunal discharge criteria

It has been noted that references in the 1959 Act to detention for "observation (with or without medical treatment)" were replaced by references to detention for "assessment (or for assessment followed by medical treatment)" in the 1982 and 1983 statutes. The new phrase also forms part of the tribunal discharge criteria. Two examples of situations in which its interpretation has been disputed and caused difficulty have been given (**233**). Whether a tribunal is obliged to discharge a patient once a diagnosis and prognosis have been reached and a programme of treatment been commenced was touched upon but not resolved in *R. v. Wessex Mental Health Review Tribunal, ex p. Wiltshire County Council.*[71] In this case, the tribunal were of the opinion that the discharge criteria were satisfied, and that a statutory duty to discharge existed, because the patient's condition was well-known and could not properly be said to require "assessment." In its application for judicial review of that decision, Wiltshire County Council contended that "no Mental Health Review Tribunal properly directing itself on the relevant law and acting reasonably could have reached the decision that the Patient should be discharged from his detention under section 2 ... The Tribunal applied an unnecessarily restrictive test when interpreting the words 'assessment' and 'assessment followed by treatment' contained in section 72(1) ..." The case was eventually determined without reference to this particular issue.

The statutory framework

The meaning of the phrase "for assessment (or for assessment followed by treatment)" in section 72 must be determined by reference to the statutory framework. Based on the observations which have already been made, it is submitted that this framework may be summarised in the following way—

---

[71] *R. v. Wessex Mental Health Review Tribunal, ex p. Wiltshire County Council; Perkins v. Bath District Health Authority* (1989) 4 B.M.L.R. 145.

- Where a patient is assessed not to be mentally disordered, the first of the reasons for detaining him has been fulfilled and the second also in that no treatment will follow what constitutes a completed assessment. Although section 23 does not expressly oblige a responsible medical officer to then discharge the patient, a duty to do so arises because continuing the patient's detention will not then be for a purpose authorised by the Act.

- Similarly, once a patient has been assessed not to suffer from any form of mental disorder that warrants compulsory treatment then both purposes are fulfilled, continued detention being warranted neither for assessment or treatment.

- Where, however, a patient has been assessed to suffer from a disorder which does warrant detention for treatment, his responsible medical officer is not thereby bound to discharge him simply because he has commenced the treatment indicated by his assessment of the patient's treatment needs. Nor is he obliged to recommend the making of a section 3 application merely because the focus of the detention has shifted from the first of the statutory purposes (assessment) to the second (treatment following assessment). The wording of section 2(2)(a) — "(or for assessment followed by medical treatment)" — and the consent to treatment provisions in Part IV are clearly intended to permit the giving of any treatment indicated by the assessment for the duration of the 28-day period.

- Indeed, it would arguably be improper for the responsible medical officer to complete a section 3 recommendation if the treatment assessed to be necessary might, in his opinion, be concluded within the 28-day section 2 period. This is because it is a condition of detention under section 3 that the treatment which the patient requires cannot be provided unless he is detained under that section.

- Bearing these points in mind, the issue about the ambit of section 72(1)(a)(i) becomes whether Parliament intended to impose on tribunals a duty to discharge a patient who the responsible medical officer is not obliged to discharge, simply because the first of two statutory purposes authorised by the application has been fulfilled.

- It would be remarkable if Parliament intended that whenever an assessment of a patient's condition demonstrates a need for compulsory treatment — that is that the assessment should be "followed by treatment" — a tribunal is then obliged by virtue of this positive finding of a serious mental disorder to discharge the patient. If this were correct a patient must be discharged both when he is assessed not to need compulsory treatment and when he is assessed to need such treatment.

- A patient who suffers from mental impairment or a psychopathic disorder may not be detained, nor his detention be renewed, unless his condition is treatable. However, a tribunal reviewing his case is not obliged to discharge him even if satisfied that his condition is untreatable. Nor is it obliged to discharge a mentally ill or severely mentally impaired patient whose

241

condition is untreatable even though there appears to be no risk of him being neglected or exploited upon release. Nor, because the discharge criteria are phrased as a double-negative, is it obliged to discharge any patient unless it is positively satisfied that the discharge criteria are made out. These features reflect the fact that, as a review body, it is only obliged to discharge a patient if persuaded that the two core grounds for making or renewing an application no longer subsist. It is therefore unlikely that Parliament intended, in this single instance, that a tribunal but not the responsible medical officer is obliged to discharge.

- For the above reasons, it is submitted that the use of the words "followed by" in section 2 are consequential upon Parliament's preference for the word "assessment." The words emphasise that where a person is detained for 28 days, those with clinical responsibility for him should not simply passively observe his mental state but actively assess his need for treatment and then commence that treatment as soon as practicable, thereby minimising the period of detention and compulsion.

- The incorporation within section 72(1)(a) of the same wording used in section 2, together with the addition of the word "then", was unfortunate and unnecessarily ambiguous. The underlying intention was to require a tribunal to consider whether it is satisfied, in the light of the evidence presented at the hearing, that the patient's condition does not, or no longer, warrants his detention for either of the statutory purposes authorised by the application, namely assessment or treatment following assessment. Insofar as the drafting is, as elsewhere in section 72, indifferent, section 72(1) should, it is submitted, be read as follows — *"(a) the tribunal shall direct the discharge of a patient liable to be detained under section 2 above if they are satisfied (i) that he is not then suffering from mental disorder or from mental disorder of a nature or degree which warrants his detention in a hospital for assessment (or for medical treatment following assessment) for at least a limited period."*

- In other words, the phrase "(or for assessment followed by medical treatment)" may properly be read as meaning "(or for medical treatment following assessment)" where treatment has already been commenced before the hearing takes place.

- It may be added that the "golden rule" of statutory interpretation allows the court to prefer a sensible meaning to an absurd if literally correct meaning. Similarly, the court may read in, ignore or alter a word in the statute being interpreted if not to do so would make the provision unintelligible, absurd, unworkable, totally unreasonable or totally irreconcilable with other provisions within the same Act.

242

EMERGENCY APPLICATIONS

In any case of "urgent necessity," an application for admission for assessment may be made under section 4, which provides that the application shall be sufficient in the first instance if founded on one of the medical recommendations required by section 2. The grounds of the application are those set out in section 2(2). The application must include a statement that it is "of urgent necessity" for the patient to be admitted and detained under section 2 and that compliance with the usual provisions relating to such applications would involve "undesirable delay." The medical practitioner who provides the supporting recommendation must verify the statement which the applicant has made. New forms were prescribed under the 1983 Act and they require information to be given clarifying the circumstances of the emergency.

USAGE

Approximately 10 per cent. of patients compulsorily admitted to hospital for assessment are initially admitted under section 4, on the strength of a single medical recommendation. During the period 1987–1983, the number of section 4 applications declined by 42 per cent., from 2180 to 1263 cases each year.

HISTORICAL NOTE

Historically, Parliament has from time to time further restricted the circumstances in which a person may be admitted to hospital on the basis of one medical recommendation. Section 30 of "An Act to regulate the Care and Treatment of Insane Persons in England" (1828)[72] provided that a medical certificate upon which an order for the confinement of any person, other than a parish patient, was given had to be signed by two medical practitioners unless "special circumstances" prevented the patient being separately visited by two medical practitioners. Where special circumstances existed, a person could be admitted to a licensed house upon the certificate of a single medical practitioner provided the certificate was signed by a second medical practitioner within seven days of the patient's admission. Section 11 of the Lunacy Act 1890 made provision for "urgency orders." Such an order might be made by a person aged 21 or over — the patient's spouse or a relative where practicable — who had "personally seen" the patient within the previous 48 hours. A statement of various prescribed particulars had to be annexed to the application and the order was sufficient if founded upon a single medical recommendation in the prescribed form. This medical certificate was given by a medical practitioner who had "personally examined" the patient within the period of two days prior to the patient's reception and included a statement that it was "expedient" that the patient be received and detained. Once made, the order remained in force for seven days, unless at the expiry of that period a petition was before the court in which case it continued in force until the petition was disposed of. The formalities relating to the making of an emergency application under section 29 of the 1959 Act were similar to those presently in force, save that the application could be made by any relative of the patient — not just by his "nearest relative" — and the applicant had to have seen the patient within the period of 72 hours prior to making the application, compared with the 24 hour period now stipulated. In only permitting a 72-hour period of confinement, this represented a further tightening of the procedures.

---

[72]   9 Geo. IV., c.41.

URGENT NECESSITY

In *Re Cathcart*,[73] Halsbury L.C. emphasised that urgency orders under the 1890 Act should only be used where instant intervention was required and, given that the statutory procedures have subsequently been further tightened, it is likely that the use of emergency applications remains confined to such cases. The *Memorandum* on the Act states that it may be necessary to admit a patient on the basis of a single medical recommendation "in exceptional circumstances."[74] The *Code of Practice* emphasises the need for a "genuine emergency."[75] This requires evidence of the existence of a significant risk of mental or physical harm to the patient or to others; and/or the danger of serious harm to property; and/or the need for physical restraint of the patient.[76]

THE APPLICATION PROCEDURES

An application may not be made under section 4 unless the applicant has personally seen the patient within the previous 24 hours. Section 14, which deals with the preparation of social reports following nearest relative applications, does not apply in such cases.

THE EFFECT OF AN EMERGENCY APPLICATION

A duly completed emergency application constitutes sufficient authority—

- for the applicant, or any person authorised by him, to take the patient and convey him to the hospital specified in the application within the period of 24 hours beginning at the time when the patient was examined by the practitioner giving the medical recommendation or the time when the application is made, whichever is the earlier;[77]

- for the managers of the hospital to admit the patient within that period and thereafter to detain him in accordance with the provisions of the Act.

DURATION

The application ceases to have effect once 72 hours have elapsed since the time of admission unless by then the managers have received the second medical recommendation required by section 2 and the recommendations together comply with the usual requirements applicable in section 2 cases.[78] Where the necessary second recommendation is provided within this period, the patient remains liable to be detained for assessment for the remainder of the 28-day detention period which

---

[73]   *Re Cathcart* [1893] 1 Ch. 466.
[74]   *Mental Health Act 1983: Memorandum on Parts I to VI, VIII and X* (D.H.S.S., 1987), para. 28.
[75]   *Mental Health Act 1983: Code of Practice* (2nd ed., 1993), para. 6.2.
[76]   *Ibid.*, para. 6.3.
[77]   The Act clearly envisages that the application may be made before the medical recommendation is given, notwithstanding that it must be "founded" on the recommendation. See also Lunacy Act 1890, s.11(2); *Archbold's Lunacy and Mental Deficiency Law* (Butterworth & Co., Shaw & Sons, 5th ed., 1915), p.191.
[78]   Apart from the necessary modification that the second recommendation may be dated later than the application: see Mental Health Act 1983, s.4(4)(b).

commenced with his admission to hospital under section 4. On a practical level, it is important that the applicant obtains a copy of any second medical recommendation later furnished. If this is not done, and the second recommendation is materially defective, the patient may be detained for 28 days in pursuance of an invalid application made by him, albeit that it was in order when he submitted it.[79]

APPLICATIONS FOR ADMISSION FOR TREATMENT

A person may be liable to be detained in hospital for treatment under section 3 in one of four ways—

- Under section 3, a person may be admitted to hospital for treatment in pursuance of an application for treatment.

- Under section 19, a person who is subject to guardianship may be transferred to hospital.

- Under Part VI of the Act and the Mental Health (Scotland) Act 1984, a person who is detained in hospital for treatment in Scotland or Northern Ireland may be removed to a hospital in England or Wales.

- Under the transitional provisions, a patient admitted to hospital for treatment prior to the implementation of the 1983 Act may be deemed to have been admitted in pursuance of an application made under section 3.

Applications under section 3

An application for admission for treatment may be made in respect of a patient on the grounds that—

a. "he is suffering from **(213)** mental illness **(060)**, severe mental impairment **(070)**, psychopathic disorder **(082)** or mental impairment **(070)** and his mental disorder is of a nature or degree **(213)** which makes it appropriate **(215)** for him to receive medical treatment **(216)** in a hospital **(131)**; and

b. in the case of psychopathic disorder or mental impairment, such treatment is likely to alleviate or prevent a deterioration of his condition **(222)**; and

c. it is necessary **(220)** for the health **(217)** or safety **(218)** of the patient or for the protection of other persons **(219)** that he should receive such treatment and it cannot be provided unless he is detained under this section **(239)**."[80]

---

[79] For example, the second recommendation is, like the first, given by a medical practitioner who is not section 12 approved or is otherwise insufficient to warrant the patient's detention.

[80] Mental Health Act 1983, s.3(2).

Transfer to hospital under section 19

Where a patient who is subject to a guardianship application is transferred to hospital under section 19 (283), the guardianship application takes effect as if it were a section 3 application and as if the patient had been admitted to hospital in pursuance of it on the date of his original reception into guardianship.

Removal under Part VI

Section 82(1) enables patients who are detained for treatment in Northern Ireland under Article 12(1) or 13 of the Mental Health (Northern Ireland) Order 1986 to be removed to a hospital in England or Wales. Where this occurs, section 82(4) of the 1983 Act provides that the patient shall be treated as if he had been admitted to hospital in pursuance of a section 3 application made on the date of his admission to hospital in England or Wales.

Removal under the Mental Health (Scotland) Act 1984

The Mental Health (Scotland) Act 1984 similarly provides that detained patients removed from Scotland to England or Wales shall be treated as if they had been detained in pursuance of an application made on the date of their arrival under the corresponding provision in the 1983 Act.[81]

Patients deemed to be liable to be detained under section 3

Section 3 derives from section 26 of the Mental Health Act 1959. Patients who were originally admitted under section 26 and have remained continuously detained since then are deemed to have been admitted in pursuance of a section 3 application. In practice, it is worth carefully checking the transitional provisions since it is common to find that the first renewal report due after the new Act came into force was not furnished within the prescribed period. If this is the case, there will have been no valid authority for the patient's detention under the 1983 Act since some date shortly after it came into force.

STATUTORY FRAMEWORK

The main differences between the grounds of application and the statutory procedures applicable under section 2 and section 3 have already been summarised (226, 228).

DURATION

An application under section 3 authorises the managers of the hospital to detain the patient for a period of up to six months beginning with the date of his admission under section 3. The authority for the detention of the patient may be renewed if appropriate for a further period of six months and thereafter at yearly intervals in accordance with the provisions of section 20. The effect of an application under section 3 in other respects is dealt with below (273 et seq.).

---

[81] Mental Health (Scotland) Act 1984, s.77(2).

GUARDIANSHIP APPLICATIONS

A patient may be received into guardianship under Part II in one of three ways—

- Under section 7, an application may be made for a patient's reception into guardianship.[82]

- Under section 19, a patient who is liable to be detained under section 2 or 3 may be transferred into guardianship.[83]

- Under Part VI and the Mental Health (Scotland) Act 1984, a patient who is subject to a guardianship application in Scotland or Northern Ireland may be removed into guardianship in England or Wales.

Guardianship applications

A guardianship application in respect of a patient may be made under section 7 on the grounds that—

a. "he is suffering from (**213**) mental disorder (**051**), being mental illness (**060**), severe mental impairment (**070**), psychopathic disorder (**082**) or mental impairment (**070**) and his mental disorder is of a nature or degree (**213**) which warrants (**215**) his reception into guardianship under this section; and

b. it is necessary in the interests of (**220**) the welfare (**217**) of the patient (**098**) or for the protection of other persons (**219**) that the patient should be so received."[84]

Transfer into guardianship under section 19

Where a patient who is liable to be detained under section 2 or 3 is transferred into guardianship, the Act provides that the application has effect as if it were a guardianship application made and accepted on the date when the patient was originally admitted to hospital for assessment or treatment, as the case may be.[85] The transfer of a patient into guardianship involves few formalities. Because no fresh application is necessary, and the effect is to end the patient's liability to detention, the nearest relative's consent and fresh medical recommendations are not required, nor need the patient be interviewed by an approved social worker. If the underlying aim is to reduce the time spent by the patient in hospital, but it is realised that compulsory readmissions will periodically be necessary, further transfers to and from hospital and guardianship may be made.

---

[82] Mental Health Act 1983, ss.7(1) and (5), 11(1) and (2).

[83] Mental Health Act 1983, paras. 19(1)(a) and (2)(b). For the prescribed procedure and forms, see the Mental Health (Hospital, Guardianship and Consent to Treatment) Regulations 1983, reg. 7(3).

[84] Mental Health Act 1983, s.7(2). There is no treatability test for guardianship. It suffices that guardianship is in the interests of the patient's general welfare or for the protection of others.

[85] Mental Health Act 1983, s.19(2)(b). Because of an oversight, a section 2 patient who is transferred into guardianship does not have a legal classification under the Act.

Removal under Part IV

Section 82(1) provides that patients subject to guardianship in Northern Ireland may be removed to in England or Wales and received into guardianship there. Where this occurs, section 82(3) provides that the patient shall be treated as if he received into guardianship in pursuance of a section 7 application made on the date he arrives at the place where he is to reside.

Mental Health (Scotland) Act 1984

The Mental Health (Scotland) Act 1984 similarly provides that a patient subject to guardianship in Scotland who is removed to England or Wales under the 1984 Act shall be treated as if he had been received into guardianship in pursuance of a section 7 application made on the date he arrives at the place where he is to reside.[86]

HISTORICAL NOTE

Although the placing of persons suffering from mental disorder under a guardian can be traced back to the middle ages,[87] guardianship in its present statutory form has its origins in the Mental Deficiency Act 1913[88] and the recommendations of the Percy Report,[89] most of which were later enacted in the Mental Health Act 1959.[90]

The Mental Deficiency Acts 1913 and 1927

The Mental Deficiency Act 1913 provided that "idiots" and "imbeciles" could be received into guardianship upon a parent furnishing a statement of statutory particulars concerning the patient, accompanied by a certificate signed by two medical practitioners, one of whom was required to be approved for the purpose.[91] Reception conferred on the guardian the powers of a father over the patient.[92] There was no court involvement in this procedure. However, as today, guardianship could be imposed by a criminal court in certain circumstances[93] and a distinctive feature of the 1913 and 1927 statutes was that such orders could also be made under a court's civil jurisdiction.[94] Some judicial involvement was required before guardianship could be imposed on less seriously handicapped individuals (the "feeble-minded") and persons who today might be classified as having a psychopathic disorder ("moral imbeciles").[95] Furthermore, as in the 1959 Act, certain age-limits applied. Mental Deficiency Rules provided for matters such as changes of residence and transfers to hospital. The legislation therefore resembled that in the 1959 Act: the abolition of the need for applications to be judicially considered aside, it is generally a myth that the civil procedures in the 1959 Act represented a clean break with the past.

---

[86]   Mental Health (Scotland) Act 1984, s.77(3).

[87]   See R. Neugebauer, "Diagnosis, Guardianship, and Residential Care of the Mentally Ill in Medieval and Early Modern England" *Amercian Journal of Psychiatry* (1989) 146:12, 580–1584.

[88]   Mental Deficiency Act 1913, implementing the recommendations of *The Report of the Royal Commission on the Care and Control of the Feeble-Minded*, Cd. 4202 (1908).

[89]   *The Report of the Royal Commission on the Law Relating to Mental Illness and Mental Deficiency*, Cmnd. 169 (1957), paras. 387, 359, 400 and 411.

[90]   Mental Health Act 1959, ss.33 and 60.

[91]   Mental Deficiency Act 1913, s.3(1).

[92]   *Ibid.*, s.10(2).

[93]   *Ibid.*, ss.4(b) and 8.

[94]   For example, upon a petition being presented under s.5(1).

[95]   However, the endorsement of the medical certificate by a Justice of the Peace often sufficed: Mental Deficiency Act 1913, ss. 2 and 3.

The Mental Health Act 1959

The 1959 Act extended the availability of guardianship to persons suffering from mental illness. It conferred on the guardian "to the exclusion of any other person all such powers as would be exercisable by ... him in relation to the patient if ... he were the father of the patient and the patient were under the age of fourteen years."[96] The guardian's duties included ensuring "that everything practicable is done for the promotion of his physical and mental health."[97] The use of guardianship under the Act declined markedly during the following years, partly due to doubts about the precise ambit of these paternalistic powers, but also because of increasing concern in some quarters that they were inappropriately wide.[98]

The White papers of 1978 and 1981

The Government re-examined the law relating to guardianship in the White Paper *"Review of the Mental Health Act 1959."*[99] After further consultations, it published a second white paper in November 1981,[100] in which it explained its proposals for revising the existing law relating to guardianship:[101]

> "43. The guardian, who is usually but not always a local social services authority, is given the powers that a father has over a child under 14. These powers are therefore very wide, as well as somewhat ill-defined, and out of keeping, in their paternalistic approach, with modern attitudes to the care of the mentally disordered. The 1978 White Paper, in discussing guardianship powers in the Mental Health Act (in Chapter 4), suggested that further consideration was needed and put forward three possible options. One option was to retain guardianship powers in more or less their present form with some minor changes, *e.g.* reducing the duration of guardianship powers in line with the proposals for detention in hospital (see para. 19 above). The second option was to introduce a range of community care orders to parallel existing compulsory hospital powers (the proposal of the British Association of Social Workers). The third was to introduce new specific powers to restrict the liberty of the individual only as much as is necessary to ensure that he receives medical treatment and social support and training— the "essential powers" approach.

> 44. The Government has considered all the issues involved and the many comments received and has decided that the third option, which was widely supported, most closely meets current needs. The Bill therefore provides that guardianship powers should be retained but that the guardian should have only the "essential powers" rather than all the powers of the father of a child under 14 as at present. The essential powers are:—

> *a.* power to require the patient to live at a place specified by the guardian;

> *b.* power to require the patient to attend places specified by the guardian for medical treatment, occupation or training;

> *c.* power to ensure that a doctor, social worker or other person specified by the guardian can see the patient at his home."

---

[96] Mental Health Act 1959, s.34(1).
[97] Mental Health (Hospital and Guardianship) Regulations 1960, reg. 6(1).
[98] *Review of the Mental Health Act 1959*, Cmnd. 7320 (1978), para. 4.8.
[99] *Review of the Mental Health Act 1959*, Cmnd. 7320 (1978).
[100] *Reform of Mental Health Legislation*, Cmnd. 8405 (1981).
[101] *Ibid.*, paras. 43 and 44.

The Mental Health (Amendment) Act 1982

The essential powers outlined in paragraphs 44(a) to (c) were enacted as paragraphs 8(a)–(c) of the Mental Health (Amendment) Act 1982 and as paragraphs 8(1)(a)–(c) of the 1983 Act, the latter being in the main a consolidating statute.

THE STATUTORY FRAMEWORK

A guardian's powers under the Act are described as "essential powers" in that they only authorise restricting the patient's liberty in the three essential ways set out in section 8.[102] The guardian's authority does not extend to exercising any control over the patient's property and finances, to consenting to medical treatment on his behalf,[103] or to any other area of his life the control of which would require the guardian to exceed these essential powers.

A GUARDIAN'S "ESSENTIAL POWERS"

8.—(1) ... the application shall, subject to regulations made by the Secretary of State, confer on the authority or person named in the application as guardian, to the exclusion of any other person—

(a) the power to require the patient to reside at a place specified by the authority or person named as guardian;

(b) the power to require the patient to attend at places and times so specified for the purpose of medical treatment, occupation, education or training;

(c) the power to require access to the patient to be given, at any place where the patient is residing, to any registered medical practitioner, approved social worker or other person so specified.

Exercising the powers

A patient who absents himself from the place where he is required to reside may be compelled to return there.[104] However, with that single exception, a guardian's power to "require" a non-compliant patient to do any act covered by section 8 falls short of being able to enforce such lawful demands. Following the patient's reception into guardianship, there is no statutory power to convey the patient to the nominated place of residence, nor to any place he is required to attend as part of his treatment and care programme. Similarly, if the patient obstructs access to him by a authorised person, he commits no offence.[105] The Act therefore limits the guardian's authority to exercising certain "essential powers," none of which authorise the patient's detention

---

[102] These three powers can be remembered as the three "A"s: accommodation, attendance, access.
[103] See, *e.g.*, the dicta of McCullough J. in *R. v. Hallstrom, ex p. W (No. 2)* [1986] 2 All E.R. 306 at 313 and of Wood J. in *T. v. T. and another* [1988] 1 All E.R. 613 at 617.
[104] Mental Health Act 1983, ss.18(3) and (4), 135(2).
[105] Mental Health Act 1983, s.129.

and most of which are widely seen as unenforceable.[106] Where a patient refuses to do some act lawfully required of him by his guardian, it has sometimes been speculated that the guardian may apply to the High Court for an order of mandamus directing the patient to do the required act. However, this seems unlikely given Parliament's decision not to include a statutory mechanism for enforcing demands made by the guardian.[107]

Limits of a patient's essential rights

Because the liberty of a patient under guardianship is subject to less interference than that of a detained patient, the Act confers on the former correspondingly fewer forms of statutory protection. The patient enjoys the full protection of the criminal law if he is ill-treated or neglected[108] and, since he is not detained, he is better placed to refuse to comply with any arbitrary demands made of him. Furthermore, the exercise of a private guardian's functions are subject to an absolute right of discharge vested in the patient's nearest relative[109] and to supervision by the local social services authority.[110] The rights granted to both groups of patients are, in

---

[106]   This absence of a power of conveyance is often relied upon by social workers who do not wish to make an application in a particular case, although they are invariably unable to give an example of a patient who refused to take up residence at the address stipulated by his guardian. It is important to compare the likely benefits of guardianship with the limitations of a purely informal arrangement — rather than to persistently repeat the fact that the guardian's powers are less than those of a detaining hospital. Because guardianship is a form of adult care order, and many patients previously in care deteriorated when they no longer had structured support, there is sometimes a real prospect of benefit. Furthermore, if no benefit accrues, nothing has been lost. The *Code of Practice* favours a flexible, fast-track, approach to guardianship: *Mental Health Act 1983: Code of Practice* (2nd ed., 1993), para. 13.3. In theory, completing a guardianship application, and obtaining a decision concerning its acceptance, should take no longer than does the acceptance of an application for his admission to hospital. When a known patient is beginning to deteriorate, this enables guardianship to be used as a last attempt at heading off the need for compulsory readmission to hospital. If the patient is aware of this, there is a considerable incentive to comply with the community-based programme. In practice, the procedures of most local authorities are so convoluted that any decision about whether to make or accept a guardianship application can take several weeks or months.

[107]   Where, following an application's acceptance, the patient refuses to take up residence at the nominated address, a more elegant argument would be that he is then absent from there without leave. Accordingly, he may be taken into custody and conveyed there under section 18. Insofar as material, section 18 provides as follows: "18—(3) Where a patient who is for the time being subject to guardianship ... absents himself without the leave of the guardian from the place where he is required by the guardian to reside, he may, subject to the provisions of this section, be taken into custody and returned to that place by any officer of a local social services authority ... (6) In this Act 'absent' without leave' means absent from any ... place and liable to be taken into custody and returned under this section, and related expressions shall be construed accordingly." The counter-argument is that the use of the phrase "returned to that place" in subsection 18(3) indicates that the patient must have "resided at that place" before he can absent himself from it and be "returned to that place." Furthermore, the inclusion of an express power of conveyance in sections 6 and 40 (in relation to applications and orders for admission to hospital), and the absence of such a power in sections 8 and 40 (in relation to guardianship cases), is significant. The Act differentiates between taking and retaking a patient. In rebuttal, it may be said that the patient is absent without leave (as defined), and the effect of the omissions in sections 8 and 40 is merely that no force may be used unless the patient is unlawfully absent from where he is required to be. It would be anomalous if the power to nominate a residence for the patient is enforceable against him if he resides there for an hour but not if he refuses to take up residence. It would likewise be anomalous if a patient who is residing at the required place can refuse to take up residence at some alternative place designated for him but, if he does so for an hour (to see what it is like), he is then unlawfully absent if he returns to his previous abode.

[108]   Mental Health Act 1983, s.127(2).

[109]   *Ibid.*, ss.23(2)(b) and 25.

[110]   Under paragraph 12(c) of the Mental Health (Hospital, Guardianship and Consent to Treatment) Regulations 1983, a private guardian is under a duty when exercising his statutory functions "to comply with such directions as that authority may give."

theory, adequate to protect them against any arbitrary or ill-founded exercise of the compulsory powers to which they are respectively subject, and commensurate with the degree of interference with their liberty. Consequently, the statutory rights of a patient under guardianship may conveniently be referred to as his "essential rights." As regards patients subject to guardianship—

- There is no prohibition against the medical practitioners who provide the recommendations for guardianship being employed at the same hospital, even if one works under the direction of the other.[111]

- An approved social worker is not required to "interview" a patient before making a guardianship application, as long as he has "personally seen" that patient within the previous 14 days.[112]

- The nearest relative may not require that the patient be assessed by an approved social worker with a view to his reception into guardianship — he may only require an assessment with a view to his admission to hospital.[113]

- Provided a guardianship application is forwarded to the local social services authority within 14 days of the date of the second medical examination, there is then no particular time within which it must be accepted. In theory, the patient could be received into guardianship some months later.[114]

- There is no duty to notify a patient received into guardianship, or his nearest relative, of their statutory rights.[115]

- The appropriate medical officer is not under a statutory duty to consult one or more persons who have been professionally concerned with the patient's treatment before furnishing a report renewing the guardianship.[116]

- If a patient subject to guardianship does not apply to a tribunal, the Act does not require that his case is periodically referred to it for consideration.[117]

- A tribunal has no power to discharge a patient from guardianship on a future date or to make recommendations.[118]

- A tribunal may refuse to discharge a patient from guardianship notwithstanding that it is satisfied that the nature or degree of any mental disorder does not warrant guardianship.[119]

- The duty to provide after-care in section 117 does not extend to patients discharged from guardianship.[120]

- The Mental Health Act Commission's statutory remit does not extend to overseeing the welfare of patients subject to guardianship.[121]

---

[111] Mental Health Act 1983, ss.12(3) (4) and (7).
[112] *Ibid.*, ss.11(5) and 13(2).
[113] *Ibid.*, s.13(4).
[114] *Ibid.*, s.8(1) and (3).
[115] *Ibid.*, ss.11(3) and 132.
[116] *Ibid.*, s.20.
[117] *Ibid.*, ss.40(4) and 145(3); Sched. 1, Part I, paras. 1 and 2.
[118] *Ibid.*, subss. 72(3) (4) and (5).
[119] *Ibid.*, s.72(4).
[120] *Ibid.*, s.117.
[121] *Ibid.*, ss.120 and 121.

DURATION

A guardianship application authorises the guardian to exercise the statutory powers for a period of up to six months beginning with the date of its acceptance. The authority may be renewed as appropriate for a further period of six months and thereafter at yearly intervals in accordance with the provisions of section 20.

LEGAL FORMALITIES CONCERNING APPLICATIONS

The legal and procedural formalities relating to the making of applications are set out in sections 2–15 of the Act and in the Mental Health (Hospital, Guardianship and Consent to Treatment) Regulations 1983. Where a patient is admitted to hospital or received into guardianship in pursuance of an application, there should in each case be (a) a written application; (b) supporting written medical recommendation(s); (c) a form recording receipt of a medical recommendation; (d) a form recording the patient's admission or reception into guardianship.

THE PATIENT

A guardianship application may not be made in respect of a child who is a ward of court or under 16 years of age.[122] An application for the admission to hospital of a minor who is a ward of court requires the court's leave.[123]

THE APPLICANT

An application under Part II may be made by an approved social worker (**160**), by the patient's nearest relative (**100**), or by the person who is exercising for the time being that relative's statutory functions (**109, 111**).[124]

Requirement that the applicant has seen the patient

An emergency application may not be made unless the applicant has personally seen the patient within the previous 24 hours. In any other case, no application shall be made unless the applicant has personally seen the patient within the period of 14 days ending with the date of the application.[125]

Applications by approved social workers

Before an approved social worker makes an application for a patient's admission to hospital, he "shall interview the patient in a suitable manner and satisfy himself that detention in a hospital is in all the circumstances of the case the most appropriate way of providing the care and medical treatment of which the patient stands in need."[126] No similar duty arises in the case of a guardianship application or in respect of any application made by the nearest relative. However, in all cases, an approved

---

[122]   Mental Health Act 1983, ss.7(1) and 33(3).
[123]   *Ibid.*, s.33(1).
[124]   *Ibid.*, ss. 11(1), 29(6), 32(2)(e); Mental Health (Hospital, Guardianship and Consent to Treatment) Regulations 1983, reg. 14.
[125]   Mental Health Act 1983, s.11(5).
[126]   Mental Health Act 1983, s.13(2).

social worker owes a duty of care to the patient and he should therefore make any necessary inquiries before applying.[127]

Duty to consult the nearest relative

Before making any section 3 or guardianship application, an approved social worker must consult with the person (if any) appearing to be the patient's nearest relative, unless it appears to that social worker that in the circumstances such consultation is not reasonably practicable or would involve unreasonable delay. Furthermore, no such application may be made if the nearest relative has notified that social worker, or the local social services authority which appointed him, that he objects to the application being made.[128]

Duty to make application

An approved social worker is under a duty to make an application in respect of a person within the area of the local social services authority which has appointed him "in any case where he is satisfied that such an application ought to be made and is of the opinion, having regard to any wishes expressed by relatives of the patient or any other relevant circumstances, that it is necessary or proper for the application to be made by him."[129] No such duty arises in the case of patients outside the appointing authority's area and, similarly, a patient's nearest relative is never under a statutory duty to make an application.

Applications to be in the prescribed form

Every application must specify the qualification of the applicant to make the application.[130] The application must be in the form set out in Schedule 1 to the Mental Health (Hospital, Guardianship & Consent to Treatment) Regulations 1983, as amended by the Mental Health (Hospital, Guardianship & Consent to Treatment) (Amendment) Regulations 1996.[131]

---

[127] The duty of care is personal and "it is the business of the duly authorised officer, rather than that of the doctor, to see that the statutory powers are not used unless the circumstances warrant it." *Buxton v. Jayne* [1960] 1 W.L.R. 783, *per* Devlin L.J. at 784. See also *R. v. Barnsley* (1849) 12 Q.B. 193; *R. v. Wakefield* 48 J.P. 326.

[128] Mental Health Act 1983, s. 11(4). It is not, however, necessary that the social worker is consulted after the social worker has interviewed the patient: *Re Whitbread (Mental patient: Habeas Corpus)*, *The Times*, 14 July 1997, C.A. In that case, the approved social worker consulted the nearest relative in August, when the nearest relative agreed that his son should be admitted to hospital. The patient then took steps to avoided being interviewed. This eventually occurred in October, following which, but without the nearest relative being further consulted, a section 3 application was made. The court held that a nexus had to exist between the consultation and the application that was subsequently made, and had to place the nearest relative in a position, if so minded, to object to it. Provided that was the case, the duty of consultation had been discharged and section 11(4) was not to be construed as imposing a particular chronological sequence. As to whether an approved social worker may authorise another approved social worker to undertake the consultation on his behalf, see *R. v. South Western Hospital Managers, ex p. M.* [1993] Q.B. 683 **(597, 457)**.

[129] Mental Health Act 1983, *s.13(1)*. The words "necessary" and "proper" are not coterminous. In *Re Mercury Model Aircraft Supplies* [1956] 1 W.L.R. 1153, it was said that work may be done by solicitors which is not necessary but which is none the less proper, even if due in some degree to over-caution or some other cause. It may therefore be proper to make an application but not necessary to do so, in the sense that another person, such as the nearest relative, could make it.

[130] Mental Health Act 1983, s.11(1).

[131] *Ibid.*, s.32(2)(a). The Mental Health (Hospital, Guardianship and Consent to Treatment) (Amendment) Regulations 1996, which came into force on 1 April 1996, prescribed new Forms 2 and 9 for section 2 and 3 applications made by an approved social worker. The other application forms remained unchanged. As to the position where the prescribed form is used, see *Re E (Mental Health: Habeas Corpus)*, 10 December 1996 and *Warren v. Warren* [1953] 1 W.L.R. 1268 **(270)**.

PRESCRIBED FORM OF APPLICATIONS

	Nearest relative applications	ASW applications
Section 2 application	Form 1	Form 2
Section 3 application	Form 8	Form 9
Section 4 application	Form 5	Form 6
Section 7 application	Form 17	Form 18

Applications to be founded upon written medical recommendations

Except in a case where it is urgently necessary that the patient be admitted to hospital for assessment, an application shall be founded on the written recommendations of two registered medical practitioners,[132] signed on or before the date of the application.[133] The recommendations may be given either as separate recommendations or as a joint recommendation signed by both practitioners[134] and shall be in the form prescribed by the regulations.[135] Neither a guardianship application or a section 3 application is of any effect unless the patient is described by both medical practitioners as suffering from the same form of mental disorder, whether or not he is described by either of them as also suffering from another form.[136]

Emergency applications

An emergency application may be made founded upon a single medical recommendation, given if practicable by a doctor who has previous acquaintance with the patient.[137] The second recommendation required by section 2 must be furnished to the managers within the period of 72 hours from the time of the patient's admission, otherwise his liability to detention lapses.

---

[132] Mental Health Act 1983, ss.2(3), 3(3), 7(3).

[133] *Ibid.*, s.12(1).

[134] *Ibid.*, s.11(7).

[135] *Ibid.*, ss.2(3), 3(3), 4(3), 7(3) and 32(2)(a). The prescribed form is that set out in Schedule 1 to the Mental Health (Hospital, Guardianship & Consent to Treatment) Regulations 1983, as amended by the Mental Health (Hospital, Guardianship & Consent to Treatment) (Amendment) Regulations 1996. The 1996 Regulations, which came into force on 1 April 1996, prescribed new forms of recommendation in all cases involving admission to hospital (Forms 3,4, 7, 10 and 11). Only the medical recommendations given in support of a guardianship application (Forms 19 and 20) remained unchanged. As to the position where the the previous prescribed form is used, see *Re E (Mental Health: Habeas Corpus)*, 10 December 1996 and *Warren v. Warren* [1953] 1 W.L.R. 1268 **(270)**.

[136] Mental Health Act 1983, ss.11(6) and 15(3). Thus, the application is invalid if one recommendation describes the patient as suffering only from "mental illness" and the other only from "mental impairment," but not if the second states that the patient suffers from "mental illness and mental impairment." It would appear, however, that an application is not *per se* invalid if the application itself states that the patient is suffering from psychopathic disorder and the two medical recommendations that he is suffering only from mental illness. Because it is the form of forms of disorder recorded on the application that constitute a patient's legal classification, the responsible medical officer would no doubt reclassify the patient on admission (see s.16(1)). Judicial review might, nevertheless, still be appropriate if an approved social worker applicant had clearly failed to have regard to the relevant law and circumstances. For example, if the effect was that he should have, but could not have, had regard to the treatability test in section 3(2)(b). Or the effect was that he could not have properly interviewed the patient or been satisfied as to the appropriateness of his detention.

[137] Mental Health Act 1983, s.4(3).

PRESCRIBED FORM OF RECOMMENDATIONS

	Joint recommendation	*Separate recommendations*
Section 2 application	Form 3	Form 4
Section 3 application	Form 10	Form 11
Section 4 application	Not applicable	Form 7
Section 7 application	Form 19	Form 20

Medical recommendations to be founded upon personal examinations

Except in a case where it is urgently necessary that the patient be admitted to hospital for assessment, the recommendations shall be given by practitioners who have personally examined the patient either together or separately. Where they examined the patient separately, not more than five clear days must have elapsed between the days on which the separate examinations took place.[138]

Medical recommendation(s) to include the prescribed information

The medical recommendation upon which an emergency application is founded shall include a statement verifying that the patient's admission and detention under section 2 is urgently necessary and that compliance with the usual provisions of Part II of the Act would involve undesirable delay.[139] Medical recommendations provided under sections 2 and 3 shall include a statement that in the signatory's opinion the patient's condition satisfies the statutory grounds for admission under that section.[140] A recommendation under section 3 shall also include the grounds for the practitioner's opinion why that is so and shall specify whether other methods of dealing with the patient are available and, if so why they are not appropriate.[141]

Recommendations to be given by practitioners who are individually and collectively qualified for the purpose

At least one of the recommendations shall be given by a medical practitioner approved by the Secretary of State under section 12 as having special experience in the diagnosis or treatment of mental disorder. Unless that doctor has previous acquaintance with the patient, the other recommendation shall, if practicable, be given by a medical practitioner who has such previous acquaintance.[142]

---

[138] Mental Health Act 1983, s.12(1) and (7). Thus, if the first doctor examines the patient on Monday and the second at the end of that week, on Sunday, that suffices. The clear days in between (Tuesday to Saturday) do not exceed five. It is the date of the examinations which is legally important in this context, not the date on which the recommendations are completed.

[139] *Ibid.*, s.4(3).

[140] *Ibid.*, s.2(3), 3(3).

[141] *Ibid.*, s.3(3). A doctor examining the patient owes him a duty to exercise reasonable care: *Hall v. Semple* (1862) 3 F. & F. 337; *Everett v. Griffiths* [1921] 1 A.C. 631, H.L.; *Harnett v. Fisher* [1927] 1 K.B. 402, C.A.

[142] Mental Health Act 1983, s.12(2) and (7). It suffices in section 4 cases that the second recommendation, following admission, is provided by an approved doctor if the first was not.

Admissions to mental nursing homes

Where the application is for the patient's admission to a mental nursing home (a "private hospital"), neither of the recommendations may be given by a medical practitioner who is on the staff of that home or by a relative of such a person.[143]

Admissions to NHS facilities

Where the application is for the patient's admission to an NHS hospital, at least one of the medical recommendations must be given by a practitioner who is not on the staff of that hospital[144] unless—

    a.   compliance with this requirement would result in delay involving serious risk to the health or safety of the patient; *and*

    b.   one of the practitioners giving the recommendations works at the hospital for less than half of the time which he is bound by contract to devote to work in the health service; *and*

    c.   where one of those practitioners is a consultant, the other does not work (whether at the hospital or elsewhere) in a grade in which he is under that consultant's directions.[145]

Other disqualified medical practitioners

A medical recommendation may not be given by any of the following persons—

    •   a relative of the patient;[146]

---

[143] Mental Health Act 1983, ss.12(3) and 12(5)(e). However, following admission, the patient's responsible medical officer may subsequently renew the authority for the patient's detention, notwithstanding that he has a financial interest in providing medical services to the patient. The Act caters for this by providing that an NHS patient receiving treatment in a "private hospital" may be discharged by the Health Authority or NHS trust funding his treatment there, as well as by his nearest relative or a tribunal. The Act also relies on the fact that professionals with no competing interest were originally satisfied as to the existence of the grounds for admission to hospital. However, many mental nursing homes take the view that doctors who have patients at the home, but who are not employees of the company which owns or manages the home, are not on the staff of the hospital. It is usually only the medical director of the home who has such a contract. Consequently, the other doctors treating patients there may, and do, provide recommendations for each other's patients. While the distinction may have some merit in the context of employment law, the interpretation seems inappropriate in the context of a statute concerning individual liberty. A further problem arises where a detained patient is transferred from an NHS hospital to a mental nursing home and a doctor on the staff of that home provided one of the medical recommendations upon which his detention is founded. Because the application is deemed to have always specified the home as the admitting hospital, it is (at least literally) the case that the application is thereby invalidated. Furthermore, the time allowed by section 15(3) for providing a second recommendation will have expired. The situation is not as uncommon as might be thought, given that a number of practitioners at an NHS hospital may undertake private work at a local mental nursing home.

[144] Mental Health Act 1983, s.12(3).

[145] A general practitioner who is employed part-time at an NHS hospital, as opposed to a mental nursing home, is not regarded as being a practitioner on its staff.

[146] For these purposes, a relative is any of the following persons: husband, wife, father, father-in-law, mother, mother-in-law, son, son-in-law, daughter, daughter-in-law, brother, brother-in-law, sister or sister-in-law.

- the applicant, a partner of the applicant, or a person employed as an assistant by the applicant, or by a relative of such a person;

- a partner or an assistant of the practitioner who has given the other medical recommendation, or by a relative of such a person;

- a person who receives or has an interest in the receipt of any payments made on account of the maintenance of the patient, or by a relative of such a person.

The application shall be addressed to and properly served on the relevant body

Every application for admission must be addressed to the managers of the hospital to which admission is sought[147] and delivered to an officer of managers of the hospital authorised by them to receive it.[148] Similarly, every guardianship application must be addressed to the local social services authority named in the application.[149] However, in this case, the application may be either delivered or sent to the authority's registered or principal office by prepaid post.[150] It must be "forwarded" to the authority within the period of 14 days beginning with the date on which the patient was last examined by a registered medical practitioner before giving a medical recommendation in support of the application.[151]

The hospital managers shall record receipt of the recommendations

The managers of the hospital to which an application is addressed are to record, in the form set out in Form 14 of Schedule 1 to the 1983 Regulations, the receipt by them of the joint medical recommendation or, where separate recommendations were completed, their receipt of the second medical recommendation, and to attach this record to the recommendation.[152] In the case of guardianship applications, Form 15 is used instead.[153]

---

[147]   Mental Health Act 1983, s.11(2). In practice, approved social workers do not always address the application to the hospital to which the patient is taken, leaving that part of the form to be completed by a hospital officer once a bed has been located for the patient. Such omissions are not new. *See Archbold's Lunacy and Mental Deficiency Practice* (Butterworth & Co., Shaw and Sons, 5th ed., 1915), pp. 175–176. Nevertheless, there is no statutory authority to take a person into custody or to convey him to a hospital until an application specifying a hospital has been duly completed. See ibid., s.6(1).

[148]   *Ibid.*, s.32(2)(b); Mental Health (Hospital, Guardianship and Consent to Treatment) Regulations 1983, reg.3(2). "Delivered" means served personally by hand and an application for a person's detention under the Act may therefore not be sent by facsimile transmission or by post.

[149]   Mental Health Act 1983, s.11(2).

[150]   *Ibid.*, s.32(2)(b); Mental Health (Hospital, Guardianship and Consent to Treatment) Regulations 1983, reg.3(1).

[151]   Mental Health Act 1983, s.8(1) and (3).

[152]   *Ibid.*, s.32(2)(a) and (c); Mental Health (Hospital, Guardianship and Consent to Treatment) Regulations 1983, reg. 4(4). A new Form 14 was prescribed by the Mental Health (Hospital, Guardianship & Consent to Treatment) (Amendment) Regulations 1996, which came into force on 1 April 1996. Previously, receipt of the recommendations was recorded on the old Form 15, and the patient's admission on the old Form 14. The two records have now been amalgamated and the revised Form 14 is to be used for both purposes in admission cases. Unfortunately, the new form is poorly drafted and a feature of many of the new forms is the draftsman's apparent inability to adhere to the statutory criteria or to the statutory framework.

[153]   Mental Health Act 1983, s.32(2)(a) and (c); Mental Health (Hospital, Guardianship and Consent to Treatment) Regulations 1983, reg. 5(4).

The patient must be admitted within the prescribed period

In cases involving admission under section 2 or 3, the authority conferred by the application to take the patient into custody, convey him to the hospital named in the application, and to admit and detain him there, lapses at the expiration of fourteen days beginning with the date of the last medical examination upon which the application is founded.[154] Where the application is made under section 4, the patient must be admitted within the period of 24 hours beginning either at the time when the patient was examined by the practitioner giving the medical recommendation or the time when the application is made, whichever is the earlier.[155] No such time limits apply in the case of guardianship. Provided the application is forwarded to the local social services authority within 14 days of the most recent medical examination, there is then no particular time within which it must be accepted. In theory, the patient could be received into guardianship some months after the application was made and the recommendations completed.[156]

Applications in respect of in-patients

Where an application, or a further application, is made in respect of someone who is already an in-patient, "the patient shall be treated ... as if he had been admitted to the hospital at the time when that application was received by the managers."[157]

APPLICATIONS IN RESPECT ON IN-PATIENTS

5.—(1) An application for the admission of a patient to a hospital may be made under this Part of this Act notwithstanding that the patient is already an in-patient in that hospital or, in the case of an application for admission for treatment that the patient is for the time being liable to be detained in the hospital in pursuance of an application for admission for assessment; and where an application is so made the patient shall be treated for the purposes of this Part of this Act as if he had been admitted to the hospital at the time when that application was received by the managers.

The admission or the acceptance of the application shall be recorded

Where a patient is admitted to a hospital in pursuance of an application , a record of his admission shall be made by the managers of that hospital in the form set out in Form 14 to Schedule 1 of the 1983 Regulations and the record shall be attached to the application.[158] Where a patient is received into guardianship, a record of the

---

[154] Mental Health Act 1983, s.6(1)(a) and (2). Thus, for example, where a section 2 application relies upon two medical recommendations based upon separate medical examinations which were conducted on 1 January and 7 January, the patient must be taken, conveyed, and admitted to hospital under that application before midnight on 20 January.
[155] Mental Health Act 1983, s.6(1)(b) and (2).
[156] See *ibid.*, s.8(1) and (3).
[157] *Ibid.*, s.5(1). See p.260.
[158] Mental Health (Hospital, Guardianship and Consent to Treatment) Regulations 1983, reg. 4(3). A new Form 14 was prescribed by the Mental Health (Hospital, Guardianship & Consent to Treatment) (Amendment) Regulations 1996, which came into force on 1 April 1996. This appears to assume that the date on which the "statutory documents" are received is necessarily the date of admission. The unfortunate consequence is that hospital administrators often mistakenly calculate the renewal date by reference to the day on which they received these documents, even if section 5(1) does not apply and the patient was admitted sometime before then.

acceptance of the application shall similarly be made, in the form set out in Form 21, and the record attached to the application.[159]

Effect on previous applications

Where a patient is admitted to hospital in pursuance of a section 2 application, any outstanding guardianship application or supervision application continues in force. Where, however, a patient is admitted to a hospital under section 3 or is received into guardianship, any pre-existing application ceases to have effect.[160] The effect of an application on a pre-existing order or direction made under Part III is more complicated and considered later (**303**).

Whether applications for admission require acceptance

A guardianship application does not take effect unless and until it is accepted by the local social services authority. It is therefore clearly no more than an application, in that it may be accepted or rejected. The position of patients already in hospital when an application is furnished lies at the opposite end of the spectrum. Section 5 provides that the patient shall be treated as if he had been admitted to the hospital at the time when the application was received, rather than accepted, by the managers. This is the case regardless of whether the patient was previously in hospital informally or in pursuance of some prior authority for his detention. The use of the phrase, "shall be treated as if he had been admitted to the hospital," implies that "admission" carries its normal, general, meaning: a patient is admitted to hospital when he becomes an in-patient but may be "treated" as having been admitted subsequently. That this is so is borne out by section 6(2) which deals with applications made in respect of patients in the community: these patients are always admitted to hospital and never "treated" as if they had been admitted there. According to that subsection, where a person in the community is admitted to the hospital specified in an application, that application authorises the managers to detain him there. The position here is therefore intermediate between that pertaining to guardianship and that pertaining to patients already in hospital: the authority to detain the patient is expressed to arise automatically if he is admitted to hospital, but the managers can refuse to admit him. The literal effect of section 6(2) is that, while the decision whether or not to admit the patient is one for the managers, whether admission is formal or informal is, as in the case of patients already there, a matter for the persons charged with implementing the compulsory procedures — approved social workers, nearest relatives and medical practitioners. As with an individual already receiving in-patient care, liability to detention derives from the conjunction of in-patient status and the receipt by the managers of a duly made application. It may be that this is what Parliament intended and is consistent with the overall framework of the Act. Not only the initial authority, but also that authority's renewal, is automatic upon the necessary documents being furnished. If so, the managers' role is limited to admitting or discharging patients in respect of whom an application has been made: they never, in any meaningful sense, accept or approve an application, merely scrutinise it to verify that it gives them the purported authority. This then is what the Act actually says. The counter argument is that admission means admission in pursuance of the application which has been made. Sections 5 and 6 are not to be interpreted in a way which conflicts with section 131, which provides that nothing in the Act shall be construed as preventing a patient from being admitted in pursuance of arrangements made in that behalf and without any application rendering him

---

[159]   Mental Health (Hospital, Guardianship and Consent to Treatment) Regulations 1983, reg. 5(3).
[160]   Mental Health Act 1983, s.6(4).

liable to be detained. That being so, a distinction must be drawn between the use of the word "furnished" in sections 5(2) and 20(8) and "received" in section 5(1). Accordingly, the managers may refuse to receive a duly completed application furnished to them if they consider that informal admission is more appropriate. The suggestion that, because an applicant specifies a particular hospital, and authorises his detention there, the managers of that hospital must either admit the patient formally or not at all runs counter to the whole tenor of mental health legislation since the Mental Treatment Act 1930. If the counter-argument is correct, applications for admission under the Act are genuinely applications. The managers may refuse to receive an application furnished to them in respect of an in-patient and admit informally any patient whose compulsory admission is sought, as well as refusing to admit him at all.

The authority conferred by the application on the managers or guardian

Provided an application for admission appears to be duly made and the patient is admitted to the specified hospital within the permitted period (or, if already an in-patient there, is treated by virtue of section 5 as if he had been so admitted), the application constitutes sufficient authority for the managers to detain the patient in the hospital in accordance with the provisions of the Act.[161] Similarly, provided a guardianship application is "duly made" and forwarded to the local social services authority within the 14-day statutory period (**259**), the authority's acceptance of it confers on the guardian the powers specified in section 8(1).[162]

Notifying the patient and the nearest relative (section 132)

Following admission, the managers must as soon as practicable take such steps as are practicable to ensure that a detained patient understands the authority for his detention and his statutory rights. The prescribed information must be given both orally and in writing.[163] Unless the patient objects, the managers must also, within a reasonable period following admission, take such steps as are practicable to furnish the nearest relative with a copy of the written information given to the patient.[164] Where this information is not provided, either because the patient was received into guardianship or because he requested otherwise, neither the managers nor the local social services authority are under any statutory duty to notify the nearest relative of the patient's admission or reception. However, an approved social worker who makes a section 2 application must take such steps as are practicable to inform the person appearing to be the nearest relative that the application is to be or has been made. Where practicable, the nearest relative must therefore be told of the application even if the patient requests otherwise. In section 3 and guardianship cases, there is no statutory duty to notify the nearest relative of the patient's admission in cases where it was not possible to consult him before making the application.[165] The statutory framework is therefore somewhat inconsistent as concerns a nearest relative's rights to information.

---

[161] Mental Health Act 1983, s.6(2). If the application appears to be duly made, the managers are justified in detaining the individual even if he is in fact not mentally disordered: *Norris v. Seed* (1849) 3 Exch. 782; *Mackintosh v. Smith* 4 Macq. H.L.C. 913.

[162] Mental Health Act 1983, s.8(1).

[163] *Ibid.*, s.132(1)–(3). The prescribed information is set out in section 132.

[164] *Ibid.*, s.132(4).

[165] In other words, although the nearest relative must generally be consulted about the making of a section 3 application, if the application was made without any such consultation taking place, there is no statutory duty to inform the nearest relative of the patient's admission or rights. See *ibid.*, s.11(3) and (4).

Scrutiny of applications

The application should be scrutinised by the hospital managers or local social services authority, or by an authorised officer on their behalf. The purpose of this is to ensure that any irregularities are identified and, where permissible, rectified within period allowed under section 15, which is 14 days from the date of the patient's admission or reception (**265**).

SCRUTINY OF APPLICATIONS AND IRREGULARITIES

The hospital managers or local social services authority are not required to verify the qualifications of the persons who completed the application and medical recommendations or the facts and opinions recited in them. This is because an application "which appears to be duly made and to be founded on the necessary medical recommendations may be acted upon without further proof of the signature or qualification of the person by whom the application or any such medical recommendation is made or given, or of any matter of fact or opinion" stated in it.[166] It is, however, necessary to scrutinise the documents to verify that they are in the required form and that the correct statutory procedures appear to have been complied with. Before the 1959 Act was in force, applications were forwarded to the Board of Control in London for scrutiny. The Percy Commission recommended that the Board should be abolished and this function performed by hospital or local health authority staff at the time of the patient's admission or reception. The Commission were of the opinion that, where the documents did not appear to be in the form required by law, the health authority should not accept them as authorising the patient's detention or guardianship. If necessary, the patient should be cared for informally, or by use of emergency procedures, while the documents were corrected or new documents prepared.[167]

IMPORTANCE OF LEGAL PROPRIETY

Applications and medical recommendations having been designated as "forms" in the regulations, there is commonly a failure on the part of social workers and doctors to distinguish between the relative importance of these forms and the many other forms which they are required by their employers to complete, such as those used to record after-care information. This laxity has been reinforced by a perception that the courts do not require strict compliance with those procedures which Parliament provided must be complied with before one person has any authority to interfere with the liberty of another.[168] The importance of observing legal formalities was most elegantly expressed by Coleridge J. in *Re Greenwood*. The following passages

---

[166] Mental Health Act 1983, ss.6(3) and 8(3). The provision only relates to applications which appear valid on their face.

[167] *Report of the Royal Commission on the Law Relating to Mental Illness and Mental Deficiency*, Cmnd. 169 (1957), para. 483. The Act provides that defective applications or medical recommendations may generally be rectified within 14 days of the patient's admission or reception into guardianship, in which case they are retrospectively deemed to have been in their amended form (**265**).

[168] *R. v. South Western Hospital Managers, ex p. M.* [1993] Q.B. 683 is the best example of what is perceived to be the modern judicial approach.

demonstrate the importance of applying first principles in matters concerning individual liberty, and remain among the most important known to English law.[169] They continue to be particularly pertinent in relation to any failure to observe the procedures set out in the body of the statute—

The Queen v. Pinder; In re Greenwood

(1855) 1 Jur. 522.   *Court of Queen's Bench, Coleridge J.*

A medical certificate was given by a medical practitioner in which he stated that he had examined the patient on 3 October 1854, at Blackburn, in the county of Lancaster. The statute then in force prohibited the reception of any lunatic into any licensed house without the medical certificates in the form set out in the Schedule to the Act. The prescribed form required the address where the examination took place to be specified ("here insert the street and number of house").

Coleridge J.

"This was an application, on the return to a writ of habeas corpus, for the discharge of William Greenwood from the custody of William Pinder, the occupier of a private house duly licensed for the reception of lunatics; and upon the reading of the return it was objected that the reception of him into this house and his subsequent detention there were unlawful, on account of a defect in the medical certificates under which he had been admitted; and this is the question which I have now first to determine .... The [Act] prohibits, in express terms, the reception of any lunatic into any licensed house without the medical certificates, according to the Form in Schedule (A), No. 2, annexed to the Act .... It is not agreeable to decide on a formal objection, where, under the circumstances of the particular case, the defect appears to have had no influence on the merits, and to have occasioned neither inconvenience nor injustice; and, so far as appears, that may be said in the present case. But decisions are precedents; and therefore in arriving at them, it is necessary to look at general principles rather than to the particular circumstances. Here the words are express. By the 4th section, to receive a lunatic except under an order in one form and with medical certificates under another is expressly forbidden; and to break the prohibition is an indictable offence. When from this enactment we turn to the schedules referred to, we find them full of minute particulars, manifestly framed with anxious carefulness, as if to secure some important object. It would seem dangerous to enter into a comparison of these, and to class some as material which must be observed, and some as immaterial which may be disregarded. We cannot be sure that we have the means of making the discrimination on any sound principles, or that we know the particular intention of the legislature as to the one or the other. It could hardly be contended that we could properly reject all; and yet, as they seem to have a necessary connexion one with the other, the same argument which would lead to the dispensing with one might in time be applied to another, and so lead to dispensing with the whole. This is a general observation; but I cannot help perceiving, in reference to this and preceding statutes upon the same subject, that the legislature has proceeded in them with the double object of protecting the public and lunatics, real or supposed; facilitating in many respects the reception of persons dangerous to themselves or others or of unsound mind into asylums, where they will be properly restrained and treated, yet guarding both their reception and continuance there

---

[169] Although some contemporary practitioners would deride his insistence on procedural propriety as "legalistic," it is necessary to specify how a "legalistic" approach differs from an insistence on doing only what is "legal."

with great, and it cannot be denied with proper, jealousy, to secure persons placed there from being improperly treated there with harshness or inconsiderateness, or detained there unnecessarily. Now, multiplied and minute forms are among the means, perhaps the necessary means, by which the desired objects are attained; they are specially a protection to the real or supposed lunatic and if neglect of any prescribed form be permitted, no one can say that some measure of that protection may not thereby be weakened or made incomplete .... If it be asked, what purpose the particular provision now in question can answer, how it is material, or what benefit can result from the statement appearing upon the face of the certificate? I think it might be enough to answer, that with such questions the Court has no concern, and that when it is clearly established that the legislature has so enacted, the only business of the Court is to give full effect to the enactment. But it seems to me that, as to the present matter it is obvious enough that it may, in a great many cases, be a guard against or lead to the detection of collusive examinations to know the exact house in which they are alleged to have taken place; and it may therefore be important that he who grants the certificate should on the face of it state that fact. If it be doubted whether any examination has taken place, whether the examinations are made separately, or if it be desired to know at what time of day, in whose presence, or under what circumstances it took place, it cannot he questioned that inquiry into all these particulars is made more easy by a statement on the face of the certificate on what day and in what house it took place. Nothing is more common than this mode of legislation. It should be remembered, this is not a case of the sufficiency of an equivalent phrase; if it were, different considerations might arise but here, that which the statute requires has been wholly omitted, and nothing substituted in its place.

Whether patient should be discharged

I come to the conclusion, then, upon principle, that the certificate is defective in a particular which I have no right to consider is immaterial ... I was urged, however, in the commencement of the argument, at all events not to discharge the alleged lunatic; and I was reminded of what had fallen from the Court on several occasions when defects of a formal nature in orders or certificates have been urged as the ground for discharging lunatics; and I still feel that in such cases when, on the affidavits, it appears clear that the party confined is in such a state of mind that to set him at large would be dangerous either to the public or himself it becomes a duty and is within the common law jurisdiction of the Court, or a member of it, to restrain him from his liberty, until the regular and ordinary means can be resorted to of placing him under permanent legal restraint. But this arises from an obvious necessity, and cannot be extended to a case like the present. Upon the facts before me, Mr. Greenwood may be of much impaired memory, of much enfeebled intellect; it may be that he cannot prudently govern a household or manage a considerable property ... but it is quite clear that he is harmless to himself and to others. Mr. Pinder has not found it needful to restrain him at home or to prevent him from rambling alone at his free will and pleasure abroad. If, therefore, his present custody is illegal, I must determine it; and the power which I possess for the public safety or the personal safety of the individual must not be strained to continue his confinement. *Discharge granted.*

KINDS OF DOCUMENTARY IRREGULARITY

Documentary irregularities fall into three broad groups—

- those which are both incapable of retrospective correction and sufficiently serious to render invalid the patient's detention or guardianship under the Act.

- those which may be rectified within the 14-day period following admission or reception but which, if not rectified, are sufficiently serious to render the application invalid at the expiration of that period.

- errors and omissions which, even if not corrected within the statutory period, are not sufficiently serious to render the application invalid.

DEFECTS AND ERRORS

Sections 8(4) and 15(1) of the 1983 Act provide a mechanism for rectifying applications or medical recommendations which are found to be incorrect or defective in any respect. "Defective" literally means to fail to do while "incorrect" indicates a mistake, a want of exactness, as compared with an omission.

Applications for admission under Part II

Section 15(1) provides that if, within 14 days of a patient's admission in pursuance of an application, the application or a supporting medical recommendation is found to be in any respect incorrect or defective, it may within that period and with the the the hospital managers' consent be amended by the person by whom it was signed. Upon such amendment being made, the application or recommendation has effect, and is deemed to have always had effect as if it had been originally made as so amended. The managers may authorise any officer (employee) or class of officers to consent to the amendment of a document on their behalf.[170]

Guardianship cases

Section 8(4) makes like provision for amending any guardianship application or supporting medical recommendation which is found to be incorrect or defective. Any amendments must be made within the 14 day period beginning with the date of the patient's reception into guardianship and require the consent of the local social services authority,[171] which authority may authorise in writing an officer, or class of officers, to consent on its behalf to the rectification of documents.[172]

---

[170] Mental Health Act 1983, s.32(3); Mental Health (Hospital, Guardianship and Consent to Treatment) Regulations 1983, reg.4(2)(a). In practice, the Mental Health Act Administrator sometimes "tidies up" the application or medical recommendations by correcting obvious inaccuracies, having first obtained the signatory's consent by telephone. The purported justification for this is usually said to be that the administrator is acting as the signatory's "agent."

[171] This is presumably a minor drafting error and meant to read "responsible social services authority."

[172] Mental Health (Hospital, Guardianship and Consent to Treatment) Regulations 1983, reg. 5(2).

The ambit of sections 8(4) and 15(1)

Section 15(1) corresponds to section 32(1) of the 1959 Act, which derived from a similar provision in the Lunacy Act 1890.[173] Section 8(4) derives from section 34(4) of the 1959 Act, which enactment was cast in identical terms. In the case of *In Re V.E. (Mental Patient)*,[174] Lord Widgery C.J. described the provisions as constituting a "slip rule" permitting the correction of accidental mistakes in the form of the documents themselves. The view expressed in the *Memorandum* is that defects which may be remedied as being "incorrect or defective" include, "the leaving blank of any spaces on the form which should have been filled in (other than the signature) or failure to delete one or more alternatives in places where only one can be correct."[175] This interpretation of the type of error caught by the subsection is repeated by Gostin,[176] Jones[177] and Hoggett.[178] Their common opinion is expressed by Hoggett:[179]

> "'Incorrect' probably means 'inaccurate' in the sense of mis-stating names, dates, places or other details which had they been correctly stated would have justified the admission. It does not mean that a document which accurately reflects the facts can be rectified if those facts do not fall within the legal requirements. For example, a frequent fault is that the medical recommendations are undated or dated later than the application ... If in fact they were signed on or before the date of the application, the mistake can be rectified. But if they were signed later, then the application is invalid and the detention illegal.
>
> 'Defective' probably means 'incomplete' in the sense that all the information required in the forms has not been given. It cannot mean that forms which are complete and accurate statements of the facts can be falsified in order to provide legal justification for detention where none exists ..."

Unauthorised amendments

The effect of an unauthorised amendment was considered in the case of *Lowe v. Fox*,[180] in which the petitioner[181] included in the statement of particulars in support of his wife's admission[182] the following answer to the question, "When and where previously under care and treatment?": "During the period of twenty years has been constantly under treatment." A few days after the admission had taken place the petitioner added to this answer the additional words, "for hysteria by [Dr. X]." The addition was not approved by the Commissioners in Lunacy, who at the time fulfilled the function, now performed by the hospital managers and the local social

---

173   Lunacy Act 1890, s.34(1): "(1) If an order or certificate for the reception of a lunatic is, after such reception, found to be in any respect incorrect or defective, such order or certificate may, within fourteen days next after reception, be amended by the person who signed the same ... (3) Every order and certificate amended under this section shall take effect as if the amendment had been contained therein when it was signed."

174   *Re V.E. (Mental Patient)* [1972] 1 W.L.R. 669 at 673.

175   *Mental Health Act 1983: Memorandum on Parts I to VI, VIII and X* (D.H.S.S., 1987), para. 54.

176   L. Gostin, *Mental Health Services — Law and Practice* (Shaw & Sons Ltd.), para. 6.05.1.

177   R. Jones, *Mental Health Act Manual* (Sweet & Maxwell, 5th ed., 1996), p.78.

178   B. Hoggett, *Mental Health Law* (Sweet & Maxwell, 4th ed., 1996), pp.90–91.

179   *Ibid.*

180   *Lowe v. Fox* 12 App. Cases 206; 51 J.P. 468.

181   A petitioner under the Lunacy Act 1890 fulfilled a role equivalent to that of a nearest relative applicant under current law.

182   The statement of particulars may be seen as equivalent to an application under Part II.

services authority, of approving any amendments to the admission documents. The Court held that the order was not invalidated by the entry, taking the view that the addition was merely a statement of something which had already appeared on the face of the documents.[183] Cast in contemporary language, the ratio is that an amendment made after admission without the sanction of the managers, but in an immaterial particular, will not invalidate the authority so as to prevent the managers of the hospital from relying on it to justify the patient's detention.[184] By material is meant that the grounds said to justify the patient's detention have been altered.

Falsification of documents

Section 126(4) makes it an offence, subject to proof of mens rea, to wilfully make a false entry or statement in any application, recommendation or other document required or authorised to be made under the Act.[185]

Summary

A technical defect in the form of an application or recommendation may, with the necessary consent, be amended within the prescribed period by its signatory. Unauthorised amendments may invalidate an application if material and a court should consider whether the authority is valid and sufficient without regard to unauthorised amendments to the original. Where a defect which is rectifiable under section 8 or 15 is not remedied within the period allowed, the effect of that failure depends upon the importance of the error or defect and whether even legally significant breaches render an application invalid or voidable, that is valid until set aside by a competent court.[186] In trivial cases, although the defect or omission may no longer be rectified after a fortnight, so that the application will never be in the correct form, nevertheless the authority conferred by the application will not be affected.

RECOMMENDATIONS INSUFFICIENT TO WARRANT DETENTION

Subsections 15(2) and (3) provide that a fresh medical recommendation may be completed during the rectification period where it appears to the managers that one of the original recommendations, or their combined effect, is insufficient to warrant the patient's detention in pursuance of the application.

---

[183] (1) "... the judgment which we are delivering rests upon the fact that the alteration was an alteration wholly immaterial and that it is not intended to cast any doubt upon the proposition that an alteration of a document of this description in a material particular, if made at all events with the privity and knowledge of the person who is relying upon it, would make it invalid and would preclude him from legally relying upon it." per Lord Herschell. (2) "If a material part of [the document] was altered so that it no longer spoke the language which it did speak when it was originally received, and upon which the detention was authorised, that vitiated the document, I think it would be a very calamitous view of the state of the law if any doubt could be entertained as to whether such a misuse of the authority given by the statute could be made with impunity. It is as well that it should be generally known that any tampering with a document of that sort would impair its validity and deprive any person professing to act under it of any protection from it." per Lord Halsbury, L.C.

[184] See *Archbold's Lunacy and Mental Deficiency Law* (Butterworth & Co., Shaw & Sons, 5th ed., 1915).

[185] Subsection (1) further provides that it shall also be an offence for a person to have such a document in his custody or under his control if he knows or believes it to be false within the meaning of Part I of the Forgery and Counterfeiting Act 1981. Under the 1981 Act, a document may be "false" both by virtue of what it omits as well as what it includes. See R. Jones, *Mental Health Act Manual* (Sweet & Maxwell, 5th ed., 1996), p.333.

[186] See Lord Denning's judgment in *D.P.P. v. Head* [1959] A.C. 83, H.L.

One of the medical recommendations insufficient

Section 15(2) provides that if within the period of 14 days beginning with the date of a patient's admission to hospital in pursuance of an application, it appears to the managers that "one of the two medical recommendations" on which the application is founded is insufficient to warrant the patient's detention they may, within that period, give notice in writing to that effect to the applicant.[187] Where such notice is given, the medical recommendation shall be disregarded,[188] but the application shall be deemed always to have been sufficient if—

    a.   a fresh medical recommendation which complies with the relevant provisions of Part II (other than those relating to the time of signature and the interval between examinations) is furnished to the managers within that period;[189] *and*

    b.   that recommendation, and the other recommendation on which the application is founded, together comply with those provisions.

Subsection (2) will be applicable where a medical recommendation does not include the information required by section 3(3) or, arguably, was furnished by a practitioner who is disqualified by section 12(5) from giving a recommendation.

Medical recommendations taken together insufficient to warrant detention

Section 15(3) applies where the recommendations appear to comply with the Act and to warrant the patient's detention when considered separately but not when considered together. Section 15(3) provides that where the medical recommendations upon which an application for admission is founded are "taken together" insufficient to warrant the patient's detention, a notice under subsection (2) may be given in respect of "either of those recommendations." The Act also provides, however, that no such notice may be given where an application is of no effect because the two recommendations do not agree on at least one form of disorder from which the patient is suffering.[190] Subsection (3) will be applicable where the recommendations are collectively insufficient because—

    •   the two examinations upon which the recommendations are founded took place more than five clear days apart; or

---

187   The managers may authorise any officer (employee) or class of officers to give the written notice on their behalf: Mental Health Act 1983, s.32(3); Mental Health (Hospital, Guardianship and Consent to Treatment) Regulations 1983, reg.4(2)(b).

188   On a strict reading of section 15(2), the original medical recommendation is disregarded upon the managers giving notice, regardless of whether their opinion that it is insufficient to warrant the patient's detention is accurate or not. Consequently, if a second medical recommendation is not received within the 14-day period, the patient automatically ceases to be liable to be detained, because the application is then founded on a single medical recommendation.

189   Necessarily, this third recommendation will be dated later than the date of the application, and the examination upon which it is based may have taken place more than a week after that upon which the other valid medical recommendation is based. The Act recognises this and provides that as long as the two medical recommendations, both individually and collectively, comply with all the other requirements in Part II relating to medical recommendations, the application shall be deemed to have always been sufficient.

190   Mental Health Act 1983, ss.11(6) and 15(3).

- neither practitioner was approved under section 12(2) of the Act; or

- both recommendations were provided by doctors on the staff of an NHS hospital although section 12(4) did not apply.

BOTH RECOMMENDATIONS INSUFFICIENT

Where both recommendations are when considered separately insufficient to warrant the patient's detention, the position is irretrievable. Section 15 only allows one substitute recommendation to be furnished.

Joint medical recommendation

Section 15(2) allows the managers to give notice where "one of the two medical recommendations" appears to them to be insufficient. Section 15(3) provides for giving notice in respect of "either" of the "recommendations" where they are "taken together" insufficient to warrant the patient's detention. However, section 11(7) provides that an application may be founded on a joint recommendation and sub-sections (2) and (3) do not seem to have been drafted with this in mind. If a joint recommendation is insufficient there is no longer even a single valid recommendation in existence and the application cannot be rectified.

MEDICAL RECOMMENDATIONS AND GUARDIANSHIP

There is no equivalent provision whereby a substitute medical recommendation may be furnished during the 14-day period following acceptance of a guardianship application. This distinction appears to be intentional since the 1959 Act similarly made no provision for this.[191] This may reflect the fact that the time which a local social services authority has to scrutinise a guardianship application *before* accepting it is unlimited. At any rate, the legal position seems clear. If a medical recommendation is, whether considered separately or in conjunction with the other recommendation, insufficient then the guardianship application cannot be retrospectively validated.

APPLICATIONS

Sections 15(2) and (3) apply only to the recommendations upon which an application is founded and not to the application itself. If an application is insufficient to warrant the patient's detention a fresh application cannot be furnished during the fortnight following patient's admission. For instance, section 15 cannot save an application which is insufficient to warrant the patient's detention because the applicant had not seen the patient within the previous 14 days.

PRESCRIBED FORMS

A form used to make an application, or to give a recommendation, may be defective for one of three reasons—

---

[191] Because that statute was in force for 24 years, there was ample time for the omission to become apparent and to be rectified in the current legislation if this was a lacuna. Moreover, the Scottish and Northern Irish legislation does make provision for a fresh medical recommendation to be furnished in guardianship cases: Mental Health (Scotland) Act 1984, s.42(2) and (3); Mental Health (Northern Ireland) Order 1986, Art. 21(2) and (3).

- An obsolete form, which is no longer the prescribed form, has been used.

- There are defects in the prescribed forms.

- A law stationer's form, the wording of which departs from the prescribed form, has been used.

Use of obsolete forms

On 1 April 1996, new forms for making applications and giving recommendations were introduced.[192] The previous prescribed forms had been in force for more than a decade. Not all practitioners had a stock of the new forms or were aware that they were in force, because the Department of Health delayed issuing them. Consequently, a number of applications were made using the old forms during the following months. This was the point in issue in *Re E (Mental Health: Habeas Corpus)*.[193] The patient was admitted to hospital under section 3 on 16 June 1995. On 27 September, a tribunal refused to review the patient's detention on the basis that his detention was unauthorised and there was no authority in existence for it to review. On 9 October, a new section 3 application was completed, using the correct forms. The patient contended that he had been unlawfully detained between 16 June and 9 October and that his detention remained irregular notwithstanding the completion of a fresh application in the prescribed form. The court held that departures which were truly *de minimis* were not intended by the Act to be taken account of. Differences between forms which were *de minimis* should be ignored unless the statute expressly or by necessary implication required it to be given effect.

Defects in the prescribed forms

Some of the current prescribed forms do not accurately recite the statutory conditions for admission or renewal. Although it is a condition of admission for treatment, and renewal, that the patient's detention is necessary for his health or safety or for the protection of others, the new forms require the responsible medical officer to consider instead whether it is necessary "in the interests" of the patient's health or safety or "with a view to" the protection of others that he should receive treatment. The very general words, "in the interests of" and "with a view to," constitute part of the looser section 2 and guardianship criteria (**221**). Using the form prescribed by the regulations made under the statute therefore involves departing from the criteria prescribed by Parliament in the statute itself.

Defective law stationers' forms

The case of *Warren v. Warren* involved the use of a printed form the wording of which departed in one respect from the prescribed form, rather than a prescribed form the wording of which departed from the statutory criteria.[194] It was held that the use of the word "declare" in place of "certify" could be regarded as equivalent and sufficient, and in substitution for it (**288**).

---

[192] By The Mental Health (Hospital, Guardianship and Consent to Treatment) (Amendment) Regulations 1996.
[193] *Re E (Mental Health: Habeas Corpus), 10 December 1996 (unreported).*
[194] *Warren v. Warren* [1953] 1 W.L.R. 1268.

RECTIFICATION OF APPLICATIONS AND RECOMMENDATIONS

Points for consideration	Irregularity	Rectification provisions	Effect of an irregularity
1. Do the application or recommendations contain any error or defect which the Act expressly provides cannot be rectified and shall render the application invalid?	▪ Medical recommendations which do not both describe the patient as suffering from at least one common form of mental disorder, *e.g.* one states the patient is suffering only from mental illness, the other only from mental impairment	Such an irregularity cannot be retrospectively rectified under section 15: see s.15(3).	*The application is "of no effect": s.15(3).*
2. Do the application or recommendations contain any error or defect which the Act implies cannot be rectified and shall render the application invalid?	▪ Application completed by a person not qualified to complete it, *e.g.* not an ASW, not the nearest relative, not a person authorised to exercise relative's functions.	The customary view is that section 15(2) does not apply because it only allows for the rectification of applications and recommendations — unsigned documents and documents completed by persons not qualified to complete them do not constitute an application or recommendation. It is not so much that the application or recommendation is insufficient, rather the document is not an application or recommendation at all.	*The conventional view is that any such application, or application which relies upon a document which is not a recommendation, is invalid and cannot be rectified under section 15. However, the point has not been determined by the courts so some caution is necessary.*
	▪ Recommendation completed by a practitioner who is not fully registered: see Medical Act 1983, ss.47 & 48.		
	▪ Recommendation completed by a practitioner disqualified under s.12(5).		
	▪ Unsigned application or medical recommendation.		
If the recommendations are signed, the next step is to scrutinise each document separately, to ensure that it complies with the various statutory formalities. **3. Is the recommendation sufficient to warrant the patient's detention in pursuance of the application?**	▪ Non-section 2 recommendations which contain insufficient grounds/reasons for the doctor's opinion that the statutory criteria are satisfied	Section 15(2) provides that the hospital managers may notify the applicant of their opinion that the recommendation is insufficient, in which case the recommendation is disregarded. The applicant may then arrange for a fresh medical recommendation to be furnished within the statutory 14-day period. Section 15(2) does not apply to guardianship applications and no provision is made for the provision of a substitute recommendation in such cases.	*If a fresh sufficient recommendation is provided within the period allowed, the application is retrospectively validated. If not, the validity of the detention depends on the correctness of the managers' opinion that the recommendation is insufficient. In guardianship cases, the guardianship is always invalid if a recommendation is insufficient.*

271

Points for consideration	Irregularity	Rectification provisions	Effect of an irregularity
If both forms when considered separately are sufficient to warrant the patient's detention, the next question to address is their combined effect. **4. When considered together, are the recommendations sufficient to warrant the patient's detention in pursuance of the application?**	▪ Neither medical practitioner is approved under s.12(2). ▪ More than five <u>clear</u> days elapsed between the days on which the doctors furnishing the two medical recommendations conducted separate examinations of the patient. ▪ Both recommendations were provided by doctors on the staff of the NHS hospital to which the patient was admitted although s.12(4) did not apply.	Section 15(3) provides that the hospital managers may notify the applicant of their opinion and, in doing so, they shall stipulate which recommendation is to be disregarded. The applicant may then arrange for a fresh medical recommendation to be furnished within the statutory 14-day period. Section 15(3) does not apply to guardianship applications and no provision is made for the provision of a substitute recommendation in such cases.	*As before, if within the 14 day period the applicant furnishes to the managers a fresh medical recommendation which, when considered together with the other remaining recommendation, is sufficient to warrant the patient's detention, the application shall be deemed to have always been valid. If not, the validity of the patient's detention depends on the correctness of the managers' opinion that the recommendations are collectively insufficient. In guardianship cases, the guardianship is always invalid in such cases.*
5. If the application and both medical recommendations are sufficient to warrant detention, whether considered separately or together, are any other errors or defects in the forms apparent?	▪ Leaving blank spaces on the form which should have been completed, other than the space for signing it or for recording the doctor's reasons for believing that the statutory criteria are satisfied. ▪ Failure to delete one or more alternative clauses in places where only one can be correct ▪ Errors in the spelling of names, addresses or places	Sections 8(4) and 15(1) provide that an application or medical recommendation which is in any respect incorrect or defective may, with the managers' consent, be amended during the 14 days following admission or reception into guardianship.	*Once the amendment has been made, the recommendation is deemed to have effect as if it had been originally made as so amended. If the error or defect is not corrected, the validity of detention or guardianship depends on the significance of the error or defect. If trivial, the authority is unlikely to be affected.*

272

The authority for a patient's detention or guardianship under Part II remains in force until it is discharged or expires (**285**) or, more rarely, the patient is transferred from hospital into guardianship, or vice-versa (**282**). Prior to then, a patient may be granted leave to be absent from the hospital where he is liable to be detained (**280**), transferred to another hospital, or placed under the care of a different guardian (**282**). A detained patient may be given treatment for mental disorder without his consent in the circumstances set out in Part IV.

TREATMENT WITHOUT CONSENT (PART IV)

Part IV of the 1983 Act, which comprises sections 56 to 64, regulates the circumstances in which a patient who is liable to be detained under the Act may be given non-consensual treatment for mental disorder.[195] Section 58 is concerned with the administration of ECT and medication and is the most important section in practice. In certain circumstances, treatment may only be given if it has been authorised by a registered medical practitioner appointed for the purpose by the Mental Health Act Commission, on the Secretary of State's behalf. These Second Opinion Appointed Doctors are commonly referred to as "SOADs."

Psychosurgery and the surgical implantation of hormones

Psychosurgery (any surgical operation for destroying brain tissue or for destroying the functioning of brain tissue) is a particularly invasive treatment and one carrying special risks. The Act therefore provides that, except in an emergency, it may not be performed on any person — including therefore informal patients and out-patients — unless the individual consents to the operation and, furthermore, his capacity to give consent, the fact that he does consent, and the likelihood of benefit have been independently verified. These special safeguards also apply to one other form of treatment, the surgical implantation of hormones for the purpose of reducing the male sex drive. As to the use made of psychosurgery and the kinds of disorder which it may be used to treat, see page 1130.

The special procedures

Unless it constitutes urgent treatment lawfully given under section 62 (**278**), no person may be given any form of section 57 treatment unless[196]—

a. he has consented to it; *and*

b. a SOAD and two other persons appointed for the purposes of section 57 have certified in writing that he is capable of understanding the nature, purpose and likely effects of the treatment in question and has consented to it; *and*

---

[195] Part IV is not merely concerned with compulsory treatment since, if a patient is incapable of consenting to or refusing treatment, there may be no need to compel him to receive the proposed treatment. It has been variously held that the phrase "medical treatment for mental disorder" is, in essence, not synonymous with "psychiatric treatment," insofar as it includes ancilliary treatments such as force-feeding a patient who suffers from anorexia nervosa (**279**).

[196] Mental Health Act 1983, s.57(2).

c. the SOAD has further certified in writing that, having regard to the like-lihood of the treatment alleviating or preventing a deterioration of the patient's condition, the treatment should be given; *and*

d. before certifying that the treatment should be given, the SOAD has first consulted two other persons who have been professionally concerned with the patient's medical treatment, one of whom is a nurse and the other neither a nurse nor a registered medical practitioner.

The statutory certificate

Certificates authorising treatment under section 57 must be in the form set out in Form 37 to the Mental Health (Hospital, Guardianship and Consent to Treatment) Regulations 1983.[197]

"Excluded patients"

Section 57 treatments aside, the provisions in Part IV of the Act only apply to treatment which is given to certain classes of patients. Another way of making the same point is that certain patients (referred to here as "excluded patients") are excluded from the operation of Part IV and so may only be given treatment to which they do not consent if its administration is justified under common law.[198] These patients therefore retain a citizen's usual right to refuse medication or ECT.

EXCLUDED PATIENTS

▪ Patients who are not liable to be detained in a hospital	*Informal patients and those living in the community under guardianship, after-care under supervision or conditional discharge*
▪ Patients awaiting admission to hospital	*Following the making of an application under ss.2–4 or the imposition of an order or direction under Part III.*
▪ Patients who are detained in a hospital under an order which lasts for 72 hours or less	*Under section 4, 5(2), 5(4), 135 or 136.*
▪ Patients sent to hospital by a criminal court only so that a medical report can be prepared	*Under section 35.*

People detained under section 2 or for treatment

Having regard to the list of excluded persons, it can be seen that the only patients who do come within the ambit of Part IV, and who therefore do not enjoy the usual right to refuse psychiatric treatment, are those admitted to hospital under an application, court order or direction which expressly authorises admission for

---

[197] Mental Health Act 1983, s.64(2); Mental Health (Hospital, Guardianship and Consent to Treatment) Regulations 1983, reg. 16(1)(b).
[198] Mental Health Act 1983, s.56(1).

treatment. The authority conferred by a section 2 application is assessment followed by any necessary treatment while, in the other cases, the statutory purpose of the admission is expressed to be solely for the purpose of giving treatment.

PATIENTS TO WHOM ALL THE PART IV PROCEDURES APPLY

- Patients detained in hospital for assessment (followed by treatment)   *Under section 2*

- Patients detained in hospital for treatment   *Under section 3, 36, 37, 38, 44, 45A, 46–48*

Different forms of treatment

When considering whether a particular patient may be given compulsory treatment for mental disorder, the first step is therefore to determine whether he is a patient to whom the procedures in Part IV apply or is excluded from its provisions. If Part IV applies, the second step is to consider the nature of the treatment which it is proposed to give him because different statutory procedures apply to different kinds of treatment. Treatments which a doctor may give a Part IV patient are divided into three categories according to whether the patient's valid consent and/or independent authorisation is required.

DIFFERENT KINDS OF TREATMENT

- Psychosurgery

- Surgical implantation of hormones to reduce the male sex drive

These treatments require **both** the patient's verified valid consent **and** a certificate authorising the treatment given by a SOAD.

- ECT at any time

- Medication without the patient's consent for longer than three months

These treatments require **either** the patient's valid consent **or** that a certificate authorising the treatment has been given by a SOAD.

- Urgent treatment given under section 62

- Medical treatments for mental disorder which do not fall within the above classes and are given under section 63 by, or under the direction of, the responsible medical officer, including medication during the initial three month period, non-invasive treatments such as nursing care, and various ancillary treatments (such as force-feeding in the case of anorexia nervosa)

These kinds of treatment **neither** require the patient's consent **nor** independent authorisation by a SOAD.

Medication during the first three months

Sections 58 and 63 provide that a patient to whom Part IV applies may, without his consent and without any need for independent authorisation, be given medication for his mental disorder for a period of three months, provided it is given by or under the direction of his responsible medical officer. The three month period begins on the day on which the patient is first given medication for mental disorder after becoming a patient to whom Part IV applies. In other words, any medication previously given to him when he was an "excluded patient" is ignored. If the patient ceases to be a patient to whom Part IV applies before the three months have expired, the doctor's right to administer compulsory medication for a period of three months by definition no longer applies, since it is a power conferred by Part IV. The patient, being now exempt from the provisions of Part IV, may only be given further medication without his consent if justified under common law. If, as not uncommonly happens, he later again becomes a patient to whom Part IV applies — for example, a further application is made after a short period of informal hospital treatment — the statutory three month period begins afresh with the reintroduction of the statutory scheme. Where, however, the authority for the patient's detention and compulsory treatment simply changes from one application, order or direction to which Part IV applies to another, without their being any break in the patient's status as a Part IV patient, the three month period is not recalculated but continues for whatever is left of it.

Examples

X has been continuously detained since 1 January and he has also been given chlorpromazine daily since then. He was detained under section 5(2) on 1 January, under section 2 on 3 January, and under section 3 on 26 January. Patients detained under section 5(2) fall outside Part IV of the Act. The treatment given on 1 and 2 January was therefore not administered under Part IV. On 3 January, the patient was both detained under section 2 and given medication for mental disorder, and the three month period therefore began to run. Because he has been continuously detained since then, the three month period during which he may be given medicine without his consent or a second opinion expires at midnight on 2 April.

Example 2

If, in the above example, no medication was administered until 14 January, in order to allow the patient's responsible medical officer to assess his condition and the need for treatment, the three month period would have commenced on that date rather than on 3 January.

Example 3

If the patient was discharged from detention on 1 March, because he undertook to take medication informally but then defaulted on that agreement, so that a further section 3 application was made on 7 March, and medication given to him, the position would be as follows. Because he was an informal patient between 1 March and 6 March, he was not during that period a patient to whom Part IV applied. When he was redetained on 7 March, a new "continuous" period of detention as a Part IV patient began. He may therefore be treated without his consent or a second opinion for a period of three months beginning from then, *i.e.* until midnight on 6 June.

Medication after three months and ECT at any time (section 58)

Once the three month statutory period has expired, further medication for mental disorder may only be administered if it is given with the patient's valid consent, or has been authorised by a SOAD, or it constitutes urgent treatment given under section 62. A consent is valid in this context if the patient understands the nature, purpose and likely effects of the proposed treatment and consents to receiving it. ECT, *whether given during or after the first three months during which a person is a Part IV patient,* may similarly only be administered if it is given with the patient's valid consent, or has been authorised by a SOAD, or it constitutes urgent treatment given under section 62.[199]

The statutory certificates (Forms 38 and 39)

It is not sufficient that the patient has given a general oral or written consent to ECT, or to medication administered after the initial three month period. A statutory certificate must be completed. Where a patient who is capable of giving a valid consent to treatment does consent to ECT, or to medication being given outside the initial three month period, that treatment may still only be given if his responsible medical officer has first certified that the patient understands the nature, purpose and likely effects of the proposed treatment and has consented to it. He does this by completing the relevant statutory certificate, Form 38.[200] Where a patient is incapable of understanding the nature, purpose and likely effects of ECT or of the medication proposed, or withholds his consent, he may then only be given that treatment if a SOAD has certified that it should nevertheless be given having regard to the likelihood of it alleviating or preventing a deterioration of the patient's condition. He authorises the treatment by completing a Form 39. Before completing that certificate, he must first consult two other persons who have been professionally concerned with the patient's medical treatment, one of whom is a nurse and the other neither a nurse nor a registered medical practitioner.[201]

Withdrawing consent to treatment

Where a patient being treated in accordance with a valid Form 38 later withdraws his consent a visit from a SOAD must be arranged so that the treatment can be authorised by him if appropriate. Prior to the completion of a Form 39, the treatment must be discontinued unless the responsible medical officer considers that its discontinuance pending a SOAD visit would cause serious suffering to the patient.[202]

Plans of treatment

A Form 38 or Form 39 may authorise a plan of treatment, such as a course of ECT or a course of specified medication.[203] If the patient later withdraws consent to further treatment before the course of treatment has been completed, section 62

---

[199] There are therefore two circumstances in which a Form 38 or 39 may be required in the case of a section 2 patient: (i) where ECT is being administered; (ii) where, following a county court application made under section 29, the patient has been detained under that section for more than three months.

[200] Mental Health Act 1983, ss.58(3)(b), 58(4), 64(2); Mental Health (Hospital, Guardianship and Consent to Treatment) Regulations 1983, reg. 16(1)(b), Sched. 1, Form 38.

[201] Mental Health Act 1983, ss.58(3)(b), 58(4), 64(2); Mental Health (Hospital, Guardianship and Consent to Treatment) Regulations 1983, reg. 16(1)(b), Sched. 1, Form 39.

[202] Mental Health Act 1983, ss.60(1) and 62(2).

[203] *Ibid.*, s.59.

similarly requires the treatment to be discontinued unless the responsible medical officer considers that its discontinuance pending a SOAD visit would cause serious suffering to the patient.[204]

Future reviews of treatment

Where a SOAD has completed a Form 39, the responsible medical officer is periodically required to report to the Mental Health Act Commission on the progress of the patient's treatment. In the case of unrestricted patients, such a report must be furnished on the next occasion on which the responsible medical officer furnishes a report renewing the patient's detention for a further period.[205] Reports are made using a non-statutory form called Form MHAC/1.

MEDICATION AFTER 3 MONTHS AND ECT AT ANY TIME

- Patients who are capable of consenting to the proposed treatment and consent to receiving it

  The responsible medical officer or a SOAD has completed a Form 38, certifying that the patient understands the nature, purpose and likely effects of the treatment and has consented to it.

- Patients who are capable of consenting to the proposed treatment but who refuse consent

  A SOAD has completed a Form 39, certifying that although the patient does not consent to the proposed treatment it should nonetheless be given having regard to the likelihood of it alleviating or preventing a deterioration of his condition.

- Patients who are incapable of giving a valid consent to the proposed treatment

  A SOAD has completed a Form 39, certifying that although the patient is incapable of understanding the nature, purpose and likely effects of the treatment, it should nonetheless be given having regard to the likelihood of it alleviating or preventing a deterioration of his condition.

- Patients who require the treatment urgently

  The treatment may lawfully be given, despite the lack of a Form 38 or Form 39, if it constitutes "urgent treatment" under section 62.

Urgent treatment

The usual procedural safeguards concerning psychosurgery, ECT and medication administered after the initial statutory period, do not apply if the particular treatment constitutes urgent treatment given under section 62. The need to give urgent treatment under section 62 most commonly arises when a patient requires ECT and it is not appropriate to delay the first application for the period of two or three days which it takes for a SOAD to attend the hospital. Section 62 provides that the usual section 57 and 58 procedures do apply to any treatment—

a. which is immediately necessary to save the patient's life; *or*

b. which (not being irreversible) is immediately necessary to prevent a serious deterioration of his condition; *or*

---

[204] Mental Health Act 1983, ss.60(2) and 62(2).
[205] *Ibid.*, ss.61(1) and 121(2)(b).

c. which (not being irreversible or hazardous) is immediately necessary to alleviate serious suffering by the patient; *or*

d. which (not being irreversible or hazardous) is immediately necessary and represents the minimum interference necessary to prevent the patient from behaving violently or being a danger to himself or to others.

Applying section 62

In practice, some practitioners may find it easier to approach the criteria for urgent treatment by firstly asking if the treatment is irreversible and then, secondly, whether it is hazardous.

URGENT TREATMENT

• Is the proposed treatment irreversible?	If so, the treatment may only be given if immediately necessary to save the patient's life.
• If not, is it hazardous?	If so, the treatment may only be given if it is either immediately necessary to save the patient's life *or* immediately necessary to prevent a serious deterioration of his condition.
• If the proposed treatment is neither hazardous nor irreversible	It may be given in any of the four circumstances referred to in section 62.

What constitutes irreversible or hazardous treatment

The Act does not specify that particular treatments, such as psychosurgery or ECT, shall be deemed to be irreversible or hazardous for the purposes of section 62. It merely provides that a "treatment is irreversible if it has unfavourable irreversible physical or psychological consequences and hazardous if it entails significant physical hazard."[206] Treatments (such as ECT) which may be hazardous for an aged patient, or a patient with some serious concurrent physical illness, will not necessarily be hazardous for a young, physically healthy, person. As to whether treatments are reversible, this is defined by reference to the consequences of the treatment rather than the procedure itself. Furthermore, only treatment which has unfavourable consequences is irreversible for these purposes. Consequently, although psychosurgery is irreversible in the sense that it involves destroying brain tissue, or the way in which such tissue functions, it does not constitute irreversible treatment in the context of section 62 unless the physical and psychological effects of the operation are both permanent and unfavourable.

Section 63

Section 63 provides that a patient's consent "shall not be required for any medical treatment given to him for the mental disorder from which he is suffering, not being treatment falling within section 57 or 58 above, if the treatment is given by or under the direction of the responsible medical officer." In *B v. Croydon Health Authority* [1995] 1 All E.R.683, the court dismissed the argument that, whilst force-feeding

---

[206] Mental Health Act 1983, s.62(3).

may be a prerequisite to a treatment for mental disorder, or it may be treatment for a consequence of the mental disorder, it cannot be said to be treatment for that disorder. The definition of medical treatment in section 145, and the term "medical treatment ... for mental disorder" in section 63, included a range of acts ancillary to the core treatment. Treatment (in the form of nasogastric feeding) to alleviate the symptoms of mental disorder (in the form of a refusal to eat in order to inflict self-harm) was just as much a part of treatment for the disorder as that directed towards remedying its underlying cause. It therefore fell within section 63 and could be administered without the patient's consent.[207] The court added that it would be strange if a hospital could, without a suicidal patient's consent, give him treatment for the underlying mental illness but not without such consent treat the consequences of the suicide attempt.[208] *Tameside and Glossop Acute Services Trust v. C.H.* [1996] 1 F.L.R. 762 concerned a pregnant woman who believed that the doctors were trying to harm her baby, with the consequence that the baby was at significant risk. The mother-to-be was detained at the time under section 3 and, relying on section 63, Wall J.gave a declaration that it would be lawful to induce labour or to perform a caesarian section. The success of the psychiatric treatment depended on the patient delivering a healthy baby and on a prompt resumption of strong antipsychotic medication and, accordingly, such interventions were part of the overall medical treatment for her mental disorder.

Seclusion

As to whether seclusion may constitute a medical treatment given to the patient for the mental disorder from which he is suffering, see page 1168.

LEAVE OF ABSENCE

The responsible medical officer may grant a patient leave to be absent from the hospital where he is liable to be detained, subject to such conditions as that officer considers necessary in the interests of the patient or for the protection of others,[209] including that he remains in custody during his absence.[210] Leave may be granted to enable a patient to reside at an address outside hospital or at another hospital.[211] Where leave is granted for a specific period, it may be further extended in the patient's absence.[212] A patient who absents himself from the hospital or place where he is required to reside as a condition of his leave is absent without leave for the purposes of the Act.[213]

---

[207]   *B v. Croydon Health Authority* [1995] 1 All E.R.683 at 687 F–G, *per* Hoffmann L.J.

[208]   *Ibid.*, at 687j–688a.

[209]   Mental Health Act 1983, s.17(1).

[210]   *Ibid.*, s.17(3). More particularly, the subs. provides that "the patient may be kept in the custody of any officer on the staff of the hospital, or of any other person authorised in writing by the managers of the hospital, or, if the person is required ... to reside in another hospital, of any officer on the staff of that other hospital." Thus, while only the responsible medical officer can grant leave and direct that the patient shall remain in custody, if the custodian is to be some person other than an NHS employee such as a nurse — for example, a police constable or social worker — only the managers can authorise that. Furthermore, while any grant of leave need not as a matter of law be in writing any such authority given to a non-NHS employee by the managers must be.

[211]   See *ibid.*, ss.17(3) and 18(2). A patient granted leave to reside at another hospital is not detained there but remains liable to be detained at the hospital from which he has leave to be absent. However, in appropriate cases, a condition that the patient shall remain in the custody of a nurse at the second hospital may be attached to the leave.

[212]   *Ibid.*, s.17(2).

[213]   *Ibid.*, s.18(1)(c) and (6).

Legal status of patients absent from hospital

The legal status of a detained patient who is absent from hospital can only be one of two things — he is either absent with leave (with his responsible medical officer's permission) or absent without leave (without that person's permission). Although patients who briefly leave the grounds to buy cigarettes at the local shop or "to pop home," sometimes with a nurse's permission, are commonly considered not to be absent from the hospital without leave, as a matter of law they are if they do not have their responsible medical officer's prior permission. Just as the statement that a person is helping the police with their enquiries is legally meaningless so too there is no intermediate legal position when it comes to being absent from hospital.

Patients kept in custody

The fact that patients granted leave may, in the circumstances stated above, remain in custody during their absence raises the question of what being in custody means. In the first place, the patient "remains" in custody because his previous detention in the hospital is also a form of legal custody. More specifically, the patient is "in legal custody"[214] and the nominated custodian is "in charge" of him.[215] The patient's custodian has certain duties to him, in particular to take reasonable care that the patient does not harm himself or others. As to his powers, if the patient attempts to escape from his custodian or does briefly escape, the latter then has authority to keep or take him back into his legal custody and, if on their way to some particular destination, to convey him to the stipulated place.[216] The position of patients granted leave to be absent from the hospital where they are liable to be detained, subject to a condition that they "reside" at another hospital but remain in custody, does, however, differ in one important respect. In contrast to patients transferred to that hospital under section 19, patients on leave there remain "liable to be detained" at the hospital from which they have leave to be absent. It is the managers of that first hospital who have authority to detain them and who remain legally responsible for them. It is to them that any reports renewing the authority for the patient's detention, and any other statutory reports, must be submitted.

Revocation and recall

Once a responsible medical officer grants leave, he may only revoke it and recall the patient to the hospital where he is liable to be detained if it is necessary to do so in the interests of the patient's health or safety or for the protection of others.[217] A patient who is on leave may not be recalled to hospital after he has ceased to be liable to be detained under the Act.[218] This is logical because there is no longer any hospital at which he is liable to be detained and to which he can be recalled. Furthermore, the authority for his detention may not be renewed unless he requires further treatment in hospital as a detained patient, and he cannot be recalled simply as a way of bringing him within the statutory conditions for renewal.[219]

---

[214] Mental Health Act 1983, s.137(1).
[215] See *ibid.*, s.17(4).
[216] See *ibid.*, ss.137 and 138.
[217] Mental Health Act 1983, s.17(4). Any revocation of leave must be by notice in writing, served on the patient or (where applicable) on his custodian. Thus, the revocation but not the grant of leave must be in writing. Where leave is revoked but the patient does not return to hospital, he is thereafter absent without leave: *ibid.*, s.18(1)(b).
[218] *Ibid.*, s.17(5).
[219] *R. v. Hallstrom, ex p W (No. 2)* [1986] 2 All E.R. 306, *per* McCullough J.

A patient is detained under section 3 on 1 January 1995. On 1 March, he is granted leave of absence subject to a condition that he resides at a different hospital. He will cease to be liable to be detained unless, prior to 30 June, the section is renewed for a further period. Since he remains an in-patient in hospital, the authority for detention may be renewed for a further period if he satisfies the renewal criteria set out in section 20(4). In particular, renewal requires that the medical treatment in hospital which it is appropriate for him to receive cannot be provided "unless he *continues* to be detained."[220]

Patients subject to guardianship

Section 17 does not apply to guardianship cases. If a guardian agrees to the patient staying at an address other than his nominated place of abode, he simply specifies the new address as the place where the patient is required to reside for the time being.[221] Thus, although patients subject to guardianship may be absent without leave from their required place of residence they are never absent from there with leave granted under section 17.

TRANSFERS AND REMOVALS UNDER SECTION 19

The transfer of a patient from one hospital to another, or from the guardianship of one person or authority to another, has no legal consequences other than to transfer the powers and duties conferred and imposed by the application from one person or body to another. The statutory provisions relating to the duration, expiry and renewal of the detention or guardianship remain unaffected.[222] This is not, however, the case where the transfer is from hospital to guardianship, or vice-versa.

Transfers from hospital to guardianship

Where a patient who is liable to be detained under section 2 or 3 is transferred into guardianship, the section 2 or 3 application takes effect as if it were a guardianship application made and accepted on the date when the patient was originally admitted to hospital for assessment or treatment, as the case may be.[223]

---

[220] Since a patient on leave is not detained in the hospital where he is residing, the renewal criteria can only be satisfied if (a) he is first transferred (b) the word "detained" in this context is read as meaning "liable to be detained," or (c) being in the custody of an officer of the hospital where the patient is residing constitutes being detained in hospital for the purposes of s.20. The conventional view, first set out in the *Mental Health Act 1959: Memorandum on Parts I, IV to VII and IX, (D.H.S.S., 1960),* was reiterated in the Department of Health's *Health Service Guidelines* HSG(96)28. This is that the renewal criteria cannot be met if the patient has leave to reside at another hospital at the relevant time, *i.e.* he is absent with leave from the hospital at which there is authority to detain him and he is therefore not detained at either hospital. Furthermore, it is unlawful to return him to the first hospital purely for the purpose of renewing his liability to detention. See also page 281.

[221] See Mental Health Act 1983, s.8(1)(a).

[222] The guardianship also continues if a private guardian relinquishes his functions and, by virtue of section 10, the guardianship thereupon vests in the local social services authority. It similarly vests in the local authority if a guardian is incapacitated, dies, or is removed by the county court on the grounds that he has exercised his functions negligently or without due regard for the patient's welfare. In any such eventuality, section 19(2)(c) applies and the guardianship is treated as having commenced on its original date, but as if the substitute guardian had been named in the original authority for guardianship. The change of guardian does not affect the patient's tribunal rights nor does it act as a deemed withdrawal of any outstanding application or reference before a tribunal.

[223] Mental Health Act 1983, s.19(2)(b). Because of an oversight, a section 2 patient who is transferred into guardianship does not have a legal classification under the Act.

Transfers from guardianship to hospital

Where a patient who is subject to a guardianship application is transferred to hospital, the guardianship application takes effect as if it were a section 3 application and as if the patient had been admitted to hospital in pursuance of it on the date of his original reception into guardianship.[224]

Example

A patient is admitted to hospital under section 2 on 1 January. He is transferred into guardianship on 18 January. As a result, he is deemed to have been received into guardianship under section 7 on 1 January. His condition deteriorates and he is transferred back to hospital under section 19 on 1 May. The effect of the transfer is that he is deemed to have been admitted to hospital under section 3 on 1 January.

Removals under section 19

Where a detained patient is removed under section 19(3) to a hospital under the same hospital managers, the statutory provisions relating to the duration, expiry and renewal of the authority for the patient's detention remain unaffected.[225]

TERMINATION OF DETENTION OR GUARDIANSHIP

A patient may be discharged from liability to detention or guardianship under the Act. Even if a patient is not discharged, the authority for his detention or guardianship may cease to have effect for one of the reasons set out in the table on page 285.

DISCHARGE OF PATIENTS

A patient who is liable to be detained or subject to guardianship under Part II may be discharged in the circumstances specified in sections 23 and 72.

Orders for discharge under section 23

Section 23 provides that a patient shall cease to be liable to be detained or subject to guardianship if an order is made discharging him from detention or guardianship. An "order for discharge" must be in writing and comply with the other requirements of the section. A number of persons may make an order for discharge: the responsible medical officer;[226] the managers of the hospital where the patient is liable to be detained; the responsible social services authority of a patient subject to

---

[224] Mental Health Act 1983, s.19(2)(d).

[225] As to the distinction between transfers and removals under section 19, see p.135.

[226] Most orders for discharge are made by responsible medical officers. There is no prescribed form. Some hospitals have devised an in-house form. Where that is not so, it may in practice be difficult to discern any entry in the case notes which is capable of constituting an *order* for discharge. The exercise of the power is personal to the responsible medical officer and cannot be delegated. Orders may sometimes be signed by junior medical officers, in effect recording decisions communicated to them orally by the responsible medical officer. The legality of this is not established. Because the Act states that such orders must be in writing and made by the responsible medical officer, discharge may well only be effective if the responsible medical officer signs the order himself.

guardianship; the nearest relative.[227] The Secretary of State may discharge a patient who is liable to be detained in a mental nursing home, as may any NHS trust or Health Authority which is financing his assessment or treatment there.[228]

Patients detained for 72 hours or less

As drafted, section 23 applies only to patients who are subject to guardianship, liable to be detained under section 3, or liable to be detained "in pursuance of an application for assessment" — which, as defined by section 2(1), excludes patients detained under section 4.[229] Indeed, the Act appears to include no mechanism for discharging patients whose detention under the Act is authorised for a period not exceeding 72 hours, whether under sections 4, 5, 135 or 136. It may be argued that the omission in section 23 of any explicit reference to section 4 is deliberate. In essence, the purpose of the patient's detention is to allow the application process to be completed within a hospital setting because its completion outside hospital would involve unacceptable risks. The period of detention is too short to make it appropriate to prescribe any formal procedure for the patient's release, in terms of a written order of discharge or a tribunal review. The patient may simply be released by the managers at their discretion if and when it becomes clear to them that no second recommendation will be forthcoming: the fact that they are authorised to detain the patient does not mean that they must do so. The Act protects the patient during this interim period by instead providing that he may not be compulsorily treated until such time (if ever) as a second recommendation is furnished. But it is only if a second recommendation is furnished is the patient placed in exactly the same position as a person admitted under section 2. Alternatively, it may be said that an emergency application is, as section 4(1) makes clear, an application for admission for assessment and the fact that it is initially founded on a single recommendation does not alter that fact. Section 23 therefore applies. The point is further considered on page 623, in the context of a section 4 patient's right to apply to a tribunal under section 66(1)(a).

Discharge by a Mental Health Review Tribunal

A Mental Health Tribunal may, and in the circumstances specified in section 72, must discharge a patient from liability to detention or guardianship under the Act (**463**).

---

[227] However, an order for discharge made by the nearest relative of a patient detained under Part II is of no effect if a report barring the patient's discharge is furnished to the managers of a hospital by the patient's responsible medical officer: see Mental Health Act 1983, s.25 (**610**).

[228] *Ibid.*, s.23(3).

[229] Section 2(1) states that an application made under section 2 is "in this Act referred to as 'an application for admission for assessment'" while section 4(1) provides that an application made under section 4 is "in this Act referred to as 'an emergency application.'" The alternative, generic, expression "an application for admission to hospital" is used where, as in section 13, a particular provision is intended to apply to all applications under sections 2, 3 and 4.

I. Patient no longer subject to compulsion under the 1983 Act — now informal

• *Patient discharged from liability to detention or guardianship*	Patient discharged under section 23 or by a tribunal under section 72.	**283**
• *Patient released by the High Court (habeas corpus, judicial review)*	Patient released due to the lack of a valid authority for his detention/guardianship.	**861**
• *Expiration of the period of detention or guardianship*	Expiration of the section 2 period or expiration of a period of liability to detention or guardianship without renewal.	**286**
• *Cessation due to the patient being absent without leave*	Patient continuously absent without leave for a period of six months or, if his period of detention or guardianship had longer than that to run when he absented himself, at the expiration of that detention or guardianship period.	**289**
• *Cessation due to the patient being in custody in pursuance of a court order*	Patient in custody in pursuance of a court order for a period of six months or, if released before being in custody for six months, has not returned or been taken into custody under the Mental Health Act within 28 days of his release.	**300**
• *Cessation following the patient's reclassification under section 16*	Untreatable patient reclassified as suffering only from a psychopathic disorder and/or mental impairment.	**302**
• *Cessation upon the patient's removal outside the jurisdiction.*	Patient removed from England and Wales under Part VI of the Act, including therefore under section 86.	**306**

II. Patient remains subject to compulsion but under a different statutory provision

• *Cessation upon a subsequent application being made in respect of him under Part II of the Act*	A s.3 application is made in respect of a patient detained under s.2 or subject to guardianship; a guardianship application is made in respect of a detained patient.	**303**
• *Cessation upon a subsequent order or direction being made in respect of him under Part III of the Act.*	The patient is received into guardianship or detained under Part III, otherwise than under ss.35, 36 or 38.	**304**
• *Patient transferred from hospital to guardianship or vice-versa*	The patient is transferred under section 19 of the Act.	**282**

Notes: Since 1 April 1996, a patient who is liable to be detained or subject to guardianship no longer ceases to be so liable or subject upon being continuously absent with leave for a period of six months: see Mental Health (Patients in the Community) Act 1995, s.3(1) **(300)**.

EXPIRATION OF PERIOD OF DETENTION OR GUARDIANSHIP

A patient will cease to be liable to be detained or subject to guardianship upon the expiration of the period of detention or guardianship authorised by the Act unless that authority can be, and is, renewed for a further period or a further application, order or direction is made prior to its expiration.

Cessation at the end of the assessment period

The authority to detain a patient which is conferred by an application for assessment normally expires after 28 days. However, a patient's liability to detention under section 2 may be extended beyond 28 days if a county court application under section 29 is pending at the expiration of that period (**112**). The conventional view is there where a section 2 patient is absent without leave during the final week of the 28 day period the effect of this is not to extend the authorised period of detention beyond 28 days (**289**). Since the tribunal hearing date initially fixed in an assessment case must be a day within three weeks of the patient's admission, these expiry and extension provisions will only ever be relevant where a hearing is adjourned because the patient is absent without leave at the time it is originally scheduled to take place.

Cessation at the end of a period of treatment or guardianship

Where a patient is detained for treatment or subject to guardianship, the authority for his detention or guardianship will expire unless periodically renewed for periods of six or twelve months at a time, in accordance with the provisions of section 20. The authority is renewed where, during the final two months of the existing period, the patient's responsible medical officer (or, in guardianship cases, his appropriate medical officer) examines him and "duly" furnishes a renewal report to the managers or authority responsible for him, stating that in his opinion the conditions for renewal are satisfied.[230]

Extended detention or guardianship due to absence without leave

The normal six and twelve month periods of detention or guardianship may be extended if a patient is, or has been, absent without leave (**292**) or detained in custody otherwise than under the 1983 Act (**300**). Furthermore, if an absent patient returns or is returned to hospital within the extended period, the authority for his detention or guardianship may be retrospectively renewed in the circumstances described below (**293 et seq.**).

Reasons for non-renewal

Non-renewal will generally be intentional and due to the fact that a patient's condition is no longer considered to be sufficiently serious that the conditions for renewal are satisfied. However, the authority will also expire if a renewal examination is conducted outside the statutory period; the renewal report is not "duly" furnished within those two months; it materially differs from the prescribed form; *or* is

---

[230] In cases involving patients who are detained for treatment, the responsible medical officer's report must be made using Form 30. In guardianship cases, the prescribed form is Form 31. Mental Health (Hospital, Guardianship and Consent to Treatment) Regulations 1983, reg.10. It was held in a Scottish case that a renewal report is "furnished" to the hospital managers when it is committed to the internal mailing system operated by those managers. *Milborrow, Applicant* (1996) S.C.L.R. 315, Sh. Ct.

otherwise insufficient to constitute a valid renewal.[231] The rectification provisions do not apply to renewal reports. Consequently, where such a report is insufficient to renew the authority for a patient's detention or guardianship, it may not be retrospectively validated once the previous period has expired.[232]

The effect of a report furnished under section 20

Section 20(8) provides that where such a renewal report is "duly" furnished, the authority for the patient's detention shall "thereby" be renewed for a further period. Unless the managers discharge the patient, they must ensure that the patient is informed that a renewal report has been furnished. It was always thought that the furnishing of a renewal report to the hospital managers instantly renewed the patient's liability for a further period: it was not necessary that the managers also consider this report, and the patient's suitability for discharge, before the existing period of detention had expired. The case of *ex p. B.* confirmed this.

R. v. Managers of Warlingham Park Hospital, ex p. B.

(1994) 22 B.M.L.R. 1   *C.A. (Sir Thomas Bingham M.R., Staughton, Kennedy L.JJ.)*

B. was detained under section 3. During the final two months of the first six-month period of detention, the responsible medical officer examined her and furnished a report to the managers, stating that in his opinion the conditions for renewal were satisfied. In due course, the managers met to consider the report and B's suitability for discharge but did so only after the initial six month period had expired. They decided not to discharge and recorded the section's renewal by signing the second part of the renewal report. The same pattern of events was repeated when the patient's detention next came to be renewed. The managers delayed reviewing B's case, and signing the renewal report, until after the period of detention authorised by the first renewal had expired.

The application for judicial review

It was submitted on the patient's behalf that regulation 10 made it clear that the responsible medical officer's report was no more than a "recommendation" for renewal.[233] Renewal required that all of the steps referred to in section 20, which together constituted the renewal procedure, were completed before the existing period of detention expired. In B's case, the authority for her detention had

---

[231] For example, the responsible medical officer must consult one or more persons who have been professionally concerned with the patient's medical treatment before furnishing a renewal report: see Mental Health Act 1983, s.20(5). In practice, consultants rarely conduct any specific statutory consultation of this kind and the statutory renewal form (Form 30) does not require confirmation that this has been done, or information about who was consulted and when.

[232] See Mental Health Act 1983, ss.8(4) and 15. In *R. v. Board of Control, East Ham Corporation and Mordey, ex p. Winterflood* [1938] 2 K.B. 366, C.A, the authority for the patient's detention was not renewed until after the previous period of detention had expired, the purported renewal therefore being a nullity. Where the defect is identified before the period of detention or guardianship has expired, there is of course time to furnish a fresh report in the prescribed form or to commence the whole process afresh, depending on the nature of the omission. In its annual report of 1989, the Mental Welfare Commission for Scotland noted that one-sixth of all guardianship cases terminated that year had unintentionally lapsed. *Mental Welfare Commission for Scotland: Annual Report for 1989*, para. 12.16.

[233] Paragraph 10(1) of the Mental Health (Hospital, Guardianship and Consent to Treatment) Regulations 1983 provides that "any report for the purposes of section 20(3) (medical recommendation for renewal of authority to detain) shall be in the form set out in Part I of Form 30." Paragraph (3) states that "any renewal of authority for detention ... under section 20(8) shall be recorded by the managers of the hospital ... in the form set out in Part II of Form 30."

already expired by the time the managers reviewed her suitability for discharge, considered and endorsed the renewal "recommendation,"and notified her that a report had been furnished. The hospital managers argued that the valid renewal of the authority for a patient's detention required only that the responsible medical officer had furnished a renewal report to them before that period had ended.

Sir Thomas Bingham M.R.

There were no grounds for holding that B had at any time been unlawfully detained and the application was therefore dismissed. The court was mindful of the fact that the case concerned the liberty of the subject and of the need to ensure that procedures relating to the detention of patients were scrupulously followed. It was also highly desirable that the managers should give timely information to the patient as soon as they had the renewal report to hand and as soon as they had taken a decision as to discharge. The authority to continue to detain B arose when the responsible medical officer furnished his renewal report to the managers; it was impossible to read "thereby" as referring to anything other than the furnishing of his report. On any reasonable reading of section 20, it was not the case that the steps required of the managers also had to be taken within the final two month period. Regulation 10 required them to do no more than "record" their decision that the patient should not be discharged. If the regulations introduced any note of ambiguity that simply demonstrated that the Secretary of State had not fully understood the effect of section 20.

Prescribed form defective

A new prescribed Form 30 came into force on 1 April 1996.[234] This was unfortunate because the old form recited the correct statutory criteria for renewal and the only changes made to it involve a failure to accurately recite the statutory conditions for renewal. Although it is a condition of renewal that further treatment in hospital is necessary for the patient's health or safety or for the protection of others, the new form requires the responsible medical officer to certify that it is necessary "in the interests" of his health or safety or "with a view to" the protection of others that he should receive that treatment. As has been noted, "in the interests of" and "with a view to" are phrases which form part of the looser section 2 and guardianship grounds and were deliberately not incorporated in the section 3 admission and renewal criteria (**221**). Using the form prescribed by the regulations made under the statute therefore involves departing from the criteria prescribed by Parliament in the statute itself. Although the case of *Warren v. Warren*[235] involved the use of a printed form the wording of which departed in one respect from the prescribed form, rather than a prescribed form the wording of which departs from the statutory criteria, the courts must be likely to adopt a similarly practical approach to the error. In that case, Mr. Commissioner Glazebrook QC, relying on *R. v. Pinder*,[236] held that the use of the word "declare" in place of "certify" could be regarded as equivalent and sufficient, and in substitution for it. The issue is one of the sufficiency of the incorrect wording of the new forms. Although the errors here are more material than that in *Warren v. Warren*, the consequences of holding otherwise are unlikely to be contemplated.

---

[234] Mental Health (Hospital, Guardianship and Consent to Treatment) (Amendment) Regulations 1996, reg. 3.

[235] *Warren v. Warren* [1953] 1 W.L.R. 1268.

[236] *R. v. Pinder, Re Greenwood* (1855) 24 L.J.Q.B. 148 (**263**).

CESSATION DUE TO ABSENCE WITHOUT LEAVE

If an unrestricted patient is absent without leave from the hospital or place where he is required to be his liability to detention or guardianship will eventually cease if he is neither taken into custody nor returns there of his own accord.[237] When considering the continued liability to detention or guardianship of any patient who is, or has been, absent without leave, it is imperative to approach the matter in two distinct stages:

1) After what period of time does the patient cease to be liable to be detained or subject to guardianship and so also cease to be liable to be taken into custody under the Act?

2) If the patient is taken into custody during the permitted period, or before its expiration returns there of his own accord, what effect does this have and what legal procedures must then be carried out?

Patients detained under section 2

Section 18 provides that a section 2 patient who is absent without leave shall "not be taken into custody" after the expiration of the period referred to in section 2(4), which (unless extended under section 29) is the usual 28 day section 2 period.[238]

The effect of recapture or return during the permitted period

Section 21 is expressed to apply to a patient who is absent without leave on the day on which he would "*apart from this section*" cease to be liable to be detained or who is absent during the preceding week. In this context, unless county court proceedings have been commenced, that means absent during the final week of the four weeks' detention authorised by section 2(4). Where section 21 applies, it provides that if such a patient is taken into custody during the time allowed by section 18 — which, in this context, means before the final week has expired — he shall not cease to be liable to be detained until the end of the period of one week beginning with the date if his return to hospital.[239]

The effect of section 2(4)

Notwithstanding the wording of section 21, the view universally taken in practice has always been that if a section 2 patient is absent without leave during the final week of the 28 day period the effect of this can never be to extend the authorised period of detention beyond 28 days. This is because section 2(4) provides that the authorised period of detention shall not exceed that period unless it has been extended by section 29 or the patient is subsequently detained for treatment under some other statutory provision — no other exception, such as that referred to in section 21, is mentioned in section 2(4). Furthermore, the purpose of the one week

---

[237]   Section 18(5) of the 1983 Act states that, "'Absent without leave' means absent from any hospital or other place and liable to be taken into custody and returned under this section, and related expressions shall be construed accordingly."

[238]   See Mental Health Act 1983, s.18(5).

[239]   See *ibid.*, s.21.

extension allowed by section 21 has always been explained, for example in the *Memorandum* on the Act, in terms of giving a responsible medical officer sufficient time to renew the authority to detain a patient for treatment. The assumption has therefore been that section 21 only applies to patients who are liable to be detained for treatment. Nevertheless, the use of the phrase *"apart from this section"* in section 21 raises the possibility that it is intended to be a further way in which the period of detention authorised following admission under section 2 may be extended. The rationale would be to allow those involved sufficient time to examine and interview the patient and to complete any necessary section 3 application. All these consequences logically follow from a literal reading of section 21. However, a literal reading of the section would also mean that absent section 4 and section 5(2) patients who are taken into custody during the 72-hour detention periods conferred by those powers could then also be further detained for a week, which is a nonsense. In summary, section 21 cannot be read entirely literally but there is an element of ambiguity as to whether it is meant to also extend to patients detained under section 2. Either section 2(4) was meant to be exhaustive, and section 21 was drafted in the belief that that had been made clear, or the draftsman believed that the phrase *"apart from this section"* in section 21 made it similarly clear that this was an additional exception.

Unrestricted patients detained for treatment or subject to guardianship

Prior to the coming into force of the Mental Health (Patients in the Community) Act 1995, section 18 provided that where an unrestricted patient who was liable to be detained for treatment or subject to guardianship had been continuously absent without leave for a period of 28 days, he ceased to be liable to be detained or subject to guardianship. The rationale was that, if a patient could remain in the community without drawing attention to himself or obviously requiring treatment for that length of time, his condition could not be sufficiently serious to warrant detention or control.

The amendments made by the 1995 Act

Section 18 now provides that where such a patient absents himself without leave from the hospital or place where he is required to reside, he only ceases to be liable to be detained or subject to guardianship after he has been continuously absent for a period of six months or, if the existing period of detention or guardianship had more than six months left to run when he absented himself, upon that period expiring.[240] The precise period for which the application, order or direction remains in force, and during which an absent patient may be taken into custody, therefore depends upon how long his period of detention or guardianship had left to run on the day he went absent —

- As has already been noted, the authority of the hospital managers or a guardian over an unrestricted patient lapses after six months unless it is renewed for a further period of six months and thereafter for periods of one year at a time.

---

[240] Mental Health Act 1983, s.18(1) and (4), as amended by s.2(1) of the Mental Health (Patients in the Community) Act 1995.

- The first year's detention or guardianship thus consists of two six-month statutory periods. Consequently, if a patient absents himself before he has been detained for treatment or subject to guardianship for a year, there will always be less than six months of the current period of detention or guardianship left to run on the day he goes missing: even if he absents himself on the second day of one of the six month periods, there will necessarily be less than six months of that period remaining.

- Where, however, a patient has been continuously detained for treatment or subject to guardianship for more than one year the last renewal of his section will have been for a period of 12 months. If the patient then absents himself during the first half of that year, there would at that time have been more than six months of the existing period of detention or guardianship left. Conversely, if he absented himself during the second half of the year there would at that time have been less than six months of the period outstanding.

- Bearing these statutory periods in mind, the authority for the patient's detention or guardianship remains in force, and he remains liable to recapture, for six months if the period of detention or guardianship in existence when he absented himself had less than six months left to run at that time. If there were more than six months left, he remains liable for the whole of the remainder of the unexpired period.

- It is therefore the period of detention or guardianship in existence when the patient absents himself which is material. For these purposes, if a patient absents himself during the final two months of a period of detention or guardianship any renewal report furnished before he went absent is ignored.[241] Thus, if a patient in his second six-month of detention absents himself in December after his responsible medical officer had furnished a report renewing from 1 January the authority to detain him, this does not mean that he can be taken into custody at any time during the following year. Rather, he remains liable to be taken into custody for a period of six months commencing from the day he went missing.

- It suffices if a patient is taken into custody during the permitted period even though he is not returned to the hospital or place where he is required to be until after that period has expired. Thus, if a patient absent from a hospital in Lancashire is recaptured by police in Devon on the last day of the prescribed period but is not returned for two days, he remains liable to be detained.[242]

---

[241] Mental Health Act 1983, s.18(4), as substituted by Mental Health (Patients in the Community) Act 1995, s.2(1).

[242] The position is similar where a warrant is issued under section 72 of the Criminal Justice Act 1967 to arrest a hospital order patient who is absent without leave. If the patient is then held in pursuance of the warrant in some country outside the United Kingdom, Channel Islands and Isle of Man, he is deemed to have been taken into custody on the date he is apprehended in pursuance of the warrant. See Mental Health Act 1983, s.21A(4).

PERIOD FOR WHICH PATIENTS REMAIN SUBJECT TO THE ACT

Class of patients	Class comprises	Recapture period, etc.
▪ Patients whose period of detention or guardianship had less than six months to run on the day they went absent without leave	▪ *Patients who were in their first or second period of detention for treatment or guardianship on the day they went absent without leave* ▪ *Patients whose detention for treatment or guardianship was last renewed for a period of one year and who then go absent during the second six months of that period.*	Patient may be recaptured for a period of six months. The managers' authority to detain the patient or the guardian's authority lapses if the patient has not been recaptured upon the expiration of this period, and he is no longer liable to be taken into custody and returned.
▪ Patients whose period of detention or guardianship had more than six months to run on the day they went absent without leave	▪ *Patients whose detention for treatment or guardianship was last renewed for a period of one year and who then go absent during the first six months of that period.*	Patient may be recaptured at any time during whatever remains of the existing period of detention or guardianship. If he is still at large upon the expiration of this period, the managers' or guardian's authority lapses.

Examples

The following examples illustrate the practical effect of the new provisions concerning the period during which an absent patient may be recaptured.

Examples

X has been subject to guardianship for between three and four years. On 1 January, the authority for his guardianship was renewed for a further period of 12 months. On 1 February, he left his required place of residence.

Under the previous provisions, he would have ceased to be subject to guardianship after 28 days if he had not by then returned, or been returned, to his nominated place of abode. Under the new provisions, he remains liable to be taken into custody for the remainder of the current period of guardianship, that is until 31 December.

The position would be different if he had absented himself during the second half of the year, when there was less than six months of the guardianship period left. He would then have been liable to be taken into custody during the following six months, *i.e.* beyond the date by which renewal would normally be necessary.

292

Example 2

X is detained under section 3 on 1 January. Unless the authority for his detention is renewed, he will cease to be liable to be detained after six months, on 30 June. On 1 February, after a month in hospital, he goes absent without leave. Under the previous provisions, he would have ceased to be liable to be detained after 28 days absence. Under the new section 18(4), he remains liable to be taken into custody for six months, until 31 July, even though this is beyond the date by which the section would normally need to be renewed to remain in force.

Effect of a patient's return during the permitted period

It can be seen that because a patient is always liable to be taken into custody for at least six months, whereas a period of detention or guardianship often expires six months from its commencement, some provision must be made for retrospectively renewing the patient's liability under the Act. Two other points must also be addressed. Firstly, the possibility that a patient might be returned so near to the end of his period of detention or guardianship that there is insufficient time to renew it before it expires. Secondly, where a patient has been absent for a prolonged period, the possibility that he no longer needs to be detained or under guardianship. With that last point in mind, different statutory procedures apply depending upon whether or not a returned patient has been absent for more than 28 days.

Patients who have been absent for 28 days or less

Where a patient is absent for 28 days or less, he would not have ceased to have been detained or subject to guardianship under the old law. In particular, there would not have been any presumption that he no longer required detention or guardianship. Consequently, the position set out in the 1983 Act as originally drafted has been retained where a patient's absence does not exceed 28 days—

- Unless the patient's return occurs during the final week of a period of detention or guardianship, or after such a period would ordinarily have expired had he not been absent, no legal consequences arise. The existing period of detention or guardianship continues in the normal way and in due course will expire unless renewed in the normal manner.

- Where, however, the patient's return takes place during the final week of a period of detention or guardianship, or occurs after the expiry of that period, section 21 provides that his liability to detention shall not cease until the expiration of one week beginning with the day of his return. This allows the patient's responsible or appropriate medical officer time to examine him and, if appropriate, to furnish a renewal report under section 20. Where a renewal report is furnished after the date on which the previous six or twelve month period of detention or guardianship would ordinarily have expired, the report is treated as if it had been furnished on the final day of that period, and future renewal and expiry dates are calculated on that basis.[243]

---

[243] Mental Health Act 1983 s.21A(3), as substituted by Mental Health (Patients in the Community) Act 1995, s.2(2).

A patient is detained under section 3 on 1 January. His liability to detention will ordinarily expire at midnight on 30 June unless it is renewed for a further period. The patient absents himself from hospital on 21 June and is not returned there until 11 July. Because he has not been absent for 28 days, the application remains in force and, furthermore, the initial period of detention is extended for a further week commencing on the day of his return. If, prior to midnight on 17 July, his responsible medical officer examines him and furnishes a renewal report to the managers, the authority for his detention is thereby renewed for a further period of six months, commencing on 1 July.

Patients absent without leave for more than 28 days

Where a patient who has been absent for more than 28 days is taken into custody or returns to the required place before the recapture period has expired, two of the problems which may then arise are the same as in cases involving patients who have been absent for less than 28 days. Firstly, there may be insufficient time remaining to examine him and to furnish a renewal report. Secondly, the last day of the period of detention or guardianship which was in force when he absented himself may already have passed so that the authority for his detention or guardianship requires retrospective renewal. However, the additional consideration referred to also comes into play. Even when the patient's absence has not upset the ordinary renewal provisions because he is returned before renewal is due, the length of his absence may indicate that he no longer needs to be detained or under a guardian. While it is no longer a statutory presumption that a patient who has been absent for more than 28 days no longer requires detention or guardianship, the possibility that this is the case must still be addressed. That being so, the 1995 Act introduced a mechanism for determining whether or not such a patient still meets the statutory conditions for detention or guardianship. In all cases, the statutory criteria used to determine this issue are the ordinary renewal criteria — irrespective of whether or not renewal is actually due. Nevertheless, the Act refers to those criteria when they are used for this purpose as "the relevant conditions." The point to bear in mind is that the relevant conditions are the renewal criteria.

Duty to examine and report on the patient

A patient who has been absent for more than 28 days may be detained for a period of one week beginning with the day of his return. During this period, his responsible medical officer is under a duty to examine him.[244] He must consider whether, in his opinion, the patient would satisfy the criteria for having his detention or guardianship renewed if renewal were due. As with the ordinary renewal procedure, before furnishing any report stating that a detained patient appears to satisfy the criteria, he must first consult at least one other person who has been professionally concerned with the patient's medical treatment. However, in this case, he must also consult an approved social worker. This additional requirement reflects the fact that where prolonged absence is followed by detention in hospital for treatment, reauthorising the patient's subsequent detention is factually rather similar to making

---

[244] The Act refers to the patient's appropriate medical officer but, except where a private guardian has been appointed, the responsible medical officer is also his appropriate medical officer.

a fresh application.[245] If, having examined the patient and consulted these other professionals, the responsible medical officer does not, during the week allowed, furnish a report stating that it appears to him that the "relevant conditions" are satisfied, the patient ceases to be liable to be detained or subject to guardianship at the expiration of that period.

Effect of furnishing a report

If, having examined the patient and consulted the relevant persons, it does appear to the responsible medical officer that the patient satisfies the relevant conditions, he is under a statutory duty to furnish a report to this effect. The precise effect of this report depends upon exactly when it is furnished in relation to the period of detention or guardianship which was in existence when the patient absented himself. Put like this, there are three possibilities. The report might be furnished:

- *Before the renewal period*   That is, at some time before the final two months of the period of detention or guardianship in force when the patient absented himself.

- *During the renewal period*   That is, at some time during the final two months of that period of detention or guardianship.

- *After the renewal period*   That is, at some time after that period of detention or guardianship would ordinarily have expired had the patient not been absent.

Section 3 admission on 1 Jan	Months 1,2,3,4 Pre-renewal	Months 5,6 Renewal period	Months 7,8 Post-renewal
	Section 21B(4)	Section 21B(7)	Section 21B(5)
1 Jan		1 May 1 July	1 Sept

Reports furnished prior to the renewal period

Where a report is furnished on a date before the final two months of the period of detention or guardianship which was in force when the patient absented himself, that period of detention or guardianship simply continues as if the patient had never been absent. However, a right to apply to a tribunal exercisable within 28 days arises if the form of mental disorder specified in the report is different to that or those previously specified, so that it has the effect of reclassifying the patient.[246]

---

245   Providing that a patient who has been absent for more than 28 days may be detained for a week following his return in order to allow a fresh application to be made would, however, leave the decision about the patient's detention to an approved social worker. A feature of the new provisions in 1995 Act is that the responsible medical officer is the key figure and approved social workers are most often merely consulted by him before exercising a particular power.

246   See Mental Health Act 1983, s.66(1)(fb), as inserted by s.2(6) of the Mental Health (Patients in the Community) Act 1995.

Example

A patient is detained under section 3 on 1 January. His liability to detention will ordinarily expire at midnight on 30 June unless it is renewed for a further period. The responsible medical officer must examine the patient and furnish a renewal report during May or June if he is to be detained beyond that date. On 1st February he absents himself from hospital without leave. He remains absent until Monday 15 April. He has been away for more than 28 days and the new provisions apply. He will cease to be liable to be detained at midnight on Sunday 21 April unless, prior to then, his appropriate medical officer has examined him, undertaken the necessary consultations, and furnished a report to the managers stating that the "relevant conditions" are satisfied. The relevant conditions are the same as the renewal criteria. However, a renewal report is still required in May or June before the patient's liability to detention may be continued beyond 30 June.

Report furnished during the renewal period

Where a report is coincidentally furnished during the final two months of a period of detention or guardianship, it may state that it shall also take effect as a renewal report. This reflects the fact that the relevant conditions are the same as the renewal criteria and in each case the responsible medical officer must consult at least one other person who has been involved in the patient's medical treatment before furnishing a report. Requiring him to repeat the procedure and certify on a similar form that the renewal criteria are made out would thus be unnecessarily bureaucratic.[247]

Example

A patient is detained under section 3 on 1 January. His liability to detention will ordinarily expire at midnight on 30 June unless it is renewed for a further period. On 1 February he absents himself from hospital without leave. He remains absent during May and June so it is not possible for him to be examined with a view to renewing the detention for a further six months. On Monday 7th June — during the final two months of the initial six month period of detention — he is returned to hospital. He has been away for more than 28 days and the new provisions apply. If the appropriate medical officer furnishes a report to the managers stating that the relevant conditions are satisfied, he may also stipulate that the report shall also take effect as the renewal report which is then due. If he does this, not only does the patient's liability to detention not lapse one week after his return but it is also renewed for a further six months from 1 July.

Report furnished after the renewal period

With regard to patients who have been absent for 28 days or less, it has already been noted that the effect of furnishing a conventional renewal report after a period of detention or guardianship would ordinarily have expired is that the authority is retrospectively renewed. The effect is essentially the same here although, because furnishing a report stating that the relevant conditions are satisfied involves taking

---

[247]   If the report does not specify that it shall have effect as a renewal report but the form of disorder specified within it is different to that previously specified, its effect is to reclassify the patient at a time other than when renewing the authority for his detention or guardianship. Accordingly, a right to apply to a tribunal within the following 28 days arises under s.66(1)(fb).

all the steps involved in a renewal, a separate conventional renewal report is not required. The report stating that the relevant conditions are satisfied automatically takes effect as a renewal report — there is no need to elect that it shall have this additional effect because, unless it does, there would be no authority for the patient's detention or guardianship after the initial one week extension expires.

Example

A patient is detained under section 3 on 1 January. His liability to detention will ordinarily expire at midnight on 30 June unless it is renewed for a further period. On 1 February he absents himself from hospital without leave. He remains absent during May and June so it is not possible for him to be examined with a view to renewing the detention for a further six months. On Monday 15 July, he is returned to hospital.

He has been away for more than 28 days and the new provisions apply. He will cease to be liable to be detained at midnight on Sunday 21 July unless, prior to then, his appropriate medical officer has examined him, undertaken the necessary consultations, and furnished a report to the managers stating that the relevant conditions are satisfied. If such a report is furnished during that week, its effect is to retrospectively renew the patient's detention for a further six months commencing on 1 July.

Double renewals

Because patients may now be absent for considerable periods of time but still remain liable to be detained, it is possible that by the time a patient is taken into custody not only will the previous authority for his detention require retrospective renewal but that retrospectively renewed further period of detention will have less than two months left to run and be due for renewal.[248]

Example

A patient is detained under section 3 on 1 January. His liability to detention will ordinarily expire at midnight on 30 June unless it is renewed for a further period. Before any renewal report is completed, the patient absents himself on 25 May. On 10 November, he is returned to hospital.

He has been away for more than 28 days and the new provisions apply. The responsible medical officer furnishes the necessary report during the week following the patient's return. This automatically retrospectively renews the authority for the patient's detention for a further six months, from 1 July until 31 December. However, the patient has been absent for so long that this period of detention is itself due for renewal since it has less than two months left. That being so, the responsible medical officer can elect that his report shall also have effect as the renewal report now due for that period. Thus, the effect of the single report is to renew the authority for the patient's detention for a period of 18 months — from 1 July until 31 December the following year.

---

[248] It is even possible that the retrospectively renewed period of detention or guardianship will itself require *retrospective* renewal and the Act provides for this. If in the example above the patient had absented himself on 28 June and been returned on 27 December, a report furnished on 2 January would retrospectively twice renew the authority for the patient's detention — once from 1 July and again from the following 1 January (the day before the report was furnished).

Summary

having regard to the above, the questions which must be asked when a patient detained for treatment or subject to guardianship is absent may be rephrased:

1) After what period of time does the patient cease to be liable to be detained or subject to guardianship and so also cease to be liable to be taken into custody under the Act?

2) If he is returned during this permitted period, was he absent for more than 28 days or for 28 days or less?

3) If for more than 28 days and within the following week his responsible medical officer furnished a report stating that the relevant conditions were satisfied, was this furnished before, during, or after the normal renewal period.

The 1997 Regulations and the prescribed forms

Because the authority to detain a patient who is returned after more than 28 days absence will lapse unless a report in the prescribed form is furnished during the following week, one would expect the 1996 Regulations to have prescribed such a form, thereby enabling such reports to be furnished as and when necessary. The more so since the new absence without leave provisions constituted a large part of the 1995 Act. This was not the case and it was not until some months after the Act's commencement that the Department of Health became aware that almost half the statute was effectively not in force. The Mental Health (Hospital, Guardianship and Consent to Treatment) Amendment Regulations 1997 now provide that a report furnished under section 21B(2) shall be in the form set out in Form 31A in relation to a patient who is liable to be detained and Form 31B in relation to a patient who is subject to guardianship. Departmental guidelines concerning the statutory provisions, and the completion of the new forms, is contained in *NHS Executive Letter EL (97)26*. Unfortunately, the printed copies of the new forms and the advice contained in the guidelines appear to be defective in several respects.

Form 31A

The form actually prescribed in the 1997 regulations is sufficient for the purpose. However, the Department of Health has added the following explanatory note at the end of the printed forms distributed to hospitals and local authorities:

> **"This form should not be used for patients who on return from absence without leave have a maximum 7 days before their liability to detention expires. Such patients have their liability to detention extended by a week on return to Hospital by virtue of section 2(1)(b). Detention may be renewed during the 7 days under section 20 using form 30."**

This cannot be correct. The statutory procedure following a patient's return after a period of absence without leave is determined by the length of his absence, not by whether the authority will expire within seven days unless renewed:

298

- If the patient was absent for 28 days or less, the prescribed procedure is that set out in section 21A, which involves completing the standard renewal report (Form 30) if renewal is both due and appropriate.

- If the patient has been absent for more than 28 days, the prescribed procedure is that set out in section 21B. This involves the appropriate medical officer examining the patient, consulting (*inter alia*) an approved social worker, and then completing and furnishing Form 31A, during the week following the patient's return.

- If the normal section 20 procedure is mistakenly adopted, with the effect that no approved social worker is consulted and no Form 31A is completed during the week allowed, the patient's liability to detention will expire at the end of that week.[249]

- However, the problem should not arise. Provided that the correct form is furnished before the end of the week (Form 31A), it automatically renews the authority for the patient's detention where that authority would otherwise have expired and, if it is due to expire shortly, the appropriate medical officer may elect that the form shall be treated as the renewal report due under section 20.

It should be emphasised that the explanatory notes at the bottom of the printed form are not part of the prescribed form, which has not itself been altered and is sufficient for the intended purpose. The solution is simply to ignore the explanatory notes and to always use Forms 31A and 31B whenever a patient is returned after more than 28 days absence without leave.

NHS Executive Letter EL (97)26

Paragraph 4 repeats the advice as to when the standard form of renewal report (Form 30) should be completed in preference to the new forms. The additional guidance given in paragraphs 8 and 9 is somewhat misleading—

- Paragraph 9 states that a patient has no right to a tribunal if the authority for his detention or guardianship is simply restored under section 21B, rather than renewed. This depends upon whether the report has the additional effect of reclassifying the patient. If it does, a right to apply to a tribunal arises under s.66(1)(fb).

---

[249] Where no report has been furnished by then, section 21B expressly provides that a patient's liability to detention or guardianship ceases at that time if it would not otherwise have expired. In the case of patients whose authority would ordinarily have expired before the week's end, because they were returned during the final week of the section or after it would ordinarily have expired, there is no need for such an express provision. No report having been furnished under section 21B which has the effect of renewing the authority,[†] there is necessarily no longer any authority for the patient's detention or guardianship.   † *by virtue of section 21B(5) or (6).*

- Paragraph 8 is concerned with the effect where a section 21B report specifies a different form of mental disorder to that in the original application: "The appropriate medical officer does not then need to submit a separate reclassification report under section 16 of the Act unless the section 21B report also serves as a section 20 renewal report."

In fact, it is not necessary to furnish a separate re-classification report under section 16 where the section 21B report also serves as a section 20 renewal report. The section 21B report has "effect as a report duly furnished under section 20(3)" and "where the form of mental disorder specified in a report furnished under subsection (3) ... is a form of disorder other than that specified in the application ... the appropriate medical officer need not ... furnish a report under section 16": *Mental Health Act 1983, ss.20(9), 21B(7)*. It is because section 20(9) automatically has this effect that it is unnecessary for section 21B(8) to expressly provide that such a report shall have such an additional effect.

CESSATION DUE TO ABSENCE WITH LEAVE

Prior to the coming into force of the Mental Health (Patients in the Community) Act 1995, if a patient has been absent with leave from the hospital where he was liable to be detained for a continuous period of six months, the authority to detain him there ceased at the expiration of that period. The position now is that a patient granted leave may not be recalled after he has ceased to be liable to be detained under the relevant application or order.[250] So, if a patient's liability to detention is renewed for twelve months and two months later he is granted leave, it is possible for that leave, and the patient's liability to recall, to continue for the remaining ten months of the period of liability to detention.[251] As to whether the responsible medical officer can renew the authority to detain a patient who is absent from hospital with his leave, see page 281.

CESSATION DUE TO A PATIENT BEING IN CUSTODY

Section 22 applies to an unrestricted patient who, while detained for treatment or subject to guardianship, is taken into custody in pursuance of an order or sentence imposed by a court in the United Kingdom. The section does not apply to patients detained for assessment. The authority to detain such a patient lapses at the normal time, even if in custody.

Custody exceeding six months

Subsection 22(1) provides that the application, order or direction shall cease to have effect where a patient has been detained in custody for a continuous period of more than six months. Successive remands in custody are treated as constituting a single continuous period of detention.

---

[250] Mental Health Act 1983, s.18(4), as substituted by the Mental Health (Patients in the Community) Act 1995, s.2(1).

[251] A patient granted leave to be absent from hospital and not subsequently recalled will nevertheless be absent without leave if he subsequently ceases to reside at the place where he is required to reside by his responsible medical officer. The effect of this may then be that he then does not cease to be liable to be detained at the expiration of the period of detention which was in force at the time he absented himself.

Subsection 22(2) deals with the situation where a patient is released before he has been in custody for a continuous period exceeding six months—

- The patient is treated as having absented himself without leave from the hospital or other place where he is required to be on the day of his release from prison.[252]

- If he is neither taken into custody under the Mental Health Act 1983, nor returns to the hospital or other place where he is required to be, within 28 days of his release, the application, order or direction ceases to have effect at the expiration of that period. Until then, it continues to have effect, whether or not it would ordinarily have expired during the patient's time in custody or during the 28 days following his release.[253]

- If the patient is taken into custody under the Mental Health Act 1983, or returns to the required place of his own accord, within 28 days of his release from prison then this may or may not have an effect on the renewal of his detention or guardianship under the Act.

- It could be that his detention or guardianship was not due for renewal during the period between his removal to prison and his return to the required place. Alternatively, it may be that his detention or guardianship would ordinarily have expired during that period or within a week of his return to the required place. Where this is the case, section 21 applies . and, upon his return, the application, order or direction remains in force for a further week.

- This allows the patient's responsible or appropriate medical officer time to examine him and, where appropriate, to furnish a renewal report under section 20. Where such a report is furnished on a day after that on which the previous period of detention or guardianship would otherwise have expired, the report is deemed to have been furnished on the final day of that period.[254] Future renewal and expiry dates are calculated on that basis.

---

[252] The word "prison" is used here so as to avoid the confusion which otherwise results from referring to patients being taken into custody — in this context that could mean custody in pursuance of the court order or being taken into custody under the Mental Health Act as a patient absent without leave. However, some patients in custody in pursuance of a court order will, of course, be detained at a place other than a prison.

[253] As can be seen, section 22 provides an alternative to sections 35 and 36 in cases where a defendant is already liable to detention under Part II. If the court grants bail instead of remanding under section 35, the patient can simply be returned to the hospital from which he is deemed to be absent without leave. This then avoids all of the problems which arise when there are two authorities for a patient's detention.

[254] Mental Health Act 1983, s.21A.

The following examples concern a patient detained under section 3 on 1st January. His liability to detention will, unless renewed, expire at midnight on 30th June. In normal circumstances, any examination for the purpose of renewal must be conducted on a day between 1 May and 30 June. Likewise, any renewal report must be furnished during the same two month period.

Example 1

The patient is remanded into custody by a magistrates' court on 1 March. He remains in prison until 1 May when he is released on bail, the effect of which is that he is treated as having absented himself from hospital without leave on that day. He will cease to be liable to be detained under section 3 if he is still absent from hospital without leave at midnight on 28 May. Section 21 is irrelevant since, if he is returned before then, the date of his return must necessarily occur on a day prior to the last week of his current period of detention. The application is therefore renewable in the ordinary way.

Example 2

The patient is, as in the first example, remanded into custody on 1 March. He remains in prison until 1 August when he is released. The effect of section 22 is that the day of his release from prison is treated as if it were 30 June, that is the last day of the six-month period of detention which commenced on 1 January, and the patient is treated as if he had absented himself on that day. If he is returned to hospital on 20 August, within 28 days of his release, the section 3 application remains in force for a further week, until midnight on 26 August. If a renewal report is furnished to the managers during that week, his section is treated as if it had been renewed in the ordinary way, that is for a further six month period beginning on 1 July.

Example 3

The patient is remanded into custody on 3 May and released on 1 November. He is returned to hospital on 21 November, that is within 28 days. A renewal report is furnished on 25 November. As before, this takes effect as if his detention had been renewed for a further six-month period on 1 July. A second renewal report could* in theory be furnished later the same day, authorising the patient's detention for a further year from 1 January.[255]

Cessation following reclassification

If a report furnished under section 16 is to the effect that a patient detained in hospital is suffering from psychopathic disorder or mental impairment, but not from mental illness or severe mental impairment, the report must also state whether, in the appropriate medical officer's opinion, further medical treatment in hospital is likely to alleviate or prevent a deterioration of the patient's condition. Where his opinion is

[255] It is possible for a patient not to be returned until the retrospectively renewed period has itself expired. If, in the above example, the patient is remanded into custody on 15 June, released on 9 December and returned to hospital on 4 January, a renewal report furnished on 8 January has the effect of renewing the section 3 application from 1 July until 31 December but that second period of detention has itself already expired. There being no provision for double renewals in section 22 (equivalent to that in section 21B(6)(b)), the patient is no longer liable to be detained.

that such treatment is not likely to have that effect, the authority of the managers to detain the patient ceases (**056**).[256]

Cessation following a subsequent application under Part II of the Act

A fresh application under Part II of the Act will in certain circumstances bring to an end any previous application but not, it seems, any pre-existing order or direction made under Part III.

Effect of guardianship applications and section 3 applications

Reception into guardianship discharges any pre-existing application made under Part II.[257] Likewise, an admission under section 3 revokes any prior section 2 application, supervision application or guardianship application.[258]

Effect of applications under section 2

Where a patient is admitted for assessment under Part II, any pre-existing guardianship application or supervision application continues in force, as therefore does any tribunal application or reference relating to that guardianship. This effect is deliberate. The Act does not similarly provide that admission under section 2 revokes any pre-existing authority for the patient's detention under section 3. In practice, the situation arises where a section 3 patient who is absent without leave is admitted for assessment to a hospital which is unaware of the fact that he is already liable to be detained for treatment elsewhere.[259]

Effect of applications under Part II on Part III orders

The Act provides that a restricted patient remains liable to be detained under the accompanying hospital order or transfer direction until an order discharging him is made.[260] It does not expressly provide that a guardianship order or an unrestricted hospital order continues to have effect notwithstanding any subsequent application in respect of the same patient. Nor, equally, does it expressly provide the opposite, namely that such an application revokes a prior order. The situation usually arises where a patient who is absent without leave is admitted to a hospital elsewhere in England and Wales which is unaware of the existence of the previous order or direction. It also arises where a section 3 application is made in respect of a patient who is subject to a guardianship order, in preference to using the somewhat laboured transfer provisions in section 19. Although the making of an application is

---

[256] Mental Health Act 1983, s.16(2).
[257] *Ibid.*, ss.8(5) and 25H(5)(b).
[258] *Ibid.*, ss.6(4) and 25H(6)(a).
[259] The three possible approaches to this problem are: (1) the second application terminates the first — the Act does not provide this; (2) the second application is ineffective because of the existence of a prior application authorising detention under section 3 — again, the Act does not provide this; (3) both applications are valid and the patient's detention under Part II in either hospital is authorised. Upon discovering that a prior application exists, the patient may be returned to the first hospital, provided that the authority to detain him there has not expired by virtue of section 18(4), because his absence has been prolonged. It is submitted that the third approach is the correct one. If so, the omission may be deliberate, and designed to ensure that the authority to detain a patient for treatment is not accidentally revoked by an application to detain him for assessment elsewhere. Similar problems do not arise when it is discovered that a treatment application has been accidentally revoked by another treatment application. The patient can simply be transferred to the original hospital under section 19, in which case the application is deemed to have always specified the hospital where there was previously authority to detain him. No further treatment application is necessary.
[260] Mental Health Act 1983, s.41(3)(a).

unnecessary in normal circumstances, because section 19 can and should be used to transfer the patient from guardianship to hospital, and vice-versa, this does not help to determine the legal effect of any subsequent application.[261]

Cessation due to a subsequent order or direction under Part III

The Act does not provide that all orders and directions made under Part III of the Act have the effect of revoking a pre-existing application.

Court orders made during criminal proceedings under ss.35, 36 and 38

Where a court makes an order under section 35, 36, or 38, that order does not revoke any hospital order, guardianship order or application previously made in respect of the same patient. This is because the order does not take effect as if the patient had been detained for treatment or received into guardianship under Part II.[262] They are interim orders made by the court in the course of the proceedings before it.

Court orders determining criminal proceedings (ss.37 and 37/41)

These orders dispose of the proceedings before the court and, subject to certain exceptions and modifications, they take effect as if the patient had been detained for treatment or received into guardianship under Part II of the Act.[263] Consequently, any previous application under Part II ceases to have effect. There is, however, a caveat to this if the hospital order or guardianship order, or the conviction on which it was made, is quashed on appeal. In such cases, the previous order or application is revived upon the order being quashed (see below).[264]

Directions made by the Secretary of State under Part III (ss.47-49)

A transfer direction, with or without restrictions, revokes any previous application made under Part II. Again, subject to certain exceptions and modifications, it takes effect as if the patient had been detained for treatment under Part II.[265]

---

[261] The possible approaches to this problem are essentially the same as in the note above: (1) the application terminates the order unless it is one made under section 2 — the Act does not expressly provide this†; (2) the application is ineffective because of the existence of a prior court order — again, the Act does not provide this; (3) both the order and the application are valid and the patient's detention in either hospital, or both his detention and guardianship, are authorised. The first interpretation is undesirable insofar as the patient's absence without leave results in the accidental termination of a court order and the acquisition by that patient's nearest relative of a power of discharge unintended by the court. The second and third interpretations both have the consequence that court orders are not revoked by applications, whether accidentally or otherwise, and their termination requires an order or direction for discharge or their non-renewal. However, the second interpretation has two disadvantages. Firstly, the Act does not provide that the subsequent application is ineffective and, secondly, such an inference means that the managers, although unaware of the prior authority, are liable for unlawfully detaining the patient in their hospital. The third interpretation avoids these disadvantages but does produce the anomaly that the same patient may be simultaneously liable to detention and subject to guardianship under the Act. The answer to that may simply be that this is an unfortunate consequence of the patient absenting himself without leave or a misguided avoidance of section 19. It is submitted that the third interpretation is correct, at least in the case of patients who have been absent without leave. † See the precise wording of section 40(4)) ("shall be treated for the purposes of the provisions of this Act mentioned in Part I of Schedule 1") and the absence of any reference to sections 2, 3, 4 and 7 in Sched. 1, Pt. I.

[262] See Mental Health Act 1983, ss.35, 36, 38, 40, 55(4) and 145(3).
[263] Ibid., ss.40(4), 41(3), and 145(3).
[264] Ibid., s.40(5).
[265] Mental Health Act 1983, ss. 40(4), 41(3), 55(4) and 145(3).

Section 37 order quashed on appeal

It has been noted that the effect of a hospital or guardianship order is that any previous authority for an unrestricted patient's detention or guardianship ceases to have effect. Section 40(5) attempts to deal with the situation where such an order, or the conviction on which it was made, is later quashed on appeal. It provides that any application, order or direction which was in force immediately prior to the making of the quashed order shall then be deemed not to have been revoked by it. Furthermore, section 22 shall have effect "as if during any period for which the patient was liable to be detained or subject to guardianship under the (quashed) order, he had been detained in custody as mentioned in that section." Section 22 refers in turn to sections 18 and 21 and the following examples illustrate the combined effect of sections 18, 21, 22 and 40(5).

Examples

A patient is received into guardianship under Part II of the Act on 1 January. Unless renewed, the authority for his guardianship will lapse on 30 June. On 1 February, he is charged with burglary but granted bail. On 30 May, he is convicted by a magistrates' court, which makes a hospital order. His admission has the effect of revoking the guardianship application. On 19 September, the Crown Court quashes the conviction, the effect of which is that the quashed hospital order is now treated as not having revoked the guardianship application. Sections 21 and 22 apply. The patient is treated—

a. as if he had continued to be subject to the guardianship application during the period from 30 May until 19 September (the period during which he was liable to be detained under the hospital order);

b. as if he had been committed to prison on 30 May (the day on which the quashed order was imposed);

c. as if he had been released from prison on the day of the successful appeal;

d. as if this notional release from prison took place on the last day of the six month guardianship period which commenced on 1 January;

e. as if on that day he had absented himself without leave from the place where he was required by his guardian to reside.

The simple effect of all this is that the guardianship will lapse if the patient is not taken into custody under the 1983 Act, or does not return himself to the place where he is required to reside, within 28 days of the date on which the hospital order was quashed.

If the patient returns or is taken into custody during the 28-day period, his appropriate medical officer has one week from the day of his return within which to furnish a renewal report under section 20(6). If he furnishes such a report during this week, the guardianship application which commenced on 1 January is treated as if it had been renewed for six months with effect from 1 July.[266]

---

[266] The only exception to this would be if the patient had been remanded in custody by the magistrates on or prior to 19 March and had remained in continuous custody until the hospital order was imposed on 30 May. In this example, he would then be deemed to have been in continuous custody for a period exceeding six months by the time the hospital order was quashed. The guardianship application which commenced on 1 January would therefore have lapsed. See s.22(1).

Example 2

If the hospital order in the previous example was imposed by a Crown Court and quashed by the Court of Appeal on 15 December, the period for which the patient was subject to it, and during which he is deemed to have been continuously in custody, extends from 30 May until 15 December and so exceeds six months. Section 40(5) therefore does not save the pre-existing guardianship application because it has lapsed by virtue of section 22(1).

Effect of a successful appeal on tribunal proceedings

Where a previous application, order or direction is reactivated as a result of a successful appeal against a hospital order or a guardianship order, the effect of 40(5) is that any tribunal application or reference which was outstanding on the date the quashed order was imposed, but which was deemed withdrawn, is also reactivated. Secondly, upon the revival of the earlier authority, the hospital's managers may be required to forthwith refer the patient's case to a tribunal under section 68.

Cessation due to removal outside the jurisdiction

Where a patient who is detained or subject to guardianship in England and Wales is removed to Scotland, Northern Ireland, the Channel Islands or the Isle of Man under Part VI of the Act, the application, order or direction under which he was previously liable to be detained or subject to guardianship in England and Wales — including any restriction order or direction — ceases to have effect.[267]

Removal to countries outside the UK, Channel Islands or Isle of Man

An application, order or direction — other than a restriction order or direction — ceases to have effect upon a patient's removal to a hospital or other institution in a country outside the United Kingdom, Channel Islands or Isle of Man in pursuance of arrangements made under section 86.[268]

---

[267] Mental Health Act 1983, s.91(1).
[268] *Ibid.*, s.91(2).

5. Orders and directions under Part III

INTRODUCTION

Part III of the Mental Health Act 1983 comprises provisions dealing with "patients concerned in criminal proceedings or under sentence." In some cases, admission to hospital under Part III gives rise to a right of application to a tribunal. Criminal proceedings involving persons suffering from mental disorder may be viewed as comprising six distinct stages: (a) the commission of an alleged offence; (b) arrest, detention and charge; (c) pre-trial procedures, including remands, jurisdiction, mode of trial, and committals; (d) the trial process, including a defendant's fitness to plead and to stand trial; (e) sentencing and disposal; (f) the post-sentencing stage. Special legal provisions apply at each stage but Part III is mainly concerned with the formalities relating to the admission and detention of persons during or following criminal proceedings.[1]

ORDERS AND DIRECTIONS UNDER PART III

The table on page 311 summarises the orders and directions which may be made under Part III, their purpose, and the ways in which a person may challenge his detention under the Act. Persons admitted to hospital under sections 35, 36 and 38 are in a fundamentally different position from persons admitted under the other orders and directions.[2] The Part II provisions concerning the duration, discharge and renewal of the authority for a patient's detention, and related matters such as leave and transfer, do not apply to them. The termination of a patient's detention under sections 35, 36 or 38 is a matter for the court with jurisdiction to deal with him.

Remands and orders under sections 35, 36 and 38

Sections 35 and 36 provide that a criminal court may remand an accused person to hospital during the course of criminal proceedings, for the preparation of a report on his mental condition or for treatment. Section 38 further provides that, before sentencing an offender, the court may direct his admission to hospital in order to assist it in determining the most appropriate way of disposing of the case. In each instance, the admission is directed by the court having jurisdiction to deal with a

---

[1] *Important Note*: The Crime (Sentences) Act 1997 received the Royal Assent on 21 March 1997. Many of its provisions came into force on 1 October 1997 (**398**). The final section of the chapter summarises the new laws concerning mandatory life sentences and the imposition of hospital directions and limitation directions. Less fundamental amendments of sections of the 1983 Act are referred to in the appropriate part of the text, or in footnotes.

[2] See *e.g.* the references to sections 35, 36 and 38 in sections 30(4)(a), 43(3), 80(1), 81(1), 85(1), 91(1), 123(1), 138(4) and 145(3) of the Mental Health Act 1983.

defendant whose case it has not yet disposed of. Because the court retains jurisdiction over the defendant, his detention in hospital is a matter for that court and Part II of the Act does not apply. If it did, the patient could be discharged from detention (including by a tribunal), or granted leave to be absent from the hospital (in effect bail), or transferred to another hospital without reference to the court. The effect would be to undermine the court's jurisdiction over the defendant and possibly to interfere with the administration of justice.

Other orders and directions

The position is different with hospital and guardianship orders, and transfer directions made by the Secretary of State. The making of a guardianship order or a hospital order is a final order which brings the criminal proceedings to an end. Consequently, the defendant may not go back to the court which imposed the order to seek its termination. Such orders are, however, orders of potentially indefinite duration. Provisions are therefore required which define their effect and enable the necessity for compulsory powers to be periodically reviewed and, if appropriate, discharged. The Act achieves this by providing that such patients are generally to be treated as if they had been admitted to hospital for treatment or received into guardianship under Part II, subject to certain necessary exceptions and modifications. They may therefore apply to a tribunal at defined intervals. Patients who are transferred from custody to hospital by direction of the Secretary of State are in a similar position insofar as their detention may be for a potentially indefinite period. Furthermore, since their detention was not ordered by a court, arrangements must be made for their detention to be judicially reviewed. The Act again provides that such patients are deemed to have been admitted under Part II, subject to necessary exceptions and modifications, and they may apply to a tribunal for a review of the justification for their detention. If the transferred patient is involved in criminal proceedings, the court with jurisdiction may also terminate the direction.

THE FOUR FORMS OF MENTAL DISORDER

The making of any order or direction under Part III requires evidence that the defendant suffers from, or is suspected to suffer from, one of the four particular forms of mental disorder set out in sub-section 1(2).[3] In contrast to the framework under Part II of the Act, mental disorder *simpliciter* never suffices. Certain orders and directions may only be made if the individual suffers from one of the two "major forms" of mental disorder: mental illness or severe mental impairment. Conversely, the new hospital and limitation directions may presently only be given in respect of offenders who suffer from a psychopathic disorder.[4]

---

[3] It should be emphasised that a person may not be classified as mentally impaired unless his handicap is associated with abnormally aggressive or seriously irresponsible conduct (**051, 078**). A mentally handicapped person therefore has the benefit of the Part III provisions if his conduct is disordered but not otherwise. The anomaly arises because, in 1982, Mind and Mencap lobbied to ensure that mentally handicapped persons could not be "sectioned" under Part II unless their conduct was disordered. This was achieved by making a conduct disorder a precondition of any statutory finding that an individual is mentally impaired. However, achieving this objective had the (presumably unintended) effect of taking handicapped people whose conduct is not disordered outside the operation of Part III — even though the absence of disordered conduct does not make such a person less vulnerable or less unfitted to prison.

[4] Mental Health Act 1983, s.45A(2)(a), as inserted by Crime (Sentences) Act 1997, s.46. The new directions are considered on p.398 *et seq.*

Mental illness and severe mental impairment

All of the orders and directions found in Part III of the Act are presently available in cases where a person suffers from, or in the case of section 35 is suspected to suffer from, a "major" form of mental disorder and the other conditions for making the particular order or direction are satisfied.

Psychopathic disorder and mental impairment

The majority of the provisions of Part III of the Act also apply to any person who is suffering from, or in the case of section 35 is suspected to suffer from, a "minor" form of mental disorder. However, there are important exceptions. Sections 36 and 48 are not available and it is therefore not possible during the course of criminal proceedings to remand or remove to hospital under Part III an unconvicted person who suffers only from psychopathic disorder or mental impairment, however urgent his need for treatment and however treatable the condition. Section 37(3) also does not apply so that a magistrates' court may not make a hospital or guardianship order in respect of a person who suffers only from a minor form of mental disorder unless it has first convicted him.

MEDICAL EVIDENCE

As with applications under Part II, the making of any order or direction under Part III requires medical evidence from one or two medical practitioners. Remands under section 35 may be founded upon the evidence of a single medical practitioner approved for the purposes of section 12 as having special experience in the diagnosis or treatment of mental disorder (**146**). In all other cases, the evidence of two practitioners is required, at least one of whom must be so approved.[5]

The medical practitioners

Section 12 does not apply to the making of orders or directions under Part III except for the requirement that evidence is received from a medical practitioner approved for the purposes of that section by the Secretary of State. A medical practitioner is not disqualified from giving evidence because he has some personal or financial interest in the matter. A court may therefore direct a defendant's admission to a private mental nursing home on the evidence of a doctor employed there. It may also order admission to an NHS hospital on the evidence of two medical practitioners employed there. However, except in the case of interim hospital orders, there is no requirement that evidence be received from a doctor on the staff of the hospital to which admission is sought.

Oral medical evidence

Court orders under Part III may be founded upon oral or written medical evidence, subject to the caveat that a restriction order may not be made unless at least one of the medical practitioners whose evidence is taken into account by the court under section 37 has given evidence orally before the court.[6] Directions under sections 48 to 49 are necessarily founded upon medical reports rather than oral evidence.

---

[5]   Mental Health Act 1983, s.54(1).
[6]   *Ibid.*, s.41(2). The doctor giving the oral evidence need not be section 12 approved.

MENTALLY DISORDER OFFENDERS AND THE COURTS

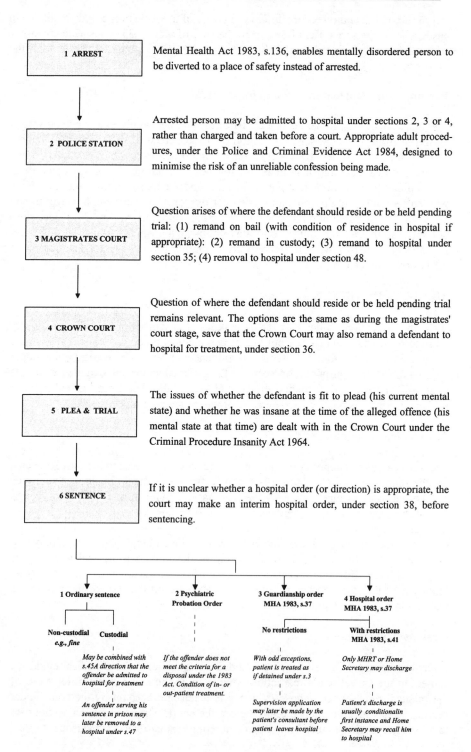

1 ARREST

Mental Health Act 1983, s.136, enables mentally disordered person to be diverted to a place of safety instead of arrested.

2 POLICE STATION

Arrested person may be admitted to hospital under sections 2, 3 or 4, rather than charged and taken before a court. Appropriate adult procedures, under the Police and Criminal Evidence Act 1984, designed to minimise the risk of an unreliable confession being made.

3 MAGISTRATES COURT

Question arises of where the defendant should reside or be held pending trial: (1) remand on bail (with condition of residence in hospital if appropriate): (2) remand in custody; (3) remand to hospital under section 35; (4) removal to hospital under section 48.

4 CROWN COURT

Question of where the defendant should reside or be held pending trial remains relevant. The options are the same as during the magistrates' court stage, save that the Crown Court may also remand a defendant to hospital for treatment, under section 36.

5 PLEA & TRIAL

The issues of whether the defendant is fit to plead (his current mental state) and whether he was insane at the time of the alleged offence (his mental state at that time) are dealt with in the Crown Court under the Criminal Procedure Insanity Act 1964.

6 SENTENCE

If it is unclear whether a hospital order (or direction) is appropriate, the court may make an interim hospital order, under section 38, before sentencing.

1 Ordinary sentence

2 Psychiatric Probation Order

3 Guardianship order MHA 1983, s.37

4 Hospital order MHA 1983, s.37

Non-custodial *e.g., fine* **Custodial**

No restrictions

With restrictions MHA 1983, s.41

May be combined with s.45A direction that the offender be admitted to hospital for treatment

If the offender does not meet the criteria for a disposal under the 1983 Act. Condition of in- or out-patient treatment.

With odd exceptions, patient is treated as if detained under s.3

Only MHRT or Home Secretary may discharge

An offender serving his sentence in prison may later be removed to a hospital under s.47

Supervision application may later be made by the patient's consultant before patient leaves hospital

Patient's discharge is usually conditionalin first instance and Home Secretary may recall him to hospital

PART III OF THE MENTAL HEALTH ACT

Section	Jurisdiction	Purpose	Appeals	

Court orders made during the course of the criminal proceedings

Section	Jurisdiction	Purpose	Appeals	
35	Magistrates or Crown Court	Remand to hospital for a report on the accused's mental condition.	Application to court for termination of the remand.	**315**
36	Crown Court	Remand of accused to hospital for treatment.	Application to court for termination of the remand.	**315**
38	Magistrates or Crown Court	Admission to hospital to determine whether a hospital order is an appropriate disposal.	Appeal against conviction or sentence. Court may terminate order.	**322**
43/44	Magistrates' court	Committal of defendant to the Crown Court with a view to a restriction order.	No right of appeal unless the committal was unlawful, in which case judicial review.	**372**

Court orders which bring criminal proceedings to an end

Section	Jurisdiction	Purpose	Appeals	
37	Magistrates or Crown Court	1. Guardianship order 2. Order directing admission to hospital	Appeal against conviction or sentence. Right to apply to a MHRT — 1. Immediate right. 2. right after six months.	**325** **328**
37/41	Crown Court	Restriction order. To protect the public from serious harm by restricting the application of the Act to a patient made the subject of a hospital order.	Appeal against conviction or sentence. Right to apply to a MHRT after six months.	**333**
51	Crown Court	Hospital (with restriction order if appropriate) made in the absence of a section 43 or 48 patient.	Appeal against conviction or sentence. Right to apply to a MHRT after six months.	**329** **374**
45A	Crown Court	Sentence of imprisonment accompanied by hospital and limitation directions; offender begins his sentence by being removed to hospital for treatment.	Appeal against conviction or sentence. Immediate right to apply to a MHRT.	**398**

Directions by warrant of the Secretary of State

Section	Jurisdiction	Purpose	Appeals	
46	Home Secretary	Transfer to hospital of services personnel detained during Her Majesty's Pleasure.	Immediate right to apply to a MHRT.	**376**
47	Home Secretary	Transfer to hospital of a person serving a term of imprisonment who is in need of treatment.	Immediate right to apply to a MHRT.	**378**
48	Home Secretary	Transfer to hospital of a non-prisoner in urgent need of treatment.	Immediate right to apply to a MHRT.	**378**

Important note: The power to give a hospital direction and a restriction direction under section 45A was brought into force on 1 October 1997 (398). However, such directions may only be given in respect of offences committed prior to that date.

Written medical evidence

In contrast to the position under section 12(1), the Act does not require that medical reports are based upon recent or proximate examinations of the person concerned, and it is not uncommon in practice for orders to be founded upon medical reports prepared several weeks or months previously, or at significant intervals.

Proof of signature and qualifications

A court may receive a written medical report in evidence without requiring proof that the signature is genuine or that the doctor who has furnished the report is a fully registered medical practitioner or approved under section 12; but the court may require the signatory of any such report to be called to give oral evidence.[7]

Disclosure of reports and patient's right to require oral evidence

Where, in pursuance of a direction of the court, a medical report is tendered in evidence otherwise than by or on behalf of the person who is the subject of the report, then—

- if that person is represented by counsel or a solicitor, a copy of the report is to be given to his counsel or solicitor;

- if that person is not represented, the substance of the report must be disclosed to him or, if he is a child or young person, to any parent or guardian of his present in court; and

- that person may require the signatory of the report to be called to give oral evidence, and evidence to rebut the evidence contained in the report may be called by or on behalf of that person.[8]

THE NEED FOR THE MANAGERS' OR THE GUARDIAN'S CONSENT

The duty of ensuring that patients are appropriately placed in hospitals which can adequately contain them generally rests with the courts in the light of their experience and the medical advice. However, a court may not make an order under Part III unless it is satisfied on evidence that arrangements have been made for the person's admission to a hospital or, as the case may be, that the proposed guardian is willing to receive the patient into guardianship. Under sections 35 and 36, the court must be satisfied that arrangements have been made for the accused's admission within the period of seven days beginning with the date of the remand.[9] In the case of hospital orders, interim hospital orders and hospital directions, the statutory period is 28 days.[10] The hospital specified in a court order may be an NHS hospital or a "private

---

[7] Mental Health Act 1983, s.54(2).

[8] *Ibid.*, s.54(3). A defendant does not have a statutory right to require a psychiatrist who has provided a report on behalf of the defence to give oral evidence, should the report be furnished to the court and he dispute some aspect of it, or later disagree with the recommendation made. Where a report relates only to arrangements for a person's admission to a hospital, that person has no right to require its signatory to give oral evidence or to rebut the evidence contained in the report. Any such report purporting to be signed by a person representing the hospital managers may be received in evidence without proof of his signature and without proof that he has the requisite authority. See *ibid.*, s.54(2).

[9] Mental Health Act 1983, ss.35(4), 36(3).

[10] Mental Health Act 1983, ss. 37(4), 37(6), 38(4). *Ibid.*, 45A(5), as inserted by Crime (Sentences) Act 1997, s.46.

hospital," that is a mental nursing home which is registered under the Registered Homes Act 1984 to receive patients detained under the 1983 Act.

Obtaining evidence as to the availability of a hospital bed

Where a court is minded to make a hospital order or an interim hospital order, or to give hospital and limitation directions, it may request the Health Authority for the region in which the defendant resides or last resided — or any other Health Authority that appears to it to be appropriate — to furnish it with such information as that Authority has, or can reasonably obtain, with respect to any hospital or hospitals in its region or elsewhere at which arrangements could be made for the defendant's admission.[11] The Authority specified must comply with any such request.[12] In *R. v. Birch*, the court observed that this power to require the Health Authority to furnish information under section 39 was not used as often as it might be.[13]

Removal to a place of safety pending admission by court order

Where a court makes any order under Part III, upon being satisfied that arrangements have been made for the defendant's admission to a particular hospital within the prescribed period, it may further direct that he be removed to, and detained in, a place of safety pending admission to that hospital.[14]

Definition of a place of safety

A "place of safety" in relation to a person aged 17 or over means a police station, prison or remand centre, or any hospital the managers of which are willing to temporarily receive the patient.[15] In the case of a person aged under 17, the expression has the same meaning as in the Children and Young Persons Act 1933 and so excludes a prison or remand centre.[16]

Persons removed to hospital by the Secretary of State

The Home Secretary is responsible for securing the admission to hospital of mentally disordered prisoners who meet the criteria in sections 47 and 48 of the 1983 Act. The Home Secretary is also responsible for securing the admission to hospital of persons found unfit to plead or not guilty by reason of insanity under the Criminal Procedure (Insanity) Act 1964.

---

[11]   Mental Health Act 1983, s.45A(8), as inserted by Crime (Sentences) Act 1997, s.46.

[12]   *Ibid.*, s.39(1). Subsection (2) provides that, in relation to Wales, references to the Health Authority refer to the Secretary of State for Wales and the words "in Wales" are to be substituted for references to "in its region or elsewhere." A local social services authority may similarly be required to furnish information to a court about the arrangements which might be made for a patient's reception into guardianship. See *ibid.*, s.39A.

[13]   *R. v. Birch* (1989) 11 Cr.App.R.(S.) 202, C.A.

[14]   Mental Health Act 1983, ss.35(4), 36(3), 37(4) and 38(4).

[15]   *Ibid.*, s.55(1). In practice, the place of safety is usually a prison or remand centre.

[16]   *Ibid.*, s.55(1). Section 107 of the Children and Young Persons Act 1933 provides that "place of safety" means "a community home provided by a local authority or a controlled community home, any police station, or any hospital, surgery or other suitable place, the occupier of which is willing temporarily to receive a child or young person."

Locating a bed for the patient

In practice, the Secretary of State will not direct a person's removal from prison to hospital unless the managers of that hospital are willing to receive him there, although, as a matter of law, their consent is unnecessary.[17] The Home Secretary generally relies on the prison medical officer to arrange a bed with a local or secure hospital before submitting the necessary medical reports with his request for a warrant authorising transfer. Once these are received, the issue of whether the placement will provide adequate security for the protection of the public is considered. In the case of remand prisoners, it is always necessary for the Home Office to make enquiries of the police or Crown Prosecution Service about the circumstances of the offence before reaching a decision. The placement of sentenced prisoners can usually be decided more easily, since reports on their offences, their behaviour in prison and prison category are usually readily available. These contain sufficient evidence to enable the Home Office to decide how dangerous they are, and how likely to abscond. As a general rule of thumb, only non-violent offenders who seem amenable to treatment are considered suitable for open conditions at local hospitals; the remainder are placed in locked wards, secure units and special hospitals.[18]

Transfer to a mental nursing home

Prior to 1 October 1997, the Act did not permit Home Secretary to remove a patient in custody to a "private hospital" under section 47 or 48. It was, however, not uncommon for him to do so (**381**). This limitation ceased to have effect when section 49(3) of the Crime (Sentences) Act 1997 was brought into force on that date, although its introduction cannot retrospectively validate transfers made before then.[19]

Power to specify hospital units

The Crime (Sentences) Act 1997 empowers a court which makes a restriction order or gives a limitation direction to specify the hospital unit to which the defendant is to be admitted.[20] The Home Secretary is given an identical power where he transfers a prisoner to hospital under sections 47 and 49.[21] The term "hospital unit" means any part of a hospital which is treated as a separate unit. Where a unit is specified, references in the Act to the patient being detained, or being liable to be detained, in a hospital are to be construed accordingly. The purpose of the new power is to prevent patients from whom the public may be at risk of serious harm from being allowed parole within the hospital grounds, or from being moved to an open ward, without the Home Secretary's consent.

APPLICABILITY OF PART III TO YOUNG OFFENDERS

There are few age limits in Part III of the Act. A guardianship order may only be made in respect of a person who has attained the age of 16 years and a child may not

---

17 See Mental Health Act 1983, ss.47 and 48.
18 See A. Pickersgill, "Balancing the public and private interest" in *Risk-taking in Mental Disorder: Analyses, Policies and Practical Strategies* (ed. D. Carson, S.L.E Publications Ltd., 1990).
19 Crime (Sentences) Act 1997, ss. 49(3), 56(2); Sched. 6.
20 Crime (Sentences) Act 1997, s.47. The power extends to restriction orders imposed under the Criminal Procedure (Insanity) Act 1964.
21 The power does not extend to persons transferred to hospital under section 48, even where a restriction direction is also given under section 49.

be committed to the Crown Court under section 43. For the purposes of Part III of the Act:

- "child" means a person under the age of 14 years and "young person" someone who has attained the age of 14 years but is under the age of 18 years.[22]

- any reference to an offence punishable on summary conviction with imprisonment is to be construed without regard to any prohibition or restriction imposed by or under any enactment relating to the imprisonment of young offenders.[23]

- the term "guardian" in relation to someone aged under 18 includes any person who has for the time being the care of that child or young person.[24]

- references to a magistrate court include references to the youth court.

REMANDS TO HOSPITAL UNDER SECTIONS 35 AND 36

Section 35 provides that, where the conditions specified in the Act are satisfied, the Crown Court or a magistrates' court may remand an accused person to a hospital for a report on his mental condition. Under section 36, the Crown Court may, instead of remanding an accused person in custody, remand him to hospital for medical treatment.

RELATIONSHIP TO PART II

Although section 35 refers to assessment, it is not the judicial equivalent of an admission for assessment under Part II. The purpose of section 35 is limited to obtaining a report on someone who is merely suspected, on the basis of a single medical opinion, to suffer from a form of mental disorder. Because nothing more than a reasonable suspicion has to be established, it does not render the individual liable to compulsory treatment. Likewise, section 36 is not equivalent to section 3 and the power to remand for treatment only arises where the Crown Court would otherwise remand in custody, not *per se* because section 3 would be appropriate if the accused was not before the court.

CRITERIA FOR IMPOSITION

The conditions imposed by the Act in respect of remands to hospital under section 35 or section 36 are set out in the table on the following page.

---

[22] Mental Health Act 1983, s.55(1); Children and Young Persons Act 1933, s.107(1). Section 99 of the 1933 Act (which relates to the presumption and determination of age) applies for the purposes of Part III of the 1983 Act: see Mental Health Act 1983, s.55(7).
[23] Mental Health Act 1983, s.55(2).
[24] *Ibid.*, s. 55(1); Children and Young Persons Act 1933, s.107(1).

The medical grounds

The same medical grounds apply under section 36 as for hospital orders under section 37. However, when a defendant who remains detained for treatment under section 36 comes to be sentenced, the court must also consider whether a hospital order is the most appropriate way of disposing of the case.

CONDITIONS OF REMANDS UNDER SECTIONS 35 AND 36

Section 35	*Section 36*
Bail is inappropriate	
• The court is of the opinion that it would be impracticable for a report on the accused's mental condition to be made if he were remanded on bail. (s.35(3)(b))	• "Instead of remanding an accused person in custody", the court may remand him to hospital under section 36. (s.36(1))
The court is satisfied as to the medical grounds	
• The court is satisfied, on the written or oral evidence of a registered medical practitioner who is approved under section 12, that "there is reason to suspect that the accused is suffering from mental illness, psychopathic disorder, severe mental impairment or mental impairment." (s.35(3)(a))	• The court is satisfied, on the written or oral evidence of two registered medical practitioners, one of whom is approved under section 12, that "the accused person is suffering from mental illness or severe mental impairment of a nature or degree which makes it appropriate for him to be detained in a hospital for medical treatment." (s.36(1))
The defendant is an "accused person"	
• The defendant is "an accused person" within the meaning of section 35(2). (s.35(2), **317**)	• The defendant is "an accused person" within the meaning of section 36(2). (s.36(2), **317**)
A hospital bed is available	
• The court is satisfied, on the written or oral evidence of the medical practitioner who would be responsible for making the report or of some other person representing the managers of the hospital, that arrangements have been made for his admission to that hospital within the period of seven days beginning with the date of the remand. (s.35(4))	• The court is satisfied, on the written or oral evidence of the medical practitioner who would be in charge of his treatment or some other person representing the managers of the hospital, that arrangements have been made for his admission to that hospital within the period of seven days beginning with the date of the remand. (s.36(3))

"ACCUSED PERSON"

A defendant may only be remanded to hospital under Part III if he is "an accused person" within the meaning of sections 35 and 36. The meaning of the term is defined in the table below.

STATUTORY DEFINITIONS OF "AN ACCUSED PERSON"

Section 35	*Section 36*
In relation to a magistrates' court	
• "any person who has been convicted by the court of an offence punishable on summary conviction with imprisonment and any person charged with such an offence if the court is satisfied that he did the act or made the omission charged or he has consented to the exercise by the court of the powers conferred by this section." (s.35(1)(b))	• *Not applicable — a magistrates' court has no power to remand under section 36.*
In relation to the Crown Court	
• any person who "is awaiting trial before the court for an offence punishable with imprisonment or who has been arraigned before the court for such an offence and has not yet been sentenced or otherwise dealt with for the offence on which he has been arraigned" other than a person who has been convicted of an offence the sentence for which is fixed by law. (s.35(1)(a) and (3))	• "any person who is in custody awaiting trial before the Crown Court for an offence punishable with imprisonment (other than an offence the sentence for which is fixed by law) or who at any time before sentence is in custody in the course of a trial before that court for such an offence." (s.36(2))

"Accused persons" and magistrates' courts

A magistrates' court may not remand a defendant to hospital for treatment and may only remand under section 35 defendants who are charged with an offence which is punishable on summary conviction with imprisonment. Accordingly, neither section 35 nor section 36 is available to magistrates in respect of a defendant who is charged with an indictable only offence. It might be argued that the final phrase of section 35(2)(b) ("or he has consented to the exercise by the court of the powers conferred by this section") is to be read disjunctively so that, if a defendant consents to being remanded under section 35, the class of offence with which he is charged is immaterial. However, a natural reading of the paragraph is against such a construction. Furthermore, although the recent emphasis on diverting mentally disordered offenders from prison often involves invoking section 35, its statutory purpose is not diversion *per se,* but to obtain a report to assist the court in relation to the defendant's fitness for trial and the most appropriate way of dealing with him. In relation to a person who is charged with an indictable only offence, only the Crown Court can deal with these matters and make these decisions.

Purpose of section 35

The purpose of section 35 is to enable a court to obtain a medical report on a defendant whose case it may dispose of, in particular to assist it in determining whether the medical grounds for making a hospital order are satisfied. Prior to the introduction of section 35, magistrates' courts could remand an accused person for the preparation of a medical report under sections 10 or 30 of the Magistrates' Courts Act 1980. Where the accused was charged with an offence punishable upon summary conviction with imprisonment, they could do so without first convicting him if satisfied that he had done the act or made the omission charged.[25] However, if the preparation of a report on an out-patient basis was inappropriate, the defendant had to be remanded in custody or granted bail with a condition of hospital residence. The Butler Committee recommended that courts should have the option of remanding an accused directly to hospital where bail was inappropriate and section 35 gave effect to this recommendation. In effect therefore, section 35(2)(b) provides that a magistrates' court may remand a person to hospital for the preparation of a report in similar circumstances to those in which it could previously have remanded him on bail or in custody for that purpose.

"Accused persons" and the Crown Court

A person charged with murder, but not convicted of it, may be remanded by the Crown Court to a hospital for the preparation of a report under section 35 but he may not be remanded there for treatment under section 36.[26] The Government's reasons for this restriction were that any court finding that a defendant satisfied the medical grounds for detention under section 36 "would inevitably prejudice any subsequent consideration of his mental state during the course of the trial ... the question of the accused's responsibility for his actions assumes a crucial importance in cases where the offence with which he is charged is one of murder and for this reason such offences have been excluded from the application of the clause."[27]

"At any time before sentence is in custody in the course of a trial"

Section 36 provides that an accused person is a defendant who is "in custody awaiting trial before the Crown Court" or who "at any time before sentence is in custody in the course of a trial before that court." In *R. v. Grant,*[28] it was said that a trial was not complete until sentence had been passed or the offender was discharged. The purpose of these rather inelegant phrases appears to be to exclude persons who have been committed for sentence to the Crown Court.

---

[25] Magistrates' Courts Act 1980, s.30. Section 10 of the Magistrates' Courts Act 1980 gave magistrates' courts a general power to adjourn a case after conviction for the purpose of enabling enquiries to be made.

[26] Following conviction, a life sentence is the only course available to the court.

[27] *Mental Health (Amendment) Bill: Notes on Clauses, House of Commons* (D.H.S.S., 1982), p.123.

[28] *R. v. Grant* [1951] 1 K.B. 500.

The customary view is that the Crown Court may not remand under Part III an accused person who is charged with an indictable only offence until after committal or transfer. It may, however, be argued that such a defendant is from the outset of the proceedings "in custody awaiting trial before the Crown Court for an offence punishable with imprisonment." Accordingly, if he is remanded in custody by a magistrates' court and applies to the Crown Court for bail, the Crown Court may remand him to hospital for treatment if bail is inappropriate. Likewise, the Crown Court may remand under section 35 an accused person charged with an indictable only offence who has appealed to it against a magistrates' court's refusal to grant bail. The problem with this view is that any further remands and any reports on the accused's mental condition prior to committal would also need to be dealt with by the Crown Court. The better view is therefore that where a mentally ill or severely mentally impaired defendant who is charged with an indictable only offence requires urgent treatment pending committal or transfer, his removal to hospital must be arranged under section 48. Nor may a court remand him to hospital for a report on his mental condition prior to committal or transfer.

Relationship between sections 35, 36 and 48

A defendant who is charged with murder may not be remanded under section 36. He may, however, be removed to hospital for urgent treatment under section 48 if he suffers from mental illness or severe mental impairment.[29] Except where the Crown Court requires a report under section 35, persons charged with murder who suffer only from psychopathic disorder or mental impairment must be dealt with under the ordinary criminal provisions pending trial, and either remanded in custody or granted bail. In non-murder cases, sections 35, 36 and 48 are all available at some stage in respect of defendants who suffer from mental illness or severe mental impairment, provided the other conditions for exercising the powers exist. However, in the case of defendants who suffer only from psychopathic disorder or mental impairment, the defendant may be remanded for the preparation of a report under section 35, if the other conditions for exercising that power are satisfied, but not admitted to hospital for treatment under either section 36 or 48.[30]

EFFECT OF THE REMAND

Where an accused person is remanded to hospital under Part III, a constable or other person directed by the court is required to convey the accused person to the specified

---

[29]   Under the 1959 Act, the Secretary of State could transfer a defendant awaiting trial or sentence who was suffering from mental illness or severe subnormality of a nature or degree which warranted his detention in hospital for medical treatment. In practice, the power was only used if a defendant was in need of urgent treatment. With the introduction of section 36, a need for urgent treatment was made a condition of giving a transfer direction under section 48, and only section 36 is available in cases where an accused's need for treatment is not urgent.

[30]   It may be thought an anomaly that a court can obtain a medical report on such a defendant under section 35 but not then remand him to hospital for treatment if that report indicates that he requires treatment. However, the purpose of reports under section 35 is to assist the court in disposing of the case and not *per se* diversion, ascertaining whether the defendant requires treatment prior to disposal. Furthermore, the fact that both sections 36 and 48 are not available indicates that Parliament did not consider that the treatment needs of defendants suffering from "minor" forms of mental disorder would be sufficiently pressing to require provision to be made for them to receive in-patient treatment prior to trial or sentence.

hospital within the period of seven days beginning with the date of the remand; and the managers of the hospital to admit him within that period and thereafter detain him in accordance with the provisions of section 35 or 36, as the case may be.[31] The court may, pending the accused's admission, give directions for his conveyance to, and detention in, a place of safety.[32]

Application of Part II of the Act

Part II of the Act does not apply to persons detained under sections 35 and 36. The responsible medical officer therefore has no authority to grant leave of absence, nor may such patients be removed or transferred to another hospital under section 19, or discharged from liability to detention under section 23.

Consent to treatment and section 35

Part IV of the Act does not apply to persons remanded to hospital under section 35[33] and they may only be given treatment to which they consent or which is justified under common law. Because section 35 patients are not liable to compulsory treatment under the Act, the practice has arisen of detaining such persons under section 2 or 3 upon their admission under section 35, the two authorities for the patient's detention existing in parallel. Jones summarises some of the objections to this practice, including several of those set out in a legal advice furnished by the author.[34]

Consent to treatment and section 36

Persons detained in hospital under section 36 are subject to Part IV of the Act and may be treated without their consent. Where a section 36 patient who is awaiting admission to the hospital specified in the remand is removed to another hospital as a place of safety, it appears that Part IV of the Act also applies to treatment given there.[35]

Effect of remands on existing applications and orders

Remands to hospital under Part III do not have the effect of bringing to an end any pre-existing application, hospital order or guardianship order in respect of the same patient. Because the remand is to hospital rather than in custody, section 22 does not apply.

DURATION OF REMAND AND FURTHER REMANDS

An accused person may not be remanded under section 35 or 36 for more than 28 days. However, a court may further remand an accused person—

---

[31] Mental Health Act 1983, ss.35(9) and 36(8).
[32] Ibid., ss.35(4) and 36(3).
[33] Ibid., s.56(1)(b).
[34] An "Advice on sections 2, 3 and 35 and other related provisions of the Mental Health Act 1983" prepared by the author is referred to in B. Chaffey, "Detaining the detained: an injustice" The Journal of Forensic Psychiatry (1991) Vol. 2 No. 3, 331–335, and summarised in R. Jones, Mental Health Act Manual (Sweet & Maxwell, 5th ed., 1996), pp.160–161.
[35] This may be a drafting error because Part IV of the Act does not apply to patients who are detained in a place of safety while awaiting admission under section 37.

- in section 35 cases, if it appears to the court on the written or oral evidence of the registered medical practitioner responsible for making the report, that a further remand is necessary for completing the assessment of the accused person's mental condition.[36]

- in section 36 cases, if it appears to the court, on the written or oral evidence of the responsible medical officer, that a further remand is warranted.[37]

The power to further remand may be exercised without the accused being brought before the court if he is represented by counsel or a solicitor and his counsel or solicitor is given an opportunity of being heard.[38] An accused person may not be remanded under section 35 for more than 12 weeks in all and the same maximum period applies in section 36 cases.[39]

Termination of the remand

The court may at any time terminate a remand under section 35 or 36 if it appears to the court that it is "appropriate" to do so.[40]

Absconders

The Act expressly provides that the court may terminate the remand upon application by the accused or upon his being brought before the court having absconded from the specified hospital.[41] If an accused person absconds from the hospital to which he has been remanded, or while being conveyed to or from that hospital, he may be arrested without warrant by any constable and shall, after being arrested, be brought as soon as practicable before the court that remanded him. The court may thereupon terminate the remand and deal with him in any way in which it could have dealt with him if he had not been remanded under the section in question.

CHALLENGING DETENTION UNDER SECTIONS 35 AND 36

A person remanded under section 35 or 36 has a statutory right to obtain at his own expense an independent report on his mental condition from a registered medical practitioner chosen by him and to apply to the court on the basis of it for his remand to be terminated.[42] In practice, the cost of any medical reports prepared by the defence is likely to be met by the legal aid fund at no cost to the accused person.

Mental Health Review Tribunals

A person remanded to hospital under section Part III may apply to the court for the remand to be terminated but has no right to apply to a tribunal for his discharge from hospital.[43] However, because section 35 patients may in practice also be detained under section 2 or 3, tribunals are sometimes called upon to deal with the cases of Part II patients who are also detained in hospital under section 35.

---

[36]   Mental Health Act 1983, s.35(5).
[37]   *Ibid.*, s.36(4).
[38]   *Ibid.*, ss.35(6) and 36(5).
[39]   *Ibid.*, ss.35(7) and 36(6).
[40]   *Ibid.*
[41]   *Ibid.*, ss.35(10) and 36(8).
[42]   *Ibid.*, ss.35(8) and 36(7).
[43]   See, in particular, *ibid.*, s.145(3).

INTERIM HOSPITAL ORDERS

Before making a hospital order or direction or dealing with an offender in some other way, the Crown Court or a magistrates' court may make an "interim hospital order" authorising his admission to hospital.[44] The purpose of the provision is to enable the court to determine whether a defendant who suffers from one of the four forms of mental disorder satisfies the criteria for making a hospital order or, more generally, whether such a disposal is appropriate.

CRITERIA FOR IMPOSITION

The following conditions are imposed by section 38—

- The person has been convicted before the Crown Court of an offence punishable with imprisonment, other than an offence the sentence for which is fixed by law, or by a magistrates' court of an offence punishable on summary conviction with imprisonment.[45]

- The court is satisfied, on the written or oral evidence of two registered medical practitioners, one of whom is approved under section 12, that "the offender is suffering from mental illness, psychopathic disorder, severe mental impairment or mental impairment and that there is reason to suppose that the mental disorder from which the offender is suffering is such that it may be appropriate for a hospital order to be made in his case."[46]

- The court is further satisfied, on the written or oral evidence of the registered medical practitioner who would be responsible for making the report or of some other person representing the hospital managers, that arrangements have been made for his admission to that hospital and for his admission to it within the period of 28 days beginning with the date of the order.[47]

Magistrates courts

A magistrates' court may in certain circumstances make a hospital order without convicting an accused person who suffers from mental illness or severe mental impairment but the making of an interim hospital order always requires that the defendant has been convicted. Accordingly, where such a defendant is unfit to plead or to be tried, and the court is not satisfied that he did the act or omission charged, it may remand him to hospital under section 35 if he consents to being so remanded; otherwise, it is no powerless to direct his admission to hospital under Part III.[48]

---

[44] Section 45A of the Mental Health Act 1983 was brought into force on 1 October 1997. It provides that the Crown Court may also make an interim hospital order in order to assist it in deciding whether to give hospital and limitation directions in connection with offences committed on or after that date. See Mental Health Act 1983, ss.38(1), 38(5) and 45A(8); Crime (Sentences) Act 1997, s.46.

[45] Mental Health Act 1983, s.38(1).

[46] *Ibid.*, s.38(1)(a) and (b).

[47] *Ibid.*, s.38(4).

[48] It may be argued that a person who is unfit for trial will also lack capacity to give a valid consent.

EFFECT OF AN INTERIM HOSPITAL ORDER

Where an interim hospital order is made, a constable or any other person named by the court is required to convey the offender to the hospital specified in the order within 28 days.[49]

Authority for the patient's detention

An interim hospital order authorises the managers of the hospital specified in the order to admit the patient at any time within the 28 day period and thereafter detain him in accordance with the provisions of section 38.[50]

Application of Part II of the Act

The provisions of Part II of the Act do not apply. The responsible medical officer therefore has no authority to grant leave of absence, nor may such patients be removed or transferred to another hospital under section 19, or discharged from liability to detention under section 23.[51]

Consent to treatment

Persons detained in hospital under an interim hospital order are subject to Part IV of the Act and so may be administered treatment without their consent in the circumstances set out in sections 56 to 63 of the Act.[52] Part IV also appears to apply to section 38 patients detained in a place of safety while awaiting admission to the specified hospital but this is probably a drafting error.[53]

Effect on previous applications and orders

The making of an interim hospital order does not have the effect of bringing to an end any pre-existing application, hospital order or guardianship order which is in force in respect of the patient.[54]

DURATION AND FURTHER ORDERS

An interim hospital order may be in force for such period, not exceeding 12 weeks, as the court may specify when making the order. It may be renewed for further periods of not more than 28 days at a time if it appears to the court, on the written or oral evidence of the responsible medical officer, that the order's continuation is warranted, but it may not continue in force for more than 12 months in all.[55] The power of renewing an interim hospital order may be exercised without the offender being brought before the court if he is represented by counsel or a solicitor and his counsel or solicitor is given an opportunity of being heard.[56]

---

[49]   Mental Health Act 1983, s.40(3)(a).
[50]   *Ibid.*, s.40(3)(b).
[51]   See, in particular, *ibid.*, ss.40(4) and 145(3).
[52]   *Ibid.*, s.56.
[53]   See the reference to s.37(4), but the absence of any reference to s.38(4), in s.56(1)(b) of the 1983 Act.
[54]   See Mental Health Act 1983, s.40.
[55]   *Ibid.*, s.38(5), as amended by Crime (Sentences) Act 1997, s.49(1). Section 49(1) of the 1997 Act, which came into force on 1 October 1997, extended the maximum duration of an interim hospital order from six months to twelve months.
[56]   *Ibid.*, s.38(6).

Termination of the interim hospital order

The court is required to terminate an interim hospital order if it makes a hospital order or decides, after considering the written or oral evidence of the responsible medical officer, to deal with the offender in some other way.[57]

Absconders

If an offender absconds from a hospital in which he is detained in pursuance of an interim hospital order, or while being conveyed to or from such a hospital, he may be arrested without warrant by a constable and shall, after being arrested, be brought as soon as practicable before the court that made the order. The court may thereupon terminate the order and deal with him in any way in which it could have dealt with him if no such order had been made.[58]

The making of a hospital order

Where an interim hospital order is in force, the court may make a "hospital order" without the offender being brought before the court if he is represented by counsel or a solicitor and his advocate is given an opportunity of being heard. It is, however, doubtful whether the court may make a restriction order in the offender's absence.[59]

CHALLENGING DETENTION UNDER SECTION 38

In contrast to the position where an accused person has been remanded under section 35 or 36, the offender has no express statutory right to apply to the court which imposed the order for its termination on the basis of an independent medical report. Rather, an interim hospital order is a sentence for the purposes of the appeal against sentence provisions in the Criminal Appeal Act 1968.[60]

Section 38 and Mental Health Review Tribunals

Because the offender's case has not been disposed of by the court, he has no right to apply to a tribunal for his discharge.

---

[57] Mental Health Act 1983, s.38(5).
[58] *Ibid.*, s.38(7).
[59] The wording used in section 51(5) — "the court may make a hospital order (with or without a restriction order) in his case in his absence" — is not adopted in s.38(2), which provides that "the court may make a hospital order without his being brought before the court". Furthermore, it would appear that hospital and limitation directions cannot be given in the offender's absence once section 45A is in force. See the references to subsections (1) and (5) of section 38 in section 45A(8) of the Mental Health Act 1983, but the absence of any reference to subsection (2).
[60] Criminal Appeal Act 1968, s.50(1). It is not, however, a sentence for the purposes of section 36(1) of the Criminal Justice Act 1988 (which provides that where it appears to the Attorney General that the sentencing of a person in the Crown Court has been unduly lenient, he may in certain circumstances refer the case to the Court of Appeal, for them to review the sentencing of that person). Criminal Justice Act 1988, s.35(5).

GUARDIANSHIP ORDERS

Under section 37, the Crown Court or a magistrates' court may by order place a person under the guardianship of a local social services authority or of such other person approved by a local social services authority as may be specified.

CRITERIA FOR IMPOSITION

The following conditions apply in all cases—

- Subject to certain exceptions, the accused has been convicted by a magistrates' court of an offence punishable on summary conviction with imprisonment[61] or has been convicted by the Crown Court of an imprisonable offence, other than one the sentence for which is either fixed by law or falls to be imposed under sections 2–4 of the Crime (Sentences) Act 1997.[62]

- the court is satisfied, on the written or oral evidence of two registered medical practitioners, one of whom is approved under section 12, that the offender is suffering from mental illness, psychopathic disorder, severe mental impairment or mental impairment of a nature or degree which warrants his reception into guardianship under the Act.[63]

- the court is of the opinion, having regard to all the circumstances including the nature of the offence and the character and antecedents of the offender, and to the other available methods of dealing with him, that the most suitable method of disposing of the case before it is by means of a guardianship order under section 37.[64]

- the offender is at least sixteen years of age.[65]

- the court is satisfied that that the proposed guardian is willing to receive the offender into guardianship and, by inference, that any proposed private guardian has been approved by the local social services authority.[66]

---

[61] A magistrates' court cannot therefore make a guardianship order if the offence is indictable only (**326**).

[62] Mental Health Act 1983, s.37(1), as amended by Crime (Sentences) Act 1997, s.55(1), Sched. 4, para. 12(1); Crime (Sentences) Act 1997, ss.2(2) and 55(2). The Crown Court may not make such an order if the sentence is one which falls to be imposed under section 2 of the 1997 Act. In other words, there are no exceptional circumstances relating to the offences or the offender which justify the court not imposing the required mandatory life sentence for a second serious offence. The new position under section 37 is, however, ambiguous as regards the order's availability where a person has been convicted of a third class A drug trafficking offence. Subs. (1) merely prohibits such an order being made if a life sentence is mandatory. However, subs. (1A) then states that nothing in sections 3(2) and 4(2) of the Crime (Sentences) Act 1997 shall prevent a court from making a hospital order under section 37(1). It does not say that nothing in those sections shall prevent a court from making an order under section 37(1), that is a hospital order *or* a guardianship order. A natural reading of section 37(1A) leads to the conclusion that sections 3 and 4 of the 1997 Act are intended to prevent a court from imposing a guardianship order if the sentence is one which falls to be imposed under either of those sections. The intention may be that, unless the nature or degree of the offender's disorder is sufficiently serious that compulsory treatment in hospital is warranted, the law should take its normal course.

[63] Mental Health Act 1983, ss.37(2)(a)(ii) and 54(1).

[64] *Ibid.*, s.37(2)(b).

[65] *Ibid.*, s.37(2)(a)(ii).

[66] *Ibid.*, s.37(6).

The need for a conviction

A magistrates' court may not make a guardianship order in respect of a patient who suffers from mental impairment or a psychopathic disorder unless it has convicted him of an offence triable on summary conviction with imprisonment. It may, if it thinks fit, make such an order without convicting a person accused of such an offence if he suffers from mental illness or severe mental impairment and the court is satisfied that he did the act or made the omission charged and the usual conditions for making such an order are satisfied.[67] As to the Crown Court's powers, it may only make a guardianship order in respect of a person who has been convicted before it of an offence punishable with imprisonment, other than an offence such as murder for which the sentence is fixed, unless the accused has been found unfit to plead or not guilty by reason of insanity.[68]

THE ORDER

A guardianship order must specify the form or forms of mental disorder from which, upon the medical evidence, the offender is found by the court to be suffering. No such order may be made unless the offender is described by each of the practitioners whose evidence is taken into account as suffering from one common form of mental disorder, whether or not he is also described by either of them as also suffering from another.[69]

Combining guardianship with other forms of sentence

Where a court makes a guardianship order, it may also make any other order which it has power to make in respect of such an offence other than a custodial sentence, a fine, a probation order, or a supervision order under the Children and Young Persons Act 1969.[70]

EFFECT OF A GUARDIANSHIP ORDER

A guardianship order confers on the guardian named in the order the same powers as a guardianship application accepted under Part II (250).[71] The patient is to be treated for the purposes of the statutory provisions mentioned in Part I of Schedule 1 to the Act as if on the date of the order he had been received into guardianship in pursuance of a guardianship application made under section 7, but subject to the exceptions and modifications specified in that Part of the Schedule.[72] These are mainly

---

[67]   Mental Health Act 1983, s.37(1) and (3). A magistrates' court only has the same power to make a guardianship or hospital order without convicting such a person as it does following conviction. Consequently, it may not make such an order if the accused is charged with an offence which is triable only on indictment: *R. v. Chippenham Magistrates, ex p. Thompson [1996] C.O.D. 195.* It may, however, make such an order without convicting the accused if he is charged with an offence triable either way, notwithstanding that he is unable to consent to summary trial. The circumstances in which it is appropriate to exercise the power are bound to be rare and will usually require the consent of those acting for the accused if he is under a disability and cannot be tried: *R. v. Lincolnshire (Kesteven) Justices, ex p. O'Connor* [1983] 1 W.L.R. 335, *per* Lord Lane L.C.J. This is so even if the accused has previously elected trial by jury: *R. v. Ramsgate Justices, ex p. Kazmarek* (1985) 80 Cr.App.R. 366.

[68]   *Ibid.*

[69]   *Ibid.*, s.37(7).

[70]   *Ibid.*, s.37(8).

[71]   *Ibid.*, s.40(2).

[72]   More particularly, the provisions of Part II concerning the duration, discharge and renewal of the guardianship, and reclassification, apply equally therefore to patients received into guardianship under Part III subject to these generally minor modifications.

minor and consequential. For example, the Schedule states that references to guardianship applications in Part II of the Act take effect as if they referred to the guardianship order. Drafting errors excepted, the only substantive differences are that—

- the patient's statutory nearest relative has no power to discharge the order.

- by way of compensation for the loss of this right, the nearest relative may instead apply to a tribunal for the patient's discharge during the year beginning with the date of the order, and thereafter make a further application during each year the order remains in force.

- where a patient subject to a guardianship order is transferred to hospital under section 19, the transfer takes effect as if a hospital order (rather than a section 3 application) had been imposed by the court on the date of the original guardianship order.[73]

Effect on previous applications and orders

Subject to the effect of any successful appeal against conviction or sentence, the making of a guardianship order has the consequence that any application, hospital order (without restrictions) or guardianship order previously in force in respect of the same patient ceases to have effect.[74]

CHALLENGING GUARDIANSHIP ORDERS

The patient may appeal against the court's sentence in the usual way. The Act expressly provides that, where the order was made by magistrates otherwise than upon conviction, the patient shall have the same right of appeal against the order as if it had been made on his conviction; on any such appeal, the Crown Court has the same powers as if the appeal had been against both conviction and sentence.[75] Such an appeal by a child or young person may be brought by him or by his parent or guardian on his behalf.[76]

Effect of a successful appeal

If the guardianship order, or the conviction on which it was made, is quashed on appeal, section 22 has effect as if during any period for which the patient was subject to guardianship under the order, he had instead been detained in custody as mentioned in that section (**304**).

Guardianship orders and Mental Health Review Tribunals

The patient's periodic rights of application are the same as those of a patient received into guardianship under Part II. The patient may make an application during the six month period beginning with the date of the order and, thereafter, make a further application during each period for which the guardianship is renewed. The nearest relative's periodic rights of application have already been described.

---

[73] Consequently, the nearest relative does not acquire a right to discharge the patient from liability to detention in hospital.
[74] Mental Health Act 1983, ss.40(4) and (5). See p.304.
[75] *Ibid.*, s.45(1).
[76] *Ibid.*, s.45(2).

HOSPITAL ORDERS

Under section 37, a court may in certain circumstances dispose of a case before it by ordering a defendant's admission to, and detention in, the hospital specified in its order.

CRITERIA FOR IMPOSITION

The following requirements must be met before a hospital order may be imposed under section 37—

- Subject to limited exceptions, the accused has been convicted by a magistrates' court of an offence punishable on summary conviction with imprisonment or has been convicted by the Crown Court of an imprisonable offence, other than one the sentence for which is either fixed by law or falls to be imposed under section 2 of the Crime (Sentences) Act 1997;[77]

- the court is satisfied, on the written or oral evidence of two registered medical practitioners, one of whom is approved under section 12, that the offender is suffering from mental illness, psychopathic disorder, severe mental impairment or mental impairment of a nature or degree of a nature or degree which makes it appropriate for him to be detained in a hospital for medical treatment;[78]

- in cases of psychopathic disorder or mental impairment, the court is further satisfied that such treatment is likely to alleviate or prevent a deterioration of his condition;[79]

- the court is of the opinion, having regard to all the circumstances including the nature of the offence and the character and antecedents of the offender, and to the other available methods of dealing with him, that the most suitable method of disposing of the case is by means of a hospital order;[80]

- the court is satisfied on the written or oral evidence of the registered medical practitioner who would be in charge of his treatment or of some other person representing the managers of the hospital that arrangements have been made for his admission to that hospital [...] and for his admission to it within the period of 28 days beginning with the date of the making of such an order.[81]

---

[77] Mental Health Act 1983, s.37(1), as amended by Crime (Sentences) Act 1997, s.55(1), Sched. 4, para. 12(1); Crime (Sentences) Act 1997, ss.2(2) and 55(2). A magistrates' court cannot make a hospital order if the offence is indictable only (**326**). Likewise, the Crown Court may not make such an order if the sentence is one which falls to be imposed under section 2 of the 1997 Act. In other words, there are no exceptional circumstances relating to the offences or the offender which justify the court not imposing the required mandatory life sentence for a second serious offence (**405**). As to the order's availability where a person has been convicted of a third Class A drug trafficking offence, see **329, 407**.

[78] Mental Health Act 1983, s.37(2)(a)(i).

[79] *Ibid.*

[80] *Ibid.*, s.37(2)(b).

[81] *Ibid.*, s.37(4), as amended by Crime (Sentences) Act 1997, Sched. 4, para. 12(3). The square brackets previously contained the words, "in the event of such an order being made by the court," but they were removed from subs. 37(4) on 1 October 1997. The purpose of the amendment seems to be to leave any decision about whether a hospital order or a hospital direction is imposed to the sentencing court. It avoids the possibility of hospital managers giving evidence that a bed is available in the event that the court makes a hospital order but not if it gives a hospital direction.

THE NEED FOR A CONVICTION

A magistrates' court may not make a hospital order in respect of a person who suffers from mental impairment or a psychopathic disorder unless it has convicted him of an offence punishable on summary conviction with imprisonment. Its power to make a hospital order without convicting a person suffering from mental illness or severe mental impairment is the same as its power to make a guardianship order in such circumstances (**325**).

Crown Court

The Crown Court may make a hospital order in respect of a person who has been convicted before it of an imprisonable offence other than one the sentence for which is fixed by law or which falls to be imposed under section 2 of the 1997 Act. It may make an order otherwise than upon conviction if —

- the accused has been removed to hospital by the Secretary of State under section 48 (**378**) and the conditions specified in section 51(5) and (6) are satisfied (**374**).

- the accused has been found unfit to plead or not guilty of the offence charged by reason of insanity.

CRIME (SENTENCES) ACT 1997

The Crown Court may not make a hospital order if it is required to impose a life sentence under section 2(2) of the 1997 Act.[82] Section 2 applies where a person is convicted of a serious offence (**405**) committed after the commencement of the section if, at the time of its commission, he was aged 18 or over and had previously been convicted within the United Kingdom of another serious offence. It requires the court to impose a life sentence unless it is of the opinion that there are exceptional circumstances relating to either of the offences or to the offender which justify it not doing so. If the circumstances are exceptional, a life sentence is not required, and the court retains its normal discretion as to the most appropriate sentence. It may therefore make a hospital order (with or without restrictions).

Third class A drug trafficking offence

The position is different in relation to offences to which section 3(2) of the 1997 Act applies. This requires a court to impose a minimum term of seven years' imprisonment for a third class A drug trafficking offence. However, in such cases, a court is not required to impose the sentence required by section 3 if the offender satisfies the medical conditions for admission to hospital under section 37. This is because the following new subsection has been inserted in the 1983 Act:

> "37.—(1A) In the case of an offence the sentence for which would otherwise fall to be imposed under subsection (2) of section 3 or 4 of the Crime (Sentences) Act 1997, nothing in that subsection shall prevent a court from making an order under subsection (1) above for the admission of the offender to a hospital."[83]

---

[82] Mental Health Act 1983, s.37(1), as amended by Crime (Sentences) Act 1997, Sched. 4, para. 12(1).

[83] *Ibid.*, s.37(1A), as inserted by Crime (Sentences) Act 1997, Sched. 4, para. 12(2). Section 4 of the 1997 Act similarly requires the imposition of a minimum term of three years' imprisonment for a third domestic burglary (**407**). However, there are no plans to bring this section into force.

THE ORDER

The hospital order must specify the form or forms of mental disorder from which the offender is found by the court to be suffering. No such order may be made unless the offender is described by each of the practitioners whose evidence is taken into account as suffering from one common form of mental disorder, whether or not he is also described by either of them as suffering from another of them.[84]

Other forms of sentence

Where a court makes a hospital order, it may also make any other order which it has power to make in respect of such an offence other than a "a sentence of imprisonment," a fine, a probation order, or a supervision order under the Children and Young Persons Act 1969.[85]

THE EFFECT OF A HOSPITAL ORDER

Section 40(1)(a) provides that a hospital order is sufficient authority for a constable, an approved social worker or any other person directed by the court to convey the patient to the hospital specified in the order within a period of 28 days.

Detention in a place of safety pending admission

The court may give directions for the patient's conveyance to, and detention in, a place of safety pending his admission to the specified hospital.[86]

Emergencies and other special circumstances

If, prior to the expiration of the 28-day period during which the patient is to be admitted to the hospital named in the order, it appears to the Secretary of State that, "by reason of an emergency or other special circumstances," it is not practicable for the patient to be received there, he may give directions for the patient's admission to such other hospital as appears to be appropriate. Where such a direction is given, the Secretary of State must cause the person having custody of the patient to be informed, and the hospital order takes effect as if the hospital specified in the directions were substituted for the hospital specified in the court order.[87]

Authority for the patient's detention

A hospital order authorises the managers of the hospital specified in the order to admit the patient at any time within the statutory 28 day period and thereafter detain him in accordance with the provisions of the Act.[88]

Effect on previous applications and orders

Subject to the effect of a successful appeal against conviction or sentence (**304**), the making of the order has the consequence that any previous application, guardianship order or unrestricted hospital order ceases to have effect.[89]

---

[84] Mental Health Act 1983, s.37(7).

[85] As to whether a "sentence of imprisonment" includes a suspended sentence, sections 47(5) and 55(6) only define what constitutes "serving" a sentence of imprisonment for the purposes of Part III.

[86] Mental Health Act 1983, s.37(4).

[87] *Ibid.*, s.37(5).

[88] *Ibid.*, s.40(1)(b).

[89] *Ibid.*, s.40(5).

Application of Part II of the Act

A patient who is admitted in pursuance of a hospital order is treated for the purposes of the provisions mentioned in Part I of Schedule 1 to the Act as if he had been admitted to hospital on the date of the order in pursuance of an application duly made under section 3, but subject to the modifications specified in that Part of the Schedule.[90]

The modifications specified in Part I of Schedule 1

These are mainly minor and consequential. For example, the Schedule states that references to section 3 applications in Part II generally take effect as if they referred to the hospital order made by the court. The only substantive differences are that—

- the patient has no right to apply to a tribunal during the period of six months beginning with the date of the order;

- the patient's statutory nearest relative has no power to discharge the hospital order;

- by way of compensation for the loss of this right, the nearest relative may instead apply to a tribunal for the patient's discharge during the period between the expiration of six months and the expiration of 12 months beginning with the date of the order, and further apply in any subsequent period of 12 months.

- if the patient is later transferred into guardianship under section 19, the transfer takes effect as if a guardianship order, rather than a guardianship application, had been made by the court on the date of its original order.[91]

Duration, discharge and renewal

As with section 3 applications, the authority to detain the patient which is conferred by a hospital order requires periodic renewal and lapses unless renewed at the statutory intervals in accordance with the provisions of section 20. The initial six-month period of detention authorised by the order commences on the date of the order rather than the date of the patient's admission to the named hospital. Apart from the fact that the patient's nearest relative has no power to make an order for discharge under section 23, the order may be discharged in the same way as an application under section 3.

Consent to treatment

The consent to treatment provisions in Part IV apply to patients detained under a hospital order although, when calculating the three month statutory period for the purposes of section 58, any medication administered while the patient is detained in a place of safety pending admission (even if another hospital) is discounted. The three month period therefore commences on the first day the patient receives medication for mental disorder following his admission to the hospital named in the

---

[90]   Mental Health Act 1983, s.40(4).
[91]   Consequently, the nearest relative may not discharge the patient from guardianship but may periodically apply to a tribunal for him to be discharged

order, provided he was not detained in hospital under some other provision of the Act to which Part IV applies immediately prior to the order's imposition.

After-care under supervision

An application for an unrestricted hospital order patient to be subject to after-care under supervision after he leaves hospital may be made in the same circumstances as may a supervision application in respect of a patient liable to be detained under section 3 (**426 et seq.**).

APPEALS AGAINST CONVICTION OR SENTENCE

The patient has the usual rights of appeal where a hospital order is imposed following conviction. For the purposes of the Criminal Appeal Act 1968, the term "sentence" includes a hospital order made under Part III.[92]

Appeals to the Crown Court

Where a magistrates' court makes a hospital order without convicting the accused, he has the same right of appeal against the order as if it had been made on his conviction; and on any such appeal the Crown Court has the same powers as if the appeal had been against both conviction and sentence. Any such appeal by a child or young person with respect to whom any such order has been made, whether the appeal is against the order or against the finding upon which the order was made, may be brought by him or by his parent or guardian on his behalf.[93]

Effect of a successful appeal

Where a hospital order is imposed, any pre-existing application, hospital order without restrictions or guardianship ceases to have effect. However, if the hospital order, or the conviction on which it was made, is quashed on appeal, section 22 has effect as if during any period for which the patient was liable to be detained under the hospital order he had instead been detained in custody as mentioned in that section (**304**).[94]

MENTAL HEALTH REVIEW TRIBUNALS

Where a hospital order is made, the patient and his nearest relative may apply to a tribunal during the period between the expiration of six months and the expiration of twelve months beginning with the date of the order, and thereafter make a further application each year the order remains in force. The patient may also ask the hospital managers to review his case, with a view to them exercising their power of discharge under section 23.

PATIENTS SUBJECT TO A NOTIONAL HOSPITAL ORDER

Where a restricted patient is an in-patient at the time his restrictions cease to have effect, he is deemed to have been admitted to hospital under a second, notional, hospital order made, without restrictions, on the day when the restrictions ceased to

---

[92]   Criminal Appeal Act 1968, s.50(1).
[93]   Mental Health Act 1983, s.45.
[94]   *Ibid.*, s.40(5).

have effect.[95] Such patients are often referred to as being subject to a "notional hospital order."[96] They are thereafter in exactly the same legal position as any other section 37 patient, with the single exception that they may apply to a tribunal for their discharge during the six month period commencing with the date of the notional hospital order.[97] This reflects the fact that they will already have been detained in hospital for same time under the hospital order imposed by the court.

RESTRICTION ORDERS

Where a hospital order is made by the Crown Court, and it appears to the court that it is necessary for the protection of the public from serious harm, the court may further order that the offender shall be subject to the special restrictions set out in section 41 of the Act, either without limit of time or during such period as may be specified in the order; and any such order is known as "a restriction order."

CRITERIA FOR IMPOSITION UNDER SECTION 41

The Act lays down the following conditions in relation to the imposition of a restriction order under section 41 —

- the Crown Court has made a hospital order;

- at least one of the registered medical practitioners whose evidence is taken into account by the court under section 37(2)(a) has given evidence orally before the court;

- it appears to the court, having regard to the nature of the offence, the antecedents of the offender and the risk of his committing further offences if set at large, that it is necessary for the protection of the public from serious harm that the offender shall be subject to the special restrictions set out in section 41, either without limit of time or during such period as may be specified in the order.

PARASITIC NATURE OF RESTRICTION ORDERS

A restriction order is parasitic in nature and cannot exist on its own. If the hospital order to which it is attached ("the relevant hospital order") ceases to have effect then so too does the attendant restriction order. In theory, the converse is not also true so that the restriction order may cease to have effect but the patient continue to be detained in hospital under the relevant hospital order. However, the Act provides that where this happens the patient is to be treated as if he had been admitted under a second, notional, hospital order made without restrictions on the date on which the restrictions ceased to have effect. In practice therefore, the cessation of either of the two orders made by the court also brings the other to an end.

---

[95] Not the date on which the hospital order or transfer direction with restrictions attached was originally made by the court or the Secretary of State.

[96] Sometimes confusingly abbreviated on the Part A statement as "not 37."

[97] Mental Health Act 1983, ss.41(5), 55(4).

RESTRICTION ORDERS WITH AND WITHOUT LIMIT OF TIME

Where a restriction order is made without limit of time, the patient remains subject to the special restrictions and liable to be detained under the relevant hospital order until such time as the restriction order is discharged. If a restriction order is made for a limited period then, subject to a single minor exception, the patient becomes an unrestricted patient at the expiration of that period. Accordingly, if he is detained in hospital at that time, he may thereafter be discharged in the same way as any other hospital order patient, without conditions and without being liable to recall by the Secretary of State. If he has already been discharged from hospital, he ceases to be liable to detained altogether. The making of restriction orders of limited duration has generally been discouraged and the Aarvold Report observed that of 232 restriction orders made by the courts in 1971 only 13 were with a time limit.[98] In *R. v. Gardiner*, Lord Parker C.J. observed that "since in most cases the prognosis cannot be certain, the safer course is to make any restriction order unlimited in point of time. The only exception is where the doctors are able to assert confidently that recovery will take place within a fixed period when the restriction order can properly be limited to that period."[99] The Butler Report of 1975 noted that it was a widely held view that a restriction order without a time limit was preferable to an order the duration of which was prescribed by the court and it approved removing from the statute the power to make orders limited in time.[100] In *R. v. Birch*, Mustill L.J. stated that "the observations of Lord Parker, C.J. in *Gardiner* (supra) as to the imprudence in any but the most exceptional case of imposing a restriction for a fixed period rather than for an unlimited period still hold good under the 1983 Act."[101] In *R. v. Haynes*, the Court of Appeal held that where a limited-term restriction order was made it was wrong to fix its term by reference to the sentence of imprisonment which would have been imposed had a custodial sentence been passed instead.[102]

THE SPECIAL RESTRICTIONS

Section 41(3) sets out the special restrictions applicable to patients who are subject to both a hospital order and a restriction order. The effect of the restriction order is to restrict the ways in which the hospital order to which it is attached may cease to have effect and, more generally, the circumstances and ways in which the patient may leave hospital. For as long as the restriction order remains in force, the authority to detain the patient which is conferred by the underlying hospital order also remains in force, requiring no periodic renewal, never lapsing through effluxion of time, its termination always requiring a positive act in the form of an order or direction discharging it. In the main, the restrictions operate only indirectly on the patient. Most often, it is the exercise of the statutory powers ordinarily granted to doctors and hospital managers in respect of detained patients which are restricted. For example, the patient's responsible medical officer cannot grant him leave to be absent from hospital without the Home Secretary's consent and nor can the hospital's managers transfer him to another hospital without that consent. Similarly, the responsible medical officer and the managers cannot discharge the patient from

---

[98] *Report on the Review of Procedures for the Discharge and Supervision of Psychiatric Patients subject to Special Restrictions*, Cmnd. 5191 (1973), para. 7.
[99] *R. v. Gardiner* [1967] 1 W.L.R. 464.
[100] *Report of the Committee on Mentally Abnormal Offenders*, Cmnd. 6244 (1975), para. 14.25.
[101] *R. v. Birch* (1989) 11 Cr.App.R.(S.) 202.
[102] *R. v. Haynes* (1981) 3 Cr.App.R.(S.) 330.

hospital under section 23 without the Secretary of State's prior consent. However, while the exercise of these legal powers is restricted, the Home Secretary has no responsibility for the patient's medical treatment or his day to day management throughout his stay in hospital. These are professional matters for the doctors, nurses, psychologists and others to decide.

Application of Part II of the Act

A patient who is admitted to hospital in pursuance of a hospital order and a restriction order is treated for the purposes of the provisions of Parts II and V of the Act mentioned in Part II of Schedule 1 to the Act as if he had been admitted to hospital on the date of the order in pursuance of an application duly made under section 3 of the Act, but subject to the exceptions and modifications specified in that Part of the Schedule.[103] The nature and effect of these exceptions and modifications are described below.

DURATION, RENEWAL AND EXPIRY OF THE HOSPITAL ORDER

None of the provisions of Part II of the Act relating to the duration, renewal and expiration of hospital orders apply during the period the restriction order remains in force. The authority for the patient's detention which is conferred by the relevant hospital order does not require periodic renewal. Nor does it cease to have effect because the patient has been absent without leave for a certain period of time; detained in custody for a continuous period exceeding six months; made the subject of a subsequent application, order or direction under the Act, including a further restriction order or restriction direction; or removed to a country outside England and Wales under section 86.[104] In short, if a restriction order is also made, the hospital order remains in force for as long as the restriction order does and a positive act is required, in the form of an order or direction for discharge, to bring the patient's liability to detention to an end.

Absence with and without leave

A restricted patient who has been absent without leave for a certain period of time does not cease to be liable to be detained[105] and the power to take a restricted patient into custody and to return him under section 18 may be exercised at any time.[106]

Restricted patients in prison, etc.

A restriction order does not cease to have effect by virtue of the fact that a restricted patient has been continuously in custody in pursuance of a sentence or court order for a period exceeding six months. Upon the patient's release from prison or some other place of custody, section 18 applies as if the patient had absented himself without leave on the day of his release.[107]

---

[103]   Mental Health Act 1983, s.41(3).
[104]   *Ibid.*, ss.41(3)(a) and 91(2).
[105]   *Ibid.*, s.41(3); Sched. 1, Pt. II, paras. 2 and 4(b).
[106]   *Ibid.*, s.41(3)(d).
[107]   *Ibid.*, s.41(3), Sched. 1, Pt. II, para. 6.

Subsequent applications, orders or directions

Section 40(5) does not apply and the making of a subsequent application, order or direction under the Act in respect of the same patient does not have the effect of discharging any pre-existing restriction order or hospital order to which it is attached.[108]

Removal under Part VI of the Act

Where, under section 86, a restricted patient is removed to a country outside the United Kingdom, the Isle of Man and the Channel Islands, the hospital order and the restriction order continue in force so as to apply to the patient if he returns to England and Wales at any time before the end of the period for which the orders would otherwise have continued in force.[109]

RESTRICTIONS AS TO LEAVE OF ABSENCE

A restricted patient's responsible medical officer may not grant him leave to be absent from hospital except with the consent of the Secretary of State.[110]

Revocation of leave and recall to hospital

Leave may be revoked and the patient recalled to hospital if it appears to the responsible medical officer *or* to the Secretary of State that it is necessary to do so either in the interests of his own health or safety or for the protection of others. Notice of the leave's revocation must be given in writing to the patient or (if he is in custody) to the person for the time being in charge of him.[111] The Secretary of State may recall the patient at any time, provided the conditions referred to above appear to him to be satisfied.[112] However, a patient's responsible medical officer may not recall him to the hospital where he is liable to be detained after the expiration of twelve months beginning with the first day of his absence from that hospital on leave.[113] Visiting friends or attending an out-patient appointment at a hospital does not bring to an end a continuous period of leave of absence since the patient does not thereby become an in-patient.[114] However, where a patient voluntarily stays overnight in hospital, this may do so.[115] For the avoidance of doubt, where a patient is absent without leave during the twelve month period, he has not been absent *with* leave for twelve months at the expiration of one year from the date on which leave was originally granted.

RESTRICTIONS ON TRANSFER TO ANOTHER HOSPITAL

A restricted patient may not be transferred from one hospital to another, in pursuance of regulations made under section 19, except with the consent of the

---

[108] Mental Health Act 1983, s.41(4).
[109] *Ibid.*, s.91(2).
[110] *Ibid.*, ss.17(1), 41(3), 41(3)(c)(i) and 145(3); Sched. 1, Pt. II, paras. 2 and 3(a). Note that the Secretary of State has no power to grant a restricted patient leave of absence.
[111] *Ibid.*
[112] *Ibid.*, ss.17(5), 41(3), 41(3)(c) and (d), 145(3); Sched. 1, Pt. II, paras. 2 and 3(c).
[113] *Ibid.*, ss.17(5), 41(3) and 145(3); Sched. 1, Pt. II, paras. 2 and 3(c).
[114] *R. v. Hallstrom, ex p W (No. 2)* [1986] 2 All E.R. 306, at 319 and 320, *per* McCullough J.
[115] *Ibid.*, at 319. An alternative view would be that a patient remains continuously absent with leave for these purposes until such time as a notice revoking that leave is served under s.17(4).

Secretary of State.[116] Where a restricted patient is transferred under section 19, the hospital order takes effect as if it were an order for his admission to the hospital to which he is transferred.

Transfer of special hospital patients

For the purposes of the Act, the special hospitals are all managed by the Secretary of State. Section 123(1) provides that the Secretary of State may direct the "removal" of a patient from one special hospital to another and, by sub-section (2), he may also direct the "transfer" of a special hospital patient to a hospital which is not a special hospital. The powers apply equally to unrestricted patients but, since the majority of special hospital patients are restricted, the power is of particular relevance in this context.[117]

Removal to a hospital under the same managers

Sections 19 and 123 both distinguish between the "removal" of a patient to another hospital (that is his removal from one hospital to another hospital under the same managers) and the "transfer" of a patient to another hospital (which is the only option available if moving a patient involves transferring the authority to detain him to different statutory managers).[118] Section 41(3)(c)(ii) provides that the "power to *transfer* a patient in pursuance of regulations under section 19" shall, in the case of a restricted patient, be exercisable only with the consent of the Secretary of State. However, prior to 1 October 1997, no similar qualification applied to removals under subsection (3). The managers were therefore able to remove a restricted patient from one hospital under their management to another without the Home Secretary's consent.[119] This lacuna has now been rectified.

CRIME (SENTENCES) ACT 1997

Prior to 1 October 1997, the legal position was that the Home Secretary's consent was not required before a restricted patient was granted ground parole; moved to an open ward within the same hospital; or removed from one hospital to another under the same statutory management (including, possibly, a community ward). However,

---

[116]   Mental Health Act 1983, ss.19(1) and (2), 41(3)(c), 145(3); Sched. 1, Pt. II, paras. 2, 5.

[117]   Parts VIII–X of the Act do not incorporate the definition given to "hospital" by section 34(2). The definition of a hospital in section 145(1), which excludes mental nursing homes ("private hospitals") therefore applies for the purposes of section 123, unless the context requires a different meaning. If the definition in section 145(1) does apply, the Secretary of State may not, under section 123, direct the transfer of a special hospital patient to a mental nursing home. It may be difficult to argue that the context requires another meaning since various other provisions in Parts VIII–X specifically refer to both hospitals and mental nursing homes. For example, sections 120 (Mental Health Act Commission), 127 (ill-treatment of patients), 131 (informal admission), 132 (duty to give information to detained patients), 133 (duty to inform nearest relative of discharge), and 135 (definition of a place of safety) refer to "hospitals" and "mental nursing homes." On the other hand, sections 117 (after-care) and 122 (pocket money for in-patients) are also expressed to apply only to hospitals, rather than to hospitals and mental nursing homes.

[118]   Section 19(3) provides that a patient who is for the time being liable to be detained may at any time be removed to any other hospital or accommodation which is managed by the same managers. Upon the patient's removal, the hospital order made by the court is deemed to have directed the patient's admission to the hospital to which he has been removed.

[119]   Section 41(3) and Part II of Schedule 1 to the Act provide that section 19 applies in relation to a restricted patient subject to the exclusions and modifications in the Schedule, neither of which related to subsection 19(3) until the Crime (Sentences) Act 1997 modified the position. Section 19(3) therefore applied in full.

the Crime (Sentences) Act 1997 enables the Home Secretary to exert greater control in some of these areas—

- The Home Secretary's consent is now required before a patient may be removed from one hospital to another hospital under the same managers.[120]

- Provided that restrictions are attached, a hospital order, section 47 transfer direction, or hospital direction, may specify the hospital unit to which the patient is to be admitted. For example, secure unit x at hospital y.[121] In this context, a "hospital unit" is "any part of a hospital which is treated as a separate unit."[122] Where a particular hospital unit is specified, any reference in the 1983 Act to a hospital — for example, in sections 17(1) and 19(3) — is to be construed accordingly. In such cases, the effect will be that the Home Secretary's consent is required before a patient who is to be detained in a specific unit may lawfully be taken, or allowed, outside that building or unit or be removed under section 19(3) to an open ward on the same site.

- However, at least initially, most restricted in-patients will not be detained in pursuance of an order or direction which specifies a particular unit. The new provisions do not prevent the managers moving these patients between a locked unit and an open ward within the *same* hospital, or granting them ground parole, without the Home Secretary's consent.

---

[120] Mental Health Act 1983, s.41(3)(c), Sched. 1, Pt. II, para. 5, as amended by Crime (Sentences) Act 1997, s.49(2) and 49(3). As amended, section 41(3)(c) reads, "the following powers shall be exercisable only with the consent of the Secretary of State, namely— ... (iii) power to transfer the patient in pursuance of regulations under section 19 above *or in pursuance of subsection (3) of that section.*"

[121] Crime (Sentences) Act 1997, s.47.

[122] Crime (Sentences) Act 1997, s.47(3). A medium secure unit located away from the main building in part of the hospital grounds is clearly treated as a separate unit, as is any specialist psychiatric intensive care unit located in the main hospital building. Whether one of several open wards can be said to be part of a hospital which is treated as a separate unit is less clear. All wards are separate units in the sense that they are self-contained and separate from the other wards. If this is the correct sense, the Home Secretary's leave will be required before a patient admitted to a specific open ward in pursuance of such an order or direction may lawfully leave, or be allowed to leave, the designated ward (for example, to go to the hospital shop or have ground parole) or be removed to another open ward within the same hospital. The alternative view is that the word "unit" denotes a separate building (as in the phrase "industrial unit") or a self-contained and separately-staffed facility which provides a specialised service for a particular class of patients (as in the phrase "intensive care unit"). The provision is not designed for patients who are considered suitable for admission to an open ward. In support of this argument, it may be argued that: (1) Parliament could not have intended that the Home Secretary's leave should be necessary before a patient on an open ward may attend the occupational therapy unit, ECT suite, hospital psychology department, and so on. Such a provision would interfere with the treatment programme, when what treatment is given in a hospital, and when, is a matter for the responsible medical officer; (2) Similarly, Parliament did not intend that the management of open wards within the same hospital should be restricted. (3) Such an interpretation is supported by an examination of the equivalent provisions in the Crime and Punishment (Scotland) Act 1997. Section 9 of that Act is, insofar as material, identical to section 47 of the Crime (Sentences) Act 1997. However, in Scotland, the Mental Welfare Commission must be notified of compulsory admissions to hospital (**170**) and section 62(2) of the Mental Health (Scotland) Act 1984, as inserted by section 7(1) of the Crime and Punishment (Scotland) Act 1997, provides as follows: "62.— (2) Where the managers of a hospital specified in a hospital direction propose to admit the patient to a hospital unit in that hospital, they shall, if that unit was not so specified, notify the Secretary of State and the Mental Welfare Commission of the patient's proposed admission to and detention in that unit; and the patient shall not be so admitted unless the Secretary of State has consented to the proposed admission." That suggests that an ordinary ward is not a hospital unit.

Limits of the Secretary of State's powers

By way of summary, the Secretary of State may direct the transfer or removal of a restricted or unrestricted patient who is detained in a special hospital but he has no power to direct the transfer of a patient who is liable to be detained in a hospital which is not a special hospital. In such cases, his power is limited to either consenting to or refusing to consent to any proposed transfer. Furthermore, unless the order or direction specified a particular hospital unit, provided that the patient remains within the grounds of the hospital where he is liable to be detained, he is not absent from that hospital, either with or without leave. Consequently, moving him from a locked ward to an open ward within the hospital, or granting him permission to spend time in the hospital grounds, whether with or without an escort ("ground parole), does not require the Secretary of State's consent.[123]

RESTRICTIONS ON TRANSFER INTO GUARDIANSHIP

A restricted patient may not be transferred into guardianship, with or without the Secretary of State's consent.[124]

RESTRICTIONS ON DISCHARGE FROM HOSPITAL

Where a patient is detained under a hospital order and a restriction order is in force, the Secretary of State or a Mental Health Review Tribunal may discharge him from hospital, either absolutely or subject to conditions.[125] This power to discharge a patient from hospital subject to conditions, and without discharging the hospital order itself, is unique to cases involving restricted patients. A restricted patient who has been conditionally discharged from hospital may be recalled to hospital at any time during the period for which the restriction order remains in force.[126]

Absolute discharge from hospital

Either the Secretary of State or a Mental Health Review Tribunal may absolutely discharge a patient who is detained under a hospital order with a restriction order

---

[123] The legal status of community wards is an interesting variation on the theme that the Home Secretary's consent is not required before a patient may be moved to another ward within the same hospital. A tribunal may not discharge a patient whom it considers should be moved to a hospital "community ward" situated away from the main institution in the local town. Because the legal status of such accommodation is that it forms part of the hospital, as much as if it were a ward within the main hospital grounds, such a direction necessarily rests on a finding that the patient requires a further period of in-patient treatment. Hence, the tribunal cannot possibly have been satisfied that the patient meets the statutory criteria for being discharged from hospital: *Secretary of State for the Home Department v. Mental Health Review Tribunal for Mersey Regional Health Authority Same v. Mental Health Review Tribunal for Wales* [1986] 1 W.L.R. 1170. However, this suggests that the Secretary of State's consent may not be required if the responsible medical officer wishes to move the patient to such accommodation, because the move does not involve (a) discharging him; (b) transferring him to another hospital; or (c) granting him leave to be absent from hospital. The Secretary of State may argue that the community ward constitutes a different hospital for these purposes so that the patient is being removed under section 19(3), since this now requires the Home Secretary's consent. Alternatively, it is possible that a court would hold that taking up residence at the ward in the community involves the patient leaving the hospital in order to undertake the journey between the two sites. Hence the Secretary of State's consent is required, because the patient requires section 17 leave to be absent from hospital for whatever time it takes him to complete the journey. See p.135.

[124] Mental Health Act 1983, ss.41(3), 40(4),145(3); Sched. 1, Pt. II, paras. 2 and 5(a).

[125] *Ibid.*, ss.42 and 73.

[126] *Ibid.*, s.42(3).

attached. Where a patient is absolutely discharged from hospital, he ceases to be liable to be detained under the relevant hospital order and the restriction order, being parasitic in nature, also ceases to have effect.[127]

Absolute discharge by a tribunal

A tribunal must absolutely discharge a patient from hospital if satisfied as to the matters specified in section 73(1) of the Act. Equally, it may not absolutely discharge a patient unless satisfied as to those matters. It has no discretion either way (**512**).

Absolute discharge by warrant of the Secretary of State

Section 42(2) provides that the Secretary of State may, if he thinks fit, by warrant absolutely discharge from hospital a restricted patient who is detained there under a hospital order. In contrast to the power of absolute discharge exercisable by a tribunal, the issue of a warrant of absolute discharge is a matter for the Secretary of State's discretion: the Act does not impose any statutory criteria by reference to which his decision is to be made.

Orders for discharge under section 23

In the case of unrestricted patients, the responsible medical officer or the managers may make an order for discharge under section 23, the effect of which is that the patient ceases to be liable to be detained under the hospital order.[128] Where a restriction order is in force, no such order may be made except with the Secretary of State's consent.[129] If the Secretary of State gives consent then, because a restriction order is parasitic in nature, discharging the hospital order has the effect of also bringing the restriction order to an end. Consequently, such an order is equivalent to a direction for the patient's absolute discharge.

Conditional discharge

Either the Secretary of State or a Mental Health Review Tribunal may direct the conditional discharge of a restricted patient who is detained under a hospital order. Where a patient is discharged from hospital subject to conditions, both the hospital order and the restriction order continue in force and the patient may by warrant be recalled to hospital by the Secretary of State at any time (**345**).[130]

Conditional discharge by a tribunal

A tribunal must conditionally discharge a patient from hospital if satisfied as to the matters specified in section 73(2) of the Act. Equally, it may not conditionally discharge a patient from hospital unless it is satisfied as to these matters. As in the

---

[127] Mental Health Act 1983, ss.42(2) and 73(3).
[128] The nearest relative has no power of discharge and the reference in section 23(1) to section 25 (and, indeed, in section 23(3) to applications for admission for assessment) is therefore a drafting error. In the case of restricted patients who are detained in a mental nursing home, the Secretary of State may himself discharge the patient under section 23 (as an alternative to discharging him under section 42) and certain other persons may also do so with his consent; namely, any health authority or NHS trust which has contracted with the mental nursing home for the patient to be treated there.
[129] Mental Health Act 1983, ss.23(1) and 2(a), 41(3) and 41(3)(c)(iii); Sched. 1, Pt. II, para. 7(b).
[130] *Ibid., s.42(3).*

case of absolute discharge, it has no discretion either way (**511**). Liability to recall is by inference a condition of the discharge and it is not necessary as a matter of law to impose any express conditions.[131]

Conditional discharge by warrant of the Secretary of State

Section 42(2) provides that the Secretary of State may, if he thinks fit, by warrant conditionally discharge from hospital a restricted patient who is detained there under a hospital order. As in the case of absolute discharge, the issue is again a matter for the Secretary of State's discretion and the Act does not impose any statutory criteria by reference to which his decision is to be made.

The conditions of discharge and their variation

Section 73(5) provides that the Secretary of State may, following a patient's conditional discharge by a tribunal, subsequently vary any of the conditions attached by the tribunal to the discharge or impose further conditions. In contrast, section 42 does not expressly provide that where the Secretary of State himself directs the patient's conditional discharge he may later vary those conditions or impose further conditions, whether more onerous or not. Although the drafting is imprecise, this may be inferred from section 73 and the general framework of the Act. Unless such an inference is drawn, patients would have to be recalled to hospital each time their conditions required variation, whereas the Act envisages a gradual relaxation of the conditions in cases where a patient settles in the community without incident and moves towards absolute discharge. Furthermore, taking any other view means that where problems are reported by a patient's supervisors the Secretary of State may only recall or not recall, even if the difficulties could adequately be dealt with by a temporary tightening of the conditions of his discharge.

Cessation of the special restrictions

It has been noted that an absolute discharge has the effect not only of discharging the patient from hospital but also of bringing to an end both the hospital order under which he was liable to be detained there and the attendant restriction order, which is incapable of independent existence. However, the option of absolute discharge is only available if the patient is ready to be discharged from hospital. A mechanism is therefore required which enables the restriction order to be brought to an end on other occasions, whether prior to a patient's discharge from hospital or following his conditional discharge from hospital.

Cessation of restrictions prior to discharge

Section 42(1) provides that if the Secretary of State is satisfied that a restriction order is no longer required to protect of the public from serious harm, he may direct that the patient shall cease to be subject to the special restrictions, in which case the restriction order ceases to have effect. Such a direction does not *per se* discharge the relevant hospital order. However, the Act provides that, where such a direction is given, the patient shall be treated as if he had been admitted to the hospital where he is liable to be detained in pursuance of a second, notional, hospital order made

---

[131] Mental Health Act 1983, s.73(4)(b). Notwithstanding the absence of the words "(if any)" from section 42(2), it is submitted that, for the same reason, the Secretary of State is not obliged as a matter of law to impose express conditions of discharge.

without restrictions on the date when the restrictions ceased to have effect. It may be noted that where a tribunal does not discharge a restricted patient from hospital, it does not have this option of directing that he shall no longer be subject to the special restrictions.

Conditionally discharged patients

Where the Secretary of State gives a direction under section 42(1) in respect of a conditionally discharged patient, the patient is deemed to have been absolutely discharged on the date when the restriction order ceases to have effect. Accordingly, he ceases to be liable to be detained under the relevant hospital order. In the case of conditionally discharged patients, a tribunal also has power to give such a direction. Section 75(3)(b) provides that where a tribunal considers the case of a patient who has been conditionally discharged, it may direct that the restriction order shall cease to have effect. Where such a direction is given, the Act provides that the patient shall also cease to be liable to be detained under the relevant hospital order.

Expiration of restriction order of limited duration

Where a restriction order is made for a limited period, it will (with one exception) cease to have effect at the expiration of the period specified by the court. The effect of the period's expiration depends upon the patient's legal status at that time. In essence, the position is identical to that where the Secretary of State gives a direction under section 42 that restrictions imposed without limit of time shall cease to have effect.

Patients detained in hospital

Where, at the time the restriction order expires, the patient is detained in hospital in pursuance of the hospital order, he is treated as if he had been admitted there under a notional hospital order made, without restrictions, on the date when the restriction order ceased to have effect.[132]

Conditionally discharged patients

Where a patient has been conditionally discharged prior to the expiration of the period for which the order was imposed, and no warrant of recall is outstanding, the patient is deemed to be absolutely discharged.[133] Where a warrant of recall is outstanding at the expiration of the period specified by the court, because the patient is still absent without leave from the hospital specified in that warrant, the period of the restriction order continues until the patient eventually returns or is returned to the hospital. Upon his return, the restriction order expires and the patient is deemed to have been admitted to the hospital specified in the warrant under a notional hospital order made, without restrictions, on the date of his return to the hospital.[134]

Summary of discharge powers

The different ways in which a restriction order and the hospital order to which it is attached, may cease to have effect are summarised in the following table.

---

[132] Mental Health Act 1983, s.41(5).
[133] *Ibid.*, ss.42(5), 73(8).
[134] *Ibid.*, s.42(3)(b).

DISCHARGE OF RESTRICTION ORDER PATIENTS : SUMMARY

Order, direction or event	Effect
• Direction of Secretary of State that the special restrictions shall cease to have effect made in respect of a patient who is liable to be detained in hospital. • Expiration of a limited-term restriction order in respect of a patient who at the time is liable to be detained in hospital.	The restriction order ceases to have effect but the patient remains liable to be detained under the relevant hospital order. However, the Act provides that the patient shall be deemed to have been admitted under a hospital order without restrictions made on the date the restriction order came to an end.
• Direction of Secretary of State or a Mental Health Review Tribunal that a detained patient shall be conditionally discharged from hospital.	Both the hospital order and the restriction order remain in force. The patient remains liable to be detained under the hospital order and may be recalled to hospital by the Secretary of State.
• Direction of Secretary of State or a Mental Health Review Tribunal that a detained patient shall be absolutely discharged from hospital. • Order for discharge under section 23. • Direction of Secretary of State or a Mental Health Review Tribunal that the special restrictions shall cease to have effect in respect of a patient who has been conditionally discharged. • Expiration of a limited-term restriction order after a patient has been conditionally discharged from hospital.	Both the hospital order and the restriction order cease to have effect.

TRANSFERS OF CONDITIONALLY DISCHARGED PATIENTS

Section 48(1) of the Crime (Sentences) Act 1997 was brought into force on 1 October 1997. It provides that responsibility for a conditionally discharged patient in Northern Ireland or Scotland may be transferred to the Home Secretary, and vice-versa. Conditionally discharged patients transferred to England or Wales are deemed to have been conditionally discharged by the Home Secretary or by a Mental Health Review Tribunal on the date of their transfer. Accordingly, the patient must wait a further year before he may apply to a Mental Health Review Tribunal. If the restriction order or direction is of limited duration, it expires on the date on which it would have expired had the patient not been transferred.

Crime (Sentences) Act 1997

Section 48(1) provides that the Mental Health Act 1983 and the Mental Health (Scotland) Act 1984 shall have effect subject to amendments in Schedule 3 to the 1997 Act concerning transfers within the British Islands of responsibility for conditionally discharged patients.

Transfers to Scotland and Northern Ireland

- Sections 80A and 81A of the 1983 Act are concerned with the transfer of conditionally discharged patients to Scotland and Northern Ireland respectively. A patient so transferred is treated as if he were subject to a restriction order, and as if he had been conditionally discharged, under the corresponding provisions in the Mental Health (Scotland) Act 1984 or the Mental Health (Northern Ireland) Order 1986, as the case may be.[135]

Transfers to England and Wales

- Section 82A provides that if it appears to the relevant Minister that it would be in the interests of a conditionally discharged patient who is subject to a restriction order or restriction direction under Article 47(1) or 55(1) of the Mental Health (Northern Ireland) Order 1986 to transfer him under that section, that Minister may, with the consent of the Home Secretary, transfer responsibility for him to the Secretary of State.

- Section 77A of the Mental Health (Scotland) Act 1984 similarly provides that if it appears to the Secretary of State for Scotland that it would be in the interests of a conditionally discharged patient subject to a restriction order under section 59 of the Criminal Procedure (Scotland) Act 1995 to transfer him under that section, the Secretary of State may, with the consent of the Home Secretary, transfer responsibility for him to the latter.

- Where responsibility for such a patient is transferred, he is to be treated as if he were subject to a restriction order or restriction direction under section 41 or 49 and as if he had been conditionally discharged under section 42 or 73 on the date of the transfer. The restriction order or direction will, if of limited duration, expire on the date on which it would have expired had the transfer not been made.

---

[135] Mental Health Act 1983, ss.80A and 81A, as inserted by Crime Sentences Act 1997, Sched. 3, Pt. I, paras. 1 and 2.

While a restriction order remains in force, the Secretary of State may at any time by warrant recall the patient to such hospital as may be specified in the warrant.[136] A conditionally discharged patient remains liable to detention in this limited sense.[137] Upon a warrant being issued, the hospital order and the restriction order have effect as if the hospital specified in the warrant were substituted for that specified in the hospital order.[138] Pending his admission to the named hospital, the patient is to be treated as absent from there without leave.[139] Section 18 applies, with the modification that the patient does not cease to be liable to be taken into custody after he has been absent for a certain length of time.[140] He may at any time be taken into custody and conveyed to the named hospital by any approved social worker, by any officer on the staff of the named hospital, by any constable, or by any person authorised in writing by the managers of the named hospital.[141] If it appears to a justice of the peace that there is reasonable cause to believe that the patient is to be found on private premises within the jurisdiction of the justice, and that admission to the premises has been refused, or that a refusal is apprehended, he may issue a warrant authorising any constable to enter those premises (if need be by force) and to remove the patient.[142]

Home Office policy concerning the recall of patients

The Home Office requires psychiatric and social supervisors to submit quarterly or six-monthly reports on the patient's mental state and ability to cope, although supervisors must also notify the Home Office of any worrying developments as soon as they occur. The Home Office's policy concerning the recall of restricted patients has been summarised by Pickersgill[143]—

- When a psychiatrist or social supervisor notifies the Home Office of problems, account is taken of any representations and supporting evidence which suggests that the patient should not be compulsorily recalled to hospital. However, while wishing to avoid any possibility of over-reacting and unnecessarily depriving a patient of his freedom, the Home Office always gives paramount consideration to the public's safety and he will exercise his power of recall whenever there is an element of doubt.

---

[136] Section 42(3) provides that, "The Secretary of State may at any time during the continuance in force of a restriction order ... by warrant recall the patient to such hospital as may be specified in the warrant." Section 73(4)(a) provides that where a patient is conditionally discharged by a tribunal under that section, "he may be recalled by the Secretary of State under subsection (3) of section 42 above as if he had been conditionally discharged under subsection (2) of that section."

[137] The phrase "liable to be detained" is used elsewhere in the Act to denote a patient who has leave to be absent from hospital under section 17 but who has not yet been discharged from hospital. Conditionally discharged restricted patients remain "liable to be detained" under the relevant hospital order in the more limited sense that, although discharged, the hospital order remains in force.

[138] Mental Health Act 1983, s.42(4)(a).

[139] *Ibid.*, s.42(4)(b).

[140] *Ibid.*, ss.18(1), 41(3) and 41(3)(d); Sched. 1, Pt. II, para. 4.

[141] *Ibid.*, s.18(1).

[142] *Ibid.*, s.135(2). Although the Home Office has been known to advise social workers that it is not necessary to first obtain a warrant before entering and searching private premises where it is suspected that an absent restricted patient is staying, the section 135 procedure applies to restricted and unrestricted patients alike.

[143] A. Pickersgill, "Balancing the public and private interests" in *Risk-taking in Mental Disorder: Analyses, Policies and Practical Strategies* (ed. D. Carson, S.L.E. Publications, 1990).

- If the patient is engaging in odd or anti-social behaviour inside or outside his home, such as threatening violence, exposing himself, or acting in a way similar to that prior to the index offence, he will normally be recalled to hospital, whether or not his supervisors advocate such action.

- Patients who come to the Home Office's attention only when they have been charged with re-offending are usually left in the community or in prison to be tried and sentenced.[144] Exceptions may be made where the patient is on bail and shows signs of committing further offences as the result of his mental state.

- There are a number of occasions when measures falling short of recall can be taken. Warning letters can be used where a patient has not kept appointments with his supervisors or is showing signs of resuming heavy drinking which played a part in his index offence. Consent may be given to the patient's readmission to hospital as an informal patient (**365**).

The exercise of the power to recall

As can be seen from the table below, patients discharged by a tribunal are more likely to be reconvicted during the following two years. However, this probably reflects the fact that the Home Secretary has, since 1984, left it to tribunals to decide whether to discharge in borderline cases, declining to do so himself. Bearing this in mind, it does not appear that the Secretary of State is more likely to recall patients whom a tribunal has discharged.

Number of conditionally discharged patients recalled and/or convicted								
Period	No. discharged		% RECALLED		% CONVICTED WITHIN 2 YEARS OF			
			within 2 years		A grave offence		Any standard list offence	
	MHRT	*SofS*	*MHRT*	*SofS*	*MHRT*	*SofS*	*MHRT*	*SofS*
1975–77	—	402	—	10.0%	—	1.7%	—	14.9%
1978–80	—	373	—	8.0%	—	2.1%	—	17.7%
1981–83	—	336	—	3.9%	—	2.7%	—	13.4%
1984–86	237	138	18.6%	13.0%	2.1%	1.5%	14.4%	8.0%
1987–89	173	142	12.1%	12.7%	1.2%	0%	5.8%	0.7%

Source: Home Office Statistical Bulletin (Home Office, 1994), Issue 18/94.

---

[144] For an example of this, see *R. v. Trent Mental Health Review Tribunal., ex p. Ryan* [1992] C.O.D. 157, D.C.

Constraints on the Secretary of State's power of recall

In *R. v. Secretary of State for the Home Department, ex p. K.*,[145] McCowan L.J. dealt with the breadth of the Secretary of State's power to recall a restricted patient to hospital—

> "Counsel for the appellant submitted that if the section is given this literal interpretation the Secretary of State would be provided with an unbridled power at his whim and without cause to deprive a conditionally discharged patient of his liberty. That is only so, however, if one ignores the public law constraints recognised by the decisions in *Associated Provincial Picture Houses Ltd. v. Wednesbury Corp.*[146] and *Padfield v. Ministry of Agriculture Fisheries and Food.*[147]

> Counsel for the appellant argues that, even if the convention cannot assist him, Padfield 's case should. The discretion given to the Secretary of State by s.42(3) can only be used to promote the policy and objects of the Act, which are, according to his submission, that persons should not be deprived of their liberty unless they are shown, on the basis of objective medical evidence, to be suffering from mental disorder of such a degree as to warrant their compulsory confinement. In our judgment, that defines the policy and objects of the Act on far too narrow a basis. We prefer the view of McCullough J.[148] ... : These are to regulate the circumstances in which the liberty of persons who are mentally disordered may be restricted and, where there is conflict, to balance their interests against those of public safety."

The Wednesbury and Padfield cases

The principles which derive from the *Wednesbury* case are that, subject to complying with the law, the discretion of a body to whom a discretion is entrusted by statute is absolute. However, it must be a real exercise of the discretion: the body must have regard to matters to which it is expressly or by implication referred by the statute conferring the discretion; it must ignore irrelevant considerations; it must not operate on the basis of bad faith or dishonestly; it must direct itself properly in law; it must act as any reasonable person would act and must not be so absurd in its actions that no reasonable person would act in that way.[149] According to *Padfield's case*, which concerned the Milk Marketing Board,[150]

> "Parliament must have conferred the discretion with the intention that it shall be used to promote the policy and objects of the Act; the policy and objects of the Act must be determined by construing the Act as a whole and construction is always a matter of law for the Court. In a matter of this kind it is not possible to draw a hard and fast line, but if the Minister, by reason of having misconstrued the Act or for any other reason, so uses his discretion, as to thwart or run counter to the policy and objects of the Act, then our law would be very defective if persons aggrieved were not entitled to the protection of the Court."

---

[145] *R. v. Secretary of State for the Home Department, ex p. K.* [1991] 1 Q.B. 270, C.A.
[146] *Associated Provincial Picture Houses v. Wednesbury Corporation* [1948] 1 K.B. 223.
[147] *Padfield v. Ministry of Agriculture Fisheries and Food* [1968] A.C. 997.
[148] *R. v. Secretary of State for the Home Department, ex p. K.* [1990] 1 W.L.R. 168 at 174.
[149] *Associated Provincial Picture Houses v. Wednesbury Corporation*, supra., at 228. See K. Bagnall Q.C., *Judicial review* (Profex, 1985), p.12.
[150] *Padfield v Ministry of Agriculture Fisheries and Food*, supra., at 1030.

The need for a material change of circumstances and medical evidence

Whether the Home Secretary must have medical evidence that the mental state of a patient conditionally discharged by a tribunal has subsequently deteriorated before he may recall him to hospital was considered in *ex p. K*. The Court of Appeal held that Parliament's intention was that the Secretary of State should, at any time during the continuance of a restriction order, be empowered in his discretion to recall a restricted patient to hospital. More particularly, there is no requirement in section 42 that the Secretary of State may not recall a patient unless he has medical evidence that the patient is suffering from mental disorder. The exercise of the power of recall is simply subject to the ordinary public law constraints recognised by the decisions in *Associated Provincial Picture Houses Ltd v. Wednesbury Corp. [1948] 1 K.B. 223* and *Padfield v. Ministry of Agriculture Fisheries and Food [1968] A.C. 997*.

Ex p. K.

According to McCullough J., in the Divisional Court, it would be unlawful for the Secretary of State to recall a patient who had been discharged the previous week by a tribunal in the absence of some fresh development: it does not matter whether one castigates such an action as irrational, illegal, or as frustrating the objects and policy of the Act. Nor would it be a proper exercise of the power of recall if the Secretary of State realised that the patient's condition was such that he would be released when his case was considered by a tribunal. However, it is, in general, sufficient that he has reason to believe that the patient's condition is such that, after recall, he might not be released by a tribunal considering his case under section 75(1). Despite a lack of medical evidence of any subsequent change in a patient's mental condition since his discharge by a tribunal, it is open to the Secretary of State to take, and act upon, the view held by him of the patient's mental state, provided he does so in a way which is consistent with the purposes of the Act.

R. v. Secretary of State for the Home Department, ex p. K.

[1990] 1 W.L.R. 168   *Q.B.D., McCullough J.*

In January 1971, the patient was convicted of the manslaughter of a neighbour's 12-year-old daughter. Her condition when found indicated that she had been raped, asphyxiated, cut with a sharp instrument and bitten. The patient had been before the courts on 11 previous occasions and had previous convictions for rape, indecently assaulting a girl aged seven, and having sexual intercourse with a girl aged between 13 and 16. He had only been out of prison for some six weeks before committing the index offence. The court was satisfied that he was suffering from a psychopathic disorder and it directed his admission to a special hospital in pursuance of a hospital order and a restriction order made without limit of time. The patient was transferred to a different special hospital in November 1981. In March 1985, a tribunal reviewed his case. A special hospital consultant gave evidence that in his opinion the patient was not a danger to himself or others and the chief psychologist there said that he was now functioning at a normal level. An experienced nursing officer well acquainted with the patient said that he would "welcome him as a next door neighbour." Given the unanimous medical evidence that the patient was not presently suffering from any form of mental disorder, but taking the view that it was appropriate for him to remain liable to recall, the tribunal conditionally discharged him from hospital.

Events following conditional discharge

In October 1985, some seven months after being discharged, the patient made an unprovoked attack on a girl of 16 whom he saw walking along a road in the afternoon. He put both hands round her throat and applied some pressure but she managed to run off. The next night, at about 11.30 pm, he attacked a young woman of 21. After speaking to her, he held her neck in an arm lock and put his hand over her mouth, pulling her into an entry and then pushing her to a crouching position. She pretended to weaken and, as he began to let her go, she screamed and he ran off. On being interviewed, the patient said only that he did not know why he had done it. A sexual motive for each assault was suspected but could not be proved. The patient's supervising psychiatrist and probation officer had not been aware of any signs of the impending violence. Subsequently, in April 1986, the patient pleading guilty in each case to assault occasioning actual bodily harm. He was described in court by his leading counsel as "so disturbed mentally that he cannot control the impulses from which he suffers." A special hospital medical report concluded that he had a severe personality disorder, probably with some psycho-sexual involvement, and an alcohol problem. However, this could not be equated with a psychopathic disorder which either needed or would respond to treatment. In the doctor's opinion, he was not suffering from a mental disorder as defined by section 1 of the 1983 Act. A disposal under Part III of the Act was therefore impossible. Having considered the medical and other evidence, the judge sentenced the patient to a total of six years imprisonment, describing him as "a very dangerous man ... in particular to young girls and young women." The patient remained conditionally discharged, notwithstanding that he was serving a sentence of imprisonment, and in 1986 he reapplied to the tribunal, again seeking his absolute discharge from the hospital and restriction orders. At the hearing in December 1986, the Home Secretary emphasised the importance of the restrictions, in that they enabled the patient to be recalled to hospital at the expiration of his current sentence, or subsequently, should that be deemed necessary in the interests of public safety. The medical evidence before the tribunal was again unanimously of the view that the patient was not suffering from any form of mental disorder. The tribunal accepted this evidence but, as before, also considered it appropriate for him to remain liable to be recalled. In particular, supervision would still be required after his release from prison and it was necessary to test his behaviour in the community before it would be appropriate to absolutely discharge him.

The issue of a warrant of recall

The patient's his earliest date of release was 24 October 1989 and, on 1 September 1989, with the prospect of release approaching, the Secretary of State issued a warrant authorising the patient's detention in a special hospital upon his release from prison. A letter of the same date informed the patient of the decision and the reasons for it: "The Home Secretary, having considered the nature of your further offences of assault occasioning actual bodily harm and wounding, of which you were convicted on 14 April 1986, has concluded that he cannot be satisfied that you no longer present a serious risk to public safety, and he has therefore authorised your recall to [a particular special hospital] under section 42(3) of the Mental Health Act 1983 when your prison sentence expires on 24 October 1989." The Secretary of State issued the warrant without seeking any further expert medical opinion. However, he had never at any time agreed with the medical opinion that the patient was not suffering from a psychopathic disorder and was of the opinion that his grave misgivings on this point had been fully confirmed by the two offences following the patient's conditional discharge.

The application for judicial review

The applicant applied for judicial review by way of (1) an order of certiorari to quash the warrant of recall dated 1 September 1989 and (2) an order of prohibition restraining the Secretary of State from so recalling him. He contended (1) that it was to be implied that the Secretary of State could only exercise his power to recall a patient to hospital on the recommendation of a medical practitioner and (2) that the Secretary of State could not exercise his power of recall in circumstances where a Mental Health Review Tribunal was obliged to order his conditional discharge because he was not suffering from any mental disorder. McCullough J. heard the application on 23 October 1989, the day before the appellant was due to be released from prison. Unless a lawful warrant of recall could be issued in the circumstances, the patient would return to the community on the following day.

McCullough J.

Although it had been contended that, because any exercise of the power of recall under section 42(3) led to a deprivation of liberty, therefore any doubt about its scope should be resolved so as to give effect to the right to liberty, that principle could only come into play if it was first apparent that there was a doubt. On its face, section 42(3) required only a patient who had been conditionally discharged and in respect of whom a restriction order was in force. Other than what might be called the ordinary public law constraints recognised by the decisions in *Associated Provincial Picture Houses Ltd v. Wednesbury Corporation [1948] 1 KB 223* and *Padfield v. Ministry of Agriculture Fisheries and Food [1968] AC 997,* the Secretary of State's discretion appeared to be unfettered. If any further restriction could be implied, it could only derive from a consideration of the Act as a whole. The policy and objects of the Act were to regulate the circumstances in which the liberty of persons who are mentally disordered may be restricted and, where there is conflict, to balance their interests against those of public safety. In relation to persons who were under sentence and subject to restrictions, Parliament had cast on the Secretary of State, and in many instances on him alone, the direct responsibility for taking decisions in each individual case. None of the Home Secretary's powers in section 41 and 42 were expressed to be exercisable only if their use had been recommended by one or more doctors. Indeed, the power of recall might sometimes need to be exercised very quickly. It was therefore clear that Parliament advisedly left the Secretary of State's power of recall uncircumscribed by the need to act on medical opinion. In requiring the Secretary of State to refer the case to a tribunal within one month of the patient's recall, rather than sooner or later, Parliament was striking a balance and intended to enable the Secretary of State to act under section 42(3) without medical evidence if he saw fit. This point also disposed of the applicant's reliance on a passage in the judgment of the European Court of Human Rights in *Winterwerp v. The Netherlands* (1979) 2 E.H.R.R. 387, 403 about the need for objective medical expertise before a person could be deprived of his liberty on the basis of unsoundness of mind. It was clear that the Secretary of State believed that the applicant presented a danger to the public and that it could not safely be said that he was no longer suffering from psychopathic disorder. His belief about the applicant's mental condition was not unreasoned. The reports which were before the tribunal of 18 December 1986 were, in the view of the Secretary of State, unsatisfactory in a number of respects. For example, one report concluded that "I do not feel that, if seen *a priori* without his previous hospitalisation history, any psychiatrist would take the view that he was psychopathically disordered within the meaning of the Act of 1983 or would attempt to admit him to hospital for treatment." Why, one might ask, should one express a view without regard to his previous hospitalisation history? The opinion of the Secretary of State as to the question of psychopathic disorder was based on reason and one did not have to be a doctor to evaluate the worth of reports which had such features. Judges, for example, had to do it all the time. So, in the exercise of a number of his functions, did the Home Secretary. Further, the confidence of the responsible medical officer and of all the others who predicted that the applicant could safely be released from hospital in March 1985 had been shown to have been misplaced, a factor which must case doubt on their overall judgment.

Limitations of Secretary of State's power

It was not entirely right to submit that the Secretary of State had power under section 42(3) to order a recall in circumstances in which a tribunal would be obliged to order the patient's conditional discharge. He could not properly exercise his power of recall if he realised that the patient's condition was such that, when his case was considered by a tribunal, he would be released. However, it was, in general, enough that the Secretary of State had reason to believe that the patient's condition was such that, after recall, he might not be released by a tribunal considering his case under section 75(1). That is, he believed the patient was or might well be mentally disordered and that, for the protection of others, he should be in hospital for treatment. If that was his state of mind then he acted in conformity with the purposes and intendment of the Act and his decision could only be open to challenge on the usual Wednesbury grounds. Thus, adopting the wording of section 73, he could, in general, properly recall if, with reason, he feared (i) that the patient was suffering from mental disorder to an extent which made it appropriate for him to be liable to be detained in a hospital for medical treatment; and (ii) that it was necessary for his own health and safety or for the protection of others that he should receive such treatment. "In general" because the observation was subject to a qualification which represented the only point which had caused His Lordship any real difficulty. This was the extent to which a tribunal's decision to conditionally discharge a restricted patient subsequently bound the Secretary of State. The point had been most tellingly made by the patient's counsel when he asked if it could be lawful for the Secretary of State, a week after a patient had been conditionally discharged by a tribunal, to exercise his power of recall in the absence of some fresh development. The answer was plainly not. It did not matter whether one castigated such an action as irrational, or illegal, or as frustrating the objects and policy of the Act. According to the patient's counsel, this was what has happened here since there was no evidence that the patient's condition has deteriorated; indeed there was no evidence about it at all. There were, no doubt, occasions when the Secretary of State had to act with speed under section 42(3) but this was not one of them. For years the applicant has been safely in prison. What the Secretary of State was in fact doing was overturning a decision with which he did not agree. His views were put to the tribunal on that occasion and they were rejected. He did not like the result so he was going to frustrate it by what could only be regarded as a misuse of section 42(3). The submission had more than a hint of *res judicata* in it and it was useful to see what was in fact decided in December 1986. The tribunal was constituted because the patient, who had earlier been discharged conditionally, wanted to be discharged absolutely. The issue in December 1986 had been confined to the issue of whether the patient should remain liable to recall and nothing was decided at that hearing which procured his conditional release. That was procured by the earlier decision of 19 March 1985 since when the events of October 1985 had occurred. Thus, insofar as considerations of *res judicata* might apply in the field (on which no submissions had been made and the court expressed no opinion), there was nothing in the tribunal's decisions to prevent

351

the Secretary of State from alleging that further events had occurred since March 1985 which had a bearing on the question of the patient's mental condition — namely the attacks of October 1985. Despite the lack of evidence of any subsequent change in the patient's mental condition, it was open to the Secretary of State to take and act upon the view held by him provided he did so in a way consistent with the purposes of the Act. It would, however, be unlawful for the Secretary of State to recall a restricted patient to hospital when only the previous week or month he had been conditionally discharged from hospital by direction of a tribunal, unless meanwhile something has happened which justified the belief that a different view might now be taken about one of the factors on which his release had depended. But that was not the situation here. The hypothetical situation would frustrate the purposes of the Act but the present one did not. The essential factual difference between December 1986 and September 1989 was that in December 1986 there was no imminent prospect of the applicant coming into contact with members of the public, in particular young females; now there was. That was why the Secretary of State did not then act but now did. In terms of the application of the Wednesbury criteria [1948] KB 223, 229, it was important for the court to remember that the Secretary of State, before exercising his power under section 42(3), must give full weight to the fact that his decision will affect the liberty of the person recalled, but his interests were not the only ones for the Secretary of State to consider. *Application dismissed.*

The Appeal

K appealed against the decision of McCullough dismissing his application for judicial review and the case was therefore considered by the Court of Appeal.

R. v. Secretary of State for the Home Department, ex p. K.

[1991] 1 Q.B. 270   *C.A. (Slade, Balcombe and McCowan L.JJ.)*

As to the facts of the case and the decision in the Divisional Court, see p.348.

McCowan L.J.

The words of section 42(3) being plain and unambiguous, it was clear from the decision in *R. v. Secretary of State for the Home Department, ex p. Brind [1990] 2 W.L.R. 787* that it was not open to courts in this country to look to the European Convention on Human Rights for assistance in their interpretation. There was no requirement in section 42 that the Secretary of State could not by warrant recall a patient unless he had medical evidence that the patient was suffering from mental disorder. The submission that a literal interpretation of the subsection gave the Secretary of State an unbridled power, at his whim and without cause, to deprive a conditionally discharged patient of his liberty was only so if one ignored the public law constraints recognised by the decisions in *Associated Provincial Picture Houses Ltd v. Wednesbury Corp. [1948] 1 K.B. 223* and *Padfield v. Ministry of Agriculture Fisheries and Food [1968] A.C. 997.* As to Padfield's case, the policy and objects were as stated by McCullough J. in the Divisional Court. There were many powers in the 1983 Act which could not be exercised except on the recommendation of one or more doctors. It was therefore no accident or omission on the part of the legislature that section 42(3) did not require that, before exercising his power of recall, the Secretary of State first be satisfied by medical evidence that the patient was suffering from mental illness, etc. The clear intention was that the Secretary of State should be empowered, at any time during the continuance of a restriction order, in his discretion to recall a patient to hospital. In exercising that discretion, the Secretary of State would no doubt find it necessary to balance the interests of the patient against those of public safety. The intention of the 1983 Act was that the interests of the patient shall be safeguarded by the provision in section 75(1) that, within one month of the patient being returned to hospital, the Secretary of State must refer his case to a tribunal. For all these reasons, counsel for the appellant had failed to persuade the court that the Secretary of State had acted contrary to *Padfield* principles.

Whether the Home Secretary's decision had been irrational

It was furthermore not factually correct that the Secretary of State had addressed his mind only to the aspect of public safety and not also to the appellant's mental condition. This was clear from his letter of 1 September. Nor could it be said that the Secretary of State's decision to recall the appellant was Wednesbury unreasonable because there had been no change of circumstances since the decision of the tribunal in December 1986; he had no medical evidence that the appellant was now suffering from any mental disorder; and, if he had had any doubts, the only proper course had been to ask the appellant to subject himself to another psychiatric examination prior to his release. Against these arguments, it was necessary to weigh, *inter alia*, the appellant's record of offences of violence against women prior to the index offence; the nature of the index offence and the manner in which it was dealt with by the court; the diagnosis that the appellant was suffering from psychopathic disorder between 1970 and 1985; his commission of two further serious offences of violence to women six months after his release from hospital; what was said by the appellant's counsel in mitigation on 14 April 1986; the unsatisfactory nature of the responsible medical officer's report before the tribunal on 18 December 1986; the fact that no tribunal had seen fit to discharge the appellant absolutely, because they thought there was a danger of him suffering a relapse; that nearly three years had passed since a tribunal last looked at the case, during which time he had been in prison; that the best method of coming to an up-to-date conclusion on his mental state and the possible danger to the public would be by another reference to a tribunal; and that the Secretary of State believed that such a tribunal might well conclude that the appellant was suffering from psychopathic disorder. Taking account of all those factors, it was impossible to say that the Secretary of State's decision had been irrational. *Appeal dismissed.*

Whether patient must have breached a condition of his discharge

The case of *Roux v. United Kingdom*,[151] which is presently before the European Court of Human Rights, raises the issue of whether a restricted patient who has not breached a condition of his discharge may be recalled to hospital by the Secretary of State. The patient was conditionally discharged by a tribunal, subject to conditions that he submit to supervision, accept any psychological treatment considered necessary, and reside at an address approved by his supervisors. He left hospital on 11 April 1994. His behaviour from that time until the issue of a warrant of recall on 25 May gave the Home Secretary and his medical supervisors cause for concern: he returned to his sheltered accommodation in a drunken and distressed state on the first night; described himself as suicidal on 16 April and was informally admitted to

---

[151] *Roux v. United Kingdom* (App. No. 25601/94), European Commission First Chamber Decision as to admissibility, 4 September 1996.

a psychiatric clinic the next day; allegedly brought a prostitute back to his flat and argued with her about money; and was exceeding the agreed levels of alcohol intake. There was particular concern that he was beginning to repeat the pattern of behaviour prior to the commission of his two offences against prostitutes and the medical opinion was that he should be recalled because his mental state was likely to deteriorate if he remained at the flat.

The complaints

The patient complained that his recall was in breach of Article 5, because there was no non-compliance with a court order and no breach of an obligation prescribed by law. In particular, he should not have been recalled as he had not breached any condition of his discharge and no court had determined the state of his mental health at the time. The Government submitted that the Secretary of State's power of recall was not limited by the conditions attached to release and there could be occasions where recall was appropriate even though no conditions had been breached. Conversely, some breaches of the conditions of discharge from hospital would not warrant recall to hospital. The Commission unanimously declared the patient's application admissible, without prejudging the merits of the case.

Domestic law

As a matter of domestic law, it must be correct that it is not a precondition of recall that a patient is in breach of one or more of the conditions of his discharge. Firstly, it was held in *R. v. Secretary of State for the Home Department, ex p. K.* [1991] 1 Q.B. 270 that Parliament's intention was that the Secretary of State should, at any time during the continuance of a restriction order, be empowered in his discretion to recall a restricted patient to hospital. Secondly, a patient may be conditionally discharged but no express conditions be imposed on his discharge: nevertheless, the patient remains liable to recall (**535**). Thirdly, a patient's recall may be justified if his mental state has deteriorated, although this does not involve any breach of a condition attached to his discharge. Fourthly, it is also the case that there will generally be grounds for recall if the patient has reoffended, although being of good behaviour is never an express condition of discharge. If the complaint is upheld, the consequence is likely to be merely that the Home Secretary will attach ever more numerous conditions to each and every discharge, to the benefit of no one.

Whether patient may be recalled to hospital where he already is

Whether a conditionally discharged patient may be recalled to a hospital to which he has already been readmitted informally or under Part II of the Act was considered in *ex p. D.* It was held that the fact that a patient is already receiving in-patient treatment in a hospital, and is liable to detention there under some other provision of the Act, does not prevent the Home Secretary from issuing a warrant under section 42(3), formally recalling him to that hospital. A warrant under section 42(3) authorises *both* the patient's compulsory readmission and detention *and* the reinstatement of the regime of control under section 41. The purpose of the Secretary of State authorising the patient's recall is so that he may resume the restrictive powers which he seeks to exercise over that patient. In short, the word "recall" should not be regarded in purely physical terms but should be viewed as reinstating the restrictive regime of control under section 41. The judgment is commented on below (**365**).

R. v. Secretary of State for the Home Department and another, ex p. D.

The Times, 1 April 1996   *Q.B.D., Hidden J.*

The patient was subject to a restriction order. In October 1993, a tribunal directed that he be conditionally discharged. He left the unit on 22 March 1994 and moved to a hospital in Brighton (*sic.*). On 10 January 1995, his condition deteriorated and he was readmitted to the regional secure unit under section 3. On 5 May, a warrant was issued by the Secretary of State, recalling him to that unit under section 42(3). The authority to detain the patient conferred by the section 3 application was not renewed in July. In November 1995, a tribunal reviewed the patient's case but did not direct his discharge from hospital.

The application for habeas corpus

The patient applied for an order of habeas corpus on the ground that the warrant of recall had been issued without jurisdiction. The question to be determined by the court was whether the Secretary of State could recall a patient to a hospital where he already was and where he was already receiving treatment. Counsel for the patient submitted that the words "recall the patient to ... hospital" had to be given their ordinary and natural meaning, which meant that the power could only be exercised if the patient was not a patient in that hospital.

Hidden J.

Section 42(4) made it clear that the hospital mentioned in the warrant might be either the hospital from which the patient had been conditionally discharged or any other hospital. The word "recall" meant "order to return, call back, permanently or temporarily." Nothing in the Act prevented the issue of such a warrant in respect of a person who was present at the relevant hospital but without there being in existence any hospital order and restriction order in relation to that hospital. The argument forwarded on the patient's behalf would mean that the hospital to which the patient was recalled could not be the hospital where he was being treated and happened to be. *Application refused.*

D. v. Mental Health Review Tribunal for the South Thames Region

The Times, 10 May 1996   *C.A. (Sir Thomas Bingham M.R., Ward and Evans L.JJ.)*

Sir Thomas Bingham M.R.

The most obvious meaning of "recall" was to authorise the bringing back of someone to where he once was. However, Parliament could not have intended the provisions to have the limited and narrow effect contended by the patient's counsel. A warrant under section 42(3) authorised both the compulsory readmission and detention of the patient *and* the reinstatement of the regime of control under section 41. That was the purpose of the Secretary of State authorising the recall, so that he could resume the restrictive powers which he sought to exercise over that patient. It would be absurd if the effect of a section 3 admission was to deny the Secretary of State powers which he might well wish to exercise pursuant to section 41. It would further be absurd if he could only exercise those powers if the patient were ceremonially allowed to leave one hospital in order that the warrant could be properly issued. It would also be absurd if the fact that he was in one hospital justified his recall to any hospital other than that hospital, not least because if he were recalled to any other hospital he could then be transferred to that hospital. *Appeal dismissed.*

The use of Part II or informal admission in preference to formal recall

The fact that *D.* was not recalled until he had been detained in hospital under Part II for some four months seems to have been accepted by the court as a valid exercise of the Home Secretary's discretion. Certainly, the Secretary of State sometimes agrees to restricted patients being admitted informally, or under section 2 or 3, as an alternative to formal recall under section 42. Similarly, on being notified that a conditionally discharged patient has been readmitted informally or under Part II, he may not always immediately recall the patient. At the same time, the Secretary of State has contended that a patient readmitted to hospital under section 2 or 3 cannot then apply to a tribunal for his discharge from hospital. This is because section 41(3)(b) provides that "no application shall be made to a Mental Health Review Tribunal in respect of a (restricted) patient under section 66 or 69(1) below." Having been informed of the Secretary of State's view, some tribunals have therefore refused to consider applications made by such patients on the basis that they are not applications authorised by the Act. All of these issues were later considered in the case of *ex p. Stewart*. It was held in the Divisional Court that Parts II and III of the Act can operate independently and in parallel; that a restricted patient readmitted to hospital under section 3 has the same rights to apply to a tribunal as any other section 3 patient; that because a restricted patient detained under section 3 is also liable to detention under the relevant hospital order, the Home Secretary may subsequently recall him to hospital under section 42(3), for example if he is discharged by a tribunal from liability to detention there under section 3. That decision was subsequently affirmed by the Court of Appeal.

R. v. Managers of the N.W. London Mental Health NHS Trust, ex p. Stewart

CO/1825/95, 19 July 1996   *Q.B.D., Harrison J.*

The patient was subject to a hospital order and a restriction order made without limit of time. He was conditionally discharged by a tribunal in July 1993. The psychiatrist in charge of his treatment was of the opinion that he required a short readmission to hospital and that recalling him under section 42 would result in an unnecessarily protracted stay in hospital. Following consultation with the relevant officer at the Home Office, the patient was readmitted to hospital under section 3 on 1 June 1995 and then released from hospital on 15 June.

The application for judicial review

The patient sought an order of certiorari, quashing the trust's decision to detain him in hospital pursuant to section 3. He also sought four declarations. Firstly, a declaration that there was no power under section 3 to detain a conditionally discharged restricted patient. Secondly, a declaration that the patient's detention by the trust was unlawful. Thirdly, a declaration that the *Notes for the Guidance of Supervising Psychiatrists*, issued by the Home Office and the Department of Health, were erroneous in law insofar as they advised that conditionally discharged restricted patients could lawfully be detained under section 3.[152] Fourthly, a declaration that the *Code of Practice*, published by the Department

---

[152]   Paragraph 49 of the *Notes of Guidance* provided that a supervising psychiatrist could decide to take immediate local action to admit a conditionally discharged patient to hospital for a short period, either with the patient's consent or using civil powers such as those under section 3. However, according to the Notes, it was generally inappropriate for such a patient to remain in hospital for more than a short time under civil powers of detention, and the Home Secretary would usually wish to consider issuing a warrant of recall if the period of in-patient treatment seemed likely to be protracted.

of Health pursuant to section 118 of the 1983 Act, was erroneous in law insofar as it contained identical advice.[153] The patient also claimed damages for false imprisonment, but it was agreed that this claim should be adjourned pending a decision as to the legality of his detention. The Secretary of State for the Home Department and the Secretary of State for Health were later joined as second and third respondents.

The patient's submissions

It was contended on the patient's behalf that the continued liability of a restricted patient to detention under the relevant hospital order was one of the special restrictions imposed by section 41(3)(a). That continuing liability necessarily excluded authority to detain him under any other statutory provision. The whole statutory scheme was founded on the basis of one source of liability to detention and the Part II and III regimes were mutually exclusive. This was clear for a number of reasons:

- In the first place, section 41(3)(a) provided that none of the Part II provisions concerning the duration, renewal and expiration of the authority for a patient's detention applied to restricted patients: such language was incompatible with the use of section 3.

- Secondly, sections 40(4) and 41(3) provided that a patient subject to a restriction order was to be treated for the purposes of the statutory provisions mentioned in Part II of Schedule 1 as if he had been admitted in pursuance of a section 3 application, subject to any modifications referred to in the Schedule. Treating a restricted patient *as if he had been* detained under section 3, in order to bring in a modified Part II regime applicable to such patients, would be unnecessary *if he had actually been* detained under section 3. Furthermore, the omission of any reference to section 3 in the Schedule 1 list of Part II provisions which applied to restricted patients in an unmodified form necessarily implied an intention to exclude the operation of section 3 in respect of a restricted patient.

- Thirdly, a conditionally discharged restricted patient could only apply to a tribunal under section 75 and that section only contemplated readmission to hospital by way of recall. That the intention was that restricted patients requiring in-patient treatment would be recalled was borne out by section 41(3)(b). That paragraph prohibited a restricted patient from applying to a tribunal under section 66. Furthermore, section 72(7) provided that a tribunal's usual section 72(1) powers in respect of section 2 and 3 patients did not apply in the case of restricted patients.

- Fourthly, if a conditionally discharged patient could be detained under section 3, the Secretary of State's control over such patients would be reduced, because the responsible medical officer could discharge the patient from hospital under section 23 without the Secretary of State's consent.

- Fifthly, it was a condition of admission under section 3 that the treatment could not be provided unless the patient was detained under that section. That indicated that Parliament had not intended section 3 to be used in such cases, because any necessary in-patient treatment could be provided by recalling the patient to hospital under section 42(3).

---

[153] The *Code of Practice* provided that, if a conditionally discharged restricted patient required hospital admission, it would not always be necessary for the Home Secretary to recall him to hospital; in some cases, it might be appropriate to consider admitting him under Part II.

- Sixthly, any ambiguity should be resolved in favour of the liberty of the subject and in a manner consistent with the European Convention on Human Rights. The statute should not be interpreted so as to deprive a restricted patient readmitted under section 3 of the right to apply to a tribunal under section 66.

The trust's submissions

On the trust's behalf, it was contended that there could be more than one source of liability to detention and the Part II powers could be exercised independently of those in Part III of the Act. More particularly—

- There was nothing in section 41(3) which expressly excluded the application of section 3 and the absence of any reference to section 3 in schedule 1 showed that section 3 was intended to operate independently from the exercise of Part III powers. A restriction order and a section 3 application had different and quite distinct purposes. The former was imposed to protect the public from serious harm, the latter made for essentially therapeutic purposes, when treatment was required for a patient's health or safety. That being so, it was questionable whether the Secretary of State could properly recall a conditionally discharged restricted patient if the public was not at risk of serious harm from him, for instance where he was suicidally depressed.

- As drafted, the exceptions and modifications referred to in Schedule 1 only applied to a patient admitted "in pursuance of a hospital order," not to a patient subject to a hospital order who was admitted to hospital in pursuance of some other authority, such as a section 3 application. Accordingly, the restrictions in section 41(3) had no application if a restricted patient who was liable to be detained in pursuance of a hospital order was in fact detained in pursuance of an application made under section 3: he was not being detained and treated in a hospital *as a* restricted patient. Consequently, the restriction in section 41(3)(b) concerning the making of a tribunal application under section 66 did not apply.

- The case of *D. v. Mental Health Review Tribunal for the South Thames Region* (355) involved a conditionally discharged patient detained in hospital under section 3 who was then recalled to that hospital by the Secretary of State. Although the question of whether his detention under section 3 was lawful was not canvassed, it provided an example of how the two regimes could operate independently, resulting in that case in the patient's detention under two separate powers.

- Where only a short admission was necessary, a more protracted admission, resulting from bureaucratic delay in obtaining the patient's further discharge, was not in his interests. The patient's interpretation would, for no good reason, frustrate the purpose of the Act by depriving doctors and conditionally discharged patients of the use of Part II powers.

Submissions of amicus curiae (instructed by the Treasury Solicitor)

There was presently a case before the European Commission for Human Rights in which the Government was arguing that the section 3 power did co-exist with the Part III powers, while conceding that a restricted patient had no right to a tribunal unless and until recalled. The Department's opinion was that, unless such a patient was recalled, there would appear to be a breach of Article 5(4) of the European convention on Human Rights. Counsel disagreed with that view. Section 41(3)(b), which disapplied section 66, only applied to a patient in his capacity as a restricted patient. Section 72(7) similarly only applied to a patient who was detained and appearing before a tribunal in his capacity as a restricted patient. The right of access to the tribunal for Part II patients under section 66 remained available. The Part II and Part III regimes were perfectly capable of coexisting independently of each other and they had different purposes. If a conditionally discharged patient became depressed and suicidal then a civil admission under section 3, for his own health or safety, would be appropriate, rather than recall to hospital as a restricted patient, the purpose of which was to protect the public from serious harm.

Harrison J.

The main issue was whether a conditionally discharged patient could lawfully be detained under section 3. There was no authority on the point but it had hitherto been common practice in appropriate cases to admit and detain such patients under that section. That practice has been endorsed by the Home Office and the Department of Health in the *Notes for Guidance* and *Code of Practice*. The rival contentions were whether, as the patient contended, the two parts of the Act were mutually exclusive or whether, as the trust contended, they could operate independently of each other.

Absence of any express prohibition

- Had Parliament intended that the exercise of Part III powers excluded the operation of the Part II powers, it might be assumed that the legislation would have expressly so provided. However, the statute did not expressly exclude the operation of Part II in the case of a restricted patient. It was therefore necessary to consider whether it was excluded by necessary implication, having regard to the various statutory provisions.

Sections 40(4) and 41(3)

- There was nothing in the language of section 41(3) to negate the trust's submission that the special restrictions set out there applied to a restricted patient only insofar as he was detained or liable to be detained in pursuance of the relevant hospital order. In other words, they applied to him *qua* restricted patient. That did not in itself exclude a liability to be detention under the separate power in, and for different purposes of, section 3.

- The wording of section 40(4), which applied Schedule 1, referred to a patient admitted to hospital "in pursuance of a hospital order." That made it clear that the section and the Schedule were not intended to relate to a person who was admitted to hospital under some other power, for instance under section 3. There was therefore nothing in section 40(4) or Schedule 1 which was inconsistent with the independent operation of the Part II or Part III regimes.

Tribunal applications

- It would be inconsistent to conclude that the Part II and Part III regimes could co-exist and operate independently and yet also hold that, if a conditionally discharged patient was admitted under section 3, the effect of the restriction order was to deprive him of his right as a section 3 patient to apply to a tribunal under section 66. Once the restriction set out in section

41(3)(b) was understood as referring only to the patient in his capacity as a restricted patient readmitted under the relevant hospital order, it had no impact on him in respect of any detention pursuant to the separate power of detention conferred by section 3.

- The purpose served by section 72(7) was simply to make it clear that a tribunal's powers under section 72(1) did not apply to a restricted patient who was detained pursuant to the relevant hospital order and who applied to the tribunal under section 70. There were, however, two separate routes to a tribunal. The route for a person detained under section 3 was via section 66 and section 72. In contrast, the route for a restricted patient detained under the hospital order was via sections 70 and 73, and via section 75 for a conditionally discharged restricted patient.

Purpose of the Part II and III powers and their parallel operation

- A restriction order was imposed because the court had decided that it was "necessary for the protection of the public from serious harm" that the special restrictions in section 41(3) should apply to the patient, having regard to the nature of his offence, his antecedents, and the risk of him committing further offences. Although the Secretary of State was not bound to direct that a restriction order cease to have effect when it was no longer required for the protection of the public from serious harm, and he also had a wide discretionary power when deciding whether to recall a conditionally discharged patient, the primary purpose of the exercise of the recall power was to protect the public from serious harm, because that was the whole purpose of making the restriction order in the first place.

- Admission under section 3 did not arise out of criminal proceedings. Admission and detention for treatment under that section had to be necessary for the health or safety of the patient or for the protection of other persons, while in the case of a restriction order it must be necessary for the protection of the public from serious harm.

- If it was necessary to compulsorily readmit a conditionally discharged patient in the interests of his own health or safety, and not for the protection of the public from serious harm, it would be appropriate to detain him under section 3 rather than to recall him. Although it was not necessary to decide the point, it was doubtful whether there would be power to recall a conditionally discharged restricted patient in those circumstances: the primary purpose of any recall should be to protect the public from serious harm from the conditionally discharged restricted patient.

- The contention that a restricted patient could not properly be admitted under section 3, because any necessary in-patient treatment could be provided without detaining him under that section, by recalling him under section 42(3), was not convincing. If the phrase "and it (such treatment) cannot be provided unless he is detained under this section (section 3)" had any significance, it did no more than make clear that the patient's admission and detention was for the purposes there specified. Those purposes would include detaining a patient whose detention was not needed to protect the public from serious harm but necessary solely for his own health or safety. The patient's admission and detention under that section might also be necessary "for the protection of other persons" without other persons being at any risk of serious harm from the patient and without the public at large being at risk, serious or not.

- The potential length of detention arising from delay obtaining a patient's discharge following recall was not a good reason for admitting a patient under section 3 rather than recalling him under section 42(3). Admission under section 3 should comply with the statutory purposes specified in section 3(2)(c) — the necessity to detain the patient for his own health and safety or the protection of others, rather than the protection of the general public from serious harm.

- The parallel operation of Part II and Part III powers was illustrated in the Court of Appeal case of *D. v. Mental Health Review Tribunal for the South Thames Region*. The then Master of the Rolls had proceeded on the implicit assumption that the two powers could co-exist. The facts of that case provided a good example of how the two regimes could co-exist and operate independently of each other, and the court had been told that no practical difficulties had arisen as a result of their dual operation.

- It was appropriate and desirable that the section 3 power should be available as well as the recall power under Part III. Parliament could not have intended to deprive a patient who needed treatment solely for his own health or safety of treatment by admission under section 3 simply because he had been convicted of an imprisonable criminal offence which resulted in him being subject to a restriction order. If he were discharged by the tribunal, it would be a discharge in relation to his liability to detention under section 3 which would in no way affect the Secretary of State's powers to recall him as a restricted patient.[154]

Decision

The various relevant statutory provisions did not demonstrate an intention on the part of the legislature to exclude the application of section 3 in respect of a conditionally discharged patient. Nor were they ambiguous so as to dictate an interpretation in favour of the liberty of the subject. Moreover, the conclusion reached did not involve the patient being deprived of his right to apply to a tribunal under section 66, so that the question of a breach of the Convention did not arise. *Application dismissed with costs. Leave to appeal allowed.*

R. v. Managers of the NW London Mental Health NHS Trust, ex p. Stewart

CO/1825/95, 25 July 1997   *C.A. (The President, Schiemann and Saville L.JJ.)*

The patient appealed on the following ground: "The learned Judge was wrong in law in holding that the Applicant could lawfully be detained pursuant to the said Section 3, notwithstanding that, at the time of his detention pursuant to the said Section 3, as a conditionally discharged restricted patient he remained liable to be detained pursuant to Sections 37 and 41 of The Mental Health Act 1983." In addition to the submissions made before the Divisional Court, the patient's counsel also relied on section 56(1), which provides that the consent to treatment provisions in Part IV apply "to any patient liable to be detained under this Act except ... (c) a patient who has been conditionally discharged ... and has not been recalled to hospital." Part IV therefore applied to section 3 patients,

---

[154] The Home Secretary's power to recall the patient might, of course, not be available in a particular case if the prior observation, that it is doubtful whether a conditionally discharged patient may be recalled unless the public are at risk, is correct. And, if section 3 is only appropriate and recall inappropriate where it is the patient's health or safety which is in issue, this would seem to mean that the Home Secretary may often not be empowered to recall a section 3 restricted patient discharged by a tribunal.

who could be subjected to compulsory treatment, but not to conditionally discharged patients, who could not be treated compulsorily. The distinction drawn there clearly indicated that the civil admission and restricted patient recall provisions were incompatible and intended to be kept distinct.

The President

The patient's case, which was that Parts II and III were mutually exclusive, with the effect that a conditionally discharged patient could not be readmitted to hospital otherwise than by way of recall under section 42, would necessarily fail if those parts were in fact capable of operating independently. On 24 April 1996 the Court of Appeal, presided over by Sir Thomas Bingham M.R., had given judgment in the case of *D. v. Mental Health Review Tribunal for the South Thames Region*. The issue there was whether, given that the patient was already in hospital, a warrant for his recall to the same hospital could properly be issued. It was noteworthy that the lawfulness of his initial admission under section 3 was not raised or queried, despite the fact that the court gave detailed consideration to the relevant provisions of Parts II and II. It was also noteworthy that both the *Code of Practice* and the Home Office's *Notes for the Guidance of Supervising Psychiatrists* sanctioned the practice of readmitting restricted patients under Part II and that guidance had been in force for some years without having previously been challenged. In the Divisional Court, the learned judge had held that nothing in any section of the Act was inconsistent with the independent operation of the Part II admission and Part III recall regimes. He had further held that a conditionally discharged patient detained under section 3 had a right to apply to a tribunal under section 66. A restricted patient recalled under section 42 was liable to more stringent restrictions than was the case following detention under section 3. As the guidance indicated that it might be convenient and in the patient's interests not to resurrect the full stringency of recall in certain cases, the flexibility given to the supervising psychiatrist was something which could operate both in the patient's interests and in the public's interests. That the Secretary of State retained his power of recall following readmission to hospital under Part II had been confirmed by the Court of Appeal in *D. v. Mental Health Review Tribunal for the South Thames Region*. Having reviewed the statutory provisions in great detail, in the context of the submissions made, Harrison J. had come to the clear conclusion that the powers provided by Part II could be invoked in the case of a conditionally discharged restricted patient. He said:

> "I accept the argument ... that the Part II and Part III powers can co-exist and operate independently of each other. The provisions relating to restricted patients relied upon by the applicant are, in my view, dealing solely with patients in their capacity as restricted patients liable to be detained pursuant to a hospital order, a capacity which is not applicable to the power of admission and detention under section 3. That power is not excluded by the provisions of Part III and the rights of a patient detained under that power exist, including those of access to the tribunal under section 66 whether or not he happens also to be a conditionally discharged restricted patient. If he were discharged by the tribunal it would be a discharge in relation to his liability to detention under section 3 which would in no way affect the Secretary of State's powers to recall him as a restricted patient. Such a conclusion ensures that patients and those treating them can take advantage of the benefits of treatment for the purposes mentioned in section 3(2)(c)."

His Lordship agreed with that conclusion and would accordingly dismiss the appeal.

Schiemann L.J.

The provisions in sections 40(4) and 41(3) did not *expressly* prevent an application being made under Part II in respect of a conditionally discharged patient and there was no advantage to anyone in holding that the subsections implicitly inhibited their use. Parliament had seen fit to make the use of the powers in Part II available in respect of individuals who had not been convicted of any crime and there was no need to inhibit their use in respect of individuals who has been convicted and were subject to orders made under sections 37 and 41.

The construction advanced on the patient's behalf would be productive of considerable harm in certain circumstances. For example, a doctor examining a person who was evidently severely mentally ill and a danger to himself or others would need to establish whether that person was subject to a conditional discharge before he could determine whether his admission to hospital under Part II would be lawful. That information might not be easily obtainable if the patient was unco-operative. If the patient was in fact subject to restrictions and the doctor proceeded he would be acting illegally. While the decision in *Re S-C (mental patient: habeas corpus)* [1996] 1 All E.R. 532 might mitigate the consequences of the illegality, it hardly dealt with the substantive point.

Lastly, even if it was correct that section 56(1)(c) made it impossible to lawfully treat a conditionally discharged patient without his consent unless and until he was recalled — and it was not necessary to decide the point — the only consequence would be that the recall procedures needed to be activated prior to treatment. That fact would not prevent the patient's detention in the meanwhile. *Saville L.J. agreed with both judgments. Appeal dismissed.*

The European Convention

Counsel as amicus in the case of *ex p. Stewart* referred to a case before the European Court of Human Rights, in which the Government was arguing that a restricted patient could be readmitted to hospital under section 3 and, if so, had no right to a tribunal unless and until recalled. The Department's opinion was said to be that, unless such a patient was recalled, there would appear to be a breach of Article 5(4) of the European Convention on Human Rights.[155] The case referred to is that of *Pauline Lines v. United Kingdom*. On 17 January 1997, the Government was still maintaining its position, notwithstanding Harrison J.'s judgment in *ex p. Stewart,* and what was there expressed to be the Department's view as to the requirements of the European Convention. The Government nevertheless indicated to the European Commission that guidance was being issued to psychiatrists requesting them not to use their powers under section 3 in respect of conditionally discharged patients: they should instead put in train the formal recall procedure, so as to ensure an early tribunal review. The European Commission unanimously declared admissible the patient's complaint that she was deprived of a tribunal by virtue of the fact that she was readmitted to hospital under section 3, rather than formally recalled.

---

[155] Article 5(4) provides that, "Everyone who is deprived of his liberty by .. detention shall be entitled to take proceedings by which the lawfulness of his detention shall be decided speedily by a court and his release ordered if his detention is not lawful."

App. No. 24519/94, 17 January 1997   *European Commission of Human Rights*[156]

The patient was detained as if subject to a hospital order and a restriction order made without limit of time. She was conditionally discharged by the Secretary of State on 30 June 1993 but, following a suicide attempt, was readmitted to hospital under section 3 on 27 July 1993. Reports on her condition and progress were received by the Home Office on 28 August 1993, 6 October 1993 (by telephone) and 18 November 1993. She was formally recalled to hospital by the Secretary of State on 3 December 1993, on the ground that her condition had not sufficiently improved to make her return to the community likely in the immediate future. On 7 December 1993, the Secretary of State referred the case to a tribunal, which heard the matter on 23 February 1994. The tribunal found that she continued to suffer from mental illness requiring detention in hospital for medical treatment, and continued to present a danger to herself and the public, and did not direct her discharge.

The complaints

The patient complained, *firstly*, that she was not entitled to apply to a tribunal whilst detained under section 3 and, *secondly*, about the length of time it took for her to have a review following admission, in both cases contrary to Article 5(4) of the Convention. The formal recall procedure would not necessarily have been any more complex or slower than the section 3 procedure, and it would have accorded the patient an entitlement to a tribunal review prior to 3 December 1993. The conduct of reviews by health professionals and Home Office officials could not constitute a "court" within the meaning of Article 5(4). Furthermore, the review which did eventually take place was not speedy, since it took place seven months after her compulsory admission to hospital in July 1993. What the tribunal subsequently decided was irrelevant: the fact that a person might not be discharged when her case was reviewed had no bearing on her entitlement to a speedy and independent review.

The Government's submissions

The Government indicated that section 3 was used to readmit some restricted patients in order to allow health professionals to retain control over the patient's treatment and thereby facilitate a possible early discharge. Use of the formal recall procedure could leave the patient with a sense of failure and delay that person's early discharge. A conditionally discharged patient readmitted to hospital under section 3, rather than by warrant of recall, was not entitled to apply for a tribunal review, because section 41(3)(b) of the 1983 Act deprived her of the rights of application granted to other section 3 patients by section 66(1). This deliberate distinction between the rights of patients liable to be detained under Parts II and III of the Act was one which the Government wished to maintain.[157] Following an admission under section 3, the case was reviewed monthly and, as soon as it became apparent that discharge might not be imminent, the patient was formally recalled and the case referred to a

---

[156]   First Chamber Decision as to admissibility.

[157]   The Government has never specified why it wishes to maintain this distinction. The reason why the Home Office has encouraged readmission under section 3 has generally been interpreted by patients as deriving from its insistence that such patients have no right to a tribunal. Furthermore, the corollary is that the responsible medical officer may not exercise his usual powers to discharge a section 3 patient or to grant him leave without the Home Secretary's consent. In other words, the distinction enables the Home Secretary to circumvent the decision in *X. v. United Kingdom* — which gave recalled patients a right to a tribunal —and to maintain absolute control over the issue of when the patient is discharged. The expectation is that the Home Secretary will now revert to the recall procedure if readmission under section 3 no longer has this advantage.

tribunal. The Home Office's policy was to recall restricted patients readmitted to hospital under section 3 well within the six month period during which an unrestricted patient detained under that provision was entitled to a tribunal review, and as soon as it was clear that their detention would be of significant duration. There was no violation of Article 5(4) provided that such a patient's case was referred to a tribunal within that six month period. The Government nevertheless recognised that it was undesirable for patients to be deprived of their entitlement to a review in such circumstances, even if the motives were good. Accordingly, guidance was being issued to psychiatrists requesting them not to use their powers under section 3 in respect of conditionally discharged patients. They should instead put in train the formal recall procedure, so as to ensure an early tribunal review. In the present case, the patient had not been immediately recalled because of evidence that her condition was likely to lead to imminent discharge. Article 5(4) had not been violated because the patient's case had been kept under constant review by both health professionals and Home Office officials. Her right to apply for a review was only deferred because it was hoped that her discharge was imminent and the formal recall procedure could be avoided. Furthermore, the patient had suffered no detriment because the tribunal subsequently found that her continued detention was necessary. Her review was speedy in that it was determined seven months after the commencement of her detention and the delay was not caused by any desire to prolong her detention, but rather to facilitate her early discharge.

The Commission's findings

The patient's period of detention between 27 July 1993 and 23 February 1994 raised serious issues under Article 5(4) which required determination on their merits. These complaints could not be dismissed as manifestly ill-founded and no other ground for declaring them inadmissible had been established. *The Commission therefore unanimously declared admissible, without prejudging the merits, the patient's complaints about the lack of entitlement to take proceedings by which the lawfulness of her detention after 27 July 1993 could be decided speedily by a court.*

Commentary

The decisions in *D. v. Mental Health Review Tribunal for the South Thames Region, ex p. Stewart*, and *Lines v. United Kingdom* do not conclusively resolve all of the issues raised in those cases. This is because the judgment of the European Court of Human Rights is still awaited. It is important to separate out the three questions of whether a restricted patient may be readmitted to hospital under Part II; whether the Home Secretary is obliged to recall a restricted patient upon being notified that he is in hospital; and whether a conditionally discharged patient detained under Part II may apply to a tribunal. As far as the domestic law is concerned, the effect of the cases is that a conditionally discharged patient may be readmitted under Part II; that the Home Secretary is not obliged to recall that patient upon being notified that he is receiving in-patient treatment; that a conditionally discharged patient detained under Part II has the same rights of application as other patients detained under the same provision. However, Harrison J.'s observations concerning the third question would appear to be *obiter* because the declarations sought concerned the lawfulness of the patient's detention. At the same time they are a necessary consequence of the declarations made and it is therefore puzzling that the Government has pursued its argument before the European Commission that such a patient has no right to apply to a tribunal. Because the issues have not all been finally resolved, it is worthwhile summarising some additional arguments concerning them.

The decisions in *D.* and *ex p. Stewart* are particular interesting because of the absence of any reference to the earlier decision in *Home Department v. Mental Health Review Tribunal for Mersey Regional Health Authority* (**516**). In that case, the court held that the word "discharge" in the context of restricted patients means release from hospital, a release which could be absolute or conditional. Accordingly, it is not possible to discharge a patient from hospital subject to a condition that he resides there: a patient cannot both be in hospital and discharged from hospital. More particularly, the fact that a tribunal is satisfied that a patient requires in-patient treatment means that it cannot also be satisfied that he meets the criteria for being discharged from hospital. The argument that discharge means merely discharge from liability to detention in hospital under the relevant hospital order (and the accompanying restrictions on leave, transfer, and so forth) was one rejected in the *Mersey case.* If a restricted patient cannot be both a discharged patient and an in-patient, it might be thought that this distinction must also apply when a discharged patient returns to hospital. Allowing the patient to reside there as an informal in-patient, or to be detained there under the ordinary civil procedures, is incompatible with his existing legal status as a discharged patient: he becomes a discharged in-patient. The underlying rationale is that the in-patient –discharge–recall regime set out in sections 42 and 73 is simple and exhaustive and, in the absence of some express provision to the contrary, should not be complicated unnecessarily by incorporating additional civil powers.

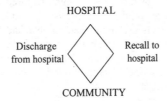

HOSPITAL

Discharge from hospital   Recall to hospital

COMMUNITY

As Part III of the Act and section 73 make clear, restricted patients always remain liable to be detained in hospital until formally discharged from there. Their status can only be one of two things — (1) that of an in-patient liable to be detained and subject to restrictions on discharge, transfer and leave; (2) that of a patient in the community following discharge who is subject to conditions and recall. The usual third possibility in unrestricted cases of being an informal or unrestricted in-patient is not an option: the purpose of the restrictions being to restrict the operation of the usual provisions concerning leave, transfer and discharge from hospital during periods when the mental state of certain patients — those from whom the Crown Court was satisfied the public are at risk of serious harm when unwell — is of a sufficiently serious nature or degree as to require them to be in hospital. That is the purpose of providing that the restrictions remain in force following conditional discharge. Until such time as the Secretary of State or a tribunal is satisfied that the public no longer need the protection of these special restrictions, decisions about whether or not the patient may be absent from hospital, or be transferred to a less secure hospital, or be discharged, are not decisions which can ever be made by his consultant or by the hospital's managers acting alone (**520**). To summarise, the Secretary of State has a discretion about whether to recall to hospital a patient who is in the community (section 42 says that he "may" issue a warrant of recall). However, if his opinion is that further in-patient treatment is appropriate, or he is notified that the patient has been taken to hospital in an emergency, he must recall the patient. He cannot deal with a restricted in-patient's case on the factual basis that he remains a discharged patient. In particular, it would be unlawful to vary the patient's condition of residence to one of residence in hospital. Accordingly, the Home Secretary has a discretion about whether to recall a patient to hospital but no discretion as to whether or not to recall to hospital a patient who, in the exercise of his discretion, he considers should be in hospital. The Act says that he may recall the patient to hospital, not that he may not recall a patient who is or needs to be in hospital, and the discretion conferred on him does not extend to waiving his duty to protect the public by vetting proposals for leave, and so forth. While the regime may seem punitive, a further warrant of conditional discharge can be speedily effected. If a patient requires only a short period in hospital, there is no legal reason why he cannot again be discharged by warrant after a few days or weeks.[158] Indeed, the reason why the Home Secretary has one month within which to refer a recalled patient's case to a tribunal is to avoid any need for him to refer the cases of patients who can be redischarged by him within that period. As concerns tribunals, the effect of the statutory scheme is that they have no jurisdiction to consider an application made under section 66 or 69(1) following readmission under Part II. Such applications are unauthorised for the very reason that Parliament never intended that restricted patients would be detained under Part II, certainly not for any longer than was necessary for the Secretary of State to take a view about the need for recall to hospital. That would allow the patient's suitability for discharge to be determined by a tribunal presided over by a lawyer who was not a member of the judiciary.

Counter-argument that there is no obligation to recall

Against the above interpretation of the law may be set at least four competing arguments. It may be argued that the exercise of the power of recall is discretionary and not fettered by any statutory criteria while the exercise by a tribunal of its power of discharge involves no discretion. It must discharge if satisfied that the patient no longer requires in-patient treatment, and that he meets the other criteria for being discharged, and it may not discharge otherwise. In contrast, the Home Secretary may direct that a person who requires further in-patient treatment shall cease to be restricted, has a discretion not to discharge a patient whom he believes a tribunal would be bound to discharge, and so is similarly not obliged to recall a patient who requires further in-patient treatment. While this sounds plausible, the reasoning is not wholly convincing. Although the Home Secretary may direct that a person shall cease to be restricted if he is satisfied that restrictions are no longer necessary to protect the public from serious harm, he, no more than a tribunal, may discharge a restricted patient on condition that he remains in hospital. If the exercise of his power to discharge a restricted patient is limited to exercising it in respect of patients who he believes no longer require to be in hospital, it is then inconsistent to contend that he may nevertheless allow a discharged patient to return to and reside in hospital — whether by varying the condition of residence to residence there or by allowing him to reside at a place other that where he is required to reside. A second argument in favour of the practice is that it is not expressly prohibited and it has

---

[158] The only formality involved in redischarging a recalled restricted patient involves drawing up a warrant of recall. These days that consists of nothing more than a signed sheet of A4 paper containing the standard wording. Accordingly, reaching such decisions is only as prolonged as the Secretary of State makes it. There is a certain inconsistency in the Home Secretary's view that patients who require a short admission may be more appropriately detained under Part II and the contention that, if the law required him to take the decision, this would be a prolonged affair. If the public are not at risk, and the responsible medical officer notifies him that the patient no longer needs in-patient treatment, why need his decision be prolonged? The risks involved are the same.

been common practice for some years. Had Parliament not intended that the Secretary of State should have this discretion, it would have made this plain in the 1983 Act. However, the fact that a practice is common does not make it lawful. It has similarly been commonplace for the Secretary of State to transfer prisoners to mental nursing homes but no one could realistically argue that the Act permits that. Furthermore, the rather tired device that "if Parliament had intended that provision x should not apply in circumstances y, it would have said so" must always be tested by reversing the proposition and seeing if there is any loss of plausibility: here there is none.[159] It may, thirdly, be argued that the statutory framework for restricted patients set out in section 42 is one where the Home Secretary recalls patients, and resubmits them to the restricted regime, if they can no longer, in his opinion, safely be allowed to remain in the community. The purpose of recall, as was made clear in *D. v. Mental Health Review Tribunal for the South Thames Region*, is merely to reinstate the regime of control under section 41. It would be punitive to formally recall restricted patients who can be treated informally or under the ordinary civil provisions. Against this, the judgment in *D.* is not wholly reconcilable with that in the *Mersey case* nor, arguably, the statutory framework. Furthermore, if it really is the case that the patient can be adequately treated, and the public adequately protected, on an informal basis, or under the ordinary civil provisions, then the Home Secretary should lift the restrictions. If, however, the patient has a potential for dangerous behaviour when mentally unwell, the restrictions are appropriate.[160] Finally, it might be said that, if a patient cannot be readmitted informally or under the ordinary civil provisions, there might be undesirable delays in cases where mental health professionals have to act urgently. Even if a patient may be readmitted under Part II in an emergency, that does not necessarily mean that the Secretary of State is not obliged to recall upon being notified of the fact.[161] Moreover, the issue of a warrant requires no medical evidence and may be communicated by telephone in urgent cases, which is a somewhat speedier process than the procedures set out in Part II for non-offenders. The Home Secretary may then review the situation during the following days and decide whether or not the patient needs to remain in hospital or can be redischarged by him. To summarise the counter-argument, a restricted patient may be readmitted informally or under Part II for in-patient treatment without special restrictions. It is a matter for the Home Secretary's discretion as to whether to reimpose the special restrictions applicable to in-patients. He may not consider that is necessary where the patient is willingly residing in hospital or being detained there under some other provision. If the patient is discharged from detention under Part II by a tribunal or, if informal, attempts to leave hospital, the option of recall may be delayed until that time.

---

[159] In this case, an alternative proposition might be, "if, having provided a particular statutory mechanism for recalling restricted patients to hospital, Parliament had intended that a restricted patient could be recalled to hospital under some civil provision unconnected with the protective framework it laid down for restricted patients, it would have said so."

[160] In other words, the Secretary of State may direct that an in-patient shall cease to be subject to the restrictions if he is satisfied that they are no longer necessary in order to protect the public from serious harm. If he is not satisfied they are unnecessary, and so they remain in force, he has no more discretion to deal with that in-patient on the basis that the special restrictions shall not apply to him for the time being than he has a discretion to deal with a conditionally discharged patient on the basis that he is in the community informally.

[161] If a conditionally discharged patient may be admitted under Part II, there exists one authority for his discharge from hospital and another authorising his detention in hospital. If he is then recalled, it might be thought that his admission in pursuance of the warrant discharges the earlier authority for his detention under Part II. However, the wording of sections 40(5), 42(4)(a) and 55(3) does not support such a construction — although it would be logical for those sections to so provide if Parliament contemplated that a patient's readmission might initially be effected under Part II.

The purpose served by section 41(3)(b)

Three views are possible concerning the ambit of section 41(3)(b): that restricted patients who require further in-patient treatment must be recalled to hospital by the Secretary of State under section 42(3), and hence the question of whether a tribunal may review their detention under Part II should not arise; that they may be readmitted under section 2 or 3 and, if so, have the normal tribunal rights of such patients; that they may be readmitted under section 2 or 3 but, if so, have no right to apply to a tribunal for their discharge. The third of these views is, it is submitted, absurd. As with the other paragraphs of the subsection, paragraph 41(3)(b) lists those provisions which apply to unrestricted patients who are *detained* in pursuance of a hospital order which do not apply, or only in a restricted way, to patients who, although also *detained* in pursuance of a hospital order, are subject to restrictions. The common feature of all the provisions set out there — transfer, leave of absence, absence without leave, discharge, tribunal applications under sections 66 and 69 — is that they are restrictions on the powers exercisable in respect of patients who are detained under the relevant hospital order. They are not restrictions on restricted patients who have been (conditionally) discharged. Consequently, if a restricted patient is recalled, and he again becomes a detained patient, the restrictions take effect. However, until a discharged patient is recalled, the restrictions referred to in section 41(3) do not come into play. The intention of section 41(3)(b) is limited to making clear that, while a detained unrestricted hospital order patient or his nearest relative may apply to a tribunal under section 66 or 69(1), neither may do so if the patient is detained in pursuance of such an order with restrictions: the patient's rights of application are then those set out in section 70. Alternatively, since section 41(3)(b) refers only to applications in respect of a patient, rather than to applications by or in respect of a patient, which is the usual statutory wording, the purpose is simply to rule out applications by nearest relatives. What, it is submitted, one cannot do is to readmit restricted patients otherwise than by recall and then claim that, not only is the Home Secretary under no statutory duty to refer their cases to a tribunal within one month of readmission, but, furthermore, they may not apply for their discharge. The concept of a patient being detained under section 2 or 3 with restrictions attached, a sort of restriction application rather than a restriction order, is one unknown to law.[162] It would mean that patients could be detained under section 3 for an indefinite period without a tribunal having any jurisdiction to review the necessity for that. Such a view is contrary to the decision in *X. v. United Kingdom*,[163] which obliged Parliament to provide for an independent judicial review of the cases of restricted patients readmitted to hospital. Because Parliament complied with that judgment by requiring the Secretary of State to refer such cases to a tribunal, he is in breach of his duty in contending that he need not recall or refer the cases of patients readmitted under Part II, and nor may they apply to a tribunal.[164]

---

[162] Although the Home Secretary argues that patients may be detained in pursuance of an application with restrictions attached, and not merely detained under a hospital order with restrictions, that proposition is untenable. If the purpose of issuing a warrant is to reintroduce the restrictions in the case of a patient initially detained under Part II (as was stated in *D. v. Mental Health Review Tribunal for the South Thames Region*), this necessarily means that he was not subject to those restrictions whilst detained only under Part II. Accordingly, his tribunal rights of application in respect of his detention under Part II cannot have been restricted *prior to* recall and the restoration of a restricted regime. The concept of being an informal patient subject to formal restrictions on leaving hospital is likewise a *non-sequitur*. The patient is either free to leave or he is not.

[163] *X. v. United Kingdom* (1981) 4 E.H.R.R. 188.

[164] It has been known for conditionally discharged patients to be readmitted under section 3 and detained in hospital for up to eight years without being formally recalled. Because such patients are notionally still conditionally discharged, their cases are not referred to a tribunal every three years.

Summary as to the Part II, recall and tribunal provisions

It has been decided in the domestic courts that restricted patients may be readmitted under Part II. Furthermore, the Home Secretary is not obliged to immediately recall the patient upon being notified of that fact. However, *obiter*, such patients are entitled to apply to a tribunal. As to the case of *Lines v. United Kingdom*, either the Secretary of State has erred in his view that he is not obliged to recall and refer or he is in error in contending that patients so admitted can be detained under a restriction application and have no tribunal rights. Either way, he is in breach of the European Convention.

The Mersey case[165]

The decision in the *Mersey case* in effect removed the words "liable to be detained" from section 72(1)(b)(i), with the consequence that a tribunal may only discharge restricted patients who no longer need to be in hospital. If it is correct — and one is presently bound to take this view — that (1) the purpose of the power of recall is to reintroduce the restrictions, (2) a restricted patient may be recalled to a hospital within which he is already detained or residing informally, and (3) a restricted patient may lawfully be both in hospital and conditionally discharged from hospital, this raises the issue of whether the *Mersey case* was correctly decided. In other words, whether tribunals may in fact conditionally discharge patients who, although requiring further in-patient treatment, do not need to be detained in the hospital in pursuance of the relevant hospital order and associated restrictions. The counter-argument is simply that the statute confers a discretion on the Home Secretary but not on a tribunal. A tribunal may not discharge a patient who requires further in-patient treatment but the Home Secretary need not recall a patient who does **(522)**. That observation takes one back to issue already raised of the meaning of the word "discharge" and whether the statutory framework requires the Home Secretary to recall a patient whom he is satisfied needs to be in hospital.

Ex p. Cooper[166]

The observations in *D.* and *ex p. Stewart* concerning the purpose of the restrictions and the power of recall raise the possibility that *ex p. Cooper* was wrongly decided. The tribunal in that case was satisfied that the patient had never posed any risk of serious harm to the public, when ill or otherwise; that this would also not be the case if he relapsed in the future; and that it was not necessary to protect the public from serious harm that he should be discharged subject to conditions and liability to recall by the Secretary of State. Nevertheless, the tribunal only discharged him conditionally. The patient applied for judicial review, contending that he had been entitled to an absolute discharge. Because the tribunal had been satisfied that the statutory purpose behind conditional discharge and recall did not apply in his case, it was by definition satisfied that liability to recall was inappropriate: it was simply using the restrictions for therapeutic purposes, as a form of community treatment order, or as a form of hospital order of indefinite duration. The issue was therefore whether a tribunal which is satisfied that it will not in future be appropriate to recall a patient to hospital in order to protect the public may nevertheless not be satisfied that it is inappropriate for him to remain liable to recall by the Home Secretary, and

---

[165] *Home Department v. Mental Health Review Tribunal for Mersey Regional Health Authority, Same v. Mental Health Review Tribunal for Wales* [1986] 1 W.L.R. 1170 **(515)**.

[166] *R. v. North West Thames Mental Health Review Tribunal, ex p. Cooper* 1990 [C.O.D.] 275 **(529)**. When assessing the objectivity and correctness of the observations which follow, the reader should be aware that the author was the solicitor in this case.

so lawfully decline to absolutely discharge him. The court refused the application, relying on dicta of Butler-Sloss L.J. in *R. v. Merseyside Mental Health Review Tribunal, ex p. K.*,[167] where it had been said that the power to impose a conditional discharge and retain residual control over patients "would appear to be a provision designed both for the support of the patient in the community and the protection of the public."

OTHER EXCEPTIONS AND MODIFICATIONS

Various other statutory provisions either do not apply to restricted patients or only in a modified way.

Reclassification

Because allowing a restricted patient to be reclassified would serve no legal purpose in terms of the duration of his liability to detention, the reclassification provisions in sections 16 and 20 of the Act do not apply.[168] This is because the authority to detain a restricted patient does not require periodic renewal and the fact that such a patient's condition proves to be untreatable never entitles him to be discharged. It is, moreover, also the case that some restricted patients have no legal classification.

Nearest relative provisions

Restricted patients do not have a statutory nearest relative and sections 26–28 do not apply to them.[169]

Consent to treatment

Part IV of the Act applies to restricted patients who are detained in hospital or who are absent with leave from hospital. It does not, however, apply to conditionally discharged patients, with the effect that they may not be administered treatment without their valid consent unless justified under common law.[170] It should, however, be emphasised that it is usually a condition of discharge that the patient takes such medication as may be prescribed by, or under the direction of, the consultant in charge of his treatment. Consequently, a patient who fails to comply with such a condition risks being recalled to hospital by the Secretary of State.

Supervision applications

A supervision application may not be made in respect of a restricted patient, the pre-existing statutory scheme for conditional discharge and recall making the new powers unnecessary.[171]

PERIODIC REPORTS

In deciding whether to exercise his powers under the Act, the Secretary of State is assisted by periodic reports furnished to him by the patient's responsible medical officer. The responsible medical officer is required to examine the patient and to

[167] *R. v. Merseyside Mental Health Review Tribunal, ex p. K.* [1990] 1 All E.R. 694.
[168] Mental Health Act 1983, ss.41(3) and 145(3).
[169] *Ibid.*, ss.41(3) and 145(3); Sched. 1, Pt. II, paras. 1 and 2.
[170] *Ibid.*, s.56(1).
[171] *Ibid.*, s.41(3)(aa), as inserted by the Mental Health (Patients in the Community) Act 1995, s.1(2) and Sched. 1, para. 5.

report on him to the Secretary of State at such intervals (not exceeding one year) as the Secretary of State may direct; and every report must contain such particulars as the Secretary of State may require.[172]

MENTAL HEALTH REVIEW TRIBUNALS

Where a court makes a restriction order, a convicted patient has no right to apply to a tribunal during the period of six months commencing with the date of the relevant hospital order.[173] This prohibition also applies to unrestricted patients admitted under a hospital order. Restricted patients have the same rights to obtain an independent medical opinion under section 76 as unrestricted persons.

The effect of section 41(3)(b)

Section 41(3) sets out the special restrictions applicable to a patient in respect of whom a restriction order is in force and paragraph (b) states that, "no application shall be made to a Mental Health Review Tribunal in respect of a patient under section 66 or 69(1) below." As to the proper interpretation of this provision in relation to conditionally discharged patients admitted under Part II, see page 365.

COMMITTALS UNDER SECTIONS 43 AND 44

A magistrates' court has no power to impose a restriction order. The Butler Committee considered whether they should be given such a power, possibly for a short limit of time, but rejected the suggestion because it considered that restriction orders should be more sparingly used in the future, rather than the provisions extended.[174] However, if the conditions for imposing a hospital order are satisfied, a magistrates' court may commit an offender to the Crown Court where it considers that, if a hospital order is made, a restriction order should also be made. Bail may not be granted and the offender is to be detained in prison custody or remanded to hospital pending sentence. Where he is remanded to hospital, he is deemed to be subject to a restriction order until such time as the Crown Court deals with his case.

CRITERIA FOR IMPOSITION

A magistrates' court may, instead of making a hospital order or dealing with an offender in any other manner, commit him in custody to the Crown Court to be dealt with by that court where the following conditions are satisfied[175]—

- the offender has been convicted of an offence punishable on summary conviction with imprisonment.[176]

---

172 Mental Health Act 1983, s.41(6).
173 *Ibid.*, s.70.
174 *Report of the Committee on Mentally Abnormal Offenders*, Cmnd. 6244 (1975), para. 14.27.
175 Mental Health Act 1983, s.43(1).
176 The magistrates may not make a hospital order and then commit the offender to the Crown Court for it to determine whether a restriction order should also be made. Because a conviction is necessary, a magistrates' court which is minded to make a hospital order under section 37(3) cannot commit the case to the Crown Court under section 43. Accordingly, if the magistrates find that the defendant is not guilty of the charge against him by reason of insanity, they may impose a hospital order but may not commit him to the Crown Court under section 43: *R. v. Horseferry Road Stipendiary Magistrate, ex p. Koncar* [1996] C.O.D. 197, D.C.

- the offender is at least fourteen years of age.

- the conditions in section 37(1) for making a hospital order are satisfied in respect of the offender.

- it appears to the court that, having regard to the nature of the offence, the antecedents of the offender and the risk of his committing further offences if set at large, that if a hospital order is made a restriction order should also be made.

PERSONS COMMITTED IN CUSTODY

Provided that the usual conditions for exercising the following powers are satisfied, an offender who has been committed in custody may, prior to the disposal of his case by the Crown Court, be—

- remanded to hospital by the Crown Court under section 35 (for the preparation of a report on his mental condition) or section 36 (for treatment).[177]

- removed to hospital by the Secretary of State for urgent treatment under section 48(2)(a).[178]

PERSONS COMMITTED TO HOSPITAL

Where a magistrates' court is satisfied, on oral or written evidence,[179] that arrangements have been made for the offender's admission to a hospital in the event of his being committed to the Crown Court under section 43 the court may, instead of committing him in custody, order his admission to that hospital, to be detained there until the case is disposed of by the Crown Court.[180] The court may give directions for his production from the hospital to attend the Crown Court by which his case is to be dealt with.[181]

Detention in a place of safety pending admission

The court may, pending the patient's admission to the hospital specified in its order, give directions for his conveyance to and detention in a place of safety.[182] If, prior to the offender's admission to that hospital, it appears to the Secretary of State that, "by reason of an emergency or other special circumstances," it is not practicable for him to be received there, he may direct the patient's admission to such other hospital as appears to be appropriate.[183] Upon the patient's admission to the hospital specified by

---

[177] Mental Health Act 1983, s.43(3).
[178] *Ibid.*, s.48(2)(a). In which case, it is mandatory to also give a restriction direction under section 49.
[179] The evidence is to be given by the registered medical practitioner who would be in charge of the offender's treatment or by some other person representing the managers of the hospital in question: Mental Health Act 1983, s.44(2).
[180] *Ibid.*, s.44(1) and (3). It is not the case that the magistrates must be satisfied that arrangements have been made for the offender's admission to hospital within 28 days.
[181] *Ibid.*
[182] *Ibid.*, ss.44(3) and 37(4).
[183] *Ibid.*, ss.44(3) and 37(5).

the court or the Secretary of State, the managers of that hospital shall thereafter detain him in accordance with the provisions of the Act.[184]

Effect of committal to hospital

Where a magistrates' court commits an offender to hospital, he is deemed to be subject to a hospital order together with a restriction order until such time as his case is disposed of by the Crown Court.[185] Notwithstanding this, the patient has no right to apply to a tribunal (**625**).

CROWN COURT'S POWERS TO DEAL WITH OFFENDER

Where an offender has been committed under section 43, the Crown Court shall inquire into the circumstances of the case and may[186]—

- exercise any power to make an interim hospital order or a hospital order (with or without restrictions) which the Crown Court would possess if the offender had been convicted by it of an offence punishable with imprisonment;[187] *or*

- deal with the offender in any other manner in which the magistrates' court might have dealt with him.

Disposal of the case in the patient's absence

In the case of a person committed to hospital under section 44, the court having jurisdiction to deal with him may make a hospital order (with or without a restriction order) in his absence if[188]—

a. it appears to the court that it is impracticable or inappropriate to bring him before the court; *and*

b. the court is satisfied, on the written or oral evidence of at least two registered medical practitioners, that the patient is suffering from mental illness or severe mental impairment of a nature or degree which makes it appropriate for him to be detained in a hospital for medical treatment; *and*

c. the court is of the opinion, after considering any depositions or other documents required to be sent to the proper officer of the court, that it is proper to make such an order.

---

[184] Mental Health Act 1983, ss.40(1) and 44(3).
[185] *Ibid.*, s.44(3).
[186] *Ibid.*, s.43(2).
[187] The Crown Court is not, however, empowered to give hospital and limitation directions under section 45A because the offender has not been convicted by it.
[188] Mental Health Act 1983, s.51(7). This power also applies to section 48 patients, according to the same criteria.

COMMITTAL TO THE CROWN COURT UNDER OTHER POWERS

Section 41 only empowers the Crown Court to make a restriction order in respect of a person convicted before that court. While section 43(1) allows it to make a restriction order in respect of a person who has been committed under the 1983 Act, specifically with a view to the making of a restriction order, it does not allow the court to make such orders in respect of a person convicted by a magistrates' court and committed to it for sentence under the ordinary criminal powers. Additional provisions are therefore required if it is to have power to impose a restriction order in such cases.

Committals under section 38 of the Magistrates' Courts Act 1980

Where a person aged 18 or over is convicted of an offence triable either way, a magistrates' court may commit him in custody or on bail to the Crown Court for sentence if it is of the opinion that—

a. the offence, or the combination of the offence and one or more offences associated with it, was so serious that greater punishment should be inflicted for the offence than the court has power to impose (s.38(2)(a)); or

b. in the case of a violent or sexual offence, that a sentence of imprisonment for a term longer than the court has power to impose is necessary to protect the public from serious harm from him (s.38(2)(b)).[189]

Mental Health Act 1983, s.43(4)

Section 43(5) provides that the power of a magistrates' court to commit an offender under section 38(2)(a) "shall also be exercisable ... where it is of the opinion that greater punishment should be inflicted as aforesaid on the offender unless a hospital order is made in his case with a restriction order." The effect of the provision is that a magistrates' court may commit an offender notwithstanding that its opinion that greater punishment is necessary is not an absolute opinion but conditional upon a restriction order not being made. It is therefore relevant where a magistrates' court considers that an ordinary hospital order is an inappropriate disposal and the case should be disposed of either by way of a restriction order or a more substantial custodial sentence than it has power to impose. The first of these alternatives does not legally constitute greater punishment than the magistrates may themselves inflict on the offender[190] although the second obviously does. Section 43(5) therefore ensures that an offender may be committed under section 38 notwithstanding that it is legally arguable that the court is not of the opinion that "greater punishment" than it has power to impose is necessary.

Purpose of committals under the 1980 and 1983 Acts

It may be asked why section 43(1) is necessary if a magistrates' court can commit an offender under section 38. The answer is that the usual committal procedure in the

---

[189] See Magistrates Courts' Act 1980, s.38; Criminal Justice Act 1967, s.56; Powers of Criminal Courts Act 1973, s.42; Criminal Justice Act 1991, ss. 25, 31, Part I; Criminal Justice Act 1993, s.66.

[190] See *R. v. Bennett* [1968] 2 All E.R. 753, where the Court of Appeal substituted a hospital order and a restriction order for a sentence of three years' imprisonment, emphasising that such an order was "a remedial order designed to treat and cure the appellant and could not be regarded as more severe than a sentence of imprisonment."

Magistrates Court Act 1980 does not cater for the situation where a magistrates' court considers that its powers of punishment are sufficient but not its powers to deal with the offender otherwise than by way of punishment under the 1983 Act.

Committal of incorrigible rogues under the Vagrancy Act 1824

The Vagrancy Act 1824 provides that where a person who is deemed to be a rogue and vagabond, because he has been convicted of an offence under section 4 of the Act, is convicted by a magistrates' court of a further offence under section 4, that court may[191] commit him to the Crown Court, either in custody or on bail, to be dealt with there as an "*incorrigible* rogue and vagabond." The Crown Court may, if it thinks fit, impose a sentence of imprisonment not exceeding one year. Section 43(5) of the 1983 Act provides that where a person has been committed as an incorrigible rogue and vagabond, the Crown Court may make a hospital order, with or without a restriction order, in the same circumstances as it can under section 41 in respect of a person who has been convicted before it of an offence.

RESTRICTION ORDERS UNDER SECTION 46

The Secretary of State may by warrant direct the removal to hospital of a person who is detained in custody during Her Majesty's pleasure in pursuance of an order made under the Service Discipline Acts. A direction under section 46 has the same effect as a hospital order together with a restriction order made without limitation of time. The transitional provisions provide that certain other patients are deemed to be subject to a restriction order of unlimited duration made under section 46.

PERSONS TO WHOM SECTION 46 APPLIES

Section 46 applies to persons who are required to be kept in custody during Her Majesty's pleasure, or until the directions of Her Majesty are known, by virtue of an order made under[192]—

- section 16 of the Army Act 1955

- section 116 of the Air Force Act 1955.

- section 63 of the Naval Discipline Act 1957.

- section 16 of the Courts-Martial (Appeals) Act 1968.

The four enactments provide that, where a court enters a finding that an accused person is unfit for trial or not guilty of an offence by reason of insanity, that person shall be kept in custody until the directions of Her Majesty are known, who may give directions for the safe custody of the accused in such place and in such manner as Her Majesty thinks fit.[193]

---

[191] Subject to section 70 of the Criminal Justice Act 1982.
[192] Mental Health Act 1983, s.46(2).
[193] The Queens Regulations for the Army (1975), the Royal Navy and the Royal Air Force contain provisions relating to the psychiatric examination of persons liable to trial by Courts-Martial.

Appeals from Courts-Martial

Appeals from Courts-Martial go to the Courts-Martial Appeal Court which is the Criminal Division of the Court of Appeal under a different name. Not surprisingly therefore, the court's powers under the Courts-Martial Appeals Act 1968 when dealing with appeals involving special findings correspond to those conferred upon the Criminal Division—

- Where, on an appeal against conviction, the Courts-Martial Appeal Court is of the opinion that the proper finding would have been that the appellant was unfit to stand trial or not guilty by reason of insanity, it must order that he be kept in custody under the relevant service Act (see above).

- Where the Courts-Martial Appeal Court allows an appeal against a finding that the appellant was unfit to stand trial then, unless it substitutes a verdict of acquittal, he may be tried for the offence with which he was charged and the court may make such orders as it thinks necessary or expedient for his continued detention pending trial.[194]

- Where, on appeal, the Courts-Martial Appeal Court substitutes a finding of not guilty for a finding that the appellant was not guilty by reason of insanity, it has the same powers as the Court of Appeal in such a case to direct that the appellant be detained for assessment under section 2 **(226)**.[195]

Directions under section 46

Section 46(1) provides that the Secretary of State may by warrant direct that a person to whom the section applies shall be detained in such hospital (not being a mental nursing home) as may be specified in the warrant and, where that person is not already detained in the hospital, give directions for his removal there.[196] Where a direction under section 46 is given in respect of a person who is already in the specified hospital, he is deemed to be admitted in pursuance of, and on the date of, the direction.[197]

Effect of a direction under section 46

A direction under section 46 has the same effect as a hospital order together with a restriction order, made without limitation of time **(334 et seq.)**.[198] A reference to a hospital order or a restriction order in sections 40, 41 or 42 or in section 69(1) is to be construed as including a reference to a direction made under section 46.[199]

---

[194]   Courts-Martial Appeals Act 1968, ss.25(1) and (4).
[195]   *Ibid.*, ss.23(1) and (2).
[196]   The prohibition on removing a patient to a mental nursing home under section 46 was not removed by section 49(3) of the Crime (Sentences) Act 1997. Section 46 is now the only application, order or direction under the 1983 Act which may not specify a mental nursing home.
[197]   Mental Health Act 1983, s.46(3).
[198]   *Ibid.*
[199]   *Ibid.*, s.55(4).

Section 46 will be revoked when Part III of Schedule 7 to the Armed Forces Act 1996 is brought into effect.[200] Section 8 of, and Schedule 2 to, that Act lay down a new statutory scheme for dealing with the issues of insanity and fitness to plead at Courts-Martial. The effect is to bring military law into line with civilian law, as set out in the Criminal Procedure (Insanity) Act 1964. Accordingly, where a person is found to be not guilty by reason of insanity, or unfit to stand trial by Court-Martial, the court may make any of the following orders: a guardianship order, an admission order, a supervision and treatment order, an order discharging him absolutely.[201] As in the case of civilians, restrictions may be attached to an order for admission but are no longer mandatory,[202] and it is the Secretary of State who specifies the hospital to which the patient is to be admitted.[203] Guardianship orders and admission orders made under the new provisions have effect as if made under section 37 of the 1983 Act, and restriction orders likewise take effect as if they had been imposed under section 41.[204]

THE 1983 ACT TRANSITIONAL PROVISIONS

It is not uncommon for a tribunal to deal with an application or reference concerning a patient who is detained under section 46. However, the majority of such patients are not former armed forces personnel. This is because the transitional provisions in the 1959 and 1983 Acts provide that certain other classes of patients shall be deemed to be subject to a direction made under section 46.[205] In particular, persons initially detained as Broadmoor patients[206] or under the following provisions: section 2 of the Criminal Lunatics Act 1800; section 2 of the Trial of Lunatics Act 1883; the Colonial Prisoners Removal Act 1884; section 5(4) of the Criminal Appeal Act 1907; section 8(4) or 9 of the Mental Deficiency Act 1913; and section 63(3) or 64 of the Criminal Justice Act 1948.

TRANSFER DIRECTIONS AND RESTRICTION DIRECTIONS

Sections 47 and 48 provide that the Secretary of State may direct the removal of a person from prison, or some other place of custody, to hospital for treatment. Any such direction is known as "a transfer direction"[207] and has the same effect as if a hospital order had been made in the patient's case.[208] Where the Secretary of State gives a transfer direction, he may — and must in the case of persons awaiting trial or sentence before the Crown Court or a magistrates' court — also direct that the

---

[200] Armed Forces Act 1996, s.35(2), Sched. 7, Pt. III.
[201] Army Act 1955, s.116A(2); Air Force Act 1955, s.116A(2); Naval Discipline Act 1957, s.63A(2).
[202] Army Act 1955, s.116B(2); Air Force Act 1955, s.116B(2); Naval Discipline Act 1957, .s.63B(2)
[203] Army Act 1955, s.116B(1); Air Force Act 1955, s.116B(1); Naval Discipline Act 1957, s.63B(1).
[204] Army Act 1955, s.116A(5); Air Force Act 1955, s.116A(5); Naval Discipline Act 1957, s.63A(5).
[205] Mental Health Act 1983, s.148(1), Sched. 5, para 37(2); Mental Health Act 1959, s.71.
[206] Other than Broadmoor patients who had been conditionally discharged under section 5 of the Criminal Lunatics Act 1884 by the time the 1959 Act came into force. These patients were deemed to also be conditionally discharged patients under the new legislation.
[207] Mental Health Act 1983, ss.47(1) and 145(1).
[208] Ibid., ss.47(3) and 48(3).

patient shall be subject to the special restrictions set out in section 41. Where restrictions are attached to the transfer, the Secretary of State's direction is known as a "restriction direction" (383). In contrast to the position where the court makes a restriction order, there is no provision in the Act for the Secretary of State to make a restriction direction for a limited period.

TRANSFER DIRECTIONS UNDER SECTIONS 47 AND 48

Section 47 provides that the Secretary of State may by warrant direct that a person serving a sentence of imprisonment may be removed to and detained in such hospital as may be specified in the warrant (not being a mental nursing home). Section 48 gives the Secretary of State a like power to remove to hospital persons detained in prison, or some other place of custody, otherwise than in pursuance of a sentence of imprisonment.

"Sentence of imprisonment"

Section 55(6) provides that references in Part III of the Act to persons serving a "sentence of imprisonment" shall be construed in accordance with section 47(5). Accordingly, for the purposes of sections 47 and 48, references to a person serving a sentence of imprisonment include—

- a person detained in pursuance of any sentence or order for detention made by a court in criminal proceedings (other than an order under any enactment to which section 46 applies);

- a person committed to custody under section 115(3) of the Magistrates' Courts Act 1980 (which relates to persons who fail to comply with an order to enter into recognisances to keep the peace or be of good behaviour); *and*

- a person committed by a court to a prison, or other institution to which the Prison Act 1952 applies, in default of payment of any sum adjudged to be paid on his conviction.

STATUTORY CONDITIONS

The table on the following page sets out the statutory conditions which must be met before a transfer direction may be given under section 47 or 48. In essence, the patient must be a patient to whom the section applies and the Secretary of State be satisfied that the patient meets the medical criteria for detention in hospital and of the opinion that it is appropriate to give such a direction.

The medical grounds

As the table indicates, it is not a condition of removal under section 47 that the patient is in urgent need of hospital treatment and section 47 applies to persons who are suffering from mental impairment or psychopathic disorder, and not merely to persons suffering from mental illness or severe mental impairment. The distinctions reflect the fact that some persons serving prison sentences will be serving life sentences or long custodial sentences.

Directions under section 47	*Directions under section 48*

Categories of patient in respect of whom a direction may be given

• Section 47(1)(a) : Persons serving a sentence of imprisonment (379)	• Section 48(2)(a) : persons detained in a prison or remand centre, not being persons serving a sentence of imprisonment or persons falling within the following paragraphs.
	• Section 48(2)(b) : persons remanded in custody by a magistrates' court.
	• Section 48(2)(c) : civil prisoners, that is to say, persons committed by a court to prison for a limited term (including persons committed to prison in pursuance of a writ of attachment), who are not persons falling within section 47.
	• Section 48(2)(d) : persons detained under the Immigration Act 1971.

Medical evidence and criteria

• The Secretary of State is satisfied, by reports from at least two registered medical practitioners (at least one of whom is approved under section 12), that the person is suffering from mental illness, psychopathic disorder, severe mental impairment or mental impairment of a nature or degree which makes it appropriate for him to be detained in a hospital for medical treatment.	• The Secretary of State is satisfied, by reports from at least two registered medical practitioners (at least one of whom is approved under section 12), that the person is suffering from mental illness or severe mental impairment of a nature or degree which makes it appropriate for him to be detained in a hospital for medical treatment and that he is in urgent need of such treatment.
• In the case of psychopathic disorder or mental impairment, the Secretary of State is further satisfied, on the reports, that such treatment is likely to alleviate or prevent a deterioration of his condition.	

Expediency ground

• The Secretary of State is of the opinion having regard to the public interest and all the circumstances that it is expedient to by warrant direct that that person be removed to and detained in the hospital specified in his direction (not being a mental nursing home).

Removal to a mental nursing home

Prior to 1 October 1997, sections 47 and 48 prohibited the Secretary of State from directing a person's removal to a mental nursing home (a "private hospital") under those sections.[209] It was nevertheless quite common for him to give the directions, although recent practice tended to involve invoking the transfer provisions in section 19 as a way of circumventing the prohibition. The usual sequence of events was for the transfer direction to direct the patient's removal to an NHS hospital, notwithstanding that the Secretary of State, and all the other involved parties, knew when the direction was given that the patient's real destination was a mental nursing home — the prison medical notes recorded this as the destination and the availability of a bed there was verified prior to removal. The direction having been given, the patient was driven to the NHS hospital. The prison van remained outside the NHS hospital's offices for the few minutes it took an administrator to complete a form authorising the patient's transfer to the home under section 19. The Home Secretary's consent to the transfer had already been given in advance. It was then contended that although the patient was not admitted to a bed at the NHS facility, and it was used as no more than a staging post, he had been "received" there for the purpose of section 47 or 48. Furthermore, the Act did not expressly prohibit the transfer to a "private hospital" of a restriction direction patient removed to an NHS hospital under section 47 or 48.[210] Whether sitting in a van parked in the courtyard of an NHS hospital constituted being received at that hospital was at best open to doubt. But, in any case, section 19(2) provides that where a patient is transferred under that section the provisions of Part II apply to him as if the direction were a direction for his removal to the hospital to which he is transferred. Thus, the direction took, and takes, effect as if the mental nursing home (rather than the NHS unit) was specified in the warrant — and such a direction could not at that time be given for a patient's removal to, and detention in, such a home. Where a patient is detained in a private hospital in pursuance of a direction given under section 47 or 48 prior to 1 October 1997, .High Court proceedings may therefore be appropriate if he wishes to be remitted to custody.

Form of the direction

A transfer direction is required to specify the form or forms of mental disorder from which the patient is, upon the medical reports, found by the Secretary of State to be suffering; and no such direction may be given unless the patient is described in each of those reports as suffering from the same form of disorder, whether or not he is also described in either of them as suffering from another form.[211]

The necessity for removal within 14 days

A transfer direction ceases to have effect at the expiration of the period of 14 days beginning with the date on which it is given unless the person to whom it relates has by then been received to the hospital specified in the direction.[212]

---

[209] The prohibition was removed on 1 October 1997 when section 49(3) of the Crime (Sentences) Act 1997 was brought into force.

[210] The Secretary of State sometimes also contended that the statutory prohibition on directing a patient's removal to a mental nursing home did not extend to section 48. However, section 48 expressly provides that the Secretary of State has the *same* power of giving a transfer direction under that section as he does under section 47.

[211] Mental Health Act 1983, ss.47(4) and 48(3).

[212] *Ibid.*, ss.47(2) and 48(3).

Sections 48 and 36 contrasted

Section 48(2)(a) provides that the Secretary of State may remove to hospital a defendant who suffers from mental illness or severe mental impairment and who is in custody awaiting trial or sentence before the Crown Court. Section 36 gives the Crown Court a similar power to remand a person who suffers from either of these forms of disorder to hospital for treatment. The two powers differ, however, in a number of respects—

- a person whose case is before a magistrates' court may be removed to hospital under section 48 but not remanded there for treatment under section 36.

- it is not a condition of a remand under section 36 that the patient is in urgent need of hospital treatment.

- the accused cannot be admitted to a mental nursing home under section 48.

- a remand for treatment under section 36 may not be made unless the court is satisfied that a bed is available whereas the Secretary of State may direct a patient's removal to a hospital under section 48.

- defendants transferred under section 48 are subject to the special restrictions set out in section 41.

- defendants detained under section 48 are entitled to apply to a Mental Health Review Tribunal.

- where a person is detained under section 48, his liability to detention in hospital may be terminated by the Home Secretary as well as by the Crown Court.

- persons detained under section 48 may, in the circumstances specified in section 51, be made the subject of a hospital order (with or without restrictions) without being brought before the court, tried or convicted of the alleged offence.

The legal effect of a transfer direction

Provided the patient is admitted within the statutory 14 day period, the Act provides that "a transfer direction ... shall have the same effect as a hospital order made in his case."[213] Unless a restriction direction is also given **(383)**, the usual provisions applicable to patients who are liable to be detained under a hospital order therefore apply **(330)**.

Effect on previous applications and orders

The giving of a transfer direction has the effect of bringing to an end any previous application or order which was in force in respect of the same patient, other than a hospital order with restriction order.[214]

---

[213] Mental Health Act 1983, ss.47(3) and 48(3).

[214] Section 55(4) provides that any reference to a hospital order in s.40(4) and (5) is to be construed as including a reference to a direction under Part III having the same effect as a hospital order.

Application of Parts II and V of the Act

Where a patient is admitted to hospital in pursuance of a transfer direction, he is treated, for the purposes of the provisions in Parts II and V of the Act mentioned in Part I of Schedule 1, as if he had been admitted on the date of the direction in pursuance of an application duly made under section 3, but subject to the exceptions and modifications specified in that Part of the Schedule.[215] These exceptions and modifications apply equally to patients admitted to hospital under a hospital order and their effect has already been summarised (**331**).

Part IV and consent to treatment

Part IV of the Act applies to patients who are liable to be detained under a transfer direction (with or without restrictions) and they may therefore be administered treatment without their consent in the circumstances there set out.[216]

Duration, renewal, expiration and discharge

Where a transfer direction only is given in respect of a patient, he is deemed to have been admitted to hospital under a hospital order made without restrictions on the date of the direction. If the patient was, prior to his removal, serving a sentence of imprisonment, the Secretary of State may not remit him to prison to serve out his sentence and usual provisions concerning the duration, renewal and discharge of hospital orders apply.[217]

Civil prisoners and persons detained under the Immigration Act 1971

The position is different where the patient is a civil prisoner or a person detained under the Immigration Act 1971. In such cases, the patient is, as before, treated as if a hospital order had been made under section 37 on the date of the transfer direction and he may not be remitted to custody by the Secretary of State. However, the transfer direction expires on the date that the patient would have ceased to be liable to be detained in the place from which he was removed had no direction been given. If the patient's mental state is such that he requires detention under the 1983 Act beyond that date then an application must be made under section 2 or 3.[218]

Mental Health Review Tribunals

The patient may apply to a tribunal during the period of six months beginning with the date of the transfer direction.[219] He may make a further application during the following six months and one application during each subsequent year that he remains liable to be detained.[220] His nearest relative may apply to the tribunal in the circumstances set out in section 69(1).

RESTRICTION DIRECTIONS UNDER SECTION 49

Section 49 provides that where the Secretary of State gives a transfer direction in respect of a patient who has been remanded in custody by a magistrates' court or

---

[215] Mental Health Act 1983, ss.47(3), 48(3), 55(4), and 40(4).
[216] *Ibid.*
[217] Section 50(1) applies only to restricted patients.
[218] See Mental Health Act 1983, s.53.
[219] *Ibid.*, s.69(2).
[220] Under section 66(1)(f).

who is detained in a prison or remand centre but who is not serving a sentence of imprisonment — generally persons awaiting trial or sentence before the Crown Court — he shall also by warrant further direct that the patient shall be subject to the special restrictions set out in section 41. In other cases, it is a matter for the Secretary of State's discretion as to whether or not to also give a "restriction direction."[221]

Whether restrictions necessary to protect public from serious harm

Given that it may be mandatory to give a restriction direction, a person may be restricted under section 49 even though it is common ground that restrictions are not necessary to protect the public from serious harm. Furthermore, where a discretion exists, the Act does not provide that restrictions may only be imposed if the Secretary of State is satisfied they are necessary for that purpose. These facts may be highly relevant to any subsequent tribunal proceedings.

THE GIVING OF A RESTRICTION DIRECTION

Mandatory	*discretionary*
Section 48(2)(a) : persons awaiting trial or sentence in the Crown Court	Section 47(1)(a) : persons serving a sentence of imprisonment (**379**)
Section 48(2)(b) : persons remanded in custody by a magistrates' court.	Section 48(2)(d) : persons detained under the Immigration Act 1971.
	Section 48(2)(c) : civil prisoners

LEGAL EFFECT OF A RESTRICTION DIRECTION

Just as the making of a transfer direction has the same effect as if a hospital order had been made in respect of the patient so a restriction direction has the same effect as a restriction order made under section 41.[222] Accordingly, for the purposes of the provisions of Parts II and V of the Act referred to in Part II of Schedule 1, the patient is treated as if he had been admitted on the date of the restriction direction in pursuance of an application duly made under section 3, but subject to the exceptions and modifications specified in that Part of the Schedule.[223] These exceptions and modifications apply equally to patients admitted to hospital following the imposition of a restriction order and their effect is set out above (**335**). In summary, unless the Act expressly provides otherwise, patients subject to a restriction direction are to be treated as if both a hospital order and a restriction order had been made on the date of the transfer direction.

Medical reports

While a person is subject to a restriction direction, the responsible medical officer must examine the patient and report to the Secretary of State at such intervals (not exceeding one year) as the Secretary of State may direct; and every report shall contain such particulars as the Secretary of State may require.[224]

---

[221] Mental Health Act 1983, s.49(1).
[222] *Ibid.*, s.49(2).
[223] *Ibid.*, ss.49(2), 55(4), 41(3) and 145(3).

Persons remanded in custody by a magistrates court

As has been noted, the Secretary of State must also give a restriction direction under section 49 in such cases. Following the giving of the directions, the court may further remand the accused in his absence provided that he has appeared before the court within the previous six months.[225] The effect of a further remand in custody is that the transfer and restriction directions continue in force. A remand on bail brings the directions to an end.[226] Committal proceedings, whether under section 6(1) or (2) of the Magistrates' Courts Act 1980, may be conducted in the accused's absence, provided he is legally represented and the court is satisfied, on the written or oral evidence of the responsible medical officer, that he "is unfit to take part in the proceedings."[227] Where the patient is committed in custody, whether for trial or sentence, he is thereafter deemed to be liable to detention in hospital pursuant to a transfer direction made under section 48(2)(b). Thereafter, the provisions of section 51, instead of those set out in section 52, apply.[228]

Alternative means of disposal available to the magistrates

A transfer direction under section 48 may only be given in respect of a person suffering from mental illness or severe mental impairment who is in urgent need of treatment. Section 37(3) provides that a magistrates' court may in certain circumstances make a hospital order without convicting such a person, unless he is charged with an offence triable only on indictment.

Persons awaiting trial or sentence before the Crown Court

Where, under section 48(2)(b), the Secretary of State directs the removal to hospital of a person who is awaiting trial or sentence before the Court Crown, he must also give a restriction direction. Consequently, all defendants who are removed to hospital by the Secretary of State during the course of criminal proceedings are subject to a restriction direction. The court having jurisdiction to try or otherwise deal with the detainee may make a hospital order (with or without a restriction order) in his absence, and without convicting him, if [229]—

a. it appears to the court that it is impracticable or inappropriate to bring him before the court; *and*

b. the court is satisfied, on the written or oral evidence of at least two registered medical practitioners, that the detainee is suffering from mental illness or severe mental impairment of a nature or degree which makes it appropriate for the patient to be detained in a hospital for medical treatment; *and*

c. the court is of the opinion, after considering any depositions or other documents required to be sent to the proper officer of the court, that it is proper to make such an order.

---

[224] *Ibid.*, s.49(3).
[225] Mental Health Act 1983, s.52(4).
[226] *Ibid.*, ss.48(2)(b) and 52(2).
[227] *Ibid.*, s.52(7).
[228] *Ibid.*, s.52(6).
[229] *Ibid.*, s.50(5)–(6).

DURATION AND DISCHARGE OF RESTRICTION DIRECTIONS

The Act provides that a restriction direction will cease to have effect upon the patient's remission to custody (**386**); the giving of a direction by the Secretary of State or a Mental Health Review Tribunal (**387**); the expiration of the direction (**389**).

TREATMENT INEFFECTIVE OR NO LONGER REQUIRED

The Act provides for the remission to prison, or some other place of custody, of restricted patients previously removed to hospital under sections 47 or 48. Both the transfer direction and the restriction direction cease to have effect upon the patient's arrival at the place to which he is remitted. The statutory criteria by reference to which a patient may be remitted to prison are the same in all cases, namely that he "no longer requires treatment in the hospital to which he has been removed" or that "no effective treatment can be given to him there."[230] Where the person removed is involved in criminal proceedings, the court with jurisdiction to deal with his case always has power to remit him.

REMISSION TO PRISON OR OTHER PLACE OF CUSTODY

	By Secretary of State	By the Court
• Patients serving a sentence of imprisonment removed under sections 47/49	Section 50(1)	Not applicable
• Civil prisoners and Immigration Act detainees	Section 53(2)	Not applicable
• Persons remanded in custody by a magistrates' court and detained under s.48(2)(b)	No power to remit	Section 52(5)
• Persons awaiting trial or sentence before the Crown Court and detained under s.48(2)(a)	Section 51(3)	Section 51(4)

Remission by the Secretary of State

With the exception of patients removed under section 48(2)(b) whose cases are still before a magistrates' court, the Secretary of State may direct that any restriction direction patient be remitted to any place in which he might have been detained had he not been removed to hospital. He may do so upon being notified by the responsible medical officer, any other medical practitioner, or a Mental Health Review Tribunal, that the patient "no longer requires treatment in the hospital to which he has been removed" or that "no effective treatment can be given to him there."[231]

---

[230] The transfer direction may therefore be terminated if no effective treatment can be given in the hospital where the patient is detained, even though effective treatment could be given in some other hospital.

[231] Mental Health Act 1983, ss.50(1), 51(3) and 53(3).

Remission by a magistrates' court

In the case of patients removed under section 48(2)(b) whose cases are still before a magistrates' court, the magistrates' court dealing with the case may direct that the restriction direction shall cease to have effect if satisfied, on the written or oral evidence of the responsible medical officer, as to either of the above grounds for remission.[232] The court may so direct notwithstanding that the period of remand has not expired or that, in the course of the same hearing, it has just committed the accused to the Crown Court for trial or sentence.[233] Unless the court then remands the patient on bail, he will necessarily be returned to custody.

Remission by the Crown Court

In the case of a patient awaiting trial or sentence before the Crown Court, that court may remit the patient to custody or release him on bail if satisfied, on the responsible medical officer's evidence, as to the existence of either of the grounds for remission.[234] In Crown Court proceedings, therefore, either the court or the Secretary of State may terminate the direction, although the court may only do so if "satisfied" upon the responsible medical officer's evidence as to the existence of either ground. In contrast, the Secretary of State's power is exercisable upon his being "notified" by the responsible medical officer, another medical practitioner, or a tribunal, that either ground exists: he would not appear to have to personally satisfy himself that this is so. A further distinction is that, whereas the Secretary of State must either remit or not remit, the Crown Court may grant bail as an alternative to remission (subject to section 25 of the Criminal Justice and Public Order Act 1994).[235] It is therefore generally in the patient's interests to encourage his responsible medical officer to report to the court rather than to the Home Secretary, if a report is to be made.

DISCHARGING THE DIRECTIONS

As drafted, the Secretary of State has the same statutory powers in respect of a patient who is subject to a restriction direction as he does in a case involving a patient who is subject to a restriction order. There are, however, a number of practical differences and a tribunal's powers are more limited when dealing with the case of a patient who is subject to a restriction direction.

Absolute discharge from hospital

Section 42(2) provides that the Secretary of State may, if he thinks fit, by warrant absolutely discharge from hospital a restricted patient who is detained under a transfer direction. A patient who is absolutely discharged ceases to be liable to be detained under the transfer direction, and the restriction direction, being parasitic in nature, accordingly also ceases to have effect. It is exceptional for a patient involved in criminal proceedings, who has been removed to hospital under section 48(2)(a) or (b), to be absolutely discharged.

---

[232]   Mental Health Act 1983, s.52(5).
[233]   *Ibid.*, s.52(5).
[234]   *Ibid.*, s.51(4).
[235]   *Ibid.*

The managers of a hospital may, with the Secretary of State's consent, order the discharge of a restricted patient who is liable to be detained there under a transfer direction. Any such order for discharge is equivalent to a direction for the patient's absolute discharge and both the transfer direction and the restriction direction cease to have effect.

Conditional discharge

The Secretary of State may direct the conditional discharge of a restricted patient who is detained under a transfer direction.[236] Where a patient is discharged from hospital subject to conditions, both the transfer direction and the restriction direction remain in force and the patient may by warrant be recalled to hospital by the Secretary of State at any time.[237]

Directions under section 42(1)

Section 42(1) provides that if the Secretary of State is satisfied in the case of any patient that a restriction direction is no longer required for the protection of the public from serious harm, he may direct that the patient shall cease to be subject to the special restrictions, in which case the restriction direction ceases to have effect. If the patient is detained in hospital at the time when such a direction is given, he is treated as if he had been admitted to that hospital in pursuance of a hospital order made without restrictions on the date when the restrictions ceased to have effect.[238] If the patient has already been conditionally discharged, he is deemed to have been absolutely discharged on the date when the restrictions cease to have effect, and accordingly ceases to be liable to be detained under the transfer direction.[239]

Home Office practice

As concerns patients involved in criminal proceedings who have been removed to hospital under section 48(2)(a) or (b), the Secretary of State will only exceptionally discharge, or consent to the discharge of, such a person, or give a direction under section 42 that the special restrictions shall cease to have effect in respect to him.[240] If the patient has recovered his health, he will generally be remitted to custody. A patient who is serving a sentence of imprisonment, and has been removed to hospital under section 47, will also generally be remitted to prison to serve out his sentence upon recovering his health. There are, however, exceptions. For example, patients whose sentences are about to expire (**558**) and persons serving life sentences whom the Secretary of State deems to be "technical lifers" and suitable for rehabilitation under the Mental Health Act 1983 (**392**).

Mental Health Review Tribunals

A tribunal's powers are limited and it either has no power to discharge a restriction direction patient from hospital or may only do so with the Secretary of State's

---

[236] Mental Health Act 1983, s.42(2).
[237] *Ibid.*, s.42(3).
[238] *Ibid.*, s.41(5).
[239] *Ibid.*, s.42(5).
[240] Since Parliament has required the Home Secretary to give a restriction direction in the case of patients involved in criminal proceedings, leaving him no discretion, it is somewhat anomalous that he may at his discretion then direct that the mandatory special restrictions shall cease to have effect.

consent **(555)**. However, once a patient has been conditionally discharged (whether by the Secretary of State or with his consent), he is in exactly the same position as any other conditionally discharged patient and a tribunal may direct that the restrictions shall cease to have effect.[241]

POWERS OF TRIBUNALS (555)

Patients who are liable to be detained in hospital

• Section 48 patients	No power to direct the patient's absolute or conditional discharge from hospital.
• Section 47 patients	Power to direct the patient's absolute or conditional discharge from hospital but only with the Secretary of State prior consent.

Conditionally discharged patients

• All restriction direction patients	Power to direct that the transfer direction and restriction direction shall cease to have effect, without the Secretary of State prior consent.

EXPIRATION OF THE DIRECTIONS

With the exception of persons serving a life sentence, both the transfer direction and the restriction direction will eventually cease to have effect through effluxion of time even if no direction is given having that effect and the patient has not been remitted to prison or some other place of custody.

EXPIRATION OF DIRECTIONS IN RESTRICTED CASES

• Patients serving a determinate sentence of imprisonment removed under sections 47/49	The restriction direction ceases to have effect on the expiration of the patient's sentence. However, unless he is a conditionally discharged patient, the patient is deemed to be admitted to hospital under a hospital order made, without restrictions, on the date of the sentence's expiration. If conditionally discharged, the patient ceases to be subject to any form of order or direction, unless a warrant of recall is outstanding.[†]
• Civil prisoners and Immigration Act detainees	Both the transfer direction and the restriction direction expire on the date on which the patient would have ceased to be liable to be detained in the place from which he was removed had no direction been given. If the patient's mental state is such that he requires detention under the 1983 Act beyond that date, an application must be made in the ordinary way under section 2 or 3.

---

[241]   Mental Health Act 1983, ss.74 and 75.

- Accused persons remanded in custody under s.48(2)(b)

Both the transfer direction and the restriction direction cease to have effect if the accused's case is disposed of by the magistrates' court otherwise than by way of committal in custody to the Crown Court. Following such a committal, the patient is deemed to be subject to a transfer direction made under s.48(2)(a) [see below].

- Persons awaiting trial or sentence before the Crown Court and detained under s.48(2)(a)

Both the transfer direction and the restriction direction cease to have effect upon the patient's case being disposed of by the court having jurisdiction to try or otherwise deal with him.

† *Where a warrant of recall is outstanding, because the patient is absent from hospital without leave at the expiration of his sentence, the transfer and restriction directions continue to have effect until the patient eventually returns or is returned to the hospital. Upon his return, the directions expire and the patient is deemed to have been admitted to the hospital specified in the warrant under a notional hospital order made, without restrictions, on the date of his return.*

LIFE SENTENCE PRISONERS

Every life prisoner must serve the penal part of his sentence (the "tariff") before there is any prospect of release. In murder cases, the Home Secretary sets the tariff if the offence was committed by a person aged 18 or over. Although he seeks recommendations from the trial judge and the Lord Chief Justice as to the appropriate term to be served, he is not bound by their advice.[242] In other cases — where an life sentence is required under section 2 of the Crime (Sentences) Act 1997, or a discretionary life sentence is imposed;[243] or a person is detained during Her Majesty's pleasure — the relevant part of the sentence which must be served is set by the sentencing judge, having regard to the seriousness of the offence.

Release into the community

If a life prisoner is transferred to hospital under sections 47 and 49 of the 1983 Act, there are three possible ways in which he may be released back into the community after the expiry of the tariff period—

- Release on life licence under the Crime (Sentences) Act 1997. This is possible because section* 50(1)(b) of the Mental Health Act provides that, if the Secretary of State is notified that a prisoner no longer requires treatment in hospital for mental disorder, or that no effective treatment can be given to him there, he may exercise any power of releasing him on licence which would have been exercisable were he in prison.

- Discharge by the Secretary of State under section 42(2) of the 1983 Act, whether absolutely or subject to conditions.

- Discharge by a tribunal under section 74(2) of that Act, upon the Secretary of State notifying it within 90 days that the patient may be discharged in accordance with its finding.

---

[242] *Doody v. Secretary of State for the Home Department* [1994] 1 A.C. 531 at 566, *per* Lord Mustill; . *R. v. Secretary of State, ex p. Hickey (No. 1)* [1995] 1 All E.R. 479 at 484, C.A.

[243] If the maximum sentence for an offence is life imprisonment, the court may impose such a sentence if the individual is dangerous and unpredictable and the offender cannot adequately be dealt with under the Mental Health Act 1983. The purpose of the sentence is to ensure that the offender is detained for as long as he may be dangerous to others. *R. v. Wilkinson* (1983) 5 Cr.App.R.(S.) 105.

A prisoner who is absolutely discharged under the 1983 Act is not subject to supervision and nor is he liable to be recalled to hospital or prison. If he is discharged conditionally, he is subject to supervision and he may be recalled to hospital, but not to prison. However, a person who has been conditionally discharged may later be absolutely discharged by a tribunal without the consent of the Secretary of State. In 1985, the then Home Secretary announced to the House of Commons that transferred life sentence prisoners would henceforth normally be discharged by way of life licence, rather than absolutely or conditionally discharged under the 1983 Act.[244] The Home Secretary's power in section 50(1)(b) of the 1983 Act would, he said, be used to release such prisoners under the same arrangements as those they would have been subject to had they remained in, or been returned to, prison. In *R. v. Secretary of State for the Home Department, ex p. S, The Times*, 19 August 1992, Henry J. held that this new policy was lawful. In exceptional circumstances, the usual policy is departed from and the Home Secretary's discretion to absolutely or conditionally discharge a prisoner under section 42, or to consent to his discharge by a tribunal, remains unfettered. Persons whom the Home Secretary is willing to treat and release under the ordinary Mental Health Act procedures for detained patients are referred to by him as "technical lifers." Experience has shown the principal categories into which these "exceptional cases" fall. According to an affidavit filed on the Home Secretary's behalf in *ex p. S.*:

> "This might be justified in a number of circumstances, for example, where evidence, not available to the sentencing court, suggests that the person was in fact suffering from a mental disorder at the time the offence was committed, or that the court had wished to make a hospital order but had been prevented from doing so because no hospital place was available. In such circumstances, as indicated in the statement, the Home Secretary would normally consult the trial judge and the Lord Chief Justice at some stage prior to the discharge decision to see whether they were content for him to treat the case as though a hospital order had been made in the first instance. If so, the Home Secretary would exercise his own power to discharge the person under section 42(2) of the Mental Health Act 1983."

Life prisoners other than those who committed murder when aged 18 or over

Section 28 of the Crime (Sentences) Act 1997 governs the release on licence of those sentenced to life imprisonment under section 2 of that Act, those serving a discretionary life sentence, and those detained during Her Majesty's pleasure. Once the prisoner has served the tariff part of his sentence he can, under section 28(7) of the 1997 Act, require the Home Secretary to refer his case to the Parole Board.[245] The Home Secretary must then release the prisoner if the Parole Board direct that but the Board may only give such a direction if satisfied that it is no longer necessary for the protection of the public that the prisoner should be detained. However, it has been held that a life sentence prisoner who continues to require detention in hospital for treatment under sections 47 and 49 has no right to have his case referred to the Parole Board.[246] The duration of his detention in hospital is governed by the

---

[244] It had previously been his practice to release such persons by way of conditional discharge under the 1983 Act.

[245] In *Thynne v. United Kingdom* [1990] 13 E.H.R.R. 666, the European Court of Human Rights held that the United Kingdom was in breach of the convention in not providing a court rather than a minister to consider at reasonable intervals the lawfulness of the continued detention of discretionary lifers. Accordingly, Parole Board discretionary lifer panels, which are somewhat similar to Mental Health Review Tribunals, were constituted to periodically consider whether a section 28 prisoner who has served his tariff still needs to be in prison or may be released on life licence.

[246] *R. v. Secretary of State, ex p. Hickey (No. 1)* [1995] 1 All E.R. 479 at 487, C.A.

procedures set down in the 1983 Act. It is only when the Home Secretary is notified, by the responsible medical officer or a tribunal, that a lifer no longer requires further treatment in hospital that the Parole Board procedures come into play. At that time, the Home Secretary will either remit the patient to prison, where he has the benefit of section 28, or, if that is inappropriate, arrange for the his case to be referred to a Parole Board panel while he remains in hospital, followed by release from hospital on life licence if the panel directs that.[247]

Life prisoners who committed murder when aged 18 or over

The position of persons convicted of a murder committed when aged 18 or over is different and is dealt with in section 29 of the 1997 Act. The Secretary of State has a broad discretion whether and when to release such a prisoner, and is not bound by judicial advice as to the tariff period.[248] Parole Board recommendations that a prisoner be released are advisory only and mandatory lifers do not have any right to a review by a judicial body, such as a Parole Board panel, either under domestic law or the Convention.[249] They do, however, have the benefit of the Home Secretary's policy in relation to life prisoners detained in hospital under sections 47 and 49. Their cases will be referred to the Parole Board if and when they no longer require, or can no longer effectively be given, hospital treatment, provided that the tariff period has expired and it is not appropriate to remit them to prison.

"Technical lifers"

The term "technical lifer" applies to any life prisoner transferred to hospital whom the Home Secretary, after consultation with the judiciary, believes should have been made subject to a hospital order and a restriction order following conviction. Insofar as possible, a "technical lifer" is dealt with by the Home Office as if he were subject to a hospital order and a restriction order. He will not be remitted to prison and eventual discharge is by way of absolute or conditional discharge under the 1983 Act, without the Parole Board playing any role.[250] The exceptional circumstances which may be considered to justify this are generally—

- that the mental disorder which led to the patient being transferred existed at the time of the offence and was relevant to it;

- that the sentencing court would have wished to dispose of the case by making a hospital order but was for some reason prevented from doing so. For example, because no hospital bed was available or because the defendant refused to raise a defence of diminished responsibility, thereby leading to his conviction for murder and a mandatory life sentence.[251]

---

[247] *Hansard* (1994) H.C. Vol. 245, col. 9.

[248] *Doody v. Secretary of State for the Home Department* [1994] 1 A.C. 531 at 566, *per* Lord Mustill; *R. v. Secretary of State, ex p. Hickey (No. 1)* [1995] 1 All E.R. 479 at 484, C.A.

[249] *Wynne v. United Kingdom, The Times,* 27 July 1994

[250] As to patients sentenced before the Criminal Justice Act 1991 was in force, the fact that punishment is inappropriate means that the tariff is incapable of certification under para. 9 of Sched. 12 to that Act. However, the Secretary of State has power to discharge such a patient from hospital under section 42(2) of the 1983 Act: see *R. v. Secretary of State, ex p. Hickey (No. 1)* [1995] 1 All E.R. 479 at 485.

[251] Home Office decisions refusing to treat a patient as a "technical lifer" are susceptible to judicial review: *R. v. Secretary of State for the Home Department, ex p. Pilditch* [1994] C.O.D. 352, Jowitt J.

28.—(l) A life prisoner is one to whom this section applies if—

(a) the conditions mentioned in subsection (2) below are fulfilled; or
(b) he was under 18 at the time when he committed the offence for which his sentence was imposed.

(2) The conditions referred to in subsection (l)(a) above are—

(a) that the prisoner's sentence was imposed for an offence the sentence for which is not fixed by law; and
(b) that the court by which he was sentenced for that offence ordered that this section should apply to him as soon as he had served a part of his sentence specified in the order.

(3) A part of a sentence specified in an order under subsection (2)(b) above shall be such part as the court considers appropriate taking into account—

(a) the seriousness of the offence, or the combination of the offence and other offences associated with it; and
(b) the effect of any direction which it would have given under section 9 above if it had sentenced him to a term of imprisonment.

(4) Where in the case of a life prisoner to whom this section applies the conditions mentioned in subsection (2) above are not fulfilled, the Secretary of State shall direct that this section shall apply to him as soon as he has served a part of his sentence specified in the direction.

(5) As soon as, in the case of a life prisoner to whom this section applies—

(a) he has served the part of his sentence specified in the order or direction ("the relevant part"); and
(b) the Parole Board has directed his release under this section, it shall be the duty of the Secretary of State to release him on licence.

(6) The Parole Board shall not give a direction under subsection (5) above with respect to a life prisoner to whom this section applies unless—

(a) the Secretary of State has referred the prisoner's case to the Board; and
(b) the Board is satisfied that it is no longer necessary for the protection of the public that the prisoner should be confined.

(7) A life prisoner to whom this section applies may require the Secretary of State to refer his case to the Parole Board at any time—
(a) after he has served the relevant part of his sentence ....

29.—(1) If recommended to do so by the Parole Board, the Secretary of State may, after consultation with the Lord Chief Justice together with the trial judge if available, release on licence a life prisoner who is not one to whom section 28 above applies.

(2) The Parole Board shall not make a recommendation under subsection (1) above unless the Secretary of State has referred the particular case, or the class of case to which that case belongs, to the Board for its advice.

Remission to prison
- On being advised that a transferred prisoner no longer requires treatment in hospital, the Home Secretary's normal course is to remit him to prison under section 50(1)(a) of the 1983 Act, where he will be eligible for a Discretionary Lifer Panel review or a Parole Board hearing in the normal manner. However, this general policy is departed from in some cases, and the patient discharged into the community without first being remitted to prison.

Release from hospital —
- A transferred prisoner subject to a restriction direction who is not remitted to prison can be discharged from hospital in three ways, each of which can be initiated only by the Secretary of State—

1. Home Secretary's direction for the patient's absolute or conditional discharge
1. Section 42(2) of the 1983 Act gives the Secretary of State power, if he thinks fit, to discharge the patient either absolutely or subject to conditions.

2. MHRT direction for the patient's absolute or conditional discharge under the 1983 Act
2. Under Section 74 of the 1983 Act, where a tribunal notifies the Home Secretary that a transferred prisoner would be entitled to be absolutely or conditionally discharged if subject to a restriction order, the tribunal must so discharge him if the Home Secretary consents but not otherwise.

3. Release from hospital under life licence
3. Under section 50(1)(b) of the 1983 Act, where the Home Secretary is notified by the responsible medical officer, any other registered practitioner, or a tribunal, that the person no longer requires treatment in hospital for mental disorder, or that no effective treatment can be given there, he may, instead of remitting him to prison, exercise any power of releasing him on life licence under the Crime (Sentences) Act 1997 which would have been exercisable if the patient had been remitted.

Release from hospital on life licence usual
- As to these three options, where the Home Secretary agrees to a transferred patient being discharged direct from hospital, his policy since 1985 has been to use the power in section 50(1)(b). That is, to authorise the offender's release on the same basis as if he had remained in prison — on life licence, post tariff, and following consideration of the case by the Parole Board and the judiciary (persons who committed murder when aged 18 or over) or the Discretionary Lifer Panel (other cases). This policy, which ensures lifelong control, was found to be lawful in *R. v. Secretary of State for the Home Department, ex. p. Stroud* [1993] C.O.D. 75.

- However, the effect of the decision in *R. v. Secretary of State for the Home Department, ex p. Hickey (No. 1)* [1995] 1 All E.R. 479 is that transferred lifers whose tariffs have expired, but who require further treatment in hospital, do not qualify for the regular Discretionary Lifer Panel and Parole Board reviews to which they would have been eligible had they remained in prison.

Exceptions to the general rule

- There are two main exceptions to the general policy that life prisoners will usually be remitted to prison and that those not remitted will be released from hospital under life licence, rather than by absolute or conditional discharge under the 1983 Act—

1. "Technical lifers"

1. If the patient has been designated a "technical lifer" by the Home Secretary then his discharge will be under section 42 or 74 — that is he will be absolutely or conditionally discharged under the 1983 Act, and recalled to hospital under that Act if necessary.

2. Other prisoners

2. The Home Secretary accepts that release on life licence direct from hospital will sometimes be appropriate even though the patient does not meet the Home Office criteria for technical lifer status—

a. Where recommended by the responsible medical officer as being the best option for the individual patient, the Home Office is willing to *consider* proposals for the patient's rehabilitation through the hospital system and, after the tariff has expired, his eventual release on life licence direct from hospital, under section 50(l)(b).

b. Where a Mental Health Review Tribunal notifies the Home Secretary under section 74(1)(a) that a patient whose tariff has expired would be entitled to be conditionally discharged if subject to a restriction order, and the tribunal also recommended that the patient should remain in hospital if not discharged, the Secretary of State will refer the case to the DLP or Parole Board while the person remains in hospital, even if he does not agree with the tribunal's recommendation.

c. The Home Secretary will normally only refer the case of a patient whose tariff has expired to the DLP or Parole Board if he has been notified by the responsible medical officer or a tribunal that the patient no longer requires treatment in hospital.

LIFERS TRANSFERRED TO HOSPITAL UNDER SECTIONS 47&49
I. PERSONS WHO COMMITTED MURDER WHEN AGED 18 OR OVER

1) Patient designated a technical lifer (342): dealt with under the 1983 Act as if a hospital order and a restriction order had been made by the sentencing court

2) Patient not designated a technical lifer

Patient no longer requires treatment in hospital or no effective treatment can be given there: MHA1983, s.50(1)

Patient continues to require treatment in hospital

Appropriate to remit the patient to prison   *Inappropriate to remit the patient to prison*

Remitted to prison under MHA 1983, s.50(1)(a)

REHABILITATION IN HOSPITAL

Secretary of Secretary considers any proposal concerning a move to a less secure hospital

Three years before the tariff, the possibility of increased leave will be considered

Responsible Medical Officer

MHRT

Patient does not meet MHA 1983 s.74 criteria for being discharged

Patient does meet the MHA 1983 s.74 criteria for being discharged

Recommends patient's release on life licence under MHA 1983 s.50(1)(b)

Remains in hospital & no reference to Parole Board

Did the tribunal also recommend that the patient remain in hospital if not discharged under MHA 1983?

Secretary of State agrees in principle to release from hospital on life licence

Case put to the Parole Board and to the judiciary — Remitted to prison — No

Secretary of State agrees to release on life licence under C(S)A 1997, s.29

Secretary of State does not agree to release on life licence

Yes

Patient remains in the hospital while case is put to Parole Board and the judiciary

Release

Patient remains in prison or hospital, as the case may be.

Source: Adapted from Home Office Mental Health Unit flowchart

LIFERS TRANSFERRED TO HOSPITAL UNDER SECTIONS 47&49
II. OTHER CASES

1) Patient designated a technical lifer (342): dealt with under the 1983 Act as if a hospital order and a restriction order had been made by the sentencing court

2) Patient not designated a technical lifer

Source: Adapted from Home Office Mental Health Unit flowchart

Patient no longer requires treatment in hospital or no effective treatment can be given there: MHA1983, s.50(1)

Patient continues to require treatment in hospital

Appropriate to remit the patient to prison

Inappropriate to remit the patient to prison

Remitted to prison under MHA 1983, s.50(1)(a)

REHABILITATION IN HOSPITAL

Secretary of Secretary considers any proposal concerning a move to a less secure hospital

Three years before the tariff, the possibility of increased leave will be considered

Responsible Medical Officer

MHRT

Patient does not meet MHA 1983 s.74 criteria for being discharged

Patient does meet the MHA 1983 s.74 criteria for being discharged

Recommends patient's release on life licence under MHA 1983 s.50(1)(b)

Remains in hospital & no reference to Parole Board

Did the tribunal also recommend that the patient remain in hospital if not discharged under MHA 1983

If Secretary of State agrees in principle to release from hospital on life licence

Case put to the discretionary lifers panel (DLP)

Remitted to prison ___ No

Yes

DLP releases on licence under C(S)A 1997, s.28

DLP does not release on licence under CJA 1991, s.34

Patient remains in the hospital while case is put to discretionary lifers panel (DLP)

Release

Patient remains in prison or hospital, as the case may be.

HOSPITAL AND LIMITATION DIRECTIONS

The Crime (Sentences) Act 1997 received the Royal Assent on 21 March 1997. Many of its provisions were brought into force on 1 October 1997, including those directly relevant to persons with mental health problems.[252] The Act requires the Crown Court to impose a life sentence for a second serious offence, unless there are exceptional circumstances. It also inserted a new power in the 1983 Act which enables the Crown Court in certain cases to impose a sentence of imprisonment and at the same time to direct the offender's removal to hospital for treatment. These new "hybrid orders" are referred to in the Act as hospital directions and limitation directions. Once made, their effect is identical to that where the Home Secretary transfers a serving prisoner to hospital for treatment by giving a hospital direction together with a restriction direction, under sections 47 and 49 (384).

INTRODUCTION

Where the Crown Court sentences an offender who suffers from a psychopathic disorder to imprisonment, it may in certain circumstances also direct that, instead of being removed to and detained in a prison, he be removed to and detained in a specified hospital ("a hospital direction") and be subject to the special restrictions set out in section 41 (a "limitation direction").[253] A hospital direction has effect as a transfer direction made under section 47[254] and a limitation direction has effect as a restriction direction made under section 49.[255] Prior to October 1997, a court sentencing an offender could impose a hospital order or a prison sentence, but could not combine the two. However, in some cases, a sentencing court is of the opinion that the circumstances of the offence merit a custodial sentence, for example because the offender's personality disorder did not greatly diminish his culpability, but it is also concerned to minimise the risk of repetition by ensuring that he is given any medical treatment likely to be beneficial. In other cases, the sentencing court may be satisfied that the defendant is mentally disordered but not satisfied that successfully treating his mental disorder will prevent further serious offending following release from hospital. A prison sentence has the disadvantage that it does not guarantee that the offender will receive the psychiatric treatment he requires. A hospital order has

---

[252]   The following provisions were, *inter alia,* brought into force on 1 October 1997: automatic life sentence for a second conviction for a serious sexual or violent offence (Section 2); mandatory minimum sentence of seven years for a third Class A drug trafficking conviction (Section 3); new provisions for the release of those sentenced to detention during Her Majesty's pleasure (Sections 28–33); abolition of consent requirements for certain community penalties (Section 38, and related paragraphs of Schedule 4); hospital and limitation directions for sentencing mentally disordered offenders (Section 46, and Schedule 4, paragraph 12); power to specify hospital units for detention of mentally disordered offenders (Sections 47, 49(2) and 49(4)); movement of conditionally discharged patients between jurisdictions in the United Kingdom (Section 48 and Schedule 3); extended maximum duration of interim hospital order (Section 49(1)); transfer of prisoners to private psychiatric hospitals for treatment (Section 49(3)). See The Crime (Sentences) Act 1997 (Commencement No. 2 and Transitional Provisions) Order 1997 (1997 S.I. No. 2200). Note that sections 38 (abolition of consent requirements for certain community penalties) and 46 (hospital and limitation directions) do not apply to offences committed before 1 October 1997. *Ibid.,* reg. 5(1)(a).

[253]   Mental Health Act 1983, s.45A(3), as inserted by Crime (Sentences) Act 1997, s.46. It is not possible for the Crown Court to impose a hospital direction without at the same time making a limitation direction ("The court may give *both* of the following directions, namely (a) ... ; *and* (b) ...").

[254]   Mental Health Act 1983, s.45B(2)(a), as inserted by Crime (Sentences) Act 1997, s.46.

[255]   Mental Health Act 1983, s.45B(2)(b), as inserted by Crime (Sentences) Act 1997, s.46.

been seen as having the disadvantage that the offender is entitled to be discharged as soon as he is no longer detainable in hospital. The aim of the new power is to combine the security of a custodial sentence with the immediate availability of medical treatment. Whatever else happens, the offender will serve his sentence securely detained unless the Home Secretary (rather than a tribunal) is satisfied that he is fit to be absolutely or conditionally discharged from hospital. The new directions are presently only available in respect of offenders who suffer from a treatable psychopathic disorder. These are the people for whom the power is thought likely to be most appropriate, because of widespread doubts about whether the risk of reoffending in such cases can be influenced through clinical treatment.

BASIC FRAMEWORK

The conditions which must be satisfied before the Crown Court may give the directions are similar to those that must exist before a hospital order and a restriction order may be made under sections 37 and 41. Similarly, the immediate effect of giving the directions, in terms of the patient's removal to a place of safety, his conveyance to hospital and admission by the hospital managers, is identical to that which follows the imposition of a hospital order (**401**). The fact that the directions are given by a court, and that they may only be given if the option of making a hospital order has been rejected, has therefore led to the general framework for making hospital and restriction orders being adopted as the basis of the court procedure. However, once the directions have been given and the offender is detained in the specified hospital, they do not take effect as a hospital order and a restriction order made under sections 37 and 41. Instead, they take effect as if the offender had initially been removed to prison, and had commenced his sentence there, and then been transferred to hospital by the Home Secretary under sections 47 and 49. The effect is that he is first-and-foremost a prisoner and only secondarily a patient. Once he no longer requires further treatment in hospital, or no effective treatment can be given there, he may be remitted to prison to serve out his sentence. Unless he has served his sentence, he has no entitlement to release into the community at that point.

PRISONERS AND THE MENTAL HEALTH ACT 1983

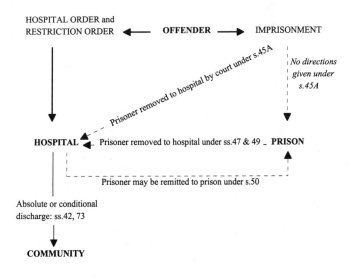

IMPOSING LIMITATION DIRECTIONS AND RESTRICTION ORDERS

Provision	S.45A	S.37/41	Notes
The defendant has been convicted before the Crown Court of an offence the sentence for which— (i) is not fixed by law (murder) (ii) does not fall to be dealt with under s.2 of the 1997 Act	s.45A(1) —	s.37(1) s.37(1)	A hospital order may not be made if a life sentence is required under section 2, but hospital and limitation directions may be given after the imposition of such a sentence.
The court is satisfied, on the written or oral evidence of two registered medical practitioners, one of whom is section 12 approved, that the offender is suffering from a psychopathic disorder of a nature or degree which makes it appropriate for him to be detained in a hospital for medical treatment	s.45A(2) s.54(1)	s.37(2) s.54(1)	*Identical requirements.*
The court is further satisfied, on that evidence, that such treatment is likely to alleviate or prevent a deterioration of his condition;	s.45A(2)	s.37(2)	*Identical requirements.*
At least one of the registered medical practitioners whose evidence is taken into account by the court in relation to (1) and (2) has given evidence orally before the court.	s.45A(4)	s.41(2)	*Identical requirements.*
The court is satisfied that arrangements have been made for his admission to the hospital specified within the period of 28 days.	s.45A(5)	s.37(4)	*Identical requirements.*
The court has imposed a sentence of imprisonment.	s.45A(1)	—	It is a condition of making a hospital order that the court is of the opinion, having considered alternative sentences such as imprisonment, that a hospital order is the most suitable method of disposing of the case: s.37(2)(b).
Except where a life sentence is required under section 2 of the Crime (Sentences) Act 1997, the court considered making a hospital order before deciding to impose a sentence of imprisonment.	s.45A(1)	—	

Provision			
It appears to the court, having regard to the nature of the offence, the antecedents of the offender and the risk of his committing further offences if set at large, that it is necessary for the protection of the public from serious harm that the patient be subject to the special restrictions.	—	s.41(1)	Restrictions must be imposed (in the form of a limitation direction) if a court gives a hospital direction — regardless of whether they appear to be necessary to protect the public from serious harm.

Effect of the orders or directions up to the time of admission

Provision			
Subject to the effect of a successful appeal, the making of the orders or directions has the consequence that any pre-existing application, unrestricted hospital order, or guardianship order ceases to have effect.	s.45B(2) s.47(3) s.49(2) s.55(4)	s.41(4)	*Identical requirements.*
Pending admission to the specified hospital within 28 days, the offender may be conveyed to, and detained in, the place of safety specified by the court.	s.45A(5)	s.37(4)	*Identical requirements.*
A constable, or any other person directed by the court, is authorised to convey the offender to the specified hospital during the 28 day period following sentence.	s.45B(1)	s.40(1)	*Identical requirements.*
Provided that the offender is admitted within that 28 day period, the managers of the specified hospital are authorised to admit him there and to thereafter detain him in accordance with the provisions of the Act.	s.45B(1)	s.40(1)	*Identical requirements.*
In an emergency or other special circumstances, the Home Secretary may give instructions/directions for the patient's admission within the 28 day period to a hospital other than that specified by the court.	s.45A(6) s.45A(7)	s.37(5)	*Identical requirements.*

401

CRITERIA FOR IMPOSITION

The following conditions must be met before the directions may be given—

- The defendant has been convicted before the Crown Court of an offence committed before 1 October 1997 the sentence for which is not fixed by law.[256]

- The court is satisfied, on the written or oral evidence of two registered medical practitioners, one of whom is approved under section 12, that the offender is suffering from a psychopathic disorder of a nature or degree which makes it appropriate for him to be detained in a hospital for medical treatment;[257]

- The court is further satisfied, on that evidence, that such treatment is likely to alleviate or prevent a deterioration of his condition;[258]

- At least one of the registered medical practitioners whose evidence is taken into account by the court in relation to (1) and (2) has given evidence orally before the court;[259]

- The court is satisfied, on the written or oral evidence of the registered medical practitioner who will be in charge of his treatment, or of some other person representing the managers of the hospital, that arrangements have been made for his admission to that hospital within the period of 28 days beginning with the date on which the directions are given;[260]

- The court has imposed a sentence of imprisonment, other than a life sentence for murder;[261]

- Except where a life sentence is required under section 2 of the Crime (Sentences) Act 1997, the court considered making a hospital order before deciding to impose a sentence of imprisonment in respect of the offence.[262]

---

[256] Mental Health Act 1983, s.45A(1), as inserted by Crime (Sentences) Act 1997, s.46; The Crime (Sentences) Act 1997 (Commencement No. 2 and Transitional Provisions) Order 1997, sub-para. 5(1)(a). A life sentence imposed under section 2 of the 1997 Act for a second serious offence is not to be regarded as a sentence which is fixed by law. Accordingly, the Crown Court may combine a life sentence under section 2 of the 1997 Act with hospital and limitation directions: Crime (Sentences) Act 1997, s.2(4); Mental Health Act 1983, s.45A(1)(b), as inserted by Crime (Sentences) Act 1997, s.46. The power to give such directions is not available to a magistrates' court, and nor may the Crown Court give them in the case of an offender who has been committed for sentence.

[257] Mental Health Act 1983, s.45A(2)(a) and (b), as inserted by *ibid.*; Mental Health Act 1983, s.54(1), as amended by *ibid.*, s.55(1), Sched. 4, para.12(6).

[258] Mental Health Act 1983, s.45A(2)(c), as inserted by *ibid.* Reaching such a decision may sometimes be difficult. Section 45A(8) therefore provides that the sentencing court may make an interim hospital order under section 38(1) before passing sentence.

[259] Mental Health Act 1983, s.45A(4), as inserted by *ibid.*

[260] Mental Health Act 1983, s.45A(5), as inserted by *ibid.*

[261] Mental Health Act 1983, s.45A(1), as inserted by *ibid.*

[262] Mental Health Act 1983, s.45A(1)(b), as inserted by *ibid.*

Commentary

The medical conditions which must be satisfied before hospital and limitation directions are given are identical to those which must exist before a hospital order is made in respect of a person who suffers from psychopathic disorder. As in the case of section 37, the court must also be satisfied that a hospital bed is available within 28 days. Where the sections do diverge is the necessary absence in section 45A of any reference to the remaining condition which must be satisfied before a hospital order is made under section 37 (with or without restrictions). As to this, section 37(2)(b) makes it a condition of imposing a hospital order that the court "is of the opinion, having regard to all the circumstances, including the nature of the offence and the character and antecedents of the offender, and to the other available methods of dealing with him, that the most suitable method of disposing of the case is by means of a hospital order." In contrast, it is a condition of giving the directions under section 45A that the court which has just sentenced the offender to imprisonment considered making a hospital order but was of the opinion (adopting the language of section 37(2)(b)) that the most suitable method of disposing of the case was by way of custodial sentence. "Considered" in this context can be taken to mean that the necessary medical reports were before the court, and a bed was available, and it was therefore in a position to consider making such an order. Where a prisoner's admission to hospital under section 45A is directed, the imposition of the special restrictions set out in section 41, in the form of a limitation direction, is mandatory. There is no requirement that such a direction may not be given unless it appears to the court that the special restrictions are necessary in order to protect the public from serious harm. Restrictions being mandatory, the individual's position in this respect diverges from that of a prisoner transferred under section 47, and is instead the same as that of a person awaiting trial who is transferred to hospital under section 48(2)(a) or (b).

EFFECT OF THE DIRECTIONS

It has been noted that a hospital direction has effect as a transfer direction made under section 47 and a limitation direction has effect as a restriction direction given under section 49.[263] The effect of these directions has already been described (**374**), including in relation to persons sentenced to life imprisonment (**390**). The following additional notes are either by way of emphasis or deal with incidental matters specific to limitation directions—

- A hospital direction and a restriction direction imposed under section 45A constitute a sentence for the purposes of the Criminal Appeal Act 1968.[264]

- Section 50 of the 1983 Act (which deals with the expiration of prisoners' sentences and also their remission to prison or release from hospital on licence) applies to patients subject to limitation directions as it applies to prisoners who are subject to restriction directions (**386 et seq.**).[265]

- The consent to treatment provisions in Part IV apply to patients detained under hospital and limitation directions as they apply to patients detained in

---

[263] Mental Health Act 1983, s.45B(2), as inserted by Crime (Sentences) Act 1997, s.46.

[264] Criminal Appeal Act 1968, s.50(1), as amended by Crime (Sentences) Act 1997, s.55(1), Sched. 4, para. 6(1)(a).

[265] Mental Health Act 1983, s.50(5), as inserted by Crime (Sentences) Act 1997, Sched. 4, para. 12(5).

pursuance of transfer and restriction directions.[266] Such patients may there-fore be given medication and other forms of treatment without their consent in the circumstances specified in that Part of the Act (**273**).

- The patient's position being identical to that of a prisoner transferred to hospital under sections 47 and 49, he may apply to a tribunal during the six month period beginning with the date of the directions, once more during the following six months, and thereafter once during each subsequent year the directions remain in force.[267]

- Persons detained in hospital in pursuance of directions given under section 45A are entitled to after-care under section 117 when they cease to be de-tained and leave hospital (**413**).[268] However, being restricted patients, a super-vision application may not be made in respect of them under section 25A.[269]

- As in other restricted cases, the responsible medical officer must at such intervals (not exceeding one year) as the Secretary of State may direct examine and report to the Secretary of State on the patient; and every report must contain such particulars as the Secretary of State may require."[270]

EXTENDING SECTION 45A TO OTHER DISORDERS

The drafting of section 45A enables a phased introduction of hospital and limitation directions. More particularly, the Secretary of State may by order extend section 45A so that such directions may also be given in respect of offenders who suffer from one or more of the other forms of mental disorder.[271] Any such order may be limited to particular classes of offenders or offences; provide that any reference to a sentence of imprisonment or to a prison includes custodial sentences and instit-utions of other descriptions; and include such supplementary, incidental or conse-quential provisions as appear to be necessary or expedient.[272]

THE NEW SENTENCING FRAMEWORK

Section 2 of the Crime (Sentences) Act 1997 requires the Crown Court to impose a life sentence for a second serious offence unless there are exceptional circum-stances. Section 3 provides that a minimum sentence of seven years' imprisonment shall be imposed for a third class A drug trafficking offence while section 4 requires a minimum sentence of three years' imprisonment for a third offence of domestic

---

[266]   Mental Health Act 1983, Part IV, as amended by Crime (Sentences) Act 1997, s.55(1), Sched. 4, para. 12(7).
[267]   Mental Health Act 1983, ss.69(2)(b), as amended by Crime (Sentences) Act 1997, s.55(1), Sched. 4, para. 12(8).
[268]   Mental Health Act 1983, s.117(1), as amended by Crime (Sentences) Act 1997, s.55(1), Sched. 4, para. 12(17).
[269]   Mental Health Act 1983, s.41(3)(aa), as inserted by Mental Health (Patients in the Community) Act 1995, s.2(1), Sched. 1, para. 5.
[270]   Mental Health Act 1983, s.45B(3), as inserted by Crime (Sentences) Act 1997, s.46.
[271]   Mental Health Act 1983, s.45A(10), as inserted by Crime (Sentences) Act 1997, s.46.
[272]   Mental Health Act 1983, s.45A(11), as inserted by Crime (Sentences) Act 1997, s.46. For example, that a hospital direction shall specify the form(s) of disorder from which the offender has been found to suffer, and shall be of no effect unless the patient is described by both medical practitioners whose evidence is taken into account as suffering from at least one common form of mental disorder.

burglary. The effect of section 45A has already been described: the Crown Court may, instead of making a hospital order, imprison an offender suffering from a treatable psychopathic disorder and then direct his removal to hospital for treatment, in which case a tribunal may not direct his release, and he will continue to be detained until *both* his sentence has expired and he no longer requires detention in hospital for treatment (**399**). Taken together, these provisions represent a significant shift in the balance between the respective needs to ensure that the public are protected from repeat offending and that effective medical treatment is given to mentally disordered offenders. The purpose served by the life sentence is to protect the public from a further repetition of the most serious kinds of sexual and violent offences and to ensure that those who commit them, for whatever reason, receive supervision for life unless the circumstances are truly exceptional. A disposal under the mental health legislation cannot achieve that because the individual must be released as soon as he no longer satisfies the criteria for detention in hospital. According to the Government, it would frustrate the purpose of the mandatory sentence, which is to protect the public, if evidence of mental disorder is regarded in itself as an exceptional circumstance which enables the life sentence to be avoided. Furthermore, a life sentence is not inappropriate for, if a conviction is arrived at by the court, some degree of culpability has been established.

Mandatory sentences for a second serious offence

Section 2 applies if a person is convicted of a serious offence committed on or after 1 October 1997 and, at the time of its commission, he was aged 18 or over and had previously been convicted in any part of the United Kingdom of another serious offence.[273] The following offences committed in England and Wales are serious offences: attempted murder, conspiracy to commit murder, incitement to murder, soliciting murder; manslaughter; wounding or causing grievous bodily harm with intent; rape, attempted rape, intercourse with a girl under 13; possession of a firearm with intent to injure, use of a firearm to resist arrest, carrying a firearm with criminal intent; robbery, if the offender had in his possession a firearm or imitation firearm.[274] If section 2 applies, the court shall impose a life sentence[275] unless it is of the opinion that there are exceptional circumstances relating to either of the offences or to the offender which justify it not doing so.[276] Where the court does not impose a life sentence, it shall state in open court that it is of the opinion that there are exceptional circumstances and what those exceptional circumstances are.[277] What

---

[273] Crime (Sentences) Act 1997, s.2(1).

[274] *Ibid.*, s.2(5). Subsections (6) and (7) list those offences committed in Scotland and Northern Ireland which are to be regarded as serious offences.

[275] A sentence of imprisonment for life in case of a person aged 21 or over; in other cases, a sentence of custody for life under section 8(2) of the Criminal Justice Act 1982. Crime (Sentences) Act 1997, s.2(2). Where a life sentenced is imposed under section 2 in respect of a serious offence, the offence is not to be regarded as an offence the sentence for which is fixed by law. See *ibid.*, s.2(4).

[276] *Ibid.*, s.2(2). Section 1(2) sets out the basis on which the court shall carry out its sentencing functions: when determining whether it would be appropriate not to impose a life sentence, the court shall have regard to the circumstances relating to either of the offences or to the offender. This is somewhat different from the basis upon which the court must carry out its sentencing functions under sections 3 and 4. More particularly, under section 2, the life sentence usually required is not required if there are exceptional circumstances which "justify" not imposing it. Under sections 3 or 4, the minimum sentence usually required is not required if the circumstances are such that such a custodial sentence would be "unjust." It is submitted that the section 2 test confers greater discretion. Although the circumstances may not be such that a life sentence would be unjust, they may be sufficiently exceptional that they justify not imposing life imprisonment. As to the meaning of "justify," see pp.221 and 485.

[277] Crime (Sentences) Act 1997, s.2(3).

constitutes "exceptional circumstances" is not defined and is a matter for judicial discretion and interpretation. Unless there are exceptional circumstances which take the case outside section 2, the sentence "falls to be imposed under section 2" and it necessarily follows that the Crown Court may not make a hospital order.[278] However, if the offender sentenced to life imprisonment under section 2 is diagnosed as having a treatable psychopathic disorder and a hospital bed is available, the court may also give a hospital direction and a limitation direction under section 45A of the 1983 Act, so that in-patient treatment can be provided. Until such time as the power to give these directions is extended to persons who suffer from the other forms of mental disorder (mental illness, mental impairment, severe mental impairment), they will be taken to prison and may only be transferred to hospital for treatment if the Home Secretary gives a transfer direction under section 47. Section 2 was brought into force on 1 October 1997.

LIFE SENTENCES AND SECTION 2

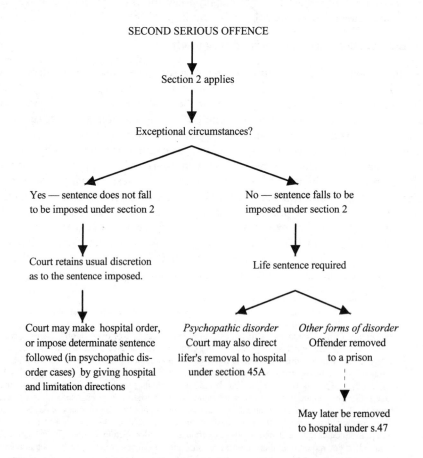

---

[278] Mental Health Act 1983, s.37(1), as amended by Crime (Sentences) Act 1997, Sched. 4, para. 12(1).

Minimum sentence for third domestic burglary

Section 4 requires a minimum sentence of three years' imprisonment for a third offence of domestic burglary. For these purposes, "domestic burglary" means a burglary committed in respect of a building or part of a building which is a dwelling. The offender must be aged 18 or over when the third burglary is committed; all three of the burglaries must have been committed after the commencement of the section; and, more particularly, the second committed after he had been convicted of the first.[279] Provided that these conditions are satisfied, the court must impose a custodial sentence for a term of at least three years except where it is of the opinion that there are specific circumstances which relate to any of the offences or to the offender which would make the prescribed custodial sentence unjust in all the circumstances.[280] Where the court does not impose such a sentence, it must state in open court that it is of the opinion that such a sentence would be unjust in all the circumstances and state what the specific circumstances are. Where there are no specific circumstances which justify not imposing the minimum sentence, the sentence "falls to be imposed under section 4." However, section 37(1A) of the 1983 Act provides that, where a sentence would otherwise fall to be imposed under section 4(2), nothing "shall prevent a court from making an order under subsection (1) ... for the admission of the offender to a hospital."[281] The Government does not presently have any plans to bring section 4 into force, given current pressures on prison capacity and available resources.

Minimum sentence for third class A drug trafficking offence

Section 3 contains similar provisions and it requires a minimum sentence of seven years' imprisonment for a third class A drug trafficking offence. The offender must be aged 18 or over when the third offence is committed and one of the prior offences must have been committed after he had been convicted of the first.[282] The remaining statutory provisions are the same as those set out in section 4. Provided that these conditions are satisfied, the court must impose a custodial sentence for a term of at least seven years except where it is of the opinion that there are specific circumstances which relate to any of the offences or to the offender which would make the prescribed custodial sentence unjust in all the circumstances.[283] Where the

---

[279] Where a person is charged with a third domestic burglary and the circumstances are such that, if he is convicted, he could be sentenced for it under section 4, the burglary is triable only on indictment.

[280] Section 1 sets out the basis on which the court shall carry out its sentencing functions: when determining whether it would be appropriate not to impose a sentence of at least three years, the court shall have regard to the specific circumstances which relate to any of the offences or to the offender *and* would make the prescribed custodial sentence unjust in all the circumstances: *Ibid.*, s.1(3).

[281] Section 37(1A) of the Mental Health Act 1983, as inserted by paragraph 12(2) of Schedule 4 to the Crime (Sentences) Act 1997. Because the courts may make a hospital order as an alternative to imposing the minimum custodial sentence, there will never be any need to establish that the offender's mental state or psychiatric history constitute exceptional circumstances before such an order can be made. As to the absence of any reference to a guardianship order in section 37(1A), see p.325.

[282] In contrast to the position under section 4, it is not necessary that all three offences have been committed after the commencement of the section. *Ibid.*, s.3(1). Where a person is charged with a third drug trafficking offence and the circumstances are such that, if he is convicted, he could be sentenced for it under section 3, the charge is triable only on indictment. *Ibid.*, s.3(4).

[283] Section 1(3) sets out the basis on which the court shall carry out its sentencing functions: when determining whether it would be appropriate not to impose a custodial sentence of at least seven years, the court shall have regard to the specific circumstances which relate to any of the offences or to the offender *and* would make the prescribed custodial sentence unjust in all the circumstances.

court does not impose such a sentence, it must state in open court that it is of the opinion that such a sentence would be unjust in all the circumstances and what the specific circumstances are. Where there are no specific circumstances which justify not imposing the minimum sentence, the sentence "falls to be imposed under section 3." However, section 37(1A) of the 1983 Act provides that, where a sentence would otherwise fall to be imposed under section 4(2), nothing "shall prevent a court from making an order under subsection (1) ... for the admission of the offender to a hospital."[284] Section 3 was brought into force on 1 October 1997.

SECTIONS 3 & 4 AND THE MENTAL HEALTH ACT 1983

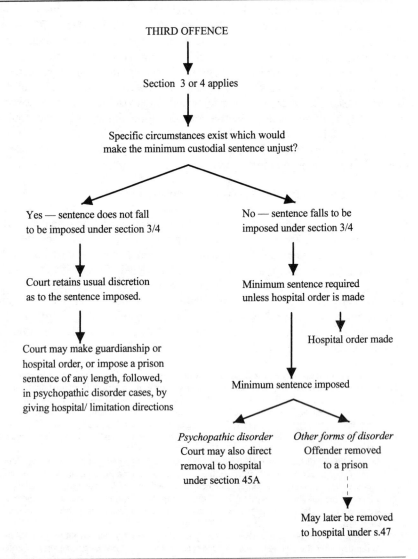

THIRD OFFENCE

Section 3 or 4 applies

Specific circumstances exist which would make the minimum custodial sentence unjust?

Yes — sentence does not fall to be imposed under section 3/4

No — sentence falls to be imposed under section 3/4

Court retains usual discretion as to the sentence imposed.

Minimum sentence required unless hospital order is made

Hospital order made

Court may make guardianship or hospital order, or impose a prison sentence of any length, followed, in psychopathic disorder cases, by giving hospital/ limitation directions

Minimum sentence imposed

Psychopathic disorder
Court may also direct removal to hospital under section 45A

Other forms of disorder
Offender removed to a prison

May later be removed to hospital under s.47

---

[284]   Section 37(1A) of the Mental Health Act 1983, as inserted by paragraph 12(2) of Schedule 4 to the Crime (Sentences) Act 1997. Because the court may make a hospital order as an alternative to the minimum custodial sentence, there will never be any need to establish that the offender's mental state or psychiatric history constitute exceptional circumstances before such an order can be made. As to the absence of any reference to a guardianship order in section 37(1A), see p.325.

- If a person has been convicted of murder then a life sentence is mandatory and the offender may only be admitted to hospital for treatment if he is later removed there by the Home Secretary under section 47.

- Under section 2 of the Crime (Sentences) Act 1997, a life sentence will now also be required if a defendant has been convicted of a second serious offence and there are no exceptional circumstances which justify not imposing such a sentence.

- Section 2 of the 1997 Act will not apply if a person awaiting trial for a second serious offence is detained in hospital under section 48, on account of the fact that he is mentally ill or severely mentally impaired, and his case is disposed of under section 51(5) of the 1983 Act, that is by making a hospital order in his absence without convicting him.

- Section 2 of the 1997 Act also does not apply where a jury is satisfied that a person has committed an act which would constitute a second serious offence if convicted of it but he is not convicted, having been found unfit to plead or not guilty of the offence by reason of insanity. In such cases, the "sentence falls to be imposed" under the Criminal Procedure (Insanity) Act 1964 rather than under the 1997 Act. The disposals available under the former do not include imprisonment, let alone life imprisonment.

- Section 2 of the 1997 Act will again not apply where a person is convicted of a serious offence and, sometime in the past, a jury found that he did an act which, had he been convicted of it, would have constituted his first serious offence, but he was not convicted because he was found to be unfit to plead or not guilty of it by reason of insanity. The defendant having only ever been convicted of one serious offence, the court retains its usual discretion as to the most appropriate sentence in such cases. The court may therefore make a hospital order. Equally, though, the fact that the sentence does not fall to be imposed under section 2 does not prevent the court from imposing a maximum sentence of life imprisonment if the circumstances make that appropriate.

- Where a person is convicted of a second serious offence, he falls to be sentenced to life imprisonment under section 2 unless the court is of the opinion that there are exceptional circumstances relating to either of the offences or to the offender which justify it not doing so.

- What constitutes exceptional circumstances is not defined in the Act and is therefore a matter for judicial discretion and interpretation.

- Although the court must have regard to the circumstances relating to the offender and the offences, the fact that the offender is mentally disordered is not without more an exceptional circumstance which empowers the court to refrain from imposing a life sentence.

- More particularly, the fact that the responsibility of an offender convicted of manslaughter on the grounds of diminished responsibility is diminished by reason of mental illness is not of itself an exceptional circumstance — it is a common feature of all such offences, not an exceptional feature.

- If there are exceptional circumstances, the court retains its usual discretion as to the appropriate sentence: it is not bound to impose a life sentence and may instead make a hospital order under section 37 (or any other order which a first offence could attract, such as a determinate sentence).

- If there are no exceptional circumstances and a life sentence is therefore imposed, the sentencing court may also give hospital and limitation directions under section 45A of the 1983 Act if the offender suffers from a psychopathic disorder and the other statutory conditions for giving such directions are satisfied. These statutory conditions are identical to those which must be satisfied before a hospital order may be made under section 37, with the single exception that the condition specified in section 37(2)(b) is necessarily absent. Having disposed of the case by way of life imprisonment, the court is not required to state its opinion that the most suitable method of disposing of the case is by means of an order under section 37, even if that is its opinion.

- If there are no exceptional circumstances and a life sentence is therefore imposed, the sentencing court will not have any power to also give those directions in respect of an offender who suffers from some other form of disorder, *i.e.* mental illness, severe mental impairment, mental impairment. Whether such an offender receives necessary treatment for his mental disorder depends on the Home Secretary later transferring him to hospital under section 47. The sentencing court may informally recommend that the Home Secretary do so but no more.

- Except for sentences passed under section 2 of the 1997 Act, the sentencing court retains the option in all cases of making a hospital order, as an alternative to imposing the minimum sentence usually required.

- More particularly, where a person is convicted of a third domestic burglary or a third Class A drug trafficking offence, the sentence does not fall to be imposed under sections 3 or 4 if specific circumstances exist, in relation to the offender or the offences, which would make it unjust to impose the minimum sentence. Those special circumstances may include the offender's mental condition.

- If the caveat applies, the court retains its usual discretion as to the appropriate sentence and may, *inter alia*, impose a hospital order, a guardianship order, or a term of imprisonment of less than the minimum length usually required.

- If there are no specific circumstances which would make it unjust to impose the minimum sentence, the fact that such a sentence would not be unjust does not prevent the court from instead making a hospital order (but not a guardianship order) under section 37.

- If, however, the minimum sentence not being unjust, the court also decides that a hospital order is not the most appropriate way of disposing of the case before it (s.37(2)(b)), it must then impose a sentence of at least the minimum length. Not having found such a sentence to be unjust, and not finding a hospital order to be appropriate, it may not at this final stage do "Solomon's justice" by imposing a prison sentence of less than the minimum.

- Where a sentence of imprisonment is imposed under sections 3 or 4 (whether for more than three or seven years or, if that would be unjust, for some lesser length), the sentencing court may also give hospital and limitation directions under section 45A of the 1983 Act if the offender suffers from a psychopathic disorder and the other statutory conditions for giving such directions are satisfied. The sentencing court does not, however, have any power to also give these directions in respect of imprisoned offenders who suffer from some other form of disorder. In their case, whether or not they receive any necessary treatment depends upon the Home Secretary later giving a transfer direction under section 47.

- Having regard to the above, and the changes introduced by the Criminal Procedure (Insanity and Unfitness to Plead) Act 1991, it may be anticipated that the defence will henceforth more often seek a special verdict in cases where the offender is charged with what will constitute a first or second serious offence if he is convicted. Furthermore, in homicide cases, a verdict of insanity will have particular advantages over a finding that the defendant is guilty of manslaughter by reason of diminished responsibility.

6. After-care and supervision applications

INTRODUCTION

Section 117 of the Mental Health Act 1983 imposes a statutory duty on Health Authorities and local social services authorities to provide after-care to patients who leave hospital having been detained there for treatment. The Mental Health (Patients in the Community) Act 1995 introduced a new power of supervised discharge. This allows an application to be made under Part II for an unrestricted patient who is liable to be detained for treatment, and therefore entitled to after-care, to be subject to "after-care under supervision" when he leaves hospital (**422**). The Act also amended the law concerning patients who are lawfully or unlawfully absent from hospital or the place where they are required to reside. Thus, the Act provides for each of the three situations in which an unrestricted patient who has been detained for treatment may be in the community — he may have leave to be absent from hospital, or he may be absent from there without leave, or he may have been discharged and no longer liable to detention.

AFTER-CARE UNDER SECTION 117

Health and social services authorities have a statutory duty under section 117 of the 1983 Act to provide after-care for patients who have been detained in hospital for treatment. More specifically, the Act provides that the duty to provide after-care under section 117 applies to persons who are detained under sections 3, 37, 45A, 47 or 48 "and then cease to be detained and *(whether or not immediately after so ceasing)* leave hospital."[1] The italicised words were inserted by the 1995 Act and they emphasise that the duty to provide after-care does not lapse because a patient who has ceased to be liable to be detained then remains in hospital for a period as an informal patient. Previously, it was sometimes argued that a patient who had been detained for treatment and then became an informal in-patient before being discharged could not be said to "then cease to be detained and leave hospital."

WHAT CONSTITUTES AFTER-CARE

The Act does not specify the extent of the statutory duty, other than that after-care services must be provided until the relevant authorities are satisfied that the patient is no longer in need of such services. What constitutes after-care and the exact nature of that duty is not defined and no regulations have been made which prescribe

---

[1]   Mental Health Act 1983, s.117, as amended by Mental Health (Patients in the Community) Act 1995, s.1(2), Sched. 1, para. 15, and Crime (Sentences) Act 1997, s.55(1), Sched. 4, para. 12(17).

how the duties are to be performed. However, the fact that the duty is confined to persons who have required detention for treatment for a potentially indefinite period suggests that the central purpose of the after-care is to minimise, as far as practicable, the risk of relapse and the need for further in-patient treatment.

SECTION 117 : AFTER-CARE

"After Care

117.—(1) This section applies to persons who are detained under section 3 above, or admitted to a hospital in pursuance of *a hospital direction made under section 45A above or* a hospital order made under section 37 above, or transferred to a hospital in pursuance of a transfer direction made under section 47 or 48 above, and then cease to be detained and *(whether or not immediately after so ceasing)* leave hospital.

(2) It shall be the duty of the Health Authority and of the local social services authority to provide, in co-operation with relevant voluntary agencies, after-care services for any person to whom this section applies until such time as the Health Authority and the local social services authority are satisfied that the person concerned is no longer in need of such services*; but they shall not be so satisfied in the case of a patient who is subject to after-care under supervision at any time while he remains so subject.*

(2A) It shall be the duty of the Health Authority to secure that at all times while a patient is subject to after-care under supervision—

(a) a person who is a registered medical practitioner approved for the purposes of section 12 above by the Secretary of State as having special experience in the diagnosis or treatment of mental disorder is in charge of the medical treatment provided for the patient as part of the after-care services provided for him under this section; and

(b) a person professionally concerned with any of the after-care services so provided is supervising him with a view to securing that he receives the after-care services so provided.

(2B) Section 32 above shall apply for the purposes of this section as it applies for the purposes of Part II of this Act.

(3) In this section "the Health Authority" means the Health Authority, and "the local social services authority" means the local social services authority, for the area in which the person concerned is resident or to which he is sent on discharge by the hospital in which he was detained.

The words in italics represent insertions and amendments made by the Mental Health (Patients in the Community) Act 1995, Sched. 1, para. 15; the Health Authorities Act 1995 (which replaced previous references to a District Health Authority with references to the Health Authority); and the Crime (Sentences) Act 1997.

WHEN THE DUTY TO PROVIDE AFTER-CARE ARISES

Section 117 imposes a duty to provide after-care services for patients who are detained for treatment and then cease to be detained and leave hospital. In *ex p. Fox*, the Divisional Court rejected a submission that the duty to provide after-care only comes into existence when the patient is discharged from hospital. The duty to provide after-care services is a continuing duty in respect of any patient who may be discharged, although it is only triggered in any particular case at the moment of discharge.

R. v. Ealing District Health Authority, ex p. Fox

[1993] 1 W.L.R. 373   Q.B.D., Otton J.

In 1988, the patient appeared at the Central Criminal Court where he was convicted of inflicting grievous bodily harm with intent and possessing a firearm with intent to commit an indictable offence. The court was satisfied that he was suffering from mental illness and psychopathic disorder and directed that he be admitted to a special hospital in pursuance of a hospital order and a restriction order made without limit of time. On 18 July 1991, a Mental Health Review Tribunal considered his case. It directed the patient's conditional discharge but deferred the discharge until such time as it was satisfied that arrangements had been made which enabled the conditions of discharge to be satisfied. In particular, it was necessary for the Health Authority to appoint a responsible medical officer to provide psychiatric supervision for the patient in the community. In the reasons for its decision, the tribunal stated that any delay in discharging the patient would cause problems in his rehabilitation. Before coming to its decision, the tribunal did not seek the views or agreement of any doctor who might, by virtue of its decision, become responsible for providing medical treatment and supervision in the community. The doctors of the Health Authority which had the duty to provide the patient with after-care following discharge were unwilling to undertake the necessary supervision. More particularly, a forensic consultant at the regional secure unit for the area within which the tribunal decided that the patient should be discharged declined to act. He stated that, "I can only properly agree to accept the role of medical supervisor in cases where I feel the patient is amenable to continuing supervision ... I do not have this confidence and it would be wrong of me to give the appearance that I have and accept the responsibility of supervising him when I feel it to be impossible." The consultant's colleagues at that unit were of the same view. Likewise, the catchment area consultant declined to act, stating that it was important to note that at no time had he been consulted by the tribunal about taking responsibility for the patient. Based on the doctors' opinions, the Health Authority concluded that the patient should instead be supervised for at least 18 months in a regional secure unit rather than in the community. Accordingly, the Health Authority did not appoint a responsible medical officer and the patient remained in hospital. In February 1992, a consultant psychiatrist not employed by the Health Authority was instructed on the patient's behalf by his solicitor. He interviewed the patient in hospital during that month. He was willing to see the patient as an out-patient privately but, for practical reasons, could not take responsibility for how the supervision might turn out. The tribunal was due to reconsider the patient's case in March 1992 but the patient cancelled the hearing, applying instead for judicial review.

The grounds of application

The patient applied for judicial review, seeking a declaration that the Health Authority had erred in law in refusing to supply psychiatric supervision in the community for the applicant; alternatively, an order of certiorari to quash the decision of the Health Authority not to provide community psychiatric supervision; and, finally, an order of mandamus to compel the Health Authority to provide the supervision. The grounds of the application were, *inter alia*, that the Health Authority had substituted the clinical judgment of its consultant psychiatrist —that it was preferable for the applicant to be supervised in a regional secure unit— for the decision of the tribunal that he should be released into supervision in the community; that the authority had thereby prevented him from fulfilling the conditions for his release; and that the authority had failed to fulfil its duty under section 117 to provide after-care services for him. The Health Authority's case was that a tribunal has no express or implied statutory power to direct a Health Authority to provide any type of health care. If the contrary proposition were correct, a Health Authority would be under such a duty to provide community medical supervision even though a patient's condition had seriously deteriorated since the tribunal decision. There would be no need for the deferral procedure unless there was a possibility that a Health Authority might lawfully decline to provide the service contemplated by the tribunal. The effect of a deferred discharge was simply to require the Health Authority to ascertain whether the conditions could be complied with and, if the tribunal was satisfied that the necessary arrangements had been made, the discharge then took effect. Furthermore, the Health Authority was not under any duty to provide after-care to the patient by virtue of section 117: that section had not been triggered because the patient had not yet left hospital.

Otton J.

1. A conditional discharge, whether immediate or deferred, was a final order and once made the tribunal had no power to revoke it. However, section 73(7) empowered a tribunal to defer its order so that arrangements could be made which enabled the conditions of the order to be fulfilled. Although the tribunal knew that no regional secure unit was available, it was entitled to decide that conditional discharge was appropriate.

2. While it might be true that there was no express statutory power to direct a Health Authority to provide a particular type of health care to a particular person at a particular time, it did not follow that it was not in breach by refusing to treat the patient within or under its aegis. Section 117(2) was mandatory. That duty was not only a general duty but a specific duty owed to the patient to provide him with after-care services until such time as the health and local social services authorities were satisfied that he was no longer in need of them. The duty did not only come into existence when the patient was discharged from hospital. The duty to provide after-care under section 117 was a continuing duty in respect of any patient falling within section 117 who might be discharged, although the duty to any particular patient was only triggered at the moment of discharge. In the alternative, such a duty could be spelt out from the general statutory framework concerning the National Health Service, which required health authorities to provide a comprehensive range of hospital and community psychiatric services, including appropriate services to meet the needs of mentally disordered offenders.

3. As to whether the Health Authority had discharged its duty to the patient, the mere acceptance by it of the doctors' opinions was not of itself a sufficient discharge of its obligation to proceed with reasonable expedition and diligence and to give effect to the arrangements specified and required by the tribunal. The effect of a tribunal's decision was not merely to require the relevant authority to determine whether it was prepared to satisfy the conditions, so as to enable the discharge to take place. The purpose of deferral was to allow time for the Health Authority to give effect to the conditions which the tribunal had already determined.[2] If the authority's doctors did not agree with the conditions which had been imposed, and were disinclined to make the necessary arrangements, the authority could not let the matter rest there. It was under a continuing obligation to make further endeavours to provide arrangements within its own resources, or to obtain them from other Health Authorities, so as to put in place the practical arrangements enabling the patient to comply with the conditions the or, at the very least, to make inquiries of other service providers.

4. If the arrangements still could not be made, the Health Authority should not permit an impasse to continue. It should refer the matter to the Secretary of State, so that he could consider exercising his power to refer the case back to the Mental Health Review Tribunal, under section 71(1). That was also the appropriate course of action where there was a subsequent deterioration of the patient's condition.[3] There was no reason, either in principle or in practice, why a Health Authority faced with such a dilemma could not of its own initiative inform the Secretary of State of the deterioration, send him its medical reports and request him to refer the case to the tribunal afresh.

5. In summary, the authority had erred in law in that it had not fulfilled its obligations. The fact that it was not prepared to take any steps other than to obtain the views of its doctors meant that it was still in breach of its duty arising from the decision of the Mental Health Review Tribunal. As to the relief sought, it was appropriate to make an order of certiorari to quash the Health Authority's decision not to provide psychiatric supervision in the community for the patient. It was also appropriate to make a declaration in the following terms:

    (1) that the authority has erred in law in not attempting with all reasonable expedition and diligence to make arrangements so as to enable the applicant to comply with the conditions imposed by the Mental Health Review Tribunal;

    (2) that a [district] Health Authority was under a duty under section 117 of the Mental Health Act 1983 to provide after-care services when a patient leaves hospital, and acts unlawfully in failing to seek to make practical arrangements for after-care prior to that patient's discharge from hospital where such arrangements are required by a Mental Health Review Tribunal in order to enable the patient to be conditionally discharged from hospital.

---

2   *R. v. Oxford Regional Mental Health Review Tribunal, ex p. Secretary of State for the Home Department* [1988] A.C. 120.

3   In *R. v. Oxford Regional Mental Health Review Tribunal, ex p. Secretary of State for the Home Department* [1988] A.C. 120 at 128, Lord Bridge said that section 73(7) "certainly enables the Secretary of State, when a deterioration in the condition of the patient is brought to his attention, to forestall the patient's discharge by exercising his power under section 71 of the Act of 1983 to refer the patient's case to the tribunal afresh."

The duty to provide after-care under section 117 does not extend to informal patients; patients detained for assessment under Part II; patients detained under any of the short-term powers of detention with a maximum duration of 72 hours or less; patients subject to guardianship, unless previously detained for treatment; Part III patients detained for treatment under sections 36 or 38; patients remanded to hospital for the preparation of a report under section 35. The rationale in the case of patients detained under section 35, 36 or 38 is that their cases have not yet been disposed of by the court. The court may later make a hospital order, in which case a statutory entitlement to after-care will arise, but equally it might deal with the offender in some other manner such as by way of a custodial sentence.

Patients detained in mental nursing homes

The Act is ambiguous with regard to patients admitted to mental nursing homes.[4] It provides that references to a "hospital" in Parts III *(mentally disordered offenders)*, V *(mental health review tribunals)* and VI *(removal and return of patients within the United Kingdom)* are to be construed as referring to "a hospital within the meaning of Part II" and therefore as including mental nursing homes which are registered to receive detained patients.[5] References to a "hospital" in Part VIII— which includes section 117 — bear instead the meaning given in section 145(1) and so exclude mental nursing homes unless the context requires a different meaning. Because this is so, certain provisions in Part VIII are expressly stated to apply both to hospitals and mental nursing homes (see ss. 116, 118 and 120) but others only to hospitals (see sections 117, 122 and 123). The question arises whether the context requires that where a section in Part VIII, such as section 117, refers only to a hospital this is nevertheless to be interpreted as referring to "a hospital within the meaning of Part II." It would seem incongruous if Parliament intended that section 117 should apply to private patients treated in an NHS hospital but not to NHS patients admitted to mental nursing homes under a contract with a Health Authority. Therefore, the absence of any reference to mental nursing homes in section 117 is probably only loose drafting. It is submitted that "hospital" in this context includes mental nursing homes, notwithstanding the definition of a hospital in section 145 and the fact that only certain sections within Part VIII of the Act are expressed to apply to mental nursing homes.

Patients detained under sections 47 and 48

The clause originally inserted in the Bill during the Third Reading in the House of Lords only provided that patients detained under what are now sections 3 and 37 had a statutory entitlement to after-care. The references to patients transferred from prison or custody were added later. Presumably, if the patient "ceases to be detained

---

[4]   The problems concerning the section's interpretation mainly arise because it was inserted during the Third Reading of the Bill, following a division in the House of Lords which the Government lost. Although the Government knew that the section was "defective in a number of respects" it did nothing to rectify those defects. See *Mental Health (Amendment) Bill: Notes on Clauses, House of Commons* (D.H.S.S., 1982), p.161.

[5]   Except where otherwise expressly provided or where the context requires a different meaning. Likewise, the references to a hospital in sections 128 (assisting patients to absent themselves without leave), 134 (correspondence of patients) and 138 (retaking of patients escaping from custody) are also to be construed according to the definition in section 34(2), and therefore encompass mental nursing homes which are registered to receive detained patients.

and leaves hospital" because he is remitted to prison rather than discharged into the community no duty to provide after-care arises or, if it does, it is not triggered at that point. Some section 47 patients remitted to prison will be serving life sentences and some section 48 patients who are remitted will later be dealt with under the ordinary sentencing provisions. From one perspective, there is little merit in distinguishing between section 36 and section 48 patients since the majority of them are defendants awaiting trial in the course of criminal proceedings. The main difference in this context is that a section 48 patient may be discharged from hospital under the Mental Health Act 1983 whereas the section 36 patient may only be released by being granted bail. The implication is perhaps that if a patient is dealt with under the ordinary criminal provisions, by way of bail or custody, no duty to provide after-care arises, that duty being limited to cases where the patient "ceases to be detained and leaves hospital" through being discharged under the 1983 Act. If so, the rationale may be that the discharged patient's circumstances reflect the fact that it is more appropriate to continue to deal with him as a patient. Conversely, the grant of bail and remission to prison both imply that it is more appropriate to again deal with the individual as an ordinary offender. An intermediate view would be that the term "leaves hospital" excludes being remitted to prison but includes section 48 patients who leave hospital and take up residence in the community as a result of being granted bail. Although the position is ultimately unclear, it is submitted that the distinguishing feature of section 3, 37, 47 and 48 patients, compared with those detained under sections 35, 36 and 38, is that the former but not the latter may be discharged under the Mental Health Act 1983. Accordingly, the duty imposed by section 117 only applies to patients who cease to be detained because they are discharged under the 1983 Act and then leave hospital.

Patients granted leave of absence

It has been noted that the duty to provide after-care is triggered when a patient previously detained for treatment then ceases to be detained and (whether or not immediately after so ceasing) leaves hospital. The wording of section 117 now makes it clear that where a patient ceases to be detained but does not immediately leave hospital this does not affect his statutory entitlement. The converse situation is that where the patient leaves hospital first, under section 17 leave, and only later ceases to be "liable to be detained." The question whether leave granted prior to a patient's discharge from liability to detention triggers the duty to provide after-care was not in issue in *ex p. Fox* (**415**) and, consequently, not canvassed. It has been contended that the duty to provide after-care to patients granted leave of absence is not triggered until such time as they are also discharged from liability to detention.[6] The view of the Mental Health Act Commission is that a literal interpretation is to be preferred and the duty is triggered when a patient is granted leave, at which point he literally ceases to be detained and leaves hospital, albeit that he remains "liable to be detained." In support of the Commission's view, it may be noted that, in *R. v. Hallstrom*,[7] McCullough J. was not convinced that the word "detained" in section 117 meant in fact "liable to be detained."[8] If this is correct, the phrase "leaves"

---

[6] By Nigel Pleming Q.C. in *R. v. Hallstrom, ex p. W.; R. v. Gardner, ex p. L.* [1986] 1 Q.B. 1090.

[7] *R. v. Hallstrom, ex p. W.; R. v. Gardner, ex p. L.*, supra.

[8] See also *Safford v. Safford* [1944] P.61, which concerned the meaning of the word "detained" in the context of leave granted under sections 55 and 275 of the Lunacy Act 1890. The word "detained," rather than the expression "liable to be detained," is also used in section 72(2), a usage which McCullough J. considered in *ex p. W.*: " ... in section 72(2) the only reference is a patient 'detained.' Presumably this is to be taken as covering one on leave of absence and only 'liable to be detained,' for discharge means not merely discharge from hospital but discharge from the authority to detain."

hospital" bears a different meaning in section 117 to that which it bears in section 25A. In other words, a person granted leave under section 17 has left hospital for the purposes of section 117 and the duty to provide after-care is triggered at this point. However, he has not left hospital for the purposes of section 25 until such time as he also ceases to be liable to be detained. It is only then that the after-care being provided under section 117 is reinforced by the statutory supervision scheme.

Duty triggered when patient leaves hospital though still liable to be detained

In favour of this construction, it may fairly be said that Parliament clearly foresaw that the period during which there exists a duty to provide after-care will commonly not correspond to any period of statutory supervision. And if, as is the case, the duty to provide after-care under section 117 may continue after any statutory supervision has been terminated so the duty to provide it may arise before any period of supervision commences. Such an interpretation ensures that detained patients who require a long period of continuous trial leave at a local social services hostel may have a statutory entitlement to such community care services. Indeed, their provision may be a necessary precondition of granting leave preparatory to eventual discharge. Furthermore, construing section 117 in this way is more consistent with the way in which it is drafted. Had the intention been to exclude patients granted leave, the wording would surely have been the reversed. As originally enacted, section 117 would instead have referred to patients who "leave hospital and then cease to be detained" rather than to patients who "then cease to be detained and leave hospital." Likewise, the duty now would apply only to patients who "leave hospital and (whether or not immediately after so leaving) then cease to be detained."

Duty triggered when patient ceases to be liable to be detained for treatment

Against the above view, it may be pointed out that leave to be absent from hospital is usually first granted for an hour only, progressing to overnight leave and then weekend leave, and building up gradually to extended leave. If leaving hospital under section 17 constitutes leaving hospital for the purposes of section 117, it is not clear whether the duty to provide after-care is continually triggered and suspended with each short additional period of absence or only triggered when leave becomes open-ended. Certainly, a social services authority will not usually be aware of each short period of leave, the grant of which is at the consultant's discretion. However, this objection, although superficially attractive, is not conclusive: the duty on the local social services authority would be to provide a patient on leave with any *necessary* after-care services. In the case of short absences, such as one hour's town leave, it is simply the case that providing social after-care services at that stage is unnecessary. Nevertheless, they must be provided when a patient requires more intensive support as the periods outside hospital become longer. A more fundamental objection is perhaps that the whole notion of after-care is directed towards a patient's situation after he has completed his medical treatment and ceased to be liable to be detained in hospital for that purpose. Thus, the National Health Service Act 1977 draws a distinction between care and after-care, authorising and in some cases requiring social services authorities to make arrangements for "the care of persons suffering from illness and for the after-care of persons who have been so suffering."[9] Moreover, the definition of medical treatment in section 145 of the 1983 Act includes rehabilitation under medical supervision. This all suggests that while

---

[9]   See National Health Service Act 1977, Sched. 8, para. 2(1).

the patient continues to receive medical treatment (including rehabilitation under section 3) it is treatment and care which is being provided rather than after-care. As to the drafting of section 117, if the intention was to include patients who leave hospital under section 17, any contention that section 117 includes patients on leave involves removing the phrase "cease to be detained." The section as originally enacted would simply have referred to "patients who then leave hospital" rather than to patients who "then cease to be detained and leave hospital." Excluding patients who have leave to be absent from hospital has the intended virtue that the phrase "leaves hospital" bears the same meaning in sections 25A and 117: the completion of systematic arrangements for the patient's after-care upon his ceasing to be liable to be detained leads to discharge from section and, if necessary, its simultaneous provision under statutory supervision.

Patients detained under other powers

It has already been noted that some patients previously detained for treatment may remain in hospital informally after their liability to detention has ended. However, this does not affect their entitlement to statutory after-care on leaving hospital. A variation of this situation occurs when a long-stay patient remains in hospital for a number of years after a section 3 application has ceased to have effect and, during part of that period he is detained under another provision of the Act to which no entitlement to after-care under section 117 attaches. For example, the patient may subsequently be detained under section 5(2) or under section 2 and then at a later date cease to be detained and leave hospital. This may happen where the local emergency social work team has a policy of not making section 3 applications in respect of patients not known to them. In practice, some long-stay patients spend years in hospital during which they are variously informal or subject to the whole gamut of applications and powers under Part II of the Act. Although the new words inserted by the Mental Health (Patients in the Community) Act 1995 arguably do not quite cater for this situation, it is submitted that the underlying statutory intention is clear. If a patient's condition has been sufficiently serious to warrant compulsory in-patient treatment for an indefinite period, a statutory duty to provide him with after-care arises upon his leaving hospital. This duty survives subsequent changes in his legal status during the remainder of what is a continuous period of in-patient treatment. The effect of holding otherwise would be to introduce an undesirable degree of arbitrariness into the statutory provisions. Some patients would lose their statutory entitlement because of the subsequent use of a certain kind of compulsory power when, if anything, the further use of compulsory powers merely emphasises the patient's continuing need for intensive support following eventual discharge from hospital.

Patients readmitted to hospital under section

A common further variation of the above situation is that of a patient previously detained for treatment whose after-care following discharge from hospital was insufficient to prevent a relapse of his condition, the consequence being readmission under section 2 or section 4. By way of amplification, a patient previously detained under section 3 may spend eight months at home, relapse, be urgently admitted under section 4, his detention continued under section 2, and he then apply to a tribunal for his discharge. Can the tribunal assume that the duty to provide statutory after-care survives readmission to hospital under a power which carries no entitlement to it? If so, the mere fact of having once been detained for treatment could in theory lead to a life-long statutory commitment in the case of patients with a continuing need for community psychiatric support, punctuated only by occasional readmissions to hospital. Conversely, holding otherwise means that if after-care arrangements break down, because a patient needed more intensive after-care than was being provided, the readmission may both demonstrate a need for increased after-care and terminate the patient's statutory right to any after-care. As to this point, it is submitted that the relevant health and social services authorities cannot reasonably be satisfied that the patient is no longer in need of the services which it has been their duty to provide following the previous admission: the fact of the subsequent admission under section 2 manifestly demonstrates that the patient remains in need of those services. Consequently, if a section 2 patient was entitled to statutory after-care at the time of his admission under that section he will be entitled to it when he again ceases to be detained and leaves hospital.

SECTION 117 AFTER-CARE UNDER SUPERVISION

The Mental Health (Patients in the Community) Act 1995 made several important changes to the Mental Health Act 1983. The Act amended the law concerning patients who are lawfully or unlawfully absent from hospital or the place where they are required to reside. A new power of supervised discharge allows an application to be made under Part II for an unrestricted patient who is liable to be detained for treatment to be subject to "after-care under supervision" when he leaves hospital, with a view to securing that he receives the after-care services provided for him under section 117 ..."[10] The supplement to the Code of Practice states that:

> "Supervised discharge is intended for patients whose care needs to be specially supervised in the community because of risk to themselves or others. This applies particularly to 'revolving door' patients who have shown a pattern of relapse after discharge from hospital. Relapses often follow the breakdown of arrangements for care in the community, for. example when a patient stops taking medication. The legal framework which supervised discharge provides should help to prevent such failures provided that the care arrangements which it underpins have been fully agreed between the agencies concerned. Its purpose is to complement and reinforce existing arrangements under the Care Programme Approach ..."[11]

THE BASIC FRAMEWORK

The basic framework may be summarised as follows. Section 117 provides that patients who are liable to be detained for treatment have a statutory entitlement to after-care when they leave hospital. However, a proportion of patients habitually refuse to receive the after-care which is provided for them in pursuance of this duty. Provided the statutory conditions are satisfied, the responsible medical officer of an

---

[10] Mental Health Act 1983, s.25A(1), as inserted by Mental Health (Patients in the Community) Act 1995, s.1(1).
[11] *Mental Health (Patients in the Community) Act 1995: Guidance on Supervised Discharge (After-care under supervision) and related provisions. Supplement to the Code of Practice* (Department of Health and the Welsh Office, 1996), para. 5.

unrestricted patient who is liable to be detained for treatment may now apply to the Health Authority for him to be supervised after he leaves hospital, with a view to securing that he receives the after-care services to be provided for him. Such applications are known as "supervision applications." Where such an application has made and accepted and the patient then leaves hospital, he is then "subject to after-care under supervision." Patients subject to after-care under supervision must at all times have a supervisor and a doctor in charge of their medical treatment who is approved under section 12(2) as having special experience in the diagnosis or treatment of mental disorder — what is referred to as a "community responsible medical officer." The Health Authority and the local social services authority which under section 117 have the duty to provide a supervised patient with after-care services ("the responsible after-care bodies") may under section 25D impose certain requirements on him. These requirements correspond to the essential powers of a guardian appointed under the Mental Health Act 1983 — they comprise require-ments of residence, attendance and access. The patient may be required to reside at a specified place; required to attend specified places at specified times for the purpose of medical treatment, occupation, education and training; and access to him by authorised persons may be required by the responsible after-care bodies. These bodies must continue to provide after-care to the patient for as long as he remains subject to after-care under supervision. The applications process reflects the statutory purpose of supervised discharge. Before making an application, the responsible medical officer must consider the after-care services to be provided for the patient and any requirements to be imposed on him under section 25D. He must also consult certain persons, both professionals and non-professionals, and take any views which they express into account. Any application which is then made must be supported by two recommendations. It must also be accompanied by details of the after-care services and any requirements to be imposed under section 25D, and by statements from the persons who are to fulfil the functions of the supervisor and the community responsible medical officer, acknowledging that they will be under-taking those duties.

TERMINOLOGY AND SECONDARY LEGISLATION

Before dealing with the substantive provisions, it is necessary to define various new statutory terms and phrases and to make some reference to the prescribed forms. The reader should also be aware that regulations have been made which enable the responsible after-care bodies to delegate the performance of many of their functions to an NHS Trust. Consequently, although the Act refers to applications being made to, and accepted by, the relevant Health Authority, the expectation is that an NHS trust will usually perform these particular functions. Because the regulations are quite technical, and it is most important to understand the primary legislation, their consideration has been postponed until the statutory scheme has been explained (**453**). For the same reasons, the precise nature of the duty to consult the interested parties before exercising a particular statutory power, and to notify them if it is then exercised, is likewise delayed until then (**455**).

NEW TERMS

The Act introduces a number of new terms and these are summarised immediately below. The references to the section of the Act within which the term is defined are references to sections of the 1983 Act.

Supervision application	An application for a person to be supervised after he leaves hospital, with a view to securing that he receives the after-care services provided for him under section 117 (ss.25A(1) & (2), 145(1)).
After-care under supervision	If a duly made supervision application has been accepted in respect of a patient who then leaves hospital, he is "subject to after-care under supervision" (ss.25A (2), 145(1A)).
Community responsible medical officer (CRMO)	The person who is in charge of medical treatment provided for a patient subject to after-care under supervision (s.34(1)). The CRMO must be approved under s.12(2) of the Mental Health Act 1983 (s.117 (2)(a))
Supervisor	The person who is supervising a patient subject to after-care under supervision (s.34(1)). The person acting as a patient's community responsible medical officer may also be his supervisor (s.34(1A)).
Responsible after-care bodies	The bodies which have (or will have) the duty under s.117 to provide after-care services for the patient, i.e. the relevant health and local social services authorities (ss. 25D, 145(1)).
	For so long as a person is subject to after-care under supervision, the responsible after-care bodies may not be satisfied that the patient no longer requires after-care services under s.117. They must therefore continue to provide such services. Furthermore, the Health Authority —not both responsible after-care bodies— shall ensure that the patient has a community responsible medical officer and a supervisor at all times (s.117 (2A)).

New statutory phrases

The 1995 Act was considerably longer than it needed to be, partly because various lengthy phrases repeatedly used in it were not also given a convenient statutory handle or title, such as the "community responsible medical officer." For the sake of brevity and convenience, the following non-statutory terms are intermittently used in the text to denote these statutory phrases.

Primary carer   A person who plays (or will play after the patient
                               leaves hospital) a substantial part in the care of the
                               patient but who is not professionally concerned with
                               any of the after-care services provided (or to be
                               provided).

Interested parties   The Act repeatedly provides that the following per-
                               sons have a statutory right both to be consulted be-
                               fore certain statutory steps are taken and to be
                               notified that they have been taken: the patient, his
                               nearest relative, any primary carers. For the sake of
                               brevity, they may be collectively referred to as the
                               "interested parties."

Essential powers   The Act further provides that the responsible after-
                               care bodies (**424**) may, under section 25D, impose
                               any of the following "requirements" on a patient who
                               is subject to after-care under supervision (or will be
                               so subject when he leaves hospital) for the purpose of
                               securing that he receives the section 117 after-care
                               services provided for him —

                               a) that the patient reside at a specified place;

                               b) that the patient attend at specified places and times
                               for the purpose of medical treatment, occupation,
                               education, or training; and

                               c) that access to the patient be given, at any place
                               where the patient is residing, to the supervisor, any
                               registered medical practitioner or any approved social
                               worker or to any other person authorised by the
                               supervisor.

                               These powers may conveniently be referred to as "es-
                               sential powers" since they are the same as the "essen-
                               tial powers" of a guardian under the 1983 Act (**250**).
                               The only difference concerns their enforcement. As
                               to this, the Act provides that a patient subject to after-
                               care under supervision may be taken and conveyed
                               by his supervisor, or a person authorised by the
                               supervisor, to a place of residence or any place which
                               he is required to attend for the purpose of medical
                               treatment, occupation, education, or training (see
                               s.25D(4)).

THE PRESCRIBED FORMS

Section 32 of the Mental Health Act 1983 provides that the Secretary of State may make regulations for carrying Part II of the Act into full effect. The regulations may in particular prescribe the form of any application, recommendation, report or order made or given under the Act.[12] They may further provide for requiring such bodies as may be prescribed by the regulations to keep such registers or other records as may be prescribed in respect of patients subject to after-care under supervision.[13] Regulation 3 of The Mental Health (After-care under Supervision) Regulations 1996 provide that applications and recommendations, and any statutory reports and directions made following an application's acceptance, shall be in the form set out in Schedule 1 to the regulations. The table below sets out which forms to be used for each purpose.

AFTER-CARE UNDER SUPERVISION — STATUTORY FORMS

- **Supervision application**   Form 1S   *Reg. 3(a)*

- **Medical recommendation**   Form 2S   *Reg. 3(b)*

- **Approved social worker's recommendation**   Form 3S   *Reg. 3(c)*

- **Report reclassifying the patient**   Form 4S   *Reg. 3(d)*

- **Report renewing the authority for the patient's**   Form 5S   *Reg. 3(e)*
  after-care under supervision

- **Report renewing the authority for the patient's**   Form 5S   *Reg. 3(f)*
  after-care under supervision

- **Direction ending after-care under supervision**   Form 6S   *Reg. 3(g)*

THE APPLICATION PROCEDURES

The application procedures differ from those common to other forms of application. In particular, a supervision application is made by the patient's responsible medical officer rather than by an approved social worker or his nearest relative. Only one of the two supporting recommendations is a medical recommendation, the other being provided by an approved social worker. Supervision applications are parasitic in nature in that an application, order or direction authorising a patient's detention for treatment must first exist to which a supervision application can then be attached.

---

[12] Mental Health Act 1983, s.32(2)(a).
[13] Mental Health Act 1983, s.32(2)(c), as amended by s.1(2), and Sched. 1, para. 2, of the Mental Health (Patients in the Community) Act 1995. The previous requirement that any such records or registers be kept by the hospital managers or by local social services authorities has been replaced by a general reference to the prescribed bodies. This allows the regulations to prescribe that registers and records be maintained by other bodies, such as organisations providing after-care services under a contract with a health or local social services authority.

THE PATIENT

If an unrestricted patient aged 16 or over is liable to be detained for treatment, and a duty exists to provide him with after-care under section 117 when he leaves hospital, an application may be made for him to be supervised after he leaves hospital, with a view to securing that he receives those after-care services.[14]

Patients not entitled to section 117 after-care

The 1995 Act did not modify the legal position concerning the supervision of informal patients and unrestricted patients subject to guardianship or detention under sections, 2, 3, 5, 35, 36, 38, 135 and 136.[15] That being so, it can be seen that unrestricted patients entitled to after-care are thereby also liable to statutory supervision while, conversely, patients not entitled to after-care are not liable to statutory supervision.

Wards of court

Where a supervision application has been made in respect of a ward of court, the provisions in the 1983 Act concerning after-care under supervision have effect in relation to the minor subject to any order which the court may make in the exercise of its wardship jurisdiction.[16] Although the supervision application and guardianship frameworks resemble each other in several respects, it is therefore the case that a supervision application, but not a guardianship application, may be made in respect of a ward of court.

Patients liable to be detained in Scotland

A supervision application may be made in respect of a patient subject to a community care order in Scotland who intends to leave that country in order to reside in England and Wales.[17] Section 117 and the supervision application provisions in the 1983 Act apply subject to the various modifications set out in The Mental Health (Patients in the Community) (Transfers from Scotland) Regulations 1996.[18]

THE APPLICANT

Although supervision applications are made under Part II of the Act, the application process is distinctive. A supervision application may only be made by the patient's responsible medical officer.[19] Applications must be supported by two recommendations but only one of them is given by another medical practitioner, the other being provided by an approved social worker (**160**).[20]

---

[14] Mental Health Act 1983, ss.25A(1) and 40(4), Sched. 1, Pt. I, para. 8A., as inserted by ss.1(1) and 1(2) of, and Sched. 1, para. 6(c) to, the Mental Health (Patients in the Community) Act 1995. This is, of course, provided that the statutory criteria for making such an application are satisfied.

[15] As to departmental guidelines concerning their supervision, see p.745 *et seq.*

[16] Mental Health Act 1983, s.33(4), as inserted by s.1(2) of, and Sched. 1 para. 3 to, the Mental Health (Patients in the Community) Act 1995.

[17] Mental Health Act 1983, s.25J(1), as inserted by s.1(1) of the Mental Health (Patients in the Community) Act 1995.

[18] *Ibid.*, s.25J(2); The Mental Health (Patients in the Community) (Transfers from Scotland) Regulations 1996. As to the reverse procedure, see The Mental Health (Patients in the Community) (Transfer from England and Wales to Scotland) Regulations 1996.

[19] *Ibid.*, s.25A(5), as inserted by s.1(1) of the Mental Health (Patients in the Community) Act 1995.

[20] Mental Health Act 1983, s.25B(6), as inserted by s.1(1) of *ibid.*

Persons to be consulted before an application is made

Before making a supervision application, the responsible medical officer must consult the persons referred to in the table on page 458 and take into account any views expressed by them.[21]

Matters to be considered before application is made

The responsible medical officer shall not make a supervision application unless he has considered the following matters[22]—

a. the after-care services to be provided for the patient under section 117; *and*

b. any "essential powers" to be imposed on him under section 25D.

There are good reasons for requiring this. The logical first step is to formulate a section 117 after-care plan in the normal way and only then to decide whether the specified services need to be reinforced by providing them under statutory supervision. Unless an after-care plan has been agreed, it will be difficult, perhaps impossible, to have a considered opinion about the grounds which must exist before an application may lawfully be made. One cannot accurately gauge a person's likely compliance with the services to be provided for him until a decision has been made about what is to be provided for him. Similarly, until a decision has been taken about what services are necessary, one cannot have a firm opinion about the precise risks which may arise if those services are not received — or whether the availability of essential powers is likely to help to ensure that the patient receives them.

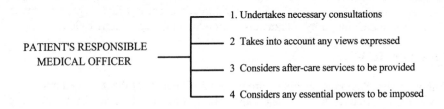

PATIENT'S RESPONSIBLE MEDICAL OFFICER

1. Undertakes necessary consultations
2. Takes into account any views expressed
3. Considers after-care services to be provided
4. Considers any essential powers to be imposed

Recommending that an application be made

A Mental Health Review Tribunal which does not discharge an unrestricted patient who is liable to be detained for treatment may recommend that the responsible medical officer considers whether to make a supervision application and further consider the patient's case if no such application is made.[23]

---

21   Mental Health Act 1983, s.25B(2)(a)–(c), as inserted by s.1(1) of the Mental Health (Patients in the Community) Act 1995.

22   *Ibid.*, s.25B(1)(b) and (4), as inserted by s.1(1) of the Mental Health (Patients in the Community) Act 1995.

23   *Ibid.*, s.72(3A), as inserted by s.1(2) of, and para. 10(2) of Sched. 1 to, the Mental Health (Patients in the Community) Act 1995.

THE GROUNDS OF APPLICATION

A supervision application may be made in respect of a patient "only" on the grounds specified in section 25(A)(4) of the 1983 Act.[24] Those grounds are set out below.

THE STATUTORY GROUNDS — SECTION 25(A)(4)

Existence of a form of mental disorder	**a.** he is suffering from one of the four forms of mental disorder specified in section 1 of the 1983 Act;
Substantial risk of serious harm	**b.** there would be a substantial risk of serious harm to the health or safety of the patient or the safety of other persons, or of the patient being seriously exploited, if he were not to receive the after-care services to be provided for him under section 117 after he leaves hospital;
Likelihood of benefit from supervision	**c.** his being subject to after-care under supervision is likely to help to secure that he receives the after-care services to be provided under section 117.

Existence of a form of mental disorder

It suffices that the patient suffers from one of the four forms of mental disorder set out in section 1 of the Act. According to the Code of Practice, while "supervised discharge is primarily intended for severely mentally ill people it may be suitable for some people suffering from other forms of mental disorder. In the case of those suffering from mental impairment or severe mental impairment the question of potential exploitation may be particularly relevant, though the RMO should then always consider whether guardianship might offer a better option for the patient's after-care."[25]

No requirement that disorder be of particular nature or degree

In contrast to the application criteria for guardianship and admission to hospital, there is no requirement that the patient's disorder be of a particular nature or degree. The rationale for this partly derives from the fact that supervision applications may be made in respect of patients who have leave to be absent from hospital under section 17. In some cases, these patients may be in remission or even symptom free and it would be difficult to satisfy a more restrictive test. Provided that there is still evidence of an underlying form of mental disorder, and the other grounds are satisfied, the patient may be made the subject of a supervision application. This

---

[24] Mental Health Act 1983, s.25A(4), as inserted by s.1(1) of the Mental Health (Patients in the Community) Act 1995.

[25] *Mental Health (Patients in the Community) Act 1995: Guidance on Supervised Discharge (After-care under supervision) and related provisions. Supplement to the Code of Practice* (Department of Health and the Welsh Office, 1996), para. 14.

reflects the fact that supervised discharge principally focuses on the risks associated with a future exacerbation of the patient's mental state rather than the present nature or degree of any disorder. That being so, the "nature and degree" qualification applicable in other cases is to some extent enshrined in the second of the supervision application grounds — albeit that the terminology of the 1995 Act fastens on to the nature or degree of the potential risk rather than the nature or degree of the disorder *per se*. Nevertheless, the first aspect (the patient's potential for dangerous behaviour) is consequential upon the second (his mental state).

Substantial risk of serious harm

The second condition requires the applicant, and the professionals providing the supporting recommendations, to consider the possible consequences if the patient does not receive the after-care services to be provided for him. A supervision application may only be made where there would be a substantial risk of serious harm to the patient's health or safety or the safety of others, or a substantial risk of the patient being seriously exploited, if he were not to receive those after-care services upon leaving hospital. A risk of serious harm does not suffice unless that risk is a substantial one. Similarly, a substantial risk of harm does not suffice unless the harm will be serious and, in the case of persons other than the patient, it is their safety, not merely their health, which will be substantially at risk. The identified substantial risk is one consequential upon failure to receive the proposed after-care services and is expressed as a future conditional. In some cases, any risk of suicide or serious harm to others may be substantial irrespective of whether the patient is receiving available after-care services. In the majority of cases, it is unlikely that this second condition will be satisfied so that most patients will, as before, receive their after-care without any formal element of supervision. Because of the need for a substantial risk of serious harm, the view expressed in the Code of Practice is that patients who meet the criteria for supervised discharge should "normally" be included in the supervision registers established in accordance with the *Health Service Guidelines* HSG(94)5 (**755**).[26]

Likelihood of benefit from supervision

If there will be a substantial risk of serious harm should the patient not receive the proposed after-care services, the third condition requires consideration to be given to the practicalities of the situation — will providing those after-care services under formal supervision be likely to help to secure that the patient receives them and so reduce the substantial risk of serious harm which has been identified?[27] This might not be the case in one of two situations. In the first place, although a failure to receive after-care would give rise to a substantial risk, the patient may be both reliable and willing to take advantage of the services being provided. Thus, the risk that the patient will not receive the after-care services arranged for him is

---

[26] *Mental Health (Patients in the Community) Act 1995: Guidance on Supervised Discharge (After-care under supervision) and related provisions. Supplement to the Code of Practice* (Department of Health and the Welsh Office, 1996), para. 6.

[27] In most contexts, the word "secure" is synonymous with the more natural "ensure," so that the third of the statutory tests can be read as referring to statutory supervision being likely to help to ensure that the patient receives the after-care services provided for him under section 117. To secure is to make fast or safe and the noun which corresponds to it is security. The preference for the word perhaps reflects the underlying idea that to secure after-care provides security against the substantial risks which will otherwise arise.

430

insignificant and formal supervision is unlikely to help to provide greater security. Secondly, there is the situation where there is a real risk that the patient will reject some part of the after-care arranged for him, and there are substantial risks associated with that, but imposing formal supervision is unlikely to help to secure that he receives the services. This may be because the only part of the after-care likely to be rejected is prescribed medication; its administration to a supervised patient cannot be compelled; and the patient has made it plain that he will not accept medication voluntarily. In this context, the Code notes that "the arrangements clearly will not work without a substantial measure of agreement on the part of those responsible for them ... While the Act does not require the patient's agreement to supervised discharge it is unlikely to be effective unless the patient, and any informal carer, has understood and accepted its terms."[28]

"Likely to help secure"

Notwithstanding the above, it should be noted that the third statutory ground is satisfied if statutory supervision is likely *to help* to secure that the patient receives the after-care services. The condition is not that such supervision is likely to secure that he does. In other words, getting the patient to accept and participate in the after-care services may largely be a matter of persuasion, professional skill, and building a good therapeutic relationship. However, it suffices that the availability of the statutory powers is likely to help this process of ensuring that after-care is received. As to whether this is likely, the courts may adopt the approach outlined in *R. v. Canons Park Mental Health Review Tribunal, ex p. A* (**223**).[29] That case revolved around the question of whether compulsory admission for treatment was likely to either alleviate or prevent a deterioration of the condition of a patient suffering from a psychopathic disorder. The patient would not accept or co-operate with the only form of treatment which might have that effect. The court held that it was not necessary that treatment be immediately likely to have such a benefit, provided there was a prospect that the patient's attitude might change, so that alleviation or stabilisation was likely over time. The fact that there might initially be some deterioration in the patient's condition, due to the patient's initial anger at being detained, did not mean that her condition was unlikely to be treatable if nursing care was likely to lead to insight being gained, co-operation enlisted, and the condition alleviated in due course. Accordingly, in this context, it probably also suffices that statutory supervision is likely over time to help to secure that the patient receives the after-care services, even though some initial lack of co-operation, due to resentment or other causes, is envisaged. Similarly, the fact that a patient will not voluntarily take medication, and any substantial risks which may arise in the future stem from this, does not mean that the third of the statutory conditions is thereby not satisfied. If refusing medication is likely to lead to a deterioration in the patient's mental state and so affect his participation in other aspects of the care plan, such as attending out-patient check-ups and specified daily activities, the essential powers associated with statutory supervision may well help to secure that he receives these after-care services — even if they do not provide complete security. It is also possible that the patient's attitude to taking medication will change over time to one of grudging acceptance although the likelihood of this is frankly negligible in most cases and so something of a legal fiction.

---

[28] *Mental Health (Patients in the Community) Act 1995: Guidance on Supervised Discharge (After-care under supervision) and related provisions. Supplement to the Code of Practice* (Department of Health and the Welsh Office, 1996), paras. 23 and 24.

[29] *R. v. Canons Park Mental Health Review Tribunal, ex p. A.* [1994] 3 W.L.R. 630.

Supervised discharge and conditional discharge

It has already been noted that the supervision application framework does not apply to restricted patients. This is because a separate supervisory framework for them already exists in the form of conditional discharge, and recall to hospital in the event of relapse, breach of a condition of discharge, or conduct placing the public at risk. It is important to realise the new legislation does not represent the creation of such a regime for unrestricted patients. The statutory grounds for supervision which must be considered in unrestricted cases are more specific than in restricted cases. Indeed, in the case of detained restricted patients, there are no limiting statutory criteria at all. Consequently, consideration is necessarily given to all likely risks to the patient and others and not merely substantial risks which come into being when after-care services are not received. Many restricted patients have a potential for dangerous conduct even if they receive after-care and the need to supervise them reflects this fact. The purpose of their statutory supervision is not merely to make it more likely that they will receive any key after-care arrangements incorporated as conditions of discharge. It also provides a framework for recalling patients in any of the circumstances just specified.

The chain of reasoning

When the grounds for after-care under supervision are examined by reference to the purpose of supervision in restricted cases, their purpose is more focused: to secure compliance with after-care arrangements made under section 117 in cases where non-compliance will give rise to a substantial risk of serious harm. Considered together, the three grounds for making a supervision application represent a single chain of reasoning:

1. Is the patient (still) mentally disordered?

2. If so, will there be a substantial risk of serious harm to the patient or others when he leaves hospital if he does not receive the mental health after-care services provided for him?

3. If so, will providing these services under statutory supervision be likely to help to secure that he receives them, so consequentially reducing the risk of serious harm being done?

The legislation therefore caters only for the situation where a substantial risk to the patient or others will arise if he does not receive the proposed after-care services. As to the chain of reasoning, it could have been, but is not, as follows:

1. Is the patient (still) mentally disordered?

2. If so, will there be a substantial risk of serious harm to the patient or others when he leaves hospital?

3. If so, will formally supervising him help to reduce this risk?

A broader set of statutory grounds along these lines would have catered for two additional situations. Firstly, the situation where substantial risks exist even if the patient receives the after-care services provided. The risk here is essentially immediate and unconditional, rather than one which will come into being if the after-care services are not received.[30] Secondly, the situation where supervision might be useful as a long-leash, if it included a mechanism for recalling a patient to hospital in any of the circumstances applicable to restricted patients, but not in terms of helping to make compliance with after-care services any more likely.

THE SUPPORTING RECOMMENDATIONS

Supervision applications must be accompanied by two written recommendations in the prescribed form, one provided by a registered medical practitioner and the other by an approved social worker.[31] A registered medical practitioner may at any reasonable time visit a patient and examine him in private for the purpose of deciding whether to make a recommendation.[32] Similarly, an approved social worker may at any reasonable time visit and interview a patient for the same purpose although, in this case, the Act does not specify any right to a private interview.[33] For the purpose of deciding whether to make a recommendation, the visiting doctor or social worker may "require the production of an inspect any records relating to the detention of the patient in any hospital or to any after-care services provided for the patient under section 117."[34]

The medical recommendation

The Act provides that the medical recommendation shall be given by "a registered medical practitioner who will be professionally concerned with the patient's medical treatment after he leaves hospital or, if no such practitioner other than the responsible medical officer will be so concerned, of any registered medical practitioner."[35] The recommendation must include a statement that "in the opinion of the medical practitioner, having regard in particular to the patient's history, all *(three)* of the conditions for making an application are complied with."[36]

The patient's history

The reference to the patient's history is clearly directed towards the phenomenon of "revolving-door patients" and intended to focus attention on the patient's record of compliance with previous after-care arrangements. However, there is no bar on making an application in respect of a patient who has not previously been detained for treatment provided there is evidence upon which the doctor can form the opinion that the statutory grounds exist. For example, the circumstances leading up to the patient's compulsory admission to hospital may demonstrate the existence of a substantial risk of serious harm when he is not in receipt of community psychiatric

---

[30]   The presumption here must be that such patients will generally not be suitable for discharge at all, whether supervised or unsupervised.

[31]   Mental Health Act 1983, s.25B(6), as inserted by s.1(1) of the Mental Health (Patients in the Community) Act 1995.

[32]   *Ibid.*, s.25C(3), as inserted by s.1(1) of the Mental Health (Patients in the Community) Act 1995.

[33]   *Ibid.*, s.25C(4), as inserted by s.1(1) of the Mental Health (Patients in the Community) Act 1995.

[34]   *Ibid.*, s.25C(5), as inserted by s.1(1) of the Mental Health (Patients in the Community) Act 1995.

[35]   *Ibid.*, s.25B(6)(a), as inserted by s.1(1) of the Mental Health (Patients in the Community) Act 1995.

[36]   *Ibid.*, s.25B(7), as inserted by s.1(1) of the Mental Health (Patients in the Community) Act 1995.

services. Moreover, his subsequently expressed views about voluntarily accepting after-care may be such that the third of the statutory grounds is also satisfied.

Prohibitions

Section 12, which applies to medical recommendations given in support of an application for admission or a guardianship application, does not apply to supervision applications. Apart from the prohibitions applicable to both recommendations, which are summarised below, the medical recommendation may not be given by the responsible medical officer since he is the applicant.[37] There is no requirement that it is provided by a doctor who is approved under section 12(2) of the Act as having special experience in the diagnosis or treatment of mental disorder. This is because it is presumed that the responsible medical officer will be approved under that section, although such approval is not a necessary condition of being the responsible medical officer.

Code of Practice

Although the Act does not prohibit the medical recommendation from being given by a doctor who works under the direction of the responsible medical officer, the Code of Practice discourages this. It states that the medical recommendation should normally be provided by the doctor who will be the patient's community responsible medical officer when he leaves hospital, unless the applicant himself will be undertaking that function. In the latter case, "if the RMO is unable to identify another doctor who will be involved in the patient's treatment after he or she leaves hospital the recommendation may be made by any other doctor, including a member of the hospital staff (but not one who works under the direction of the RMO)."[38] Nevertheless, if a junior member of the responsible medical officer's team will be the only other doctor concerned with patient's treatment after he leaves hospital, the Act does state that this doctor "shall" provide the recommendation, in preference to a doctor unconnected with the patient.

The social work recommendation

A recommendation provided by an approved social worker must include a statement that "in the opinion of the social worker (having regard in particular to the patient's history)" the second and third of the three grounds of application are complied with.[39] It is therefore the two medical practitioners involved in the application process — the responsible medical officer within the application itself and the doctor providing the supporting medical recommendation — who certify that the first, medical, ground exists.

Conditions and prohibitions applicable to both recommendations

Because section 12 does not apply, it is not necessary that the application and the medical recommendation are based on medical examinations which have taken place

---

[37] Mental Health Act 1983, s.25C(9)(a), as inserted by s.1(1) of the Mental Health (Patients in the Community) Act 1995.

[38] *Mental Health (Patients in the Community) Act 1995: Guidance on Supervised Discharge (After-care under supervision) and related provisions. Supplement to the Code of Practice,* (Department of Health and the Welsh Office, 1996), para. 30.

[39] Mental Health Act 1983, s.25B(6)(b), as inserted by s.1(1) of the Mental Health (Patients in the Community) Act 1995.

together or, if separately, not more than five clear days apart. Nor is it necessary that the application is made within 14 days of the date of the second recommendation. Nor is there any requirement that the application is accepted within fourteen days of it being made, which condition applies to applications for admission though not to guardianship applications. Nor is there any prohibition against the application or medical recommendation being provided by a doctor on the staff of a mental nursing home at which the patient is liable to be detained. Again, no such prohibition applies in the case of guardianship. The result is that the statutory prohibitions are confined to forbidding recommendations being given by persons with a close familial or other interest in the matter. Specifically, a recommendation may not be given[40] —

- by a "close relative" of the patient, the applicant (responsible medical officer), or the person who has provided the other recommendation; *or*

- by a person who receives or has an interest in the receipt of any payments made on account of the maintenance of the patient or a "close relative" of such a person; *and*

- for these purposes, a person's close relatives are his spouse, parents, children and siblings and those individuals married to them.[41]

The Act does not prohibit a responsible medical officer from making an application because he is closely related to the patient or has an interest in payments made on account of the patient's maintenance or is a close relative of someone with such an interest. Secondly, on a strict reading, a person is not prohibited from providing a recommendation because he will or may have a future interest in such maintenance payments when the patient leaves hospital. However, the courts are unlikely to adopt a strict reading on that point since the statutory purpose is clear.

FORM OF THE APPLICATION

The Act provides that a supervision application must *inter alia* state the names of the persons who are to be the patient's "community responsible medical officer" and the "supervisor" when he leaves hospital, and also the names of any primary carers consulted before the application was made.

Documents in support of the application

Section 25B(9) of the 1983 Act provides that, the medical and social work recommendations apart, a supervision application must be accompanied by the documents specified in the following table.[42]

---

40   Mental Health Act 1983, s.25C(9), as inserted by s.1(1) of the Mental Health (Patients in the Community) Act 1995.

41   A relative is a "close relative" if he or she is the "husband, wife, father, father-in-law, mother, mother-in-law, son, son-in-law, daughter, daughter-in-law, brother, brother-in-law, sister or sister-in-law" of the person concerned: *Ibid.*, s.25C(10), as inserted by s.1(1) of the Mental Health (Patients in the Community) Act 1995.

42   *Ibid.*, s.25B(9), as inserted by s.1(1) of the Mental Health (Patients in the Community) Act 1995.

Community responsible medical officer's written statement	**a.**	a statement in writing by the person who is to be the "community responsible medical officer" after the patient leaves hospital that "he is to be in charge of the medical treatment provided for the patient as part of the after-care services provided ... under section 117 ...";
Supervisor's written statement	**b.**	a statement in writing by the person who is to be the "supervisor" after the patient leaves hospital that "he is to supervise the patient with a view to securing that he receives the after-care services so provided";
Details of after-care services	**c.**	details of the after-care services to be provided for the patient under section 117;
Details of requirements under s.25D.	**d.**	details of any requirements to be imposed under section 25D ("essential powers")

The application (Form 1S)

The application must be in the prescribed form. As prescribed, the application is in three parts. Part I is to be completed by the applicant who must certify that in his opinion the statutory grounds for making such an application exist. Part II consists of the statements made by the persons who will be the patient's community responsible medical officer and supervisor when he leaves hospital, acknowledging that they are to undertake these duties. Part III is completed by the Health Authority upon accepting the application. Its acceptance of the application, the fact that the local social services authority was consulted before it was accepted, and the fact that the necessary persons have been notified of its acceptance, must all be recorded here. In this respect, the application form follows the format adopted under the 1959 Act, since the application's acceptance and the patient's admission are recorded on the application rather than by completing a separate document. Although section 25B(9) specifies that a number of additional statements must "accompany" the application, it can be seen that two of these are incorporated within the application form itself. This leaves the details of the after-care services to be attached to the application, which is no doubt normally done simply by appending a copy of the after-care plan to it. The only other requirement imposed by section 25B(9) is that the application made in respect of the patient shall be accompanied by "details of any requirements to be imposed on him under section 25D," what have been referred to as the essential powers. As to this, Part I of the application includes a space to be completed by the responsible medical officer which begins, "I consider that the patient should be subject to the following requirements:– ...." Whether simply completing this part of the application satisfies the statutory requirement is considered below (**439**).

436

To whom the application is made

A supervision application must be addressed to the Health Authority which will have the duty under section 117 to provide the after-care services for the patient "after he leaves hospital."[43] In practice, it will normally be furnished to the NHS trust responsible for the hospital where the patient is liable to be detained (**453**).

Informing persons that an application is being made

On making an supervision application, the responsible medical officer must inform the interested parties (**425**) of the following matters: that an application is being made; the section 117 after-care services to be provided; any essential powers to be imposed on the patient under section 25D; and the names of the persons who are to be the patient's community responsible medical officer and supervisor after he leaves hospital.[44]

ACCEPTANCE OF APPLICATIONS

The local social services authority which has the corresponding duty to provide after-care must be consulted by the Health Authority before the latter accepts an application for after-care to be provided under supervision.[45] As with guardianship, there is no maximum period within which an application must be accepted.

Informing persons of an application's acceptance

Where Health Authority accepts a supervision application, it must inform the patient, both orally and in writing, that the application has been accepted and of its effect in his case, including what rights he has to apply to a Mental Health Review Tribunal.[46] Any nearest relative or primary carer consulted by the responsible medical officer before making the application must also be informed by the Health Authority of its acceptance. In the case of a nearest relative, this information must be given in writing but need not also be given orally. A primary carer must simply be "informed," so the notification may be oral or written.[47]

Whether an application can be accepted in respect of an informal patient

According to section 25A(1), a supervision application may be made in respect of a patient who is liable to be detained in hospital. This raises the possibility that the application could be accepted after the patient has ceased to be liable to be detained for treatment provided it was made while he was so liable: there is no statutory period within which an application must be accepted. The situation might arise where the patient is discharged from detention under section 3 by his nearest relative or a tribunal before the Health Authority has had sufficient time to consult the local social services authority and decide whether to accept the application. However, the wording of the statute suggests that an application may not be accepted

---

[43] Mental Health Act 1983, s.25A(6), as inserted by s.1(1) of the Mental Health (Patients in the Community) Act 1995.

[44] *Ibid.*, s.25A(10)–(11), as inserted by s.1(1) of the Mental Health (Patients in the Community) Act 1995.

[45] *Ibid.*, s.25A(7), as inserted by s.1(1) of the Mental Health (Patients in the Community) Act 1995.

[46] *Ibid.*, s.25A(8)(a), as inserted by s.1(1) of the Mental Health (Patients in the Community) Act 1995.

[47] *Ibid.*, s.25A(8)(b) and (c), as inserted by s.1(1) of the Mental Health (Patients in the Community) Act 1995.

after the patient has left hospital. For example, section 25A(2) states that where an application "has been duly made and accepted ... in respect of a patient and he has left hospital, he is ... 'subject to after-care under supervision.'"[48] This implies that the acceptance of the application must precede the patient's leaving hospital, as does section 25A(7). This provides that before accepting a supervision application a Health Authority shall consult the local social services authority which "will" also have the duty to provide after-care to the patient under section 117. If an application could be accepted after the patient had left hospital, the reference would be to the social services authority which "has or will have" that duty. Furthermore, any other construction would be incompatible with the wording of section 25G(1) concerning the duration and renewal of the authority for a patient's supervision. This provides that a patient subject to after-care under supervision shall initially be so subject for the period (a) beginning when he leaves hospital; and (b) ending with the period of six months beginning with the day on which the supervision application was accepted. If a patient on section 17 leave is discharged from liability to detention under section 3 on 1 January, but a supervision application is not accepted until 8 January, any view that the application could be so accepted would mean that he was subject to after-care under supervision during the week prior to its acceptance, which is a nonsense. Section 25G(1) therefore only makes sense if the acceptance of the application must precede the patient leaving hospital. This still leaves open the possibility that a supervision application could be accepted after an in-patient had ceased to be liable to be detained if he then remained in hospital as an informal patient. He would not yet have left hospital.

DEFECTIVE APPLICATIONS AND THEIR RECTIFICATION

A supervision application is of no effect unless the form of mental disorder specified in it by the responsible medical officer (or at least one of them) is also specified in the medical recommendation.[49] Section 25C(6) provides for the rectification of incorrect or defective applications or recommendations during the 14 day period following the application's acceptance. Documents may only be amended with the Health Authority's consent and only by the person who completed the document which is considered to be incorrect or defective in some respect.[50] Where an application or recommendation is duly amended within the statutory period, it has effect as if it had been originally made or given in its amended form.[51]

Defects and errors

Section 25C(6) corresponds to sections 8(4) and 15(1) of the 1983 Act, which allow for the rectification of defective or incorrect applications and recommendations made or given in respect of an application for admission to hospital or reception into guardianship. The view expressed in the *Memorandum* is that defects which may be remedied as being "incorrect or defective" include "the leaving blank of any spaces on the form which should have been filled in (other than the signature) or failure to

---

[48]   Mental Health Act 1983, s.25A(2), as inserted by s.1(1) of the Mental Health (Patients in the Community) Act 1995.

[49]   *Ibid.*, s.25C(2), as inserted by s.1(1) of the Mental Health (Patients in the Community) Act 1995. This provision corresponds to that set out in section 11 for other applications, with the necessary caveat that it is the (medical) application and the medical recommendation which must specify a common form of mental disorder.

[50]   *Ibid.*, s.25C(6), as inserted by s.1(1) of the Mental Health (Patients in the Community) Act 1995.

[51]   *Ibid.*, s.25C(7), as inserted by s.1(1) of the Mental Health (Patients in the Community) Act 1995.

delete one or more alternatives in places where only one can be correct."[52] As with guardianship applications, there is no provision equivalent to subsections 15(2) and (3), which only apply to applications for admission to hospital. These subsections provide that a fresh medical recommendation may be completed during the rectification period where it appears to the managers that one of the two original recommendations, or their combined effect, is insufficient to warrant the patient's detention in pursuance of the application. Consequently, in the case of supervision applications, if the application or a recommendation is insufficient to warrant the patient's supervision, *or* this is the combined effect of the recommendations, *or* of the application considered together with the medical recommendation, a further application or recommendation cannot be obtained during the rectification period. Consequently, the particular application cannot be retrospectively validated.[53]

IMPOSING ESSENTIAL POWERS UNDER SECTION 25D

The requirements specified in section 25D may only be imposed on a patient by both the responsible after-care bodies or by some person or body authorised to act on their behalf.[54] However, the statutory scheme is not as clear as it might be. It has been noted that the requirements which may be imposed under section 25D correspond to the essential powers of a guardian appointed under the Act. In the case of guardianship, these powers arise upon the application's acceptance and are exercisable by the guardian as the need arises.

Statutory references to the requirements

The references in the Act to these requirements are as follows. The responsible medical officer shall not make a supervision application unless he has considered any requirements "to be imposed".[55] If a supervision application is then made by him, it shall be accompanied by details of any requirements "to be imposed" on the patient.[56] On making such an application, the responsible medical officer shall inform the interested parties of the requirements "to be imposed."[57] Where "a patient is subject to after-care under supervision (or, if he has not yet left hospital, is to be so subject after he leaves hospital) "the responsible after-care bodies have power "to

---

[52] *Mental Health Act 1983: Memorandum on Parts I to VI, VIII and X* (D.H.S.S., 1987), para. 54.

[53] As in the case of guardianship, this reflects the fact that the time which a local social services authority has to scrutinise a guardianship application before accepting it is unlimited. However, in the case of supervised discharge, it is also the case that many of the defects which sections 15(2) and (3) cater for are irrelevant, there being no requirement that the two examining doctors examined the patient not more than five clear days apart; or that at least one of them was approved under section 12(2) of the Act; or that not more than one of them was (except in an emergency) provided by doctors on the staff of the same NHS hospital. Furthermore, since supervision applications are accompanied by, rather than founded on, two supporting recommendations, and do not have to be furnished within 14 days of the second recommendation, it is arguable that (1) where a recommendation is defective, the original application can be resubmitted with fresh, valid, recommendations and (2) where an application is defective a fresh application relying on the same recommendations as before can be submitted. This assumes, of course, that the patient is still liable to be detained.

[54] If an NHS trust has been authorised to act on behalf of the Health Authority in this respect but not by the local social services authority, it will be for that NHS trust and the social services authority to decide whether to impose any of the requirements. If the NHS trust has been authorised by both authorities it can impose the requirements acting alone.

[55] Mental Health Act 1983, s.25B(1)(b) and 25B(4)(b), as inserted by s.1(1) of the Mental Health (Patients in the Community) Act 1995.

[56] *Ibid.*, s.25B(9)(d), as inserted by s.1(1) of the Mental Health (Patients in the Community) Act 1995.

[57] *Ibid.*, s.25B(10) and (11), as inserted by s.1(1) of the Mental Health (Patients in the Community) Act 1995.

impose" any of the requirements for the purpose of securing that he receives the after-care services.[58] Any requirements "imposed" on a patient who is (or who is to be) subject to after-care under supervision shall be kept under review and, where appropriate, modified by the responsible after-care bodies.[59] Where the responsible after-care bodies modify any of the requirements "imposed" on the patient they must inform the interested parties of this fact.[60]

Interpretation of the provisions

Although the responsible medical officer has no power to impose requirements on the patient nevertheless he may not make an application unless he has considered any requirements "to be imposed" on him. If he then makes an application it must be accompanied by details of any requirements "to be imposed" and he must inform the interested parties of the requirements "to be imposed." However, it is only when the application has been accepted that any power to actually impose these requirements, or any others, actually arises and this power is one for the responsible after-care bodies, rather than the responsible medical officer, to exercise. The alternative construction, that the after-care authorities can impose them on a patient who is to be subject to after-care under supervision before an application for him to be so subject is made, and it is these requirements which are being referred to by the responsible medical officer in his application, seems weak. There can be no power to impose anything on the patient until an application in respect of him has been accepted. Nor can it be said that he "is to be subject to after-care under supervision" until an application for him to be subject to after-care under supervision has first been made and accepted. Moreover, the application is not accompanied by details of requirements already imposed on the patient but by requirements which are to be imposed. Bearing these points in mind, the statutory scheme appears to be as follows—

1. The responsible medical officer and the other professionals involved in the patient's case will agree an after-care plan, setting out the services to be provided for him.

2. The responsible medical officer will consider these services in the context of the statutory criteria and form a personal opinion as to whether their provision needs to be reinforced by imposing requirements on the patient under section 25D. However, before actually making any application which might have that effect, he must consult the various other professionals and non-professionals specified in the Act. Furthermore, a community responsible medical officer and a supervisor will need to be found and two supporting recommendations obtained. If the responsible medical officer does proceed, it is likely that there will be broad professional agreement about what requirements are appropriate.

3. If, after all this, the responsible medical officer makes an application, it must be accompanied by details of any requirements which, having consulted the necessary persons and taken their views into account, he considers should be imposed on the patient if the application is accepted.

---

[58]   Mental Health Act 1983, s.25D(1), as inserted by s.1(1) of the Mental Health (Patients in the Community) Act 1995.

[59]   *Ibid.*, s.25E(1), as inserted by s.1(1) of the Mental Health (Patients in the Community) Act 1995.

[60]   *Ibid.*, s.25E(8), as inserted by s.1(1) of the Mental Health (Patients in the Community) Act 1995.

4. The responsible after-care bodies will then consider whether to accept the application, having regard, *inter alia*, to the information contained within it as to the after-care services to be provided, the perceived risks and benefits, and the requirements which the applicant considers should be imposed by them on the patient if they accept the application.

5. If the Health Authority accepts the application, the responsible after-care bodies will impose any necessary requirements on the patient. These are likely to be the requirements specified in the application, since it was acceptable to them, but not necessarily so. They can be imposed prior to the patient leaving hospital provided that the application has been accepted. For example, a requirement that the patient resides at a hostel may be imposed, so that there is a power to convey him there when the authority to detain him lapses.

AFTER THE APPLICATION'S ACCEPTANCE

The Act provides for certain situations which may or will occur after the application has been accepted and the patient leaves hospital. During the period between the application's acceptance and the day he leaves hospital, the patient is someone who "is to be subject to after-care under supervision after leaving hospital."

THE COMMENCEMENT OF AFTER-CARE UNDER SUPERVISION

Where a supervision application has been accepted in respect of a patient, he becomes subject to after-care under supervision on the day he leaves hospital.[61] If someone other than the persons specified in the application is to be the patient's prospective supervisor or community responsible medical officer, the responsible after-care bodies must inform the interested parties of this change in the arrangements.

The meaning of "leaves hospital"

What constitutes leaving hospital for these purposes is defined in section 25A(9)—

"**25A.**–(9) Where a patient in respect of whom a supervision application is made is granted leave of absence from a hospital under section 17 above (whether before or after the supervision application is made), references in—

(a) this section and the following provisions of this Part of this Act; and

(b) Part V of this Act,

to his leaving hospital shall be construed as references to his period of leave expiring (otherwise than on his return to the hospital or transfer to another hospital)."

---

[61] Mental Health Act 1983, s.25A(2), as inserted by s.1(1) of the Mental Health (Patients in the Community) Act 1995.

Effect of the sub-section

The effect of the subsection is that a patient in respect of whom a supervision application has been accepted only becomes subject to after-care under supervision when he has both left hospital and ceased to be liable to be detained. More particularly—

- A supervision application may be made in respect of a patient who has leave to be absent from hospital under section 17. If so, he does not become subject to after-care under supervision until such time as he ceases to be liable to be detained.

- Similarly, where a supervision application is made in respect of a detained patient who is later granted leave of absence, he does not become subject to after-care under supervision until the day on which he also ceases to be liable to be detained.

- Where, however, a patient is still in hospital on the day he ceases to be liable to be detained, receiving further treatment there as an informal patient, he does not become subject to after-care under supervision until the day on which he does eventually leave hospital.

Who is in charge of the patient's medical treatment

Patients who are *to be* subject to after-care under supervision when they leave hospital, including informal in-patients, have a responsible medical officer but no community responsible medical officer.[62] This is because only a patient who has actually left hospital, as defined above, has a community responsible medical officer.[63] This has the important consequence that, until the patient leaves hospital, only a tribunal has authority to terminate his liability to statutory supervision or to reclassify him. During this interregnum, neither the doctor in charge of his treatment, nor any other person or body, may direct that the patient shall not be subject to supervision upon leaving hospital.

KEEPING THE ARRANGEMENTS UNDER REVIEW

The responsible after-care bodies are required to keep under review and, where appropriate modify, both the after-care services provided under section 117 and any requirements imposed on the patient.[64]

PATIENT REFUSING OR NEGLECTING TO RECEIVE AFTER-CARE

Where a patient who is subject to supervision "refuses or neglects" to receive any or all of the after-care services provided for him, or to comply with any of the

---

[62] The definition of the responsible medical officer in section 34(1)(a) was amended by section 2(1) of, and paragraph 4(3)(b) of Schedule 1 to, the Mental Health (Patients in the Community) Act 1995. It now covers patients who remain in hospital informally following the acceptance of a supervision application. However, that doctor has no statutory functions to perform once the patient has ceased to be liable to be detained so the amendment is superfluous to this extent.

[63] See *e.g.* Mental Health Act 1983, ss.25E(9) and 25H(1), as inserted by s.1(1) of the Mental Health (Patients in the Community) Act 1995, and s.34(1) , as inserted by s.1(2) of, and Sched. 1 para 4(2) to, the 1995 Act.

[64] *Ibid.*, s.25E(1), as inserted by s.1(1) of the Mental Health (Patients in the Community) Act 1995.

requirements imposed under the essential powers, the responsible after-care bodies must do four things[65]—

a. review the after-care services and any requirements imposed on the patient under section 25D.

b. consider whether it is appropriate to modify any of the after-care services provided or requirements imposed and, having consulted the interested parties (425) and taken their views into account, make any modifications which are appropriate.

c. consider whether it might be appropriate for the patient to cease to be subject to after-care under supervision and, if they conclude that it might be, inform the community responsible medical officer.

d. consider whether it might be appropriate for the patient to be admitted to a hospital for treatment and, if they conclude that it might be, inform an approved social worker.

Duty to notify interested persons of any modifications

The responsible after-care bodies must notify the patient and any of the interested parties who were consulted about modifying the after-care services or requirements of any modifications then made (458).[66]

CHANGE OF STATUTORY OFFICERS

The interested parties must be informed of any change of supervisor or community responsible medical officer (459). This must be done at the time when the patient leaves hospital if the community responsible medical officer or the supervisor is to be someone other than the individuals specified in the application. Similarly, the interested parties must be notified of any subsequent changes. Perhaps surprisingly, the new medical officer or supervisor is not also required to sign a statement of the kind set out in Part II of the application.

APPLICATION OF OTHER PROVISIONS IN PARTS II AND IV

The application to patients receiving after-care under supervision of the reclassification, consent to treatment, transfer, leave of absence, absence without leave, and nearest relative provisions are considered here.

Reclassification

The Act provides that the community responsible medical officer may reclassify a patient who is suffering from a form of disorder other than the form or forms specified in the application.[67] As with other kinds of application, reclassification is

---

[65]   See Mental Health Act 1983, s.25E(2)–(7), as inserted by s.1(1) of the Mental Health (Patients in the Community) Act 1995.

[66]   *Ibid.*, s.25E(8), as inserted by s.1(1) of the Mental Health (Patients in the Community) Act 1995.

[67]   Mental Health Act 1983, s.25F, as inserted by s.1(1) of the Mental Health (Patients in the Community) Act 1995.

automatic if a renewal report specifies a form of disorder other than that, or those, specified in the application,[68] and a tribunal may also reclassify the patient.[69] Reclassification other than by a tribunal or at the time of renewal gives rise to a right of application to a Mental Health Review Tribunal (**608**). However, as with guardianship, it has no bearing on the statutory criteria which are applied when the patient is next examined with a view to renewing the authority for a further period.

Consent to treatment

The consent to treatment provisions in Part IV of the Act do not apply to patients who are only subject to after-care under supervision.[70] Accordingly, the patient cannot be given medication or ECT without his valid consent unless justified under common law. He may, however, be required to attend out-patient appointments on a regular basis.

Transfers to hospital or into guardianship

The transfer provisions in Part II do not apply to patients subject to after-care under supervision. It is thus not possible to transfer such a patient to hospital or into guardianship under section 19 and a fresh application is necessary to achieve either of those ends.

Patients moving to Scotland

The situation is governed by The Mental Health (Patients in the Community) (Transfer from England and Wales to Scotland) Regulations 1996, and involves making an application to the sheriff for a community care order.[71]

Leave of absence

The leave of absence provisions in section 17 do not apply to patients who are subject to after-care under supervision and the position is identical to that applicable in guardianship cases (**282**). If the responsible after-care authorities agree to the patient temporarily residing elsewhere, they simply specify the new address as the place where he is required to reside for the time being under section 25D.

Absence without leave

The lack of any specific provisions concerning absence without leave is considered below (**282**).

County court applications under section 29

Because the nearest relative has no power to prevent the making of a supervision application, or to discharge a patient once an application has been accepted, it will

---

68 Mental Health Act 1983, s.25G(9), as inserted by s.1(1) of the Mental Health (Patients in the Community) Act 1995.
69 *Ibid.*, s.72(5), as amended by s.1(2) of, and Sched. 1 para. 10(4) to, the Mental Health (Patients in the Community) Act 1995.
70 *Ibid.*, s.56(1).
71 Mental Health (Scotland) Act 1984, s.35A(1), as inserted by Mental Health (Patients in the Community) Act 1995, s.4(1), as substituted by The Mental Health (Patients in the Community) (Transfer from England and Wales to Scotland) Regulations 1996, reg. 3.

be rare for any application to be made under section 29 for the appointment of an acting nearest relative. Such an application could only be made on one of the "no fault" grounds in section 29(3)(a) or (b) — that is, on the basis that the patient has no identifiable nearest relative or that the person entitled is incapacitated by illness. The duration of the order would need to be specified, otherwise it would normally lapse after three months. The main purpose for applying would be to ensure that there is some individual authorised to exercise any tribunal rights of application under section 66. It may also be noted that where a section 3 patient's nearest relative was previously displaced by the county court under section 29, that order ceases to have effect when the patient ceases to be liable to be detained for treatment.[72] From then onwards, the relative is entitled to be consulted about matters such as the renewal or termination of the authority, unless the usual caveat applies (**456**).

DURATION AND TERMINATION OF SUPERVISION

The Act provides that a patient who leaves hospital subject to after-care under supervision shall initially be so subject for the period of six months beginning with the day on which the supervision application was accepted (not the day on which he leaves hospital as defined above). The authority conferred by a supervision application remains in force until it lapses in the absence of a valid renewal, is terminated by the community responsible medical officer or a tribunal, or is revoked by virtue of the patient being admitted to hospital otherwise than as an informal patient or under section 2 or 4. It will, less commonly, also lapse if the patient has been in custody for a certain length of time. Where a person ceases to be subject to after-care under supervision, the responsible after-care bodies must inform the interested parties.

RENEWING THE AUTHORITY FOR A PATIENT'S SUPERVISION

The renewals framework is similar to that applicable in guardianship cases. The authority conferred by an application lapses after six months unless before then it is renewed for a further period of six months and therefore for further periods of one year at a time. Renewal requires that the community responsible medical officer examines the patient during the final two months of the period of supervision which is drawing to a close and furnishes a report stating that it appears to him that the conditions for renewal ("the renewal criteria") are satisfied. Such reports are furnished to the responsible after-care bodies.[73] The renewal criteria are the same as the original grounds for making a supervision application. As in the case of applications which authorise detention or guardianship, the relevant medical officer is under a statutory duty to furnish such a report if he is of the opinion that the conditions for renewal exist. Similarly, and as with other kinds of application, reclassification is automatic where a renewal report specifies a form of disorder other than that, or those, specified in the application, and a separate report reclassifying the patient need not be submitted.[74]

---

[72] Mental Health Act 1983, s.30(4).
[73] Not, as with the original application, to the Health Authority alone.
[74] *Ibid.*, s.25G(9)–(10), as inserted by s.1(1) of the Mental Health (Patients in the Community) Act 1995.

Duty to consult and notify other professional and non-professional carers

Before furnishing a renewal report, the community responsible medical officer must consult and take into account the views of the following persons: the patient; his supervisor; unless no other person is professionally concerned with the patient's medical treatment, one or more persons who are so concerned; one or more persons who are professionally concerned with the after-care services (other than medical treatment) provided under section 117; any person believed to be a primary carer; and the patient's nearest relative unless the statutory caveat applies (**456**).[75] Where a renewal report is furnished, the responsible after-care bodies must inform the interested parties (the patient and any primary carer or nearest relative consulted before the report was furnished) of that fact.[76]

When the first six month period commences

The initial six month period commences from the day on which the supervision application is accepted, albeit that the patient does not actually become subject to after-care under supervision until he leaves hospital. Consequently, by the time the patient leaves hospital, the authority for his supervision will often have less than six months left to run and may require renewal soon after he leaves. It will be remembered that, in this context, leaving hospital means that the patient has both left hospital and ceased to be liable to be detained there.

Example

X is detained under section 3. The authority for his detention was renewed on 1 January for a period of six months. On 1 February a supervision application in respect of him was accepted by the local NHS trust on behalf of the Health Authority. On 1 April he was discharged from liability to detention under section 3 and left hospital. He therefore became subject to after-care under supervision on that day. The authority for his supervision will lapse after four months, at midnight on 31 July, unless before then it is renewed for a further period of six months.

Patients who do not leave within six months of the application's acceptance

It is quite possible that a patient does not leave hospital in the statutory sense during the six month period following the application's acceptance. The question arises whether the authority for his supervision may be renewed before he has become subject to after-care under supervision. Having regard to the renewal process set out in section 25G, it would appear not. This is because subsection (1) provides for renewing the authority to supervise a patient who is, rather than who is to be, subject to after-care under supervision; and subsection (2) refers to renewing the authority of a patient "already" subject to after-care under supervision for a second period of six months. Furthermore, unless and until the patient has ceased to be liable to be detained and is subject to after-care under supervision, it will be impossible to conduct the consultations which are necessary before a renewal report can be furnished.

---

[75] Mental Health Act 1983, s.25G(5), as inserted by s.1(1) of the Mental Health (Patients in the Community) Act 1995.

[76] *Ibid.*, s.25F(8), as inserted by s.1(1) of the Mental Health (Patients in the Community) Act 1995.

In particular, no one will be professionally concerned with the after-care services provided under section 117 (as opposed to those to be provided). Indeed, the patient does not yet have a supervisor or even a community responsible medical officer who could furnish such a report.

Examples

X is detained under section 3. The authority for his detention was renewed on 1 January for a period of 12 months. On 1 February a supervision application in respect of him was accepted by the local NHS trust on behalf of the Health Authority. The authority for him to be subject to after-care under supervision when he leaves hospital will cease at midnight on 31 July unless it is renewed for a further period of six months. Accordingly, if he is still in hospital or is still liable to be detained, on that date, the authority conferred by the supervision application will lapse. A further application will then be necessary.

On 1 March, the patient was granted extended leave of absence under section 17. This does not constitute leaving hospital for the purposes of the supervision provisions and the patient does not become subject to after-care under supervision on that date. The leave of absence granted under section 17 may continue for the remainder of the 12 month period of liability to detention which began on 1 January: until 31 December. However, if it continues beyond 31 July then, unless a fresh supervision application is made, there will be no authority to supervise the patient upon his eventually "leaving" hospital. Renewal of the supervision application accepted on 1 February is not possible, since the patient has not yet become subject to after-care under supervision.

Example 2

If the patient in the above example was not granted leave of absence but, following the supervision application's acceptance, he was discharged from liability to detention under section 3 on 1 April, and he then remained in hospital as an informal patient, the position would be as follows. The authority conferred by the supervision application would lapse unless he had left hospital by midnight on 31 July. So, for example, if he remained in hospital as an informal patient until 15 August, there would by then be no authority to supervise him.

Delaying acceptance of the application

Having regard to the above, Health Authorities will no doubt consider delaying acceptance of an application until immediately before the patient is ready to leave hospital. However, they will need to balance this consideration against the possibility of the patient being unexpectedly discharged from liability to detention before then by his nearest relative, a tribunal, or by the managers of the NHS trust. The Act does not preclude accepting an application made many months previously, nor therefore one based on examinations and consultations conducted many months previously. However, it remains to be seen whether any such acceptance might be judicially reviewable if there was evidence before the Health Authority of a subsequent material change in the patient's condition, or a change in the opinions of those previously consulted, which it took no account of before accepting the application.

Absence without leave

If a patient who is subject to after-care under supervision absents himself from the place where he is required to reside by the responsible after-care bodies, he is as a matter of logic absent from there without leave. However, section 18, which provides that a patient does not cease to be liable to be detained or subject to guardianship until he has been absent for at least six months, does not apply to supervised patients. Nor does any person appear to be authorised to take him into custody under section 18 or 138.[77] Nor do sections 21 and 21A apply. They provide for the retrospective renewal of the authority conferred by an application where an absent patient is returned after the date on which the authority for his detention or guardianship would ordinarily have expired. Accordingly, if it is impossible to renew the authority for a patient's supervision for a further period, because he is absent during the final two months of the period of supervision which was in force when he went absent, he ceases to be so subject at the expiration of that period. Whether these omissions are deliberate, or instead represent a significant oversight on the draftsman's part, is unclear.

Examples

X was detained under section 3 on 1 January. On 1 February a supervision application in respect of him was accepted by the local NHS trust on behalf of the Health Authority. On 1 March he ceased to be liable to be detained and left hospital, taking up residence at a local hostel in accordance with a requirement imposed on him by the responsible after-care bodies. The authority for his supervision, including authority to require him to reside there, will cease at midnight on 31 July unless it is renewed for a further period of six months. This requires that the community responsible medical officer examines him during June or July and furnishes a report renewing the authority for a further six-month period. X absents himself from the hostel on 15 May, not being located or returning there until 10 August. The authority conferred by the supervision application has lapsed. He can longer be required to reside there unless a guardianship application is made.

Example 2

X was detained under section 3 on 1 January. The authority to detain him will ordinarily expire at midnight on 30 June unless renewed for a further period. On 1 February a supervision application in respect of him was accepted by the local NHS trust on behalf of the Health Authority. The authority for him to be subject to after-care under supervision when he eventually leaves hospital will cease at midnight on 31 July unless it is renewed for a further period of six months. On 15 April he absents himself from hospital without leave. Although the authority for his detention can be renewed if he is taken into custody at any time before midnight on 14 October (**292**), the authority for his subsequent supervision will lapse if he is not returned by 31 July. A fresh supervision application will therefore be necessary if he is taken into custody and returned to hospital during the period from 1 August until 14 October.

---

[77] Although not specifically an absence without leave provision, s.25D(4) could be used by the supervisor, or by a person authorised by him, such as a police constable, to take and convey an absent patient to the required place. However, it does not appear that a police constable may take an absent supervised patient into custody unless authorised to do so by the supervisor.

Effect of a subsequent application or order under the 1983 Act

The authority conferred by a supervision application is revoked if the patient is admitted to hospital for treatment under section 3, *or* in pursuance of a hospital order or transfer direction, *or* he is received into guardianship in pursuance of a guardianship application or order.[78] The interested parties must be informed that the patient has ceased to be so subject (**459**).[79] Admission as an informal patient, or under section 2 or 4, does not have the effect of terminating the after-care under supervision, nor does admission under sections 35, 36 or 38.

Detention under section 2

While a patient who is subject to after-care under supervision is detained under section 2 he is not required during this period to receive any after-care services provided for him under section 117 or to comply with any requirements previously imposed on him under section 25D.[80] If the patient would ordinarily have ceased to be subject to after-care under supervision during the period he is detained under section 2, or during the 28 day period beginning with the day he ceases to be detained under that provision, he does not cease to be so subject until 28 days have expired from the time he ceased to be detained under section 2.[81] Any renewal report furnished during this extended period is valid and, where necessary, may have retrospective effect.

Example

On 1 January a supervision application made in respect of X, a patient detained under section 3, was accepted by the local NHS trust on behalf of the Health Authority. On 1 March he ceased to be liable to be detained and left hospital, at which point he became subject to after-care under supervision. The authority for his supervision was renewed for a further period of six months commencing on 1 July. This authority will ordinarily expire on 31 December unless before then it is renewed for a further period of twelve months. Renewal requires that the community responsible medical officer examines him during November or December and furnishes a report renewing the authority.

On 25 November, and before any such report has been furnished, X is admitted to hospital under section 2. He is discharged from liability to detention under section 2 on 18 December. His community responsible medical officer then has 28 days — until midnight on 14 January — within which to examine the patient, consult the necessary persons, and furnish a report renewing the authority for the patient's supervision. Thus, if he furnishes such a report on 8 January, it has retrospective effect and the authority for the patient's supervision is thereby renewed for a period of 12 months beginning on 1 January. If no report has been furnished by midnight on 14 January, the patient ceases to be subject to after-care under supervision at that time.

---

[78]   Mental Health Act 1983, ss.25H(5), 40(4), 55(4), 145(3), Sched. 1 Pt. I para. 1, as inserted by s.1(1) and (2) of, and Sched. 1 para. 6(a) to, the Mental Health (Patients in the Community) Act 1995.

[79]   *Ibid.*, s.25H(6), as inserted by s.1(1) of the Mental Health (Patients in the Community) Act 1995.

[80]   *Ibid.*, s.25I(1)(b) and (2), as inserted by s.1(1) of the Mental Health (Patients in the Community) Act 1995. The same presumably applies to patients admitted under sections 4, 35, 36 and 38.

[81]   *Ibid.*, s.25I(3)–(5), as inserted by Mental Health (Patients in the Community) Act 1995, s.1(1).

Patients taken into custody (prison)

The authority to supervise a patient may similarly be extended, and retrospectively renewed, if he is taken into custody in pursuance of a sentence or order passed by a court within the United Kingdom, including an order remanding him in custody. If the patient is released from custody before he has been in custody for a period of six months and during that period, or within 28 days of his release, he would ordinarily have ceased to be subject to supervision because of a failure to renew the authority for a further period, he nevertheless continues to be subject to after-care under supervision for a period of 28 days beginning with the date of his release from custody. Any renewal report which is furnished during this extended period has effect as if it had been furnished during the final two months of the period of supervision which was in force when the patient was taken into custody.[82]

Example

X was detained under section 3 on 1 January. On 1 February, a supervision application in respect of him was accepted by the local NHS trust on behalf of the Health Authority. On 1 March he ceased to be liable to be detained and left hospital, thereby becoming subject to after-care under supervision. The authority for his supervision will ordinarily cease at midnight on 31 July unless it is renewed for a further period of six months.

On 1 April he is charged with burglary and remanded in custody. He is released after five months, on 1 September. He remains subject to supervision for a further 28 days, until midnight on 28 September. If no renewal report is furnished before then he ceases to be subject to after-care under supervision at that point. If, however, a renewal report is furnished during that period it has retrospective effect. Thus, a report furnished on 14 September will renew the authority for the patient's supervision for a period of six months commencing on 1 August.[83]

DIRECTING THAT THE AUTHORITY CEASE TO HAVE EFFECT

Although many of the provisions which apply to patients subject to after-care under supervision mirror the pre-existing guardianship provisions, the discharge powers differ. Following the acceptance of a supervision application, the authority to supervise the patient is not dischargeable by the responsible medical officer; the managers of the hospital at which he is liable to be detained or residing; the Health Authority; the local social services authority; the nearest relative; the Secretary of State. Thus, neither the patient's nearest relative nor the responsible after-care bodies have power to terminate the supervision. Apart from the patient's community responsible medical officer, only a tribunal may direct that a patient subject to after-care under supervision shall cease to be so subject. Moreover, until the patient leaves hospital and the supervision actually commences, *only* a tribunal may

---

[82] Mental Health Act 1983, s.25I, as inserted by s.1(1) of the Mental Health (Patients in the Community) Act 1995. Note that, in contrast to section 22, a patient whose supervision was last renewed for a period of 12 months does not automatically cease to be subject to after-care under supervision by virtue only of the fact that he has been in custody for more than six months.

[83] It may briefly be noted that section 25I does not provide for double renewals or for double retrospective renewals of the kind found in section 21B6(b) and (7). See p.297 for an illustration of the point.

terminate his liability to supervision. Furthermore, until then, the Secretary of State has no power to refer his case to a tribunal. And, once the patient has left hospital, if the responsible after-care bodies review the after-care arrangements and any requirements imposed on him, and conclude that statutory supervision is no longer justified, their only available course of action is to notify the community responsible medical officer of their opinion (**442**).

Direction by the community responsible medical officer

The responsible community medical officer may at any time direct that a patient subject to after-care under supervision shall cease to be so subject.[84] Such a direction is equivalent to an order for discharge under section 23 in respect of a patient who is liable to be detained or subject to guardianship. However, before giving any such direction, the community responsible medical officer must first consult the same classes of professional and non-professional persons as must be consulted before a supervision application is renewed for a further period and take their views into account (**459**).[85] Where a direction terminating the statutory supervision is given, the responsible after-care bodies (not the community responsible medical officer) must inform the interested parties of this fact (**459**).[86] There should therefore be written evidence of the fact that a direction has been given, although the Act does not expressly provide that such a direction itself must be in writing.

Discharge by a Mental Health Review Tribunal

Following the application's acceptance, the patient's rights to apply to a tribunal, and the tribunal's powers, are similar to those in cases involving guardianship. And, as with guardianship cases, there is no duty to periodically refer the patient's case to a tribunal if no application has been made for a certain period of time.

Rights of application

The patient's rights of application correspond to those of a patient subject to guardianship. However, the nearest relative's rights are more limited that those of the nearest relative of a patient subject to a guardianship order. As can be seen from the table on the following page, the patient may in many cases prevent his nearest relative from acquiring a right to make an application to a tribunal in respect of him. To this extent, and quite uniquely in the overall context of the Act, the nearest relative's rights are rights subject to the patient's discretion, rather than absolute rights vesting in the relative by virtue of his relationship to the patient.

Tribunal's powers

Where a tribunal considers the case of an in-patient in respect of whom a supervision application has been accepted, the tribunal must direct that the application shall cease to have effect if they are satisfied that the grounds for making such an application "are not complied with" (**508**). If not satisfied as to this, the tribunal may still revoke the application at its discretion (as in guardianship cases) and, where it does not direct that the application shall cease to have effect, reclassify the patient.

---

[84] Mental Health Act 1983, s.25H(1), as inserted by Mental Health (Patients in the Community) Act 1995, s.1(1).

[85] *Ibid.*, s.25H(2)–(4), as inserted by Mental Health (Patients in the Community) Act 1995, s.1(1).

[86] *Ibid.*, s.25H(6) as inserted by s.1(1) of the Mental Health (Patients in the Community) Act 1995. It appears to be assumed that the CRMO will notify these bodies that he has directed that the patient shall cease to be subject to after-care under supervision.

Where a patient has left hospital, and so is receiving after-care under supervision, the position is essentially the same, except that the duty to revoke the application arises if the tribunal are satisfied that the criteria for renewing supervision applications are not complied with. However, apart from minor and inconsequential modifications, the renewal criteria are the same as the original grounds for making a supervision application.

TRIBUNAL RIGHTS OF APPLICATION

Right of application	Who may apply	When they may apply
• **Following the acceptance of a supervision application made under s.25A (s.66(1)(ga).**	*The patient or, subject to the note below, his nearest relative*	During the six-month period beginning with the date of the application's acceptance.
• **Following the furnishing of a report under s.25F reclassifying the patient (s.66(1)(gb)**	*The patient or, subject to the note below, his nearest relative*	During the 28 day period beginning with the day on which the applicant is informed the report has been furnished.
• **Following the furnishing of a report under s.25G renewing the authority for the patient's supervision for a further period (s.66(1)(gc)**	*The patient or, subject to the note below, his nearest relative*	During the additional six or twelve month period of supervision authorised by the report.

Notes concerning the nearest relative: In each case above, the nearest relative only has a right to make an application if he has been, or was entitled to be, informed under the Act of the application's acceptance or, as the case may be, that a report renewing the authority or reclassifying the patient has been furnished. If the patient requests that the nearest relative not be informed of his reclassification, the nearest relative is not entitled to be informed. If the patient requests that the nearest relative not be consulted about whether a supervision application should be made or renewed, that relative will not be consulted unless the patient has a propensity to violent or dangerous behaviour and the medical officer in charge of his treatment considers that consultation is appropriate. Unless this caveat applies, the nearest relative is not entitled to be consulted unless he is also one of the patient's primary carers (456). If the nearest relative is not entitled to be consulted about whether an application should be made, or the authority renewed, then neither is he entitled to be informed that such an application or authority has been made or renewed. Consequently, he has no right to apply to a tribunal upon the application being accepted or the authority conferred by it renewed.

MENTAL HEALTH ACT COMMISSION

Patients subject to after-care under supervision do not fall within the Commission's remit. However, patients in respect of whom a supervision application has been accepted, but who remain liable to be detained, will come within the Commission's jurisdiction for so long as they remain liable to be detained for treatment. The Act provides that the Code of Practice shall include guidance on after-care under supervision.

DELEGATION AND CONSULTATION

This final section of the chapter deals with two important but technical areas, the delegation of statutory functions and the extent of the duty to consult various interested parties before exercising some statutory power.

DELEGATION OF FUNCTIONS

As has been noted, section 32 of the 1983 Act provides that the Secretary of State may make regulations for carrying Part II of the Act into full effect. The regulations may in particular determine the manner in which the functions under Part II of the hospital managers, local social services authorities, Health Authorities and National Health Service Trusts are to be exercised. They may also specify the circumstances in which, and the conditions subject to which, "any such functions" may be performed by officers of, or other persons acting on behalf of, those managers and authorities.[87]

The Mental Health (After-care under Supervision) Regulations 1996

The Mental Health (After-care under Supervision) Regulations 1996 have been made under section 32 and they came into force on 1 April 1996.[88] They provide that functions under what are referred to as the "relevant provisions" may in the circumstances prescribed be performed by some other body or person on behalf of a Health Authority or local social services authority.[89] The "relevant provisions" are those set out in Schedule 1 to the regulations.[90]

SCHEDULE 1 Regulation 2(1)

PROVISIONS OF THE ACT CONFERRING FUNCTIONS ON
HEALTH AUTHORITIES AND LOCAL SOCIAL SERVICES AUTHORITIES

(1) Provision of the Act	*(2) Subject matter*
Section 25A(6), (7) and (8)	Supervision applications— acceptance etc.
Section 25C(6)	Supervision applications—consent to amendment
Section 25D(1)	Imposition of requirements
Section 25E(1), (3), (4), (6), (8) and (11)	Review and modification of requirements imposed
Section 25F(1) and (4)	Receipt of reclassification report
Section 25G(3) and (8)	Receipt of renewal report and notification
Section 25H(6)	Ending of after-care under supervision and notification

---

[87] Mental Health Act 1983, s.32(3).
[88] The Mental Health (After-care under Supervision) Regulations 1996 (1996 No. 294).
[89] *Ibid.*, reg. 2.
[90] *Ibid.*, reg. 2(1).

Functions the performance of which cannot be delegated

Regulation 2 expressly provides that nothing in the regulations shall permit a Health Authority or local social services authority to authorise a person or body to exercise the relevant functions under section 25E(1) and (3) of the 1983 Act so far as they relate to review and modification of after-care services provided (or to be provided) to a patient under section 117.[91] What this means is that the health and local social services authorities must themselves review and where necessary modify the after-care services being provided under section 117. They may, however, in the circumstances prescribed by the regulations, authorise another body or a person not employed by them to undertake the process of reviewing and modifying any essential powers previously imposed under section 25D. Thus, the regulations separate out the processes of reviewing and modifying the after-care services comprised in the after-care plan (which may not be delegated) and of reviewing and modifying the way in which the new statutory powers are being exercised to secure the receipt of those services (which may be delegated).

Who may be authorised to perform one of the relevant provisions

Subject to the above caveat, the regulations authorise the making by a health or local social services authority of the following arrangements with regard to the performance of those functions referred to in the "relevant provisions" —

1. A Health Authority may "make arrangements" for its functions under the relevant provisions to be exercised on its behalf by an officer of that authority or by a committee or sub-committee of that authority.[92]

2. A Health Authority may "make arrangements" for its functions under the relevant provisions to be exercised on its behalf by another Health Authority; or by an officer, committee or sub-committee of another Health Authority, including a Special Health Authority; or for their exercise by a joint committee or joint sub-committee of the Health Authority and another Health Authority.[93]

3. A Health Authority which "makes an arrangement" with an individual, an NHS trust, or some other person or body such as a voluntary organisation, for the provision of psychiatric and related services to the patient may also "authorise that person or body to perform on its behalf its functions under the relevant provisions" in respect of him.[94]

---

[91] The Mental Health (After-care under Supervision) Regulations 1996, reg. 2(5).

[92] The Mental Health (After-care under Supervision) Regulations 1996, reg. 2(3); National Health Service Act 1977, s.16, as substituted by s.2(1) of, and Sched. 1 para. 7 to, the Health Authorities Act 1995. The term "an officer" means an employee.

[93] The Mental Health (After-care under Supervision) Regulations 1996, reg. 2(3); National Health Service Act 1977, s.16, as substituted by s.2(1) of, and Sched. 1 para. 7 to, the Health Authorities Act 1995. A Health Authority does not appear to have authority to make arrangements for its functions under the relevant provisions to be exercised by a joint-committee of the Health Authority and a local social services authority.

[94] The Mental Health (After-care under Supervision) Regulations 1996, reg. 2(2); National Health Service and Community Care Act 1990, s.4; National Health Service Act 1977, s.23.

4. Where the Health Authority has authorised or arranged for its statutory functions under the relevant provisions to be exercised by some other some person or body, the local social services authority with the corresponding duty under section 117 to provide the patient with after-care services "may authorise the same person or body to perform all of" its functions under the relevant provisions in respect of him."[95]

Summary

The intention behind the regulations is to enable statutory powers and duties which specifically relate to the element of statutory supervision in a patient's after-care plan, rather than to the provision or delivery of those services, to be exercised on behalf of the responsible after-care bodies by some agreed person or body. While Health Authorities will no doubt routinely delegate the exercise of these functions to NHS trusts from which they have purchased health services, it must be emphasised that a local social services authority is not obliged to follow suit — it is merely lawful for it to do so. Indeed, many social services authorities may wish to retain joint control with the NHS trust in relation to the way in which any essential powers under section 25D are imposed and modified.

DUTIES TO CONSULT AND NOTIFY OTHER PERSONS

When contrasted with applications for guardianship under Part II, a noteworthy feature of the statutory framework for after-care under supervision is that many powers are solely vested in the responsible medical officer or, once the patient leaves hospital, the community responsible medical officer. The acceptance of an application does not require the consent of the patient's statutory nearest relative or the local social services authority and they have no power to later terminate the authority. In part compensation for this, the Act imposes an extensive range of duties on those doctors (and others) to consult various interested parties before exercising any statutory power, to take their views into account, and to notify them of any statutory steps which are then taken. These duties are set out on page 458.

The basic framework

The basic framework may be summarised in the following way—

- Where a statutory power is one for the medical practitioner in charge of the patient's treatment to exercise and involves the authority for after-care under supervision (making an application, furnishing a renewal report, terminating the supervision), he must consult a range of professionals and non-professionals (the interested parties) involved in the case before exercising it.

- Where the exercise of a statutory power is vested in both responsible after-care bodies (modifying the after-care services or any essential powers imposed under section 25E), the statute only imposes a duty to consult relevant non-professionals (the interested parties). Such collective professional decisions mean that the professionals involved are doing the consulting rather than being consulted.

---

95 The Mental Health (After-care under Supervision) Regulations 1996, reg. 2(4).

- Upon a statutory power being exercised, whether by the doctor in charge of the patient's treatment or by the after-care bodies, the duty is to inform the relevant non-professionals (the interested parties) of this fact, it being assumed that persons professionally involved will be notified as a matter of course. The basic rule of thumb is that if an interested party was consulted before the particular step was taken he must also be informed if it is then taken.[96]

The nearest relative's right to be consulted and kept informed

The general rule is that, unless the nearest relative is also a primary carer, he generally need not be consulted about some proposed statutory step if the patient objects to that. However, if the doctor in charge of the patient's treatment is of the opinion that he has a propensity for violent or dangerous behaviour towards others and, by virtue of this, it is appropriate to consult the relative about the step in question then that person may be consulted.

When the caveat does not apply

The caveat represents a recognition that the relative may be a potential victim of the feared behaviour and so should be consulted and kept informed about the supervisory process. However, it does not apply in two situations. The patient's right to "request" that his nearest relative is not informed of any reclassification is not qualified in this way. Consequently, the relative's right to apply to a tribunal following reclassification becomes one exercisable only with the patient's consent. This represents a departure from the position in respect of detained patients and those subject to guardianship. Here, the nearest relative's right to be told of any reclassification, and to then apply to a tribunal, is a personal one: it is his right and not one for the patient to grant. The second exception is that where the patient's community responsible medical officer or supervisor changes, the Act simply provides that the nearest relative shall be informed of this unless the patient has requested otherwise. Accordingly, if the caveat would apply on the facts, the absurd position is reached that patient cannot prevent the nearest relative from being informed of who is to be the community responsible medical officer and supervisor when the application is made, but can prevent him being told that they are no longer performing those duties. This must be a drafting error so that, under the "golden rule" of statutory construction, the caveat may be read as applying here also.

Whether doctors must personally undertake statutory consultations

The Code of Practice states that the responsible medical officer and, by implication, the community responsible medical officer is not obliged to personally undertake all consultations but the responsibility should be delegated only with his express agreement.[97] No authority is given for this statement and, indeed, the Act does not itself authorise delegating the statutory duty to another person, such as a junior

---

[96] Strictly speaking, if it was not practicable to consult the nearest relative about some proposed step before the event it is not then necessary to notify him that it has been taken after the event, even though that would be practicable.

[97] *Mental Health (Patients in the Community) Act 1995: Guidance on Supervised Discharge (After-care under supervision) and related provisions. Supplement to the Code of Practice* (Department of Health and the Welsh Office, 1996), para. 5.

doctor or administrator.[98] In the absence of an express provision of the kind found in section 5(3), the customary view has always been that a responsible medical officer may not delegate the performance of his statutory functions. For example, he must personally examine the patient and furnish statutory reports required under section 20 and 58, and only he within the medical team has authority to discharge a patient or grant him leave of absence under section 17. Likewise, he must personally consult another person professionally involved in the patient's medical treatment before furnishing a renewal report or a report reclassifying him. In the absence of any express provision to the effect that the duties vested in him may be undertaken by another individual not specified by Parliament, it must therefore be assumed that the same principles apply. Accordingly, the responsible medical officer must, likewise, personally consult his professional colleagues before making a supervision application, renewing it, or terminating it. Otherwise the personal exercise of the powers vested in him by Parliament becomes divorced from the personal duties imposed on him by Parliament, by which the exercise of those powers is kept in check. And, if he must conduct professional consultations personally, there appears to be no logical reason why the non-professionals are only entitled to be consulted vicariously. Indeed, the extensive nature of the duty to consult others reflects the concentration of several powers in a single pair of hands, counter-balances this, and compensates persons such as the nearest relative for their relatively limited statutory rights. Often, these rights consist *only* of this right to be consulted by the person who is contemplating exercising one of his powers. While the need to conduct a series of consultations is time-consuming — and the understandable unpopularity of the prospect with some consultants appears to have been the motivation for the advice in the Code — there is nevertheless nothing in the Act to support such a view. It involves reading every reference to the medical officers in charge of a patient's treatment as referring not in fact to them but to them or any authorised person: that is not what the Act says. Indeed, if professional convenience is allowed to dictate such an interpretation, the ambit of many other protective provisions would be thrown into doubt, with significant consequences for the liberty of the subject. Approved social workers might claim that their corresponding statutory duty to consult the nearest relative before making an application is satisfied if vicariously performed. And a similar latitude might be claimed in respect of consulting others before renewing a patient's detention, reclassifying him, or authorising compulsory treatment under section 58. Better therefore to emphasise that the law requires consultants who are over-worked to distinguish between their statutory and non-statutory duties, when deciding what duties may properly be delegated to junior members of their team.[99]

---

[98] Nor do the regulations provide for such a delegation of his statutory functions. Indeed, it is noteworthy that while section 34(2)(e) and (3) allow for the performance by a third party of the statutory functions of nearest relatives, and the delegation of functions vested in the hospital managers, local social services authorities, and NHS trusts, no such provision is made in respect of the responsible medical officer's functions.

[99] Support for a counter-argument derives from dicta of Laws J. in *R. v. South Western Hospital Managers, ex p. M.* [1994] All E.R. 161 at 175–176, where His Lordship said that an approved social worker's duty to consult the nearest relative before making a section 3 application could be performed vicariously. Since part of that decision has since been overruled, there are difficulties with other parts of it (**593**), and no reasons were given for the opinion expressed there, it is submitted that the conventional view about an approved social worker's duties being personal should be adhered to until the courts firmly decide otherwise.

CONSULTATION AND NOTIFICATION OF INTERESTED PARTIES

Provision	Subject matter	The duty to consult or notify
S.25B(1)–(3)	• **Consultation prior to making an application**	The RMO shall consult the patient; one or more persons who have been professionally concerned with the patient's medical treatment in hospital; one or more persons who will be professionally concerned with the after-care services to be provided under s117; any person whom he believes will be a primary carer after the patient leaves hospital; where practicable, the person (if any) appearing to be the nearest relative unless the patient has requested otherwise, and neither of the following caveats apply. The first caveat is that the patient has a propensity to violent or dangerous behaviour towards others and the RMO considers it is appropriate to take such steps as are practicable to consult that relative about making an application. The second caveat is that the nearest relative will also be a primary carer and so, despite the patient's wishes, is entitled to be consulted in that capacity.
S.25B(10)–(11)	• **Notification that an application has been made, etc.**	The RMO shall inform the following persons that he had made an application: the patient (orally and in writing); any nearest relative (in writing) and primary carer (not specified) consulted before it was made. The persons notified shall also be informed of the after-care services to be provided for the patient, of any essential powers to be imposed on him; and of the persons who are to be his CRMO and supervisor.
S.25A(7)	• **Consultation before an application is accepted**	Before accepting an application, the Health Authority must also consult the local social services authority which constitutes the other responsible after-care body.
S.25A(8)	• **Notification of the application's acceptance**	The Health Authority shall inform the patient (orally and in writing), any person whom the RMO stated in the application was consulted before it was made as a primary carer (not specified) or nearest relative (in writing). The patient must also be informed orally and in writing of the application's effect, including his rights of application to a Mental Health Review Tribunal. Strictly speaking, there is no similar statutory duty to inform the local social services authority of the application's acceptance.
S.25E(1)–(7)	• **Consultation about modifying the after-care services or essential powers**	The responsible after-care bodies must first consult the following persons about the proposed modifications: the patient; any person whom they believe is a primary carer; where practicable, the person (if any) appearing to be the nearest relative unless, subject to the same caveats as before, the patient has requested otherwise. The first caveat in this context is that the patient has a propensity to violent or dangerous behaviour towards others and the RMO (or the person who is to be the CRMO) considers that it is appropriate to take such steps as are practicable to consult that relative about the modifications.
S.25E(8)	• **Notification of modifications to the after-care services or essential powers**	The responsible after-care bodies shall inform the following persons of the modifications: the patient (orally and in writing); any nearest relative (in writing) and primary carer consulted before they were made.

S.25E(9)–(11)	• **Notification of change of CRMO or supervisor**	Where at the time the patient ceases to be liable to be detained a person other than those named in the application becomes the CRMO or supervisor, or at a later date some other person assumes one or both of those roles, the responsible after-care bodies shall notify the following persons of the name of the person assuming the role: the patient (orally and in writing); any person whom the bodies believe is a primary carer; where practicable the person (if any) appearing to be the nearest relative unless the patient has requested otherwise (in writing). The first caveat previously referred to does not apply in this case.
S.25F(1)–(3)	• **Consultation prior to any reclassification**	Unless no other person is professionally concerned with the patient's medical treatment, the CRMO shall before furnishing a report reclassifying a patient consult one or more persons who is so concerned.
S.25F(4)	• **Notification of reclassification**	Where a report reclassifying a patient is furnished, the responsible after-care bodies shall notify the following persons of this fact: the patient (orally and in writing); where practicable, the person (if any) appearing to be the nearest relative unless the patient has requested otherwise (in writing). Both of the caveats previously referred to do not apply and there is no duty to inform a person believed to be a primary carer since he has no right to a tribunal following reclassification.
S.25G(1)–(7)	• **Consultation prior to furnishing a renewal report**	Before considering whether the statutory grounds exist for renewing the authority conferred by a supervision application, the CRMO shall consult the following persons: the patient; the supervisor; unless no other person is professionally concerned with the patient's medical treatment, one or more persons who is so concerned; one or more persons who are professionally concerned with the section 117 after-care services (other than medical treatment); any person whom the CRMO believes is a primary carer; where practicable the person (if any) appearing to be the nearest relative unless, subject to the same two caveats as before, the patient has requested otherwise. The caveat is that the patient has a propensity to violent or dangerous behaviour towards others and the RMO considers that it is appropriate to take such steps as are practicable to consult that relative about renewing the authority.
S.25G(8)	• **Notification of renewal of the authority**	Where the CRMO furnishes a renewal report, the responsible after-care bodies shall notify the following persons of this fact: the patient (orally and in writing); any nearest relative (in writing) and primary carer (not specified) consulted before it was made. The patient shall also be informed of the also be informed orally and in writing of the renewal report's effect, including his rights of application to a Mental Health Review Tribunal.
S.25H(1)–(5)	• **Consultation about the ending of after-care under supervision**	The CRMO shall not direct that a patient shall cease to be subject to after-care under supervision unless he has first consulted the same classes of persons who must be consulted prior to any renewal and has taken any views expressed by them into account. The caveats concerning the need to consult the nearest relative similarly apply.
S25H(6)–(7)	• **Notification of the ending, cessation or expiration of after-care under supervision**	Where the CRMO directs that a patient shall cease to be subject to after-care under supervision, or the patient ceases to be subject for any other reason, the responsible after-care bodies shall notify the same persons of this fact as must be notified of any report renewing the authority for a further period. That is to say the patient (orally and in writing); any nearest relative (in writing) or primary carer consulted before it was made.

459

A tribunal's powers

7. A tribunal's powers in unrestricted cases

INTRODUCTION

This chapter deals with a tribunal's powers in respect of unrestricted patients. These patients comprise —

For a brief summary and comparison of a tribunal's powers in these cases, see the introduction. As to whether a tribunal may have regard to irregularities in the authority for the patient's detention, guardianship or supervision, see page 574.

PATIENTS DETAINED UNDER SECTION 2

A tribunal's powers when dealing with the case of a patient who is liable to be detained for assessment are specified in section 72, the relevant parts of which are set out on the following page.

SUMMARY OF POWERS

A tribunal must discharge a section 2 patient whom it considers satisfies the statutory criteria for being discharged set out in section 72(1)(a) — "mandatory discharge." Where the mandatory discharge criteria are not satisfied, it may still discharge the patient at its discretion if it considers that is appropriate having regard to all the circumstances of the case — "discretionary discharge." A tribunal which discharges a patient may direct that the discharge take effect on a specified future date, rather than forthwith, regardless of whether discharge is mandatory or discretionary. A tribunal which does not discharge may, with a view to facilitating a patient's discharge on some future date, recommend that he be granted leave of absence, transferred to another hospital, or transferred into guardianship. In the event that its recommendation is not complied with, the tribunal may further consider the case. In summary, a tribunal is obliged to discharge if the relevant statutory criteria are satisfied, may in other cases discharge at its discretion and, where it does not discharge, may make certain statutory recommendations with a view to facilitating discharge in the future.

POWERS OF TRIBUNALS IN SECTION 2 CASES

Discretionary discharge

72.—(1) Where application is made to a Mental Health Review Tribunal by or in respect of a patient who is liable to be detained under this Act, the tribunal may in any case direct that the patient be discharged, and

Mandatory discharge

(a) the tribunal shall direct the discharge of a patient liable to be detained under section 2 above if they are satisfied—

(i) that he is not then suffering from mental disorder or from mental disorder of a nature or degree which warrants his detention in a hospital for assessment (or for assessment followed by medical treatment) for at least a limited period; or
(ii) that his detention as aforesaid is not justified in the interests of his own health or safety or with a view to the protection of other persons.

Future discharge

(3) A tribunal may under subsection (1) above direct the discharge of a patient on a future date specified in the direction;

Recommendations

and where a tribunal do not direct the discharge of a patient under that subsection the tribunal may—

(a) with a view to facilitating his discharge on a future date, recommend that he be granted leave of absence or transferred to another hospital or into guardianship; and
(b) further consider his case in the event of any such recommendation not being complied with.

References

(6) Subsections (1) to (5) above apply in relation to references to a Mental Health Review Tribunal as they apply in relation to applications made to such a tribunal by or in respect of a patient.

TERMINOLOGY

As to the meaning of the words used in the admission and discharge criteria, see "discharge" (**466**); "patient" (**098**); "liable to be detained" and "detained" (**467, 585**); "satisfied" (**567**); "then" (**466**); "suffering from" (**213**); "mental disorder" (**051**); "nature or degree" (**213**); "warrants" (**215**); "detention" (**215**); "hospital" (**131**); "assessment" (**231**); "treatment" (**216**); "for at least a limited period" (**226**); "ought to be so" and "justified in the interests of"" (**221, 227, 466**); "health" (**217**); "safety" (**218**); "protection of other persons" (**219**). By way of summary—

464

- A person whose symptoms are merely controlled by medication still "suffers from" mental disorder. Furthermore, the fact that a person is in remission, and there are no longer any obvious symptoms or signs of mental disorder, is not proof that the underlying disorder is not of a severe nature.

- The words "nature" and "degree" are not interchangeable. The word "degree" focuses attention on the present manifestations of any mental disorder which exists. The word "nature" focuses attention on precisely that: the characteristics of the patient's condition, its historical course and chronicity, and the prognosis associated with any diagnosis made. A condition may be severe because it is acute (of a severe degree) or because it is chronic or progressive and difficult to treat (of a severe nature).

- "Warrants" denotes a condition the nature or degree of which is sufficiently serious to require the use of the particular compulsory power. The "the unsoundness of mind, whose presence is essential to justify a compulsory order, manifestly means more than mental illness which qualifies a person to be a voluntary patient ... in ordinary language "certifiable" is perhaps more likely to be used to express the same idea."[1]

- "Detention" refers to the case of a person lawfully held against his will, one who is not free to depart when he pleases.

- "Assessment" involves assessing from a clinical viewpoint the patient's need for prolonged treatment and assessing from a legal viewpoint the necessity of prolonged and potentially indefinite compulsory treatment.

- "Medical treatment," unless the context otherwise requires, "includes nursing, and also includes care, habilitation and rehabilitation under medical supervision."[2]

- "Health" may be described as the standard of physical and mental functioning necessary for a person to perform the activities which are expected of him, according to the norms of the society in which he lives; all *disabling* disease, illness and handicap must be absent.

- "Safety" denotes freedom from physical harm. A patient's safety may be at risk because of his own acts (dangerous conduct towards himself), his omissions to act (self-neglect), how others act towards him (exploiting or ill-treating him), or omit to act towards him (failing to care for him).

- The expression "protection of other persons" indicates a need to protect other persons from the consequences of the patient's actions, including psychological injury and damage to property resulting from his mental state.

- "Justified in the interests of" means that the patient "ought to be detained"[3] because of the possibility of harm to himself or others if he is not.

---

[1] *Buxton v. Jayne* [1960] 2 All E.R. 688 at 697, *per* Devlin L.J.
[2] Mental Health Act 1983, s.145(1).
[3] The expression used in the section 2 admission criteria.

MANDATORY DISCHARGE

The discharge criteria closely correspond to the original grounds for admission under section 2 or 4. The expression "ought to be detained" in section 2(2)(b) is, however, replaced in section 72(1)(a)(ii) by a reference to the patient's detention being "justified." In both cases, the contrast is between that which is necessary (detention under section 3) and that which ought to be done and can be justified (detention under section 2). The other difference is the addition of the word "then" in the discharge criteria, the effect of which is that a tribunal must discharge a patient if it is satisfied that there are no grounds for detention under section 2 at the time of the hearing — the tribunal is not reviewing whether such grounds existed at the time of the patient's admission to hospital. The word should not, however, be interpreted so literally as to mean that a tribunal must therefore disregard the history of the patient's condition or recent fluctuations in his mental state. These are relevant because they define the nature of his present condition. The point generally arises where there is good evidence that a patient who presents very well at the hearing was floridly ill a day or two previously. This may indicate a qualitative improvement in his mental health but it may also be evidence merely that his mental state fluctuates markedly over short periods of time. Likewise, the fact that a person behaved violently towards a nurse a week before the hearing may, in the absence of evidence that circumstances have materially changed, be an indication that detention continues to be justified with a view to protecting others.

The meaning of "discharge"

In assessment cases, "discharge" means to discharge the patient from his liability to detention under section 2, not discharge from hospital (**571**). Consequently, a tribunal must discharge a patient who requires in-patient assessment or in-patient treatment if it is satisfied that his condition does not warrant detention for either of these purposes or that his detention in hospital is not justified with a view to his health or safety or the protection of others.

Completed "assessments"

Section 72(1)(a)(i) requires a tribunal to "discharge" a patient detained under section 2 if they are satisfied that he is not "then" suffering from mental disorder "or from mental disorder of a nature or degree which warrants his detention in a hospital for assessment (or for assessment followed by a medical treatment) for at least a limited period." The extent of this obligation has caused considerable debate, leading some tribunals to conclude that a duty to discharge arises if the assessment of a patient's need for treatment has been concluded prior to the hearing. The meaning of "assessment" in this context has already been considered in some detail (**231**). By way of summary, it has been submitted that where a patient is assessed not to be mentally disordered, the first of the reasons for detaining him has been fulfilled and the second also in that no treatment will follow what constitutes a completed assessment. Similarly, both statutory purposes have been fulfilled once a patient has been assessed not to suffer from any form of mental disorder which warrants compulsory treatment, continued detention being warranted neither for assessment or treatment. Where, however, a patient has been assessed to suffer from a disorder which does warrant detention for treatment, neither his responsible medical officer nor a tribunal is thereby bound to discharge him simply because the former has commenced the treatment which the patient has been assessed to need. It would be remarkable if Parliament intended that whenever an assessment of a patient's condition demonstrates a need for compulsory treatment — that is that the assessment should be "followed by treatment" — a tribunal is then obliged to discharge the patient by virtue of this positive finding of a serious mental disorder. If this were correct a patient must be discharged both when he is assessed not to need compulsory treatment and when he is assessed to need such treatment. Insofar as the drafting is indifferent, the phrase "(or for assessment followed by medical treatment)" may properly be read as meaning "(or for medical treatment following assessment)" where treatment has already been commenced before the hearing. Accordingly, section 72(1)(a)(i) should be read as follows —

> *"(a) the tribunal shall direct the discharge of a patient liable to be detained under section 2 above if they are satisfied (i) that he is not then suffering from mental disorder or from mental disorder of a nature or degree which warrants his detention in a hospital for assessment (or for medical treatment following assessment) for at least a limited period."*

Patients not requiring in-patient assessment or treatment

Section 72 requires a tribunal to discharge a patient who is "liable to be detained" under section 2 if it is satisfied either that his mental disorder is not of a kind which warrants his "detention in a hospital ..." or that "his detention as aforesaid" is not justified for one of the permitted purposes. In contrast, a tribunal is only obliged to discharge a section 3 patient where satisfied that his mental disorder is not of a kind which makes it appropriate for him to be "liable to be detained in a hospital ..." As McCullough J. noted in *ex p. W*,[4] those "liable to be detained" are those who are detained and those who have leave to be absent from hospital. Consequently, a tribunal is not obliged to discharge a section 3 patient merely because he is not presently receiving in-patient treatment — the issue is whether his condition makes it appropriate for him to remain liable to detention. The question arises whether the use in the section 2 discharge criteria of the word "detained" in preference to "liable to be detained" is simply loose drafting or is intended to require tribunals to discharge patients who do not presently require in-patient assessment or in-patient treatment.

The argument that "detained" means "liable to be detained"

Section 72(3) provides that a tribunal which does not "discharge" a section 2 patient may recommend that he be granted leave of absence, with a view to facilitating his "discharge" on a future date. This suggests that a tribunal is not invariably under a duty to discharge a section 2 patient who does not presently need to be detained in hospital. Otherwise, the fact that a tribunal considers leave appropriate would oblige it to discharge and the option of recommending leave as a way of facilitating discharge would not exist. The "assessment" includes assessing whether any treatment assessed to be necessary can be given outside hospital, and the words "detained" and "detention" in section 72(1)(a) mean "liable to be detained" and "liable to detention" respectively.[5]

---

4   *R. v. Hallstrom, ex p. W. ; R. v. Gardner, ex p. L.* [1986] 2 All E.R. 306.

5   The word "detained" in mental health legislation has often been interpreted as including persons who have leave to be absent from hospital. See *e.g. Safford v. Safford* [1944] P.61. The word "detained" is also used in section 72(2), a usage which was considered in *ex p. W.* : "Presumably this is to be taken as covering one on leave of absence and only 'liable to be detained,' for discharge means not merely discharge from hospital but discharge from the authority to detain."

The argument that "detained" means "detained"

The counter-argument is simply that the draftsman's use of the word "detained" in relation to the section 2 criteria for discharge, and "liable to be detained" in relation to the section 3 criteria, must be deliberate. Section 72(1)(a) and (b) both commence with a common initial reference to patients who are liable to be detained. In both cases, the phrase does not form part of the criteria for discharge. Its purpose is to emphasise that a patient must be liable to be detained, in the sense that his detention is legally authorised, before he can be discharged by a tribunal. The Act then goes on to use the word "detention" twice in the discharge criteria for section 2 patients but not at all in the criteria which determine whether a section 3 patient must be discharged. This is because there is no obligation to discharge a patient previously detained for treatment if his condition justifies no more than a period of trial leave outside hospital. However, in section 2 cases, the purpose of the admission is more specific. It is to detain a person in order to assess his need for in-patient treatment and to provide any in-patient treatment assessed to be necessary. If, on a proper assessment of the patient's mental state, a tribunal is satisfied that his condition does not presently warrant detention in hospital, or that his detention there is not justified for his health or safety or to protect others, the limited purpose of the admission has been completed. In other more finely-balanced cases, the phrasing of the discharge criteria as a double-negative comes into play. If a tribunal is *not* satisfied that a section 2 patient's detention is unwarranted or unjustified, it is not obliged to discharge him. In this case, it may recommend that he be granted leave, which may help to facilitate his future discharge by establishing whether further detention and treatment in hospital is unwarranted or unjustified. Nevertheless, it does not follow from the fact that a tribunal may recommend (some) leave in finely balanced cases, where the patient cannot overcome the double-negative, that it need not discharge a patient if it *is* satisfied that his condition does not presently warrant detention, or it is satisfied that his detention there is not presently justified.

Summary

The argument is finely balanced. However, it is submitted that a tribunal must discharge a section 2 patient if it is satisfied that the nature or degree of his mental disorder is not at present so serious that detention in hospital is warranted, either for assessment or treatment. Likewise, if it is satisfied that detention in hospital is not presently justified for one of the three statutory purposes. This will generally be the case if open-ended, "extended", leave has been granted, unless the tribunal's opinion is that this leave is inappropriate in the light of the patient's condition.

DISCHARGE ON A FUTURE DATE

Section 72(3) not only empowers a tribunal to postpone the discharge of a patient whom it has discharged at its discretion, but also to delay the discharge of a patient who is entitled to be discharged. A tribunal's power to defer making a direction for a restricted patient's conditional discharge should not be confused with this power to direct that an unrestricted patient shall be discharged on a specified future date. In the former case, the patient's discharge may never be directed. In the latter case, the tribunal's direction that the patient be discharged is complete and in force the moment it is made: it is not provisional upon future events.[6]

---

[6] In *Grant v. The Mental Health Review Tribunal for the Trent Region; R. v. The Mersey Mental Health Review Tribunal, ex p. O'Hara, The Times*, 26 April 1986 (**549**), McNeill J. observed that the power is one "wholly different" to deferred discharge under section 73(7).

Postponing mandatory discharge

Because of the tribunal's finding that there were no longer any statutory grounds for the patient's detention, it was previously sometimes argued that a mandatory discharge could not be postponed under section 72(3): once it had been established that there were no legal grounds for detaining him, he had to be immediately set at liberty.[7] This was always a somewhat weak argument. The paramount rule of statutory construction is that "every statute is to be expounded according to its manifest and expressed intention"[8] and all other rules of interpretation are subordinate to it.[9] As Crane pointed out, since section 72(3) clearly shows that the legislature intended to allow a discharge to be postponed for a specified period of time, section 72(1) must be interpreted in this light. If there was any ambiguity about section 72(3), it needed to be pointed out.[10] That a tribunal which is under a duty to direct a patient's discharge may direct that he be discharged on a future date, rather than forthwith, was recently confirmed in *R. v. South Thames Mental Health Review Tribunal, ex p. P.* The case is also quite interesting as an example of the operation of section 72(1)(b)(iii) (**491**) and of rule 18, which allows two tribunal applications concerning the same patient to be joined (**637**).

R. v. Mental Health Review Tribunal for North Thames Region, ex p. P

CO/1467/96, 20 May 1997   *Q.B.D., Harrison J.*

On 29 April 1996, a tribunal considered two applications made in respect of the same patient, who was detained under section 3. One of them she had herself made and the other had been made by the statutory nearest relative under section 66(1)(g), following the issue of a report barring discharge. The tribunal received two written reports from the responsible medical officer's senior house officer. These indicated that the patient's medication had been increased following a relapse and that the administration of compulsory ECT under section 58 would need to be considered during the following fortnight if her depression did not respond. The tribunal heard evidence from the patient's new responsible medical officer, who stated his opinion that it was necessary to detain her in the interests of her health and safety, but not in order to protect others. To the best of his knowledge, she had never tried to harm herself and had not admitted to any suicidal ideation or intent. He was, however, concerned that she would, if discharged, further withdraw, refuse medication and harm herself. A nursing report confirmed that the patient had at no time been an actual or potential danger to herself or to others, and that she was compliant with medication. The patient's evidence was that, if discharged, she would return to live with her mother and would take her medication, attend out-patient appointments and see a social worker. She was, however, opposed to receiving ECT. Her mother, who was the nearest relative, indicated that she would like her daughter to be discharged so that she could come home as soon as possible.

---

[7] In *R. v. Oxford Mental Health Review Tribunal, ex p. Stoddard* (January 1994, unreported), a tribunal directed that a patient who satisfied the criteria for mandatory discharge be discharged in four months' time. This was in order to enable a care assessment to be carried out and a care plan put in place. In the opinion of Treasury Counsel, the power to postpone discharge was only available where the patient was being discharged under the tribunal's discretionary power. Moreover, any other construction might contravene Article 5(1) of the European Convention on Human Rights. The application for judicial review was therefore conceded by the tribunal.

[8] *Attorney-General for Canada v. Hallett & Carey Ltd.* [1952] A.C. 427 at 449, *per* Lord Radcliffe.

[9] *Prince Ernest of Hanover v. Attorney-General* [1956] Ch. 188 at 201, *per* Evershed M.R.

[10] M. Crane, "Discharge under MHA 1983" in *LAG Bulletin*, November 1995.

The tribunal's decision in respect of the patient's application

In relation to the patient's application, the tribunal did not direct her discharge. Expressing their findings as a double negative, they were not satisfied as to existence of the grounds for mandatory discharge. As to their discretionary power of discharge, the patient's depression was unlikely to lift spontaneously and to return her to the community would be doing her a great disservice.

The tribunal's decision in respect of the nearest relative's application

In relation to the nearest relative's application, the tribunal directed that the patient be discharged on 20 May 1996. As to the additional ground for mandatory discharge in such cases, set out in section 72(1)(b)(iii), the tribunal was satisfied that the patient would not, if released, be likely to act in a manner dangerous to other persons or to herself: "Accordingly, the mother's application must succeed but we postpone discharge pursuant to section 72(3) until 20 May so that the patient may receive such further treatment as the RMO thinks appropriate, which may include ECT."

The application for judicial review

On 8 May 1996, Popplewell J. granted the patient leave to apply for judicial review and he further granted an interim injunction restraining the responsible medical officer from administering ECT pending the hearing of the application. The issue was whether a tribunal which has a duty to discharge a patient under section 72(1)(b) may, under section 72(3), direct that that discharge shall take place on a future date. On the patient's behalf, it was submitted that the power of postponement was only available when a tribunal exercised its discretionary power of discharge. If a patient was entitled to be discharged, any deferral of that discharge was inconsistent with the duty to discharge which had arisen.

Harrison J.

Section 72(3) provided that a tribunal which discharged a patient under section 72(1) could direct that this discharge take place on a future date specified in its direction. A direction to discharge under section 72(1) could be a discretionary discharge or a mandatory discharge and section 72(3) did not in any way confine the power to cases of discretionary discharge under section 72(1). There was no ambiguity and, if Parliament had intended the power to apply only to such cases, it could and would have said so. The argument advanced on the patient's behalf involved reading the word "forthwith" into section 72(1)(b) and also some limiting phrase, such as "when exercising the discretionary power to direct the discharge of a patient," into section 72(3).The way section 72 operated was that a tribunal had, first of all, to apply the statutory criteria for discharge and decide whether it was obliged to discharge the patient (mandatory discharge) and then, secondly, if it was not obliged to do so decide whether to discharge the patient at its discretion (discretionary discharge). Having decided that it either had to or would direct the patient's discharge, it thirdly had to consider whether that discharge should be immediate or whether it should —pursuant to section 72(3)— be on a future date specified in the direction.

Purpose of the deferment

The legislation did not specify the circumstances in which, or the purposes for which, deferment of discharge could or should he directed. There was force in the point that one would not normally expect to delay a discharge if the patient was entitled to it. It was of paramount importance that the power to defer discharge should not be used so as to circumvent the obligation to discharge if the statutory criteria in section 72(1)(a) or (b) were met. If there was such a misuse of the power, the remedy of judicial review would be available. As to the present case, the application for judicial review had been based on the proposition that there was no power to defer discharge if a duty to discharge existed. However, during the course of argument, the patient's counsel had raised the question of whether, if such a power existed, it might have here been exercised for an unlawful purpose. In particular, the power had, it was said, been exercised in order to enable her to receive compulsory treatment, rather than for some purpose connected with the statutory issue raised by section 72(1)(b)(iii), *i.e.* whether she would, if released, be likely to act in a manner dangerous to other persons or to herself. That was an argument worthy of serious consideration. However, the judicial review hearing was taking placed on the day set by the tribunal for the patient's discharged and she would no longer be detained when the parties were in a position to fully argue the point. It was therefore not practicable to determine it. Although the point could not be decided, and it would not be right for the court to express any concluded view on this aspect of the case, His Lordship harboured grave reservations about whether the exercise of the power in this case was lawful.

Summary

On a proper construction of section 72(3), a tribunal had power to direct the discharge of a patient on a future date in circumstances where there was a mandatory duty to discharge the patient under section 72(1)(b)(iii). It followed that the application must be dismissed. *Application dismissed and interim injunction discharged.*

Postponement must be for purpose of discharge

In *ex p. P.*, the issue of precisely when the power of postponement might not be available was raised but not resolved. It is submitted that the position is as follows.

1. Provided that a tribunal has sufficient information to determine the patient's current suitability for discharge, it must determine whether or not it is satisfied that he is presently entitled to be discharged. It may not adjourn the hearing to see if his condition improves, with a view to discharge at a later reconvened hearing.[11] Nor may it may defer a restricted patient's discharge under section 73(7) in the hope that he may be suitable for discharge by the time the conditions of discharge are met.[12] Nor therefore may it direct, under section 72(3), that a patient shall be discharged on a specified future date in the hope or expectation that his mental state will by then have improved sufficiently for discharge to be mandatory or appropriate.

2. It follows that a direction that a patient shall only be discharged after further compulsory in-patient treatment is given is incompatible with a finding that he is not presently suffering from a mental disorder which warrants further detention for treatment or which makes it appropriate for him to remain liable to such treatment. It is similarly incompatible with a finding that further treatment in hospital is unnecessary for the patient's health or safety or to protect others.[13]

---

[11] *R. v. Nottingham Mental Health Review Tribunal, ex p. Secretary of State for the Home Department, R. v. Northern Mental Health Review Tribunal, ex p. Secretary of State for the Home Department, The Times,* 25 March 1987, Q.B.D.; *The Times,* 15 September 1988, C.A.

[12] See *e.g., R. v. Oxford Regional Mental Health Review Tribunal, ex p. Secretary of State for the Home Department* [1988] 1 A.C. 120.

[13] This was, of course, not the case in *ex p. P.* since the tribunal refused the patient's application.

3. However, in some cases, a tribunal's finding that the patient is entitled to be discharged rests on the evidence which it has received about the arrangements which can be made for him outside hospital. As to this, Lord Bridge stated in the Oxford case that a tribunal "may perfectly properly be satisfied that hospital detention is no longer necessary provided that [a restricted patient] can be placed in a suitable hostel and required to submit to treatment as an out-patient by a suitable psychiatrist. These are matters to be secured by imposing appropriate conditions."[14]

4. In unrestricted cases, a tribunal may similarly decide that it is under a duty to discharge the patient because arrangements can be made for his treatment and care outside hospital which, once made, mean that continued liability to detention in hospital is unwarranted, inappropriate, or unnecessary having regard to his present mental condition. If it is the case that it is only when those arrangements have been made that further liability to detention is inappropriate, unjustified, or unnecessary, the date of discharge may be postponed. So, for example, if it will take a fortnight to make these arrangements, postponing the discharge for that period is not incompatible with the tribunal's finding that the patient is entitled to be discharged: those arrangements constitute the basis of his entitlement.

5. The power to direct a patient's discharge on a future date is quite different from that set out in section 72(3), which enables a tribunal to defer giving a direction that the patient shall be discharged. The fact that a discharge date must be specified indicates that the power is intended to be used where a tribunal which has sufficient information to make a decision is satisfied that arrangements can be made which entitle the patient to be discharged or which make discretionary discharge appropriate.

6. In ex p. P., the postponement was unlawful having regard to the statutory framework relating to applications under section 66(1)(g). This is that the nearest relative has a right to discharge the patient unless the responsible medical officer bars that discharge under section 25, on the ground that the patient is likely to behave dangerously if released, and a tribunal is not satisfied that that is not the case. The nearest relative's right to order the patient's discharge in such circumstances cannot be barred under section 25, or postponed under section 72, on the lesser ground that further detention and treatment is necessary for the patient's health.

Postponing discharge to enable section 3 application to be made

In *ex p. Wiltshire County Council*, Nigel Pleming Q.C. submitted that a tribunal cannot direct a section 2 patient's discharge on a future date merely so as to give the relevant professionals an opportunity to decide whether to make a further application authorising his detention under section 3.[15] The point was not conceded or

---

[14]   *R. v. Oxford Regional Mental Health Review Tribunal, ex p. Secretary of State for the Home Department* [1988] 1 A.C. 120, at 127.

[15]   "Mr. Pleming is also prepared to concede that a Mental Health Review Tribunal cannot defer discharge under section 72(3) of the Act in order to allow the authorities to decide whether there is some basis for his detention other than that which he is currently detained. That concession is not accepted by the County Council and, that being so, it would be wrong for us to endorse Mr. Pleming's concession without further argument." *R. v. Wessex Mental Health Review Tribunal, ex p. Wiltshire County Council* (1989) 4 B.M.L.R. 145., *per* Lord Donaldson M.R.

ruled upon. Nevertheless, the function of tribunals is to review the justification for compulsory powers. Their powers do not include a power to authorised a patient's detention pending the completion of an application under Part II — a sort of judicial section 5(2). Furthermore, the statutory purpose of the power of postponement is to bring about the patient's discharge from liability to detention, not to prolong the period for which he may be detained. The problem should, in any case, not arise if the mandatory discharge grounds in section 72(1)(a) are properly construed. In other words, the tribunal in *ex p. Wiltshire County Council* was wrong in its opinion that it was obliged to discharge the patient from liability to detention under section 2 because he was no longer being assessed in some restrictive sense. Had they not discharged, there would have been no need to resort to such a device as a way of enabling him to be further detained while a new application was made.

Further application prior to the patient's discharge

In *ex p. M*, the patient's case was heard by a tribunal on 14 December 1992. The tribunal was satisfied that she was not suffering from mental disorder of a nature or degree which warranted her detention in a hospital for assessment and so directed her discharge. However, the tribunal directed that the discharge be deferred until 17 December in order that social services could make arrangements for a suitable support programme. During the period between the tribunal's direction and the date on which it was to come into effect, the patient was detained under section 3. Laws J. said that he could see no basis for construing the statute so as to produce the result that the duty and discretion of the approved social worker to make the section 3 application were to any extent impliedly limited or abrogated by the existence of an earlier tribunal decision to discharge (**593**).

Future discharge and section 29 applications

A point considered, but not determined, in *ex p. Wiltshire County Council* was whether the making of a county court application, under section 29, during the period between the date on which the tribunal directed the patient's discharge and the date fixed by it for his discharge has the effect of extending the section 2 period and overriding the tribunal's outstanding direction for the patient's discharge.[16] The answer must be that it does not. A tribunal cannot postpone a patient's discharge until midnight on the 28th day because this would be equivalent to a direction that he not be discharged, that the existing authority for his detention be allowed to run its full course. It must therefore specify a date prior to the authority's expiration, whereas section 29(4) only has effect if the patient is still detained under section 2 at the moment immediately before the usual 28-day period expires.[17]

STATUTORY RECOMMENDATIONS

A tribunal which does not direct the discharge an unrestricted patient who is liable to be detained in hospital may, with a view to facilitating his discharge on a future date,

---

[16]   *R. v. Wessex Mental Health Review Tribunal, ex p. Wiltshire County Council; Perkins v. Bath District Health Authority* (1989) 4 B.M.L.R. 145.

[17]   Section 29(4) provides that the usual 28-day section 2 period shall be extended "if, immediately before the *expiration* of the period for which a patient is liable to be detained by virtue of an application for admission for assessment," an application under section 29(3)(c) or (d) is pending. That the period referred to is the 28-day period is clear from the use of the word "expiration" and the fact that the 1959 Act included an identical provision, albeit that tribunals had no power to discharge such patients.

recommend that he be granted leave of absence, or transferred to another hospital, or into guardianship.[18] It may further consider his case in the event that such a recommendation is not being complied with.[19] The power to make these recommendations also applies to unrestricted patients who are liable to be detained for treatment. Indeed, because the treatment which a section 2 patient requires is usually still being assessed, it is relatively rare for tribunals to make statutory recommendations about their future care or treatment. Moreover, the short duration of section 2 applications means that it will generally not be feasible for a tribunal to further consider the case if its recommendation is not being complied with.

Recommendations and the 1983 Rules

Although the Act provides that a tribunal "may" further consider a patient's case if its recommendation is not being complied with, the rules provide that a tribunal "shall" specify the period at the expiration of which it "will" further consider the patient's case if its recommendation is not complied with.[20] The rules then state that if, after making appropriate inquiries of the responsible authority, it appears to the tribunal that its recommendation has not been complied with, it may reconvene the proceedings after giving the parties the required notice.[21] Notwithstanding the rules, it is clear from the statute that a tribunal is not obliged to further consider the case at the expiration of any period stipulated under the rules.

Recommending leave of absence

A tribunal may recommend that a patient be granted leave of absence with a view to facilitating his discharge on a future date. It is then up to the responsible medical officer to decide whether suitable arrangements can be made for the patient's absence from hospital and what conditions of leave should be imposed. Leave is most often granted so that a patient can reside, or spend time, outside hospital. However, it may also be granted to enable a patient to reside at a hospital other than that in which he is liable to be detained. This is usually done as a step preparatory to formal transfer, although the power may also be used if treatment is required at a general hospital. Two points may be noted. Firstly, the actual grant of leave and the imposition of any conditions of leave, such as a condition of residence or a condition that the patient remains in custody during his absence, are matters for the responsible medical officer. Similarly, whether the patient should be in the custody of a person other than a hospital employee is a matter for the hospital managers. All a tribunal may do is to recommend leave generally. Secondly, the purpose of recommending leave must be to facilitate the patient's discharge on a future date, rather than to enable him to undergo an operation or to attend some function.

Recommending transfer to another hospital

A tribunal which does not discharge a patient may recommend that he be transferred to another hospital with a view to facilitating his discharge on a future date. Thus, as Mann J. observed in *Secretary of State for the Home Department v Mental Health Review Tribunal for Mersey Regional Health Authority*, provision is made

---

[18]   Mental Health Act 1983, s.72(3)(a).
[19]   *Ibid.*, s.72(3)(b).
[20]   Mental Health Review Tribunal Rules 1983, r.24(4) and 33.
[21]   *Ibid., rr.25(2) and 33.*

for the achievement of an interim regime preparatory to discharge.[22] In assessment cases, the power may be used to recommend a patient's transfer to a unit with special expertise in assessing and treating conditions of the kind from which he is suspected to suffer. In other cases, the power may be used to recommend a patient's transfer from a high or medium secure unit to his local catchment area hospital. It may, of course, be the case that the nominated hospital is unable to accommodate the patient so that the recommendation cannot be implemented. Because the recommendation may only be made with a view to facilitating the patient's future discharge, it is unlawful for a tribunal to recommend transfer from a local hospital to a special hospital because of concerns for the public's safety. Notwithstanding this, it has been known for such recommendations to be made with that purpose in mind.

Recommending transfer into guardianship

Where a section 2 patient is transferred into guardianship, he is treated as if he had been received into guardianship in pursuance of a guardianship application accepted on the date of his admission to hospital under section 2. However, patients detained for assessment are not recorded as suffering from a particular form of mental disorder and no provision is made for a form of mental disorder to be recorded at the time of transfer. Following transfer, such patients also have no right to apply to a tribunal until the next period of guardianship has commenced, which in section 2 cases will necessarily not be for at least five months.

The rationale of recommendations for transfer into guardianship

The effect of a transfer into guardianship is necessarily that the patient ceases to be liable to be detained for treatment. Consequently, it might be argued that if the tribunal's opinion was that the nature or degree of the patient's condition warranted guardianship, rather than continued liability to detention in hospital, it was in fact under a legal duty to discharge him. However, the criteria for discharge in section 72 are essentially relative, rather than absolute. Whether a tribunal is satisfied that a patient's detention is no longer warranted or appropriate often depends upon what alternative arrangements exist or can be made. Similarly, whether further in-patient treatment is justified or necessary for the patient's health or safety, or to protect others, can often only be determined by reference to the availability of a structured package of care in the community. If there is a viable alternative, the risk of early relapse or non-compliance with treatment may be slight but not otherwise. Furthermore, on a technical point, a transfer under section 19 does not involve the patient being discharged: the effect of the recommendation is to facilitate his future discharge from the authority conferred by the application or order being reviewed.

Whether the tribunal can discharge on reconvening

Where a tribunal's recommendation is not being complied with, and it reconvenes the proceedings, whether it can then direct the patient's discharge was recently considered in the unreported case of *Mental Health Review Tribunal v. J.J.H.* Before considering that case, it is worthwhile briefly summarising the historical origins of the power and the main arguments for and against a power to reconsider the original decision not to direct discharge.

---

[22]   *Secretary of State for the Home Department v Mental Health Review Tribunal for Mersey Regional Health Authority* [1986] 1 W.L.R. 1170.

Historical origins of the power

Under the Mental Health Act 1959, a tribunal had no statutory power to make recommendations. It could only discharge or not discharge a patient and, if the latter, reclassify him in appropriate cases. Paragraph 6.5 of the Government's 1978 White Paper[23] dealt with the proposals, set out in an earlier consultative document,[24] for extending the powers of tribunals in unrestricted cases—

> "There has been general endorsement of the Consultative Document's proposals for extending the powers of Tribunals to enable them to order delayed discharge (for up to three months) and to recommend trial leave, transfer to another hospital or conditional discharge. The distinction between ordering and recommending is an important one and takes account of the need for the agreement of others, *e.g.* the receiving hospital or social services department. It is proposed to adopt the suggestion that a Tribunal should be informed if any of their recommendations are not accepted and why, and that, if not implemented within a specified time, the Tribunal should be able to make an alternative finding. Recommendations by Tribunals for trial leave and transfer to another hospital do not entail legislative change. The Act does not however make express provision for the conditional discharge of unrestricted patients from hospital ... The purpose of conditional discharge would generally be to ensure that on discharge the patient remained resident in a particular place or continued to undertake some specified form of treatment. "

Mental Health (Amendment) Act 1982

In accordance with these proposals, the 1982 Act made provision for statutory recommendations and discharge on a future date. The idea of recommending conditional discharge in unrestricted cases was, however, rejected and replaced by a power to recommend transfer into guardianship.[25] Initially, Parliament envisaged that the power to make recommendations would be set out in the Mental Health Review Tribunal Rules but in the event the power was placed on a statutory footing.[26]

"Further consider the patient's case"

Although the White Paper of 1978 envisaged that tribunals would be able to make an alternative finding, the proposals set out there did not reach the statute book in their envisaged form. The matter is one of statutory intent and the rules cannot be used to construe the statute.[27] The question is whether the words "further consider the patient's case" can properly be interpreted as meaning or including "further consider its decision" or "further consider the patient's case and make any decision which it may make under section 72(1)." The case law concerning restricted patients indicates that a tribunal's decision as to whether or not to discharge is a final

---

[23]   *Review of the Mental Health Act 1959*, Cmnd. 7320 (1978).

[24]   *A Review of the Mental Health Act 1959* (D.H.S.S., 1976), paras. 8.12–8.17.

[25]   See *e.g. Hansard*, H.L. Vol. 426, col.783, *per* Lord Sandys, who said with regard to the non-implementation of recommendations: "The Committee may say that recommendations are all very well, but recommendations are not always implemented, so that the tribunal's wishes may not be put into effect. But we intend to provide for this eventuality also by setting down in the rules that if the tribunal's recommendations are not implemented within a certain period — say three months — then the tribunal should reconvene to consider why this is and whether another course of action now seems preferable."

[26]   See e.g. *Hansard*, H.L. Vol. 426, col. 784.

[27]   In any case, rule 25(2) is poorly drafted and of little assistance. It refers to giving notice of the reconvened hearing to the Secretary of State although a tribunal has no power to make such recommendations in restricted cases. To this extent, the rule would appear to be ultra vires: *R. v. The Mersey Mental Health Review Tribunal, ex p. O'Hara, The Times*, 26 April 1986 **(549)**.

decision, one which cannot later be reconsidered if arrangements cannot be made fulfilling the conditions imposed.[28] Against this, the powers of tribunals in unrestricted cases are clearly far wider and allow for the exercise of discretion. More particularly, whilst section 73(7) does not provide that a tribunal may reconsider the patient's case if satisfactory arrangements are not made, section 72(3) expressly confers a discretionary power to further consider the patient's case.

Arguments concerning a power of discharge upon reconvening

The main arguments in favour of a power of discharge upon reconvening are as follows: (1) the ambit of the words is deliberately as broad as possible, leaving the issue of how to proceed to the tribunal's discretion; (2) the natural meaning of to further consider someone's case is that the body concerned should review his overall circumstances, including his mental condition and whether compulsory powers are still required; (3) if Parliament had intended that tribunals should have no power to discharge, it would have made that explicit, since the words used in the statute clearly make that interpretation possible; (4) though not strictly relevant, there is some evidence that Parliament intended that tribunals should have the option of reaching an alternative finding; (5) it is clearly unsatisfactory, and hence probably not what Parliament intended, that a tribunal which further considers a patient's case should have no power to discharge him at the end of the reconvened hearing if it is of the opinion that he is entitled to be, or should be, discharged; (6) the *Oxford case* can be distinguished because of the absence in section 73(7) of any power to further consider a restricted patient's case and the absence of any discretion in restricted cases; (7) the use of the words "further consider" in preference to "reconsider" indicates that the tribunal is not reconsidering its earlier decision but may at its discretion make a further decision; (8) the words "further consider his *case*" should be read together with the words "the tribunal may in any *case* direct that the patient be discharged" in section 72(1); (9) accordingly, a tribunal which reconvenes can further consider discharge but cannot be required to further consider it. The main arguments against a power of discharge are: (1) Parliament cannot have intended that patients may have a further opportunity to be discharged if a tribunal's recommendation is not complied with but not if it is complied with; (2) section 72(3) provides that the power to make a recommendation facilitating future discharge arises only where a tribunal "do not direct the discharge of a patient" under section 72(1); thus, the tribunal has already determined the patient's application to be discharged; (3) had Parliament intended to empower tribunals to discharge a patient in such circumstances, it would have made this explicit by the use of some phrase such as "further consider the patient's case, including its decision not to discharge him"; (4) the purpose of a recommendation is to facilitate future discharge if it is complied with, not discharge if it is not complied with; (5) the words "further consider the patient's case" mean to consider why its recommendation is not being complied with and to take or encourage any action which may lead to existing obstacles to its implementation being overcome.

Mental Health Review Tribunal v. J.J.H.

Although not all of these arguments were referred to in *Mental Health Review Tribunal v. J.J.H.*, and the historical origins of the power appear not to have been considered, the court held that a tribunal which further considers a patient's case under section 72(3) has precisely the same powers as it had at the original hearing.

---

[28]   *R. v. Oxford Regional Mental Health Review Tribunal, ex p. Secretary of State for the Home Department*, [1988] 1 A.C. 120.

Mental Health Review Tribunal v. J.J.H.

CO/3946/96, *10 July 1997*   *Q.B.D., Kay J.*

The patient was detained under section 3. On 9 July 1996, his application was heard by a tribunal. Having not directed his discharge, the tribunal recommended his transfer to another hospital. The recommendation was not complied with and the question arose as to what were its powers at the reconvened hearing. The tribunal reluctantly concluded that it had no power to reconsider its original decision; all it could do was to consider the reasons for the failure to comply with its recommendation. The patient challenged the ruling.

Kay J.

There was no authority on the point and it was therefore necessary to apply the normal rules of statutory interpretation. On the face of it, the use of the words "his case" in section 72(3)(b) suggested that the tribunal could consider the whole matter again. "His case" must mean his application for discharge: that was the case that had been considered and therefore the case that was to be further considered. If it had been Parliament's intention to restrict the tribunal's further consideration of the case to the recommendations made by it, the subsection could very readily have been worded "further consider such recommendation." Bearing in mind that the subection dealt with the liberty of the subject, it would require some very compelling reason to read it in a way that was unfavourable to the patient. Three main arguments had been advanced against the interpretation suggested by him: (1) It was contended that the wording of the subsection contradicted such a straightforward interpretation. The first clause of subsection 72(3) required a tribunal to make a decision as to the patient's release on a future date. It was only when that direction was ruled out that the question of whether a recommendation should be made arose. Hence, the further consideration involved considering the case in the light of a decision already made, namely that he was not entitled to be, and should not be, discharged. The only further consideration allowed was the making of some other recommendation. With regard to this argument, there seemed to be no justification for reading the subsection in this restricted way. It seemed clear that Parliament, having regard to the patient's rights, wished to put in place a meaningful safeguard for the situation where a tribunal's recommendations were not followed. (2) It was then said that to interpret the subsection as giving power to make any of the decisions permitted at the original hearing placed such a patient in a more favourable position than one in respect of whom a tribunal's recommendation had been complied with. That was in a sense true but it was not a reason to interpret the provision in a way that placed him at a disadvantage vis-à-vis a patient whose recommendation had been given effect. (3) The final argument was that the patient's interpretation left uncertainty as to when the tribunal's decision became final. That could not be so. When the tribunal's recommendation was implemented, the decision became final. If the recommendation was not followed, and the matter came back before the tribunal for further consideration, it would become final either then or when any alternative recommendation made by it was implemented. If there was a dispute as to whether or not the recommendation had been implemented, the tribunal would first of all resolve that issue. There was, in any case, a real sense in which such a decision was never final because the patient was entitled to periodically apply for his discharge. The only question was whether following one hearing his eligibility to be discharged should not be further considered unless and until fresh proceedings were commenced. For the reasons given, a tribunal had the same powers when it further considered a patient's case under section 72(3) as it had at the original hearing, and subject to the same statutory criteria and principles. *Tribunal's decision quashed.*

UNRESTRICTED PATIENTS DETAINED FOR TREATMENT

Where a tribunal determines the case of an unrestricted patient who is liable to be detained in hospital for treatment, its powers are specified in section 72, the relevant parts of which are set out in the table on pages 481–482. Unrestricted patients liable to be detained for treatment are detained under one of the following sections: 3, 37 (hospital orders), 47 or 48 (transfer directions).

SUMMARY OF POWERS

The majority of patients detained in hospital for treatment are not subject to special restrictions. Whatever the original authority for such a patient's detention, the Act provides that tribunals shall apply the same discharge criteria and have the same powers in all cases involving unrestricted patients detained for treatment. A tribunal's powers are similar to those in respect of patients detained for assessment, so that the cases of all unrestricted in-patients are dealt with in a comparable way. In particular, a tribunal is required to discharge a patient who satisfies the statutory criteria for being discharged set out in section 72(1)(b), may at its discretion discharge a patient where this is not so and, if it does not discharge, may make the same kinds of recommendations as in a section 2 case. Discharge may, as before, either be forthwith or on a specific future date. There are, however, three important differences. When deciding whether to exercise its discretionary power of discharge, a tribunal must have regard to certain statutory matters set out in section 72(2). Furthermore, a tribunal which does not discharge may recommend that a supervision application be made; and it may also direct that the form of mental disorder from which the patient is recorded as suffering on the authority for his detention be amended, so as to show that he is suffering from some other form. A similar power of reclassification would be superfluous in section 2 cases because all patients detained for assessment are classified as suffering from "mental disorder" generally, rather than from one or more of its particular forms.

STATUTORY FRAMEWORK

The statutory criteria which determine whether a tribunal must discharge a patient who is liable to be detained for treatment do not correspond to the criteria which regulate their admission to hospital and any renewal of the authority to detain them. The respective criteria are set out in the table on page 483 and the differences illustrate the relatively limited nature of a tribunal's functions. In particular, a tribunal is not bound to discharge such a patient merely because it is satisfied that his condition is not treatable in the statutory sense and takes the view that, as matters presently stand, the criteria for later renewing the authority for his detention are not satisfied. Likewise, a tribunal is not bound to discharge a mentally ill or severely mentally impaired patient merely because it is satisfied that his condition is not treatable and he would not be vulnerable if discharged (**492**).

Historical development of powers

The present statutory framework is also exposed by considering a tribunal's powers under the previous statute and the amendments made to it. Under the Mental Health Act 1959, a tribunal had a like duty to discharge if satisfied as to the statutory criteria and it could discharge at its discretion where this was not the case. There were, however, no issues which, as a matter of law, it had to have regard to before exercising its discretion to discharge. Moreover, a tribunal which discharged a patient could not discharge him on a future date and, if it did not discharge, it had no power to make any statutory recommendations of the kind which it may now make, although it could reclassify. The discharge grounds were set out in section 123 of that Act and they were materially different to the present criteria in relation to the two universal grounds for mandatory discharge—

Mental Health Act 1959	*Mental Health Act 1983*
123.—(1) Where application is made to a Mental Health Review Tribunal by or in respect of a patient who is liable to be detained under this Act, the tribunal may in any case direct that the patient be discharged, and shall so direct if they are satisfied—	**72.** —(1) Where application is made to a Mental Health Review Tribunal by or in respect of a patient who is liable to be detained under this Act, the tribunal may in any case direct that the patient be discharged, and (b) the tribunal shall direct the discharge of a patient ... if they are satisfied—
(a) that he is not then suffering from mental illness, psychopathic disorder, subnormality or severe subnormality; or	(i) that he is not then suffering from mental illness, psychopathic disorder, severe mental impairment or mental impairment <u>or from any of those forms of disorder of a nature or degree which makes it appropriate for him to be liable to be detained in a hospital for medical treatment</u>; or
(b) that it is not necessary in the interests of the patient's health or safety or for the protection of other persons <u>that the patient should continue to be liable to be detained</u>;	(ii) that it is not necessary for the health or safety of the patient or for the protection of other persons <u>that he should receive such treatment</u>;

As can be seen—

- Under the 1959 Act, unless a tribunal was satisfied that the patient was not mentally disordered, it was only obliged to discharge him if it was satisfied that it was unnecessary in the interests of his health or safety, or for the protection of others, that he "should continue to be liable to be detained. "

- The previous reference in the second ground as to whether or not it is necessary for the patient to continue to be liable to be detained has been replaced by a reference to whether or not it necessary for his health, etc., that he should receive "such treatment." Different views are taken about whether the reference to "such treatment" in section 72(1)(b)(ii) is a reference to the necessity of treatment in a hospital as a detained patient or simply a reference to the necessity of treatment in a hospital (**488**).

- Conversely, a reference to the patient's detainability has been added to the first ground, which now requires a tribunal to consider whether it appropriate that the patient should remain liable to be detained in a hospital for medical treatment.

THE STATUTORY CRITERIA — UNRESTRICTED PATIENTS DETAINED FOR TREATMENT

Discretionary discharge

72. —(1) Where application is made to a Mental Health Review Tribunal by or in respect of a patient who is liable to be detained under this Act, the tribunal may in any case direct that the patient be discharged, and

Mandatory discharge

(b) the tribunal shall direct the discharge of a patient liable to be detained otherwise than under section 2 above if they are satisfied—

Criteria applicable in all cases

(i) that he is not then suffering from mental illness, psychopathic disorder, severe mental impairment or mental impairment or from any of those forms of disorder of a nature or degree which makes it appropriate for him to be liable to be detained in a hospital for medical treatment; or

(ii) that it is not necessary for the health or safety of the patient or for the protection of other persons that he should receive such treatment; or

Additional criteria where a nearest relative applies following a report barring discharge

(iii) in the case of an application by virtue of paragraph (g) of section 66(1) above, that the patient, if released, would not be likely to act in a manner dangerous to other persons or to himself.

Matters which a tribunal must have regard to in determining whether to exercise its discretionary power of discharge

(2) In determining whether to direct the discharge of a patient detained otherwise than under section 2 above in a case not falling within paragraph (b) of subsection (1) above, the tribunal shall have regard—

"Treatability test"

(a) to the likelihood of medical treatment alleviating or preventing a deterioration of the patient's condition; and

"Vulnerability test"

(b) in the case of a patient suffering from mental illness or severe mental impairment, to the likelihood of the patient, if discharged, being able to care for himself, to obtain the care he needs or to guard himself against serious exploitation.

Future discharge

(3) A tribunal may under subsection (1) above direct the discharge of a patient on a future date specified in the direction;

481

Recommendations with a view to facilitating discharge

and where a tribunal do not direct the discharge of a patient under that subsection the tribunal may—

(a) with a view to facilitating his discharge on a future date, recommend that he be granted leave of absence or transferred to another hospital or into guardianship; and

(b) further consider his case in the event of any such recommendation not being complied with.

Other recommendations

(3A) Where, in the case of an application to a tribunal by or in respect of a patient who is liable to be detained in pursuance of an application for admission for treatment or by virtue of an order or direction for his admission or removal to hospital under Part III of this Act, the tribunal do not direct the discharge of the patient under subsection (1) above, the tribunal may—

(a) recommend that the responsible medical officer consider whether to make a supervision application in respect of the patient; and

(b) further consider his case in the event of no such application being made.

Reclassification

(5) Where application is made to a Mental Health Review Tribunal under any provision of this Act by or in respect of a patient and the tribunal do not direct that the patient be discharged ... the tribunal may, if satisfied that the patient is suffering from a form of mental disorder other than the form specified in the application, order or direction relating to him direct that that application, order or direction be amended by substituting for the form of mental disorder specified in it such other form of mental disorder as appears to the tribunal to be appropriate.

References

(6) Subsections (1) to (5) above apply in relation to references to a Mental Health Review Tribunal as they apply in relation to applications made to such a tribunal by or in respect of a patient.

STATUTORY CRITERIA FOR ADMISSION, RENEWAL AND DISCHARGE CONTRASTED

Grounds for detention under section 3	*Grounds for renewal — s.3,37,47, 48 patients*	*Tribunal criteria for discharge — s.3,37,47, 48 patients*
An application may be made in respect of a patient on the grounds that—	It appears to the responsible medical officer that—	The tribunal shall direct the discharge of a patient if they are satisfied—
▪ he is suffering from mental illness, severe mental impairment, psychopathic disorder or mental impairment of a nature or degree which makes it appropriate for him to receive medical treatment in a hospital;	▪ the patient is suffering from mental illness, severe mental impairment, psychopathic disorder or mental impairment, and his mental disorder is of a nature or degree which makes it appropriate for him to receive medical treatment in a hospital;	▪ that he is not then suffering from mental illness, psychopathic disorder, severe mental impairment or mental impairment or from any of those forms of disorder of a nature or degree which makes it appropriate for him to be liable to be detained in a hospital for medical treatment;
—and—	—and—	—or—
▪ it is necessary for the health or safety of the patient or for the protection of other persons that he should receive such treatment and it cannot be provided unless he is detained under this section.	▪ it is necessary for the health or safety of the patient or for the protection of other persons that he should receive such treatment and that it cannot be provided unless he continues to be detained;	▪ that it is not necessary for the health or safety of the patient or for the protection of other persons that he should receive such treatment
—and—	—and either—	*In determining whether to exercise its discretionary power of discharge a tribunal shall have regard—*
▪ in the case of psychopathic disorder or mental impairment, such treatment is likely to alleviate or prevent a deterioration of his condition.	▪ such treatment is likely to alleviate or prevent a deterioration of his condition	▪ to the likelihood of medical treatment alleviating or preventing a deterioration of the patient's condition; and
	—or—	—and—
	▪ in the case of mental illness or severe mental impairment, the patient, if discharged, is unlikely to be able to care for himself, to obtain the care which he needs or to guard himself against serious exploitation.	▪ in the case of a patient suffering from mental illness or severe mental impairment, to the likelihood of the patient, if discharged, being able to care for himself, to obtain the care he needs or to guard himself against serious exploitation.

TERMINOLOGY

For the meaning of the words used in the admission and discharge criteria, see—
"discharge" (485) and "released" (491); "patient" (098); "detention," "detained" and
"liable to be detained" (215, 487, 585); "satisfied" (567); "then" (466); "suffering
from" (213); "mental illness" (060); "psychopathic disorder" (082); "severe mental
impairment" (070); "mental impairment" (070); "nature or degree" (213); "appropriate" (490); "hospital" (131); "medical treatment" (216); "necessary" (221, 485);
"health" (217); "safety" (218); "protection of other persons" (219); "dangerous"
(218). By way of summary—

- A person whose symptoms are merely controlled by medication still "suffers
  from" mental disorder. Furthermore, the fact that a person is in remission,
  and there are no longer any obvious symptoms or signs of mental disorder,
  is not proof that the underlying disorder is not of a severe nature.

- The words "nature" and "degree" are not interchangeable. The word "degree" focuses attention on the present manifestations of any mental disorder
  which exists. The word "nature" focuses attention on precisely that: the
  characteristics of the patient's condition, its historical course and chronicity,
  and the prognosis associated with any diagnosis made. A condition may be
  severe because it is acute (of a severe degree) or because it is chronic or progressive and difficult to treat (of a severe nature).

- "Appropriate" in the context of the section 3 admission criteria refers to a
  person whose condition makes in-patient treatment appropriate, irrespective
  of whether detention is necessary for that purpose. However, the test in section 72(1)(b)(i) is whether liability to detention in hospital for treatment is
  appropriate. The "the unsoundness of mind, whose presence is essential to
  justify a compulsory order, manifestly means more than mental illness
  which qualifies a person to be a voluntary patient ... in ordinary language
  "certifiable" is perhaps more likely to be used to express the same idea."[29]

- Patients who are "liable to be detained" for treatment are those who are detained in hospital and those who have leave to be absent from hospital under
  section 17. Accordingly, a tribunal is not obliged by virtue of section
  72(1)(b)(i) to discharge a patient who has leave to reside at home or in a
  hostel, or who it considers should be granted leave of absence, unless it is
  also satisfied that it is inappropriate for him to remain liable to be detained
  in a hospital for further medical treatment.

- "Medical treatment," unless the context otherwise requires, "includes nursing, and also includes care, habilitation and rehabilitation under medical
  supervision."[30]

- "Health" may be described as the standard of physical and mental functioning necessary for a person to perform the activities which are expected of
  him, according to the norms of the society in which he lives; all *disabling*
  disease, illness and handicap must be absent.

---

[29] *Buxton v. Jayne* [1960] 2 All E.R. 688 at 697, *per* Devlin L.J.
[30] Mental Health Act 1983, s.145(1).

484

- "Safety" denotes freedom from physical harm and a patient's safety may be at risk because of his own acts (dangerous conduct towards himself), his omissions to act (self-neglect), how others act towards him (exploiting or ill-treating him), or omit to act towards him (failing to care for him).

- The expression "protection of other persons" indicates a need to protect other persons from the consequences of the patient's actions, including psychological injury and damage to property resulting from his mental state.

- "Necessary" is stronger than the phrase "justified in the interests of" which is used in relation to section 2. Many things which are not necessary may nevertheless be justified.

THE CRITERIA FOR MANDATORY DISCHARGE

The customary view is that discharge in relation to unrestricted patients means merely discharge from liability to detention for treatment while, in relation to restricted patients, it means discharge both from hospital and from liability to detention for the time being (**571**). Accordingly, a tribunal is under a duty to discharge an unrestricted patient who requires further treatment in hospital if it is satisfied that it is not appropriate for him to be liable to be detained there for that treatment. In other words, it is appropriate for him to receive any further in-patient treatment as an informal patient.

The two common discharge grounds

In all cases, a tribunal must discharge a patient if it is satisfied that he is entitled to be discharged on one of two grounds—

- The first of them, which is set out in section 72(1)(b)(i) and is sometimes referred to as the "diagnostic question," requires the tribunal to consider whether the patient is suffering from a mental disorder the nature or degree of which makes it appropriate for him to be liable to be detained for in-patient treatment.

- The second ground, which is set out in section 72(1)(b)(ii), requires considering whether such treatment is "necessary" for the patient's own health or safety or to protect others. The criteria which comprise the second ground are therefore directed towards the issue of risk: the likelihood of undesirable consequences if the individual does not receive necessary medical treatment. The risks may consist of a likelihood of significant deterioration in his health, a risk to his physical safety, or a risk to others.

The combined effect of the two grounds is that a tribunal must terminate a patient's liability to detention in a hospital for treatment if it is satisfied that it is unnecessary for his health or safety or to protect others that he receives further in-patient treatment *or* it is satisfied that it is no longer appropriate for him to be liable to be detained in a hospital in order to receive treatment there.

THE NATURE OR DEGREE OF DISORDER AND SECTION 72(1)(b)(i)

The nature or degree of mental disorder which makes admission, removal or renewal appropriate is different from that which determines whether a tribunal is bound to discharge a patient under section 72(1)(b)(i).

Section 3 patients and section 72(1)(b)(i)

The admission grounds and the renewal criteria require only that the patient's condition is such that in-patient medical treatment is appropriate.[31] Accordingly, the first of the statutory grounds for detention or renewal exists if this is so regardless of whether detention for in-patient treatment is also appropriate. The issue of whether the patient's detention is necessary forms part of the second universal ground for making an application or renewing the authority conferred by it — this requires both that in-patient treatment is necessary for the patient's health or safety or for protection of others and that it cannot be provided unless he is detained.

Admission and renewal criteria	*Tribunal discharge criteria*
• The patient is suffering from a form of mental disorder the nature or degree of which makes it appropriate for him to receive medical treatment in a hospital.	• The patient is not suffering from a form of mental disorder the nature or degree of which makes it appropriate for him to be liable to be detained in a hospital for medical treatment.

The reasons why the admission and renewal grounds separate out the two issues of the appropriateness of in-patient treatment and the necessity for detention have already been explained (**215**). However, in this context, the important point is that the tribunal discharge criteria do not adhere to the same format: a patient must be discharged if the nature or degree of his condition makes it inappropriate that he should remain liable to be detained for further in-patient treatment. The issue is the appropriateness of liability to detention rather than actual detention. It does not suffice that in-patient treatment is appropriate but, equally, it is not essential that a patient presently requires in-patient treatment if it is nevertheless appropriate that he should remain liable to be detained for further in-patient treatment. That being so—

1. Even if further in-patient treatment is appropriate, a tribunal must discharge a patient under the first ground if it is satisfied that his condition no longer makes it appropriate for him to be liable to be detained for that purpose.

2. Conversely, a tribunal is not obliged to discharge a patient who has extended leave to be absent from hospital unless it is satisfied that his condition makes it inappropriate for him to be liable to be detained for further in-patient treatment. This is so even though it is necessarily of the opinion that he could not currently be admitted afresh under section 3 and nor could the authority to detain him be renewed if renewal was due.

---

[31]   See Mental Health Act 1983, ss.3(2)(a) and 20(4)(a).

Part III patients and section 72(1)(b)(i)

In contrast to the first ground for detention under section 3, admission for treatment under sections 37, 47 and 48 requires that the court or the Secretary of State is satisfied that the patient is suffering from a form of mental disorder the nature or degree of which makes it appropriate for him to be "detained" in a hospital for medical treatment. This reflects the absence in Part III of any requirement that the patient's admission for treatment is necessary for his health or safety or to protect others and it cannot be provided unless he is detained. However, following admission, the same renewal and tribunal discharge criteria apply to all unrestricted patients who have been detained for treatment. In the case of Part III patients, the first of the grounds for renewal is less stringent than the original admission ground. This is because renewal is possible provided his condition makes further in-patient treatment appropriate, regardless of whether continued detention in hospital is appropriate. As to a tribunal's duties, it has already been noted that a tribunal must discharge an in-patient whom it is satisfied no longer needs to be liable to be detained. Conversely, it need not discharge a patient who is no longer in hospital unless satisfied that it is inappropriate for him to remain liable to detention for further in-patient treatment. With regard to section 48 patients, while removal requires that their condition necessitates urgent treatment, whether or not this remains the case is irrelevant insofar as the renewal and tribunal discharge criteria are concerned.

Whether and when liability to detention is appropriate

The use of a "liability to detention" test takes account of three possible situations encountered in practice. Firstly, it may not be appropriate to continue to detain or to compulsorily treat some in-patients. Secondly, it may be appropriate for some in-patients who have been seriously ill to initially leave hospital on a trial basis and to be liable to recall during the current period of detention if further in-patient treatment is indicated. Thirdly, it may similarly be appropriate for some patients already no longer in hospital to remain liable to recall for further in-patient treatment because of the risk of relapse.

Patients who are receiving in-patient treatment

Although it is sometimes said that the test set out in section 72(1)(b)(i) is whether it is appropriate to physically detain the patient in hospital, this is something of a simplification. The existence of an authority to detain a patient not only empowers the managers to detain him in the hospital, using restraint if necessary. It also has the necessary consequence that the patient may only leave the ward or hospital with permission and, where necessary, only then with an escort or subject to conditions. The administration of treatment without his consent is also authorised. Accordingly, it may be appropriate for an in-patient to remain "liable to be detained" even though he would not otherwise immediately leave hospital. For example, because he might otherwise refuse prescribed medication; intermittently absent himself in a way that undermines the treatment programme or puts himself or others at risk; or intermittently require restraint. This is, of course, provided that in-patient treatment is necessary for his health or safety or to protect others. Bearing these points in mind, the responsible medical officer should always be asked to clarify why a power of detention is appropriate: is it because the patient may need to be restrained; that he requires a period of trial leave before it can be established that further detention for treatment is inappropriate; or that he would otherwise discharge himself from hospital, refuse necessary treatment, or intermittently absent himself?

Patients who have extended leave of absence

As to patients who are not receiving in-patient treatment at the time of their tribunal hearing, different considerations apply. Whether the patient would deviate from his prescribed medication if free to do so is not strictly the issue. The statutory test is not whether it is appropriate to compel him to take medication at home but whether his condition makes it appropriate for him to be liable to detention in a hospital for further medical treatment *there*. Furthermore, some degree of non-compliance may not be likely to give rise to any need for further treatment in hospital, in which case the purpose served by the admission has been completed.

THE RISK GROUND AND SECTION 72(1)(b)(ii)

Section 72(1)(b)(ii) provides that a tribunal shall discharge a patient if it is satisfied that it is not necessary for his health or safety or to protect others "that he should receive such treatment." In the *Oxford case*, Lord Bridge said in passing that this phrase "must here mean treatment under detention."[32] Consequently, in practice, the phrase is often taken by tribunals to refer back to sub-paragraph (i) and to mean that it is unnecessary for the patient to remain liable to be detained in a hospital for medical treatment. However, that is not actually what section 72 says and textbook opinion on the point varies. Jones' note reads as follows: "Compare with the criterion set out in para. (a)(ii). The patient will not gain his discharge if he satisfies the tribunal that treatment under detention is not necessary: he must show that medical treatment is not necessary."[33] Similarly, Gostin and Fennell comment: "Thus if the tribunal is not satisfied that the patient does not need in-patient care in the interests of his own health, it is not required to discharge him even if satisfied that detention is not necessary for his safety or for the protection of others."[34] However, Gostin writing on his own states: "Criterion (ii) is set in the disjunctive. Thus, the patient need not be discharged if detention is necessary for his health or safety or the protection of others."[35] The *Memorandum* on the Act is of no assistance, completely confusing the two grounds for discharge.[36] It is submitted that Jones' interpretation, and that of Gostin and Fennell collectively, is the correct one. The phrasing of section 72(1)(b)(ii) materially differs from that used in section 123(1)(b) of the 1959 Act, and in sections 3(2)(c), 20(4)(c) and 72(1)(a)(ii) of the 1983 Act, and the omission from section 72(1)(b)(ii) of any reference to the necessity of detention must be deliberate. The correct approach is to decide first of all whether further in-patient treatment is unnecessary. If it is, it cannot possibly be appropriate for an individual to remain liable to detention in a hospital when further treatment there is unnecessary. If, however, the tribunal is not satisfied that further in-patient treatment is unnecessary, the issue becomes whether it is nevertheless satisfied that the patient's condition is not of a nature or degree which makes it appropriate for him to remain liable to detention in hospital for the purpose of giving him any in-patient treatment which is or may be necessary.

---

32   *Campbell v. Secretary of State for the Home Department* [1988] 1 A.C. 120, at 127.
33   R. Jones, *Mental Health Act Manual* (Sweet & Maxwell, 5th ed., 1996), p.256.
34   L. Gostin and P. Fennell, *Mental Health: Tribunal Procedure* (Longman, 2nd ed., 1992), p.88.
35   L. Gostin, *Mental Health Services — Law and Practice* (Shaw & Sons), para. 18.08.2.
36   *Mental Health Act 1983: Memorandum on Parts I to VI, VIII and X* (D.H.S.S., 1987), para. 214.

Patients detained under section 3 and section 72(1)(b)(ii)

It is a condition of admission under section 3, and of any renewal, that it is necessary for the patient's health or safety or for the protection of others that he receives in-patient treatment and "it cannot be provided unless he is detained under this section" or, in the case of renewal, "continues to be detained." The tribunal discharge criteria are, however, different. They require a tribunal to discharge only if they are satisfied "that it is not necessary for the health or safety of the patient or for the protection of other persons that he should receive such treatment."

Admission and renewal criteria	Tribunal discharge criteria
• The patient's mental condition makes it appropriate for him to receive medical treatment in a hospital.	• The patient is not suffering from a form of mental disorder the nature or degree of which makes it appropriate for him to be liable to be detained in a hospital for medical treatment.
• ... such treatment is likely to alleviate or prevent a deterioration of his condition.	
• It is necessary for the health or safety of the patient or for the protection of other persons that he should receive such treatment *and it cannot be provided unless he is detained under this section/continues to be detained.*	• It is not necessary for the health or safety of the patient or for the protection of other persons that he should receive such treatment.

It can be seen that the additional admission and renewal condition, that "such treatment" cannot be provided unless the patient continues to be detained, is omitted from the tribunal discharge criteria. Equally, it is not replaced by a requirement that such treatment cannot be provided unless he continues to be *liable to be detained.* The reason given for this at the time was that a tribunal might otherwise be obliged to discharge a patient because necessary in-patient treatment could be provided without him being liable to be detained.[37] The change also ensured that the two issues of the need for in-patient treatment and the need for compulsion remained separate (**215**).

Whether further in-patient treatment is or may be necessary

Section 72(1)(b)(ii) is therefore concerned with the issue of whether further in-patient treatment is or may be necessary for one of the statutory purposes, the references to "such treatment" in sections 3, 20 and 72 being references to the necessity of medical treatment in hospital, rather than the necessity of *compulsory* in-patient or out-patient treatment.[38] Unless a tribunal is satisfied that further in-patient treatment is unnecessary, it has not been demonstrated that the purpose of the patient's admission, which was for him to receive necessary in-patient treatment, has been fulfilled. Even if he is not presently in hospital, in order to establish if he can now cope or be treated outside hospital, whether this trial absence will prove to be permanent or temporary, and whether a tribunal can be satisfied that further in-patient treatment is no longer necessary, may often be unclear. Whether it is appropriate for the patient to be continued to be liable to be detained for medical treatment in a hospital is a separate matter, to be considered under sub-paragraph (i).

---

[37] See *Mental Health (Amendment) Bill: Notes on Clauses, House of Commons* (D.H.S.S., 1982), p.150.

[38] See also the different form of words used in section 72(1)(a)(ii) in relation to section 2 patients.

The significance of the distinction

The effect of the omission in section 72(1)(b)(ii) is that the appropriateness of in-patient treatment constitutes the first ground for admission and renewal, while the necessity for compulsion forms part of the second universal ground, but the position is reversed when it comes to the tribunal discharge criteria. The reversal is significant for two reasons—

1. Firstly, while compulsory admission and renewal requires that the in-patient treatment considered to be necessary cannot be provided unless the patient is detained — in other words detention is also necessary — a tribunal is not required to consider if this is in fact the case. If it is not satisfied that further in-patient treatment is unnecessary, it is only obliged to discharge the patient if it is satisfied that it is inappropriate for him to remain liable to be detained for that purpose. Whether a tribunal considers that liability to detention is "appropriate" is a much looser and more subjective test than considering whether further in-patient treatment cannot be provided unless the patient remains liable to be detained. What is appropriate in any particular situation involves balancing several, often competing, considerations. The issue is therefore whether the patient's health or safety or the need to protect others necessitates further in-patient treatment, rather than whether those considerations necessitate his further detention: the issue there is not whether his continued liability to detention is unnecessary but whether it is inappropriate in all the circumstances.

2. The second consequence relates to the fact that tribunals sometimes deal with cases involving patients on extended leave in terms of whether compulsory out-patient treatment is necessary for the patient's health or safety or to protect others. However, a tribunal must discharge a patient under paragraph (b)(ii) if it is satisfied that further in-patient treatment is unnecessary for one of the permitted purposes. This is so however convenient or beneficial it is to be able to enforce out-patient treatment, in particular medication, during what remains of the current period of detention. The statutory test is whether further in-patient treatment is or may be necessary, not whether the patient should be liable to compulsory treatment in the community. Of course, the two issues will be factually related if it is likely that the patient will immediately cease medication and relapse if discharged, so that further in-patient treatment is necessary. However, that is often not the case.[39]

---

[39] Again, section 72 accords with the statutory framework. Admission and renewal require that in-patient treatment or further in-patient treatment is necessary. If further in-patient treatment may be necessary during the current period of detention then a further renewal is a possibility and a tribunal is not required to discharge the patient. If further treatment in hospital does then prove to be necessary, the authority to detain him may be renewed. If, however, a tribunal is satisfied that further in-patient treatment will not be necessary, the purpose served by section 3, which was to admit the patient to hospital for medical treatment, has been served. Thereafter, one is simply allowing the section to continue as a community treatment order.

Part III patients and section 72(1)(b)(ii)

It is not a ground of admission for treatment under Part III that it is necessary for the patient's health or safety, or to protect others, that he receives in-patient treatment and it cannot be provided unless he is detained under that section. Section 37 requires instead that the court is of the opinion that a hospital order is the most appropriate way of disposing of the case, having regard to all the circumstances including the nature of the offence, the character and antecedents of the offender, and the other available methods of dealing with him. Transfer directions under sections 47 and 48 require that the Secretary of State is of the opinion that it is expedient to direct the person's removal to hospital for treatment, having regard to the public interest and all the circumstances. However, following admission, the same renewal and tribunal discharge criteria apply to all unrestricted patients detained for treatment. Consideration must then be given to whether in-patient treatment *is* necessary for the patient's health or safety or to protect others and, in the case of renewal, to whether it can be provided without the patient being detained. Whether the patient's presence in hospital is in the public interest, and the other matters referred to in original criteria for making such orders and directions, are irrelevant except insofar as they are evidence of the appropriateness of the patient's detention.

Summary

A tribunal must terminate a patient's liability to detention in a hospital for in-patient treatment if it is satisfied that it is unnecessary for his health or safety or to protect others that he receives further in-patient treatment or it is satisfied that it is no longer appropriate for him to be liable to detention in a hospital in order to receive treatment there.

NEAREST RELATIVE APPLICATIONS AND S.72(1)(b)(iii)

Where a tribunal application is made under section 66(1)(g) — that is by the nearest relative following the issue of a report barring him from ordering a section 3 patient's discharge — the criteria for mandatory discharge include a third ground. In such cases, a tribunal must also discharge the patient where satisfied that "the patient, if released, would not be likely to act in a manner dangerous to other persons or to himself." This ground therefore corresponds to the statutory ground upon which the patient's discharge was barred (**610**). The Act therefore distinguishes between detention which is necessary or justified for the patient's own health or safety, or to protect others, and the likelihood of dangerous behaviour. What constitutes dangerous conduct has already been considered (**218**) and it may simply be noted here that the Butler Committee equated "dangerousness with a propensity to cause serious physical injury or lasting psychological harm."[40]

"If released"

As to why section 72(1)(b)(iii) refers to the patient being dangerous "if released," rather than dangerous "if discharged," the reason for the substitution is not readily apparent.[41] The ground upon which an order barring discharge may be made, which

---

[40] *Report of the Committee on Mentally Abnormal Offenders*, Cmnd. 6244 (1975), para. 4.10.
[41] The word "release" is only used in three other places in the Mental Health Act 1983: ss. 50(1), 51(4), and Sched. 5, para. 35(1). Its use was more common in the 1959 Act, the usage there ("released from the hospital") corresponding to that in Sched. 5, para. 35(1).

is the act giving rise to the tribunal, is that the responsible medical officer believes that the patient would "if discharged" be likely to act in a dangerous manner. Logically, the tribunal are considering the same question, namely whether it is satisfied that this is not the case: Is the patient likely to act in a dangerous manner if the tribunal directs his discharge, that is releases him? Unless it can be said that the tribunal must discharge such a patient if he is no longer in hospital — release meaning release from hospital — there would seem to be no significance in the use of the word in preference to "discharge."

DISCRETIONARY DISCHARGE AND SECTION 72(2)

Another significant difference between the admission and renewal criteria on the one hand, and the tribunal discharge criteria on the other, concerns what are by custom known as the patient's treatability and vulnerability. The authority to detain a patient may only be renewed for a further period if it appears to the responsible medical officer *either*—

a. that medical treatment in a hospital is likely to alleviate or prevent a deterioration of his condition; *or*

b. that a mentally ill or severely mentally impaired patient would, if discharged, be unlikely to be able to care for himself, to obtain the care which he needs or to guard himself against serious exploitation.

However, while these two conditions form part of the mandatory renewal criteria — that is, the patient cannot be further detained unless one of them appears to be satisfied — they are excluded from the tribunal grounds for mandatory discharge. Instead, they are matters which a tribunal must have regard to when it decides whether to exercise its discretion to discharge a patient who does not satisfy the (correspondingly narrower) grounds for mandatory discharge in section 72(1)(b).[42]

Mandatory conditions for renewal	*Discretionary discharge by a tribunal*
MHA 1983, s.20(3)	*MHA 1983, s.72(2)*
The authority to detain a patient may only be renewed for a further period if it appears to the responsible medical officer either—	In determining whether to discharge a patient who does not satisfy the discharge grounds set out s.72(1)(b), a tribunal shall have regard—
• that medical treatment in a hospital is likely to alleviate or prevent a deterioration of his condition; or	• to the likelihood of medical treatment alleviating or preventing a deterioration of the patient's condition; and
• that a patient suffering from mental illness or severe mental impairment would, if discharged, be unlikely to be able to care for himself, to obtain the care which he needs or to guard himself against serious exploitation	• in the case of a patient suffering from mental illness or severe mental impairment, to the likelihood of the patient, if discharged, being able to care for himself, to obtain the care he needs or to guard himself against serious exploitation.

---

[42] That this is so was confirmed in *R. v. Canons Park Mental Health Review Tribunal, ex p. A* [1994] 3 W.L.R. 630 (**223**).

Patients suffering only from psychopathic disorder or mental impairment

Insofar as tribunals are concerned, a person who suffers only from mental impairment or psychopathic disorder may not be compulsorily admitted to hospital for treatment unless in-patient treatment is likely to alleviate or prevent a deterioration of his condition ("the treatability test"). Nor may the authority for his detention be renewed for a further period unless it appears to his responsible medical officer that further in-patient treatment is likely to confer such a benefit.[43] Whether and when treatment may be said to be likely to alleviate or prevent a deterioration of a patient's condition was considered by the Court of Appeal in the case of *ex p. A* (**223**). While the treatability test forms part of the mandatory conditions for admission or renewal, it does not form part of the statutory criteria for mandatory discharge by a tribunal. Instead, it is a matter which must be taken into account by a tribunal when deciding whether or not to exercise its discretionary power of discharge. Accordingly, a tribunal is not bound to discharge such a patient merely because it is satisfied that his condition is not treatable in the statutory sense and takes the view that, as matters presently stand, the criteria for later renewing the authority for his detention are not satisfied. Consequently, if the tribunal decides not to exercise its discretion in favour of discharge, the patient's responsible medical officer may later renew the authority for a further period if he disagrees with the tribunal's assessment of the patient's treatability — and this may have been part of his evidence to the tribunal. Indeed, he will be under a duty to furnish a renewal report if this is his opinion and the other conditions are satisfied. Thus, if the patient is not entitled to be discharged on some other ground, the tribunal can decline to interfere with the responsible medical officer's opinion concerning the patient's treatability and lawfully allow the patient's liability to detention to continue.[44]

Patients suffering from mental illness or severe mental impairment

It has been noted that where the responsible medical officer's opinion is that a patient suffers only from psychopathic disorder or mental impairment, he may only renew the authority for his detention if it appears to him that medical treatment in hospital is likely to alleviate or prevent a deterioration of the patient's condition ("the treatability test"). Where, however, his opinion is that the patient suffers from mental illness or severe mental impairment, renewal is permissible on the alternative ground that he would, if discharged, be unlikely to be able to care for himself, to obtain the care which he needs, or to guard himself against serious exploitation ("the vulnerability test"). The grounds for renewing the detention of a patient who suffers from mental illness or severe mental impairment are therefore somewhat broader. As to the circumstances in which a tribunal must discharge a patient, the position is similar to that just outlined. While the treatability and vulnerability tests form part of the mandatory conditions for renewing the authority to detain a person who suffers

---

[43]   See Mental Health Act 1983, s.20(4).

[44]   The point may be particularly relevant where a patient is reclassified by his responsible medical officer under section 16 with the effect that he is then recorded as suffering only from psychopathic disorder or mental impairment. The authority to detain him immediately ceases unless that doctor is of the opinion that his condition is treatable in the statutory sense. If he considers that the patient's condition is treatable, the patient remains liable to be detained but may apply to a tribunal. If the tribunal which then reviews the patient's case disagrees, being of the opinion that his condition is not in fact treatable, it is nevertheless not obliged by virtue of this finding to direct the patient's discharge. The right to a tribunal following reclassification is thus fundamentally different from that which arises following the issue of a barring report, where the tribunal must discharge if it is satisfied that the grounds for barring discharge do not apply.

from mental illness or severe mental impairment, they are not part of the statutory criteria for mandatory discharge. Instead, they are matters which must be taken into account when a tribunal decides whether to exercise its discretionary power of discharge. Accordingly, a tribunal is not bound to discharge a mentally ill or severely mentally impaired patient merely because it is satisfied that his condition is not treatable and he would not be vulnerable if discharged. And, as before, if a tribunal decides not to exercise its discretion in favour of discharge, and the patient's responsible medical officer disagrees with its assessment of the patient's treatability or vulnerability, he will later be under a duty to furnish a renewal report if this remains his opinion and the other conditions are satisfied.

Summary

While the above considerations define when a tribunal is under an obligation to discharge, they do not represent the whole picture. When a tribunal is considering whether to exercise its discretion to discharge a section 2 patient, there are no matters which it must have regard to as a matter of law. That being so, the purpose of section 72(2) is clearly to require a tribunal to address the issue of whether the patient's detention could be continued if renewal was due — whether he is still detainable in that loose sense. If the tribunal is of the opinion that further in-patient treatment will be of no benefit, and the patient will not be vulnerable if discharged, it is clearly required to carefully consider what possible justification there might be in permitting his detention in hospital for further treatment. The tribunal's view as to the patient's treatability and vulnerability also has some bearing on both of the grounds for mandatory discharge — that is, whether liability to detention is still appropriate and whether in-patient treatment is necessary for the patient's health or safety or to protect others. Why ineffective in-patient treatment is necessary needs to be spelt out.[45]

DISCHARGE ON A FUTURE DATE

Where a tribunal discharges a patient, section 72(3) provides that it may direct his discharge on a future date specified in the direction. As to whether a tribunal is obliged to discharge forthwith a patient who satisfies the statutory criteria for discharge, and who is therefore legally entitled to be discharged, see page 469. It has been known for a tribunal to direct that a patient shall be discharged on a date after the end of the current period of detention. In some cases, this is because the tribunal's decision that the patient must or should be discharged is founded on a finding that adequate alternative arrangements can be made for the patient's treatment and care outside hospital but these arrangements will not be concluded prior to the expiration of the period of detention which is drawing to a close. One argument would be that the tribunal's finding is essentially that the patient's detention under the existing authority is not unwarranted and should be allowed to run its full course. Accordingly, its finding necessarily leads to a decision not to discharge the patient. Whether the detention continues beyond then is a matter for the responsible medical officer.

---

[45] Most often, the reasons will be that (1) it is necessary that the patient receives nursing and care in hospital in order to protect other people, and (2) it is appropriate for him to be liable to be detained there for such treatment because his untreatable mental disorder is of a severe nature and degree, manifesting itself from time to time in violent conduct.

RECOMMENDATIONS TO FACILITATE DISCHARGE

If a tribunal does not direct that a patient shall be discharged, the natural next question is whether there are any other powers it may exercise short of discharging the patient. In this respect, a tribunal's power to make recommendations under section 72(3) with a view to facilitating a patient's future discharge, is the same as in section 2 cases (**474**). The tribunal may recommend that the patient be granted leave of absence, transferred to another hospital, or transferred into guardianship. If its recommendation is not being complied with, it may further consider the patient's case. The limits of the power to make recommendations, and whether a tribunal which reconvenes may then direct the patient's discharge, have already been considered (**476**). However, two further points may be noted. Firstly, the authority to detain a patient who is liable to be detained for treatment will lapse if he is granted extended leave of absence and is not recalled to hospital prior to the expiration of the current period of detention (**281**). Secondly, a patient who is transferred into guardianship is treated as if he had been received into guardianship on the date of his original admission to hospital under section 3 or, as the case may be, the date on which the hospital order was made. One effect of this is that the authority for his guardianship will immediately be due for renewal if, at the time of transfer, the existing authority for his detention was due to expire within two months.

OTHER RECOMMENDATIONS

Subsection 72(3A) was inserted into the 1983 Act by the Mental Health (Patients in the Community) Act 1995. It empowers a tribunal which does not discharge a patient who is liable to be detained for treatment to recommend that his responsible medical officer considers whether to make a supervision application in respect of him. The tribunal may later further consider the patient's case in the event that no supervision application is made.

Whether recommendation must be with a view to facilitating discharge

It seems quite probable that the new power will in due course be the subject of an application for judicial review. The essence of the application is likely to be that a recommendation under section 72(3A) may only be made in the same circumstances in which a recommendation may be made under section 72(3), namely with a view to facilitating the patient's discharge on a future date. In support of this contention, the argument may be forwarded that the statutory function of a tribunal is to review whether compulsory powers are necessary and it is never involved in the process of imposing compulsory powers. With the coming into force of the Mental Health Act 1959, patients could henceforth be detained for treatment without the need for any judicial order. Tribunals were therefore constituted which would enable patients who were detained to have the need for compulsory powers independently reviewed. Parliament cannot have intended that these judicial bodies — set up to protect the liberty of the subject and with the sole function of reviewing whether there were grounds for using compulsory powers — would also be involved in the process of imposing additional compulsory powers by recommending that a further application be made. Any departure from the principle that a patient may apply to a tribunal safe in the knowledge that, if his application is refused, he will not at any rate be in a worse position would require clear evidence that this was Parliament's intention. To hold otherwise would seriously undermine the very raison d'être of the tribunal system. Patients would then be disinclined to exercise their right to a review, because of a fear that the tribunal might not only not lift the existing compulsory powers but also recommend the use of further powers upon eventual discharge. Recommending that a fresh application be made is qualitatively different in this respect from recommending transfer into guardianship. In the latter case, the existing application becomes a guardianship application and the patient is only subject to guardianship for whatever remains of the period of detention previously authorised. There is no further application and he does not thereby become liable to compulsory powers for any greater period of time.

The statutory framework

Upon first reading the new provision, the purpose of inserting a whole new subsection after section 72(3) appears simply to be to clarify that a tribunal may only recommend that a supervision application be considered if the patient is liable to be detained for treatment. This reflects the fact that an application, order or direction authorising detention for treatment must first exist before a supervision application may be made. Because section 72(3) also applies to patients detained under section 2, a reference to a supervision application being made in some cases but not others could not easily have been added to the existing list of recommendations without making it so lengthy as to be virtually unreadable. However, this point does not cater for the fact that section 72(3A) does not similarly qualify the circumstances in which such a recommendation may be made by including the same words, "with a view to facilitating his discharge on a future date." That phrase could, as with section 72(3), easily have been added after the words "the tribunal may ..." but was not. It must be presumed that the omission was deliberate since the likelihood of any draftsman missing such an obvious point, when deliberating over whether to simply amend section 72(3) or to construct a new subsection along similar lines, must be virtually nil. It would clearly be illogical for a tribunal to recommend that a supervision application be considered unless it was of the opinion that there were grounds for making such an application. From the tribunal's viewpoint, the first of the statutory grounds will necessarily exist in every case where it makes the recommendation because it would otherwise have directed the patient's discharge. The second ground requires that there would be a substantial risk of serious harm to the health or safety of the patient or the safety of other persons, or of the patient being seriously exploited, if he were not to receive the after-care services provided under section 117 after he leaves hospital. The final ground is that providing those after-care services under supervision is likely to help to secure that the patient receives them. Given its opinion that a supervision application should be considered, the tribunal's reasons for not discharging the patient are likely to include a belief that there will be a substantial risk of serious harm if the patient leaves hospital and does not receive necessary after-care. Hence, the patient is not suitable for discharge and, by implication, will not be suitable for as long as this remains the case. However, the making of a supervision application would be likely to help to secure that he receives those services, thereby reducing those substantial risks, and so making discharge more likely. In many cases therefore, the effect of making of a supervision application will necessarily be to facilitate the patient's discharge. Furthermore, it may be contended that recommending that an application is made is not qualitatively different from recommending a patient's transfer into guardianship. In both cases, the underlying purpose is to hasten the end of his liability to detention in hospital by encouraging the bringing into being of a statutory scheme for the patient's supervision and care outside hospital. While all this may often be the case, so that the tribunal's main purpose in making the recommendation will be to facilitate discharge, by making it a more realistic option, it will not always be so straight-forward. It is only a matter of time before a tribunal recommends that a supervision application be considered with the primary purpose of protecting the public from serious harm. For example, the patient may be on leave, and his current period of detention drawing to a close at the time of the hearing, so that he will soon cease to be liable to be detained. The responsible medical officer may not consider that recall is presently justified but nevertheless wish him to remain on leave for what remains of the existing period. In this situation, a tribunal which considers that the patient will probably not co-operate with after-care or take medication once he can no longer be compelled to do so, and believes that he will then relapse and there be a substantial risk of serious harm to others, may wish to recommend that a supervision application be made. This will not advance discharge because the patient will shortly cease to be liable to be detained anyway and that will not, of course, be the purpose behind the recommendation. In other cases, the responsible medical officer may indicate that he himself plans to discharge the patient in a few weeks time and the tribunal be similarly concerned by this prospect. It has a different view as to the patient's likely compliance and potential dangerousness. In yet other cases, it may simply be clear from the reasons for the tribunal's decision that it considers that the conditions for an application are satisfied and it would be prudent to make such an application, in order to ensure that a statutory scheme is in place when the patient is eventually released. However, again, it may be obvious that the primary concern is to ensure that the public are protected if the patient is discharged, for example by his nearest relative, rather than to facilitate his discharge. Virtually all that can usefully be said with regard to these situations is to repeat the fact that the likelihood of any draftsman forgetting to insert the words "with a view to facilitating discharge" in section 72(3A), when deciding whether to amend section 72(3) or to construct a new sub-section along similar lines, must be virtually nil. The omission must therefore be deliberate and reflect the intention behind the Mental Health (Patients in the Community) Act 1995. This was not to introduce additional safeguards in response to public concern that the liberty of detained patients was being unjustifiably infringed. Rather, it was to respond to their concerns that the existing safeguards against serious harm resulting from patients being in the community were in-sufficient. As to this, a person who has been detained for treatment may later be in the community in one of three ways — upon ceasing to be liable to be detained, upon being granted leave to be absent from hospital, upon being absent from hospital without leave — and the Act tightened the existing framework, and extended the element of control over patients in all three of these areas. Empowering a tribunal which considers that not only is the patient not suitable for discharge, but also that his discharge will lead to a substantial risk of serious harm, to recommend that the new power of supervised discharge be considered is therefore not inconsistent with the overall aims of the Act which created this new power. In the alternative, because any recommendation will often serve more than one purpose, both protecting the patient and others from serious harm and so also facilitating his discharge, the omission of the words is simply designed to avoid endless challenges based on the contention that the *primary* purpose behind the recommendation was not to facilitate discharge. Either way, even if the new power is ill-considered, it is submitted that Parliament's intention is clear. A recommendation is not invalid because it is made with a view to some purpose other than facilitating the patient's discharge.

Recommendation that consideration be given to the matter

It has been noted that a tribunal may further consider the patient's case in the event that no supervision application is made. If the responsible medical officer notifies the tribunal that he has considered but rejected making a supervision application then, even though he has complied with its recommendation, the tribunal may nevertheless still further consider the case. This is, of course, provided that the patient remains liable to be detained. If he is no longer so liable, the time for making a supervision application has passed and the tribunal application will in any case be deemed to have been withdrawn.

Power of supervised discharge already considered

Where the responsible medical officer indicates in his evidence that he has already considered and ruled out the need for a supervision application, whether the tribunal may still make the recommendation has not been decided. Strictly speaking, it would then be asking him not to consider the matter but to reconsider the decision which he has made. However, this may be too literal an approach for two reasons. Firstly, most consultants will have previously considered the matter in the limited and literal sense that they have reflected upon whether there are grounds for making an application. If "consider" in this context meant only that, it would virtually never be possible for a recommendation to be made under section 72(3A). Consequently, it is more likely that the word in this context means to consider making an application having first taken the various steps which must be taken before making an application may be considered. These preparatory steps involve consulting the various professional and non-professional persons referred to in section 25B, taking their views into account, and considering both the after-care services to be provided and any essential requirements which should be imposed under section 25D. Secondly, the contention that some general prior deliberation of the matter rules out the recommendation does not take account of the fact that the making of any recommendation entitles a tribunal to later reconvene to examine the reasons why the particular step has not been taken. The person or authority which has not carried the recommendation into effect can then be obliged to furnish the tribunal with an account of the reasons for not taking the recommended course of action. Thus, whether or not the matter has been previously considered in some general way, the purpose served by any recommendation is that the particular matter must be systematically considered, and the tribunal given reasons if the recommendation is rejected after proper consideration. Unless this view is taken, there would be little point in providing that a tribunal can further consider the case at that point. The intention therefore appears to be to require the responsible medical officer to consult the relevant persons, to consider the statutory issues, to then form an opinion about whether an application should be made, and to notify the tribunal of his view. The tribunal may then itself further consider the matter, reconvening if it finds the reasoning unconvincing or it wishes to further explore the issue.

RECLASSIFICATION

Apart from making recommendations, a tribunal has one other power in respect of patients whom it does not discharge. Section 72(5) provides that a tribunal which does not discharge a patient may in the circumstances specified direct that the authority for his detention shall be amended by substituting for the form of mental disorder specified in it such other form of mental disorder as appears to the tribunal to be appropriate.

72.—(5) Where application is made to a Mental Health Review Tribunal under any provision of this Act by or in respect of a patient and the tribunal do not direct that the patient be discharged *or, if he is (or is to be) subject to after-care under supervision, that he cease to be so subject (or not become so subject)*, the tribunal may, if satisfied that the patient is suffering from a form of mental disorder other than the form specified in the application, order or direction relating to him, direct that that application, order or direction be amended by substituting for the form of mental disorder specified in it such other form of mental disorder as appears to the tribunal to be appropriate.

(6) Subsections (1) to (5) above apply in relation to references to a Mental Health Review Tribunal as they apply in relation to applications made to such a tribunal by or in respect of a patient.

Issues arising from section 72(5)

Several questions naturally arise from any consideration of the subsection—

1. What is the purpose served by reclassification?

2. What are the legal consequences of reclassification?

3. Does the giving of a direction reclassifying the patient ever have the effect that the patient must be immediately discharged?

4. If a tribunal is satisfied that a patient's classification is erroneous, why is a direction reclassifying him not mandatory?

5. Is the power of reclassification merely one of substitution?

6. Does the power extends to restricted cases?[46]

In order to make sense of these questions, it is necessary to first summarise the legislative history.

Mental Health Act 1959

The 1959 Act provided that an application, other than one for observation, could describe the patient as suffering from more than one form of mental disorder."[47] Similarly, an order or direction was required to specify the form "or forms" of disorder from which the patient was found to be suffering.[48] The responsible medical officer could reclassify an unrestricted patient who appeared to him to be suffering from "a form" of disorder other than "the form or forms" specified in the authority.[49] A tribunal which did not discharge an unrestricted patient had the same power to reclassify a patient whom it did not discharge as now conferred by section 72(5).

---

[46] Consideration of this last question is postponed until later (**551**).
[47] Mental Health Act 1959, s.26(4), 33(5).
[48] *Ibid.*, ss.60(5), 72(5), 73(3).
[49] *Ibid.*, ss. 38(1), 63(3), 147(4), Third Sched.

It could, if satisfied that he was suffering from "a form" of disorder other than "the form" specified, direct that the authority be amended by substituting for "the form" specified such "other form" as appeared to it to be appropriate.[50] In contrast to the present position, reclassification could never be effected through the furnishing of a renewal report, no doubt because the renewal criteria did not refer to the form of disorder from which the patient was then suffering.[51] Consequently, the original classification stood unless and until the responsible medical officer or a tribunal exercised their discretionary power of reclassification. As to why reclassification might be desirable, the form of disorder recorded could have a bearing on whether the compulsory powers had effect after the patient reached the age of 25. What was important in this respect was whether the patient suffered only from a minor (psychopathic disorder or subnormality) or a major (mental illness or severe subnormality) form of disorder.

Patients subject to guardianship

The ordinary renewal criteria were the same in all cases and made no reference to the form of disorder recorded, or its nature or degree.[52] However, where a guardianship application was in force, the patient ceased to be subject to guardianship when he attained the age of 25 if he was recorded as suffering only from a minor disorder.[53] If the effect of reclassifying a patient aged under 25 was that he was now recorded as suffering from a major disorder, the application became capable of having effect after he reached that age. Conversely, if the effect was that the patient was recorded as now suffering only from a minor disorder, he immediately ceased to be subject to guardianship if aged over 25, otherwise the authority ceased when he reached that age. Different rules applied to patients subject to a guardianship order: such orders did not cease to have effect upon the patient attaining that age, regardless of the form of disorder specified in it.[54] Reclassification by the responsible medical officer gave rise to a right to apply to a tribunal in all cases. This was so notwithstanding even though it necessarily had no bearing on renewal, nor any legal consequences at all if the patient was subject to a guardianship order.

Unrestricted patients detained for treatment

The renewal criteria were, as with guardianship, the same in all cases, making no reference to the form of disorder from which a patient was recorded as suffering or its nature or degree. If the effect of amending an application was that a patient aged under 25 was then recorded as suffering only from a minor disorder, he ceased to be liable to be detained on attaining that age unless, during the two months prior to that birthday, the responsible medical officer furnished a report stating that he would, if released, be likely to act in a manner dangerous to himself or others. Where reclassification was in the other direction, so that an application no longer recorded that a patient under 25 years of age was suffering only from a minor disorder, the consequence was to render him liable to be detained after he reached that age, regardless of whether he was dangerous. Reclassification gave rise to a right to apply to a tribunal in all cases, notwithstanding that it had no bearing on the likelihood of renewal nor, in hospital order cases, any legal consequences for the order's duration.

---

50   Mental Health Act 1959, s.123(3).
51   *Ibid.*, s.43.
52   *Ibid.*, s.43(4).
53   *Ibid.*, s.44(1).
54   *Ibid.*, s.63(3)(b).

The significance of a patient's classification, and thus of reclassification, under the 1959 Act may be summarised as follows: (1) it was irrelevant for renewal purposes; (2) it had no bearing on the duration of a hospital order, guardianship order or transfer direction; (3) it might have a bearing on the duration of a guardianship application or an application for admission for treatment, but not necessarily so. Notwithstanding points (1)–(3), (4) all unrestricted patients could be reclassified by their responsible medical officer or a tribunal; (5) reclassification was, however, discretionary; (6) where a patient was reclassified by his responsible medical officer, that gave rise in all cases to a right to apply to a tribunal; (7) there was no power to reclassify restricted patients.

Mental Health Act 1983

The conditions for renewing the authority for a patient's detention or guardianship now require the patient's medical officer to give his opinion of the form of disorder from which the patient appears to be suffering, and the renewal criteria differ according to the form specified. The careless references to the form or forms of disorder recorded have been carried over into the present legislation. An application, other than one made under section 2, may describe the patient as suffering from "more than one of the ... (four) forms of mental disorder ..."[55] Likewise, an order or direction made under Part III shall specify the "form or forms" of disorder from which the patient is found to be suffering.[56] Where the responsible medical officer furnishes a renewal report and "the form" of disorder specified therein is a form "other than that" previously specified, the authority "shall have effect as if that other form of mental disorder were specified in it ..."[57] Similarly, if at any other time it appears to the patient's responsible medical officer that the patient is suffering from a form of disorder other than "the form or forms" specified, he may furnish a report to that effect, whereupon the application, order or direction shall have effect "as if that other form of mental disorder were specified in it."[58] As can be seen the drafting is inconsistent. The Act provides that the authority for a patient's detention or guardianship may specify more than one form of disorder and the power to reclassify under section 16 clearly contemplates and deals with the possibility. However, the drafting of sections 20 and 72 are materially different insofar as they contemplate a single form of disorder being recorded, whether as the original classification or following an earlier reclassification. Furthermore, while the power in section 72 is expressed as one of substitution, that given to the responsible medical officer is one of adding a further form to that or those specified, although section 16(2) then partly contradicts this by suggesting that the power there is one of substitution.

---

[55] Mental Health Act 1983, s.11(6).

[56] *Ibid.*, ss.37(7), 47(4), 48(3).

[57] *Ibid.*, ss.20(9), 40(4), 55(4), 145(3), Sched. 1, Pt. I, para. 6(b). Strictly speaking, it is the appropriate medical officer who furnishes such reports. However, the responsible medical officer will also be the patient's appropriate medical officer in all cases except those where a private guardian has been appointed under the Act.

[58] Mental Health Act 1983, ss.16(1), 40(4), 55(4), 145(3), Sched. 1, Pt. I, para. 3. However, section 16(2) immediately contradicts section 16(1), because it is clear that, following such a reclassification, the patient may no longer be recorded as suffering from any major form of mental disorder. Thus, the responsible medical officer may also remove a form of disorder from the pre-existing classification.

The purpose served by reclassification

Reclassification under the 1959 Act frequently had important legal consequences in terms of the duration of the compulsory powers. Following the abolition of the age-limits, and given that it is the form of disorder from which the patient is found to be suffering at the time of renewal which is determinative, it is a largely pointless exercise nowadays as far as tribunals are concerned. The rationale behind providing a tribunal right of application in *all* cases can be summarised in the following way (**053, 608**). Where during the course of a period of detention, a patient's mental state, or his responsible medical officer's assessment of it, is so materially different from that upon which the current period of detention was authorised as to require legal reclassification, the continuance of the detention for the remainder of the authorised period should always be susceptible to independent review. Similarly where a patient is subject to guardianship or after-care under supervision.

The legal consequences of reclassification

The legal consequences of reclassification by a responsible medical officer are that it may necessitate the patient's immediate discharge and, in other cases, a right to apply to a tribunal arises (**302, 608**). Subject to the decision in *Re. V.E.*, the legal consequences of reclassification by a tribunal are now negligible.

Whether reclassifying ever obliges the tribunal to discharge

In *Re V.E. (mental health patient),*[59] the application for the patient's admission to hospital for treatment stated that she was suffering from mental illness. E applied to a tribunal for her discharge. The tribunal did not discharge but concluded that her condition had been wrongly diagnosed and directed under section 123(3) of the 1959 Act — which sub-section is repeated in the 1983 Act as section 72(5) — that the application for her admission be amended so as to substitute "psychopathic disorder" for "mental illness." Under the 1959 Act, an application for treatment could not be made in respect of a patient aged over 21 if she suffered only from that form of disorder. The patient was aged 40. The question arose whether the tribunal's direction that the patient be reclassified was incompatible with its direction that she not be discharged. Did its reclassification have the effect that she must be discharged on the ground that, as a person over 21 suffering from psychopathic disorder, no application could be made for her detention under the 1959 Act? The Court of Appeal held that the application remained throughout the only authority for the patient's compulsory detention. Consequently, if an amendment of the application so altered its averments that they no longer alleged circumstances which would justify detention, the patient had to be discharged. Accordingly, since the amended application alleged no more than psychopathic disorder in a patient aged 40, her continued detention could not be justified under the Act and she was entitled to be discharged. In any event (*per* Lord Widgery C.J.), she was entitled to discharge by reason of the fact that on a proper diagnosis she had never qualified for detention at all. Under the present statute, there is only one circumstance in which precisely the same legal situation may arise. That is where a tribunal do not discharge an unrestricted patient detained under section 48 but reclassify the form of mental disorder recorded to psychopathic disorder or mental impairment. A transfer direction cannot be made under section 48 in respect of a person suffering only from

---

[59]   *Re V.E. (mental health patient)* [1973] 1 Q.B. 452 (**577**).

such a "minor" form of mental disorder and, hence, according to *Re V.E.*, the patient must be immediately discharged.

Why directing reclassification is not mandatory

The power to reclassify conferred by section 72(5) is permissive rather than obligatory and section 16(1) provides that the responsible medical officer has a similar discretion. As drafted, neither a tribunal nor a responsible medical officer would seem to be obliged to effect reclassification, even though satisfied that the present classification is incorrect. So, for example, a tribunal which does not discharge a patient recorded as suffering from mental illness, because it is satisfied that that he suffers from a serious psychopathic disorder, is not obliged to reclassify him. The original reasons for conferring such a discretion may well have been twofold. Firstly, because reclassification had no legal consequences in terms of renewal, and often no bearing at all on the duration of the powers, it was left to the tribunal's discretion whether to reclassify if no purpose would be served by doing so.[60] Secondly, a discretion not to reclassify avoided a tribunal being obliged to discharge a patient aged over 25 because it was of the opinion that he suffered only from a minor disorder (see *Re V.E.*, **577**). Similarly, the fact that the power remains discretionary may reflect the fact that reclassification rarely fulfils any useful legal purpose and, when it does, a tribunal might prefer not to exercise the power.

Whether the power is one of substitution only

Section 72(5) is more restrictively drafted than sections 16 and 20 insofar as it explicitly provides that the tribunal's power is one of substitution — it may substitute for the form of disorder specified such other form as appears to the tribunal to be appropriate. As drafted, the provision does not extend to many situations in which a tribunal might be minded to alter a patient's formal classification. For example, a tribunal may wish to delete one of two forms of disorder recorded without substituting another form for it. Conversely, it might wish to add a form of mental disorder to that already specified, rather than in substitution for it. Thus, in *ex p. Hinsley*, which was not proceeded with for reasons unknown, the patient sought judicial review of the tribunal's decision to add a further form of mental disorder to the original classification. The question arises whether the power is one of substitution only or also empowers a tribunal to add or delete a form of disorder which it is satisfied is incorrect. One view is simply to acknowledge that the drafting is inconsistent and to take a practical approach. This is that Parliament must have intended that both a tribunal and the responsible medical officer may adjust a patient's classification in whatever way is necessary in order to ensure that it accurately reflects their opinion concerning the legal basis of his detention. The alternative approach is that Parliament must have had some reason for formulating the tribunal's power in such a distinctive and limited way. For example, where a patient's detention as authorised solely on the ground of mental illness, the lawfulness of his continued detention might be open to challenge if a tribunal had found that he was not mentally ill and could not substitute an alternative form of disorder for that recorded in the application. In that situation, a tribunal which found him to be suffering from some other form of disorder might wish to make a single substitution, so as to ensure that his further detention was authorised. Ultimately, the very precise terms of section 72(5) make it difficult to argue that there is any ambiguity in the drafting, only an unnecessary limitation spelt out at some length.

---

[60] See *Mental Health Act 1959: Memorandum on Parts I, IV to VII and IX* (D.H.S.S., 1960), para. 90.

PATIENTS SUBJECT TO GUARDIANSHIP

A tribunal's discharge powers when reviewing the case of a patient subject to guardianship are set out in section 72(4) of the Act.

PATIENTS SUBJECT TO GUARDIANSHIP

Discretionary discharge

72.—(4) Where application is made to a Mental Health Review Tribunal by or in respect of a patient who is subject to guardianship under this Act, the tribunal may in any case direct that the patient be discharged,

and shall so direct if they are satisfied—

Mandatory discharge

(a) that he is not then suffering from mental illness, psychopathic disorder, severe mental impairment or mental impairment; or
(b) that it is not necessary in the interests of the welfare of the patient, or for the protection of other persons, that the patient should remain under such guardianship.

Reclassification

(5) Where application is made to a Mental Health Review Tribunal under any provision of this Act by or in respect of a patient and the tribunal do not direct that the patient be discharged, the tribunal may, if satisfied that the patient is suffering from a form of mental disorder other than the form specified in the application, order or direction relating to him direct that that application, order or direction be amended by substituting for the form of mental disorder specified in it such other form of mental disorder as appears to the tribunal to be appropriate.

References

(6) Subsections [(4)] to (5) above apply in relation to references to a Mental Health Review Tribunal as they apply in relation to applications made to such a tribunal by or in respect of a patient.

TERMINOLOGY

For the meaning of the words used in the criteria for reception and discharge, see— "discharge" (**571**); "patient" (**098**); "subject to guardianship" (**250**); "satisfied" (**567**); "then" (**466**); "suffering from" (**213**); "mental illness" (**060, 068**); "psychopathic disorder" (**082**); "severe mental impairment" (**070**); "mental impairment" (**070**); "necessary in the interests of" (**221, 485**); "welfare" (**217**); "protection of other persons" (**219**). For a short summary of the meaning of many of these terms, see page 484. "Welfare" is not statutorily defined. While any arrangement which is necessary for a patient's health and safety may also be said to be necessary in the interests of his welfare, the latter has a wider ambit and includes matters such as social functioning, education, training and the other matters referred to in section 8.

SUMMARY OF POWERS

Section 72(4) provides that a tribunal shall discharge a patient from guardianship if the criteria set out there are satisfied. As in other unrestricted cases, a tribunal also possesses a discretionary power to discharge a patient whom it does not consider satisfies the criteria for mandatory discharge. Because a guardianship application or order specifies the form of disorder from which the patient has been found to suffer, a tribunal has the same power to reclassify a patient whom it does not discharge from guardianship as it does an unrestricted patient detained for treatment. There the similarities end. A tribunal has no power to direct a patient's discharge from guardianship on a specified future date so that any discharge must take effect forthwith. Moreover, a tribunal which does not discharge a patient from guardianship has no power to make statutory recommendations with a view to facilitating his future discharge from guardianship. In part, this is because the recommendations which a tribunal may make when reviewing a patient's liability to detention would be irrelevant or inappropriate in guardianship cases. Recommending leave of absence would be otiose because a guardianship patient cannot be granted leave of absence. Similarly, recommending transfer to hospital would contravene the statutory premise that a tribunal's functions in unrestricted cases are limited to discharging patients or facilitating their discharge. Except in so far as recently provided for by the 1995 Act, a tribunal has no power to further restrict a person's freedom.

THE CRITERIA FOR MANDATORY DISCHARGE

The main point to note in relation to the criteria for mandatory discharge is the absence of any "nature or degree" test. Under section 72(4)(a), a tribunal is not obliged to discharge a patient unless it is satisfied that he is no longer suffering from a form of mental disorder.[61] This is so notwithstanding that it is satisfied that he is not then suffering from a form of disorder which is of a nature or degree warranting guardianship. For two reasons, it is not possible to argue that this is a drafting error. Firstly, there is similarly no "nature or degree" test in relation to conditionally discharged patients and those subject to after-care under supervision. The position is therefore the same for all patients subject to powers of supervision in the community whose cases a tribunal may consider (**068**). Secondly, the current position repeats that set out in section 123(2)(a) of the Mental Health Act 1959. That Act was in force for 23 years. If this was a lacuna, there was ample time for it to become apparent and for the omission to be remedied in the present legislation.

DISCRETIONARY DISCHARGE

There are no matters which a tribunal must have regard to as a matter of law before determining whether to exercise its discretionary power of discharge.

RECLASSIFICATION

As to the power of reclassification conferred by section 72(5), see page 499. It has already been noted that where a section 2 patient is transferred into guardianship he does not have a classification under the Act. Unless the pragmatic view is taken that

---

[61] As to whether a very mild disorder of mind can constitute mental illness for the purposes of section 72, see p.68.

a patient may be classified, and not merely reclassified, under section 20(9) or 72(5), there is little that can be done about this.

CASE LAW

In *ex p. E*,[62] the guardianship application was invalid and the patient was being detained at the place where she was required to reside by the local authority. The patient applied for habeas corpus, for judicial review of the guardianship application, and for judicial review of the tribunal's decision that she not be discharged from the guardian's authority over her. In the event, the local authority itself discharged the guardianship several months later, a matter of days before the applications were due to be heard.

SUPERVISION APPLICATION CASES

A tribunal's discharge powers when reviewing the case of a patient who is, or who is to be, subject to after-care under supervision are set out in section 72(4A) of the Act.

SUMMARY OF POWERS

Where a tribunal reviews the case of a patient who is, or who is to be, subject to after-care under supervision, its range of powers are the same as in guardianship cases. The tribunal must direct that the patient shall cease to be subject to after-care under supervision, or liable to supervision upon leaving hospital, if it is satisfied that the relevant statutory criteria are not complied with. Where this is not the case, it may still at its discretion direct that the patient shall cease to be subject to after-care under supervision or not become subject to it upon leaving hospital. A tribunal which does not direct that the patient shall cease to be subject or liable to supervision may reclassify the form of disorder from which he is recorded as suffering. As with guardianship, it has no power to make any statutory recommendations with a view to facilitating a patient's discharge from statutory supervision at a later date.

TERMINOLOGY

As to the meaning of the words used in the application and discharge criteria, see "patient" **(098)**; "after-care under supervision" **(422)**; "leaves hospital"; **(441)**; "complied with" **(508)**; "satisfied" **(567)**; "suffering from **(213)**; "mental illness" **(060)**; "psychopathic disorder" **(082)**; "severe mental impairment" **(070)**; "mental impairment" **(070)**; "substantial risk of serious harm" **(430)**; "health" **(217)**; "safety" **(218)**; "serious exploitation" **(219)**; "after-care services under section 117" **(413)**; "likely to help to secure" **(431)**.

---

[62] *R. v. South East Thames Mental Health Review Tribunal, ex p. E*, CO/1096/89 (unreported). See also p.581.

Discretionary discharge

72.—(4A) Where application is made to a Mental Health Review Tribunal by or in respect of a patient who is subject to after-care under supervision (or, if he has not yet left hospital, is to be so subject after he leaves hospital), the tribunal may in any case direct that the patient shall cease to be so subject (or not become so subject),

Mandatory discharge

and shall so direct if they are satisfied—

Patients not yet subject to after-care under supervision

(a) in a case where the patient has not yet left hospital, that the conditions set out in section 25A(4) above are not complied with; or

"25A(4). A supervision application may be made in respect of a patient only on the grounds that—

(a) he is suffering from mental disorder, being mental illness, severe mental impairment, psychopathic disorder or mental impairment;
(b) there would be a substantial risk of serious harm to the health or safety of the patient or the safety of other persons, or of the patient being seriously exploited, if he were not to receive the after-care services to be provided for him under section 117 below after he leaves hospital; and
(c) his being subject to after-care under supervision is likely to help to secure that he receives the after-care services to be so provided."

Patients subject to after-care under supervision

(b) in any other case, that the conditions set out in section 25G(4) above are not complied with.

"25G(4) The conditions [for renewal] referred to in subsection (3) above are that —

(a) the patient is suffering from mental disorder, being mental illness, severe mental impairment, psychopathic disorder or mental impairment;
(b) ; and there would be a substantial risk of serious harm to the health or safety of the patient or the safety of other persons, or of the patient being seriously exploited, if he were not to receive the after-care services provided for him under section 117 below
(c) his being subject to after-care under supervision is likely to help to secure that he receives the after-care services so provided."

Reclassification

(5) Where application is made to a Mental Health Review Tribunal under any provision of this Act by or in respect of a patient and the tribunal do not direct that ... if he is (or is to be) subject to after-care under supervision, that he cease to be so subject (or not become so subject), the tribunal may, if satisfied that the patient is suffering from a form of mental disorder other than the form specified in the application ... relating to him direct that that application ... be amended by substituting for the form of mental disorder specified in it such other form of mental disorder as appears to the tribunal to be appropriate.

References

(6) Subsections [(4A)] to (5) above apply in relation to references to a Mental Health Review Tribunal as they apply in relation to applications made to such a tribunal by or in respect of a patient.

WHEN PATIENT BECOMES SUBJECT TO SUPERVISION

By way of summary as to when a patient becomes subject to after-care under supervision—

- Where a supervision application is accepted, the patient is then "to be subject" to after-care under supervision "after he leaves hospital." For these purposes, a patient does not leave hospital, and so does not become subject to after-care under supervision, until he has *both* ceased to be liable to be detained for treatment (*i.e.* his liability to detention has been discharged or has lapsed) *and* has left hospital in the conventional sense that he has ceased to be an in-patient.

- By way of amplification, two situations will be commonly encountered. Firstly, a supervision application may be accepted in respect of a patient who is then discharged from detention under section 3 or 37 but who remains in hospital for a further period as an informal patient. He has not left hospital and does not become subject to after-care under supervision until he actually leaves hospital. Secondly, a supervision application may be accepted in respect of a patient who has leave to be absent from hospital or who is subsequently granted such leave. He has not left hospital for these purposes, and does not become subject to after-care under supervision, until such time as he also ceases to be liable to be detained for treatment. In both cases, the patient has not yet left hospital in the statutory sense and the tribunal criteria to be applied are those in section 72(4A)(a).

- In the case of patients who have not yet left hospital, no person or body other than a tribunal has power to "terminate" the supervision application.

THE MANDATORY CRITERIA

Where a patient is not yet subject to after-care under supervision, the tribunal must consider whether it is satisfied that, as matters now stand, a supervision application could not be made because it is satisfied that one or more of the three grounds for making such an application do not apply. In the case of patients who are subject to after-care under supervision, it must decide whether it is satisfied that one or more of the conditions which must exist before the authority for a patient's supervision can be renewed do not exist as matters presently stand.[63]

"Satisfied that the conditions are not complied with"

The use of the words "complied with" might at first sight seem to require a tribunal to review whether the conditions for making the supervision application, or for renewing it, were complied with at the time when the application was accepted or last renewed. That this is not so is clear if one considers the position of a patient who, having ceased to be liable to be detained, immediately returns home two

---

[63] If a tribunal applied the wrong criteria, it is arguable that the High Court might not set aside their decision solely on this ground because the criteria in section 25A(4) and 25G(4) are virtually identical. On the other hand, it might be said that the tribunal's grasp of the patient's legal position was so tenuous that it must be doubtful whether the decision it reached was correctly arrived at.

months after the supervision application's acceptance. Even though the authority conferred by the application has not yet been renewed, so that it is impossible for a tribunal to retrospectively consider whether there had been grounds for renewal, the discharge criteria to be applied by the tribunal are the renewal conditions set out in section 25G(4) — not the grounds in section 25A(4) upon which the application had been made. Thus, the tribunal is not reviewing whether the authority for the patient's current period of supervision was validly made or renewed. It must instead adopt the customary approach of looking at matters as they stand at the time of the hearing. The use of the phrase "are complied with," rather than "were complied with," in paragraphs (a) and (b) of section 72(4A) confirms this.

Supervised patients subsequently readmitted to hospital

Where a patient who is not receiving in-patient treatment ceases to be liable to be detained for treatment he thereupon becomes subject to after-care under supervision. If he is later readmitted to hospital as an informal patient, or under section 2 or 4, he nevertheless remains subject to after-care under supervision. However, he has still left hospital for the purposes of section 72(4A) and the criteria to be applied by a tribunal which then hears his case in hospital are the renewal conditions set out in section 72(4A)(b).

No requirement that disorder be of particular nature or degree

It suffices for the purposes of making or renewing a supervision application that the patient suffers from one of the four statutory forms of mental disorder. There is no requirement that this disorder be of a particular nature or degree.[64] This reflects the fact that supervised discharge principally focuses on the risks associated with a future exacerbation of the patient's mental state rather than the present nature or degree of any disorder. That being so, a "nature or degree" qualification is to some extent enshrined in the second of the supervision application grounds, albeit that the Act fastens on to the nature and degree of the potential risks rather than the nature or degree of the patient's disorder *per se*. Nevertheless, the first aspect (his potential for dangerous behaviour) is consequential upon the second (his mental state). See page 429.

Substantial risk of serious harm

The second condition requires the tribunal to consider the possible consequences if the patient does not receive the after-care services which are being provided, or will be provided, for him. Insofar as words can define anything, the test could not be more stringent. In terms of making a supervision application or renewing the authority, a risk of serious harm does not suffice unless that risk is a substantial one. Similarly, a substantial risk of harm does not suffice unless the harm will be serious and, in the case of persons other than the patient, it is their safety rather than merely their health which will be substantially at risk. Likewise, a tribunal must terminate the patient's liability to statutory supervision if it is satisfied that any risk of serious harm is insubstantial; or that any harm which is substantially likely does not amount to serious harm; or any serious harm to others would involve serious harm to their health rather than to their safety. The second ground is expressed as a future

---

[64]   As to whether a very mild disorder of mind can constitute mental illness for the purposes of section 72, see p.68.

conditional so that a supervision application may only be made where there will be a substantial risk of serious harm *if* the patient were not to receive the after-care services provided for him. In some cases, a substantial risk of suicide, or of serious harm to others, may exist regardless of whether the patient receives those services. In practice, the courts may take the view that if there will or may be a substantial risk of serious harm if the patient does not receive after-care, it is irrelevant that such a risk currently exists even though he is receiving after-care.

Likelihood of benefit from supervision

If there will or may be a substantial risk of serious harm should the patient not receive the proposed after-care services, the third condition requires consideration to be given to the practicalities of the situation — will providing those after-care services under formal supervision be likely to help to secure that the patient receives them and so reduce the substantial risk of serious harm which has been identified? As to the third ground and, in particular, the phrase "likely to help secure," see page 430 *et seq.*

DISCRETIONARY DISCHARGE

There are no matters which a tribunal must have regard to as a matter of law before determining whether to exercise its discretionary power of discharge.

RECLASSIFICATION

As to the power of reclassification conferred by section 72(5), see page 499. For two reasons, reclassification has no legal consequences in terms of the likelihood of renewal. Firstly, the renewal criteria are the same whatever the form of mental disorder which the patient suffers from. Secondly, whether or not a patient is suffering from a particular form of disorder at the time a renewal report is furnished is a matter for the patient's community responsible medical officer to determine; he is not bound by any previous reclassification (**057**).

8. A tribunal's powers in restricted cases

INTRODUCTION

This chapter deals with a tribunal's powers in respect of restricted patients. These patients comprise —

- Patients who are liable to be detained for treatment in pursuance of a **511** hospital order and a restriction order, under sections 37 and 41 or section 46.

- Patients who are liable to be detained for treatment in pursuance of a **555** transfer direction and a restriction direction, made under sections 47 and 49 or 48 and 49, or a hospital direction and a limitation direction imposed under section 45A.

- Patients who are subject to a restriction order or a restriction **560** direction but have been conditionally discharged from hospital by a tribunal or by the Secretary of State.

DETENTION SUBJECT TO A RESTRICTION ORDER

A tribunal's powers when dealing with the case of a patient who is liable to be detained in hospital and subject to a restriction order are set out in section 73 of the Act. Section 72 does not apply except insofar as the criteria for discharge set out in section 72(1)(b) are incorporated within section 73.[1]

SUMMARY OF POWERS

The essence of a restriction order is that the usual powers by which a patient who is liable to be detained for treatment in pursuance of a hospital order may be discharged or granted greater freedom are restricted. This principle extends to tribunals so that its usual powers either do not apply or only in a restricted way. The single superficial similarity is that a tribunal must discharge a patient who satisfies

[1]   Mental Health Act 1983, s.72(7); *Grant v. The Mental Health Review Tribunal for the Trent Region; R. v. The Mersey Mental Health Review Tribunal ex p. O'Hara, The Times*, 26 April 1986 **(549)**.

the same statutory criteria that apply to unrestricted patients who have been detained for treatment. However, "discharge" in this context means discharge from hospital, not merely discharge from liability to detention in hospital for the time being. The effect is that a tribunal may not discharge a restricted patient who requires further treatment in hospital.[2] That being so, although the same statutory discharge criteria set out in section 72(1)(b) apply to all patients who are liable to be detained for treatment, those criteria only apply to restricted patients in a restricted way. Furthermore, a tribunal has no discretionary power of discharge in restricted cases. It must discharge a patient whom it is satisfied meets the criteria for being discharged and not discharge a patient unless it is satisfied that is the case.[3] Where a patient is entitled to be discharged, the discharge may be absolute or subject to conditions.

Absolute discharge

Absolute discharge is mandatory if a tribunal is also satisfied that it is not appropriate for a patient whom it must discharge to be liable to be recalled to hospital for further treatment by the Secretary of State. Its effect is to bring both the hospital order and the attendant restriction order to an end. If a patient is entitled to be absolutely discharged, the tribunal's direction has immediate effect and it cannot direct that his absolute discharge take effect only on a specified future date.[4] A tribunal is not obliged to absolutely discharge a patient whom it must discharge merely because it is satisfied that he is not presently suffering from a form of mental disorder. The patient may relapse and later require recall to hospital for further treatment.[5] Nor, in the case of restriction orders imposed under the 1959 Act, is it obliged to absolutely discharge a patient whom it must discharge even though it is satisfied that the protection of the public does not require that he be subject to conditions of discharge and recall. Consequently, once a restriction order is in force, it is not inappropriate for a patient to be subject to recall for further treatment by the Secretary of State solely for therapeutic reasons associated with his own personal health and safety.[6]

---

2   See *Secretary of State for the Home Department v. Mental Health Review Tribunal for Mersey Regional Health Authority, Same v. Mental Health Review Tribunal for Wales* [1986] 1 W.L.R. 1170 (**516, 365**).

3   See *R. v. Oxford Regional Mental Health Review Tribunal, ex p. Secretary of State for the Home Department* [1988] 1 A.C. 120 (**544**). Although it is sometimes thought that limited term restriction orders are invariably of short duration, this is not the case. For example, restriction orders of 40 and 44 years' duration were imposed in the *R. v. Sowle* (*The Times*, 20th October 1960) and *R. v. Upchurch* (*The Times*, 25th March 1965). However, where a limited term restriction order has been imposed, a tribunal's powers, and the statutory criteria to be applied, are the same as in cases involving restriction orders made without limit of time. Similarly, because the statutory criteria are determinative, and because a restriction order is not a form of punishment, there can be no element of retribution or of a tariff operating in discharge decisions. As to this, the tribunal in *ex p. M.A.R.C.* (1989, unreported) conceded an application for judicial review because there was an element of retribution in its decision.

4   See Mental Health Act 1983, s.73(1) and (7). In *ex p. M.S.* (1991, unreported), the tribunal directed that absolute discharge be deferred for 12 months so that arrangements could be made for the patient's future care. Judicial review was granted by consent.

5   *R. v. Merseyside Mental Health Review Tribunal, ex p, K.,* 20 May 1988, Q.B.D. (unreported) (**527**); [1990] 1 All E.R. 694, C.A. (**529**). Such a patient must, however, be discharged: see Mental Health Act 1983, s.73(1). In *ex p. Gill* (CO/180/85, unreported), the tribunal found the patient not to be suffering from mental disorder but did not discharge him. By consent, its decision was quashed and the tribunal was ordered to consider and direct the patient's absolute or conditional discharge.

6   *R. v. North West Thames Mental Health Review Tribunal, ex p. Cooper* [1990] C.O.D. 275 (**530**).

Conditional discharge

Where a restriction order patient satisfies the criteria for mandatory discharge, but the tribunal is not also satisfied that it is inappropriate for him to remain liable to recall for further treatment, it must direct his conditional discharge. The effect of conditional discharge is that both orders remain in force and the patient must comply with any conditions imposed on his discharge. The conditions of discharge are initially a matter for the tribunal's discretion although the Secretary of State may later vary those conditions or impose further conditions. Common conditions include a condition of residence and further conditions that he be supervised by, and attend appointments with, a nominated psychiatrist and a supervising social worker or probation officer. If the patient later relapses, or fails to comply with the conditions of his discharge, or the public may be at risk from him, he may be recalled to hospital for further treatment by the Secretary of State.

Deferred conditional discharge

Provided satisfactory arrangements outside hospital are in place which enable the conditions imposed on a patient's discharge to be satisfied forthwith, the direction for his discharge takes effect forthwith and, as with absolute discharge, may not be postponed to a specified future date. However, where a patient is conditionally discharged, it may be impossible for the conditions imposed on his discharge to be satisfied immediately. For example, where it is a condition of discharge that he resides at a supervised hostel but no suitable place is available. The Act therefore provides that a tribunal may defer a direction for a patient's conditional discharge until such time as it is satisfied that suitable arrangements have been made which meet the conditions imposed — "deferred conditional discharge." The tribunal will reconsider the patient's case upon being notified that suitable arrangements have been made and, if satisfied with them, it may direct his discharge. If it transpires that arrangements cannot be made which allow the conditions attached to the patient's discharge to be satisfied, the fact that the tribunal has already determined the application means that it may not reconvene or reconsider its decision to discharge him on those conditions. The tribunal's direction for his discharge will eventually be deemed never to have been made.[7] A tribunal's power in restriction order cases to defer its direction for a patient's conditional discharge should not be confused with its power to direct the discharge of an unrestricted patient on a specified future date. In the latter case, the tribunal's direction discharging the patient is effective and complete the moment it is made: it is not provisional upon future events.

Duty to determine suitability for discharge if sufficient information available

Provided a tribunal has sufficient information to determine the patient's current suitability for discharge, it must determine whether or not it is satisfied that he is presently entitled to be discharged. It may not adjourn the hearing to see if his condition improves, with a view to discharge at a later reconvened hearing.[8] Nor can it defer a direction that a patient be conditionally discharged in the expectation or hope that he will be suitable for discharge by the time the conditions can be met.

---

[7]   Mental Health Act 1983, s.73(7).
[8]   *R. v. Nottingham Mental Health Review Tribunal, ex p. Secretary of State for the Home Department; R. v. Northern Mental Health Review Tribunal, ex p. Secretary of State for the Home Department, The Times*, 25 March 1987, Q.B.D.; *The Times*, 15 September 1988, C.A. (**818**)

Tribunal's powers short of directing discharge

It has been noted that a tribunal is obliged to discharge a patient subject to a restriction order if satisfied that the criteria for mandatory discharge exist. Furthermore, if it is not satisfied that the patient is entitled to be discharged, it may not discharge him, for it has no discretionary power of discharge. Further still, a tribunal which does not discharge such a patient from hospital has no power to make recommendations of the kind it may make in unrestricted cases.[9] Specifically, it cannot, with a view to facilitating his discharge on a future date, recommend that he is granted leave to be absent from hospital, or transferred to a different hospital or into guardianship — nor, necessarily, if it makes such a recommendation in error may it further consider his case if that recommendation is not complied with. It is unlikely that a tribunal has any power to reclassify a restricted patient (**551**).

RESTRICTION ORDER PATIENTS LIABLE TO BE DETAINED

Mandatory absolute discharge

73.—(1) Where an application to a Mental Health Review Tribunal is made by a restricted patient who is subject to a restriction order. or where the case of such a patient is referred to such a tribunal, the tribunal shall direct the absolute discharge of the patient if satisfied—

[(a)(i) that he is not then suffering from mental illness, psychopathic disorder, severe mental impairment or mental impairment or from any of those forms of disorder of a nature or degree which makes it appropriate for him to be liable to be detained in a hospital for medical treatment; or

(ii) that it is not necessary for the health or safety of the patient or for the protection of other persons that he should receive such treatment;] and

(b) that it is not appropriate for the patient to remain liable to be recalled to hospital for further treatment.

Mandatory conditional discharge

(2) Where ... the tribunal are satisfied as to the matters referred to in paragraph (a) [above] but not as to the matter referred to in paragraph (b) ... the tribunal shall direct the conditional discharge of the patient.

Deferred conditional discharge

(7) A tribunal may defer a direction for the conditional discharge of a patient until such arrangements as appear to the tribunal to be necessary for that purpose have been made to their satisfaction; and where by virtue of any such deferment no direction has been given on an application or reference before the time when the patient's case comes before the tribunal on a subsequent application or reference, the previous application or reference shall be treated as one on which no direction under this section can be given.

---

[9] *Grant v. The Mental Health Review Tribunal for the Trent Region; The Queen v. The Mersey Mental Health Review Tribunal ex p. O'Hara, The Times*, 26 April 1986 (**549**).

TERMINOLOGY

For the meaning of the words used in the admission and discharge criteria, see—"discharge" (515); "patient" (098); "detention" (215); "detained" and "liable to be detained" (487); "satisfied" (567); "then" (466); "suffering from" (213); "mental illness" (060); "psychopathic disorder" (082); "severe mental impairment" (070); "mental impairment" (070); "nature or degree" (213); "appropriate" (490); "hospital" (131); "medical treatment" (216); "necessary" (221, 485); "health" (217); "safety" (218); "protection of other persons" (219); "recall" (345, 768); "absolute discharge" and "conditional discharge" (340). For a short summary of the meaning of many of these terms, see page 484.

THE CRITERIA FOR MANDATORY DISCHARGE

Section 72(1)(b)(i) requires a tribunal to discharge a patient who is liable to be detained for treatment if satisfied that he is not then suffering from a form of mental disorder "of a nature or degree which makes it appropriate for him to be liable to be detained in a hospital for medical treatment." Section 72(1)(b)(ii) requires a tribunal to discharge such a patient if satisfied that it is not necessary for his health or safety or for the protection of others that he should receive such treatment.

The meaning of "discharge" in unrestricted cases

The effect of these provisions in unrestricted cases is that a tribunal must terminate a patient's liability to detention in hospital if it is satisfied that it is either not necessary for his health or safety or to protect others that he receives further in-patient treatment or it is satisfied that it is no longer appropriate for him to be liable to be detained there for treatment (485 et seq.). Discharge in this context therefore means "discharge from liability to detention" rather than "discharge from hospital." Because the Act provides that the same criteria for discharge shall apply to restricted patients who are liable to be detained for treatment, without any qualification or amendment, it might be thought that Parliament intended that they would be entitled to be discharged in identical circumstances. However, this is not the case for the reasons given below.

The meaning of "discharge" in restricted cases

Section 73(7) provides that a tribunal "may defer a direction for the conditional discharge of a patient until such arrangements as appear to the tribunal to be necessary for that purpose have been made to their satisfaction." Section 73(4) further provides that a patient who has been conditionally discharged by a tribunal may be "recalled" by the Secretary of State under section 42(3). Section 42(3) is more specific still and it states that the Secretary of State may "by warrant recall the patient to such hospital as may be specified in the warrant." Where a patient is subsequently recalled, section 75(1) requires the Secretary of State to refer his case to a tribunal. Sections 42 and 75 distinguish between discharge from hospital and a termination of the restrictions. As can be seen, these provisions specific to restricted patients imply that discharge in their case does actually entail discharge from hospital. If so, the provisions are at least superficially at variance with the criteria for mandatory discharge: those criteria oblige a tribunal to discharge a patient if satisfied that it is not appropriate for him to be liable to be detained in a hospital for medical treatment. In

515

unrestricted cases, continued liability to detention has always been considered inappropriate where the patient is both reliable and willing to receive any necessary in-patient treatment informally and without compulsion. This apparent contradiction was considered by the Divisional Court in the following case.

Secretary of State for the Home Department v. Mental Health Review Tribunal for Mersey Regional Health Authority Same v. Mental Health Review Tribunal for Wales

[1986] 1 W.L.R. 1170   *Q.B.D., Mann J.*

Secretary of State for The Home Department v. Mental Health Tribunal for Wales

The patient was detained in Ely Hospital in pursuance of a hospital order together with a restriction order made without limitation of time. His case was reviewed by a Mental Health Review Tribunal on 21 December 1983. Section 72(1)(b)(i) requires a tribunal to discharge a restricted patient whom it is satisfied is not suffering from a form of mental disorder "of a nature or degree which makes it appropriate for him to be liable to be detained in a hospital for medical treatment." The tribunal was satisfied that the patient was suffering from severe mental impairment of a degree which made it appropriate that he should continue to receive treatment in the form of rehabilitation, supervision and guidance as to personal hygiene, and training in elementary social skills. However, the patient was entitled to be conditionally discharged because—

a. the supervision, guidance and rehabilitation which the patient required could be given in a hostel or other suitable community provision — it did not necessarily have to be given by nursing or medical staff, or under medical supervision and, in the tribunal's opinion, thus did not constitute "medical treatment" as defined by section 145(1); and

b. it was appropriate that the patient should remain liable to be recalled to hospital for further treatment.

There were no suitable residential placements available which would provide the sort of supervision and rehabilitation treatment which the patient needed. Since it was necessary that the patient reside in some place where he could be supervised, and he could not in common humanity be turned out of the hospital which had been his home for over 21 years without some alternative placement being available, the tribunal directed that he be conditionally discharged subject to a condition of residence at Ely Hospital. Should a suitable hostel become available, the Secretary of State could vary the condition of residence imposed by the tribunal.

Mann J.

Mann J. held as follows—

a. As defined by section 145(1), the expression "medical treatment" includes "nursing, and also includes care, habilation and rehabilitation under medical supervision ..." The tribunal had misdirected itself in holding that the treatment which the patient required (supervision and guidance as to personal hygiene, and rehabilitation in training in elementary social skills) did not constitute medical treatment as defined.

b. Given that the patient required "medical treatment," and given the tribunal's finding that it was appropriate to impose a condition that he reside in hospital, it could not by definition have been satisfied under section 72(1)(b)(i) that his mental disorder was not of a nature or degree which made it appropriate for him to be liable to be detained in a hospital for medical treatment. There was an obvious inconsistency between (a) a tribunal being satisfied that the patient's condition no longer made it appropriate for him to be liable to be detained in a hospital for medical treatment and (b) its imposition of a condition that he continue to reside in hospital.

c. The word "discharge" in sections 72 to 75 could only mean release from hospital, a release which could be absolute or conditional. It was therefore not possible to discharge a patient from hospital subject to a condition that he reside in a hospital. Section 73(4)(a), with its reference to "recall" strongly supported the inconsistency of such a condition with the concept of discharge.

Secretary of State for the Home Department v. Mental Health Review Tribunal for Mersey Regional Health Authority

The patient was detained in a special hospital under a hospital order with a restriction order attached, the form of mental disorder recorded being psychopathic disorder. The tribunal stated that it was satisfied as to the statutory criteria for discharge in both section 72(1)(b)(i) and (ii). However, on the facts, it was satisfied that the patient would be unable to cope if discharged from a special hospital directly into the community. He first needed to spend a period of time in a local hospital, namely Winwick Hospital. The tribunal directed that the patient be discharged on condition that he accept psychiatric and social services supervision for two years. It deferred its direction for his discharge until arrangements had been made for the patient's admission to Winwick Hospital "with a view to his subsequent discharge to a local hostel or to his home."

Mann J.

Mann J. held as follows—

a. Section 73(7) provides that a tribunal "may defer a direction for the conditional discharge of a patient until such arrangements as appear to the tribunal to be necessary for that purpose have been made to their satisfaction." The word "discharge" means release from hospital and the statutory purpose of deferral is to enable "arrangements" for the patient's *discharge* from hospital to be made. In this case, the tribunal deferred the patient's "discharge" until arrangements had been made for his admission to another hospital rather than for his discharge from hospital. Once the arrangements had been made the period for which the patient's discharge from hospital was deferred came to an end. However, those arrangements, being for his admission to another hospital, ensured not his discharge from hospital but his continued detention in hospital. Thus, although the tribunal's direction purported to discharge the patient from hospital, the arrangements to be made were inconsistent with the direction that he be discharged.

517

b. The fact that the tribunal was satisfied that the patient's condition was such that he required a further period of medical treatment in hospital before discharge was appropriate was inconsistent with its purported finding that the statutory criteria for discharge from hospital were satisfied.

Commentary

It seems clear that the tribunal in *Secretary of State for the Home Department v. Mental Health Review Tribunal for Mersey Regional Health Authority* was not satisfied that the patient met the criteria for being discharged. It was merely satisfied that his condition was no longer such that medical treatment in a special hospital was necessary. Accordingly, he should be transferred to a less secure hospital "with a view to his subsequent discharge to a local hostel or to his home." Because a tribunal which does discharge a restricted patient has no power to direct or recommend his transfer to another hospital, with a view to facilitating his discharge in the future, it in effect attempted to use the power to defer conditional discharge under section 73(7) as a mechanism for effecting the patient's transfer. The decision in *Secretary of State for The Home Department v. Mental Health Tribunal for Wales* is more problematic. The tribunal was found to have misdirected itself both as to what constituted medical treatment and in thinking that it could impose as a condition of discharge a condition of residence in hospital. The other question of law stated for the court's determination was whether, given that the treatment which the patient required was medical treatment,

> "the tribunal could have been satisfied under section 72(1)(b)(i) ..., on the facts found by it, that the patient's mental disorder was not of a nature or degree which made it appropriate for him to be liable to be detained in a hospital for medical treatment when at the same time it decided that it was appropriate for him to remain in hospital as the condition of his discharge."

The court answered that question "no." However, to say that because the tribunal imposed a condition of hospital residence, and found that the patient required medical treatment, therefore it could not have been satisfied that it was no longer appropriate for him to be *liable to be detained* in a hospital for medical treatment is, arguably, looking at the matter the wrong way round. The tribunal's finding was essentially that the patient could be discharged to a suitable hostel if one was available and liability to detention in a hospital was not appropriate. Faced with the unavailability of suitable accomodation, the appropriate course was to direct the patient's discharge subject to a condition of residence at a suitable hostel and to then defer its direction until satisfactory arrangements could be made. However, faced with this problem that suitable accomodation was not immediately available, and considering that the patient could not in common humanity be turned out of hospital, the tribunal instead directed his immediate conditional discharge, subject to a condition of residence in hospital. It did this with a view to the Home Secretary later varying that condition if a suitable place became available. In other words, the inconsistency lay not in the finding that the discharge criteria were satisfied — the tribunal was entitled to find that medical treatment in a hospital was no longer *necessary*[10] — but in the fact that, having come to that finding, it considered it

---

[10]   See *R. v. Oxford Regional M.H.R.T., ex p. Secretary of State for the Home Department* [1988] 1 A.C. 120, *per* Lord Bridge: "The tribunal may perfectly properly be satisfied that hospital detention is no longer necessary provided that the patient can be placed in a suitable hostel ... These are matters to be secured by imposing appropriate conditions."

necessary to discharge forthwith and, in the absence of alternative arrangements, to impose a temporary condition of residence in hospital. In short, the imposition of a condition of hospital residence may have been an error but it was not evidence that the patient's mental state made residence in hospital appropriate or necessary, only unavoidable until suitable arrangements for his discharge could be made.

Applying the section 72(1)(b) criteria in restricted cases

The legislation is unsatisfactory insofar as a natural reading of the discharge criteria appears to oblige a tribunal to "discharge" a patient if his mental condition is no longer of a nature or degree which makes it appropriate for him to be "liable to be detained" in a hospital for medical treatment — including therefore persons for whom further in-patient treatment, but not compulsory in-patient treatment, is appropriate. It might be thought that if "discharge" means "discharge from hospital" then a tribunal has no option but to discharge from hospital a patient who no longer requires detention there notwithstanding that informal in-patient treatment is more appropriate than medical treatment in the community. However, Mann J. came to the opposite conclusion, namely that a tribunal which discharged a restricted patient subject to a condition that he resides in hospital could not have been satisfied that the criteria for discharge were made out. One view is that this involves rewriting section 72(1)(b)(i) so that the words "liable to be detained" are omitted and a duty to discharge arises only if a tribunal are satisfied that an in-patient is not suffering from a disorder "of a nature or degree which makes it appropriate for him to be ... in a hospital for medical treatment." Since the second ground for discharge is that it is not necessary for the patient's health or safety or for the protection of others that he receives such treatment, the difference between the two grounds becomes rather indistinct. For patients already no longer in hospital, because they have been granted leave of absence, the criteria in section 72(1)(b) are presumably to be given their natural and literal meaning, in which case "discharge" means discharge both from hospital and from liability to detention for the time being. The effect of the decision is, at any rate, that a restricted patient who requires further in-patient treatment, or a trial period of leave before being discharged from hospital, is suffering from a mental disorder of a nature or degree which makes it appropriate for him to be "liable to be detained" for treatment. Having regard to the *Mersey case*, it would seem that section 72(1)(b) must be construed in restricted cases in the following way—

- *A tribunal must discharge a restricted patient if it is satisfied that it is not necessary for his health or safety or to protect others that he should receive further in-patient treatment.*

If the patient is temporarily absent from hospital on trial leave, a tribunal may not discharge him unless it is satisfied that the period of in-patient treatment which began when he was admitted to hospital, or most recently recalled, has been completed. In other words, further treatment in hospital is unnecessary in this sense.[†] Similarly, a tribunal which considers that an in-patient requires a period of trial leave before it can be satisfied that further treatment in hospital is unnecessary may not discharge him.

- *A tribunal must discharge a restricted patient if it is satisfied that he is not then suffering from a form of mental disorder the nature or degree of which makes it appropriate for him to be liable to be detained in a hospital for medical treatment.*

If an in-patient requires further treatment in hospital, a tribunal cannot be satisfied that it is inappropriate for him to be detained for that purpose — quaere whether the statute therefore requires that restricted in-patients are detained and subject to those restrictions. If the patient is not in hospital because he is on trial leave, it may be too early to say whether or not it is appropriate for him to remain liable to be detained in the hospital for further treatment there.

The common theme is therefore whether the period of in-patient treatment brought about by the patient's admission or recall to hospital has been completed.

† *It cannot be the case that the tribunal is being asked to consider whether it is satisfied that further treatment in hospital for the target condition will never be necessary, i.e. that the patient is cured.*

Reconciling the apparent contradictions

Various explanations may be advanced in an attempt to reconcile any apparent contradictions in the drafting:

1.) The statutory framework is such that if a restricted patient requires treatment in hospital he must necessarily be subject to restrictions on leaving that hospital, transfer, discharge, etc.

2.) The *Mersey case* was wrongly decided, having regard to the decisions in *ex p. D.* and *ex p. Stewart*. "Discharge" means discharge from liability to detention in pursuance of the relevant hospital and restriction orders. Accordingly, there is nothing to prevent a tribunal from discharging a restricted patient subject to a condition of residence in hospital and, if no (or no alternative) condition of residence is imposed, the patient may reside in hospital informally. Similarly, the law does not prevent a patient who does leave hospital from being readmitted informally or under Part II.

3.) Although "discharge" means discharge from hospital, and neither the Home Secretary nor a tribunal may discharge a patient from hospital on the basis that he remains in hospital, the Home Secretary has a discretion as to whether or not to recall to hospital a discharged patient who requires treatment there, even one sufficiently ill to require detention there.

First interpretation: restricted in-patient must always be restricted

Until the decisions in *ex p. D.* and *ex p. Stewart* (**355 et seq.**), the decision in the *Mersey case* was most satisfactorily explained by holding that the matter turned on the statutory framework for restricted patients and, more particularly, the fact that the absolute-conditional discharge regime was in force before tribunals ever acquired a power to discharge such patients. They remained liable to be detained in hospital until such time as the Secretary of State considered it appropriate to discharge them or to consent to their discharge. If they merely had leave to be absent from hospital and were in the community on a trial basis, they had not been discharged from hospital. Whatever the hospital records might show, they remained in-patients on trial leave. When tribunals then also acquired a power to discharge such patients, it was unfortunate that the discharge criteria used for ordinary hospital order patients, and other unrestricted patients detained for treatment, were adopted without any sort of qualification. This appeared to put restricted patients on exactly the same footing in terms of their entitlement to be discharged when this was not in fact the case. As Part III of the Act and section 73 made clear, restricted patients always remained liable to be detained in hospital until formally discharged from there. Their status could only be one of two things — (1) that of an in-patient liable to be detained and subject to restrictions on discharge; (2) that of a patient in the community following discharge who was subject to conditions and recall. The usual third possibility in unrestricted cases of being an informal in-patient, or a patient detained without restrictions, was not an option. If a restricted patient's mental state was sufficiently unstable for him to need to be in hospital he could not leave that hospital without the Secretary of State's consent. Whether he could have leave to be absent from there, or be transferred to a less secure hospital, or be discharged, were not decisions which could ever be made by his consultant or by the hospital's managers acting alone. The terminology in section 72(1)(b) had to be understood in the context of this framework. Unless a tribunal was satisfied that it was unnecessary for an in-patient to receive further treatment in hospital, it could not by definition be satisfied that it was appropriate for him not to be detained there — the statutory framework being such that all restricted in-patients are necessarily detained and subject to special restrictions on being granted leave, transferred, or discharged. Thus, a consequence of the original court's finding that hospital treatment under special restrictions was necessary to protect the public from serious harm was that a tribunal had no jurisdiction in relation to the patient's legal status during any period for which in-patient treatment was or might be necessary. Its powers were limited to determining his suitability to be discharged from hospital. While the Secretary of State could direct that a restricted in-patient cease to be subject to the restrictions, so enabling him to receive informal treatment there, a tribunal did not have this option. From this, it could be inferred that Parliament intended that the functions of tribunals should be confined to determining whether the patient was actually suitable for discharge.

Second interpretation: Mersey case wrongly decided

An alternative explanation is that the decision in the *Mersey case* is wrong, having regard to the subsequent Court of Appeal decisions in *ex p. D.* (355) and *ex p. Stewart* (356). If it is correct — and one is presently bound to take this view — that (1) the purpose of the power of recall is to reintroduce the restrictions, (2) a restricted patient may be recalled to a hospital within which he is already detained or residing informally, and (3) a restricted patient may lawfully be both in hospital and conditionally discharged from hospital, then it must also be the case that (4) a tribunal may conditionally discharge a patient who, although requiring further in-patient treatment, does not presently need to be detained in the hospital in pursuance of the relevant hospital order and associated restrictions. Using the language adopted in *ex p. Stewart*, where a tribunal discharges a patient from his present liability to detention in pursuance of the relevant hospital order (to which the restrictions attach), he is thereby discharged from liability to detention there *qua* restricted patient. That does not prevent him from remaining there informally or in accordance with any condition of residence imposed by the tribunal, nor, where necessary, in pursuance of an application made under Part II at some later time.

Third interpretation: Home Secretary's discretion

The counter-argument to the position just advanced is that neither the Home Secretary nor a tribunal have a discretion to discharge a patient who requires further in-patient treatment but the Home Secretary does have a discretion not to recall to hospital a discharged patient who requires further in-patient treatment. This seems to be the effect of the case law and, if so, one is presently bound to hold that this is the correct interpretation. Perhaps the best way of reconciling the three cases is as follows. The fact that the Home Secretary may not discharge a restricted patient on the basis that he remains in hospital does not affect the fact that who is discharged and who is recalled is *otherwise* a matter for his discretion: he need not discharge a patient whom he could legally discharge, or who a tribunal would be bound to discharge, and need not recall a patient whom he could legally recall. However, tribunals have no discretion and, in their case, the decision in the *Mersey case* is the only one of the three that is relevant. The third interpretation does produce the anomaly that that the Home Secretary may not "discharge from hospital" a patient who needs to be in hospital but need not "recall to hospital" a patient who needs to be in hospital.

Whether further treatment in hospital is necessary or appropriate

Although the statutory test in restricted cases is essentially whether the patient's condition makes a further period of treatment in a hospital unnecessary or inappropriate, whether treatment in hospital remains necessary, and whether liability to detention for treatment remains appropriate, is not uncommonly relative. The determining factor is often whether safe alternative arrangements can be made for the patient's supervision, management and treatment outside hospital. Thus, Lord Bridge said in the leading case on tribunals that their "satisfaction or lack of satisfaction as to ... the paragraph (b) matters will ... inevitably be coloured by the conditions they have in mind to impose. Thus the answers to the questions ... may be vitally influenced by the conditions which are to be imposed to regulate his life style upon release into the community ... the tribunal may perfectly properly be satisfied that hospital detention is no longer necessary provided that the patient can be placed in a suitable hostel and required to submit to treatment as an out-patient by a suitable psychiatrist. These are matters to be secured by imposing appropriate conditions ..."[11]

The importance of the statutory definition of a hospital

Whether the patient's condition makes further treatment in a hospital appropriate, and whether in-patient treatment is necessary for his health or safety or to protect

---

[11]   *R. v. Oxford Regional Mental Health Review Tribunal, ex p. Secretary of State for the Home Department* [1988] 1 A.C. 120, *per* Lord Bridge.

others, must also be understood in the context of the statutory definition of a hospital.[12] This definition is a broad one (131) and it includes mental nursing homes which are registered to receive detained patients. It also includes community-based facilities attached to the main hospital (137). These outlying units are often referred to as hospital hostels or as community wards. Consequently, if a tribunal believes that the appropriate next step is for the patient to reside in such a facility, that amounts to a finding that further in-patient treatment remains necessary and appropriate. Even if the unit is several miles from the main hospital and has the outward appearance of not being part of a hospital, the tribunal may not discharge the patient on condition that he resides there. It is therefore crucially important to verify the legal status of any hostel-type place being proposed.

The importance of the statutory definition of medical treatment

Just as the statutory definition of a hospital is a broad one, so too is that given to the term "medical treatment" (216). The definition includes nursing and care so that, for legal purposes, all in-patients are necessarily receiving medical treatment. This makes it impossible to successfully judicially review a tribunal decision on the basis that the patient was merely being detained in hospital and there was no evidence that it was necessary that he should receive further treatment in hospital. The point usually arises in cases where an in-patient classified as having a psychopathic disorder is not receiving any medical treatment in the form of medication or psychotherapy. Adopting the statutory phraseology, if the need to protect others means that he requires nursing care in secure conditions, it cannot be said that there was no evidence before the tribunal that it was appropriate for him to remain liable to detention in hospital *for medical treatment* and that *such treatment* is necessary to protect others. The point arose in the case of *ex p. Ryan*.

R. v. South East Thames Mental Health Review Tribunal, ex p. Ryan

CO/98/87, 30 June 1987   *Q.B.D., Watkins L.J. and Mann J.*

In June 1970, the patient was convicted at the Central Criminal Court of arson He was found to be suffering from a psychopathic disorder and the court directed his admission to a special hospital in pursuance of a hospital order with a restriction order attached. The patient was detained in a local hospital when a tribunal reviewed his case in 1986. The tribunal found that although he had not recently been a management problem in the structured environment of the hospital his behaviour continued to be unpredictable. He had very little insight into his own condition and was liable to react impulsively when frustrated. Before any discharge could be contemplated, a period of trial leave in a suitably supervised hostel needed to be considered. The tribunal concluded that the patient "continues to suffer from psychopathic disorder of such a nature and degree which makes it appropriate for him to be liable to be detained in a hospital for medical treatment which is necessary for his own health and safety and the protection of other persons." The patient applied for judicial review of the tribunal's decision not to discharge him. He submitted that although he was receiving care in hospital he was not receiving any medical treatment. By implication, it could not be the case that it was necessary for him to be in hospital for treatment or that it was appropriate to detain him for that purpose.

---

[12]   Unless the context otherwise requires, the definition of a hospital given in section 34(2) applies for the purposes of tribunal proceedings: Mental Health Act 1983, s.79(6).

Watkins L.J.

The question for the tribunal was whether the applicant was still suffering from a psychopathic disorder the nature or degree of which made it appropriate for him to continue to be liable to be detained. The challenge to the decision rested on the basis that it was arrived at without the requisite evidence being available to the tribunal. The Tribunal consisted of, among others, a consultant psychiatrist. It was therefore well equipped to reach the conclusion that the patient still needed to be kept in a hospital for the benefit of himself and for the protection of the public and that he was in need of treatment as defined in section 145.

Medical treatment

It had been submitted that the tribunal had misdirected itself in considering the definition of "medical treatment" in section 145. The court was referred to *Minister of Health v. Royal Midland Counties Home for Incurables, Leamington Spa, General Committee* (1954) 2 W.L.R. 755, and to words used by Lord Evershed, M.R. at page 760 as to the definition of the word "treatment." It was, however, to be noted that Denning L.J. at page 165 said of that word:

> "The key to the legal position lies in the fact that the Act draws a sharp distinction between 'treatment ' and 'care '..... If an institution is provided for the reception and 'treatment' of incurables, it is a hospital and is to be taken over by the State; but if it is provided only for the reception and 'care' of them it is not. Where is the line, then, to be drawn in this regard between 'treatment' and 'care'? Neither is defined in the Act, but 'treatment' means, I think, the exercise of professional skill to remedy the disease or disability, or to lessen its ill effects or the pain and suffering which it occasions; whereas 'care' is the homely art of making people comfortable and providing for their well-being so far as their condition allows. 'Nursing', too, is not defined, but it covers, I think, both treatment and care."

That seemed admirably to explain the meaning of those different words, in the context of the Act in which they appeared and which the court in that case was considering. It was, however, of no assistance in the present case, notably because in section 145 Parliament has deliberately provided that treatment and care shall not be different but that treatment shall include care, nursing, habilitation and rehabilitation under medical supervision. As defined, the patient unhappily still needed to be kept and cared for in the setting of a mental hospital. *Application dismissed.*

Patients whose conditions are untreatable

In unrestricted cases, the treatability of the patient's condition and whether he would be vulnerable if discharged are matters relevant to the renewal criteria and the exercise of a tribunal's discretionary power of discharge. When it comes to restricted cases, the authority for their detention never requires periodic renewal and may never lapse, whether because their conditions prove to be untreatable or for any other reason. Furthermore, a tribunal has no discretionary power of discharge. Consequently, the fact that a restricted patient who is not vulnerable is untreatable has no legal effect on the exercise of its discharge power. If the nature of the patient's disorder is such that further medical treatment in a hospital is both appropriate and necessary in order to protect other people, because nursing in secure conditions prevents him from harming them, he may not be discharged even though

524

that treatment is neither alleviating his condition nor preventing its deterioration. It is at least alleviating the consequences of his deteriorating condition. The application of the discharge criteria in relation to restricted patients who are being detained for treatment, but whose conditions are untreatable, was considered in *ex p. D*. The case covers some of the same ground as *ex p. Ryan*. However, in addition, the tribunal was of the opinion that the patient's treatment in a special hospital was neither alleviating nor preventing a deterioration of his condition. Since treatment in hospital was wholly ineffective, the issue was raised of whether it had been open to the tribunal to find, firstly, that it was nevertheless appropriate for him to be detained there for treatment and, secondly, that such treatment was necessary for his health or safety or to protect others.

R. v. Mersey Mental Health Review Tribunal, ex p. D

The Times, 13 April 1987   *Q.B.D., Russell L.J. and Otton J.*

D. had been detained in a number of special hospitals since 1939, following a finding that he was insane in relation to a charge of murder. During the first ten years in hospital he was involved in some aggressive incidents but these had no sexual connotation. Much later, in 1969, it was reported that he had been involved in sexual acts with men of "infantile mentality" involving a measure of violence on his part. On two occasions he had placed his hands around the throats of his partners, causing one of them to become unconscious. The patient admitted to being attracted to young boys and, in March 1984, was found to have a photograph of a boy wearing swimming trunks in his possession. D. himself did not wish to be discharged from the hospital where he was detained.

The patient's case was considered by the Mersey Mental Health Review Tribunal on 1 August 1986. The tribunal heard evidence from the responsible medical officer and a psychologist both of whom were of the opinion that he no longer suffered from a psychopathic disorder. Notwithstanding this evidence, the tribunal stated that it was satisfied that the patient was suffering from a psychopathic disorder of a nature or degree which made it appropriate that he remain liable to be detained in a hospital for medical treatment. Furthermore, although such treatment would neither alleviate nor prevent a deterioration of his condition, it was necessary for his own health or safety or for the protection of others.

The tribunal's decision finished with a passage under the heading "Other comments." In this the tribunal stated that it sympathised with those responsible for the patient's care in that they found themselves unable to adopt any form of treatment other than containment in conditions of high security. However, the index offence and the patient's subsequent conduct had led the tribunal to the conclusion that "such containment was the only course open in the case of one from whom the community needs to be protected." The patient applied for judicial review of the tribunal's decision.

Russell L.J.

The tribunal included a psychiatrist. Having listened to the evidence, it had the task of making its own assessment of it. It did not accept the views of the responsible medical officer and psychologist. Given the patient's behaviour between January 1969 and July 1971, and the discovery of the photograph as recently as 1984, he could not be described as suffering only from a tendency towards sexual deviation (**089**). The patient's counsel had realistically conceded that this finding was open to it. It had then been submitted that the tribunal's "other comments" indicated that it had misdirected itself concerning the discharge criteria set out in section 72(1)(b)(i). That passage, it was said, did not make it plain that the tribunal had had proper regard to the question of medical treatment. It gave the impression that the tribunal considered that the patient's continued detention was appropriate simply because, having regard to the history, he ought to be contained in conditions of high security. The test was, however, whether it was appropriate for him to be liable to be detained there for medical treatment. As to this submission, medical treatment as defined in section 145(1) included nursing and care under medical supervision. The Act did not require the patient's discharge simply because such treatment was not likely to alleviate or prevent a deterioration of his condition. Although it was unfortunate that the tribunal's other comments were phrased in the way that they were, there was no evidence that the tribunal had misdirected itself.

Otton J.

The tribunal's "other comments" had to be seen in context. They did not go to the heart of the tribunal's decision nor form any part of it. They were not used by way of explanation or enlargement of the decision but simply in recognition of the difficulty which the patient's case presented for the hospital authorities. When using the expression "containment in conditions of high security," the tribunal would inevitably have known that this meant containment in a special hospital which would provide medical treatment within section 145(1) of the 1983 Act. *Application dismissed.*

WHEN A PATIENT MUST BE ABSOLUTELY DISCHARGED

If a patient is entitled to be discharged, a tribunal must absolutely discharge him if it is also satisfied that "it is not appropriate for the patient to remain liable to be recalled to hospital for further treatment." As to this obligation, the courts have held that a tribunal is not obliged to absolutely discharge a patient whom it must discharge simply because it is satisfied that he is not presently suffering from any form of mental disorder: *R. v. Merseyside Mental Health Review Tribunal, ex p. K.* (527). Nor, even though the sole statutory purpose of the restriction order regime and of the Secretary of State's involvement is to protect the public from serious harm, is it obliged to absolutely discharge a patient whom it is satisfied has never posed a risk of serious harm to the public and who, if he relapsed, would not pose such a risk. Notwithstanding that the restrictions and the Secretary of State's involvement are designed to ensure that the public are protected from such harm, it is not inappropriate or unlawful for him to remain liable to recall by the Secretary of State for therapeutic reasons associated only with his own personal health and safety: *R. v. North West Thames Mental Health Review Tribunal, ex p. Cooper* (529).

Ex p. K.

In ex p. K, the patient raised the technical argument that because the tribunal had been satisfied that he was not then suffering from mental disorder, he was not a patient within the meaning of the Act, and the Act no longer applied to him. Since he was no longer a patient, he could not be a conditionally discharged patient and so was entitled to be absolutely discharged.

CO/532/88, 20 May 1988   *Q.B.D., Parker L.J. and Simon Brown J.*

In January 1971, the patient was convicted of the manslaughter of a neighbour's 12-year-old daughter. Her condition when found indicated that she had been raped, asphyxiated, cut with a sharp instrument and bitten. The patient had been before the courts on 11 previous occasions and had previous convictions for rape, indecently assaulting a girl aged seven, and having sexual intercourse with a girl aged between 13 and 16. He had only been out of prison for some six weeks before committing the index offence. The court was satisfied that he was suffering from a psychopathic disorder and it directed his admission to a special hospital in pursuance of a hospital order and a restriction order made without limit of time. In March 1985, a tribunal reviewed his case. A special hospital consultant gave evidence that in his opinion the patient was not a danger to himself or others and the chief psychologist there said that he was now functioning at a normal level. An experienced nursing officer well acquainted with the patient said that he would "welcome him as a next door neighbour." Given the unanimous medical evidence that the patient was not presently suffering from any form of mental disorder, but taking the view that it was appropriate for him to remain liable to recall, the tribunal conditionally discharged him from hospital.

In October 1985, some seven months after being discharged, the patient made an unprovoked attack on a girl of 16 whom he saw walking along a road in the afternoon. He put both hands round her throat and applied some pressure but she managed to run off. The next night, at about 11.30 pm, he attacked a young woman of 21. After speaking to her, he held her neck in an arm lock and put his hand over her mouth, pulling her into an entry and then pushing her to a crouching position. She pretended to weaken and, as he began to let her go, she screamed and he ran off. On being interviewed, the patient said only that he did not know why he had done this. A sexual motive for each assault was suspected but could not be proved. The patient's supervising psychiatrist and probation officer had not been aware of any signs of the impending violence. Subsequently, in April 1986, the patient pleaded guilty in each case to assault occasioning actual bodily harm. He was described in court by his leading counsel as "so disturbed mentally that he cannot control the impulses from which he suffers." A special hospital medical report concluded that he had a severe personality disorder, probably with some psycho-sexual involvement, and an alcohol problem. However, this could not be equated with a psychopathic disorder which either needed or would respond to treatment. In the doctor's opinion, he was not suffering from a mental disorder as defined by section 1 of the 1983 Act and any disposal under Part III of the Act was therefore impossible. Having considered the medical and other evidence, the judge sentenced the patient to a total of six years imprisonment, describing him as "a very dangerous man ... in particular to young girls and young women."

The patient remained conditionally discharged notwithstanding that he was serving a sentence of imprisonment. In 1986 he reapplied to the tribunal, again seeking his absolute discharge from the hospital and restriction orders. The medical evidence before the tribunal was again unanimously of the view that the patient was not suffering from any form of mental disorder. The tribunal accepted this evidence but, as before, also considered it appropriate for him to remain liable to be recalled. In particular, supervision would still be required after his release from prison and it was necessary to test his behaviour in the community before it would be appropriate to absolutely discharge him.

The application for judicial review

The patient sought judicial review of the tribunal's decision on the ground that it was wrong in law. As soon as the tribunal had found that he was not suffering from mental disorder he ceased to be a "patient" within the meaning of the Act because a "patient" was defined in section 145(1) as a person suffering or appearing to suffer from mental disorder. Having found that the patient was not suffering from mental disorder, the tribunal had been under a statutory duty to absolutely discharge him from the restriction order. The Act no longer applied to him.

Parker L.J.

Section 145(1) provided that the definition of a patient given there applied unless the context required a different meaning. That permitted the word to bear a different meaning in Part V if the context required that. The basic dispute was whether the definition of a "patient" in section 145(1) did or did not apply to the tribunal discharge provisions set out in sections 72–75. The patient's counsel accepted that if the word "patient" in those sections meant a person who is or had been a patient then both of the decisions of the tribunal were beyond challenge.

Turning to the statutory framework, it was useful to consider the consequences of the argument forwarded on the patient's behalf. It would mean that, even if there was ample evidence before the tribunal that the patient was liable to have a relapse at some time in the future, the tribunal would be obliged to let him loose upon the public. That was not a conclusion at which one would readily arrive unless the wording of the Act was plain.

In fact, the wording of the Act was plain, but plain in the opposite sense. It was plain that the initial tribunal properly applied the wording of the section and did what it would appear was intended by Parliament — namely maintain the right to recall and make the discharge subject to conditions so that there could be some measure of control over the patient, albeit that at the particular time he was not suffering from any mental condition. That this was plainly Parliament's intention was clear from the fact that someone should remain subject to conditional discharge unless a tribunal was satisfied that it was no longer appropriate that he should remain liable to recall.

As to the meaning of "patient" in Part V of the Act, it also seemed clear that the context did require that a different meaning be given to the word. Once a restriction order is made in respect of an offender he is then a patient. There is then a provision that that person, who now is referred to as a 'patient', shall not be discharged save under certain sections. He is thereafter referred to as a 'patient' but it is the same person. Since it was provided in the Act that the patient shall not be discharged unless certain conditions were satisfied, and they plainly were not, that was the end of the matter.

Brown J.

I agree. Were the patient's counsel correct in his central contention, and a tribunal was under a duty to absolutely discharge a restricted patient who is not then suffering from any relevant mental disorder, one would have expected the legislation both to say so with crystal clarity and also to impose upon the tribunal a clear requirement to reach a specific finding upon that basic question. *Application dismissed.*

[1990] 1 All E.R. 694   *C.A. (Kerr, Butler-Sloss L.JJ. and Sir Denys Buckley)*

As to the facts of the case and the decision in the Divisional Court, see above. The Court of Appeal dismissed the appeal for the following reasons.

Kerr and Butler-Sloss L.JJ.

Having regard to the purpose of the 1983 Act, which was to lay down a framework for the admission and detention of persons convicted of crimes who were found to be suffering from mental disorder and were capable of being treated, and to provide a procedure designed to give them the opportunity of being discharged back into the community by making an application to an independent body, namely a Mental Health Review Tribunal, an offender became a restricted patient when he was detained under an order made under section 41 and he remained a patient until he was discharged absolutely, if at all, by the tribunal under section 73(1). The term "patient" in section 145(1) was to be interpreted accordingly.

While the offender remained a patient, the tribunal had the statutory power to make an order that his discharge be subject to conditions. Section 73 gave to the tribunal power to impose a conditional discharge and retain residual control over patients not then suffering from mental disorder or not to a degree requiring continued detention in hospital. That would appear to be a provision designed both for the support of the patient in the community and the protection of the public, and was an important discretionary power vested in an independent tribunal, one not lightly to be set aside in the absence of clear words. Accordingly, the tribunal had been acting within its statutory powers in imposing a conditional discharge under section 73(2).

Sir Denys Buckley

There was no irregularity in the tribunal's decision since it did not effect any discharge of the patient but merely suspended the operation of the 1985 tribunal's conditional discharge so long as he remained in prison. From the moment the 1985 tribunal imposed conditions, the patient ceased to be a restricted patient subject to a restriction order and became instead, and continued to be, a person subject to the conditions imposed and to the powers of recall vested in the Home Secretary.

Ex p. Cooper

In *R. v. Mental Health Review Tribunal, ex p. Cooper*, the patient had been admitted to Broadmoor following his conviction for a passport offence in 1963. He was one of the many old-style "Eaton and Toland patients" who ended up in special hospitals on restriction orders because they were social nuisances and their petty thefts, and the like, were seen as harmful to the public's interests.[13] The case again involved an application for judicial review founded on the ground that a patient conditionally discharged by a tribunal had been entitled to an absolute discharge.

---

[13]   *R. v. Eaton* (1975) Current Sentencing Practice F.2.4(d), C.A.; *R. v. Toland (Michael Henry)* (1973) Current Sentencing Practice F.2.4(b).

R. v. North West Thames Mental Health Review Tribunal, ex p. Cooper

[1990] C.O.D. 275   *Q.B.D. Rose J.*

In 1963, following his conviction for making a false statement for the purpose of obtaining a passport, the applicant was detained in Broadmoor Hospital pursuant to a hospital order with restrictions under sections 60 and 65 of the Mental Health Act 1959. His admission to a special hospital was considered to be appropriate because there was a risk that he might abscond from a local hospital and he would benefit from the recreational facilities at Broadmoor. On 12 February 1985, he was transferred to Ealing Hospital. In September 1985, a tribunal which considered his case specifically referred to the fact that he was not a danger to others while in April 1986 it was recorded that violence towards the individual was not part of his pattern of behaviour. On 17 February 1989, the matter again came before a tribunal, which directed that he be conditionally discharged. The reasons given for the tribunal's decision were that the patient had for some years been in substantial but not total remission. He had, since September 1985, been free to come and go by day and throughout that time there had been no serious incident of anti-social behaviour nor any relapse in his condition. However, after 30 years of institutional care, re-integration into the community would be stressful and the tribunal was therefore satisfied that for his own health and safety he should have the protection of continued treatment and supervision and of liability to recall should his condition deteriorate.

The application for judicial review

The patient applied for judicial review of the tribunal's decision on the ground that, since it was not necessary to protect the public from serious harm that he should be discharged subject to conditions and be liable to recall by the Secretary of State, he was entitled to be discharged absolutely under section 73. The restriction order had been imposed under the 1959 Act. Paragraph 14.24 of the Butler Report had referred with concern to the fact that restriction orders under that statute had sometimes been imposed for trivial matters in respect of persons who were essentially nothing more than social nuisances.[14] This was such a case. As a result of such concerns, a requirement that such an order be necessary to protect the public from serious harm was introduced by virtue of section 28(1) of the Mental Health (Amendment) Act 1982. Paragraph 10(1) of Schedule 5 to the 1982 Act expressly provided that that amendment applied in relation to existing restriction orders made under the 1959 Act. When a hospital order was imposed, the same discharge criteria applied regardless of whether the patient was restricted or unrestricted. The purpose of a hospital order was therapeutic and it put the patient in essentially the same position as a section 3 patient. An unrestricted hospital order patient was entitled to be unconditionally discharged once it was no longer necessary for his health or safety or to protect others that he receive further in-patient treatment. However, if a restriction order had been attached, because that was necessary to protect the public against a risk of future serious harm, the position was fundamentally different. The criteria which determined whether the patient was detained or discharged were the same as in a section 3 or ordinary hospital order case. The patient was *inter alia* entitled to be discharged once it was no longer necessary for his health or safety or to protect others that he receive further in-patient treatment. However, because of the restriction order, the patient could be discharged on conditions and be liable to recall by the Home Secretary. The purpose of this conditional discharge regime was, as the Butler Report and many court judgments made clear, to protect the public against the possibility of serious

---

[14]   *Report of the Committee on Mentally Abnormal Offenders*, Cmnd. 6244 (1975).

harm following the patient's return to the community. It ensured that patients who might, when ill, cause the public serious harm were subject to proper supervision in the community and could be recalled if there were any grounds for concern about the possibility of such behaviour — *inter alia*, because they were becoming unwell and again required to be in hospital so as to avoid harm to others being caused. Whether liability to recall was appropriate, and what conditions should be imposed, were matters for the tribunal's discretion but subject to the policy and objects of the Act. A tribunal which was dealing with one of the old "social nuisance" cases, and which was satisfied that the patient had never posed any risk of serious harm to the public, when ill or otherwise, and was further satisfied that this would not be the case if he relapsed in the future, was by definition satisfied that liability to recall by the Home Secretary was inappropriate. For it was satisfied that the statutory purpose behind conditional discharge and recall did not apply in his case. It was then simply using the restrictions for therapeutic purposes, as a form of community treatment order or as a form of hospital order of indefinite duration.

Rose J.

It had been submitted that the tribunal were seeking to direct a conditional discharge solely for therapeutic reasons. The powers exercisable over a conditionally discharged patient, to supervise and recall him, were not necessary for the protection of the public. Furthermore, it was contended that the maintenance of liability to recall under section 73(1)(b) could only be proper if the applicant posed some danger to others. Accordingly, the tribunal had taken into account an immaterial consideration and failed to take into account that a restriction order could not be made now because the patient did not pose a serious risk to others. However, Butler-Sloss L.J. had said in *R. v. Merseyside Mental Health Review Tribunal, ex p K* [1990] 1 All E.R. 694 at 699, 700 that section 73 gave a tribunal "power to impose a conditional discharge and retain residual control over patients not then suffering from mental disorder or not to a degree requiring continued detention in hospital. This would appear to be a provision designed both for the support of the patient in the community and the protection of the public, and is an important discretionary power vested in an independent tribunal, one not lightly to be set aside in the absence of clear words." The application would therefore be dismissed.

Kerr L.J.

Mr. Pleming, on behalf of the tribunal, relied upon dicta of Butler-Sloss L.J. in *ex p. K*. It was possible for a tribunal to be satisfied that no serious harm to others was anticipated or likely but not to be satisfied that it is not appropriate for him to remain liable to be recalled to hospital. He emphasised that a tribunal had no power to order that a patient shall cease to be subject to a restriction order. That was a power which by virtue of section 42(1) was vested in the Secretary of State and it was to the Secretary of State that a patient must in appropriate cases seek a cessation of the restriction order. Furthermore, Ackner L.J. had said in *R. v. Hallstrom, ex p. W.* [1986] 1 Q.B. 824 at 846 that a tribunal had no power to consider the validity of the admission which gave rise to the liability to be detained. Having regard to the material before the tribunal and the above judgments, the argument that the tribunal's conclusion was irrational could not be sustained. The words of the statute plainly permitted, and indeed only permitted, the tribunal, if it was in the state of mind with regard to satisfaction which this tribunal was, to make a conditional discharge order. The decision of a tribunal was one which the courts would be reluctant to interfere with unless challenge on the well-known lines had been substantiated. No such challenge had been substantiated. *Application dismissed.*

It seems unsatisfactory to take the short passage in *ex p. K* as constituting authority for the proposition that it is not inappropriate for a passport offender to be liable to recall for purely therapeutic purposes.[16] As another Court of Appeal decision involving K made clear, the policy and objects of the Act in restricted cases are to regulate the circumstances in which the liberty of persons who are mentally disordered may be restricted and, where there is conflict, to balance their interests against those of public safety.[17] K's case involved a patient who was highly dangerous and, although presently not mentally disordered, had previously committed serious offences while on conditional discharge. The support of the patient in the community in that case was therefore necessary to protect the public and the two issues went together.[18] While a tribunal has no power to direct that a patient who requires further in-patient treatment shall cease to be subject to restrictions, it has power to direct that a patient who does not require in-patient treatment shall not be subject to recall — in order words, it may absolutely discharge him. If he does not satisfy the criteria for being detained in pursuance of the hospital order, the issue then becomes whether liability to recall is inappropriate. If that issue is not to be determined by reference to the statutory purpose and function of liability to recall, and the policy and objects of the Act, then it is difficult to see by what other test it is to be determined. The decision in *Hallstrom* is plainly irrelevant since the lawfulness of the original order was not being challenged. It was simply factually relevant that the public had never been at risk of serious harm from the patient, the order having been made at a time when that was not a precondition of such orders. The issue was instead whether the patient, once entitled to be discharged, was entitled to be absolutely discharged given the law as it stood on the day of the tribunal's decision and its finding on the facts — *viz.*, that (1) it was possible that readmission for treatment might be necessary in the future for the patient's own health or safety but (2) if he relapsed, there was no likelihood of a risk of serious harm to the public. The decision is unfortunate because it simply gives credence to the arguments of those lawyers who contend that restricted patients are never entitled to be absolutely discharged, however harmless. As to whether the case might be decided differently today, see page 370.

CONDITIONAL DISCHARGE

Where a tribunal conditionally discharges a patient, he must comply with such conditions as may be imposed at the time of discharge by the tribunal or at any subsequent time by the Secretary of State. The latter may from time to time vary any

---

[15] When assessing the objectivity and correctness of the observations which follow, the reader should be aware that the author was the solicitor in this case and he formulated the case outlined above.

[16] Furthermore, what Butler-Sloss L.J. said was that the provision made for conditional discharge would appear to be a provision designed *both* for the support of the patient in the community and the protection of the public.

[17] *R. v. Secretary of State for the Home Department, ex p. K.* [1991] 1 Q.B. 270, *per* McCowan L.J., approving dicta of McCullough J. in *R. v. Secretary of State for the Home Department, ex p. K.* [1990] 1 All E.R. 703 at 709, [1990] 1 W.L.R. 168 at 174.

[18] As to this point, see the Home Office's own guidelines: "The purpose of formal supervision resulting from conditional discharge *is to protect the public from further serious harm in two ways*: first by assisting the patient's successful reintegration into the community ... second, by close monitoring of the patient's mental health or of a perceived increase in the risk of danger to the public so that steps can be taken to assist the patient and protect the public." *Supervision and After-Care of Conditionally Discharged Restricted Patients— Notes for the Guidance of Supervising Psychiatrists* (DHSS and the Home Office, 1987), paras. 7 and 8.

condition imposed by the tribunal at the time of discharge or by him. The patient may be recalled to hospital by the Secretary of State in the same way as if he had conditionally discharged the patient himself and his powers under section 42 are not affected by those given to a tribunal under section 73.[19]

Effect of conditional discharge by a tribunal

73.—(4) Where a patient is conditionally discharged under this section—

(a) he may be recalled by the Secretary of State under subsection (3) of section 42 above as if he had been conditionally discharged under subsection (2) of that section; and

(b) the patient shall comply with such conditions (if any) as may be imposed at the time of discharge by the tribunal or at any subsequent time by the Secretary of State.

(5) The Secretary of State may from time to time vary any condition imposed (whether by the tribunal or by him) under subsection (4) above.

(8) This section is without prejudice to section 42 above.

The conditions of discharge

Common conditions of discharge include a condition of residence; a condition that the patient submits to supervision by, and attends appointments with, a supervising social worker or probation officer; a condition that he similarly be supervised by, and attend appointments with, a supervising psychiatrist; and a condition that he complies with any treatment prescribed by the latter.

Conditions of residence

The condition of residence is usually expressed in terms "that the patient shall reside at accommodation approved by his responsible medical officer."[20] The terminology is unfortunate because a conditionally discharged patient has no responsible medical officer. The underlying rationale is presumably either that the consultant is better placed to decide what accommodation is suitable or that phrasing the condition in this way avoids the need to later vary the condition if the patient moves. The legal justification for the practice presumably rests on a literal construction of section 73(4)(b), which merely requires the patient to comply with any conditions imposed by the tribunal at the time of his discharge. That paragraph being silent on all other matters, it is not necessary to impose a condition of residence and, equally, if a condition of residence is imposed, it is not necessary that the tribunal itself specifies the residence. Section 73 leaves such decisions entirely to its discretion. It suffices that the tribunal has considered whether it is necessary for the patient to be subject to

---

[19]   Mental Health Act 1983, s.73(8).
[20]   According to the *Memorandum*, "The Conditions which *the Home Secretary* would normally think it appropriate to attach to a conditional discharge are that the patient shall live in a particular household ..." *Mental Health Act 1983: Memorandum on Parts I to VI, VIII and X* (D.H.S.S., 1987), para. 164.

a condition of residence and, if so, whether it should itself specify a particular address for him. If, having considered those issues, it is satisfied that the patient is entitled to be discharged without a particular place of residence being specified, such as a specialist hostel, the decision about where the patient shall live may properly be left to a supervisor's judgement, rather than the patient's. Indeed, the tendency with such legislation is for supervisors to nominate a residence. Furthermore, if the other common conditions of discharge can be cast in that form — those requiring the patient to accept any treatment, and to attend any out-patient appointments and other activities, prescribed by his supervisors — then so too may conditions which relate to decisions about where he shall live.

Whether common practice lawful or advisable

The practice of leaving the decision about where the patient lives to his consultant is not beyond objection, notwithstanding that conditions phrased in this way have been referred to without comment in several law reports. The Act requires the patient to comply with any conditions imposed by the tribunal discharging him or by the Secretary of State, who may later vary any existing conditions. In contrast, the patient's responsible medical officer has no power to impose conditions of discharge on the patient, or to vary them, and the patient cannot therefore be required to comply with any conditions that he does impose. The statutory intention is arguably that the patient shall reside at an address specified by the tribunal or by the Secretary of State unless it is inappropriate to impose a condition of residence. In this respect, their respective roles mirror those performed by them when the patient was in hospital: the patient's consultant may propose that the patient be given greater freedom, including that he have leave to reside at an address outside hospital, but any actual decision having that effect requires the Secretary of State's consent or, in the case of discharge, a judicial direction. That being so, a patient discharged by a tribunal and living in a hostel cannot move into his own flat simply because his consultant consents to that. Although that would not involve breaching the tribunal's direction, if phrased in the above form, the prior question is whether the tribunal had power to phrase the condition in a way which vested in the consultant a decision vested in the Secretary of State. As to the justification that the phraseology avoids any need to vary the condition if the patient moves, the purpose of section 73(5) in this context may therefore be precisely to ensure that a patient cannot move unless an existing condition of residence is first varied. This restriction ensures that any such proposals must first be approved by the Secretary of State or, if his consent is withheld, by a tribunal under section 75. In terms of the practicalities, the position is unsatisfactory if a tribunal does not specify the place of residence and the responsible medical officer does not agree to the patient residing at the address which the tribunal had in mind when it reached its finding that he was entitled to be conditionally discharged. It may be difficult to be sure that the tribunal would have been satisfied that liability to detention in hospital was no longer necessary or appropriate had the alternative arrangement been canvassed.[21] From the patient's viewpoint, the position will be unsatisfactory if, as has been known, the responsible medical officer withholds his approval to the patient immediately taking up residence outside hospital, so that the patient is still languishing in hospital some

---

[21] " ... the tribunal's satisfaction or lack of satisfaction as to ... the paragraph (b) matters may be vitally influenced by the conditions which are to be imposed to regulate his life style upon release into the community ... The tribunal may perfectly properly be satisfied that hospital detention is no longer necessary provided that the patient can be placed in a suitable hostel ... These are matters to be secured by imposing appropriate conditions." *R. v. Oxford Regional Mental Health Review Tribunal, ex p. Secretary of State for the Home Department* [1988] 1 A.C. 120, at 127, *per* Lord Bridge.

weeks after the tribunal directed his discharge. A tribunal in those circumstances has no power to reconvene to specify an address if the supervisor interprets the decision as being conditional in the sense that discharge is to be effected once the conditions of discharge are satisfied, which involve him being satisfied that a particular address outside hospital is suitable.

Summary

Regardless of whether it is lawful to leave the issue of where the patient resides to his supervisors, the Home Office's practice of nominating the place where the patient shall reside has much to commend it. It ensures that the supervisors' proposals are properly vetted and prevents any possibility of the patient's discharge being delayed because no residence is immediately specified. It is perhaps noteworthy that where a tribunal defers giving a direction for the patient's discharge, because suitable accommodation is not immediately available, its direction is deferred "until such arrangements *as appear to the Tribunal* to be necessary for that purpose have been made to *their* satisfaction."[22] It must likewise be the case that a tribunal which discharges forthwith must first have satisfied itself about the suitability of the arrangements which may immediately be made for the patient's discharge. And if, having satisfied themselves that suitable arrangements have been made for the patient in the community, including a suitable residence, it is arguably at best poor practice not to specify the conditions upon which its discharge decision rests, leaving the decision about what will in fact happen to the doctor's judgment and discretion.

Whether any express conditions must be imposed

It is clear from section 73(4)(b) that it is not mandatory for a tribunal which conditionally discharges a patient to impose any express conditions of discharge. The patient's discharge is still conditional because the orders remain in force and he may be recalled to hospital. A failure to appreciate this led to the lawfulness of the warrant of recall issued in the following case being challenged.

R. v. Secretary of State for the Home Department, ex p. Didlick

The Times, 30 March 1993   *Q.B.D., Watkins L.J., Rougier J.*

In 1973, the patient was conditionally discharged, subject initially to the usual conditions as to supervision and residence. In January 1979, he received a letter from the Home Office which included the following statement: "I am pleased to inform you that the Home Secretary has now decided that the conditions attaching to your discharge from hospital on 5 September 1973 may be allowed to lapse. As Doctor C. has already explained, your liability to recall to hospital remains but this power would only be exercised should you again be in need of compulsory long-term in-patient treatment ..." In December 1991, the Secretary of State issued a warrant under section 42(3), revoking the conditional discharge granted in 1973 and recalling the patient to hospital.

The application for judicial review

The patient applied for judicial review, submitting that the revocation of the conditions in 1979 brought the conditional discharge to an end, at which time the discharge being no longer conditional became absolute and the restriction

---

[22]   Mental Health Act 1983, s.73(7).

order came to an end. Consequently, no order existed in January under which a warrant could be issued recalling the patient to hospital. The warrant of recall was therefore unlawful and certiorari should issue to quash it.

Rougier J.

Before a restriction order can be brought to an end, the Secretary of State must either make a direction to that effect or must discharge the patient absolutely. Each of these is a positive act. There is no room for the situation whereby a restriction order ceases to have effect by inference or implication. It followed that by merely allowing the conditions under which the patient was discharged to lapse, the Secretary of State did not thereby bring to an end the operation of the restriction order. It further followed that the issue of the warrant was *intra vires* the Secretary of State and valid. *Application dismissed.*

Whether any conditions may not be imposed

A condition of residence in hospital cannot be specified.[23] Apart from this, there is no case law on the issue of whether there are certain conditions which may not be imposed by a tribunal, or indeed by the Secretary of State. Conditions which are sometimes imposed in practice include that the patient shall not take drugs; that he shall not consume alcohol; that he shall not frequent a particular address, such as the former matrimonial home or a school; that he shall not enter a particular locality; and that he shall not communicate directly or indirectly with his spouse or children, save via his legal representatives. Some of these conditions might be objected to on the grounds that they are equivalent to a civil injunction or, in the case of consuming alcohol, interfere with a lawful activity. Others have essentially the same quality as conditions of bail, although this is not objectionable *per se* since the individual's liberty in both cases is conditional and an alternative to lawful custody. Some of them also resemble conditions imposed as part of a probation order. Perhaps all that can be said is that the purpose of such conditions must be the statutory purpose of protecting the public from harm, whether by helping to ensure that the patient's mental state and behaviour are properly supervised; or that he receives any treatment and care necessary for his mental health; or that he avoids any particular conduct or situations believed to be associated with the existence of a risk to others.[24] It is obviously desirable that the conditions are unambiguous so that the patient and his supervisors are clear about what is required of the patient and whether any condition has been broken. Requiring that a patient refrains from the excessive consumption of alcohol is ambiguous because what is excessive is largely subjective.

Whether the conditions may be immediately changed

If a tribunal directs a patient's immediate discharge, the Home Office's Mental Health Unit are notified of the after-care details and the conditions of discharge imposed by the tribunal. According to Pickersgill, the Home Office will then consider whether the detailed arrangements are satisfactory, consulting as necessary the patient's responsible medical officer or the newly appointed supervisors, before reaching a decision. The Home Secretary might vary the conditions, for example

---

[23]   *Secretary of State for the Home Department v. Mental Health Review Tribunal for Mersey Regional Health Authority; Same v. Mental Health Review Tribunal for Wales* [1986] 1 W.L.R. 1170.

[24]   The conditional discharge regime is unique to restricted patients and it is one of the main ways in which the public is protected against the risk of serious harm identified by the court.

changing the condition of residence or imposing supervision conditions where none were imposed by the tribunal.[25] This practice can be objected to as amounting to reviewing and redrafting the terms of a court's order, with reliance being placed on dicta in *ex p. Fox*[26] and *ex p. K.*[27] In the latter case, McCullough J. said that it would be unlawful for the Secretary of State to recall a patient who had recently been conditionally discharged by direction of a tribunal, unless something had happened which justified the belief that a different view might now be taken about one of the factors on which his release had depended. The conditions of discharge form part of the tribunal's direction and are often inseparable from the factors upon which the patient's release depended.[28] The tribunal's decision and direction is that the patient is entitled to be discharged subject to, and on, those conditions. If the Home Secretary is able to immediately vary those conditions, the patient is then not entitled to apply to a tribunal for those conditions to be varied back, so as to accord with the original conditions, until he has been discharged for a year. Where a tribunal imposes a condition that the patient resides in unsupervised lodgings, and the Home Secretary immediately varies that condition by requiring residence in a supervised hostel, it is certainly arguable that the practice is objectionable for the reasons given by McCullough J. As to the statute, section 73 provides that the Secretary of State may "from time to time" vary any condition imposed by the discharging tribunal and may impose additional conditions "at any subsequent time." Having set out a tribunal's power of conditional discharge, section 73 therefore immediately provides that any conditions imposed on the discharge may be varied by the Secretary of State, who is then the person responsible for the discharged patient. Because the effect of the tribunal's decision is that the Home Secretary becomes responsible for a patient in the community who he considers should be in hospital, he is clearly given broad powers to tailor the conditions when he considers that is necessary in order to properly discharge his statutory function of protecting the public. However, it is notable that the powers to impose and vary conditions are not exercisable on precisely the same terms. There must be some difference between a power which may be exercised "at any subsequent time" and one set out in the same subsection which is exercisable "from time to time." The imposition of a further condition, which may be done at any subsequent time, is not *per se* inconsistent with any condition imposed by the tribunal itself and does not involve any variation of the terms of its order. The variation of a condition imposed by the tribunal is, however, inconsistent with that part of its decision; those conditions form part of the decision and cannot be severed from it. This may be why the power is expressed not to be exercisable "at any subsequent time" but only from "time to time." The phrase is that used in section 12 of the Interpretation Act 1978, which provides that where a statute confers a power then, unless the contrary intention appears, it may be exercised from time to time "as occasion requires." That, it is submitted, means that the conditions can be varied as and when something happens which requires that but not if the occasion remains unchanged.

---

[25]   A. Pickersgill, "Balancing the public and private interests" in *Risk-taking in Mental Disorder; Analyses, Policies and Practical Strategies* (ed. D. Carson. S.L.E. Publications, 1990).

[26]   *R. v. Ealing District Health Authority, ex p. Fox* [1993] 1 W.L.R. 373 (**415**).

[27]   *R. v. Secretary of State for the Home Department, ex p. K* [1990] 1 W.L.R. 168 (**348**).

[28]   See *R. v. Oxford Regional Mental Health Review Tribunal, ex p. Secretary of State for the Home Department* [1988] 1 A.C. 120, *per* Lord Bridge: " ... the tribunal's satisfaction or lack of satisfaction as to ... the paragraph (b) matters may be vitally influenced by the conditions which are to be imposed to regulate his life style upon release into the community." See also *Pickering v. Liverpool Daily Post and Echo Newspapers plc & others* [1991] 2 A.C. 370 (**850**), where it was held that a direction that a patient be discharged, either absolutely or conditionally, was analogous to a formal court order.

DEFERRED CONDITIONAL DISCHARGE

If it is not possible for a patient to be immediately discharged from hospital because arrangements in the community need to be made before the conditions imposed on the patient's discharge can be complied with, the tribunal may defer its direction for the patient's discharge.[29]

Duties arising following deferred conditional discharge

The obligations of those involved in making the necessary arrangements following deferred conditional discharge were set out by Lord Bridge in *R. v. Oxford Regional Mental Health Review Tribunal, ex p. Secretary of State for the Home Department:*[30]

> "Whoever is responsible for making the arrangements should then proceed with all reasonable expedition to do so and should bring the matter to the attention of the tribunal again as soon as practicable after it is thought that satisfactory arrangements have been made. Pursuant to rule 25 the tribunal may then decide that the arrangements are to their satisfaction without a further hearing."

Duty to provide after-care under section 117

The above judgment was applied in *R. v. Ealing District Health Authority, ex p. Fox.*[31] In that case, a tribunal directed the patient's conditional discharge but deferred discharge until such time as it was satisfied that arrangements had been made which enabled the conditions of discharge to be satisfied. In particular, it was necessary for the Health Authority to appoint a responsible medical officer to provide psychiatric supervision for the patient in the community. Because the consultants in the relevant catchment area were not willing to supervise the patient, the Health Authority did not appoint a responsible medical officer and the patient remained in hospital. The tribunal was due to reconvene in March 1992, in order to reconsider the patient's case, but the patient cancelled the hearing, applying instead for judicial review. The High Court held that the mere acceptance by the Health Authority of its doctors' opinions was not of itself sufficient discharge of its obligation to proceed with reasonable expedition and diligence to give effect to the arrangements by the tribunal; that where the doctors did not agree with the conditions imposed by the tribunal and were unwilling to make the necessary arrangements, the Health Authority was under an obligation to endeavour to provide arrangements from its own resources or to obtain them from other appropriate Health Authorities; that the Health Authority's obligations were not ended by any intervening deterioration in the patient's condition; and, accordingly, the authority had erred in law in failing to fulfil its obligations. Accordingly, it was appropriate to make a declaration in the following terms:

---

[29]   In practice, immediate discharge is not always immediate. Implementing the arrangements may, as with any move, take a few days to implement. However, no further arrangements need to be made and submitted to the tribunal for approval. The arrangements already made simply required the tribunal's say-so to be put into effect.

[30]   *R. v. Oxford Regional Mental Health Review Tribunal, ex p. Secretary of State for the Home Department* [1988] 1 A.C. 120 (**544**).

[31]   *R. v. Ealing District Health Authority, ex p. Fox* [1993] 1 W.L.R. 373 (**415**).

(1) that the authority had erred in law in not attempting with all reasonable expedition and diligence to make arrangements so as to enable the applicant to comply with the conditions imposed by the Mental Health Review Tribunal;

(2) that a [district] Health Authority is under a duty under section 117 of the Mental Health Act 1983 to provide aftercare services when a patient leaves hospital, and acts unlawfully in failing to seek to make practical arrangements for after-care prior to that patient's discharge from hospital where such arrangements are required by a Mental Health Review Tribunal in order to enable the patient to be conditionally discharged from hospital."

Whether decision to discharge final or provisional

Although such a decision is described in the tribunal rules as a "provisional decision" that is only so in the limited sense that whether or not the direction is eventually given is provisional upon future events, that is whether arrangements can be made which satisfy the tribunal that the conditions attached to the discharge can now be fulfilled. The tribunal's actual decision, that the patient be conditionally discharged, is a final decision which cannot be reversed or amended. These points were all considered in a series of cases which ended in the House of Lords.[32] As will be seen, two judgments of the Divisional Court were heard together on appeal, and reversed, and the House of Lords then upheld the decision of the Court of Appeal. It is nevertheless useful to summarise briefly the judgments in the Divisional Court because they provide the context for what followed.

R. v. Oxford Regional Mental Health Review Tribunal and Campbell, ex p. the Secretary of State for the Home Office

CO/576/85, 8 November 1985   *Q.B.D., Woolf J.*

The Home Secretary applied for an order of certiorari in respect of the tribunal's decision on 12 February 1985 that the patient be conditionally discharged. The grounds of the application were that the Secretary of State was not provided with a copy of a psychiatric report commissioned on behalf of the patient and furnished to the tribunal in support of his application to be discharged, and nor was he given notice of the hearing. In consequence, he had no opportunity to submit supplementary observations on that report which might have affected the tribunal's decision and was unable to seek the tribunal's leave to be represented at the hearing or to make oral representations to it.

---

[32] There have also been a number of unreported cases in which tribunals which deferred a direction for the patient's conditional discharge later reconvened and directed the patient's absolute discharge: *e.g. ex p. Hughes, ex. p. Cummings, ex p. Stowell, and ex p. Tinnion*. In all of these cases, the tribunal's decision was quashed. Although the practice is not uncommon, the rules do not authorise a tribunal to reconvene because satisfactory arrangements which comply with the conditions imposed by it have not been made. Rule 25(1), which applies to deferred conditional discharge decisions ("provisional decisions"), simply provides that a further decision can be made without a further hearing. The power conferred by rule 25(2), to reconvene upon giving notice to the parties, applies only where a tribunal has made a recommendation under section 72(3). Consequently, unless an implied power to reconvene can be inferred from section 73(7) itself, there is no power to reconvene following deferred conditional discharge.

Woolf J.

The Secretary of State had a very important role to play in tribunal proceedings, ensuring that matters relevant to the public's interests were placed before the tribunal, so that it was in a proper position when exercising its jurisdiction not only to do what was in the patient's interests but also to do what was in the public's interests.

The Mental Health Review Tribunal Rules 1983 and the Mental Health Act 1983 made it clear that a decision which resulted in discharge being deferred was a truly provisional decision: it was a decision in principle and not a final decision. A tribunal could later consider any change in the patient's mental state and circumstances before deciding whether to make a direction discharging him. Equally, if the arrangements envisaged by it could not be made, but satisfactory alternative discharge arrangements could, the provisional nature of its decision meant that it could discharge the patient on conditions based on those alternative arrangements. Moreover, because a decision under section 73(7) was a provisional decision, the Secretary of State still had an opportunity to put before the tribunal those matters which, through an unfortunate error, he was prevented from putting before the tribunal at the original hearing. Rule 28 of the Mental Health Review Tribunal Rules 1983, which dealt with procedural irregularities, was wide enough to deal with such a situation albeit that it was not exhaustive, because it did not cover breaches of natural justice which did not necessarily involve a breach of the rules.

A tribunal's direction for a patient's deferred conditional discharge stood unless good reason was shown for re-opening the matter. Unless there was an exceptional change of circumstances, or an occurrence of the sort that occurred in this case, a tribunal would be perfectly entitled not to re-open matters that had been subject to a provisional decision. It would only do so if it considered that necessary so as to comply with the intent of the Act, and the rules then allowed matters to be re-opened that had previously been decided. Although rule 25 gave a tribunal a discretion to dispense with a further hearing where it had made a provisional decision, that discretion had to be exercised in a responsible and proper manner. Where there was a need for a further hearing, to enable the Secretary of State properly to perform his statutory responsibilities, the tribunal had to ensure that there was ample opportunity for him to put forward those matters which he wanted to. In this case, there was therefore an alternative and more appropriate remedy than judicial review open to the Secretary of State and the application was therefore dismissed.

R. v. Yorkshire Mental Health Review Tribunal, ex p. Secretary of State for the Home Department (Mollie Lord)

CO/936/85, 21 January 1986   *Q.B.D., Kennedy J.*

The patient was subject to a restriction order without limit of time. On 23 January 1985, a tribunal reviewed the patient's case, adjourning the hearing for three months to see if a hostel place could be found. However, no hostel place had been found by the time the tribunal met again on 1 April 1985. The tribunal directed that the patient be conditionally discharged but that its direction be deferred until the following arrangements had been made to their satisfaction: 1. that the patient be received and accommodated in a supervised hostel; 2. that she be subject to such periodic psychiatric out-patient treatment as may be advised; and 3. that she remain under the supervision of an officer of the relevant social services department. The tribunal further directed that, if the necessary arrangements had not been made within the following six months, it would reconvene to reconsider the case and, in the light of the patient's progress, whether its conditional discharge decision could be perfected without the attachment of any specified arrangements: "there is always a possibility that at that time we may feel able to conclude that the statutory criteria for conditional discharge without deferment have been satisfied." It was that part of the tribunal's decision which the Secretary of State objected to and upon which his application for judicial review was based.

The application for judicial review

It was submitted on the Secretary of State's behalf that the proper exercise of the power of deferral conferred by section 73(7) required that a final decision that the patient be conditionally discharged had first been taken. The effect of deferral was simply that the normal consequence of that decision — the patient's actual discharge — was postponed until the arrangements thought to be necessary by the tribunal had been made. The power to defer a direction for a patient's discharge was not to be confused with a simple power to adjourn the decision as to whether or not the patient should be discharged. Once a tribunal had reached a finding that a patient satisfied the criteria for being discharged it had no option but to discharge. The wording of section 73(7) pointed to the same conclusion since it spoke of arrangements being made "for that purpose," which would be inappropriate if it was intended to convey a power to postpone the decision about whether there should be a conditional discharge at all. More significantly, section 73(7) provided no mechanism for deciding at a later date what, if any, form of discharge there should be. If a tribunal was still free to consider the basic question of whether or not there should be a discharge, it could under the rules do so without a further hearing, without notice to the parties or the Secretary of State, and without recording what it decided. In fact, the power to reconsider the case of a patient granted a deferred conditional discharge conferred by rule 25(1) was confined to approving or not approving the arrangements for the patient's discharge made during the intervening period.

Kennedy J.

His Lordship referred to the conclusions reached by Woolf J. in R. v. Oxford Mental Health Review Tribunal and Campbell, ex p. Secretary of State for the Home Department.

When a tribunal exercised its power to defer, its decision in favour of conditional discharge was provisional in the limited sense that it was ineffective until the necessary arrangements had been made to the tribunal's satisfaction. It was clear in the present case that the tribunal never had in mind any disposal other than conditional discharge and that the tribunal's decision as to that was complete. However, if the arrangements originally considered to be necessary could not be made, the tribunal could upon reconvening the proceedings consider if any other arrangements were appropriate. If the tribunal was minded to significantly alter or to revoke the arrangements originally considered to be necessary then, since it must act judicially, it would no doubt consider a further hearing to be necessary unless all parties agreed otherwise. Whether or not there was a further hearing, the tribunal would be making a further decision and it would be a decision determinative of the application. In accordance with rule 23(3), the decision would have to be in writing and supported by reasons.

As to the facts of the present case, the position was that (1) the tribunal at its hearing on 1 April 1985 decided that the patient should be conditionally discharged, being satisfied as to the criteria for discharge; (2) nothing in the tribunal's reasoning or the directions it gave led to the conclusion that the tribunal envisaged ever reconsidering its decision that the patient be conditionally discharged; (3) the tribunal did envisage reconvening if necessary to reconsider, in the light of the patient's progress, whether the direction for conditional discharge could be given without the arrangements being made which at the time of deferring the tribunal considered to be necessary. The tribunal was entitled to act in that way without exceeding the powers granted to it by section 73(7).

The power of deferral could not be used just to see how the patient progressed so that, when it was used, it must be used by a tribunal which had determined — as this tribunal did — that the patient should be conditionally discharged if certain specified arrangements could be made to the tribunal's satisfaction. Once the power was exercised, it was inevitable that time would pass and during that period it might well emerge that the arrangements originally envisaged were unnecessary, or could not be made, or that other satisfactory arrangements could be made in their place. If that emerged, it was still open to the tribunal to heed the additional information and, having altered the arrangements it originally specified so as to take account of developments, to direct the patient's conditional discharge. *Application dismissed.*

R. v. Oxford Regional Mental Health Review Tribunal, ex p. Secretary of State for the Home Department; Same v. Yorkshire Mental Health Review Tribunal, ex p. Same

[1986] 1 W.L.R. 1180   *C.A. (Lawton and Stephen Brown L.JJ., Sir John Megaw)*

Lawton L.J.

Both cases substantially raised the same point, namely the powers of a tribunal under section 73(2) of the Mental Health Act 1983.

R. v. Oxford Regional MHRT

The Secretary of State ˙was entitled to notice of the hearing and also to early notice of any psychiatric reports relied upon by the patient. The Secretary of State did not receive either prior to the hearing on 12 February 1985 when the tribunal directed the patient's conditional discharge. When the Secretary of State was sent a copy of the tribunal's decision, it was apparent that there had been a very serious breakdown in the administrative arrangements contained in the Mental Health Review Tribunals Rules 1983 and he therefore applied for judicial review. Woolf J. broadly held that, because the tribunal could reconvene and reconsider the position, the Secretary of State had an opportunity to make his representations to the tribunal at that time and this provided a more appropriate remedy than judicial review.

R. v. Yorkshire MHRT

On 1 April 1985, the tribunal considered the patient's case and directed that she be conditionally discharged. However, the tribunal directed that, if the necessary discharge arrangements could not be made within six months, it would reconvene to reconsider the case and whether the patient's progress during the intervening period enabled its direction to be perfected without the specified arrangements being attached.

Deferred conditional discharges

The problem turned on the construction of the 1983 Act and the ordinary canons of construction applied. Under that Act, the Secretary of State was the guardian of the public welfare. As a consequence, the Act gave him certain powers and the rules made pursuant to it envisaged that he was entitled to make representations to a tribunal. It was clear that the intention of Parliament under section 72(1)(b) was that people should not be detained in hospital if it was no longer appropriate that they should be there for medical treatment. Under section 73(1) and (2), discharge was mandatory if a tribunal was satisfied that a patient meets the criteria for discharge and, equally, it could not discharge unless it was satisfied that was the case. Although it had been submitted that a tribunal were entitled to look at the need for social support when considering whether those criteria have been established, that meant writing something into the section which was not there. The tribunal had to ask themselves whether the criteria had been established to their satisfaction and confine their attention to those criteria; they were not entitled to look at any other matter. Thus, a tribunal had only three options: to grant an absolute discharge, to grant a conditional discharge, to refuse discharge. Section 73(7) provided for deferring a direction for the conditional discharge of a patient until such arrangements as appeared to the tribunal to be necessary for that purpose had been made to their satisfaction. The Oxford tribunal decided that the first of the criteria applicable in subsection (2) had been established and they directed conditional discharge. That was their decision. In the case of Miss Lord, the Yorkshire tribunal persuaded themselves that they could go back over the whole case again if she made progress during the time she was waiting for suitable arrangements to be made. However, once they had decided that the patient was entitled to a conditional discharge they could not go back on that part of the order. The arrangements referred to in section 73(7) were solely for the purpose of conditional discharge, not for reconsidering whether there should be conditional discharge at all. In neither case had there ever existed a power to reconsider the decision to discharge made by the tribunal. Once a decision had been made, a tribunal must stand by it and all that they were concerned with thereafter was the approval of such arrangements as they thought necessary for accomplishing conditional discharge. In Miss Lord's case, the tribunal misdirected themselves in thinking that they had power to reconsider her case, and, accordingly, to that extent their decision was wrong and could, and should, be remedied by the court.

Failure to give notice in the Oxford case

The fact that the Secretary of State was not given an opportunity of making representations to the Oxford tribunal was a classic case of a failure of natural justice entitling the court to intervene by ordering judicial review. In order to avoid such a mishap recurring in cases where the Home Secretary was not represented, tribunals should, before starting to hear the application, inquire and note whether he had been given notice of the application and when. As to the application of rule 28, which dealt with procedural irregularities, once the tribunal had made the decision which they made on 12 February 1985, the irregularity could not be cured. The Secretary of State had lost his right to make any representations about the patient's suitability to be discharged and, as the tribunal had no power to reconvene to reconsider its finding in this respect, it followed that there was nothing that the Secretary of State could do. *Appeals allowed.*

Campbell v. Secretary of State for the Home Department

[1988] 1 A.C. 120   *House of Lords (Lord Bridge of Harwich, Lord Brandon of Oakbrook, Lord Ackner, Lord Oliver of Aylmerton and Lord Goff of Chieveley)*

The patient involved in the case of R. v. Oxford Regional Mental Health Review Tribunal appealed against the decision of the Court of Appeal.

Lord Bridge of Harwich

It was common ground that the tribunal's decision had been made in breach of the 1983 rules. What was more important was that there had been a breach of the most fundamental rule of natural justice, in that the Secretary of State, as a vitally interested party, was denied a hearing. It was difficult to see how the tribunal's decision could properly stand. Such a fundamental flaw as vitiated the proceedings leading to the tribunal's decision called for a complete rehearing *de novo*. If every issue remained open for decision under section 73(7), and that provided the appropriate occasion for the rehearing, the earlier purported decision was at best irrelevant, at worst an embarrassment which the tribunal would have to do their best to put out of mind, but which would make it difficult for justice to be seen to be done at a rehearing before them. There was an inherent inconsistency in the argument forwarded on the patient's behalf. That argument accepted, on the one hand, that the tribunal proceedings were defective and relied on a rehearing under section 73(7) to cure that defect whilst claiming, on the other hand, that he was entitled to rely on the earlier decision in his favour. If the construction adopted by the Court of Appeal was right, and there was no power under subsection (7) to re-open any issue already decided under subsection (2), the earlier decision must be quashed. That would enable the rehearing to take place before a differently constituted tribunal.

The construction of section 73

As to the true construction of section 73, the first issue which a tribunal must address was whether they were satisfied as to one or other of the matters referred to in section 72(1)(b). If they were so satisfied and also satisfied that the patient need not remain liable to recall it was mandatory to direct his absolute discharge. If the tribunal thought that the patient should remain liable to recall, they could only contemplate a conditional discharge. Here, the tribunal's satisfaction or lack of satisfaction as to one or other of the matters in section 72(1)(b) would inevitably be coloured by the conditions they had in mind to impose. Whether or not the tribunal was satisfied that the patient's disorder was not of a nature or degree which made it appropriate for him to be liable to be detained in hospital for medical treatment, or that it was not necessary for his own health or safety or for the protection of others that he should receive such treatment, might be vitally influenced by the conditions which are to be imposed to regulate his life style upon release into the community. To take obvious examples suggested by the decision of the tribunal in this case, the tribunal might perfectly properly be satisfied that hospital detention was no longer necessary provided that the patient could be placed in a suitable hostel and required to submit to treatment as an out-patient by a suitable psychiatrist. These were matters to be secured by imposing appropriate conditions. Once the tribunal was satisfied as to one or other of grounds for discharge it was mandatory to direct his conditional discharge. But if the tribunal was only able to be so satisfied by the imposition of conditions on the patient's release, it was obvious that in many cases some time must elapse between the decision that conditional discharge was appropriate and the effective order directing the patient's discharge — the purpose being to enable the necessary practical arrangements to be made which would enable the patient to comply with the conditions, *e.g.* securing a suitable hostel placement for him and finding a suitable psychiatrist who was prepared to undertake his treatment as an out-patient.

Whether tribunal's decision was provisional or merely the implementation of it

The words of section 73(7) reserved to the tribunal the further decision as to whether the necessary arrangements had "been made to their satisfaction" but they were wholly inapt to indicate a deferment of the decision as to whether the tribunal was or could be satisfied that the patient must be discharged according to the statutory criteria. If the contrary argument were right, and a tribunal could not make a decision about whether it was satisfied as to the criteria for conditional discharge unless and until suitable discharge arrangements were in place, the two stage procedure contemplated by sections 73(2) and (7) would not seem to serve any useful purpose at all. However, the wording of section 73(7) clearly contemplated the possibility that it might not be possible to make suitable arrangements which complied with the conditions, in which case the decision that the patient was entitled to be discharged was deemed never to have been made. This clearly indicated a two stage process and the provision would be otiose if the decision as to whether the patient should be discharged was only one made once satisfactory arrangements had been made.

Patients who deteriorate while the arrangements are being made

Since a tribunal had no power to re-open the issue of a patient's suitability to be discharged under subsection (2) and must direct his discharge once satisfactory arrangements enabling the conditions to be met had been made, the question arose whether they could be compelled to discharge a patient whose condition had deteriorated during the intervening period. It might be that the second part of section 73(7) was designed to meet this very contingency. Whether that was so or not, it certainly enabled the Secretary of State, when a deterioration in the condition of the patient was brought to his attention, to forestall the patient's discharge by exercising his power under section 71 to refer the patient's case to the tribunal afresh.

Deferring discharge to a specified future date

Neither the Act nor the rules provided any authority for deferring the conditional discharge of a patient to a specified future date. It was impossible for a tribunal which deferred a direction to predict how long it would take to make the necessary arrangements. The decision should simply indicate that the direction was deferred until the necessary arrangements had been made to the satisfaction of the tribunal and specify what arrangements were required, which could normally be done, no doubt, simply by reference to the conditions to be imposed. Whoever was responsible for making the arrangements should then proceed with all reasonable expedition to do so and should bring the matter to the attention of the tribunal again as soon as practicable after it was thought that satisfactory arrangements had been made. Pursuant to rule 25, the tribunal could then decide that the arrangements were to their satisfaction without a further hearing. *Lord Brandon of Oakbrook, Lord Ackner, Lord Oliver of Aylmerton and Lord Goff of Chieveley agreed. Appeal dismissed.*

Commentary

The House of Lords decision in the *Oxford case* is the most important case on a tribunal's powers when reviewing the case of a restricted patient who is liable to be detained in a hospital. Apart from ruling on the nature of the power to defer conditional discharge, it also established the fact that the criteria for discharge are essentially relative, rather than absolute. Lawton L.J. took the opposite view in the Court of Appeal, stating that this was reading something into section 72(1)(b) that was not there. However, according to the decision in the House of Lords, whether or not a tribunal is satisfied that a patient's mental disorder is not of a kind which makes it appropriate for him to remain liable to detention in a hospital for medical treatment will often depend on the conditions of discharge it has in mind. Similarly, whether a tribunal is satisfied that it is not necessary for a patient's health or safety, or for the protection of others, that he receives such treatment will often depend upon the conditions to be imposed. Consequently, to take the Mollie Lord case, the tribunal could not later reconsider or revise the conditions of discharge if the arrangements originally envisaged could not be made: that amounted to reconsidering the decision as to whether she should be discharged at all. The tribunal's decision was that, on the conditions imposed by it, it was not appropriate or necessary for her to be further detained in hospital. Reconsidering those conditions necessarily involved reconsidering whether she should be discharged, that is whether she might satisfy the criteria for discharge on other conditions. Thus, the tribunal was reopening the issue already determined of her entitlement to be discharged under section 73.[33]

Patient's condition deteriorating before arrangements completed

The problem of what to do if a patient's condition declines prior to the arrangements for his discharge being completed was canvassed in each of the above cases, at each stage of the appeals process. Counsel for the Secretary of State submitted to Woolf J. that there was always the Home Secretary's power to recall a patient where that was necessary. On the assumption that a patient cannot be recalled to hospital until he has been discharged from it, and that to attempt to do so before then would be to interfere with the uncompleted judicial process, this was presumably a reference to the patient being immediately recalled upon leaving hospital — the equivalent of a prison gate arrest.[34] The position then forwarded by the Secretary of State in the Court of Appeal was that those responsible for the patient and for making the arrangements would be aware of any deterioration and there would be "no need to do anything more than to say that, in all the circumstances, the arrangements are not satisfactory." That, as Lawton L.J. pointed out, was a pragmatic approach to the problem. It was also a contradictory one because, as the same counsel pointed out at some length, the tribunal's role on reconsidering the case is limited to considering whether satisfactory arrangements which comply with the conditions imposed have been made, not whether the patient is entitled to be discharged. The approach

---

[33]   Where arrangements complying with the conditions imposed by the tribunal cannot be made, there is, of course, nothing to prevent the Home Secretary discharging the patient on alternative conditions: see Mental Health Act 1983, s.73(8).

[34]   The Secretary of State's power of recall under section 42(3) is exercisable in respect of a patient "who has been conditionally discharged." As section 73(7) makes clear, a patient is not discharged under section 73 unless and until arrangements for his discharge have been made to the tribunal's satisfaction. Furthermore, discharge may only be deferred until the necessary arrangements have been made, and for no longer and for no other purpose.

amounts to reconsidering the decision to discharge. The answer then given in the House of Lords was that the Secretary of State could refer the patient's case to the tribunal, in which case the direction that he be discharged would be deemed never to have been given. However, it is only when the case actually comes before a fresh tribunal that the previous decision is deemed not to have been made. There are strict limits as to the extent to which any new hearing may be expedited and the patient would be unlikely to consent to the time limits being abridged. So the question might then become whether it was lawful for the previous tribunal to deliberately delay the matter, by refusing to consider whether the conditions it had imposed were now met, in effect subverting its own final decision that the patient be discharged by refusing to implement it. Not to allow it to do so might damage public confidence in the tribunal system by seeming to place the public at unnecessary risk. To allow it to do so might damage public confidence in the tribunal system, by seeming to undermine the impartiality of the tribunal and allowing it to resile on its decisions — the tribunal would be colluding in the patient not being discharged. It seems better therefore to take the position set out by McCullough J. in *R. v. Secretary of State for the Home Department, ex p. K.*[35] In that case, a patient previously conditionally discharged by a tribunal was recalled at the prison gate upon serving a prison sentence for two offences committed following his discharge. It was submitted that what the Secretary of State did was to overturn a decision with which he did not agree. His views were put to the tribunal on that occasion and they were rejected. He did not like the result so he was going to frustrate it by what could only be regarded as a misuse of section 42(3). McCullough J. held that it would be unlawful for the Secretary of State to recall a restricted patient to hospital when only the previous week or month he had been conditionally discharged from hospital by direction of a tribunal, unless meanwhile something has happened which justified the belief that a different view might now be taken about one of the factors on which his release had depended. However, in K's case, there was nothing in the tribunal's decision to prevent the Secretary of State from alleging that further events had occurred since the tribunal's decision which had a bearing on the question of his mental condition, namely the commission of two serious offences. Accordingly, it was lawful to detain K. at the prison gate and to recall him to hospital. Similarly, if a patient's condition on leaving the hospital gate is such that there is evidence that his condition requires his immediate recall to hospital, recalling him is no more groundless than recalling him two weeks, two months or two years later on exactly the same grounds. All three situations are factually the same in the one material respect — his condition has significantly deteriorated during the period since the decision to discharge him was made and it is unlikely that the same tribunal would now discharge him if his case was before it. They are factually different in one immaterial respect, which is simply how long it has taken the patient to deteriorate since the discharge decision was made. The advantages of this approach are several:

1.) it leaves the power of recall where it belongs, in the Secretary of State's hands, rather than involving tribunals in the recall process, which would undermine the confidence of patients in their impartiality;

2.) it leaves the tribunal's functions as being to discharge patients, including reviewing the justification for their recall to hospital, and discharging them again if appropriate;

---

[35]   *R. v. Secretary of State for the Home Department, ex p. K.* [1990] 1 W.L.R. 168, McCullough J.

3.) it allows for a speedy hearing of the justification for such an exceptional recall — the Secretary of State can immediately refer the patient's case back to the tribunal and both he and the patient can consent to the usual time limits being abridged, so that a speedy hearing is held;

4.) it may be possible for the satisfactory arrangements already made for the patient's discharge to be kept open if the case can be dealt with quickly;

5.) it represents a reasonable balance of the need to protect the public and the need to protect the patient's interests, and to generally give effect to tribunal decisions in all but the most exceptional circumstances.

Secretary of State's powers prior to discharge

During the deferral period, the patient remains liable to be detained and the Secretary of State has his usual powers in respect of such patients. In particular, he may consent to the patient being granted leave of absence while the necessary arrangements for his discharge are being made. Although he has power to impose further conditions of discharge or to vary the conditions of discharge, these powers are not exercisable until the patient has actually been discharged.[36] Thus, the Home Secretary cannot impose further conditions or vary the conditions while the arrangements stipulated by the tribunal are being made. That would throw the process into complete confusion. On considering whether satisfactory arrangements had been made which complied with the conditions imposed by it, the tribunal would find that those conditions no longer existed and that alternative arrangements had been made.

RECOMMENDATIONS AND RESTRICTED CASES

Unless a tribunal is satisfied that the patient comes within the statutory grounds for discharge set out in section 73(1), it may not discharge the patient. This limitation naturally leads on to the issue of whether a tribunal has any powers short of discharge. In particular, whether it may recommend under section 72(3) that the patient be granted leave of absence, transferred to another hospital, or transferred into guardianship, and further consider his case in the event that its recommendation is not complied with.

Application of section 72(3) in restricted cases

Section 72(7) provides that section 72(1) shall not apply in the case of a restricted patient except as provided in sections 73 and 74. The wording is superficially ambiguous insofar as it implies that the other subsections in section 72 do apply, including, where a patient is not discharged, the power to make recommendations and to reclassify him. The point was considered in the following cases and it was resolved that this is not in fact so. Consequently, a tribunal's powers are limited to those conferred by section 73. It has a duty to discharge in certain circumstances, otherwise no powers at all. The subsections of section 72 referred to in the judgment below are set out on pages 482 and 483.

---

[36]   If a tribunal's direction for a patient's conditional discharge has been deferred then, by definition, he has not yet been conditionally discharged. Consequently, subsections 73(4) and (5) do not apply.

Grant v. The Mental Health Review Tribunal for the Trent Region
The Queen v. The Mersey Mental Health Review Tribunal ex p. O'Hara

The Times, 26 April 1986   *McNeill J.*

The two matters raised substantially the same point and were heard together, with the parties' consent.

Grant

In Grant, the tribunal received evidence that the patient, who was detained at a special hospital, would be accepted on transfer at a local NHS hospital. The tribunal's view was that such a transfer was appropriate. However, it did not consider that it had any statutory power to make such a recommendation and declined to do so. The tribunal was asked to state a case, pursuant to section 78(8) of the Mental Health Act 1983. The question of law for the opinion of the court was whether a tribunal considering an application made by a restricted patient had the power to make a statutory recommendation for his transfer to another hospital under section 72(3) and to further consider his case in the event that its recommendation was not complied with.

O'Hara

In O'Hara's case, the patient's solicitor conceded at the outset that he was not in a position to put forward evidence which would justify the patient's discharge. However, the responsible medical officer recommended his transfer from the special hospital where he was detained to a local NHS hospital. The question again raised was whether, when dealing with a restricted patient, a tribunal had power to go beyond the express provisions of section 73 — including such parts of section 73 as expressly incorporated provisions of section 72 — and to exercise the power to make a recommendation in section 72(3).

McNeill J.

Although an advisory role in terms of a power to make recommendations existed under section 74 in the case of patients subject to restriction directions, and there was a similar power to make recommendations in respect of unrestricted patients under section 72(3), there was no similar provision in section 73. It therefore seemed that Parliament did not intend tribunals to have such an advisory role when considering the case of a detained patient who was subject to a restriction order.

MHA 1983, s.72(6)

Section 72(6) provided that subsections (1) to (5) — which dealt with the mandatory and discretionary discharge of patients and the making of recommendations and reclassification of those not discharged — "apply in relation to references to a Mental Health Review Tribunal as they apply in relation to applications made to such a tribunal by or in respect of a patient." The effect and purpose of the subsection was nothing more than that if the preceding subsections applied to tribunal proceedings commenced by application, they applied equally to those commenced by way of reference. The intention was not that the whole of section 72 applied to restricted patients.

MHA 1983, s.72(7)

Section 72(7) provided that subsection (1) "shall not apply in the case of a restricted patient except as provided in sections 73 and 74 below." The intended effect was not that all of the subsections in section 72 other than subsection (1) applied to restricted patients. The effect was simply to make it clear that, subject to the express incorporation of sub-paragraphs 72(1)(b)(i) and (ii) in section 73, section 72(1) only applied to applications made by or in respect of a "patient." It did not to applications made by "restricted patients" as defined by section 79.

MHA 1983, s.72(5) — reclassification

Although it had been contended that the power of reclassification conferred by section 72(5) was relevant both to unrestricted and to restricted patients, and its applicability in all cases was suggested by the absence of any comparable provision in section 73, such a provision would be unnecessary in unrestricted cases. A restriction order was "a further order" upon a hospital order and a change in a patient's mental condition did not involve any variation of a restriction order. Moreover, even if section 72(5) did apply to restricted patients, it did not support the contention that section 72(3) did.

MHA 1983, s.72(3) — recommendations

It was noteworthy that the subsection 72(3) authorised a tribunal to direct the patient's discharge on a future date and it was only if immediate or future discharge was declined that the power to make a recommendation under that subsection arose. That section 72(3) did not apply in restricted cases was clear given that this power of future unqualified discharge was irreconcilable with the power conferred on tribunals under section 73(7) to defer giving a direction for a restricted patient's discharge. Parliament plainly intended to repose wider powers on a tribunal dealing with an unrestricted patient.

MHRT Rules 1983, r.25

Although rule 25 provided for a tribunal reconvening a restricted patient's case if its recommendation was not complied with, this apparent inconsistency in a statutory instrument could not confer a jurisdiction not given in the governing statute. Nor could the wording of the rules be a guide to the construction of the statute. While rule 25(2) was not *ultra vires*, its effect was limited to the circumstances in which the statute empowered making a recommendation and to an extent it was procedural. In summary, the statute neither expressly nor by implication empowered a tribunal dealing with the case of a restricted patient to exercise the power given to it by section 72(3) in unrestricted cases. While the Secretary of State could request, or a tribunal offer, informal advice, there was no statutory power requiring or authorising that. *Applications dismissed*

Commentary

The 1983 Act was a consolidating Act and the present provisions repeat those set out in Schedule 1 to the Mental Health (Amendment) Act 1982. The benefit of consulting that statute is that the drafting is much clearer. All of the tribunal provisions which apply to restricted patients are set out in the Schedule while those which apply to unrestricted patients are set out in the body of the Act. Thus, there can be little confusion about which powers apply in which type of case. It is noticeable that the Schedule does not include any power to make recommendations and the decision in *Grant* was therefore clearly the correct one. Furthermore, since a restricted patient cannot be transferred into guardianship, it is difficult to see how any other interpretation is tenable.[37]

---

[37]   That being one of the recommendations that can be made under section 72(3). See Mental Health Act 1983, ss. 41(3), 55(4) and 145(3); Sched. 1, Pt. II, paras. 2 and 5.

RECLASSIFICATION IN RESTRICTED CASES

Apart from the power to make recommendations, the other power possessed by a tribunal which does not discharge an unrestricted patient is that of reclassifying his condition. The nature and limits of this power have already been considered (**499**). However, a further issue, to be addressed here, is whether that power extends to tribunal proceedings involving restricted patients.

RECLASSIFICATION — SECTION 72(5)

72.—(5) Where application is made to a Mental Health Review Tribunal under any provision of this Act by or in respect of a patient and the tribunal do not direct that the patient be discharged *or, if he is (or is to be) subject to after-care under supervision, that he cease to be so subject (or not become so subject)*, the tribunal may, if satisfied that the patient is suffering from a form of mental disorder other than the form specified in the application, order or direction relating to him, direct that that application, order or direction be amended by substituting for the form of mental disorder specified in it such other form of mental disorder as appears to the tribunal to be appropriate.

(6) Subsections (1) to (5) above apply in relation to references to a Mental Health Review Tribunal as they apply in relation to applications made to such a tribunal by or in respect of a patient.

(7) Subsection (1) shall not apply in the case of a restricted patient except as provided in sections 73 and 74.

Case law

The question of whether a tribunal may reclassify a restricted patient was touched upon but not resolved in *Grant v. The Mental Health Review Tribunal for the Trent Region* (**549**). However, McNeill J. appeared to have reservations about whether such a power existed. More recently, leave to apply for judicial review of a tribunal's decision on the ground that it had reclassified a restricted patient when it had no such power was refused.

R. v. South West Thames Mental Health Review Tribunal, ex p. P.D.

FC3 95/6604/D, 12 June 1996   *C.A. (Aldous, Phillips and Potter L.JJ.)*

The patient was liable to be detained in pursuance of a hospital order and a restriction order. The form of disorder recorded on the hospital order was mental impairment. In December 1992, a tribunal which did not discharge the patient considered and rejected the responsible medical officer's argument that he should be reclassified as suffering only from a psychopathic disorder. According to the written reasons for its decision, the tribunal was satisfied that the patient continued to suffer from mental impairment and there were no grounds for reclassification. Another tribunal considered the patient's case in September 1994 and it had before it reports from the patient's new responsible medical officer and from a psychiatrist instructed by the patient. The tribunal did not direct the patient's discharge but it did direct that "the patient be reclassified by substituting for the present form of mental disorder, namely mental impairment, psychopathic disorder."

The patient's application for judicial review

The patient's application for judicial review was founded on three principle grounds. Firstly, that a tribunal has no power to reclassify a restricted patient as suffering from some form of mental disorder other than that specified by the sentencing court in the original hospital order. Secondly, if it had such a power, it was nevertheless bound by the decision of the earlier tribunal to the contrary because there had been no change of circumstances or new evidence of psychopathic disorder since that time. Thirdly, the reasons given for the tribunal's decision to reclassify were inadequate and/or were Wednesbury unreasonable. Leave to apply for judicial review on these grounds was refused and the patient appealed against this refusal.

Aldous L.J.

The first submission was that the tribunal had no power to reclassify a restricted patient. Although section 72 was in wide terms, the powers to deal with restricted patients were to be found in section 73. The judge considered that submission and said that the submission that the exercise of jurisdiction by the tribunal under section 72(5) was *ultra vires* was, in his opinion, an unarguable proposition: "It seems to me having regard to the total terms in which that section is couched and having regard to the remainder of the relevant provisions of the statute, section 72(5) is the appropriate vehicle for dealing with the reclassification of patients detained in a mental hospital, whether under compulsory detention by way of order of the court or otherwise." That seemed to be the right conclusion, particularly when one took into account section 72(7).

Whether the patient should have been exercised

The argument that any power to reclassify the patient should not have been exercised in the absence of some new circumstances amounted to a submission that the earlier tribunal's conclusion concerning the patient's condition constituted a judicial finding that was *res judicata* or analogous thereto. There could not be res judicata in these cases. A tribunal had its statutory duty to perform and it could not avoid that by accepting a submission that it was bound to follow another tribunal's decision, even if there had been no change of circumstances. It must apply itself and come to its own decision. In each case there must inevitably be an update on the patient's condition. It was right that a tribunal should apply its mind to the matters before it and not feel itself fettered by a previous decision, but of course pay due regard to it.

Whether the reasons for the decision were adequate

A decision to reclassify a patient was an important decision and the tribunal set out five paragraphs of reasons as to why it had decided to do so. However, it was arguable that the reasons given for reclassifying the patient were inadequate or, if adequate, showed that the tribunal had not turned its mind to the relevant legal matters that had to be considered under the statute. The matter was sufficiently arguable for leave to be granted. *Phillips and Potter L.JJ. agreed. Leave to appeal granted.*

Commentary

Whether the court was referred to the decision in *Grant*, in particular in relation to the effect of section 72(7), and what arguments were advanced, is not recorded in the Court of Appeal transcript. However, for the reasons given below, it is submitted that the decision on the substantive point of whether a restricted patient may be reclassified is extremely difficult to sustain. The point therefore deserves to be fully argued.

Mental Health Act 1959

Restricted patients could not be reclassified under the 1959 Act, whether by their responsible medical officer, the Secretary of State, or by a tribunal advising the Home Secretary as to the exercise of his powers.[38] The reason for this limitation cannot have been that a restricted patient's classification had no bearing on the duration of the orders, that liability not requiring periodic renewal. This is because a patient's classification similarly had no bearing on the duration of a hospital order without restrictions and the renewal criteria did not refer at all to the form of disorder from which an unrestricted patient was suffering. The main reason for extending the provisions to unrestricted hospital order patients appears to have been to enable them to apply to a tribunal for their discharge if the original grounds for their detention were considered to no longer hold good (**499**). Restricted patients had no power to apply to a tribunal under the 1959 Act and tribunals had no power to discharge them. Their only right was to periodically require the Secretary of State to refer their cases to a tribunal for advice. There was, however, no point in giving advice about the correctness of the patient's formal classification, because neither the Secretary of State nor any other person had any power to reclassify.

Mental Health (Amendment) Act 1982

The 1982 Act conferred tribunals with power to discharge restricted patients, so the issue becomes whether, in giving tribunals this power, Parliament also intended to confer on them a power to reclassify restricted patients whom they did not discharge.

The argument in favour of such a power

In favour of the contention that tribunals have a power of reclassification in restriction order cases is the reference in section 72(5) to applications made "under any provision of this Act by or in respect of a patient" — although, according to the *Grant case*, the use of the term a "patient" in section 72 but a "restricted patient" in section 73 is significant and represents a deliberate limitation.

The arguments against such a power

Notwithstanding the refusal of leave in *ex p. P.D.*, there are weighty arguments against any interpretation that the statute empowers tribunals to reclassify restricted patients—

- In the first place, it remains the case that neither the Secretary of State nor a restricted patient's responsible medical officer have any power to reclassify. Hence, one needs to establish some reason why Parliament intended that restricted patients should only be reclassified by tribunals. That is because the limitation that only a tribunal had a certain power would be unique within the statutory framework.

---

[38]   Mental Health Act 1959, ss. 38(1), 65(3), 66(6), 123(4), 147(4), Third Schedule.

- Secondly, in *Grant v. Mental Health Review Tribunal*,[39] the court held that section 72(7) did not have the effect that section 72(3) — the power of a tribunal to make recommendations in unrestricted cases — was incorporated into section 73: the powers specified in section 72 were powers expressed to be exercisable in respect only of "patients," not "restricted patients" as defined by section 79. The section was only relevant to restricted patients insofar as expressly incorporated by subsequent sections specifying a tribunal's powers in respect of them. Furthermore, as Neill J. observed, although there was no comparable reclassification provision in section 73, that was because such a provision would be unnecessary. It is difficult to see how section 72(7) can possibly be read as stating that subsection 72(5) but not subsection 72(3) applies to cases determined under section 73.

- Thirdly, the proper construction of the statute tends against any such view. The 1983 Act was a consolidating Act and the present provisions repeat those introduced by Schedule 1 to the Mental Health (Amendment) Act 1982. The benefit of consulting that statute is that the new tribunal powers concerning restricted patients were set out in the schedule while those applicable in unrestricted cases were set out in the body of the Act. Thus, there could be little confusion about which powers applied to which type of case. Section 28(4) of the 1982 Act provided that Schedule 1 had effect "for enabling persons who are subject to restriction orders or restriction directions to be discharged by Mental Health Review Tribunals ..." Schedule 1 conferred on tribunals the present power to discharge, absolutely or conditionally, but no power to reclassify restricted patients who were not so discharged. Section 28(4) did not state that Schedule 1 had effect for enabling restricted patients "to be discharged" by tribunals and the pre-existing power to reclassify unrestricted patients in subsection 123(3) was also to be lifted out from that section and added to the new powers specified in the schedule.

- Fourthly, it seems clear that section 72(5) does not apply to cases dealt with under section 74. A tribunal's powers in such cases are limited to notifying the Secretary of State whether the patient meets the statutory grounds for discharge and a power which arises only when a tribunal does not discharge cannot possibly apply. One therefore needs to establish some reason why Parliament intended that a patient subject to a restriction order, but not a patient subject to a restriction direction, may be reclassified by a tribunal. There appears to be no reason and, indeed, one would expect the opposite to be the case if any distinction was to be drawn.[40]

- Fifthly, restricted patients dealt with under the Criminal Procedure (Insanity) Act 1964 have no classification under the 1983 Act. Although tribunals quite often do it, it is difficult to see how these patients can be "reclassified."

[39] *Grant v. The Mental Health Review Tribunal for the Trent Region; R. v. The Mersey Mental Health Review Tribunal ex p. O'Hara, The Times,* 26 April 1986 (**549**).

[40] This is because only patients who suffer from a major form of mental disorder may be transferred to hospital under section 48. Hence, the patient's classification might be of some relevance in such cases. See *Re V.E. (mental health patient)* [1973] 1 Q.B. 452 (**577**). Likewise, when section 45A is brought into force, that power is only exercisable in respect of offenders who suffer from a psychopathic disorder.

- Sixthly, the power of reclassification in section 72(5) is a discretionary power and the general view is that a tribunal's powers in restricted cases do not permit the exercise of any discretion. They have a duty to discharge in certain circumstances, otherwise no powers at all. All in all, one is drawn to the conclusion that it is highly improbable that Parliament intended to confer on tribunals a power to reclassify restricted patients.

DETAINED PATIENTS SUBJECT TO RESTRICTION OR LIMITATION DIRECTIONS

- *Section 45A provides that where the Crown Court sentences an offender who suffers from a psychopathic disorder to imprisonment, it may in certain circumstances also direct that, instead of being removed to and detained in a prison, he be removed to and detained in a specified hospital ("a hospital direction") and be subject to the special restrictions set out in section 41 (a "limitation direction") (398).*[41]

- *Section 47 provides that the Secretary of State may by warrant direct the transfer to hospital of a patient who is serving a sentence of imprisonment. Section 48 similarly provides that the Secretary of State may remove to hospital certain other categories of detained persons, such as defendants remanded in custody pending trial. In each case, the Secretary of State may, and in some cases must, also give a restriction direction under section 49 (383).*

A tribunal's powers are further restricted when it deals with the case of a patient who is subject to a restriction direction and, following the implementation of section 45A, a limitation direction. The reason for this is that there are two authorities for the patient's detention — the earlier of them authorising his detention in prison or some other place of custody, the later authorising his removal from that place and his detention in a hospital for treatment. The fact that a tribunal is satisfied that the usual statutory grounds for detaining and treating such a person in hospital are no longer satisfied may be a reason for not further detaining him there. However, the fact that he no longer requires hospital treatment is not a reason *per se* for also releasing him from the prior authority for his detention in prison.

STATUTORY POWERS

A tribunal's powers in such cases are set out in section 74 of the Act, which is set out below.

---

[41] Mental Health Act 1983, s.45A(3), as inserted by Crime (Sentences) Act 1997, s.46. The section was brought into force on 1 October 1997 (**398**).

All patients

74.—(1) Where an application to a Mental Health Review Tribunal is made by a restricted patient who is subject to [a limitation direction or] a restriction direction, or where the case of such a patient is referred to such a tribunal, the tribunal—

Notification of whether the criteria for absolute or conditional criteria are satisfied

(a) shall notify the Secretary of State whether, in their opinion, the patient would, if subject to a restriction order, be entitled to be absolutely or conditionally discharged under section 73 above (**514**); and

Recommendations concerning patients who satisfy the criteria for conditional discharge

(b) if they notify him that the patient would be entitled to be conditionally discharged, may recommend that in the event of his not being discharged under this section he should continue to be detained in hospital.

Section 47 patients

Secretary of State giving notice that patient may be discharged

(2) If in the case of a patient not falling within subsection (4) below—

(a) the tribunal notify the Secretary of State that the patient would be entitled to be absolutely or conditionally discharged; and

(b) within the period of 90 days beginning with the date of that notification the Secretary of State gives notice to the tribunal that the patient may be so discharged,

the tribunal shall direct the absolute or, as the case may be, the conditional discharge of the patient.

Transfer to prison where no such notice is given unless tribunal recommended otherwise in the case of a patient who satisfied the criteria for conditional discharge

(3) Where a patient continues to be liable to be detained in a hospital at the end of the period referred to in subsection (2)(b) above because the Secretary of State has not given the notice there mentioned, the managers of the hospital shall, unless the tribunal have made a recommendation under subsection (1)(b) above, transfer the patient to a prison or other institution in which he might have been detained if he had not been removed to hospital, there to be dealt with as if he had not been so removed.

Section 48 patients

Immediate remission to custody of patients satisfying absolute discharge criteria and, unless tribunal has recommended otherwise, of patients who satisfy the criteria for conditional discharge

(4) If, in the case of a patient who is subject to a transfer direction under section 48 above, the tribunal notify the Secretary of State that the patient would be entitled to be absolutely or conditionally discharged, the Secretary of State shall, unless the tribunal have made a recommendation under subsection (1)(b) above, by warrant direct that the patient be remitted to a prison or other institution in which he might have been detained if he had not been removed to hospital, there to be dealt with as if he had not been so removed.

SUMMARY OF POWERS

A tribunal must approach the case as if the patient was subject to a restriction order rather than a restriction or limitation direction. It must therefore apply the section 73 discharge criteria applicable in such cases and reach a finding as to whether, if that was the case, it would be obliged to direct the patient's absolute or conditional discharge (**515 et seq.**). It must notify the Home Secretary of its finding. What then happens depends upon whether the patient is serving a sentence of imprisonment or is instead detained under section 48.

Restriction direction patients detained under section 48

Where a tribunal notifies the Home Secretary that a restricted patient detained under section 48 satisfies the criteria for absolute discharge, the Secretary of State must direct that the patient be remitted to prison or such other institution in which he might have been detained had he not been removed to hospital. Where a tribunal instead notifies the Home Secretary that the patient satisfies the criteria for conditional discharge then, similarly, the Secretary of State shall remit him to custody under section 74 unless the tribunal also "recommended" that the patient should continue to be detained in hospital.

The rationale behind the tribunal's powers

While it may be appropriate to return to prison a patient who satisfies the criteria for being discharged from the hospital to which he was removed, there is often an important distinction between patients who meet the criteria for absolute discharge and those who only satisfy the criteria for conditional discharge. In the latter case, the patient may merely be in remission. Returning him to the prison where his health deteriorated may only serve to bring about a relapse and a second removal to hospital in .the not too distant future. The Act therefore enables a tribunal to "recommend" that the patient remains in hospital rather than be remitted to custody. In other cases, the main reason for a tribunal's finding that the patient would, if subject to a restriction order, only be discharged on conditions does not stem from any fear that his health will deteriorate if he is returned to prison. It reflects instead a belief that conditions of residence and supervision would be necessary in order to protect the public if the patient was in the community. Consequently, a tribunal is not bound to recommend that a patient not be remitted to prison.

Restriction direction patients detained under section 45A or 47

Serving prisoners are in a somewhat more favourable position. Where a tribunal notifies the Secretary of State that the patient satisfies the criteria for absolute discharge, the tribunal shall so discharge the patient if, within the following 90 days, the Secretary of State serves notice on the tribunal that the patient may be absolutely discharged. Otherwise, at the expiration of that period, the managers of the hospital must transfer the patient to prison, or to such other institution in which he might have been detained had he not been removed to hospital. Where a tribunal notifies the Secretary of State that a patient satisfies the criteria for conditional discharge, it may also "recommend" that he continue to be detained in hospital if the Secretary of State does not give notice that he may be conditionally discharged by the tribunal. If the Secretary of State serves notice on the tribunal within 90 days that the patient may be so discharged, the tribunal shall direct his conditional discharge. Failing this, the managers must transfer the patient to prison at the expiration of that period, unless the tribunal "recommended" otherwise. A tribunal which directs a patient's conditional discharge in accordance with the Secretary of State's notice may where necessary defer its direction until satisfactory arrangements have been made which enable the conditions of discharge to be complied with.

The rationale behind the tribunal's powers

It can be seen that the Act distinguishes between persons serving a sentence of imprisonment and persons in custody for some other reason. In the former case, the prisoner may be nearing the end of his sentence by the time a tribunal considers his case, in which case the restrictions will shortly cease to have effect anyway. If he is fit to be absolutely discharged from hospital, it may be inappropriate to return him to prison to serve out the short residual part of his sentence, the more so because that is the place where his mental health broke down. In other cases, there may be advantages in conditionally discharging a prisoner into the community under the 1983 Act rather than under licence. Allowing a patient to be discharged under the supervision of the professionals with experience in dealing with people who have psychiatric problems may, in particular, confer a greater measure of protection for the public. The position of patients transferred under section 48 is materially different. Most of these patients will have been transferred to hospital during the course of criminal proceedings before the Crown Court or a magistrates court and still be awaiting trial or sentence.

The effect of absolute discharge

Where a patient detained under section 45A or 47 is absolutely discharged under section 74, he ceases to be liable to be detained by virtue of the relevant hospital or transfer direction and the restrictions accordingly also cease to have effect.[42] The patient not having been remitted to prison to serve out his sentence, he is discharged into the community.

The effect of conditional discharge

The effect of conditional discharge is the same as that where a patient subject to a restriction order is conditionally discharged. The patient remains liable to recall to hospital for further treatment and he must comply with any conditions of discharge imposed by the tribunal or subsequently by the Secretary of State.[43] The latter may from time to time vary any existing conditions of discharge.[44] Unless the patient is serving an indeterminate (life) sentence, his sentence will eventually expire. If the patient is still conditionally discharged at that time, because he has not been recalled to hospital during the intervening period, he is deemed to be absolutely discharged on that day.[45] If, having been recalled, he is again liable to be detained in hospital for treatment, the restrictions cease to have effect on that date.[46] However, in this case, the patient remains liable to be detained in hospital for treatment. More particularly, he is treated as if he had been admitted to that hospital under a "new" notional hospital order made without restrictions on the date his sentence expired.[47] He may

---

[42] Mental Health Act 1983, ss.74(6) and 73(3).
[43] *Ibid.*, ss.74(6) and 73(4).
[44] *Ibid.*, ss.74(6) and 73(5).
[45] *Ibid.*, ss.74(6) , 73(6), 50(2)–(4).
[46] *Ibid.*, s.50(2).
[47] Mental Health Act 1983, ss.41(5) and 55(4).

apply to a tribunal during the following six months[48] and, if the hospital order is then renewed, he may thereafter make one further tribunal application during each six or twelve month period he remains liable to be detained. The final situation to be considered is that where a restriction or limitation direction patient is recalled to hospital prior to the expiration of his sentence. He is again liable to be detained subject to restrictions and the Home Secretary must refer his case to a tribunal.[49] The somewhat unsatisfactory effect is that the tribunal must again deal with his case under section 74. Consequently, his transfer back to prison at this late stage again becomes a possibility albeit that it was not a possibility while he was discharged.[50]

RESTRICTION DIRECTION CASES — SUMMARY OF PROVISIONS

Tribunal's findings, etc.	Section 45A & 47 patients	Section 48 patients
• *Patient does not satisfy the discharge criteria.*	Patient remains in hospital.	
• *Patient satisfies criteria for conditional discharge — MHRT recommends that patient not be remitted to custody as a result of its finding.*	Tribunal directs patient's conditional discharge if Secretary of State gives notice within 90 days that it may do so; otherwise patient remains in hospital.	Patient remains in hospital.
• *Patient satisfies criteria for conditional discharge — MHRT makes no recommendation about remission to custody.*	Tribunal directs patient's conditional discharge if Secretary of State gives notice within 90 days that it may do so; otherwise patient transferred to prison.	Patient remitted to custody — 90 day rule does not apply.
• *Patient satisfies the criteria for absolute discharge.*	Tribunal directs patient's absolute discharge if Secretary of State gives notice within 90 days that it may do so. Otherwise patient transferred to prison.	

The effect of remission to prison

Where a restricted patient detained under section 45A, 47 or 48 is transferred or remitted to prison under section 74, the transfer direction and the restriction direction, or the hospital direction and the limitation direction as the case may be, cease to have effect on his arrival in the prison or other institution.[51]

---

[48]   *Ibid.*, s.69(2)(a). It is submitted that any tribunal application outstanding on the date the restrictions cease is deemed to have been withdrawn (**648**).

[49]   *Ibid.*, s.75(1)(a).

[50]   See the wording of section 75(1)(b).

[51]   Mental Health Act 1983, s.74(5).

Recommendations and reclassification

It is clear that a tribunal which deals with the case of a patient who is subject to a restriction or limitation direction has no power to make recommendations. Nor would it seem to have any power to reclassify the patient (**554**).

THE HOME SECRETARY'S POWERS

The Home Secretary's powers under sections 42 and 50–53 apply in the usual way to patients who are not discharged under section 74.[52] This means that a patient who is not discharged under section 74 may still be absolutely or conditionally discharged by the Secretary of State under section 42, and he may similarly direct that the restriction or limitation direction shall cease to have effect in respect of a patient who has not been discharged. Conversely, if the patient is not discharged or remitted to prison under section 74, he may still be remitted to prison by the Secretary of State under sections 50–53 in the circumstances set out there. One of these circumstances is that he has been notified by a tribunal that the patient "no longer requires treatment in hospital for mental disorder or that no effective treatment for his disorder can be given in the hospital to which he has been removed" (**386**).[53] This must be why section 74 refers to a tribunal recommending, rather than directing, that a patient shall not be remitted to prison.

LIFE SENTENCE PRISONERS

It has been noted that where a person serving a determinate sentence is removed to hospital, the restriction direction will cease to have effect on the date on which the sentence expires. In the case of persons serving a sentence of life imprisonment it is necessarily the case that the restrictions cannot lapse in this way. The patient therefore remains subject to the restriction or limitation direction unless and until he is either absolutely discharged, remitted to prison or released on licence. The matter is further complicated by the fact that the release into the community of persons serving life imprisonment is usually by way of life licence. There are therefore two possible routes back into the community: (1) release on life licence; (2) absolute or conditional discharge under the 1983 Act. The inter-relationship of the two schemes has already been summarised (**390**).

CONDITIONALLY DISCHARGED PATIENTS

The powers of a tribunal when determining an application or reference by a conditionally discharged patient are set out in section 75(3) of the Act. The tribunal may vary the existing conditions, impose a fresh condition of discharge, or direct that the restriction order or direction shall cease to have effect, in which case the patient also ceases to be subject to the associated hospital order or transfer direction.[54] A further

---

[52]   Mental Health Act 1983, ss. 74(6), 74(7) and 73(8).

[53]   In this respect, patients remanded in custody by a magistrates court and then removed to hospital under sections 48 and 49 are in a more favourable position than other restriction direction patients. Prior to committal to the Crown Court, the Secretary of State cannot remit them to prison except in the circumstances permitted by section 74.

[54]   As to whether this power to terminate the restrictions, and thereby to bring the relevant orders or directions to an end, extends to patients subject to limitation directions, see page 563.

option is, of course, to give no direction at all, in which case the existing conditions of discharge will continue as if there had been no tribunal hearing at all.

CONDITIONALLY DISCHARGED PATIENTS

Tribunal's discretionary powers   "**75.**—(3) Sections 73 and 74 shall not apply to an application [by a conditionally discharged patient] under subsection (2) above but on any such application the tribunal may—

(a) vary any condition to which the patient is subject in connection with his discharge or impose any condition which might have been imposed in connection therewith; or

(b) direct that the restriction order or restriction direction to which he is subject shall cease to have effect;

and if the tribunal give a direction under paragraph (b) above the patient shall cease to be liable to be detained by virtue of the relevant hospital order or transfer direction."

THE ABSENCE OF STATUTORY CRITERIA

Section 75 provides that sections 73 and 74 shall not apply to applications by conditionally discharged patients. A patient who has already been conditionally discharged cannot, strictly speaking, then be absolutely discharged so neither of the discharge powers exercisable under section 73(1) are relevant to the patient's situation. Nevertheless, it is noteworthy that section 75 does not impose a duty on a tribunal to direct that the restrictions shall cease to have effect even where satisfied that it is not appropriate for the patient to remain liable to be recalled to hospital for further treatment. The drafting of section 75(3) carefully avoids giving the patient any entitlement to have the restrictions terminated. There is no statutory test which, if satisfied, obliges their termination and the section avoids using any of the words previously used in section 72 or 73 which might require a tribunal to give a particular direction — "shall," "necessary," "appropriate," "justified," and so forth. Given the absence of any statutory criteria, no burden of proof can exist because there is no statutory issue to be determined to which it could relate. It is not a case of being satisfied or not satisfied about certain issues or facts. The tribunal may simply do or not do any of the things listed in section 75(3) and which kind of order it makes, if any, is a matter for the tribunal's discretion. That discretion is completely unfettered by statute and its scope is similar to that vested in the Home Secretary when exercising his powers, which are similarly unfettered by statute. Provided that a tribunal does not exercise its discretion in a manner which is "Wednesbury unreasonable" or wholly inconsistent with the purposes and objects of the statute, its decision is not susceptible to judicial review. The question arises of why the "appropriateness of liability to recall" test in section 73(1)(b) is not incorporated into section 75, given that decisions about what is appropriate are largely subjective and, as *ex p. Cooper* shows, virtually unreviewable. As a matter of logic, Parliament must have conceived of some situation in which the facts might seem to a tribunal to require it to terminate the restrictions because it was not appropriate for the patient

561

to remain liable to recall to hospital *for further treatment*. The most likely explanation is that Parliament had in mind the case of a patient who, although said to have been "cured" of his mental disorder and therefore not to be in need of further in-patient treatment in the future, nevertheless remained dangerous. A similar predicament might arise if the condition of a person suffering from a psychopathic disorder was not now considered to be treatable in a hospital. It might also arise as a result of legal as well as clinical changes; as where, a sex offender dealt with under the 1959 Act was not considered to suffer from a psychopathic disorder as defined by the 1983 Act.[55] The tribunal's opinion in each case being that there was no possibility of the patient requiring further in-patient treatment in the future, it might feel constrained to take the view that it could not possibly be appropriate for him to remain liable to be recalled to hospital for further treatment. It might then consider itself to be under a duty to terminate the restrictions — even though it was also of the opinion that the patient was dangerous and that the protection of the public required his continued supervision in the community. Whether the restrictions should be terminated is therefore a matter for the tribunal's unfettered discretion. The fact that events since the patient has left hospital demonstrate that further in-patient treatment is unnecessary is not determinative.

VARYING OR IMPOSING CONDITIONS

A tribunal which decides that a patient should remain conditionally discharged may vary any condition to which he is subject in connection with his discharge or impose any condition which might have been imposed in connection therewith. Two points may be noted. Although a tribunal cannot direct a patient's recall to hospital, it would appear to be lawful for it to impose a more stringent regime of supervision in the community. This is necessarily the effect of imposing an additional condition on him. That being so, it must also be the case that it may tighten up the regime by varying an existing condition of his discharge. For example, by requiring him to attend out-patient appointments weekly instead of monthly. The only argument that can be advanced against this proposition is that the Act in its original form demonstrates a principle that tribunals cannot further restrict a person's freedom. They can only relax the element of compulsion to which he is subject or leave it unchanged. This always used to be the position in relation to unrestricted patients, who could apply to a tribunal safe in the knowledge that, if their application was refused, they would not at any rate be in a worse position. This was, and to the extent that it still holds good is, an extremely valuable principle, because patients might otherwise be afraid to apply to the very judicial body set up to safeguard their liberty. Nevertheless, the wording of section 75 is clear and the statutory framework for restricted patients is distinctive. The policy and objects of the Act in their case are to regulate the circumstances in which the liberty of persons who are mentally disordered may be restricted and, where there is conflict, to balance their interests against those of public safety.[56] It seems probable that section 75 is to be understood as representing a similar balance of these competing interests. On the one hand, the tribunal may not cancel the patient's status as a discharged patient and it may direct

---

[55]   See *R. v. Secretary of State for the Home Department, ex p. K.* [1991] 1 Q.B. 27 for an illustration of this type of case. The medical evidence in that case was unanimously of the view that the patient did not have a psychopathic disorder as defined by the 1983 Act but he had a history of serious sexual offending, which included recent offences.

[56]   See *R. v. Secretary of State for the Home Department, ex p. K.* [1991] 1 Q.B. 27, *per* McCowan L.J., approving dicta of McCullough J. in *R. v. Secretary of State for the Home Department, ex p. K.* [1990] 1 W.L.R. 168 at 174.

that he shall cease to be subject to the special restrictions. On the other hand, if he is to remain in the community as a supervised patient, it may impose further conditions or vary the existing conditions. There is no qualification of the kind found in section 72(3), namely that the conditions may only be varied with a view to facilitating the patient's absolute discharge on a later date. Furthermore, while the imposition of a more stringent regime may often be resented, and seem punitive to the patient, it is in his interests that such a power exists if the imposition or variation of conditions is necessary in order to minimise the possibility of relapse, or of an incident or concerns arising which would lead to his recall. The second point to note is that while a tribunal may vary an existing condition, or impose an additional condition, on a strict reading of section 75(3) it may not direct that an existing condition shall cease to have effect. However, on a similarly strict reading of the statutory provisions, the Home Secretary similarly has no such power, nor indeed may he vary conditions previously imposed by himself under section 42. Varying the conditions must therefore be given a general meaning and taken to include directing that a particular condition or conditions shall no longer have effect.

Whether any conditions cannot be varied

For reasons already given, it is necessarily the case that a tribunal cannot vary the conditions of discharge by directing that the patient shall cease to be liable to recall by the Secretary of State. Such liability is part of the statutory scheme and means that the discharge of any restricted patient is always conditional, even if he is not subject to any express conditions of discharge (535). Accordingly, in *ex p. Ruff,* a tribunal's direction that the conditions of a patient's discharge be varied, so that he no longer be liable to recall, was quashed by consent.[57]

Patients in prison

Where a conditionally discharged patient reoffends, the Home Secretary usually allows the consequential criminal proceedings to run their course unless the patient is granted bail. This may mean that a future tribunal hearing takes place in prison. *R. v. Secretary of State for the Home Department, ex p. K*[58] contains an example of the kind of approach taken in such circumstances. The decision of the tribunal in that case was that "no direction be made, save that the conditions of discharge be varied to provide that the conditions as to residence, attendance for out-patient treatment, and supervision by a Probation Officer and Consultant Psychiatrist be suspended until the day of the patient's release from prison."

PATIENTS SUBJECT TO LIMITATION DIRECTIONS

Insofar as relevant, section 75(1)(b) of the 1983 Act, as amended by the Crime (Sentences) Act 1997, provides that, following a restricted patient's recall to hospital, "section 70 above shall apply to the patient as if the relevant hospital order, *hospital direction* or transfer direction had been made on that day."[59] That subsection has been amended by inserting the italicised words. Those words both involve and represent a recognition that some conditionally discharged patients recalled to hospital will henceforth be patients subject to the new hospital and limitation direc-

---

[57]   *R. v. Mental Health Review Tribunal, ex p. Ruff* (CO/99/86, unreported).
[58]   *R. v. Secretary of State for the Home Department, ex p. K* [1990] 1 W.L.R. 168.
[59]   Mental Health Act 1983, s.75(1)(b), as amended by Crime (Sentences) Act 1997, s.55(1), Sched. 4, para. 12(13).

tions. However, when one reads on and considers the position of conditionally discharged patients who have not been recalled to hospital, no similar insertion has been made as regards a tribunal's powers. Subsection (3) still provides as follows:

> "75.—(3)... the tribunal may—
> (a) vary any condition to which the patient is subject in connection with his discharge or impose any condition which might have been imposed in connection therewith; or
> (b) direct that the restriction order or restriction direction to which he is subject shall cease to have effect;
> and if the tribunal give a direction under paragraph (b) above the patient shall cease to be liable to be detained by virtue of the relevant hospital order or transfer direction."

In particular, no reference to a patient subject to hospital and limitation directions has been inserted inside the references to patients subject to hospital and restriction orders or hospital and restriction directions. Because subsection (1) has been amended, as indeed has section 74 with regard to a tribunal's powers in cases involving *undischarged* section 45A patients, this leads to a strong presumption that the omission is deliberate. Such a reference could easily have been added, as in section 74 and 75(1)(b), but was not, and the likelihood of any draftsman missing such an obvious point when he obviously had regard to section 75 must be virtually nil. Furthermore, if the terms of the section are not ambiguous then it matters not what Parliament's reasons were for so providing. When it is clearly established that the legislature has so enacted, the only business of the court is to give full effect to the enactment.[60] Nevertheless, the distinction may reflect the fact that there is a distinction to be drawn between the class of prisoners removed to hospital under section 45A and those removed under section 47. As enacted, the power conferred by section 45A is confined to persons suffering from a psychopathic disorder and the underlying premise is that the public are particularly at risk from such persons **(399)**. The new power give courts the option in their case of combining the immediate provision of hospital treatment with the security of a custodial sentence. The effect is that the offender will serve his sentence securely detained in one place or another unless the Home Secretary, rather than a tribunal, is satisfied that he is fit to be absolutely or conditionally discharged from hospital. Where the Home Secretary does conditionally discharge the patient, further providing that only he may bring the directions to an end until the offender has served the term of imprisonment imposed by the court is not inconsistent with the overall aims of the Act which created this new power. The omission must therefore be deliberate and reflect the intention behind the Crime (Sentences) Act 1995, which, with its provision for mandatory life sentences and limitation directions, was to respond to public concern about the release of dangerous offenders. It is also significant that the Mental Health (Patients in the Community) Act 1995, passed in the same Parliament, gave tribunals a power to recommend that a patient whom it does not release should not only not be released but should be subject to a further order restricting his liberty upon eventually being released. The new limitation concerning a tribunal's powers under section 75 is not at odds with the thrust of recent legislation in this area, which has seen an increase in the powers of tribunals to restrict individual liberty whilst not conferring any additional powers to restore liberty **(495)**. Accordingly, even if the new power is viewed as misguided, Parliament's intention would seem to be clear.

---

[60] See judgment of Coleridge J. in *Re Greenwood* **(263)**.

Because of the consequences of a literal interpretation of the subsection, in terms of a tribunal's powers in respect of conditionally discharged patients, it is possible to raise quite strong arguments against the position just advanced, arguments which deserve to be fully aired before the courts. The essence of the attack will no doubt be along very familiar lines: that the omissions constitute a drafting error; that it can be inferred from the overall statutory framework, and in particular from sections 45B(2) and 75, that Parliament intended to place limitation direction patients in a position identical to that of restriction direction patients; that, in the alternative, the fact that limitation directions are referred to in subsection (1) but not in subsection (3) creates an ambiguity which should be resolved in favour of the liberty of the subject; that any contrary interpretation would involve a breach of the European Convention on Human Rights. More particularly, the following submissions may be made:

1.) Section 45B(2) of the 1983 Act, as inserted by the 1997 Act, provides that a hospital direction shall have effect as a transfer direction made under section 47 and a limitation direction shall have effect as a restriction direction given under section 49.[61]

2.) Accordingly, the references to a hospital direction and a restriction direction in section 75(3) include patients subject to hospital and limitation directions.

3.) Alternatively, there is no other provision in the 1983 Act (as amended) that does not apply identically to all prisoners removed to hospital for treatment under special restrictions. Consequently, the absence of any reference in section 75(3) to section 45A patients must be an oversight.

4.) Either way, had Parliament intended to provide that tribunals were to have no power to terminate the limitation directions, so as to create this single but fundamental exception to the general position brought about by section 45B(2), it would have done so by including such a provision in the body of the Act. More particularly, if Parliament intended to break with precedence by distinguishing two classes of conditionally discharged patients, each with different rights, it would have made this explicit in the body of the statute by including such an amendment in section 49 of the 1997 Act.

5.) As it is, the paragraph said to have the effect complained of is to be found in Schedule 4. Section 55(1) of the 1997 Act provides that those enactments in the 1983 Act mentioned in Schedule 4 shall have effect subject to the amendments there specified, "being minor amendments and amendments consequential on the provisions of this Act." An amendment to the effect that a tribunal may not absolutely discharge a conditionally discharged patient if he is subject to a limitation direction is not a minor amendment of the position set out in section 45B(2). Nor is it one consequential upon the provisions set out in the body of the Act, for section 45A provides that limitation direction patients are to be treated as

---

61 Mental Health Act 1983, s.45B(2), as inserted by Crime (Sentences) Act 1997, s.46.

if subject to a restriction direction. Unless one takes the view that Parliament was being devious, which is not permissible, one is bound to hold that the paragraph complained of must be interpreted in a way which is minor and inconsequential, *i.e.* in a way which is consistent with section 55(1) and does not violate section 45B(2).[62]

6.) There is a presumption that Acts of Parliament are not intended to derogate from the requirements of international law and the interpretation complained of would mean that the United Kingdom is in breach of the European Convention on Human Rights. Indeed, section 75 was enacted because the fact that restricted patients previously had no right to a tribunal which could order their release was held to constitute a violation of the Convention.[63] Furthermore, if and when the Convention is incorporated into English and Welsh law, as is the present Government's intention, the effect will be that the limitation must be then be ruled to be unlawful.[64]

7.) To summarise, although only persons classified as having a psychopathic disorder may be made the subject of the new directions, once made their effect is the same as if the prisoner had initially commenced his sentence in prison and had then been transferred to hospital by the Secretary of State (**398**). Parliament's intention must have been that if the Home Secretary consented to some of them being released under the 1983 Act, rather than being remitted to prison or released on licence, they would then be dealt with in the same manner as other conditionally discharged patients.

Summary

The paramount rule of statutory construction is that "every statute is to be expounded according to its manifest and expressed intention"[65] and all other rules of interpretation are subordinate to it.[66] Because sections 74 and 75(1) have been amended, so as to refer to hospital and limitation directions, this leads to a strong presumption that the apparent failure to confer on tribunals a power to remove the directions is deliberate. The fact that the amendment having this apparent effect was expressed to be a minor amendment or one consequential on the provisions of this Act would seem to be the strongest argument for giving full effect to section 45B(2). Even so, it must be doubtful whether there is any real ambiguity.

---

[62] The alternative view would be that, although the principal purpose served by Schedules is to enable the presentation of the main sections of the enactment uncluttered by material of secondary or incidental importance, the Schedule is as much part of the enactment as is the section introducing it or any other section. See G.C. Thornton, *Legislative Drafting* (Butterworths, 3rd ed., 1987), pp. 332–333; *A-G v. Lamplough* (1878) 3 Ex D 214 at 229, C.A.; *I.R.C. v. Gittus* [1921] 2 A.C. 81, H.L.

[63] *X. v. United Kingdom* (1981) 4 E.H.R.R. 181.

[64] The argument against this is that, because the patient is still serving a prison sentence, neither section 74 nor section 75(3) infringes the Convention.

[65] *Attorney-General for Canada v. Hallett & Carey Ltd.* [1952] A.C. 427 at 449, *per* Lord Radcliffe.

[66] *Prince Ernest of Hanover v. Attorney-General* [1956] Ch. 188 at 201, *per* Evershed M.R.

9. The limits of a tribunal's powers

INTRODUCTION

This chapter is concerned with legal technicalities which are mainly of interest to lawyers. More particularly, it deals with the following legal issues—

THE BURDEN AND STANDARD OF PROOF

In all cases other than those involving conditionally discharged patients, a tribunal must decide whether it is "satisfied" that the statutory grounds for discharge exist. The reference to a tribunal being "satisfied" has given rise to considerable debate in practice about the onus and standard of proof in tribunal cases.

THE ONUS OR BURDEN OF PROOF

Assuming that the concepts are relevant to inquisitorial proceedings of this kind,[1] the onus of proof lies on the applicant in all proceedings except those involving conditionally discharged patients, where no burden can exist either way because there is no statutory issue to be determined. Because sections 72 and 73 are unambiguous in this respect, attempts to argue that a different construction may or must be inferred from the overall statutory framework, or from the terms of the European Convention on Human Rights, have met with failure. In *ex p. Hayes,*[2] Ackner L.J. said that in his judgment counsel had "rightly" not pursued in the Court of Appeal his submission in the Divisional Court that the onus of satisfying the

---

[1]   Because it is for the tribunal to satisfy itself whether the grounds for discharge exist, it may be argued that the concept of a burden of proof lying on a particular party or person is not germane. Furthermore, there is not always an applicant and the patient may occasionally not even attend. In restricted cases, the responsible authority and the applicant may jointly support the latter's discharge. Nevertheless, the reality is usually that the applicant is seeking to be discharged and so to satisfy the tribunal that the grounds for his detention advanced by the detaining authority are legally insufficient. The risk of non-persuasion lies with him.

[2]   *R. v. The Mental Health Review Tribunal, ex p. Hayes*, 9 May 1985, C.A. (unreported) (**066**).

tribunal was not upon the patient. And, in *ex p. A.*,[3] Kennedy L.J. observed that the first thing to be noted about the duty to discharge in section 72(1)(b) was that the tribunal is only required to direct discharge if it is satisfied of a negative: if the patient may be suffering from a form of mental disorder of the requisite nature or degree then the obligation to discharge under sub-paragraph (i) does not arise. His Lordship added that "the approach is not surprising, because the tribunal is not intending to duplicate the role of the responsible medical officer. His diagnosis stands until the tribunal is satisfied that it is wrong." Because a tribunal is not obliged to discharge if it is *not* satisfied that the patient is *not* suffering from a disorder of the requisite nature or degree, the statutory test is sometimes referred to as the "double-negative," and many decisions not to discharge are phrased in this way. Thus, while the tribunal discharge criteria are cast as a double-negative, the admission and renewal criteria are not.

European Convention on Human Rights

As to whether the statutory provisions violate the European Convention on Human Rights, the domestic law is most vulnerable in relation to the non-judicial detention of citizens under Part II. The central issue is whether it is lawful to require a citizen who has been deprived of his liberty otherwise than by judicial process to prove to a judicial authority that there are no lawful grounds for depriving him of his liberty before he is entitled to be released. Stated differently, if those detaining a person cannot satisfy a judicial authority that there are lawful grounds for his detention is it nevertheless lawful to continue to detain him because he cannot demonstrate the absence of such grounds? Although a tribunal may discharge a person at its discretion if the facts are finely balanced, this does not affect the fact he is not entitled to be set at liberty.[4]

THE STANDARD OF PROOF

Because a patient is only entitled to be discharged if the tribunal reviewing his case is satisfied that the grounds obliging it to discharge exist, the natural next question is what standard of proof is imposed by the word "satisfied"? Given that the onus is on the patient, to what degree must a tribunal be persuaded by the evidence before it can be satisfied and so under an obligation to discharge? Does "satisfied," it is sometimes said, mean satisfied beyond all reasonable doubt or satisfied on the balance of probabilities? One senior legal member used to take the view that a tribunal may never be satisfied because the word implies certainty or virtual certainty and that is *never* possible when dealing with mental disorder. However, if this were true then restricted patients could never be discharged and such an approach is unlawful. The issue was touched upon in *ex p. Hayes,*[5] where Ackner L.J. observed that the patient's counsel had "sought to raise questions as to the standard of proof required." In that case, His Lordship could find nothing in the decision which indicated that the tribunal had imposed any undue standard of proof upon the patient, nor therefore any arguable point of law. In *ex p. Ryan,*[6] Nolan J. referred to the "double-negative" aspect of the discharge test, saying:

---

[3]   *R. v. Canons Park Mental Health Review Tribunal, ex p. A* [1994] 3 W.L.R. 630 (**223**).

[4]   It is noteworthy that, prior to 1959, it was generally for the applicant to satisfy a court that the statutory grounds for detention existed rather than for the citizen to satisfy a court, in the form of a tribunal held after the event, that there were no grounds for detention.

[5]   *R. v. The Mental Health Review Tribunal, ex p. Hayes, supra.*

[6]   *R. v. Trent Mental Health Review Tribunal, ex p. Ryan* [1992] C.O.D. 157, D.C (**839**).

"The negative form of the requirement required them to be satisfied — a fairly strong word — that the patient was not suffering from psychopathic disorder. So far as the clinical and medical evidence was concerned, it seems to me that they were entitled to say they were not satisfied and in so far as they went on to conclude that his conduct towards young females has been seriously irresponsible resulting from the psychopathic disorder... Once again there was material upon which the tribunal could properly link the two."

"Satisfied"

Although a tribunal which is satisfied that a patient is entitled to be discharged has no discretion about whether or not to discharge him, in deciding whether or not it is satisfied that he is entitled to be discharged, it has a very broad discretion. Hence, in reality, the effect of the double-negative test is that almost all decisions to discharge are discretionary. It has been variously held in relation to legislation not concerned with mental health that "satisfied" means to be persuaded[7]; to make up one's mind, coming to a conclusion on the evidence which, together with its other conclusions, leads to the judicial decision[8]; to be satisfied beyond reasonable doubt[9]; that there must be solid grounds upon which the court can found a reliable opinion[10]; that the term is indicative of judicial discretion[11]; and that the word simply says on whom the burden of proof rests, leaving the court itself to decide what standard of proof is required in order to be satisfied.[12]

The use of the word "satisfied" elsewhere in the Act

The word "satisfied" is used in many places in the 1983 Act. It is the duty of an approved social worker to make an application under Part II in any case where he is satisfied that such an application ought to be made.[13] A patient's responsible or appropriate medical officer is under a duty to furnish a report renewing the authority for the patient's detention or guardianship for a further period if it appears to him that the criteria for renewal are "satisfied."[14] A criminal court may authorise a patient's detention or guardianship under Part III if "satisfied" on medical evidence as to the statutory criteria for detention or guardianship[15] and no such order may be made unless the court is also satisfied that a bed is available or, as the case may be, that a proposed guardian consents to acting in that capacity.[16] In the case of detention under section 35 or 37, a magistrates court must in certain circumstances additionally be "satisfied" that the patient did the act or omission charged.[17] Similarly, the Secretary of State may remove a patient to hospital for treatment where he is satisfied on medical evidence as to the medical criteria for transfer.[18] Under section 42, the Secretary of State may direct that a patient shall cease to be

---

[7]   See *Briginshaw v. Briginshaw* (1938) 60 C.L.R. 336, *per* Dixon J.
[8]   See *Blyth v. Blyth* [1966] 1 All E.R. 524 at 541, H.L., *per* Lord Pearson.
[9]   See *Preston-Jones v. Preston-Jones* [1951] A.C. 391. In general, however, the legislature is quite capable of inserting the words "beyond all reasonable doubt" if it means that.
[10]   See *R. v. Liverpool City Justices, ex p. Grogan, The Times*, 8 October 1990.
[11]   *Birch v. County Motor & Engineering Co.* [1958] 1 W.L.R. 980, C.A.
[12]   See *Blyth v. Blyth* [1966] 1 All E.R. 524 at 536, H.L., *per* Lord Denning.
[13]   Mental Health Act 1983, s.13(1).
[14]   *Ibid.*, ss.20(3)(b), 20(6)(b).
[15]   *Ibid.*, ss.35(3)(a), 36(1), 37(2), 38(1)(a), 43(1)(a).
[16]   *Ibid.*, ss.35(4), 36(3), 37(4), 37(6), 38(4), 44(1).
[17]   *Ibid.*, ss.35(2)(b), 37(3).
[18]   *Ibid.*, ss.47(1), 48(1).

restricted if he is satisfied that a restriction order is no longer required for the protection of the public from serious harm.[19] The court with jurisdiction to deal with a defendant who has been transferred to hospital under section 48 may remit him to custody where satisfied on medical evidence that he no longer requires in-patient treatment or that no effective treatment can be given.[20] A magistrates court may commit such a defendant in his absence if satisfied on medical evidence that the accused is unfit to take part in the proceedings.[21] The functions of the judge under Part VII of the Act are also exercisable where, after considering medical evidence, he is satisfied that a person is incapable, by reason of mental disorder, of managing and administering his property and affairs.[22] A receiver shall be discharged on the judge being satisfied that that patient has later become capable.[23] The duty to provide after-care under section 117 applies until such time as the relevant health and social services authorities are satisfied that the person is no longer in need of such services.[24]

Other qualifying words — satisfied about what?

It should be noted that the criteria for discharge include other qualifying words, which vary according to the particular authority being reviewed. For example, a tribunal must discharge a patient detained under section 3 if it is satisfied that it is not "necessary" for his health or safety, or for the protection of others, that he receives treatment in hospital. In relation to section 2 patients, the duty to discharge arises if the tribunal is satisfied that the patient's detention is not "justified" in the interests of his health or safety or for the protection of others. Many things which are not necessary may nevertheless be justified. Similarly, while a tribunal must discharge a section 3 patient if it is satisfied that continued liability to detention is not "appropriate," it must discharge a section 2 patient if satisfied that his detention is not "warranted" for assessment or treatment following assessment. Whether the use of a power is appropriate is again rather more subjective than whether or not it is warranted. The use in the criteria of words such as "appropriate" and "justified" means that it is not particularly meaningful to approach the criteria for discharge in terms of being satisfied beyond reasonable doubt or on the balance of probabilities. One cannot easily talk of a course of action being appropriate beyond all reasonable doubt and whether something is or is not justified may have little to do with probability. The tribunal must therefore act judicially and give proper consideration to all of the evidence, ensuring that it has sufficient evidence concerning the statutory matters before reaching its decision. For example, adequate evidence about whether the patient is or may still be mentally disordered and whether his health or safety or other persons would be at risk if set at liberty.[25] The finding reached must be based on some material that tends logically to show the existence of facts supportive of the finding and the reasoning behind the finding must be internally consistent. Beyond that, the tribunal must simply be persuaded, content in their own minds on the evidence before them, that there are no longer any grounds for de-

---

[19] Mental Health Act 1983, s.42(1).
[20] *Ibid.*, ss.51(4), 52(5).
[21] *Ibid.*, s.52(7)(a).
[22] *Ibid.*, s.94(2). The position is essentially the same with periodic payments made under s.142(1).
[23] *Ibid.*, s.99(3).
[24] *Ibid.*, s.117(2).
[25] In *Shepherd*, the Secretary of State asked the tribunal to state a case in December 1984 but later decided not to proceed. The issue was whether a tribunal which conditionally discharged a patient had given adequate consideration to the requirement in s.41 to protect the public from serious harm.

tention, guardianship or supervision. If the patient's detention followed the commission of very serious offences, it will clearly be more difficult for them to be satisfied that his detention is no longer necessary to protect others or that it is not appropriate for him to remain liable to be detained. However, the fact that it will be more difficult to persuade the tribunal that there are no longer any grounds for his detention does not involve any elevation of the standard of proof. The basic need to be persuaded remains the same. The fact that a particularly persuasive argument is necessary in order to rebut a particularly persuasive argument for continued detention does not involve any alteration in the meaning of the word "satisfied," nor therefore increasing the standard of proof in such cases.

THE MEANING OF DISCHARGE IN UNRESTRICTED CASES

In the context of a restricted case, Mann J. said that "the word 'discharge,' as employed in sections 72 to 75 ... means, and in my judgment can only mean, release from hospital ...."[26] In the context of an unrestricted case, McCullough J. observed that "discharge means not merely discharge from hospital but discharge from the authority to detain."[27] If either of these constructions is correct, tribunals have been misinterpreting the provisions since they came into force. The customary view is that discharge in relation to unrestricted patients means merely discharge from liability to detention while, in relation to restricted patients, it means discharge both from hospital and liability to detention.

THE CRITERIA FOR DISCHARGE

Section 72(1)(b), which applies to undischarged restricted and unrestricted patients, provides that a tribunal shall direct the discharge of a patient who is liable to be detained for treatment if they are satisfied either that he is not then suffering from any form of mental disorder the nature or degree of which "makes it appropriate for him to be liable to be detained in a hospital for medical treatment" or that it is neither necessary for his health or safety or for the protection of others "that he should receive such treatment" (**485**).

Patients absent from hospital with leave

As McCullough J. observed in *ex p. W*,[28] those "liable to be detained" are those who are detained and those who have been granted leave of absence. The reference to the appropriateness of liability to detention in section 72(1)(b) means that a tribunal is not bound to discharge a patient who has indefinite leave to be absent from hospital, or an in-patient whom it considers should be granted such leave, solely because his condition does not presently make in-patient treatment appropriate. It is only obliged to discharge him if it is satisfied that his mental state no longer makes it appropriate for him to be liable to further detention in a hospital for medical treatment.

---

[26]   *Secretary of State for the Home Department v. Mental Health Review Tribunal for Mersey Regional Health Authority, Same v. Mental Health Review Tribunal for Wales* [1986] 1 W.L.R. 1170 (**516**).

[27]   *R. v. Hallstrom, ex p. W.; R. v. Gardner, ex p. L.* [1986] 1 Q.B. 1090.

[28]   *Ibid.*

Patients in hospital

The converse situation is that of an unrestricted in-patient who, although in need of further hospital treatment, no longer requires compulsory treatment because he has recovered sufficiently to appreciate his need for treatment. Adopting the language of section 72(1)(b)(i), the nature or degree of his disorder remains sufficiently serious for further treatment in hospital to be appropriate but not so serious that it is appropriate for him to be "liable to be detained" there for that purpose.

THE ARGUMENT THAT THE WORD BEARS THE SAME MEANING

A plausible argument may be advanced for saying that the word "discharge" bears the same meaning in restricted and unrestricted cases, and tribunals chaired by members of the judiciary have been known to proceed on this basis—

- It may be said that Parliament would not have defined the discharge criteria in restricted cases by incorporating without qualification the criteria applied in unrestricted cases if it intended that the words in section 72(1)(b) should bear a different meaning in such cases.

- Furthermore, the framework of section 72 suggests that discharge means discharge from hospital.

- Subsection (2) provides that a tribunal shall, when considering whether to discharge at its discretion, have regard to the likelihood of a mentally ill or severely mentally impaired patient "if discharged" being able to care for himself, to obtain the care he needs or to guard himself against serious exploitation — considerations which are not pertinent unless the patient is being discharged from hospital.

- Section 72(3) then provides that a tribunal may direct the "discharge" of a patient on a future date, which suggests the making of arrangements outside hospital prior to discharge from hospital.

- The same subsection then states that a tribunal which does not discharge a patient may, "with a view to facilitating his discharge on a future date," recommend that he is granted leave of absence or is transferred to another hospital or into guardianship. A patient on leave, although no longer an in-patient, is therefore not "discharged" and, accordingly, discharge means both discharge from hospital and discharge from liability to detention. Similarly, the purpose of recommending transfer to another hospital can only be to facilitate the patient's future "discharge from hospital." And, as to a patient's reception into guardianship, this necessarily involves discharge both from hospital and from liability to detention.

- Finally, it is noteworthy that in guardianship cases a tribunal has no power to discharge on a future date nor, where it does not discharge, any power to make statutory recommendations with a view to facilitating the patient's discharge in the future. This must be because Parliament considered that, since the patient was already in the community, the section 72(3) powers — being exclusively concerned with making arrangements for "discharge" into the community — were irrelevant.

Customary usage aside, the view that the word "discharge," and the statutory criteria for discharge, are to be interpreted differently in unrestricted cases relies both on the statutory framework and a natural and literal reading of section 72(1).

- Under the Mental Health Act 1959, a tribunal's powers of discharge were limited to discharging unrestricted patients who were liable to be detained for treatment or subject to guardianship. Patients who were liable to be detained and patients subject to guardianship were in an identical position: the tribunal was under a duty to discharge forthwith where the statutory criteria were satisfied; could discharge forthwith at its discretion if this was not the case; or not discharge.[29] Fairly clearly, therefore, discharge meant the same in both cases, that is discharge from the compulsory powers to which the patient was then subject.

- Consistent with this, section 47 was cast in similar terms to the current section 23 and it provided that various other persons and bodies could make "an order for discharge." According to section 47, "a patient who is for the time being liable to be detained or subject to guardianship ... shall cease to be so liable or subject if an order in writing discharging him from detention or guardianship (in this Act referred to as an order for discharge) is made in accordance with the following provisions ..."

- That is what one would expect given the historical context. It is inconceivable that, when repealing the Mental Treatment Act 1930, Parliament intended to impose a more restrictive regime whereby patients, once compulsorily admitted, were to remain subject to compulsion until such time (if ever) as sufficiently well to leave hospital. Furthermore, there is nothing in the present statute to indicate that Parliament intended that "discharge" was henceforth to bear a different meaning in unrestricted cases to that which it had borne in the 1959 Act.

- The purpose of extending the range of a tribunal's powers in 1982 was simply to enable them to deal more effectively with different situations frequently encountered by them. So, for example, a patient's discharge could be postponed *if* the patient wanted to immediately leave hospital but arrangements for this first needed to be made.

- Even if "discharge" means discharge from hospital, it can only mean "deemed discharge" in this context. In other words, just as an informal in-patient is deemed for the purposes of the Act to have been admitted to hospital on the date the application is received, so he is deemed to have been discharged from hospital for statutory purposes when an order for his discharge is made, notwithstanding that he remains in hospital informally.[30]

---

[29] A tribunal could not discharge on a future date and, if it did not discharge, it had no power to make statutory recommendations with a view to facilitating the patient's discharge in the future.

[30] See Mental Health Act 1983, s.5(1), **260**.

Conclusion

In unrestricted cases, discharge means discharge from guardianship or from liability to detention. That this is so is beyond doubt.

THE LEGALITY OF THE APPLICATION OR ORDER

The conventional view is that the function of a tribunal in both restricted and unrestricted cases is to review the grounds for the patient's detention or guardianship at the time of the hearing. Accordingly, a tribunal has no power to determine whether the original admission was lawful and it has no power to deal with complaints about matters such as the effects of a particular treatment, consent to treatment, and the use of restraint, except insofar as they relate to the exercise of the tribunal's powers under the Act. More particularly, a tribunal cannot be competent to review the validity of an order made by a criminal court, which is subject to appeal following sentence.[31] Nor can it quash an application made under Part II or determine the *vires* of a person's admission. These are matters for the High Court.

RESTRICTED PATIENTS

Because a tribunal has no discretionary power of discharge in restricted cases, it clearly may not consider the lawfulness of the patient's detention. Section 73 makes it clear that a tribunal must discharge a restricted patient who satisfies the criteria for discharge set out there and not discharge him unless that is so. It has no other powers and may not discharge on any other basis.

UNRESTRICTED PATIENTS

As regards these patients, a tribunal must likewise discharge if satisfied that the conditions for discharge exist, which involves considering their mental state and the risks involved in discharge. However, the tribunal may also discharge the patient at its discretion, because section 72 commences by stating that a tribunal may "in any case" direct a patient's discharge before going on to set out the circumstances in which it is obliged to discharge. The question arises whether a tribunal may have regard to any irregularities in the authority for a patient's detention when it decides whether to exercise its discretionary power of discharge. If so, a tribunal could not be obliged to discharge a patient simply because it was of the opinion that the use of

---

[31] Where the order is defective because it does not accurately reflect the order made by the court, judicial review will also lie if no other remedy is available. In *R. v. Reading Crown Court, ex p. Norris*, a case dealt with by the author during 1991–1992, the copy of the judge's order made by the clerk to the court indicated that a restriction order had been imposed and it was sent to the Home Office. For various reasons, the patient's solicitor at a tribunal held some six years later entertained the thought that the clerk might have mistakenly forgotten to cross through the section of the printed form which stated that restrictions had been attached to the hospital order. Lengthy enquiries revealed this to be the case. Judicial review proceedings were commenced and the order was amended by consent to show that only a hospital order had been imposed.

compulsory powers had not been properly authorised. However, it could take that possibility into account, along with all of the other relevant circumstances, such as any risks involved in discharging the patient.

Unrestricted Part II patients

The statutory framework in relation to patients admitted to hospital by court order is manifestly different from that pertaining to citizens admitted under Part II without any prior court order or judicial involvement. The nature of these civil procedures is unique within English law in that a British citizen is deprived of his liberty upon the completion of procedures involving the exercise of powers which in other contexts would be regarded as judicial or executive. These procedures cannot properly be described as administrative because, in constitutional terms, they involve the detention or restraint of one of the Queen's subjects but, equally, it would be inaccurate to describe them as a judicial process since no judicial authority is involved. It would therefore not be altogether surprising if tribunals, being judicial bodies, could take into account an apparent lack of authority for such a patient's detention when deciding whether to direct his discharge.

Unrestricted Part III patients

The discretionary power of discharge extends to cases involving unrestricted patients admitted to hospital or received into guardianship under Part III. In the case of admission in pursuance of a hospital order, no tribunal application may be made during the following six months. By that time, the statutory period for challenging the order, if its validity is contested, will have expired. In the case of guardianship orders, the patient may immediately apply to a tribunal although, by the time any tribunal sits, the order will be before an appeal court or the time for disputing its validity have passed.

CASE LAW

The authority invariably given for the proposition that a tribunal may not grant relief to an unrestricted patient who is not lawfully detained is *ex p. Waldron*. According to dicta of Ackner L.J. in that case, a tribunal's jurisdiction "is limited to entertaining applications made by a person who is liable to be detained under the Act."[32] However, Glidewell and Slade L.JJ. declined to express a view and expressly left the point open.[33] Notwithstanding this, the dicta of Ackner L.J. have since routinely been cited by counsel without *ever* drawing to the court's attention the reservations of these two eminent Lord Justices. Accordingly, the case cannot without more be considered as authority for the proposition commonly derived from it. It is also noteworthy that no consideration was given in *ex p. Waldron* to the earlier decision of the Court of Appeal in *Re V.E* (577). In that case, the court held that a tribunal had been obliged to discharge a patient because there was no lawful authority for her detention. Thus, against the dicta of Ackner L.J. must be set this decision and the fact also that the two other judges in *ex p. Waldron* left the point open.

---

[32]   *R. v. Hallstrom and another, ex p. W.* [1986] 1 Q.B. 824 at 846, *per* Ackner L.J.
[33]   *Ibid.*, at 848, *per* Neill L.J., and at 852-53, *per* Glidewell L.J.

[1986] 1 Q.B. 824   *C.A. (Ackner, Neill and Glidewell L.JJ.)*

W. was admitted to hospital under section 3 on the basis of medical recommendations submitted by Dr. Hallstrom and Dr. Morgan (the doctors). The patient contended that the application was unlawful and she applied to the Court of Appeal for leave to apply for judicial review, in the form of an order of certiorari quashing it.

Prior to making that application, she had unsuccessfully applied to a tribunal for her discharge. At that hearing, her solicitor had submitted to the tribunal that they should quash the original application for admission because it was invalid, being founded on a written recommendation which did not in fact represent the opinion held by Dr. Hallstrom at any material time.

Ackner L.J.

It was apparent from the tribunal's reasons for its decision that it did not fully grasp the point which the solicitor was seeking to make. That was not altogether surprising since it was being said that the patient was not liable to be detained and yet the section under which the discharge of such liability was being made provided only for applications being made "by or in respect of a person who was liable to be detained under this Act." Counsel for the doctors maintained that a person who considered that her admission for treatment was a nullity, having been made without jurisdiction, and who considered that she was not a person who was liable to be detained under the Act, could apply to a tribunal, as the patient had done. If dissatisfied with the tribunal's decision, the patient could then ask the tribunal to state a question of law for determination by the High Court. However, the jurisdiction given to the tribunal was limited to entertaining applications made by a person who was liable to be detained under the Act. The tribunal's powers were thus confined to granting or refusing relief to persons liable to be detained. It had no power to consider the validity of the admission which gave rise to the liability to be detained. The tribunal could not be used where it was sought to challenge the underlying validity of the admission, as a route to the High Court.

Counsel for the doctors sought to rely on section 66(1)(b) to get over this difficulty. That subsection provided that where a patient was admitted in pursuance of an application for admission for treatment an application could be made to a tribunal within the relevant period. However, section 77(1) prohibited an application being made to a tribunal except in such cases and at such times as were expressly provided by the Act. The section 66(1)(b) case had to be a person who was liable to be detained under the Act because he had been admitted in pursuance of a section 3 application and that required the fulfilment of the conditions specified in that section. Such an applicant, being admitted to the hospital in pursuance of such an application, thereby acquired a liability to detention. That a section 66(1)(b) patient was necessarily a person liable to be detained was recognised by section 6(4), which dealt with the effect of an application for admission. It provided that where a patient was admitted in pursuance of an application any previous application under Part II by virtue of which he was liable to be detained, or subject to guardianship, ceased to have effect. It followed that the applicant was not entitled to seek from the tribunal a decision as to the *vires* of her admission. It had no jurisdiction to entertain such an application.

Neill L.J.

"I agree with the order proposed by Ackner L.J. I intend to confine my decision, however, to the question whether the High Court has jurisdiction to entertain the applicant's claim for judicial review ... For my part I do not consider ... it would be appropriate at this stage to express any view as to the possibility of obtaining some effective relief in a case such as the present from the mental health review tribunal itself."

Glidewell L.J.

If the court decided that section 139(1) did not prevent a challenge by way of judicial review, there might be a second question, namely whether leave should nevertheless be refused because there was an alternative procedure by which the same question could be decided? That procedure was an application to a tribunal under section 66, followed by a case stated on a point of law for the decision of the High Court under section 78(8). However, in the circumstances, counsel for the doctors accepted that, if the court decided the section 139 point against Dr. Hallstrom, leave should be granted. There was clearly an important point at issue as to the limits of a doctor's power under section 3. Moreover, the tribunal in this case had not dealt directly with the section 139 point. Instead, its decision rose another point of law with which the court was not concerned, namely whether, even if an original application under section 3 was invalid, a patient may nevertheless be "liable to be detained" within section 72(1)(b) of the Act at the time the tribunal hears his application. It had always been a principle that certiorari would go only where there was no other equally effective and convenient remedy. Whether the alternative statutory remedy would resolve the question at issue fully and directly, whether the statutory procedure would be quicker or slower than procedure by way of judicial review, whether the matter depended on some particular or technical knowledge which was more readily available to the alternative appellate body, were some of the matters which a court should take into account when deciding whether to grant relief by way of judicial review when an alternative remedy was available. Counsel as amicus argued that the procedure by way of an application to a tribunal and a case stated was not apt to decide the question whether the powers of the Act had been exceeded. That, he said, was not a question with which the tribunal was or could be concerned. If he was correct (and it was not necessary to decide whether he was), there was, of course, no alternative remedy available in any case such as this. *Leave to apply for judicial review granted.*

Re V.E.

In *Re V.E. (mental health patient)*,[34] the application for the patient's admission to hospital for treatment stated that she was suffering from mental illness. V.E. applied to a tribunal for her discharge. The tribunal did not discharge but concluded that her condition had been wrongly diagnosed and directed under section 123(3) of the 1959 Act — which subsection is repeated in the 1983 Act as section 72(5) — that the application for her admission be amended so as to substitute "psychopathic disorder" for "mental illness." Under the 1959 Act, an application for treatment could not be made in respect of a patient aged over 21 if she suffered only from that form of disorder. The patient was aged 40. The question arose whether the tribunal's direction that the patient be reclassified was incompatible with its direction that

---

[34]   *Re V.E. (mental health patient)* [1973] 1 Q.B. 452.

she not be discharged. Did its reclassification have the effect that she must be discharged on the ground that, as a person over 21 suffering from psychopathic disorder, no application could be made for her detention under the 1959 Act? The tribunal stated a case for the High Court's determination.[35] The Court of Appeal held that, as the application remained throughout the only authority for the patient's compulsory detention, if an amendment of the application so altered its averments that they no longer alleged circumstances which would justify detention, the patient had to be discharged. Accordingly, since the amended application alleged no more than psychopathic disorder in a patient aged 40, her continued detention could not be justified under the Act and she was entitled to be discharged. In any event (*per* Lord Widgery C.J.) she was entitled to discharge by reason of the fact that on a proper diagnosis she had never qualified for detention at all.[36]

Re V.E. (mental health patient)

[1973] 1 Q.B. 452   *C.A. (Lord Widgery C.J., Willis and Bridge JJ.)*

On 11 June 1971, the patient was admitted to hospital under section 26. Both recommendations recorded the opinion that the patient was suffering from mental illness. At the hearing on 14 January 1972, the responsible medical officer's evidence was that she was not suffering from mental illness, nor had she been when her detention was authorised. The tribunal was, however, satisfied that the patient was suffering from psychopathic disorder. Having decided not to discharge, it directed that the application be amended by substituting "psychopathic disorder" for "mental illness." One of the questions of law stated by the tribunal for the High Court's determination was whether, by reason of the substitution of "psychopathic disorder" for "mental illness," the patient might thereafter be detained pursuant to the Act.

Lord Widgery C.J.

The question of law to be considered was whether, notwithstanding that the tribunal had refused to order the patient's discharge on medical grounds, she was nevertheless entitled to be discharged on the ground that as a person over 21 suffering from psychopathic disorder she was never liable to be detained under the Act at all. The argument for the hospital board was that if a patient was once detained by virtue of a valid application, his detention could be continued so long as he continued to suffer from some mental disorder and his release was undesirable in his own or the public interest. While it would not be wholly surprising if the Act had this effect, His Lordship was satisfied that it did not. To begin with it was clear that the application and its supporting recommendations must specify the particular form of mental disorder relied on and that, if the relevant disorder was psychopathic disorder, an application could not be made if the patient was over 21. In deciding whether a particular patient was detained "as a psychopath," one's attention was directed to the form of the application, and, what was more significant, that provision was made for

---

[35] Section 124(5) of the 1959 Act was identical to section 78(8) of the present statute. It stated that a tribunal tribunal "may, and if so required by the High Court shall, state in the form of a special case for determination by the High Court any question of law which may arise before them."

[36] Although the Law Report states this as being the opinion of Widgery C.J., it would seem that Bridge J. was also of that view. He said that unless the patient was entitled to be discharged, a patient detained on the basis of an erroneous diagnosis, who could not have been lawfully detained at all if correctly diagnosed at the outset, would have no redress under the Act if the error was only discovered and corrected at a later stage.

the amendment of the application as necessary. If it was intended that a re-classification under section 123(3) might itself produce a situation requiring the discharge of the patient, it was strange that this was not specifically recognised. However, there was no reason why reclassification by a tribunal under section 123(3) should have a different effect from one made under section 38 by the responsible medical officer. The conclusion must be that if an amendment of the application so altered its averments that they no longer alleged circumstances which would justify detention, the patient must be discharged. In the present case the amended application alleged psychopathic disorder in a patient aged 40. This was not a situation which justified detention under the Act and the patient was entitled to be discharged. His Lordship concluded,

"Even if I had taken a different view of the general scheme of the Act I should have held that this patient was entitled to discharge by reason of the fact that on a proper diagnosis she never qualified for detention under section 26 at all. It was one thing to say that a patient once properly detained can remain in detention notwithstanding a change in circumstances, and quite a different thing to say that an initial mistake in diagnosis can be upheld. I would answer the question put by saying that the patient must be discharged."

Willis J.

It seemed clear that the necessary medical recommendations on which the original application was based were erroneous. It followed that if what the tribunal found in January 1972 to be the correct diagnosis had been the medical view in June 1971 there would have been no lawful basis for the application made under section 26. The question arose whether the amendment of the application by the tribunal had effectively invalidated its authority for the patient's continued detention. The application for admission, in its original form or as amended, remained throughout the only lawful authority for a patient's compulsory detention in hospital. As soon as that application ceased to reflect the type of mental disorder on which a patient could have been lawfully admitted and detained under section 26(2), so soon did there cease to exist any lawful authority for that patient's continued detention.

Bridge J.

Although the duration of the authority to detain a patient conferred by an application, order or direction could be renewed from time to time as provided by the Act, it was nevertheless the application, order or direction which remained the essential foundation for that authority throughout its duration. There were four forms of mental disorder and it was convenient to refer to two of them as "major disorders" (mental illness and severe subnormality) and to the second pair as "minor disorders" (psychopathic disorder and subnormality). This dichotomy was certainly of crucial importance to the initial liability to detention of a person in respect of whom an application, order or direction was to be made. It had been argued for the hospital board that the reclassification of a patient over 40 years of age and the consequential amendment of the application, to substitute a minor for a major disorder, had no effect on the application as a continuing authority for her detention in hospital. However sensible that result might be in the particular circumstances of this case, there was no basis for the contention in the provisions of the Act and much greater anomalies were involved in accepting the argument. A patient detained, as here, on the basis of an erroneous diagnosis, who could not have been lawfully detained at all if correctly diagnosed at the outset, would have no redress under the Act if the error was only discovered and corrected at a later stage. The problem of construction, which looked so formidable at first blush, arose from the absence of any express provision in sections 38(1) or 123(3) indicating that amendment might lead to *immediate* discharge. The explanation of that drafting peculiarity must lie in the fact that reclassification and amendment could have a variety of different consequences in different circumstances, none of which were spelt out in those sections but must be sought elsewhere in the Act. The draftsman might have sacrificed clarity to economy of language but, if one looked at the Act as a whole, there could be no real doubt of his legislative intent. *Determination accordingly.*

Commentary

Under section 123 of the 1959 Act, a tribunal was required to discharge an unrestricted patient who was liable to be detained for treatment if satisfied either (a) that he was not then suffering from mental illness, psychopathic disorder, subnormality or severe subnormality; or (b) that it was not necessary in the interests of his health or safety, or for the protection of other persons, that he should continue to be liable to be detained. In *Re V.E.*, the tribunal was not satisfied as to either of those grounds for mandatory discharge. Nevertheless, the court held that the patient was entitled to be immediately discharged because the effect of the tribunal's finding was that there was no lawful authority for her detention. Furthermore, the point was resolved by way of a tribunal, followed by that tribunal stating a case. It is possible to distinguish the case from *ex p. Waldron* on the basis that the effect of the tribunal's finding concerning the statutory criteria in *Re V.E.* was that there was *no longer* any authority for the patient's detention. There was authority to detain her at the commencement of the hearing and the tribunal did not involve itself in reviewing whether the application procedures had been complied with. Nevertheless, against this, three things must be acknowledged: (1) the patient was entitled to be immediately discharged even though she did not satisfy the statutory criteria for mandatory discharge; (2) this was because there was no lawful authority for her continued detention under the Act; and (3) she was apparently also entitled to be discharged because "she never qualified for detention under section 26 at all" (*per* Widgery C.J.) and "could not have been lawfully detained at all if correctly diagnosed at the outset" (*per* Bridge J.). That immediate discharge meant discharge by the tribunal is clear both from the use of the case stated procedure and the subsequent enactment of the Mental Health (Amendment) Act 1975, which removed any obligation on a tribunal to discharge if the circumstances should arise again.

THREE APPROACHES ADOPTED BY TRIBUNALS

The illegality of a guardianship application or an application for admission is occasionally obvious. For example, the doctors providing the medical recommendations have failed to specify a common form of mental disorder or the authority was not renewed during the prescribed period. In clear-cut cases, a tribunal could, and sometimes does, refuse to hear a patient's application on the basis that there is no existing authority to discharge. Although having no power to quash the application, the tribunal is nevertheless considering its validity to the extent of verifying that it has jurisdiction. If habeas corpus or judicial review is later refused, because the tribunal was mistaken in its ruling, or because of the discretionary nature of the remedy, the situation is unsatisfactory.[37] Likewise, if the patient is immediately released by the managers in the light of the tribunal's decision. Consequently, other tribunals proceed on the basis that there is authority to detain the patient, holding that the sufficiency of the application is wholly irrelevant. Liability to detention is presumed. In section 2 cases, where a copy of the section papers must be furnished to the tribunal, and presumably therefore read, the approach can seem artificial if the patient's detention has clearly not been properly authorised. Yet other tribunals adopt a third approach, which is that issues concerning the lawfulness of the patient's detention and treatment (whether those issues relate to a failure to observe the formalities set out in Parts II and IV or the conditions of detention) are relevant to the exercise of its discretion. However, in most cases, such as that in *ex p. Waldron*, the sufficiency of the application, and whether or not the patient is lawfully detained, is a matter of dispute.[38] Moreover, in section 2 cases, the application may be defective and invalid in its present form but the rectification period not have expired. Sometimes, the lawfulness of the detention or guardianship cannot be separated out from the issues which comprise the mandatory discharge criteria. For example, in *ex p. E*,[39] a mentally impaired patient was, with the approval of her guardian, being detained in the residential care home where she was required to reside. It was said on the guardian's behalf that the efficacy of the guardianship programme depended upon staff being able to detain her there. Given the patient's detention, and the fact that the application was being enforced in an unlawful manner, the patient's solicitor argued that it could not be the case that the guardianship was "necessary in the interests of the welfare of the patient." It was contrary to her welfare that she should be subject to the authority of a guardian which was abusing its powers over her and the tribunal should discharge her from that authority. In the event, the patient was discharged by the guardian a matter of days before the subsequent habeas corpus and judicial review proceedings were due to be heard by the Divisional Court.

QUESTIONS TO BE DETERMINED

It is clear that a tribunal has no power to quash any application, order or direction. Only the High Court has jurisdiction to determine the lawfulness of an application made under Part II. The purpose of the case stated procedure in section 78 is limited to enabling patients to apply to the High Court where it is contended that a tribunal's decision was based on some mistaken understanding of the law — in the case of *Re V.E.*, the fact that the patient was entitled to be immediately discharged by the tribunal. However, while a tribunal may not *determine* the lawfulness of a Part II

---

[37]   For an example of the dangers of this approach, see *Re E (Mental Health: Habeas Corpus), 10 December 1996 (unreported)*. In that case, a tribunal sitting on 27 September refused to review the patient's detention on the basis that his detention under section 3 was not authorised and there was no authority in existence for it to review. The High Court later refused to grant habeas corpus, being satisfied that his detention under the Act was authorised.

[38]   Although it is not uncommon to find that 20 per cent of applications at a particular hospital are incorrect or defective in some respect, on average only some 2–3 per cent of them are so grossly irregular as to be obviously invalid. The reference to the admission documents in the 1983 regulations as "forms" has led to a widespread failure to distinguish their importance from non-statutory forms, such as after-care forms. Furthermore, while their effect is the same as that of a warrant committing a person to prison, in that total deprivation of liberty is effected, the modern judicial approach has tended not to insist on strict compliance with the law, which of course leads to there being no strict compliance with the law. See *e.g. R. v. South Western Hospital Managers, ex p. M* [1993] Q.B. 683 (**597**).

[39]   *R. v. London Borough of Lewisham, R. v. South East Thames Mental Health Review Tribunal, ex p. E* (CO1094/89, 1095/89,1096/89).

application, in the sense of quashing it or awarding damages for unlawful imprisonment, that does not necessarily mean that it is not obliged to direct the release of a patient if *it* is of the opinion that his detention is unauthorised.[40] Nor that it may not have regard to the possibility that the patient's detention is unauthorised when deciding whether to direct his discharge at its discretion. The fact that section 72 provides that a tribunal may in any case direct that the patient (rather than the application or order) shall be discharged allows for the interpretation that it may order a patient's release because his detention appears to be irregular, without quashing the application or order, or legally determining the point. The issues are essentially fourfold—

- Firstly, whether an application however defective remains in force until it is quashed or until an order or direction is given releasing the patient from any liability to detention in pursuance of it.[41]

- Secondly, whether a patient who is, or may be, unlawfully detained can still apply to a tribunal for his discharge.

- Thirdly, if the patient is or appears to be unlawfully detained, whether any authority exists for a tribunal to review and discharge or whether "discharge" means simply "to direct the release of."

- Fourthly, whether Parliament, in conferring a discretionary power of discharge on tribunals in unrestricted cases, nevertheless intended that they should have no discretion to take account of any defects in the authority for the patient's detention. In other words, whether it intended that they should confine their attention to the issues mentioned in section 72, reserving the power to finely balanced cases where the patient could not satisfy the statutory criteria because they are phrased as a double-negative.

Before considering these questions it is necessary to consider the historical development of a tribunal's functions and how they came to have a discretionary power of discharge.

HISTORICAL DEVELOPMENT OF THE TRIBUNAL'S POWERS

It is pertinent to briefly summarise the origins of the tribunal system, with particular regard to a tribunal's duty to discharge in certain circumstances and its discretion to discharge in all cases. The history of tribunals dates back to the Percy Commission of 1954–57, which reviewed the law relating to mental illness and mental deficiency.[42] Prior to 1959, the order of a justice of the peace, or other judicial authority, was generally necessary before a person could be compulsorily admitted

---

[40] According to *Re V.E.*, once the tribunal's finding was that there was no authority for the patient's detention, or that there never had been, it should have discharged the patient. Although it generally has a discretion as to whether or not to discharge a patient whose medical condition and circumstances do not come within the specified grounds, it has no discretion if the patient's liability to detention was unauthorised.

[41] If the application may only be quashed by certiorari, and the patient only released from detention in pursuance of an application which has not been quashed by habeas corpus or an order or direction for his discharge, then a tribunal must necessarily consider the patient's application.

[42] *Report of the Royal Commission on the Law relating to Mental Illness and Mental Deficiency*, Cmnd. 169 (1957).

to hospital or received into guardianship. The Percy Commission advocated the repeal of these certification procedures. In their place, it recommended that a person's detention or reception into guardianship should be authorised if an application supported by two medical recommendations was accepted by the hospital to which admission was sought or, in the case of guardianship, was accepted by the social services authority concerned. Because the proposed new procedures did not involve any judicial body, the Percy Commission recommended that, if a patient then wished the justification for his detention to be formally reviewed, rather than merely to apply to the hospital's own management committee or the local authority to exercise its power of discharge, this need should be met by the establishment of a new independent review body. The functions of such a tribunal would be to review the continuing need for compulsion:[43]

> "We should make it clear that these review tribunals would not be acting as an appellate court of law to consider whether the patient's mental condition at the time when the compulsory powers were first used had been accurately diagnosed by the doctors signing the recommendations, or whether there had been sufficient justification for the use of compulsory powers at that time, nor to consider whether there was some technical flaw in the documents purporting to authorise the patient's admission ... The review tribunal's function would be to consider the patient's mental condition at the time when it considers his application, and to decide whether the type of care which has been provided by the use of compulsory powers is the most appropriate to his present needs, or whether any alternative form of care might now be more appropriate, or whether he could now be discharged from care altogether."

Scrutiny of statutory documents

Prior to the introduction of the 1959 Act, applications were forwarded to the Board of Control for scrutiny and it had a discretion to direct the patient's discharge if unamended statutory documents were materially defective.[44] The Percy Commission recommended that the Board should be abolished and this function performed by hospital or local health authority staff at the time of the patient's admission. It stated that where the admission documents did not appear to be in the form required by law, the hospital or health authority should not accept them as authorising them to detain the patient or exercise powers of guardianship. If necessary, the patient

---

[43] *Report of the Royal Commission on the Law relating to Mental Illness and Mental Deficiency*, Cmnd. 169 (1957), pp.150-151.

[44] See Lunacy Act 1890, s.34(2). It was not unlawful on the part of an asylum to detain a patient until they had proper authority for his discharge, even if he was of sound mind at the time of his admission: *Mackintosh v. Smith* 4 Macq. H.L. 913. The word "discharge" in the 1890 Act seems to have meant "to order the release of," the patient remaining liable to be detained until the order was quashed or he was discharged. As in *Re V.E.*, no particular significance was attached to the objection that there was, on a literal view, no authority in existence to be discharged. Rather, the patient was being discharged, not the order. While an irregular order for a patient's detention could only be discharged by the High Court (in the sense of being declared unlawful and set aside), various persons and bodies could make an order for his discharge (in the sense of releasing him from the effects of that order). Thus, the Board of Control had a discretion to order a patient's discharge if a certificate seemed incorrect or defective (which did not involve determining the issue) or the patient appeared to be detained without sufficient cause. If the patient's discharge was ordered, this had the effect of prospectively annulling the order, that is reducing it to nothing, whatever was its status before — which is somewhat different from legally determining the issue of whether it ever had any status in law. In other cases, the Board of Control and its predecessors sometimes recommended the discharge of the patient otherwise than by their own order, with a view that the patient should be immediately re-certified: *Archbold's Lunacy and Mental Deficiency Practice* (ed. J.W. Greig & W.H. Gattie, Butterworth & Co./Shaw & Sons, 5th ed., 1915), p.195.

should be cared for informally, or by use of emergency procedures, while the documents were corrected or new documents prepared.[45] The 1959 Act adopted this particular recommendation and it is clear that the function of scrutinising documents, in order to ensure that they conferred the necessary authority, was one transferred to the managers, rather than to tribunals, under the new scheme. This was perhaps not surprising because many patients detained under the civil procedures would not have a tribunal hearing, nor therefore would tribunals have an opportunity to scrutinise their statutory documents. It may be noted that the function of scrutinising documents was not restored in 1983 to the body which is the modern day successor of the Board of Control, namely the Mental Health Act Commission.

Mental Health Act 1959 and discretionary discharge

As originally drafted, the 1959 Bill only required a tribunal to consider the matters set out in the criteria for mandatory discharge and to discharge if satisfied that the grounds for detention did not exist, not discharging otherwise. The Minister of Health explained the functions of tribunals by reference to the above passages from the Royal Commission's report.[46] However, later on during the Bill's passage, a discretionary power of discharge was added, for reasons given by the then Minister of Health—

> "The Clause as it stands in the Bill requires a tribunal to discharge when satisfied on the criteria ... but it does not permit it discretionally to discharge in other circumstances. In the Amendment, we propose to give the tribunal discretion to discharge in any case, and to require it to discharge if it is satisfied in respect of the criteria which are specified in the Bill. I think that is the right approach, because the other people who have the power to discharge, that is to say, the nearest relative, the hospital managers, the responsible medical officer and so on, have complete discretion to discharge if they think fit. So it is right that these tribunals, which we are carefully constituting with balanced representation and which have judicial or quasi-judicial functions to perform, should not be at a disadvantage, and that, in addition to having a duty to discharge when satisfied of the criteria, should have a discretion to discharge in any case."[47]

In contrast to the present position, there were never any matters which a tribunal constituted under the 1959 Act had to consider before deciding on whether to exercise its discretion to order a patient's discharge. Its discretion was unfettered, subject to the usual need to act in accordance with the statutory framework. Likewise, there was, and is, nothing to prevent the managers, or the patient's nearest relative, from making an order for discharge under section 23, on account of their concerns about the validity of the authority. Albeit that the managers could alternatively take the view that no order for discharge is necessary if they conclude that they have no authority to detain the patient. This, though, assumes that an order for patient's discharge is not the same thing as an order for his release: If an order for discharge is an order discharging a patient from an existing liability to detention then it is not necessary to make such an order if the managers correctly conclude that the application being considered did not authorise them to detain the patient in the first place. If, however, an application once accepted remains in force, and so renders the patient liable to detention, until the High Court quashes the application (by judicial

---

[45]   *Report of the Royal Commission on the Law Relating to Mental Illness and Mental Deficiency*, Cmnd. 169 (1957), para. 483.

[46]   The Minister for Health, Mr. Derek Walker-Smith M.P., *Hansard*, Standing Committee E Official Report, cols. 705–707 (14 April 1959).

[47]   The Minister for Health, Mr. Derek Walker-Smith M.P., *Hansard*, H.C. Vol. 605, col. 331 (5 May 1959).

review) or some authorised body orders the patient's release (by habeas corpus or an order or direction for his discharge) then, the defective authority not having been quashed, the managers should order the patient's discharge in such a case.[48]

DEALING WITH APPLICATIONS MADE UNDER SECTION 66

Sections 66 and 77 do not refer to applications being authorised if made by patients who are liable to be detained in pursuance of an application for admission for treatment.[49] On a natural reading of section 66, a patient admitted under section 3 is being detained in pursuance of the application made to and accepted by the managers of the relevant hospital. "Pursuant to" simply means to follow on from and his detention follows on from the application. He is not being detained in pursuance of any purported common law authority. Since the patient has been admitted in pursuance of the application, he may therefore apply to a tribunal during the relevant period. Likewise, where a report is furnished under section 16 or 20, he may make an application during the relevant period. All these applications are applications made in cases and at times expressly provided by the Act and hence, according to a similarly natural reading of section 77, authorised applications. The purpose of a tribunal is to "deal" with applications and references made by and in respect of patients under the statutory provisions.[50] Nowhere in Part V does it state that it may or shall not deal with an application if it becomes apparent that the authority being reviewed is, or may be, invalid. That, arguably, constitutes part of the review in the case of a Part II patient, since there has been no prior judicial scrutiny of the justification for the citizen's detention. Given the wording of section 66(1), it is submitted that if it is the case that a tribunal may not consider applications made by patients who are, or may not be, liable to be detained then this limitation cannot be discerned from this section.

LIABILITY TO DETENTION AND SECTION 72

The next question is whether the terms of section 72 prevent a tribunal from hearing, or continuing to hear, an application if it becomes apparent immediately before or

---

[48]   In this context, mention must be made of Lord Denning's judgment in *D.P.P. v. Head* [1959] A.C. 83. In that case, His Lordship said that "if the original order was only voidable, then it would not be automatically void. Something would have to be done to avoid it. There would have to be an application to the High Court for certiorari to quash it .. And being only voidable, the court would have a discretion whether to quash it or not. It would do so if justice demanded it, but not otherwise. Meanwhile the order would remain good and a support for all that had been done under it." Furthermore, a defective application could be cured by a valid renewal (what was then known as a continuation order). Clearly, if the authority conferred by an application is valid until set aside by the High Court, the patient remains liable to be detained under it for the purposes of any prior tribunal hearing and a tribunal may review his case. However, Lord Denning's view is not now the conventional view and Lord Somervell distanced himself from it in that case: "I am not satisfied that the order was not void. On the wording of section 9 of the Mental Deficiency Act, 1913, I think the certificates may well be for this purpose part of the order to be looked at in order to see whether it is good on its face. If they are not part of the order it might, I think, be maintained that they afford no evidence on which the order could validly have been based. In either case I would wish to reserve the question whether the order would not be void rather than voidable." Lord Reid and Lord Tucker concurred with these reservations but Viscount Simmonds did not.

[49]   Section 66(1) *inter alia* provides that where (b) a patient is admitted to a hospital in pursuance of an application for admission for treatment; or (c) a patient is received into guardianship in pursuance of a guardianship application; or (d) a report is furnished under section 16 above in respect of a patient; or (f) a report is furnished under section 20 above in respect of a patient and the patient is not discharged; an application may be made to a Mental Health Review Tribunal within the relevant period.

[50]   Mental Health Act 1983, s.65(1).

during the hearing that the authority for the patient's detention, guardianship or supervision is flawed. Insofar as material to the present question, section 72(1) provides as follows:

> "**72.** —(1) Where application is made to a Mental Health Review Tribunal by or in respect of a patient who is *liable to be detained* under this Act, the tribunal may in any case direct that the patient be discharged, and
>
> (a) the tribunal shall direct the discharge of a patient *liable to be detained* under section 2 above if they are satisfied—
>
> (i) that he is not then suffering from mental disorder or from mental disorder of a nature or degree which warrants his *detention* in a hospital for assessment (or for assessment followed by medical treatment) for at least a limited period; or
>
> (ii) that his *detention* as aforesaid is not justified in the interests of his own health or safety or with a view to the protection of other persons.
>
> (b) the tribunal shall direct the discharge of a patient *liable to be detained* otherwise than under section 2 above if they are satisfied—
>
> (i) that he is not suffering from mental illness, psychopathic disorder, severe mental impairment or mental impairment or from any of those forms of disorder of a nature or degree which makes it appropriate for him to be *liable to be detained* in a hospital for medical treatment;" ..."

The phrase "liable to be detained" is not used in the statute in any one universal way but, insofar as section 72(1) is concerned, three views are possible:

- If the two references in paragraph 72(1)(b) to patients who are "liable to be detained" bear the same meaning, and are both simply meant to embrace patients who have leave, it is unlikely that the opening references in section 72 to patients who are liable to be detained bear a different meaning.

- The word "detained" embraces patients who have leave of absence whereas the word "liable" means that a legal authority to detain the patient exists.[51]

- The three opening references to patients who are liable to be detained in section 72(1), 72(1)(a) and 72(1)(b), which do not form part of the criteria for discharge, refer to patients who are liable *in law* to be detained, while the subsequent reference in section 72(1)(b)(i) bears a different meaning, referring to patients either detained or on leave.

If the last view is correct, and it is perhaps the strongest interpretation, a tribunal may not review the case of a patient whose detention seems to it to be unauthorised unless it is the case that a patient remains liable to detention in pursuance of the application or order made under the Act until (a) such time as the High Court quashes it or (b) such time as the High Court orders his release or his release is ordered or directed under section 23 or 72.

---

[51] This construction is supported by various cases prior to 1959, such as *Safford v. Safford* [1944] P.61, but contradicted by the use of the word "detained" in section 72(1)(a)(i) and (ii) but "liable to be detained" in section 72(1)(b)(i).

Arguments against any power to take account of irregularities

The main arguments in favour of the now customary views that a tribunal may either not hear a patient's case if it is satisfied that his detention is not authorised or, if it may, that it may not have regard to any irregularities in the authority giving rise to the tribunal proceedings, may be summarised as follows—

1. The function of a tribunal at a hearing is to review the patient's current mental condition, and the risks associated with it, not to review whether his detention, guardianship or supervision is authorised.

2. The dicta of Ackner L.J. in *ex p. Waldron* accurately state the legal position and have, in effect, subsequently been adopted as such by the courts, albeit that the reservations of Glidewell and Slade L.JJ. were regrettably never brought to their attention.

3. In those places where the phrase "liable to be detained" does not form part of the statutory criteria, it refers to a patient whose detention is legally authorised. This is clear from a reading of both sections 20 and 72. If a patient is not liable to be detained, or subject to guardianship or supervision, there is no authority in existence for a tribunal to review or discharge.

4. A tribunal must either proceed on the basis that there is authority for the use of the compulsory powers being reviewed or, alternatively, it may take a view as to the sufficiency of that authority, but only to the extent of determining if it has jurisdiction to hear the application or reference.[52]

5. The underlying statutory purpose of discretionary discharge is to enable a tribunal to discharge a patient who cannot displace the double-negative test, that is a person who cannot demonstrate that there are no grounds for his detention, but whose mental state and circumstances make discharge appropriate.

6. If the contrary view were correct, a tribunal might discharge a patient subject to a guardianship order because it was of the opinion that the order was irregular in some material respect. This would involve reviewing the order of a criminal court and a tribunal has no jurisdiction to do that.

---

[52] Paragraphs (3) and (4) are not entirely compatible. If, as was stated by Ackner L.J. in *ex p. Waldron*, a tribunal "has no power to consider the validity of the admission" then its lawfulness must be presumed, unless "to consider" means "to legally determine." Unless it means this, the dicta cannot be reconciled with a second observation made in that case, namely that an application is only authorised, and so may only be dealt with, if the patient is actually liable to detention. For, unless a tribunal can consider and come to a view about the validity of the admission, it cannot establish if the patient is actually liable to detention and his tribunal application is authorised. However, if its view on the point is not determinative, because only the High Court can determine the validity of the admission, it has no authority to refuse to hear his case on the ground that, in its opinion, he is unlawfully detained and his application is unauthorised. Ackner L.J.'s two observations therefore seem to be contradictory. Thus, the dicta of Ackner L.J. in fact lead to the conclusion that the patient remains liable to be detained until the application is quashed, habeas corpus is granted, or an order or direction for discharge is made under section 23 or 72. The only outstanding question becomes whether the tribunal may have regard to any irregularities it is aware of when deciding whether to exercise its power of discharge under section 72.

7. Furthermore, because the same discretionary power of discharge applies equally to all unrestricted patients, it cannot be correct that there is a discretion to take account of irregularities in applications but not irregularities in court orders.

Arguments in favour of a power to take account of irregularities

The main arguments in favour of the proposition that a tribunal may have regard to irregularities in the authority can be summarised as follows—

1. *Re V.E.* is authority for the proposition that a tribunal which is satisfied that a civil patient's detention is not authorised under the Act is obliged to direct his discharge, notwithstanding that it is not satisfied that he is entitled to be discharged according to the statutory criteria for mandatory discharge.[53]

2. A patient's detention may not be authorised under the Act but the hospital managers nevertheless be entitled to act upon the application. And, if the managers may act upon an application which appears to be duly made, and so detain the patient in pursuance of it, that patient thereby becomes liable to detention by them notwithstanding that there is no authority for his detention under the Act. For it can hardly be said that the managers are entitled to act on the application but the patient is not thereby liable to detention by them. Furthermore, if they may detain him in pursuance of that application, it must also be the case that he may apply to a tribunal in respect of his detention in pursuance of the application.[54]

---

[53] This proposition is, of course, incompatible with the contention that flaws in the authority are matters relevant *only* to the exercise of the discretionary power of discharge. The more restrictive ratio of the decision in *Re V.E.* is that a tribunal must discharge the patient if the effect of a direction which it may lawfully make is that there is, or was, no authority to detain the patient.

[54] Section 6 deals with the effect of applications made under Part II. Subsections (1) and (2) provide that a "duly completed" application for admission constitutes sufficient authority for the patient's conveyance to, and detention in, the hospital named in the application. Subsection (3) then provides that an application for admission "which appears to be duly made and to be founded on the necessary medical recommendations may be acted upon without further proof of the signature or qualification of the person by whom the application or any such medical recommendation is made or given or of any matter of fact or opinion stated in it." The effect of these subsections was considered by Laws J. in *R. v. Managers of South Western Hospital, ex p. M.* [1993] Q.B. 683 at 700 and then by Sir Thomas Bingham M.R. in *Re S.-C. (Mental Patient: Habeas Corpus)* [1996] W.L.R. 146 at 156–157. Laws J. observed that an application which is not "duly completed" may nevertheless "appear to be duly made" on its face, as where an approved social worker applicant states that the nearest relative has not objected to the application being made when in fact he has. He then said that it followed that "although the managers were not authorised to detain the patient by section 6(2) standing alone, they were entitled to act upon the application, and thus to detain the patient, by virtue of section 6(3). Accordingly, the applicant's detention is not unlawful." As to this, the then Master of the Rolls said that he "would accept almost everything in that passage as correct with the exception of the last sentence. The judge goes straight from a finding that the hospital managers were entitled to act upon an apparently valid application to the conclusion that the applicant's detention was therefore not unlawful. That is, in my judgment, a non-sequitur. It is perfectly possible that the hospital managers were entitled to act on an apparently valid application, but that the detention was in fact unlawful. If that were not so the implications would, in my judgment, be horrifying."

3. If only the High Court has jurisdiction to quash an application made under Part II, it follows that, until then, the application continues to have an existence and the patient's detention is in pursuance of it. It is not in pursuance of any common law authority. While an irregular application may only be discharged by the High Court (in the sense of being quashed), various persons and bodies may make an order or direction for the patient's discharge under sections 23 and 72 (in the sense of releasing him from his detention pursuant to that application).

4. No particular significance is to be attached to the objection that if a patient's detention is unauthorised then there is no authority in existence for a tribunal to review. It has already been explained that the managers may lawfully act on an application and detain the patient even though his detention is not authorised. Furthermore, it is the patient who is being discharged, not the application or order. In the context of unrestricted cases, to order or direct a patient's discharge means to authorise his release. If the patient's discharge is ordered, this has the effect of prospectively annulling the application, that is reducing it to nothing, whatever was its status before — which is different from legally determining the issue of whether it ever had any status in law.

5. To authorise a person's release, because that seems to be appropriate in all the circumstances, including the possibility that his detention is not authorised, is therefore not the same thing as judicially determining the lawfulness of his detention. That is no more so than it was when the Board of Control could make an order for a patient's discharge having regard to mistakes and defects in a reception order. Just as the Board had a discretion to order a patient's discharge on that basis, but only the High Court could determine the issue, tribunals (which inherited the Board's discharge functions) have a discretion to discharge that basis, but only the High Court can determine the issue.[55]

6. In any case involving an unrestricted patient, a tribunal may at its discretion direct that the patient shall be discharged. Although, in some cases, the Act requires a tribunal to have regard to certain matters before exercising that power, in no case does it provide that there are certain matters which it may not have regard to. That was because it was of the opinion that a tribunal should not be at a disadvantage vis-à-vis the other persons and bodies who may make an order for the patient's discharge under section 23. If the hospital managers, and the nearest relative of a Part II patient, may have regard to the possibility that a patient's detention is unauthorised, when deciding whether to exercise their discretion to make an order for his discharge, there is no reason why a tribunal's discretion should be interpreted as being any narrower in this respect.

---

[55] In *Re Shuttleworth*, Lord Denman C.J. remarked that, if the patient was dangerous, it was better that she should remain in custody till the commissioners acted. *Re Shuttleworth* (1846) 9 Q.B. 651 at 662. The commissioners, and later the Board of Control, had a discretion to discharge a patient whose detention appeared to be irregular or without good cause and tribunals arguably inherited this independent discretionary power of discharge in 1959.

7. The fact that it is not the duty of tribunals to scrutinise all applications following their acceptance is irrelevant. Tribunals could not possibly have been charged with such an administrative function. Moreover, it does not logically follow from the fact that it is not their duty to rectify defective documents that they may not take account of evidence that the use of compulsory powers is unauthorised.

8. Mandatory discharge by a tribunal aside, every other statutory power to discharge an unrestricted patient is discretionary. That is because no person can be required to order or direct a patient's release if to do so would place him or others at risk. He may in effect be required to seek a determination from the High Court that his detention is unauthorised.

9. The objection that such a discretion might mean that a tribunal may have regard to the fact that a hospital or guardianship order was apparently not imposed in accordance with the requirements of Part III is not as significant as first appears. In the first place, it is indisputably the case that a tribunal, or the managers, can lawfully discharge a patient from guardianship immediately after the order was imposed even though there has been no change of circumstances. That in effect involves overturning an order made by a criminal court. Secondly, the standard section 37 form completed by the clerk to the court, and sent to the hospital, is merely a record of the order made by the judge. It is equivalent to the Form 14 completed in Part II cases following the acceptance of an application. Hence, one can never proceed on the basis that a patient's detention is unauthorised simply because this form is defective (see *ex p. Norris*, **574**). Thirdly, it may be that, unless the patient avails himself of his statutory right of appeal in respect of an order, he cannot in any subsequent legal proceedings question its validity, including within tribunal proceedings.[56] And, if an appeal to a superior criminal court was dismissed, that is conclusive proof that the irregularity was immaterial. Fourthly, and in the alternative, if the detaining authority or local authority can properly have regard to any obvious irregularities in the authority for a Part III patient's detention, whether in terms of the order or subsequent renewals, it is unclear why their discretion should be unfettered in this respect but a tribunal's be fettered. Furthermore, there can in justice be no objection to a tribunal having a discretion to release a patient from the effect of an order which is subsequently shown to be invalid. Better that than that injustice should prevail because a person was too mentally incompetent to query the order at the relevant time.

10. In summary, subject to the precise effect of the decision in *Re V.E.*, a tribunal may, but may not be required to, discharge a patient whose mental condition does not entitle him to be discharged, having regard to all the circumstances of the case, including any evidence of a lack of authority for his detention, supervision or guardianship. That is not in any sense the same thing as determining the validity of the application. It involves going no further than directing the patient's discharge and finding the irregularity to be a material circumstance.

---

[56] See *Re Corke* [1954] 1 W.L.R. 899.

CONCLUSION AND SUMMARY

The issue is quite finely balanced. However, as to the four questions previously raised, it is submitted that—

1. For the purposes of the 1983 Act, a patient remains liable to be detained in pursuance of an application until it is quashed, the High Court orders his release, his release is ordered or directed under sections 23 or 72, or the application is not renewed.

2. Accordingly, until the patient's release is authorised, or those entitled to detain him lose their entitlement because the authority is not renewed, the patient is liable to be detained in pursuance of the application and may apply to a tribunal. A tribunal's function is to deal with applications duly made under section 66, *e.g.* within 28 days of a report reclassifying the patient, not to deal merely with those applications authorised under section 66 which are made by persons whose detention is duly authorised.

3. Since only the High Court may quash a Part II application, so rendering it *void ab initio*, an authority exists for a tribunal to review. However, the point is not of central importance because a patient detained following the acceptance of an application is liable to be detained in pursuance of it; the managers may be entitled to detain him although the application does not authorise that; and "discharge" means "to order the release of".

4. A tribunal's discretion is unfettered by statute and it is objectionable that its discretion should be impliedly fettered when that of a person acting under section 23 is not. Accordingly, it may have regard to the possibility that the patient's detention is unauthorised when exercising its power to discharge a patient at its discretion.

With the passing of years, this is very much a personal opinion. Although the Court of Appeal's judgment in *Re V.E.* has disappeared from view, and both counsel and textbooks have failed to acknowledge the reservations of Slade and Glidewell L.JJ. in *ex p. Waldron*, so that the dicta of Ackner L.J. have taken hold in a rather unconsidered fashion, that does not mean that the view expressed by him does not state the law. Only that the statement has not been subjected to proper scrutiny. Most tribunals are likely, and would be wise, to adhere to Ackner L.J.'s statement that they may not consider applications made by patients whose detention under the Act is not authorised. Nevertheless, because the practice of refusing to hear an application on account of the tribunal's opinion that the patient's detention is unauthorised is fraught with danger, and full of contradictions, other tribunals will no doubt continue to proceed on the assumption, or presumption, that the patient is liable to detention, with which issue the tribunal is not concerned. Assuming that the author's opinion will be held to be wrong, it does indeed seem preferable to deal with applications on the basis that (1) the authority is valid until such time, if ever, as the High Court determines otherwise; (2) the patient remains liable to detention in pursuance of it until the application is quashed or his release is ordered, either by the High Court or by virtue of an order or direction made under sections 23 or 72; and (3) the tribunal must confine its attention to those matters expressly referred to in section 72.

THE EXTENT TO WHICH DIRECTIONS ARE BINDING

The extent to which a tribunal's direction that a patient shall be discharged is binding on those who may reauthorise his detention under the Act was considered in the cases of *ex p. K* and *ex p. M*.

Ex p. K.

In *ex p. K*, a restricted patient who had been conditionally discharged by a tribunal was later recalled to hospital by the Secretary of State. McCullough J said that it would be unlawful for the Secretary of State to recall a patient who had recently been conditionally discharged by direction of a tribunal, unless something had happened which justified the belief that a different view might now be taken about one of the factors on which his release had depended.

R. v. Secretary of State for the Home Department, ex p. K.[57]

[1990] 1 W.L.R. 168   *Q.B.D. McCullough J.*

In January 1971, the patient was convicted of the manslaughter of a neighbour's 12-year-old daughter. The court was satisfied that he was suffering from a psychopathic disorder and it directed his admission to a special hospital in pursuance of a hospital order and a restriction order made without limit of time. In March 1985, a tribunal reviewed his case. Given the unanimous medical evidence that the patient was not presently suffering from any form of mental disorder, but taking the view that it was appropriate for him to remain liable to recall, the tribunal conditionally discharged him from hospital. In October 1985, some seven months after being discharged, the patient made an unprovoked attack on a girl of 16 whom he saw walking along a road in the afternoon. The next night, at about 11.30 pm, he attacked a young woman of 21. A sexual motive for each assault was suspected but could not be proved. Subsequently, in April 1986, the patient pleading guilty in each case to assault occasioning actual bodily harm. Having considered the medical and other evidence, the judge sentenced the patient to a total of six years imprisonment. In 1986 and whilst in prison, the patient reapplied to the tribunal. At the hearing in December 1986, the medical evidence was again unanimously of the view that the patient was not suffering from any form of mental disorder. The tribunal accepted this evidence but, as before, also considered it appropriate for him to remain liable to be recalled. The patient's earliest date of release was 24 October 1989 and, on 1 September 1989, with the prospect of release approaching, the Secretary of State issued a warrant authorising the patient's detention in a special hospital upon his release from prison. The applicant applied for judicial review by way of an order of certiorari to quash the warrant of recall dated 1 September 1989 and an order of prohibition restraining the Secretary of State from so recalling him.

McCullough J.

The only point which had caused real difficulty was the extent to which a tribunal's decision to conditionally discharge a restricted patient subsequently bound the Secretary of State. The point had been most tellingly made by the patient's counsel when he asked if it could be lawful for the Secretary of State, a week after a patient had been conditionally discharged by a tribunal, to exercise

---

[57]   For a fuller summary of the judgment, see page 348.

his power of recall in the absence of some fresh development. The answer was plainly not. It did not matter whether one castigated such an action as irrational, or illegal, or as frustrating the objects and policy of the Act. According to the patient's counsel, this was what has happened here since there was no evidence that the patient's condition has deteriorated; indeed there was no evidence about it at all. There were, no doubt, occasions when the Secretary of State had to act with speed under section 42(3) but this was not one of them. For years the applicant has been safely in prison. What the Secretary of State was in fact doing was overturning a decision with which he did not agree. His views were put to the tribunal on that occasion and they were rejected. He did not like the result so he was going to frustrate it by what could only be regarded as a misuse of section 42(3). The submission had more than a hint of *res judicata* in it and it was useful to see what was in fact decided in December 1986. The tribunal was constituted because the patient, who had earlier been discharged conditionally, wanted to be discharged absolutely. The issue in December 1986 had been confined to the issue of whether the patient should remain liable to recall and nothing was decided at that hearing which procured his conditional release. That was procured by the earlier decision of 19 March 1985 since when the events of October 1985 had occurred. Thus, insofar as considerations of *res judicata* might apply in the field (on which no submissions had been made and the court expressed no opinion), there was nothing in the tribunal's decisions to prevent the Secretary of State from alleging that further events had occurred since March 1985 which had a bearing on the question of the patient's mental condition — namely the attacks of October 1985. Despite the lack of evidence of any subsequent change in the patient's mental condition, it was open to the Secretary of State to take and act upon the view held by him provided he did so in a way consistent with the purposes of the Act. It would, however, be unlawful for the Secretary of State to recall a restricted patient to hospital when only the previous week or month he had been conditionally discharged from hospital by direction of a tribunal, unless meanwhile something has happened which justified the belief that a different view might now be taken about one of the factors on which his release had depended. But that was not the situation here. The hypothetical situation would frustrate the purposes of the Act but the present one did not. The essential factual difference between December 1986 and September 1989 was that in December 1986 there was no imminent prospect of the applicant coming into contact with members of the public, in particular young females; now there was. That was why the Secretary of State did not then act but now did. In terms of the application of the Wednesbury criteria [1948] KB 223, 229, it was important for the court to remember that the Secretary of State, before exercising his power under section 42(3), must give full weight to the fact that his decision will affect the liberty of the person recalled, but his interests were not the only ones for the Secretary of State to consider. *Application dismissed.*

In re M

In *ex p. M*, the patient, who was detained under section 2, applied to a tribunal which heard the matter on 14 December 1992. The tribunal was satisfied that she was not suffering from mental disorder of a nature or degree which warranted her detention in a hospital for assessment and accordingly directed her discharge. However, the tribunal directed that she be discharged on 17 December in order that social services could first make arrangements for a suitable support programme. During the period between the giving of the direction and the date fixed by the tribunal for the patient's discharge, she was detained under section 3. Laws J. said that he could see no basis for construing the statute so as to produce the result that an approved social worker's duty or discretion to make a section 3 application was to any extent impliedly limited or abrogated by the existence of an earlier tribunal decision to discharge. There was no sense in which those concerned in making a section 3 application were at any stage bound by an earlier tribunal decision.

R. v. South Western Hospital Managers, ex p. M.

[1993] Q.B. 683   *Q.B.D, Laws J.*

The patient was admitted to hospital under section 4 on 30 November 1992. The admission took effect as a section 2 application on 1 December 1992, upon receipt of the second medical recommendation. On 14 December, a tribunal reviewed her case. Before the tribunal was a medical report prepared by the responsible medical officer, Dr. Lawrence, and a social circumstances report prepared by a social worker. The medical report stated that the patient had an 11 year history of bipolar affective disorder; was currently manic and without insight; had endangered her life and the lives of others by setting fires within the past two weeks; was unwilling to stay in hospital or to accept medication; and that the doctor therefore planned to place her under section 3. The tribunal received oral evidence from the writers of the two reports, the patient's uncle (a priest), and a friend of the patient. The responsible medical officer was excused from the hearing after giving his evidence and being questioned on it, but before the other oral evidence was taken. Having considered all the evidence, the tribunal was satisfied that the patient was not suffering from a mental disorder of a nature or degree which warranted her detention in a hospital for assessment and, accordingly, discharged her.[58] It postponed the date of her discharge until 17 December so that the social services could make arrangements for a suitable support programme for both her and her family. The recorded reasons for the decision stated that, although the tribunal did not accept that the patient's behaviour leading to her admission was merely eccentric, "there was, however, no firm evidence that her children were at risk and she had a good deal of support from neighbours and relatives when in her own home. We were per-suaded to accept her undertaking that she would co-operate with a programme of treatment organised for her by the hospital and would take medication as advised and attend hospital when required."

The patient's admission under section 3

The tribunal's decision and the reasons for it were communicated to Dr. Lawrence on the day of the hearing. Having received a copy of the decision, Dr. Lawrence saw the patient but did not carry out a further medical examination. Having seen her, he completed a medical recommendation for her compulsory admission under section 3, that recommendation being based on an examination conducted earlier that day prior to the hearing. He took into account the tribunal's decision but "remained concerned that the patient would not take her medication or fulfil her undertaking to the tribunal because she continued to insist both during and after the tribunal hearing that she was not mentally ill." Furthermore, after the tribunal hearing, he had been informed by a ward nurse that the patient was pretending to take her medication, but in fact hid it under her tongue and spat it out afterwards. The second medical recommendation was provided on the following day by a General Practitioner from the practice at which the patient was registered. She described bizarre behaviour, incoherence, and pressure of speech on the patient's part, and was of the opinion that someone who considered it normal to light a fire in their home was not fit to be

---

[58]   The tribunal's decision was silent as to whether the patient was also entitled to be discharged under sub-paragraph 72(1)(a)(ii).

discharged and to look after her children. She was not aware of the tribunal's decision but stated that, had she known of it, it would not have affected her recommendation. She had been told that the patient had refused to accept medication. On the same day, the case was referred to an approved social worker, who interviewed the patient and was told by her that she was not taking her medication but was hiding it under her tongue. Her assessment was that the patient would refuse out-patient treatment, continue to not take her medication, and continue to act in a bizarre manner and to threaten her neighbours. That evening, she was informed by another social worker that the latter had been in touch with the patient's mother in the Republic of Ireland. That social worker had been informed by the mother that she had no objection to the section 3 process. It was, of course, the case that the patient's mother was disqualified from being the statutory nearest relative because she was ordinarily resident outside the United Kingdom, the Channel Islands and the Isle of Man (see s.26(5)(a)). The patient's uncle, who was the statutory nearest relative, was also consulted by the second social worker, although not in his capacity as nearest relative. He disagreed with the tribunal decision. The section 3 application was accepted by the managers on 17 December.

The applications for judicial review and habeas corpus

On 22 December 1992 an application for leave to move for judicial review was refused by Potts J. The patient then applied for a writ of habeas corpus.

Laws J.

The patient had been refused leave to apply for judicial review. Since that was done after a hearing, His Lordship had no power to grant such leave and no renewed application had been made to him. However, the court would deal with the merits and substance of the argument. Although it had been contended that there had been an abuse of the process of the court, the application process under Part II did not involve any step within court proceedings. The argument was therefore misconceived. The suggestion that the section 3 process was unlawful because the issue with which it purported to deal was *res judicata* had rightly been abandoned by counsel. As to issue estoppel, it could only apply in a second set of proceedings where an issue had been conclusively decided in an earlier set of proceedings. Here, there was no second set of proceedings. Ultimately, the principal argument depended on the proposition that, on the true construction of the Act, the hospital managers had no power to detain a patient under section 3 if a tribunal had recently decided that the patient be discharged and there had been no change of circumstances since that decision. So regarded, the question became one of pure statutory construction.

Statutory construction

The construction advanced on the patient's behalf could not be sustained, not least because section 13 imposed a duty on an approved social worker to make a section 3 application in the circumstances which the section specified. That duty was not abrogated or qualified in a case where there had been a recent tribunal decision directing discharge. If that were the case, it would say so. Accordingly, the managers were obliged to consider on its merits any application made by an approved social worker in pursuance of his or her duty. The existence of a recent tribunal decision could no more fetter this obligation than it could the social worker's own express duty under section 13. Furthermore, if the legislature had intended otherwise one would expect a clear qualification to have been imposed within the terms of sections 3, 6 or 13. It could not sensibly be suggested that if the intention was that a patient should not be liable to detention under section 3 in cases where there was a recent tribunal decision to discharge and no change of circumstances, that would not be clear and express on the face of the statute. The patient's counsel had then submitted that some period of time must be allowed to elapse after a tribunal decision, at least while there was no significant change in the patient's condition and circumstances, before a section 3 application was permissible. Alternatively, there must be a significant change in the condition or circumstances of the patient before a further application could be made. That could not be right. Honest and responsible doctors and other experts would differ upon such questions as the significance of any apparent change in a patient's condition. To make the legality of a detention depend upon issues of that sort would be to abandon any claim in the area to a reasonable degree of legal certainty and would put the experts involved in individual cases in an invidious if not impossible position. Nor was there anything in the statute to suggest that such a state of affairs was intended. The court had been referred to dicta of McCullough J. in *ex p. K* (**592**). However, the Act expressly gave the Secretary of State a power to recall to hospital a patient who has been conditionally discharged by a tribunal. There was therefore a plain nexus between the Secretary of State's power to recall and a tribunal's power to conditionally discharge. Even if the legality of a warrant of recall depended upon the Secretary of State having had regard to the basis of the earlier tribunal decision, so as to avoid any frank inconsistency with it, no such reasoning could apply to the relationship between the section 3 regime and the tribunal's functions under sections 66 and 72(1). There was no cross-reference between them and no basis for construing the statute so the duty and discretion of the approved social worker to make a section 3 application, and the function of the managers in considering it, were impliedly limited or abrogated by the existence of an earlier tribunal decision to discharge.

Multiple applications

In theory, the legal position outlined by the court might produce an impasse with a section 3 patient being alternately discharged and readmitted a number of times in quick succession. In reality, that was highly unlikely to happen, given good faith and the procedures and safeguards which coloured the section 3 process. Moreover, the public law safeguards enshrined in the *Wednesbury* and *Padfield* rules applied to all exercises of administrative power (**347**).

Alternative ground for refusing the application

The reasons for the tribunal's decision stated that they were persuaded to accept the patient's undertaking that she would co-operate with a programme of treatment organised for her by the hospital and would take medication as advised. On the facts there had been a change of circumstances since the tribunal's decision. It had become apparent that she was not taking her medication but hiding it under her tongue. Even though the tribunal was clearly told, and by the patient herself, that she had refused much of her medication in hospital, and this was borne out by the contemporary hospital notes, the fact was that the situation continued after the tribunal hearing. Thus, even if a section 3 application was only be good in the event of some change of circumstances or fresh development since an earlier tribunal decision to discharge, that was sufficiently established in this case.

Habeas corpus and judicial review

For all of the above reasons, the primary argument that the patient's detention under section 3 was flawed, because it was inconsistent with the tribunal's decision to discharge, must be rejected. That argument would in any event go to judicial review and not to habeas corpus. The reason was that, by section 6, if an application appeared to be duly made the managers could act upon it. That meant that the managers were not bound to investigate the possibility that there might be a latent defect in the application caused by a failure to respect a recent tribunal decision. A sufficient return to a writ of habeas corpus was made where it was shown that there existed *ex facie* a statutory authority for the detention.

Summary

There was no sense in which those concerned in a section 3 application were at any stage bound by an earlier tribunal decision. The doctors, social worker, and managers must under the statute exercise their independent judgment whether or not there was an extant tribunal decision relating to the patient. They would no doubt wish to have regard to any such decision, where they knew of it, in order to ensure that they had the maximum information about the facts of the case. But it could not confine or restrict their own exercise of the functions which the Act conferred on them. *Application dismissed.*

COMMENTARY

The judgment in *ex p. M.* must be approached with caution because the basis on which the court rejected the patient's application for habeas corpus has since been disavowed.[59] As to the other half of the judgment, it is noteworthy that, having decided that the question of the effect of a tribunal's direction was one "of pure statutory construction," the court managed to construe the statute without once referring to Part V of the Act. At no stage did it consider for a moment what inferences might be drawn from the tribunal framework and the powers vested in them, confining its attention to the powers vested in doctors and prospective applicants. Nor did it contemplate the fact that the European Convention on Human Rights requires that persons detained on the ground of unsoundness of mind must have access to an independent and impartial court which can speedily determine the issue and direct their release.[60] A tribunal's powers under section 72 are of two sorts. It has power to direct (discharge and reclassification) and power to recommend (leave of absence,

---

[59] The court held that a patient's detention was lawful provided that the application on its face appeared to be duly made. The patient could be detained on the basis of a medical examination conducted prior to a judicial decision that he be discharged (without that doctor further examining the patient) together with a recommendation given by a second doctor who was not informed that a judicial direction for the patient's discharge was outstanding. Nor did it matter that the application was then made by a person who did not consult the nearest relative, or correctly identify that relative, but arranged for another relative to be consulted by another person not making the application, or that those accepting it knew that it was defective because the nearest relative had not been consulted. The court's remarks were *obiter* and the opinion that a writ of habeas corpus is not available if an application appears on its face to be duly made was criticised by the Court of Appeal in *Re S-C (Mental patient: habeas corpus)* [1996] W.L.R. 146 (**866**). Sir Thomas Bingham M.R. said that the implications of such an interpretation were "horrifying" and would mean that a patient's detention was lawful "even though every statutory safeguard built into the procedure was shown to have been ignored and violated."

[60] Article 5(4) of the Convention provides that "Everyone who is deprived of his liberty ... shall be entitled to take proceedings by which the lawfulness of his detention shall be decided speedily by a court and his release ordered if the detention is not lawful." Lawful in this context means both the substantive and technical lawfulness of the patient's detention. As to this, if a decision on the substantive lawfulness of a patient's detention (the facts/merits) is not binding then, by definition, it is not a decision — the substantive lawfulness of the patient's detention has not been decided. It may be noted that it was the breach by the United Kingdom of Article 5(4) that led to the domestic law having to be revised, as a result of which section 2 patients acquired a right to apply for their discharge to a tribunal.

transfer, supervision). The difference is that a direction must be given effect to while a recommendation need not be complied with.[61] To direct means to order, to rule, to command, and section 72 empowers a tribunal to "direct that the patient be discharged." The power is not one limited to recommending the patient's release to the hospital managers or notifying them of the tribunal's opinion about whether grounds for detaining him exist. In contrast, a tribunal's power in restriction direction cases is so limited by statute, the decision as to whether the patient is actually discharged lying elsewhere. The tribunal's direction that a patient is released is one addressed to those detaining him, the hospital managers. It is therefore difficult to see how the managers in ex p. M, being in possession of an outstanding court order directing them to discharge the patient on 17 December, could properly accept any application which authorised them to detain a patient whom they had been directed to release. It is similarly difficult to see how a social worker could be satisfied that an application "ought to be made" for the patient's detention in the very hospital from which his release had been ordered, the more so because the section 3 admission criteria are more stringent than in section 2 cases. Furthermore, as McCullough J. observed in *ex p. K.*, one cannot rule out that some principle similar to res judicata applies. Since the application process is unique, and nowadays involves an application made to a body other than a court, it is not irrational to suppose that such a body may be bound by a recent judicial finding on the same issues any less than was the case when such applications were actually made to a court. Finally, the contention that, if Parliament had intended that a patient could not be readmitted before being discharged in accordance with a judicial direction, then it would have said so, is wholly unconvincing.[62] It is therefore submitted that the correct position is that set out by McCullough J. in *ex p. K.*, the observations there holding good for restricted and unrestricted patients alike. If a tribunal directs a patient's discharge, he must be discharged. A further application may not be made in the absence of some fresh development. Some further event must occur which has a bearing on the question of the patient's mental condition and justifies the belief that a different view might now be taken about one of the factors on which his release had depended. Where this is not the case, any further application frustrates the objects and policy of the Act. In this context, they are that a person who is detained in pursuance of an application or order is entitled to have the substantive justification for his detention reviewed and decided by a court. Tribunals review decisions to make applications, applicants do not review tribunal decisions. They have no power to review or overturn the decision of a court, otherwise it is not a decision, and the issue of whether existing circumstances constitute grounds for the patient's detention has not been determined. Any other view means that the law has moved not only

[61]   Thus, a recommendation under section 72(3) that a patient be granted leave of absence does not oblige the responsible medical officer to grant leave. Similarly, a recommendation that a patient be transferred does not bind the hospital managers. In both cases, the tribunal may reconvene to further consider the patient's case if its recommendation is not complied with but it may not direct that the patient be granted leave or transferred.

[62]   Any proposition to the effect that "if Parliament had intended that provision x should not apply in circumstances y, it would have said so" should always be tested by reversing it, so that it reads "if Parliament had intended that provision x should apply in circumstances y, it would have said so," and then seeing if there is any loss of plausibility. In this case, an alternative proposition might be, "if Parliament had intended that a patient whose discharge had been directed by a judicial body, because it was satisfied that there were no grounds for detention, could be readmitted before he had been discharged, it would have said so." Or, less fairly, "if Parliament intended that a doctor could give evidence in the morning to a court which was reviewing the grounds for a patient's detention and then, in the afternoon, sign a medical recommendation on being notified of that court's finding that his evidence had been rejected and the patient was entitled to be discharged, and do that on the basis of an examination conducted prior to the hearing, it would have said so."

from the position that a court order is required before a person can be denied his liberty to the position that he has a right to have the justification for his detention judicially reviewed after the event, but to the further position that such retrospective decisions do not entitle the person concerned to be set at liberty. Social workers and doctors become the ultimate judges of when a person may be detained when that is for judges of law to decide. If this is what Parliament's intended, that really is something one would have expected it to make clear.

Tribunal procedure and practice

10. Commencing the proceedings

INTRODUCTION

A patient may apply to a tribunal or his case may be referred to a tribunal. Section 65(1) provides for the establishment of Mental Health Review Tribunals for the purpose of dealing with applications and references made by and in respect of patients. Where authorised by the statute, an application may be made by a patient, by his nearest relative, by the person presently exercising the nearest relative's statutory functions, or by the High Court in the case of a ward. In certain circumstances, the Act imposes on the managers of a hospital or the Secretary of State a duty to refer a patient's case to a tribunal (**632**), and it also provides that the Secretary of State may at his discretion make such a reference at any other time (**637**).

MATTERS ARISING

On receipt of an application or reference, the tribunal is required to give notice of it to the persons specified in the rules and, where an assessment application has been made, to hear it within the following seven days (**638**). The tribunal will decide whether it may and should postpone its consideration of an application (**641**) and also whether to appoint a representative for the patient (**878**). If a prior application or reference is outstanding in respect of the same patient, it will decide whether to join the proceedings (**639**). If the patient moves to the area of another tribunal during the proceedings, his case may be transferred to that tribunal (**648**). Because assessment applications must be heard within seven days of their receipt and their consideration may not be postponed, these joinder and transfer provisions are rarely relevant in such cases. In certain circumstances, an application of reference may be withdrawn (**649**) or deemed to be withdrawn (**650**).

RIGHTS OF APPLICATION

Applications must be in writing and should include the information prescribed by the Mental Health Review Tribunal Rules 1983 (**619**). The application must be authorised by statute and no application may be made by or in respect of a patient except in such cases and at such times as are expressly provided by the Act.[1] The rights of application vary according to the authority for the patient's detention, guardianship or supervision. The tables on pages 614 and 615 summarise the rights conferred by the Act, other than an unrestricted patient's right to apply following reclassification. The relevant sections of the Act are set out in full in Appendix IA.

---

[1]   Mental Health Act 1983, s.77(1).

DIFFERENT KINDS OF AUTHORISED APPLICATION

Most patients, and sometimes their nearest relatives also, are entitled to periodically apply to a tribunal for the patient's discharge. However, there are in essence two kinds of authorised application. Firstly, these periodic general rights of application, which arise simply because the person is liable to be detained or is subject to guardianship or supervision, and, secondly, various contingent rights of application, the acquisition of which is dependant upon one of the additional events specified in paragraphs 66(1)(d)(fb)(g)(gb)(h) first occurring.[2] These events are—

• the furnishing under section 16, 21B or 25F of a report reclassifying the form of mental disorder from which an unrestricted patient is recorded as suffering — the common feature and consequence of these reports is to reclassify the patient in between renewals.	*Relevant to all unrestricted patients.*
• the furnishing by a responsible medical officer of a report under section 25, preventing the nearest relative of a section 3 patient from making an order for his discharge.	*Applies only where the patient is liable to be detained under section 3.*
• the making of an order by a county court under section 29, directing that the functions of the patient's nearest relative be exercisable by some other person or authority.	*Relevant only to Part II patients: those liable to be detained under section 2 or 3 or subject to guardianship under section 7.*

Who acquires the right of application

Only the first of these events results in the patient acquiring an additional right of application, although the patient's nearest relative may jointly acquire a right to apply (**610**). The second event gives rise to a right of application which is exercisable by the nearest relative who has been prevented from ordering the patient's discharge. In relation to the third event, which involves the appointment of an acting nearest relative, it is the patient's actual nearest relative ("the displaced nearest relative") who acquires the right, this right being in substitution for the loss of his right to personally order the patient's discharge. Thus, in the second and third cases, the right to apply is acquired by the person whose statutory powers have been interfered with or curtailed in some way.

The importance of the distinction

The usefulness of distinguishing between general and contingent rights of application is that it simplifies the statutory scheme—

---

[2] Since these events can never occur in the case of restricted patients, consequently they possess only the periodic rights of application set out in sections 69,70 and 75.

- A restricted patient has only general periodic rights of application and the person who would ordinarily be his nearest relative has no rights of application at all.

- If an unrestricted patient is or is to be subject to after-care under supervision, or he is liable to be detained or subject to guardianship under Part III, both the patient and his nearest relative have the right to periodically apply to a tribunal. However, unless the patient is reclassified, no additional right to apply can ever arise.

- Lastly, if the patient is liable to be detained or subject to guardianship under Part II, the occurrence of any of the three events set out above will give rise to a right to apply to a tribunal and applications may only ever be made by the patient unless one of these events has occurred.

Number of applications authorised

Where a right of application is granted by the Act it must be exercised during the period specified. This is referred to in section 66 as "the relevant period."[3] Section 77(1) states that where under the Act any person is authorised to make an application within a specified period, not more than "one such application" may be made by him within that period. However, for these purposes, any application previously made by him during the same period which was later withdrawn is to be disregarded.[4]

"One such application"

The defining phrase in section 77(1) is "one *such* application." While each right of application may only be exercised once during the period prescribed for exercising *such* a right, each separate right has its own period during which it may be exercised once. For example, if a section 3 patient in his first six months of detention has already exercised his general right to apply to a tribunal during that initial period of detention (which right arises under section 66(1)(b)), he may still make a further application if he is reclassified during that period. As to his right under section 66(1)(b), he has made one *such* application during the period specified for making *such* an application. And, as to section 66(1)(d), he has similarly made only one *such* application during the period prescribed for exercising that right. Conversely, therefore, if he is reclassified before he has exercised his general right of application for that period of detention, and he applies as a result of being reclassified, he may later apply again during the current period of detention. However, it should be noted that a tribunal may often postpone its consideration of an application which is made shortly after the determination of a previous application or reference (**641**).

---

[3] Where a supervision application is accepted in respect of a hospital order patient, it is clear from the Act that he may immediately apply to a tribunal. However, a drafting error means that no relevant period for making this initial application is prescribed. Nevertheless, it is clear from the statutory framework that the tribunal application may be made at any time during the six-month period following the Health Authority's acceptance of the supervision application. See Mental Health Act 1983, ss.40(4), 55(4), 66, 145(3), Sched. 1, Pt. I, para. 9, as amended by Mental Health (Patients in the Community) Act, s.1(2) and Sched. 1, paras. 6, 7, and 14.

[4] Mental Health Act 1983, s.77(2).

UNAUTHORISED APPLICATIONS

The effect of sections 65(1) and 77(1) is that patients and their nearest relatives have no implied rights of application and tribunals have no jurisdictional discretion to "deal with" applications not expressly authorised by the statute. Since in law no application has been made none can have been received for a tribunal to consider.

Examples of unauthorised applications

An application will be unauthorised if no right to apply exists or if the person making the application is not an eligible applicant and so not entitled to exercise any right which does exist. More particularly, an application will *inter alia* be unauthorised if no right of application exists[5]; the application has been made outside the prescribed time limits[6]; the same right of application has already been exercised and determined during the relevant period[7]; the person applying is not the nearest relative as defined by sections 26–28[8]; the person applying has not been properly authorised by the nearest relative to exercise his statutory functions[9]; the patient is a ward of court and his nearest relative has not obtained the court's leave to make the application.[10]

Ambiguities and anomalies

Ambiguities in the drafting mean that it is not always immediately apparent whether or not a person has a general right to periodically apply to a tribunal. However, in order to avoid confusion, consideration of these ambiguities and anomalies is postponed until after the general scheme has been explained. See page 623.

Irregular applications, orders or directions

According to dicta of Ackner L.J. in the case of *ex p. Waldron*, a tribunal's jurisdiction following a patient's admission to hospital "is limited to entertaining applications made by a person who is liable to be detained under the Act."[11] That being so, if a section 2 or 3 application is so irregular as not to confer any legal authority for the patient's detention, no liability to detention under the Act can exist for a tribunal to review. The appropriate course is for him to apply for habeas corpus. It should, however, be noted that Glidewell and Slade L.JJ. declined to express a view on the matter and expressly left the point open.[12] The issue is considered in greater detail on pages 574 *et seq.*

---

5   Mental Health Act 1983, s.77(1).
6   *Ibid.*
7   *Ibid.*, s.77(2).
8   Various duties imposed by the Act require an approved social worker or the managers of a hospital to consult or notify the person "appearing to be" the patient's nearest relative. See *e.g.* Mental Health Act 1983, ss. 11(3) and (4), 132(4), 133(1). However, Part V of the Act does not similarly allow a tribunal to deal with an application by a person who appears to be the patient's nearest relative. Only applications made by the "actual" nearest relative are authorised.
9   Where, in accordance with the 1983 regulations, a patient's nearest relative authorises some other person to exercise his functions under Part II, the person authorised may also exercise the former's tribunal rights of application — notwithstanding that, in contrast to the wording used in section 29(1) and (6), a person authorised under section 32 is superficially authorised only to exercise the nearest relative's functions under Part II, not those exercisable under Part V. See p.110.
10   Mental Health Act 1983, s.33(2). This limitation does not appear to apply to the nearest relative of a Part III patient: Mental Health Act 1983, ss.40(4), 55(4), 145(3), Sched. 1, Part I.
11   *R. v. Hallstrom and another, ex p. Waldron* [1986] 1 Q.B. 824 at 846, *per* Ackner L.J.
12   *Ibid.*, at 848, *per* Neill L.J., and at 852–53, *per* Glidewell L.J.

GENERAL PERIODIC RIGHTS OF APPLICATION

In the cases prescribed by Part V, a patient or his nearest relative may periodically apply to a Mental Health Review Tribunal. Section 77(2) provides that where a person is authorised to make an application to a tribunal within a specified period, not more than one *such* application shall be made by that person within that period, but for that purpose there shall be disregarded any application which is withdrawn in accordance with rule 19. Rights of application not exercised during the periods in which they arise cannot be accumulated and carried forward.

Patients admitted to hospital for assessment

A patient admitted to hospital in pursuance of an application for assessment may make an application to a tribunal during the 14 day period beginning with the date of his admission for assessment. Because a patient's liability to detention under section 2 may not be renewed for a further period upon the expiration of the 28 day period of detention, the Act does not provide such patients with any further periodic rights of application.[13]

Patients detained for treatment or subject to guardianship or supervision

Patients admitted to hospital for treatment, or placed under guardianship or statutory supervision, remain subject to the compulsory powers for a potentially indefinite period, albeit that the authority for an unrestricted patient's detention, guardianship or supervision requires periodic renewal. That being so, the Act provides that they may apply for their discharge at periodic intervals.

Applications during the first six months

The general rule is that all such patients, both restricted and unrestricted, may apply to a tribunal during the six month period beginning with—

- In the case of Part II patients, the date of their admission for treatment or the date on which the guardianship or supervision application was accepted;

- In the case of Part III patients, the date of the order or direction authorising their admission, removal or reception into guardianship.

The only patients who may not make an application during this initial six month period are persons admitted for treatment under a hospital order (made with or without restrictions) imposed by a criminal court following conviction or, not having been convicted, under section 37(3) or 51(5).[14]

---

[13] In particular, no further right to apply arises if a section 2 patient's liability to detention is extended beyond 28 days because an application is made to the county court under section 29 (see ss. 2(4) and 29). In practice, this may have the effect of extending the section 2 period by several weeks or, if an appeal is then lodged in respect of the court's order, by several months. Where the delay is protracted, the appropriate remedy will usually be to ask the Secretary of State (for Health) to refer the patient's case to a tribunal under section 67(1).

[14] The rationale for this is often said to be that a court in England and Wales has already recently reviewed and approved the necessity for the use of compulsory powers. However, a patient may apply during the six month period following the making of a guardianship order or an order imposed under the Criminal Procedure (Insanity) Act 1964.

Subsequent applications

Where a patient remains liable to detention for treatment or subject to guardianship or supervision for longer than six months, the Act places all patients in the same position. A patient may make an application to a tribunal during his second six month period of detention, guardianship or supervision and thereafter make an application during each subsequent twelve month period he remains so liable.

Conditionally discharged patients

A conditionally discharged restricted patient may not make an application during the first year following his discharge from hospital.[15] He may apply during the second year and thereafter make an application during each subsequent two year period. If he is subsequently recalled to hospital, he may apply during the second six month period following his return and make a further application during each subsequent year. This is because a recalled patient is treated for these purposes only as if the hospital order and restriction order, or the transfer direction and restriction direction, had been made on the day of his return to hospital.[16]

Periodic applications by nearest relatives

The underlying principle is that if the Act gives the nearest relative a power to order the patient's discharge under section 23 then that relative has no right to periodically apply to a tribunal for his discharge: the right is unnecessary since he may himself discharge. Where, however, the nearest relative of an unrestricted patient has no such power, the Act compensates him for this limitation, and protects the patient's position, by periodically allowing him to apply to a tribunal for the latter's discharge. Since a restricted patient has no statutory nearest relative, it is necessarily the case that the person who would be that relative if restrictions had not been imposed possesses no rights of application whatsoever.[17]

Patients liable to be detained or subject to guardianship under Part II

The nearest relative of a patient who is liable to be detained or subject to guardianship under Part II may himself order that patient's discharge. It is presumed that he will resort to this power in the first instance, rather than apply to a tribunal for the patient's discharge. Consequently, the Act does not give that relative any general right to periodically apply to a tribunal and such a person may only make an

---

[15] Where a tribunal defers its direction for the patient's conditional discharge, the one year waiting period necessarily commences only from the day (if any) on which the tribunal brings the period of deferment to an end and actually directs his discharge. Until then, he is not a conditionally discharged patient. The point was considered in *R. v. Canon's Park Mental Health Review Tribunal, ex p. Martins* (1995) 26 B.M.L.R. 134. In that case, Ognall J. said that the year begins on the day of the patient's actual release, meaning the date on which the tribunal gave the direction and ordered the patient's release. As with directions for a patient's immediate conditional discharge, the patient may in practice remain in hospital for a further day or two after the tribunal's direction has been given, so that practical arrangements, such as transport, can be finalised.

[16] See Mental Health Act 1983, s.75(1). It should be noted that future application periods are calculated by reference to the date of the patient's return to hospital rather than the date of the warrant of recall. Following the issue of a warrant, the patient is thereafter absent from hospital without leave until such time as he returns or is returned to hospital. See *ibid.*, s.42(4)(b).

[17] As to this, the exceptions and modifications of Part II of the Act mentioned in Sched. 1, Pt. I, para 1 may be compared with those listed in Sched. 1, Pt. II, para 1. Sections 26–28, which define who is a patient's statutory nearest relative, apply to unrestricted hospital order patients but not to those subject to restrictions.

application if one of the events specified in s.66(1)(d), (fb), (g) or (h) has occurred. In guardianship cases, the relative's power to order discharge is unfettered. In the case of section 3 patients, the responsible medical officer may bar the discharge in certain circumstances and, where this happens, this event gives rise to the right to apply under section 66(1)(g) (**612**).

Unrestricted patients subject to a hospital or guardianship order or to supervision

The nearest relative of a Part III patient, or a patient in respect of whom a supervision application has been accepted, is in a different position. He may not make an order terminating the authority for the patient's detention, guardianship or supervision. Consequently, the Act gives him certain rights to apply to a tribunal for the authority's termination, these rights being compensatory and in lieu of a power of discharge—

- Following the acceptance of a supervision application, the nearest relative may make one application to a tribunal during each six or twelve month period the authority remains in force, provided he was entitled to be consulted about the application being made or last renewed, as the case may be.

- Upon the making of a guardianship order, the patient's nearest relative may apply to a tribunal once during each year the order is in force, beginning with the date of the order.

- Where a hospital order is made, the nearest relative may make an application during the second six-month period following the date of the order and thereafter apply once during each subsequent period of 12 months.

- As can be seen, the nearest relative's entitlement is the same in all of these cases once a supervision application, guardianship order or hospital order has been in force for one year — he may make an application during each subsequent twelve month period the order remains in force.

CONTINGENT RIGHTS OF APPLICATION

It has been noted that, in addition to any general rights to periodically apply to a tribunal, an additional or substitutional right to apply may arise if one of three events occurs. These are the reclassification of the form of mental disorder from which an unrestricted patient is recorded as suffering otherwise than in the course of renewal; the furnishing of a report by the responsible medical officer barring the discharge of a patient detained under section 3; the making of an order under section 29 directing that the nearest relative's statutory functions shall be exercisable by some other person or authority. With regard to the table below, unless a section 29 order has been made, the person exercising the nearest relative's functions will be the nearest relative himself or the person authorised by him under section 32. If a section 29 order has been made authorising some other person to exercise the nearest relative's functions, the displaced nearest relative loses the right to apply following reclassification or the issue of a barring report.

	Patient	Person exercising nearest relative's functions	Displaced nearest relative
Reclassification of an unrestricted patient under s.16	•	•	
Reclassification of a patient subject to after-care under supervision under s.25F	•	see note below	
Reclassification of an unrestricted patient previously absent without leave under s.21B(8)	•		
Issue of report barring the discharge of a patient detained under s.3		•	
Making of county court order under s.29 in respect of a patient detained or subject to guardianship under Part II			•

Caveat: In the case of patients subject to after-care under supervision, the nearest relative only acquires a right of application following reclassification if he is entitled to be informed that the report reclassifying the patient has been furnished. See p.451.

RECLASSIFICATION UNDER SECTION 16, 21B OR 25F

With three exceptions, where a patient is admitted to hospital for treatment or placed under guardianship or supervision, the application, order or direction authorising this will specify the form or forms of mental disorder from which he has been found to suffer.[18] If it later appears that an unrestricted patient is suffering from a form of disorder other than the form(s) specified, the Act provides various mechanisms for amending the application, order or direction (**054**). This process is known as "reclassification."

Reclassification under the 1983 Act

Where the form or forms of disorder specified in a renewal report differ from that or those previously specified, sections 20, 21B(7) and 25G provide for the patient's automatic reclassification (**054**). Such automatic reclassification in the course of renewal does not give rise to any additional right of application to a tribunal. This is because a right to apply arises anyway by virtue of the renewal of the authority, albeit that it is not one exercisable until the new period of detention, guardianship or supervision has actually begun.

---

[18]   The exceptions are (1) where an order is made under the Criminal Procedure (Insanity) Act 1964; (2) where a section 2 patient is transferred into guardianship under section 19; (3) where a hospital direction is given under section 45A. As to the third exception, such a direction may only be given in respect of a person who suffers from a psychopathic disorder and the Act therefore does require the form of disorder to be specified in it.

Reclassification otherwise than during renewal

Sections 16, 21B(7)–(8) and 25F enable an unrestricted patient's condition to be reclassified at a time other than when furnishing a report renewing the authority for the compulsory powers.[19] Because the justification for compulsion has materially changed since the present period of detention, guardianship or supervision was authorised, the Act provides that the patient, and in some cases his nearest relative also, may apply to a tribunal within 28 days of being informed of the reclassification.[20] This takes account of the fact that the patient may already have used his general right to make an application during the existing period, and might otherwise not be entitled to have the justification for the compulsory powers again reviewed for some months. It may also give a nearest relative who would not have consented to the application being made had it been made on the newly revised grounds the option of having the new reasons for using the powers independently reviewed.

Reclassification under section 16 or 25F

Where a report is furnished under section 16 or 25F, sections 66(1)(d) and 66(1)(gb) respectively provide that an application may be made to a tribunal "by the patient or ... by his nearest relative if he has been (or was entitled to be) informed under this Act of the report."[21] This application must be made within the relevant period, which is "28 days beginning with the day on which the applicant is informed that the report has been furnished."[22] The 28 day period for making the application therefore begins on the day the prospective applicant "is informed" that a report has been furnished, rather than on the date of the reclassification. Where the managers, the responsible after-care bodies or the guardian initially omit to notify either or both prospective applicants, the right may therefore be exercisable some time after the event.

"by the patient or ... by his nearest relative"

Hoggett has noted that the reference in section 66 to the effect that an application may be made by the patient or by his nearest relative suggests that one or the other of them may apply under section 66(1)(d) or (gb) but not both. However, as she implies, the wording is ambiguous.[23] Section 77(2) states that where under the Act any person is authorised to make an application to a tribunal "not more than one such application shall be made *by that person* within that period." The most natural reading of this provision is that both the patient and the nearest relative may apply

---

[19]   Under the 1959 Act, the same renewal criteria applied whatever the form of mental disorder recorded in the application, order or direction and, indeed, the criteria made no reference to the form of mental disorder from which a patient was recorded as suffering. A patient could only be reclassified by his responsible or appropriate medical officer under what is now section 16 and therefore a right of application to a tribunal always arose upon reclassification. This is not now the case.

[20]   The present rationale may be inferred from the fact that the reclassification provisions do not apply to restricted patients, whose detention does not require periodic renewal, and from the fact that no right of application arises if reclassification occurs in the course of renewal. It may more precisely be formulated in the following way: Where during the course of period of detention, a patient's mental state, or his responsible medical officer's assessment of it, is so materially different to that upon which the current period of detention was authorised as to require legal reclassification, the continuance of that detention for the remainder of the authorised period should always be susceptible to independent review. Similarly where a patient is subject to guardianship or after-care under supervision.

[21]   Mental Health Act 1983, s.66(1)(d)(i) and (gb)(i). As to whether the nearest relative is entitled to be informed in supervision application cases, see page 451.

[22]   Mental Health Act 1983, s.66(2)(d).

[23]   B. Hoggett, *Mental Health Law* (Sweet & Maxwell, 4th. ed., 1996), p.178.

and, where this happens, the rules provide for hearing both applications together. If both apply, both have the rights of an applicant.

Reclassification under section 21B

Rather anomalously, where a patient who has been absent without leave for more than 28 days is reclassified under section 21B upon his return, and a right to apply to a tribunal arises, this is exercisable only by the patient. There seems to be no logical reason for distinguishing this situation from other reclassifications between renewals so the omission may be unintentional.

ISSUE OF A SECTION 25 REPORT BARRING DISCHARGE

The nearest relative of a Part II patient may make an order directing his discharge from detention or guardianship under the Act.[24] In guardianship cases, the power is absolute and no notice is required. However, where the patient is detained under section 2 or section 3, section 25 provides that an "order for discharge" may not be made by his nearest relative except after giving 72 hours notice to the managers of the hospital.[25] If, during that period, the patient's responsible medical officer furnishes to the managers a report certifying that in his opinion the patient would "if discharged .. be likely to act in a manner dangerous to other persons or to himself," any order made at the expiration of that period is of no effect.[26] "No further order" for discharge shall then be made by "that relative" during the six months beginning with the date of the responsible medical officer's report.[27] Where no "barring report" is served within 72 hours, any order for discharge made after the expiration of that period takes effect.[28]

Right of application to a tribunal

Where a "barring report" is furnished to the managers of a hospital in respect of a section 3 patient, they are under a duty to ensure that the nearest relative is informed

---

[24] The order must be in writing and served on the managers or the responsible local social services authority. It "may be" in the form set out in Form 34 or 35 of Schedule 1 to the Mental Health (Hospital, Guardianship and Consent to Treatment) Regulations 1983. See Mental Health Act 1983, s.23(1) and (2)(b), s.32(2)(a) and (b); Mental Health (Hospital, Guardianship and Consent to Treatment) Regulations 1983, regs. 2(1) and 15.

[25] Mental Health Act 1983, s.25(1). There is no prescribed form for giving this notice.

[26] A report furnished under section 25 by the responsible medical officer must be in the form set out in Part I of Form 36 to Schedule 1 to the Mental Health (Hospital, Guardianship and Consent to Treatment) Regulations 1983. Receipt of the form by the managers must take place within the 72–hour period and be recorded in Part II of the same form. See sections 25(1) and (2)(a), s.32(2)(a) and (b), and regulations 2(1) and 15(3). On a literal reading of the section, it suffices that the patient is likely to be dangerous even if the patient is no longer mentally disordered or any likely dangerous conduct is not a consequence of the fact that he is mentally disordered. For example, a patient with previous convictions for robbery may be likely to reoffend for reasons entirely unconnected with his psychiatric condition. However, unless psychopathy is an issue, it is submitted that a barring report based on a patient's likely dangerousness must relate to dangerousness associated with or arising from mental disorder.

[27] Mental Health Act 1983, s.25(1)(b). Where, therefore, a different person becomes the patient's nearest relative during the following six months, he is not debarred from making an order for discharge within that period.

[28] Any order for discharge completed by the nearest relative following the expiration of the 72 hours must be in writing and served upon the managers of the hospital where the patient is liable to be detained. The order for discharge "may be" in the form set out in Form 34 of Schedule 1 to the Mental Health (Hospital, Guardianship and Consent to Treatment) Regulations 1983. See section 23(1) and (2)(a), section 32(2)(a) and (b), and regulations 2(1) and 15(1).

of that fact.[29] The reason for this is because section 66(1)(g) provides that the nearest relative may apply to a tribunal for the patient's discharge during the 28 day period beginning with the day on which he was informed that the report had been furnished. If he does, the discharge criteria which then apply are more favourable to discharge than in any other kind of tribunal proceedings. Specifically, the tribunal which determines the application is required to discharge the patient if it is satisfied that he would not, "if released, ... be likely to act in a manner dangerous to other persons or to himself."[30]

Patients who are liable to be detained for assessment

No right of application arises where a barring report is issued in respect of a patient who is detained for assessment.[31] However, the fact that the nearest relative has attempted to discharge the patient from detention under section 2 will generally mean that he also objects to the patient being detained under section 3. Where this is so, the patient may not be detained beyond the 28 day section 2 period unless an application is first made to the county court on the ground that the nearest relative's objection to admission under section 3 is, viewed objectively, unreasonable.

COUNTY COURT ORDERS UNDER SECTION 29

Section 29 of the Act provides that the county court may appoint a person or local social services authority to exercise a nearest relative's statutory functions on one or more of four grounds: that a patient has no ascertainable nearest relative; that a patient's nearest relative is incapacitated; that the nearest relative has unreasonably objected to the making of a guardianship application or an application under section 3; or that the nearest relative has exercised "without due regard to the welfare of the patient or the interests of the public his power under Part II to discharge the patient from hospital or guardianship, or is likely to do so" (**111**).

Duration of county court orders

An order made under section 29 lapses if the patient is not placed under guardianship or admitted or removed to hospital for treatment under Part II or III (otherwise than under section 36 or 38) within three months of the date of the court's order. If the patient becomes so liable during that three month period, or was already under guardianship or so detained when the court order was made, the order remains in force until the patient ceases to be liable to be detained or subject to guardianship.[32] For this purpose, transfers under section 19 are to be ignored.

Effect of section 29 orders on tribunal proceedings

Where an order under section 29 is in force, the nearest relative's ordinary rights of application under sections 66 and 69 are exercisable by the court appointee. However, section 66(1)(h) gives the displaced nearest relative a right to apply to a tribunal during the "12 months beginning with the date of the order, and in any subsequent period of 12 months during which the order continues in force."

---

[29] Mental Health Act 1983, s.25(2).

[30] Mental Health Act 1983, s.72(1)(b)(iii).

[31] Thus, a nearest relative's objection to a patient's detention under section 2 does not preclude such an admission nor, where dangerousness is an issue, its continuance.

[32] There are two possible exceptions to this rule although they are rare. They are where the order is made for a specified period (**112**) or where it is discharged by the court prior to the patient ceasing to be liable to be detained or subject to guardianship (**113**).

PATIENTS' GENERAL PERIODIC RIGHTS OF APPLICATION

Authority for the patient's detention or guardianship	First six months	Subsequent rights
PART II PATIENTS		
• **Patients detained for assessment** (including patients admitted under s.14A of the Criminal Appeal Act 1968 and assessment patients removed to England or Wales under Part IV or under the Mental Health (Scotland) Act 1984)).	During first 14 days, s.66(1)(a).	Not applicable.
• **Patients detained for treatment under s.3**	Yes, s.66(1)(b).	The patient may make an application during the second six months and during each subsequent 12 month period: ss.66(1)(f) and (gc), 70(a) and 75(1)(b). In the case of Part II patients, the application periods are calculated by reference to the date on which the existing application for the patient's detention, guardianship or supervision under Part II was accepted. In the case of Part III patients, the tribunal application periods commence from the date on which the order or direction was made by the court or the Secretary of State.
• **Patients received into guardianship under s.7** (including section 2 or 3 patients transferred into guardianship under s.19 and guardianship patients removed to England or Wales under Part VI or the Mental Health (Scotland) Act 1984)	Yes, s.66(1)(c).	
• **Patients in respect of whom a supervision application made under s.25A has been accepted**	Yes, s.66(1)(ga)	
• **Part II patients transferred from guardianship to hospital under s.19**	Yes, s.66(1)(d).	
PART III PATIENTS		
• **Part III patients transferred from guardianship to hospital under s.19**	Yes, s.66(1)(d)	
• **Detained Part III patients (including restricted patients) removed to a hospital in England or Wales under Part VI of the 1983 Act or under the Mental Health (Scotland) Act 1984**	Yes, s.69(2)(a)	
• **Patients received into guardianship under s.37** (including hospital order patients transferred into guardianship under s.19 and guardianship patients removed to England or Wales under Part VI or the Mental Health (Scotland) Act 1984))	Yes, s.69(1)(b)(i)	
• **Patients (including restricted patients) removed to hospital under s.45B(2), 46, 47 or 48**	Yes, s.69(2)(b)	
• **Patients deemed to have been admitted under a notional hospital order after the cessation of restrictions**	Yes, s.69(2)(a)	
• **Patients admitted to hospital under s.5(1) of the Criminal Procedure & Insanity Act 1964.**	Yes, s.69(2)(a)	
• **Patients made the subject of a hospital order** (including restricted patients) otherwise than above.	No	
• **Conditionally discharged patients who have been recalled to hospital**		
• **Conditionally discharged restricted patients**		In second year after discharge and during each subsequent 2 years.

614

NEAREST RELATIVES' RIGHTS OF APPLICATION

Authority for the patient's detention or guardianship	Person exercising the nearest relative's functions under Part V			Displaced nearest relatives
	Right to make periodic applications	*Right to apply following reclassification*	*Right to apply following a barring report under s.25*	*Right to make periodic applications*
Patients detained for assessment	No	No (not applicable)	No	A displaced relative may apply in the year following the date of the court order and in each subsequent year it remains in force.
Patients liable to be detained under s.3	No		Within 28 days of being informed that a report has been furnished.	
Patients received into guardianship under s.7		Within 28 days of being informed that a report has been furnished. *In the case of patients subject to statutory supervision, if the nearest relative is not entitled to be informed that a report has been furnished then no right to apply arises.*		No
Patients in respect of whom a supervision application made under s.25A has been accepted	The nearest relative may make one application during each six or 12 month period the application remains in force if previously entitled to be consulted about the application being made or renewed.			
All unrestricted patients admitted to hospital under Part III (including patients transferred to hospital under ss.19, 47 or 48 and detained Part III patients removed to England or Wales under Part VI or the Mental Health (Scotland) Act 1984))	The nearest relative may apply during the period of 6 and 12 months beginning with the date of the order or direction and in each subsequent year.			
All patients subject to a guardianship order (including those transferred into guardianship under s.19 and guardianship patients removed under Part VI or the Mental Health (Scotland) Act 1984)	The nearest relative may apply in the year beginning with the date of the order and in each subsequent year.			
All restricted patients		No (not applicable)	No (not applicable)	

A restricted patient's nearest relative has no rights of application.

APPLICANTS' RIGHTS TO INFORMATION AND ADVICE

Section 132 requires the managers of a hospital or mental nursing home to take such steps as are practicable to ensure that every patient who is detained understands what rights of applying to a tribunal are available to him. Those steps are to be taken as soon as practicable after the commencement of the patient's detention under the provision in question and must include giving him the information both orally and in writing.[33] The managers are not under a corresponding duty to inform the person who appears to be the nearest relative of his rights of application. However, unless the patient has requested otherwise, they must furnish him with a copy of the written information given to the patient setting out the latter's rights.

Guardianship

Section 132 does not impose a duty on a guardian or local social services authority to inform patients who are received, or transferred, into guardianship of their rights of application.

European Convention on Human Rights

Article 5(2) of the Convention, which provides that everyone who is arrested shall be informed promptly, in a language which he understands, of the reasons for his arrest and of any charge against him, applies to persons detained under Part II. This arguably imposes a wider obligation on hospitals than does section 132 and requires patients to be notified of the reasons for their detention and not merely the consequences of being detained, the statutory authority for that detention, and the methods of challenging it.[34]

MEDICAL ADVICE AVAILABLE TO PROSPECTIVE APPLICANTS

Any patient entitled to apply to a tribunal may authorise a registered medical practitioner to visit and examine him in private for the purpose of advising him whether to make an application.[35] Likewise, where the patient's nearest relative, or a person exercising his functions, is entitled to make an application, he may similarly authorise such a practitioner to visit and examine the patient for the purpose of advising whether an application should be made.[36] A prospective applicant may instruct some other person, such as a solicitor, to authorise a medical practitioner on his behalf. Any person who without reasonable cause refuses to allow a medical practitioner so authorised to visit, interview or examine a patient, or who refuses to withdraw when required to do so by that practitioner for the purpose of enabling him

---

[33] The Department of Health publishes patients' rights leaflets which are commonly used by hospitals to provide patients with the written information required by section 132. It is questionable whether these leaflets fully comply with the requirements of the section and, in any case, most of them are inaccurate in a number of respects. The information is also available in Braille and spoken versions are available on cassettes for those who require them.

[34] See *Van der Leer v. The Netherlands* (1990) 12 E.H.R.R. 567–575. The court held that the word "arrest" in Article 5(2) embraces a deprivation of liberty on the ground of unsoundness of mind (see paras. 27-28). Any person who is entitled to take proceedings to have the lawfulness of his detention speedily decided cannot make effective use of that right unless he is promptly and adequately informed of the reasons why he has been deprived of his liberty" (at para. 28). The requirement would probably be satisfied by giving the patient a copy of the application. As to a patient's right to a copy of the application, see *Re Dell* (1891) 35 Sol. Journ. 783.

[35] Mental Health Act 1983, s.76(1).

[36] *Ibid.*

to examine a patient in private, or who otherwise obstructs him in the exercise of his functions, commits an offence.[37] Despite its wording, section 76 applies to all tribunal applications without modification, including those concerning Part III patients, whether restricted or not.[38] It does not extend to proceedings commenced by reference. No regulations have been made under section 32 regulating the conduct of the medical examination or the production of records.

INDEPENDENT MEDICAL ADVICE AND OPINIONS

Visiting and examination of patients

76.—(1) For the purpose of advising whether an application to a Mental Health Review Tribunal should be made by or in respect of a patient who is liable to be detained or subject to guardianship *or to after-care under supervision (or, if he has not yet left hospital, is to be subject to after-care under supervision after he leaves hospital)* under Part II of this Act or of furnishing information as to the condition of a patient for the purposes of such an application, any registered medical practitioner authorised by or on behalf of the patient or other person who is entitled to make or has made the application—

(a) may at any reasonable time visit the patient and examine him in private, and
(b) may require the production of and inspect any records relating to the detention or treatment of the patient in any hospital *or to any after-care services provided for the patient under section 117 below.*

(2) Section 32 above shall apply for the purposes of this section as it applies for the purposes of Part II of this Act.

The italicised words were inserted by the Mental Health (Patients in the Community) Act 1995, s.1(2) and Sched. 1, para.11.

Production and inspection of records

Provided that their production is required for one of the statutory purposes, the medical practitioner may require the production and inspection of "any records relating to the patient's detention or treatment in any hospital."[39] "Hospital" in this context includes a mental nursing home which is registered to receive detained patients. Any person who without reasonable cause refuses to produce a document or record for inspection the production of which is *duly* required of him by an authorised medical practitioner, commits an offence.[40]

---

[37] Mental Health Act 1983, s.129(1)(b).
[38] *Ibid.*, ss.40(4), 55(4), Sched.1, Pt. I, para.1., etc.
[39] *Ibid.*, s.76(1). He is not, however, empowered to take copies of those documents unless such a right is implied by the right of inspection. Section 76 derives from section 37(1) of the Mental Health Act 1959 and from section 9(2) of the Mental Health (Amendment) Act 1982. Under the 1959 Act, a medical practitioner authorised under what is now section 76 had no power to require the production or inspection of any records relating to the patient's detention or treatment in any hospital. Section 9(1) of the Mental Health (Amendment) Act inserted in section 37 the provision now found in section 76(1)(b).
[40] Mental Health Act 1983, s.129(1)(c). The prosecution must prove, *inter alia*, that the production of the documents or records in issue was required for the purpose of giving advice under section 76.

"Any records relating to the patient's detention or treatment in any hospital"

Insofar as detained patients are concerned, the phrase could hardly be broader. The sole qualification is that the medical practitioner may only require the production of records which he requires either (1) for the purpose of giving advice about the making of an application or (2) if an application has already been made, for the purpose of furnishing the applicant with information as to his own or the patient's condition. Subject to this caveat, the words are wide enough to cover records held at a hospital other than that where the patient is then liable to be detained, including records relating to previous periods of detention; documents which would not be disclosable to the prospective applicant under the Access to Health Records Act 1990; records held by social services authorities concerning the patient's detention; and various records held off the ward, such as occupational therapy records, clinical complaints files, incident and accident reports.

Patients subject to guardianship

The words "any records relating to the patient's detention or treatment in any hospital" are of limited relevance in such cases. As drafted, the authorised medical practitioner may not require the production of any records relating to the guardianship, not even a copy of the application or order. Many of the other records he would wish to inspect will relate to care which the patient receives in the community rather than to any treatment in a hospital. For example, files held at a social services area office and records kept at a residential home where the patient is required to reside or at a training centre he is required to attend. Where a patient is receiving psychiatric treatment, that is more likely to involve his attending a clinic run by a community mental health team than a hospital.[41] Moreover, if he has a private guardian, his nominated medical attendant may well be a general practitioner rather than a hospital-based consultant.

Restricted patients who are detained

According to Schedule 1 to the Act, section 76 applies without qualification to restricted patients. As drafted, the phrase "*any* records *relating to* the patient's detention or treatment in any hospital" is wide enough to cover records in the possession of the Secretary of State which relate to the patient's detention or treatment in any hospital. For example, periodic reports submitted under section 41(6), documentation concerning the imposition of the order or direction, and arguably written advice concerning a patient's continued detention or treatment tendered by the Aarvold Board (**165**).[42]

Conditionally discharged patients

A conditionally discharged patient remains liable to be detained in a hospital under the hospital order or transfer direction by virtue of which he was originally admitted. However, the records disclosable under section 76 are those which relate to his "detention or treatment in any hospital" rather than his liability to detention in

---

[41] It should be noted that the statutory definition of a "hospital" in the Act includes clinics, dispensaries and out-patient departments maintained in connection with an institution for the reception and treatment of persons suffering from mental disorder: see Mental Health Act 1983, s.145(1); National Health Service Act 1977, s.128(1).

[42] Section 76 empowers the authorised doctor to require the production and inspection of "any records relating to the patient's detention or treatment in any hospital." This power did not exist under the 1959 Act when the High Court reached its decision in *R. v. Secretary of State for the Home Department, ex p. Powell* concerning the confidentiality of reports prepared by the Board (**167**).

hospital. In some cases, the production of records compiled by a social supervisor may not, on a strict interpretation, be duly "required."

Disclosure of information

In deciding what information gathered in the course of his interview, examination and inspection should be disclosed to a prospective applicant in support of any advice tendered, the medical practitioner will owe that person and, in certain cases, third parties a duty of care. In exceptional circumstances, it may be lawful for a medical practitioner to disclose information arising from his interview with a patient to some other person or body against his client's wishes.[43] No action will lie against a medical practitioner if he acts in good faith and with reasonable care.[44]

OTHER RELEVANT ENACTMENTS

Section 24 provides that a nearest relative who is considering whether to exercise his power to make an order for discharge has a similar right to obtain an independent medical report on the patient. The powers of a medical practitioner under section 24(2) are identical to those conferred by section 76.

FORM AND CONTENTS OF THE APPLICATION

There is no prescribed form. A letter therefore suffices provided it is clear that an application is being made and it includes wherever possible the information specified in the rules. However, tribunals have drafted forms which may be used to make an application and they are generally available from tribunal offices, hospitals and social services authorities.

ASSESSMENT APPLICATIONS (SECTION 2 CASES)

An assessment application must be in writing and signed by the patient or any person authorised by him to do so on his behalf.[45] The application must indicate that it is made by or on behalf of a patient detained for assessment,[46] the reason being so that the tribunal is aware of the need to hear the case within seven days of its receipt. Wherever possible, an assessment application shall include the following information[47]—

- the name of the patient;

- the address of the hospital or mental nursing home where the patient is detained;

- the name and address of the patient's nearest relative and his relationship to the patient;

---

[43] See *W. v. Egdell and others* [1990] Ch 359, [1990] 2 W.L.R. 471 (**711**).
[44] Mental Health Act 1983, s.139.
[45] Mental Health Act 1983, s.77(3); Mental Health Review Tribunal Rules 1983, r.30(1).
[46] Mental Health Review Tribunal Rules 1983, r.30(2).
[47] *Ibid.*

- the name and address of any representative authorised by the patient in accordance with rule 10 **(877)** or, if none has yet been authorised, whether the patient intends to authorise a representative or wishes to conduct his own case.

Applications not including the specified information

If any of the above information is not included in the assessment application, the rules provide that, where requested by a tribunal, it shall in so far as is practicable be provided by the responsible authority.[48]

ALL OTHER APPLICATIONS

The application must be in writing[49] and signed by the applicant or any person authorised by him to do so on his behalf.[50] It shall wherever possible include the information specified in rule 3(2)—

- the name of the patient;

- the patient's address, which shall include —

  i. the address of the hospital or mental nursing home where the patient is detained; or

  ii. the name and address of the patient's private guardian; or

  iii. in the case of a conditionally discharged patient or a patient to whom leave of absence from hospital has been granted, the address of the hospital or mental nursing home where the patient was last detained or is liable to be detained; together with the patient's current address;

- where the application is made by the patient's nearest relative, the name and address of the applicant and his relationship to the patient;

- the section of the Act under which the patient is detained or is liable to be detained;

- the name and address of any representative authorised in accordance with rule 10 or, if none has yet been authorised, whether the applicant intends to authorise a representative or wishes to conduct his own case.

Applications relating to after-care under supervision

In the case of a patient who is, or who is to be, subject to after-care under supervision, the application shall also contain the following information in addition to that just specified[51]—

---

[48] Mental Health Review Tribunal Rules 1983, r.30(3).
[49] Mental Health Act 1983, s.77(3); Mental Health Review Tribunal Rules 1983, r.3(1).
[50] Mental Health Review Tribunal Rules 1983, r.3(1).
[51] Mental Health Review Tribunal Rules 1983, r.3(2)(e), as inserted by Mental Health Review Tribunal (Amendment) Rules 1996, r.3.

- the names of the persons who are (or who are to be) the patient's supervisor and community responsible medical officer;

- the name and address of any place at which the patient is (or will be) receiving medical treatment;

- where the patient is subject to after-care under supervision, his current address;

- where the patient is not yet subject to after-care under supervision, the address of the hospital where he is, or was last, detained or is liable to be detained.

Applications not including the specified information

As in the case of assessment applications, if any of the information specified above is not included in the application, it shall in so far as is practicable be provided by the responsible authority or, in the case of a restricted patient, the Secretary of State, at the request of the tribunal.[52]

SUBMITTING THE APPLICATION

The Act provides that the application shall be addressed to the tribunal for the area in which the hospital where the patient is detained is situated.[53] Where the application relates to a conditionally discharged patient, or a patient who is subject to guardianship or after-care under supervision, it shall be made to the tribunal for the area in which the patient resides.[54] Only the tribunal to which the application is required to be addressed has jurisdiction to deal with it.[55]

Patients granted leave of absence

Where the application involves a patient who has leave to be absent from hospital, rule 2(1) provides that the tribunal with jurisdiction is that for the area in which the hospital where the patient is liable to be detained is situated. A patient may, of course, be granted leave to reside at a hospital other than that where he is liable to be detained. The power is often used to enable a special hospital patient to spend a period of trial leave at a regional secure unit with a view to his formal transfer there. Where a patient is residing in a hospital under leave of absence, he is not liable to be detained there. Rather, until such time as he is transferred, he remains liable to be detained at the hospital from which he has leave to be absent. Similarly, his responsible medical officer remains unchanged and it is the managers of that hospital who have authority to detain him and who are therefore the responsible authority for the purpose of the tribunal proceedings. According to section 77(3) and rule 2, applications in such cases should be made to the hospital from which the patient is on leave since that is the hospital where he is liable to be detained — he is neither detained, nor liable to be detained, at the hospital where he is residing.[56]

---

52 Mental Health Review Tribunal Rules 1983, r.3(3).
53 Mental Health Act 1983, s.77(3)–(4), as amended by Mental Health (Patients in the Community) Act 1995, s.1(2) and Sched. 1 para. 12; Mental Health Review Tribunal Rules 1983, r.2(1).
54 Mental Health Act 1983, s.77(3); Mental Health Review Tribunal Rules 1983, r.2(1).
55 Mental Health Act 1983, s.66(1); Mental Health Review Tribunal Rules 1983, r.2(1).
56 See the Memoranda on the 1959 and 1983 Acts. *Mental Health Act 1983: Memorandum on Parts I to VI, VIII and X*, (D.H.S.S., 1987), para. 83; *Mental Health Act 1959: Memorandum on Parts I, IV to VII and IX*, (D.H.S.S., 1960), para. 100.

Applications by patients not yet subject to after-care under supervision

Where the patient is not yet subject to after-care under supervision, the Act provides that the application shall be made to the tribunal for the area in which he is to reside on becoming so subject after leaving hospital.[57] It is that tribunal which has jurisdiction to deal with the case.[58] If the patient will be residing some distance away from the hospital where he is liable to be detained, this necessarily creates some problems. For example, if he is in a private hospital in the Midlands and will be returning home to Devon when he leaves hospital, the hearing will either have to be held in the Midlands (with the South & West Tribunal members travelling there) or the patient, the responsible medical officer, and the like, will need to travel to Devon for the hearing.

Regional offices

Although there exists a tribunal for each health service region, several tribunals share the same office. Applications should therefore be forwarded to the following administrative offices and addressed to the clerk for the particular regional tribunal.[59] Applications concerning patients detained at Ashworth Hospital are dealt with by the Liverpool office; those concerning Rampton Hospital patients by the Nottingham office, and those concerning Broadmoor patients by the Hinchley Wood (London South) office.

THE MENTAL HEALTH REVIEW TRIBUNALS

• South Thames • South & West	London South Office, Hinchley Wood, Block 3, Crown Offices, Kingston-By-Pass Road, Surbiton, Surrey KT6 5QN. Tel.: 0181 398 4166. Fax 0181 339 0709.
• North Thames • Anglia & Oxford	London North Office, Canons Park, Government Buildings, Honeypot Lane, Stanmore, Middlesex HA7 1AY. Tel: 0171 972 2000. Fax 0171 972 3731.
• Trent • Northern & Yorkshire	Nottingham Office, Spur A, Block 5, Government Buildings, Chalfont Drive, Western Boulevard, Nottingham NG8 3RZ. Tel: 0115 9294222. Fax 0115 9428308.
• North West • West Midlands	Liverpool Office, Cressington House (3rd Floor), 249 St Mary's Road, Garston, Liverpool, Lancs L19 0NF. Tel: 0151 494 0095. Fax 0151 270133.
• Wales	MHRT for Wales, 1st Floor, Crown Buildings, Cathays Park, Cardiff CF1 3NQ. Tel: 01222 825111. Fax 01222 823117.

---

[57]   Mental Health Act 1983, s.77(3), as amended by the Mental Health (Patients in the Community) Act 1995, s.1(2) and Sched. 1 para. 12.

[58]   Mental Health Review Tribunal Rules 1983, r.2(1).

[59]   As to the areas covered by each regional tribunal, see p.192. It is not safe to make assumptions. For example, South Yorkshire is in the Trent region rather than the Northern & Yorkshire Region.

Some of the provisions which deal with patients' periodic rights of application are ambiguous, obtuse or have somewhat anomalous consequences. In order to avoid confusion, their consideration was postponed until this stage. They are now considered here.

PATIENTS DETAINED UNDER SECTION 4

Section 66(1)(a) provides that "a patient who is admitted to hospital in pursuance of an application for admission for assessment" may apply to a tribunal during "the relevant period," which section 66(2)(a) defines as "14 days beginning with the day on which the patient is admitted as so mentioned." Opinion varies as to whether a patient who is detained for assessment using the emergency procedure in section 4 may apply under section 66(1)(a). Jones, Gostin and Fennell take the view that they may not, Hoggett that they may.

The case against a right of application

Section 2(1) provides that applications for assessment made under that section are "in this Act referred to as 'an application for admission for assessment'," while section 4(1) states that an admission for assessment made under that section "is in this Act referred to as 'an emergency application.'" Those definitions extend to Part V of the Act.[60] The alternative, generic, expression "an application for admission to hospital" is used where, as in section 13, a particular provision is intended to apply to all applications under sections 2, 3 and 4. Consequently, section 66(1)(a) only confers a right of access to a tribunal following admission under section 2. That this is so is clear from reading the mandatory discharge criteria in section 72(1)(a) which state that "a tribunal shall direct the discharge of a patient liable to be detained under section 2 above ..." This reference to section 2 is then repeated twice in the section. Such an interpretation is consistent with a statutory framework which provides that section 2 and section 4 applications have different legal consequences. In particular, section 56 provides that a section 4 patient shall not be given treatment without his consent: it is in this way that Parliament decided to protect such patients, and other patients detained for 72 hours or less, rather than by giving them a right of application to a tribunal.

The case for a right of application

Section 4 provides that, in cases of urgent necessity, "an application for admission for assessment may be made in accordance with the following provisions of this section." A patient who is admitted under section 4 is therefore "admitted to hospital in pursuance of an application for admission for assessment" and, accordingly, is entitled to apply to a tribunal under section 66(1)(a). Section 145(1) provides that the term "an application for admission for assessment" is not to be interpreted according to the meaning given in section 2(1) if "the context otherwise requires." Case law demonstrates that a word or phrase used in the context of Part V may require a different meaning.[61] The references to section 2 in section 72 simply acknowledge the fact that if the patient is still detained when the tribunal hearing

---

[60] Mental Health Act 1983, s.145(1).

[61] See *R. v. Merseyside Mental Health Review Tribunal, ex. p. K.* [1990] 1 All E.R. 694 at 699, *per* Butler-Sloss L.J.

takes place the second medical recommendation will by then have been furnished. Section 66(2)(a) makes it clear that the 14 day period for making a tribunal application under section 66(1)(a) commences, like the 28 day detention period, from the date of admission for assessment. Where the emergency procedure is used, a patient's date of admission for assessment is the date of his admission under section 4. Therefore he may apply to a tribunal on that day. The alternative view has the effect that section 4 patients lose up to three days during which to make a tribunal application and leads to an unnecessarily complicated position: if the second recommendation is received on the day following admission, a patient may apply between the second and fourteenth days following admission and so forth. The right of application, and the speed with which the detention is reviewed, becomes dependant upon the speed with which the second recommendation is furnished. As a matter of policy, a person should not be prejudiced because their admission for assessment is founded upon one rather than two medical recommendations unless the Act makes it clear that this was Parliament's intention.

Summary

It may be noted that essentially the same problem arises in terms of the construction of section 23, which empowers various persons or bodies other than tribunals to discharge a patient (**284**). On a strict reading of this section, a section 4 patient may not be discharged under section 23. This is because it only provides for making an order for discharge in respect of a patient who is liable to be detained in pursuance of "an application for admission for assessment." Likewise, section 23 does not apply to other civil patients detained for 72 hours or less under sections 5(2), 135 and 136. The purpose of these short-term powers is to authorise a person's detention for a period of time sufficient to enable the application procedures to be undertaken or completed. In the case of detention under section 4, the patient may not be compulsorily treated until such time (if ever) as a second recommendation is furnished. Its purpose is to allow the application process to be completed within a hospital setting where its completion outside hospital would involve unacceptable risks. Only if a second recommendation is furnished is the patient in exactly the same position as a person admitted under section 2. If no second recommendation is furnished within 72 hours, the patient ceases to be liable to be detained at the expiration of that period. Otherwise he may be detained for up to 28 days and, being then in the same position as any other section 2 patient, may apply to a tribunal. Although the matter is finely balanced, it is submitted that the Act differentiates patients detained for more than 72 hours from those detained for lesser periods in the context of tribunal rights, discharge, and liability to compulsory treatment—

• *Detention for 72 hours or less under sections 4, 5, 135 and 136*	Patient not liable to compulsory treatment under Part IV and he has no right of application to a tribunal. No formal statutory mechanisms for discharging the patient's liability to detention.
• *Detention for up to 28 days or more, under sections 2, 3 and 37*	Patient liable to compulsory treatment under Part IV but he has a right to apply to a tribunal. Various formal statutory mechanisms for discharging the patient's liability to detention.

"INTERIM RESTRICTION ORDERS" UNDER SECTION 44(3)

Where a magistrates court commits an offender to hospital pending sentence by the Crown Court, he is deemed to be subject to a hospital order together with a restriction order until such time as his case is disposed of.[62] In practice, even if such a patient has a right of application to apply to a tribunal, his case is likely to be disposed of before he has been subject to the restrictions for a period of six months. However, it might be argued that if a restriction order is subsequently made by the Crown Court, the six month waiting period is to be treated as having commenced on the date of the magistrates court's order rather than on the day when his case is disposed of. Throughout this whole period the patient has been subject to a restriction order. Similarly, if he does not then apply to a tribunal, the date on which his case must eventually be referred to a tribunal is to be calculated by reference to the former date. It is submitted that this view is incorrect. The six months referred to in section 70 relates to the "relevant hospital order," *i.e.* that imposed by the Crown Court.[63] Furthermore, the definition of a restricted patient in section 79 appears to exclude persons *treated as* subject to a restriction order by virtue of section 44.

UNCONVICTED HOSPITAL ORDER PATIENTS

Where an unconvicted person is admitted for treatment under a hospital order imposed under section 5(1) of the Criminal Procedure (Insanity) Act 1964, he may apply to a tribunal during the six month period beginning with the date of the order. This is so whether or not a restriction order was also made. However, where a patient's case is disposed of without trial under the 1983 Act, by way of a hospital order made pursuant to section 37(3) or 51(5), no such right arises. Although unconvicted, the patient must still wait for six months before he is entitled to apply to a tribunal.

CONDITIONALLY DISCHARGED PATIENTS AND PART II

The Home Office for many years argued that a conditionally discharged restricted patient who was readmitted to hospital under section 2 or 3, rather than by way of recall under section 42(3), was not entitled to apply to a tribunal for his discharge. The Court of Appeal has now determined that this is not the case.[64] The effect of recent case law is that a conditionally discharged patient may be readmitted under Part II; that the Home Secretary is not obliged to recall that patient upon being notified that he is receiving in-patient treatment; that a conditionally discharged patient detained under Part II has the same rights of application as other patients detained under the same provision (**365**).

PATIENTS TRANSFERRED TO HOSPITAL UNDER SECTION 19

Section 66(1)(e) provides that a patient who is transferred from guardianship to hospital may apply to a tribunal during the six month period beginning with the day of his transfer. One consequence of this is that his rights of application do not initially correspond to the renewal periods under Part II. This is because his detention is deemed to have commenced on the date of his original reception into guardianship

---

[62] Mental Health Act 1983, s.44(3).
[63] *Ibid.*, s.79(2). Note the significance of the word "is" in the subsection.
[64] *R. v. Managers of the North West London Mental Health NHS Trust, ex p. Stewart* (CO/1825/95), 25 July 1997, C.A.

but his initial general right to apply to a tribunal following transfer is calculated by reference to the transfer date. Similarly, the managers' duty to refer his case if no application is made under section 66(1)(e) arises six months after the date of his transfer. This has the consequence that the patient's detention may be renewed, and a further right of application come into being, before the time for exercising the right conferred by the transfer has expired. Furthermore, on a strict reading of section 68(1), if the right to apply following a renewal is exercised within six months of the transfer, but not the right of application under section 66(1)(e), the managers must still refer his case to a tribunal at the expiration of that period.

Example

A patient is received into guardianship under section 7 on 1 January. On 1 March, he is transferred to hospital under section 19. This takes effect as if he had been admitted to hospital under section 3 on 1 January. The patient's detention is later renewed for six months with effect from 1 July. His rights of application are as follows—

a. He has a right of application under section 66(1)(e) during the six months following his transfer, *i.e.* during the period between 1 March and 31 August.

b. Following the section's renewal for what is deemed to be a second period of detention, he also acquires a right of application under section 66(1)(f), *i.e.* between 1 July and 31 December.

Accordingly, during the period 1 July to 31 August, the patient has two concurrent rights of application. On a strict reading of the Act, the managers must refer his case to a tribunal if he does not exercise his right to apply under section 66(1)(e) by 1 September, whether or not he has made a previous application under section 66(1)(f).[65]

TRANSFERS INTO GUARDIANSHIP UNDER SECTION 19

A transfer in the opposite direction — from hospital into guardianship — similarly takes effect as if the original application, order or direction which authorised the patient's admission to hospital were a guardianship application or order.[66] However, it is noticeable that, although section 66(1)(e) specifically provides that a patient who is transferred from guardianship to hospital may apply to a tribunal during the

---

[65] Section 68(1) requires the managers to refer a patient's case unless by that date an application has been made under paragraphs 66(1)(e), (d), (g) or (h). Applications under section 66(1)(f) are not counted, probably because the draftsman missed the point. Because a patient transferred under section 19 is deemed to have been admitted to hospital under section 3 on the date of his original reception into guardianship, it might be contended that the patient in the above example is also entitled to make an application under section 66(1)(b) prior to 1 July. However, the wording of section 68(1) indicates that the rights of application under paragraphs 66(1)(b) and 66(1)(e) are mutually exclusive and the proposition is untenable.

[66] A first reading of section 19(2)(b) might suggest that the patient is deemed to have been received into guardianship on the date of his transfer rather than the date on which the original application was made. This is because paragraphs 19(2)(a), (c) and (d) all conclude by referring to the time when the application was originally accepted whereas paragraph (b) provides instead that the provisions of Part II apply to the patient "as if the application were a guardianship application duly accepted at the said time." However, consideration of section 41(2)(b) of the 1959 Act, and of Sched. 1, Pt. I, para. 5 to the 1983 Act, makes it clear that this is not so and any ambiguity is unintentional.

following six months, it does not confer such a right of application following transfer from hospital into guardianship.[67] The reason for the distinction can be discerned from the fact that, under both the 1959 and the 1983 Acts, the tribunal rights of a patient transferred from one hospital or guardian to another are also unaffected by any transfer.

Additional right to apply arises	*No additional right to apply arises*
▪ Transfer from guardianship to hospital	▪ Transfer from one guardian to another
	▪ Transfer from one hospital to another
	▪ Transfer from hospital into guardianship

The distinction reflects the fact that, whereas a transfer from hospital into guardianship involves few formalities and represents a relaxation of the pre-existing regime, with the patient ceasing to be liable to detention and compulsory treatment, the transfer to hospital procedures essentially duplicate those for making a fresh application under section 3, and have the same consequences. Accordingly, as regards the patient's tribunal rights of application, he is in this respect also placed in a position identical to that of a patient admitted afresh under section 3 — he may apply during his first six months of detention in hospital and his case must be referred to a tribunal after six months if no such application has by then been made. This appears to be the most sensible construction and the two anomalies which result from it are best viewed either as drafting omissions or as the natural secondary consequences of the draftsman's primary aim. The first anomaly has already been referred to. Where a patient is transferred from guardianship to hospital, a further right of application will arise upon any renewal of the authority for the patient's detention before the time for exercising the right of application which arose upon his transfer has expired. The second anomaly is that where a section 2 patient who has exercised his right of application under section 66(1)(a) is transferred into guardianship, he may not apply to a tribunal during what remains of the initial six-month period of guardianship. As to this, it seems likely that Parliament simply missed the point, just as it failed to address the fact that such a patient has no legal classification under the Act.

Summary

A patient who is transferred from one hospital or guardian to another may apply to a tribunal during what remains of the existing period of detention or guardianship if he has not already done so. Similarly, it would seem that a patient who is transferred from hospital to guardianship may apply to a tribunal if he has not already exercised his general right to apply once during that period, but not otherwise. If he did exercise that right, he will not be entitled to reapply until the second six-month period of guardianship has commenced, unless he is reclassified before then. For a further consideration of the point, see page 654.

---

[67] At first sight, the reason for the distinction may seem to be consequential upon the mandatory reference provisions in section 68(1), which refer back to section 66(1)(e). In other words, the purpose served by section 66(1)(e) is to avoid imposing any duty on the managers to immediately refer the case of a patient who had been under guardianship for more than six months but not had a tribunal. In fact, this cannot be the reason. The 1959 Act included no mandatory reference provisions yet it also provided for a patient applying to a tribunal within six months of being transferred if the transfer was from guardianship to hospital but not if it was in the opposite direction (Mental Health Act 1959, s.41(5)). Section 66(1)(e) of the 1983 Act merely repeats the pre-existing provision.

UNRESTRICTED PATIENTS ABSENT WITHOUT LEAVE

The Mental Health (Patients in the Community) Act 1995 rather unnecessarily introduced the following provisions into section 66—

> **66.**—(1) Where ... (fa) a report is furnished under subsection (2) of section 21B above in respect of a patient and subsection (5) of that section applies (or subsections (5) and (6)(b) of that section apply) in the case of the report ... an application may be made to a Mental Health Review Tribunal within the relevant period ... (i) by the patient.

> (2) In subsection (1) above "the relevant period" means ... (f) in the case mentioned in paragraph ... (fa) of that subsection, the period or periods for which authority for the patient's detention or guardianship is renewed by virtue of the report;

Statutory framework

The law concerning absence without leave and its effect on the individual's liability to detention or guardianship under the Act has already been considered (**289**). The table on the following page summarises the tribunal rights of patients who are returned after a period of absence.

Patients absent without leave for 28 days or less

Although section 21 has been redrafted, where a patient is absent without leave for 28 days or less the position set out in the 1983 Act as originally enacted has been retained—

- Unless the patient's return occurs during the final week of a period of detention or guardianship, or after such a period would ordinarily have expired had he not been absent, no legal consequences arise. The existing period of detention or guardianship simply continues in the normal way. If the patient had not exercised his right to apply to a tribunal before absenting himself, he may do so upon his return during whatever remains of that period.

- If the patient's return within 28 days occurs during the final week of a period of detention or guardianship, or after it would ordinarily have expired, a renewal report may be furnished after the period would ordinarily have expired.

- Where this happens, the effect of the report is to retrospectively renew the authority for a further period and the new period of detention or guardianship is deemed to have commenced on the day it would have began had the patient never been absent. The patient then has exactly the same right to apply to a tribunal as any other patient whose detention or guardianship has been renewed. Pursuant to section 66(1)(f), he may make one application during the new six or twelve month period of detention or guardianship.

Patient absent for 28 days or less and renewal reports furnished under s.20

No retrospective renewal of the authority for the patient's detention or guardianship not necessary.

- No consequences. If he has not already applied, patient may exercise his usual right to apply during whatever remains of the period of detention or guardianship in existence both when he left and returned.

Retrospective renewal of the authority for the patient's detention or guardianship necessary.

- The patient has the ordinary right to make one application to a tribunal during (whatever remains of) what is now the current period of detention or guardianship.

Patients absent for more than 28 days and reports furnished under s.21B

Report furnished prior to the final two months of the period of detention or guardianship which was in force when the patient absented himself.

- No consequences unless patient also reclassified. If he has not already applied, patient may exercise his usual right to apply during whatever remains of the period of detention or guardianship in existence both when he left and returned.

- If the report has the secondary effect of reclassifying the patient, a right to apply does arise by virtue of this fact (**630**).

Report furnished during the final two months of the period of detention or guardianship which was in force when the patient absented himself.

- If the report provides that it shall also have effect as a renewal report furnished under s.20, patient has the ordinary right to make one application to a tribunal once the new period of detention or guardianship has commenced.

- If the report does not provide that it shall also have effect as a renewal report furnished under s.20 but has the effect of reclassifying the patient, a right to apply arises by virtue of this fact (**631**).

Report furnished after the period of detention or guardianship which was in force when the patient absented himself would ordinarily have expired

- The patient has the ordinary right to make one application to a tribunal during (whatever remains of) the period of detention or guardianship which, following the report, is now the current period of detention or guardianship.

- If the report also has the effect of renewing the authority for the patient's detention or guardianship for a further year upon the expiration of what is now the current period of detention or guardianship, once that further period has commenced the patient has the ordinary tribunal rights of application of any renewed patient.

629

Patients absent without leave for more than 28 days

The new provisions introduced by the 1995 Act concern patients who are taken into custody or who return to the required place after having been absent without leave for more than 28 days. The authority for the patient's detention or guardianship will lapse after one week unless his appropriate medical officer has furnished a report stating that it appears to him that the patient satisfies the "relevant conditions."

The effect of a report furnished under section 21B

The precise effect of such a report in terms of the patient's continued liability to detention or guardianship depends upon exactly when it is furnished in relation to the period of detention or guardianship which was in force when he absented himself. Put like this, there are three possibilities. The report might be furnished—

- prior to the final two months of that period (before any renewal report was due);

- during the final two months of that period (at a time when a renewal report can legally be furnished); or

- after that period of detention or guardianship would ordinarily have expired (after the time when a renewal report would ordinarily need to be furnished).

The effect of a report in terms of the patient's tribunal rights

A patient's tribunal rights similarly depend upon within which of these three periods the report is furnished. The effect in each case is as follows—

- Where the report is furnished on a date before the final two months of the period of detention or guardianship which was in force when the patient absented himself, that period of detention or guardianship simply continues as if the patient had never been absent. He may apply to a tribunal during what remains of the existing period of detention or guardianship if he had not already exercised that right before absenting himself. No additional right to apply to a tribunal arises simply because a report has been furnished authorising his continued detention or guardianship. However, if the form of mental disorder specified in the report is different from that previously specified, the report has the secondary effect of reclassifying the patient. In this case a right to apply does arise, but it arises by virtue of the fact that the patient's condition has been reclassified otherwise than during the course of renewal.[68]

- Where the report is furnished during the final two months of a period of detention or guardianship, it *may* also provide that it shall take effect as the renewal report which is now due. If so, the effect is the same as with any other renewal report. Under section 66(1)(f), the patient may make one application during the new six or twelve month period of detention or

---

[68]   The right to apply following such a reclassification is conferred by section 66(1)(fb).

guardianship. Furthermore, as with all other renewals, even if the report has the secondary effect of reclassifying the patient no additional right to apply to a tribunal arises by virtue of this fact: he is already entitled to apply once the new period authorised by the report has begun. However, if the report does not also provide that it shall also take effect as the renewal report now due, but has the secondary effect of reclassifying the patient, an additional right to apply to a tribunal does arise. However, as before, it arises by virtue of the fact that the patient's condition has been reclassified otherwise than during the course of renewal.[69]

- Where the report is furnished after the date on which the period of detention or guardianship in existence when the patient absented himself would ordinarily have expired, it automatically has the effect of retrospectively renewing the authority for the patient's detention or guardianship. It is this retrospective renewal which gives rise to the new right of application referred to in section 66(1)(fa). That right is exercisable during whatever remains of what is, following the report, now the current period of detention or guardianship. Because the report automatically has the effect of renewing the authority for the patient's detention or guardianship, and so gives rise to a right to apply to a tribunal by virtue of that fact, no additional right to apply arises if it also has the secondary effect of reclassifying the patient.

- It has just been noted that if a report is furnished after the date on which the statutory period in existence when the patient absented himself would ordinarily have expired, the authority for the patient's detention or guardianship is thereby retrospectively renewed for a further period of six or twelve months. However, it is possible that there will already be less than two months left of that new period of detention or guardianship or that period may itself have already expired. The Act allows for this by providing that the single report may renew the patient's detention or guardianship for two further periods if necessary. This is why section 66(2)(f) provides that the right to apply to a tribunal under section 66(1)(fa), following retrospective renewal, is exercisable during the "period or periods" for which authority for the patient's detention or guardianship is renewed by virtue of the report.

Summary

The above provisions may seem unnecessarily complicated to some people and this is indeed the case. It is simply bad drafting. The same effect could have been achieved by providing that, if the authority for a patient's detention or guardianship is retrospectively renewed for a further period or periods, he may make one application to a tribunal under section 66(1)(f) during what is then his current period of detention or guardianship. Secondly, if the effect of a report is not to renew his detention or guardianship but to reclassify him, he may apply to a tribunal during the following 28 days under section 66(1)(d). This is certainly the easiest way to remember the logic of these verbose provisions.

---

[69] The right to apply following such a reclassification is conferred by s.66(1)(fb).

REFERENCES

In certain circumstances, the Act imposes a duty on the managers of a hospital or the Secretary of State to refer a patient's case to a tribunal ("mandatory references") or allows the Secretary of State to refer a case at his discretion ("discretionary references"). Where a reference is made, the tribunal is required to deal with it as if the patient had in fact made an application, subject to certain modifications of the rules relating to pre-hearing matters.[70]

THE REFERENCE PROVISIONS

Unrestricted patients

- Mandatory references in respect of patients who are liable to be detained in a hospital   Section 68

- Discretionary references in respect of such patients and other unrestricted patients (those subject to guardianship or after-care under supervision)   Section 67

Restricted patients

- Mandatory references in respect of patients who are liable to be detained in a hospital   Sections 71, 75

- Discretionary references in respect of such patients and other restricted patients (those who have been conditionally discharged)   Section 71

AUTHORISED AND UNAUTHORISED REFERENCES

Section 77(1) provides that no application shall be made to a tribunal except in such cases and at such times as are expressly provided by the Act. Although it is therefore silent as to references, the wording of section 65 and the 1983 Rules[71] makes it clear that tribunals may only deal with references made in accordance with the statutory provisions, that is authorised references. A tribunal therefore has no discretion to consider a reference made by hospital managers in respect of a patient whose case falls outside the terms of section 68 nor, for example, a reference by a local social services authority in respect of a patient subject to guardianship.

MANDATORY REFERENCES

In the circumstances prescribed by Part V, the case of a patient who is liable to be detained in hospital for treatment must be referred for review to a Mental Health Review Tribunal.

---

[70]   See Mental Health Review Tribunal Rules 1983, r.29. The rules relating to adjournments (r.16), the hearing procedure (rr.21–22), the recording and communication of the tribunal's decision (rr. 23–24), and the legal effect of any failure to comply with the rules apply equally to applications and references. Rules 3,4,9 and 19 do not apply and rules 5,6,7 apply as modified by rule 29(c).

[71]   Rule 2 defines a reference as meaning a reference which is made under sections 67, 68, 71 or 75.

Patients detained under Part II

Where the conditions specified in section 68 exist, the managers of a hospital are required to refer to a tribunal the case of a patient who is liable to be detained for treatment there under Part II.

MANDATORY REFERENCES UNDER SECTION 68

Duty of managers of hospitals to refer cases to tribunal

68.—(1) Where a patient who is admitted to a hospital in pursuance of an application for admission for treatment or a patient who is transferred from guardianship to hospital does not exercise his right to apply to a Mental Health Review Tribunal under section 66(1) above by virtue of his case falling within paragraph (b) or, as the case may be, paragraph (e) of that section, the managers of the hospital shall at the expiration of the period for making such an application refer the patient's case to such a tribunal unless an application or reference in respect of the patient has then been made under section 66(1) above by virtue of his case falling within paragraph (d), (g) or (h) of that section or under section 67(1) above.

(2) If the authority for the detention of a patient in a hospital is renewed under section 20 or 21B above and a period of three years (or, if the patient has not attained the age of sixteen years, one year) has elapsed since his case was last considered by a Mental Health Review Tribunal, whether on his own application or otherwise, the managers of the hospital shall refer his case to such a tribunal.

Upon the commencement of a second period of detention (s.68(1))

Section 68(1) applies to patients who are admitted to hospital under section 3 or transferred from guardianship to hospital under section 19. It provides that if such a patient has not exercised his general right to apply to a tribunal within the following six months, the managers shall refer his case to a tribunal at the expiration of that period, unless an application or reference was made in respect of him by some other person during that period.[72] Applications or references previously made but subsequently withdrawn are to be discounted.[73] If the managers did not refer a patient's case because an application or reference was pending at the commencement of the second six month period of detention, but it is subsequently withdrawn, they must refer the patient's case to a tribunal as soon as possible after its withdrawal.[74]

---

[72] However, section 68(1) is imprecisely drafted. Unless some other person has applied, the duty to refer the patient's case arises if he has not applied during the first six months "by virtue of his case falling within" section 66(1)(b) or (e). However, it is possible for a patient to apply during that period under various other provisions. He may apply under s.66(1)(f) if he has been transferred from hospital to guardianship; and under section 66(1)(fb) if he has been reclassified on returning to hospital after more than 28 days absence without leave. As drafted, the exercise of either of these rights has no bearing on the matter. Consequently, the managers must refer the patient's case after six months unless one takes the pragmatic view that *any* application made during the first six months releases the managers from the obligation.

[73] Mental Health Act 1983, s.68(5).

[74] *Ibid.*

Subsequent references (s.68(2))

Subsection (2) provides that where the authority for the detention of a patient is "renewed" under section 20 or 21B and a period of three years (or if the patient has not attained the age of sixteen years, one year[75]) has elapsed since his case was last considered by a tribunal, whether on his own application or otherwise, the managers of the hospital shall refer his case to a tribunal.[76]

"Renewed"

The authority for a patient's detention is renewed on the day his responsible medical officer furnishes a report to the managers stating that the statutory conditions for renewal are satisfied.[77] Such a report may be furnished on any day during the final two months of the period of detention which is then drawing to a close. The wording in subsection (2) is therefore materially different to that in subsection (1). The managers' duty to refer a patient's case under subsection (1) arises on the day the second six-month period of detention commences, not on the day the responsible medical officer furnishes his report authorising that further period of detention. Conversely, when calculating the three year period under subsection (2), the material date is that on which the renewal report was furnished.[78]

Example

A patient has been detained under section 3 since 1 January 1990. His case was last considered by a tribunal on 15 November 1990. The position on 1 November 1993 is that the authority for his detention will expire on 31 December unless his responsible medical officer furnishes a report under section 20(3) during the following two months. If he furnishes the report on 3 November, three years will not have elapsed since a tribunal had last considered the patient's case and no reference will be due for another year or thereabouts. If, however, he furnishes his report on or after 15 November 1993, the managers are required to refer the patient's case to a tribunal at that time.

Renewals under section 21B

Section 21B applies to unrestricted patients who, being liable to detention for treatment or subject to guardianship, are returned after having been absent without leave for more than 28 days. If the patient's appropriate medical officer then furnishes a report under section 21B, its effect may be to renew the authority for the patient's detention or guardianship for a further period or periods. If the report has

---

[75]   The material factor is the minor's age on the day the authority is renewed and the authority is (literally) renewed on the day the renewal report is furnished.

[76]   Mental Health Act 1983, s.68(2), as amended by s.2(7) of the Mental Health (Patients in the Community) Act 1995.

[77]   Mental Health Act 1983, subss. 20(3) and (8).

[78]   As to retrospective renewals, the renewal is deemed to take effect on the last day of the previous period of detention or guardianship (see sections 21A and 21B). In such cases, that is therefore the relevant date, not the date on which the report is actually furnished. Although the view expressed in the text equates to what section 68 says, the above example illustrates that the position is unsatisfactory. There is therefore room to argue that a patient's detention for these purposes is not renewed until he has actually commenced the renewed period of detention. On this basis, the managers who receive a report renewing the detention or guardianship should wait to see if the patient applies during what remains of the existing period and refer the patient's case if no application has been made by the time it expires.

this effect, and the patient's case was last considered by a tribunal three or more years ago, the managers must refer the patient's case to a tribunal under section 68(2).[79]

"Since his case was last considered by" a tribunal

Where the previous tribunal made a recommendation under section 72(3) and later "further considered" his case because that recommendation was not implemented, it is not entirely clear when the patient's case was last considered for these purposes. If a tribunal reconvenes because its recommendation has not been complied with, and then further considers whether the patient must or should be discharged, it is strictly speaking considering his case at that second hearing. However, it may be argued that this is too literal an interpretation of the reference provisions, and the three-year period commences from the initial determination required under the Act.

Unrestricted patients detained under Part III

Section 68(1) does not apply to patients who are subject to a hospital order or a transfer direction, other than patients who are deemed to be subject to a hospital order following their transfer from guardianship under section 19.[80] The better view is that section 68(2) does apply.[81] The managers are required to refer to a tribunal the case of any hospital order patient whose detention is renewed "if three years (or, in the case of a patient aged under 16, one year) have elapsed since his case was last considered by a tribunal." The final phrase is unfortunate in Part III cases because the patient's case may never have been considered by a tribunal: there may be no last occasion. The words, "and his case has not been considered by a tribunal during the previous three years," are presumably to be substituted for the offending phrase in subsection (2).[82]

---

[79] In the case of retrospective renewals, the relevant date (when determining whether a tribunal has considered the patient's case during the past three years) appears to be the last day of the previous period of detention or guardianship, not the date on which the report is actually furnished. See s.21B(6).

[80] See Mental Health Act 1983, ss.19(2), 40(4), 66(1)(e), 68(1), Sched. 1, Pt. I, paras. 2, 5, 9.

[81] The drafting is again imprecise. In the first place, sections 66–68 are expressed to be concerned with "applications and references concerning Part II patients" and sections 69–71 with "applications and references concerning Part III patients." Section 145(3) then provides that any reference in the Act to an enactment in sections 66 and 67, shall be construed as a reference to that enactment as it applies by virtue of sections 40(4) and 55(4), and some of the provisions are extended to Part III patients.. Sections 40(4) and 55(4) provide that a patient who is detained under a hospital order or a transfer direction shall be treated for the purposes of the provisions mentioned in Part I of Schedule 1 to the Act as if he had been admitted for treatment under Part II, subject to any modifications specified. The schedule provides that section 66 (applications) shall apply to hospital order patients subject to various modifications and section 67 (discretionary references) without modification. Section 68(2) (mandatory references after three years) is not mentioned as applying to hospital order patients, either with or without modification. The answer is probably that any lack of clarity only arises because of the ambiguous cross-headings and recent cases suggest that English courts are not prepared to take account of them when construing a statute. When one reads section 68 without reference to them, the words used in subsection 68(1) are applicable to hospital order patients who have been transferred under section 19 and subsection 68(2) applies to any patient whose detention is renewed and who has not had a tribunal for the specified period. A reading of section 40(2) of the Mental Health (Amendment) Act 1982, and the provisions in section 71 concerning restricted patients, supports this view.

[82] If this is correct, the subsection in effect reads as follows: "(2) If the authority for the detention of a patient in a hospital is renewed under section 20 or 21B above *and his case has not been considered by a Mental Health Review Tribunal during the previous three years* (or, if the patient has not attained the age of sixteen years, one year), whether on his own application or otherwise, the managers of the hospital shall refer his case to such a tribunal."

Mandatory references and restricted patients

The Secretary of State is required to refer to a tribunal the case of any restricted patient detained in a hospital whose case has not been considered by a tribunal within the last three years.[83] Where a conditionally discharged patient is recalled to hospital, the Secretary of State is also required to refer his case to a tribunal within one month of the date of his return to hospital.

MANDATORY REFERENCES UNDER SECTION 71

References by Secretary of State concerning restricted patients

71.—(1) The Secretary of State may at any time refer the case of a restricted patient to a Mental Health Review Tribunal.

(2) The Secretary of State shall refer to a Mental Health Review Tribunal the case of any restricted patient detained in a hospital whose case has not been considered by such a tribunal, whether on his own application or otherwise, within the last three years.

(3) The Secretary of State may by order vary the length of the period mentioned in subsection (2) above.

(4) Any reference under subsection (1) above in respect of a patient who has been conditionally discharged and not recalled to hospital shall be made to the tribunal for the area in which the patient resides.

(5) Where a person who is treated as subject to a hospital order and a restriction order by virtue of an order under section 5(1) of the Criminal Procedure (Insanity) Act 1964 does not exercise his right to apply to a Mental Health Review Tribunal in the period of six months beginning with the date of that order, the Secretary of State shall at the expiration of that period refer his case to a tribunal.

Conditionally discharged patients

There is no corresponding duty to refer to a tribunal the case of a conditionally discharged patient. Since patients subject to guardianship or after-care under supervision are in the same position in this respect, the rationale would seem to be that the mandatory reference provisions are intended to protect patients who are liable to be detained and subject to compulsory treatment.

Patients found insane or unfit to plead

Section 71 makes special provision for patients who are treated as subject to a restriction order under by virtue of an order under section 5(1) of the Criminal Procedure (Insanity Act) 1964, following a finding of insanity or unfitness to plead. Where such a patient does not apply to a tribunal during the six month period

---

[83]   In contrast to the position set out in section 68(2), no special provision is made for children subject to restrictions and the usual three-year rule applies to them.

beginning with the date of the order, the Secretary of State is required to refer his case at the expiration of that period.[84] Where no such reference is made because at the expiry of that period an application is under consideration by a tribunal, but the patient later withdraws it, the Secretary of State must refer his case as soon as possible after that date.[85]

Patients subject to guardianship and after-care under supervision

The duty, under Section 68, to refer to a tribunal the case of a patient who has not applied for a tribunal for a certain period of time is one imposed only on hospital managers and therefore only relevant to patients who are liable to be detained. No corresponding duty is imposed on a guardian, responsible social services authority or Health Authority in respect of patients who are subject to guardianship or after-care under supervision. They are therefore not entitled to a mandatory reference if no application has been made for a certain period of time.

DISCRETIONARY REFERENCES

Section 67(1) provides that the Secretary of State may, if he thinks fit, at any time refer to a tribunal the case of an unrestricted patient, including a patient who is subject to guardianship or to after-care under supervision under Part II of the Act.[86] Section 71(1) contains a similar power in respect of restricted patients, including conditionally discharged patients. Tribunal proceedings under section 86 are commenced by way of a discretionary reference under sections 67 or 71.

FORM AND CONTENTS OF THE REFERENCE

Rule 29 of the 1983 Rules does not specify any particular form which a reference shall take nor specify any information which it shall wherever possible include.[87] The form which the reference takes is therefore a matter for the managers', or the Secretary of State's, discretion.

SUBMITTING THE REFERENCE

Although section 77 does not extend to references, rule 2(1) provides that the tribunal which has jurisdiction to deal with a reference is that which has jurisdiction in the area in which the patient is detained or liable to be detained. If the discretionary reference relates to a conditionally discharged patient, or a patient subject to guardianship or after-care under supervision, the tribunal with jurisdiction is that for the area in which the patient resides.[88]

---

[84] However, the Secretary of State is not required to refer the case of a patient who is admitted to hospital for treatment under s.5(1) but without any restriction order also being made.

[85] Mental Health Act 1983, s.71(6).

[86] Mental Health Act 1983, ss.67(1), 40(4) and 55(4), s.67(1), as amended by the Mental Health (Patients in the Community) Act 1995, s.1(2) and Sched. 1, para. 8. As drafted, there is, however, no power to refer the case of a patient who "is to be" subject to after-care under supervision on leaving hospital.

[87] Nor do the Act or rules expressly say that the reference must be made in writing unless this may be inferred from the use of the word "receipt" in rule 29(a).

[88] Mental Health Review Tribunal Rules 1983, r.2(1); Mental Health Act 1983, s.71(4).

PROCESSING THE APPLICATION OR REFERENCE

On receipt of an application or reference, the tribunal is required to give notice of it to the persons specified in the rules and, where an assessment application has been made, to arrange to hear it within the following seven days (**638**). If a prior application or reference is outstanding in respect of the same patient, the tribunal will decide whether to join the proceedings (**639**). It will also consider whether its consideration of an application may be postponed (**641**) and whether a representative should be appointed for the patient (**878**). If the patient moves to the area of another tribunal during the proceedings, his case may be transferred to that tribunal (**648**). In certain circumstances, an application of reference may be withdrawn (**649**) or deemed to be withdrawn (**650**).

NOTICE OF THE APPLICATION, etc.

The purpose of giving notice of the application or reference is to notify the persons responsible for preparing reports of the proceedings and, where relevant, to inform a patient that an application or reference has been made concerning him. In assessment cases, the notice of application also constitutes the notice of hearing.

Assessment applications

On receipt of an assessment application, a tribunal is required to fix a hearing date, being one within the following seven days, and to give notice of the date, time and place fixed for the hearing to the patient, the responsible authority, the nearest relative (where practicable),[89] and any other person who, in the opinion of the tribunal, should have the opportunity of being heard. The members appointed to deal with the case are appointed by the regional chairman. Upon receiving notice of the application, or a request from the tribunal, whichever may be the earlier, the responsible authority is required to furnish the tribunal with copies of the admission papers and the various reports required under the rules (**663**).[90]

Other applications

Following receipt of the application, the tribunal sends notice of the application to the patient, unless he made the application, the "responsible authority" and, if the patient is a restricted patient, to the Secretary of State.[91] The notice of application must be sent whether or not the tribunal exercises any power to postpone its consideration of the application (**641**).[92]

Notifying the nearest relative

An application by a patient is not required to specify the person who is his nearest relative and the rules do not require notice of the application's receipt to be sent to that person. However, the responsible authority must furnish this information and the nearest relative is given notice of the proceedings at a later stage, once the reports have been received. (**779**).[93]

---

[89] Mental Health Review Tribunal Rules 1983, r.31. An "assessment application" is one made under section 66(1)(a) by a patient who is detained for assessment. The rules are drafted on the basis that a nearest relative will not apply in respect of a patient who is detained for assessment.
[90] Mental Health Review Tribunal Rules 1983, r.32(1).
[91] *Ibid.*, r.4(1).
[92] *Ibid.*, r.4(2).
[93] *Ibid.*, r.7(d).

References

Where a reference is made by the Secretary of State, the tribunal is required to send notice of the reference to the responsible authority and to the patient. Where it is made by the managers of a hospital, the tribunal send notice of its receipt to the patient and a request to the managers for a copy of the authority's statement in respect of the patient (**664**).[94]

TWO OR MORE OUTSTANDING APPLICATIONS OR REFERENCES

When an application or reference is made, it may happen that there is already an application or reference outstanding in respect of the same patient. Where this is the case, the rules provide that a tribunal may consider more than one application or reference in respect of a patient at the same time, including in due course conducting a single hearing.[95] Furthermore, where a tribunal has previously postponed its consideration of an earlier application, it may direct that the latter be determined at the same time as the subsequent application or reference.[96] Where more than one applicant is involved in tribunal proceedings, each has the same rights under the rules as he would have if he were the only applicant.[97]

Nearest relative applications

The existence of concurrent applications or references usually results from applications having been made by both a patient and his nearest relative. Where this is the case, they will need to consider whether it would be preferable from their point of view for one of them to withdraw his application. This may then allow that right of application to be exercised at a later date in the event that the application which proceeds does not result in the patient's discharge. However, no purpose is served by withdrawing a right of application which will then lapse before there is an opportunity to exercise it, and consideration will also need to be given to the effect of the postponement provisions in rule 9 (**641**). Where the nearest relative's application is made under section 66(1)(g), following the issue of a barring report, that application should not be withdrawn since the discharge criteria to be applied will be more favourable to discharge than those which apply in respect of the patient's application (**491**).

References

A mandatory reference may not be withdrawn. From a prospective applicant's viewpoint, it will generally be a waste of a right of application to exercise it before the date on which any pre-existing mandatory reference is determined.

Assessment and guardianship applications

An application for assessment does not discharge any pre-existing guardianship application or order. Where a patient under guardianship makes a tribunal application and he is then admitted to hospital for assessment, he may make a further

---

[94] Mental Health Review Tribunal Rules 1983, r.29(b).
[95] *Ibid.*, rr.18(1) and 29.
[96] *Ibid.*, r.9(6).
[97] *Ibid.*, r.18(2).

application in respect of his detention. This subsequent application must be heard within seven days. Generally, it will be preferable to hear the two applications separately and to deal first with the question of the patient's liability to detention. Significant problems are likely to result from any attempt to deal with the two matters together. There will be two responsible authorities, two responsible medical officers (and possibly a nominated medical attendant also), two sets of reports, different discharge criteria and different rules applicable in respect of each application.

Patients in respect of whom a supervision application has been accepted

An unrestricted patient who is liable to be detained in hospital for treatment may generally apply to a tribunal once during each statutory period of detention. If a supervision application is then accepted in respect of him, he does not actually become subject to after-care under supervision until he has both ceased to be liable to be detained and left hospital in the conventional sense. However, upon the supervision application being accepted, he may apply to a tribunal for it to terminate the authority to supervise him upon leaving hospital. If the tribunal does not terminate the authority conferred by the supervision application, it will in any case lapse if he has not both ceased to be liable to be detained for treatment and left hospital within six months of its acceptance. During that six months, a tribunal may receive two applications from the same patient — one made under section 66(1)(b) or (f) concerning his liability to detention and one made under section 66(1)(ga) concerning the power to supervise him. These applications could be considered together or separately but, neither having yet been determined, it may not be possible to postpone the consideration of either. As to what will generally be the most suitable course of action the following points may be borne in mind. The area within which the patient is to reside on leaving hospital may be different from that where the hospital is located, in which case the two applications must be made to different tribunals (**621, 622**). Apart from being generally unsatisfactory, this means that the applications cannot be joined. The required content of the medical and social circumstances reports are identical in all material respects so that the same reports could suffice for the purposes of both applications. The factual information required under Parts A and E of Schedule 1 to the rules differ but these basic statements of the case history complement each other and would not *per se* necessitate hearing the applications separately. Details of the after-care services to be provided, and of any requirements imposed or to be imposed under section 25D, must also be furnished where tribunal proceedings relate to a supervision application. Again, this is not an onerous obligation and the former will generally consist of a copy of the already prepared after-care plan. In terms of preparing the cases for hearing, the very real problems associated with joining tribunal applications made by a patient subject both to detention under section 2 and guardianship may therefore often not apply. The first main determinant when deciding whether to join the applications is likely to be whether there would then be unacceptable delay in hearing the earlier of the applications. However, this must be balanced against the benefit of hearing the later application speedily upon the same reports. The second main factor is likely to be the fact that different statutory criteria will apply when determining the two applications. The evidence will need to be taken with this in mind, which might be confusing for the patient. Balancing this, the tribunal will be able to decide whether liability to detention is still appropriate in the context of the arrangements made for the patient's supervised discharge. If those arrangements seem to be sound and in place, this may be a very telling reason why continued liability to detention is no longer appropriate, or no longer necessary for the patient's health or safety or to protect others. If they will soon be in place, it might alternatively be a telling reason for discharging the patient's liability to detention on a defined future date. Having regard to the above, where the timescale permits the two applications to be heard together, there are perhaps two main arguments as to whether or not this is possible or desirable—

1. Firstly, it might be contended that the ambit of rule 18 is limited to enabling a joint hearing of two applications made by the same patient, or applications made by him and his nearest relative, in relation to the same authority. It is not intended to enable tribunals to simultaneously hear applications which concern different authorities, and so involve applying different statutory criteria, and making two decisions. Consequently, if the timescale permits, the ideal is for the same tribunal to hear both applications during the same day, one after the other. The applications may largely be determined on the basis of the same reports, and the duplication of evidence can be minimised in this way, but the parties to the proceedings will be different, as may the persons giving oral evidence. Most importantly, it ensures that the statutory issues are separately considered.

2. Secondly, there is no reason why the applications must be heard separately and, if heard together, applying the different statutory criteria does not cause any particular problems. Considering whether the patient is entitled to be (or should be) discharged from liability to detention, and then whether his after-care should be provided under statutory supervision, is straightforward. Indeed, separating the two issues by requiring them always to be addressed at separate hearings will often be artificial and the rules do not require that.

It is submitted that the first approach is preferable. While the second approach has certain advantages, experience suggests that hearing the issues together might well degenerate into chaos. Where the timescale permits, it would seem better to hear the supervision application case first. That way the tribunal will be clear about whether the patient, if discharged, will be being discharged subject to supervision.

POSTPONING CONSIDERATION OF A REFERENCE

A tribunal cannot postpone its consideration of a reference.[98]

POSTPONING CONSIDERATION OF AN APPLICATION

A tribunal may postpone its consideration of certain classes of application if it has determined a previous application or reference in respect of the same patient within the previous six months. The power is exercisable by the regional chairman, or by another member of the tribunal appointed to act on his behalf, but is rarely used.[99]

---

[98]   Mental Health Review Tribunal Rules 1983, r.29(a).
[99]   *Ibid.*, rr.2(1) and 5.

The basic framework

On receipt of an application, the issue of postponement may be approached in four stages—

1.   Is there a power of postponement? (**643**)

2.   If yes, for how long may consideration be postponed? (**645**)

3.   Is postponement in the patient's interests? (**647**)

4.   If yes, for how long should consideration be postponed? (**647**)

POSTPONEMENT: MHRT RULES 1983, r.9

Powers to postpone consideration of an application

9.—(1) Where an application or reference by or in respect of a patient has been considered and determined by a tribunal for the same or any other area, the tribunal may, subject to the provisions of this rule, postpone the consideration of a further application by or in respect of that patient until such date as it may direct, not being later than—

(a) the expiration of the period of six months from the date on which the previous application was determined; or

(b) the expiration of the current period of detention, whichever shall be the earlier.

(2) The power of postponement shall not be exercised unless the tribunal is satisfied, after making appropriate inquiries of the applicant and (where he is not the applicant) the patient, that postponement would be in the interests of the patient.

(3) The power of postponement shall not apply to—

(a) an application under section 66(1)(d) *or (gb)* of the Act;

(b) an application under section 66(1)(f) of the Act in respect of a renewal of authority for detention of the patient for a period of six months *or an application under section 66(1)(gc) of the Act in respect of a report furnished under section 25G(3) concerning renewal of after-care under supervision,* unless the previous application or reference was made to the tribunal more than three months after the patient's admission to hospital, reception into guardianship *or becoming subject to after-care under supervision*;

(c) an application under section 66(1)(g) of the Act;

(d) any application where the previous application or reference was determined before a break or change in the authority for the patient's detention or guardianship *or his being (or being about to be) subject to after-care under supervision* as defined in paragraph (7).

(4) Where the consideration of an application is postponed, the tribunal shall state in writing the reasons for postponement and the period for which the application is postponed and shall send a copy of the statement to all the parties and, in the case of a restricted patient, the Secretary of State.

(5) Where the consideration of an application is postponed, the tribunal shall send a further notice of the application in accordance with rule 4 not less than 7 days before the end of the period of postponement and consideration of the application shall proceed thereafter, unless before the end of the period of postponement the application has been withdrawn or is deemed to be withdrawn in accordance with the provisions of rule 19 or has been determined in accordance with the next following paragraph.

(6) Where a new application which is not postponed under this rule or a reference is made in respect of a patient, the tribunal may direct that any postponed application in respect of the same patient shall be considered and determined at the same time as the new application or reference.

(7) For the purposes of paragraph (3)(d) a breach or change in the authority for the detention or guardianship *or his being (or about to be) subject to after-care under supervision* of a patient shall be deemed to have occurred only—

(a) on his admission to hospital in pursuance of an application for treatment or in pursuance of a hospital order without an order restricting his discharge; or
(b) on his reception into guardianship in pursuance of a guardianship application or a guardianship order; or
(c) on the application to him of the provisions of Part II or Part III of the Act as if he had been so admitted or received following—
(i) the making of a transfer direction or
(ii) the ceasing of effect of a transfer direction or an order or direction restricting his discharge; or
(d) on his transfer from guardianship to hospital in pursuance of regulations made under section 19 of the Act.
(e) on his ceasing to be subject to after-care under supervision on his reception into guardianship in accordance with section 25H(5)(b).

Mental Health Review Tribunal Rules 1983, as amended by the Mental Health Review Tribunal (Amendment) Rules 1996, r.7.

Whether a power of postponement exists

Whether a power of postponement exists depends upon the right of application being exercised and whether there has been a break in the authority for the patient's detention, supervision or guardianship since the previous application or reference was determined.

Restricted patients

Where an application is made by a restricted patient and a previous application or reference concerning him has been determined during the previous six months, a tribunal may always postpone its consideration of the new application if it is satisfied that is in the patient's interests.

Patients detained for assessment

The postponement provisions do not apply to an "assessment application," that is an application made by a patient who is detained for assessment.[100]

---

[100]   Mental Health Review Tribunal Rules 1983, rr.33 and 2(1). The rules do not take account of the possibility that an application may be made by the nearest relative of a section 2 patient.

Unrestricted patients detained for treatment or subject to guardianship

The general rule is that each time a tribunal determines an application or reference, the consideration of any application made during the following six months concerning that patient may be postponed. However, the rule does not apply if the patient was a restricted patient at the time of the previous determination or subject to a application, order or direction different from that to which the new application relates.[101] Even where there has been no such break in the authority for the patient's detention or guardianship, a tribunal may not postpone its consideration of certain types of application, however recent its last determination. It may not postpone an application arising from a patient's reclassification (under section 66(1)(d)) or the barring of his discharge (under section 66(1)(g)). Similarly, an application made by a patient under section 66(1)(f) during his second six month period of detention or guardianship may only be postponed if it is made during the first three months of that period and the previous application or reference was made during the final three months of the first period of detention or guardianship.[102] Once these exceptions and modifications to the general rule have been accounted for, it may be seen that consideration of the following types of application may always be postponed where that is in the patient's interest and there has been a determination during the previous six months: applications made by a nearest relative under section 69 in respect of a Part III patient; applications made by the displaced relative of a Part II patient under section 66(1)(h); applications made under section 66(1)(f) by a patient who has been detained or subject to guardianship under the same provision of the Act for one year or more; applications made under section 66(1)(fa) or (fb) by a patient who has returned to hospital or the place where he is required to be after more than 28 days absence without leave.[103]

Proceedings involving after-care under supervision

The consideration of a tribunal application made by the patient or his nearest relative may be postponed in the following circumstances—

- Where a tribunal application is made under section 66(1)(ga) during the six month period following the supervision application's acceptance, its consideration may apparently be postponed if a previous application or reference in

---

[101] Mental Health Review Tribunal Rules 1983, rule 9(7). There is one exception to this rule. Where a patient is transferred from hospital into guardianship under section 19 and an application or reference has been determined within the past six months while the patient was detained in hospital, this does give rise to a power of postponement following transfer.

[102] The opening words in rule 9(3) ("the power of postponement") refer back to rule 9(1). In other words, the previous application or reference must have been determined before consideration may be given to postponing an application made during the first three months of the second period of detention or guardianship. Applications or references made during the first six months which have not been determined, including applications which were withdrawn, are therefore ignored and so do not give rise to any power of postponement.

[103] Where a patient who is liable to be detained or subject to guardianship returns to the hospital or place where he is required to be after more than 28 days absence without leave, a right to apply to a tribunal will arise either (1) under section 66(1)(fa), if the authority for his detention or guardianship is *retrospectively* renewed for a further period or periods or (2) under section 66(1)(fb), if he is reclassified otherwise than in the course of *prospectively* renewing the authority for a further period. The failure to insert in rule 9(3)(a) a reference to applications made under section 66(1)(fb) following such a reclassification is odd, as is the failure to insert a reference to section 66(1)(fa) in rule 9(3)(b). It seems likely that the draftsman did not understand the effects of these provisions since there is no logical reason for dealing with renewal or reclassification under section 21B in a different manner to applications under section 66(1)(d), (gb), and (f). Indeed, all of the amendments to rule 9 made by the Mental Health Review Tribunal (Amendment) Rules 1996 appear to make little legal or grammatical sense.

respect of the patient has been considered during the past six months. The intention may be to enable a tribunal to postpone considering a patient's case until he has left hospital or to enable it to postpone its consideration of a supervision application made in response to its own recent recommendation.[104]

- Where the authority for a patient's supervision is renewed, section 66(1)(gc) provides for a further application during each subsequent six or twelve month period the authority remains in force. Consideration of such an application may be postponed if a previous application or reference was determined during the past six months unless that application or reference was made during the three months following the acceptance of the supervision application.

- Where a patient or his nearest relative applies under section 66(1)(gb) following the patient's reclassification, consideration of such an application may not be postponed.

- Where a patient who is or has been subject to after-care under supervision becomes liable to be detained for assessment or treatment, or is received into guardianship, any tribunal application previously made under sections 66(1) (ga)–(gc) in respect of his liability to statutory supervision is never a ground for postponing the consideration of any tribunal application then made in respect of his detention or guardianship.[105]

The maximum period of postponement

The maximum period of postponement is set out in rule 9(1). Because the drafting of the paragraph is ambiguous, it is worth considering it alongside the enactment in the 1960 Rules from which it derives—

MHRT Rules 1960, r.4(1)	*MHRT Rules 1983, r.9(1)*
"4.—(1) Where an application by or in respect of a patient has been considered and determined by a tribunal for the same or any other area, the tribunal ... may, subject to the provisions of this rule, postpone the consideration of a further application by or in respect of that patient until such time as they or he may direct, not being later than the expiration of the period of twelve months from the date on which the previous application was determined."	"9.—(1) Where an application or reference by or in respect of a patient has been considered and determined by a tribunal for the same or any other area, the tribunal may, subject to the provisions of this rule, postpone the consideration of a further application by or in respect of that patient until such date as it may direct, not being later than— (a) the expiration of the period of six months from the date on which the previous application was determined; or (b) the expiration of the current period of detention, whichever shall be the earlier."

---

[104] However, since no person or body other than a tribunal may terminate the liability to supervision of a patient who is to be subject to supervision upon leaving hospital, and since the consideration of a first tribunal application cannot usually be postponed, the drafting is suspicious. It must therefore be doubtful whether a power to postpone the consideration of a first application made by a patient who is to be subject to supervision would be *intra vires* section 78.

[105] This is the combined effect of rr.9(7)(a)–(e) and 33. The insertion of r.9(7)(e) appears to be superfluous since reception into guardianship always constitutes a break or change of authority: see r.9(7)(b). It seems unlikely that r.9(7)(e) is meant to imply that where a patient ceases to be subject to after-care under supervision because he is admitted to hospital for treatment in accordance with s.25H(5)(a), this does not constitute a break or change, so that consideration of any application then made under s.66(1)(b) may be postponed. Again, such a provision would seem to be *ultra vires*.

The phrases "previous application" and "further application"

Gostin and Fennell suggest that rule 9(1)(a) does not apply if the previous determination involved a reference, and the postponement period is by default that specified in rule 9(1)(b): "the expiration of the current period of detention." However, restricted patients by definition do not have a current period of detention. It appears in fact that an error was made when the previous rule was redrafted in 1983 to take account of the introduction of the new automatic reference provisions. The old rule was both simple and coherent: where a "previous application" had recently been determined, consideration of a "further application" could be postponed. The continued use in the new rules of the word "further," in the phrase "further application," can only be an omission on the part of the draftsman. There may have been no "previous application," the previous determination being of a reference.[106] This tends to suggest that both the continued use of the phrase "further application" and the failure to add the words "or reference" after "previous application" are two consequences of a single oversight on the draftsman's part; the continued inclusion of the phrase "new application" in rule 9(6) being a third. The ambiguous terms of rule 9(3)b) reinforce the impression of indifferent draftsmanship.[107] The likelihood of a drafting error is further strengthened if one considers the application of the present rules to restricted patients.

Restricted patients

In any case where a previous application or reference has been determined within the past six months, a tribunal may postpone its consideration of any further application until the expiry of that six-month period.

Unrestricted patients

The effect of rule 9(1) is that the consideration of a reference cannot be postponed but the consideration of an application involving an unrestricted patient may be postponed for up to six months from the date on which the previous application or reference was determined or until the expiration of the current statutory period, whichever is the earlier.

"Determination"

An application is determined by a tribunal when it makes its decision as to whether a patient is to be discharged.[108] Consequently, an application may not be postponed because an undetermined application or reference has been considered during the preceding six months. For example, one which was subsequently withdrawn, has yet to be heard, or stands adjourned. In such cases, a decision should be taken as to whether the proceedings should be considered together. Similarly, where a tribunal defers a direction for conditional discharge or makes a recommendation under

---

[106]   It cannot be argued that the purpose of the phrase "further application" is to indicate that the consideration of an application may only be postponed if the previous determination related to a reference. Had that been the intention, the rule would not have been changed and the inclusion of the word "reference" in the opening line would be meaningless.

[107]   As enacted, rule 9(3)(b) provided that, "The power of postponement shall not apply to ... an application made under section 66(1)(f) in respect of the renewal of authority for *detention* of the patient for a period of six months, unless the previous application or reference was made to the tribunal more than three months after the patient's *admission to hospital or reception into guardianship.*"

[108]   See rules 23(2) and (3) and *R. v. Oxford Regional Mental Health Review Tribunal, ex p. Secretary of State for the Home Department* [1988] 1 A.C. 120.

section 72(3), and it later reconvenes the proceedings or further considers the patient's case, the period after the substantive hearing is to be discounted when calculating whether a power of postponement exists.[109]

Whether postponement is in the patient's interests

The power of postponement may not be exercised unless the tribunal is satisfied, after making "appropriate" inquiries of the applicant and (where he is not the applicant) the patient, that postponement would be in the interests of the patient.[110] Where no such inquiries are made before the power is exercised, the appropriate remedy in the first instance will be to invite the tribunal to cure that irregularity by making the necessary inquiries. Only the patient's interests are relevant: whether a nearest relative applicant is from his point of view acting reasonably in exercising his right of application, and whether he has applied before, is ultimately academic.

Relevant factors

The following considerations are likely to be relevant in determining whether postponement is in the patient's interests: whether the current application is made by the patient or by his nearest relative; the patient's attitude to any application by his actual or acting nearest relative; whether the previous proceedings were commenced by reference; where a patient has applied, whether he made the previous application; the length of time which has elapsed since the previous application or reference was determined; whether the new application is likely to merely duplicate the issues considered at the previous hearing; the tribunal's decision on the previous occasion (in particular its recorded reasons for not discharging and any recommendations made under section 72); the period for which consideration may be postponed.

The specified period of postponement

The factors to be considered when deciding what period of postponement to direct will necessarily be similar to those which are relevant when determining whether to exercise the power at all and reflect the reasons for deciding to exercise the power.

Giving notice of the postponement and the reasons for it

Where a tribunal postpones consideration of an application, it must state in writing the period for which consideration of the application is postponed and the reasons for postponement[111]; and serve that statement on the parties[112] and, in the case of a restricted patient, the Secretary of State. It must also still serve the notice of application required under rule 4.

---

[109] By way of example, take the case of a patient who on 1 January 1990 was detained under section 3. On 3 March 1993, a tribunal does not direct that he be discharged and makes a recommendation under section 72(3). This is not complied with and, on 9 September 1993, the tribunal reconvenes the hearing. If the patient then makes a further application on 2 January 1993, its consideration may not be postponed because more than six months have elapsed since the last determination.

[110] Mental Health Review Tribunal Rules 1983, r.9(2).

[111] Mental Health Review Tribunal Rules 1983, r.9(4). Proper and adequate reasons must be given which deal with any substantial points raised and enable the parties to determine whether the tribunal has made any error of law in making its decision. See *Bone v. Mental Health Review Tribunal* [1985] 3 All E.R. 330, 333; *Re Poyser and Mills' Arbitration* [1964] 2 Q.B. 467; *Alexander Machinery Ltd. v. Crabtree (N.I.R.C.)* [1974] I.C.R. 120.

[112] At this stage of the proceedings, the "parties" will be the applicant, the patient (if he is not the applicant), and the responsible authority: see Mental Health Review Tribunal Rules 1983, r.2(1).

Commencing consideration of the application

If the application is withdrawn or deemed to be withdrawn before the postponement period expires, no further steps need be taken.[113] Where a further application is made during the postponement period by or in respect of the same patient and its consideration is not postponed, the tribunal may direct that the postponed application be considered and determined at the same time as the new application.[114] In all other cases, the tribunal is required to send a further notice of application under rule 4 not less than 7 days prior to the expiry of the postponement period and "consideration of the application shall proceed thereafter."[115]

PATIENTS WHO ARE TRANSFERRED DURING THE PROCEEDINGS

The rules provide that where, in the course of the proceedings, a patient moves within the jurisdiction of another tribunal, the proceedings shall be transferred to that other tribunal if the chairman of the tribunal originally having jurisdiction over those proceedings so directs.

TRANSFERRING THE PROCEEDINGS: MHRT RULES 983, r.17

Interpretation

2.—(1) "tribunal" in relation to an application or a reference means the Mental Health Review Tribunal constituted under section 65 of the Act which has jurisdiction in the area in which the patient, at the time the application or reference is made, is detained or is liable to be detained or is subject to guardianship or is (or is to be) subject to after-care under supervision, or the tribunal to which the proceedings are transferred in accordance with rule 17(2), or in the case of a conditionally discharged patient, the tribunal for the area in which the patient resides.

Transfer of proceedings

17.—(1) Where any proceedings in relation to a patient have not been disposed of by the members of the tribunal appointed for the purpose, and the chairman is of the opinion that it is not practicable or not possible without undue delay for the consideration of those proceedings to be completed by those members, he shall make arrangements for them to be heard by other members of the tribunal.

(2) Where a patient in respect of whom proceedings are pending moves within the jurisdiction of another tribunal, the proceedings shall, if the chairman of the tribunal originally having jurisdiction over those proceedings so directs, be transferred to the tribunal within the jurisdiction of which the patient has moved and notice of the transfer of proceedings shall be given to the parties and, in the case of a restricted patient, the Secretary of State.

---

[113] Mental Health Review Tribunal Rules 1983, r.9(5).
[114] *Ibid.*, r.9(6). This would generally happen where the subsequent application was of a kind the consideration of which may not be postponed. As to the tribunal's general power to direct that two or more outstanding applications or references be considered together, see rule 18.
[115] *Ibid.*, r.9(5). A minor drafting error. For obvious reasons, rule 4(1)(b) should be read in this context as referring to, "the applicant and (where he is not the applicant) the patient."

Application of rule 17(1)

A patient may move within the jurisdiction of another tribunal because he is transferred from one hospital to another under section 19 or 123; or is granted leave to reside at another hospital or outside hospital under section 17; or because the place of residence of a conditionally discharged patient, or a patient subject to guardianship or after-care under supervision, changes. Mental Health Review Tribunal proceedings pending in Northern Ireland at the time of a patient's removal to England and Wales may not been transferred to a tribunal in England and Wales.

WITHDRAWING AN APPLICATION OR REFERENCE

An application or a discretionary reference may be withdrawn, but not a mandatory reference.

WITHDRAWAL OF APPLICATION : MHRT RULES 1983, r.19

Withdrawal of Application

19.—(1) An application may be withdrawn at any time at the request of the applicant provided that the request is made in writing and the tribunal agrees.

(2) If a patient ceases to be liable to be detained or subject to guardianship *or after-care under supervision* in England and Wales, any application relating to that patient shall be deemed to be withdrawn.

(2A) Where a patient subject to after-care under supervision fails without reasonable explanation to undergo a medical examination under rule 11, any application relating to that patient may be deemed by the tribunal to be withdrawn.

(3) Where an application is withdrawn or deemed to he withdrawn, the tribunal shall so inform the parties and, in the case of a restricted patient, the Secretary of State.

Mental Health Review Tribunal Rules 1983, as amended by the Mental Health Review Tribunal (Amendment) Rules 1996, r.10.

Withdrawing an application

A request by an applicant to withdraw his application must be made in writing and its withdrawal requires the tribunal's consent.[116] Such a consent may be given by the regional chairman.[117] Where an application is withdrawn, the tribunal is required to notify the parties of this.[118] Applications which have been withdrawn are discounted for the purpose of determining whether an applicant has exercised his right to apply to a tribunal during a specified period.

---

[116]   Mental Health Review Tribunal Rules 1983, r.19(1).
[117]   *Ibid.*, r.5.
[118]   *Ibid.*, r.19(3).

The need for the tribunal's consent

As sections 68(5) and 71(6) make clear, withdrawing an application may in certain circumstances simply result in the patient's case being immediately referred to the same tribunal by the hospital managers or by the Secretary of State. Providing that withdrawal requires the tribunal's consent allows proceedings which are shortly to be heard, and in respect of which reports have already been received, to proceed if their discontinuance would simply result in the same matter immediately coming back before the tribunal. The provision also has the secondary benefit of ensuring that applications are not withdrawn because of any undue pressure on the patient or his nearest relative.

Withdrawing a reference

A discretionary reference may be withdrawn by the Secretary of State at any time before it is "considered" by the tribunal and, where a reference is withdrawn, the tribunal shall inform the patient and the other parties of that fact.[119] The word "considered" is inconsistently used in the tribunal rules. Its use in this context suggests that it refers to the commencement of the hearing.

DEEMED WITHDRAWAL OF AN APPLICATION OR REFERENCE

Rule 19(2) provides that an application or reference "shall be deemed to be withdrawn" if the patient "ceases to be liable to be detained or subject to guardianship or after-care under supervision in England and Wales."[120] Where an application is deemed to have been withdrawn, the tribunal shall notify the parties of this.[121] As drafted, the rule appears to provide that an application or reference shall not be deemed withdrawn merely because during the proceedings the patient becomes liable to be detained or subject to guardianship under a different statutory provision. The various ways in which a patient may generally cease to be detained or subject to guardianship under a particular statutory provision have already been considered (**283 et seq.**). For these purposes, four distinct situations can be identified and the correct approach must be to try to discern the statutory framework rather than to construe the statute according to what the rules say. In any case, it seems clear that a literal reading of rule 19 does not cater for all of the possible eventualities.

Patients ceasing to be subject to any form of compulsion under the Act

In many cases, the effect of an order discharging the patient is that he ceases to be subject to any application, order or direction under the Act. In unrestricted cases, this will also be the effect of not renewing the authority for his detention, guardianship or supervision, of his being absent without leave or in judicial custody for a certain period of time, and of his removal outside the jurisdiction under Part VI. In all these cases, the effect of rule 19 is to allow the tribunal to cease its consideration of the application or reference and to close the file. The effect is therefore procedural in that the rule simply confirms what would still be the case if it did not exist, namely that there is no longer any authority in existence for the tribunal to review.

---

[119]   Mental Health Review Tribunal Rules 1983, r.29(d).
[120]   *Ibid.*, r.19(2).
[121]   *Ibid.*, r.19(3).

Patients who are subject to more than one provision

A patient who is liable to be detained or subject to guardianship or supervision may become subject to a second application, order or direction but this not have the effect of discharging the earlier authority which a tribunal is reviewing. Examples of this second situation are the making of a supervision application in respect of an unrestricted patient who is liable to be detained for treatment; the admission for assessment of a patient subject to guardianship or after-care under supervision; the making of a further application, order or direction in respect of a restricted patient; and the making of an order under section 35, 36 or 38. In all these cases, the patient continues to be subject to the earlier authority which the tribunal is reviewing and it is clear that the application or reference cannot be deemed to be withdrawn.

One provision ceasing to have effect upon another coming into effect

The third situation is that where a patient whose case is being considered by a tribunal ceases to be subject to that particular authority because of a subsequent application, order or direction. There are many ways in which this may happen although the most common of them is that a patient ceases to be detained under section 2 upon the acceptance of a section 3 application. Other examples are that a section 2 or section 3 patient is received into guardianship; a hospital order or a guardianship order is made in respect of an unrestricted patient; a patient subject to after-care under supervision is admitted to hospital for treatment or received into guardianship; or a patient subject to guardianship is admitted to hospital for treatment. In none of these cases has the patient, in the words of rule 19, "ceased to be liable to be detained or subject to guardianship or after-care under supervision in England and Wales." In most cases, however, he will have ceased to be subject to whichever particular form of compulsion gave rise to the tribunal application — detention, guardianship or supervision — and now be subject to one of the other two forms.

Change in what is authorised by the application, order or direction

The final situation is that where a patient is transferred from hospital to guardianship or vice-versa. In these cases, the application or order which gave rise to the tribunal proceedings continues in existence but the form of compulsion authorised by it has changed. Here, therefore, the patient has ceased to be liable to be detained or subject to guardianship without the authority or order being discharged or lapsing. In contrast, a transfer from one hospital or guardian to another involves no change in the form of compulsion which is authorised.

A tribunal's powers under Part V

The next stage is to consider whether an application is to be deemed withdrawn in the last two of these situations. This involves examining the terms of Part V and then considering the consequences of deeming, or not deeming, an application to be withdrawn in the particular situations. As to the first step, the following sections seem particularly relevant—

- Section 72(4) commences: "Where application is made to a Mental Health Review Tribunal by ... a patient who is subject to guardianship under this Act, the tribunal may ..." This suggests that the application must have been made by a patient subject to guardianship, not merely that the patient is subject to guardianship at the time of the hearing.

651

- Section 72(4A) commences: "Where application is made to a Mental Health Review Tribunal by or in respect of a patient who is subject to after-care under supervision (or, if he has not yet left hospital, is to be so subject after he leaves hospital), the tribunal may ..." This subsection similarly suggests that the application must have been made by a patient who was subject to supervision, not merely that he is being supervised at the time of the hearing.

- Section 73(1) commences, "Where an application to a Mental Health Review Tribunal is made by a patient who is subject to a restriction order, ... the tribunal shall ..." Again, this subsection points in the same direction. The patient must both be subject to such an order at the time of the hearing and have made the application at a time when he was so subject.

- Section 74(1) commences, "Where an application to a Mental Health Review Tribunal is made by a patient who is subject to a restriction direction, ... the tribunal shall ..." A natural reading leads to the same conclusion.

- Section 75(3) sets out a tribunal's powers in respect of applications made under subsection (2), which again suggests that the patient must also have been a conditionally discharged patient when he applied for the review.

- Section 78(2) provides that rules made under that section may in particular make provision (c) for restricting the persons qualified to serve as members of a tribunal *for the consideration of any application, or of an application of any specified class*; (d) *for enabling a tribunal to dispose of an application* without a formal hearing where such a hearing is not requested by the applicant. Again, the wording of these paragraphs suggests that it is the particular application authorised by the Act which is being considered and disposed of.

Although one must bear in mind that any general rule may be subject to exceptions, the general intention seems to be that a tribunal may only deal with an application or reference if the patient is subject to the particular compulsory power which gave rise to the right to a review of the justification for that power. Whether this is correct and, if it is, whether there are any exceptions to the rule, leads to the second step. This is to consider the consequences of deeming, or not deeming, an application to be withdrawn following the power's revocation or a patient's transfer.

Patients detained for treatment under Part II

Ignoring various fanciful possibilities, a patient will cease to be liable to be detained for treatment under section 3 if he is received into guardianship or, having become involved in criminal proceedings, is admitted to hospital for treatment under section 37 or 48. Unless restrictions have been attached, the status of a patient admitted for treatment under either of those provisions will be virtually unchanged. However, unless he is reclassified, a patient who is admitted under section 37, whether with or without restrictions, is not entitled to apply to a tribunal during the initial six month period of detention authorised by the court. If, however, he is entitled to proceed with a tribunal application previously made whilst detained under section 3, because it is not deemed to have been withdrawn, the effect of this will necessarily be that his liability to detention under section 37 is reviewed during the first six months. For two reasons, the statutory intention must be that the tribunal application ceased to have effect at the time when the patient ceased to be liable to be detained under the provision to which the right of application attached. Firstly, it is clear that patients detained under a hospital order, with or without restrictions, are not entitled to have the present justification for their detention reviewed by a tribunal during the initial period of detention authorised by the court. Secondly, if one allows tribunal applications previously in force to continue then hospital order patients would, if previously detained under section 2, 3 or 48, be entitled to a review during the first six months by virtue of that fact, rather than by virtue of their detention under the relevant hospital or restriction order. However, patients previously detained for treatment under section 36 or 38 would still need to wait the full six months. There is nothing in the Act to suggest that Parliament intended that some patients are entitled to a review within six months of the order's imposition, and others not, depending on their previous legal status. Indeed, such a scheme would introduce an unwelcome degree of unfairness into the matter.[122]

Patients detained under section 48

The point just made is perhaps best illustrated by reference to the position of defendants who, pending trial, are detained in hospital for treatment under sections 48 and 49. Under section 69(2)(b), such a patient may immediately apply to a tribunal in respect of his detention in pursuance of those directions. However, it is not always the case that the tribunal can determine that application before the criminal proceedings are concluded and, not infrequently, the court disposes of the case by making a hospital order *and* a restriction order. Sections 51(2) and 52(6) provide that the transfer direction ceases to have effect when the case is disposed of and the attendant restriction direction, being parasitic in nature, also ceases to have effect at that time. The patient may not apply to a tribunal during the initial six month period of detention authorised by the court unless he is entitled to proceed with his outstanding application, because it is not deemed to have been withdrawn by him. Again, it cannot have been Parliament's intention that patients who were previously detained in hospital for treatment under section 48 should be entitled to an early review of the hospital and restriction orders but not patients who were detained for treatment there under section 36 or 38. Accordingly, the right conferred by section 69(2)(b) must be a right to have the present justification for the patient's transfer to hospital reviewed in accordance with section 74.[123] If the criminal proceedings are concluded before that can be done, section 69(2)(b) does not give rise to a right to an immediate review of the justification for any hospital order or restriction order then imposed. Unless the patient appeals against the sentence imposed, he must wait for six months, along with all other patients detained under the same provision. Indeed, the contrary notion seems absurd and, insofar as rule 19 implies otherwise, the draftsman must have misunderstood Parliament's intention.

---

[122] The position must be the same where a court imposes a hospital order in respect of an unrestricted patient who was already detained under a previous hospital order, in which case the second order discharges the first. Where a hospital order and a restriction order is made in respect of a patient who is already subject to a hospital order and a restriction order, the earlier orders continue in force as does any tribunal application relating to them. In practice, the Home Secretary sometimes rationalises the position by absolutely discharging the patient from one of the pairs of orders.

[123] Similarly, where a patient who is liable to be detained ceases to be subject to restrictions, because they were imposed for a limited term or his sentence of imprisonment expires, any outstanding tribunal application is deemed withdrawn. The Act in effect acknowledges this by giving the patient notionally detained under a new hospital order an immediate right to apply to a tribunal.

Patients subject to after-care under supervision

A patient who is subject to after-care under supervision ceases to be so subject if he is admitted to hospital for treatment or received into guardianship. The issues affecting liability to detention and guardianship on the one hand and supervision on the other are sufficiently distinct that different reports are required under the rules and different responsible authorities are required to furnish them. Some of the parties will also be different. For example, notices will have been served on the community responsible medical officer and the supervisor although, following readmission, the patient no longer has any such officers. Furthermore, if the outstanding tribunal application had been made by the nearest relative, he will no longer be an authorised tribunal applicant — allowing the application to proceed would involve the tribunal hearing an application concerning the patient's detention by a person not authorised to apply for it's review. Likewise, if the outstanding application was made following reclassification, it is difficult to see how that gives rise to any right to an independent review following admission — it is then the patient's classification on the admission documents which is relevant and that has not been amended. And, where a patient who has been detained in pursuance of a hospital order for less than six months applies to a tribunal because he is to be subject to after-care under supervision upon leaving hospital, it must be the case that the tribunal is not entitled to also review his liability to detention. In other words, the tribunal's jurisdiction is limited to reviewing the justification for the power upon which the right of application is founded. It may only exercise those powers under section 72 which relate to the specific right of application exercised under section 66. For all these reasons, it is therefore difficult to believe that the consequence of readmission for treatment or reception into guardianship can ever be anything other than the deemed withdrawal of any pre-existing tribunal application concerning the patient's supervision.

Patients transferred to a different guardian or hospital

Where a patient subject to guardianship is transferred into the guardianship of another person or authority, the original application or order continues in force and it is treated as if it had always specified the new person or authority as being the person's guardian. The patient has therefore never ceased to be subject to guardianship, his rights to apply to a tribunal are unaffected, and any outstanding tribunal application cannot be deemed withdrawn. The consequences are the same where a patient who is liable to be detained is transferred to another hospital. Transfers of this kind may involve a change of responsible authority, and they may necessitate transferring the proceedings to another tribunal and the commissioning of further reports, but their effect is not that the existing application or reference is deemed to be withdrawn. The application, order or direction being reviewed continues to have effect and the form of compulsion authorised by it has not changed.

Patients transferred from guardianship to hospital

The position is similar where the transfer is from guardianship to hospital insofar as the application or order is deemed to have always been in its amended form. The effect is that the guardianship application or order is treated as if it had always been a section 3 application or a hospital order. However, following a transfer to hospital, a fresh right of application arises under section 66(1)(e) which is exercisable during the following six months. The intention here must be to place such patients, insofar as is practical, in exactly the same position as those admitted under section 3. The logical consequence of conferring a new right of application following transfer is that any rights of application exercisable under the pre-existing scheme cease to have effect. Although the rules are not conclusive, the fact that a tribunal may not postpone its consideration of an application made under section 66(1)(e) supports this view. Holding otherwise would mean that some detained patients are entitled to two hearings during their first six months in hospital whilst others are only entitled to one. Furthermore, any other interpretation gives rise to anomalies which suggest that Parliament did not intend that an existing application should continue to have effect. For example, where a Part III patient is transferred from guardianship to hospital during the initial six-month period, any outstanding application made by his nearest relative must be deemed withdrawn — that person has no right to apply during what is now the first six months of the patient's detention under a hospital order.

Patients transferred from hospital into guardianship

Transfers from hospital into guardianship similarly take effect as if the original application, order or direction which authorised the patient's admission to hospital had always been in its amended form. The original authority has not ceased to have effect but now has a different effect, in that the patient is no longer liable to detention in a hospital. However, in this case no new right of application is conferred and the statutory scheme becomes unclear, as the following diagram illustrates.

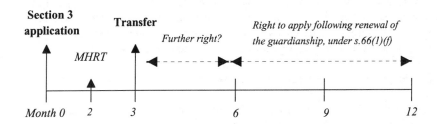

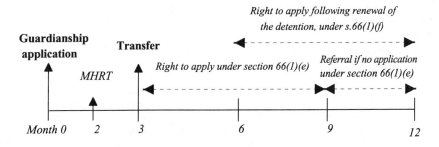

In particular, it is unclear whether (1) any pre-existing tribunal application made in respect of the patient's detention is meant to continue to have effect; and (2) whether a previous determination in relation to the patient's detention, during what is now the current six or twelve month period of guardianship, prevents a further application being made during that period.[124] Two views are possible. The first is that a patient transferred from hospital to guardianship has not previously applied to a tribunal for a review of his guardianship during what is now the current period of guardianship. Accordingly, he has yet to exercise his right of application under section 66(1)(c) or (f) and may do so following the transfer. Any previous application in relation to his detention in hospital, whether determined or pending, is ignored — in the latter case, it is deemed withdrawn. This view has the consequence that a hospital order patient transferred within six months of the order's imposition, who had no right to apply before, may apply during what remains of that period.[125] The second view is simply that a patient who is admitted to hospital for treatment under Part II may make one application during the following six months, and a patient admitted under Part III none, and no different rights having been provided following transfer, the patient's position is unaffected by any transfer. If the patient has already had a tribunal during the current period, he is not entitled to make a further application until the authority is next renewed.[126] The corollary is that any outstanding tribunal not disposed of prior to the transfer continues and is not deemed withdrawn. In support of this interpretation, it may be said that it is consistent with sections 19(2)(b) and 72(4).[127] Furthermore, there would be little need for section 66(1)(e) if this were not the case. The purpose of that paragraph is to ensure all detained patients have a right to a tribunal during their first six months of detention, even if they have already had a tribunal during the current period of the authority. The patient always has the same right to a review of his detention following transfer as he would have had he been detained for treatment in pursuance of an application. The point of prescribing a new, fresh, right of application in such cases must be to modify the usual position following transfer, that is to vary the logical consequences of transfer in terms of tribunal rights. Here one is dealing with the unmodified position. It is submitted that the second view is correct, primarily because this must be the position if the transferred patient had previously been detained for more than six months, and section 66(1)(e) would otherwise unnecessarily complicate the scheme set out in section 66 without serving any purpose which compensated for that.

Section 2 patients detained under section 3

It sometimes happens that a section 3 application is accepted in respect of a section 2 patient before that person's application to a tribunal under section 66(1)(a) has been determined. The usual approach over the years has been for the tribunal to still review the case on the appointed date but to determine the application according to the criteria for discharge in section 72(1)(b). The justification for doing so is essentially four-fold: (1) the application was made during the relevant period for making such an application and the patient was authorised to make it; (2) section 72(1) is expressed to apply where an application has been made by a patient who is

---

[124] Note that these questions have already been touched upon (**625 et seq.**).

[125] Note that where a transfer is the other way, and a guardianship order patient is transferred to hospital, he may in fact apply under section 66(1)(e), even though he is now deemed to be a hospital order patient in hospital during what is now the initial period of detention.

[126] This must be the position after the initial six-month period has expired. All applications then made are made under section 66(1)(f). In other words, if a patient in his second year of detention had a tribunal prior to being transferred, he will already have exercised his right to apply under paragraph (f) for that period.

[127] Section 72(4) commences: "Where application is made to a Mental Health Review Tribunal by ... a patient who is subject to guardianship under this Act, the tribunal may ..." Since the patient is deemed to have been subject to guardianship both at the time he made his application and at the time of the hearing so the tribunal must determine it.

liable to be detained; (3) the application having been authorised, and the tribunal's powers under that subsection being exercisable in respect of a person who is liable to be detained, the application must be determined; (4) combining a tribunal's powers in section 2 and 3 cases within a single subsection, and uniquely avoiding any reference to the patient's status at the time he made the application, must have been designed to achieve this unique effect. In short, provided that the patient's application was authorised at the time it was made, the tribunal must determine it and which of the paragraphs in section 72(1) it applies — paragraph (a) or paragraph (b) — depends upon his status at the time the application is dealt with. As to the patient's rights of application, the view taken was that, because the patient has not exercised his right to make an application during the six-month period following the admission under section 3, he could make a further application during that period — in this case, under section 66(1)(b).[128]

The counter-argument

Until recently, there were several grounds upon which exception could be taken to the argument just outlined or to any contention that a patient could not be detained under section 3 whilst a section 2 tribunal was pending —

- Firstly, it had been held that an approved social worker's duty or discretion to make a section 3 application is in no way impliedly limited or abrogated by the existence of an earlier tribunal decision to discharge: there is no sense in which those concerned in making a section 3 application are at any stage bound by an earlier tribunal decision. If this is correct, and the approach is open to criticism (**597**), holding that a section 2 patient cannot be admitted under section 3 until the tribunal has reviewed his detention does not necessarily confer any practical benefit on him. The relevant mental health professionals being of the opinion that the criteria for detention under section 3 exist, they can still make that application, albeit that any tribunal decision in favour of discharge should cause them to reconsider the necessity for that.

- Secondly, there is no reason why a patient detained under section 3 should be entitled to two reviews of the present authority for his detention if he was previously detained under section 2 but only one review if admitted under section 3 at the outset.

- Thirdly, if the tribunal does not vacate the hearing date, but invites the patient to lodge an application under section 66(1)(b), and proceeds on the basis of the reports which have already been prepared, the patient is not thereby to be taken as having been deprived of a right to a hearing later on during the initial six-month period of detention. Rather, in an ideal world, every patient's detention under section 3 would be reviewed as quickly as possible after it had been authorised.

- Fourthly, while some consultants undoubtedly do all they can to avoid a tribunal hearing, if the tribunal deals with the patient's section 66(1)(b) on the date originally set aside for the section 2 hearing, there will then be no incentive for them to attempt to delay hearings in this way.

---

[128] See the wording of section 66(1)(a) and (b).

- Fifthly, it is necessary to separate out the two issues of the law concerning section 3 applications and a tribunal's jurisdiction under Part V. Insofar as some consultants are guilty of bad practice in this area, the protection afforded by the Act lies with approved social workers and the patient's nearest relative. If a tribunal hearing is pending, the nearest relative may quite properly object to a section 3 application being made until the outcome of the tribunal is known. Insofar as section 29 is relevant, there is nothing unreasonable about that person objecting to the patient's admission for an indefinite period of treatment until he has the benefit of the tribunal's findings. Similarly, it would be quite lawful, and often good practice, for an approved social worker to conclude that he is not satisfied that such an application ought to be made at present because the patient is safely detained, receiving treatment, and an independent judicial review of the merits of his detention is pending.[129]

- Sixthly, the equivalent provisions in the 1959 Act suggest that any ambiguity in section 72(1) is unintentional.[130] Only patients detained for treatment could apply to have their cases reviewed under section 123 of that Act and, giving that scheme, the drafting was sufficiently precise. The right to a review for patients detained for 28 days was one introduced by the Mental Health (Amendment) Act 1982. The draftsman effected this amendment by inserting what is now section 72(1)(a) after the word "and." However, one cannot easily conclude from that a deliberate intention to place section 2 patients in a unique position.

Ex p. M.

The position of section 2 patients who are detained under section 3 before the tribunal hears their application was recently considered in *R. v. South Thames Mental Health Review Tribunal, ex p. M.*[131] It is understood that Collins J. held that the approach customarily adopted by tribunals was the correct one. The patient's application having been authorised by section 66(1)(a), the tribunal must deal with it. Which criteria the tribunal apply, and what powers it possesses, are determined by section 72. The patient in this instance being detained for treatment at the time of the hearing, the criteria in section 72(1)(b) must be applied. In essence, therefore, the sections 66 and 72 deal with completely different matters (a patient's rights of application and a tribunal's powers) and the answer to the issue raised requires that they be kept distinct.

---

[129] See Mental Health Act 1983, s.13(1).

[130] "123.—(1) Where application is made to a Mental Health Review Tribunal by or in respect of a patient who is liable to be detained under this Act, the tribunal may in any case direct that the patient be discharged, and shall so direct if they are satisfied—
(a) that he is not then suffering from mental illness, psychopathic disorder, subnormality or severe subnormality; or
(b) that it is not necessary in the interests of the patient's health or safety or for the protection of other persons that the patient should continue to be liable to be detained."

[131] *R. v. South Thames Mental Health Review Tribunal, ex p. M.*, CO/2700/97, 3 September 1997. The transcript had not been printed by the time this book was published. Prior to *ex p. M.*, High Court proceedings concerning the point had previously been initiated but not determined. In *J.M.S. v. Mental Health Review Tribunal*, the tribunal dealt with an application made at a time when the patient was detained under section 2 but applied the discharge criteria in section 72(1)(b). The patient asked the tribunal to state a case as to whether this was the correct approach. However, because the patient was discharged by the tribunal, the matter was academic. In the case of *J.O.L.*, the tribunal dealt with the matter in the same way but did not discharge the patient.

Summary

Although it is particularly important that provisions for the benefit of people with mental health problems should be plain and unambiguous, that is rarely the case with Part V and the rules, and no more so than here. However, it is submitted that—

- The Act provides a particular right of application, exercisable within a particular period of time, for each distinct form of authority for a person's detention, guardianship or supervision.

- The general statutory rule is that a tribunal's jurisdiction to deal with an application ceases if the patient ceases to be subject to the authority to which the right of application attaches. Similarly, although rule 19 does not apply to mandatory references, a tribunal has no jurisdiction to consider a reference made under section 68 if a further application, order or direction is made which has the effect of discharging the earlier authority.

- There are, however, two exceptions to the general rule. Firstly, an application made by a section 2 patient is not deemed to be withdrawn if he is detained under section 3 before it is determined. The rationale appears to be that section 2 is a precursor of section 3 and section 72(1) does not contain any qualifying words to the effect that a tribunal's powers under paragraph (b) are only exercisable if the application was made by a patient who was detained for treatment. The second exception involves patients who are transferred under section 19: unless the transfer is from guardianship to hospital, which gives rise to a new right of application, any outstanding tribunal application should be determined (*transfer from one hospital or guardian to another, or from hospital into guardianship*).[132]

Supervised patients not attending medical examination

Rule 19(2A) was inserted by the Mental Health Review Tribunal (Amendment) Rules 1996. It provides that where a patient subject to after-care under supervision fails without reasonable explanation to undergo a medical examination under rule 11, any application relating to that patient may be deemed by the tribunal to be withdrawn. The provision has such a punitive flavour, so wholly out of keeping with the traditional tolerance of tribunals towards the occasional shortcomings of people suffering from mental ill-health, that it is tempting to say that the provision is *ultra vires*. There seems to be nothing in the Act which entitled the draftsman to single out patients subject to after-care under supervision from other patients who may be residing in the community — patients subject to guardianship, conditionally discharged patients, and those absent from hospital with leave — and to lay down that their applications may be deemed withdrawn if they fail to attend the medical examination, but not those of other patients.[133] The fact that an application can be

---

[132] The alternative interpretation here is that if the effect of a transfer is to terminate the form of compulsion previously authorised by the application, order or direction then the tribunal application is deemed to have been withdrawn, but not otherwise

[133] Mental Health Act 1983, section 78(5) allows the rules to make different provisions in different cases. However, that must mean that some rules may apply to section 2 cases and others to restricted cases, and so forth, as the particular features of each kind of case dictates. It cannot have been Parliament's intention that the rules would be selective in this sense, *i.e.* arbitrary.

deemed withdrawn if the patient fails, rather than refuses, to attend a medical examination is highly unsatisfactory. Apart from the fact that the patient may not have received the letter of appointment, there are many reasons associated with a person's mental condition which might reduce his ability to attend an examination. Not all of those grounds would necessarily be reasons for not terminating the supervision application which it is the tribunal's duty to review. It is also highly unsatisfactory that the power can be exercised if the patient has not provided a reasonable explanation for his failure, not where the tribunal has reason to believe that he has refused to attend without good cause. In summary, the Act does not expressly provide that the rules may deem an application to be withdrawn, so rule 19 should be interpreted restrictively. It is one thing for the rules to provide that an application shall be deemed withdrawn if the patient is no longer subject to the particular provision. That is essentially procedural. It is quite another for them to empower a tribunal to withdraw an application by a patient who may still wish it to deal with his case. There is nothing in the statute to suggest that tribunals may do so or that the rules can single out a certain class of patient for such treatment. The appropriate and polite course is to ask the patient to contact the tribunal about fixing a date for the examination and the hearing and to await his response, thereafter appointing a representative, or adjourning the proceedings *sine die,* until contact is established. It is submitted that the rule is *ultra vires* the Act.

11. Obtaining reports on the patient

INTRODUCTION

Where an application or reference has been made to a tribunal, the Mental Health Review Tribunal Rules 1983 impose on the "responsible authority" and, in cases involving restricted patients, the Secretary of State a duty to furnish to the tribunal a statement about the patient.[1] The precise nature of this obligation, and the information and reports which the statement must include, are set out in the rules. The persons whom the authority or the Secretary of State has asked to write the reports should be aware of the need in certain circumstances to prepare the report in two separate parts or to indicate clearly whether part of the report should be withheld from a particular person (**702**).

THE "RESPONSIBLE AUTHORITY"

Rule 2(1) defines the body or authority which is the "responsible authority" for the purposes of the tribunal proceedings—

- In cases involving patients who are liable to be detained in a hospital or mental nursing home, the managers of the hospital or home are the "responsible authority."[2]

- In the case of patients subject to guardianship, the "responsible authority" is the "responsible local social services authority," that is the local authority which is the patient's guardian or, where a private guardian has been appointed, the local social services authority for the area within which the guardian resides.[3]

- In relation to a patient subject to after-care under supervision, the "responsible authority" is "the Health Authority which has the duty under section 117 of the Act to provide after-care services for the patient."[4]

- In cases involving conditionally discharged patients, there is no "responsible authority" but the rules require the Secretary of State to furnish a statement.[5]

---

[1]   This power to require a statement derives from Mental Health Act 1983, s.78(2)(g).

[2]   Mental Health Review Tribunal Rules 1983, r.2(1); Mental Health Act 1983, s.145(1).

[3]   Mental Health Review Tribunal Rules 1983, r.2(1); Mental Health Act 1983, s.34(3).

[4]   Mental Health Review Tribunal Rules 1983, r.2(1), as inserted by the Mental Health Review Tribunal (Amendment) Rules 1996, r.2(c).

[5]   This is because conditionally discharged patients are not liable to be detained in any specific hospital and the Secretary of State is never a party to, nor the responsible authority in, tribunal proceedings.

Patients not yet subject to after-care under supervision

The definition of the responsible authority in proceedings relating to after-care under supervision should be noted. The Act and the rules distinguish between a patient "subject to after-care under supervision" and a patient who "is to be" subject to after-care under supervision.[6] In the latter case, the patient is still liable to be detained or in hospital, or both, and hence he is not yet subject to supervision.

The tribunal with jurisdiction

Section 77(3) provides that a tribunal application made by a patient who *is to be* subject to after-care under supervision is to be made to the tribunal for the area in which he is to reside when he leaves hospital and becomes subject to supervision. It is this tribunal which has jurisdiction to deal with the case.[7] The patient may, of course, be detained in a hospital situated outside that tribunal's area. If so, and he has also appealed against his liability to detention, a separate application will be pending before a different tribunal.

The responsible authority

The application must therefore be made to the tribunal for the area where the patient is to reside, and it is the Health Authority for that area which will be responsible for providing him with after-care and which will be the responsible authority in any tribunal proceedings held after he has left hospital. However, rule 2(1) provides that the Health Authority is only the responsible authority in relation to a patient "subject to after-care under supervision" — not one who *is to be* so subject — whereas the managers of the relevant hospital are the responsible authority in cases involving patients who are liable to be detained. As drafted, the main problem arising from the definition is that there is no responsible authority if the patient is residing in hospital informally before becoming subject to supervision. In practice, the managers will no doubt be asked to fulfil this role. The alternative construction, that the Health Authority is always the responsible authority in any proceedings involving after-care under supervision, is difficult to reconcile with the drafting. This is because the other rules do distinguish between patients subject to after-care under supervision and those who are to be so subject. There will be a change of responsible authority if the patient leaves hospital before the proceedings are determined, but this also happens in the case of hospital transfers and so is nothing new.

THE BASIC FRAMEWORK

The 1983 Rules prescribe the information and reports to be furnished following the commencement of tribunal proceedings and they refer to Schedule 1, Parts A to F of which specify the precise information which each statement or report is to include and any documents to be furnished. In all cases except assessment cases the basic obligation to provide the tribunal with certain information and reports is specified in rule 6. As to the disclosure of reports, see page 702. As to the submission of observations on reports furnished, see pages 710 and 928. As to the commissioning of reports by or on behalf of the patient or a nearest relative applicant, see pages 711 and 926. As to the giving of directions that further information or reports be furnished, see page 783.

---

[6] See *e.g.* Mental Health Act 1983, ss.25A(2) and (6), 25D(1) and (2).
[7] Mental Health Review Tribunal Rules 1983, r.2(1), as amended by the Mental Health Review Tribunal (Amendment) Rules 1996.

Patients liable to be detained for treatment or subject to guardianship

6.—(1) The responsible authority shall send a statement to the tribunal and, in the case of a restricted patient, the Secretary of State, as soon as practicable and in any case within 3 weeks of its receipt of the notice of application; and such statement shall contain—

(a) the information specified in Part A of Schedule 1 to these Rules, insofar as it is within the knowledge of the responsible authority; and
(b) the report specified in paragraph 1 of Part B of that Schedule; and
(c) the other reports specified in Part B of that Schedule, in so far as it is reasonably practicable to provide them.

Additional statement if patient restricted

(2) Where the patient is a restricted patient, the Secretary of State shall send to the tribunal, as soon as practicable and in any case within 3 weeks of receipt by him of the authority's statement, a statement of such further information relevant to the application as may be available to him.

Conditionally discharged patients

(3) Where the patient is a conditionally discharged patient, paragraphs (1) and (2) shall not apply and the Secretary of State shall send to the tribunal as soon as practicable, and in any case within 6 weeks of receipt by him of the notice of application, a statement which shall contain—

(a) the information specified in Part C of Schedule 1 to these Rules, insofar as it is within the knowledge of the Secretary of State; and
(b) the reports specified in Part D of that Schedule, in so far as it is reasonably practicable to provide them.

Proceedings in respect of supervision applications

(3A) Where the patient is (or is to be) subject to after-care under supervision paragraph (1) shall not apply and the responsible authority shall send a statement to the tribunal as soon as practicable, and in any case within 3 weeks of the responsible authority's receipt of the notice of application, and this statement shall contain—

(a) the information specified in Part E of Schedule 1 to these Rules, in so far as it is within the knowledge of the responsible authority;
(b) the reports specified in Part F of that Schedule;
(c) the details of the after-care services being (or to be) provided under section 117 of the Act; and
(d) details of any requirements imposed (or to be imposed) on the patient under section 25D of the Act;

and shall be accompanied by copies of the documents specified in paragraph 3 of Part E of that Schedule.

Patients detained under section 2

32.—(1) On receipt of the notice of an assessment application, or a request from the tribunal, whichever may be the earlier, the responsible authority shall provide for the tribunal copies of the admission papers, together with such of the information specified in Part A of Schedule 1 to these Rules as is within the knowledge of the responsible authority and can reasonably be provided in the time available and such of the reports specified in Part B of that Schedule as can reasonably be provided in the time available.

PATIENTS LIABLE TO DETENTION OR UNDER GUARDIANSHIP

Where a patient is liable to be detained in hospital for treatment or is subject to guardianship, rule 6(1) provides that the "responsible authority" shall as soon as practicable, and in any case within three weeks of its receipt of notice of the application, send a statement to the tribunal and, in the case of a restricted patient, to the Secretary of State. There will, of course, be no notice of application if the proceedings were commenced by reference. If the patient's case was referred by the Secretary of State, the tribunal gives notice of the reference to the responsible authority and the three-week period begins with the day on which this notice is received. If the patient's case was instead referred to a tribunal by the managers of the hospital in which he is detained, those managers are also the responsible authority for the purposes of the ensuing tribunal proceedings. No notice of the reference will be given to them, for the obvious reason that they are fully aware that the reference has been made. The rules provide instead that the tribunal shall, on receiving the reference, send to the managers a request for the usual statement and the three-week period begins with the day on which the request is received.

The responsible authority's statement

This information and reports which collectively constitute the authority's statement are specified in Parts A and B of Schedule 1. In addition to providing this statement, the responsible authority must, if practicable and upon being requested to do so by the tribunal, also provide it with any of the information specified in rule 3(2) or 30(2) which was not included in the written application (**620**).

Patients who are liable to be detained in hospital or subject to guardianship

---

Responsible authority's statement

▪ Factual statement ("Part A statement")	Sched. 1, Pt. A	**671**
▪ Medical report	Sched. 1, Pt. B, para. 1	**680**
▪ Social circumstances report	Sched. 1, Pt. B, para. 2	**682**
▪ The views of the authority on the suitability of the patient for discharge	Sched. 1, Pt. B, para. 3	
▪ Any other information or observations on the application which the authority wishes to make	Sched. 1, Pt. B, para. 4	

Additional statement required in restricted cases

▪ Secretary of State's statement	No prescribed format	**700**

The Part A statement

The information specified in Part A of Schedule 1 (known as the "Part A statement") comprises basic factual information about the patient, such as his date of birth, the authority for his detention or guardianship, and details of persons involved in his treatment. The duty here is to provide the specified information insofar as it is within the knowledge of the responsible authority and, in the case of patients detained for assessment, in so far as it can reasonably be provided in the time available.

The medical report

The duty to provide a medical report is unqualified in all cases except those involving patients detained for assessment. In their case, such a report must still be provided if it "can reasonably be provided in the time available"[8] and it is exceptional for there not to be a report. Any medical report must be up-to-date, prepared for the tribunal, and include the relevant medical history and a full report on the patient's mental condition. Patients who have a private guardian will have both an appropriate medical officer/nominated medical attendant and a responsible medical officer. In such cases, it is for the responsible social services authority to decide which of them should prepare the medical report. The tribunal may, however, direct that a further medical report is provided by the other practitioner and that both of them attend the hearing in due course.[9]

The other reports which comprise the authority's statement

The other reports which make up the responsible authority's statement must be provided "in so far as it is reasonably practicable to provide them" and, in the case of patients detained for assessment, in so far as they can reasonably be provided in the time available.[10] These reports are an up-to-date social circumstances report containing the information specified in the schedule, the views of the authority on the suitability of the patient for discharge,[11] and any other information or observations on the application or reference which the authority wishes to make.

Patients detained for assessment

It can be seen that, in the case of patients detained for assessment, the rules provide that, if time permits, the responsible authority shall provide the tribunal with the same reports and information as are required under rule 6 in cases involving other patients liable to detention in hospital. However, in addition, the tribunal must be furnished with a copy of the admission papers and this requirement takes account of the likelihood in practice that the reports and information furnished will be less comprehensive than in other types of case.

Organising the responsible authority's statement

The responsible authority usually asks the hospital's Mental Health Act Administrator to prepare the factual Part A statement; the patient's responsible medical officer to provide the medical report; and requests that the relevant social services authority nominates a social worker to undertake the social circumstances report. The rules do not, however, require that the medical report is prepared by the responsible medical officer, nor that a social worker writes the social circumstances report. In practice, medical reports are not infrequently written by junior medical staff on the consultant's team.

---

[8]   Mental Health Review Tribunal Rules 1983, r.32(1).
[9]   *Ibid.*, rr.14(1) and 15(1).
[10]   *Ibid.*, r.32(1).
[11]   The equivalent provision in the 1960 Rules was rather more pointed and required the responsible authority to set out the reasons why it was not itself willing to discharge the patient.

Restricted cases — the Secretary of State's statement

Because the Secretary of State also has a responsibility for restricted patients, rule 6(2) provides for an additional statement to be furnished in such cases, comprising any further information relevant to the proceedings as may be available to him. The usual form and contents of this statement are dealt with later (**700**).

Provision of separate statements

In cases other than those involving patients detained for assessment, rule 6(4) provides that if the responsible authority or the Secretary of State is of the opinion that part of their statement should be withheld from the applicant or (where he is not the applicant) the patient, on the ground that its disclosure would "adversely affect the health or welfare of the patient or others," that part shall be made in a separate document in which shall be set out the reasons for believing that disclosure would have that effect (**704**). In assessment cases, because of the limited time for preparing even a single report, the rules provide instead that the responsible authority shall indicate if any part of the admission papers or reports should, in their opinion, be withheld from the patient on any of these grounds (**704**).

Service of statements

The rules provide that statements provided under rule 6 may be served either by delivering them by hand or by sending them by pre-paid post to the tribunal office or, as the case may be, the Home Office.[12] It may be noted that the Secretary of State's duty to furnish a statement, and the time limits for doing so, are only activated upon receipt by him of the responsible authority's statement.

Time limits

The primary duty imposed on the responsible authority and the Secretary of State is to send the prescribed statement to the tribunal "as soon as practicable." Rule 26 deals with requests for extensions of time limits prescribed by the rules. Where the statement has not been sent by the time the three week period expires, and no extension of the three week time limit has been applied for, rule 28 applies and it makes provision for dealing with procedural irregularities (**806**). In practice, responsible authorities rarely observe the three-week time limit but, equally, applications for an extension of that time limit are exceptional. Where, in a case involving an unrestricted patient, no medical report has been furnished after five weeks, this is often a good indication that the responsible medical officer intends, or hopes, to himself discharge the patient prior to the hearing. A decision not to furnish a report in such circumstances reflects his opinion that it is unproductive to prepare reports for hearings which are unlikely to take place. Occasionally, the responsible medical officer may defer writing the report for the alternative reason that it will be out of date by the time of the hearing. Although it is for the tribunal, not the responsible authority, to extend time limits if it thinks fit, the absence of effective sanctions has resulted in a relaxed view being taken in practice. Which, in matters concerning individual liberty, is to be deplored.

---

[12]   Mental Health Review Tribunal Rules 1983, r.27.

The rules state that the responsible authority shall "provide" the tribunal with the required reports and information and this takes account of the fact that the reports will often be handed to the Clerk to the Tribunal shortly prior to the commencement of the hearing, rather than sent or delivered to the tribunal's regional office.[13]

Postponement of proceedings

A tribunal is required to send notice of an application to the responsible authority whether or not it postpones consideration of that application.[14] Where consideration is postponed, a further notice of application is sent at least seven days before the expiration of the postponement period.[15] It would appear therefore that the three-week period during which the responsible authority must send their statement commences afresh upon receipt of the second notice of application, even if this is received prior to the expiration of the postponement period.

CASES INVOLVING CONDITIONALLY DISCHARGED PATIENTS

Where an application is made by a conditionally discharged patient, rule 6(3) provides that the Secretary of State shall send a statement to the tribunal as soon as practicable, and in any case within 6 weeks of receipt by him of the notice of application. Not all of the information specified in Parts A and B would be relevant to cases involving conditionally discharged patients, who may have been living in the community without being subject to compulsory powers for some time. In their case, the rules provide that the statement shall instead include the basic factual information specified in Part C of Schedule 1 and the reports specified in Part D. The Part C statement corresponds to the Part A statement required in other cases while the reports specified in Part D are similar to those set out in Part B and also include the observations of the Secretary of State.

Conditionally discharged patients		
Secretary of State's statement		
▪ Factual statement ("Part C statement")	Sched. 1, Pt. C	**675**
▪ Medical report	Sched. 1, Pt. D, para. 1	**680**
▪ Supervisor's report	Sched. 1, Pt. D, para. 2	**682**
▪ Report on patient's home circumstances	Sched. 1, Pt. D, para. 3	**682**
▪ The views of the Secretary of State on the suitability of the patient for absolute discharge	Sched. 1, Pt. D, para. 4	**680**
▪ Any other observations on the application which the Secretary of State wishes to make	Sched. 1, Pt. D, para. 5	**700**

---

[13]   Mental Health Review Tribunal Rules 1983, r.32(1).
[14]   *Ibid.*, r.4(2).
[15]   *Ibid.*, r.9(5).

The Part C statement

As with a Part A statement, the obligation is to provide the information specified in so far as it is within the knowledge of the Secretary of State.

The medical report

Where there is a medical practitioner responsible for the care and supervision of the patient in the community, the statement must in so far as it is reasonably practicable include an up-to-date medical report prepared for the tribunal, including the relevant medical history and a full report on the patient's mental condition. In practice such a report is invariably furnished.

The other reports

Where there is a social worker or probation officer responsible for the patient's supervision in the community, the statement must insofar as is reasonably practicable include an up-to-date report prepared for the tribunal on the patient's progress in the community since discharge from hospital. Again, in practice, there is invariably such a report, which also includes the required details of the patient's home circumstances, and it is equivalent to the social circumstances report provided in other kinds of case. The other matters referred to in the schedule are then furnished in a single separate document completed by the Home Office. These are the views of the Secretary of State on the suitability of the patient for absolute discharge and any other observations on the application which the Secretary of State wishes to make.

Providing separate statements

Rule 6(4) applies to proceedings involving conditionally discharged patients as it applies to restricted patients who are liable to be detained. The Secretary of State may therefore provide the statement in two parts if of the opinion that any part of his statement should be withheld from the applicant on the ground that its disclosure would "adversely affect the health or welfare of the patient or others" (**704**).

Discretionary references

There is necessarily no notice of application where the Secretary of State refers the case of a conditionally discharged patient to a tribunal. Following such a reference, no provision is made in the rules for the Secretary of State's statement to be provided within a particular period.[16]

CASES CONCERNING SUPERVISION APPLICATIONS

As with proceedings involving patients who are liable to be detained in hospital for treatment or subject to guardianship, the responsible authority must send a statement to the tribunal as soon as practicable, and in any case within three weeks of its receipt of the notice of application.[17] And that statement must include a basic factual statement and an up-to-date medical report. However, in this case, details of the

---

[16] Mental Health Review Tribunal Rules 1983, rr.2(1), 6(3), 29(b) and (c). This is probably a drafting error and, in practice, the Secretary of State will no doubt endeavour to provide his statement within the usual six week period.

[17] Mental Health Review Tribunal Rules 1983, r.6(3A), as inserted by Mental Health Review Tribunal (Amendment) Rules 1983, r.4.

after-care services being (or to be) provided under section 117 and of any essential requirements imposed (or to be imposed) on the patient under section 25D must also be provided, together with copies of certain documents. These are the supervision application, any renewal reports, and any record of the modification of the after-care services provided. The precise kind of social report provided depends on whether the patient is in the community subject to after-care under supervision or still waiting to leave hospital.

Tribunal proceedings concerning after-care under supervision

Responsible authority's statement

▪ Factual statement ("Part E statement") including	Rule 6(3A), Sched. 1, Pt. E	**677**
▪ Details of the after-care services provided (or to be provided) and of any essential requirements imposed under section 25D; and		
▪ Copies of the supervision application, any renewal reports, and any record of the modification of the after-care services provided		
▪ Medical report	Sched. 1, Pt. F, para. 1	**680**
▪ Social circumstances report if patient has not yet left hospital	Sched. 1, Pt. F, para. 2	**670** **682**
▪ Supervisor's report if patient has left hospital	Sched. 1, Pt. F, para. 3	**670**

The Part E statement and supporting documents and details

The documents referred to in Part E must be provided, as must details of the after-care services and any essential requirements imposed on the patient. In addition, such of the other information specified in Part E which is within the knowledge of the responsible authority must be furnished to the tribunal.

The medical report

As with cases involving liability to detention and guardianship, the duty to provide a medical report is unqualified. It must be up-to-date, prepared for the tribunal, and include a full report on the patient's mental condition. If the patient has left hospital he will have a community responsible medical officer and this doctor must prepare the report. Thus, in contrast to other kinds of proceedings, the responsible authority cannot ask a doctor other than the person in charge of the patient's treatment to prepare it and nor may the community responsible medical officer delegate the function to a junior member of his team. Nor is it enough for the doctor in charge to sign a report prepared by a junior doctor in his team. He must actually prepare it himself. If the patient has not yet left hospital he will not yet have a community responsible medical officer. In this case, the report is to be prepared by his responsible medical officer or, where there is none, his last responsible medical officer. Again, this duty cannot be delegated. The reference to the patient's last responsible medical officer clearly refers to the situation where a patient has remained in hospital after ceasing to be liable to be detained there for treatment. Since he is no longer detained he does not have a responsible medical officer but, equally, since he is not yet subject to after-care under supervision he does not yet have a community responsible medical officer.

The other reports

Where the patient has not yet left hospital he will similarly not yet have a supervisor. Nor will there be any progress in the community to report on. The rules therefore provide that the statement shall include a social circumstances report the contents of which are in all material respects identical to those of a social circumstances report prepared in respect of a person who is detained or subject to guardianship. This report is to be prepared "by a person professionally concerned with the nature of the patient's social circumstances." That qualification is new, as is the fact that such a report must be provided. The responsible authority cannot assert that it is not reasonably practicable to provide such a report and this reflects the fact that the relevant social services authority as well as health service professionals should all by now be involved in the discharge process. Where the patient has left hospital, a report is required from the patient's supervisor. Again, the question of the practicality of that does not arise and the report must be prepared by that person rather than by any other person willing to act. The new specificity in the rules reflects the fact that there must at all times be a community responsible medical officer and a supervisor, and the duty to provide these reports reflects their central role in the supervision process. The content of the supervisor's report must include details of the patient's progress in the community and home circumstances, as with conditionally discharged patients. It must also include an assessment of the effectiveness of the supervision, together with details of the attitude of the nearest relative and any non-professional primary carers. This reflects the fact that, the tribunal apart, only the community responsible medical officer can terminate after-care under supervision but the patient's nearest relative and any primary carers are generally entitled to be consulted about statutory developments. If the supervisor and non-professionals have reservations about the efficacy of supervision, this requirement ensures that the tribunal knows that the community responsible medical officer's view is not shared by the other relevant individuals. The age-old general requirement that the authority's statement shall include any observations it wishes to make, including its view about the patient's suitability to be discharged, has been omitted. Presumably, this reflects the fact that it has no power to terminate the authority for the patient's supervision.

MHRT RULEs 1983 AND REPORTS : SUMMARY OF PROVISIONS

• Patients detained for assessment	Rule 32, Sched. 1, Pts. A and B.
• Supervision application proceedings	Rule 6(3A), Sched. 1, Pts. E and F.
• All other unrestricted patients	Rule 6(1), Sched. 1, Pts. A and B.
• Conditionally discharged patients	Rule 6(3), Sched. 1, Pts. C and D.
• All other restricted patients	Rule 6(1) and (2), Sched. 1, Pts. A and B.

FACTUAL STATEMENTS

It has been noted that in every kind of tribunal proceedings a factual statement must be provided to the tribunal, setting out basic information about the patient and the history of his detention, guardianship and supervision since the application, order or direction being reviewed was made.

FACTUAL STATEMENT REQUIRED

Patient's status	Statement required
Application or reference concerning patient who is liable to be detained or subject to guardianship	▪ Part A statement
Application or reference concerning conditionally discharged patient	▪ Part C statement
Application or reference concerning patient who is, or is to be, subject to after-care under supervision	▪ Part E statement

---

FORM AND CONTENT OF A "PART A STATEMENT"

The purpose of the Part A statement is to provide the tribunal with certain basic factual information about the patient, including the authority for his detention or guardianship, and details of persons involved in his treatment and care. As under the 1960 Rules, the duty imposed on the responsible authority is limited to providing information which is within its knowledge. There is no requirement that it takes reasonable steps to acquire the information. However, if the statement is inadequate, the tribunal may direct that the responsible authority shall obtain further information about the patient.[18] Part A of Schedule 1 comprises thirteen different paragraphs[19] —

1. The full name of the patient

The Part A statement commences with the patient's full name. In some cases, this may differ from that given on the tribunal application form or the authority for the patient's detention or guardianship. This may be because the patient has changed his name by deed poll, a practice which is not uncommon in special hospital cases and may be an early indication that the circumstances surrounding the index offence attracted widespread publicity or local hostility at the time. Alternatively, an adopted name may be a pointer to the patient's mental state and reflect a delusional belief held by him. Of greater legal significance, the patient may have married or divorced since the time of admission, in which case there will have been a change of nearest relative. The person now qualified to exercise those functions may be willing to

---

[18]   Mental Health Review Tribunal Rules 1983, r.15(1).

[19]   Paragraphs 1 to 6 derive from and, with minor modifications, repeat corresponding provisions in the 1960 Rules. Paragraphs 7–13 were introduced by the 1983 Rules. Under the 1960 Rules, if the responsible authority considered that the applicant was not entitled to make the application, it was also required to state its reasons for this opinion. This particular provision was not re-enacted, although the present rules do allow the authority to include in its statement any additional information or observations it wishes to make.

make an order for the patient's discharge under section 23 but, not having been given a statutory rights leaflet, be unaware of his power to do so. Where a patient's name is incorrectly spelt on a Part II application, or in the supporting medical recommendations, this will generally be inconsequential in terms of the legal validity of his detention. Rarely, a Part II application may not give the name of the person being detained, stating only "a person unknown." Inevitably, this tends to reflect the severity of the patient's condition at the time of his admission.

2. The age of the patient

In guardianship cases, the authorised representative should verify that the patient was aged 16 or over at the time of his reception into guardianship. In any proceedings involving a patient aged under 18, the representative should ascertain whether the patient has a guardian under children's legislation, is in care, or the subject of a residence order. If so, the usual provisions as to who is his nearest relative will not apply (**106**). Where the person who has been treated as the nearest relative is not in fact the nearest relative, any tribunal proceedings commenced by that person will be invalid, as may be any Part II application under which the patient is detained or subject to guardianship. A guardianship application may not be made in respect of a ward of court. Nor may any other application under Part II, or a tribunal application, be made except with the court's leave.

3. The date of admission of the patient to the hospital or mental nursing home in which the patient is currently detained or liable to be detained, or of the reception of the patient into guardianship.

When considered together with paragraph (5), the date of admission recorded in paragraph (3) enables a tribunal to know whether the patient has been transferred under section 19 or section 123 and, in many cases, whether he was originally admitted to hospital as an informal patient.

4. Where the patient is treated in a mental nursing home under contractual arrangements with a health authority, the name of that authority.

In non-assessment cases, the Health Authority and the registration authority of that home will be parties to the proceedings and must, on receipt of the authority's statement by the tribunal, be given notice of the proceedings.[20] The Health Authority itself has power to discharge the patient and either he or his authorised representative may wish to invite it to do so.[21]

5. Details of the original authority for the detention or guardianship of the patient, including the Act of Parliament and the section of that Act by reference to which detention was authorised and details of any subsequent renewal or change in authority for detention.

Apart from providing basic information about the history of the patient's detention or guardianship, paragraph 5 serves three purposes. When considered with paragraph (9), it enables the tribunal to ascertain whether the application or reference is

---

[20] Mental Health Review Tribunal Rules 1983, rr.2(1), 7(a) and (e).
[21] Mental Health Act 1983, ss.23–24. For the same reason, details of any NHS trust contracting with a mental nursing home should be included here. Otherwise, the reference to such a trust in rule 7, which was inserted by the Mental Health Review Tribunal (Amendment) Rules 1996, is ineffective.

authorised (**604**), to identify any break in the authority for the patient's detention and also, therefore, to know whether consideration of the application may be postponed (**641**).

6. The form of mental disorder from which the patient is recorded as suffering in the authority for detention [including amendments, if any, under section 16 or 72(5) of the Act, but excluding cases within section 5 of the Criminal Procedure (Insanity) Act 1964[22]].

Although not required by paragraph 6, details of any reclassification effected under section 20 and 21B may also be entered here, in order to ensure that the tribunal is aware of the patient's present classification and of all previous reclassifications.[23]

7. The name of the responsible medical officer and the period which the patient has spent under the care of that officer.

The functions of the patient's responsible medical officer have already been summarised (**147**). Renewal reports furnished under section 20 and any outstanding Form 38 should be checked by an authorised representative, to confirm that they were completed by the responsible medical officer.

8. Where another registered medical practitioner is or has recently been largely concerned in the treatment of the patient, the name of that practitioner and the period which the patient has spent under his care.

If a private guardian has been appointed, he is required to appoint a "nominated medical attendant" for the patient, who is the "appropriate medical officer" for the purposes of sections 16 (reclassification) and 20 (renewals of guardianship). Where a patient is residing in a hospital under leave of absence, a situation which most commonly arises in cases involving special hospital patients, the name of the doctor in charge of the patient's treatment at the hospital where he has leave to reside should appear here. The responsible authority may sometimes provide details of the registrar who has been involved in the patient's treatment; of the patient's General Practitioner; or of the consultant psychiatrist usually responsible for the patient's treatment (in cases where all patients on a locked ward, or an admission ward, temporarily have the same responsible medical officer).

9. The dates of all previous tribunal hearings in relation to the patient, the decisions reached at such hearings and the reasons given. (In restricted patient cases this requirement does not relate to decisions before September 30, 1983[24]).

When considered in conjunction with paragraph (5), the information will enable the tribunal to determine whether the application or reference is authorised or its consideration may be postponed. Where the previous tribunal deferred a direction for the conditional discharge of a restricted patient until suitable arrangements could

---

[22] Patients detained under section 5 of the Criminal Procedure (Insanity) Act 1964 do not have a classification although the responsible authority often states here that the patient suffers from "mental illness." Because of this, tribunals have reclassified such patients.

[23] The paragraph has been copied from the 1960 Rules and so fails to take account of the additional reclassification provisions introduced in sections 20(9) and 21B of the 1983 Act.

[24] On account of the fact that, prior to 30 September 1983, tribunals had no power to discharge a restricted patient.

be made for him in the community, but those arrangements have not been made by the time his case next comes before a tribunal, its decision is treated as never having been made.[25]

10. Details of any proceedings in the Court of Protection and of any receivership order made in respect of the patient.

Where the patient's financial affairs are subject to the Court of Protection, the Court must, on receipt of the authority's statement by the tribunal, be given notice of the proceedings and, accordingly, becomes a party to those proceedings.[26] The court will sign legal aid forms on the patient's behalf and need to authorise any legal fees incurred by an authorised representative if a private arrangement is contemplated. Where a patient is both subject to guardianship under the Act and under the Court of Protection, it may be possible for the authorised representative to argue that the guardianship is superfluous to the patient's welfare.[27]

11. The name and address of the patient's nearest relative or of any other person who is exercising that function.

The person exercising the functions of the nearest relative must, unless he made the application, be given notice of the proceedings and thereupon becomes a party to them.[28] The information should be carefully verified with the patient since mistakes are commonplace. Where the person recorded as exercising the functions is a person appointed by the county court under section 29 (**111**) or authorised under regulation 14 of the 1983 regulations (**109**), a copy of the relevant court order or authority should be obtained. Social workers sometimes believe that a county court order made under section 29 remains in force until discharged by the court and section 3 applications may be made over a number of years on this assumption, without the patient's nearest relative being consulted. Similarly, some social workers believe that a nearest relative may informally delegate his functions to another person without using the procedure set out in regulation 14. In the case of Irish patients, any relatives ordinarily resident in the Republic must be discounted unless the patient himself ordinarily resides there.[29]

12. The name and address of any other person who takes a close interest in the patient.

Persons recorded here may include other relatives, friends, or an advocate appointed for the patient under a local scheme. They may be willing to give oral evidence or to provide a letter in support of the patient's application for discharge, or be able to provide support if the patient is discharged. With the patient's permission, the authorised representative will usually wish to discuss the case with any person whose details are recorded here.

---

[25] Mental Health Act 1983, s.73(7).
[26] Mental Health Review Tribunal Rules 1983, rr.2(1) and 7(c).
[27] If the main purpose behind the guardianship is to require a patient who neglected himself when living alone to reside in supported accommodation, it is often unlikely that the court will approve the payment of rent to a private landlord, in which case the patient will be unable to move even if the guardian's authority is rescinded.
[28] Mental Health Review Tribunal Rules 1983, rr.2(1) and 7(d).
[29] Mental Health Act 1983, s.26(5)(a).

13. Details of any leave of absence granted to the patient during the previous 2 years, including the duration of such leave and particulars of the arrangements made for the patient's residence while on leave.

The details of any leave of absence which has been granted should be scrutinised. If the patient has leave to reside at a hospital other than that where he is liable to be detained, the hospital where he is liable to be detained is the responsible authority for the purposes of the tribunal proceedings.[30] Furthermore, the conventional view is that an unrestricted patient's liability to detention cannot be renewed if he has leave to reside at another hospital (**282**). Any unrestricted patient who, on a day prior to 1 April 1996, was continuously absent from hospital with leave for a period of six months, ceased to be liable to be detained at the expiration of that period (**300**).

FORM AND CONTENT OF A "PART C STATEMENT"

Not all of the information required in a Part A statement would be relevant to cases involving conditionally discharged patients, since they are living in the community without being subject to compulsory powers.[31] In their case, the rules provide that the more limited factual information specified in Part C of Schedule 1 shall be furnished instead. However, in addition to the limited information specified in Part C, a tribunal may direct that further information be furnished.[32] The authorised representative will usually wish to obtain the following supplementary information contained in Part A statements insofar as it is not provided under Part D: details of any other medical practitioners who are or have been recently concerned with the patient's treatment; the dates of all previous tribunal hearings in relation to the patient (so as to verify his entitlement to make the application and to know the reasons for previous decisions); details of any proceedings in the Court of Protection and of any receivership order made in respect of the patient; details of any persons who take a close interest in the patient. The representative will also wish to see a copy of the restriction order and he will require details of the original conditions of discharge and any subsequent variations of them.

1. The full name of the patient.

Paragraph 1 of the Part C statement is the same as paragraph 1 of the Part A statement (**671**).

2. The age of the patient.

Paragraph 2 of the Part C statement is also the same as the corresponding paragraph of the Part A statement (**672**). A person under the age of 14 may not be committed to the Crown Court under section 43(1) with a view to the making of a restriction order. That limitation apart, a restriction order may be made in respect of an offender of any age.

---

[30]   Mental Health Act 1983, ss.17–18; Mental Health Review Tribunal Rules 1983, r.2(1).
[31]   They cannot be compelled to adhere to the conditions of discharge although the option of recall is, of course, available to the Secretary of State.
[32]   Mental Health Review Tribunal Rules, r.15(1).

3. The history of the patient's present liability to detention including details of offence(s), and the dates of the original order or direction and of the conditional discharge.

A conditionally discharged patient is liable to be detained in the sense that the relevant hospital order or transfer direction remains in force notwithstanding his discharge from hospital and he may be recalled to hospital for further treatment. The details of the index offence should enable the representative to obtain the court papers or the trial solicitor's file. This is particularly important if the patient's case was disposed of following a finding that he was not guilty by reason of insanity or unfit to plead. It may still be possible to hold a trial, although this is rare following conditionally discharge. If the restrictions cease to have effect during the proceedngs, the patient is deemed to be absolutely discharged and his tribunal application is similarly deemed withdrawn.[33] This will be the effect if a limited-term restriction order, or the prison sentence of a patient liable to detention under section 45A or 47, expires. If the patient is recalled prior to the hearing then his application is deemed withdrawn. However, if he is admitted to hospital informally or under Part II, any tribunal proceedings initiated under section 75 continue until such time as he is formally recalled to hospital under section 42.

4. The form of mental disorder from which the patient is recorded as suffering in the authority for detention. (Not applicable to cases within section 5 of the Criminal Procedure (Insanity) Act 1964.)

Paragraph 4 of the Part C statement corresponds to paragraph 6 of the Part A statement (**673**). However, the reclassification provisions in sections 16, 20 and 21B do not apply to restricted patients. The fact that a restricted patient is not for the time being suffering from mental disorder does not mean that he is entitled to be absolutely discharged.[34]

5. The name and address of any medical practitioner responsible for the care and supervision of the patient in the community and the period which the patient has spent under the care of that practitioner.

Conditionally discharged patients do not have a responsible medical officer. However, it will almost invariably be a condition of discharge that the patient attends appointments with a medical practitioner (his medical supervisor) and complies with any programme of treatment prescribed by him. Failure to do so may lead to the patient's recall to hospital. The medical supervisor will be asked to prepare a report for the tribunal (**663, 681**).

6. The name and address of any social worker or probation officer responsible for the care and supervision of the patient in the community and the period which the patient has spent under the care of that person.

It will generally be a condition of discharge that the patient submits to supervision by a social worker or probation officer and attends appointments with that person. He will also be required to prepare a tribunal report (**663, 682**).

---

[33] Mental Health Review Tribunal Rules 1983, r.19(2).
[34] See *R. v. Merseyside Mental Health Review Tribunal, ex p. K.* [1990] 1 All E.R. 694, C.A. (**527**)

FORM AND CONTENT OF A "PART E STATEMENT"

Where the tribunal proceedings involve a patient who is subject to after-care under supervision, or is to be so subject when he leaves hospital, the factual statement required is that set out in Part E. The statement must be accompanied by the various documents referred to in paragraph 3 below (**436, 663, 668**).

1. The full name, address and age of the patient.

As in the case of guardianship, a supervision application may not be made in respect of a patient under 16 years of age.[35] If the patient's address is not one within the area of the tribunal dealing with the case, the most likely explanation is that the patient's application has been sent to the wrong tribunal. If so, the tribunal has no jurisdiction.[36]

2. The date of the acceptance of the supervision application in respect of the patient.

A supervision application may not be accepted after the date on which the patient leaves hospital in the statutory sense, that is after the day on which he has both ceased to be liable to be detained for treatment and ceased to be an in-patient. Conversely, if a patient does not leave hospital in this statutory sense during the six month period following the application's acceptance, the authority to supervise him ceases at the expiration of that period.

3. A copy of the original supervision application, details of the after-care services provided (or to be provided) under section 117 of the Act, details of any requirements imposed (or to be imposed) under section 25D(1) of the Act, a copy of any report furnished under section 25G(3)(b) of the Act in relation to renewal of the supervision application and a copy of any record of modification of the after-care services provided.

According to the Act, a supervision application must be "accompanied" by details of the after-care services to be provided and of any requirements to be imposed under section 25D. The details of the after-care services will no doubt usually consist of a copy of the after-care plan which was attached to the application. As to the imposition of essential requirements, the prescribed application form includes a space for setting out the requirements which the responsible medical officer personally considers should be imposed. However, he has no power to impose any requirements on the patient by virtue of his position as the patient's responsible medical officer. Such requirements may only be imposed after the application has been accepted and then only by both responsible after-care bodies acting jointly — unless they have authorised some other body, such as an NHS trust, to undertake this function on their behalf. If the after-care services and any requirements imposed on the patient have subsequently been modified, the tribunal is to be furnished with any record of those modifications so that it knows the present position. Authorised representatives will wish to scrutinise the application and to ensure that the persons

---

[35]   Mental Health Act 1983, s.25A(1)(b), as inserted by s.1(1) of the Mental Health (Patients in the Community) Act 1995. It was the date when the application was made rather than the date on which it was accepted which was material.

[36]   Mental Health Act 1983, s.77(3).

entitled to be consulted prior to any application, renewal report or modifications being made were consulted (**455**).

4. Any reclassification of the form of mental disorder from which the patient is recorded as suffering in the supervision application reported in accordance with section 25F(1) of the Act.

Reclassification under section 25F gives rise to a right to apply to a tribunal (**611**). However, it has no consequences in terms of the duration of the authority for the patient's supervision or the likelihood of it being renewed for a further period: the renewal criteria are the same in all cases, whatever the form of disorder recorded. Where, after the date of any report reclassifying the patient under section 25F(1), the authority for the patient's supervision has been renewed then his current classification will be the form or forms of disorder specified on the last renewal report.

5. The name of the person who is (or is to be) the community responsible medical officer and the period (if any) during which he has been in charge of the patient's medical treatment.

According to the Act, a supervision application must be "accompanied" by statements from the persons who are to be the patient's community responsible medical officer and supervisor, stating that they are to fulfil those statutory roles. However, these statements have been incorporated into the supervision application form. Part II of the application form comprises these signed statements. If the patient is subject to after-care under supervision, a medical report prepared by the community responsible medical officer will form part of the responsible authority's statement. If the arrangements have changed by the time the patient leaves hospital, the interested parties must be informed of this fact when he leaves hospital and, similarly, they must be notified of any subsequent changes (**443**).

6. The name of the person who is (or is to be) the patient's supervisor.

See **424**. If the patient is subject to after-care under supervision, a report prepared by the supervisor will form part òf the responsible authority's statement.

7. Where a registered medical practitioner other than the community responsible medical officer is or has recently been largely concerned in the treatment of the patient, details of the name and address of the practitioner and the period which the patient has spent under his care.

If the patient has not yet left hospital, it will be appropriate to provide details here of who is his responsible medical officer. While a supervised patient's community responsible medical officer must be approved under section 12 of the Act, his General Practitioner may nevertheless also be involved in providing treatment. Until the patient leaves hospital only a tribunal may terminate the authority to supervise him.

8. The name and address of any place where the patient (if he has been discharged) is receiving medical treatment.

This is likely to be the out-patient department of the local psychiatric unit or a community mental health centre managed by the same NHS trust.

9. The name and address of the hospital where the patient was detained or liable to be detained when the supervision application was made.

This information somewhat duplicates paragraph 3 because the supervision application includes these details.

10. The dates of any previous tribunal hearings in relation to the patient since he became subject to after-care under supervision, the decisions reached at such hearings and the reasons given.

Although a patient does not become subject to after-care under supervision until he has ceased to be liable to be detained and left hospital, it would clearly be useful to include here particulars of any hearings concerning the same supervision application which took place before the patient left hospital. Likewise, if the supervision application was made in response to a recommendation made by a tribunal under section 72(3A), it would be important to know that and the reasons given by the previous tribunal for its recommendation. Even if these points do not apply, the reasons why previous tribunals did not discharge the patient from liability to detention for treatment may contain important information about the perceived risks to his health and safety, or to others, outside hospital.

11. Details of any proceedings in the Court of Protection and of any receivership order made in respect of the patient.

Where the patient's financial affairs are subject to the Court of Protection, the Court must, on receipt of the Part A statement by the tribunal, be given notice of the proceedings and, accordingly, becomes a party to those proceedings (**779**).[37]

12. The name and address of the patient's nearest relative or of any other person who is exercising that function.

The person who appears to be the patient's nearest relative must, unless he made the application, be given notice of the proceedings and thereupon becomes a party to them.[38] This new rule is inconsistent with the statutory framework. The Act itself provides that, unless dangerousness is an issue, the patient may prevent his nearest relative from being consulted about a statutory step being taken, in which case that relative is not to be told that it has been taken (**456**). It may therefore often be the case that, in accordance with the patient's wishes and rights, the nearest relative has not been told of the supervision application's acceptance or notified of subsequent developments, in terms of modifications to the after-care plan, and so forth. Nevertheless, the rules provide that the relative automatically becomes a party to any subsequent tribunal proceedings and so is made aware of the fact that the patient is subject to statutory supervision. The *vires* of the rule is therefore open to question insofar as it seems to require the service of such a notice in all cases. It should be noted that any county court order previously made under section 29(3)(c) or (d) ceases to have effect when the patient ceases to be liable to be detained. Accordingly, the authority of the person appointed by the county court to exercise the nearest relative's functions also ceases at that time, and the actual nearest relative's functions are again exercisable in person.

---

[37]   Mental Health Review Tribunal Rules 1983, rr.2(1) and 7(c).
[38]   Mental Health Review Tribunal Rules 1983, rr.2(1) and 7(bb), as inserted by r.5(a) of The Mental Health Review Tribunal (Amendment) Rules 1996.

13. The name and address of any other person who takes a close interest in the patient.

Non-professionals who are considered to play a substantial part in the patient's care, or will do when he leaves hospital, have quite extensive statutory rights to be consulted before any statutory step other than reclassification is taken. In particular, they must be consulted before an application is made or before the authority conferred by it is renewed or terminated. In keeping with this, once the patient has left hospital, the report prepared for the tribunal by his supervisor must include a report on the attitude of such a person to the supervision. As to other persons who may be listed here, see page 674.

THE MEDICAL REPORT

A medical report must be provided in all cases except those involving conditionally discharged patients who do not have a doctor. However, this caveat is of theoretical interest only and in a practice a medical report is always prepared. The content of any psychiatric report is the product of two things: the content of the patient's mind interpreted by the content of the doctor's mind. The evidence of mental disorder consists of facts (things actually said to or observed by the writer), inferences from these facts, hearsay (facts communicated to the doctor), inferences from hearsay, assumptions and suppositions about matters not reported or observed, and presumptions about what causes and alleviates severe mental distress. Many matters presented as fact are nothing more tangible than suppositions or inferences based on the assumed content of the patient's mind. The quality and accuracy of health service records, and of Home Office records relating to the index offence, are highly variable and necessarily mostly hearsay. There is often scope for hearsay gradually to acquire by virtue of frequent repetition the status of hard fact, or for established facts to become distorted, and the Mental Health Act Commission has been involved in several cases where serious errors have crept into a case history.[39] While a report or case note will record any symptoms or signs of mental disorder, it will not specify all of the questions asked and the matters raised which, when dealt with, were indicative of normal mental functioning. That being so, a report or note may conceal a great deal of normal mental phenomena and the greater truth is sometimes to be found not in what a report says but in what it does not say. The representative must seek out and draw attention to this silent evidence.

Patients liable to be detained or subject to guardianship

A medical report provided under rule 6 or 32 must be up-to-date; prepared for the tribunal; include the relevant medical history; and include a report on the patient's mental condition.[40] The obligation to furnish such a report in respect of a patient who is subject to guardianship or detained otherwise than for assessment is absolute and not qualified by words such as "insofar as it is reasonably practicable."[41] In section 2 cases, a medical report is required if it can reasonably be provided in the time available. Exceptionally, only oral medical evidence is given.[42]

---

[39]   Mental Health Act Commission, *Second Biennial Report 1985–87* (H.M.S.O., 1987), para. 18.4.
[40]   Mental Health Review Tribunal Rules 1983, Sched. 1, Pt. B, para. 1; Sched. 1, Part D para. 1.
[41]   As was the case with the other reports specified in Part B of the Schedule.
[42]   Mental Health Review Tribunal Rules 1983, r.32(2).

Conditionally discharged patients

A medical report is required if it is reasonably practicable for the Secretary of State to provide one.[43] In theory, there might be no medical practitioner responsible for the patient's care and supervision in the community, in which case a report is not required.[44]

Patients subject to after-care under supervision

An up-to-date medical report prepared for the tribunal, and including the relevant medical history and a full report on the patient's mental condition, must be provided. In the case of patients subject to after-care under supervision, this must be prepared by the patient's community responsible medical officer. In the case of patients who have not left hospital and who are therefore not yet subject to after-care under supervision, it must be prepared by the patient's responsible medical officer or, where there is none, his last responsible medical officer (**669**).

MEDICAL ISSUES

Medical issues are largely dealt with in Part II of this book and the reader is referred to the following material relevant to any consideration of the medical report. Chapter 17 examines basic concepts such as disorder, disease, illness, psychosis, and what constitutes normal mental health. Chapter 18 explains the assessment process, in particular the mental state examination and special procedures such as EEGs and blood tests. Part of this chapter is devoted to explaining medical terms used in psychiatric reports, and the various terms are listed in the index. Chapter 19 then deals with the diagnosis and classification of medical disorders. The various treatments for mental disorder are outlined in chapter 20, which includes details of the common side-effects of medication, abbreviations used in prescribing, and the reasons why treatment may be ineffective. The remaining chapters in Part III focus on particular forms of mental disorder and their treatment: personality disorders (chapter 21); mood disorders (chapter 22); schizophrenia and related psychoses (chapter 23); and organic disorders, such as dementia (chapter 24). Chapter 16 deals with the role of the authorised representative and includes advice on taking a case history and matters such as questions to put to medical witnesses. Risk assessment and health service guidelines concerning discharge from hospital are considered in chapter 12.The organisation and management of the National Health Service and the functions of professionals employed within that service were covered in chapter 3. Defective or inadequate medical reports (**783**), directions for the preparation of further reports (**783**), the commissioning of independent medical reports (**711, 926**), and the medical member's examination (**793**) are considered where indicated.

---

[43] Mental Health Review Tribunal Rules 1983, r.6(3)(b). The exemption from furnishing a report where it is not reasonably practicable to provide one does not extend to medical reports concerning detained patients. The purpose of the phrase appears to be to provide for events outside the control of the responsible authority. Although the hospital managers may require a medical practitioner to prepare a report, ultimately they may only request that a local social services authority instructs a social worker to prepare the social circumstances report. Similarly, the Secretary of State relies on the willingness of medical and social supervisors to prepare tribunal reports at his request. Thus, where such requests are not complied with, or not within the specified time limits, the responsible authority or the Home Secretary is not *per se* in breach of rule 6. The appropriate remedy is for the tribunal to then direct that the missing report be furnished, under rule 15(1).

[44] *Ibid.*, Sched. 1, Pt. D, para. 1.

SOCIAL CIRCUMSTANCES AND SUPERVISORS' REPORTS

The main purpose of a social circumstances report is to inform the tribunal of what are likely to be the patient's circumstances if he is discharged and no longer subject to compulsion. In particular, what medical and social services, and other kinds of support, will be available to him. These matters not only have a bearing on the tribunal's discretionary power of discharge but also affect whether the criteria for mandatory discharge are fulfilled. This is because whether a tribunal is satisfied that further treatment in hospital is unnecessary, or that continued liability to detention there is inappropriate, may depend on the existence of a viable alternative. As to this, health and social services authorities have a duty under section 117 of the 1983 Act to provide after-care to patients who have been detained in hospital for treatment. The nature of this obligation was considered in chapter 6. The existence of separate health and social services authorities and concern about the premature discharge of patients has resulted in there being a number of enactments, directions, guidelines and codes concerning the discharge of patients and their after-care. The most important of them, and the way in which they interrelate, are summarised in the following chapter (**745 et seq.**). As to inadequate social circumstances reports, and the commissioning of further reports, see pages 783 and 926.

CONDITIONALLY DISCHARGED PATIENTS

If there is a social worker or probation officer responsible for the patient's care and supervision in the community, the rules provide that an up-to-date report shall be prepared for the tribunal on the patient's progress in the community since discharge from hospital and also a report on the patient's home circumstances. The role of a supervisor is not the same as that of a key-worker or social worker although in practice the same person fulfils all of those functions. Supervision literally means to oversee and this function is one of monitoring the patient's mental state, functioning and behaviour in the community and ensuring that appropriate action is taken if his circumstances appear to be unsatisfactory. A social worker may therefore be both the agent of the local authority, in terms of co-ordinating and providing after-care, and an agent of the Home Secretary, in terms of reporting on the patient's progress and any developments which have a bearing on the exercise of the latter's functions.

AFTER-CARE UNDER SUPERVISION

A patient who has not yet left hospital will not yet have a supervisor. Nor will there be any progress in the community to report on. The rules therefore provide that the statement shall include a social circumstances report the contents of which are in all material respects identical to those of a social circumstances report prepared in respect of a person who has appealed against his detention or guardianship. This report is to be prepared "by a person professionally concerned with the nature of the patient's social circumstances." Where the patient has left hospital, a report is required from the patient's supervisor. The content of the supervisor's report must include details of the patient's progress in the community and home circumstances, as with conditionally discharged patients. It must also include an assessment of the effectiveness of the supervision, together with details of the attitude of the nearest relative and any non-professional carers. As to the precise nature of the obligation to provide a social circumstances or supervisor's report, and the reasoning behind the drafting, see page 670.

Mental Health Review Tribunal Rules 1983, Schedule 1, Part F

REPORTS RELATING TO PATIENTS SUBJECT (OR TO BE SUBJECT)
TO AFTER-CARE UNDER SUPERVISION

2. Where the patient is subject to after-care under supervision an up-to-date report prepared for the tribunal by the patient's supervisor including reports on the following—

(a) the patient's home and family circumstances, including the attitude of the patient's nearest relative or the person so acting and the attitude of any person who plays a substantial part in the care of the patient but is not professionally concerned with any of the after-care services provided to the patient;

(b) his progress in the community whilst subject to after-care under supervision including an assessment of the effectiveness of that supervision.

3. Where the patient has not yet left hospital an up-to-date social circumstances report prepared for the tribunal by a person professionally concerned with the nature of the patient's social circumstances including reports on the following—

(a) the patient's home and family circumstances, including the attitude of the patient's nearest relative or the person so acting;
(b) the opportunities for employment or occupation and the housing facilities which would be available to the patient upon his discharge from hospital;
(c) the availability of community support and relevant medical facilities;
(d) the financial circumstances of the patient.

ALL OTHER CASES

In any case involving a patient who is liable to be detained or subject to guardianship, the responsible authority is required to provide the tribunal with a social circumstances report insofar as that is reasonably practicable and, in the case of patients detained for assessment, insofar as it can reasonably be provided in the time available.[45] The various reports collectively referred to as the "social circumstances report" serve to inform the tribunal of the alternatives to in-patient treatment and the patient's likely circumstances should he be discharged by the tribunal and leave hospital. The social circumstances report should include evidence of discharge and after-care planning even if the view of those responsible for the patient's treatment and care is that discharge is presently inappropriate.

Legal requirements

Any social circumstances report shall be up-to-date, prepared for the tribunal, and include reports on the following [46]—

---

[45]   Mental Health Review Tribunal Rules 1983, r.32(1).
[46]   *Ibid.*, Sched. 1, Pt. B, para. 2. The equivalent provision in the 1960 Rules required the responsible authority only to provide an account of the facilities available for care of the patient if the authority for detention or guardianship were discharged.

a. the patient's home and family circumstances, including the attitude of the patient's nearest relative or the person so acting (**687**);

b. the opportunities for employment or occupation and the housing facilities which would be available to the patient if discharged (**687, 690**);

c. the availability of community support and relevant medical facilities (**687, 690**);

d. the financial circumstances of the patient (**692**).

FORMAT OF THE REPORT

Before considering these different requirements, and any legal provisions relating to them, it is useful to set out a sample report illustrating the basic format. The following example includes material not required under the rules, in particular details of the medical history. This is partly because the medical report is often wholly inadequate but mainly because it is important to set out the basis of any opinion that the patient can or cannot be treated or cared for in the community, whether informally or under guardianship or statutory supervision. Ultimately, however, it is a matter of personal preference as to whether the report goes further than merely detailing the factual information specified in the Schedule.

MENTAL HEALTH REVIEW TRIBUNAL

Social circumstances report dated 1 March 1997

John Smith	*Date of birth: 05.04.62*
Pinel Ward, Metropolitan Hospital	*Section 3*
Address at time of admission	*45 Clove Gardens, London N5*

Introduction

The relevant statutory events, in terms of the use made of compulsory powers, should first be briefly recited. The information given here should include the date of the patient's admission to hospital; the sections of the Act under which he has been detained during the present period of continuous detention; the date on which the present authority to detain him was last renewed; any transfers to different hospitals; and any extended leave of absence which is still in force.

Brief example

John Smith was admitted to the Metropolitan Hospital as an informal patient on 3 January 1995. On 6 January 1995, he was detained under section 2 and a section 3 application was then accepted on 21 January 1995. The current authority for his detention will expire at midnight on 20 January 1998, unless he is discharged before then or the authority is renewed for a further period.

Sources of information

The next paragraph should set out the sources of the information referred to in the report, the writer's position and involvement in the case, and any legal responsibilities of the local authority employing him.

Brief example

I am an approved social worker employed by [authority], which is the local social services authority which will be responsible for providing after-care to this patient under section 117 when he leaves hospital. The patient's case has been allocated to me. My report is based on interviews with the patient on 20 February and 26 February. I have recently spoken at length with Dr. Richard Smith, the patient's consultant and responsible medical officer, and with Mrs. Rachel Smith, the patient's mother and nearest relative. I have also spoken to ward staff and have had access to medical, nursing and social work notes.

The current admission

Events surrounding the patient's admission and the present use of compulsory powers should be summarised early on in the report since they provide the context for what follows. For convenience, the recent history can be dealt with in three stages: the events leading up to the admission, the admission itself, and the developments since admission. The future provision of treatment and after-care requires knowing for how long the patient has been ill, what triggered the present illness or relapse, whether he unilaterally stopped treatment, and his attitude to voluntary treatment. With compulsory admission, matters usually come to a crisis and some event occurs which persuades family members or professionals that there is no other realistic course of action. It is important to identify what occurred immediately prior to the decision to invoke compulsory powers. Having established the general history and the circumstances preceding and surrounding the use of compulsory powers, the way in which matters have developed since admission should briefly be dealt with. It is particularly important to highlight any matters which have a bearing on the suitability of any facilities in the community which the report later refers to: compliance with treatment in hospital, periods of absence without leave, episodes of violence or self-harm, etc.

Home and family circumstances

The rules require a report on the patient's home and family circumstances including information about the attitude of the nearest relative. These details enable the tribunal to know the level of family support likely to be available to the patient if discharged; why the nearest relative has not exercised any personal power to discharge the patient; alternatively, whether he would discharge the patient if he had that power. It is useful to list here close family members (any spouse or partner, parents, children, and siblings), and to specify their ages and relationship to the patient, in order to verify that the nearest relative has been correctly identified. That person's views can then be summarised.

Accommodation

The rules require a report on the patient's home circumstances and the housing facilities available to him if discharged. If the client has no accommodation to go to but is detained for treatment, he will be entitled to after-care under section 117 on leaving hospital. If he needs to reside in supported accommodation, but is reluctant to do so, guardianship, after-care under supervision, or conditional discharge may need to be considered.

Employment and occupational opportunities

The rules require a report on the patient's opportunities for employment or occupation if discharged. The client's employment history may reveal information about the duration and causes of any illness or relapse; may help to define the severity of any illness or disability; is often a good, if not wholly reliable, yardstick against which to assess his current level of mental functioning; and a pointer to the likely opportunities for him in the immediate future. Improving his underlying mental state and self-esteem, as opposed to merely suppressing the worst symptoms, often necessitates improving his social situation and opportunities. There remains a tendency to regard people with schizophrenia as unfit for any sort of employment or training which does not involve mundane tasks. However, it is often better to emphasise the importance of accepting medical treatment and supervision as ways of achieving stability and maximising the prospect of returning to some activity which interests the client and which he finds fulfilling. The risk of non-compliance with treatment and relapse may well be greater if the message is that insight and treatment involves living the life of an invalid. For most people, treatment is a means to an end and there is little incentive in accepting that one is ill and would benefit from medication if the benefits of doing so are put in these terms.

Financial circumstances

The rules require a report on the patient's financial circumstances. This part of the report should set out his savings, assets and sources of income; the benefits currently being received; his entitlement to benefits following discharge; all known financial liabilities; any litigation, current or pending, concerning debts; and any arrangements which have been made for managing his financial affairs, *e.g.* the appointment of a receiver or appointee or the execution of a trust or an enduring power of attorney.

Client's physical health

Any relevant medical history should be briefly summarised. Although the rules require the responsible authority to furnish a medical report which includes the relevant medical history, it is important to highlight any physical illnesses or disabilities which may necessitate special social services provision in the community, or which may undermine the effectiveness of any programme of treatment and care outside hospital, *e.g.* addiction to drugs or alcohol.

Forensic history

Because social services authorities are involved in providing after-care, it is important to draw attention to any evidence which suggests that the client may require careful supervision following discharge or be unsuitable for discharge. In restriction order cases, the circumstances of the index offence should be explored, paying particular attention to the considerations considered by the Home Office to be relevant when assessing a patient's suitability to be discharged. The forensic history is an important indicator of the likelihood of harm to others associated with mental disorder, although people with mental health problems may be predisposed to crime as much as any other individual from the same background. Because diverting people away from the criminal courts is now widely encouraged, the absence of criminal convictions does not necessarily reflect an absence of criminal conduct.

Psychiatric history

Any proposals about after-care, and the suitability of resources outside hospital, should take account of the success or failure of previous arrangements made for the patient. In general terms, events in the past reveal the nature of any illness, and the patient's response to it and to treatment, and the purpose of taking any history is to look for patterns of events which have an explanatory or predictive value. The link may be that the patient tends to default on treatment and then relapses, that the illness is cyclical in nature, or that particular anniversaries or kinds of event precipitate periods of illness. It is helpful to obtain a clear idea of the duration of any periods which the client has spent outside hospital relative to periods spent as an in-patient. If all or most of the periods of in-patient treatment are relatively short or relatively prolonged, the discharge process and tribunal case can be approached with that in mind.

After-care, community support and medical facilities

The rules require a report on the availability of community support and relevant medical facilities. These should be summarised in detail. The report should then analyse whether the community resources are a viable alternative detention and treatment in hospital. If further time is required to perfect a realistic programme of after-care, it may nevertheless be the case that the client is willing to remain in hospital informally while these arrangements are made.

Conclusion and recommendations

The report should conclude by summarising (a) the most important conclusions drawn in the course of the report and (b) the writer's recommendations.

HOME AND FAMILY CIRCUMSTANCES

The details of the patient's home and family circumstances should reveal who is the nearest relative. Having ascertained that, any Part II application should be examined to verify that the nearest relative was correctly identified at the time of admission. If the report indicates that the nearest relative considers that a Part II patient should be discharged, it may be that he is not aware of his power to make an order for discharge under section 23 (**610**). If the patient was residing with a family member prior to admission but that family member is not willing for him to return then, unless the patient has a right of occupancy, alternative accommodation will be required (**692**). It may, of course, be the case that the patient is unaware of this or cannot accept that his parents, or other relatives, will not allow him to return home.

EMPLOYMENT, OCCUPATION AND COMMUNITY SUPPORT

A number of statutes require or authorise social services authorities to make arrangements for promoting the welfare of persons suffering from mental disorder, including making provision for the employment or occupation of such persons.

National Assistance Act 1948, s.29

Local authorities are required to publish a plan for the provision of "community care services" in their area, including therefore services which an authority may provide, or arrange to be provided, under Part III of the National Assistance Act 1948.[47] Section 29 provides that a local authority may with the Secretary of State's approval, and to such extent as he directs shall, make arrangements for promoting the welfare of persons ordinarily resident in the authority's area who, being aged 18 or over, suffer from mental disorder of any description.[48] Arrangements may in particular be

---

[47]   National Health Service and Community Care Act 1990, s.46.
[48]   National Assistance Act 1948, s.29.

made for providing them with recreational facilities and with suitable work, including providing workshops and hostels where persons engaged in workshops may live.[49] A local authority may employ as their agent any voluntary organisation or any person carrying on, professionally or by way of trade or business, activities which consist of or include the providing these services.[50] Every local authority is required to inform itself of the number of persons within its area to whom section 29 applies,[51] to keep registers of such persons,[52] to inform itself of the need to make arrangements for them under section 29,[53] to periodically publish general inform-ation as to the services provided,[54] and to inform users of any of its services of any section 29 service which in its opinion is relevant to their needs.[55] Where it appears to a local authority that a person may be in need of *any* service which it may provide or arrange under section 29, the authority is required to assess the individual's need for such services and to decide whether his needs call for it to provide such a ser-vice.[56] More particularly, where a local carries out such an assessment of a person's need for community care services, or a person to whom section 29 applies so re-quests, it shall decide whether his needs call for the provision by it of the following kinds of welfare services : practical assistance in his home; assistance in arranging for carrying out works adapting his home; the provision of meals in his home or elsewhere; the provision of lectures, games, outings or other recreational facilities outside his home, or assistance in taking advantage of available educational facil-ities; the provision of a telephone, wireless, television, library or similar recreational facilities, or assistance in obtaining them; the provision of facilities for travelling to and from home for the purpose of participating in any services provided under sec-tion 29, or assistance with such travel.[57] Where the authority is satisfied that any such arrangements are necessary in order to meet the needs of that person, it is their duty to make those arrangements under section 29.[58]

National Health Service Act 1977, s.21 and Sched. 8

Section 21(1) states that the services described in Schedule 8 to the Act in relation to prevention, care and after-care are functions exercisable by local social services authorities. The schedule provides that a local authority may with the Secretary of State's approval, and to such extent as he directs shall, make arrangements for the provision of centres or other facilities for training or keeping suitably occupied persons who require care or after-care as a result of illness.[59] The Secretary of State has directed local authorities to provide centres or other facilities (including day centres, training centres and domiciliary establishments) for training or occupa-

---

49   The Secretary of State has directed authorities to make arrangements to provide such advice and support as may be needed for people in their own homes or elsewhere, and facilities for social rehabilitation and for occupational, social, cultural and recreational activities: *D.H.S.S. Circular No. 13/74*, paras. 8(1) and 9.

50   National Assistance Act 1948, s.30. Unless the context otherwise requires, the expression "voluntary organisation" means "a body the activities of which are carried on otherwise than for profit, but does not include any public or local authority": *ibid.*, s.64(1).

51   Chronically Sick and Disabled Persons Act 1970, s.1.

52   National Assistance Act 1948, s.29(4)9(g); *D.H.S.S. Circular No. 13/74*, paras. 8(1) and 9.

53   Chronically Sick and Disabled Persons Act 1970, s.1.

54   *Ibid.*, s.1(2)(a).

55   *Ibid.*, s.1(2)(b).

56   National Health Service and Community Care Act 1990, s.47(1).

57   Disabled persons (Services Consultation and Representation) Act 1986, ss.4(a) and 16; Chronically Sick and Disabled Persons Act 1970, s.2(1); National Health Service and Community Care Act 1990, s.47(1), (2) and (7).

58   Chronically Sick and Disabled Persons Act 1970, s.2(1).

59   National Health Service Act 1977, s.21(1) and Sched. 8, para. 2(1)(b).

Patients' homes

According to the handbook, home care is unsuitable for those at significant risk to themselves or others and people who live in markedly adverse social circumstances. However, day hospitals provide alternatives to hospitalisation for even quite psychotic patients and are suitable settings for group therapies and more intensive support for out-patients. A person cared for at home may be supported by regular visits from a community psychiatric nurse, his key worker or a social worker, receive medical treatment as an out-patient or as a day-patient, and receive additional medical treatment from his General Practitioner. Arrangements may be made for him to attend a day centre or drop-in centre. In most areas there will be a multidisciplinary community mental Health centre or resource centre.

Unstaffed group homes

Unstaffed group homes or "flatlets" supported by regular visits from relevant professionals, included designated domiciliary home care workers, may be available.

Adult placement schemes

If private board and lodging houses are used for accommodation, those arranging the service should ensure that it is close to friends, family, or the user's previous residence, and that quality standards. The of selection of carers and patients, and the provision of training and continuing support, particularly in emergencies, are crucial to the success of such schemes. The quality of the service should be monitored on an ongoing basis by the key worker or care manager.

Residential care homes

Small groups of patients need the support of group homes within which staff are present either continuously or for extended periods of the day. Sleeping-in staff provide the least restrictive option for many patients who require a high level of support. Some schemes have developed on a "core and cluster" model with staff from the more highly staffed hostels also supporting those which are more independent. Care homes should be local to friends and families or to the user's previous residence. Voluntary sector organisations such as Turning Point, Making Space, the Guidepost Trust, the Mental After Care Association, and the Richmond Fellowship have particular experience in this area.

Mental nursing homes

Mental nursing homes provide an asylum for extended periods. Care should be provided in as domestic a setting as possible. If the home is registered to receive detained patients, it is a hospital for the purposes of tribunal proceedings. A patient may therefore be transferred there under section 19, or given leave to reside there, as an alternative to discharging him from liability to detention under the Act.

24 hour NHS residences

Hospital hostels may be suitable for younger people. Permanently staffed residences tend to be more appropriate for "revolving-door" patients than repeated admissions to acute wards. Although the hostels are situated away from the mother hospital,

691

sometimes in converted hotel or bed and breakfast premises, they remain part of the "mother" hospital. Whatever appearances may suggest, the legal position is therefore that the patient remains an in-patient.

Homeless persons

It may be that a person does not require supportive accommodation and could be treated from home but is homeless. Whatever treatment setting is appropriate, if a patient has no fixed abode then problems may arise in terms of obtaining the agreement of a health or social services authority to assess him and to accept responsibility for providing services following discharge. If the patient's district of residence is in dispute, reference may be made to section 117(3) and to the following guidelines: *Ordinary residence* (Local Authority Circular (93)7), *Establishing District of Residence* (Department of Health, 1993).

THE PATIENT'S FINANCIAL CIRCUMSTANCES

The majority of patients receive income support while in hospital and are likely to remain dependent on benefits for a period of time following discharge. If necessary, a person may be appointed to administer any benefits to which the patient is entitled. In the case of persons who were in employment or receiving a pension immediately prior to admission, various statutes provide for arrangements to be made for their payment to a third party during any period for which the recipient is incapable of managing his property and affairs (**696**). A patient who has significant capital may object to a proposal to discharge him to residential or nursing home accommodation, because the cost of the accommodation is means-tested. The fees will quite rapidly erode capital which he has saved over the years. The property of a patient who has significant capital may be under the authority of the Court of Protection, in which case the court will need to approve any discharge arrangements which involve private expenditure.

Benefits and appointees

The most important benefits to which a patient may be entitled are set out in the table on the following pages. An appointee may be authorised under the relevant statute to receive benefits on the patient's behalf. An appointee's functions include finding out what benefits the patient is entitled to claim, completing claim forms, cashing benefits, using the benefit to pay bills and to buy food and any other necessary items, dealing with correspondence from the Benefits Agency, and notifying it about changes in the patient's financial circumstances. The proposed appointee fills in a standard the form available from agency, following which both he and the patient are visited. If it is agreed that the patient needs an appointee, the agency confirms this in writing. An appointee may resign after giving the agency one month's notice and the patient should notify it if he no longer needs an appointee or the arrangement is not working.

BENEFITS FOR PATIENTS

Non-means-tested contributory benefits

Statutory Sick Pay

This is paid by the patient's employer during the first 28 weeks he is unable to work because of illness, at the standard rate of £55.70 per week. After this, the patient will need to claim incapacity benefit, which is payable for the following 28 weeks at the higher short-term rate — also £55.70 per week. If the person is still unable to work after a year, IB is then payable at the long-term rate. SSP is taxable and taken into account if the patient claims Income Support.

The standard rate is £55.70 per week.

Incapacity benefit

Payable to persons who are incapable of work, including persons who are certified by the Benefits Agency Medical Service as having a severe learning disability or a severe mental illness. Persons with a regular occupation during the previous 21 weeks who are not entitled to statutory sick pay receive incapacity benefit at the short-term lower rate for 28 weeks from the beginning of their illness, provided they have paid sufficient national insurance contributions. The higher short-term rate is payable after 28 weeks and the long-term rate after one year on IB. IB is taken into account for the purposes of income support and other income-related benefits. Those on the long-term rate do, however, qualify for a disability or severe disability premium in respect of any income support, housing benefit or council tax benefit payable. The benefit is taxable except when paid at the short-term lower rate.

The short-term benefit is paid at two rates: higher (£55.70), lower (£47. 10). The long-term rate is £62.45, with age-related additions of £6.60 per week for those aged between 35 and 44 and £13.15 for those aged under 35. Additional amounts are payable if there are child dependants.

Non-means-tested, non-contributory benefits

Severe Disablement Allowance

This is a weekly benefit paid to people aged 16–64 who are incapable of work and who became so incapable before the age of 20 for a period lasting at least 28 weeks. Alternatively, the person must be 80% disabled and have been so disabled for a consecutive period of 28 weeks. SDA is not taxable but is fully taken into account for income support purposes, although it does entitle the IS claimant to a disability or severe disability premium. Days spent in prison or other legal custody do not count towards the 28 weeks (SS(SDA)Regs., reg.7).

The allowance is payable at a basic rate of £37.75 per week, with age-related additions of £13.15 for persons aged under 40; £8.30 for persons aged between 40 and 49, and £4.15 for those aged between 50 and 59.

693

Disability living allowance

The person must be 65 or under when he first claims. DLA consists of two components: a mobility component and a care component. The lower mobility rate is payable to a person who is sufficiently mentally or physically disabled that, familiar routes aside, he is unable to walk outdoors for most of the time without guidance or supervision. The higher mobility rate is payable inter alia to people who cannot walk and to severely mentally impaired persons with severe behavioural problems who qualify for the highest rate of DLA. The lower rate care component is payable to persons aged 16 or over who are not receiving institutional care in a hospital or home but who are so severely mentally or physically disabled that they could not prepare a cooked main meal for themselves if given the ingredients. It is also payable to persons who, not being in an institution, are so severely disabled physically or mentally that they require attention or supervision from another person. The person must have continuously satisfied at least one of the attention and supervision conditions during the three months preceding the claim and be likely to continue to do so for the next six months. In this case, the care component is payable at three different rates, depending on how much care or supervision is needed. DLA ceases after 28 days in hospital although there is a concession for recipients who had been in hospital informally for one year when this restriction was introduced in July 1996. As to the tax position and effect on other benefits, see the brief note on attendance allowance.

The mobility component is payable at two rates: higher (£34.60), lower (£13.15). The care component is payable at three rates: higher (£49.50 per week), middle (£33.10), lower (£13.15).

Attendance Allowance

This is a weekly benefit paid to people aged 65 or over who need a lot of looking after. The rules concerning entitlement are similar to those for the higher and middle rate DLA care component. Both AA and DLA are not taxable and are additional benefits, i.e. they are not taken into account as income and, indeed, other benefits such as IS are paid with a premium if the individual is in receipt of AA or DLA. Invalid care allowance may also be payable if the AA or DLA care component is being paid at the middle or higher rate.

The higher rate is £49.50 per week, the lower rate £33.10 per week.

Invalid Care Allowance

This is a weekly benefit paid to people who look after someone getting Attendance Allowance or the Disability Living Allowance Care at the middle or higher rate. The carer must regularly look after the person being cared for at least 35 hours per week and earn less than £50 p.w. after expenses.

Invalid care allowance is payable at a rate of £37.35 per week.

694

Income Support and Income-based job-seeker's allowance

In general, a person must be aged 18 or over to claim IS although 16-17 year-olds with mental health problems will usually be eligible. People in receipt of AA, DLA, SDA or IB at the long-term rate are entitled to an additional disability premium payment. Persons entitled to income support who first entered a residential care home or nursing home after 31 March 1993 only receive a residential allowance of £54 a week towards the home's fees (£60 in Greater London). They must therefore apply to the local social services authority for funding. If this is forthcoming, the local authority will then claw back most benefits paid to the assisted person by Central Government. For those who have to look for work in order to qualify for benefit, Jobseeker's Allowance (JSA) replaced income support on 7 October 1996.

The basic personal allowance is £38.90 for a single person aged 18-24 and £49.15 for a person aged 25 or over. For a couple both aged over 18 the personal allowance is £77.15. Additional allowances are paid in respect of dependant children. The disability premium for a single person is £20.95 and the severe disability premium £37.15.

Housing benefit

Persons on low incomes who pay rent may be entitled to housing benefit if their savings and other capital do not exceed £16,000.

Council tax benefit

Persons living alone who are severely mentally impaired are exempt from paying the council tax. Persons on low incomes with savings and other capital of £16,000 or less may eligible for council tax benefit.

Community Care Grants and crisis loans

A person entitled to income support or income-based Jobseeker's Allowance may be eligible for a community care grant if he is moving from hospital or residential care into his own home, needs to buy an item or service, or needs help with fares. Mentally handicapped and mentally ill people are a priority group. If the claimant has savings of over £500, only part of the item's cost may be met. People leaving hospital may also be entitled to a crisis loan from the Benefits Agency if rent has to be paid in advance to a private landlord.

Notes: levels of benefit are revised annually. Sources: National Welfare Benefits Handbook, 27th Ed. (1997/98), Child Poverty Action Group, London 1997; Rights Guide to Non-Means Tested Benefits, 20th ed. (1997/98), Child Poverty Action Group, London 1997.

695

Payment of salaries and pensions

Where the statutory requirements are satisfied, periodic payments (including pensions) may be administered on behalf of a mentally disordered person by the Court of Protection, by a government department (under section 142 of the 1983 Act), or by a local authority (under section 118(3) of the Local Government Act 1972).

Government salaries and pensions

Where a salary or employment-related pension is payable directly from monies provided by Parliament, or payable by a government department, the body by whom the sum in question is payable, if satisfied after considering medical evidence that the patient is incapable by reason of mental disorder of managing and administering his property and affairs, may instead of paying the sum to the patient—

- pay the sum, or such part of it as they think fit, to the institution or person having the care of the patient, to be applied for his benefit;

- pay the remainder (if any), or part of it, to or for the benefit of members of the patient's family,[72] or towards the patient's debts.

Local authority payments and pensions

Section 118(3) of the Local Government Act 1972 confers upon a local authority limited powers to administer any remuneration or pension payable to an officer or pensioner of that authority who is mentally disordered. The authority must be satisfied on medical evidence that the person to whom the monies would ordinarily be payable is by reason of mental disorder incapable of managing and administering his property and affairs. Before exercising the power, the local authority must give notice to the patient and to the Court of Protection, specifying the funds involved and how it intends to administer them.

Services pensions

A services pension may be administered on the patient's behalf in a manner similar to that above, under powers granted by Royal Warrant.

The Court of Protection

The property of some patients is subject to the jurisdiction of the Court of Protection. The Court is an office of the Supreme Court situated at Stewart House, 24 Kingsway, London WC2B 6JX. It comprises the Master of the Court of Protection, the Assistant Master, a Legal Officer and Registrar.

Public Trust Office

A body called the Public Trust Office, situated a the same address, carries out the administrative functions of the court. Part VII of the 1983 Act deals with the Court of Protection.

---

[72] Or to other persons for whom the patient might be expected to provide if he were not mentally disordered.

Functions of the Judge

The functions of the judge under Part VII are exercisable where, after considering medical evidence, he is satisfied that a person is "incapable, by reason of mental disorder, of managing and administering his property and affairs."[73] The judge's functions under the Act are exercisable by the Lord Chancellor, by any nominated Judge, and (subject to certain statutory exceptions) by the Master of the Court of Protection, the Public Trustee (subject to the Master's directions), and by any nominated officer (subject to the Master's directions and so far only as provided by the instrument by which he is nominated).[74] The judge may by order appoint a specified person or the holder for the time being of a specified office as the patient's receiver.[75] Any receiver so appointed shall do all such things in relation to the patient's property and affairs as the judge orders or directs him to do and may do any thing in relation to the patient's property as the judge authorises him to do.[76] In normal circumstances, the patient's nearest relative should be proposed as the receiver. However, if no one personally connected with the patient is willing or able to act, a professional person may be appointed in appropriate cases or, failing all else, the Public Trustee. The appointment of joint receivers is not favoured.

Applications for the appointment of a receiver

The application is usually made by the patient's nearest relative. If some other individual, such as an officer of a local authority, makes the application then the reason for this should be clearly stated. The prescribed forms to be lodged by the applicant are a notice of application, a certificate of family and property, and a medical certificate. An application fee is payable and relatives of a degree equal to, or nearer than, the applicant must be notified of the application. When the application is issued, it is normally stamped, "Attendance not required unless notified," and the order is then made without the holding of a hearing. The order appointing a receiver will include directions as to the management of the patient's estate. The receiver opens a separate bank account ("J. Smith as receiver for P.Smith") and collects in all cash belonging to the patient. Any Notice of Appeal in respect of the appointment of a receiver must be served within eight days of the order. If the patient later recovers, an application for an order "determining the proceedings" should be made in the prescribed form, supported by a medical certificate and a certificate of the funds in court. Legal aid is not available for proceedings in the Court of Protection.

The powers exercisable over the patient's property

Section 95 empowers the Judge to do, or to secure the doing of, all things as appear to be necessary or expedient for the patient's maintenance or benefit; for his family's maintenance or benefit; for providing for other persons whom the patient might be expected to provide if not mentally disordered; for providing for purposes which the patient might be expected to provide if not mentally disordered; or for administering his affairs.[77] Without prejudice to the generality of these powers, the judge may in particular make orders or directions for the control and management of his property; the acquisition, sale, exchange, or disposal of any property; the execution for the patient of a will; the carrying on by a suitable person of any profession, trade

---

[73]   Mental Health Act 1983, s.94(2).
[74]   *Ibid.,* s.94(1).
[75]   *Ibid.,* s.99(1).
[76]   *Ibid.,* s.99(2).
[77]   *Ibid.,* s.95(1).

or business of the patient; the dissolution of a partnership of which the patient is a member; the carrying out of any contract entered into by the patient; the conduct of legal proceedings in the patient's name or on his behalf; and the reimbursement of money applied by any person in payment of his debts or for the maintenance of him or his family.[78]

When it may not be necessary to appoint a receiver

It may not be necessary to apply to the Court for the appointment of a receiver in the following circumstances: where the patient's only income is in the form of social security benefits (**692**); where the patient's only asset consists of a pension or salary payable by a Government department (**696**); where the patient's only asset consists of a service pension (**696**); where the patient's only asset consists of a local authority pension (**696**); where the property is subject to a trust; where an Enduring Power of Attorney exists (*infra*); where the patient's needs are otherwise being provided. If an application is required but the estate is small, it may be possible to make all the necessary arrangements by way of a single order, thereby avoiding the need to appoint a receiver. For example, the order may direct that periodic payments be made to the hospital where the patient is receiving treatment, to be applied for his benefit.

Powers of attorney

A power of attorney is a particular form of agency. The person giving the power is known as the "donor" and the recipient of the power as the "attorney" or "donee." Unlike a trust, the donor remains the owner of the property. However, the attorney may deal with the property subject to the terms of the power granted. The problem with an ordinary power of attorney of this kind is that the powers granted come to an end if the donor later becomes incapable by reason of mental disorder of personally supervising or directing his attorney. These limitations led to the enactment of the Enduring Powers of Attorney Act 1985.

Enduring Powers of Attorney

The 1985 Act provided for the creation of enduring powers of attorney which survive the onset of mental incapacity. It is, of course, still necessary that a person is mentally capable when he grants the power. EPAs must be made on special forms and they may be expressed to come into force immediately or upon a specified occasion. The donor may consider limiting the property covered by the instrument, the transactions which may be undertaken, and the purposes for which his property may be used. This is because a general Enduring Power of Attorney confers authority on the attorney to do on the donor's behalf anything which a donor can lawfully do by his attorney.

Donor becoming mentally incapable

If the attorney has reason to believe that the donor is, or is becoming, mentally incapable, he must as soon as practicable apply to the court for the registration of the instrument creating the power. The effect of actual incapacity is to prevent the attorney from taking any action under the power until an application for registration has been made. Because an application can generally be made only after various notices have been given, there will be a period during which the attorney's powers are suspended. However, the 1985 Act empowers the court to give directions

---

[78]   Mental Health Act 1983, s.96(1).

concerning the management of the donor's affairs prior to the making of an application if of the opinion that it is necessary to do so.[79] Necessary means more than merely desirable or convenient; there must be some real urgency. Once registration has been applied for, the attorney acquires a limited power to act pending the initial determination of the application. He may take action to maintain the donor or to prevent loss to his estate. However, it is only after registration that the attorney's previous authority is, at least in principle, restored. At that point, he has the same powers under the instrument as he had prior to the onset of mental incapacity, but subject now to the court's power to give directions.

The application procedure

A medical report is not necessary. Notice of the intention to apply for registration must be given in Form EP1 to the donor in person and also by first-class post to those relatives entitled to receive such notice by virtue of Schedule 1 Part I to the 1985 Act. All notices must be served within 14 days of each other. The application, in Form EP2, must be lodged with the Public Trust Office not later than 10 days after the date on which the last of the necessary notices was given. The application fee is £50.00 and the application must be accompanied by the original instrument. Five weeks after the last notice was given, the Court will consider whether there have been any valid objections. The valid grounds for objection are that the instrument is invalid, that it no longer subsists, that the application is premature,[80] that fraud or undue pressure was used on the donor to create it, or that the attorney is unsuitable. If there are no objections, and the Court has no reason to believe that there might be if inquiries were made, it must register the instrument. Having registered and sealed the instrument, the Public Trustee returns the original to the attorney (with any office copies requested). The donor may revoke an EPA prior to registration but, thereafter, revocation requires the Court's confirmation.

The effect of registration

The general intention behind the statute is that registration will usually make little difference to the attorney's authority and duties. The court will not normally act in the same manner as if a receiver had been appointed. Spot checks, investigations and the scrutiny of the attorney's management of the donor's affairs are not routine. Nevertheless, the court has wide powers to supervise the conduct of the attorney . It may require him to furnish information or to produce documents or things in his possession as attorney; give any consent or authorisation to act which the attorney would have been able to obtain from a mentally capable donor; (subject to any conditions or restrictions in the instrument) authorise him to act beyond the statutory powers so as to benefit himself or persons other than the donor; and relieve him wholly or partly from any liability which he has or may have incurred on account of a breach of his duties. It may also give certain directions as to the management or disposal of the donor's property and affairs; the rendering of accounts; and the remuneration or expenses of the attorney, whether or not in accordance with any provision made by the instrument. An attorney is bound to keep proper accounts of transactions involving the donor's money and must keep such money separate from his own. However, the statutory scheme is that an attorney (unlike a receiver) is not required as a matter of routine to prepare accounts in a special form. The attorney

---

[79]   The procedure is set out in *Practice Direction — Mental Health (Enduring Powers of Attorney: Applications Prior to Registration)* [1986] 2 All E.R. 42. Any application prior to registration must inter alia be accompanied by the original instrument.

[80]   That refers to the donor not becoming, rather than not actually being,, mentally disordered.

may initially apply for some form of relief or determination by letter, which letter must include including the attorney's name and address (as the applicant); the donor's name and address, the form of relief or determination required, and the grounds for the application. Any subsequent disclaimer of the attorneyship is not valid unless and until the attorney has given notice both to the donor and the court.

The Enduring Power of Attorney Rules 1994

The Court of Protection (Enduring Powers of Attorney) Rules 1994 (S.I. 1994 No. 3047) came into force on 22 December 1994. Rule 6(1) provides that the Public Trustee may exercise the functions of registering an instrument and giving directions under section 6(3) of the Act. The Public Trustee may refer such a matter to the court for determination. The address is: Protection Division, Public Trust Office, Stewart House, 24 Kingsway, London WC2B 6JX).

THE SECRETARY OF STATE'S STATEMENT

Where a patient detained for treatment is subject to restrictions, the Secretary of State is required to furnish to the tribunal a statement of such further information relevant to the application or reference as may be available to him. The documentation within the Home Secretary's file commonly includes witness statements concerning the index offence, a copy of the restriction order, a record of previous convictions, the medical recommendations relied upon by the court imposing the order, and other documentation subsequently received, such as the periodic reports on the patient's progress from his responsible medical officer, decisions of previous tribunals, records of case conferences, and so forth.

Cases involving restricted patients who are liable to be detained

If the responsible authority's statement relates to a restricted patient who is liable to be detained, it must also send a copy of the statement to the Secretary of State.[81] The rules provide that the Secretary of State shall, as soon as practicable, and in any case within three weeks of receipt of the authority's statement, then send to the tribunal "a statement of such further information relevant to the application or reference as may be available to him" (known as "the Secretary of State's statement"). As to the disclosure of the statement to the patient, see page 702.

Proceedings involving conditionally discharged patients

There is no responsible authority in cases involving conditionally discharged patients. Where an application is made by such a such a patient, the rules require the Secretary of State to send a statement to the tribunal as soon as practicable and in any case within six weeks of receipt by him of the notice of application. This statement must include the statement and reports referred to in Schedule 1 (**667**).

FORMAT OF THE STATEMENT

There are no other formal requirements as to the format of the Secretary of State's statement but the standard format is as follows.

---

[81]   Mental Health Review Tribunal Rules 1983, r.6(1).

The statement by the responsible authority in respect of the below-named patient's case was received in the Home Office on (date)

The Home Secretary offers the following information and observations for consideration by the Tribunal.

Patient's name:
Name and address of hospital in which the patient is currently detained:

The Home Secretary has no objection to this statement being disclosed to the patient/considers that the information in the attached document should be withheld from the patient.

A. Circumstances of the offence leading to admission to hospital

On (date) at the [name of court] Mr -- was convicted of --.

On (date) [at (name of court if different to that convicting the patient)] he was reported to be suffering from [form of mental disorder] and the court made an order under section -- of the [statute] authorising his detention in -- Hospital, [together with an order under section --- of the Act making him subject to the special restrictions set out in that section for an unlimited period.]

[By virtue of para. 3 of Sched. 5 of the Mental Health Act 1983, the patient is now detained as if he were subject to an order under sections 37 and 41 of the 1983 Act.]

Details of the offence or alleged offence leading the order being imposed —

It was reported that ... *the summary of the index offence is commonly 100–200 words in length and highlights any aspects of it which, in the Secretary of State's opinion, were particularly significant or grave and which, in his role as guardian of the public's safety, require to be in the forefront of the tribunal's mind when assessing the patient's suitability for discharge and the risks such a decision might involve.*

B. Observations on Part A of the responsible authority's statement

This may involve correcting factual inaccuracies in the responsible authority's statement, for instance an incorrectly spelt name or date of birth, or providing details required under Part A but which the authority itself did not provide or was unable to do so. For instance, dates of leave of absence. It is generally a short section within the statement, often taking the form of brief numbered points.

C. Observations on Part B of the responsible authority's statement and the Secretary of State's observations on the patient's suitability for discharge

The Home Secretary has read the reports of [responsible medical officer's name] and of [name of social worker providing the social circumstances report] and is satisfied that Mr -- continues to suffer from [form of mental disorder]. *If the reports recommend the patient's discharge then the Home Secretary's objections to this will be set out here.*

Enclosures

A record of the patient's recorded convictions is attached.

CONTENT OF THE HOME SECRETARY'S STATEMENT

Home Office statements provide factual information about the patient, including a full list of convictions and an account of the circumstances of the index offence(s) — or the reported circumstances of the alleged offence if the patient is awaiting trial or was found to be under a disability. The account is normally based on information provided by the police, the courts, or the Crown Prosecution Service. Where appropriate, the tribunal's attention is drawn to issues such as the patient's fitness to plead, the position of life sentence prisoners in relation to the Parole Board, the arrangements for repatriating a patient under section 86, the reasons for making any discretionary reference, and any relevant High Court judgments. The Home Office statement represents the Home Secretary's principal opportunity to seek to ensure that a restricted patient is not discharged where it is believed that his continued detention is necessary for the protection of the public. The cases in which the Home Secretary wishes particularly to influence the tribunal are those where it appears that discharge is a likely outcome and the Home Office has already reached a decision not to grant discharge or those where, although no firm decision has been reached in the Home Office, there are grounds for believing that the patient could still be dangerous. If the responsible medical officer has reported to the tribunal that the patient would be dangerous if discharged, the Home Office is unlikely to disagree and might only wish to support that view with additional evidence from their files. The most important points the Home Office looks for in a responsible medical officer's assessment of a patient's dangerousness are whether there is an adequate understanding of how the patient came to commit the index offence and any previous serious offences, and sound evidence that the patient and circumstances have changed in such a way as to make the repetition of such offences unlikely. The key issue is whether the recommendation for discharge is soundly based and adequate arrangements have been made to ensure public safety. If the responsible medical officer's report does not cover these points to the Home Office's satisfaction, it draws this inadequacy to the tribunal's attention and conveys the Home Secretary's view that in the absence of such evidence it would not be safe to conclude that the patient's detention in hospital is unnecessary for the protection of the public. Home Office statements may also comment on any discharge plans contained in the responsible authority's statement, including the adequacy of proposed accommodation and supervision; compliance with medication; the importance of day-time occupation; and possible future alcohol or drug abuse. Because of his paramount responsibility for public safety, the Home Secretary errs on the side of caution.

DISCLOSURE OF STATEMENTS

Section 78(2)(h) of the Act provides that the rules may in particular make provision for making available to a patient or applicant copies of any documents obtained by or furnished to the tribunal in connection with the application, except where the tribunal considers it undesirable in the interests of the patient or for other special reasons. The grounds upon which part of a statement may be withheld from a patient or a nearest relative applicant under the 1983 rules are the same in all cases, namely that the material's disclosure would adversely affect the health or welfare of the patient or others. A tribunal must always consider whether disclosing a document to a patient or applicant would have this effect, irrespective of whether a request has been made for the document, or part of it, to be withheld.

Statements by the responsible authority and the Secretary of State

6.—(4) Any part of the authority's statement or the Secretary of State's statement which, in the opinion —

(a) (in the case of the authority's statement) the responsible authority; or
(b) (in the case of the Secretary of State's statement) the Secretary of State,

should be withheld from the applicant or (where he is not the applicant) the patient on the ground that its disclosure would adversely affect the health or welfare of the patient or others, shall be made in a separate document in which shall be set out the reasons for believing that its disclosure would have that effect.

(5) On receipt of any statement provided in accordance with paragraph (1), (2) or (3), the tribunal shall send a copy to the applicant and (where he is not the applicant) the patient, excluding any part of any statement which is contained in a separate document in accordance with paragraph (4).

Disclosure of documents

12.—(1) Subject to paragraph (2), the tribunal shall, as soon as practicable, send a copy of every document it receives which is relevant to the application to the applicant, and (where he is not the applicant) the patient, the responsible authority and, in the case of a restricted patient, the Secretary of State and any of those persons may submit comments thereon in writing to the tribunal.

(2) As regards any documents which have been received by the tribunal but which have not been copied to the applicant or the patient, including documents withheld in accordance with rule 6, the tribunal shall consider whether disclosure of such documents would adversely affect the health or welfare of the patient or others and, if satisfied that it would, shall record in writing its decision not to disclose such documents.

(3) Where the tribunal is minded not to disclose any document to which paragraph (1) applies to an applicant or a patient who has an authorised representative it shall nevertheless disclose it as soon as practicable to that representative if he is—

(a) a barrister or solicitor;
(b) a registered medical practitioner;
(c) in the opinion of the tribunal, a suitable person by virtue of his experience or professional qualification;

provided that no information disclosed in accordance with this paragraph shall be disclosed either directly or indirectly to the applicant or (where he is not the applicant) to the patient or to any other person without the authority of the tribunal or used otherwise than in connection with the application.

Note: There is a minor drafting error in rule 6(5). The paragraph should clearly be read as referring also to statements provided in accordance with paragraph (3A).

703

NON-ASSESSMENT CASES

In non-assessment cases, rule 6(4) provides that, if either the responsible authority or the Secretary of State is of the opinion that part of their statement should be withheld from the applicant or (where he is not the applicant) the patient on the stated grounds, that part shall be made in a separate document in which shall be set out the reasons for believing that disclosure would have that effect. Upon receiving a statement prepared in two parts, the tribunal shall send a copy of it to the patient or applicant excluding that part contained in the separate document.

ASSESSMENT APPLICATIONS

The rules take account of the fact that it will generally be impractical for the responsible authority to provide its statement in separate documents. Where the responsible authority provides a tribunal with admission papers and other documents in connection with an assessment application, it shall indicate if any part of them should, in their opinion, be withheld from the patient[82] on the ground that disclosure would adversely affect the health or welfare of the patient or others, and shall state their reasons for believing that its disclosure would have that effect. Rule 32 provides that the tribunal shall make available to the patient papers and documents which it receives "excluding any part indicated by the responsible authority."

DISCLOSURE OF REPORTS AND DOCUMENTS: ASSESSMENT CASES

Provision of admission papers, etc.

32.—(1) On receipt of the notice of an assessment application, or a request from the tribunal, whichever may be the earlier, the responsible authority shall provide for the tribunal copies of the admission papers, together with such of the information specified in Part A of Schedule 1 to these Rules as is within the knowledge of the responsible authority and can reasonably be provided in the time available and such of the reports specified in Part B of that Schedule as can reasonably be provided in the time available.

(2) The responsible authority shall indicate if any part of the admission papers or other document supplied in accordance with paragraph (1) should, in their opinion, be withheld from the patient on the ground that its disclosure would adversely affect the health or welfare of the patient or others and shall state their reasons for believing that its disclosure would have that effect.

(3) The tribunal shall make available to the patient copies of the admission papers and any other document supplied in accordance with paragraph (1), excluding any part indicated by the responsible authority in accordance with paragraph (2).

General procedure, hearing procedure and decisions

33.(a) rule 12 shall apply as if any reference to a document being withheld in accordance with rule 6 is a reference to part of the admission papers or other documents supplied in accordance with rule 32 being withheld.

---

[82]   The rules presume that in practice an application will not be made by the nearest relative of a section 2 patient, although such applications are legally possible.

CONSIDERATION OF THE REASONS FOR NON-DISCLOSURE

The effect of the above provisions is to release a tribunal from the usual requirement that it shall as soon as practicable disclose to a patient and an applicant any reports and information which it receives. That is all. Rule 12(2) requires the tribunal to then consider whether the material's disclosure would, in its opinion, adversely affect the health or welfare of the patient or others.[83] Unless the tribunal is satisfied that disclosure would have such an effect, it must direct the disclosure of the previously withheld material.

"Adversely affect the health or welfare of the patient or others"

The previous rules provided for withholding a document on the grounds that its disclosure would "be undesirable in the interests of the patient" or for "other special reasons."[84] The criteria under the 1983 rules are rather more specific, namely that disclosure would "adversely affect the health or welfare of the patient or others." Documents must be disclosed unless the tribunal is satisfied that disclosure would have this effect so that, where non-disclosure is sought, the onus is on the person seeking non-disclosure to satisfy the tribunal as to the grounds. This is an example of a "double-negative" phrased in the patient's favour. However, as drafted, the tribunal has no discretion if it is satisfied that disclosure would have such an effect. This is because the present rules do not expressly refer to the interests of the patient generally, such as his interest in being discharged, or to other special reasons such as the interests of justice. According to the rules, these are not factors to be balanced against those specified. If the tribunal is satisfied that non-disclosure would be contrary to the interests of justice, it nevertheless cannot disclose the material if it is also satisfied that to do so would adversely effect some person's health or welfare. As to this, the tribunal must act judicially and the rules must be interpreted in accordance with, and are subservient to, the interests of justice. The rule must therefore be read as requiring the tribunal not to disclose material which would adversely affect the health or welfare of the patient or others unless of the opinion that the interests of justice require its disclosure. To the extent that rule 12 goes further than the restrictions on disclosure envisaged by section 78(2)(h), it is submitted that that part of it is *ultra vires*. It may be noted that in practice it is extremely rare for a tribunal to withhold part of a document from the patient, notwithstanding that an objection has been made to its disclosure.[85] The rule is therefore interpreted in a way which is consistent with the interests of justice, even if the justification given is that a high standard of proof is required before a tribunal can be satisfied that the grounds for non-disclosure exist.

DISCLOSURE TO AUTHORISED REPRESENTATIVES

Where, on considering the issue of disclosure, a tribunal "is minded" not to disclose a document to the patient or applicant, it must nevertheless disclose it as soon as practicable to any authorised representative of that person who is a solicitor or barrister, a registered medical practitioner or, in the tribunal's opinion, a "suitable

---

[83] Prior to the hearing, the regional chairman may exercise the tribunal's powers under rule 12. Mental Health Review Tribunal Rules 1983, rr. 5, 12(2) and 33(a).

[84] Mental Health Review Tribunal Rules 1983, rr.6(1) and 13(1). The rule therefore precisely matched the wording in the statute, now set out as section 78(2)(h) of the 1983 Act.

[85] Confidentiality is perhaps most often sought for that part of the social circumstances report setting out the views of the patient's family and that part of the medical report which includes the diagnosis. Only rarely are such objections accepted as grounds for non-disclosure.

person by virtue of his experience or professional qualification" — provided that the information shall not be disclosed "either directly or indirectly to the applicant or ... the patient or to any other person without the authority of the tribunal or used otherwise than in connection with the application."[86] The consequence of this provision is that a suitable authorised representative always receives all relevant documents and, furthermore, receives sensitive material before any final decision as its disclosure to his client is made. This allows the representative an opportunity to make representations before a decision is reached.

DECISIONS NOT TO DISCLOSE INFORMATION

Where, having considered the issue including any representations, a tribunal is satisfied as to the statutory grounds, it must record in writing its decision not to disclose the document or information to the patient and/or the applicant.[87] The rules provide only that the decision shall be recorded in writing, not the reasons for the tribunal's opinion.[88] Having decided that information should be withheld in a case involving an unrepresented patient, it is important that the tribunal goes on to consider the effect of its decision on the future conduct of the proceedings, proceeding on the basis that the reasons for non-disclosure will remain valid until the case is disposed of. The patient (or other applicant) will have to be excluded from the hearing when the significance of the information withheld from him is considered, and the reasons for the tribunal's discharge decision avoid any reference to that evidence.[89] If the information is relevant to the discharge issue (and the fact of its disclosure to other parties suggests relevance[90]), the possibility immediately arises that the patient may not be discharged for reasons he is unaware of, being reasons based on evidence the accuracy of which he has had no opportunity to contest or rebut. In such circumstances, a tribunal should, where possible, authorise a representative to act on the relevant person's behalf, to ensure the fair conduct of the proceedings.[91]

DOCUMENTS RECEIVED LATER ON DURING THE PROCEEDINGS

Documents provided under rule 6 or 32 aside, a tribunal may receive supplementary reports or documents about the patient later on during the proceedings. For example, reports which it has directed shall be obtained (under rule 15) or letters from

---

[86] Mental Health Review Tribunal Rules 1983, rr.12(3) and 33(a).

[87] Non-disclosure is mandatory where the tribunal (or the chairman) is satisfied as to the criteria for withholding the material. Although the rules do not explicitly provide for the situation where a tribunal decides that only part of the material for which confidentiality is sought should be withheld, it may direct under rule15 that a supplementary report be submitted which includes the information specified by it.

[88] This is in contrast to the position under rule 21(1), which provides that a tribunal shall record in writing its "reasons" to hold a hearing in private and inform the patient of those reasons, and rule 21(4), which provides that a tribunal shall inform any person excluded from a hearing of its "reasons" and record those "reasons" in writing. The rationale may be that it would be difficult, if not impossible, to give the person affected any meaningful explanation of the reasons for non-disclosure without revealing the nature of the material which it has been decided he should not see, for his own sake or that of others. On the other hand, the rule could, but does not, provide for the reasons to be recorded and communicated to any suitable authorised representative. However, he will have seen the separate document, and any reasons set out therein as to why the material should be withheld, and may therefore infer that those arguments have been preferred to any representations which he has made.

[89] See Mental Health Review Tribunal Rules 1983, rr.21–22 and 24(2).

[90] The tribunal is only required to furnish the responsible authority and the Secretary of State with documents relevant to the application or reference, which can only mean relevant to the statutory matters which a tribunal must consider when reaching its discharge decision.

[91] See Mental Health Review Tribunal Rules 1983, r.10(3).

relatives of the patient. The general rule is that the tribunal shall, as soon as practicable, send a copy of every document it receives which is relevant to the proceedings to the applicant, the patient (where he is not the applicant), the responsible authority and, in the case of a restricted patient, the Secretary of State, and any of those persons may submit comments thereon in writing to the tribunal.[92] However, before disclosing the document to a patient or applicant, the tribunal is required to consider whether its disclosure would adversely affect the health or welfare of the patient or others. Again, if satisfied that it would, it must record in writing its decision not to disclose it. The rules do not provide for documents not forming part of the responsible authority's or the Secretary of State's statement to be provided in two parts, nor for disclosing only part of any document received.

STATUTORY RIGHTS OF ACCESS TO INFORMATION

Authorised representatives sometimes apply as their client's agent for access to his health or social work records, with the specific aim of obtaining more detailed information than is provided in the reports prepared under the 1983 rules. The provisions relating to access to personal information are complicated, and their detailed consideration lies outside the scope of this work, but they are briefly summarised below. In the case of long-stay patients or those with chronic problems, it will paradoxically often be more important to see the first volume of case notes, too often filed away unread for up to thirty years, than to read the current volume. The recent material is often uninformative, referring to the individual in terms such as "a long-stay chronic schizophrenic with negative symptoms first admitted to hospital in 1962." Only if one knows the beginning can one understand the man, the causes of his breakdown, his suffering, the lost opportunities, the forgotten treatments which helped him, his undiminished desire to be a freeman, and the esteem with which his desire for liberty should be held. The gratitude at being treated as a human being, rather than as a biological organism, is in most cases truly pathetic.

ACCESS TO HEALTH AND SOCIAL WORK RECORDS

	Manual records	*Computerised data*
Health service records	Access to Health Records Act 1990.	Data Protection Act 1984; The Data Protection (Subject Access Modification) (Health) Order 1987.
Social work records	Access to Personal Files Act 1987; The Access to Personal Files (Social Services) Regulations 1989.	Data Protection Act 1984; The Data Protection (Subject Access Modification) (Social Work) Order 1987.
Medical reports for employment/insurance purposes	Access to Medical Reports Act 1988.	Not applicable.

---

[92] A court, authority or person given notice of the proceedings under rule 7 thereby becomes a party to the proceedings and may be represented and appear at the hearing. However, rule 12 does not provide that they shall, as parties to the proceedings, be sent copies of documents which the tribunal receives and given an opportunity to comment on them. The Home Secretary, who is not a party, must, however, be sent documents received as soon as practicable.

Data Protection Act 1984

The Data Protection Act 1984 applies to computerised health service and social work personal data. In general, an individual is entitled to be told whether a data user has personal data of which he is the subject and, where that it the case, to be supplied with a copy of that information.[93] However, section 29 provides that the Secretary of State may modify the usual access provisions where the personal data consists of information about the subject's mental health and orders have been made to this effect.[94]

Access to Personal Files Act 1987

The 1987 Act applies to non-computerised personal information held by local social services authorities. It provides that "accessible personal information" shall be disclosed to a person in the circumstances specified by regulations made under the Act.[95] Accessible personal information" is any information contained in records kept by a local social services authority for the purpose of any past, current or proposed exercise of its social services functions (153) and which relates to a living individual who can be identified from that information (or from that and other information in the authority's possession), including expressions of opinion about the individual but not any indication of the authority's intentions with respect to him.[96] Information is not accessible personal information if recorded before 11 November 1987, except to the extent that access to it is required to make intelligible information recorded on or after that date.[97]

Access to Medical Reports Act 1988

The Act provides that an individual has a general right of access to any medical report relating to him which is to be, or has been, supplied by a medical practitioner for employment or insurance purposes.[98]

Access to Health Records Act 1990

The 1990 Act provides a general right of access to health records, or any part of such records, made before 1 November 1990, other than those held on a computer.[99] A health record in this context is a record which consists of information relating to the physical or mental health of an individual and has been made by or on behalf of a health professional in connection with the care of that individual.[100] The definition of a "health professional" is a broad one and includes a registered medical

---

[93]   Data Protection Act 1984, s.21(1).
[94]   The Data Protection (Subject Access Modification) (Health) Order 1987 and The Data Protection (Subject Access Modification) (Social Work) Order 1987.
[95]   Access to Personal Files Act 1987, s.1(1).
[96]   Ibid., s.2 and Sched. 1, para.4.
[97]   Ibid., s.2(4).
[98]   Access to Medical Reports Act 1988, s.1(1).
[99]   Access to Health Records Act 1990, ss.1(1), 3(2), 5(1)(b) and 12(2). Access to any part of a health record made before 1 November 1990 may, however, be given if the holder of the record considers that necessary in order to make intelligible information recorded on or after that date (s.5(2)).
[100]   Access to Health Records Act 1990, ss.1 and 11. "Care" includes examination, investigation, diagnosis and treatment. It may be noted that section 11, in which various expressions are defined, does not commence with the words, "unless the context otherwise requires."

practitioner, registered pharmaceutical chemist, registered nurse, registered occupational therapist, clinical psychologist, art therapist, or music therapist, employed by a health service body.[101] The effect of the statutory definitions is that virtually any record relevant to tribunal proceedings which was made after 31 October 1990 in connection with a patient's medical treatment will be a "health record" for the purposes of the 1990 Act. [102]

Grounds for refusing access

Where a general statutory right of access exists, access may nevertheless be refused in any case on the ground that the information's disclosure would be likely to cause serious harm to the physical or mental health of the patient or, computerised health records apart, be likely to have such consequences for a third party.[103] Access may also be refused to any part of a record which is likely to enable the patient to identify or deduce the identity of another person referred to (unless he consents to the information's disclosure) or the source of the information, unless that third party is a health or social work professional involved in the care of the patient.[104]

Access and Mental Health Review Tribunals

Because statutory applications made to a local authority or health service body for access to personal records take around 40 days to process, there is no point in applying if the sole purpose is to obtain information which might support a tribunal application made by a section 2 patient. In other cases, the grounds upon which a document received by the tribunal may be withheld from the patient (that disclosure would adversely affect the health or welfare of the patient or others) are wider than those generally applicable under the legislation governing access to personal records (that disclosure would be likely to cause serious harm to the physical or mental health of the patient or others), leaving open the possibility that access might be gained to the same information under one of the above enactments.[105] However, the existence of an alternative "confidentiality" ground for withholding information under the legislation — that access would allow a third party or the source of information to be identified — is likely to prevent the disclosure of information concerning the patient given in confidence to a health service professional or a social worker by a third party and furnished in turn to a tribunal. In practice, because of the

---

[101] Access to Health Records Act 1990, s.2(1). Subsection (4) states that the Act applies to health professionals in the public service of the Crown as it applies to other health professionals.

[102] The extent to which a patient may have a general common law right of access to medical records compiled before 1 November 1990 was touched upon, but not determined, by the Court of Appeal in R. v. Mid-Glamorgan Family Health Services and Another, ex. p. Martin, The Times, 16 August 1994.

[103] Access to Health Records Act 1990, s.5(1)(a)(i); Access to Medical Reports Act 1988, s.7(1); Data Protection (Subject Access Modification) (Health) Order 1987, Art. 4(2)(a); Data Protection (Subject Access Modification) (Social Work) Order 1987, Art. 4(3)(a); Access to Personal Files (Social Services) Regulations 1989. In the case of computerised social work records, an additional ground exempting access is that serious harm to the "emotional condition" of the patient or a third party would be likely to be caused.

[104] Access to Health Records Act 1990, s.5(1) and (2); Access to Medical Reports Act 1988, s.7(2) and (3); Data Protection (Subject Access Modification) (Health) Order 1987, Arts. 4(2)(b) and (3); Data Protection (Subject Access Modification) (Social Work) Order 1987, Arts. 4(3)(b), (4) and (6); Access to Personal Files (Social Services) Regulations 1989.

[105] Moreover, section 1(5) of the Access to Personal Files Act 1987 specifically provides that the obligation to give access under the Act applies notwithstanding any enactment or rule of law authorising the withholding of information.

paperwork involved in dealing with formal applications under the 1990 Act, access is often agreed between the responsible medical officer and the patient, or his authorised representative, on an informal basis. The patient's case notes may also be inspected by an independent psychiatrist instructed by the patient or his representative.[106] Misunderstandings are only likely to arise if a representative obtains access to the case notes without first obtaining proper authorisation and then seeks to cross-examine the responsible medical officer by persistent, detailed, references to entries in those notes. Although the practice take places, it is unbefitting conduct for a solicitor to inspect case notes given to him by a nurse or junior doctor who is clearly under the impression that solicitors engaged in a tribunal case automatically have access to them under the 1983 Act or rules.[107]

COMMENTING ON THE AUTHORITY'S STATEMENT

Subject to the power in rule 12(2) not to disclose certain documents to the patient or the applicant, rule 12(1) provides that any person to whom a tribunal sends a copy of a document which it has received in connection with the proceedings may submit comments in writing to the tribunal.

COMMENTS ON DOCUMENTS RECEIVED BY THE TRIBUNAL

12.—(1) Subject to paragraph (2), the tribunal shall, as soon as practicable, send a copy of every document it receives which is relevant to the application to the applicant, and (where he is not the applicant) the patient, the responsible authority and, in the case of a restricted patient, the Secretary of State and any of those persons may submit comments thereon in writing to the tribunal.

The accuracy of the reports

Rule 12 is a highly useful rule because it enables the issues and any matters in dispute to be clarified and itemised in advance of the hearing. From the patient's point of view, it ensures that when the tribunal members receive the authority's statement in advance of the hearing they will read this with his observations as to their accuracy and with the benefit of any counter-balancing points helpful to discharge. Because the responsible authority's statement is necessarily adverse to discharge, the written observations therefore ensure that the members do not come to the hearing aware only of the reasons for not discharging and perhaps with an unconscious inclination against discharge. Early observations may also allow the medical member to be aware of the issues likely to be canvassed at the hearing and he can then examine the patient with these in mind before forming his preliminary opinion. If the patient has difficulty communicating his opinion and feelings, or is likely to have difficulty understanding some questions put to him at the hearing, perhaps because he is severely mentally impaired or has a poor grasp of English, it is also fairer to him to take the time to set out his case in writing.

---

[106] Mental Health Act 1983, s.76.
[107] Solicitors' Practice Rules 1990, rule 1(a) and (d).

OBTAINING FURTHER REPORTS AND INFORMATION

Apart from the reports which must be furnished by the responsible authority or the Secretary of State under the rules, there are a number of other ways in which a tribunal may receive medical evidence and other information about the patient—

- If the reports are inadequate in some respect, the tribunal may direct that further reports or information are provided (**783**)

- Following the appointment of a tribunal to hear the case, the medical member is required to examine the patient and to take such other steps as he considers necessary to form an opinion of the patient's mental condition. The medical member may see the patient in private, examine his medical records, and take such notes and copies of them as he may require for use in connection with the proceedings (**793**).

- The patient, or his authorised representative, may commission a medical report or a social circumstances report from a practitioner of his choosing (*infra*).

- Similarly, where the patient's nearest relative is the applicant that person may commission reports on the patient (*infra*).

REPORTS PREPARED FOR A PATIENT OR APPLICANT

Following the commencement of tribunal proceedings, a patient or applicant will often wish to instruct a medical practitioner, generally a psychiatrist, to prepare a report on the patient's mental health. Section 76 provides that, for the purpose of furnishing information as to the patient's condition for the purposes of an application, any registered medical practitioner authorised by or on behalf of the patient or a nearest relative applicant may at any reasonable time visit the patient and examine him in private, and may require the production of and inspect any records relating to the detention or treatment of the patient in any hospital (**616, §926**). An unrestricted patient whose case is referred to a tribunal has a similar right to authorise a doctor to examine both him and his records, but not it seems a restricted patient whose case is referred.[108]

Confidentiality of reports

The extent to which a medical report prepared on behalf of the patient or a nearest relative applicant is confidential was considered in *W. v. Egdell*. Under section 76, the relationship between doctor and patient is contractual and whether the report's disclosure without the patient's consent amounts to a breach of contract turns not on what the doctor thinks but on what the court rules. The law recognises an important public interest in maintaining professional duties of confidence. The fact that a patient has a strong private interest in barring a report's disclosure does not affect this fact. However, such duties are not absolute and are liable to be overridden where there is a stronger public interest in disclosure. The breadth of the doctor's duty therefore depends on the circumstances. In a case involving a restricted patient

---

[108]   Mental Health Act 1983, ss.67, 68, 71 and 76.

who has committed very serious crimes of violence, the crucial question is how, on the special facts of the case, the balance should be struck between the public interest in maintaining professional confidences and the public interest in protecting the public against possible violence. If the doctor becomes aware of information which *properly* leads him to fear that a decision about the patient's release may be made on the basis of inadequate information, with a real risk of consequent danger to the public, he is entitled to take such steps as are reasonable in all the circumstances to communicate the grounds of his concern to the responsible authorities. In making its ruling the court will give such weight to the considered judgment of the psychiatrist as seems in all the circumstances to be appropriate.

W. v. Egdell and others

[1989] 2 W.L.R. 689   *Chancery Division, Scott J.*

W. had been detained in special hospitals for some ten years under a restriction order without limit of time. The circumstances of the index offence were that he had shot and killed five people and wounded two others. In March 1985, his responsible medical officer recommended to the Secretary of State that he be transferred to a regional secure unit and a place for him became available in June 1986. A previous tribunal had supported this recommendation but the Home Secretary's consent to transfer had not been granted. In April 1987, the patient again applied to a tribunal.

Tribunal medical report prepared by responsible medical officer

The responsible medical officer's report of 19 May 1987 repeated her earlier recommendation that W. be transferred to a regional secure unit. She stated that he suffered from schizophrenia but had been stable on medication for the past 5 years. He had considerable insight into his mental state, accepted the need to continue medication, and realised that his mental state required close and careful monitoring.

The Home Secretary's statement and observations

The Home Secretary remained unwilling to consent to the patient's transfer. He considered that the case called for the utmost caution and W. would first need to show a very long period of stable behaviour, bearing in mind his history of indiscriminate violence. In particular, his interest in weapons needed to be more fully explored and explained. The Home Secretary would be prepared to reconsider the issue of transfer in about 18 months' time following such exploration. He would in all probability wish to refer any future proposals to the Advisory Board on Restricted Patients.

Independent medical report prepared under section 76

The patient instructed a solicitor to act as his authorised representative. As provided for by section 76, they commissioned a report on his behalf from a consultant psychiatrist, Dr. Egdell. Dr. Egdell's ten-page report of 29 July 1987 contained new information concerning the risk to the public. The patient had described to him a life-long interest in making and exploding home made bombs, which he called "fireworks." He was aware of the precautions necessary to avoid injury to himself but, in relation to the index offence, had been prepared to use them to "scare people off " with no apparent regard for the risk of injury to others. His interest in guns was similarly profound, prolonged and, in the last years before the offence, manifestly abnormal. While agreeing that the patient was suffering from a mental illness at the time of the index offences, Dr. Egdell referred to the possibility first raised in July 1984 that the illness might be a paranoid psychosis rather than paranoid schizophrenia. The relevance of the distinction was that medication would be less effective in the former case in protecting against a relapse. He was not convinced that the patient really had insight into his illness and there was a striking lack of remorse. For example, the wife at the garage "made a fuss" so she was shot. He showed no concern for those who were wounded, their relatives or the effects of his offence on his own family. Although reluctant to say on the basis of one interview that he suffered from a psychopathic personality, he clearly had an abnormal personality. All these issues needed to be highlighted and resolved before a decision was made on his departure from the special hospital. Consequently, Dr. Egdell concluded by strongly recommending that W. not be considered for transfer, let alone discharge, until this had been done.

Withdrawal of tribunal application and disclosure of report

On considering Dr. Egdell's report, W. withdrew his tribunal application on 18 August 1987 and his solicitors did not disclose the report to the tribunal or to any third party. On learning of the non-disclosure, Dr. Egdell telephoned the assistant medical director at the secure hospital. He explained his concern that important matters relating to W.'s interest in firearms and explosives had not been properly explored. It was his opinion that a copy of the report ought to be supplied to the Home Office because it contained evidence to suggest that W.'s interest in guns and explosives was long standing and pre-dated his illness, which were pointers to a psychopathic disorder. The assistant medical director indicated that additional information was always helpful but asked Dr. Egdell to contact W.'s solicitors as a matter of courtesy, to see if they would agree to the report's disclosure. In accordance with their client's instructions, the solicitors declined to agree. Dr. Egdell pressed his case with the hospital and was eventually asked to forward a report of his concerns to the assistant medical director. This he did by sending a copy of his tribunal report, having simply substituted the assistant director's name for that of the solicitors who had commissioned it. In November 1987, copies of the report were then sent by the hospital to the Home Office and the Department of Social Security, upon Dr. Egdell indicating that he would have no alternative but to do this himself if the hospital did not comply with his request. The Home Secretary then referred W.'s case to the tribunal, as he was required to do under section 71(2), and forwarded a copy of the report to it.

The writs

On 22 December 1987, W. issued a writ against Dr. Egdell, seeking an injunction restraining him from further disclosure of the contents of his medical report; delivery up of all copies of the report; and damages for breaching his duty of confidentiality. On 19 July 1988, he issued a second writ against the Secretary of State for Social Services, the Home Secretary, the relevant Hospital Board and the Mental Health Review Tribunal, all of whom had received a copies of the report, seeking an injunction to restrain them from disclosing the contents of Dr. Egdell's report; delivery up of all copies of the report; and, as against the Home Secretary and the hospital board, damages for breach of the duty of confidentiality.

Relevant guidelines

At the time, paragraphs 80–81 of the General Medical Council's "Advice on Standards of Professional Conduct and of Medical Ethics" included the following guidance on the principles which should govern the confidentiality of information relating to patients—

80. It is a doctor's duty, except in the cases mentioned below, strictly to observe the rule of professional secrecy by refraining from disclosing voluntarily to any

713

third party information about a patient which he has learnt directly or indirectly in his professional capacity as a registered medical practitioner. The death of the patient does not absolve the doctor from this obligation.

81. The circumstances where exceptions to the rule may be permitted are as follows—

(a) If the patient or his legal adviser gives written and valid consent, information to which the consent refers may be disclosed.

(b) Confidential information may be shared with other registered medical practitioners who participate in or assume responsibility for clinical management of the patient. To the extent that the doctor deems it necessary for the performance of their particular duties, confidential information may also be shared with other persons (nurses and other health care professionals) who are assisting and collaborating with the doctor in his professional relationship with the patient. It is the doctor's responsibility to ensure that such individuals appreciate that the information is being imparted in strict professional confidence.

(g) Rarely, disclosure may be justified on the ground that it is in the public interest which, in certain circumstances such as, for example, investigation by the police of a grave or very serious crime, might override the doctor's duty to maintain his patient's confidence.

Scott J.

It was important to notice that the nature of a hearing before a mental health review tribunal was inquisitorial, not adversarial. That appeared particularly from rules 11, 14, 15(1) and 22(2), which concerned medical examinations, evidence, further information, and hearing procedures. It was open to W. and his solicitors, having received the report, to decide not to use it. The basis of W.'s case was that his interview with Dr. Egdell on 23 July 1987, and the report written by Dr. Egdell on the basis of that interview was, or ought to have been, protected from disclosure. It was claimed that Dr. Egdell was in breach of his duty of confidence in telling the assistant medical director about the report, in sending a copy of the report to him and in urging the despatch of a copy to the Home Office. The hospital ought to have recognised the confidential character of the report, that it came under a duty not to disclose it and that it broke that duty by sending a copy to the Home Office. The Home Office likewise came under a duty to respect the confidential character of the report and broke that duty by sending a copy to the tribunal. The claim against the Secretary of State for Health and against the tribunal was for an order that each be required to deliver up or destroy the copies of the report that each held. The case against each defendant was therefore based on the confidential character of the communication between W. and Dr. Egdell and of Dr. Egdell's report because of the doctor–patient relationship. It was clear from *A-G v. Guardian Newspapers Ltd*[109] that the duty to maintain confidentiality was not necessarily the same in relation to third parties who became possessed of confidential information as it was in relation to the primary confidant. The reason was that the third party recipient could be subject to some additional and conflicting duty which did not affect the primary confidant or might not be subject to some special duty which did affect that confidant. That being so, the cases against the respective defendants were not identical and the breadth and nature of the duty of confidence that affected each of them had to be separately assessed.

---

[109]   *A.-G. v. Guardian Newspapers Ltd. (No 2)* [1988] 2 W.L.R. 805 at 873.

It was plain that the circumstances imposed a duty of confidence on Dr. Egdell. The question here was not whether he was under a duty of confidence but the breadth of that duty. It was well established that the public interest in the preservation of confidences could be outweighed by some other countervailing public interest which favoured disclosure. The General Medical Council's advice did not provide a definitive answer to the question raised but was valuable in showing its approach to the breadth of a doctor's duty of confidence. It showed that the duty though important was not absolute. The duty of confidence did not prevent a doctor from disclosing confidential information to other doctors charged with the care or treatment of the patient or, in rare cases, where the public interest overrode this duty. The duty of confidence owed by Dr. Egdell to W. was both created and circumscribed by the particular circumstances of the case. They were that W. had killed five people and seriously wounded two others. He had been diagnosed as suffering from mental illness and had been ordered to be detained without limit of time. The psychiatrist responsible for his treatment regarded him as no longer a danger to the public provided he remained on suitable medication. She regarded the index offences as having been occasioned by mental illness from which he had been cured. The circumstances did not impose on Dr. Egdell a duty not to disclose his opinions and his report to the assistant medical director at the hospital since the doctor's opinions were relevant to the nature of the patient's treatment and care there.

The duties owed by Dr. Egdell

The duty owed to W. was not Dr. Egdell's only duty. W. was not an ordinary member of the public. He was, consequent on the killings he had perpetrated, held in a secure hospital subject to a regime whereby decisions concerning his future were to be taken by public authorities — the Home Secretary or the tribunal. W.'s own interests would not be the only nor the main criterion in the taking of those decisions. The safety of the public would be the main criterion. A doctor called on to examine a patient such as W. owed a duty not only to his patient but also a duty to the public. His duty to the public would require him to place before the proper authorities the result of his examination if, in his opinion, the public interest so required. This would be so whether or not the patient instructed him not to do so.

W.'s interest only a private interest

W. had a strong private interest in barring disclosure of the report to the Home Office and, probably, to the hospital authorities as well. The public interest in non-disclosure had been put in terms that in about 80 per cent. of the tribunal cases independent psychiatric reports were submitted. If patients were held to be unable to suppress unfavourable reports, they would be unwilling to commission such reports or might not be wholly frank when being examined. The value of the independent reports would then be reduced. Those propositions did not seem to have much weight. The possibility of a lack of frankness was always present and the suggestion that the commissioning of independent reports would be reduced did not seem in the least self-evident. If the private interest of W. was set in the balance against the public interest served by disclosure, the weight of the public interest prevailed.

Conclusions regarding Dr. Egdell's liability

If a patient in W.'s position commissioned an independent psychiatrist's report, the duty of confidence on the doctor making the report did not bar him from disclosing the report to the hospital charged with his care if the doctor judged the report to be relevant to the patient's care and treatment. Nor did it bar him from disclosing the report to the Home Secretary if the doctor judged the report to be relevant to the exercise of the Home Secretary's' discretionary powers in relation to that patient. That was an inevitable result of the circumstances that led to W. being subjected to a restriction order. This limitation of W.'s rights was justified by the need for the following bodies to be fully informed about him: (1) the hospital in charge of his clinical management; (2) the Home Secretary, in whom very important discretionary powers were reposed; and (3) the tribunal on whom an obligation to order his discharge was placed in certain circumstances.

Legal privilege

There was a clear and important distinction to be drawn between instructions given to an expert witness and the expert's opinion given pursuant to those instructions. In the case of expert witnesses, the rule was that legal professional privilege attached to confidential communications between the solicitor and the expert. The instructions were covered by that privilege and the expert could be barred when giving evidence of his opinion from referring to documents which, in the solicitors' hands, would be covered by legal professional privilege. However, legal professional privilege did not attach to the chattels or documents on which the expert based his opinion or to the independent opinion of the expert himself. There was no property in an expert witness any more than there was in any other witness. The court was entitled, in order to ascertain the truth, to have the actual facts which the expert has observed adduced before it in considering his opinion. The information acquired from W. formed part of the facts on which the opinion expressed by Dr. Egdell in his report was based. Neither Dr. Egdell's opinion, nor the facts on which it was based, were privileged.

The hospital's liability

The hospital's legal position had to be considered on the hypothesis that the disclosure of the report to it was a breach by Dr. Egdell of the duty of confidence he owed to W. The restriction order scheme set out in the 1983 Act required co-operation between the Home Secretary and the hospitals in which patients were held. The Home Secretary, when deciding whether or not to exercise any of his discretionary powers, depended on the hospital in which the patient was held to supply him with relevant information about that patient. It could never be right for the authorities of such a hospital to withhold from the Home Secretary relevant information about a patient subject to a restriction order. The importance for public safety that the Home Secretary should be fully informed required that that be so. Accordingly, even if Dr. Egdell were in breach of duty in disclosing his report to the hospital authority, that authority was not in breach of any duty in forwarding it to the Home Secretary. On the contrary, the hospital had a duty to send a copy to him. *A fortiori*, the Home Secretary was under a duty to send a copy of the report to the tribunal. Rule 6(2) of the 1983 rules placed a statutory obligation on the Home Secretary to send to it a statement of such further information relevant to the application as might be available to him. The Home Secretary's statutory duty under rule 6(2) overrode any confidentiality attaching to the report.

The tribunal's liability

As to the position of the tribunal, it was entitled to retain its copies and to make such use of them as it thought fit at the hearing. Both the public interest in a tribunal being fully informed and the inquisitorial nature of its proceedings overrode any confidentiality attaching to the report.

The actions failed because Dr. Egdell's report was relevant material to be taken into account by the hospital, by the Home Office and by the tribunal in the discharge of their respective functions and because, in the very special circumstances of W.'s case, the duty of confidence owed by Dr. Egdell to his patient did not bar disclosure of the report to those recipients. It was for those recipients of the report to attribute to it such weight as they thought it merited. *Actions dismissed.*

W. v. Egdell and others

[1990] Ch. 359   *C.A. (Sir Stephen Brown P., Bingham L.J., Sir John May)*

In the Court of Appeal, W.'s counsel acknowledged that there were two competing public interest considerations. However, he submitted that the dominant public interest was the duty of confidence owed to W. The burden of proving that that duty was overridden by public interest considerations rested fairly and squarely on Dr. Egdell. Where the public interest relied on to justify a breach of confidence was alleged to be the reduction or elimination of a risk to public safety, it must be shown (a) that such a risk was real, immediate and serious; (b) that it would be substantially reduced by disclosure; (c) that the disclosure was no greater than was reasonably necessary to minimise the risk; and (d) that the consequent damage to the public interest protected by the duty of confidentiality was outweighed by the public interest in minimising the risk. Furthermore, in common with other professional men, the doctor was under a duty not to disclose without his patient's consent any information which he had gained in his professional capacity, save in very exceptional circumstances.

Sir Stephen Brown P.

This appeal raised in an unusually stark form the question of the nature and quality of the duty of confidence owed to a restricted special hospital patient by an independent consultant psychiatrist who had been engaged on his behalf in connection with a forthcoming tribunal. In this case, the number and nature of the killings committed by W. inevitably gave rise to the gravest concern for the safety of the public. The authorities responsible for his treatment and management must be entitled to the fullest relevant information about his condition. It was clear that Dr. Egdell did have highly relevant information about W.'s condition which reflected on his dangerousness. The position therefore came within the terms of rule 81(g) of the General Medical Council's rules. The suppression of the material contained in his report would have deprived both the hospital and the Secretary of State of vital information directly relevant to questions of public safety. Insofar as the judge referred to the private interest of W., that passage in his judgment did not accurately state the position. There were two competing public interests. This was not a case of legal professional privilege although it was relevant as part of the background which gave rise to the issue of confidentiality. Dr. Egdell was clearly justified in taking the course that he did.

Bingham L.J.

The philosophy underlying the statutory regime was clear. A man who committed crimes, however serious, when subject to severe mental illness was not to be treated as if he were of sound mind. Although he required treatment in hospital, not punishment, he might represent a great and continuing danger to the public. So his confinement in hospital could be ordered to continue until the

Home Secretary, as guardian of the public safety, adjudged it safe to release him or relax the conditions of his confinement. But a decision by the Home Secretary adverse to the patient was not conclusive. The patient had recourse to an independent tribunal which, if certain conditions were satisfied, must order his discharge, and it could also make non-binding recommendations. Lest an inactive patient be forgotten, the patient's case must be reviewed by the tribunal at three-yearly intervals. These provisions represented a careful balance between the legitimate desire of the patient to regain his freedom and the legitimate desire of the public to be protected against violence. The heavy responsibility of deciding how the balance should be struck in any given case at any given time rested in the first instance on the Home Secretary and in the second instance on the tribunal. It was only by making a careful and informed assessment of the individual case that the potentially conflicting claims of humanity to the patient and protection of the public could be fairly and responsibly reconciled.

The duty of confidence

It had never been doubted that the circumstances imposed on Dr. Egdell a duty of confidence to W. The breadth of that duty was dependent on the circumstances. The decided cases very clearly established (1) that the law recognised an important public interest in maintaining professional duties of confidence but (2) that the law treated such duties not as absolute but as liable to be overridden where there was held to be a stronger public interest in disclosure. Thus, the public interest in the administration of justice might require a clergyman, a banker, a medical man, a journalist or an accountant to breach his professional duty of confidence. Likewise, a solicitor's duty of confidence towards his clients was held to be overridden by his duty to comply with the law of the land, which required him to produce documents for inspection under the Solicitors' Accounts Rules. Those qualifications of the duty of confidence arose not because the duty was not accorded legal recognition but because of the overriding public interest.

The public interest in W.'s right to confidence

It was nevertheless important to insist on the public interest in preserving W.'s right to confidence because the court of first instance had concluded that, while W. had a strong private interest in barring disclosure of Dr. Egdell's report, he could not rest his case on any broader public interest. Here, the judge fell into error. W. had a strong personal interest in regaining his freedom and no doubt regarded Dr. Egdell's report as an obstacle to that end. So he had a personal interest in restricting the report's circulation. But those private considerations should not be allowed to obscure the public interest in maintaining professional confidences. The fact that Dr. Egdell as an independent psychiatrist examined and reported on W. as a restricted mental patient under section 76 did not deprive W. of his ordinary right to confidence, underpinned, as such rights are, by the public interest. But it did mean that the balancing operation fell to be carried out in circumstances of unusual difficulty and importance.

Advice of the General Medical Council

Rule 81 of the General Medical Council's advice listed the exceptions to the rule of professional secrecy. The judge had regarded rule 81(b) as accurately stating the law and held that Dr. Egdell's disclosure in the present case fell squarely within it. However, that paragraph was directed towards the familiar situation in which consultants or other specialised experts report to the doctor with clinical responsibility for treating or advising the patient. The second sentence showed that the doctor whose duty was in question was regarded as having a continuing professional relationship with the patient. It was doubtful if the draftsman of paragraph (b) had in mind a consultant psychiatrist consulted on a single occasion but it was not necessary to reach a final view. In any case, the judge preferred to rest his conclusion on the exception set out in rule 81(g) and, if the disclosure could not be justified under that exception, it would be unsafe to justify it under any other. It was this exception which the judge upheld and applied when he held that a doctor called on to examine a patient such as W. owed a duty not only to his patient but also a duty to the public. This duty to the public would require him to place before the proper authorities the result of his examination if, in his opinion, the public interest so required, whether or not the patient instructed him not to do so. Counsel for W. had criticised that passage as wrongly leaving the question of whether disclosure was justified or not to the subjective decision of the doctor. He made the same criticism of the judge's opinion that, if a patient in W.'s position commissioned an independent psychiatrist's report, the duty of confidence on the doctor did not bar him from disclosing the report to the hospital charged with his care if he, the doctor, judged the report to be relevant to that care and treatment. Nor, the judge had said, did it bar him from disclosing the report to the Home Secretary if the doctor judged the report to be relevant to the exercise of his discretionary powers. Those criticisms were just. Where, as here, the relationship between doctor and patient was contractual, the question was whether the doctor's disclosure was or was not a breach of contract. The answer to that question must turn not on what the doctor thought but on what the court ruled. In making its ruling the court would give such weight to the considered judgment of a professional man as seemed in all the circumstances to be appropriate.

The balance to be struck between the two public interests

The crucial question was how, on the special facts of the case, the balance should be struck between the public interest in maintaining professional confidences and the public interest in protecting the public against possible violence.

Submissions of counsel for W.

Counsel for W. had submitted that the following features of the case indicated that the public interest in maintaining confidences was shown to be clearly preponderant—

(1) Section 76 of the 1983 Act showed a clear parliamentary intention that a restricted patient should be free to seek advice and evidence for the specified purposes from a medical source outside the prison and secure hospital system. Section 129 ensured that the independent doctor could make a full examination and see all relevant documents. The exa mination could be in private, so that the authorities did not learn what passed between doctor and patient.

(2) The proper functioning of section 76 required that a patient should feel free to bare his soul and open his mind without reserve to the independent doctor he had retained. This he would not do if a doctor was free, on forming an adverse opinion, to communicate it to those empowered to prevent the patient's release from hospital.

(3) Although the present situation was not one in which W. could assert legal professional privilege, and although tribunal proceedings were not strictly adversarial, the considerations which had given rise to legal professional privilege underpinned the public interest in preserving confidence in a situation such as the present. A party to a forthcoming application to a tribunal should be free to unburden himself to an adviser he had retained without fearing that any material damaging to his application would find its way without his consent into the hands of a party with interests adverse to his.

(4) Preservation of confidence was conducive to the public safety: patients would be candid, so that problems such as those highlighted by Dr. Egdell would become known, and steps could be taken to explore and if necessary treat the problems without disclosing the report.

(5) It was contrary to the public interest that patients such as W. should enjoy rights less extensive than those enjoyed by other members of the public.

The first of these considerations was a powerful consideration in W.'s favour. A restricted patient who believed himself unnecessarily confined had, of all members of society, perhaps the greatest need for a professional adviser who was truly independent and reliably discreet. The second consideration was also accepted, subject to the comment that, if the patient was unforthcoming, the doctor was bound to be guarded in his opinion. If the patient wished to enlist the doctor's wholehearted support for his application, he had little choice but to be (or at least convince an expert interviewer that he was being) frank. There was great force in the third of the points. Only the most compelling circumstances could justify a doctor in acting in a way which would injure the immediate interests of his patient, as the patient perceived them, without obtaining his consent. The fourth point did not, however, impress His Lordship. It appeared to suggest that the problems highlighted by Dr. Egdell could be explored and if necessary treated without the hospital authorities being told what the problems were thought to be. This was not very satisfactory. As to the final submission, His Lordship agreed that restricted patients should not enjoy rights of confidence less valuable than those enjoyed by other patients save in so far as any breach of confidence could be justified under the stringent terms of rule 81(g).

Submissions of counsel for Dr. Egdell

Counsel for Dr. Egdell justified his client's disclosure by relying on the risk to the safety of the public if the report were not disclosed. The steps of his argument, briefly summarised, were as follows. Dr. Egdell believed that W. had had a long-standing and abnormal interest in dangerous explosives dating from well before his period of acute illness; this interest had been overlooked or insufficiently appreciated by those with clinical responsibility for W.; this interest could throw additional light on W.'s interest, also long-standing and in this instance well documented, in guns and shooting; that exploration of W.'s interest in explosives, and further exploration of W.'s interest in guns, and shooting might lead to a different and more sinister diagnosis of W.'s mental condition. Dr. Egdell's opinions in these respects although not accepted were not criticised as ill-founded or irrational. Dr. Egdell believed that these explorations could best be conducted in the secure hospital where W. was; that W. might possibly be a future danger to members of the public if his interest in firearms and explosives continued after his discharge; and that these matters should be brought to the attention of those responsible for W.'s care and treatment and for making decisions concerning his transfer and release. While W. would no doubt be further tested, such tests would not be focused on the source of Dr. Egdell's concern, which he quite rightly considered to have received inadequate attention up to then. Dr. Egdell had to act when he did or not at all.

The decisive consideration

There was one consideration which weighed the balance of public interest decisively in favour of disclosure. It could be shortly put. Where a man had committed multiple killings under the disability of serious mental illness, decisions which might lead directly or indirectly to his release from hospital should not be made unless a responsible authority was properly able to make an informed judgment that the risk of repetition was so small as to be acceptable. A consultant psychiatrist who became aware, even in the course of a confidential relationship, of information which led him, in the exercise of what the court considered a sound professional judgment, to fear that such decisions might be made on the basis of inadequate information, and with a real risk of consequent danger to the public, was entitled to take such steps as were reasonable in all the circumstances to communicate the grounds of his concern to the responsible authorities. There was no doubt that the judge's decision in favour of Dr. Egdell was right on the facts of this case. Nor could it be said that if Dr. Egdell was entitled to make some disclosure he should have disclosed only the crucial paragraph of his report and his opinion. An opinion, even from an eminent source, could not be evaluated unless its factual premise was known, and a detailed 10-page report could not be reliably assessed by perusing a brief extract.

European Convention on Human Rights

No reference had been made in argument to the European Convention on Human Rights. However, the court's decision appeared to be in accordance with it. Article 8(2) envisaged that circumstances might arise in which a public authority could legitimately interfere with the exercise of a legal right against the disclosure of information protected by the duty of professional secrecy where necessary in a democratic society in the interests of public safety or the prevention of crime. There was here no interference by a public authority. *Appeal dismissed.*

12. Risk assessment and discharge planning

INTRODUCTION

The statutory criteria for detention or guardianship under Part II of the Act and the criteria to be applied when determining whether any patient must be discharged always comprise at least two grounds. The first of these grounds (the "diagnostic question") requires considering whether the patient is suffering from a mental disorder the nature or degree of which makes in-patient treatment appropriate or, as the case may be, warrants his reception into guardianship or detention for assessment. The second ground requires considering whether further treatment or the individual's detention or restraint is "necessary" or "justified" on his own account (specifically for his health, safety or welfare) or that of others (in order to protect them). The criteria which comprise the second ground are therefore directed towards the issue of risk — specifically, the likelihood of undesirable consequences if the individual is allowed a citizen's usual freedom to decide how to act and what medical treatment or social care to accept. The risks involved in restoring a patient's liberty to him may consist of a likelihood of significant deterioration in his health, a risk to his physical safety, or a risk to others. In some cases, others may be at risk from the individual quite independently of whether or not he is mentally disordered at a given moment in time. There may be a general risk of domestic violence and an offender cured of his mental disorder may still be disposed to commit crime. Hence, the need for both statutory grounds and, unless psychopathy is an issue, the duty to release a person who though a threat to others is not mentally disordered or, if he is, the danger does not arise from this fact. Assessing risk in the context of mental disorder therefore also requires forming a judgement about the extent to which any identified risks are a feature or consequence of mental disorder (the first, diagnostic, question). Whether a patient's detention is justified or necessary in a particular case will often partly depend upon what arrangements have been, or can be, made for his treatment outside hospital. In non-restricted cases, the patient's willingness to accept appropriate treatment as an informal in-patient, and his capacity to adhere to an agreed treatment programme and discharge plan, will also be highly relevant.

RISK ASSESSMENT

It can be seen that the assessment of risk is an integral part of any decision to invoke or to rescind compulsory powers and tribunals must assess the likely risk to the patient's health and safety and the risk to others if he is discharged. Strictly speaking, risk is simply the probability that an event will occur but the word is most often used to signify the probability of an unfavourable outcome.[1] Risk-benefit analysis involves analysing and comparing the expected positive and negative results of a given action. For example, considering whether to discharge a patient involves balancing the benefits of liberty against the risks arising from allowing the patient his liberty. The key issue in cases involving mental illness is often that of the patient's judgement, the way he is likely to use his liberty if it is restored to him and he is again free to make his own decisions, including to refuse supervision or medical advice. Few people, whether mentally disordered or not, are unconditionally dangerous. Consequently, it is not enough to simply consider whether an individual's present behaviour is aggressive, threatening or self-injurious. Most people are only capable of violence, towards themselves or others, if certain events or phenomena occur either in conjunction or in succession. Large changes in a situation may result from small changes in some critical variable. Just as a sudden change in the physical state of water into steam or ice occurs with the rise or fall of temperature beyond a critical level, so the addition of a small additional stress on an individual may have a profound effect on his mental state or behaviour. In practice, unless the individual's propensity for violence has an unusually simple and readily understandable trigger, it is impossible to identify all of the relevant situations. Indeed, some of them lie in the future and will not yet have been encountered by the patient during his life. It is therefore essential to define as far as possible the circumstances in which a person has been or may be dangerous. However, because future events can never be predicted, it is equally important to put in place an adequate system for supervising any individual whose own safety may potentially be at risk or who may pose a threat to the safety of others. This maximises the likelihood of obtaining early warning that the person is drifting into a situation known to be risk-laden, or one which may be dangerous albeit that the particular constellation of events was not foreseen or planned for prior to discharge. In essence, the approach is based on the assumption that most attacks do not erupt like thunderstorms from clear skies, so that the individual can be brought inside until the gathering storm has passed. Unfortunately, as with weather systems, only the pattern for the next 24 hours can usually be forecast with some accuracy, and contact with supervisors is much less regular than that.

Explanation and prediction

The difference between explanation and prediction cannot be over-emphasised. Explanation relies on hindsight, prediction on foresight, and the prediction of future risk therefore involves more than an explanation of the past. No person who commits suicide has previously committed suicide and the vast majority of people who commit homicide have not previously done so. While it is quite common for risk assessments to focus only on the circumstances (if any) in which the patient has previously been dangerous, understanding those situations and avoiding their repetition may merely lead to a false sense of security about the future. While life is understood backwards, it must be lived forwards and once the past has changed it is a past guide to future events. Although reading the history is preferable to gazing into a crystal ball, it is nevertheless an unreliable guide. As Russell once put it, the man who has fed the chicken every day throughout its life at last wrings its neck instead.

---

[1]   *A Dictionary of Epidemiology* (ed. J.M. Last, International Epidemiological Association/ Oxford University Press, 3rd ed., 1995), p.148.

THE FOUR STAGES OF RISK ASSESSMENT

At its simplest, risk assessment can be seen as consisting of four steps: (1) identifying the hazard; (2) characterising the risk; (3) assessing the likelihood of exposure to the hazard; (4) estimating the risk. By way of example, the hazard in the case of a restricted patient with previous convictions for sexual assaults on young boys is unsupervised contact with young children. The particular risk is characterised by the fact that the patient has a psychopathic disorder with abnormal sexual drives and interests which he has historically been unable to control. If the patient is discharged he is likely at some stage to be exposed to contact with unsupervised young children. Therefore the risk of further similar offending must be high unless either his exposure to potentially dangerous situations can be avoided (which is difficult to foresee given the number of children in society) or his characteristic sexual interests and behaviour are reformed or controlled by pharmacological means.

ACTUARIAL AND CLINICAL APPROACHES

Predictions are most often founded on retrodiction, not fact,[2] and all violence takes place in the present, not in the past or the future. The current departmental guidelines acknowledge that there "have been a number of cases which demonstrate how difficult it can be in the present state of knowledge to make accurate judgements about future risks." All professional staff can do is "to recognise these difficulties and make an honest and thorough assessment based on best possible practice and taking account of all the known circumstances of each case."[3] There are two main, contrasting, approaches to assessing the risk of violence, whether by the patient to himself or to others: the clinical model and the actuarial (statistical) approach. It should, however, be emphasised that there is no evidence that psychiatrists are better able to predict future offending behaviour than other professionals who spend their time working with offenders. Hence, tribunals and the Aarvold Board comprise professionals from a number of disciplines. Whether a risk is acceptable must be a judicial decision based on the medical and other relevant evidence.

The clinical model

A psychiatrist who uses the clinical model of risk assessment approaches the issue in three distinct steps[4]—

a. determining whether the patient has a demonstrable mental disorder;

b. determining the connection between any disorder and any aggressive, potentially aggressive, or feared behaviour;

c. spelling out how any connection comes about and what aspects of the disorder are behind any violent behaviour.

---

[2]   Predictions of what will occur in the future are based on "retrospective predictions" of what has occurred in the past. In philosophy, this is a form of retrodiction.

[3]   Department of Health, *Health Service Guidelines HSG (94)27*, para. 26.

[4]   J. Gunn, "Clinical approaches to the assessment of risk" in *Risk-taking in Mental Disorder: Analyses, Policies and Practical Strategies* (ed. D. Carson, S.L.E. Publications, 1990), p.15.

If the mental disorder is the decisive factor which defines the individual's potential for dangerous behaviour, the management of that disorder is also the management of the potential dangerousness. Understanding that, and spelling it out, are useful pointers for rehabilitation and for a reduction of risk in the future. The choice of procedural safeguards will depend upon the nature of the danger to be guarded against. If the patient is released under supervision then recurrence of the illness can be monitored. This gives some confidence about the release in a planned, supervised, way and provides information about what to do if things start to go wrong. The clinician therefore makes predictive judgments rather than simple predictions. He "is not asking the statistician's simple question: How likely is it that a man like this will cause grave harm? His is the more complex question: In what circumstances would this man now be going to cause grave harm, and what is the strength or persistence of his inclination to do so in such circumstances? And, in order to make a prediction, the clinician must ask the supplementary question: How likely is it that this man will find himself in such circumstances in the foreseeable future."[5]

RISK ASSESSMENT — GUNN'S CLINICAL MODEL

---

1. Assessment

1. Detailed history
2. Substance abuse or not
3. Sexual interests and attitudes
4. Criminal history
5. Intelligence and personality
6. Mental state
7. Treatment

2. Demography

1. Age
2. Sex
3. Race
4. Previous violence
5. Previous sexual assaults
6. Socio-economic status
7. Substance abuse
8. Intelligence
9. Marital status

3. Environment

1. Family supports
2. Personal relationships
3. Employment
4. Accommodation

4. Interests and attitudes

1. Sexual
2. Violence
3. Cruelty
4. Social domination
5. Racism

5. Context

1. Availability of victims
2. Availability of weapons
3. Availability of drugs and alcohol

6. Declared intentions

1. To potential victims (including self)
2. To potential future victims
3. To caring staff

Source : Clinical approaches to the assessment of risk, John Gunn, in Risk-taking in Mental Disorder; Analyses, Policies and Practical Strategies. Ed. by David Carson. S.L.E. Publications Ltd., 1990, pp.15–16.

---

5   J. Floud, "Dangerousness in social perspective" in *Psychiatry, human rights and the law* (ed. M. Roth and R. Bluglass, Cambridge University Press, 1985), p.90.

Actuarial approaches

In theory, a sound statistical statement can be made concerning the correlation between two events and the relationship expressed as a frequential probability. Advocates of an actuarial approach to risk assessment argue that it is more scientific and objective. Consequently, it produces more consistent decisions than the present system which essentially relies on subjective judgement based on experience. However, statistical statements lack certainty when applied to the individual occasion,

> "A sound statement can be made to the effect that when a coin is tossed 1000 times, it will come down heads approximately 500 times, and the limitation of this approximation can be stated precisely. What statistics cannot do is to tell you whether the coin will come down heads or tails next time it is tossed, and yet this is precisely the type of information usually required. It is in the hope of rectifying this uncertainty that we seek a chain of causation."[6]

The limits of the actuarial approach are largely obvious. Although one can say for a group of persons what the likely figures will be there are too many variables in the individual case. Many events and processes cannot be predicted by conventional mathematical theorems or laws because small, localised perturbations have widespread general consequences. Examples include long-range weather changes, the performance of racehorses, and human behaviour. However, basic actuarial information may have significant implications which can be taken into account alongside the other things. Occasionally, this information may reduce the time and effort needed to reach decisions by confining attention to a relatively small number of key factors. Statistical patterns also direct attention to what may be key areas in a particular case, so helping to ensure that relevant considerations are not ignored. The general view is that the one approach complements the other although the features of the particular case must always be paramount.

AVOIDING TAKING RISKS

Risk cannot be avoided. All decisions to discharge or not to discharge involve the assumption of a risk. In the case of a decision to discharge, the risk is that the individual will use his greater freedom in a way which is injurious to himself or others. The risks involved in not discharging may similarly include an increased likelihood of harm to the patient or others but, more often, consist of the possibility that a citizen is detained who could safely be discharged. In other words, there is a risk of injustice. A tribunal which declines to discharge cannot be faulted insofar as no one will ever know whether its assessment of the patient's case was right or wrong. The person who is not released is thereby prevented from demonstrating that if released he would have resettled safely in the community. However, the converse is not also true. A tribunal which discharges risks catastrophe and, if the patient then either attempts or commits suicide or a serious offence against a third party, public criticism. Yet, however careful the assessment of the nature and extent of the risks involved in discharge, it is inevitable that some patients will later take their own lives or, more rarely, commit a serious offence outside hospital. These events also happen in hospitals, and in respect of patients granted leave or discharged by their consultants. The occurrence of such tragedies does not *per se* demonstrate any error

---

[6]   G.W. Bradley, *Disease, Diagnosis and Decisions* (John Wiley & Sons, Chichester, 1993), p.41.

of judgement on the part of those who discharged or supervised the patient. The public cannot be made entirely safe from the risk of reoffending and, arguably, cannot properly expect any higher measure of protection before offenders committed to hospital are released compared with those sent to prison. It must also be borne in mind that all in-patients are members of the public and themselves at increased risk of being victims of violence for as long as they are detained on a psychiatric ward. Thus, the tribunal system aims to ensure both that members of the public are not unnecessarily detained and also that members of the public are protected from people who must necessarily be detained. Balancing these different considerations is a formidable task.

Freedom to take risks and to make mistakes

While the public must be realistic about the problems involved in assessing risk and deciding what is an acceptable risk, it is equally important that tribunal members do not add to their burden in cases involving non-offenders by balancing risks which are constitutionally matters for the citizen to weigh in his own mind. The purpose of invoking compulsory powers is not to eliminate that element of risk in human life which is simply part of being free to act and to make choices and decisions. Rather, their purpose is to protect the individual and others from a particular and somewhat limited kind of risk — that which arises when a citizen is of unsound mind and his judgement of risk, or his capacity to control behaviour he knows puts himself or others at risk, is in consequence of this markedly impaired. The key issue is the patient's judgement and appreciation of his situation, the way in which he will use his liberty if it is restored to him and he is again free to make decisions for himself. It cannot be over-emphasised that a citizen who has not offended against society is generally entitled to place a high premium on his liberty, even to value it more highly than his health. Within certain limits, he is as entitled as the next person to make what others may regard as errors of judgement and, in particular, to behave in a way which a doctor regards as irrational in the sense that it does not best promote his health. Thus, a person may chain-smoke cigarettes even though the risks involved in this activity, both to the individual and others, are significant and potentially life-threatening. Even though the individual's judgement is partially impaired by his addiction, nevertheless he is able to fully comprehend the medical advice and so, in this sense, is able to rationally assess the risks involved, when exercising his freedom to follow or ignore that advice. Likewise, a patient who has been receiving treatment for mental disorder is not to be compelled to follow medical advice simply because he disagrees with all or part of that advice, provided the choices he proposes making if set at liberty are not manifestly irrational. Accordingly, if the medical opinion is that a patient needs to continue taking medication and this should be given in depot form, it is not irrational *per se* for the patient to prefer to take prophylactic medication orally simply because from a medical viewpoint this is the treatment of second choice. If the patient can rationally explain that for him the slightly increased risk of relapse is outweighed by the disadvantages for him of injections, and other persons are not at risk, such a way forward represents a reasoned balance of the risks involved.

THE RISK OF SUICIDE

Mental illness accounted for 18,286 recorded deaths in 1991. Suicide is phenomenologically related to homicide and the two may occur together. However, in statistical terms, the risk that a mentally ill person will kill himself is substantially higher than the risk that he will kill another person.[7] Suicide accounts for approximately one per cent. of all deaths annually. Of the people who commit suicide, 90 per cent. have some form of mental disorder, 33 per cent. have expressed clear suicidal intent, and 25 per cent. are psychiatric out-patients. People who have attempted suicide in the past are at increased risk, the risk being approximately one hundred times greater in the year after an attempt.[8] In the case of short-term in-patients, there is evidence of a significant clustering of suicides soon after discharge from psychiatric care.[9]

GOVERNMENT STRATEGY

In *The Health of the Nation White Paper* published in July 1992, the Government set targets of reducing the overall suicide rate by at least 15 per cent. by the year 2000 (from 11.0 per 100,000 population in 1990 to no more than 9.4) and the suicide rate of severely mentally ill people by at least 33 per cent. by then (from a life-time estimate of 15 per cent. in 1990 to no more than 10 per cent.). The Department of Health also established a Confidential Inquiry into Homicides and Suicides by Mentally Ill People, with the twin purposes of eliciting avoidable causes of death and determining best practice by a detailed examination of the circumstances surrounding such events. The inquiry has been led by the Royal College of Psychiatrists and its first report was published in 1996.[10] According to that report, whereas:

> "some mentally ill or mentally disordered people can make unimpaired judgements, ... the broadly held assumption is that their ability to make unemotional and objective judgements is likely to be impaired. It is therefore not appropriate to take a relaxed attitude to suicide within this group or to take the view that death by suicide is inevitable. The safety of people who are mentally ill or mentally disordered must remain a central issue for the psychiatric services."[11]

THE CONFIDENTIAL INQUIRY

The Confidential Inquiry's terms of reference include enquiring into the circumstances leading up to and surrounding the suicides of people discharged by the specialist psychiatric services. The first report was based on a detailed examination of 240 suicides, involving 154 out-patients (64 per cent.), 53 in-patients (22 per

---

[7] See *e.g.* W. Böker and H. Häfner, *Crimes of violence by mentally disordered offenders* (Cambridge University Press, 1982). The incidence of homicidal violence for persons suffering from schizophrenia was five per 10,000, with the risk of suicide one hundred times greater than that of homicide. Amongst those suffering from an affective disorder, the rate of homicidal violence was six per 100,000, with a risk of suicide one thousand greater than that of homicide.

[8] *Health of the Nation* (Department of Health, 1992), Appendix 1.3.

[9] M. Goldacre, *et al.*, *Lancet* (1993) 342, 283–286.

[10] *Report of the Confidential Inquiry into Homicides and Suicides by Mentally Ill People* (Royal College of Psychiatrists, 1996).

[11] *Ibid.*, p.84. Although it is clearly erroneous to associate being objective or rational with being unemotional, the basic point remains. To deliberately allow a person who is seriously mentally ill to commit suicide when there is a realistic prospect that he may later feel differently is to deprive him of the rewarding future which he may still have.

cent.), and 33 patients discharged from specialist care during the year preceding death (14 per cent.). The most common life event during the period of care preceding suicide was the breakdown of a marriage or partnership. Two-thirds of those individuals whose marital status was known were living alone. Social and employment problems were relatively common and barely a quarter of all the patients were employed, self-employed or in full-time education. Other life events often mentioned as relevant included the patient's reaction to the involvement of psychiatric services; bereavement; physical illness; and financial problems. The most common diagnoses were schizophrenia (men 31 per cent., women 17 per cent.), affective illness (men 29 per cent., women 47 per cent.) and personality disorder (men 18 per cent., women 7 per cent.). Previous self-harm was reported in around half the total cases and some degree of aggressive behaviour in 32 per cent. Slightly more than half of the out-patients had previously been in-patients and 22 per cent. of them had been admitted on five or more occasions. Two-fifths had been in-patients earlier in the episode of illness leading up to the suicide but only 30 per cent. of them had been detained at some stage during that illness. Three-quarters of the in-patients committing suicide were in wards designated as acute and one-quarter were detained at the time of death. All of the 19 per cent. of in-patients who died in their home were on leave at the time. A further 47 per cent. died somewhere else outside hospital and just over one-quarter committed suicide in hospital. It was evident that in many cases the suicide had come as a surprise to the clinical team. Although 52 per cent. of all patients had given clear intention of suicidal intent at some stage during the final episode of illness, staff felt that the danger had receded in most cases. Less than 25 per cent. of raters said that they "often" or "nearly always" thought during the period of care that the patient might try to commit suicide. In many reviews it was concluded that nothing could have reduced the likelihood of death, either because there had been no sign of likely danger or because all practical measures of supervision were in place. In only 24 per cent. of all cases were difficulties recorded in maintaining contact with the patient during the follow-up and in only 27 per cent. of cases were lapses in taking medication reported — neither problem was reported in 60 per cent. of the cases. As to those in contact, many were reported as showing poor co-operation, being seen as solitary, isolated, sometimes rigid and inflexible, and unable to build up a relationship with staff. 95 per cent. of raters were of the opinion that the treatment being offered was still relevant. Despite the general feeling that all practical supervisory measures were in place, only 40 per cent. of the out-patients who had previously been in-patients had a care plan and less than one-fifths of all out-patients had an operational care plan. Furthermore, only 38 per cent. of all patients had been provided with specialist social work contact at some stage prior to suicide. It is clearly too early to draw any conclusions but the report makes for depressing reading. While the act of suicide may sometimes have been impulsive, the background circumstances of marital breakdown, social isolation, bereavement, lack of employment, relatively low social work input and poor care planning all suggest an underlying mental deterioration or hopelessness about the future against a perception of relevant treatment and supervision and consequential surprise at the final act. From a tribunal point of view, the lesson is to pay more heed to the patient's view about whether his treatment is relevant to his situation and to be cautious about the ability of medication to resolve suicidal feelings which occur in the setting of unalleviated personal and social isolation.

EPIDEMIOLOGY

Strahan pointed out over a century ago the logical impossibility of ever knowing the mental state of the suicide just before his act. Consequently, he felt that reliable statistics were necessarily unobtainable and those that were obtained were meaningless.[12] While some knowledge of those groups of people statistically at greater risk of suicide is useful, because it directs attention to cases which might otherwise be missed, a psychiatrist cannot make an elderly white single man at lower risk on these factors with any known intervention.[13] Moreover, the vast majority of people in those groups do not commit suicide.

Gender

Rates of suicide are twice as high in men as in women and the difference is increasing. Although motherhood does not protect against depression, mothers of young children are less likely to commit suicide. However, as the following table shows, rates of suicide are higher amongst females in some cultural groups.

Suicide and Undetermined Injury by Gender and Country of Birth.
England and Wales 1970-78, Persons aged 20-69 years

Gender and Country of Birth	Proportional Mortality Ratio
Indian sub-continent : males	87
Indian sub-continent : females	120
Caribbean commonwealth : males	80
Caribbean commonwealth : females	47
African commonwealth : males	110
African commonwealth : females	120

Source: OPCS Immigration Mortality

Mental disorder

Serious mental disorder has a marked effect on lifetime suicide rates. They are estimated at schizophrenia 10 per cent., affective disorder 15 per cent., personality disorder 15 per cent.

Age

Suicide has risen by 75 per cent. in young men aged 15–24 since 1982 and it is the second most common cause of death in 15-34 year old males. Suicide rates for men under the age of 45 are now higher than those of older men, apart from men aged 75 and over. In contrast, rates for women remain lower in women aged 45 and under.

---

[12] S.A.K. Strahan, *Suicide & Insanity* (Sawn & Sonnenschein & Co., republ. 1983). See *Report of the Confidential Inquiry into Homicides and Suicides by Mentally Ill People* (Royal College of Psychiatrists, 1996), p.85. A point also made by Jack London in his novel *Martin Eden*, whose eponymous hero's suicide foretold the author's own: "and with that thought he ceased to think."

[13] W.J. Fremouw, *Suicide Risk: Assessment and Response Guidelines* (Pergamon Press, 1990), p.87.

Social Class and employment status

Suicide rates are higher amongst the unemployed, although the relationship is complex, and also highest in social class V (unskilled workers).

Suicide and Undetermined Injury by Social Class
England & Wales. 1979-80, 1982-83, Persons aged 20-69 years

Social Class	Standardised Mortality Rate
I	77
II	65
IIIN	86
IIIM	75
IV	115
V	220

Source: OPCS Occupational Mortality

Family status

The ending of marriages or partnerships — whether by divorce or death — has a direct impact on suicide rates. It may also have a delayed effect on children whose parents separate, leading to mental illness or suicide in later life.

Season

Suicide rates are highest in the spring and early summer, notably April, May and June.

Alcohol abuse

Alcohol abuse has a marked effect on the lifetime suicide rates. 15 per cent. of persons dependant on alcohol are estimated to commit suicide. The presence of psychiatric illness and alcoholism increases the risk of completed suicide.[14]

Access to means

The availability of easy and relatively painless methods of suicide is an important factor in influencing suicide rates. Self-poisoning has declined with reduced prescriptions for barbiturates but still accounts for 66 per cent. of suicides amongst women, paracetamol being commonly used. The inhalation of car exhaust fumes causes 33 per cent. of male suicides.

Health and social services support

Cramer estimated that suicides amongst hospital in-patients account for only 5 per cent. of the overall number of suicides.[15] However, recent research has highlighted

---

[14]   J.H.J. Bancroft and P. Marsack, *British Journal of Psychiatry* (1977) 131, 394.
[15]   J.L. Cramer, "The Special Characteristics of Suicide in Hospital In-Patients" *British Journal of Psychiatry* (1984) 145, 460–463.

the hitherto unrecognised frequency of suicide in traditional services.[16] Each mental health sector team can expect between 6 and 12 suicides per annum for a catchment area population of 50,000 to 100,000, of whom 2–5 persons will have been patients of the team. Each health authority responsible for a population of 500,000 persons can expect 50-60 such deaths per annum. The statistics demonstrate the importance of proper after-care arrangements since, although 10–15 per cent. of patients with a major mental disorder can be expected to take their own lives, the vast majority will do so in the community and, in the case of detained patients, following discharge.

SUICIDE — SOME RESEARCH FINDINGS

B. Barraclough, et al., British J. of Psych. (1974) 125, 355–373.	Between one-third and half of those persons who commit suicide were found to have a history of previous attempts. See also Kreitman , *infra.*
J.H.J. Bancroft and P. Marsack, Brit. J. of Psych. (1977) 131, 394.	The presence of psychiatric illness and alcoholism increases the risk of completed suicide.
A.R. Beisser and J.E. Blanchette, Diseases of the Nervous System (1961) XXII, 7, 365–369.	Repeated suicide attempts are most common during the three month period following an attempt.
S. Ganzler, et al., Life-threatening behaviour (1971) 1, 184–202.	There is a marked association between attempted suicide rates and living in an area of relative social deprivation.
K. Hawton and J. Catalan, Psychiatric management of attempted suicide patients. Brit. J. of Hosp. Med.	Approximately 90% of suicide attempts involve deliberate self-poisoning, the rest being self-injuries or a combination of both. Approximately half of male attempters have serious employment problems.
K. Hawton, et al., Journal of Neurology, Neurosurgery and Psychiatry (1980) 43, '168.	High rates of attempted suicide are found in many patients with epilepsy. See also Mackay, *infra.*
N. Kreitman, Parasuicide (John Wiley, 1980).	1–2% of persons who attempt suicide kill themselves within the following year.
H.G. Morgan, et al., Brit J. of Psych. (1975) 127, 564.	Non-opiate analgesics (for example salicylates) are used in a quarter of attempted suicides and in considerably more of the attempts of young persons.
A. Mackay, Brit. J. of Psych. (1979) 134, 277.	High rates of attempted suicide are found in many patients with epilepsy. See also Hawton, *et al.*, 1980.
I.M.K. Ovenstone, Brit. J. of Preventive and Soc. Medicine (1973) 27, 27.	There is a considerable overlap between those who commit suicide and those who attempt it but do not die.
E.S. Paykel, et al., Arch. of Gen. Psych. (1975) 32, 327.	The majority of suicide attempters have recently experienced threatening or undesirable life events, usually in the nature of inter-personal problems.
J. Roberts and K. Hawton, Brit. J. of Psych. (1980) 137, 319.	An association has been demonstrated between child abuse and attempted suicide.
P. Sainsbury, Brit. J. of Hosp. Medicine (1978) 19, 156.	Characteristics disproportionately common to persons who commit suicide include being male, of older age, living alone, and being recently bereaved.
P. Urwin and J.L. Gibbons Psychol. Medic. (1979) 9, 501.	Formal psychiatric disorders requiring treatment are found in a minority of attempted suicide patients.

---

[16]   *Health of the Nation* (Department of Health, 1992), para. 6.16.

ASSESSING THE RISK OF SUICIDE

To predict which individual out of one hundred people who has attempted suicide will die during the next year is necessarily extremely difficult. Even if those persons could be identified with 80 per cent. accuracy, two attempters per thousand will die during that time and many more be identified incorrectly as likely suicides. There is, of course, no evidence that the population can be discriminated with anything near 80 per cent. accuracy; and it would generally not be considered appropriate to continue to detain someone not thought to be in any immediate danger because events in ten months' time may take a decisive turn for the worst.[17]

Assessment following a suicide attempt

Hawton and Catalan developed a semi-structured interview schedule which includes obtaining a detailed account of events in the 48 hours preceding the attempt (degree of planning, isolation, suicide note, motives, actions after attempt, whether alcohol was taken, previous attempts) and clarifying the nature of the patient's problems and their duration. In assessing psychiatric disorders, particular attention should be paid to symptoms suggestive of depression and alcoholism.[18] Assessment following self-poisoning or self injury should include evaluation of risk of suicide; evaluation of risk of repetition; identification of psychiatric disorder; clarification of current problems faced by the patient; obtaining information from other sources, including the general practitioner, family and friends; and making arrangements for appropriate help following discharge from hospital. According to Hawton and Catalan, in-patient treatment is generally indicated for people with serious psychiatric disorders, those at risk of suicide, and those who require a short period of respite.[19] Compulsory admission is often necessary for patients who refuse help but are clearly suffering from serious depression with loss of insight and those judged to be at risk of suicide who cannot give satisfactory assurances about their intentions.

Scales for assessing the risk

Bluglass and Horton developed a six-item scale for predicting the risk of a further attempt, the scales being problems in the use of alcohol; a diagnosis of sociopathy; previous in-patient psychiatric treatment; previous out-patient psychiatric treatment; a previous attempt leading to hospital admission; and not living with relatives. A patient is given one point for each item applicable to him. The higher the score, the greater the risk of repetition. They found that a patient scoring nought had a probability of repetition within one year of five per cent while a patient with a score of five or six had a repetition probability of 48 per cent.[20] Further attempts by some individuals may be characterised by an increase in suicidal intent. The Beck Suicidal Intent Scale is often used to evaluate this.

---

[17] An American study of 4,800 war veteran patients over 4–6 years managed to identify one-half of the actual suicides while misidentifying 1,206 false positives. Of the total group identified as being those who would commit suicide, only 2.8 per cent. were identified correctly. See A.D. Pokorny, "Prediction of suicide in psychiatric patients" *Archives of General Psychiatry* (1983) 40, 249–257.

[18] For example, severe mood disturbance, forgetfulness, impaired concentration, feelings of hopelessness and guilt, loss of interest, and impaired libido.

[19] K. Hawton and J. Catalan, *Attempted suicide: a practical guide to its nature and management* (Oxford University Press, 2nd ed., 1987).

[20] D. Bluglass and J. Horton, "A scale for predicting subsequent suicidal behaviour" *British Journal of Psychiatry* (1974) 124, 573–578.

ASSESSMENT OF PATIENTS

General questions following deliberate self-poisoning or self-injury

What is the explanation for the attempt in terms of likely reasons and goals?

What was the degree of suicidal intent?

Is the patient at risk of suicide now, or is there an immediate risk of further overdose or self-injury?

What problems, both acute and chronic, confront the patient? Did a particular event precipitate the attempt?

Is the patient psychiatrically ill, and if so what is the diagnosis and how is this relevant to the attempt?

What kind of help would be appropriate, and is the patient willing to accept such help?

Issues concerning the degree of suicidal intent

Whether the attempt was impulsive or planned; if the latter, the duration of the plans.

Whether the patient was alone, or whether someone was present or within easy access.

Whether the patient was likely to be found soon after the attempt.

The nature of any precautions taken to prevent or ensure discovery.

The drugs taken, including the quantity, and whether other drugs were available but not taken; this includes the consumption of alcohol during or preceding the attempt.

The patient's expectation regarding the effect of the drugs or injury.

The presence of a suicide note or message, including tape-recorded statements.

The patient's efforts to obtain help after the attempt, and events leading to admission to hospital.

Assessment of current problems

Relationship with partner or spouse

Relationship with other family members, particularly young children

Employment or studies; Financial matters; housing

Legal, including pending court proceedings

Social isolation, relationship with friends

Psychiatric and physical health

Use of alcohol and drugs

Sexual adjustment

Bereavement and impending loss

Source: Adapted from K Hawton and J Catalan, Attempted suicide: a practical guide to its nature and management (Oxford University Press, 2nd ed., 1987).

Factors associated with subsequent suicide

Factors found to be associated with subsequent suicide include an age of 45 or over; male sex; being unemployed or retired; being separated, divorced, or widowed; living alone; poor physical health; having received medical treatment within six months; psychiatric disorder, including alcoholism; having used violent methods such as hanging, shooting, jumping, or drowning; the presence of a suicide note; and a history of previous attempts. As to these eleven factors, Tuckman and Youngman found that the risk of actual suicide increased in proportion to the number of predictors present. Attempters with two to five factors had a suicide rate of 6.98 per 1000 while those with ten or eleven had a suicide rate of 60 per 1000.[21] It can be seen that one weakness of some scales is that they concentrate only on things which tend towards hopelessness, despair, and thoughts of death. In concentrating on what the person does not have, his problems, they do not count how many things he still has left which predispose him to want to live — persons dear to him, opportunities for the future, and so forth.

SHORT-TERM CLINICAL SUICIDE RISK FACTORS

		Low	*Moderate*	*High*
1	**Recent losses**	None	Within last month	Within days of loss
2	**Depression-Anxiety**	Mild	Moderate	Severe
3	**Isolation-Withdrawal**	Regular social contacts	Some social contact	Socially isolated
4	**Hostility**	Mild	Moderate	Severe
5	**Hopelessness**	Mild	Moderate	Severe
6	**Disorientationdisorganisation**	None	Moderate	Severe
7	**Alcohol/drug abuse**	None to little	Frequent to excess	Chronic abuse
8	**Change in clinical features**	None		Unexplained improvements
9	*Suicide plan*			
9.1	**Method**	Undecided	Decided	Decided
9.2	**Availability**	No	Yes	Yes
9.3	**Time-place**	Not specific	Not specific	Yes
9.4	**Lethality**	Low None	Moderate	High
10	**Final arrangements**	None	Some planning	Written note, wills, possessions given away

Source: W.J. Fremouw, Suicide Risk: Assessment and Response Guidelines (Pergamon Press, 1990), p.38.

---

[21]   J. Tuckman and W.F. Youngman, "A scale for assessing suicide risk of attempted suicides" *Journal of Clinical Psychology* (1968) 24, 17–19. See K. Hawton and J. Catalan, *Attempted suicide: a practical guide to its nature and management* (Oxford University Press, 2nd ed., 1987), p.66.

The short-term risk

Motto studied a sample of 3000 hospitalised patients who were severely depressed or in a suicidal state, 38 of whom committed suicide within 60 days of the assessment.[22] The following nine factors were identified as indicators of short-term risk among this already high risk group of hospitalised patients: (1) prior psychiatric hospitalisation; (2) contemplation of suicide by hanging or jumping; (3) severe, moderate, or questionable suicidal impulses; (4) divorced marital status; (5) threat of financial loss; (6) sense of being a burden to others; (7) the interviewer having a mixed or negative reaction to the patient; (8) severe crying or inability to cry; (9) severe or moderate ideas of persecution or ideas of reference. The presence of any of the first four factors increased the risk of suicide three times within the next sixty days while the remaining factors increased the risk at least twofold. Motto reported that when four or more factors were present, 71 per cent. of the suicides were correctly identified while correctly excluding 81 per cent. of the non-suicides.

Levels of supportive observation

As a final note on the subject, it is worth referring to the different levels of observation in hospital. The following levels of observation are described by Morgan and Owen and it will be found in most cases that a similar three-tier structure is practised.[23]

OBSERVATION LEVELS

- Level 3   *Known place observation*   Patient not actively suicidal and judged free from immediate significant suicidal risk.

- Level 2   *15 minute observation*   Close relationship has been established with the patient who is judged not to be actively suicidal, but is considered to be at significantly increased suicidal risk compared with the average psychiatric inpatient.

- Level 1   *Constant observation*   Patient is expressing active suicidal intent, particularly if no close relationship has been established with him. Unpredictable psychotic states or recent deliberate self-harm with apparent serious suicidal intent may indicate this level of supportive observation.

FURTHER READING

There is an extensive literature on the subject of suicide, the following articles being but a small sample of those available: L. Appleby, "Suicide in psychiatric patients: risk and prevention" *British Journal of Psychiatry* (1992) 161, 749–75; C.V.R. Blacker, *et al.*, "Assessment of deliberate self harm on medical wards" *Psychiatric*

---

[22]   J.A. Motto, "Nine short-term predictors of suicide identified" *Clinical Psychiatry Newsletter*, June 1988. See W.J. Fremouw, *Suicide Risk: Assessment and Response Guidelines* (Pergamon Press, 1990), p.88.

[23]   H.G. Morgan And J.H. Owen, *Persons at risk of suicide: Guidelines on good clinical practice* (Boots, 1990).

Bulletin (1992) 16, 262–263; K. Hawton, "Assessment of suicide risk" *British Journal of Psychiatry* (1987) 150, 145–153; H.G. Morgan, "Suicide prevention. Hazards on the fast lane to community care" *British Journal of Psychiatry* (1992) 160, 149–153; H.G. Morgan and J.H. Owen, *Persons at risk of suicide. Guidelines on good clinical practice* (Boots, 1990); H.G. Morgan and P. Priest, "Suicide and other unexpected deaths among psychiatric in–patients. The Bristol confidential inquiry" *British Journal of Psychiatry* (1991) 158, 368–374; J.C. Rossiter, "Suicidal patients – effect on staff" *Psychiatric Bulletin* (1989) 13, 495–6; J.C. Rossiter, "Suicide" *Psychiatric Bulletin* (1991) 15, 674–5; P.M. Marzuk, *et al.*, "The effect of access to lethal methods of injury on suicidal rates" *Archives of General Psychiatry* (1992) 49, 451–8; N. Kreitman, "The coal gas story: UK suicide rates 1960–71" *British Journal of Preventative & Social Medicine* (1976) 30, 86–93; N.L. Farberow, *et al.*, "Case history and hospitalisation factors in suicides of neuropsychiatric hospital patients" Journal of Nervous and Mental Diseases (1966) 142, 32–44; C. Perris, *et al.*, "Some remarks on the incidence of successful suicide in psychiatric care" *Social Psychiatry* (1980) 15, 161–166; A. Prasad and G.G. Lloyd, "Attempted suicide by jumping" *Acta Psychiatrica Scandinavica* (1983) 68, 394–396; Warlingham Park Hospital (1974/75), Report of the Committee of Inquiry, Croydon Health Authority; C.P. Seager and R.A. Flood, "Suicide in Bristol" *British Journal of Psychiatry* (1965) 111, 919–932; A. Sims and K. O'Brien, "Autokabelesis: an account of mentally ill people who jump from buildings" *Medicine Science and the Law* (1979) 19, 195–198; I.W. Sletten, *et al.*, "Suicide in mental hospital patients" *Diseases of the Nervous System* (1972) 33, 328–334; E. Robins, *et al.*, "Some clinical considerations in the prevention of suicide, based on 134 successful suicides" *American Journal of Psychiatry* (1959) 49, 888–898; B. Rorsman, "Suicide in psychiatric patients: a comparative study" *Social Psychiatry* (1973) 8, 55–66; D.R. Chambers, "The Coroner, the Inquest and the Verdict of Suicide" *Medicine, Science and the Law* (1989) 29(3).

RISK TO SAFETY OF OTHERS

Although research findings tend to demonstrate a positive relationship between mental illness and offending, including violence, this must be seen against the general level of prevailing violence in homes and public houses and on the roads.[24] Mentally ill people contribute proportionately very little to the general problem of dangerous behaviour and the preventive confinement of dangerous offenders is of only marginal value as a protective device. Measured against the full range of modern social hazards, its contribution to public safety is tiny, as also is the likely impact on the rates at which serious offences are committed.[25]

---

[24] E. Fottrell, "Violent behaviour by psychiatric patients" in *Contemporary Psychiatry* (ed. S. Crown, Butterworths, 1984), pp.19–20.

[25] See J. Floud and W. Young, *Dangerousness and Criminal Justice* (Heinemann, 1981). A point endorsed by Sir Leon Radzinowicz in "Dangerousness and Criminal Justice: a few Reflections" (1981) *Criminal Law Review* 756. In 1976, the Howard League set up a committee under Floud's chairmanship to inquire into the protective sentencing of dangerous offenders in England and Wales other than those provided for under the Mental Health Act 1959.

RISK AND DANGER

A risk can in theory be measured and is the basis of actuarial prediction — in theory because in practice all of the critical variables never are known. While the risk depends on the situation, all of the situations in which the patient may find himself in the future can only be speculated upon. Danger is sometimes said to incorporate the weighting that people put on different kinds of risk. A situation is often viewed as dangerous when there is an unknown risk or a small known risk of a catastrophic outcome, such as suicide or homicide, or a significant risk of an adverse outcome involving significant physical harm. Thus, Floud has written that risks are perceived as dangers when fear is present.[26] It is the fear that the behaviour of people when mentally ill is unpredictable and not situation specific which mainly gives them such a high dangerousness rating, not danger as assessed by some objective criterion.[27] While people tend to ignore the risk of driving on a motorway or being killed by their spouse, they are fearful of the actuarially much smaller risks of flying or being injured by a dangerous offender. Although the actual risk posed by a person is static at any given time, the sense of danger is heightened if the situations in which that risk arises are not understood. No human event is ever truly random and terms such as "random violence" simply describe the predictable outcome of an unpredictable sequence of events, some of which take place in the person's mind. What level of uncertainty is tolerable is ultimately for the courts, including tribunals, to decide.

THE CONFIDENTIAL INQUIRY

The first report of the Confidential Inquiry into Homicides and Suicides by Mentally Ill People was published in 1996.[28] The terms of reference include enquiring into the circumstances leading up to and surrounding homicides committed by people discharged by the specialist psychiatric services. The first report was based on detailed consideration of 39 cases of homicide. 19 of the patients had previously been in-patients and five of them had been detained at some stage during the episode of illness leading up to the homicide. Three of these patients had been detained during the previous six months. The primary diagnoses of the patients were schizophrenia (males 55 per cent., females 8 per cent.); affective disorder (males 19 per cent., females 75 per cent.); personality disorder (males 26 per cent., females 17 per cent.). A secondary diagnosis of personality disorder was made in the cases of five men suffering from schizophrenia or paranoid psychosis. Two-thirds of the victims were family members. Nine of the 12 women killed their own children, eight of the nine being diagnosed as having a depressive disorder. Two-thirds of the offenders had been involved in earlier episodes of violent or aggressive behaviour and 26 per cent. had criminal convictions for violence. However, no aggression had

---

[26] J. Floud, "Dangerousness in social perspective" in *Psychiatry, human rights and the law* (ed. M. Roth & R. Bluglass, Cambridge University Press, 1985), p.82.

[27] J. Gunn, "Clinical approaches to the assessment of risk" in *Risk-taking in Mental Disorder: Analyses, Policies and Practical Strategies* (ed. D. Carson, S.L.E. Publications, 1990); M. Roth and R. Bluglass, "A postscript on the discussions at the Cambridge Conference on Society, Psychiatry and the Law" in *Psychiatry, human rights and the law, supra*, p. 232. This is one reason why the view that "if a person frightens you, he is probably dangerous" is so dangerous. As one of the Commissioners, Jeremy Walker, has pointed out, the important thing is that each mental health professional understands whether he is naturally over-anxious or under-anxious, a risk-avoider or a risk-taker, and then makes allowance for that.

[28] *Report of the Confidential Inquiry into Homicides and Suicides by Mentally Ill People* (Royal College of Psychiatrists, 1996).

been reported in 41 per cent. of cases during the period of care leading up to the death. Violent behaviour in other family members was noted in 11 cases. Only 16 per cent. of the out-patients had a care plan and in half the cases it was reported that no care plan had been implemented. There were problems with the administration of medicines in 41 per cent. of cases. Staff often said that the homicide had been totally unpredictable and that there had been no indicators of possible violence. Certain information about when patients were last seen by a doctor prior to the homicide appears to have been omitted from the published report.

PREDICTING VIOLENCE TOWARDS OTHERS

Having reviewed the literature, Steadman concluded that nowhere was there any documentation that clinicians can predict dangerous behaviour beyond the level of chance.[29] However, he has suggested five factors that may be risk markers for violence: the characteristics of social support available to the patient; impulsiveness; reactions to provocation; ability to empathise; and the nature of any hallucinations and delusions.[30] However, Crichton's recent review of the literature demonstrates that neither statistical models nor clinical skills are reliable predictors of future violence[31] and Monahan drew the following conclusions about assessments of dangerousness in the context of mental disorder[32]—

- The upper bound of accuracy that even the best system of risk assessment system could achieve was in the order of .33 so that for each mentally disordered person predicted to be violent two would not be.

- The best demographic predictors of violence among the mentally disordered were the same for the non-mentally disordered, *i.e.* age, gender, social class and history of offending.

- The poorest predicting factors among the mentally disordered were diagnosis, severity of disorder and personality traits.

The patient's mental state

The poorest predictors of violence include diagnosis and the severity of the disorder. In illnesses with a paranoid component, it is important to consider how a rational person would respond to the events which the patient believes are real if they were real, and to establish how he is likely to deal with these perceived threats. Most people who are sexually interfered with, or whose spouses are unfaithful, or whose

---

[29] See *e.g.* H.J. Steadman, "Predicting Dangerousness" in Rage, Hate, Assault and Other Forms of Violence (ed. D.J. Madden & J.R. Lion, Spectrum, 1976).

[30] H.J. Steadman, *et al.*, "From Dangerousness to Risk Assessment: Implications for Appropriate Research Strategies" in *Mental Disorder and Crime* (ed. S. Hodgins, SAGE Publications, 1993).

[31] See *e.g.* Crichton; P.D. Scott, "Assessing dangerousness in criminals" *British Journal of Psychiatry* (1977) 313, 127–142; T.R. Litwick, *et al.*, "The assessment of dangerousness and predictions of violence: recent research and future prospects" *Psychiatric Quarterly* (1993) 64, 245–273. See also J.J. Cocozza and H. J. Steadman, "Prediction in Psychiatry: an example of misplaced confidence in experts" *Social Problems* (1978) 25(3), 245–276; S. Winter, "Psychiatry in the Witness Box" *Social Work Today* (1981) 12,14.

[32] J. Monahan, "Risk assessment of violence among the mentally disordered: generating useful knowledge" *International Journal of Law and Psychiatry* (1988) 11, 249–257.

property is being stolen, or whose food is being poisoned, do not idly let this happen. Some people resort to litigation, others report the matter to the police, others move house or leave their job, or become reclusive, or make their home more secure, or confront their persecutors and angrily take the law into their own hands. In this respect, people who subjectively believe that these events are happening to them show a similar range of responses. Likewise, the person who thinks people are talking about him is as likely as anyone else to feel hurt about this and to respond meekly or violently. Similarly, some people who are dying take their lives, as do some people who only believe they are dying. If violence has not previously been a feature, predicting future violence depends on assessing the likelihood of the subjective events recurring and the ways in which the patient is likely to protect himself, as determined by his personality. According to Taylor, the range of risks have to be assessed in terms of their seriousness, immanence and likelihood. Relevant historical data, current dispositions (*e.g.* empathy and anger), symptomatology (*e.g.* delusions) and environmental stressors (including alcohol) all need to be considered.[33]

The importance of the personality

The underlying personality may be the determining factor in deciding whether the end result of an aggressive thought or fantasy is a violent act.[34] Megargee distinguished between "under-controlled" and "over-controlled" aggressors. He hypothesised that extreme assaultors are typically weak, mild-mannered people, with excessively high levels of inhibition about acting violently.[35] Psychometric measures of impulsivity have been shown to have a positive correlation with assaultativeness and with a tendency to "fail" subsequent to discharge from a special hospital. Blackburn concluded that in schizophrenia the patient's premorbid personality was more important in determining hostile behaviour than the illness.[36] Fottrell's view is that Brill and Malzburg's opinion that "an attack of mental illness with hospitalisation does not tend to leave an inclination towards criminal activity greater than that which existed prior to the illness" remains valid today.[37] Indeed, Sir Denis Hill considered that there were strong counterforces within the personalities of persons suffering from schizophrenia that prevented the expression of aggressive drives and this led to withdrawal and preoccupation with delusional ideas.[38]

Personality traits

Although it is commonsense that an individual's personality lays as large a part in determining how he responds to a subjectively threatening situation as it would if that event was actually taking place, it is nevertheless not possible to devise a list of personality traits which account for such variability of behaviour:

---

[33]   P. Taylor, Rehabilitation of Mentally Disordered Offenders conference, Oxford, 20 January 1993.

[34]   E. Fottrell, "Violent behaviour by psychiatric patients" in *Contemporary Psychiatry* (ed. S. Crown, Butterworths, 1984), p.20.

[35]   E.I. Megargee, "Uncontrolled and overcontrolled personality type in extreme antisocial aggression" *Psychological Monographs* (1966) 80, No. 3.

[36]   R. Blackburn, "Personality in relation to extreme aggression in psychiatric offenders" *British Journal of Psychiatry* (1968) 114, 821.

[37]   H. Brill and B. Malzburg, *Statistical Report on the Arrest Record of Male Ex-patients. aged 16 and over, Released from New York State Mental Hospitals during the period 1946–1948* (New York State Department of Mental Hygiene, 1954); E. Fottrell, "Violent behaviour by psychiatric patients," *supra*, p.21.

[38]   D. Hill in *The Natural History of Aggression* (ed. J.D. Corth & F.J. Ebbing, Academic Press, 1964).

"research has failed to show as much personality consistency as theorists would lead us to believe ... Studies which have looked at general traits such as anxiety or hostility have found that individual differences in the strength of a trait account for little of the variability of behaviour. What appears to matter most is the interaction of the differences in individuals with the differences in situations. In other words, it is not very useful to talk about general traits such as anxiety or hostility without considering the situation in which they may be exhibited. The importance of this in helping people with personality disorders is that one's efforts may be much more fruitfully directed towards finding situations in which the individual behaves less deviantly than in trying to change personality with psychotherapy."[39]

That being so, Powell has emphasised the importance of considering the underlying traits, then stating clearly the specific behaviour causing concern, and then describing the social context in which the personality problems exhibit themselves.[40]

Personality trait ⟶ Specific behaviour ⟶ Social context

The internalisation of acceptable behaviour

In personality disorder cases, some psychiatrists consider that the internalisation of acceptable behaviour is essential and reliance on external control is insufficient. This reflects the fact that people with a persistent impulse to act or react in a certain way are by definition prone to acting without much thought for the consequences. Indeed, the impulse to behave in that way may be triggered by finding themselves in a uncontrolled setting where there seems to be little prospect of detection.

The importance of the situation

Together with the individual's personality, the other factor which is always important is the particular situation. As to this, the Butler Report observed that dangerous behaviour depends in the majority of cases not only on the personality of the person concerned but also on the circumstances in which he finds himself:

"The practice of referring to some individuals as 'dangerous' without qualification creates the impression that the word refers to a more or less constantly exhibited disposition, like left-handedness or restlessness. It is true that there are people in whom anger, jealousy, fear or sexual desire is more easily aroused and whose reactions are more extreme than in most people, prompting them to do extremely harmful things. But these emotions are aroused and lead to harmful behaviour only in certain situations. A persistent housebreaker may go right through his criminal career without physically harming anyone; but if one day he is surprised, he may have it in him to commit an offence of violence. For some people drugs, alcohol or the excitement of a crowd may be a precipitating factor. The situation and circumstances which are potentially dangerous can often be defined, and sometimes foreseen and avoided or prevented. The individual who spontaneously 'looks for a fight' or feels a need to inflict pain or who searches for an unknown sexual victim is fortunately rare, although such people undoubtedly exist. Only this last group can justifiably be called 'unconditionally dangerous.'"[41]

---

[39] C.P.L. Freeman, "Personality disorders" in *Companion to psychiatric studies* (ed. R.E. Kendell & A.K. Zealley, Churchill Livingstone, 1993), p.591.

[40] G.E. Powell, "Personality" in *Scientific principles of psychopathology* (ed. P. McGuffin, *et al.*, Academic Press, 1984).

[41] *Report of the Committee on Mentally Abnormal Offenders*, Cmnd. 6244 (1975), para. 4.5.

The importance of supervision

It is crucial to assess the range of situations which might trigger the patient to behave violently given his personality and the likelihood of exposure to them. As to this, the Butler Report commented that those who discharged restricted patients had a responsibility to ensure that they "were subject to reassessment and control appropriate to their needs, that is to say having regard to the particular situations in which they may find themselves, and their possible reactions to them."[42]

Alcohol and drug-taking

A high percentage of murderers and their victims are intoxicated at the time of the crime. Lewis concluded that whilst the use of particular drugs in drug-dependent individuals may be associated with violent crime it is likely that a particular type of personality is necessary to produce violence.[43]

Arson

Persons suffering from schizophrenia may set fire to their home in response to auditory hallucinations and other patients may set fire to their property when manic or depressed. In a study of arsonists in a special hospital, McKerracher and Dacre found that as a group they had a higher psychotic morbidity level and a more marked history of attempted suicide than the other patients in the hospital.[44]

Past behaviour

Not surprisingly, there is evidence that the more violent offences a person has committed, the more chance there is that he will commit another. Although repeated offending is likely to be further repeated, the majority of offenders convicted of a single violent offence are not again convicted of violence.[45] Thus, while it is sometimes said that nothing predicts behaviour like behaviour, the approach has strict limitations (**724**).

CHARACTERISTICS OF VIOLENT IN-PATIENTS

Crichton has comprehensively reviewed the literature, drawing together the findings of various studies concerning the characteristics of violent in-patients.[46] A common feature of the studies was that a small number of patients were responsible for a significant proportion of the violent incidents reported. The highest rates of violence were in locked wards and intensive care units. In one special hospital, there was more than one life threatening incident per week.[47] The Health Services Advisory

---

42 *Report of the Committee on Mentally Abnormal Offenders*, Cmnd. 6244 (1975), *para. 4.6.*

43 A.J. Lewis, *Cannabis — A Review of the International Clinical Literature* (Home Office Advisory Committee on Drug Dependence), p.40.

44 D.W. McKerracher and A.J. Dacre, *British Journal of Psychiatry* (1966) 112,1151; See E. Fottrell, "Violent behaviour by psychiatric patients" in *Contemporary Psychiatry* (ed. S. Crown, Butterworths, 1984), p.23.

45 All that distinguishes a violent offender who does not reoffend from a non-violent person may be that a particular combination or sequence of events which causes both of them to react violently has actually taken place in the case of one of them but not the other. Hence, attempts to differentiate them from "normal" people have generally been unsuccessful.

46 J.M.H. Crichton, *Violence caused by psychiatric in-patients and its prediction: An introductory paper prepared for the Robinson Inquiry Seminar Day* (1994).

47 E. Larkin, *et al.*, "A preliminary study of violent incidents in a Special Hospital (Rampton)" *British Journal of Psychiatry* (1988) 153, 226–231.

Committee survey found that about one-tenth of psychiatric in-patients commit violent assaults against staff and NHS staff are three times more likely to suffer injury than industrial workers, mainly because of assault.[48] There is some evidence that recorded rates of in-patient violence are increasing.[49]

Diagnosis, gender and race

Although active psychotic symptoms are associated with an increased risk of violence,[50] the studies did not collectively establish a higher rate of violence among persons with a diagnosis of schizophrenia.[51] They tended to show either an equal rate of violence between the sexes or a greater rate of violence in female patients.[52] This was particularly so in secure settings such as special hospitals and prisons.[53] There was no consensus concerning the relationship between in-patient violence and race.

Structural factors

Violence appears to be more common where there is little structured activity.[54] Factors reported as being significant include poor staffing levels, the use of temporary staff, unpredictable ward programmes, and patients being under-occupied.

Antecedents of violence

Powell found that violence was commonly preceded by a high state of arousal (31 per cent. of cases), restrictions placed on patients (21 per cent.), and provocation by others (19 per cent.).[55]

---

[48]   *Violence to staff — Report of D.H.S.S. Advisory Committee on violence to staff* (D.H.S.S., 1988).

[49]   J.H.M. Crichton, Violence caused by psychiatric in-patients and its prediction (1994); R.M. Haller and R.H. Deluty, Assaults on staff by psychiatric in-patients *British Journal of Psychiatry* (1988) 152, 174–179; A.K. Shah, *et al.*, "Violence among psychiatric in-patients" *Acta Psychiatrica Scandinavica* (1991) 84, 305–309; D.V. James, *et al.*, "An increase in violence on an acute psychiatric ward: A study of associated factors" *British Journal of Psychiatry* (1990) 156, 846–852; P. Noble and S. Roger, "Violence by psychiatric in-patients" *British Journal of Psychiatry* (1989) 155, 384–390; Z. Walker and R. Seifert, "Violent incidents in a psychiatric intensive care unit" *British Journal of Psychiatry* (1994) 164, 826–828.

[50]   See J.M.H. Crichton, *Violence caused by psychiatric in-patients and its prediction, supra;* J. Monahan, "Risk assessment of violence among the mentally disordered: generating useful knowledge" *International Journal of Law and Psychiatry* (1988) 11, 249–257.

[51]   Various early studies conducted between 1965 and 1986 had failed to take into account the higher proportion of patients with schizophrenia found in hospital compared with other diagnoses.

[52]   See *e.g.* P. Noble and S. Roger, "Violence by psychiatric in-patients" *British Journal of Psychiatry* (1989) 155, 384–390; L. Binder and E. McNeil, "The relationship of gender to violent behaviour in acutely disturbed psychiatric patients" *Journal of Clinical Psychiatry* (1990) 51, 110–114; E. Fottrell, "A study of violent behaviour among patients in psychiatric hospitals" *British Journal of Psychiatry* 136 (1980) 216–221; E. Larkin, *et al.*, "A preliminary study of violent incidents in a Special Hospital (Rampton)," *supra.*

[53]   See *e.g.* E. Larkin, *et al.*, "A preliminary study of violent incidents in a Special Hospital (Rampton)," *supra;* T. Maden, "Women as violent offenders and violent patients" in *Violence in Society* (ed. P.J. Taylor, Royal College of Physicians, 1993); R.P. Dobash, *et al.*, *The Imprisonment of Women, Penal Regimes* (Blackwell Publications, 1986).

[54]   See *e.g.* M. Pearson, *et al.*, "A Study of violent behaviour among in-patients in a psychiatric hospital" *British Journal of Psychiatry* (1988) 149, 232–235; E. Fottrell, "A study of violent behaviour among patients in psychiatric hospitals," *supra.* Crichton also draws attention to the Torpy and Hall's study, which found virtually no violence in areas designated for occupation or therapy: D. Torpy and M. Hall, "Violent incidents in a secure unit" *Journal of Forensic Psychiatry* (1993) 4, 517–544.

[55]   G. Powell, *et al.*, "What Events Precede Violent Incidents in Psychiatric Hospitals?" *British Journal of Psychiatry* (1994) 165, 107–112;; G.J.M. Aiken, "Assaults on staff in a locked ward: prediction and consequences" *Medicine Science and the Law* (1984) 24, 199–207.

DISCHARGE AND AFTER-CARE PLANNING

The existence of separate health and social services authorities, and concern about the premature discharge of patients, has resulted in a plethora of enactments, directions, guidelines and codes concerning the discharge of patients and their after-care. The most important of them, and the way in which they inter-relate, are briefly summarised below before being considered in greater detail. For the sake of clarity, it is important to distinguish between statutory and non-statutory provisions and also between those which require only an assessment of a person's need for after-care; those which impose a duty to provide after-care; and those which are simply systems for carrying out assessments and delivering care.

MENTAL HEALTH ACT 1983, S.117 (413)

Health and social services authorities have a duty under section 117 of the 1983 Act to provide after-care for patients who have been detained in hospital for treatment. What constitutes after-care and the exact nature of that duty is not defined and no regulations have been made which prescribe how the duties are to be performed. The ambit of section 117 has already been considered (**418**).

DISCHARGE OF PATIENTS FROM HOSPITAL, HC(89)5 (750)

The Health Circular, "*Discharge of Patients from Hospital*," was issued in 1989 in response to criticism by a Select Committee of the lack of up to date guidance on discharge arrangements. It emphasises the need to provide families with information about after-care and to inform relevant community-based professionals of the patient's potential needs in time for them to be met. Planning should begin at an early stage. In non-emergency cases, where it is known that support will be required on discharge, discharge planning should start before admission. In emergency cases, it should be commenced as soon as possible after admission. No patient should be discharged without the authority of the doctor responsible for him, nor until the doctors concerned have agreed, and management is satisfied, that everything reasonably practicable has been done to organise the necessary care in the community.

CARE PROGRAMME APPROACH, HC(90)23 (752)

The care programme approach, set out in *Health Circular* (90)23, applies to all mentally ill patients who require psychiatric treatment or care, including persons residing in the community.[56] The purpose of the circular is to ensure the development of "systematic arrangements" and "effective systems" for assessing, reviewing, and meeting the health and social care needs of patients who can potentially be treated in the community. The circular emphasises that it is for professional staff to decide whether available resources enable acceptable arrangements to be made for treating a specific patient in the community and, where that is not the case, in-patient treatment should be provided or continued. The circular recommends that individual care programmes be co-ordinated and monitored by key-workers, who may come

---

[56] As drafted, the care programme approach circular only applies to persons suffering from mental illness but many authorities also apply the same approach to persons who suffer from mental impairment or psychopathic disorder, *e.g.* the Special Hospitals Services Authority.

from any discipline. In essence, the care programme approach is, as its name suggests, a non-statutory system for assessing and delivering communitybased health and social care. Because section 117 imposes a duty to provide after-care but no system for delivering it, the care programme approach has generally been used as the framework for providing after-care to such patients.[57]

CARE MANAGEMENT AND ASSESSMENT, NHS&CCA 1990 (156)

The 1990 Act requires local authorities to conduct community care assessments in certain circumstances. Section 47(1) states that, where it appears to a local authority that a person may be in need of "community care services", the authority is required to carry out an assessment of his need for those services and, having regard to that assessment, to decide whether his needs call for the provision by them of any such services. Although section 117 after-care is a "community care service," it should be emphasised that its provision to patients coming within the section is mandatory. There can be no question of unmet need with regard to such patients. "Care management" involves carrying out an assessment under section 47(1) and, where indicated, designing and implementing a "care package" agreed with the patient, his carers, and contributing agencies. "Care managers" undertake all or most of the "core tasks" of care management and act as brokers for services across the statutory and independent sectors; in theory, they are not involved in providing services.

Care management and the care programme approach

Departmental guidance stresses the need to ensure that social services care management systems are effectively integrated with the care programme approach, the development of which is primarily the responsibility of Health Authorities.[58] The Department of Health's present view is that multi-disciplinary assessment under the care programme approach will, if properly implemented, fulfil the statutory duties of social services departments to assess patients' needs for community care services under section 47.[59] To this extent, the care programme approach may be seen as a specialist variant of care management for people with mental health problems. Authorities should be aiming for a situation in which the appointed key worker carries out the overlapping care management functions of co-ordinating, monitoring and reviewing an agreed care plan.[60] Where the key-worker (provider) and care manager (purchaser) functions are vested in a single person, that person is expected to separate out his service provider and service purchasing roles as far as possible. However, if the two roles are combined, the care programme approach principle that the key worker not only co-ordinates care programmes but also provides services is not ultimately reconcilable with the care management principle that a care manager

---

[57]   Section 117 planning is sometimes said to have been "subsumed" within the care programme approach, with the provision of after-care to all in-patients being assessed under the latter system. Because resources are finite, after-care services may then be allocated to an informal patient or a section 2 patient in preference to a patient who has a statutory entitlement to them. It is difficult to see how the provision of after-care under s.117 can ever be "subsumed" within the care programme approach, since the first is a statutory duty and the second a mechanism for providing it. Insofar as the two overlap at all, to contend that the greater can be subsumed within the lesser is both contrary to logic and the meaning of the verb.

[58]   *Department of Health Executive Letter EL(93)119*, para. A8.

[59]   *NHS Management Executive Guidelines HSG(94)27*, para. 16.

[60]   *The Health of the Nation Key Area Handbook: Mental Illness* (Department of Health, 2nd ed., 1994), paras. 9.14–9.23.

is not involved in providing care. The duties of local authorities under the 1990 Act have already been considered (**154**). The important thing to remember here is that, in practice, the social services assessment of an in-patient's need for community care services is conducted as part of the overall care programme approach process.

SUPERVISION REGISTERS, HSG(94)5 (755)

Health Service Guidelines HSG(94)5,[61] issued on 1 February 1994 and in force from 1 April 1994, "requires" all Health Authorities to ensure through their contracts for mental health services that providers draw up, maintain and use supervision registers. The register is intended first and foremost for patients being cared for outside hospital. Supervision registers represent an extension of the care programme approach and are now an integral part of it. The purpose of the registers is to enable NHS trusts (and other NHS "provider units") to identify all individuals known "to be at significant risk of committing serious violence or suicide or of serious self-neglect as a result of severe and enduring mental illness," and who should therefore receive the highest priority for care and active follow-up.[62] For the purpose of the guidelines, "mental illness" includes people with a diagnosed personality disorder (psychopathic disorder).[63]

GUIDANCE ON DISCHARGE, HSG(94)27 (758)

On 10 May 1994, the NHS Executive issued further health service guidelines on the discharge of mentally disordered people and their continuing care in the community. The guidance in HSG(94)27[64] was part of the Secretary of State's ten point plan announced in August 1993. The other elements included the introduction of supervision registers and the proposed new power of supervised discharge, now known as after-care under supervision. The guidance set out in this circular includes advice on risk assessments and a recommended after-care form in the format of a check-list.

INTRODUCTION OF AFTER-CARE FORM (760)

In February 1995, the Department of Health circulated to health and local authorities, and other relevant organisations, an after-care form designed to be used for all patients discharged from psychiatric in-patient treatment, including those subject to section 117 of the Mental Health Act 1983. This should appear in the case notes.

AFTER-CARE UNDER SUPERVISION (422)

It has been noted that section 117 of the Mental Health Act 1983 imposes a statutory duty on Health Authorities and local social services authorities to provide after-care to patients who leave hospital having been detained there for treatment. The Mental Health (Patients in the Community) Act 1995 introduced a new power of supervised discharge. This allows an application to be made under Part II for an unrestricted

---

61   *NHS Management Executive Health Service Guidelines HSG(94)5.*
62   *Ibid.*, Annex A, para. 2.
63   *Ibid.*
64   "Guidance on the discharge of mentally disordered people and their continuing care in the community," *NHS Management Executive Health Service Guidelines HSG*(94)27.

patient who is liable to be detained for treatment, and therefore entitled to after-care under section 117, to be subject to "after-care under supervision" when he leaves hospital. The supplement to the Code of Practice states that the new power is primarily intended for patients whose care needs to be specially supervised in the community because of risk to themselves or others. This applies particularly to revolving door patients who have shown a pattern of relapse following discharge. The Act also amended the law concerning patients who are lawfully or unlawfully absent from hospital or place where they are required to reside. Thus, the Act provides for each of the three situations in which an unrestricted patient who has been detained for treatment may be in the community — he may have leave to be absent from hospital, or he may be absent from there without leave, he may have been discharged and no longer liable to detention. The new after-care under supervision provisions have already been considered. The important point to remember is that if an unrestricted patient is entitled to statutory after-care under section 117, he is now liable to receive it under statutory supervision. If he is not entitled to statutory after-care then nor is he liable to statutory supervision.

SUMMARY

Given the number of circulars issued since 1989, add to this the new legislation in 1995, and it is not surprising that most practitioners are confused about the precise inter-relationship between the different provisions and guidelines. The following table indicates which of them applies to each kind of detained patient. Because of public concern about incidents following the discharge of some patients, the Department of Health "requires" that supervision registers include where necessary persons suffering from a personality disorder. To this extent, the care programme approach has by implication also been extended to such persons.

DISCHARGE AND AFTER-CARE PROVISIONS

Authority for detention	Form of disorder	s.117	H.C. (89)5	C.P.A	Assess NHS&CCA	Register	1995 Act
Sections 3, 37, 47, 48	Mental illness	•	•	•	•	•	•
	Psychopathic disorder	•	•	?	•	•	•
	Mental impairment	•	•		•		•
Section 2	Mental illness		•	•		•	
	"Personality disorder"		•	?		•	
	Mental impairment		•				

The various enactments and guidelines do not ultimately form an entirely coherent framework. However, the guidelines require that all adults suffering from mental illness must have the benefit of proper discharge planning under the care programme approach. Beyond this, if confusion is to be avoided, it is important—

- to distinguish between statutory provisions, which have the force of law, and non-statutory guidelines issued by the Department of Health, which do not.

- to appreciate that the care programme approach confers no right to after-care and is simply a practical framework for assessing, delivering and co-ordinating medical treatment and social care in the community.

- to realise that, although section 117 after-care is a community care service for the purposes of the 1990 Act, the local authority cannot assess the patient as not requiring it and, furthermore, such assessments are in practice conducted as part of the overall care programme approach process.

- to note that the after-care under supervision legislation is an addendum to the duty to provide after-care under section 117 (the two statutory provisions in the 1983 Act form part of one framework) while supervision registers are an addendum to the care programme approach, and together form part of one non-statutory framework.

Bearing these points in mind, it can be seen that the following different situations can be identified.

Patients detained for assessment

Patients detained for assessment have no statutory entitlement to after-care under the 1983 Act but, equally therefore, they are not liable to after-care under supervision. The need for after-care services of patients considered to be mentally ill or to have a personality disorder should be assessed and, as necessary, delivered using the non-statutory care programme approach framework. Such patients should also be considered for placement on the supervision register where indicated. Although, as drafted, the care programme approach does not apply to patients whose only problem is mental handicap, it is almost invariably the case that hospitals apply the same care programme approach principles.

Unrestricted patients detained for treatment

Patients detained for treatment have a statutory entitlement to after-care under the Mental Health Act 1983 but, consequently, they may also be required to receive those services under statutory supervision. What the 1983 Act lacks is any framework for assessing the after-care services such patients need and for co-ordinating and delivering those services. The non-statutory care programme approach, which it is the primary responsibility of Health Authorities to implement, provides that practical framework. As long as the local social services authority which also has the duty to provide the patient with after-care is fully involved in that process, its involvement will also satisfy its obligation to assess the patient's need for after-care under the 1990 Act — after-care being a community care service. In the process of applying the care programme approach framework, the Health Authority will also determine whether a patient who is mentally ill or has a psychopathic disorder should be placed on the supervision register. Because of the way the statutory criteria for after-under under supervision are drafted, the Government's expectation is that if a supervision application is accepted in respect of a patient then he will normally also be placed on the supervision register. While the purpose of supervised discharge is to provide some statutory control over a patient in the community, the main purpose of the register is to record warning signs and other practical information about the identified risks in the particular case.

Restricted patients detained for treatment

The important point to remember in this case is that the after-care under supervision legislation does not extend to restricted patients. The pre-existing statutory framework, which provides for conditional discharge and recall, makes it unnecessary.

DISCHARGE PLANNING, HC(89)5

Health Circular (89)5 was issued in response to criticism of the Select Committee on the Parliamentary Commissioner for Administration. The Select Committee drew attention to the lack of up-to-date guidance on discharge arrangements and emphasised the need to provide families with information about care following discharge; to check the patient's mental state on the day of his planned departure from hospital; and to inform the patient's general practitioner and other relevant professionals of the patient's potential needs in time for them to be met. The circular emphasises the importance of ensuring that, before patients are discharged, proper arrangements are made for their return home and for any continuing care which may be necessary. The aim should be to encourage and restore independence in the home wherever possible or to facilitate the smooth transfer of the patient to alternative care in the community where this has been agreed.[65] The circular's particular importance in the context of tribunal proceedings lies in the emphasis which it places on the need to begin discharge planning at an early stage, involving where appropriate the primary health care team, local authority social services and others. In non-emergency cases, where it is known that support will be required on discharge, planning should start before admission.[66] In emergency cases, it should start as soon as possible after admission.[67] To ensure that all arrangements have been completed, responsibility for checking that the necessary action has been taken before a patient leaves the hospital should be given in one member of the staff caring for that patient.[68] No patient may be discharged without the authority of the doctor with responsibility for him[69] nor should any patient be discharged until the doctors concerned have agreed, and management is satisfied, that everything reasonably practicable has been done to organise the care which the patient will need in the community.[70] Relevant paragraphs of the circular are reproduced on the following page.

---

[65] Department of Health Circular HC(89)5, para. 3.
[66] *Ibid.*, para. 2.
[67] *Ibid.*, para. 2.
[68] *Ibid.*, para. 6.
[69] *Ibid.*, para. 4.
[70] *Ibid.*, para. 5.

HEALTH CIRCULAR (89) 5

February 1989

DISCHARGE OF PATIENTS FROM HOSPITAL

Background

2 ... Planning should begin at an early stage and involve, where appropriate, the primary health care team, local authority social services and others. For non-emergency cases where it is known that support will be required on discharge, planning should start before admission. For emergency cases it should start as soon as possible after admission. Lack of early and effective planning for services required after discharge can lead to "blocked beds" and unplanned readmission to hospital.

Discharge arrangements

5. Patients should not be discharged until the doctors concerned have agreed and management is satisfied that everything reasonably practicable has been done to organise the care the patient will need in the community. This includes making arrangements for any follow-up treatment, travel to, and any necessary support in, the home or other place in the community to which they are being discharged. They or their relatives must also be fully informed, and important points confirmed in writing, about such things as medication, lifestyle, diet, symptoms to watch for and where to get help if it is needed. Their ability to cope and access to emergency services and out-of-hours advice must be taken into account.

6. A number of staff (medical, nursing, therapy, social work, etc) may be involved in the preparations for discharge. To ensure that all arrangements have been completed, responsibility for checking that the necessary action has been taken before a patient leaves the hospital should be given in one member of the staff caring for that patient. The member of staff should have a check-list of what should have been done. If the completed check-list is filed in the patient's notes it will provide a permanent record of action taken before discharge. In many cases the patient, family or friends, will be capable of making all the arrangements for the return home. All that will be required of the nominated member of the hospital staff will be to ensure that they and the general practitioner have been given all the information they need. In other cases much more will be required, a range of services will have to be organised in advance and several agencies involved.

Local authorities and discharge planning

Local Authority Circular LAC(89)7 draws the attention of local authorities to *Health Circular* (89)5 and asks them to review their existing procedures, to ensure that people do not leave hospital without adequate arrangements being made for their support in the community. Local authorities are asked to co-operate with Health

Authorities in planning jointly for the discharge of patients from hospital and to ensure that relevant local authority staff have a clear understanding of their respective roles and responsibilities. The circular states that local authorities have a key role to play in ensuring that a range of services are available for patients who will need care and support on a continuing basis which cannot be provided by family and carers alone. Social services departments are responsible for a range of services which may be needed on discharge, including domiciliary help and care, day care services and the provision of disability equipment and adaptations. The services of local authority occupational therapists and rehabilitation officers may be required in some cases. In such cases, social services staff should be involved in assessing the patient's social care needs and home circumstances at an early stage before discharge. Social workers can advise on the particular package of services available from both statutory and non-statutory suppliers which will best meet the patients needs and preferences. They therefore have an important role to play in determining readiness for discharge and providing information, advice and counselling. Suitable accommodation is essential if people are to be able to resume independent living in the community. Social services departments should make sure that local authority housing departments are involved at an early stage in the planning process if the patient is not able to return to his or her former home or if it requires major adaptations. Any adaptations immediately necessary should have been made, or at least a firm timetable agreed, before the patient leaves hospital. Some patients may require a higher level of support which can best be provided through residential or nursing home care. Social services staff should be fully involved in assessing the need for residential care. If residential care is judged to be appropriate and is acceptable to the patient (and his or her family or corer if appropriate), close liaison with the staff of the residential care home, whether in the public, private or voluntary sector, should be established at an early stage in order to plan ahead for admission.

CARE PROGRAMME APPROACH, HC(90)23

The requirement to implement a care programme approach derives from the joint *Health/Social Services Circular* HC(90) 23/LASSL(90)11.[71] The care programme approach applies to all patients who require psychiatric treatment or care, including persons residing in the community. It requires health and social services authorities to develop care programmes based on proper "systematic arrangements" for treating patients in the community rather than by way of admission to hospital.[72] As its name suggests, it is a general scheme and does not give rise to a statutory duty towards any individual patient.

Aims of the Care Programme Approach

The care programme approach was developed with two purposes in mind. Firstly, to seek to ensure that patients treated in the community receive the health and social care they need, by introducing more systematic arrangements for deciding whether patients referred to the specialist psychiatric services can, given available resources, realistically be treated in the community. Secondly, to ensure that proper

---

[71] "The Care Programme Approach for People with a Mental Illness referred to the Specialist Psychiatric Services" *Department of Health Circular HC(90)23/LASSL(90)11.*

[72] *Ibid.*, Annex, para. 6.

arrangements are made for the continuing health and social care of those patients who can be treated in the community. The underlying purpose is therefore to ensure the support of mentally ill people in the community, thereby minimising the risk of them losing contact with services and maximising the effect of any therapeutic intervention.

Key elements of the care programme approach

Although the exact form which the care programme approach takes locally is largely a matter for individual Health Authorities, in discussion with social services authorities, all care programmes should include the following key elements—

- systematic arrangements for assessing the health care needs of patients who can potentially be treated in the community and for regularly reviewing the health care needs of those being treated in the community.

- systematic arrangements, agreed with social services authorities, for assessing and regularly reviewing the social care such patients need, in order to give them the opportunity of benefiting from treatment in the community.

- effective systems for ensuring that agreed health and social care services are provided to those patients who can be treated in the community.

It is essential to obtain the agreement of all professional staff and carers who are expected to contribute to a patient's care programme that they are able to participate as planned.

Resources

Proper arrangements should be in place for determining whether any services assessed as being necessary can be provided within available resources. It is for health and social services staff to decide whether the resources available enable acceptable arrangements to be made for treating specific patients in the community. If a patient's minimum needs for treatment in the community — both in terms of continuing health care and any necessary social care — cannot be met, in-patient treatment should be offered or continued. Health authorities should ensure that any reduction in the number of hospital beds does not outpace the development of alternative community services.

Key workers

Once an assessment has been made of the continuing health and social care needs of a patient who can be treated in the community, and all those expected to contribute have agreed that it is realistic, it is necessary to have effective arrangements for monitoring that the agreed services are provided and for maintaining contact with the patient. In the Department of Health's view, the most effective means of under-taking this work is through named individuals, called key-workers. Where this can be agreed between the relevant health and social services authorities, the ideal is for one named person to be appointed as the patient's key worker. His role will be to keep in close touch with the patient and monitor that the agreed health and social care is given. The key worker can come from any discipline but should be sufficiently experienced to command the confidence of colleagues from other disciplines. A particular responsibility of the key worker is to maintain sufficient contact with the patient to advise professional colleagues of changes in circumstances which might require review and modification of the care programme. When the key worker is unavailable, proper arrangements should be made for an alternative point of contact for the patient and any carer(s).

Maintaining contact with patients

Every reasonable effort should be made to maintain contact with the patient and, where appropriate, his carers, to find out what is happening, to seek to sustain the therapeutic relationship and, if this is not possible, to try to ensure that the patient and carer knows how to make contact with his key worker or the other professional staff involved. It is particularly important that the patient's general practitioner is kept fully informed of a patient's situation, and especially of his withdrawal from a care programme, and that day care, residential and domiciliary staff are given sufficient information to enable them to fulfil their responsibilities to the patient. The general practitioner will continue to have responsibility for the patient's general medical care if he withdraws from the care programme. Where a patient wishes to withdraw from part of a care programme only, the programme should be sufficiently flexible to accept such a partial withdrawal.

Supplementary guidelines

The "essential elements" of an effective care plan are systematic assessment, a care plan, the allocation of a key worker, and regular review. Supplementary departmental guidelines stress that the professionals responsible for making discharge decisions must be satisfied that these conditions are fulfilled before any patient is discharged.[73] The patient and others involved (including, as necessary, the carer, health and social services staff, and the patient's General Practitioner) should be aware of the contents of the care plan and should have a common understanding of — its first review date; information relating to any past violence or assessed risk of violence on the part of the patient; the name of the key worker; how the key worker or other service providers can be contacted if problems arise; what to do if the patient fails to attend for treatment or to meet other requirements or commitments.[74]

Mental Health Review Tribunals

Where a patient has applied for a tribunal, it is important that the "essential elements" of the care programme approach have been considered and can be put into operation if the patient is discharged, and that the key worker is made immediately aware of any conditions imposed.[75]

---

[73]   "Guidance on the discharge of mentally disordered people and their continuing care in the community," *NHS Management Executive Health Service Guidelines HSG*(94)27, para. 10.
[74]   *Ibid.*, para. 11.
[75]   *Ibid.*, para. 19.

SUPERVISION REGISTERS, HSG(94)5

Health Service Guidelines HSG(94)5[76] "requires" all Health Authorities to ensure through their contracts for mental health services that providers draw up, maintain and use supervision registers. The register is intended first and foremost for patients being cared for outside hospital. Supervision registers represent an extension of the care programme approach and are now an integral part of it.

Purpose of the supervision registers

The purpose of the registers is to enable NHS trusts (and other NHS "Provider Units") to identify all individuals known "to be at significant risk of committing serious violence or suicide or of serious self-neglect as a result of severe and enduring mental illness," and who should therefore receive the highest priority for care and active follow-up.[77] For the purpose of the guidelines, "mental illness" includes people with a diagnosed personality disorder (psychopathic disorder).

Administrative arrangements

Consideration for inclusion on the supervision register should take place as a "normal part" of discussing a patient's care programme before he leaves hospital and at care programme reviews following discharge. The decision as to whether a patient is included in the register rests with the consultant psychiatrist responsible for the patient's care. The decision should be taken in consultation with other members of the mental health team, including the social worker.

Criteria for inclusion

Patients should be included if they are suffering from a "severe" mental illness or a personality disorder and "are, or are liable to be at significant risk of committing serious violence or suicide or of serious self-neglect in some foreseeable circumstances which it is felt might well arise in this particular case (e.g. ceasing to take medication, loss of a supportive relationship or loss of accommodation)."[78] Judgements about risk should be based on detailed evidence, that evidence recorded in written form and available to relevant professionals.

Criteria for deregistration

The criteria for deregistration are that there is no longer considered to be a significant risk. The Health of the Nation Key Area Handbook includes guidelines about the possible need for registration of patients based upon their need for support.[79]

Categorisation

Patients entered on the register should be assigned to one or more of the three risk categories (significant risk of suicide, significant risk of serious violence to others, significant risk of severe self-neglect).

---

[76]   *NHS Management Executive Guidelines HSG(94)5.*

[77]   *Ibid.*, Annex A, para. 2.

[78]   *Ibid.*, Annex A, para. 3.

[79]   The Health of the Nation Key Area Handbook: Mental Illness (Department of Health, 2nd ed., 1994), p.100.

Group	Patient characteristics	Register
High support group	Individuals with severe social dysfunction (*e.g.* social isolation and/or difficulty with skills of daily living) as a consequence of severe or persistent mental illness or disorder. In particular individuals with the following difficulties will be identified for high levels of support— • current or recent serious risk to self or to others or of self-neglect • severe behavioural difficulties • high risk of relapse • history of poor engagement with mental health services • little contact with other providers of care • precarious housing (*e.g.* bed and breakfast) • require staff : patient ratio of about 1:15	✓ ?
Medium support group	Individuals with a moderate degree of social disability arising from mental illness or disorder, *e.g.* those able to work at least part-time and/or to maintain at least one enduring relationship. This group will also include the following individuals: • those likely to recognise and to seek help when early in relapse • those receiving appropriate services from other agencies	x
Low support group	Individuals who, following assessment, have been found to have specific and limited mental health-related needs which do not require extensive, multi-disciplinary input. In general, such individuals are likely to respond to brief or low-intensity intervention. For example: • patients with psychosis in remission • moderately severe personality disorder	x

Content of the registers

The Annex to *Health Service Guidelines* HSG(94)5 sets out the required contents of supervision registers, which are set out on the following page.

Challenging registration

In *ex p. M.*,[80] Waite J. granted certiorari quashing the entries on a council's child abuse register purporting to identify M. as the known or suspected abuser of a child K His Lordship stated that he was satisfied that it is not the law that local authorities are free to exercise arbitrary control over the entry of names of alleged abusers on a child abuse register with total immunity from supervision by the courts. Any such

---

[80]   *R. v. Norfolk County Council, ex p. M.* [1989] 2 All E.R. 359, *per* Waite J.

immunity would seriously erode the rights of the citizen. If similar principles to those propounded in *ex p. M.* are applied to supervision registers, an NHS provider unit has a legal duty to act fairly towards a patient whom it is considering registering. An entry on the register will be reviewable in the courts if that duty is breached, the entry was made in bad faith, or the decision to register was unreasonable within the limited sense of that term approved in *Associated Provincial Picture Houses Ltd. v. Wednesbury Corp.* 1 K.B. 223. Health service professionals will, however, enjoy a sensible latitude when deciding how the requirements of fairness are best to be satisfied in each case. Provided the registration procedure adopted represents a genuine attempt which is reasonable in the circumstances to reconcile the different interests, the courts will not substitute their judgement for that of health service professionals on the question of whether a significant risk exists.[81]

REQUIRED CONTENTS OF REGISTERS

Part 1. Identification

i.   Patient's full name, including known aliases, home address including postcode (or "no fixed address"), sex, and date of birth

ii. Patient's current legal status in respect of the Mental Health Act (*i.e.* whether on leave, under guardianship or subject to supervised discharge when available).

Part 2. Nature of risk

i.   Category of risk and specific warning indicators.

ii. Evidence of specific episodes of violent or self-destructive behaviour (including relevant criminal convictions) or severe self-neglect.

Part 3. Key worker and relevant professionals

i.   Name and contact details for patient's key worker.

ii. Name and contact details of other professionals involved in the care of the patient including the consultant responsible for his care.

Part 4. Care Programme

i.   Date of registration.

ii.   Date of last review.

iii. Date of next programmed review.

iv.   Components of care programme.

---

[81]   As to art. 17 of the European Convention on Human Rights, see *A. v. Norway* (unreported, January 1996), which involved the issues of whether a mental health register should be destroyed because it lacked the necessary basis in law and whether a registration provision contravened the Convention.

GUIDANCE ON DISCHARGE AND RISK ASSESSMENT, HSG(94)27

On 10 May 1994, the NHS Executive issued further health service guidelines on the discharge of mentally disordered people and their continuing care in the community. The guidance in HSG(94)27[82] was part of the Secretary of State's ten point plan announced in August 1993. The other elements included the introduction of supervision registers (755) and the proposed new power of supervised discharge (422). The guidance seeks to ensure that psychiatric patients are discharged only when and if they are ready to leave hospital; that any risk to the public or to patients themselves is minimal; and that when patients are discharged they get the support and supervision they need from the responsible agencies.

Discharge from hospital

The guidelines note that risk is a prime consideration in discharge decisions[83] and that, "generally speaking, mentally disordered people are much more likely to harm themselves or to harm others."[84] It is thus fundamental that full account is taken of the following three issues when deciding whether a person should be discharged from in-patient care: (1) whether, with adequate medication, care, and community supervision, he could still present any serious risk to himself or to others; (2) whether his need for therapy, supervision, sanctuary, or security requires continuing in-patient treatment; and (3) whether he can be cared for effectively and safely in the community, if necessary in staffed or supported accommodation.[85] Where discharge is indicated, it is essential that arrangements for discharge and continuing care are agreed and understood by the patient and everyone else involved, including private carers.[86] In particular, they should have a common understanding of the community care plan's first review date; information relating to any past violence or assessed risk of violence; the name of the key worker (prominently identified in clinical notes, computer records and the care plan); how the key worker or other service providers can be contacted if problems arise; and what to do if the patient fails to attend for treatment or to meet other requirements or commitments.[87]

Mental Health Review Tribunals

The guidelines state that where a patient has applied for a tribunal, it is "important" that the "essential elements" of care programme approach have been considered and can be put into operation if the patient is discharged, and that the key worker is immediately aware of any conditions imposed.[88]

Advice on risk assessment

The guidelines emphasise that patients "with longer term, more severe disabilities and particularly those known to have a potential for dangerous or risk-taking

---

[82]   "Guidance on the discharge of mentally disordered people and their continuing care in the community," *NHS Management Executive Health Service Guidelines HSG*(94)27.
[83]   *Ibid.*, para. 3.
[84]   *Ibid.*, para. 2.
[85]   *Ibid.*, para. 1.
[86]   *Ibid.*, para. 4.
[87]   *Ibid.*, para. 11.
[88]   *Ibid.*, para. 19.

behaviour need special consideration both at the time of discharge and during follow-up in the community. No decision to discharge should be agreed unless those taking the clinical decisions are satisfied that the behaviour can be controlled without serious risk to the patient or to other people. In each case it must be demonstrable that decisions have been taken after full and proper consideration of any evidence about risk."[89] There must be a full risk assessment prior to discharge.[90] Although the progress of many people after discharge can be monitored adequately by attendance at an out-patient clinic to see a psychiatrist, and/or by visits by a community mental health nurse, "this is unlikely to be sufficient for those patients presenting a complex range of needs. They are likely to need regular and, at times, possibly urgent multi-disciplinary re-assessments by the community based team ... Where an urgent problem arises, one responsible person (preferably the key worker or another professional in consultation with the key worker) should take the necessary immediate action followed by a wider consultation as soon as possible."[91]

Risk assessment

The guidelines include very brief notes on four stages in the assessment of risk: (1) ensuring that relevant information is available; (2) conducting a full assessment of risk; (3) seeking expert help; and (4) assessing the risk of suicide.

Making sure relevant information is available

A proper assessment cannot be made in the absence of information about a patient's background, present mental state and social functioning, and also his or her past behaviour. It is essential to take account of all relevant information, whatever its source. Too often, it has proved that information indicating an increased risk existed but had not been communicated and acted upon.[92]

INFORMATION ABOUT RISK — THE KIRKMAN INQUIRY

- the past history of the patient

- self reporting by the patient at interview

- observation of the behaviour and mental state of the patient

- discrepancies between what is reported and what is observed

- psychological and, if appropriate, physiological tests

- statistics derived from studies of related cases

- prediction indicators derived from research

Source: Report of the Panel of Inquiry Appointed to Investigate the Case of Kim Kirkman; West Midlands Regional Health Authority, 1991; Health Service Guidelines (94)27, para. 28.

---

[89] "Guidance on the discharge of mentally disordered people and their continuing care in the community," *NHS Management Executive Health Service Guidelines HSG*(94)27, para. 23.
[90] *Ibid.*, para. 24.
[91] *Ibid.*, para. 25.
[92] *Ibid.*, para. 28.

Conducting a full assessment of risk

According to the Kirkman Inquiry, "the decision on risk is made when all these strands come together in what is known as clinical judgement; a balanced summary of prediction derived from knowledge of the individual, the present circumstances and what is known about the disorder from which he suffers."[93]

Defining situations and circumstances known to present increased risk

Research has established that there are particular situations and circumstances which may indicate an increased level of risk, examples being when drug or alcohol misuse co-exist with a major mental disorder or when a patient has multiple psychiatric diagnoses.[94] Based on past experience, it is often possible to identify circumstances under which it is likely that an individual will present an increased risk; to indicate what must change to reduce this risk; to propose how these changes might be brought about; and to comment on the likelihood of interventions successfully reducing risk. Some examples are when a patient stops medication; when a person who has previously offended under the influence of alcohol or drugs starts drinking again or enters an environment where drugs are commonly available; when a person whose aggression has been apparent in one particular situation, *e.g.* in the context of a close relationship, enters another similar relationship.[95]

Seeking expert help

Expert forensic help should always be accessible to local psychiatric teams and should be used in difficult or doubtful cases.

Assessing the risk of suicide

The guidelines note that two-thirds of people committing suicide previously mentioned their suicidal ideas and a third had expressed clear suicidal intent. Most people who kill themselves have had recent contact with health care professionals. Among adolescents the most significant predictor in males is attempted suicide (possibly with a mood disorder or substance misuse) and, in females, a mood disorder. The period around discharge from hospital is a time of particularly high risk of suicide, which emphasises the need for proper assessment prior to discharge and effective follow-up afterwards."[96]

INTRODUCTION OF AFTER-CARE FORM

In February 1995, the Department of Health circulated to health and local authorities, and other relevant organisations, an after-care form designed to be used for all patients discharged from psychiatric in-patient treatment, including those subject to section 117. The use of the form, though not mandatory, was strongly recommended as constituting good practice and was devised in response to a recommendation of the *Inquiry into the Care and Treatment of Christopher Clunis.*[97]

---

[93]   *Report of the Panel of Inquiry Appointed to Investigate the Case of Kim Kirkman* (West Midlands Regional Health Authority, 1991); "Guidance on the discharge of mentally disordered people and their continuing care in the community," *NHSME Health Service Guidelines HSG(94)27*, para. 28.

[94]   *NHS Management Executive Health Service Guidelines (94)27*, para. 28; J. Swanson, *et al.*, Violence and psychiatric disorder in the community: Evidence from the Epidemiologic Catchment Area Surveys" *Hospital and Community Psychiatry* (1990) 41, 761–770.

[95]   *NHS Management Executive Health Service Guidelines (94)27*, para. 28.

[96]   *Ibid.*, para. 31.

[97]   *Report of the Inquiry into the Care and Treatment of Christopher Clunis* (H.M.S.O., 1994).

Those parts of the form particularly relevant to tribunal decision-making are presented below. In many cases, it will be appropriate to require the responsible authority to furnish the tribunal with the form, as a convenient summary of where the discharge process has reached. The following parts of the form are not reproduced: 1 About the patient; 2 Patient's nominated contact; 3 Key worker's details; 7 Review; 8 Transfer of responsibility for patient's after-care; 9 Discharge from after-care.

CHECKLIST FOR THE AFTER-CARE OF PSYCHIATRIC PATIENTS

4 After-care plan

(a) an after-care plan was agreed with the patient on	*give date*
(b) patient agrees with the after-care plan	*yes / no*
(c) the patient is subject to section 117 of MHA 1983	*yes /no*

5 Information to be included in the after-care plan

If any of the following apply to the patient, details must be recorded in the after-care plan

(a) in receipt of local authority care management	*yes / no*
(b) on supervision register	*yes / no*
(c) subject to conditional discharge	*yes / no*
(d) subject to statutory supervision by probation service	*yes / no*
(e) subject to statutory supervision by probation service	*yes / no*
(f) subject to guardianship	*yes / no*
(g) subject to CPIA 1991	*yes / no*
(h) subject to supervised discharge	*yes / no*

6 Availability of information

Where any of the following information is not available a full explanation must be recorded in the patient's after-care plan

(a) full contact list of those involved in the patient's care	*yes / no*
(b) patient's health and social needs identified	*yes / no*
(c) patient's health and social needs addressed in the after-care plan	*yes / no*
(d) risk assessment carried out	*yes / no*

Patient's after-care plan contains

(e) details of signs and symptoms suggesting likely relapse	*yes / no*
(f) steps to be followed in the event of relapse	*yes / no*
(g) steps to be followed if the patient fails to attend for treatment or meet other commitments	*yes / no*
(h) action to be taken if the patient's relative or carer can no longer provide assistance and support	*yes / no*

DISCHARGE PLANNING AND RESTRICTED PATIENTS

The assessment of risk in a restricted case is often, but not exclusively, concerned with the probable repetition of the conduct comprising the index offence, since a person is likely to be labelled as dangerous only if such behaviour is expected to continue.[98] In deciding whether detention is no longer necessary for the protection of other persons, tribunals will inevitably have particular regard to the likelihood of future serious offending. The impossibility of certain prediction is the central problem. Much of the research has concentrated on the actuarial use of information about people's past behaviour, ages, circumstances, psychological and social characteristics, as well as assessments of them by other people with relevant training or experience. Prediction of this kind assigns individuals to probability groups with differing rates of offending but it is impossible to predict with certainty that a given individual will or will not offend in future. A patient who is a model of conformity and good behaviour and exhibits no symptoms of mental disorder in hospital over a period of years may behave differently after release, given the greater opportunities to do harm which freedom in the community brings. Because assessments of risk are unreliable, most restricted patients will be granted leave of absence before being discharged from hospital subject to conditions, including supervision by a psychiatrist and social supervisor. Patients detained in special hospitals are usually rehabilitated into the community via regional secure units or local hospitals. Very few are conditionally discharged from a special hospital to independent or supervised accommodation. Responsibility for arranging transfer to conditions of lesser security rests with the hospital managers and the patient's doctor.

THE USUAL DISCHARGE PROCESS

While each case must necessarily be considered on its own merits, the general pattern of progression from detention in conditions of maximum security to absolute discharge is most often as follows. After progressing through the special hospital system to a pre-discharge ward, the patient will spend a period of leave of absence at a regional secure unit. If this is successful, and it is likely that he can be discharged from there within eighteen months to two years, he will be formally transferred to the hospital. Prior to being discharged, the patient may spend a period of time on an open ward in the local hospital, gradually being granted increasing periods of leave in the community. Leave is usually granted subject to an escort in the first instance. Discharge from hospital is initially subject to conditions and recall. In most cases, serious consideration will be given to a conditionally discharged patient's absolute discharge if he remains well and there are no other problems for a period of between two and five years. Prior to then, the conditions may be gradually relaxed but the patient remains liable to be recalled to hospital for a further period of in-patient treatment. Before a special hospital patient can realistically expect to be discharged,

---

[98] *Report of the Committee on Mentally Abnormal Offenders*, Cmnd. 6244 (1975), para. 4.9. It should be emphasised that it was not a condition of imposing a restriction order under the 1959 Act that restrictions were necessary to protect the public from serious harm. Furthermore, prior to 1991, a restriction order was mandatory if a person's case was disposed of under the Criminal Procedure & Insanity Act 1964. Under the present provisions, it is similarly the case that a restriction direction is mandatory if a person remanded in custody in criminal proceedings is removed to hospital under section 48. In all these cases, therefore, there is no "serious harm" requirement.

it is therefore often necessary for him to first be transferred to a less secure hospital and to have trial periods of leave in the community. However, a tribunal has no power to direct that a patient be transferred or granted leave with a view to facilitating his discharge on a later date. Similarly, it does not possess any statutory power to recommend that such a step be taken and to reconsider the patient's case in the event that its recommendation is not complied with. In practice, this means that, if the Secretary of State considers that a patient should remain in a special hospital, or does not consent to a patient having trial leave in the community, it will often be difficult for a tribunal to be satisfied that he meets the criteria for being discharged from hospital. In short, the Home Secretary has sole control over the steps preparatory to discharge and sole control over the patient's recall to hospital once discharged.

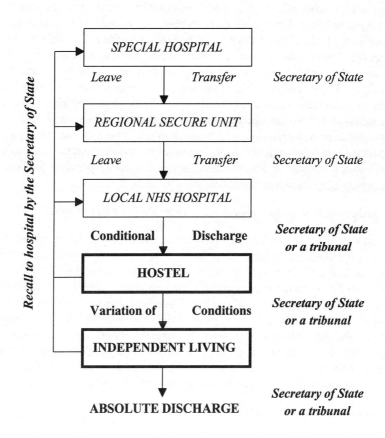

HOME OFFICE POLICY AND PROCEDURES (162, 334)

The Home Office's policies and procedures in relation to proposals for transfer, leave and discharge have been summarised by Pickersgill.[99]

---

[99]   A. Pickersgill, "Balancing the public and private interests" in *Risk-taking in Mental Disorder; Analyses, Policies and Practical Strategies* (ed. D. Carson, S.L.E. Publications, 1990).

Proposals for transfer or leave to reside at another hospital

The Home Secretary will only agree to a patient being moved to another hospital if he is satisfied that this will not give rise to any unacceptable risk. In reaching his decision, he takes account of information provided by the police and psychiatrists at the time of the index offence and information on the patient's condition and progress contained in subsequent reports from the responsible medical officer, including the periodic reports which the latter must submit at yearly intervals. He does not operate a "tariff" system on the length of time for which individual patients, or types of offender, should be detained. Nor does he try to second guess medical opinions, because he is not qualified to do so. The Home Office does, nevertheless, scrutinise transfer proposals closely, in order to verify that account has been taken of all the relevant factors; that there is an adequate understanding of how the patient came to commit his index offence; and that there is sufficient evidence to suggest that he has changed in hospital and is unlikely to abscond or reoffend if treated in less secure conditions. If the Home Office is not persuaded by the responsible medical officer's arguments in favour of transfer, or there appear to be serious gaps in his knowledge, it normally writes to him and invite his further comments before reaching a final decision. While recognising that assessing a person's mental condition and potential risk to the outside world is extremely difficult, the Home Office's concern is always to satisfy itself that the apparent risk to the public is low enough to be acceptable, and that everything possible will be done to minimise that risk if the patient moves to less secure conditions or into the community. It is these considerations which may lead to a proposal for transfer being refused if the responsible medical officer is unable to allay the initial doubts about its validity.[100]

Consideration of proposals for leave to be absent from hospital

Following transfer to a less secure hospital, the Home Office monitors the patient's progress closely to see how he settles into the new environment. Once it is satisfied that he has settled, consent is usually given to any reasonable leave arrangements which the responsible medical officer may propose.[101] These vary depending on the type of hospital and the individual's response to further treatment. While his escorted leave and group outings take place from special hospital, unescorted leave is extremely rare. However, patients at regional secure units are normally given gradually increasing freedom, working through escorted leave and short periods of unescorted leave to longer periods of unescorted leave, involving overnight or weekend absences, or regular absences to attend a training course or to take a job.

Proposals for conditional discharge

Proposals for a restricted patient's conditional discharge are considered with a similar or even greater degree of caution than transfer proposals. However, the Home Office recognises that no decision can be completely without risk and it has never sought to detain any patient until such an unlikely state is reached.[102] In particularly difficult cases, the Secretary of State seeks the views of the Advisory Board on Restricted Patients (**165**). Consideration of a patient's suitability for

---

[100] A. Pickersgill, "Balancing the public and private interests" in *Risk-taking in Mental Disorder; Analyses, Policies and Practical Strategies* (ed. D. Carson, S.L.E. Publications, 1990).

[101] *Ibid.*

[102] *Ibid.*

conditional discharge involves a complete reappraisal of the case, including scrutinising all the reports on the patient from the time of his arrest, and assessing the likely effectiveness of the proposed placement and supervision arrangements in terms of reducing the risk of relapse or reoffending. As with transfers, the key factors are that the Home Office wishes to be satisfied that the circumstances and motivation for the index offence are fully understood and that there is strong evidence to suppose that the patient is no longer the person he was when the offence occurred. Consideration is always given to the type and location of the proposed placement and the degree of supervision which will be provided. The supervising psychiatrist and social worker are given as much information as possible about his background and the offence and sent copies of the relevant Home Office guidance.

The form of disorder from which the patient suffers

The type of disorder from which the patient suffers often has a bearing on how difficult it is to assess his suitability for discharge. According to Pickersgill—

- A number of people with schizophrenia who attack other people because of delusions they suffer when unwell respond to medication. Consideration of proposals for the discharge of such patients therefore tends to be relatively straightforward as long as the Home Office is satisfied that the offences stemmed solely from the mental illness and will not be repeated as long as the patient takes his medication. A more cautious approach has to be exercised where such patients have little insight into their illness and the need for medication unless they receive depot injections and will be closely supervised in independent accommodation or a hostel setting.

- The suitability for discharge of patients suffering from mental impairment, severe mental impairment or psychopathic disorder, on the other hand, can be extremely difficult to assess, since the motive for the index offence in such cases is not always readily understood. This is especially so if a patient's mental handicap means that he cannot readily explain his thoughts and feelings at the relevant time. It is also extremely difficult to assess the degree of response to treatment. A number of these patients will require hospital care for the rest of their lives, in their own interests as well as the interests of others. Where possible, they can be discharged to sheltered housing if they have clearly become less explosive, less impulsive and better behaved with prolonged training.

- The word of patients suffering from psychopathic disorder cannot always be relied on, which poses similar problems in trying to gauge their motives and the extent to which psychotherapy and other treatment has successfully addressed their personality problems. The factors which the Home Office looks for include signs of a greater maturity, more stable behaviour, a greater tolerance of frustration and stress, together with evidence that the patient has some insight into his condition, a realistic conception of his life in the community, and a willingness to co-operate with his supervisors. Evidence of an ability to abstain from drugs, and to reduce or stop his intake of alcohol, can also be an important precondition to discharging a patient where these substances clearly contributed to the index offence.

The Home Office Checklist

The Secretary of State sends a checklist of relevant considerations to the responsible medical officer each year when a report is due on a restricted patient's progress. The questions comprised within it are an excellent aide-mémoire for tribunals and advocates when it comes to dealing with considerations of public safety.

THE HOME OFFICE CHECKLIST

---

1. Has any information come to light since the last report which increases understanding of the circumstances surrounding the index offence?

2. Is the motivation for behaviour that has put others at risk understood?

3. Is there any evidence that the patient has a persistent preoccupation with a particular type of victim or a particular type of violent/sexual/ arsonist activity?

4. What are the chances of circumstances similar to those surrounding the offence arising again and similar offences occurring?

5. In cases of mental illness, what effects have any prescribed drugs had? Do any symptoms remain? How important is the medication for continued stability? Has stability been maintained in differing circumstances? Does the patient have insight into the need for medication?

6. In cases of mental impairment, has the patient benefited from training? Is the patient's behaviour more socially acceptable? Is the patient explosive or impulsive?

7. In cases of personality disorder, is the patient now more mature, predictable and concerned about others? Is he more tolerant of frustration and stress? Does he now take into account the consequences of his actions? Does he learn from experience?

8. Does the patient now have greater insight into his condition? Is he more realistic and reliable?

9. Have alcohol or drugs affected the patient in the past? Did either contribute towards his offences?

10. Has the patient responded to stressful situations in the hospital in the past and how does he respond now — with physical aggression or verbal aggression?

11. If the patient is a sex offender, has he shown in the hospital an undesirable interest in the type of person he has previously been known to favour as his victim? What form has any sexual activity taken? What have been the results of any psychological tests?

12. What views do members of the clinical team have about the patient's continuing dangerousness?

13. Is it considered that the patient should/should not continue to be detained? For what reasons?

14. If so, is it considered that detention in conditions of special security is necessary?

PATIENT'S MENTAL STATE AND INDEX OFFENCE

When determining whether a patient meets the criteria for discharge, and the conditions of discharge, a tribunal will have particular regard to the circumstances of the index offence, the patient's mental state, his personality, the circumstances in which the public might be at risk, and (having regard to all of these matters) the management and supervision of the patient if discharged.

Prins' approach

Prins has suggested nine questions which may help in deciding whether to relax control and supervision of a mentally disordered offender who has a proven history of past violence.[103]

PRINS' NINE QUESTIONS

---

1. Have past precipitants and stresses in the patient's background been removed or sufficiently alleviated?

2. What is the patient's current capacity for dealing with provocation?

3. Have the clues to the patient's self image been explored at sufficient depth?

4. How vulnerable and fragile does the patient seem to be? Were the circumstances of the original offence the last straw in a series of stressful events, or does the individual see everybody else as hostile?

5. Was the behaviour person-specific or aimed at society in general?

6. Has the patient come to terms, in part if not in toto, with their offending act?

7. Have the details about the original offence been examined?

8. Has the health care institution monitored the patient's reaction to stress and temptation?

9. Has it been borne in mind that the patient's denial of the original offence may reflect the truth?

Other issues to be addressed

In various other publications, Prins has recommended that the following questions also be asked where consideration is being given to the release of a restricted patient—

---

[103]   H. Prins, "Social factors affecting the assessment of risk; with special reference to offender patients" in *Risk-taking in Mental Disorder; Analyses, Policies and Practical Strategies* (ed. D. Carson, S.L.E. Publications, 1990).

- How well has the patient used the various therapeutic opportunities in hospital? Is there a reasonable degree of consensus about progress? If not, what conclusions can be drawn from this fact?

- If mental illness contributed to the commission of the index offence, is it now under control? If there is a clear need for medication after discharge, how reliable are estimates of the individual's capacity to co-operate with those responsible for its administration upon discharge?

- Have the circumstances that contributed to the original offence changed substantially? If not, how much oversight may be needed to combat the resurgence of stressful events?

- Is it possible to gauge the degree of empathy the patient has for others? This question is particularly important in relation to patients suffering from a psychopathic disorder and those who have committed serious sexual offences, particularly against children.

- If alcohol or illicit drugs played a key role in the commission of the index offence, what is his likely response to them following release? A graded or phased return to the community in which opportunities for controlled and observed ingestion may be indicated.

THE MANAGEMENT OF DANGEROUS BEHAVIOUR

Because it is impossible to accurately predict the circumstances in which a person who has previously behaved dangerously might again behave dangerously, a cautious approach is taken to discharge. Consequently, many people are not discharged who could safely be discharged because there is no compelling evidence that they are now safe. More particularly, it is usually difficult to determine whether the improved behaviour of a previously violent patient in a secure hospital is attributable to natural remission or maturation, successful treatment or skilful management. That being so, there is generally a presumption that the person may still be dangerous in certain circumstances and this possibility is explored by gradually reintroducing him into the community, and monitoring his behaviour in different situations.

The three Ss

Professor John Gunn has emphasised the three "Ss" involved in the management of risk: security, supervision and support.[104]

Security

Security involves considering the necessity for detention in locked accommodation, the need for specialist services, and the level of nursing support. Decisions about the degree of security required will be affected by the seriousness of previous aggression; the seriousness of the disorder; and the nature of the disorder. The aim should be for the minimum level of security which is compatible with good management.

---

[104]   J. Gunn, "Clinical approaches to the assessment of risk" in *Risk-taking in Mental Disorder; Analyses, Policies and Practical Strategies* (ed. D. Carson, S.L.E. Publications, 1990), pp.16–17.

Supervision

It is usually a condition of any discharge that the patient is supervised by a social worker or a probation officer. Supervision is the continuous assessment of risk with a readiness to intervene if the risk increases in some way. It requires resources, good relationships between supervisors and the other persons in contact with the patient, and an in-depth knowledge of the individual and his environment. The majority of restricted patients require considerable supervision following discharge and each person involved in the process needs to be fully informed about his background and present situation.[105] The assessment of the likely effectiveness of subsequent control must be a major consideration when the decision whether or not to release is taken.[106] Supervision "cannot provide, and is not intended to provide, physical surveillance hour by hour and day by day, and it is evident that control over the personal relationships of a person who is subject to supervision entails particular difficulty."[107] However, the "supervising officer is sometimes in a position to recognise that the discharged patient may be moving into a similar situation to that which originally precipitated an offence of violence; or to perceive other signs indicating the likelihood of a repetition of dangerous behaviour. Where this is so he can take steps to warn the patient and if necessary arrange for him to be recalled to hospital."[108] If a patient is recalled as soon as a difficulty or risk arises, he is not helped to deal with the situation, suffers a positive set-back and a fresh interruption of his life, and his attitude towards his supervising officer is likely to be seriously undermined. However, the consequences of failure to recall in a deteriorating situation may be serious. The Butler Committee had "no doubt that in general the presumption on the part of the hospital should be in favour of supporting the supervising officer by readily agreeing to accept a patient on recall, even if only for a brief period of observation."[109]

Support

Support entails a strong commitment to an individual, mutual trust, and an acceptance of him without acceptance of his behaviour. It means being available at inconvenient hours and making special arrangements for him, such as having an emergency admission policy.

Sex offenders

Sexual behaviour is very difficult to alter but sometimes very potent in creating aggressive or risky behaviour.[110] It is unwise to discharge a child-sex offender to unsupervised accommodation in close proximity to a park or school, with no pre-arranged activities to occupy him during those hours when children will be in the vicinity.

---

[105]   *Report on the Review of Procedures for the Discharge and Supervision of Psychiatric Patients subject to Special Restrictions* (Cmnd. 5191, 1973), para. 43.

[106]   *Report of the Committee on Mentally Abnormal Offenders*, Cmnd. 6244 (1975), para. 4.7. In the Iliffe case, in which it was known that if the patient remarried there might then be a specific risk to his wife. In the event, he remarried without the knowledge of the supervising officer.

[107]   *Ibid.*, para. 4.30.

[108]   *Ibid.*

[109]   *Ibid.*, para. 4.31.

[110]   J. Gunn, "Clinical approaches to the assessment of risk" in *Risk-taking in Mental Disorder; Analyses, Policies and Practical Strategies* (ed. D. Carson, S.L.E. Publications, 1990), p.15.

PREPARING FOR DISCHARGE

The Home Office and Department of Health guidelines for staff of the discharging hospital are set out below.[111] The guidelines are particularly useful when it comes to considering whether any conditional discharge should be deferred.

Notes for the guidance of hospitals preparing for conditional discharge

Summary of recommendations for staff of the discharging hospital

1. Preparation for discharge should begin as soon as such an outcome seems likely.

2. The multi-disciplinary clinical team should instigate an individual programme of treatment and rehabilitation and reach a common view about the patient's expected approximate length of stay.

3. The hospital social work department should maintain links with outside individuals and agencies who may be able to offer support to the patient after discharge.

4. The multi-disciplinary team should have a clear idea of the arrangements in the community which will best suit the patient.

5. The potential supervisors should be involved as early as practicable in the multi-disciplinary team's preparations for the patient's discharge, with an opportunity to attend a case conference and meet the patient.

6. After the identification of supervision and after-care arrangements best suited to the patient's needs, nominated members of the multi-disciplinary team should be responsible for arranging the various elements to be provided.

7. Where the choice of supervision between the probation service or the social services department is clear cut, a request for the nomination of an individual social supervisor, accompanied by information about the patient, should be made to the Chief Probation Officer or Director of Social Services, as appropriate.

8. Where the choice of supervising agency is not clear cut or cannot be resolved quickly, information about the patient should be sent to both the Chief Probation Officer and the Director of Social Services with an invitation to send representatives to a case conference for discussion of the issue.

9. The responsible medical officer, after consultation with the other members of the multi-disciplinary team, is responsible for arranging psychiatric supervision by a local consultant psychiatrist.

10. Responsibility for arranging suitable accommodation should be allocated by the multi-disciplinary team to a named social worker or probation officer.

---

[111] *Supervision and after-care of conditionally discharged restricted patients: Notes for the guidance of hospitals preparing for the conditional discharge of restricted patients* (Home Office/Department of Health and Social Security, 1987), Annex A.

11. The views of the multi-disciplinary team should be taken into account and the question of accommodation discussed in a pre-discharge case conference, attended by both supervisors.

12. It is important to identify suitable accommodation and to specify which types of accommodation would not be appropriate for individual patients.

13. There should be no question of a patient going automatically to unsuitable accommodation simply because a place is available and equal care is necessary whether the proposal for accommodation is to live with family or friends, or in lodgings or a hostel.

14. A member of staff of a proposed hostel should meet the patient and discuss the patient's needs with hospital staff.

15. The patient should visit and possibly spend a period of leave in a hostel before the decision is taken to accept an available place.

16. There are a number of important factors to be considered in the selection of a hostel for a particular patient.

17. The warden of the hostel should be given detailed information about the patient, including information which he may need about medication. He should be encouraged to contact the two supervisors and, if necessary, the social work department of the discharging hospital, for further information or advice.

18. Certain written information about the patient should be sent by the hospital social work department to supervising and after-care agencies on admission, as soon as discharge is in view and when nomination of a social supervisor is requested.

19. Supervisors should receive comprehensive, accurate and up-to-date information about a patient before he is discharged to their supervision. A standard package of information should be provided to both social and psychiatric supervisors as soon as they have been nominated.

20. Copies of supervisors' reports to the Home Office should be sent to the discharging hospital for a period of one year after discharge, for information.

21. After the conditional discharge of a patient, supervisors may sometimes seek information, guidance or support from those who know the patient well. It is hoped that discharging hospitals will be able to respond helpfully to such requests.

THE EXERCISE OF THE POWER OF DISCHARGE

Only the Home Secretary could discharge a restricted patient under the 1959 Act. During each year of the period from 1976 until 1983, about 6 per cent. of detained restricted patients were first conditionally discharged by the Home Secretary. During the first two years the new provisions were in force, the percentage of patients first conditionally discharged rose to approximately 8 per cent., presumably because some of them had never posed a risk of serious harm to the public. Subsequently, the overall rate has dropped to around 5 per cent. The general position is therefore that tribunals and the Secretary of State together release proportionately fewer patients than the Secretary of State did when acting alone. Absolute discharge is rare and it has historically been the case that more restricted patients die each year than are absolutely discharged.[112] Although the statistical bulletins provide no evidence that patients have benefited from an independent review, it remains possible that this is so. The introduction of a serious harm requirement means that more restricted patients these days have committed serious offences, so it is possible that the Home Secretary acting alone would today discharge fewer patients still. It is also possible that patients are being discharged sooner than was previously the case, although the bulletins no longer provide that information.

NUMBER OF PATIENTS CONDITIONALLY DISCHARGED : 1981-1990

Year	Detained population	Number of persons first discharged		
		By Home Secretary	By MHRT	Total
1981	1864	127 (6.81%)	—	127 (6.81%)
1982	1812	112 (6.18%)	—	112 (6.18%)
1983	1816	97 (5.34%)	—	97 (5.34%)
1984	1780	55 (3.09%)	93 (5.22%)	148 (8.31%)
1985	1705	52 (3.05%)	82 (4.81%)	134 (7.86%)
1986	1691	31 (1.83%)	62 (3.67%)	93 (5.50%)
1987	1758	38 (2.16%)	49 (2.79%)	87 (4.95%)
1988	1828	46 (2.52%)	48 (2.63%)	94 (5.15%)
1989	1879	58 (3.09%)	76 (4.04%)	134 (7.13%)
1990	1909	37 (1.94%)	59 (3.09%)	96 (5.03%)
1991	1996	24 (1.20%)	60 (3.01%)	84 (4.21%)

Notes: The percentage of patients first conditionally discharged by the Home Secretary during the period 1976-80 was virtually identical to that in 1981. The percentage of patients discharged has been calculated by reference to the number of detained restricted patients as at 31 December the previous year. Source: Home Office Statistical Bulletins.

RECONVICTION FOLLOWING DISCHARGE

Reconviction following discharge is relatively rare. However, the emphasis on diversion in recent years has led to some discrepancy between levels of reoffending and rates of reconviction.[113] The term "grave offence" covers mainly offences of

---

[112] Because death previously constituted an absolute discharge for statistical purposes, it used to be said that a "St. Peter's discharge" was a detained patient's best hope of being unconditionally released. The cynics refused to believe this, claiming that the Secretary of State would find some ground for recalling the patient.

[113] The number of (unproven) offences reported to the Home Office may be twice as high as the number of reconvictions. See S. Dell and A. Grounds, *The discharge and supervision of restricted patients* (Institute of Criminology, 1996), p.85.

homicide, serious wounding, rape, buggery, robbery, aggravated burglary, and arson. Standard list offences include these offences and also matters such as theft and drug offences, and some summary offences.

Reconviction rates for tribunals and the Home Secretary

The table below indicates that patients discharged by a tribunal are more likely to be reconvicted during the following two years than those discharged by the Secretary of State. However, if the statistics concerning patients discharged by tribunals since 1984 are compared with those concerning patients discharged by the Secretary of State before then, the reason for this appears to be that the Secretary of State now leaves it to tribunals to discharge patients whom he would previously have discharged himself. When only the Home Secretary could discharge a restricted patient, he could not avoid decisions about the need to rehabilitate those for whom he had sole responsibility. With the introduction of an independent review, he has been freer to focus his attention on the issue of public safety, leaving it to tribunals to decide whether a patient should be discharged if the competing considerations are more finely balanced. As a result, "consultants are likely to be highly selective in choosing cases to recommend to the Home Secretary, and from these the Home Office can pick the best cases for release."[114]

Number of conditionally discharged patients recalled and/or convicted

| Period | No. discharged | | % recalled within 2 years | | % convicted within 2 years of | | | |
| | | | | | A grave offence | | Any standard list offence | |
	MHRT	SofS	MHRT	SofS	MHRT	SofS	MHRT	SofS
1975–77	—	402	—	10.0%	—	1.7%	—	14.9%
1978–80	—	373	—	8.0%	—	2.1%	—	17.7%
1981–83	—	336	—	3.9%	—	2.7%	—	13.4%
1984–86	237	138	18.6%	13.0%	2.1%	1.5%	14.4%	8.0%
1987–89	173	142	12.1%	12.7%	1.2%	0%	5.8%	0.7%

Source: Home Office Statistical Bulletin, Issue 18/94, Home Office, London, July 1994.

Reconviction and the form of mental disorder

As can be seen from the table below, patients classified as suffering from mental illness or severe mental impairment are much less likely to be reconvicted than those suffering from psychopathic disorder or mental impairment. It is noteworthy that no patient classified as being mentally ill who was conditionally discharged by a tribunal between 1984 and 1989 was convicted of a grave offence during the following two years.

---

[114] S. Dell and A. Grounds, *The discharge and supervision of restricted patients* (Institute of Criminology, 1996), p.84.

Patients reconvicted after conditional discharge by a tribunal

Discharged during period 1984-1989

Form of mental disorder	% convicted of a grave offence		% convicted of any standard list offence	
	within 2 yrs	within 5 yrs	within 2 yrs	within 5 yrs
Mental illness	0%	3%	4%	11%
Mental impairment	2%	5%	15%	29%
Psychopathic disorder	5%	7%	22%	41%

Notes: Mental impairment includes severe mental impairment but none of the 19 severely mentally impaired patients discharged during the period 1977-86 were reconvicted within five years of a grave offence and only one of them of a standard list offence. Source: Home Office Statistical Bulletin, Issue 18/94, Home Office, London, July 1994.

Reconviction rates for ordinary prisoners

The information concerning the number of patients who reoffend upon being returned to the community has to be seen in the context of the reconviction rates for other kinds of offender. In general terms, the public has relatively little to fear from the mentally ill offender compared with violent young men considered not to have mental health problem.

Reconviction rates for prisoners and restricted patients

Percentage of persons reconvicted of a standard list offence within two years of release

Category of offender	% reconvicted
Adult males released from prison in 1987	50%
Adult males released from prison following a sentence of imprisonment imposed for a violent offence in 1987	45%
Patients classified as suffering from psychopathic disorder conditionally discharged between 1984-89	20%
Patients classified as suffering from mental illness conditionally discharged between 1984-89	4%

Source: Home Office Statistical Bulletin, Issue 18/94, Home Office, London, July 1994

FURTHER READING

D. Murray, *Review of research on re-offending of mentally disordered offenders* (Home Office, Research Unit Paper No.55); L.S. Penrose, "Mental Disease and Crime: Outline of a comparative study of European statistics" *British Journal of Medical Psychology* (1939) 18, 1–15; D. Ward, *The validity of reconviction prediction score* (Home Office, Research and Planning Unit Paper No. 94, 1987); C.D. Webster, *et al.*, *Dangerousness: Probability and prediction, psychiatry and public policy* (Cambridge University Press, 1985); G.K. Sturup, "Will this man be dangerous?" in *The Mentally Disordered Offender* (A Ciba Foundation Blueprint, J. & A. Churchill Ltd.,1968); E.I. Megaree, "The prediction of dangerous behaviour" *Criminal Justice and Behaviour* (1970) 3(1); H. Prins, "A danger to themselves and others *British Journal of Social Work* (1975) 5(3), 297–309; P.D. Scott, "Assessing dangerousness in criminals" *British Journal of Psychiatry* (1977) 131, 127-142; J.G. Rabkin, "Criminal Behaviour of Discharged Mental Patients: a critical appraisal of the research" *Psychol. Bulletin* (1979) 86(1), 1–27; D. Hepworth, "The influence of the concept of danger on the assessment of danger to self and others" *Medicine Science and the Law* (1982) 22, 245–254; D. Hepworth, *Assessment of Danger to Self and Others: A Study of MHRTs' interpretations of dangerousness* (Ph.D. thesis, University of Nottingham, 1980); S. Dell and A. Grounds, *The discharge and supervision of restricted patients* (Institute of Criminology, Cambridge, 1996).

13. Directions and other pre-hearing matters

INTRODUCTION

Following receipt and disclosure of the responsible authority's statement or that of the Secretary of State, the other formal stages in the proceedings prior to the hearing involve giving notice of the proceedings (**779**); directing that further information or reports be furnished where appropriate (**783**); giving any other directions necessary to ensure the speedy and just determination of the application (**784**); appointing the tribunal members (**788**); conducting the pre-hearing medical examination (**793**); and giving notice of the hearing (**794**). Each tribunal has a legal chairman whose most important functions are to exercise the tribunal's powers under the rules in relation to such preliminary or incidental matters.

FUNCTIONS OF THE REGIONAL CHAIRMAN

The Act provides that one of the legal members of each Mental Health Review Tribunal shall be appointed by the Lord Chancellor as its chairman.[1] Subject to the Mental Health Review Tribunal Rules 1983, the members who are to constitute a Mental Health Review Tribunal for the purposes of any proceedings are to be appointed by the chairman or, if for any reason he is unable to act, by another member of the tribunal appointed for the purpose by him.[2] Where the chairman of the tribunal is included among the persons appointed to consider an application or reference, he shall be president of the tribunal.[3]

PRELIMINARY AND INCIDENTAL MATTERS

Section 78(2) provides that rules made under that section may in particular make provision for enabling a tribunal, or the chairman of a tribunal, to postpone the consideration of applications[4] and for enabling any functions of a tribunal which relate to matters preliminary or incidental to an application to be performed by the chairman.[5] Rule 5 provides that certain powers of a tribunal may be exercised by the regional chairman prior to the hearing of an application or reference. Any functions conferred on the chairman by the Mental Health Review Tribunal Rules 1983 may, if for any reason he is unable to act, be exercised by another member of that tribunal appointed by him for the purpose.[6]

---

[1]   Mental Health Act 1983, s.65(2), Sched. 2, para. 3.
[2]   *Ibid.*, s.65(2), Sched. 2, para. 4.
[3]   *Ibid.*, s.65(2), Sched. 2, para. 6.
[4]   *Ibid.*, s.78(2)(a).
[5]   *Ibid.*, s.78(2)(k).
[6]   *Ibid.*, s.78(6).

Assessment applications

Rule 5 applies to references, subject to the necessary modifications set out in rule 29,[7] and to assessment applications "in so far as the circumstances of the case permit."[8]

THE CHAIRMAN'S POWERS : MHRT RULES 1983, r.5

Preliminary and incidental matters

5.— As regards matters preliminary or incidental to an application, the chairman may, at any time up to the hearing of an application by the tribunal, exercise the powers of the tribunal under rules, 6, 7, 9, 10, 12, 13, 14(1), 15, 17, 19, 20, 26 and 28.

The preliminary or incidental matters

The "powers" referred to in rule 5 are the powers to send copies of the documents forming the responsible authority's or the Secretary of State's statement to the applicant or patient, excluding any part contained in a separate document;[9] the power to give notice of the proceedings, including to any person who "in the opinion of the tribunal, should have the opportunity of being heard"[10]; the power to postpone consideration of a further application in the circumstances permitted by the rules[11]; the power to appoint an authorised representative for a patient who does not desire to conduct his own case and to direct that a patient or other party may not be accompanied at a hearing by a person of his choice[12]; the power to withhold a document forming part of the responsible authority's or the Secretary of State's statement from a patient or other applicant[13]; the power to give directions to ensure the speedy and just determination of the proceedings[14]; the power to subpoena any witness to appear before the tribunal or to produce documents[15]; the power to direct that further information or documents be provided and to give directions as to the manner in which, and by whom, the information or reports shall be furnished[16]; the power to make arrangements for an application or reference to be heard by members of the tribunal other than those originally appointed or to transfer the proceedings to a different regional tribunal[17]; the power to agree to an application being withdrawn[18]; the power to give notice of the hearing[19]; the power to extend or abridge time limits specified in the rules[20]; and the power to take steps to cure irregularities.[21]

---

[7]   Mental Health Review Tribunal Rules, r.29.
[8]   *Ibid.*, r.33.
[9]   *Ibid.*, r.6.
[10]   *Ibid.*, r.7.
[11]   *Ibid.*, r.9.
[12]   *Ibid.*, r.10.
[13]   *Ibid.*, r.12.
[14]   *Ibid.*, r.13.
[15]   *Ibid.*, r.14.
[16]   *Ibid.*, r.15.
[17]   *Ibid.*, r.17.
[18]   *Ibid.*, r.19.
[19]   *Ibid.*, r.20.
[20]   *Ibid.*, r.26.
[21]   *Ibid.*, r.28.

Delegation of functions

The Act provides that any functions conferred on the chairman by the Mental Health Review Tribunal Rules 1983 may, if for any reason he is unable to act, be exercised by another member of that tribunal appointed by him for the purpose.[22] Similarly, where the chairman is for any reason unable to act, the members who are to constitute a tribunal in a particular case may be appointed by another member of the tribunal appointed for the purpose by him.[23] Not all of the statutory functions referred to in rule 5 as "powers" exercisable by the regional chairman or his appointee constitute powers in the normal sense of that word. The provision of the authority's statement to the patient and the service of notices under rules 7 and 20 are more in the nature of duties and these routine matters can clearly be undertaken by administrative staff of a tribunal without reference to the chairman or his appointee. The other preliminary and incidental matters do involve exercising a power and making a decision as to whether and how a particular power should be exercised. These decisions may in practice be taken by executive or administrative staff within a tribunal office, either on their own initiative or by way of delegation. However, it is submitted that the Act makes it clear that the powers may only be exercised by the chairman or his appointee and powers exercised by other persons are *ultra vires*.

GIVING NOTICE OF THE PROCEEDINGS

In the case of patients detained under section 2, the usual procedure is abridged. On receiving an application, the tribunal immediately fixes a hearing date and gives notice of its receipt and the hearing date to the responsible authority, the patient, and his nearest relative. The responsible authority must then endeavour to have the necessary reports prepared within the limited time available. In all other cases, a tribunal which receives an application must give notice of its receipt to the responsible authority, to the patient if it was made by his nearest relative, and to the Secretary of State if made by a restricted patient.[24] The responsible authority and the Secretary of State must then furnish their statements to the tribunal during the period prescribed by the rules. Where the proceedings are commenced by reference, the tribunal gives notice of its receipt to the patient and, if a discretionary reference or one involving a restricted patient, to the responsible authority also, since it might otherwise not be aware of the proceedings and of the need for it to prepare a statement.[25] The purpose of the initial notice of application or reference is therefore limited to notifying the patient and the Secretary of State of the proceedings and obtaining reports from the responsible authority. The other persons or bodies with a possible interest in the proceedings are not notified of them until the responsible authority's statement has been received or, in restricted cases, until the Secretary of State's statement has been received by the tribunal, which will be some three weeks later still. Rule 7 sets out who is to be given notice of the proceedings at this stage and it should be noted that the persons or bodies who receive notice thereby become parties to the proceedings.[26]

---

[22] Mental Health Act 1983, s.78(6).
[23] *Ibid.*, s.65(2), Sched. 2, para. 4.
[24] Mental Health Review Tribunal Rules 1983, r.4(1).
[25] *Ibid.*, r.29.
[26] *Ibid.*, r.2(1).

Notice to other persons interested

7.—(1) On receipt of the authority's statement or, in the case of a restricted patient, the Secretary of State's statement, the tribunal shall give notice of the proceedings—

(a) where the patient is liable to be detained in a mental nursing home, to the registration authority of that home;

(b) where the patient is subject to the guardianship of a private guardian, to the guardian;

(bb) where the patient is, or will upon leaving hospital be, subject to after-care under supervision, to the person who appears to be the patient's nearest relative, and the persons who are, or will be, the patient's supervisor and community responsible medical officer and in the case of a patient who has not yet left hospital, the person who has prepared the medical report referred to in paragraph 1 of Part F of Schedule 1 to these Rules;

(c) where the patient's financial affairs are under the control of the Court of Protection, to the Court of Protection;

(d) where any person other than the applicant is named in the authority's statement as exercising the functions of the nearest relative, to that person;

(e) where a health authority *or National Health Service trust* has a right to discharge the patient an under the provisions of section 23(3) of the Act, to that authority *or trust;*

(f) to any other person who, in the opinion of the tribunal, should have an opportunity of being heard.

Mental Health Review Tribunal Rules 1983, as amended by the Mental Health Review Tribunal (Amendment) Rules 1996, r.5.

Necessary information provided in the authority's statement

It is, of course, impossible to give notice of the proceedings to bodies such as a registration authority or the Court of Protection unless the tribunal is aware of their involvement in the patient's case. A tribunal therefore relies on the information given to it in the responsible authority's Part A, C or E statement, which is designed to elicit such details (**663, 671**).

Giving notice to the nearest relative

Rule 7(d) provides that where any person other than the applicant is named in the authority's statement as exercising the functions of the nearest relative, that person must be given notice of the proceedings. The paragraph can easily be misread as referring only to a person authorised by the county court, or by the nearest relative himself, to exercise those statutory functions — the more so since the new paragraph (bb) refers to the person who appears to be the patient's nearest relative. In fact, as the definition of a nearest relative in rule 2(1) makes clear, the person referred to in rule 7(d) is the patient's actual nearest relative if he is personally exercising his statutory functions. However, where a county court order under section 29 is in force, or the nearest relative has authorised some other person to act for him, that person is the person entitled to notice under paragraph (d). In which case, unless the proceedings involve after-care under supervision (see below), the tribunal then has a discretion to give the actual nearest relative notice under paragraph (f), as a person who ought to be heard.

Cases involving after-care under supervision

In cases involving supervision applications, rule (bb) literally provides that the person appearing to be the nearest relative must always be given notice. Because rule 7(d) already provided that the nearest relative is a party unless a county court order has been made, paragraph (bb) is superfluous in this respect unless it's intended effect is that a displaced nearest relative is always a party. Whether or not that is so, the nearest relative being a party as of right is inconsistent with the statutory framework, because he may not be entitled under the statute to be notified of the existence of the supervision application. Because the rule has the consequence that the patient cannot prevent the nearest relative from being informed about the supervision, and from participating in the proceedings, the *vires* of the rule is questionable (**679**).

Restricted cases

A restricted patient does not have a nearest relative for the purposes of the Act and the person who would be entitled to notice under paragraph 7(d) if no restrictions existed must therefore rely on being given notice by the tribunal under paragraph (f), as a person who ought to be heard.[27]

Supervision applications and paragraph (bb)

Although the professionals who provide the medical and social reports which constitute the main part of the responsible authority's statement have hitherto been viewed simply as persons involved in presenting the authority's case, generally giving oral evidence on its behalf as well, the rules now depart from that approach where the proceedings involve after-care under supervision. While the responsible authority is a party from the outset, the persons whom it asks to prepare its case by writing the necessary reports then receive personal notice of the proceedings and become parties in their own right. The new provision must partly reflect the pivotal and personal nature of the community responsible medical officer's and supervisor's statutory functions. Where the patient is not yet subject to the supervision, making the doctor in charge of his treatment a party presumably serves the purpose of giving him a continuing status in the proceedings if the patient leaves hospital before the hearing takes place.

The rights of a party to the proceedings

The rights of a party to the proceedings are more limited than they are in most legal proceedings and not all of the parties are on the same footing. The rights of persons with some interest in the proceedings fall into three categories. In the first category are the patient, any nearest relative applicant, the responsible authority and, although not a party, the Secretary of State in a restricted case. They have all the rights of a party but they also have a general right to receive copies of all documents and reports concerning the patient, to hear each other's evidence, to call witnesses, and to questions persons attending the hearing. In the second category are persons who are parties by virtue of the fact that, once reports have been filed, they are entitled to notice of the proceedings under rule 7. However, the rules do even allow the tribunal a

---

[27]   The exceptions and modifications of Part II of the Act mentioned in Sched. 1, Pt. I, para 1 may be compared with these listed in Sched. 1, Pt. II, para 1. Sections 26–28, which define who is the nearest relative, apply to unrestricted hospital order patients but not to those subject to restrictions.

discretionary power to disclose reports about the patient to them and, in consequence, they have no right to make observations about them. They are entitled to notice of the hearing and notice of any step taken which affects whether and where the hearing will take place. They also have the right to be represented, to attend the hearing (subject to the tribunal's general power to exclude persons), and to be notified of the decision and the reasons for it. However, they have no general right under the rules to hear the evidence, to put questions, or to call witnesses. In the third category are persons who are not parties but who have some interest in the proceedings, legitimate or otherwise. They may merely with the tribunal's permission appear at the hearing and take such part as the tribunal thinks proper, subject again to the tribunal's power of exclusion.

RIGHTS OF THE PARTIES UNDER THE 1983 RULES

Rule 2—(1). Unless the context otherwise requires, "party" means the applicant, the patient, the responsible authority, any other person to whom a notice under rule 7 or rule 31(c) is sent or who is added as a party by direction of the tribunal.

	Right	*Rule*
Right to notice	A copy of the written reasons for postponement and period of postponement must be sent to all the parties, although at this stage no notices will have been given under r.7.	9(4)
	Where the proceedings are transferred to another tribunal, notice of the transfer of proceedings shall be given to the parties.	17(2)
	Where an application is withdrawn or deemed to he withdrawn, the tribunal shall so inform the parties.	19(3)
	Where a discretionary reference is withdrawn by the Secretary of State, the tribunal shall inform the parties of this.	29
	The tribunal shall give at least 14 days' notice of the hearing to all the parties, unless all of the parties consent to shorter notice.	20
	Before resuming a hearing adjourned sine die, the tribunal shall give not less than 14 days' notice to the parties unless they have consented to shorter notice.	16(4)
	Where a tribunal wishes to reconvene the proceedings because a recommendation made by it has not been complied with it shall first give all parties not less than 14 days' notice unless they all consent to shorter notice.	25(2)
Representation	Any party may be represented in the proceedings.	10(1)
Hearing	Unless the tribunal otherwise directs, any party appearing before the tribunal may be accompanied by such other person or persons as he wishes, in addition to any authorised representative.	10(6)
	Subject to rule 21(4), which gives the tribunal a power to exclude persons from a hearing, any party may appear at the hearing and take such part in the proceedings as the tribunal thinks proper. The tribunal must in particular hear and take evidence from the applicant, the patient, and the responsible authority who may hear each other's evidence, put questions to each other, call witnesses and put questions to any witness or other person appearing before the tribunal.	22(4)
Decision	The written decision of the tribunal, including the reasons, shall be communicated in writing to all the parties subject to any conditions it may think appropriate as to the disclosure thereof to the patient.	24

Summary

The persons who are parties from the outset have greater rights than other parties, as does the Secretary of State although not a party. In practice, it is worth noting that parties who do not, on receiving notice, express any interest in the proceedings are often not later consulted about the abridgement of notice periods. However, the rules do not permit such a selective approach and all the parties must consent to short notice. Similarly, all of them should receive a copy of the tribunal's decision.

FURTHER INFORMATION AND REPORTS

The Act states that the rules may in particular provide for regulating the methods by which information relevant to an application or reference may be obtained by or furnished to a tribunal and confer on tribunals such ancillary powers as the Lord Chancellor thinks necessary for the purposes of the exercise of their functions.[28] Rule 15 provides that a tribunal may prior to or during a hearing call for such further information or reports as it may think desirable. The power may be used as a way of curing omissions in the responsible authority's statement or that of the Secretary of State or, if the hearing is substantially delayed, as a means of obtaining supplementary, up-to-date, reports. Rule 15 does not correspond to any previous provision in the 1960 Rules. It was added because tribunals considered that they should not need to rely wholly on the reports furnished under what is now rule 6. However, before rule 15 is of any assistance, the reports must first be received. If one or more of the reports is not furnished within the prescribed period, and no application has been made for an extension of the time limit, the tribunal may give a direction under rule 13 (**784**) that the missing report or reports be filed within a specified certain period of time. However, it is exceptional for the tribunal to do this, or to check the adequacy of the authority's statement upon receipt, and the absence of any sanctions means that the rules are frequently not adhered to.

FURTHER INFORMATION, MHRT RULES 1983, r.15

Further information

15.—(1) Before or during any hearing the tribunal may call for such further information or reports as it may think desirable, and may give directions as to the manner in which and the persons by whom such material is to be furnished.

(2) Rule 12(1) shall apply to any further information or reports obtained by the tribunal.

Inadequate medical reports

The standard of medical reports varies markedly in practice. Some are limited to no more than three-quarters of a page, do not include the relevant medical history, and cannot be said to constitute a "full" report on the patient's medical condition.

---

[28]   Mental Health Act 1983, s.78(2)(g) and (j).

Although the authorised representative may apply to the tribunal for a direction that a further report be provided, the preparation of the patient's case is necessarily hindered by a poor report unless access to his medical records can be agreed. Other reports are not "prepared for the tribunal," being first written for a managers' hearing with the original heading changed and a brief addendum added. Quite often, the report is written by a junior member of the responsible medical officer's team. Although the rules do not prohibit this, the report should ideally be counter-signed by the responsible medical officer, so that it is clear that it accurately reflects his reasons for not discharging the patient.

Inadequate social circumstances reports

The most common fault with the social circumstances report is simply that the writer was obviously unaware of the required content of such reports. Where this occurs, the tribunal may direct that the responsible authority furnishes it with a supplementary report. It is also not uncommon for a previous social circumstances report prepared by some other person to be submitted with an additional paragraph added at the end and the date changed. This is objectionable because the reporter is giving the impression that the views expressed are his own.[29] If the report indicates that no social worker has been allocated to the patient's case, the local authority should be reminded of its obligations under section 117, the National Assistance Act 1948, the National Health Service & Community Care Act 1990, and the relevant departmental guidelines (**745**). In appropriate cases, the representative may wish to consider commissioning an independent social circumstances report.

DIRECTIONS UNDER RULE 13

The Act provides that the rules may in particular make provision for conferring on tribunals such ancillary powers as the Lord Chancellor thinks necessary for the purposes of the exercise of their functions under this Act.[30] Rule 13 confers on tribunals a general power to give directions where that is necessary to ensure the speedy or just determination of an application or reference.[31] By inference, a tribunal direction that a person be added as a party to the proceedings is one given under rule 13.[32] There was no equivalent provision in the 1960 Rules. One of the main aims behind the rule was that it would help to ensure that tribunal hearings were heard within a reasonable time, the European Commission having previously declared admissible a complaint concerning the delay in holding a hearing.

DIRECTIONS UNDER RULE 13

13.—Subject to the provisions of these Rules, the tribunal may give such directions as it thinks fit to ensure the speedy and just determination of the application.

---

[29] The laziness is normally betrayed by the fact that the stated ages of the patient's relatives are now incorrect and information relating to the current admission is confined to the concluding paragraphs.

[30] Mental Health Act 1983, s.78(2)(j).

[31] Mental Health Review Tribunal Rules 1983, rr.13, 29.

[32] See *ibid.*, r.2(1).

Delays in holding hearings

The number of applications made to tribunals tripled between 1984 and 1995, from 4,321 to 13,390. This tremendous strain on their resources has prevented them from making headway in reducing the time taken to hear applications. Indeed, the situation deteriorated in 1995. The majority of special hospital restricted cases took more than 20 weeks to hear and the waiting times in non-special hospital cases, both restricted and unrestricted, increased.

WAITING TIMES FOR TRIBUNAL HEARINGS: 1994, 1995

Restricted cases

	Under 12 weeks		13–20 weeks		Over 20 weeks	
	1994	*1995*	*1994*	*1995*	*1994*	*1995*
Special hospitals	16	6	77	38	55	51
Other hospitals	46	23	87	95	33	74
Total	62	29	164	133	88	125

Unrestricted cases (excluding section 2 cases)

	Under 8 weeks		9–12 weeks		Over 12 weeks	
	1994	*1995*	*1994*	*1995*	*1994*	*1995*
Special hospitals	2	0	9	14	20	30
Other hospitals	476	325	266	309	42	78
Total	478	325	275	323	62	108

The figures above are for the last quarter of 1994 and the last quarter of 1995, as given in the Annual Reports of the Mental Health Review Tribunals for England and Wales.

Historical background

Although the waiting times lengthened in 1995, the problem of delays is not a new one. In its First Biennial Report, the Mental Health Act Commission referred to the high incidence of delays and the consequent erosion of detained patients' rights.[33] The Second Biennial Report returned to the theme, observing that the main reason for the delays at that time was a shortage of tribunal staff. Although precise figures were difficult to collate, the average delay between the application and the hearing was said to be over 14 weeks in the Southern region. In the North Western region, 30 per cent. of cases involved delays of between three and six months, and there had been cases where the authority for a patient's detention had expired before the tribunal was able to sit. As to the special hospitals, 42 cases had been pending for more than six months. In the majority of these cases, there was one report outstanding, usually the social circumstances report. The Commission urged that the matter be given urgent attention and that tribunal offices be given the staff necessary to carry out their task promptly.[34] Subsequently, the Commission has been

---

[33]   Mental Health Act Commission, *First Biennial Report 1983–85* (H.M.S.O., 1985), p.29.
[34]   Mental Health Act Commission, *Second Biennial Report 1985–87* (H.M.S.O., 1987), para. 18.3.

discouraged from commenting on tribunal issues, although it has a statutory duty to address them. In its various annual reports, the Council on Tribunals has previously identified a shortage of clerks and judicial members as causes of delay.[35]

The Blumenthal Report

In 1992, the Department of Health commissioned research into the area, the result of which was a report written by Blumenthal and Wessely. The report concluded that the pattern of delay primarily reflected the complexity of the cases. The other important factor was the request for an independent psychiatric report.[36] There was also a correlation between the time taken to prepare the medical and social circumstances reports and the time taken to hear the application. The points are not mutually exclusive. If the medical report is submitted late in the day, there may then be insufficient time to obtain an independent psychiatric report. A survey carried out by the Law Society's Mental Health Sub-Committee in 1990 similarly highlighted the problem of the late submission of medical reports by the responsible authority. It also raised the problems arising from the fact that the allocation of judges' time is beyond the tribunal's control.

Delay and the European Convention

Article 5(4) of the Convention provides that, "Everyone who is deprived of his liberty by arrest or detention shall be entitled to take proceedings by which the lawfulness of his detention shall be decided speedily by a court and his release ordered if his detention is not lawful." Lawful in this context includes "substantive lawfulness." In other words, the holding of a hearing concerning the merits of an individual's detention under the statutory provision which authorises that. On 9 December 1981, the European Commission declared admissible an application which alleged that a delay of 18 weeks between the making of an application and its determination by the tribunal contravened Article 5(4).[37] The Government, seeking a settlement from the Commission, suggested 13 weeks as a reasonable target time. It has clearly failed to meet this target, the majority of special hospital restricted cases currently taking over 20 weeks to hear. Put bluntly, it has dishonoured its part of the understanding upon which that case was settled. Subsequently, a number of patients

---

[35] As to this, the answer must lie in re-examining whether it is always necessary for a judicial member to hear restricted cases. There are many ways in which such cases could be graded. For example, one might provide that tribunals dealing with the cases of conditionally discharged patients could be presided over by a non-judicial member, leaving it to judicial members to determine whether patients should be released into the community. Or one could distinguish cases according to the type of index offence, whether the case had ever been before the Aarvold Board, or the type of hospital in which the patient is detained (maximum or medium secure units and open wards). Alternatively, one could provide that the Regional Chairman is to determine whether a judicial member is necessary but the Home Secretary may, when filing his statement, require that the case be so allocated. A further option would be for non-judicial members to preside in section 74 cases where the tribunal's power is limited to making a recommendation — this was considered acceptable to the public prior to 1983. Yet another approach would simply be greater flexibility, allowing the Lord Chancellor to authorise suitably experienced non-judicial members to hear restricted cases. Finally, the volume of cases could be reduced by conferring a power of discharge on Mental Health Act Commissioners (the Board of Control had such a power and the Mental Welfare Commission for Scotland still does), by requiring the managers to consider exercising their power of discharge once a tribunal application has been made, and by at least occasionally making use of rule 9.

[36] S. Blumenthal and S. Wessely, *The pattern of delays in Mental Health Review Tribunals* (H.M.S.O., 1994).

[37] *Barclay-Maguire v. United Kingdom*, App. no. 9117/80. See L. Gostin, "Human Rights, Judicial Review and the Mentally Disordered Offender" (1982) C.L.R. 777.

have sought judicial review in relation to delayed hearings but a ruling has been avoided by offering them an earlier date, necessarily at the expense of other patients.[38] In *Koendjbiharie v. The Netherlands*, the European Court of Human Rights recently held that the extension of a patient's detention more than four months after he had lodged an application constituted a breach of Article 5(4).[39] In *Lines v. United Kingdom*,[40] a conditionally discharged patient was readmitted to hospital under section 3 on 27 July 1993. She was formally recalled to hospital by the Secretary of State on 3 December 1993 and her case then referred to a tribunal. The tribunal heard the matter on 23 February 1994, some seven months after her compulsory admission to hospital. The patient complained that the delay was contrary to Article 5(4) of the Convention. The Government opposed the application, submitting that her review had been "speedy." On 17 January 1997, the European Commission unanimously held that the complaint raised serious issues under Article 5(4) which required determination on their merits. Subsequently, the Government has undertaken to amend the 1983 Rules so that when a conditionally discharged patient is recalled to hospital there must be a tribunal hearing within two months of the date on which the case is referred to a tribunal.[41]

Delays involving section 3 cases

The domestic law is particularly vulnerable with regard to delay in the hearing of unrestricted cases. This is because the 1959 Act abolished the previous requirement that the issue of whether a citizen's detention was justified must be determined in advance by a judicial authority, compensating citizens for this loss by enabling them to have the justification reviewed after the event. However, whereas a person could not previously be detained for a prolonged period of treatment unless a judicial order was first obtained, it is now not uncommon for more than half the authorised period of detention to have expired before there is a judicial determination of the merits. Consequently, the detention of many patients is brought to an end before a judicial hearing takes place, the average period of detention in many hospitals being significantly less than six months.

Final note

It has recently been suggested that the frequency with which patients are entitled to have a hearing might be reviewed, including the entitlement of all section 2 patients to a hearing within a fortnight of admission. However, given that some tribunals discharge up to 40 per cent. of patients at such hearings, the price would be unnecessarily prolonged detention in a significant number of cases. Furthermore, the idea that the problem of delayed access to courts should be solved by curtailing access to courts is unacceptable for many people. It has also been suggested that the new power of supervised discharge will significantly contribute to the workload of tribunals, but it must be unlikely that much use will be made of supervision applications.

---

[38] See *e.g.* the judicial review applications made in *R. v. Mental Health Review Tribunal, ex p. Hudson* (unreported, 1986) and *R. v. Mental Health Review Tribunal, ex p. Mitchell* (unreported, 1985). In the latter case, a hearing had been fixed for the day after the expiration of the authority for the patient's detention.

[39] *Koendjbiharie v. The Netherlands*, Judgments of the European Court of Human Rights, Series A, Case No. 185–B.

[40] *Pauline Lines v. United Kingdom* (App. No. 24519/94), European Commission of Human Rights, First Chamber Decision as to admissibility, 17 January 1997 (**364**).

[41] See App. No. 27560/95, which was resolved in 1997 on the basis of this undertaking and upon the Government agreeing to pay the applicant £2000 by way of compensation, plus costs. On 12 March 1997, The NHS Management Executive circularised the proposals for comment.

APPOINTMENT OF THE TRIBUNAL MEMBERS

The Act provides that, subject to the rules, the members who are to constitute a tribunal for the purposes of any proceedings (or class or group of proceedings) shall by appointed by the chairman or, if for any reason he is unable to act, by another member of the tribunal appointed for the purpose by him.[42]

CONSTITUTION

Of the members so appointed, one or more shall be appointed from the legal members[43]; one or more from the medical members[44]; and one or more from members who are neither legal nor medical members.[45] Where the chairman of the tribunal is among the persons appointed, he is the president of the tribunal.[46] In other cases, the legal member is the president or, if more than one has been appointed, the legal member nominated by the chairman.[47] It is, however, extremely rare for more than three members to hear a particular case. The present rule derives from rule 8 of the 1960 rules.

APPOINTMENT OF TRIBUNAL MEMBERS : MHRT RULES 1983, r.8

Appointment of the tribunal

8.—(1) Unless the application belongs to a class or group of proceedings for which members have already been appointed, the members of the tribunal who are to hear the application shall be appointed by the chairman.

(2) A person shall not be qualified to serve as a member of a tribunal for the purpose of any proceedings where—

(a) he is a member or officer of the responsible authority or of the registration authority concerned in the proceedings; or
(b) he is a member or officer of a health authority *or National Health Service trust* which has the right to discharge the patient under section 23(3) of the Act; or
(c) he has a personal connection with the patient or as recently treated the patient in a professional medical capacity.

(3) The persons qualified to serve as president of the tribunal for the consideration of an application or reference relating to a restricted patient shall be restricted to those legal members who have been approved for that purpose by the Lord Chancellor.

Mental Health Review Tribunal Rules 1983, as amended by the Mental Health Review Tribunal (Amendment) Rules 1996, r.6.

---

[42]   Mental Health Act 1983, s.65(2), Sched. 2, para. 4.
[43]   *Ibid.*, para. 4(a).
[44]   *Ibid.*, para. 4(b).
[45]   *Ibid.*, s.65(2), Sched. 2, para. 4(c).
[46]   *Ibid.*, s.65(2), Sched. 2, para. 6.
[47]   *Ibid.*

Restricted cases

The rules may provide for restricting the persons qualified to serve as members in relation to proceedings of a specified class[48] and make provision for restricting the persons qualified to serve as the president of a tribunal dealing with the case of a restricted patient.[49] Rule 8(3) provides that, "The persons qualified to serve as president of the tribunal for the consideration of an application or reference relating to a restricted patient shall be restricted to those legal members who have been approved for that purpose by the Lord Chancellor." The reasons given in Parliament for this restriction were summarised by Lord Belstead. The Government believed that the power to release restricted patients who might have been convicted of very serious crimes carried with it a "formidable responsibility." It was "essential" that the exercise of the power was vested in those who had the "confidence of the public and of the judiciary" — the latter being responsible for the imposition of restriction orders. Accordingly, it was felt that the tribunals making these decisions should be chaired by lawyers with "substantial judicial experience in the criminal courts."[50]

Persons disqualified from serving

Rule 8(2) *inter alia* provides that a tribunal member shall not be qualified to serve in a particular case if he is a member or officer of the responsible authority, has a personal connection with the patient, or has "recently" treated the patient in a professional medical capacity.[51] The rules do not define what constitutes having "recently" treated the patient. In any case involving a patient who is liable to be detained in a mental nursing home, a tribunal member is also disqualified if he is a member or officer of the Health Authority responsible for registering and inspecting the home or of a Health Authority or NHS trust which has contracted with the home for the patient to be treated there.

The rule against bias

Where application is made that a tribunal's decision should be quashed on account of the alleged bias of one or more tribunal members not disqualified from serving by virtue of rule 8, the proper test is whether there was a real danger of injustice having occurred as a result of the alleged bias. The test is one of real danger rather than real likelihood so as to ensure that the issue is approached in terms of the possibility rather than the probability of bias: *R. v. Gough (Robert)*.[52] In *ex p. Mackman*, objection was made to the appointment of a president who had presided at a recent tribunal involving the same patient.[53] The ratio of the case is often said to be that a president who has dealt with a patient's case may preside at a subsequent tribunal. However, the issue is the danger of bias and it is possible that a president would be disqualified if his conduct of the earlier hearing had been exceptional.

---

[48]   Mental Health Act 1983, s.78(2)(c).
[49]   *Ibid.*, s.78(4).
[50]   See *Hansard*, Vol. 426, cols. 759–764 (25 January, 1982).
[51]   The disqualification of a medical practitioner who has recently treated the patient in a professional medical capacity was not a feature of the 1960 Rules.
[52]   *R. v. Gough (Robert)*, *The Times*, 24 May 1993, H.L.
[53]   It should be noted that the test of bias applied in *Mackman*, which case pre-dated *R. v. Gough (Robert)*, was whether a reasonable and fair-minded person present at the tribunal and knowing all the relevant facts would have a reasonable suspicion that a fair hearing would not be possible.

R. v. Oxford Regional Mental Health Review, ex p. Mackman

The Times, 2 June 1986   *Q.B.D., McNeill J.*

The patient was detained in pursuance of a restriction order. On 16 January 1985, his case was considered by the Oxford Mental Health Review Tribunal. The tribunal, presided over by His Honour Judge Schindler, did not direct that he be discharged. The reasons for the tribunal's decision stated that it had preferred the responsible medical officer's evidence to that of the psychiatrist instructed by the patient. Although the patient appeared to have made considerable progress since admission, it was "far too early to form a clear picture of his condition and what the prognosis may be." His future progress needed to be very carefully monitored "and it would be beneficial to him if he co-operated with his RMO in the treatment be advises." The patient then made a further application to the Oxford tribunal. The case was due to be heard on 21 November 1985 and His Honour Judge Shindler was again appointed to sit as the president. When the patient was informed of this, he was concerned that he might not receive a fair and impartial hearing. He later deposed that the president had "very recently formed certain unfavourable views about me and my case ... I knew that he had formed an adverse view of my case just ten months ago, and I could not believe that I would have a fair hearing this time round. I felt that he would be bound to recollect my case from the previous hearing, and consciously or unconsciously to be affected by what he knew or remembered of it, and the stance he had taken. He would be bound to know that he had found against me last time." Moreover, the rules required that copies of previous tribunal decisions and the reasons for those decisions be furnished to any later tribunal. It seemed to the patient that his "only chance of winning His Honour Judge Schindler round lay in what had occurred since January 1985." At the hearing, the patient's counsel applied for the matter to be adjourned so that a different president could sit. He pointed out that the hearing would cover a good deal of the ground which had been covered at the last tribunal. Any person who had sat on such a recent tribunal would be bound to hear echoes of matters considered and opinions discussed when the previous tribunal deliberated on its decision. The tribunal refused the application but was willing to adjourn the hearing until later that day, to give the patient and his legal representatives further time to prepare. The tribunal stated that it was differently constituted, in that different medical and lay members had been appointed, and the independent medical report had been furnished by a different doctor from that whose opinion had been rejected in January. The hearing proceeded in the absence of the patient and his counsel.

Decision of the tribunal

The decision reached was again to refuse discharge. The tribunal's reasons for its decision stated that the patient had made further progress since his last tribunal. However, it was concerned that he still refused to undergo psychotherapy and showed little, if any, insight into his condition and the grave index offence. The patient would present a real danger to the public were he to be discharged.

The application for judicial review

The patient applied for an order quashing: (i) the tribunal's decision to hear and determine the application under the presidency of His Honour Judge Schindler; (ii) the decision of the tribunal on the application consequent upon their decision to hear and determine it in the patient's absence.

The tribunal's case

According to the learned judge's affidavit, the tribunal had discussed the matter fully, taking into account the representations made on behalf of the patient, and whether or not it would be unfair, or could be seen to be unfair, for him to continue as president. Although he remembered the patient from his previous hearing, and had consulted the notes which he made at that hearing, the president denied that his consideration of the case was affected by what had previously occurred and been decided. In every case the tribunal had before it the patient's history and details of previous hearings. It was by reference *inter alia* to these documents that a tribunal was able to assess what progress (if any) a patient had made since the previous hearing. The intendment of the Act was simply that each application should receive fresh adjudication, separate and distinct from the determination of any previous applications. However, that did not mean that there should be a new president for each application. It was thus not the case that the president's previous involvement had denied the patient a fair hearing.

McNeill J.

A president who sat on an applicant's case was not statutorily barred from sitting on a later case involving the same applicant. Reference had been made to *R. v. McElligott, ex p. Gallagher and Seal.*[54] That was a case in which one of the stipendiary magistrates had before him applicants charged with loitering with intent who had been before him on previous occasions. The court went out of its way to say that, although it might be desirable in those circumstances for a different magistrate to hear the matter, there was no point of law which disqualified him from doing so. The proper test was whether a reasonable and fair-minded person sitting in court, and knowing all the relevant facts, would have a reasonable suspicion that a fair hearing was not possible. That proposition was most conveniently expressed in the case of *R. v. Liverpool City Justices, ex p. Topping,* in which Ackner L.J. said that "the correct test to apply is whether there is the appearance of bias, rather than whether there is actual bias."[55] At the end of the day, could the reasonable and fair minded person sitting in court and knowing all the facts have a reasonable suspicion that a fair hearing would not be possible? No such person could have formed that view. Indeed, there were arguably certain advantages in a president sitting on the recurring applications of a particular patient, since one of the important features was to monitor the progress of a patient, as happened here. While it was understandable that the patient with his condition might form the view which he did, that was not the appropriate test. It was not his subjective view which mattered. It was the reasonable and fair-minded person's objective view of the situation. It would be quite wrong for the court to lay down that the constitution of the tribunal or the person presiding must as a matter of law be changed each time. That was not the law and it would be quite wrong to put that obligation upon either the approved legal members or upon those responsible for the tribunal's administration. Whether or not that extended to the membership, other than the president, was not for the court to decide in this case. *Application dismissed.*

---

[54]   *R. v. McElligott, ex p. Gallagher and Seal* [1972] Crim L.R. 332.
[55]   *R. v. Liverpool City Justices, ex p. Topping* [1983] 1 W.L.R. 119 at 122G to 123D.

Commentary

The court left open the question of whether different considerations might apply where it was the medical member who sat on the previous tribunal. The legal issue must still be whether there had been a real danger of injustice. However, the inquisitorial nature of the medical member's role, which involves the taking of other steps deemed *by him* to be necessary to form an opinion, may lend itself more easily to unfairness. The more so because his examination is conducted in private in the absence of the other members, who must rely on him to take all steps necessary to form a medical opinion of the patient's *present* condition. While the evidence presented at the hearing will be heard by a differently constituted tribunal, its constitution for the purposes of the medical examination is necessarily the same as before. There is a difference between a tribunal member who has sat before being able to confine himself to the evidence and arguments presented at the hearing and a medical member not taking those steps to obtain relevant information which he would usually undertake. One can therefore foresee a situation where it is asserted that a medical member did not in any meaningful sense examine the patient, as required by the rules, because he had examined him some months before and had already formed an opinion about his mental condition. While the Act requires a tribunal to consider whether it is satisfied that the patient's condition "then" meets the criteria for discharge, there was a real danger that it was interpreting the evidence according to the same examination and opinion as caused the previous tribunal to reject the medical evidence presented in favour of discharge.

When the members are appointed

Where the proceedings involve a patient who is detained for assessment, the chairman is required to appoint the members upon receipt of the application.[56] In other cases, it is a matter for the chairman's discretion as to when during the proceedings he appoints the members.

Members unable to dispose of the case

The rules provide that where the regional chairman is later of the opinion that it is not practicable or not possible without undue delay for the consideration of the case to be completed by the members appointed, he shall make arrangements for them to be heard by other members of the tribunal.[57]

ARRANGING FOR OTHER MEMBERS TO DISPOSE OF CASE

Transfer of proceedings

17.—(1) Where any proceedings in relation to a patient have not been disposed of by the members of the tribunal appointed for the purpose, and the chairman is of the opinion that it is not practicable or not possible without undue delay for the consideration of those proceedings to be completed by those members, he shall make arrangements for them to be heard by other members of the tribunal.

---

[56] Mental Health Review Tribunal Rules 1983, r.31.
[57] *Ibid.*, r.17(1).

THE PRE-HEARING MEDICAL EXAMINATION

The Act states that the rules may in particular authorise the members of a tribunal, or one or more of them, to visit and interview in private the patient.[58] Rule 11 requires the medical member of a tribunal to examine the patient prior to the hearing.[59] It applies to references and assessment applications but, in the latter case, only "in so far as the circumstances of the case permit."[60]

MEDICAL MEMBER'S EXAMINATION : MHRT RULES 1983, r.11

Medical examination

11.— At any time before the hearing of the application, the medical member or, where the tribunal includes more than one, at least one of them shall examine the patient and take such other steps as he considers necessary to form an opinion of the patient's mental condition; and for this purpose the patient may be seen in private and all his medical records may be examined by the medical member, who may take such notes and copies of them as he may require, for use in connection with the application *and in the case of a patient subject to after-care under supervision this rule shall also apply to such other records relating to any after-care services provided under section 117 of the Act.*

Mental Health Review Tribunal Rules 1983, as amended by Mental Health Review Tribunal (Amendment) Rules 1996, r.9.

Taking notes and copies of the medical records

Rule 11 provides that the medical member may inspect the patient's medical records and take such notes and copies of them as he may require for use in connection with the application. Rule 12 provides for the disclosure by a tribunal of every document it receives which is relevant to the application. Where the medical member obtains photocopies of medical notes, the question arises whether those documents are thereby received by the tribunal and come within the ambit of rule 12. Where a medical member makes a hand-written note of some entry in the medical records, that note is self-evidently not a document received by the tribunal but one created by a member of the tribunal as an *aide-mémoire*. It may therefore be said that where a copy rather than a note is taken of a document in the case notes, for example a previous medical report or a psychological assessment, the same principle applies. It is no more than a labour-saving device, a way of avoiding the time of making a hand-written record, and the copy does not thereby become a document disclosable under rule 12. The purpose of the rule is to ensure that documents furnished by the parties or the Secretary of State prior to the hearing are seen by the other parties.

---

[58]   Mental Health Act 1983, s.78(2)(g).
[59]   Rule 11 derives from rule 11 of the 1960 Rules, the only material difference being the addition of the final phrase in the present rule ("who may take such notes and copies of them as he may require, for use in connection with the application."). The 1960 rules also provided that a non-medical member could visit the patient prior to the hearing.
[60]   Mental Health Review Tribunal Rules 1983, rr.29, 33.

This ensures that all the parties have a copy of all the written evidence tendered to the tribunal and so avoids unnecessary adjournments, as well as helping to define in advance the respective cases for and against discharge. The rules are, however, ultimately less important than the general principles of natural justice. If further copies of reports copied by the medical member are taken for the other members, this can only be because they are considered to be particularly relevant to the decision to be made. Moreover, they are no longer a record made merely for such use as "he requires" but for the use of all the members. It is also difficult to think that a particular report would be copied if its contents were adequately summarised in any medical report previously prepared for the tribunal. There is then a risk that the tribunal's decision may rest on some fact or opinion recorded in the copied document which is not adequately summarised in the reports furnished under rule 6. A point considered in the following case.

Ex p. Clatworthy

In *ex p. Clatworthy*,[61] the Divisional Court quashed a tribunal decision because the reasons given for it did not enable one to see why the medical evidence before the tribunal had not been accepted. Mann L.J. noted that it might be suggested that the tribunal had proceeded on the basis of the medical member's opinion rather than the opinions laid before the tribunal. While there was no explicit suggestion that was the case, His Lordship said that, "Where a tribunal desires to proceed on the basis of some point which has not been put before it and which on the face of the matter is not in dispute, it is in my view in the highest degree desirable that the person whose case is being considered by the tribunal should be alerted to the possibility" **(805)**. The same approach must apply if a tribunal has relevant information which is not available to the applicant and which he does not know is in its possession.

GIVING NOTICE OF THE HEARING

Rules 31 (assessment applications) and 20 (all other cases) provide for giving notice of the date, time and place fixed for the hearing.

Assessment cases

Rule 31 provides that on receipt of an application, the tribunal shall give notice of the date, time and place fixed for the hearing to the patient, the responsible authority, the nearest relative (where practicable) and any other person who, in the opinion of the tribunal, should have an opportunity of being heard. Any person to whom such notice is given becomes a party to the proceedings.[62]

Non-assessment cases

Rule 20 provides that the tribunal shall give at least 14 days' notice of the date, time and place fixed for the hearing (or such shorter notice as all the parties may consent to) to all the parties and, in restricted cases, the Secretary of State. The parties are the patient, the responsible authority, any person to whom notice of the proceedings was given under rule 7, and, where relevant, a nearest relative applicant.

---

[61]   *R. v. Mental Health Review Tribunal, ex p. Clatworthy* [1985] 3 All E.R. 699, *per* Mann J.
[62]   Mental Health Review Tribunal Rules 1983, r.2(1).

794

Notice of hearing

20.—The tribunal shall give at least 14 days' notice of the date, time and place fixed for the hearing (or such shorter notice as all parties may consent to) all the parties and, in the case of a restricted patient, the Secretary of State.

Assessment applications

31.—On receipt of an assessment application the tribunal shall—

(a) fix a date for the hearing, being not later than 7 days from the date on which the application was received, and the time and place for the hearing;
(b) give notice of the date, time and place fixed for the hearing to the patient;
(c) give notice of the application and of the date, time and place fixed for the hearing to the responsible authority, the nearest relative (wherever practicable) and any other person who, in the opinion of the tribunal, should have an opportunity of being heard;

and the chairman shall appoint the members of the tribunal to deal with the case in accordance with rule 8."

The venue

Hearings usually take place in the board-room or committee room of the hospital where the patient is liable to be detained or, in cases involving conditionally discharged patients, was detained prior to discharge. In guardianship cases, the hearing may be held at the offices of the local authority appointed as the patient's guardian or, where appropriate, at the hostel where the patient resides. In the case of in-patients who are detained on a locked ward, the hearing may occasionally be held in a side-room on the ward. The authorised representative should resist this if the arrangements give a false impression of the patient's mental state and, in other cases, discuss with staff the appropriateness of any arrangements for escorting a patient to a board-room hearing. On the positive side, the holding of ward-based hearings may have the benefit that the non-medical tribunal members, who often have little or no experience of visiting psychiatric wards, are more acutely aware of the loss sustained by a detained person and the limitations of the ward environment. Wherever possible, an ante-room should be provided for the parties and witnesses or, at the very least, chairs set out in the corridor outside the board-room. Not infrequently, the patient and the parties wait standing in the corridor, although this is rarely an appropriate venue for holding final discussions and taking final instructions, and can also cause the patient unnecessary distress.

The time of the hearing

Conventionally, hearings are scheduled to take place at "10.00am for 10.30am" or at "2.00pm for 2.30pm." This means that those attending are to be present and available to the tribunal at the earlier time but the hearing will not commence until the later time. During the half-hour before the hearing, the medical member will inform the other members of his examination of the patient. Procedural matters may also be dealt with and, in section 2 cases, the reports read. In particular, the social worker attending the hearing will often bring his report with him, rather then send it to the tribunal or responsible authority in advance. The time of the hearing may affect a patient's ability to participate in the proceedings or the manner in which he gives his evidence and so, in practice, also affect the decision made. For example, the mood of many depressed patients is subject to diurnal variation and lifts as the day progresses. In other cases, where medication is due immediately prior to or during the hearing, the patient may be unduly sedated or become aroused as time passes. Similar problems arise if the hearing takes place shortly before or after depot medication is administered.

Failure to give notice of the hearing

The importance of giving notice was emphasised in the *Oxford case*.[63] In that case, the tribunal determined an application by a restricted patient having failed to give notice of the hearing to the Secretary of State. Lord Bridge described the tribunal's omission as "a breach of the most fundamental rule of natural justice, in that the Secretary of State, as a vitally interested party, was denied a hearing ... Such a fundamental flaw as vitiated the proceedings leading to that decision must surely call for a complete rehearing de novo." Previously, in the Court of Appeal, Lawton L.J. had described the tribunal's failure as "a classic case of a failure of natural justice entitling the court to intervene by ordering judicial review," adding that in future "tribunals, before starting to hear any application when the Secretary of State is not represented, should inquire, and note, whether he has been given notice of the application and when."

Failure to give notice to a party

Although it is well established that a tribunal's decision will be quashed if the Secretary of State did not receive notice of the hearing, it is unclear whether a failure to give notice of the hearing to a party listed in rule 7 would have the same consequence. Their role in the proceedings is less fundamental and they have no right under the rules to see the reports or to take a full part at the hearing, in terms of calling evidence and questioning witnesses. The effect of their absence would rarely be so material as to affect the decision reached, although one can never be entirely sure. On the other hand, the main reason for designating them as parties appears to be to entitle them to notice of the hearing, and of any step which affects whether and where a hearing will take place, so the omission is fundamental in this respect. Judicial review being a discretionary remedy, it may be that the court would simply look at any affidavit setting out the evidence which the absent party would have given, compare this with the reasons for the decision reached, and then decide whether the omission may have affected the decision reached and whether the matter is in any case now academic.

---

[63]   *R. v. Oxford Regional Mental Health Review Tribunal, ex p. Secretary of State for the Home Department* [1988] 1 A.C. 20.

14. The hearing

INTRODUCTION

Hearings take place at the hospital where the patient is liable to be detained, most often in the board-room or a committee room. That is also the normal venue if the case involves a patient who has been conditionally discharged or who is subject to after-care under supervision. In guardianship cases, the hearing takes place at the offices of a local authority guardian or, if convenient, at a hostel where the patient is required to reside. Rules 21 and 22 set out the basic hearing procedure but, more importantly, the proceedings must be conducted in a way which is fair and accords with the principles of natural justice. From a legal viewpoint, the issues to be considered in relation to the hearing are whether it should or must be held in private or public (**797**); who is entitled or may be required to attend or appear at the hearing (**800**); who may be excluded from the hearing (**801**); the pre-hearing deliberations (**805**); the hearing itself and the taking of evidence (**807**); the effect of irregularities in the conduct of the proceedings, including failure to comply with the rules (**806, 816**); the power of adjournment (**817**); and sanctions (**826**).

ATTENDANCE AT THE HEARING

The rules provide that a tribunal shall sit in private unless the patient requests a hearing in public and the tribunal is satisfied that a hearing in public would not be contrary to his interests.[1] In practice, it is exceptional for a patient to request a public hearing and virtually all hearings are held in private.

THE RIGHT TO A PUBLIC HEARING

The onus is on the patient to satisfy the tribunal that a public hearing would not be contrary to his interests. Persons other than the patient, including a nearest relative applicant, have no right to request a public hearing. Equally, the fact that a public hearing would be contrary to some other person's interests is not a material

---

[1]   Mental Health Review Tribunal Rules 1983, r.21(1). The test under the 1960 Rules was different. Rule 24(1) required a tribunal to hold a public hearing if the patient requested one provided it was satisfied that such a hearing "would not be detrimental to the interests of the patient and would not for any other reason be undesirable." This provision was considered in the case of *R. v. Mental Health Review Tribunal, ex p. Royston* (CO517/83), 10 May 1983, in which the court held that "detrimental" did not refer to the patient's relationship with his responsible medical officer and there had been no specific reason why one should not be held.

consideration: the sole test is whether a public hearing is contrary to the patient's interests. The statutory test differs from that applicable to decisions about withholding documents from the patient, which is whether their disclosure would be likely to adversely affect his health or welfare or that of others.[2] Consequently, a public hearing will be justified if any detriment to the patient's health is outweighed by the benefits to him of such a hearing.

Giving reasons for refusing a public hearing

Where the tribunal refuses a request for a public hearing or directs that a hearing begun in public shall continue in private, it is required to record its reasons in writing and to inform the patient of them.[3] It may be inferred from rule 21 that the grounds upon which a tribunal may discontinue hearing a case in public are that it is no longer satisfied that a public hearing is not contrary to the patient's interests. For example, because of the effect on his mental health or because of the adverse consequences *for him* of any publicity which the hearing is attracting.

PUBLIC AND PRIVATE HEARINGS : MHRT RULES 1983, r.21

Privacy of proceedings

21.—(1) The tribunal shall sit in private unless the patient requests a hearing in public and the tribunal is satisfied that a hearing in public would not be contrary to the interests of the patient.

(2) Where the tribunal refuses a request for a public hearing or directs that a hearing which has begun in public shall continue in private the tribunal shall record its reasons in writing and shall inform the patient of those reasons.

(3) When the tribunal sits in private it may admit to the hearing such persons on such terms and conditions as it considers appropriate.

(4) The tribunal may exclude from any hearing or part of a hearing any person or class of persons, other than a representative of the applicant or of the patient to whom documents would be disclosed in accordance with rule 12(3), and in any case where the tribunal decides to exclude the applicant or the patient or their representatives or a representative of the responsible authority, it shall inform the person excluded of its reasons and record those reasons in writing.

(5) Except in so far as the tribunal may direct, information about proceedings before the tribunal and the names of any persons concerned in the proceedings shall not be made public.

(6) Nothing in this rule shall prevent a member of the Council on Tribunals from attending the proceedings of a tribunal in his capacity as such provided that he takes no part in those proceedings or in the deliberations of the hearing procedure.

---

[2] Mental Health Review Tribunal Rules 1983, r.12(2).
[3] *Ibid.*, r.21(2).

The nature of a public hearing

Unless a case has attracted public attention, the holding of a public hearing usually means no more than that the doors to the hospital room where the hearing is taking place are left open, so that other persons may listen to the evidence and observe the proceedings if they so wish. Because a tribunal which sits in public has a general power to exclude persons or classes of persons from the hearing or part of it and, conversely, may admit persons to a private hearing on such terms and conditions as it considers appropriate, it might be thought that the distinction between the two is academic. However, that is not the case. Whether it is appropriate to admit persons who are not parties to a private hearing depends on whether they have some interest in the case being considered other than as general members of the public. For example, a person who is not a party to the proceedings may nevertheless have relevant information to impart and be admitted to part of the hearing in order to enable him to assist the tribunal. It is also usually considered appropriate to admit as an observer a person who is applying for some professional qualification which, once obtained, will involve him in undertaking tribunal cases. In both instances, the individuals admitted will be bound by the normal legal provisions which protect the essential privacy of those proceedings. The nature of a public hearing is fundamentally different. It is that all members of the public may observe the hearing unless there is some cogent reason why a particular person or class of persons should be differentiated from other members of the public and excluded on that basis. The intendment of paragraph (4) cannot be that a tribunal which is obliged to hear a patient's case publicly nevertheless retains the same discretion to exclude interested members of the public as it does in the case of a private hearing — the hearing would not then be a public hearing. Although the reference to a class of persons being excluded is most often taken to mean that the press may invariably be excluded from a public hearing, that must be doubtful. Section 12 of the Administration of Justice Act 1960, which concerns the publication of information relating to the proceedings, applies only to hearings held in private. Furthermore, the usual prohibition in rule 21(5), that information about the proceedings and the persons concerned shall not be made public unless the tribunal otherwise directs, cannot apply once a tribunal has directed that the matters be heard publicly — the information is already public by virtue of the fact that a public hearing is being held. If the issues must be publicly heard, to prohibit what is publicly heard from being publicised is contradictory. A tribunal must reflect on all of these considerations before deciding if it is satisfied that a public hearing will not be contrary to the patient's interests, and then be clear about whether it is holding a public or a private hearing, and the implications of that.

The construction of rule 21

Having regard to the above, it is submitted that paragraphs (1) and (2) of rule 21 go together: their effect is that a tribunal may cease to sit in public if it is no longer satisfied that continuing in public is not contrary to the patient's interests. Paragraphs (4) and (5) primarily relate to paragraph (3) and private hearings. However, paragraph (4) also empowers a tribunal to exclude a person or class of persons from a public hearing if they are interfering with, or likely to interfere with, the proper conduct of the proceedings. Their exclusion on this basis would not affect the fact that the hearing remains generally open to the public. Nevertheless, that the main purpose of paragraph (4) is to enable confidential matters to be dealt with in private can be inferred from the fact that it would be inappropriate to exclude the parties and their representatives from a public hearing while allowing the public to remain.

Publicising the proceedings

Rule 21(5) provides that, except in so far as the tribunal may direct, information about proceedings before the tribunal and the names of any persons concerned in the proceedings shall not be made public. This provision is considered later in relation to publication of the tribunal's decision but, as the case law summarised in the following chapter shows, it can be relevant prior to the hearing if the case is attracting publicity.

RIGHT TO APPEAR AT THE HEARING

If a hearing is held in public then, by definition, members of the public have a general right to attend the hearing as observers and to hear the evidence. They do not, of course, have any right to "appear" at the hearing nor any right to observe a hearing held in private.

Right of the parties to appear

According to the rules, the parties must be given notice of the hearing and they may appear at the hearing and take such part in the proceedings as the tribunal thinks proper.[4] This limitation reflects the inquisitorial aspect of tribunal proceedings. The following persons or bodies are parties—

- in the case of assessment applications (section 2 cases), the patient, the responsible authority, any person to whom notice of the hearing was "sent" under rule 31(c), and any other person added as a party by direction of the tribunal.[5]

- in all other cases, the patient, any nearest relative applicant, the responsible authority, any person to whom notice of the proceedings was given under rule 7, and any other person added as a party by direction of the tribunal.[6]

Rights of other persons to appear or attend

Persons who are not parties may, with the permission of the tribunal, also appear at the hearing and take such part in the proceedings as the tribunal thinks proper.[7] This includes the Secretary of State in restricted cases and, in assessment cases, persons on whom it has not been possible to send notice of the hearing during the time available. It is, however, axiomatic that the Secretary of State, although not a party, must be allowed to appear if he wishes and to take a full part in the proceedings. In addition to the parties and other persons wishing to appear and take part, a tribunal may admit other persons to a hearing held in private on such terms and conditions as it considers appropriate.[8] As has been noted, these persons may include solicitors observing a tribunal as part of their preparation for panel membership, trainee doctors, researchers, or social workers training for approval under the 1983 Act.

---

4   Mental Health Review Tribunal Rules 1983, r.22(4).
5   *Ibid.*, r.2(1).
6   *Ibid.*, r.2(1).
7   *Ibid.*, r.22(4).
8   *Ibid.*, r.21(3).

Privacy of proceedings

21.—(3) When the tribunal sits in private it may admit to the hearing such persons on such terms and conditions as it considers appropriate.

(4) The tribunal may exclude from any hearing or part of a hearing any person or class of persons, other than a representative of the applicant or of the patient to whom documents would be disclosed in accordance with rule 12(3), and in any case where the tribunal decides to exclude the applicant or the patient or their representatives or a representative of the responsible authority, it shall inform the person excluded of its reasons and record those reasons in writing.

Hearing procedure

22.—(4) Subject to rule 21(4), any party and, with the permission of the tribunal, any other person, may appear at the hearing and take such part in the proceedings as the tribunal thinks proper; and the tribunal shall in particular hear and take evidence from the applicant, the patient (where he is not the applicant) and the responsible authority who may hear each other's evidence, put questions to each other, call witnesses and put questions to any witness or other person appearing before the tribunal.

The status of those attending or appearing

The rights of persons to appear at or attend a hearing fall into four categories. In the first category are the patient, any nearest relative applicant, the responsible authority and, although not a party, the Secretary of State in a restricted case. They have all the rights of a party (**781**) but they also have a general right to receive copies of all documents and reports concerning the patient, to hear each other's evidence, to call witnesses, and to question persons attending the hearing. In the second category are persons who are parties by virtue of the fact that they were entitled to notice of the proceedings. They are entitled to notice of the hearing, to appear at it and to be represented. However, they are not entitled to copies of reports and they have no general right under the rules to hear the evidence, or to put questions, or to call witnesses. In the third category are persons who are not parties but who have some interest in the proceedings, legitimate or otherwise. They may with the tribunal's permission appear at the hearing and take such part as the tribunal thinks proper. In the fourth category are people present as observers — members of the public who attend a public hearing, members of the Council on Tribunals, and those admitted to a private hearing at the tribunal's discretion.

EXCLUDING PERSONS FROM A HEARING

Notwithstanding the general right of the parties to appear and participate at the hearing, a tribunal which sits in private may exclude from the hearing, or part of it, any person or class of persons other than a representative of the applicant or the patient to whom documents would be disclosed in accordance with rule 12(3).[9]

---

[9]   Section 78(2)(e) merely states that the rules may in particular provide for enabling a tribunal to exclude members of the *public*, or any specified class of members of the *public*, from any proceedings of the tribunal. The statutory authority for this rule, if there is any, therefore appears to be para. (j), which simply provides that the rules may confer on tribunals such ancillary powers as the Lord Chancellor thinks necessary for the purposes of the exercise of their statutory functions.

Necessarily therefore, a solicitor, barrister or registered medical practitioner who is representing a patient or nearest relative applicant can never be excluded from part of the hearing but the representative of any other party or person may.[10] The power of exclusion is often used to temporarily exclude a patient while his relatives give evidence. This may be because they have requested a confidential interview or because it is clear from their responses to questions that they are inhibited by the patient's presence from giving detailed answers of the kind necessary to enable the tribunal to obtain all relevant evidence. Likewise, if the patient requests his relatives' exclusion while he gives evidence, his request will usually be granted.[11] A patient or nearest relative applicant will also be excluded when the tribunal considers the evidence contained in any documents withheld from them, unless circumstances have materially changed since the decision not to disclose was made. It must be emphasised that the parties have a general right to appear at the hearing and to be represented, and some of them a general right also to hear and call evidence and to put questions. Consequently, the discretion to exclude parties from a hearing or part of it may not be used without good cause.

Giving reasons for excluding persons

If a tribunal excludes a person from the hearing, or part of it, it is not generally under a duty to explain and record its reasons for doing so. However, where a tribunal excludes any of the following persons, it must inform the person excluded of its reasons and record those reasons in writing: the patient; a nearest relative applicant; a representative of the responsible authority; the representative of a patient or applicant to whom documents have not been disclosed under rule 12(3).[12]

PAYMENT OF ALLOWANCES TO THOSE ATTENDING

Section 78(7) of the Act provides that a tribunal may pay allowances in respect of travelling expenses, subsistence and loss of earnings to any person attending the tribunal as an applicant or witness, to the patient if he attends otherwise than as the applicant or a witness, and to any person (other than counsel or a solicitor) who attends as the representative of an applicant. A tribunal is therefore authorised to pay an allowance to any medical practitioner who represents the applicant, covering his loss of earnings and other expenses. Where, however, a patient refuses to sign legal aid forms or to instruct a solicitor, and the tribunal appoints a solicitor to act for him, there is no authority to pay that person's professional fees. Similarly, there is never any authority to pay an allowance to a person representing the patient unless he is also the applicant.

ENFORCING ATTENDANCE OF WITNESSES

The Act states that the rules may in particular provide for regulating the methods by which information relevant to an application may be obtained by or furnished to a tribunal[13] and confer on tribunals such ancillary powers as the Lord Chancellor thinks necessary for the purposes of the exercise of their functions.[14] Rule 14

---

[10] Mental Health Review Tribunal Rules 1983, r.21(4). Rule 21(6) also provides that the rule shall not prevent a member of the Council on Tribunals from attending provided that he takes no part in those proceedings or in the deliberations of the tribunal.
[11] See also Mental Health Review Tribunal Rules 1983, r.22(2).
[12] *Ibid.*, r.21(4).
[13] Mental Health Act 1983, s.78(2)(g).
[14] Mental Health Act 1983, s.78(2)(j).

provides that a tribunal may subpoena any witness to appear before it or to produce documents. However, no person may be compelled to give any evidence, or to produce any document, which he could not be compelled to give or produce on the trial of an action.

Use made of the power

In general, the rule is only invoked as a last resort, and a warning that the power is available almost invariably suffices to bring about the desired action. When the power is occasionally used, it is most often used upon adjourning, to require a local social services authority to arrange for an officer of the authority to attend the hearing in order to give oral evidence as to the patient's social circumstances or to produce relevant documents.

SUBPOENAS : MHRT RULES 1983, r.14

Evidence

14.—(1) For the purpose of obtaining information, the tribunal may ... subpoena any witness to appear before it or to produce documents, and the president of the tribunal shall have the powers of an arbitrator under section 12(3) of the Arbitration Act 1950 and the powers of a party to a reference under an arbitration agreement under subsection (4) of that section, but no person shall be compelled to give any evidence or produce any document which he could not be compelled to give or produce on the trial of an action.

Writ of subpoena

A writ of subpoena ad testificandum or a writ of subpoena duces tecum in aid of a tribunal may be issued out of the Crown Office and no court order is necessary.[15] Issue takes place upon the writ being sealed by an officer of the Crown Office.[16] The writ has effect until the disposal of the tribunal proceedings at which the attendance of the witness is required.[17] Where there is disobedience to a subpoena duces tecum, the Court has jurisdiction to enforce obedience by committal, even though the disobedience is not wilful.[18]

Service of the writ

The writ must be served personally.[19] Unless it is served on the person to whom it is directed not less than four days (or such other period as the court may fix) before the day on which his attendance before the tribunal is required by the writ, that person is not liable to any penalty or process for failing to obey it.[20] An application to set aside the writ may be heard by a Master of the Queen's Bench Division.[21]

---

[15]   R.S.C. 1965, O.38, r.19; *Soul v. Inland Revenue Commissioners* [1963] 1 W.L.R. 112.
[16]   R.S.C. 1965, O.38, rr. 14, 19(1).
[17]   R.S.C. 1965, O.38, r.19(2).
[18]   *R. v. Daye* [1908] 2 K.B. 333.
[19]   R.S.C. 1965, O.38, r.19(3).
[20]   R.S.C. 1965, O.38, r.19(4).
[21]   R.S.C. 1965, O.38, r.19(5).

Form of the writ

A writ of subpoena must be in the form specified in Appendix A to the Rules of the Supreme Court 1965.[22] Form No.30 sets out a specimen form and should be modified as necessary (for example, where a subpoena is to be limited to compelling the production of certain documents).

Form No. 30 — Writ of subpoena issued under an enactment

In the matter of C.D. a patient
and
In the matter of the Mental Health Act 1983
and
In the Matter of the Arbitration Act 1950

ELIZABETH THE SECOND, by the Grace of God, of the United Kingdom of Great Britain and Northern Ireland and of Our other realms and territories Queen, Head of the Commonwealth, Defender of the Faith.

To [*name of witness*]

We command you to attend before the Mental Health Review Tribunal constituted under the Mental Health Act 1983 at [*address where tribunal will be sitting*] on the day of 199 at o'clock and so from day to day until the application in the above matter is heard, to give evidence on behalf of [And we also command you to bring with you and produce at the time and place aforesaid *describe documents or things to be produced*].

Witness Lord High Chancellor of Great Britain the day of 199—

Issued on the day of 199— by

The powers of an arbitrator

Apart from subsections 12(3) and 12(4), the Arbitration Act 1950 does not apply to proceedings before a Mental Health Review Tribunal.[23] The incorporated provisions merely reinforce what can already be discerned from the rule itself. It has been noted that rule 14 provides that a tribunal may subpoena any witness to appear before it (writ of subpoena *ad testificandum*) or to produce documents (writ of subpoena *duces tecum*) and, for that purpose, the president has the powers of a party to a reference under an arbitration agreement under section 12(4) of the Arbitration Act 1950. Insofar as material, that subsection provides that such a party "may sue out a writ of subpoena *ad testificandum* or a writ of subpoena *duces tecum*, but no person shall be compelled under any such writ to produce any document which he could not be compelled to produce on the trial of an action, and the High Court or a Judge thereof may order that a writ of subpoena *ad testificandum* or of subpoena *duces tecum* shall issue to compel the attendance before an arbitrator of a witness wherever he may be within the United Kingdom. For attendance before an arbitrator, a subpoena therefore issues as of course without order.

---

[22] R.S.C. 1965, O.38, r.14(1). See R.S.C. 1965, Appendix A, Forms No. 28, 29 and 30.
[23] Mental Health Act 1983, s.78(9); Mental Health Review Tribunal Rules 1983, r.14.

PRE-HEARING DELIBERATIONS

The tribunal members meet approximately half an hour before the commencement of the actual hearing in order to discuss and agree preliminary matters. These may include questions of privacy, disclosure, exclusion and conflict of interest; the order in which witnesses should give evidence; and, if appropriate, which of the tribunal members should lead the questioning of particular witnesses. This period also provides an opportunity for the tribunal to identify the issues likely to be relevant. The medical member, who will already have seen the patient, will often have a good idea of what they are likely to be and of any difficulties which might affect the patient's ability to give evidence. However, it is now not usually considered appropriate to ask the medical member about his opinion of the patient's mental condition at this stage.[24]

THE MEDICAL MEMBER'S OPINION

Notwithstanding the above, the approved custom until recently was for the medical member, during the half-hour prior to the hearing, to summarise for the benefit of the other members any information relevant to the proceedings arising out of his examination of the patient, his inspection of the case notes, and other steps taken by him to form an opinion of the patient's mental condition (**793**). According to recent annual reports of the tribunals, it is usually more appropriate for the medical member to confine his pre-hearing report to factual matters, reserving his opinion until after the evidence has been taken so that it forms part of the deliberative process.

Ex p. Clatworthy

The importance of not proceeding on the basis of some information or opinion known only to the tribunal members themselves was considered in the *ex p. Clatworthy*. The underlying principle is that if a tribunal has information which is relevant to the decision it is to make but which does not appear in the reports, or the medical member's opinion of the patient's mental condition differs significantly from that of the responsible medical officer, so that there may be grounds for his detention which he is not aware of, these matters must be brought into the open in the course of the tribunal's questioning.[25]

R. v. Mental Health Review Tribunal, ex p. Clatworthy

[1985] 3 All E.R. 699   *Q.B.D., Mann J.*

The medical evidence received by the tribunal was that the applicant was not suffering from a form of mental disorder as defined by section 1 of the Act. The tribunal did not direct the patient's discharge and the applicant sought judicial review of its decision.

Mann J.

The reasons given for the tribunal's decision did not show why the medical evidence presented to the tribunal had not been accepted. It might be suggested that there was a medical member of the tribunal who had made his own

---

[24]   *Mental Health Review Tribunals for England and Wales, Annual Report 1994* (Department of Health, 1995), Appendix 13.

[25]   *Ibid.*

examination of the patient and the tribunal had proceeded on the basis of his opinion rather than on the basis of the opinions laid before the tribunal. While there was no explicit suggestion that was the case, if a tribunal desired to proceed on the basis of some point which had not been put before it, and which on the face of the matter was not in dispute, it was in the highest degree desirable that the person whose case was being considered should be alerted to the possibility. In *Mahon v. Air New Zealand Ltd* [1984] 3 All ER 201 at 210, [1984] AC 808 at 821, Lord Diplock referred to the rules of natural justice, one of which was the rule which—

> 'requires that any person represented at the inquiry who will be adversely affected by the decision to make the finding should not be left in the dark as to the risk of the finding being made and thus deprived of any opportunity to adduce additional material of probative value which, had it been placed before the decision-maker, might have deterred him from making the finding even though it cannot be predicated that it would inevitably have had that result.'

Were it the case that the tribunal had proceeded on some basis unknown to others but known to themselves, then His Lordship would have regarded the decision as flawed by reference to that principle of natural justice.

PROCEDURAL IRREGULARITIES

Prior to the hearing, it is important to verify that all persons entitled to notice of the hearing have received notice of it and to consider whether any procedural irregularities have occurred which may have prejudiced the patient or any other person.[26]

IRREGULARITIES: MHRT RULES 1983, r.28

28.— Any irregularity resulting from failure to comply with these Rules before the tribunal has determined an application shall not of itself render the proceedings void, but the tribunal may, and shall, if it considers that any person may have been prejudiced, take such steps as it thinks fit before determining the application to cure the irregularity, whether by the amendment of any document, the giving of any notice, the taking of any step or otherwise.

Curing irregularities

Rule 28 provides that any irregularity resulting from a failure to comply with the rules before the tribunal has determined the case shall not render the proceedings void. The tribunal may, and shall, if it considers that any person may have been

---

[26] The Secretary of State must receive copies of all reports furnished to the tribunal and have an opportunity to comment on them. If professionals seek to submit supplementary reports immediately prior to the hearing, these may, if only brief up-dates, sometimes be sent by fax to the Home Office. The Secretary of State often has no further observations to make, so the hearing can proceed. In other cases, the reports are refused and the evidence is given orally. This is not satisfactory if the report contains information materially different to that set out in the reports possessed by the Secretary of State, since it amounts to circumventing his right to receive relevant written information about the case.

prejudiced, take such steps as it thinks fit before determining the case to cure the irregularity, whether by the amendment of any document, the giving of any notice, the taking of any step or otherwise. The rule applies only to a failure to observe the rules, not to a failure to comply with the basic principles of natural justice or the provisions of the Act itself. Its effect is therefore mainly confined to failure to observe time limits or to serve required notices, provided the omissions are discovered prior to the application being determined. If the proceedings must be adjourned in order to cure an irregularity, a tribunal has no jurisdiction to award costs against a party. In general, the only consequence is that the patient is detained, perhaps unnecessarily, for a further period of time.

Case law

In *Crozier*,[27] a tribunal had adjourned a restricted patient's case in order to monitor his progress. The High Court held that, once it had all the evidence necessary to determine the patient's mental state and had concluded that section 73(1) had not been satisfied, it was then its duty to refuse the application. Farquharson J. dealt briefly with the submission that, because rule 28 enabled a tribunal to correct its own irregularities, therefore judicial review was not appropriate because an alternative remedy was available: the error went beyond mere irregularity and involved the exercise of a power not conferred by statute. In the *Oxford case*,[28] the tribunal failed to give the Secretary of State notice of the hearing of a restricted patient's case. In the Court of Appeal, Lawton L.J. observed that rule 28 had no applicability once an application had been determined while, in the House of Lords, Lord Bridge of Harwich said that such a fundamental flaw as vitiated the proceedings leading to the tribunal's decision called for a complete rehearing *de novo*.

THE HEARING PROCEDURE

Subject to the rules of natural justice, rule 22 gives the tribunal a wide discretion as to how to conduct the hearing, which has been described as being inquisitorial, rather than adversarial, in nature.[29]

FORMALITY AND INFORMALITY

It is often said that the rules require the hearing to be conducted "informally" in the sense in which persons other than lawyers use the word. In fact, rule 22(1) provides that the tribunal may conduct the hearing in such manner as it considers most appropriate bearing in mind the health and interests of the patient and it shall, so far as appears to it appropriate, seek to avoid formality in its proceedings.[30] This is

---

[27] *R. v. Nottingham Mental Health Review Tribunal, ex p. Secretary of State for the Home Department (Thomas); R. v. Northern Mental Health Review Tribunal, ex p. Secretary of State for the Home Department (Crozier), The Times*, 25 March 1987 (**818**).

[28] *R. v. Oxford Regional Mental Health Review Tribunal, ex p. Secretary of State for the Home Department* [1986] 1 W.L.R. 1180, C.A.; [1988] 1 A.C. 120, H.L. (**544**).

[29] By Scott J. (as he then was) in *W. v. Egdell and Others [1989] 2 W.L.R. 689* (**712**). Nevertheless, the proceedings cannot properly be described as exclusively inquisitorial in nature.

[30] The 1960 Rules provided for informally determining cases in certain circumstances (see rr.17–20).

rather different and it may sometimes be quite inappropriate to avoid formality. A distinction must be drawn between maintaining an informal atmosphere, which reassures the patient, and following a formal approach to the taking of the evidence, which is not only essential to the proper discharge of the tribunal's powers but also reassures the patient that his liberty is highly regarded. The reference to avoiding formality must be understood in the historical context of the, now obsolete, distinction made in the 1960 Rules for determining applications either informally or by way of formal hearing. The provision previously made for disposing of cases informally was found not to be helpful. The 1983 Rules now provide only for what used to be called a formal hearing but also, because of this and by way of uneasy compromise, that tribunals shall seek to avoid formality so far as is appropriate. As to the general approach, "questioning should always be conducted politely and courteously: searching questions can be asked without being abusive or threatening, and members should bear in mind that nothing should be done to undermine profess- ional and family relationships. A tribunal hearing is a judicial procedure which needs to be structured, although in a relatively informal way, and it should be more inquisitorial than adversarial. However, it is neither a case conference nor a seminar. Needless to say, members should be objective and impartial."[31]

HEARING PROCEDURE : MHRT RULES 1983, r.22

Hearing procedure

22.—(1) The tribunal may conduct the hearing in such manner as it considers most suitable bearing in mind the health and interests of the patient and it shall, so far as appears to it appropriate, seek to avoid formality in its proceedings.

(2) At any time before the application is determined, the tribunal or any one or more of its members may interview the patient, and shall interview him if he so requests, and the interview may, and shall if the patient so requests, take place in the absence of any other person.

(3) At the beginning of the hearing the president shall explain the manner of pro- ceeding which the tribunal proposes to adopt.

(4) Subject to rule 21(4), any party and, with the permission of the tribunal, any other person, may appear at the hearing and take such part in the proceedings as the tribunal thinks proper; and the tribunal shall in particular hear and take evidence from the applicant, the patient (where he is not the applicant) and the responsible authority who may hear each other's evidence, pub questions to each other, call wit- nesses and put questions to any witness or other person appearing before the tribunal.

(5) After all the evidence has been given, the applicant and (where he is not the ap- plicant) the patient shall be given a further opportunity to address the tribunal.

---

[31] *Mental Health Review Tribunals for England and Wales, Annual Report 1994* (Department of Health, 1995), Appendix 13.

EXPLAINING THE PROCEDURE

The rules provide that at the beginning of the hearing the president shall explain the manner of proceeding which the tribunal proposes to adopt.[32] The main differences in procedure adopted by presidents relate to the order in which the evidence is taken and the order in which the tribunal members and any representatives ask questions of each witness in turn. On some occasions, a medical or other witness may need to be released, or the tribunal will need to be updated on the present situation because of the age of the reports, and these necessities will dictate the order of the evidence. Hearing from the responsible medical officer first also enables the patient to know the present reasons for detaining him, so that he can then seek to satisfy the tribunal that those grounds do not in fact apply. In other cases, hearing the patient first may save time or be more appropriate. For example, if it is likely to be rapidly apparent that he is very seriously ill. Or because the absence of any symptoms will enable the tribunal to rapidly focus on the real issue of the likelihood of relapse and whether liability to detention, rather than actual detention, is appropriate. It also allows the patient to give his evidence while he can, and to then return to the ward if necessary, when he is heavily sedated, agitated, unable to concentrate, or unable to settle and remain quiet. In unrestricted cases, the president will often ask the patient's representative if he or the patient has a preference as to the order in which evidence is taken. Apart from the fact that enlisting the representative's view may serve to shorten the proceedings, for the reasons just given, such inquiries also convey the impression that the tribunal is anxious to ensure that the patient has every opportunity to present his case for discharge effectively. Even if the patient is later disappointed by the tribunal's decision, he generally retains the impression of a hearing fairly and impartially conducted and is more likely to apply for a further review in future. The order in which the evidence is taken is therefore a matter for the tribunal's discretion and there is no requirement that the applicant is heard from first. There are very good reasons for not imposing such a requirement and to insist on this because it is the procedure adopted in the county court, when the rules do not, is not appropriate.

ABSENCE OF THE PATIENT

The patient occasionally does not attend, most often where his case has been referred to the tribunal or where it is being held following an application by the nearest relative. Less frequently, a patient who has applied but who does not wish to present his case personally simply asks his representative to present that case in his absence, in accordance with his instructions. It is obviously important that the patient is advised that this approach is likely to undermine the application but the point also arises as to whether a tribunal can proceed in the patient's absence. This is because rule 22(4) provides that a tribunal "shall in particular hear and take evidence" from the patient. Some presidents view this requirement as a bar to proceeding in such circumstances unless some other rule can be invoked which empowers them to proceed. They therefore attempt to resolve the problem by formally excluding the patient from the hearing under rule 21(4). The reasoning seems dubious because the purpose of that rule in this context is to exclude a patient who wishes to appear and be present, as can be seen from the requirement that he be given reasons for his exclusion. The correct position has to be inferred from the statutory framework, supported by the rules insofar as they are not inconsistent with it. That framework is essentially that a patient's case must be periodically reviewed by an

---

[32] The 1960 Rules contained no equivalent provision.

independent tribunal whether he desires that or not; often not since by definition he has not himself applied to the tribunal for some time. Furthermore, a nearest relative's right to apply is not dependent on having the patient's consent and that right would be undermined if the patient could prevent the application from being determined simply by not attending the hearing of it. As to the position where the patient does not attend on his own application, the Act itself envisages the possibility of an application being disposed of without a formal hearing[33] and the rules still provide for this to a limited extent. In particular, rule 22(2) provides that, at any time before the application is determined, the tribunal or any one or more of its members may interview the patient and shall interview him if he so requests. The normal practice in such cases is to visit the patient on the ward and to offer him the opportunity of making any points which he wishes to make in support of his application. Rule 21(4) simply provides that a party (the patient being a party) *may* appear at the hearing and take such part in the proceedings as the tribunal thinks proper. The rest of the rule, after the semi-colon, sets out the position where the party does appear. In *ex p. Mackman*,[34] the patient applied for an adjournment and, when this was refused, he withdrew. He applied for judicial review of the tribunal's decision to hear and determine his application in his absence and the absence of his counsel. The point does not appear to have been actively pursued in the Divisional Court. At any rate, the court did not decide that the proceedings had to be adjourned when the patient withdrew. It is submitted therefore that if the patient does not attend the hearing the tribunal must ascertain the reasons for that and should offer him an interview in private with them. They must then consider whether they have sufficient information with which to determine the application and whether it would be fair and just to determine it in all the circumstances. In other words, they should consider the need to adjourn the proceedings *sine die*. An adjournment has the benefit that the patient's right to appear at the hearing of his application is preserved and this will be more appropriate if he has simply had a temporary attack of nerves.[35] However, ultimately, a tribunal has a discretion to proceed in the applicant's absence where he declines to attend but their discretion must not be abused.[36]

EVIDENCE AND QUESTIONING

The rules provide that, subject to the power to exclude a person from a hearing or part of it, a tribunal shall in particular hear and take evidence from a nearest relative applicant, the patient and the responsible authority, who may hear each other's evidence, put questions to each other, call witnesses, and put questions to any witness or other person appearing before the tribunal.[37] A tribunal may call for further information and reports during the hearing, adjourn the hearing if necessary

---

[33] Mental Health Act 1983, s.78(2)(d).

[34] R. v. Oxford Regional Mental Health Review, ex p. Mackman, The Times, 2 June 1986, Q.B.D.

[35] Rule 16(3) provides that where the patient requests that an adjourned hearing be resumed, the hearing shall be resumed provided that the tribunal is satisfied that resumption would be in the interests of the patient.

[36] R. v. Seisdon Justices, ex p. Dougan [1982] 1 W.L.R. 1476. See also ex p. S.B.R. (CO/89/3908, unreported).

[37] The 1960 Rules provided as follows: "25.—(2) The tribunal shall give an opportunity to the applicant to address the tribunal, to give evidence and call witnesses; and the responsible authority, and with the permission of the tribunal any other person, may put questions to the applicant or to any witness called by him or on his behalf. (3) The tribunal shall give the responsible authority and any other person notified of the hearing ... an opportunity to address them, to give evidence and to call witnesses and may permit any other person whom they think fit to do so; and the applicant and the responsible authority, and with the permission of the tribunal any other person, may put questions to any person giving evidence before the tribunal."

for that purpose, and give directions as to the manner in which and the persons by whom the material is to be furnished. It may, for the purpose of obtaining inform-ation, take evidence on oath[38] and subpoena a witness to appear before it; but it may not compel a person to give evidence which he could not be compelled to give on the trial of an action. Similarly, a tribunal may subpoena a witness to produce docu-ments but not compel a witness to produce a document which he could not be compelled to produce on the trial of an action.

Evidence and the rules of natural justice

The rules provide that a tribunal may receive in evidence documents and oral evidence which would be inadmissible in a court of law, including hearsay. Further-more, the technical rules of evidence form no part of the rules of natural justice, which allow a tribunal to use evidence from other hearings, so long as the parties have an opportunity to deal with it.[39] Tribunals are therefore entitled to act on any material which is logically probative even though it would not be admissible as evidence in a court of law. Evidence is relevant if it is logically probative or disprobative of some matter which requires proof and all relevant evidence is *prima facie* admissible.[40] Its weight is determined by the degree of probability, both intrinsically and inferentially, which is attached to it by the tribunal once it is established to be relevant and admissible.

Allowing the patient an opportunity to deal with evidence

Fairness to the patient normally requires that the factual basis of expert medical opinion is open to challenge, both by cross-examination and by evidence. It is unfair, and so contrary to the rules of natural justice, to prevent cross-examination of the responsible medical officer about the factual basis for his conclusions and to prevent evidence being led by the patient on the same topic. If the factual basis of the expert opinion cannot be tested in this way then the patient is unable to conduct his case in a proper manner with any prospect at all of success. More particularly, where the expert opinion that other persons are at risk is founded on an assumption that allegations of recent offending are true, a tribunal cannot simply exclude any consideration of, or evidence, about the factual basis upon which such the expert has arrived at his opinion. Although it will not usually be practical to conduct a quasi-trial of the alleged offence, and there must be limits as to the extent of any cross-examination on such matters, it is nonetheless possible to hear second-hand evidence about what is alleged to have happened, to consider any relevant documents available, and to hear the patient's version of what happened. If the tribunal does not allow that then it is bound to be indirectly assuming that the patient did commit the alleged acts if the medical opinion was based on an assumption that he had committed them. To summarise the position, the patient must be given a proper opportunity to challenge the evidence upon which is founded the opinion that he is mentally disordered and that he or others are at risk. [41]

---

[38] The terms "'oath' and 'affidavit' include affirmation and declaration, and "swear" includes affirm and declare."

[39] *R. v. Deputy Industrial Injuries Commissioner, ex p. Moore* [1965] 1 Q.B.D. 456.

[40] *D.P.P. v. Kilbourne* [1973] A.C. 729, *per* Lord Simon. Evidence may be excluded. *i.e.* not admitted, if its prejudicial effect grossly exceeds its probative significance.

[41] The rules of natural justice are further considered on page 858.

CO3519/96, 22 April 1997   *Q.B.D., Keene J.*

Having been convicted in 1984 of arson, being reckless as to whether life would be endangered, the patient was detained at a special hospital in pursuance of a hospital order together with a restriction order made without limit of time. On 14 June 1995, a mental health review tribunal conditionally discharged him to a hostel under medical supervision. On 11 September 1995, the patient was arrested on suspicion of criminal damage, involving throwing a brick through the window of a public house. He denied the allegation. On 30 September 1995, he was again arrested, this time on suspicion of having assaulted women on 18 and 29 September 1995. Again, he denied the allegations. Subsequent to his arrest it was suggested that he had attempted to kiss the leg of a female member of staff at a day centre in August of that year. Once more he denied that suggestion. On 12 October 1995, he absconded from his hostel but returned of his own accord, following which, on 14 October 1995, he was recalled to the special hospital by the Secretary of State. His case was referred to a tribunal under section 75.

The tribunal hearing

At the tribunal hearing in August 1996, the president ruled that it was not within the tribunal's jurisdiction to consider the correctness or otherwise of the decision to recall. The only matter which the tribunal had to consider and decide upon was whether the patient should be conditionally discharged or recommended for transfer to a regional secure unit, as suggested in the psychiatric report filed by the patient. Although the patient's solicitor sought to submit evidence from the patient that he had not committed the various offences for which he had been arrested, the president indicated that the tribunal was not the forum to decide such issues. Similarly, when questions were raised about the degree of supervision which the patient had actually received outside hospital, the president said that such matters could not go to whether the patient suffered from a mental disorder such that he required hospital treatment. The president also intervened when the tribunal's medical member asked a number of questions of the patient about events following his recall, on the basis that such matters were irrelevant to the issue of whether or not he should be discharged. The tribunal did not discharge the patient. As to its reasons, the tribunal was satisfied on the responsible medical officer's evidence, the reports of the psychiatrist instructed by the patient, and the other medical evidence, that the patient suffered from psychopathic disorder. Furthermore, since his recall there had been several incidents which had caused disquiet. The tribunal agreed with the responsible medical officer that it was necessary to investigate the patient's sexual attitudes although that would be difficult in view of the patient's present reaction to his recall. In the meantime, the tribunal was satisfied that he was appropriately detained in the special hospital. According to the affidavit subsequently filed by the president, the medical member was also of the view that further treatment in hospital was required before the patient could be considered for discharge; the tribunal was satisfied on the evidence and the responsible medical officer's report that the patient was properly and appropriately detained in hospital; and the tribunal did not proceed on the basis that the patient might have been guilty of any offence or might have attempted suicide.

The application for judicial review

The patient applied to quash the tribunal's decision, principally on the basis that the hearing was unfair and in breach of the rules of natural justice. It was contended that, while it was not for the tribunal to consider the correctness of the Secretary of State's decision to recall, the circumstances leading up to that recall could not be ignored by the tribunal when considering the patient's condition at the time of the hearing. The tribunal was required to decide whether he was suffering from a psychopathic disorder of a nature and degree which made it appropriate for him to be detained in hospital for medical treatment, and whether it was necessary for his own health and safety or for the protection of others that he should receive such treatment. The patient's behaviour, or alleged behaviour, whilst on conditional discharge was plainly relevant to those issues. The tribunal could not ignore what had happened to the patient while he was on conditional discharge, because the questions about his current condition at the date of the hearing could not be dealt with in a vacuum. More particularly, the tribunal was wrong to exclude evidence and to prevent cross-examination in relation to the events prior to recall, including the degree of supervision afforded, and likewise to prevent exploration of the behaviour of the patient following recall. The patient was prevented from giving evidence about those matters and the responsible medical officer was allowed to decline to answer certain questions on those matters in cross-examination. Although it might be difficult to deal with alleged criminal conduct which has not been the subject matter of a trial, the medical reports upon which the tribunal relied, particularly those from the responsible medical officer, were predicated on the basis that the patient had behaved in a particular way both before and after his recall. Yet those facts about his behaviour were in dispute. Consequently, the tribunal in failing to hear the patient's side of the case was acting unfairly. As to the degree of supervision which the patient had received when in the community, had the issue been explored the tribunal might have concluded that with a more structured and high level of supervision the patient would have been able to cope on a conditional discharge basis.

The tribunal's case

Counsel for the tribunal made essentially three points. Firstly, the patient's solicitor had outlined his case by saying that the Secretary of State's recall was not justified or necessary and it was therefore understandable that the president ruled that the tribunal was not sitting in judgment on the correctness of that recall. Secondly, since conditional discharge was, on the expert evidence, not in issue, the tribunal was entitled to rule that the matters which the patient's representative sought to explore were irrelevant. Thirdly, once the primary question of whether or not the patient was entitled to be discharged had been determined against the patient, the tribunal did not need to go into the conditions, whether those be conditions of supervision or of any other kind.

Keene J.

The patient's application before the tribunal was that he should be conditionally discharged. That application, therefore, raised as issues those matters set out in section 73(1)(a), which incorporated the statutory discharge criteria set out in section 72(1)(b)(i) and (ii). In general terms, events leading up to a patient's recall might be irrelevant to the issues arising under those paragraphs, which were essentially concerned with his mental state at the time of the hearing, and with his health or safety and the protection of others then and in the future. However, on the other hand, the events prior to a patient's recall might be relevant. The diagnosis and opinions about the matters referred to in the relevant statutory paragraphs were not arrived at by ignoring events which had happened. The patient's behaviour might very well be material to the diagnosis and such opinions. It would depend, at least partly, on how the expert witness or witnesses had arrived at their conclusions. In the present case, the responsible medical officer's reports for the tribunal placed considerable reliance on his alleged behaviour prior to recall. They referred to the alleged suicide attempt prior to recall; to a number of occasions when he was said to have drunk excessively; to his alleged offending; to reports concerning the alleged offences furnished by the police. From this behaviour, the responsible medical officer had formed the opinions expressed in his report, namely that it was reasonable to believe that the patient had committed the alleged sexual offences, and possibly also criminal damage; that his denial of the offences precluded a full risk assessment; that it was therefore appropriate that he remain detained in hospital, primarily to protect others; that the sexual behaviour was a new development which needed to be clearly understood before any transfer to conditions of lesser security could be recommended; that he had recently shown his inability to cope with the freedom in the community despite living in a staffed hostel under supervision; that he suffered from psychopathic disorder. It would not usually be practical for a tribunal to conduct a quasi-trial of an alleged offence and there had to be limits as to the extent of any cross-examination on such matters. Since the responsible medical officer was not himself a witness of fact to the alleged actions but appeared to assume that most of the allegations were true, he could no doubt fruitfully be asked what his opinion would be if they were not. Nonetheless, it was difficult to see that the tribunal could simply exclude any consideration of, or evidence, about the factual basis upon which such an expert witness arrived at his opinion. It would be possible for a tribunal in such cases to hear evidence, albeit second-hand, about what was alleged to have happened. It would no doubt have a number of relevant documents available and could also hear the patient's version of what had happened. If it did not do so, the tribunal was bound to be indirectly assuming that the patient did commit the alleged acts if the medical opinion was based on an assumption that he had committed them. Normally, therefore, fairness to the patient required that the factual basis for the expert medical opinion was open to challenge, both by cross-examination and by evidence. Otherwise the patient would feel a justifiable sense of grievance and there would be a breach of the rules of natural justice. Although the medical evidence may have meant that the patient's application to be conditionally discharged was unlikely to succeed, it was going too far to submit that conditional discharge was not really an issue before the tribunal. The affidavit submitted by the president made it clear that that was not how the tribunal itself saw it. Furthermore, the report submitted by the psychiatrist instructed by the patient did not expressly exclude conditional discharge as an outcome. It was open to the tribunal, had it considered it appropriate, to decide that conditional discharge was an appropriate order. If that was so, the basis for the responsible medical officer's opinion became highly relevant, since he was clearly and firmly recommending against conditional discharge. There was no doubt that the tribunal attached great weight to his evidence and report. The issue before the tribunal was one upon which his evidence was highly material, and the basis for his opinion was very much to be found in his beliefs about the patient's behaviour before and after recall. It was therefore unfair procedurally of the tribunal to prevent cross-examination of the responsible medical officer about the factual basis for his conclusions and to prevent evidence being led by the patient on the same topic. If the factual basis for the responsible medical officer's expert opinion could not be tested in that way, one could only wonder how it was that the patient would be able to conduct his case in a proper manner with any prospect at all of success. Given the circumstances, the tribunal acted in a way which was contrary to the rules of natural justice and its decision was therefore *ultra vires*. Because of the passage of time since the tribunal's decision a further review had already been arranged. *Application granted — certiorari and declaration that the tribunal's decision was not reached according to law.*

Rejecting evidence

A tribunal is always entitled to take note of the fact that it finds evidence unsatisfactory, not least when it is provided by the person upon whom the burden of proof rests; that burden lying on the patient (or a nearest relative applicant) in all cases except those involving conditionally discharged patients, where it lies unallocated. More particularly, a tribunal is always entitled to reject medical evidence which it receives provided its decision is not irrational; is supported by adequate reasons; and those affected are alerted to the possibility that it desires to proceed on the basis of some point which has not been put before it and which appears not to be in dispute.[42] The fact that medical evidence is involved in the definition of psychopathic disorder is not in itself a reason why the issue of whether a patient has such a disorder should not be decided by the tribunal members in the light of their own expertise and examination of the patient.[43]

Taking evidence on oath

It is virtually unheard of for evidence to be taken on oath. However, rule 14 provides that the tribunal may do, although no person may be compelled to give any evidence which he could not be compelled to give on the trial of an action.

EVIDENCE : MHRT RULES 1983, r.14

14.—(1) For the purpose of obtaining information, the tribunal may take evidence on oath and subpoena any witness to appear before it or to produce documents, and the president of the tribunal shall have the powers of an arbitrator under section 12(3) of the Arbitration Act 1950 and the powers of a party to a reference under an arbitration agreement under subsection (4) of that section, but no person shall be compelled to give any evidence or produce any document which he could not be compelled to give or produce on the trial of an action.

(2) The tribunal may receive in evidence any document or information notwithstanding that such document or information would be inadmissible in a court of law.

The powers of an arbitrator

The reference in the rule to the powers of an arbitrator under the 1950 Act merely reinforces what can already be discerned from the rule itself. Section 12(3) simply provides that an arbitrator shall have power to administer oaths to, or take the affirmations of, the parties to and witnesses on a reference under an agreement. As to what evidence a person may not be compelled to give, the mere statement by a witness of his belief that his answer to a question will tend to criminate him is not sufficient to excuse him. The court or tribunal must see from the circumstances of the case and the nature of the evidence required that there is reasonable ground to apprehend danger to the witness if he is compelled to answer.[44]

---

42   *R. v. Mental Health Review Tribunal, ex p. Clatworthy* [1985] 3 All E.R. 330; *R. v. Mental Health Review Tribunal (Mersey Region), ex p. Davies* (CO/1723/85), 21 April 1986; *R. v. Royse* (1981) 3 Cr.App.R.(S) 58.

43   *R. v. Trent Mental Health Review Tribunal, ex p. Ryan* [1992] C.O.D. 157, D.C..

44   *Ex p. Reynolds* (1882) 20 Ch.D. 294; *Triplex Safety Glass Co. v. Lancergaye Safety Glass (1934) Ltd.* [1939] 2 K.B. 395; *Rio Tinto Zinc Corp. v. Westinghouse Electric Corp.* [1978] A.C. 547.

INTERVIEWING THE PATIENT IN PRIVATE

Before an application or reference is determined, the tribunal or one or more of its members may interview the patient, and shall interview him if he so requests, and that interview may take place in the absence of any other person.[45] The provision represents something of a compromise between those tribunal members who wished to retain a power to dispose of cases informally and those who did not.[46] Its main function now is to emphasise that the patient has an unqualified right to speak privately with the tribunal, notwithstanding that it "shall" in any case hear and take evidence from him and "may" while doing so exclude other persons from that part of a hearing.[47]

IRREGULARITIES

Once a tribunal has determined the proceedings, it will be too late to cure any irregularity by the use of rule 28 (**544**). Before the parties disperse, it is therefore important that a tribunal verifies that it has observed all procedural requirements. Provided that those entitled received notice of the hearing, the most common omissions are not notifying the patient of his right to be interviewed by one or more tribunal members in the absence of any other party; not giving or recording reasons for excluding the patient or a nearest relative applicant[48]; and considering supplementary reports brought to a restricted hearing and then determining the matter without the Secretary of State having seen or had an opportunity to comment on them. The rules aside, the most common error is to fail to ascertain the legal status of the hostel where it is proposed that a restricted patient should reside as a condition of discharge. It is preferable to review the situation before any closing address, otherwise further evidence may be taken after the patient's representative has summed up his case, which is unsatisfactory and can be a cause of embarrassment.

CLOSING ADDRESS

The rules provide that after all the evidence has been given the applicant and (where he is not the applicant) the patient shall be given a further opportunity to address the tribunal.[49]

---

[45] Mental Health Review Tribunal Rules 1983, r.22(2). Section 78(2)(g) provides that "the rules may in particular provide for authorising the members of a tribunal, or any one or more of them, to *visit and interview* in private any patient by or in respect of whom an application has been made."

[46] The rule derives from rule 12(1) of the 1960 Rules but that rule only applied to cases which did not proceed to a formal hearing. Rule 25(4), which related to formal hearings of the kind now held in all cases, empowered the tribunal to interview the patient or to take his evidence in private if they considered that was desirable in the interests of his health. The power to informally determine an application was not carried over to the present rules but rule 12(1) rather than 25(4) was incorporated in the revised hearing procedures.

[47] See rules 21(4) and 22(4).

[48] Rule 9(4) provides that a tribunal which postpones considering an application shall state in writing the reasons for postponement, and the period for which the application is postponed, and send a copy of the statement to all the parties and, in the case of a restricted patient, the Secretary of State. Rule 21(2) requires a tribunal which refuses a request for a public hearing, or directs that a hearing which has begun in public shall continue in private, to record its reasons in writing and inform the patient of those reasons (not any other party). Rule 21(4) requires a tribunal which excludes the applicant or the patient or their representatives or a representative of the responsible authority, from a hearing, or part of a hearing, to inform the person excluded of its reasons and record those reasons.

[49] Note that the 1960 Rules contained no equivalent provision.

ADJOURNMENTS

The decisions which a tribunal may reach, its powers, are regulated by statute. The manner in which it reaches its decision, the recording of that decision and the reasons for it, and their communication to the parties, are regulated by the rules. However, the first "decision" for any tribunal to make is whether it has sufficient information to determine the proceedings. If not, it should adjourn and rule 16 provides for this. Before determining the application or reference, it should also satisfy itself that there have been no irregularities in the proceedings themselves which may have a bearing on the validity of any determination.

ADJOURNMENTS

A tribunal may at any time adjourn a hearing for the purpose of obtaining further information or for such other purposes as it may think appropriate.[50] A tribunal which adjourns may do so *sine die* or it may specify a date for the hearing's resumption. Before adjourning, the tribunal may give such directions as it thinks fit for ensuring the prompt consideration of the application at an adjourned hearing.[51]

ADJOURNMENTS : MHRT RULES 1983, r.16

16.—(1) The tribunal may at any time adjourn a hearing for the purpose of obtaining further information or for such other purposes as it may think appropriate.

(2) Before adjourning any hearing, the tribunal may give such directions as it thinks fit for ensuring the prompt consideration of the application at an adjourned hearing.

(3) Where the applicant or the patient (where he is not the applicant or the responsible authority requests that a hearing adjourned in accordance with this rule be resumed, the hearing shall be resumed provided that the tribunal is satisfied that resumption would be in the interests of the patient.

(4) Before the tribunal resumes any hearing which has been adjourned without a further hearing date being fixed it shall give to all parties and ,in the case of a restricted patient, the Secretary of State, not less than 14 days' notice (or such shorter notice as all parties may consent to) of the date, time and place of the resumed hearing.

Use of the power to adjourn

The power is most often used where the prescribed reports have not been prepared, further reports are necessary, the patient is absent, no person is available to present the responsible authority's medical or social work evidence, or legal representation is appropriate. More rarely, the proceedings must be adjourned because the Secretary of State or some other party has not received notice of the hearing, or because some

---

[50] Mental Health Review Tribunal Rules 1983, r.16(1). Rule 26(1) of the 1960 Rules provided only for adjourning a formal hearing where it appeared that was desirable in order to obtain further information on a particular matter.
[51] Mental Health Review Tribunal Rules 1983, r.16(2).

other material irregularity needs to be cured. Assessment cases are not infrequently adjourned to enable the patient to obtain an independent psychiatric report, but it is not mandatory to do so. In the case of section 48 patients awaiting trial, the representative should already have considered whether it is appropriate to proceed, bearing in mind that the patient's answers to questions may prejudice the conduct of his defence at the subsequent trial or make a certain disposal more or less likely.

Adjournment must be for an authorised purpose

Where a tribunal requires further information about a patient's present state of mental health, it may properly exercise its power of adjournment in order to obtain that information. However, a tribunal has no power to adjourn the proceedings in order to allow an opportunity for a restricted patient's condition to improve, or to ascertain if an improvement already made is sustained, so as to see if such developments may enable it to change its mind. Provided a tribunal has all the evidence necessary to determine the patient's current mental state, and his entitlement to be discharged according to the statutory criteria, it is under a duty to determine the application.

R. v. Nottingham Mental Health Review Tribunal, ex p. Secretary of State for the Home Department (Thomas)

R. v. Northern Mental Health Review Tribunal, ex p. Secretary of State for the Home Department (Crozier)

The Times, 25 March 1987   *Q.B.D., Farquharson J.*

The applications were heard together with the consent of the parties. In both cases, the Home Secretary sought declarations that the tribunal's decisions to adjourn the proceedings were contrary to law.

Thomas

The tribunal heard the application on 4 August 1986 when it was accepted by all of the parties that the patient continued to suffer from mental illness. The tribunal considered that the only possible alternative to the patient's continued detention in a special hospital was to ascertain whether it was appropriate to recommend to the Home Secretary that he be transferred to a regional secure unit. Because the patient had been involved in an attack upon another patient two months before the hearing, the responsible medical officer felt unable to advise transfer at that time. The tribunal therefore adjourned the hearing for six months and gave the following reasons—

> "1. On the medical evidence the patient's illness is such that an episode of violence might recur and indeed has occurred as recently as the 7 June 1986. The tribunal accepted the responsible medical officer's evidence and that contained in the nursing notes of the events of that day.
>
> 2. Likewise in the medical evidence and in the opinion of the medical tribunal member, it is premature to recommend the patient's transfer to another hospital. The patient requires, in his own and the public's interests, further treatment at (a secure hospital) before he could be transferred to a less secure hospital which is the next objective in his rehabilitation."

Crozier

A tribunal heard the patient's application for discharge on 20 August 1986. The responsible medical officer gave evidence of a recent and considerable improvement in the patient's mental health since the commencement of lithium treatment. He wished to have an opportunity to monitor the patient's further progress as a result of the treatment and all the parties requested an adjournment. The tribunal granted an adjournment for a period not exceeding six months to enable the patient's further progress to be monitored. It was clear on the evidence before it that the tribunal could not properly have discharged the patient, either absolutely or conditionally.

The Secretary of State's case

Relying on the judgment of Lawton L.J. in *R. v. Oxford Regional Mental Health tribunal* [1986] 1 W.L.R. 1180, the Secretary of State contended that the powers granted to a tribunal by section 73(1) enabled it to come to one of only three decisions: (i) to grant the applicant's discharge absolutely; (ii) to grant the applicant's discharge conditionally; or (iii) to refuse the application. The tribunal had no discretion to refuse discharge if satisfied as to the criteria for discharge; similarly, once a decision had been made that the tribunal was not so satisfied, it had no choice but to refuse the application. The power of adjournment granted by rule 16 existed for the purposes of the exercise of the tribunal's functions under the Act. The reality of the matter was that each of the tribunals had arrogated to itself a supervisory power which enabled it to monitor the progress of the patient. That was not its proper function, which is to enable patients to be released when there were no grounds for them remaining in hospital, so as to prevent their illegal detention. They had no continuing function. Any intermediate release of a patient between applications was the business of the Home Secretary under section 42. Tribunals had to grant adjournments from time to time where reports were incomplete and further reports or information was required but that was for the purpose of determining the application before them. It was perfectly clear that the tribunals had concluded that they could not discharge on the evidence before them. Accordingly, it was not open to them to adjourn the cases for up to six months in the hope that the conditions of the patients might improve.

The case for the tribunals and the patients

The argument advanced by the Secretary of State was a far too restrictive construction of the Act and misunderstood the functions of tribunals. They were not courts in the ordinary sense but a meeting of experts to discuss the best interest of the patient in an informal setting, where the usual rules of evidence were ignored and the tribunal members and the parties worked towards a solution in the best interests of the patient. Although tribunals were bound by the mandatory provisions of section 73(1), their powers of adjournment were much wider than contended by the Home Secretary. There were many occasions when the interests of the patient were best served by a period of delay, in order to ascertain the effects of the treatment being provided. The work of tribunals would be fettered by the constraints suggested. In neither case was it said that the exercise of the power to adjourn had been capricious or unreasonable on *Wednesbury* principles.[52] The adjournments were granted with the assent of all sides and nobody was prejudiced or suffered as a result.

---

[52] *Associated Provincial Picture Houses v. Wednesbury Corporation* [1948] 1 K.B. 223.

Farquharson J.

The scheme of the Act cast tribunals in a judicial rather than an administrative role. Their task was to decide, on the basis of the reports and other available evidence, whether the patient should be released conditionally or otherwise or whether his application should be refused. The power of adjournment given by rule 16 was limited to what was necessary for the tribunal to fulfil this function, as set out more specifically in section 73(1). If a tribunal had all the evidence necessary to determine the patient's mental state, and concluded that the requirements of section 73(1) had not been satisfied, it was then its duty to refuse the application. If it was necessary to grant an adjournment in order to determine the patient's *present* suitability for discharge that must be on the basis that the further information would throw more light on his *existing* mental state. What a tribunal could not do was to adjourn a case for a period to see if his mental state altered or improved, whether as a result of further treatment or otherwise. A tribunal which took such a course would be delaying the completion of the case to see if any later developments would enable it to change its mind. The tribunal could not adjourn in the hope that a projected or existing course of treatment would at some point in the future cause a sufficient improvement to enable them to discharge the patient before he made a further application. Any alteration in the patient's condition between applications which would justify discharge must be dealt with by the Secretary of State, who could exercise his own power of discharge under section 42 or refer the case again to the tribunal. It was evident that in the case of Thomas the tribunal had concluded that the requirements of section 73(1) had not been met. In those circumstances, it was obliged to dismiss the application: it had no power to postpone the disposal of the case in the hope that, after a period of up to six months, his condition would have improved sufficiently for it to be able to recommend his transfer. In any case, the Act did not empower a tribunal to make such a recommendation. Similarly, in the case of Crozier, the tribunal was not empowered to adjourn his application to monitor his progress. As the applicants were not seeking an order of certiorari, having regard to the lapse of time, the court would make a declaration in the terms of the motion. *Declaration granted.*

R. v. Nottingham Mental Health Review Tribunal, ex p. Secretary of State for the Home Department (Thomas)

R. v. Northern Mental Health Review Tribunal, ex p. Secretary of State for the Home Department (Crozier)

The Times, 12 October 1988   *C.A. (Balcombe, Woolf, Russell L.JJ.)*

The tribunals appealed in respect of the declaration granted by Farquharson J. As to the facts, *see above.*

Balcombe L.J.

The two appeals raised the single issue of whether a tribunal which accepted that the statutory criteria for discharge were not presently satisfied could adjourn the application so as to give an opportunity for the patient's condition to improve. Mr Pleming, for the appellants, had submitted that what happened in the case of Mr. Crozier was a request for further information within rule 16. The Secretary of State accepted that a tribunal which required further information as to the present state of the mental health of a patient could properly exercise its power of adjournment. But that was not the purpose for which the Trent tribunal had adjourned Mr. Crozier's case. They adjourned it not to monitor it themselves, as apparently was at one time suggested, but to enable the responsible medical officer to monitor it and, in particular, to see whether the improvement in that state brought about by the introduction of lithium was maintained. That could not properly be described as an adjournment for the purpose of obtaining further information within rule 16(1). In both cases, Mr Pleming then relied on the second limb of rule 16, namely the power of a tribunal to adjourn a hearing "for such other purposes as it might think appropriate." As to this, the rules had to be construed in the light of the Act and, in particular, in the light of the powers contained in the Act to make rules. Section 78(2)(j) provided that rules might be made "conferring on the tribunals such ancillary powers as the Lord Chancellor thinks necessary for the purposes of the exercise of their functions under this Act ..." So it became necessary to consider what were their functions under the Act. The question was simply: did they have power under the Act and under the rules to adjourn the applications for the purposes for which they did adjourn them? In the court's judgment, the Act did not give a tribunal any such powers. It had no general supervisory function over the progress of a restricted patient. That was the function of the Secretary of State. It has certain specific judicial powers to be exercised in relation to the application before it. Where a tribunal was satisfied that the criteria for discharge in section 73 were not then fulfilled, it had no power to adjourn the proceedings in order to give the condition of the patient an opportunity to improve or, as in the Crozier case, an opportunity to see if an improvement already made was sustained. Its powers to adjourn under rule 16 were primarily for the specific purpose of obtaining further information. There might well be other matters which would entitle a tribunal within those powers to grant an adjournment but not for the purpose of seeing whether a patient's condition improved or an improvement was sustained. Woolf L.J. and Russell L.J. agreed. *Appeals dismissed.*

Commentary

Some of the reasons why a tribunal may not adjourn a restricted patient's case, so as to monitor his condition and entitlement to be discharged, clearly do not extend to unrestricted cases. Most obviously, the fact that a tribunal has no general supervisory function over the progress of a restricted patient, and that it is the Home Secretary's function to monitor, supervise and discharge such patients between applications, is irrelevant. There can be no question of a tribunal which adjourns an unrestricted patient's case arrogating to itself a function which statutorily belongs to the Secretary of State. Secondly, a tribunal's powers in restricted cases are limited to discharging a patient whom it is satisfied meets the criteria for being discharged and not discharging otherwise. In unrestricted cases, a tribunal has a discretionary power of discharge, a power to make recommendations about matters such as leave and transfer, and a power to reconvene if its recommendations are not complied with. To this extent, it does have a supervisory function. It is therefore arguable that a tribunal could say "yes, we had sufficient information at the hearing to determine whether the patient was then entitled to be discharged but that is not the end of the matter in an unrestricted case. We could not determine whether or not to exercise our discretionary power of discharge. We wanted to see whether his improvement was sustained before deciding whether to exercise that discretion in favour of discharge. How we exercise a discretion vested in us by Parliament doesn't involve us arrogating any function given to someone else. The Act makes it clear that it is a matter for our discretion." Or, alternatively, a tribunal might say that it required

821

further information before deciding whether to exercise its discretionary power to recommend that the patient be granted leave of absence. That discretionary power having been given to it by Parliament, the adjournment was for a permitted statutory purpose: it is not simply a question of entitlement to discharge in such cases. Against this argument, it may be said that (1) the intention of the Act is still that tribunals must determine the application if they have sufficient information about the patient's present mental state to reach a decision about his current entitlement to, and suitability for, discharge; (2) postponing the decision amounts to having determined that it was not appropriate to direct the patient's discharge given his present mental state — adjourning the hearing involves not postponing the exercise of its discretion but later reconsidering the way it has exercised its discretion; (3) if a tribunal can adjourn, this means that it may either make its decision in two parts (the patient is not entitled to be discharged but we will determine at a later hearing whether to exercise our discretion to discharge him) or it may later reconsider its decision about his entitlement to be discharged — the Act allows for neither (4) functions such as granting patients leave or transferring them between applications are statutorily matters for the hospital managers and the responsible medical officer. The Act allows patients to make periodic applications, so that their suitability for discharge can be periodically determined. It would be intolerable if tribunals had a continuing involvement in, or a watching brief over, a patient's progress and the Act does not contemplate this.

Adjournment a matter for the tribunal's discretion

Provided that an adjournment is for a permitted purpose, and any refusal to adjourn is not contrary to the rules of natural justice, decisions to adjourn are decisions which, on well recognised authority, are within the discretion of a tribunal. Such a decision may only be faulted if that discretion can be shown to have been exercised wrongly according to the principles set out in *Associated Provincial Picture House v. Wednesbury Corporation* [1948] K.B. 223. Where an adjournment sought on the ground that a witness is absent or cannot be located is refused, the matter must be looked at in the light of the evidence which that witness would have given, in order to determine whether the effect of the decision was a material factor likely to have affected the conclusion to which the tribunal came.

R. v. Oxford Regional Mental Health Review, ex p. Mackman

The Times 2 June 1986   *Q.B.D., McNeill J.*

The tribunal refused to adjourn a hearing so that the patient could seek judicial review of its decision to hear the application notwithstanding that the president had presided over a previous tribunal concerning the same patient some 10 months previously.

McNeill J.

A decision to adjourn was one which, on well recognised authority, was within the discretion of a tribunal. Such a decision could only be faulted if it was shown to be exercised wrongly according to the Wednesbury principles (*Associated Provincial Picture House v. Wednesbury Corporation* [1948] KB 223, [1947] 2 All ER 680). There was no evidence of that and the application was refused.

R. v. Mental Health Review Tribunal, ex p. C.

6 July 1988 (unreported)   *Q.B.D. (Macpherson J.)*

9 December 1988 (unreported).   *C.A. (May, Croom-Johnson, Glidewell L.JJ.)*

21 March 1989 (unreported)   *Q.B.D. (Popplewell J.)*

28 June 1989 (unreported)   *C.A. (Dillon, Russell, Butler-Sloss L.JJ.)*

The Facts

On 17 March 1987, the patient was transferred from prison to hospital under section 47 of the Mental Health Act 1983 and a restriction direction was also made. A three day special hospital psychological assessment of the patient in May 1987 did not indicate that he suffered from mental illness and a second-opinion approved doctor appointed by the Mental Health Act Commission was of the opinion that there was no basis for administering antipsychotic drugs. The patient applied to a tribunal and the hearing was scheduled to commence on 22 February 1988. On 4 January 1988, the patient's solicitors wrote to the clerk to the tribunal, stating that the patient "would like" various persons to attend the hearing to give oral evidence, including two prison doctors whose names were not known. One of them was a female doctor who, following a disciplinary offence, had examined the patient on 13 and 15 December 1986 at HMP Gartree and adjudged him fit to receive three days solitary confinement in a prison cell. The other doctor, who examined him at Wandsworth Prison on 27 January 1987, had also found him fit to remain in a prison cell. Further and quite extensive correspondence was entered into concerning the doctors' attendance during the pre-hearing period. The position reached on 22 February was that, despite making extensive enquiries of the prisons and of the Medical Director to the Home Office, it had been impossible for the patient's solicitors to obtain the doctors' names and that information, if it was available, had not been divulged either to them or their client.

The tribunal hearing

The hearing took four days. The tribunal asked its clerk to make enquiries at the Home Office regarding the existence of reports which the doctors had apparently completed in December 1986 and January 1987. The president notified the clerk that, if the reports could be located, she was to arrange for them to be sent by fax and to enquire as to the availability of the doctors to attend the hearing. During the lunch interval on the first day, the tribunal clerk spoke to one of the principals of C3 Division at the Home Office, who made enquiries but later telephoned to say that it was impossible within the time available to identify either doctor or to locate their reports. This information was conveyed to the tribunal. The tribunal received evidence from a Dr. Cooper, whom the patient cross-examined, on a variety of matters including the role, duties and findings of Prison Medical Officers. The evidence was that the patient would have been seen by Prison Medical Officers on a number of occasions during his detention in various prisons. Most prison medical officers were general practitioners and there were no psychiatrists on the medical staff of Gartree. Prison medical officers should, and would, bring to the attention of their superiors a suspicion of mental illness which arose from their examination. He had not seen or heard any evidence that they had done so. On the last day of the hearing, the patient sought the attendance of the still unidentified prison doctors and a charge nurse and a psychologist. The tribunal granted the last application but refused the others. The tribunal also refused an application that the hearing be adjourned until the two missing medical reports were available.

The decision of the tribunal ran to some 13 or more pages and was that the patient would not, if subject to a restriction order, be entitled to be discharged. In its reasons, the tribunal stated that in coming to its finding it had assumed in the patient's favour that the many prison doctors who had examined him had not considered that his mental condition required treatment or investigation. It concluded that any doctor who examined the patient for general purposes, without hearing his wider allegations, would have no reason to question his mental health. He functioned normally and well on all aspects of daily life other than the area of delusion. The tribunal considered that it had heard sufficient evidence. It had received the written and oral evidence of three consultant psychiatrists and a consultant physician. In addition, the medical member had spent many hours interviewing the patient, whose evidence the tribunal had heard at length. It was not minded to grant an adjournment of what was a long outstanding and long-running application to enable unknown evidence of unidentified witnesses to be located when it was most unlikely that such evidence would take the matter further than, if as far as, the concessions made by Dr Cooper.

Applications for leave to apply for judicial review

The patient applied for leave to apply for judicial review, on the ground that he had not been permitted to call the two prison doctors and the charge nurse to give evidence before the tribunal. Macpherson J. had refused the application, holding that the matter was one for the discretion of the tribunal provided that discretion was properly exercised. There was a formidable body of psychiatric evidence before the tribunal indicating that the patient was suffering from mental illness and he had cross-examined those witnesses. It was impossible to call every doctor who had seen the patient, or someone in his position, and there was nothing in the point that the prison doctors were not called. The tribunal had taken account of the silent evidence of the many prison doctors and concluded in favour of the patient that the prison doctors would not have indicated that he was suffering from mental illness. Similarly, whether or not to call the charge nurse was ultimately the decision of the president: a great deal of the nurse's information about the patient's mental health must come from the doctors who had spoken to him and the charge nurse was not qualified to give his opinion as to a person's mental health. The patient appealed against the refusal of leave. On 9 December 1988, the Court of Appeal (May, Croom-Johnson, Glidewell L.JJ.) granted leave on the single ground that the two prison doctors were not allowed to attend or submit reports on the patient's mental condition. May L.J. said that the circumstances in which those witnesses were not enabled to attend and give evidence justified inquiry and were sufficient to entitle the patient to leave to apply for judicial review. The matter was later heard by Popplewell J.

Popplewell J. (CO/819/88)

As a matter of fact, it was clearly impossible for the two doctors to be called on the final day of the hearing. They had not then been identified nor had their reports, if there were reports, been located. The question therefore arose whether the president's failure to allow an adjournment was a breach of natural justice which entitled the patient to have the tribunal's finding quashed. The matter had to be looked at in the light of the evidence which those witnesses would have given in order to determine whether the effect of the decision not to allow them to be called was a material factor likely to have affected the conclusion to which the tribunal came. The patient pointed out, with a good deal of force, that he had been the subject of some 155 adjudications in prison and that in none of those adjudications had any medical officer ever written anything casting doubt about his mental ability. It was on this matter that the two doctors would have spoken if they had been allowed to give evidence. Nevertheless, the hearing lasted four days, took evidence from a considerable number of witnesses, and various medical reports and other documents were received in evidence. When the matter was looked at in the round, would the evidence of the two doctors — saying "We have examined this applicant on one or more occasions and we found nothing wrong with him" — have made any difference to the tribunal's conclusion? In the light of the evidence before the tribunal, including its acceptance of the "silent evidence" of the absent doctors, it was impossible to say that the tribunal in any way acted unreasonably in refusing the adjournment. There was nothing unreasonable in the tribunal saying that it did not need to hear the two doctors because it accepted the evidence that they would have given in the applicant's favour. *Application dismissed. The patient appealed.*

Dillon L.J. (Court of Appeal)

The tribunal had been faced with a difficult decision in a difficult case. The crux of the question was the validity of the decision to refuse an adjournment. The patient argued that in a matter so important as the "certification" of a man as "insane" all possibly relevant evidence should be heard and it was one of the functions of a review tribunal to ensure that this was done. On the other hand, the hearing had been adjourned several times and there was no knowing how long it would take to trace the two doctors, obtain their reports and arrange, if appropriate, for them to give oral evidence before a reconvened tribunal It was a difficult decision but that did not mean that it was one to be automatically quashed on judicial review. The course which the tribunal took was one open to it in difficult circumstances. They were endeavouring to give full benefit to the patient, by assuming that the two doctors would give the evidence indicated by him, in the knowledge that the doctors would have been general practitioners rather than specialist psychiatrists. Russell and Butler-Sloss L.JJ. agreed. *Appeal dismissed.*

Resumption of the hearing

Where the patient, a nearest relative applicant, or the responsible authority requests that an adjourned hearing be resumed, the hearing shall be resumed provided the tribunal is satisfied that its resumption is in the interests of the patient.[53] Before the tribunal resumes any hearing adjourned *sine die*, it shall give to all parties and, in the case of a restricted patient, the Secretary of State, not less than 14 days' notice (or such shorter notice as all parties may consent to) of the date, time and place of the resumed hearing.[54]

Transfer of patient prior to resumption of the hearing

As to the position where a patient is transferred to a hospital within the jurisdiction of another tribunal prior to the hearing's resumption, see rule 17 (**648**) and Schedule 2, para. 5 of the 1983 Act (**988**).

---

[53] Rule 26(2) of the 1960 Rules provided that the hearing be resumed if either (a) the tribunal considered that was desirable or (b) its resumption was requested by the applicant or the responsible authority. If the current discretionary power not to reconvene is *intra vires*, the circumstances in which a patient-applicant could lawfully be denied a resumption and a determination of his application must be exceptional.

[54] Rule 16(4) should be read as if the following italicised words were inserted: "(or such shorter notice as all the parties *and the Secretary of State* may consent to)."

It has been noted that a tribunal has power to issue subpoenas, to take evidence on oath, and to take any steps necessary to cure an irregularity where a party may have been prejudiced by a failure to comply with the rules. As a final note, mention must be made of other sanctions which a tribunal has recourse to if the fair and proper conduct of the proceedings is interfered with. It is appropriate to deal with these matters in the form of a final note, otherwise they might convey the impression that tribunal proceedings have the same imposing nature as proceedings in the criminal and civil courts. They do not and it would be virtually unheard of for a tribunal to have to contemplate resort to the following provisions.

CONTEMPT OF COURT

For the purposes of the Contempt of Court Act 1981, the word "court" includes a mental health review tribunal.[55] Where contempt of court is committed in connection with "proceedings in an inferior court," an order for committal may be made only by a Divisional Court of the Queen's Bench Division. In *Peach Grey & Co. (a Firm) v. Sommers*, it was held that the Divisional Court has jurisdiction to punish contempt of an industrial tribunal, which is an inferior court within Order 52.[56] It was established by Parliament, has a legally qualified chairman appointed by the Lord Chancellor, power to compel the attendance of witnesses and to administer oaths, and a duty to give reasons for its decisions. It satisfied the three tests propounded in *Attorney-General v. BBC*[57] and was a body which discharged judicial functions. The definition of a court in section 19 of the Contempt of Court Act 1981 pointed to the same conclusion. These points are all equally applicable to mental health review tribunals and, having regard to the decision and the judgments of the Court of Appeal and the House of Lords in *Pickering v. Liverpool Daily Post & Echo Newspapers plc*,[58] there is little doubt that a mental health review tribunal is also a court for the purposes of Order 52.

Types of contempt

Civil contempt includes disobedience to a judgment or order to do any act within a specified time.[59] Criminal contempt includes contempt in the face of the court (*e.g.* a solicitor deceiving the court[60]); words, written or spoken calculated to interfere with the course of justice; acts calculated to prejudice the due course of justice (*e.g.* interference with witnesses[61]); impeding the service of process[62]; and disobedience

---

55 Contempt of Court Act 1981, s.19; *Pickering v. Liverpool Daily Post & Echo Newspapers plc* [1990] 2 W.L.R. 494, C.A.; [1991] 1 All E.R. 622, H.L.
56 *Peach Grey & Co. (a Firm) v. Sommers, The Times*, 16 February 1995. The respondent had improperly sought to influence a witness in industrial tribunal proceedings to withdraw his evidence "on the basis of favours for favours." The Divisional Court committed him to prison for one month.
57 *Attorney-General v. BBC* [1981] A.C. 303.
58 *Pickering v. Liverpool Daily Post & Echo Newspapers plc* [1990] 2 W.L.R. 494, C.A.; 1 All E.R. 622, H.L. (**850**).
59 Casual or unintentional disobedience to an order will not justify an order for committal; it must be contumacious (*Fairclough v. Manchester Ship Canal Co.* [1897] W.N. 7, C.A.; *Steiner Products Ltd. v. Willy Steiner Ltd.* [1966] 1 W.L.R. 986).
60 *R. v. Weisz* [1951] 2 K.B. 661.
61 *Bromilow v. Phillips* (1891) 40 W.R. 220; *Att.-Gen. v. Butterworth; Chapman v. Honig* [1963] 2 Q.B. 502, C.A.; *Peach Grey & Co. (a Firm) v. Sommers, The Times*, 16 February 1995.
62 *Price v. Hutchison* (1870) L.R. 9 Eq. 534; *Lewis v. Owen* [1894] 1 Q.B. 102.

to a subpoena *ad testificandum* or *duces tecum*.[63] In the context of mental health review tribunal proceedings, refusing to forward an application for a detained patient with the intention of interfering with a right of application, inducing a patient by threats to withdraw an application,[64] interfering with a witness, persuading a patient to give false evidence, disobeying a subpoena, refusing to answer a question which a witness may lawfully be compelled to answer, and wilful disobedience to a direction given by a tribunal, may all be contempt.

PERJURY AND FALSE EVIDENCE

It has been held that perjury committed in an arbitration under the Workmen's Compensation Act was perjury at common law and punishable as such.[65] The Mental Health Act 1983 provides that any person who wilfully makes a false statement in a report or other document required or authorised to be made for any purpose of the 1983 Act is guilty of an offence.[66]

STATUTORY OFFENCES

Various statutory sanctions are set out in Part IX of the Act. In particular, the Act provides that any person who without reasonable cause obstructs or refuses to allow the visiting, interviewing or examination of any person by a person authorised in that behalf by or under the Act shall be guilty of an offence.[67] Similarly, any person who refuses to produce for the inspection of any person so authorised any document or record the production of which is duly required by him commits an offence.[68]

---

[63] Disobedience to a subpoena *ad testificandum* or *duces tecum* though not wilful (R. v. Daye [1908] 2 K.B. 333) or refusal of a witness to answer a question (*ex p. Fernandez* (1861) 30 L.J.C.P. 321; and see *Att.-Gen. v. Clough* [1963] 1 Q.B. 773) may be contempt.

[64] By analogy, see *e.g. R. v. Martin, The Times*, 23 April 1986, which concerned a person seeking by threats to induce a prosecutor to withdraw a private prosecution.

[65] *R. v. Crossley* (1909) 100 L.T. 463, C.A.

[66] Mental Health Act 1983, s.126(4)(a).

[67] *Ibid.*, s.129(b) and (d).

[68] *Ibid.*, s.129(c).

15. The tribunal's decision and appeals

INTRODUCTION

The decisions by which a tribunal may determine an application or reference — its powers — are limited by statute. The manner in which it reaches its decision, the recording of that decision and the reasons for it, and their communication to the parties, are subject to various procedural requirements set out in the rules. A decision may be set aside if the tribunal had no power to make it, it was founded on an error of law, it was reached in an unfair manner, it was irrational, or the reasons given for it were inadequate or unintelligible. If a tribunal's decision is legally flawed, it may be challenged by asking it to state a point of law for the High Court's determination (**854**) or by way of judicial review (**857**).

THE TRIBUNAL'S DECISION AND REASONS

Rule 23(2) requires a tribunal to record its discharge decision and any recommendations; to state whether it was satisfied that the statutory grounds requiring discharge exist; and to record its reasons for being, or not being, satisfied. The material comprised in the third of these tasks constitute the "reasons" for the decision.

THE TRIBUNAL'S DECISION & REASONS : MHRT RULES 1983, r.23

23.—(1) Any decision of the majority of the members of a tribunal shall be the decision of the tribunal and, in the event of an equality of votes, the president of the tribunal shall have a second or casting vote.

(2) The decision by which the tribunal determines an application shall be recorded in writing; the record shall be signed by the president and shall give the reasons for the decision and, in particular, where the tribunal relies upon any of the matters set out in section 72(1), (4) *or (4A)* or section 73(1) or (2) of the Act, shall state its reasons for being satisfied as to those matters.

(3) Paragraphs (1) and (2) shall apply to provisional decisions and decisions with recommendations as they apply to decisions by which applications are determined.

Mental Health Review Tribunal Rules 1983, as amended by the Mental Health Review Tribunal (Amendment) Rules 1996, r.11.

THE DECISION OF THE TRIBUNAL

Rule 23(1) states that any decision of the majority of the members of a tribunal shall be the decision of the tribunal and, in the event of an equality of votes, the president of the tribunal shall have a second or casting vote. It would appear from the wording that a vote must be taken, that each member must cast a vote and that abstentions are not permitted. Consequently, an equality of votes may only arise where an even number of members, being at least four in number, have been appointed to deal with a case and not because one of the usual panel of three members has abstained. The decision by which the tribunal determines an application or reference shall then be recorded in writing and the record signed by the president.[1] There is no prescribed form but tribunals have devised their own standard forms for each type of case. The use of these forms is, however, not mandatory.[2]

THE REASONS FOR THE TRIBUNAL'S DECISION

A tribunal's record of its decision shall give the reasons for the decision and, in particular, where the tribunal relies upon any of the matters set out in section 72(1), (4) or (4A), or section 73(1) or (2) of the Act — the mandatory discharge criteria — the record shall state its reasons for being satisfied as to those matters.[3] Any statement of the reasons for a decision forms part of the decision and shall be taken to be incorporated in the record.[4] There is no prescribed form but the standard forms in use include space for recording the reasons for the decision.[5] As to the need for reasons to be adequate and intelligible, and to refer to any substantial points raised by the parties, see page 833 *et seq.* As to the publication of the decision and the reasons for it, see page 843.

PROVISIONAL DECISIONS AND RECOMMENDATIONS

Rule 23(3) provides that the requirements imposed by paragraphs 23(1) and 23(2) above, that a tribunal records its decision and the reasons for that decision, apply to provisional decisions and decisions with recommendations as they apply to decisions by which applications are determined. Rule 23(3) does not expressly provide that paragraphs 23(1) and 23(2) extend to directions for a patient's reclassification made under section 72(5). However, the decisions in *Bone* (**833**) and *ex p. P.D.* (**551**) suggest that reasons must be given for any direction of this kind.

---

[1] Mental Health Review Tribunal Rules 1983, r.23(2). The Interpretation Act 1978 provides that the term "writing" includes typing, printing, and other modes of representing or reproducing words in a visible form.

[2] Previously, rule 27(2) of the Mental Health Review Tribunal Rules 1960 did prescribe a specific form for recording the decision, which was set out in the Fourth Schedule. This basic form consisted of alternative clauses, for deletion or otherwise, specifying whether or not the tribunal had directed the patient's discharge or reclassification.

[3] Mental Health Review Tribunal Rules 1983, r.23(2).

[4] Tribunal and Inquiries Act 1992, s.10(6). It will therefore be difficult to argue that although the reasons are defective, the decision itself discloses no error of law.

[5] Rule 27(4) of the Mental Health Review Tribunal Rules 1960 did prescribe a form for recording the reasons for the tribunal's decision, which was set out in the Fifth Schedule. However, this form merely provided a space for doing so, prefaced by a short parenthetical note in italics stating that the tribunal's reasons should indicate whether it was or was not satisfied as to the criteria for discharge referred to in section 123. That apart, the form contained only alternative clauses for recording whether or not the tribunal considered that it was undesirable that the recorded reasons for its decision should be communicated on request to the applicant or to the responsible authority.

Decisions with recommendations

Unless the context otherwise requires, a *"decision with recommendations"* means a decision with recommendations made in accordance with section 72(3)(a) or (3A)(a) of the Act.[6] A tribunal must therefore record any statutory recommendations which it makes and the reasons for making such recommendations. Where a tribunal makes a decision with recommendations, the decision shall specify the period at the expiration of which the tribunal will consider the case further in the event of those recommendations not being complied with.[7] The tribunal has a discretion to reconvene, on giving proper notice to the parties, if its recommendation is not being complied with.[8]

Provisional decisions

Unless the context otherwise requires, a *"provisional decision"* includes a deferred direction for conditional discharge under section 73(7) and a notification to the Secretary of State in accordance with section 74(1) of the Act."[9] Where a tribunal defers a direction for a patient's conditional discharge, or notifies the Secretary of State whether a detained patient subject to a restricted direction satisfies the statutory criteria for absolute or conditional discharge, it must therefore record that "decision" and the reasons for it.

THE DUTY TO GIVE REASONS FOR THE DECISION

It has been noted that a tribunal's record of its decision must give the reasons for the decision. In particular, where the tribunal relies upon any of the matters set out in section 72(1), (4) or (4A), or section 73(1) or (2) — the mandatory discharge criteria — the record shall state its reasons for being satisfied as to those matters.

FIRST PRINCIPLES

Since 1983, there have been a number of cases where the adequacy of the reasons given for a tribunal's decision has been challenged. The first of them was *Bone v. Mental Health Review Tribunal* [1985] 3 All E.R. 330. Just over a fortnight later, Nolan J.'s judgment in Bone was referred to in the case of *R. v. Mental Health Review Tribunal, ex p. Clatworthy* [1985] 3 All E.R. 699. R. v. Mental Health Review Tribunal, ex p. Pickering [1986] 1 All E.R. 99 was then decided some four months after Clatworthy, although not reported until the following year. These three reported cases are the best known, and the most often cited, cases on the need to give reasons and the following principles can be extracted from them. The overriding test must always be whether the tribunal is providing both parties with the materials which will enable them to know that the tribunal has made no error of law in

---

[6] Mental Health Review Tribunal Rules 1983, r.2(1), as amended by the Mental Health Review Tribunal (Amendment) Rules 1996, r.2. The recommendations are that leave of absence be granted, that the patient be transferred into guardianship or to another hospital, that a supervision application be considered. There is no power to make such recommendations in restricted cases.

[7] Mental Health Review Tribunal Rules 1983, r.24(2). The Act itself does not require this **(474)**.

[8] *Ibid.*, r.25(2) **(474, 853)**.

[9] *Ibid.*, r.2(1).

reaching its finding of fact.[10] The patient must know why the case advanced in detail on his behalf had not been accepted.[11] Proper, adequate and intelligible reasons should be given which grapple with the important issues raised and can reasonably be said to deal with the substantial points that have been raised.[12] However, the reasons for the decision cannot be read "in the air". Although the reasons may not be clear or immediately intelligible on their face, the decision is addressed to parties, who are an informed audience and so well aware of what issues were raised and the nuances raised by those issues.[13] Nor should the reasons be subjected to the analytical treatment more appropriate to the interpretation of a statute or a deed. The necessity for giving reasons is often underscored by the fact that it is often very important to know the reason why an application has been turned down. The doctor in charge of a restricted patient's treatment may often be the initiator of an application for discharge and he should know why the application has been refused. He may be particularly interested in the diagnostic question and want to know why his view as to the correct diagnosis was rejected.[14]

CASE LAW

The case law falls into distinct classes: whether there is an obligation to give reasons at all; whether the reasons are adequate in the sense that they enable the applicant to know why his case was rejected; whether the reasons are intelligible and comprehensible, in that one can discern the tribunal's reasons for not being satisfied about each of the statutory grounds which entitle a patient to be discharged; whether the reasons disclose that the tribunal misdirected itself as to the law.

THE NEED TO GIVE REASONS AT ALL

In *Bone v. Mental Health Review Tribunal*,[15] the tribunal's decision included no reasons for its finding that the statutory discharge criteria were not satisfied. The case is therefore best seen as resolving the issue of whether a tribunal which does not discharge a patient has a duty to give reasons at all, rather than as a case dealing with the adequacy of the reasons — since none were given. Nolan J. held that the requirement imposed by the first part of rule 23(2) ("The decision by which the tribunal determines an application ... shall give the reasons for the decision") was unambiguous. The following words starting "and, in particular" were words of

---

10   *Bone v. Mental Health Review Tribunal* [1985] 3 All E.R. 330; *Alexander Machinery (Dudley) Ltd. v. Crabtree* [1974] I.C.R. 120 at 122. In *ex p. O'Hara*, it was not clear if the tribunal had addressed the question of whether it had power in a restricted case to make a statutory recommendation under section 72(3). If it had considered the issue, and answered it adversely to the applicant, then no reasons were given in the decision and, given the decisions in *Bone*, *ex p. Clatworthy*, and *ex p. Pickering*, it was common ground that the decision should be quashed. See *Grant v. The Mental Health Review Tribunal for the Trent Region*; *R. v. The Mersey Mental Health Review Tribunal ex p. O'Hara, The Times*, 26 April 1986, *per* McNeill J. **(549)**.

11   *R. v. Mental Health Review Tribunal, ex p. Clatworthy* [1985] 3 All E.R. 699.

12   *R. v. Mental Health Review Tribunal, ex p. Pickering* [1986] 1 All E.R. 99; *Bone v. Mental Health Review Tribunal* [1985] 3 All E.R. 330; *Seddon Properties Ltd. v. Secretary of State for the Environment* (1978) 42 P. & C.R. 26; *Re Poyser and Mills's Arbitration* [1964] 2 Q.B. 467 at 478.

13   *R. v. Mental Health Review Tribunal, ex p. Pickering* [1986] 1 All E.R. 99. The importance of not reading a decision in a vacuum was seen in *ex p. Ryan*, where Nolan J. accepted that although the tribunal did explicitly state why the patient's detention was necessary for his health or safety or to protect others— the second limb of the statutory test for discharge — the tribunal's overall view on that matter appeared with complete clarity from their reasons. *R. v. Trent Mental Health Review Tribunal, ex p. Ryan* [1992] C.O.D. 157.

14   *R. v. Mental Health Review Tribunal, ex p. Pickering [1986] 1 All E.R. 99.*

15   *Bone v. Mental Health Review Tribunal* [1985] 3 All E.R. 330.

elaboration and emphasis. They in no way limited or derogated from the overall obligation imposed by the paragraph that reasons be given for a decision whichever way it went, including therefore decisions not to discharge a patient.

Bone v. Mental Health Review Tribunal

[1985] 3 All E.R. 330   *Q.B.D., Nolan J.*

The tribunal did not discharge the patient, who was subject to a restriction order, from which it could be inferred that it was not satisfied as to the statutory criteria for discharge set out in section 72(1)(b)(i) and (ii). The tribunal's "reasons" for its decision did not more than recite this fact: "The Tribunal are not satisfied that the patient is not suffering from mental impairment which makes it appropriate for him to be liable to be detained. The Tribunal are not satisfied that it is not necessary for the health and safety of the patient or for the protection of other persons that the patient should receive medical treatment in hospital." The president contended that rule 23 required only that a tribunal give reasons in cases where it was satisfied, on applying the mandatory discharge criteria, that a patient was entitled to be discharged — it did not did not require that reasons be given as to why a tribunal decided that those criteria were not satisfied. The question of law stated for the High Court's determination was whether the reasons given for the tribunal's decision were "adequate and/or satisfy the requirement of Rule 23(2) Mental Health Review Tribunal Rules 1983 ... bearing in mind that the above reasons give to an applicant no further information than that which he can infer from the fact that the Tribunal decided not to discharge him."

Nolan J.

The president's construction of rule 23(2) was wrong. The requirement imposed by the first part of the paragraph ("The decision by which the tribunal determines an application ... shall give the reasons for the decision") was unambiguous. The following words starting "and, in particular" were words of elaboration and emphasis. They in no way limited or derogated from the initial obligation imposed by the paragraph that reasons be given for a decision, whichever way the decision went. That, strictly speaking, disposed of the question stated for the court's determination but it was right to amplify the nature of the requirement that reasons be given by reference to two very well-known authorities. The first was a passage from the judgment of Megaw J. in *Re Poyser and Mills's Arbitration* [1963] 1 All E.R. 612 at 616, [1964] 2 Q.B. 467 at 478, where he said: "... Parliament having provided that reasons shall be given, in my view that must clearly be read as meaning that proper, adequate, reasons must be given; the reasons that are set out ... must be reasons which not only will be intelligible, but also can reasonably be said to deal with the substantial points that have been raised ..." The second case was *Alexander Machinery (Dudley) Ltd. v. Crabtree* [1974] I.C.R. 120 at 122 where Donaldson P said: 'It is impossible for us to lay down any precise guidelines. The overriding test must always be: is the tribunal providing both parties with the materials which will enable them to know that the tribunal has made no error of law in reaching its finding of fact?"

REASONS WHICH DO NOT DISCLOSE WHY CASE WAS REJECTED

The decision in *Bone* was referred to in *ex p. Clatworthy*, which was heard just over a fortnight later. In *Clatworthy*, the patient suffered from sexual deviancy but the 1983 Act included a new prohibition that no person was to be dealt with under the

Act as suffering from any form of mental disorder by reason only of sexual deviancy. Given this new state of affairs, the unanimous medical evidence before the patient's tribunal was that he was not suffering from a psychopathic disorder. The tribunal stated that the patient's condition included features of psychopathic disorder, as defined in the 1983 Act, but without specifying what these were. Mann J. quashed the tribunal's decision. In doing so, he described the tribunal's reasons as a bare traverse of the circumstances in which discharge could be contemplated. Looking at the reasons, one was compelled to conclude that the patient would not know why the case advanced in detail on his behalf had not been accepted.

R. v. Mental Health Review Tribunal, ex p. Clatworthy

[1985] 3 All E.R. 699   *Q.B.D., Mann J.*

Following the expiration in 1972 of a limited-term restriction order, the patient had been liable to be detained as an unrestricted patient under a notional hospital order imposed under section 37 of the 1983 Act. At the time of his tribunal in April 1984, he was detained in a medium secure unit. The medical evidence before the tribunal, given by the responsible medical officer and a psychiatrist instructed by the patient, was that he was not suffering from a psychopathic disorder (or from any other form of disorder) as defined by section 1 of the Act, subsection (3) of which provides that a person shall not be dealt with as suffering from a psychopathic disorder by reason only of sexual deviancy. The tribunal's decision was that the patient not be discharged, its reasons being as follows: "...the rmo is concerned that the change in definition of "psychopathic disorder" in the 1983 Mental Health Act and in particular the terms of Section subs. (3) of the Act puts the patient outside the provisions of the 1983 Act. We do not agree that this is so ... he shows sexual deviancy but he also has the features of psychopathic disorder as defined in the Act and repeatedly diagnosed by doctors while he was detained in a special hospital. We see no change in his condition from the time he was first admitted to (that special hospital) in 1967."

Mann J.

The two consultant psychiatrists who gave evidence spoke in one voice as to the statutory matters which fell to the tribunal to consider. Thus apparently stood the matter at the hearing but the conclusion of the hearing was a decision that the patient not be discharged. The reasons given by the tribunal were not satisfactory and a bare traverse of a circumstance in which discharge could be contemplated. The grounds for those reasons did not enable one to see why the medical evidence was not accepted and immediately invited the question: what are the features of psychopathic disorder as defined by the 1983 Act apart from sexual deviancy? The evidence was that there was no other feature and sexual deviancy was to be discounted under the Act. Although the tribunal referred to psychopathic disorder as defined in the Act and repeatedly diagnosed by doctors when the patient was in a special hospital, the present definition of psychopathic disorder was one first introduced in 1983. Those earlier repeated diagnoses were not diagnoses which were the subject of exposition before the tribunal. They were terse and, in some instances, it could reasonably be questioned whether they were properly diagnoses of psychopathic disorder. Standing back and looking at the reasons for the decision, one was compelled to conclude that the patient would not know why the case advanced in detail on his behalf had not been accepted.

Cases since ex p. Clatworthy

The tribunal in *ex p. Davies* also rejected unanimous medical evidence that a patient with a history of sexual offending involving children did not suffer from a psychopathic disorder as defined in the 1983 Act. Although reliance was placed on the observations of the Secretary of State, those observations appear to have been confined to the likely consequences of releasing the patient given his sexual deviancy. If attention is confined to the adequacy of the reasons given for the decision, the case can be distinguished from *ex p. Clatworthy* in that the tribunal certainly spelt out why it had rejected the patient's case and the unanimous medical evidence. As to whether there was evidence entitling the tribunal to its finding, the tribunal did refer to characteristics other than sexual deviancy which in its opinion were consistent with such a diagnosis, namely sullen, morose and disruptive behaviour and an inability to learn from past events. Again, the tribunal in *ex p. Clatworthy* did not do this. Whether repeated sexual offending against children can properly be categorised as "sexual deviancy" must also be considered (**089**).

R. v. Mental Health Review Tribunal (Mersey Region), ex p. Davies

CO/1723/85, 21 April 1986   *Q.B.D., Russell J.*

In May 1967, the patient was convicted of "an offence or offences" of indecent assault. The patient had many previous convictions, including malicious damage by fire and other offences of indecent assault on girls. The court imposed a hospital order and a restriction order and he was admitted to a special hospital. He remained there until December 1982 when he was transferred to a less secure hospital. Having then been granted leave of absence, he resided with his mother. However, whilst on leave, he was observed to approach some children and to show them a pornographic magazine. As a result, his leave was revoked and he was transferred back to the special hospital in April 1983. His case was considered by a tribunal in July of that year.

The evidence before the tribunal

The medical reports prepared for the tribunal by two psychiatrists both concluded that the patient was not suffering from mental illness or psychopathic disorder, or from any other form of mental disorder, as defined by section 1 of the 1983 Act. One of the doctors further noted that he was not receiving any formal treatment and was of the opinion that he did not require treatment, was not a significant danger to anybody else, and was being inappropriately detained. In his statement, the Secretary of State observed that special hospital medical reports concerning the incident in April 1983 had described the patient as a danger to others by reason of his inability to control his deviant sexual impulses and his total lack of insight. He was conscious that the incident was not thought by those then responsible for his care to be a spontaneous act of foolishness but a serious, sinister, premeditated attempt to lure the girls away. The Secretary of State was satisfied that the patient continued to suffer from a form of mental disorder of the requisite nature or degree and that he required further treatment in hospital; was unconvinced that he had made sufficient progress to reduce appreciably his potential dangerousness towards young girls; and was of the opinion that rehabilitation should take place with extreme caution, preferably via transfer to a local hospital, where his sexual attitudes could be closely monitored.

The tribunal's decision and reasons

On 29 July 1985, the tribunal considered the patient's case and directed that he not be discharged. The tribunal expressed its finding as an affirmative, rather than as a double-negative, stating that it was satisfied that the patient was suffering from a psychopathic disorder of a nature or degree which made it appropriate for him to remain liable to be detained in a hospital for medical treatment. Such treatment was necessary for the protection of other persons. The reasons stated that the tribunal was not satisfied that the patient could overcome the enormous problems he would be faced with if released into the community without giving way to the uncontrollable impulses which resulted in the offence in 1967. The tribunal rejected the medical opinions of the two psychiatrists that the patient was not suffering from psychopathic disorder: "We accept the observations contained in the statement of the Secretary of State. We have considered the history of the applicant and his conduct in hospital since the making of the order ... The applicant's conduct whilst on leave in 1983 which resulted in his return to (the special hospital), and in recent months when he has become sullen and morose and been disruptive is consistent in the view of the Tribunal of one suffering from psychopathic disorder. The incident in [April] 1983 demonstrates an inability to learn from past events ... We take the view that the psychopathic disorder is of a nature and degree which makes it appropriate for him to be liable to be detained in a Hospital for medical treatment. In the light of the applicant's conduct as recently as [April] 1983 it is necessary for the protection of other persons that the applicant should receive medical treatment in Hospital."

Russell L.J.

Counsel had agreed that, for the purposes of the case, the effective questions which confronted the tribunal were two in number. The tribunal had to ascertain from the evidence whether the applicant was suffering from a treatable psycho-pathic disorder and whether it was satisfied that it was necessary for the protection of other persons that the applicant should be detained. The tribunal was entitled to reject the evidence of the two psychiatrists in the light of the totality of the evidence, coming as it did not only from those two eminent practitioners, but also from the observations of both the Secretary of State and the tribunal itself during the course of the hearing, when the applicant was cross-examined by the psychiatric member of the tribunal. The crucial issue was whether, in reaching those conclusions, the tribunal expressed its reasons adequately. Each case must, to a substantial extent, depend upon its own facts and that comment could be applied to the three authorities to which the court's attention was directed — Bone v. Mental Health Review Tribunal, ex p. Clatworthy, ex p. Pickering. On the facts of this case, the reasons were adequate and there was no unfairness: those affected by the reasons were adequately told of the basis of the decision. Application dismissed.

Ex p. G.

The following case is best viewed as wholly misconceived. It is axiomatic that it is not a tribunal's function to direct that a patient shall be prescribed certain medication or to give reasons why a particular drug should be prescribed. It seems to have been perfectly clear from the responsible authority's case what treatment it was proposed to give the patient and why that treatment was considered to be necessary for her health and safety.

R. v. South East Thames Mental Health Review Tribunal, ex p. G.

Unreported, 4 May 1993   *C.A. (Ralph Gibson, McCowan, Steyn L.JJ.)*

The medical evidence before the tribunal was unanimously of the view that the patient suffered from a very serious mental illness which had had devastating consequences for her health, safety and general welfare. One of the medical reports indicated that it was unlikely that any amount of medication would have any influence on her very systematised delusions. A later medical report, prepared by the responsible medical officer, stated that unless she was detained it would be impossible to offer her the opportunity of receiving clozapine, the most modern antipsychotic drug available. The tribunal did not discharge the patient. It's reasons included the fact that no previous treatment had alleviated or improved her mental state and her condition was likely to deteriorate and her vulnerability increase without treatment. The patient applied for judicial review on the basis that the reasons for the decision were inadequate, in that the tribunal did not specify the particular drug that she was to be given. Macpherson J. refused leave and the patient renewed her application for leave before the Court of Appeal.

The application for leave to apply for judicial review

McCowan L.J. said that the fact that any amount of medication would not influence the patient's systematised delusions did not mean that medication was contra-indicated. It might at the very least prevent the patient's condition deteriorating. There was no statutory requirement that a tribunal should specify the drug which a patient was to be given and that might very well be unwise. The statement that "without treatment her condition is likely to deteriorate and increase her vulnerability" gave perfectly sufficient information as to the reason why the application was refused. The patient's chances of succeeding with the application for judicial review were absolutely minimal. *Steyn L.J.* said that he had more difficulty in that the reasons were not very informative. Nevertheless, having read the reasons in the context of what was common ground on the medical evidence, there was no realistic prospect of success. *Ralph Gibson L.J.* agreed. *Application for leave to apply refused.*

REASONING UNINTELLIGIBLE OR INCOMPREHENSIBLE

The following case in many ways represents a high-water mark in terms of a tribunal's obligation to give proper reasons for its statutory findings. A patient is always entitled to be discharged on at least two alternative statutory grounds. Hence it is, or should be, necessary for a tribunal to set out in turn the reasons why it was not satisfied that each of those grounds were met. In *ex p. Pickering*, Forbes J. therefore held that it should be clear from the decision to which of the statutory grounds each reason was directed. Otherwise, it is impossible to know what (if any) were the tribunal's reasons for rejecting each one of the discharge grounds.

R. v. Mental Health Review Tribunal, ex p. Pickering

[1986] 1 All E.R. 99   *Q.B.D., Forbes J.*

The patient, who was a restricted patient, had been detained in special hospitals since his conviction and sentence in 1972. On 1 August 1984, a tribunal refused an application for discharge made by him. The written evidence before the tribunal included four psychiatric and psychological reports. Apart from a caveat entered by one of the psychiatrists, the general psychiatric opinion was that the patient was not suffering from a psychopathic disorder. The unanimous finding of the tribunal members was, however, that they were not satisfied as to the existence of any of the statutory criteria for discharge set out in section 72(1)(b). Many of the matters set out in the tribunal's reasons for its decision related either to the patient's history between 1960–1972 or were consequential on its finding that he suffered from a psychopathic disorder, e.g. "it cannot yet be foreseen when the danger of his psychopathic disorder will diminish sufficiently for his release." The reasons which might have been intended as the tribunal's explanation of why it rejected the evidence that the patient no longer suffered from psychopathic disorder referred to it not being persuaded that it necessarily followed from his improved behaviour within a secure hospital setting that such behaviour would be maintained in the community.

Forbes J.

It was accepted that one of the major issues in the case was whether or not the patient was then suffering from psychopathic disorder: "the diagnostic question." The tribunal also had to consider whether it was necessary for the protection of others (it was not suggested it was necessary for his own protection) that he should continue to receive medical treatment in hospital: a question which had a medical content but was to some extent a policy question of whether it was safe to discharge him. It was essential for a tribunal to bear in mind the distinction between the two matters to which they were directing their attention. The fact that the tribunal was not persuaded that the patient's improved behaviour over a short period of time in a strict, special hospital setting necessarily meant that such behaviour would be maintained in the community could be a legitimate reason for not being satisfied that he no longer suffered from psychopathic disorder. Equally, it was capable of being a valid reason for not being satisfied that his continued detention was unnecessary in order to protect others. It was perfectly open to the tribunal to come to either or both of those conclusions. However, it was impossible to detect from the passage whether what was said was directed to the diagnostic issue or a wholly different issue, the necessity for the protection of other persons that the applicant be detained in hospital. Either interpretation was equally possible. As such, the reasons did not grapple with the diagnostic issue of whether or not the patient was still suffering from a psychopathic disorder. *Certiorari granted.*

Cases since Pickering

It is impossible to reconcile the decision in *ex p. Pickering* with that in the following case and it must be said that *ex p. Ryan* much more closely reflects the very unsatisfactory quality of the reasons often given for tribunal decisions. The reality may simply be that pragmatism dictates that a low standard is set, otherwise the number of tribunal decisions susceptible to review would become an embarrassment. Whether or not this is now the position, the decision-making process in *Ryan*, involving as it did the liberty of the subject, seems to have been grossly inadequate. For example, the tribunal "was not satisfied that the patient was not suffering from a psychopathic disorder" but "it was satisfied that the patient was suffering from a psychopathic disorder of a nature or degree which made it appropriate for him to remain liable to be detained." Furthermore, the decision wholly failed to state whether or not the tribunal was satisfied that in-patient treatment was not necessary for the patient's health or safety or to protect others. It is difficult to see how the conclusion could be avoided that the tribunal's decision gave rise to a real risk that it had failed to properly address the statutory criteria which should determine such decisions.

[1992] C.O.D. 157   *Q.B.D., Nolan L.J., Potts J.*

The patient was convicted in 1972 of three offences of indecent assault on young girls and a hospital order was made together with a restriction order. In 1973, he was convicted of a burglary committed whilst absent from hospital without leave and the court again made a hospital order and a restriction order, this time authorising his detention in a special hospital. He was conditionally discharged at the end of 1981. In October 1986, he was sentenced to four years' imprisonment for burglary and a year's consecutive imprisonment for indecent assault. When his sentence expired, his conditional discharge was revoked, he was recalled to the special hospital, and his case referred to a tribunal.

The evidence before the tribunal

The tribunal received medical reports and oral evidence from two consultant psychiatrists, extracts from previous medical reports, and a letter from a senior clinical psychologist. The responsible medical officer's first medical report concluded that there was little doubt that the patient's condition fell within the broad definition of psychopathic disorder in section 1 of the 1983 Act. He had shown seriously irresponsible behaviour in his behaviour towards young children, was egocentric, had an alcohol problem, a long history of house-breaking, and difficulties in sustaining satisfactory interpersonal relations. The responsible medical officer's second and more recent report was equally clear that the patient was suffering from a "sociopathic personality disorder" but more guarded about whether he satisfied the legal classification of psychopathic disorder, which involved making a value judgment — whether his conduct was seriously irresponsible or abnormally aggressive. The second psychiatrist whose evidence the tribunal received stated that the patient was not suffering from a psychopathic disorder as statutorily defined.

The tribunal's decision and reasons

The tribunal directed that the patient not be discharged. Its findings were that — (i) it was not satisfied that the patient was not suffering from a psychopathic disorder and (ii) it was satisfied that the patient was suffering from a psycho-pathic disorder of a nature or degree which made it appropriate for him to re-main liable to be detained in a hospital for medical treatment. Its decision did not expressly state that it was not satisfied that such treatment was not necess-ary for the patient's health or safety or to protect others. The tribunal's reasons for its first finding were that, having reminded itself of the statutory definition in section 1(2), it could not be satisfied that the patient was not suffering from psychopathic disorder — "His conduct towards young females has been 'seri-ously irresponsible' resulting from the psychopathic disorder." As to its second finding, the patient had resisted all attempts to co-operate in psychological treatments and denied the need for help of any kind and there was a danger of repetition of offences against young females which treatment might cure.

Nolan J.

The court was referred to a passage in the judgment of Forbes J. in *R. v. Mental Health Review Tribunal, ex p. Pickering* [1986] 1 All E.R. 99, in which his Lordship criticised, and indeed quashed, the decision of a tribunal because of the inadequacy of the reasons given for it. He criticised, in particular, the manner in which the tribunal had dealt with the evidence relating to the exist-ence or otherwise of a psychopathic disorder. He took the view that the tribunal had among other things not clearly distinguished between the diagnostic question on the one hand (whether the patient suffered from a psychopathic disorder) and the questions of whether it was necessary for his health or safety or the protection of others that he should receive medical treatment, these being quite plainly separate questions under the statute. However, it seemed that the definition of a psychopathic disorder in section 1(2) imported questions which were not strictly of a clinical or medical nature because part of the definition consisted of the words, "which results in abnormally aggressive or seriously irresponsible conduct on the part of the person concerned." No doubt whether the conduct was the result of the disorder was again a medical question; whether it amounted to seriously irresponsible or abnormally aggressive behaviour raised questions other than of a purely clinical nature. So far as the clinical and medical evidence was concerned, the tribunal were entitled to say they were not satisfied that he did not suffer from a persistent disorder or disability of mind. And, insofar as they then concluded that his conduct towards young females has been seriously irresponsible resulting from the psychopathic disorder, there was material upon which the tribunal could properly link the two. The fact that the patient tended to play down the severity of his sexual offending was material capable of justifying a finding that his conduct towards young females had been seriously irresponsible. It was undoubtedly open to the tribunal to conclude that his disorder was of a nature and degree which made it appropriate for him to be liable to be detained in hospital because of the danger of repetition against young females. The tribunal contemplated further treatment involving psychological counselling, psychiatric counselling, nursing with a view to helping him live with other people without conflict, and rehabilitation under medical supervision. The tribunal was entitled to reach their findings and the reasons for their decision were adequate. The critical question was put succinctly by Mann J. in *ex p. Clatworthy* [1985] 3 All E.R. 699, 704: "Standing back and looking at these reasons and asking, would the applicant from those reasons know why the case advanced in detail on his behalf had not been accepted?" Although the tribunal did not express their decisions in terms of the necessity to detain the patient for his own health or to protect others, the view of the tribunal appeared with complete clarity from their reasons and the omission did not afford a ground for quashing the decision. *Application refused.*

RECORDING OTHER COMMENTS

The standard forms used to record and communicate tribunal decisions have for many years concluded with a space for recording "any other comments" which a tribunal wishes to make. Care needs to be taken to ensure that any further comments do not appear to undermine, or to be at variance with, the decision and the reasons just recorded. In *ex p. D*, the tribunal's "other comments" included the statement that it "sympathised with those responsible for the patient's care in that they found themselves unable to adopt any form of treatment other than containment in conditions of high security." Russell L.J. described it as unfortunate that the tribunal's other comments had been phrased in that way but there was no evidence that the tribunal had misdirected itself. Otton J. said that the comments had to be seen in context, did not go to the heart of the decision, nor formed part of it.[16] In *ex p. Merrils*, the "other comments" concerned unsubstantiated and strongly contested allegations about the patient's past behaviour. The tribunal amended it's decision by adding that the allegations had been wholly disregarded, as a result of which no further steps were taken to proceed with the judicial review.[17]

---

[16] *R. v. Mersey Mental Health Review Tribunal, ex p.* D, *The Times*, 13 April 1987, Q.B.D. (**525**).
[17] *R. v. Mental Health Review Tribunal, ex p. Merrils*, April 1994 (unreported). There would not appear to be any provision in the rules which enables a tribunal to amend its decision.

SUMMARY

The *Bone, Clatworthy* and *Pickering* decisions firmly established a requirement to give proper, adequate and intelligible reasons for all tribunal decisions. Subsequently, no unreported case based on the supposed inadequacy of the reasons for a decision has been successful. However, in a number of other cases, the existence of an arguable case led to leave to apply for judicial review being granted but the case was not heard because the remedy sought became academic.[18]

COMMUNICATING THE DECISION AND REASONS

Rule 24, which concerns the communication of the tribunal's decision and reasons, applies to provisional decisions and decisions with recommendations as it applies to decisions by which applications and references are determined. The decision by which a tribunal determines an application may, at the discretion of the tribunal, be announced by the president immediately after the hearing of the case. This is not uncommon in section 2 cases.

COMMUNICATION OF DECISIONS : MHRT RULES 1983, r.24

Communication of Decisions

24.—(1) The decision by which the tribunal determines an application may, at the discretion of the tribunal, be announced by the president immediately after the hearing of the case and, subject to paragraph (2), the written decision of the tribunal, including the reasons, shall be communicated in writing within 7 days of the hearing to all the parties and, in the case of a restricted patient, the Secretary of State.

(2) Where the tribunal considers that the full disclosure of the recorded reasons for its decision to the patient in accordance with paragraph (1) would adversely affect the health or welfare of the patient or others, the tribunal may instead communicate its decision to him in such manner as it thinks appropriate and lay communicate its decision to the other parties subject to any conditions it may think appropriate as to the disclosure thereof to the patient; provided that, where the applicant or the patient was represented at the hearing by a person to whom documents would be disclosed in accordance with rule 12(3), the tribunal shall disclose the full recorded grounds of its decision to such a person, subject to any conditions it may think appropriate as to disclosure thereof to the patient.

(3) Paragraphs (1) and (2) shall apply to provisional decisions and decisions with recommendations as they apply to decisions by which applications are determined.

(4) Where the tribunal makes a decision with recommendations, the decision shall specify the period at the expiration of which the tribunal will consider the case further in the event of those recommendations not being complied with.

---

[18] See *e.g. Coates v. M.H.R.T.* (1986), *ex p. Stevenson* (1987), and *ex p. S.B.R.* (1989).

WRITTEN COMMUNICATION OF THE DECISION

Unless the tribunal considers that the full disclosure of the recorded reasons for its decision to the patient would adversely affect his health or welfare or that of others, the written decision of the tribunal, including the reasons for its decision, must be communicated in writing within seven days of the hearing to all the parties and, in the case of a restricted patient, the Secretary of State.[19] In section 2 cases, the period within which the written decision must be communicated is three days.[20]

DISCLOSURE OF THE TRIBUNAL'S REASONS

In *Pickering v. Liverpool Daily Post and Echo Newspapers plc and others*,[21] Lord Bridge of Harwich observed that the 1960 Rules previously empowered a tribunal to prohibit the publication of the text or a summary of the whole or part of their decision or of their reasons.[22] However, the present rule no longer gave them a general power to prohibit publication. It merely released them from the duty to disclose the reasons to the patient in certain circumstances.[23] In practice, it is virtually unheard of for the full reasons for the tribunal's decision not be disclosed to the patient. However, where a tribunal considers that the full disclosure of the recorded reasons for its decision to the patient would adversely affect his health or welfare or that of others, the tribunal may communicate its decision to him in such manner as it thinks appropriate and to the other parties subject to any conditions it thinks appropriate as to their disclosure to the patient. The tribunal must disclose the full reasons to a solicitor acting for the patient, but again subject to any conditions deemed appropriate as to their disclosure to the patient.[24] The rules do not authorise a tribunal to limit the disclosure of the reasons for its decision to a nearest relative applicant or to the nearest relative of a patient. As drafted, the decision and reasons must be communicated to all of the parties referred to in rule 7 (**779**).

Informing persons of the patient's discharge

Where a patient who is liable to be detained is to be discharged otherwise than by his nearest relative, the managers must take such steps as are practicable to inform the person who appears to be the nearest relative of that fact. The information shall, if practicable, be given at least seven days before the date of discharge.[25]

---

19 Mental Health Review Tribunal Rules 1983, r.24(1).

20 *Ibid.*, r.33(d).

21 *Pickering v. Liverpool Daily Post and Echo Newspapers plc and others* [1991] 2 AC 370, [1991] 1 All E.R. 622, [1991] 2 W.L.R. 513, 6 B.M.L.R. 108.

22 Mental Health Review Tribunal Rules 1960, r.27(6).

23 Rule 27 of the 1960 Rules required the tribunal to communicate its decision in writing within seven days. However, the rules also provided that the applicant or the responsible authority could, within three weeks of receiving written notice of the decision, request the tribunal to give their reasons for it. The tribunal was obliged to comply with such a request except where they considered that it would be undesirable to do so in the interests of the patient or for other special reasons." That rule closely corresponded to the statutory authority for it, which was cast in identical terms to the present section 78(2)(i). The paragraph provides that the rules may in particular make provision for requiring a tribunal, if so requested in accordance with the rules, to furnish such statements of the reasons for any decision as may be prescribed by the rules, subject to any provision made by the rules for withholding such a statement from a patient or any other person in cases where the tribunal considers that furnishing it would be undesirable in the interests of the patient or for other special reasons. As can be seen, the present rule 24 departs from the position envisaged in the Act.

24 Mental Health Review Tribunal Rules 1960, rr.24(2) and 33.

25 Mental Health Act 1983, s.133(1). The requirement does not apply if the patient or his nearest relative has "requested" that such information should not be communicated to the latter.

Issues concerning confidentiality, privacy and the disclosure of information may arise in various contexts during the proceedings. The confidentiality of psychiatric reports prepared on behalf of an applicant was considered in *W. v. Egdell and others* (**712**) and that of records of the Aarvold Board in *ex p. Powell* (**167**). As to solicitor's obligations where there is a conflict between the client's instructions and his safety or that of the public, see page 886. Various legislation has been passed concerning the confidentiality and disclosure of medical and social services records (**708**): Data Protection Act 1984, Access to Personal Files Act 1987, Access to Medical Reports Act 1988, Access to Health Records Act 1990. The question of whether there exists a common law right of access to medical records was considered in *R. v. Mid-Glamorgan Family Health Services and Another, ex. p. Martin* (**709**). Section 12 of the Administration of Justice Act 1960 is concerned with the publication of information about proceedings before a Mental Health Review Tribunal (*infra*). As to the Mental Health Review Tribunal Rules 1983, rule 12 deals with the disclosure of documents furnished to a tribunal (**702**), rule 21(5) with the publication of information about the proceedings (**798, 844**), and rule 24 with the disclosure of the reasons for a tribunal's decision (**841**).

THE PUBLICATION OF INFORMATION

The two most important provisions concerning the publication of information relating to tribunal proceedings are section 12 of the Administration of Justice Act 1960 and rule 21(5) of the Mental Health Review Tribunal Rules 1983.

The Administration of Justice Act 1960

Section 12 of the Administration of Justice Act 1960 is concerned with the publication of information relating to proceedings in private. Insofar as material, it provides that—

"(1) The publication of information relating to proceedings before any court sitting in private shall not of itself be contempt of court except in the following cases, that is to say—

(a) where the proceedings relate to the wardship or adoption of an infant or wholly or mainly to the guardianship, custody, maintenance or upbringing of an infant, or rights of access to an infant

(b) where the proceedings are brought under Part VIII of the Mental Health Act 1983, or under any provision of that Act authorising an application or reference to be made to a Mental Health Review Tribunal or to a county court ...

(e) where the court (having power to do so) expressly prohibits the publication of all information relating to the proceedings or of information of the description which is published.

(2) Without prejudice to the foregoing subsection, the publication of the text or a summary of the whole or part of an order made by a court sitting in private shall not of itself be contempt of court except where the court (having power to do so) expressly prohibits the publication.

(3) In this section references to ... a tribunal and to any person exercising the functions of a court, a judge or a tribunal and references to a court sitting in private include references to a court sitting in camera or in chambers.

(4) Nothing in this section shall be construed as implying that any publication is punishable as contempt of court which would not be so punishable apart from this section."

The 1983 Act and rules

Section 78(2)(e) provides that the tribunal rules may prohibit the publication of reports of tribunal proceedings or the names of any persons concerned in such proceedings. Rule 21(5) of the Mental Health Review Tribunal Rules 1983 provides that, "Except in so far as the tribunal may direct, information about proceedings before a tribunal and the names of any persons concerned in the proceedings shall not be made public."[26]

THE PICKERING CASES

The issue of the private nature of tribunal proceedings, and whether the publication of certain information relating to those proceedings constitutes contempt, was extensively considered in the 1980s as a result of the Home Office practice of leaking information about pending proceedings to the press, presumably with a view to influencing the outcome since no other purpose could conceivably be served by doing so. The matter came to a head in a series of cases involving a restricted patient called Pickering. The patient's case was referred to in the Annual Report of the Council on Tribunals for the year 1985–86, in which the Council emphasised that it was "most important that tribunals make decisions on the basis of evidence before them and that they are not influenced or thought to have been influenced by comments made elsewhere, for example in Parliament or in the Press."[27] The report also contained details of an agreement reached between the Council and the responsible Minister at the Home Office concerning the Home Office's disclosure of information about patients to the press. The Mental Health Act Commission's Second Biennial Report reported that a further similar case had been brought to the Commission's attention, details of which had been referred to the Council on Tribunals and the Attorney-General. The Commission deplored "the occurrence of such leaks which inevitably have the effect of prejudicing a fair hearing and are almost certain to work in a manner adverse to the interests of detained patients, without any countervailing advantages to anyone."[28]

Chronology and facts of the Pickering cases

The chronology and facts of the cases are difficult to assimilate because the events spanned seven years, and more than one set of tribunal proceedings, and they are therefore summarised on the opposite page.

---

[26] Rule 27(6) of the Mental Health Review Tribunal Rules 1960 provided as follows: "Subject to the provisions of this rule, the tribunal may, where they think it proper to do so, prohibit the publication of the text or a summary of the whole or part of their decision or of their reasons, or direct that the text or summary may be published only to such persons and on such conditions as they may prescribe."

[27] *Annual Report of the Council on Tribunals 1985-86* (H.M.SO.,1986), para. 4.21.

[28] Mental Health Act Commission, *Second Biennial Report, Session 1985-87* (H.M.S.O., 1987), para. 18.4.

7 December 1984	The patient applied to the Mental Health Review Tribunal.
23 August 1985	A hearing date of 11 November 1985 was fixed.
2 November 1985	Two newspaper articles were published, relating to the patient's forthcoming tribunal—

(i) 'Storm over bid to free sex killer' published in the Daily Mail newspaper, the editor (Sir David English) and owners (Associated Newspapers Group plc) of which later became the first respondents in the subsequent contempt proceedings;

(ii) 'Storm over sex killer', published in the Liverpool Echo newspaper, the editor (Christopher John Oakley) and owners (Trinity International plc) of which later became the second respondents in the subsequent contempt proceedings.

11 November 1985	The hearing commenced as scheduled but was adjourned part-heard on the second day as a result of the publicity which the proceedings had attracted following the publication of the newspaper articles.
24–26 March 1986	The tribunal hearing was resumed on the 24 March. The tribunal directed that the patient not be discharged and also made the following statement :

"The Tribunal has been severely hampered by ill informed and irresponsible media coverage before and during its hearings. This coverage persisted after the Tribunal had drawn attention to the fact that the proceedings are private in their nature and that such privacy is the result of Rules approved by Parliament and which only allow for media coverage to the extent permitted by the Tribunal. Such privacy is essential for the proper conduct of necessarily difficult matters pertaining to the mental health of an individual as well as to the protection of the public. The nature and extent of coverage in this case put unreasonable pressure upon all the parties before the Tribunal and creates a wholly false impression that the result of a Tribunal may be influenced by pressure of this kind."

22 January 1987	The Divisional Court (Watkins L.J. and Macpherson J.) granted the Attorney-General leave to commence proceedings for orders of committal in respect of contempts allegedly committed by the first and second respondents in publishing the articles of 2 November 1985.
27 January 1987	The motions for contempt were initiated.
May 1988	Before the contempt proceedings were determined, the patient made a further application to the tribunal for his discharge, due to be heard in November 1988 — the publication in the press of further information about the patient ahead of the hearing of this second application became the subject of separate court proceedings: *Pickering v. Liverpool Daily Post and Echo Newspapers plc and others*.
7, 8 and 26 July 1988	The substantive hearing took place, at the conclusion of which Mann L.J. announced that the applications would be dismissed for reasons to be given later.
20 October 1988	The judgments were delivered.

Pickering v. Liverpool Daily Post and Echo Newspapers plc and others, CA.

October and November 1988	Following the decision of the Divisional Court, "a number of newspapers, believing that they were not now in danger of being held in contempt in respect of anything they said about the proceedings before the tribunal, published in October and November 1988 a series of more or less sensational articles amounting to nothing less than a chorus of protest against the possible release from detention in hospital of a man with the plaintiff's appalling record of violent sexual crimes. The hearing of the plaintiff's application was again postponed."

5 May 1989	The tribunal hearing was rescheduled for 17/18 July 1989. The patient instituted proceedings seeking a declaration and injunctions designed to prevent the defendant newspaper publishers from publishing any information whatever relating to his outstanding tribunal application. Simon Brown J. granted the patient an injunction restraining the defendants, (1) Liverpool Daily Post and Echo Newspapers plc, (2) Associated Newspapers Holdings plc and (3) Yorkshire Post Newspapers Ltd, from publishing and disseminating any information about the patient's application to the Mersey Mental Health Review Tribunal, including the names of any persons concerned with the proceedings. It may be noted that the first and second defendants were also respondents in the initial action brought by the Attorney-General.
12 May 1989	Roch J. refused to continue the interlocutory ex p. injunction granted by Simon Brown J. on 5 May 1989. Roch J. held that the plaintiff was not entitled to injunctive relief on the grounds, first, that he had no cause of action against the defendants and, secondly, that the matters which the defendants intended to publish were not within the ambit of the prohibition imposed by r 21(5). He nevertheless continued the interlocutory injunction to the extent necessary to enable the plaintiff to apply to the Court of Appeal, which the plaintiff did on the same day. Because the patient's tribunal hearing was scheduled to take place in five days' time and there was no possibility of the appeal being properly heard and determined prior to the scheduled tribunal hearing, the Court of Appeal continued the injunction granted by Simon Brown J. until the determination of the appeal and ordered the tribunal not to hear the plaintiff 's application until the expiration of seven days after the court had given judgment.
11,12, 13 July 1989	At the commencement of the substantive hearing, the court made a further injunctive order to preserve the rights of the parties pending the court's decision.
27 July 1989	The Court of Appeal held that a mental health review tribunal was a court for the purposes of s.19 of the Contempt of Court Act 1981 because it was a 'tribunal .. exercising the judicial power of the State', that the plaintiff had sufficient locus standi to bring proceedings and that he was entitled to an injunction prohibiting the defendants from publishing the date of the hearing and the actual decision of the tribunal but not the fact that he had applied for his discharge or the result of the proceedings.

Pickering v. Liverpool Daily Post and Echo Newspapers plc and others, H.L.

3, 4, 5, 6, 10 December 1990	Appeals and cross-appeals in respect of the decision of the Court of Appeal were heard by the House of Lords.
31 January 1991	Their Lordships delivered their judgments.

Summary of the final judgment

The decision ultimately reached by the House of Lords as to what information may be published can be summarised as follows—

1. The publication of the fact that a named patient, whether a restricted patient or not, has applied to a tribunal does not disclose any information about the proceedings which ought to be kept secret.

2. The essential privacy afforded by each of the exceptions in section 12(1) attaches to the substance of the matters which the court has closed its doors to consider, not to the fact that the court will sit, is sitting or has sat at a certain date, time or place behind closed doors to consider those matters.

846

3.   To the extent that the recorded reasons for the decision disclose the eviden-
     tial and other material on which it is based, that falls within the protected
     area. It is not contempt to publish the fact that a tribunal has directed that a
     patient shall be absolutely or conditionally discharged. However, the
     conditions imposed on the discharge of a restricted patient are matters rel-
     evant to the patient's mental condition which ought by their nature to re-
     main subject to protection from publication.

4.   Where a newspaper threatens to publish part of the evidence, whether the
     patient is entitled to obtain an injunction restraining it from committing
     that threatened contempt, without the intervention of the Attorney General,
     was not resolved.

5.   It could be expected that a repetition of the kind of inflammatory matter
     which characterised some of the newspaper articles published in October
     and November 1988 would be calculated to create a substantial risk of seri-
     ous prejudice to the course of justice.

The cases

It should be emphasised that the first case referred to below no longer accurately
states the law but is briefly summarised because it provides the context of what
followed.

Attorney General v. Associated Newspapers Group plc and others

[1989] 1 W.L.R. 322   *Q.B.D., Mann L.J., Henry J.*

The respondents, who were the editors and publishers of two newspapers,
published articles about a patient shortly before a tribunal was due to hear an
application for his release, those articles being partly based on information and
opinions communicated to the newspapers by the Home Office. The tribunal
hearing was subsequently adjourned part heard because of the publicity that had
been aroused. The Attorney General applied for an order that the two papers
were guilty of contempt of court because the articles had tended "to interfere
with the course of justice in particular legal proceedings," within section 1 of
the Contempt of Court Act 1981.

Mann L.J.

Section 19 of the 1981 Act provided that references to a court in the Act
included "any tribunal or body exercising the judicial power of the State" and
the expression "legal proceedings" is to be construed accordingly. The live
issues before the court were twofold: (1) whether a mental Health Review
Tribunal was a "tribunal ... exercising the judicial power of the State" and
therefore a court for the purposes of the Contempt of Court Act 1981? (2) Was
there a substantial risk of prejudice? It was axiomatic that such a tribunal must
act judicially in discharging its functions otherwise it would be susceptible to
judicial review but that fact was not in any way indicative of whether it was a
court. The fact that tribunals were inheritors of an executive function, reviewed
a patient's position against specified criteria on an annual basis, and could not
deprive a person of liberty were powerful contra-indications to the suggestion
that they dealt with the liberty of the subject. With that in mind, and the caution

847

which the House of Lords had admonished the Divisional Court to observe on the matter of extending the law of contempt to tribunals, the Divisional Court concluded that a Mental Health Review Tribunal was not a court for the purposes of the 1981 Act. In the alternative, any risk of prejudice to the tribunal's proceedings created at the time publication occurred had on the facts been remote. It followed that the Attorney General's application would be dismissed.

Pickering v. Liverpool Daily Post and Echo Newspapers plc & others

[1990] 2 W.L.R. 494   *C.A., Lord Donaldson of Lymington M.R.,*
                                          Glidewell and Farquharson L.JJ.

In 1988, the patient (plaintiff) made a further application to the tribunal for his discharge. Pending the hearing, he applied to the High Court under rule 21(5) of the Mental Health Tribunal Rules 1983 for an injunction restraining the defendants from publishing in their newspapers any information about his application to the tribunal. The Attorney General had been invited to lend his name to relator proceedings but had refused. The plaintiff contended that rule 21(5) conferred on him a private right breach of which could be restrained by injunction. The Divisional Court held that he had no such right or remedy and refused an injunction. The plaintiff appealed. At the hearing in the Court of Appeal, the defendants asserted that they had no wish or intention to report what took place at the hearing before the tribunal. The plaintiff conceded that the defendants were entitled to publish information which was in the public domain but sought to prevent them from publishing— (i) that he had made an application, (ii) the date of the hearing, and (iii) the tribunal's decision.

Whether a Mental Health Review Tribunal is a court

The Court of Appeal held unanimously that a mental health review tribunal is a court for the purposes of the contempt of court provisions. Lord Donaldson M.R. said that under the 1983 Act, tribunals were given the functions of applying statutory criteria and, on the basis of their findings, ordering or refusing to order the release of restricted patients from detention to which they had been subjected by courts. Such tribunals were also given power to summon witnesses by subpoena. Given the absence of any indication that the word "court" bore a different meaning in the Convention from that in English law, if a tribunal was not a "court" for all purposes then the European Human Rights Convention was not being complied with. Contrary to what was said in the *Newspaper Group case* (**847**), such tribunals did not inherit an executive function: they were given a new and quite different function. There appeared to be no reason why the touchstone for determining whether a body was a court should be its ability to deprive a citizen of his liberty. Insofar as *A-G v. Associated Newspapers Group plc* decided that a Mental Health Review Tribunal was not a court, it was wrongly decided.

Glidewell L.J.

The reference in section 12(1)(b) of the Administration of Justice Act 1960 to the publication of information relating to proceedings before such a tribunal being an exception to the normal rule that publication of information is not in itself a contempt suggested that tribunals had, since 1959, been courts.

Farquharson L.J.

Tribunals were independent of the state and they did not exercise a purely administrative function; they were required to act judicially and made their findings on the basis of the evidence submitted to them; they could administer an
oath to witnesses called before them; and had the power to release patients
detained under the Mental Health Act. Decisions of such consequence, affecting
the release of patients subject to hospital orders made by the criminal courts,
came within the description of "any tribunal ... exercising the judicial power of
the State."

What is prohibited — "information concerning the proceedings"

The court was also unanimous in holding that the defendants were not prohibited from publishing the fact that the plaintiff was applying to the tribunal.

The majority (Lord Donaldson M.R. and Farquharson L.J.) also held that publishing the hearing date and the tribunal's decision were matters the publication
of which was prohibited by rule 21(5), although this did not prevent publishing
the fact that the plaintiff had or had not been discharged, inferentially as a result
of the tribunal's decision.

Glidewell L.J. held that all of the information which the defendants wished to
publish, including the date of hearing of the plaintiff's application, fell outside
the ambit of the prohibition imposed by rule 21(5) and that the intended publication involved no contempt under section 12 of the 1960 Act. He would
accordingly have dismissed the appeal.

Plaintiff's cause of action for breach of r.21(5)

Lord Donaldson M.R. and Glidewell L.J. held that the plaintiff could sue in his
own name.[29] Rule 21(5) was enacted for the benefit of all persons concerned in
tribunal proceedings, the benefit of privacy being something generally accepted
as appropriate in matters concerning the mental health of individuals. A statutory prohibition was so enforceable where the prohibition was imposed for the
benefit or protection of a particular class of individuals.[30] The rights of individual citizens were not any less because a statute provided no machinery for a
prohibition's enforcement.

Farquharson L.J. rejected the view that rule 21(5) gave the plaintiff any such
right.

Plaintiff's entitlement to an injunction

Lord Donaldson M.R. and Glidewell L.J. were of the opinion that an injunction
should be issued arising from the plaintiff's cause of action.

Lord Donaldson M.R. and Farquharson L.J. held that the court could grant an
injunction under section 37 of the Supreme Court Act 1981, Lord Denning M.R.
having held in *Chief Constable of Kent v. V.*[31] that it enabled the court to grant
injunctive relief to anyone who had "a sufficient interest" if it appeared just and
convenient so to do. The plaintiff satisfied this test. Glidewell L.J. did not find it
necessary to consider the plaintiff's entitlement to an injunction on this basis.

---

[29]   Glidewell L.J. would, of course, have dismissed the appeal.
[30]   *Lonrho Ltd. v. Shell Petroleum Co. Ltd.* [1982] A.C. 173 at 185.
[31]   *Chief Constable of Kent v. V.* [1982] [1983] Q.B. 34 at 42.

[1991] 2 A.C. 370　　　　　　　　*House of Lords — Lord Bridge of Harwich, Lord Brandon of Oakbrook, Lord Templeman, Lord Goff of Chieveley, Lord Lowry.*

The defendants appealed to the House of Lords and the plaintiff cross-appealed.

Lord Bridge of Harwich

When men convicted of serious sexual crimes against young girls were ordered to be detained indefinitely in a secure mental hospital, the question whether and when they could safely be released was a matter of great public concern. The question of what criteria ought to be applied in determining whether such an offender should be released was controversial and an entirely proper subject for public debate. It was important that any restraints which the law imposed to ensure that a tribunal was not impeded in the proper discharge of its functions by media reports or comments should be clearly defined and should be effective.

The Administration of Justice Act 1960, s.12

The enactment of central importance to the issues raised was section 12 of the Administration of Justice Act 1960. The general rule was that it was not a contempt to publish information relating to proceedings in court merely because the proceedings were heard in private. But the exceptions to that rule expressed in paragraphs (a) to (d) of subsection (1) indicated that it was, at least *prima facie*, a contempt to publish information relating to proceedings in the cases indicated, including therefore proceedings before a mental health review tribunal. These exceptions to the broad principle that courts must administer justice in public reflected the yet more fundamental principle that the chief object of Courts of Justice must be to secure that justice was done. The proceedings before a mental health review tribunal were, for obvious reasons, included in the exceptions as proceedings which required for their just and effective conduct the same cloak of privacy as the common law had always drawn around proceedings in the other categories mentioned. The inclusion of such proceedings in section 12(1)(b) was an unequivocal indication that Parliament always intended that the tribunal should be a court to which the law of contempt applied. The reasoning of Lord Donaldson MR in the Court of Appeal led equally cogently to the same conclusion.

MHRT Rules 1960 and 1983

Under the Mental Health Review Tribunal Rules 1960, the prohibition now found in rule 21(4) applied only to formal hearings although the need for privacy in proceedings determined informally was the same. It followed that the functions previously served by rule 24(4) were: *Firstly*, to ensure that where a tribunal conducted a formal hearing the cloak of privacy, backed by the sanction of the law of contempt, was not lifted (unless the tribunal so directed). *Secondly*, to indicate that "the names of any persons concerned in the proceedings" fell within the protection of that cloak of privacy. That explained why the rules themselves contained no sanction for a breach of the rule: the draftsman contemplated that the only sanction necessary was that afforded by the law of contempt to which section 12(1)(b) of the 1960 Act had made the proceedings subject. The purpose now served by rule 21(5) was that previously served by rule 24(4) of the 1960 rules: to ensure that the protection given by the law of contempt to the privacy of the proceedings generally applied to the subject matter of the hearing, including the names of persons concerned, except insofar as the tribunal directed otherwise.

The scope of the prohibition in section 12

In *Re F (a minor) (publication of information)*,[32] Scarman L.J. said that what was protected from publication by section 12 "was the proceedings of the court: in all other respects a ward enjoyed no greater protection against unwelcome publicity than other children. If the information published related to the ward, but not to the proceedings, there was no contempt ..." As to what was meant by "proceedings," Geoffrey Lane L.J. had said—

> "Obviously a report of the actual hearing before the judge or part of it was included. But the words must include more than that, otherwise it would have been unnecessary to use the expression 'information relating to proceedings ...' The object was to protect from publication information which the person giving it believes to be protected by the cloak of secrecy provided by the court. 'Proceedings' must include such matters as statements of evidence, reports, accounts of interviews and such like, which are prepared for use in court once the wardship proceedings have been properly set on foot. Thus in the instant case the reports of the Official Solicitor and the social worker were clearly part of the proceedings and were protected by section 12."

Whether embargo was necessarily perpetual

The embargo on publication of matters disclosed in a private hearing was not necessarily perpetual. Silence should only be enforced for so long as was necessary to protect the interests of those for whose benefit the rule was made.

Publication of the fact that an application has been made

There was nothing in the judgments in *Re F* to suggest that publication of the fact that wardship proceedings were or had taken place in relation to an identified ward fell within the protection of section 12, and, in *Re W. (wards) (publication of information)*,[33] Sir Stephen Brown P. held that publication of the name and address of a ward did not amount to a contempt at common law or under section 12 in the absence of an express order of the court prohibiting such publication. The mere disclosure that a child was a ward disclosed nothing within the mischief which the cloak of privacy in relation to the substance of the proceedings was designed to guard against. By parity of reasoning the publication of the fact that a named patient, whether a restricted patient or not, had applied to a tribunal did not disclose any information about the proceedings which ought to be kept secret. Although rule 21 of the Mental Health Review Tribunal Rules 1983 referred to "the names of any persons concerned in the proceedings," it was concerned only with proceedings at the hearing. If it had been intended to prohibit publishing the fact that an application or reference had been made, it was likely this would have been made clear and, in any case, it was highly doubtful that any such ban would be *intra vires*.

Information about the date, time or place when proceedings are to be or have been heard

Information as to the date, time or place when proceedings of any kind were to be or had been heard was in one sense information relating to those proceedings. In a wardship case, in which no express prohibition was imposed on publication of the ward's name, it would be no contempt to publish the fact that there was to be, or had been a hearing, at the Royal Courts of Justice at 10.30 am on a certain date. The essential privacy afforded by each of the exceptions in section 12(1) attached to the substance of the matters which the court had closed

---

[32] *Re F (a minor) (publication of information)* [1977] 1 All E.R. 114.
[33] *Re W (wards) (publication of information)* [1989] 1 F.L.R. 246.

its doors to consider, not to the fact that the court would sit, was sitting or had sat at a certain date, time or place behind closed doors to consider those matters. Accordingly, it was not possible to agree with the majority of the Court of Appeal on this issue.

Publication of the decision of the tribunal

The publication of the tribunal's decision might be of no great practical importance since the only matter likely to be of public interest was whether the patient had been released from detention. It was common ground that publication of this fact was not prohibited. Section 12(2) of the 1960 Act contemplated that the formal order made by a court, as distinct from its reasoned judgment, would not normally be such as to disclose information relating to the proceedings. However, the phrase "without prejudice to the foregoing sub-section" recognised the possibility that it might do so. In the ordinary case, therefore, the formal order of the court could be published in the absence of an express prohibition, as the subsection provided. Rule 24(2) of the Mental Health Review Tribunal Rules 1983 enabled a tribunal to restrict disclosure of the recorded reasons for its decision to the patient if it considered that such disclosure would adversely affect his health or welfare or that of others. However, there was no general power to prohibit the decision's publication of the kind previously found in r.27(6) of the Mental Health Review Tribunal Rules 1960. To the extent that the recorded reasons for the decision disclosed the evidential and other material on which it was based, there was no difficulty in holding that that fell within the protected area. However, a direction given by a tribunal that a patient be discharged, either absolutely or conditionally, was analogous to the kind of formal court order which section 12(2) excluded from the protected area. It would therefore not be a contempt to publish the fact that such a direction had been given. On the other hand the conditions imposed on the discharge of a restricted case were matters relevant to the patient's mental condition which ought by their nature to remain subject to protection from publication.

Summary as to the scope of section 12

The above considerations led to the conclusion that, whether or not the plaintiff was competent to seek an injunction, there was no ground on which the defendants could properly be enjoined from publishing any of the information which they intended and claimed to be entitled to publish. On this ground, the appeal was allowed and the cross-appeal dismissed.

Restraining publication by injunction

It was not necessary to decide whether, if the defendants had been threatening to publish part of the evidence, they could have been restrained by injunction from committing such a threatened contempt at the instance of the plaintiff and without the intervention of the Attorney General. It was, however, impossible to construe that rule 21(5) gave a cause of action for breach of statutory duty in respect of the unauthorised publication of information about the proceedings. Although the publication of such unauthorised information might in one sense be adverse to the patient's interest, it was incapable of causing him loss or injury of a kind for which the law awards damages.

Contempt of Court Act 1981

The strict liability rule under the Contempt of Court Act 1981 related to contempt of a different kind. The conclusion that the media may, so far as section 12 of the 1960 Act and the 1983 rules were concerned, report the fact that a tribunal application had been made, the date and place of hearing, and any order made directing discharge was very far from asserting that they had unlimited freedom to comment on those circumstances. The plaintiff was understandably apprehensive that the media would use their freedom to mount another campaign of public protest against his release. It was impossible to determine in advance what kind of public comment on pending proceedings would create a substantial risk of the course of justice being seriously impeded or prejudiced. However, editors and publishers would be well advised to exercise great care not to overstep the mark in this regard. Although one would not expect tribunal members or medical witnesses to allow their judgment to be consciously influenced by the media, it by no means followed that a media campaign against the release of a patient would not create a substantial risk of serious prejudice to the course of justice. It could certainly be expected that a repetition of the kind of inflammatory matter which characterised some of the newspaper articles published in October and November 1988 would be calculated to do just that. *Lords Brandon of Oakbrook, Templeman, Lord Goff of Chieveley, and Lord Lowry agreed.*

FURTHER CONSIDERATION OF THE CASE

Where a tribunal makes a decision with recommendations or a provisional decision, the effect is that the proceedings have not been concluded in the sense that some further step will or may still be necessary.

TAKING FURTHER STEPS: MHRT RULES 1983, r.25

Further Consideration

25.—(1) Where the tribunal has made a provisional decision, any further decision in the proceedings may be made without a further hearing.

(2) Where the tribunal has made a decision with recommendations and, at the end of the period referred to in rule 24(4), it appears to the tribunal after making appropriate inquiries of the responsible authority that any such recommendation has not been complied with, the tribunal may reconvene the proceedings after giving to all parties and, in the case of a restricted patient, the Secretary of State not less than 14 days' notice (or such shorter notice as all parties may consent to) of the date, time and place fixed for the hearing.

Decisions with recommendations

Where a tribunal makes a statutory recommendation under section 72(3) in respect of an unrestricted patient, the Act provides that it may further consider his case in the event that its recommendation is not being complied with.[34] The rules made under the Act give the tribunal a discretion to reconvene the proceedings in cases of non-compliance. Where, under section 72(3A), a tribunal recommends that consideration be given to making a supervision application in respect of an unrestricted

---

[34] These recommendations are that the patient be granted leave of absence or be transferred into guardianship or to another hospital.

patient, it may similarly reconsider his case if no such application is made, even though its recommendation has been complied with. The nature and limits of these powers, and whether a tribunal may discharge the patient at a reconvened hearing, have already been considered (**474, 495**).

Provisional decisions

Where a tribunal directs that a patient be conditionally discharged or, in the case of a patient subject to a restriction direction, recommends to the Secretary of State that a patient be discharged, its decision is final. However, its decision is provisional in the sense that whether or not it has effect is contingent upon future events, which may or may not come to pass. If it later becomes possible for the decision to take effect, rule 25.(1) allows for this by providing that any further decision in the proceedings may be made without a further hearing. It should be noted that the rules do not provide for reconvening the proceedings on proper notice (**539, 853**).

APPEAL BY WAY OF CASE STATED

Section 78 of the Mental Health Act 1983 provides that a tribunal may state a point of law for determination by the High Court and shall do so if required by the court. The procedure is governed by Order 56 of the Rules of the Supreme Court 1965 and the jurisdiction of the High Court is exercisable by a single Judge of the Queen's Bench Division. Judicial review (**857**) is an alternative procedure and the two are not combined.

CASE STATED PROCEDURE: MENTAL HEALTH ACT 1983, s.78

78.—(8) A Mental Health Review Tribunal may, and if so required by the High Court shall, state in the form of a special case for determination by the High Court any question of law which may arise before them.

THE REMEDY

The court will determine the question of law stated for its determination. If it is of the opinion that the decision of the tribunal on the question of law was erroneous, it may give any direction which the tribunal "ought to have given" under Part V of the Act.[35] Accordingly, in appropriate cases, the court may direct the patient's discharge.

REQUESTS TO STATE A CASE

The patient or other party writes to the clerk to the tribunal specifying the point of law upon which a determination is sought. The case must be signed by the president of the tribunal and served on the party at whose request the case was stated. The tribunal must give notice to every other party to the tribunal proceedings that the case has been served on the party named on the date specified in the notice.[36] For

---

[35] R.S.C. 1965, O.94, r.11(6). As drafted, the court may not give any recommendation under section 72(3) or 72(3A) which the tribunal could have given.
[36] RSC 1965, O.56, r.9(3).

these purposes, the parties are the patient, the responsible authority, any nearest relative applicant, and (in restricted cases or those commenced by discretionary reference) the Secretary of State.[37] The court proceedings must be begun by originating motion by the person on whom the case was served.[38] The applicant is required to serve notice of the motion, together with a copy of the case, on the clerk to the tribunal and every party as defined above.[39] That notice of motion must set out the applicant's contentions on the question of law raised.[40] The motion must be entered for hearing, and the notices served, within 14 days after the case stated was served on the applicant.[41] The motion shall not be heard sooner than seven days after service of the notice of motion unless the court otherwise directs.[42] The tribunal is entitled to appear and to be heard at the hearing determining the case[43] and it would appear that the president has a separate personal entitlement to this.[44]

APPLICATIONS TO REQUIRE A TRIBUNAL TO STATE A CASE

An application to the High Court for an order directing the tribunal to refer a question of law to the court by way of case stated must be made by originating motion.[45] Notice of motion must be served on the clerk to the tribunal and every party to the proceedings to which the application relates.[46] The notice must state the grounds of the application, the question of law on which it is sought to have the case stated, and any reasons given by the tribunal for its refusal to state a case.[47] No party may apply for such an order unless within 21 days after the tribunal's decision was communicated to him he made a written request to the tribunal to state a case and either the tribunal failed to comply with that request within 21 days or refused to comply with it.[48] The period for entering the originating motion, and for service of the notice of motion, is 14 days after receipt by the applicant of notice that his request has been refused or, if the tribunal simply failed to comply with the request

---

[37]   RSC 1965, O. 94, r.11(2).

[38]   RSC 1965, O.56, r.10(1). The form of a notice of originating motion prescribed by RSC 1965, O.1, r.9(1) is Form No. 13 in Appendix A to the Rules of the Supreme Court 1965. Although the contrary has occasionally been contended, it seems unlikely that the procedure constitutes civil proceedings for the purposes of section 139(2). It is the tribunal which is stating the case, not the patient. Furthermore, if application is made to require a tribunal to state a case, whether the point being raised has any possible merit can be determined at that stage. Section 139 would merely duplicate this procedural filter. In any case, determining a point of law concerning a tribunal's powers has nothing to do with individual liability, and involves no assertion of negligence or *mala fides*, and one could not readily accept that it is implied that the law may only be determined if there is evidence of negligence or bad faith. There seems to be no evidence in the case law that leave under section 139(2) has ever been considered to be a prerequisite.

[39]   RSC 1965, O.56, r.10(2). The form of a notice of motion prescribed by RSC O.1, r.9(1) is Form No. 38 in Appendix A to the Rules of the Supreme Court 1965.

[40]   RSC 1965, O.56, r.10(3).

[41]   RSC 1965, O.56, r.10(4). The 14-day period may be extended by order of the court: RSC 1965, O.56, r.10(5). Applications for orders extending time may be made to any Judge or a Master of the Queen's Bench Division: O.56, r.13. If the applicant fails to enter the motion within the 14–day period, any other party may, within the following 14 days, bring proceedings for the determination of the case: RSC 1965, O.56, r.10(5).

[42]   RSC 1965, O.56, r.10(7). The provisions of *Practice Directions* [1987] 1 W.L.R. 232 and [1991] 1 W.L.R. 280 which govern applications for expedited hearings apply in relation to all cases stated which are required to be entered in the Crown Office list.

[43]   RSC 1965, O.94, r.11(5).

[44]   RSC 1965, O.56, r.12.

[45]   RSC 1965, O.56, r.8(1).

[46]   RSC 1965, O.56, r.8(1).

[47]   RSC 1965, O.56, r.8(2).

[48]   RSC 1965, O.94, r.11(3).

within the 21 day period referred to, 14 days after the expiration of that period.[49] If the court orders the president to state a case, the case must be signed by him and must be served on the party as a result of whose application to the court the case was stated.

TRIBUNAL STATING CASE WITHOUT ANY REQUEST

It would appear that a tribunal may state a case of its own motion, without any request being made to it by a party to the proceedings.[50] The case must be served on such party to the tribunal proceedings as the tribunal thinks appropriate and notice given to every other party that the case has been served on the named party on the date specified in the notice.[51] The proceedings must be begun by originating motion by the secretary to the tribunal.[52]

FORM OF THE CASE

The form of the case is simply a short statement of the point of law for determination. For example, the question of law stated in *Grant*[53] was whether a tribunal considering an application made by a restricted patient had the power to make a statutory recommendation for his transfer to another hospital under section 72(3) and to further consider his case in the event that its recommendation was not complied with. The court hearing a case may amend the case or order it to be returned to the tribunal for amendment, and may draw inferences of fact from the facts stated in the case.[54]

CASE STATED OR JUDICIAL REVIEW

In *Bone v. Mental Health Review Tribunal*, Nolan J. suggested that the judicial review procedure should be considered as an alternative to a case stated because it allowed a broader consideration of the issues and offered a much more comprehensive range of reliefs.[55] However, the case stated procedure continues to be used and has two particular benefits. Firstly, it avoids disputes as to the tribunal's finding on the facts and any need for affidavit evidence. Secondly, it ensures that a point of general importance is ruled upon. It is not uncommon for the court to decline to judicially review a tribunal's decision if the patient has since been discharged or is entitled to reapply to a tribunal. This is because the remedy sought (that the tribunal's decision be quashed or the patient's discharge be directed) is now academic.[56] Furthermore, the court may direct a patient's discharge under the case stated procedure and that is usually the only remedy of interest to him. If he is indeed entitled to apply for a further tribunal, certiorari carries no personal benefit.

---

49   RSC 1965, O.94, r.11(4).
50   Mental Health Act 1983, s.78(8); RSC 1965, O.56, r.9(2). Section 78(8) does not provide that a case may only be stated if requested by a party to the proceedings. It has also been contended that a tribunal may state a special case prior to determining an application or reference. This seems unlikely because an application to require a tribunal to state a case must be made within 21 days of the tribunal's *decision* being communicated to the party.
51   RSC 1965, O.56, r.9(3).
52   RSC 1965, O.56, r.10(1).
53   *Grant v. The Mental Health Review Tribunal for the Trent Region, The Times*, 26 April 1986.
54   RSC 1965, O.56, r.11.
55   *Bone v. Mental Health Review Tribunal* [1985] 3 All E.R. 330 at 334, *per* Nolan J.
56   A consequence of this is that there is no case law on a tribunal's powers in section 2 proceedings and very little guidance as to their powers in respect of other unrestricted patients.

Judicial review is the means by which the High Court exercises a supervisory jurisdiction over inferior courts. It is a public law remedy, not an appeal against the tribunal's finding on the facts.[57] The court will only interfere if the tribunal's decision was defective because it acted unlawfully (it made a material error of law); irrationally (no reasonable tribunal could have made the decision); or improperly (the tribunal failed in its duty to act fairly).[58] The facts determined by the tribunal are rarely open to review and the court will not substitute its judgment or discretion for that of the tribunal. No application for judicial review based on the assertion that a tribunal or the Secretary of State acted irrationally, or abused a discretion vested in them under the 1983 Act, has been successful. Almost every successful application concerning that statute has involved a tribunal exceeding its jurisdiction (exercising a power which it did not have) or failing to give adequate and proper reasons for its decision.[59] The procedure is governed by Order 53 of the Rules of the Supreme Court 1965.

THE GROUNDS

It has been noted that the three grounds upon which judicial review may be granted are those of illegality, irrationality, and procedural impropriety.

Illegality

Any error of law that is material to a particular decision is susceptible to judicial review.[60] Judicial review may lie if a tribunal adjourns a patient's case for an excessive period; refuses to reconvene an adjourned hearing on being requested to do so by the patient; or postpones the date of an unrestricted patient's discharge for a period which either (i) exceeds that reasonably necessary to give effect to the arrangements which, once in place, entitled the patient to be discharged or (ii) is irreconcilable with the direction for his discharge.[61]

Irrationality and the exercise of discretion

The court will not substitute its judgment or discretion for that of the body under review and the facts determined by that body are rarely open to review.[62] The test is

---

[57] Judicial review applies to any body of persons having legal authority derived from public law to determine questions affecting the rights of subjects whether that right is derived from statute or from the common law.

[58] *Council of Civil Service Unions v. Minister for the Civil Service* [1985] A.C. 314, *per* Lord Diplock at 410.

[59] *Bone v. Mental Health Review Tribunal* [1985] 3 All E.R. 330; *R v. Mental Health Review Tribunal, ex p Clatworthy* [1985] 3 All E.R. 699; *R v. Mental Health Review Tribunal, ex p Pickering* [1986] 1 All E.R. 99.

[60] See *R. v. Greater Manchester Coroner, ex p. Tal* [1985] Q.B. 67 at 81.

[61] See *e.g. R. v. Southampton Justices, ex p. Lebern* (1907) 71 J.P. 332.

[62] If there was no evidence reasonably capable of supporting a conclusion, review is available under the "no evidence" rule laid down in *Edwards v. Bairstow*. "The facts — except where the claim that a decision was invalid on the ground that the statutory tribunal ... failed to comply with the procedure prescribed by the legislation under which it was acting or failed to observe the fundamental rules of natural justice or fairness — can seldom be a matter of relevant dispute on an application for judicial review, since the tribunal or authority's findings of fact, as distinguished from the legal consequences of the facts that they have found, are not open to review by the court in the exercise of its supervisory powers except on the principles laid down in *Edwards (Inspector of Taxes) v. Bairstow* [1956] 1 W.L.R. 1302]." *Per* Lord Diplock in *Reilly v. Mackman* [1983] 2 A.C. 237.

whether a tribunal directing themselves on the relevant law and acting reasonably could have made a particular decision.[63] A decision, such as a very prolonged postponement of discharge, which strays outside discretionary limits whilst remaining within the technical ambit of statute, will be amenable to review.[64] Although a positive finding of mental illness must be founded upon some medical evidence, a tribunal is not otherwise bound to follow medical advice or opinion.[65]

Procedural impropriety and unfairness

Judicial review is the appropriate remedy if there has been a breach of natural justice.[66] The twin pillars of natural justice are the rule against bias and the right to be heard (*audi alteram partem*). Instances of bias susceptible to judicial review include those where a decision-maker had a pecuniary or personal interest in the outcome[67] or there was there was prejudging.[68] If the applicant knew of the risk of bias at the hearing but made no objection, review may be refused.[69] Parliament is presumed not to have intended that a tribunal should be authorised to act in contravention of the *audi alteram partem* principle.[70] The patient must be given a fair opportunity of hearing the case for his detention and of presenting his case and have a reasonable opportunity for preparation.[71] The right to be heard may be violated if a person entitled to be heard did not receive notice of the date, time and place of hearing,[72] or he was not given full disclosure or proper notice of anything affecting the way in which his case was presented.[73] A tribunal would appear to have a discretion to proceed in the patient's absence, if he declines to attend, but their discretion must not be abused.[74] There is no rule that parties must be allowed to call every witness they wish to call.[75] As to breaches of the tribunal rules, it is a question of construction, to be decided by the court, whether a particular procedural provision is mandatory, so that its non-observance makes the subsequent decision a nullity, or merely directory, so that the statutory tribunal has a discretion not to comply with it if, in its opinion, exceptional circumstances justify departing from it.[76]

A discretionary remedy

The Divisional Court has not infrequently held that the issue raised by an application for judicial review has become academic because the patient has acquired a

---

[63]   *Associated Provincial Picture Houses Ltd. v. Wednesbury Corporation* [1948] 1 K.B. 233, *per* Lord Greene M.R. (**347**).

[64]   See *e.g. R v. Tottenham Justices ex p. Dwarkados Joshi* [1982] 1 W.L.R. 631.

[65]   *R. v. Royse* (1981) 3 Cr.App.R.(S.) 58.

[66]   *Rigby v. Woodward* [1957] 1 All E.R. 391.

[67]   *R v. Sussex Justices, ex p. McCarthy* [1924] 1 K.B. 256.

[68]   *R v. Halifax Justices, ex p. Robinson* (1912) 76 J.P. 233.

[69]   *R v. Nailsworth Licensing Justices, ex p. Bird* [1953] 1 W.L.R. 1046.

[70]   *O'Reilly v. Mackman and others* [1983] 2 A.C. 237.

[71]   See *R. v. Merseyside Mental Health Review Tribunal, ex p. P.K.*, CO/3519/96, 22 April 1997, Q.B.D., Keene J. (**812**).

[72]   See *R. v. Oxford Regional Mental Health Review Tribunal, ex p. Secretary of State for the Home Department* [1988] 1 A.C. 120 (**544**).

[73]   *R. v. Mental Health Review Tribunal, ex p. Clatworthy* [1985] 3 All E.R. 330 (**794, 805**); *R. v. Leyland Justices, ex p. Hawthorn* [1979] Q.B. 283.

[74]   *R. v. Oxford Regional Mental Health Review, ex p. Mackman, The Times*, 2 June 1986, Q.B.D (**790**).; *R v. Seisdon Justices, ex p. Dougan* [1982] 1 W.L.R. 1476. See also the unreported case of *ex p. S.B.R.* (1989).

[75]   *R v. Grays Justices, ex p. Ward, The Times*, 5 May 1982. See also *R. v. Mental Health Review Tribunal, ex p. C.*, unreported, 28 June 1989, C.A. (**823**).

[76]   *O'Reilly v. Mackman and others* [1983] 2 A.C. 237.

further right to apply to a tribunal. The possibility also exists that this might be the effect of the Secretary of State referring the patient's case to a tribunal under section 67 or 71, at least if he undertakes not to later withdraw the reference. The discharge of the patient or agreement to a consent order may also serve to avoid any decision which would bind the party concerned and so restrict the practice complained of. The point was well illustrated in the unreported case of *ex p. E.* (**581**). From the patient's point of view, judicial review has these serious weaknesses and the need often to show irrationality on the part of the decision-maker further limits its usefulness. The case stated procedure is therefore most often to be preferred. It was some time ago predicted by Richard Gordon QC that the refusal to grant relief on the basis that the remedy sought had been rendered academic by subsequent events might, if taken too far, result in judicial review being held by the European Court not to constitute an adequate safeguard for patients in certain circumstances. The recent decision of the European Commission of Human Rights in the case of *A.T. v. United Kingdom* is interesting in this context.[77] The Government contended that the applicant's complaints should not be admitted because Article 26 required him to first exhaust all domestic remedies and he had not applied for judicial review. The Commission rejected the argument because of the limited nature of judicial review based on grounds of irrationality or *Wednesbury* unreasonableness. Judicial review will no doubt continue to be granted to patients on rare occasions but, more often, its main value for restricted patients may simply be to ensure that all domestic remedies are first exhausted before an application is made to the European Court of Human Rights.

THE ORDERS

Any application for an order of certiorari, prohibition, or mandamus shall be made by way of an application for judicial review. An application for a declaration or an injunction may also be made by judicial review. The High Court may stay the tribunal's direction pending the outcome of the review.[78]

Certiorari

Certiorari is an order which brings up into the High Court a decision of a tribunal for it to be quashed. Where certiorari is granted, the court has power to remit the matter to the tribunal, with a direction to reconsider it and to reach a decision in accordance with the judgment given by the court. In *ex p. A.*, Roch L.J. said that the court could take note of the medical member's affidavit in deciding whether to remit the case for a fresh hearing or to remit with a direction to discharge.[79] There has, however, never been a reported case of judicial review resulting in a direction for the patient's discharge. Indeed, there appears to be no reported case of a patient's application for judicial review of a tribunal's decision ever having succeeded other than on the limited ground that adequate reasons were not given by the tribunal for refusing his application.

Prohibition

Prohibition is an order restraining a tribunal from acting outside its jurisdiction. It may be invoked before the tribunal has made any decision. It would appear to be of

---

[77]   *A.T. v. United Kingdom, LAG Bulletin*, January 1996, p.19.

[78]   RSC 1965, O.53, r.3(10)(a); *R. v. Wessex Mental Health Review Tribunal, ex p. Wiltshire County Council; Perkins v. Bath District Health Authority* (1989) 4 B.M.L.R. 145, C.A.

[79]   *R. v. Canons Park Mental Health Review Tribunal, ex p. A* [1994] 3 W.L.R. 630.

limited relevance to Mental Health Review Tribunals, except when the tribunal is dealing with an unauthorised application (**606**).

Mandamus

Mandamus is an order requiring a tribunal to carry out its judicial duty. For example, to compel it to hear an authorised application which it erroneously considers is unauthorised or to compel it to record its adjudication.

Declarations

There are isolated examples of the Divisional Court making a judicial declaration as to the powers and duties of tribunals or of those involved in such proceedings. For example, *ex p. Fox*[80] and what is usually referred to as the *Crozier case*.[81]

PROCEDURE

All applications must be filed in the Crown Office. The applicant must first apply ex parte for leave and must do so promptly and in any case within three months of the decision complained of. This is done by filing Form 86A, supported by an affidavit and the requisite fee. The leave application is normally dealt with initially by a single judge without a hearing, and a copy of the order made is sent to the applicant by the Crown Office. Where leave is granted, the substantive application is made by originating motion.[82] Within 14 days of the date on which leave was granted, the applicant must serve the notice of motion, Form 86A and affidavit on any other parties interested in the decision and enter the matter for hearing. This is done by lodging with the Crown Office an affidavit of service and a copy of the originating motion. The application will proceed to a substantive hearing unless it is withdrawn by the applicant; conceded by the tribunal beforehand; or subsequent events render the granting of any relief academic. Unless the court ordered that the proceedings be expedited, and abridged the time for filing any affidavit in reply, the tribunal has 56 days from the date of service of the motion on it within which to file an affidavit. The fact that it does not do so does not preclude it from contesting the application.

JUDICIAL REVIEW AND PART II

Tribunal decisions aside, judicial review has also been used to quash applications or renewals made under Part II of the Act (**869**).

---

[80]   *R. v. Ealing District Health Authority, ex p. Fox* [1993] 1 W.L.R. 373, *per* Otton J. (**415**).

[81]   *R. v. Nottingham Mental Health Review Tribunal, ex p. Secretary of State for the Home Department (Thomas); R. v. Northern Mental Health Review Tribunal, ex p. Secretary of State for the Home Department (Crozier), The Times*, 25 March 1987 (**818**).

[82]   If leave is refused without a hearing, the applicant may renew his application by lodging in the Crown Office Form 86B (Notice of renewal) within ten days of being served with notice of the refusal.

The writ of habeas corpus *ad subjiciendum* (commonly known as habeas corpus) remains of the highest constitutional importance, for by it the liberty of the subject is vindicated and his release from any manner of unjustifiable detention is assured. It is a writ familiar to the common law at least as long ago as the thirteenth century, and its efficiency has been furthered by a number of statutes (the Habeas Corpus Acts of 1640, 1679 and 1816). It is a writ of right and granted *ex debito justitiae*, but not as of course and it may be refused where another remedy lies whereby the validity of the restraint can be effectively questioned.[83] The jurisdiction enables the court to demand an account of the restraint and, where unjustified or unlawful, to put an end to it by an order for release. The writ itself requires the production before the court of the person restrained and is directed to the person having custody of him. The only accepted occasion when an action lies against any Judge of the Supreme Court in respect of any act done by him in his judicial capacity is in the case of denial of a writ of habeas corpus under the Habeas Corpus Act 1679. Habeas corpus is declaratory in that it does not quash the impugned decision but it does result in an order for release. Applications for habeas corpus take precedence over all other court business.

THE BASIC PROCEDURE

The procedure concerning applications for a writ of habeas corpus is governed by Order 54 of the Rules of the Supreme Court 1965. The application is made ex parte to a judge in court[84] and must be supported by an affidavit by the person restrained showing that it is made at his instance and setting out the nature of the restraint.[85] Three copies of the affidavit are required for the use of the court, to be lodged, if possible, the day before the application.[86]

The classical procedure

The court may make an order forthwith for the writ to issue, in which case the court or judge shall give directions as to the court or judge before whom, and the date on which, the writ is returnable. However, this is only done if the facts and law are clear or there is a likelihood that delay may defeat justice. There must be served with the writ of habeas corpus (Form 89) a notice (Form 90) stating the court or judge before whom, and the date on which, the person restrained is to be brought, and that in default of obedience proceedings for committal of the party disobeying will be

---

[83]   The term "*ex debito justitiae*" refers to that which an applicant is entitled to as of right — the court may only properly refuse relief on the grounds that there is no legal basis for the application and habeas corpus may never be refused on discretionary grounds such as inconvenience. A writ of right is a writ obtainable as a matter of right, as contrasted with a prerogative writ, granted in the exercise of the royal prerogative as a matter of discretion only. "Not as of course" means that the writ cannot be had for the asking upon payment of a court fee, but will only be issued where there appear to be proper grounds. There is a long established practice of having a preliminary hearing to determine whether there is sufficient merit in the application to warrant bringing in the other parties. See R.J. Sharpe, *The Law of Habeas Corpus* (Clarendon Press, 2nd. ed., 1989), p.58.

[84]   It may be made to a judge otherwise than in court at any time when no judge is sitting in court.

[85]   Where the person restrained is unable for any reason to make the affidavit, the affidavit may be made by some other person on his behalf and that affidavit must state that the person restrained is unable to make the affidavit himself and for what reason.

[86]   Affidavits must be supplied to other parties on demand.

taken. The return to a writ of habeas corpus must be indorsed on or annexed to the writ and must state all the causes of the detainer of the person concerned.[87] The court has power to examine by affidavit evidence the truth of the facts alleged in the return. At the hearing of the writ, the return to the writ is first read. Motion is then made for discharging or remanding the person restrained, or amending or quashing the return. The patient's counsel is heard first, then any counsel for the Crown, and then one counsel for the person restrained in reply. If the return discloses a lawful cause, the detainee is remanded; if the return is insufficient or unlawful, he is released.

The adjournment procedure

In most cases, if the court is satisfied that there is an arguable case for the writ, the matter is adjourned for notice to be served on such persons as the court directs (using Form 88).[88] Upon the adjourned hearing, the respondent produces the alleged justification for the restraint by affidavit and full argument from all sides is presented. The procedure avoids having to deal with formal returns. If the application succeeds, the writ may be ordered to issue, in which case its function here is limited to having the patient brought up and formally released. More often, the court hearing the application simply orders that the person restrained be released and such order is sufficient warrant to any person for the release of the person under restraint. In this case, the writ is not formally issued; the Master of the Crown Office writes directing his discharge.

Further applications for habeas corpus

Where an application for habeas corpus has been made, no further application may be made on the same grounds in respect of the same person unless fresh evidence is adduced in support of the application.[89]

Appeals in civil cases

Appeal lies to the Court of Appeal (Civil Division) and is by way of rehearing. Leave is not required. An appeal lies both against an order for the release of the person restrained as well as against refusal of such an order.[90] However, the lodging of an appeal does not affect the right of the person restrained to be discharged in pursuance of the order under appeal and to remain at large regardless of the decision on appeal.

---

[87] By analogy, it is doubtful that a return which simply states that the patient is being detained under section 3 of the Mental Health Act 1983 is sufficient: see *R. v. Secretary of State for the Home Department, ex p. Iqbal* [1978] Q.B. 264.

[88] Where an application is made to a judge in court, he may alternatively direct that an application be made by originating motion to a Divisional Court, in which notice of the motion (Form 87) must be served on the person against whom the issue of the writ is sought and on such other persons as the court or judge may direct. Unless otherwise directed, there must then be at least eight clear days between the service of the notice and the date named therein for the hearing of the application. Where no judge is sitting in court and an application is made to a judge outside court, that judge may similarly direct that an application be made by originating motion to a Divisional Court, or he may direct that an originating summons for the writ be issued. Either way, the same provisions as to service and the number of clear days required after service apply.

[89] Administration of Justice Act 1960, s.14(2).

[90] *Ibid.*, s.15(1).

Criminal causes

With two exceptions, if the applicant is detained in pursuance of an order or direction made under Part III of the 1983 Act, the application for habeas corpus is deemed to constitute a criminal cause or matter.[91] This means that an order for his release may only be refused by a Divisional Court, whether application is made in the first instance to such a court or to a single judge. However, it also means (1) that a patient may only appeal against any refusal of habeas corpus by a Divisional Court to the House of Lords, and this requires the leave of either court; and (2) if the prosecutor is granted leave to appeal, or gives notice that he intends to apply for leave, the court may order that the patient shall not be released pending appeal, or only on bail.

Civil cause or matter	Criminal cause or matter
• Patients detained under Part II of the Act	• Patients detained in pursuance of an order or direction made under Part III of the Act, otherwise than under s.48(2)(c) or (d)
• Patients subject to guardianship under s.7 or 37.	
• Patients detained under s.48(2)(c) or (d) [civil prisoners and persons detained under the Immigration Act 1971]	

Further applications under Part II of the Act

It has been held that it is possible to supply a new and better cause for the detention as the court commences the hearing.[92] Sharpe concludes that it would seem that as long as material proffered tends to show present justification, it will be accepted by the court at any stage of the proceedings.[93]

The need for representation or a next friend

In *Pharaoh*, a patient detained under section 3 submitted an application for habeas corpus challenging the psychiatric diagnosis. The Health Authority declined to produce him for the purpose of the hearing unless directed to do so by the court. The court refused to order his production but invited the Official Solicitor to produce a report which disclosed that in 1985 the patient had been made subject to an order of the Court of Protection. In refusing his application, Schiemann J. expressed himself satisfied that the patient was lawfully detained, but in any event the patient was not entitled to apply for habeas corpus because (i) he was a patient of the Court of Protection and thus, by operation of Ord.80, r.2, he could only bring proceedings by his next friend and (ii) he was not represented by counsel.[94] It is submitted that Sharpe gives the correct position:[95]

---

[91] Administration of Justice Act 1960, s.14(3).

[92] *Anon* (1673) 1 Mod. 103.

[93] R.J. Sharpe, *The Law of Habeas Corpus* (Clarendon Press, 2nd ed., 1989), p.182. See *R. v. Secretary of State for the Home Department, ex p. Iqbal* [1978] Q.B. 264; *R. v. Governor of Durham Prison, ex p. Hardial Singh* [1984] 1 W.L.R. 704. Section 15 of the 1983 Act also allows for the rectification of incorrect or defective applications during the fortnight following admission.

[94] *Re Pharaoh*, CO/1279/87 (unreported). See *The Supreme Court Practice 1995* (Sweet & Maxwell, 1995), vol. 1, p.878. Litigants may with sufficient reason be allowed to apply in person.

[95] R.J. Sharpe, *The Law of Habeas Corpus* (Clarendon Press, 2nd ed., 1989), p.221.

"Any person restrained may apply for the writ. There are no restrictions based on lack of capacity to sue. The technical reason for this is the prerogative nature of the writ. This was explained in a Canadian case where it was objected that a minor could not bring proceedings: 'As the writ issues in the King's name, the status of the petitioner is immaterial, and his detention may be inquired into even if legal disabilities would prevent his taking an action for the enforcement of civil rights.'"

Medical evidence of the patient's condition

In *Pharaoh*, the Official Solicitor was invited to prepare a report and there is a history of obtaining medical evidence in cases involving detained patients. In *R. v. Turlington*, where it was alleged that the applicant was improperly held in a madhouse, Lord Mansfield said that, "The court thought it fit to have previous inspection of her, by proper persons, physicians and relations; and then to proceed, as the truth should come out upon such inspection."[96]

Whether the patient would be dangerous if released

There is no agreement about whether the likelihood of the patient acting in a dangerous manner if released is a factor which entitles the court to refuse habeas corpus and, if so, on what basis, since it is not a discretionary remedy. The two competing arguments are, *firstly*, that it must be shown that the detention was improper *and* that the applicant is not dangerous and, *secondly*, that the principle that no one can be deprived of his liberty except by due process of law must be vindicated. The often repeated authority for the first view is *Re Shuttleworth*, where Lord Denman C.J. said:[97]

> "If the Court thought that a party, unlawfully received or detained, was a lunatic, we should still be betraying the common duties of members of society if we directed a discharge. But we have no power to set aside the order, only to discharge. And should we, as Judges or individuals, be justified in setting such a party at large? It is answered that there may be a fresh custody. But why so? Is it not better, if she be dangerous, that she should remain in custody till the Great Seal or the commissioners act? Therefore, being satisfied in my own mind that there would be danger in setting her at large, I am bound by the most general principles to abstain from so doing; and I should be abusing the name of liberty if I were to take off a restraint for which those who are most interested in the party ought to be the most thankful."

Because habeas corpus is not a discretionary remedy, the only way in which the two positions can be reconciled is by reference to the common law. This is because the existence of some vitiating defect in the statutory procedure for detaining the patient will not entitle him to be discharged if his detention or restraint is not unlawful because it justified for the moment at common law. Thus, in *Re Shuttleworth*, Erle J. said that, "The prohibition is that no one shall be received or detained in a licensed house as a lunatic, without an order and certificates. It is not a general prohibition against confining lunatics. That is left as at common law." In *Re Greenwood*, Coleridge J. concluded that the proper statutory requirements had not been complied with and, after considering *Re Shuttleworth* (to which he had been a party), said:[98]

---

[96] *R. v. Turlington* (1761) 2 Burr. 1115.
[97] *Re Shuttleworth* (1846) 9 Q.B. 651 at 662.
[98] *R. v. Pinder, re Greenwood* (1855) 24 L.J.Q.B. 148 at 152. **(263)**.

"I was reminded of what had fallen from the Court on several occasions when defects of a formal nature in orders or certificates have been urged as the ground for discharging lunatics; ... in such cases when, on the affidavits, it appears clear that the party confined is in such a state of mind that to set him at large would be dangerous either to the public or himself, it becomes a duty and is within the common law jurisdiction of the Court ... to restrain him from his liberty, until the regular and ordinary [statutory] means can be resorted to of placing him under permanent restraint."

Having found that the patient was not dangerous, Coleridge J. ordered his discharge under habeas corpus on the ground that, "If ... his present custody is illegal, I must determine it; and the power which I possess for the public safety of the individual must not be strained to continue his confinement." Having regard to these cases, there are two situations in which the common law recognises as lawful actions in relation to patients which, in the case of fully competent adult, would be tortious as constituting false imprisonment or trespass to the person: (1) it is lawful at common law to restrain, and if need be detain, a "furious" or "dangerous" lunatic whose state of mind is such that he is a standing danger to himself and others[99]; (2) it is lawful to administer to a patient who "lacks the capacity to give or to communicate consent to that treatment whatever treatment,"[100] judged by the Bolam test,[101] is in the best interests of the patient as being "necessary to preserve the life, health or well being of the patient" or "to ensure improvement or prevent deterioration in his physical or mental health."[102] The position appears to be therefore that (1) habeas corpus is not a discretionary remedy and always lies if a patient's detention is unlawful; but (2) the fact that there is no statutory authority for his detention does not invariably mean that his detention is unlawful. His restraint is within the law for that short period necessary for the proper statutory procedures to be effected.[103]

WHEN HABEAS CORPUS MAY BE GRANTED

The leading recent case is *Re S-C (Mental health patient: habeas corpus)*.[104] This restored habeas corpus to its proper constitutional place after the decision in *R. v. South Western Hospital Managers, ex p. M.*[105] It has the weight of having been delivered by Sir Thomas Bingham M.R., whose judgments in mental health cases are highly esteemed, and rank equivalent to those of Coleridge J. in the nineteenth century. Where the prescribed statutory procedures are not followed, there are grounds for habeas corpus: *R. v. Pinder, re Greenwood* (1855) 24 L.J.Q.B. 148; *R. v. Board of Control, East Ham Corporation and Mordey, ex p. Winterflood* [1938] 2 KB 366, C.A.; *Re Dell* (1891) 91 L.T.O.S. 375; *R. v. Rampton Board of Control, ex p. Barker* [1957] Crim L.R. 403. Where the statute has been misconstrued, there are similarly grounds: *Re Steneult* (1894) 29 L.Jo. 345; *Re Wilkinson* (1919) 83 J.P. Jo. 422; *R. v. Board of Control and Others, ex p. Rutty [1956] 2 Q.B. 109.*[106]

---

99 *Brookshaw v. Hopkins* (1772) Lofft. 240 at 243; *Anderton v. Burrows* (1830) 4 Car. & P. 210 at 213; *R. v. Pinder, re Greenwood* (1855) 24 L.J.Q.B. 148; *Fletcher v. Fletcher* (1859) 1 El. & El. 420; *Scott v. Wakem* (1862) 3 F. & F. 328 at 333; *Symm v. Fraser* (1863) 3 F. & F. 859 at 882–883; *Re Shuttleworth* (1846) 9 Q.B. 651; *Re Gregory* (1901) A.C. 128; *Black v. Forsey and others*, 1987 S.L.T. 681.

100 *Re F* [1989] 2 W.L.R. 1025 at 1054E and 1065E.

101 *Bolam v. Friern Hospital Management Committee* [1957] 1 W.L.R. 582.

102 *Re F* [1989] 2 W.L.R. 1025.

103 The issue arose in the case of *ex p. Ede*, which was not heard because the remedy sought became academic, but which enabled the author to receive advice from James Munby Q.C.

104 *Re S-C (Mental health patient: habeas corpus)* [1996] 1 All E.R. 532, C.A.

105 *R. v. South Western Hospital Managers, ex p. M* [1993] Q.B. 683 (**597**).

106 *R. v. Board of Control and Others, ex p. Rutty* [1956] 2 Q.B. 109.

[1996] 1 All E.R. 532   *C.A. (Sir Thomas Bingham, M.R.; Neill and Hirst L.JJ.)*

On July 10, 1995 the patient was admitted to Victoria Hospital under section 3 following an application made by an approved social worker employed by Lancashire County Council. At that time the patient's nearest relative was his father. The applicant knew that and also that the patient's father objected to the application being made. Nevertheless, she stated on the application form that she had consulted the patient's mother who, to the best of her knowledge and belief, was his nearest relative and who had not objected to the application being made. Following admission, the patient was transferred to a different hospital for which Warrington Community Health Care was responsible, then transferred back to the Victoria and later placed on home leave. The patient applied for the issue of a writ of habeas corpus and his application was dismissed by Turner J. He appealed.

The grounds of the application

The patient's argument was that: (1) the nearest relative objected to the patient's admission and detention; (2) no order was made overriding the nearest relative's right to object; (3) the application was made despite the prohibition in section 11(4); (4) it was accordingly not in pursuance of an application made in accordance with section 3; (5) there was therefore no authority to detain the patient; and (6) since the patient sought to show an absence of jurisdiction, not to overturn an administrative decision, habeas corpus was an appropriate remedy. Counsel for the local authority acknowledged that the patient's detention was unlawful but questioned the appropriateness of habeas corpus, inviting the court to proceed by way of judicial review.

Sir Thomas Bingham, M.R.

No adult citizen was liable to be confined in any institution against his will save by the authority of law. The law sanctioned detention in various situations, such as in the cases of those suspected or convicted of crime and of those who were unlawful immigrants. In each situation, the powers to arrest and detain were closely prescribed, by statute and the common law in the first case and by primary and subordinate legislation in the second. Mental patients presented a special problem since they might be liable, as a result of mental illness, to cause injury to themselves or others, but the very illness which was the source of the danger might deprive the sufferer of the insight to ensure access to proper medical care. The 1983 Act contained a panoply of statutory powers combined with detailed safeguards for their protection. In particular,

- section 11(4) provided that that no application under section 3 was to be made by an approved social worker except after consultation with the person appearing to be the nearest relative, nor if the nearest relative had notified that social worker, or the relevant local social services authority, that he objected to the application being made;

- section 6(1) and (2) provided that an application duly completed in accordance with the Act was sufficient authority for the patient to be conveyed to the hospital and the hospital managers to detain him; *and*

- section 6(3) provided that any application which appeared to be duly made and to be founded on the necessary medical recommendations might be acted on without further proof of the matters contained in the application.

Section 6 plainly protected the hospital. It was not obliged to act like a private detective but could take the documents at face value. Provided they appeared to conform with the statutory requirements, the hospital was entitled to act on them.

Notwithstanding that fact, the approved social worker knew that the patient's nearest relative was his father, that he objected to the application, that the mother therefore was not the nearest relative and accordingly did not have such rights. Any delegation of the father's role under the 1983 Regulations was required to be in writing and the approved social worker knew that there was no written document by the father authorising the mother to act in his place or delegating his role to her. The approved social worker's statement on the application form was accordingly entirely false.

Whether habeas corpus appropriate

In *R. v. Secretary of State for the Home Department, ex p. Muboyayi* [1992] Q.B. 244, 254, 267–268), the applicant's challenge had lain to an underlying administrative decision to deport him, not to the jurisdiction to detain under the Immigration Act 1971. In the present case, there was no attempt to overturn any administrative decision, the object simply being to show that there never had been jurisdiction to detain the patient in the first place. That was a which, on agreed evidence, appeared to be plainly made out. In principle, an application for habeas corpus was appropriate.

Whether patient's detention was unlawful

In *R. v. Managers of South Western Hospital, ex p. M [1993] Q.B. 683*, Laws J., having found that the requirements of section 11(4) had not been followed and having held that the hospital managers had been entitled to act on the application by virtue of section 6(3), concluded that the detention was not unlawful. That conclusion was a *non sequitur*. It was perfectly possible that the hospital managers were entitled to act on an apparently valid application, but that the detention was in fact unlawful. Otherwise the implications would be horrifying. It would mean that an application which appeared to be in order would render the detention of a citizen lawful even though it had been shown or admitted that the approved social worker purporting to make the application was not so, that the registered medical practitioners, whose recommendations had founded the application, were not so and had not signed the recommendations, that the approved social worker had not consulted the nearest relative, or had done so and that that relative had objected. In other words, it would mean that the detention was lawful even though every statutory safeguard built into the procedure was shown to have been ignored or violated. Bearing in mind what was at stake that conclusion was wholly unacceptable. On present facts an application for habeas corpus was an, and possibly even the, appropriate course to pursue.

Since the trust responsible for the hospital were not before the court the matter would be adjourned to enable them to show cause why the patient should not be released from their control. *Lord Justice Neill delivered a concurring judgment and Lord Justice Hirst agreed with both judgments.*

On the adjourned hearing, eight days later, at which there were no appearances, the court made no order, having been informed by the managers of the hospital that they had read the court's judgment and had released the patient.

Whether the face of the Part II application must be defective

It was previously sometimes said that habeas corpus is limited to reviewing whether an application or renewal made under Part II of the Act is good on its face.[107] *Re S-C* makes it clear that habeas corpus provides an appropriate remedy if there is good evidence that mandatory requirements of Part II have not been complied with.[108] This is also the classical position. For example, in *Goldswain's Case*, the court "declared that they could not wilfully shut their eyes against such facts as appeared on the affidavits, but which were not noticed upon the return."[109]

Affidavit evidence to show want of jurisdiction

Section 3 of the Habeas Corpus Act 1816 provides that, criminal cases aside, the judge is empowered to inquire into the truth of the facts set forth in the return: "In all cases provided for by this Act, although the return to any writ of habeas corpus shall be good and sufficient in law, it shall be lawful for the justice or baron, before whom such writ may be returnable, to proceed to examine the truth of the facts set forth in such return by affidavit or by affirmation." As to this, Sharpe states that the intended effect was probably to encompass all situations in which the detention did not rest on a judicial determination or order.[110] In *ex p. Rutty*, the court held that it could receive affidavit evidence to enable it to decide whether there had been any evidence before the judicial authority which would justify his finding. It therefore examined the return in the light of the affidavits, in order to ascertain whether, on a proper construction of the Act, there was any evidence on which the judicial authority could properly, that is as a matter of law, find that she was a person who could be made the subject of the order. It was not enough that the judicial authority should rely on the necessary two medical certificates to give him jurisdiction.[111]

The burden of proof

One "of the pillars of liberty is that in English law every imprisonment is *prima facie* unlawful and that it is for the person directing the imprisonment to justify his act."[112] Where a person's detention has not been judicially authorised, the leading

---

107   See *R. v. South Western Hospital Managers, ex p. M* [1993] Q.B. 683.

108   According to *ex p. Choudhary*, where the order for detention is completely in order, it is *prima facie* good. The burden is then on the applicant for habeas corpus to challenge its validity and to show that he is being unlawfully detained: *R. v. Secretary of State for the Home Department, ex p. Choudhary* [1978] 1 W.L.R. 1177, C.A. Similarly, in *ex p. Hassan*, it was said that if the return to the writ on its face shows a valid authority for the detention, it is for the applicant to show that the detention is *prima facie* illegal: *R. v. Governor of Risley Remand Centre, ex p. Hassan* [1976] 1 W.L.R. 971.

109   *Goldswain's Case* (1778) 2 Wm. Bl. 1207 at 1211. The fact that a return is not now usually required does not affect the basic principle. The law's first duty is to release subjects from unlawful detention, not to justify unlawful detention by adopting a posture of wilful blindness.

110   According to Lord Scarman in *Khawaja v. Secretary of State for the Home Department* [1984] A.C. 74, section 3 marks "the beginning of the modern jurisprudence the effect of which is to displace, unless Parliament by plain words otherwise provides, the Wednesbury principle in cases where liberty is infringed by an act of the executive." If so, habeas corpus might provide an alternative to judicial review as a means of challenging decisions under the 1983 Act by the Secretary of State. In *ex p. Rutty*, Lord Goddard C.J. attributed to the 1816 Act the power to inquire into a particular fact in that case. However, Sharpe states that, "the courts have never really been prevented by the common law rule from reviewing facts essential to the jurisdiction or authority underlying the order for detention." See R.J. Sharpe, *The Law of Habeas Corpus* (Clarendon Press, 2nd ed., 1989), p.70.

111   *R. v. Board of Control and Others, ex p. Rutty [1956] 2 Q.B. 109.*

112   *Liversidge v. Anderson* [1942] A.C. 206, *per* Lord Atkin at 245 (dissenting).

case on the burden of proof is *ex p. Ahsan*. The crucial issue in that case was whether the prisoner had been examined within twenty-four hours of his arrival in England. It was only in that circumstance that the statute authorised the detention order. It was held that the legal burden was cast upon the party called upon to justify the imprisonment. Since the burden rested with the authorities, and as it could not decide the question of fact one way or the other, the issue had to be decided in the prisoner's favour.[113] Where proceedings are taken to challenge the legality of imprisonment, whether by way of habeas corpus or judicial review, the rules derived from habeas corpus are to be applied. Hence the scope of review of the factual inquiry and the burden of proof will be applied consistently according to a common principle. Whatever the formal nature of the proceedings, the burden will be on the party seeking to uphold the detention.[114]

Habeas corpus and guardianship

Sharpe notes that a person's liberty may be curtailed, yet not completely taken away[115] and the distinction is of particular importance as regards patients who are on leave or subject to guardianship, after-care under supervision, or conditional discharge. As to whether habeas corpus is available to patients who are unlawfully restrained, rather than illegally detained, the remedy was granted in *ex p. Rutty*. This was so notwithstanding that the patient had for some time been living with her family on residential licence: she was not to be let out of the house alone and was to be returned to the institution on written request by the medical superintendent. The remedy was also granted in *Re S-C*, where the patient had leave to be absent from hospital. Other possible remedies in such cases are judicial review (**857**) and obtaining relief from a mental health review tribunal (**574**).

Habeas corpus or judicial review

In *Re S-C (Mental health patient: habeas corpus)*,[116] Sir Thomas Bingham MR held that habeas corpus is an appropriate remedy in cases where the statutory preconditions for detention under Part II do not exist. Such an application does not involve attempting to overturn any administrative decision, the object simply being to show that there never had been any jurisdiction to detain the patient in the first place. The essence is the absence of some essential fact upon which the validity of the detention depends, rather than the exercise of an administrative decision, such as an irrational exercise of discretion.[117] A "writ of habeas corpus will issue where someone is detained without any authority or the purported authority is beyond the powers of the person authorising the detention and so is unlawful. The remedy of judicial review is available where the decision or action sought to be impugned is within the powers of the person taking it but, due to procedural error, a misappreciation of the law, a failure to take account of relevant matters, or taking account of irrelevant matters or the fundamental unreasonableness of the decision or action, it should never have been taken."[118]

---

[113]   *R. v. Governor of Brixton Prison, ex p. Ahsan* [1969] 2 Q.B. 222. See R.J. Sharpe, *The Law of Habeas Corpus* (Clarendon Press, 2nd ed., 1989), pp.86–87.

[114]   *Khawaja v. Secretary of State for the Home Department* [1984] A.C. 74. See R.J. Sharpe, *The Law of Habeas Corpus, supra*, p.90.

[115]   See R.J. Sharpe, *The Law of Habeas Corpus, supra*, p. 163.

[116]   *Re S-C (Mental health patient: habeas corpus)* 1 All E.R. 532, C.A.

[117]   *R. v. Secretary of State for the Home Department, ex p. Khawaja* [1984] A.C. 74.

[118]   *R. v. Home Secretary, ex p. Cheblak* [1991] 1 W.L.R. 890, *per* Lord Donaldson M.R. at 894.

THE EUROPEAN CONVENTION ON HUMAN RIGHTS

The European Convention on Human Rights and Fundamental Freedoms may provide a remedy where all effective national remedies have been exhausted. The convention has not been incorporated into English law by Act of Parliament, although the present Government has stated its intention to do so. There is a judicial presumption that Parliament intends the United Kingdom to fulfil its international treaty obligations. When interpreting ambiguities in the Mental Health Act 1983, the English and Welsh courts may use the Convention as an aid to judicial interpretation. However, there must first be an ambiguity and *ex p. Brind* is authority for the proposition that, where an English statute is plain and unambiguous, it is not open to the courts to look to the Convention for assistance in its interpretation.[119]

European Convention of Human Rights

Article 3 3. No one shall be subjected to torture or to inhuman or degrading treatment or punishment.

Article 5 5(1). Everyone has the right to liberty and security of person. No one shall be deprived of his liberty save in the following cases and in accordance with a procedure prescribed by law;

(a) the lawful detention of a person after conviction by a competent court;

(b) the lawful arrest or detention of a person for non-compliance with the lawful order of a court or in order to secure the fulfilment of any obligation prescribed by law;

(e) the lawful detention .. of persons of unsound mind, alcoholics or drug addicts or vagrants;

5(2). Everyone who is arrested shall be informed promptly, in a language which he understands, of the reasons for his arrest and of any charge against him.

5(4). Everyone who is deprived of his liberty by .. detention shall be entitled to take proceedings by which the lawfulness of his detention shall be decided speedily by a court and his release ordered if his detention is not lawful.

Article 6 6(1). In the determination of his civil rights and obligations or of any criminal charge against him, everyone is entitled to a fair and public hearing within a reasonable time by an independent and impartial tribunal established by law.

6(2). Everyone charged with a criminal offence shall be presumed innocent until proved guilty according to law.

Article 8 8(1). Everyone has the right to respect for his private and family life, his home and his correspondence.

---

[119] *R. v. Secretary of State for the Home Department, ex p. Brind* [1990] 1 All E.R. 469.

2. There shall be no interference by a public authority with the exercise of this right except such as in accordance with the law and is necessary in a democratic society in the interests of .. public safety .., for the prevention of disorder or crime, for the protection of health or morals, or for the protection of the rights and freedoms of others

Article 13   Everyone whose rights and freedoms as set forth in this Convention are violated shall have an effective remedy before a national authority notwithstanding that the violation has been committed by persons acting in an official capacity.

PROCEDURE

Provided that all effective domestic remedies have been exhausted, the patient may apply to the European Commission of Human Rights for it to hear a petition against the United Kingdom, based on an alleged breach of one or more of the articles set out in the Convention. The application must be made within six months of the final decision made by the domestic courts on the issue in dispute. The Commission will consider whether the complaint is admissible, which requires establishing a *prima facie* case that a right protected by the Convention has been violated. At this stage, some complaints will be dismissed as "manifestly ill-founded" and, indeed, the vast majority do not proceed any further. If the complaint is declared admissible, the Commission will ascertain the facts by examination of the oral and written pleadings of the parties. It will then try to broker a friendly settlement between them. This may involve the payment of compensation and an undertaking to amend domestic legislation. If a friendly settlement cannot be reached, the Commission sends a report to the Committee of Ministers, containing its opinion on the alleged breaches of the Convention. Within three months of that report's submission, the case may be referred by the Commission, or by the United Kingdom itself, to the European Court of Human Rights. The court is concerned with the application and interpretation of the Convention. Its procedure is governed by rules and the patient may be separately represented before it. The court's decision is final and compensation may be ordered if the patient can prove pecuniary loss. Where a case is not referred to the court within the three-month period, it is decided by the Committee of Ministers. The Commission's report is considered by the committee *in camera* and the individual can neither attend nor be represented. In contrast, the Government representative on the Committee of Ministers may comment on the report and cast a vote. The Government gave an undertaking when signing the convention that it will comply with judgments of the European Court of Human Rights and decisions of the Committee of Ministers.

Legal aid

A legal aid scheme ("Legal Fund") is administered by the Secretariat of the European Commission in respect of cases brought before the Commission. Legal aid is automatically extended to cover proceedings before the European Court.

CASE LAW

Space precludes any detailed consideration of the decisions of the European Court of Human Rights. However, cases involving psychiatric patients which have been determined by the court are briefly summarised in the following table.

Case No.	Judgment Date	Case Name	Issue	Art.	Whether violated
93	28.5.85	Ashingdane v. UK	Continued confinement in secure rather than ordinary hospital	5.1e	No
				5.4	No
				6.1	No
244	24.9.92	Herczegfalvy v. Austria	Detention and psychiatric treatment of a person of unsound mind	5.1	No
				5.3	No
				5.4	Yes
				3	No
				8	No
				10	Yes
185C	25.10.90	Keus v. Netherlands	Extension of psychiatric confinement after hearing held in absentia (patient absent without leave)	5.2	No
				5.4	No
185B	25.10.90	Koendjbiharie v. Netherlands	Extension of psychiatric confinement decided more than 4 months after lodging of relevant application	5.4	Yes
75	23.2.84	Luberti v. Italy	Lawfulness of psychiatric confinement — speed of determination (18 months, 10 days)	5.1 ·	No
				5.4	Yes
237A	12.5.92	Megyeri v. Germany	Failure to appoint lawyer to assist patient in proceedings concerning his possible release from detention.	5.4	Yes
144	28.11.88	Nielsen v. Denmark	Hospitalisation for 25 weeks of 12-year old child in psychiatric ward by virtue of decision of mother, sole holder of parental rights	27.2	Yes — technical point
170	21.2.90	Van der Leer v. Netherlands	Confinement in a psychiatric hospital authorised without hearing or informing the person concerned	5.1	Yes
				5.2	Yes
				5.4	Yes
185A	27.9.90	Wassink v. Netherlands	Confinement in psychiatric ward ordered after questioning of persons by telephone and following a hearing held without a registrar	5.1	Yes
				5.4	No
				5.5	No
33	24.10.79	Winterwerp v. Netherlands	Psychiatric detention procedures; no means to challenge detention.	5.1	No
				5.4	Yes
				6.1	Yes
46	5.11.81	X v. United Kingdom	Review procedures involving psychiatric detention	5.1	No
				5.4	Yes
Commission —18.5.95		Johnson v. United Kingdom	Legality of power to defer discharge under s.73(7)	5.1e	Admiss.
				5.4	Admiss.

Source: Gomien, Judgments of the European Court of Human Rights, Human Rights Information Centre, Council of Europe Press, 1995.

The authorised representative

16. The authorised representative

INTRODUCTION

Legal representation before tribunals is the norm and approximately 90 per cent. of patients in Wales are now legally represented.[1] The other chapters of this book are written in the form of a textbook, seeking to give a balanced and impartial account of the legal and medical considerations relevant to all practitioners. The representative's role is not at all neutral. It is to present a case for discharge in accordance with his client's instructions and this chapter is prepared with that perspective in mind. It is arranged in the following way.

---

[1]   *Mental Health Review Tribunals for England and Wales, Annual Report 1994* (Department of Health, 1995), p.18.

AUTHORISED REPRESENTATIVES

Section 78 of the Mental Health Act 1983 states that the rules may provide for regulating the circumstances in which, and the persons by whom, applicants and patients may, if not desiring to conduct their own case, be represented in tribunal proceedings.[2] Rule 10 of the Mental Health Review Tribunal Rules 1983 is concerned with representation. In relation to the proceedings, an authorised representative may take all such steps which his client is required by the rules to take and do all such things as his client is authorised by them to do.[3]

NOTIFYING THE TRIBUNAL OFFICE

The rules provide that an application shall wherever possible include the name and address of any representative authorised in accordance with rule 10 or, if none has been authorised, state whether the applicant intends to authorise a representative or wishes to conduct his own case.[4] Insofar as the information is not given in the application, it shall insofar as is practicable be provided by the responsible authority at the request of the tribunal.[5] Any representative authorised to represent the patient or any other party to the proceedings is required to notify the tribunal of his authorisation and postal address.[6]

---

[2]   Mental Health Act 1983, ss.78(2)(f) and 78(3).
[3]   Mental Health Review Tribunal Rules 1983, r.10(4).
[4]   *Ibid.*, rr.3(2)(e), 30(2)(d).
[5]   *Ibid.*, rr.3(3), 30(3).
[6]   *Ibid.*, r.10(2).

Representation, etc.

10.—(1) Any party may be represented by any person whom he has authorised for that purpose not being a person liable to be detained or subject to guardianship *or after-care under supervision* under the Act or a person receiving treatment for mental disorder at the same hospital or mental nursing home as the patient.

(2) Any representative authorised in accordance with paragraph (1) shall notify the tribunal of his authorisation and postal address.

(3) As regards the representation of any patient who does not desire to conduct his own case and does not authorise a representative in accordance with paragraph (1) the tribunal may appoint some person to act for him as his authorised representative.

(4) Without prejudice to rule 12(3), the tribunal shall send to an authorised representative copies of all notices and documents which are by these Rules required or authorised to be sent to the person whom he represents and such representative may take all such steps and do all such things relating to the proceedings as the person whom he represents is by these Rules required or authorised to take or do.

(5) Any document required or authorised by these Rules to be sent or given to any person shall, if sent or given to the authorised representative of that person, he deemed to have been sent or given to that person

(6) Unless the tribunal otherwise directs, a patient or any other party appearing before the tribunal may be accompanied by such other person or persons as he wishes, in addition to any representative he may have authorised.

Mental Health Review Tribunal Rules 1983, as amended by the Mental Health Review Tribunal (Amendment) Rules 1996, r.8.

CHOICE OF AUTHORISED REPRESENTATIVE

A party may not be represented by a person who is liable to be detained or who is subject to guardianship or after-care under supervision under the 1983 Act, or by a person receiving treatment for mental disorder at the same hospital or mental nursing home as the patient. Subject to this limitation, a party may be represented by any person whom he has authorised for the purpose. Apart from solicitors, alternative sources of legal representation include Citizens Advice Bureaux; law centres, hospital advocacy workers; mental health organisations; and the local Community Health Council.

Representative's rights under the rules

The choice of representative can have three important consequences in terms of the representative's rights under the tribunal rules—

1. Where the tribunal is minded not to disclose a document to the patient or a nearest relative applicant, rule 12(3) nevertheless requires it to disclose the document as soon as practicable to that person's authorised representative if he is a solicitor or barrister, a registered medical practitioner or, in the tribunal's opinion, "a suitable person who virtue of his experience or professional qualification" (702).[7]

2. A tribunal may not exclude from a hearing or part of a hearing a representative of the applicant or of the patient to whom documents would be disclosed in accordance with rule 12(3).[8]

3. A tribunal must disclose the full recorded reasons for its decision to a representative of the applicant or of the patient to whom documents would be disclosed in accordance with rule 12(3).[9]

There are therefore potential disadvantages in not authorising a qualified solicitor, barrister or medical practitioner. In practice, many representatives are chosen for the patient by the detaining hospital's Mental Health Act Administrator. However, it is preferable for the appointment to be made by the tribunal in accordance with rule 10 if the patient has no solicitor willing to act.

APPOINTMENT OF REPRESENTATIVE BY THE TRIBUNAL

Rule 10(3) provides that, as regards the representation of any patient who does not desire to conduct his own case and does not authorise a person to represent him, the tribunal may appoint some person to act for him as his authorised representative. A hearing may be adjourned and a representative appointed if it is obvious that the patient is incapable of following the proceedings or presenting a case for discharge but would prefer to be an informal patient. In the case of patients whose cases are referred to a tribunal, they may not wish to be represented anymore than they wish to be present at the hearing. If they will not see a solicitor, or sign legal aid forms, the tribunal occasionally authorises the payment of a solicitor's fees from the tribunal's own budget although there is no authority to do this. The alternatives are for the solicitor to attend at his own expense without instructions, fulfilling the role of an amicus curiae and ensuring that the case for detention is properly tested, or holding that the patient's lack of interest is determinative. Although rule 10 permits a tribunal to appoint a representative for a person who does not wish to conduct his own case, and who has not appointed anyone to do so on his behalf, that implies that he has a case which he wishes to present and that he wishes to be represented. While a tribunal may appoint a representative for a patient who wants one, the intention is not that a tribunal may require a person to be represented against his wishes.

THE MENTAL HEALTH REVIEW TRIBUNAL PANEL

The panel is non-exclusive and open to all admitted solicitors, trainee solicitors, solicitors' clerks, and Fellows and Members of the Institute of Legal Executives. Membership is initially for a term of three years. Under the terms of The Law

---

[7]   Mental Health Review Tribunal Rules 1983, r.12(3).
[8]   *Ibid.*, r.21(4).
[9]   *Ibid.*, r.24(2).

Society's General Regulations 1987, the Post Qualification Casework Committee deals with applications for panel membership and other related matters. The membership conditions are that the applicant has attended an approved course, an interview, and four tribunal hearings (whether as an observer or representative), of which at least one concerned a patient detained under section 2, one a section 3 patient, and one a restricted patient. The candidate must also agree that references may be sought by the Committee if that is deemed necessary and undertake to both prepare cases and conduct tribunal hearings personally. One-day approved courses deal with relevant aspects of mental health law, tribunal procedure, medical terminology, case studies, reports, evidence, and the role of the authorised representative. Panel interviews last approximately 45 minutes and are partly based on the discussion of case studies. Where the interviewers recommend acceptance, the candidate will normally be accepted. Where deferral or rejection is recommended, the recommendation goes before the Post Qualification Casework Committee. If the committee then decides not to accept the application, the applicant is entitled to appeal against this decision. Deferral involves reinterview after any conditions of deferral have been met, such as attending a further course, observing or conducting further hearings, or undertaking further specified reading. The office may also appoint a "mentor" to help the applicant to attend further hearings and to discuss with him those areas requiring further attention.

DISCLOSURE AND SERVICE OF DOCUMENTS

Rule 10(4) provides that, without prejudice to rule 12(3), the tribunal shall send to an authorised representative copies of all notices and documents which are by the rules required or authorised to be sent to the person whom he represents.

Service of documents

Any document required or authorised by the rules to be sent or given to a person shall, if sent or given to the authorised representative of that person, he deemed to have been sent or given to that person.[10] Documents may be sent by prepaid post or delivered to the last known address of the person to whom the document is directed.[11]

OTHER FORMS OF SUPPORT

Unless the tribunal otherwise directs, a patient or any other party appearing before the tribunal may be accompanied by such other person or persons as he wishes, in addition to any representative he may have authorised.[12]

FINANCING REPRESENTATION

Patients and nearest relative applicants are entitled to apply for financial help with regard to legal costs and disbursements incurred in providing them with legal advice, assistance and representation. The relevant legislation is set out in Part III of

---

[10]   Mental Health Review Tribunal Rules 1983, r.10(5).
[11]   *Ibid.*, r.27(b).
[12]   *Ibid.*, r.10(6).

the Legal Aid Act 1988 and Part III of the Legal Advice and Assistance Regulations 1989. The Legal Aid Board has the statutory functions of "securing" that advice, assistance and representation are available in accordance with the Legal Aid Act 1988 and of administering that Act. The introduction of a franchise scheme in relation to mental health review tribunal work is presently under consideration. Development work began in April 1997 and application forms were circulated in October 1997.

LEGAL ADVICE AND ASSISTANCE

Patients and nearest relative applicants are entitled to initial advice and assistance under the means-tested "green form scheme."[13] The application is made to the solicitor, who completes the form and assesses the client's means.[14] If a patient's means fall outside the prescribed limits, the usual alternatives are for the patient to immediately apply for ABWOR (**882**) in respect of the initial interview (since this form of legal aid is not means-tested) or for the solicitor to waive his fee for that interview. In exceptional circumstances, where a capable client with substantial savings has chosen to pay private hospital fees of some £350 per day, rather than to be treated under the National Health Service, the solicitor might be disposed to ask for a fee in respect of the first interview, payable at the usual legal aid hourly rates.

Applying for green form advice and assistance

The regulations provide that an application for advice and assistance "shall be made ... to the solicitor from whom the advice and assistance is sought"[15] and "shall be made by the client in person"[16] unless he "cannot for good reason attend on the solicitor ... (in which case) ... he may authorise another person to attend on his behalf."[17] A solicitor may not provide advice and assistance under the scheme until

---

[13]   The Legal Aid Board's present interpretation of the work covered by the green form scheme is quite restrictive. "Where ABWOR is available for proceedings, the green form should be used to take sufficient instructions in order to make that application. A statement of case is permissable (*sic*) to be drafted under the green form scheme if it is necessary to support the ABWOR application." Once the ABWOR application is pending, the green form should only be used if further work is necessary so that the client's position is not prejudiced. *Letter to the author*, 4 February 1997.

[14]   Information in the text about income and capital financial limits under the green form scheme represent the limits currently in force for the year commencing 7 April 1997. The limits are revised annually and revisions may also be made during the financial year.

[15]   Legal Advice and Assistance Regulations 1989, reg.9(1). According to section 43 of the Legal Aid Act 1988, the term "a solicitor" means "a solicitor of the Supreme Court." The Legal Aid Board has not yet objected to the practice of applications being made to an unqualified person, such as a solicitor's clerk who is a member of the tribunal panel. If the practice is ever challenged, whether the statutory intention is that unqualified persons may accept applications must be open to doubt.

[16]   Legal Advice and Assistance Regulations 1989, reg.9(3). This therefore precludes green forms being posted and signed in advance of a hospital appointment.

[17]   Legal Advice and Assistance Regulations 1989, reg. 10(1). In *Legal Aid Board costs appeals committee decision LAA 10*, asylum seeks held in detention under the Immigration Act instructed a solicitor's clerk to sign the green form for them. Following the certification of a point of principle by an area committee, the costs appeal committee considered whether this was permissible. It noted that regulation 10 could be used are where the client was unable to attend upon the solicitor "for good reason." This included mental patients and persons detained by immigration officers. If good reason could be established, the reason should be recorded and the client could then authorise "another person" to attend on the solicitor on his behalf. That other person had to be in a position to provide the information necessary to complete the green form. If an employee of the solicitor's firm was authorised to be that "other person" a full note of the authorisation/telephone attendance and physical attendance would need to be filed. The extent to which the committee's decision applies in relation to patients detained under the 1983 Act was not made clear but in principle, if there are no friends or relatives who can attend the solicitor's office, it is difficult to draw any distinction between the two types of detainee. *Law Society Gazette*, 94/21, 29 May 1997, p.34.

the prescribed form has been signed by or on the client's behalf and he has assessed the client's disposable income and disposable capital.[18] Either the client or the person authorised by him shall use a form approved by the Board[19] to "provide the solicitor with the information necessary to enable the solicitor to determine" (a) the client's disposable capital; (b) whether he is receiving income support, income-based job-seeker's allowance, disability working allowance or family credit; (c) if he is not receiving such a benefit, his disposable income.[20]

Clients directly or indirectly in receipt of income support

If the solicitor is satisfied that the client is "directly or indirectly in receipt of in-come support," he shall treat that person as if his disposable income and capital do not exceed the level entitling him to free advice and assistance under the scheme.[21]

Assessing and aggregating the client's means

In conducting the means assessment, the solicitor must aggregate the client's disposable income and disposable capital with that of any spouse unless the spouse has a "contrary interest in the matter," they are living "separate and apart," or it would "in all the circumstances... be inequitable or impractical to do so."[22] The capital and income of any person the client lives with "in the same household as husband and wife" is similarly to be assessed as if it was the applicant's own capital and income,[23] subject to the same exceptions.[24] Having where appropriate aggre-gated any spouse's or cohabitee's resources, the solicitor must then calculate the client's disposable capital and disposable income by deducting from those gross sums any deductions or allowances permitted under the regulations.[25]

Capital and disposable capital

"Capital" means "the amount or value of every resource of a capital nature."[26] It includes the value of any resources the client has disposed of for the purpose of making himself financially eligible for green form assistance. It excludes the value of the first £100,000 equity of the main or only dwelling in which he resides; a spouse's capital if it would be inequitable or impractical to assess it as his; his household furniture and effects; and the tools and implements of his trade. "Disposable capital" is the client's capital calculated as above, less certain fixed amounts which may be deducted.

---

[18] Legal Advice and Assistance Regulations 1989, reg. 13(5). Because the solicitor usually has to travel to the hospital to see his client and to complete the application, the Legal Aid Board's interpretation is that the time spent travelling to the hospital, and any initial advice given by letter or telephone, are not chargeable to the legal aid fund. Whether this interpretation is lawful or the regulation is *ultra vires* the Legal Aid Act 1988 in this respect might usefully be judicially reviewed. However, if the procedure outlined in the footnote immediately above extends to persons detained under the 1983 Act, the need for a challenge may now be less pressing.

[19] Legal Advice and Assistance Regulations 1989, regs. 9(6) and 10(4).

[20] *Ibid.*, regs. 9(4) and 10(2).

[21] *Ibid.*, reg. 13(2) and 13(3).

[22] *Ibid.*, reg. 13(1); Sched.2, para. 7(2). If the nearest relative has not exercised his power to discharge the patient, or did not object to the admission, then he necessarily has a contrary interest.

[23] *Ibid.*, reg. 13(1); Sched.2, para.2.

[24] *Ibid.*, Sched.2 para 7(2)(i).

[25] *Ibid.*, Sched.2, para 4.

[26] *Ibid.*, Sched.2, para 1.

Income and disposable income

"Income" means "the total income from all sources which the person whose disposable income is being assessed has received or may reasonably expect to receive in respect of the seven days up to and including the date of his application."[27] As with the capital assessment, it includes income which the client has "directly or indirectly" deprived himself of for the purpose of making himself eligible for green form assistance.[28] Unless one of the exemptions applies, to this sum is added the income of any spouse or cohabitee over the same seven day period, the total arrived at representing the client's gross income. "Disposable income" represents the client's gross income *less* (a) income tax paid or payable on the combined income; (b) national insurance contributions estimated by the solicitor to have been paid in respect of it; (c) an allowance of £27.30 in respect of a spouse or cohabitee who lives with the client, regardless of whether their incomes have been aggregated; (d) any allowances in respect of the maintenance of dependant children or relatives in the same household[29]; (e) payments of disability living allowance or certain kinds of attendance allowance and any payment from the social fund.

The current financial limits

Green form assistance is not available if the client's disposable capital exceeds £1000 (client with no dependants); £1335 (client with one dependant); £1535 (client with two dependants).[30] Provided the client is within the capital limits, he will be entitled to free legal advice and assistance if his disposable income, as defined above, does not exceed £77. If it does exceed that sum, green form assistance is not available. A green form extension must be obtained from the Legal Aid Board before a solicitor's expenditure under the scheme may exceed £88 (£93 in the London area).

Advice and assistance from more than one solicitor

A solicitor may not advise or assist a person under the green form scheme without the prior authority of the Area Director if the person concerned has already received advice under the scheme from another solicitor for the same matter.[31]

THE ABWOR SCHEME

The green form scheme does not extend to representation and the usual practice is to complete an application for assistance by way of representation (ABWOR) at the initial interview. This is then submitted to the Legal Aid Board and granted within one week. In urgent cases, particularly section 2 cases, ABWOR may be granted by telephone. Once granted, the certificate covers all reasonable legal costs and

---

[27] Legal Advice and Assistance Regulations 1989, Sched.2, para 1.
[28] *Ibid.*, Sched.2, para 6.
[29] £16.90 for each dependent child or dependent relative of the household under 11 years of age; £24.75 for each such person aged 11–15; £29.60 for each such person aged 16 or 17; £37.90 for each such person aged 18 or over. These are the rates for the year commencing 7 April 1997.
[30] A further £100 capital allowance should be added for each additional dependant.
[31] Legal Advice and Assistance Regulations 1989, reg. 16(1). Where a solicitor is told by the client that he has not previously received green form advice from another solicitor, but it transpires that he has, a payment may not be made under the Legal Advice and Assistance Regulations. However, it may be appropriate for an extra-statutory payment to be made. *Legal Aid Board costs appeals committee decision LAA 11*, reported in the *Law Society Gazette* 94/21, 29 May 1997, p.34.

disbursements incurred in the proceedings from that point onwards, although prior authority is required for medical and other expert reports. ABWOR is no longer means-tested.[32] A nearest relative applicant may also receive ABWOR, again without reference to means.[33] ABWOR is not conditional upon a green form having previously been signed.[34]

Psychiatric and other expert reports

An application for prior permission must be made to the Area Director of the Legal Aid Board if a solicitor wishes (a) to obtain a report or opinion from an expert; (b) to tender expert evidence; or (c) to perform an act which is either unusual in its nature or involves unusually large expenditure.[35] Form ABWOR 6 is the prescribed form. A typical fee for a report from a consultant psychiatrist is £400 (five hours at £80 per hour), plus any fares incurred or a mileage allowance, and in some cases travelling time at £35–40 per hour. Independent social circumstances reports generally cost between £200 and £250.

Legal Aid Board rulings

The Legal Aid Board has issued the following points of principle of general importance:

- There is no authority to pay a solicitor's costs at an enhanced rate[36];

- In deciding whether a claim for travel is reasonable, the Board shall consider all the relevant circumstances of the case, including (i) any legitimate expectation of the assisted person of specialist representation, *i.e.* by a mental health review tribunal panel member; (ii) the availability of panel members; and (iii) the undertaking which is required to be given by a panel member to conduct such cases personally[37];

- ABWOR for a tribunal does not cover work only carried out for a hospital managers' appeal, including representation on the appeal itself. However, if work is properly carried out in preparation for representation at the tribunal, it should not be disallowed if it incidentally assists at the hospital managers' appeal.[38]

- Following a deferred conditional discharge decision, the tribunal proceedings are not concluded until either the direction lapses by effluxion of time or the tribunal directs that the patient may be so discharged. The ABWOR approval will therefore continue until the first of these events occurs.[39]

---

[32] Legal Advice and Assistance Regulations 1989, reg. 5A.
[33] Legal Advice and Assistance (Scope) Regulations 1989, reg. 9(a). Where the nearest relative applies, the patient who is the subject of the proceedings is also entitled to be represented under the ABWOR scheme.
[34] Persons with mental health problems are occasionally detained under section 47 of the National Assistance Act 1948. It should be noted that on 7 April 1997 ABWOR was extended to cover proceedings of this type. However, the client's eligibility is subject to the usual means-test and the solicitor's fees are payable at the ordinary ABWOR rate.
[35] Legal Advice and Assistance Regulations 1989, reg. 22(7).
[36] Legal Aid Board Reference ABWOR 3.
[37] Legal Aid Board Reference ABWOR 7.
[38] Legal Aid Board Reference ABWOR 9.
[39] Legal Aid Board Reference ABWOR 11.

GENERAL PRINCIPLES

Before dealing with the first interview, it is useful to refer to some general principles concerning the preparation and presentation of a client's case.

FORMALITY AND MANNER

Practitioners new to the field are often anxious about how they should approach and deal with people who have a serious mental health problem. In terms of professional conduct, the principles are the same as for any client attending the office: to serve the client without compromising the solicitor's integrity or his overriding duty to the court and the judicial process. On a personal level, being able to take proper instructions, helping the client to formulate what it is he wants, and then pursuing those objectives in a constructive way, may require more empathy than is usually necessary in most other legal fields. It should be borne in mind that detained patients often feel uncomfortable and disadvantaged in a formal situation such as a interview. They may have low self-esteem since much mental ill-health takes root in such ground and, in other cases, a poor self-image is a necessary fertiliser of disease. The individual's false belief that his opinions are of no significance is potentially reinforced by being detained and so compelled to accept the views of others; by his subordinate status as a layman in discussion with a professional adviser; and his status as an ill and irrational patient receiving a rational, sane, visitor. The client may be perplexed by the recent turn of events or by the ward routine. Containment on an acute psychiatric ward is a frightening, and in itself largely untherapeutic, experience at the best of times, the more so if the person is unfamiliar with the environment. Helping the client to relax and gaining his trust, by appreciating his predicament, and treating him at all times respectfully and as an equal, are therefore prerequisites to making progress. The ways of responding to the individual's sense of humiliation at being categorised as mentally abnormal depend very much on how he himself has reacted to this slight. In some cases it helps to acknowledge that mental health is, like physical health, a relative term and that we are all at some level both well and ill, normal and abnormal, at any one time. With people who are seriously depressed, their feelings are often best understood as a bereavement: in some cases, the death of another important person but more often their own death or the loss of something important within them. In cases involving mania, it is similarly valuable to appreciate that grandiosity cloaks feelings of inadequacy or depression — time and again, people in a manic phase say that they are not truly careless or content whatever their behaviour may superficially suggest. Whatever social approach is adopted, the use of medical adjectives to define the person rather than the condition affecting him is insulting, and akin to describing a person with leprosy as a "leper." To refer to someone as a "schizophrenic" or as a "paranoid schizophrenic" is to imply that his personality has been so distorted by the illness that the latter is now the feature which most tellingly defines him as a person. By implication, it is more accurate to describe him in this way than to say that he is a person who has an illness called schizophrenia. From there, it is quite easy for a lawyer to drift into seeing his contribution, and legal presumptions about human liberty, as having only a marginal relevance. To summarise, the usual principles governing the solicitor-client relationship apply and few problems will arise provided the solicitor is courteous and avoids being patronising.

It is generally possible to take detailed instructions. However, if the client is particularly restless or agitated, he may initially only be able to cope with a short interview. This limitation is quite rare and mainly seen in section 2 cases where there is still evidence of mania. Most often, if any difficulty is encountered, the consequence is merely that a long interview or several interviews is necessary in order to obtain the required information. It is important to persevere and to be thorough because poor preparation produces poor performance.[40] A detailed interview avoids unpleasant surprises later. By observing and listening to the client and others, the representative can be aware of the strengths and weaknesses of his case, the likely content of the reports and oral evidence, and any inconsistencies between client's account and objectives and what is observed. This enables him to anticipate the likely objections to discharge and to plan questions and submissions which cater for those eventualities. Developing a trust and rapport with the client will later help him to give his evidence in an intelligible and structured way because he will trust the solicitor to make appropriate interventions for him. It also enables the solicitor to explore the possibility of compromise in relation to medication and treatment. Quite often, the patient is more willing to openly discuss the possibility that he has an illness, and needs some medication or treatment, with his solicitor (who is seen as being on his side) than he is with his doctor (who is seen as having deprived him of his liberty, forced injections on him, and to have no interest in or insight into the anxieties and problems which triggered the illness). Most people welcome discussing their beliefs and perceptions in an honest way provided that they do not feel that the only purpose of the discussion is to form a diagnosis and to prescribe compulsory medication. Hence, it is sometimes said that psychiatrists must elicit symptoms whereas other people have no need to.

Taking notes and recording interviews

When time permits, it is useful to maintain a reasonably comprehensive case summary. The form at the end of this chapter can be copied and revised to suit, or simply used as an *aide-mémoire* when taking instructions. It will rarely be possible, or appropriate, to attempt to obtain from a single, systematic, interview all of the information necessary to complete the summary. The aim should be to cover the areas in as natural and conversational a way as possible before the hearing, transferring relevant information to the case summary after interviews. The benefit of case summaries is that they minimise the risk of oversights, are appreciated by experts commissioned to prepare reports, and ensure continuity of legal care if a client who is not discharged later reapplies to the tribunal.

The use of tape recorders

The occasional practice of tape-recording interviews with clients has little to commend it. It risks undermining the professional relationship by seeming to compromise its confidential basis, inhibits honest and frank discussion of sensitive subjects, and carries the additional risk of the solicitor becoming incorporated into a paranoid construction of events.

---

[40] Sometimes referred to as the lesson of the five p's.

PROFESSIONAL ETHICS

The usual rules governing the solicitor-client relationship and the solicitor's duty to the court apply and the following observations are by way of amplification.

Practising the client

The tendency of a few solicitors to practice their clients must be deplored. This form of contempt consists of telling the client the questions invariably asked by tribunals and medical examiners and also the answers to them commonly interpreted as pointers towards discharge. Having been informed by the client that he has no intention of continuing medication if free to refuse it, and that he would immediately leave hospital, the representative emphasises the importance of the client telling the tribunal that he accepts that he has been ill, will take medication for as long as it is prescribed, and remain in hospital for as long as advised. Protestations about future compliance with medication are always unconvincing if at variance with the other facts and merely taint the genuine pointers towards discharge. If not discharged, the approach leaves the client dissatisfied with the outcome, and feeling that he did not have a fair hearing, because he was in effect instructed by his solicitor rather than his case presented on the basis of his instructions to that solicitor.[41] Moreover, if the tribunal members suspect that a particular solicitor favours this approach that must prejudice future applications made by other patients, because it reduces the likelihood of their genuine undertakings being given the weight which they deserve. It brings the profession into disrepute and constitutes a serious breach of the solicitor's overriding duty not to mislead the court. Once trust has been established, if the client's assessment of his situation is clearly implausible and at variance with the facts, the correct approach must be to question his assessment in the same way that a tribunal probes and examines those issues, in the hope that some genuine reassessment emerges prior to the hearing. This is not as unlikely as it sounds. If the client likes his solicitor, trusts him, feels that he understands his resentment, sees him as being on his side, and knows that their conversation is confidential and will not be recorded in the case notes, he will normally welcome discussing his views, and more often than not seriously consider alternative explanations.

The duty of confidentiality

Whether departing from a solicitor's duty of confidentiality may ever be justified is disputed. Because many clients are willing to discuss their mental experiences more freely with their solicitor, partly because of the cloak of privacy, it is often the case that the solicitor is aware of mental phenomena not recorded in the case notes and not aired at the hearing. The general view is that a solicitor remains bound in all situations by the normal duty of confidentiality. If the solicitor knows that the patient is experiencing certain symptoms of mental disorder, he may not positively assert that that is not the case, even if this is the responsible medical officer's evidence. That would amount to misleading the tribunal. Accordingly, the position is analogous to that where a solicitor knows that a defendant in criminal proceedings has previous convictions. He may not describe him as being of good character

---

[41] The practice usually emerges when a patient not discharged from detention under section 2 then appeals against his subsequent detention under section 3 and, being dissatisfied, instructs a new solicitor to represent him. The Solicitors Complaints Bureau used to be unwilling to investigate the matter on the ground that the only evidence of impropriety was the word of a detained patient. Whether the Office for the Supervision of Solicitors takes a different view has yet to be seen.

simply because the court knows of none. The qualified view is that in wholly exceptional circumstances a solicitor would be justified in disclosing something told to him in confidence. For example, if a tribunal was clearly proceeding on the erroneous basis that there was no immediate significant risk of suicide or homicide. The solicitor's obligations then become similar to those of a medical practitioner as defined in the case of *W. v. Egdell* (**711**): onerous but not absolute.

Professional guidance

The *Guide to the Professional Conduct of Solicitors* states that a solicitor is under a duty to keep confidential a client's affairs.[42] The guide, and the commentaries that form part of it, then set out certain exceptions to this duty but these are mainly statutory.[43] The previous edition of the guide included a further exception, which the Law Society still refers to when appropriate. This was that a "solicitor may reveal information which would otherwise be confidential to the extent that he believes necessary to prevent the client from committing a criminal act that the solicitor believes on reasonable grounds is likely to result in serious bodily harm." Suicide is, of course, no longer a crime but, as to this, rule 1(c) of the Solicitors' Practice Rules 1990 provides that a solicitor owes a duty to act in the best interests of the client. As to how to approach any problems in practice, the current view of The Law Society's Mental Health Sub-Committee is set out below.

Advice of the Law Society's Mental Health Sub-committee

1 So far as possible, the solicitor should act in accordance with the client's instructions, and the solicitor's own morality or religious beliefs should not affect this.

2 The solicitor should, so far as possible, make clear to the client any limits to his duty of confidentiality at the outset, before taking instructions.

3 When placed in a situation where the solicitor has concerns as to the client's mental capacity, and where the client may pose a risk to himself or others, the solicitor should seek advice from the Professional Ethics division in relation to the particular circumstances of the case.

4 Where the solicitor feels it is essential to disclose information confided in him by the client, the solicitor should advise the client that unless the client agrees to disclosure, the solicitor will cease to act.

5 That clients have the right to be heard, and for their views (however bizarre) to be represented.

6 Each case must be considered on its own merits having regard for all the facts.

THE USE OF COUNSEL

It is possible for a representative to have two tribunal cases at different hospitals listed for hearing at the same time. This most often occurs in relation to section 2 cases. When deciding whether or not to accept such instructions, all that can be done is to assess the likelihood of conflicting hearings and to advise the client of the possibility. Where two hearings do coincide, it is preferable to arrange an agency with another panel member rather than to use counsel, unless a particular barrister has a proven competency in the field.

---

[42] *The Guide to the Professional Conduct of Solicitors* (The Law Society, 6th ed., 1993), para. 16.01.
[43] *Ibid.*, para. 16.04.

THE FIRST INTERVIEW — 1. INITIAL STEPS

In this case of existing clients, the initial preparation for the first interview involves retrieving old files from storage. Even if they do not relate to previous tribunal applications, they may contain useful biographical details, information about the client's medical and forensic history, and so forth. The steps which can be taken without the client's express consent are, however, limited and most must be held over until he has seen the solicitor and provided him with instructions.

THE PURPOSE OF THE FIRST INTERVIEW

It is important to be clear about the purpose of the first interview. In assessment cases, where time is of the essence, it is necessary to obtain a full history from the initial interview. However, this may difficult if a recently admitted client remains acutely ill and is, for example, in the manic phase of an illness. In other cases, where reports will be available before any hearing date, and there will be further opportunities to meet the client, more time can be spent simply allowing him to raise and develop his concerns, with the aim of gaining a reasonable understanding of the underlying anxieties and objectives. Where possible, questions should be open-ended, information seeking, and non-judgemental, covering general topics such as schooling, family background, physical health, ward activities, and so forth. It is usually unhelpful to immediately probe, dissect and confront a client's personal beliefs and attitude to treatment. Too challenging an approach leads to resentment and guardedness, and a poor working relationship. Furthermore, because the development of false, irrational, beliefs may for some people be a necessary survival mechanism, a frontal assault on these defensive positions by the forces of logic may also be dangerous for the individual's mental health. In restricted cases, preliminary discussion about the index offence can initially be limited to obtaining factual information about the trial court, the dates of conviction and sentence, the offence charged, the plea, the essence of the prosecution case, the identity of the patient's solicitors in the proceedings, whether an appeal was lodged, and details of other convictions. It is particularly important to be positive and reassuring at the first interview, without making false promises. Some acute wards are very frightening places for those confined in them so the client may be afraid and desperate to be allowed home. A client whose case has been referred to the tribunal, or who has applied unsuccessfully in the past, may also be unduly pessimistic about his chances.

MAKING THE ARRANGEMENTS

Appointments are generally agreed both with the client and the nurse in charge of the ward on which he is detained. It is sensible to verify that the appointment does not interfere with meal-times, other prior appointments, leave arrangements, family visits, and therapeutic activities such as ward rounds and occupational therapy. It is particularly wise to check any weekend leave arrangements if the plan is to see the client during a Monday morning or a Friday afternoon. If an interview early in the day is necessary, perhaps at 8.30am prior to a morning hearing, it is important that the client still has a full breakfast if he is to be at his best. The Legal Aid Board's interpretation of the green form regulations is that a solicitor cannot claim a fee for the time and expense incurred travelling to hospital for the first visit, because no green form signed by the patient yet exists. This restriction should therefore be borne in mind when making the initial appointment. It may be that the hospital can be visited at either end of the day, on the way to or from the office, or the appointment can be combined with a previously scheduled visit to another client there.

Confirming the appointment

Whatever the arrangements, it is advisable to telephone the ward before departing for the hospital, in order to confirm that the patient is present and that he has not been regraded to informal status. It is not unknown for nurses to forget to enter an appointment in the ward diary or to fail to alert colleagues on another shift of the visit. A final check also ensures that another solicitor has not already visited the patient, because more than one person was making arrangements on his behalf.

EXAMINING THE AUTHORITY FOR THE PATIENT'S DETENTION

It cannot be assumed that there is a valid authority for the patient's detention. Accordingly, the first task on arriving at the hospital is to examine the original application or order, which is usually held by the Mental Health Act Administrator, and to obtain a copy of it. Although it is normal practice to keep copies of statutory documents in the patient's case notes on the ward, their inspection is not a safe substitute for scrutinising the originals. This is because the ward copies are often made at the time of admission and do not show any amendments made during the following fortnight, pursuant to section 15 of the Act (**265**). Even where the one is a perfect copy of the other, it may be impossible to know from the photocopies whether a particular entry is in different coloured ink and is a subsequent addition. In general terms, the representative will wish to verify that the statutory requirements were complied with, to note the reasons for invoking the compulsory powers, and to check whether the client was an informal in-patient at the time or was subject to some prior authority for his detention. Any periodic renewals of the authority should be similarly scrutinised. If the authority is materially irregular but the rectification period has not yet expired, the client may prefer to let it expire before the point is canvassed on his behalf. Procedural requirements and irregularities were considered in Chapter 4 (**253, 271**). Possible remedies include an application for habeas corpus (**861**) or judicial review (**857**), or submitting that a tribunal may have regard to the irregularity when determining whether to exercise its discretionary power of discharge (**574**).

ARRIVING ON THE WARD

If the door to an open ward is locked, this is normally because nursing staff shortages preclude continuously observing a patient who has previously absented himself without leave. Careful observation on entering the ward, and during the short walk to the nurses' office, often yields relevant information. It will be apparent whether the ward is an acute facility. Asleep or drowsy patients slumped across communal sofas or chairs indicate the use of relatively high doses of medication, and often also that patients' rooms are locked during the day, in order to encourage participation in ward activities. A disturbed ward atmosphere may reflect a restricted programme of recreational activities or be attributable to the limited availability of non-medicinal therapies. Occasionally, a neglected patient may be obviously distressed and in need of nursing assistance. These, and similar, general impressions should be noted in case they later assume a relevance in the context of the tribunal proceedings — for example, a plea to the tribunal to exercise its discretionary power of discharge or to recommend that the patient is granted leave or transferred to another hospital.

The patients' board

On entering the ward office, the information on the patients' board should be examined. This usually lists the age, gender, legal status, responsible medical officer and key nurse of each patient. It may also specify the date of compulsory applications and orders, which patients are on leave, the level of bed occupancy, whether any seclusion room is in use, and each patient's observation and pass status (*e.g.* that a patient is subject to continuous observation or that he has escorted ground leave). The information recorded on the board is therefore a useful guide to the nature of the ward, the pressures on staff and ward resources, the use made of compulsory powers, and staff decisions about managing detained patients based on perceptions of their mental states and the associated risks.

DISCUSSING THE CASE WITH NURSING STAFF

The consultant's contact with a patient may be limited to attending the weekly ward round and, consequently, nursing and junior medical staff are often better placed to comment on his mental state. They should be able to summarise the ward activities; the patient's conduct and progress since admission; his treatment plan and compliance with it; relevant developments in terms of leave; the stage which discharge and after-care planning has reached; and any historical trends about response to medication and the acceptance of informal treatment and after-care. It is therefore useful to ascertain the views of nursing staff, the more so if hospital practice is to provide a nursing report for tribunal hearings. It may, however, be more prudent to do this after first meeting the patient and explaining the need to discuss his case with staff. The client will have misgivings about the independence of a solicitor who was chosen for him by an officer of the detaining authority if he is first observed chatting amiably to nurses with whom he is clearly acquainted.

INSPECTING THE CASE NOTES

The majority of consultants have no objection to the patient's solicitor reading the case notes and it may even be ward policy to allow nurses a broad discretion about making them available to representatives. However, if the notes are proffered by a nurse who mistakenly believes that the solicitor is entitled to inspection under the tribunal rules, accepting them without more amounts to taking unfair advantage of that person's inexperience, and so may constitute professional misconduct. If there is any possibility of misunderstanding, the representative should explain the correct position. This is that the rules confer no right of inspection but it would be helpful to see the notes and also save professional time, by avoiding the need to make a statutory application. The nurse can then refer the matter to the charge nurse, or a doctor in the consultant's team, who can decide how to respond to the request.

BEING INTRODUCED TO THE PATIENT

The representative will need to be introduced to his prospective client and require the use of a private room. It may be suggested that a nurse is present during the interview if the client is thought to be unpredictably aggressive but the confidentiality of the solicitor-client relationship precludes this. It is impossible to overemphasise the importance of greeting the client warmly and confidently, approaching him with an outstretched hand. This demonstrates a friendly and receptive approach, a determination not to prejudge the man on the basis of facts or opinions reported by others, and a lack of any apprehension. In terms of personal safety, such first impressions are important because aggressive or violent conduct, while very rare, is most often triggered by a perception that the prospective victim is at some level a threat, or hostile, or is susceptible to physical intimidation.

COMMENCING THE INTERVIEW

A positive and helpful way of beginning the interview is for the representative to stress that he is legally qualified; independent of the hospital; there to act as the patient's advocate, by helping him to formulate and present a case for discharge; that he therefore wishes to hear how he can help; and that what is discussed is confidential unless the client wishes the point to be advanced on his behalf. Possible alternative remedies and the essential features of tribunal proceedings should then be outlined, the client's broad aims elicited (**924**), and legal aid forms (and any necessary tribunal application form) completed (**879, 619**).

Explaining and exploring alternative remedies

It is important not to assume that a tribunal application is the best or only way forward simply because proceedings have been commenced or the visit was arranged in order to complete such an application. The alternative ways of being discharged from liability to detention must be summarised and discussed at the outset, and the client's entitlement to make the tribunal application verified. A note to contact the nearest relative should be made if there is any possibility that he may be willing to complete an order for discharge. In practice, the nearest relative is often unaware that he possesses this power, partly because of ambiguities in the Department of Health's statutory rights leaflets. High Court proceedings or a concurrent appeal to the hospital managers (**144**) may be appropriate depending upon the facts.

Explaining the tribunal proceedings

The representative should explain that tribunals are independent bodies which exist to ensure that citizens are not detained or liable to compulsory treatment for any longer than is necessary. Legal help is free of charge and this assistance usually includes obtaining necessary expert reports from doctors and other professionals independent of the detaining hospital. In non-restricted cases, it is worth mentioning that a tribunal which does not discharge a patient may still make certain recommendations with a view to facilitating his future discharge (**474, 495**). If the patient's case has been referred to the tribunal then who has taken this action, and why, should be made clear. The risks of making a tribunal application should also be explained. The general principle in civil cases is that a tribunal can only lead to a relaxation of the current regime. It has no power to further restrict the patient's liberty and there is therefore nothing to be lost. However, if the client is detained for treatment, there is now the possibility if he is not discharged that the tribunal will recommend that a supervision application is made. Different caveats apply to restricted patients. Any previous tribunal decision for the patient's conditional discharge which was deferred will lapse (**513**) and there is the risk of a return to prison custody if the client is subject to a restriction or limitation direction (**386, 556**). Similarly, if the client is detained under section 48 and involved in on-going criminal proceedings, there will be a risk of evidence emerging at the hearing which is adverse to the criminal trial or the preferred disposal.

The client's aims and expectations

The client may not have been aware of the range of decisions which a tribunal may make following the hearing. Conversely, if a restricted patient, he may have mistakenly believed that a tribunal has power to order or recommend his transfer to another hospital or that it has a general power to review any compulsory treatment being administered. While the explanation of the tribunal's powers is still fresh in an *unrestricted* client's mind, it is worthwhile obtaining his preliminary thoughts about which of the various alternatives he would regard as an improvement on his current situation: leave of absence at home; a transfer to a different hospital; living in the community under a guardian. Some clients object to being liable to detention, others to being in hospital, others to both. Is therefore useful to establish whether it is more important to be at home, even if on section, or to be off section even if in hospital. Where the client's concerns lie outside the tribunal's remit, for example obtaining a second opinion about medication, the appropriate remedy should be explained and any necessary help offered.

Completing legal aid forms

If the client has not already applied to the tribunal and, having been advised, now wishes to do this, the necessary form or letter of application should be signed. An application for Assistance by way of Representation (ABWOR) and, where necessary, a green form should also be completed. It may sometimes be necessary to telephone the Legal Aid Board from the ward, either to obtain an immediate grant of ABWOR or an extension of the green form limit (**880**). If the client has significant savings, he should be asked whether his financial affairs are subject to the jurisdiction of the Court of Protection (**696**) or a power of attorney (**698**).

The client's account of his financial circumstances, etc.

The way in which the legal aid forms are completed and signed, especially the financial part of the form, may be informative and an early, if unreliable, guide to some of the areas of concern which led to the client's compulsory admission. If the client is unable to sign his name, this may reflect limited intellectual ability, a cognitive deficit, or educational deprivation. A woefully misdirected signature, located some considerable distance from the place indicated, is significant. Marked tremor and a shaky signature may be due to the side-effects of medication or some other condition affecting the client's co-ordination. The client may have an excellent recollection of his personal and financial circumstances, knowing his national insurance number, post code, the precise amount which he receives each week, and so forth. Alternatively, at its worst, there may be a rudimentary or chaotic understanding of his financial position, perhaps in a person who previously managed his own business and who is therefore functioning well below his optimum level. The client may not even have been receiving state benefits prior to admission because of the developing chaos and the absence of anyone to help him overcome such difficulties. The basic information recorded on the form will, of course, tell the solicitor whether the client is married, has children, and whether he has substantial savings (and could afford private medical care). Asking about debts may reveal poverty, substantial credit card bills and excessive spending during a manic phase, and pending litigation in connection with unpaid liabilities such as rent arrears. These stresses may have been instrumental in causing the client to break down or be the consequence of his breakdown. Either way, it is often a case of surveying the wreckage.

FIRST INTERVIEW — 2. PRELIMINARY OBSERVATIONS

The nature of the proceedings means that it is important to be observant and to record any distinctive features which may provide a clue to the client's state of health or be relevant to the conduct and outcome of the case. As with any social situation, quite important information and preliminary impressions are conveyed before any meaningful conversation actually takes place. By the time any interview commences, a legal representative or other observer may already have gathered quite a lot of information relevant to the case—

- In rare cases, the client's consciousness may be obviously impaired (**894**). This is, however, exceptional and generally only ever seen following a mandatory reference or an application by the nearest relative.

- Where the client's consciousness is not obviously impaired, the first thing to strike the visitor on seeing him may be his level of activity; he is either markedly over-active or under-active (**894**).

- If the client is sitting or standing relatively still when he is approached, this provides an opportunity to observe his posture, which may be unremarkable or idiosyncratic (**895**).

- On being introduced to the client, certain aspects of his general appearance may be noticeable. More specifically, certain mannerisms or gestures may be striking or there may be evidence of poor self-care (**896**).

- On walking with the client to the interview room, and getting settled there, some type of involuntary movement may be conspicuous (**898**).

Recording and describing what is observed

Observations of these kinds will inevitably lead the representative to make a mental note to ask certain questions, or to explore certain areas, later during the interview or, if more natural, on another occasion. The medical terminology used to describe abnormalities in these different areas of functioning is dealt with later but, where necessary, the main points are briefly summarised in this chapter.

PRELIMINARY OBSERVATIONS

• consciousness	• mannerisms and gestures
• responsiveness	• appearance
• level of activity	• self-care
• posture (the relative position of the parts of the body at rest)	• gait (style or manner of walking)

IMPAIRED CONSCIOUSNESS

Consciousness is the awareness of one's own internal thoughts and feelings together with the ability to recognise one's external environment. To be unconscious is to have no subjective experience. Consciousness is a continuum with full alertness and awareness at one end and brain death at the other. **Clouding of consciousness** describes impairment of orientation, perception and attention and it is seen in organic mental disorders. There is difficulty with thinking, attention, perception, memory and usually drowsiness but sometimes excitability.

Full alertness/ awareness	Clouding of Consciousness	Sopor	Coma	Brain death

Disorientation, attention and concentration

Disorientation is an impaired awareness of oneself in relation to time (the date or time of day), place (where one is) and identity (whether one's own or others), as a result of which speech and behaviour tend to be muddled. To be attentive is to be alert, aware and responsive while to concentrate is to focus and sustain mental activity on a task. Usually, it will quite quickly be obvious whether or not a client is disorientated. If not, it is worthwhile asking the patient the time of day since commonly this is the first element of orientation to suffer in cases of mild impairment of consciousness or of intellectual impairment. The client may also be asked to complete the legal aid form himself, or simply asked for the date. If it is apparent that the patient may not be orientated, he may be asked to give the date, year, time, day of the week, name of the hospital, county the hospital is situated within, and (if applicable) the floor on which the ward is situated.

Causes of disorientation, etc.

Disorientation may be the product of clouding of consciousness, due to a head injury or chronic brain disorder such as dementia, or the result of intoxication. Relatively minor impairment of consciousness may only become apparent, if at all, after the interview's commencement as a result of difficulty obtaining adequate instructions due to impaired concentration or attention. Poor attention and concentration are usually the products of tiredness or disinterest.[44] However, in some cases, they may be more pervasive, reflecting a general lowering of alertness and awareness or an incapacity to focus and sustain mental activity. This may be because of emotional disturbance, mental impairment, an illness such as schizophrenia or depression, or clouding of consciousness.

---

[44] There are many reasons why a client may not adequately answer a series of simple questions clearly aimed at obtaining from him a basic factual account of past events. Most often, the problem is simply a lack of enthusiasm for questions asked on countless previous occasions. In the context of the tribunal proceedings, the professionals involved in making the original application, the doctor who prepares the medical report for the tribunal, the social worker who prepares the social circumstances report, the nurse preparing any nursing report, the medical member of the tribunal, and concerned family members may all have recently spoken with the patient about his circumstances at some length. The solicitor must explain that he may not be able to examine the notes and it is essential that he knows in advance of any relevant information which may be raised at the hearing.

CLIENT UNRESPONSIVE

Stupor denotes awareness accompanied by profound lack of responsiveness. A person may be fully conscious and yet profoundly unresponsive to his immediate environment. While terms such as coma and sopor describe a substantial impairment of consciousness, stupor describes a profound lack of responsiveness to external stimuli and the environment, rather than profound unawareness of it. The two components of stupor are a voluntary absence of any movement (akinesia) and a voluntary absence of any speech (muteness). Where a state of stupor appears to form part of a catatonic schizophrenic illness, it is usually described as catatonic stupor.

SLOWED OR INCREASED ACTIVITY

Retardation is a general slowing down of the conscious patient's mental and bodily functions — a slowing of his thoughts, speech, actions, reactions and movement. Over-activity for substantial periods of time, evidenced by over-talkativeness, restlessness, pacing rapidly up and down, constant talking or loud singing is known as **pressure of activity**. In manic states, such pressure of activity is often accompanied by correspondingly accelerated speech, grandiosity and elation. The term **catatonic agitation** is preferred in the ICD glossary, where it refers to a state in which the psychomotor features of anxiety are associated with catatonic syndromes. Here, the patient's restlessness and activity are associated with his abnormal ideas and perceptions rather than his mood (the degree of elation or depression present).

	Normal range of responsiveness	Psychomotor Retardation	Stupor
Catatonic excitement			Catatonic stupor

Is the client over-active for substantial periods of time, as evidenced by being over-talkative, restless, pacing rapidly up and down, constantly talking or singing loudly?

CLIENT'S POSTURE OR ATTITUDE

A patient's posture may sometimes be described as manneristic or stereotyped. Conventionally, **manneristic postures** differ from **stereotyped postures** in that the former are not rigidly maintained. The term **catatonic posturing** describes the voluntary assumption of an inappropriate or bizarre posture which is usually held for a long period of time. For example, a patient standing with arms out-stretched as if he were Jesus on the cross. The terms **catalepsy, catatonic waxy flexibility and flexibilitas cerea** are synonymous and they describe a physical state of sudden onset in which the muscles of the face, body and limbs are maintained by increased muscle tone in a semi-rigid position, possibly for several hours and during which time neither expression or bodily position will change.

MANNERISMS, GESTURES, RITUALS, COMPULSIONS

Mannerisms are gestures or expressions peculiar to a person, such as an odd way of walking or eating. They differ from spontaneous, involuntary, movements (dyskinesias, **1065**) in that they are voluntary, if idiosyncratic, movements. They differ from stereotyped behaviour in that the latter is carried out in an unvarying, repetitive, manner and is not goal-directed. Stereotyped behaviour, or **stereotypy**, is the constant, almost mechanical, repetition of an action. For example, pacing the same circle each day or repetitive hand movements. A **compulsion** is an irresistible impulse to perform an irrational act which the individual recognises is irrational or senseless and which he attributes to subjective necessity rather than to external influences. Performing the act may afford some relief of tension. Compulsive behaviour may be attributable to obsessional ideas. The terms **"obsession"** and "compulsion" are not synonymous. The former refers to a thought and the latter to an act. A thought may properly be described as obsessional if a person cannot prevent himself from repeatedly, insistently, having that thought albeit that the content of the thought is not delusional in nature. Obsessive thoughts lie behind compulsive acts and stereotyped, manneristic behaviour but they may exist without being externally manifested in the form of an objectively observable repetitive action.

Does the client may exhibit a repetitive pattern of speaking, moving or walking? Does he imitate or copy the movements of another person (echopraxia)? Does he carry out actions in response to an impulse which he has a desire to restrict, or knows is absurd or gratuitous, but nevertheless feels impelled to execute? Does this impulse come from within him or from some body or force outside him? Does he believe that repeatedly carrying out the particular action is in any way strange or odd? Is he obsessed with certain thoughts albeit that the thought itself is not delusional in nature? Is he able to exercise control over those thoughts or do they control him so that he cannot prevent himself from having them?

GENERAL APPEARANCE

The client's physical appearance may give a clue as to why he is in hospital even if he does not raise the matter himself. There may be signs of recent physical injury, possibly sustained during a suicide attempt leading to the client's admission. These injuries may suggest jumping or contact with a motor vehicle. However, superficial, multiple lacerations of the arms and wrists are most often not indicative of attempted suicide but a way of relieving acute tension. Facial cuts and bruises may result from head-banging or other forms of self-abuse, such as punching oneself in the face, or be due to recent falls caused by medication-induced hypotension. "Track-marks" on the arms may indicate the use of injectable street drugs. Other irregularities of appearance which will be readily apparent to any observer are those relating to the client's weight and unusual facial characteristics, *e.g.* nystagmus, tics, and oedema. As to the possible significance, and therefore the reason for recording, such characteristics, see page 1068. In yet other cases, some part of the client's body is obviously misshapen. This may cruelly be referred to as a physical deformity and sometimes, for that very reason, relevant to the client's mental health, because it grossly undermines his self-confidence and self-esteem.

Are there any signs of physical injury, unusual facial characteristics, disfigurement, or significant weight loss?

Self-care

It may seem that the client has neglected his appearance. For example, he has not washed or shaved or changed his clothes recently, or he is inadequately dressed given the temperature and other conditions on the ward. These signs may be evidence of recent or long-standing difficulties with self-care attributable to an incapacitating mental disorder. If so, the legal relevance of such self-neglect will be two-fold. Firstly, as an indicator that the client suffers from a mental disorder the nature or degree of which is sufficiently severe to affect not only higher human functions but also basic self-care skills. Secondly, a tribunal which is considering whether to discharge at its discretion must often have regard to the likelihood of the patient then being able to care for himself or to obtain the care he needs. In tribunal proceedings, poor self-care is most often seen in cases involving long-stay patients with chronic schizophrenia marked by profound negative symptoms and social withdrawal. However, self-neglect may be a consequence of many other medical conditions: delusional beliefs about washing, often with a religious content (*e.g.* the client has let his beard grow and cultivated a Jesus-like appearance); depression with retardation or stupor; dementia; mental impairment; and obsessive-compulsive disorders.[45] There are, however, many reasons why a client's appearance may be poor apart from mental disorder. The sedative effects of medication may be profoundly disabling and render him incapable of attending to even the most basic tasks of daily living. In the case of older people thought to confused and to have dementia, their appearance may have relatively little to do with their own mental state. The laundry service may be deficient, soiled clothes bundled together without being properly marked, and so gradually lost or returned to owners in a chaotic manner. Other confused patients may have appropriated the client's clothes, believing them and the client's room to be their own. If the client was not admitted from home, his appearance may reflect the admission circumstances and a lack of consideration for his welfare. It may be that, although detained a week ago, he still has only the clothes which he is wearing; no one has gone back to his flat to collect spare clothing, toiletries, and shaving materials. Lastly, the effects of poverty should never be underestimated. It may be that the client cannot afford to spend more on self-care and his mental state, if abnormal at all, has deteriorated because of this rather than vice-versa.

Is there anything to suggest that the client has difficulty caring for himself, whether because of illness, the sedative effects of medication, or some other reason such as mental impairment or advanced age. Does he noticeably neglect his appearance? Does he maintain a reasonable level of hygiene? Is the client in any way concerned about his appearance? What reasons does the client give for his appearance? When absolutely necessary, can the client get up at a required time?

Clothes and artefacts

The other thing which may be immediately striking about the client is his clothes or the artefacts he has with him. It may be clear that some colour or possession has a particular importance for him and this is associated with the cause of his detention.

---

[45]   For example, the client who spends 20 minutes putting on each sock and shoe, not moving on until he is satisfied that each item has been put on perfectly.

ABNORMAL GAIT AND PROBLEMS CO-ORDINATING MOVEMENTS

If there is nothing distinctive about the client's appearance, posture or his level of activity, it may be that the way he moves is distinctive. Some uncontrollable movement of the body, affecting the face, head, trunk or limbs, is apparent.

INVOLUNTARY MOVEMENTS (1062)

- **Ataxia**
  An inability to co-ordinate muscles in the execution of voluntary movement. The typical ataxic gait is lurching and unsteady like that of a drunkard, with the feet widely placed and a tendency to reel to one side.

- **Tremor**
  A rhythmic, repetitive movement of some part of the body which results from the alternating contractions of opposing muscle groups.

- **Dystonia**
  Dystonia is an abnormal muscular rigidity causing painful and sustained muscle spasms of some part of the body, unusually fixed postures, or strange movement patterns. Dystonic movements usually take the form of a twisting or turning motion of the neck, the trunk, or the proximal parts of the extremities, and they are therefore powerful and deforming, grossly interfering with voluntary movement and perverting posture.

- **Spasms**
  Spasms are powerful contractions of a muscle or muscles, experienced as pronounced, spasmodic jerks of the muscles. Hiccups, cramp, tics and habit-spasms are types of muscular spasm.

- **Clonus**
  Muscles usually respond to being stretched by contracting once and then relaxing. Where stretching sets off a rapid series of muscle contractions, this is referred to as clonus (a word meaning "turmoil").

- **Athetosis**
  Slow, irregular, and continuous twisting of muscles in the distal portions of the arms and legs. These sinuous movements are bilateral (evident on both sides of the body); symmetric (both sides of the body are similarly affected); and most evident at the extremities — with exaggerated writhing motions of the fingers spread in a manner reminiscent of a snake-charmer, alternate flexion and extension of the wrists, and twisting of the muscles in the hands, fingers, feet and toes.

- **Chorea**
  Chorea is characterised by quick, irregular, spasmodic and jerky involuntary movement of muscles, usually affecting the face, limbs and trunk. The movements resemble voluntary movements but are continuously interrupted prior to being completed. There is a general air of restlessness and, characteristically, impaired ability to maintain a posture. Those parts of the limbs closest to the trunk (the proximal portions) are more affected than those further away (the distal portions). Choreic and athetosis movements may exist in conjunction, when their combined effect is referred to as choreo-athetosis.

- **Tardive dyskinesia**
  A movement disorder which appears late in treatment, characteristically after long-term treatment with antipsychotic drugs. Involuntary, slow, irregular movements of the tongue, lips, mouth, and trunk, and choreo-athetoid movements of the extremities are common.

- **Akathisia**
  A restless inability to sit still ("a motor restlessness") and, specifically, a feeling of muscular quivering, often seen as a side-effect of neuroleptic medication or a complication of Parkinson's disease.

Dyskinesia (literally, bad or difficult movement) is a general term used to describe difficult or distorted voluntary movements. It covers various forms of abnormal movement, including tremor, tics, ballismus, chorea, habit-spasm, torticollis, torsion-spasm, athetosis, chorea, dystonia, and myoclonus. Such conditions typically involve uncontrollable movements of the trunk or limbs which cannot be suppressed and impair the execution of voluntary movements. The whole body may be involved or the problem restricted to a particular group of muscles.

- *Is there any evidence of involuntary movements?*

- *Does the problem appear to be one of lack of co-ordination?*

- *Are the movements repetitive?*

- *Do they seem to consist of muscle spasms?*

- *Are the movements bilateral (evident on both sides of the body)?*

- *Are they symmetric (both sides of the body are similarly affected)?*

- *Are they most evident at the extremities (the hands, fingers, feet and toes)?*

- *Is the trunk involved?*

INTERVIEW — 3. TAKING THE CASE HISTORY

Before discussing in detail any alleged abnormal mental phenomena with the client it is best to take a full and systematic case history. This will reveal many of the areas which need to be explored and it ensures that relevant information is not overlooked. It is also less contentious than launching straight into a discussion of the client's beliefs and other experiences. It gives the representative an opportunity to first get to know the client and to form an impression of the most sensitive way of exploring sensitive issues. If it is not possible to take a detailed case history, and this is not likely to be possible within the time available because of the client's level of functioning, access to the case notes should be sought. The references alongside the headings below are references to the relevant part of the case summary form printed as an appendix to this part of the book.

BASIC FACTUAL INFORMATION (1)

In order to save time later, the first task is to obtain basic biographical information and details of relevant addresses and telephone numbers. The representative will wish to know who is the patient's responsible medical officer, who is his social worker and primary nurse, and to verify his legal status. Details will then be required of the patient's nationality and of his family circumstances, including what level of support they do or can offer him. This information will also enable the representative to ascertain whether the nearest relative has been correctly identified.

Family composition and family relationships

The patient's relationship with his family is often quite difficult and there may be little family support to draw upon. Again, it is worthwhile obtaining general background information about the client's childhood relationships with his parents and siblings and the general atmosphere at home. Also, if relevant, when these relationships began to deteriorate and the reasons for that. Histories of sexual abuse, parental divorce or separation, and general family problems, are disproportionately common amongst people compulsorily admitted to hospital. In the context of schizophrenia, the family environment may contribute both to its development and to the likelihood of relapse (**1264**). The family history may reveal highly distressing events, such as the death of a relative shortly prior to admission, or a family history of mental ill-health.

What contact does the client have with his parents and siblings? Do they know he is in hospital and, if so, have they visited him? Have they expressed any concern about his health or behaviour during recent months?

Attitude of client's spouse

Not uncommonly, separation or divorce proceedings are ongoing at the time of admission. Apart from the psychological distress, this raises the question of whether the spouse was the nearest relative at the time of the admission and, hence, the issue of the application's legality. At any rate, the spouse may now be disqualified and the person now entitled willing to consider making an order for discharge. The attitude of the patient's spouse may be that the patient cannot return home or that the children have suffered psychologically because of the client's illness. In such cases, the calling in of a social worker, or the spouse's willingness to make the application, may be affected by the fact that committal to hospital is an easier way of ousting the patient from his home than taking proceedings in the county court. However, in terms of section 72, it is not necessary to deprive a person of his liberty to be in the community if there are other ways of protecting family members.

IDENTIFYING THE NEAREST RELATIVE (2)

Having taken the family details, it should be possible to identify the nearest relative and to record the necessary information about him. Before doing so, the representative should verify that no county court order is in force. If the client says that some other person other than his statutory nearest relative is acting in that capacity, the ward staff and hospital Mental Health Act Administrator should be asked if any written authority has been given under regulation 14. As to ascertaining who is the nearest relative, see page 100. If the nearest relative may be willing to order the patient's discharge, he should be contacted forthwith. However, not too much reliance should be placed on the client's assessment of the likelihood of this and he should be warned that most relatives feel bound by the medical advice. It is important not to build up his expectations in any way and to ensure that family relationships are maintained.

Who is the nearest relative? Was the nearest relative correctly identified on the application? If not, what are the legal consequences of this? If the nearest relative was not consulted prior to a section 3 application being made, did either of the exceptions referred to in section 11(4) apply? Is the nearest relative now willing to order the patient's discharge if he has that power?

ACCOMMODATION (3)

The next area to explore is the issue of accommodation. When a person's mental state is deteriorating, it is not uncommon for rent or mortgage instalments to go unpaid, for problems with neighbours to arise, or for a landlord's property to be damaged. It is therefore important to ascertain whether any debts or court proceedings are outstanding which may affect the client's ability to return home following discharge. If the client has no accommodation to go to but is detained for treatment then he will be entitled to after-care upon leaving hospital. The issue of a patient's entitlement to be rehoused has already been dealt with in the context of after-care and the social circumstances report (**413, 690, 745**). The social worker dealing with the case should be approached about this. In some cases, the local after-care bodies may wish to place the client in supervised accommodation but there be a resistance to this suggestion. If so, guardianship may be being considered.

Does the client have accommodation to go to? Are there any rent arrears and/or possession proceedings pending which need to be sorted out? Is the accommodation currently fit for human habitation?

EDUCATION, TRAINING AND EMPLOYMENT (4)

The client's educational and employment history are important because they help to define how severe are the effects of any illness or disability, point to the likely opportunities for him in the immediate future, and are a good indicator of social and economic deprivation. Not surprisingly, many more poor people suffer mental ill-health, just as they do physical ill-health. While medication offers symptomatic relief, those symptoms were only ever surface phenomena, the superficial manifestations of the mental disorder or conflict. Improving the patient's underlying mental state and self-esteem, as opposed to merely suppressing the worst symptoms, often necessitates improving his social situation and opportunities.

Education

The client's educational history is often a good, if not totally reliable, yardstick against which to assess his current level of mental functioning. It may also yield information about the duration and possible causes of any illness or relapse. Where a dementing process is suspected in an older person, it is the relative decline in which one is particularly interested and which provides the context for interpreting the results of psychometric testing. A disproportionate number of detained patients relative to the population at large will have attended a special school for children with behavioural difficulties. In some cases, a careful history will reveal that the individual first experienced auditory hallucinations or other distressing mental phenomena from a very early age and this information is often not recorded in the case notes or psychiatric report.[46] For example, the client may say that he had the feeling that graffiti on the blackboard contained some special message for him, or that the violent conduct which led to his being removed from school was a response to voices commanding him to act in that way. He may say that he felt an outsider at school, different from the other children, had few friends or, alternatively, that he

---

[46] The received wisdom is that children very rarely have these experiences and hence they are rarely sought or recorded.

enjoyed his schooling, and did well until reaching a certain age when his performance and interest declined. All of this information will be relevant in determining the nature of his illness and its effect on his health.

How well, if at all, can the client read and write? Is there any suggestion that his intelligence is significantly below average? When did he leave full-time education and why? If he left school early, did he then manage to obtain work? Did the client ever see an educational psychologist while at school? Was his behaviour at school disturbed and did he attend a special school? Is his current level of intellectual functioning substantially below what one would expect given his education?

Employment history

The benefits of obtaining details of the client's employment history are similar. Quite often, the pattern will be that the client has never been in regular employment since leaving school; has not worked for many years since he was first admitted to hospital; or had a stable employment record over a period of time until perhaps a year prior to his first admission. In the latter case, there is often evidence of a decline in performance and professional relationships leading up to an indefinite period of sick leave, resignation, suspension, or dismissal. Sometimes this is in the context of a feeling that colleagues at work were conspiring against the client. There is still an unfortunate tendency to regard people with schizophrenia as unfit for any sort of employment or training which does not involve mundane tasks such as putting flights on darts or packing boxes. However, it is usually more beneficial not to advise the client to jettison unfulfilled ambitions and opportunities simply because he is or has been ill. Better to emphasise the importance of accepting medical treatment and supervision as ways of achieving stability and maximising the prospect of a return to some activity which interests the client and he finds fulfilling. It is hardly surprising that so many able clients become disabled if they are encouraged all the time not to exercise their abilities. This is nothing more than what used to be called institutionalisation, and the risk of non-compliance with treatment and relapse may well be greater if the message is that insight and treatment involves living the life of an invalid. Even if it does keep the client well, well for what? For most people, treatment is a means to an end and there is little incentive in accepting that one is ill and would benefit from medication if the benefits of doing so are put in these terms. Although one would not think it from listening to medical evidence at tribunals, there are worse things than relapse, one of which is to lapse into invalidity.

- *Viewed historically, does his work record reveal any pattern? How long has he been in each post? Was he dismissed from any jobs? If he is unemployed, for how long? Has he undertaken any employment training courses, other than as a condition attached to receiving benefits? Are there currently any employment opportunities for him?*

- *Has the client's situation at work, school or college been a source of anxiety or worry for him? Has any particular event occurred which has caused him undue distress? Has there been any criticism of his performance? If the client is in work, is his job at risk because of his compulsory admission to hospital? For how long is the job likely to be kept open for him?*

Social and intellectual interests

Apart from being an interesting way of getting to know the client, discussing his social and intellectual interests often provides useful information about his mental health. If a person is inactive on the ward, this may reflect the limited range of available activities; that the prescribed medication affects his concentration and makes him drowsy; that he is depressed and has lost interest in activities which previously gave him pleasure; that his attention and concentration is impaired by auditory hallucinations and other abnormal perceptions; that he is dispirited at being detained; that he is frightened to participate because of the behaviour of other patients; or that his interest in intellectual and social activities has declined over the years, as institutionalisation or the negative symptoms of schizophrenia have set in. A limited range of social activities in the community prior to admission may have similar causes but there are also other possible explanations. A lonely existence may be due to financial or transport problems. If the former, the client's financial position needs to be reassessed and, if the latter, he may be entitled to a bus pass or to reapply for the restoration of a driving licence revoked on medical grounds. If the client's social interests have always been solitary ones, this suggests a natural shyness and introversion, perhaps a sensitivity to criticism, and a tendency to see the world as slightly hostile. On other occasions, it may be more the case that the client had virtually ceased to venture outdoors at all. This may be because of apathy, depression, stupor, agoraphobia, claustrophobia (sic), panic attacks, the disabling effects of compulsive dressing rituals, or a preoccupation with inner voices. He may have believed that neighbours or passers-by were surveying him or plotting against him, and have been frightened to go out, or be protecting his home from burglary, in the mistaken belief that there have been intruders. The loss of items misplaced by him in a confused state, or finding household appliances turned on which he did not remember leaving on, may be taken as evidence of this. If the client does go out and regularly visits certain clubs, this raises the possibility of a drug-induced psychosis in a person with no prior history of admissions.

Client's preoccupations

Details of books read in the past establish the likely extent of the client's vocabulary and this may be relevant if it is suspected that a degree of mental impairment is present or that he is now developing dementia. The subject-matter of any books or newspaper articles which he is reading may be illuminating. For example, whether they suggest a morbid interest in violence or pornography or are concerned with mysticism, the occult or political conspiracies. This may lead into a discussion about the role of supernatural forces and political forces in the events which culminated in the client's admission. More generally, the programmes which the client regularly watches again give an idea of his interests and educational background. If the client watches television or listens to the radio, he may be asked if any programmes have been of particular interest or relevance to his situation. It is not uncommon for someone with schizophrenia to believe that the programmes contain special messages or signs for him.

Did the client have an active social life previously or was he shy and reserved, preferring his own company and a more solitary existence? Was he active in any clubs or societies? What pursuits and intellectual activities did the patient previously enjoy? What were his hobbies and leisure interests? What books has he read?

FINANCIAL CIRCUMSTANCES (5)

The question of an in-patient's entitlement to state benefits following discharge from hospital has been dealt with in the context of the social circumstances report (**692**). Reckless spending leading to substantial financial liabilities at the time of admission is not uncommon during manic phases if the client was previously credit-worthy. This inevitably has serious repercussions for the family's economic welfare if it is now impossible to pay the mortgage, rent or other regular outgoings, and the client cannot return to work. There may well be court proceedings on the horizon, with summonses, or letters before action from credit control agencies, lying unopened at home. Whether it is possible to set some of the contracts aside should be considered although the circumstances which allow this are limited.[47] However, in all cases it is essential to clarify the client's liabilities and to take any necessary legal steps on his behalf, either by coming to an arrangement for their repayment, by threatening bankruptcy proceedings, or by trying to avoid the contracts. In the case of unpaid rent, any order for possession can usually be suspended on terms. Less often, there is evidence of financial exploitation. The client may have made a significant gift to someone or allowed him control of his bank account. If so, an application for the property's return or a Mareva injunction may be necessary.[48] If the client's mental state is little changed, the risk of further debts being accumulated remains and, if in remission, the possibility of future similar behaviour must still be borne in mind. An application to the Court of Protection or the execution of an Enduring Power of Attorney may therefore need to be discussed (**696, 698**).

Where are the client's liabilities? Over what period of time did these arise? How are the debts to be paid? Can any of the liabilities be avoided? Are there any court proceedings pending? Is the client getting all the benefits to which he is entitled? Is it necessary to consider making alternative arrangements for the management of the client's financial affairs?

PHYSICAL HEALTH (6)

It is crucial to obtain details of the client's physical health (**1067, 1094, 1294**). Physical health problems may, of course, be real or imaginary and the product of a person's mental state rather than its cause. A conversion symptom is a loss or alteration of physical functioning which suggests a physical disorder but is actually a direct expression of a psychological conflict or need. The disturbance is not under

---

[47]   To have capacity to contract, the patient must be capable of understanding the nature and effect of the contract in question. A contract entered into by a mentally disordered person is enforceable by the other party unless it can be shown that, at the time the contract was entered into, the former was mentally incapable and the other party knew of that incapacity. Where the other party knew that the patient was incapacitated at the time, the contract is not void but merely voidable at the option of the mentally disordered person.. The burden of proof as to both issues is on the mentally disordered party and there is a general legal presumption of sanity. Special provisions apply to contracts for "necessaries." Under section 3 of the Sale of Goods Act 1979, an incapacitated person must pay a reasonable price for "necessaries," that is goods suitable to his condition in life and to his actual requirements at the times of sale and delivery.

[48]   The courts will set aside a gift if the patient did not have sufficient capacity to make it or acted under duress. The "degree (of understanding) required varies with the circumstances of the transaction. Thus, at one extreme, if the subject-matter and value of a gift are trivial in relation to the donor's other assets, a low degree of understanding will suffice. At the other, if its effect is to dispose of the donor's only asset of value ... then the degree of understanding required is as high as that required of a will." *Re Beaney (deceased)* [1978] 2 All E.R. 595.

voluntary control and is not explained by any physical disorder. Hypochondriasis denotes an unrealistic belief or fear that one is suffering from a serious illness despite medical reassurance.

Family medical history

The client should be asked about any serious physical health problems from which family members have suffered, in case any of these are of an hereditary nature or have triggered his present distress.

Did the client have any problems with his physical health as a child or during adolescence other than the ordinary childhood illnesses such as measles? Has he ever suffered any head injuries, been unconscious, been hospitalised, or undergone an operation? Did he notice any physical changes during the months preceding admission or during the period preceding his first psychiatric admission? Has he recently been in hospital for the investigation or treatment of a physical condition? When did he last see a General Practitioner? Is there any evidence of malnutrition or weight-loss?

DRUGS AND ALCOHOL (7)

Various conditions attributable to the consumption of alcohol or drugs mimic psychiatric conditions such as schizophrenia or may trigger such a condition in someone already predisposed to it. Some of these drug and alcohol-induced conditions are briefly described in chapter 24 (**1302**). If the client is dependant on alcohol or has taken illegal drugs, the details must therefore be carefully noted. For the same reasons, a note should also be made of any medication which the patient is or was taking for a physical condition.

Is there any evidence that the client was consuming an excessive amount of alcohol prior to admission or that he was taking prescribed or non-prescribed drugs?

FORENSIC HISTORY (8)

The representative will require details of all previous convictions and periods in custody and will need to know the circumstances of any offences of violence. The forensic history is an important indicator of the likelihood of harm to others associated with mental disorder. If there is no apparent temporal link between a patient's history of offending and his history of mental illness, this may lead to a classification of psychopathic disorder. As to assessing the risk of further violence, see pages 723 and 738. A record of drug-related offending draws attention to the possibility of drug-induced psychosis although, more often, the illegal drugs simply act as a trigger in someone already predisposed to that illness. Two basic points must always be borne in mind when considering the forensic history. Firstly, it cannot be overemphasised that people with mental health problems may be predisposed to crime as much as any other individual from the same background. Psychiatrists have an unfortunate tendency to interpret all violent behaviour as inevitably linked in some way to the client's mental illness, even if the facts clearly suggest it occurred in a setting well known to criminal lawyers. For example, it may naively be assumed by a psychiatrist unacquainted with the ordinary business of the criminal courts that a known patient who "sorts out" someone who offended his manliness in some trivial way must have been responding to abnormal mental phenomena — the more so if he later suffers a relapse on being confined in prison pending trial and is then observed to be hearing voices and so forth. The psychiatrist may pride himself on eliciting this imaginary connection not obvious to untrained criminal lawyers. Secondly, because diverting people away from the criminal courts is now widely encouraged, the absence of criminal convictions does not necessarily reflect an absence of criminal conduct. Not uncommonly, serious assaults on staff are either dealt with internally or, if reported to the police, not prosecuted. Violent or threatening behaviour may also be viewed as something of a norm on acute admission wards so that assaults by one patient on another do not lead to the involvement of the police unless serious injury results. Even if a client has no convictions, it is therefore important to ask whether he has ever been arrested by the police or placed in seclusion and, if so, the reasons for this.

Restriction order cases

The circumstances of the index offence should be explored, paying particular attention to the considerations considered by the Home Office to be relevant when assessing a patient's suitability to be discharged (**766**). If the patient's case was disposed of without trial, because he was under a disability, it cannot be assumed that he would have been convicted if tried. It is therefore important to establish what evidence would have been available to the court and to bear in mind that it was never tested by cross-examination. The solicitor will need details of the solicitors who dealt with the criminal proceedings, so that he can obtain their file and check that the Home Secretary's summary is fair and accurate. A note signed by the client authorising the file's release will be necessary. If the trial solicitor's file has been destroyed, copies of the depositions should still be held by the court itself, unless the papers have been sent to the Lord Chancellor's Department or county archives, and the Home Office will itself have a set.

Restriction and limitation direction cases

The representative should explain that the tribunal's powers are very limited and the hearing may result in remission to prison. This may, of course, be what the client wants and in his own interests. There is also a risk that a patient held under section 48 will make admissions during the course of the tribunal proceedings which will prejudice his chances of later being acquitted at the trial of the criminal action. In cases involving patients serving a determinate sentence of imprisonment, knowing their date of release will be important since any restrictions cease to have effect on that day (**389**).

Does the client have any previous convictions or any criminal proceedings pending? Has he ever had to be physically restrained or placed in seclusion while in hospital? Has any person taken civil proceedings against him for an injunction forbidding him from having contact with them or entering the family home? If he is a restricted patient, what were the circumstances of the index offence?

The solicitor will need details of previous admissions and periods of out-patient treatment and to establish whether the patient ceased treatment during the weeks or months prior to the present admission. If there is no prior history of mental disorder, the immediate biomedical aim will be to explain the present (the pathology) by reference to the past (the aetiology) and so to predict the future (the prognosis). The purpose of taking *any* history is to look for patterns of events which have an explanatory or predictive value. The link may be that the patient relapses when he stops treatment, or that the illness is cyclical in nature (remitting and returning at definable intervals of time), or that particular anniversaries or kinds of event precipitate periods of illness. It may be that all or most of the patient's periods of in-patient treatment are relatively short or relatively prolonged and the tribunal case can be planned with that in mind. In general terms, events in the past reveal the nature of the illness and the patient's response both to it and to treatment. For example, multiple admissions to different hospitals usually suggests an unstable, possibly vagrant, lifestyle marked by poor compliance with after-care programmes. Reasons given for frequent changes of address, and consequential moves between catchment areas, may be essentially paranoid and involve a history of repeated persecution by neighbours. In taking the history, it is important to distinguish between objective facts and their subjective interpretation. Although a single patient may acquire many different diagnoses over time, these are rarely explicable in terms of any corresponding objective changes in his condition. Most often, the different diagnoses reflect only different diagnostic fashions and practices, the fact that different symptoms were (reliably or unreliably) considered to be present or absent and, if present, prominent or not prominent. The client should be asked if he has had routine investigations, such as blood or urine tests. If the diagnosis is doubtful, his stay in hospital has been lengthy, or there have been repeated admissions, more extensive investigations, such as an EEG, will probably have been conducted.

Out-patient treatment

It is helpful to obtain a clear idea of the duration of any periods which the client has spent outside hospital relative to periods spent as an in-patient. As already noted, there may be evidence that the periods outside hospital have become fewer or shorter over time or, conversely, that greater stability has been achieved in recent years. There are many possible explanations for either pattern. For example, it may be that the illness is taking a chronic course and that each successive episode is less complete, with residual symptoms remaining. Greater stability may reflect a change of treatment or the personnel involved in treatment; natural curative processes; maturation and the resolution of underlying personality problems; happier family circumstances characterised by less emotional conflict; a reduction in pressure outside hospital; better compliance with medication; the development of a better understanding of the patient's needs; a wider range of community care facilities; or a reduction in community support. In the last case, the appearance of greater stability is illusory, the product of a failure to identify continuing problems and to intervene.

Is this the client's first admission to hospital? How many times has he previously been in hospital? Has he received out-patient treatment in the past? Is there any pattern to his admissions or periods of remission? Does he have a history of stopping treatment against medical advice following discharge from hospital?

THE CURRENT ADMISSION (11)

For convenience, the recent history can be dealt with in three stages: events leading up to the admission, the admission itself, and the developments since admission.

Events preceding the admission

Much of the relevant information will already be apparent from the information about the patient's family circumstances, accommodation, employment history, financial position, and medical history. The solicitor needs to know for how long the patient has been ill, what triggered that illness or relapse, whether he unilaterally stopped treatment, and what his attitude was to any suggestions by family members or professionals that he undergo voluntary treatment. If the client unilaterally ceased taking medication, when and why he did so needs to be established. Most often, the reason is that the patient thought that he no longer needed it, did not want to become dependent on it, or the side-effects were intolerable. Depending on the evidence available to him and the degree of suffering, discontinuance may or may not have been a reasonable risk to take at the time. If he had not previously stopped treatment against medical advice or been detained, it may be that he is now aware that the medication was merely suppressing the symptoms and it continues to be necessary. As to possible precipitants, these are listed below. This involves some repetition but it is convenient at this stage to get an overall picture of the problems.

STRESSORS AND TRIGGERS

Conjugal	*Is there any matrimonial friction and, if so, did this contribute to-wards any deterioration of the client's mental health? Does the spouse's behaviour exacerbate his condition? Is there any evidence of domestic violence or pending matrimonial proceedings?*
Parental	*Has the client's relationship with his parents been problematic? Are his parents over-critical? Has he only recently left home?*
Occupational	*Have there been any problems at work? Has the client's perform-ance been criticised?*
Accommodation	*Is the client now living alone and lonely? Has he been homeless or been threatened with homelessness? Has he recently moved from an area where he had strong community ties? Are there any neigh-bourhood disputes?*
Financial	*Is the client or his family substantially in debt? If so, have there been any court proceedings?*
Forensic	*Has the client recently been involved, or is he currently involved, in any criminal proceedings? To what extent did he feel humiliated as a result? Did the involvement reflect a prior decline in his mental health or did it trigger that decline?*
Medical	*Has the client recently suffered any significant physical injuries or illnesses?*
Bereavement	*Have any close relatives been very ill or recently died? How long ago was this?*

At what point did the client's mental health begin to deteriorate? Had he previously stopped taking medication prescribed to prevent that? Is there any evidence that stressful events of the sort referred to above triggered the present episode of illness, or were any such problems consequences not causes of his illness?

The admission

With compulsory admission, matters usually come to a crisis and some event occurs which persuades family members or professionals that there is no other realistic course of action. This may involve the police and the client's arrest or detention under section 136; an attempt by an informal patient to discharge himself from hospital or to refuse medication; an incident of self-harm or harm to others; serious self-neglect; complaints by neighbours; or extremely bizarre behaviour at home. It is important to identify what occurred immediately prior to the decision to invoke compulsory powers and which caused that decision to be made. If the client is not forthcoming, the grounds recorded on the admission papers can be read to him as an *aide-mémoire.*

Admission initially voluntary or informal

If the admission was originally on a voluntary basis, this demonstrates some appreciation of the need for assessment or treatment. However, such an admission is sometimes more informal than voluntary and it may have been made clear that an application would be made if informal admission was refused. In other cases, the client's willingness to be admitted may have had little to do with any appreciation of the need for treatment. The motivation may be a desire for accommodation and regular meals or a familiar environment. If the original admission was informal or voluntary, the subsequent use of compulsory powers may indicate that the patient's mental state has deteriorated; that it is more serious than was first believed; that some serious incident has since occurred; that different opinions are held about the necessity of a particular kind of treatment, such as antipsychotics, or their administration by injection; that the patient lacks insight into his need for intensive treatment; that his consultant lacks insight into the patient's situation or condition; that the consultant has made no real effort to enlist co-operation or to achieve a compromise: the choice has never been anything but informal or formal treatment on the consultant's terms.

- *What events or concerns gave rise to the admission? Why do the client's doctor or nurses say that admission and compulsion was necessary?*

- *What were the circumstances immediately preceding the decision to invoke compulsory powers which led to that decision being taken? Did those circumstances justify the conclusion that the client was mentally disordered and that his admission was justified or necessary for his own health or safety or to protect others?*

- *Does the client accept that he was mentally unwell at the time of admission and/or that he needed to be in hospital? If the client accepts that at the time of his admission he did require medical help, in what way? Why does he think that he became unwell? How would he describe that illness? What were the symptoms, the exact way in which he was unwell? Did anything happen before he came to hospital which contributed to his becoming ill?*

- *Does he consider that his mental state is now different? If so, in what way? Does he consider that he still needs in-client treatment? If so, for how much longer? Has any one explained why other people consider that he still needs to be in hospital? Do his parents or relatives agree about this?*

- *If the client believes that his admission was unnecessary but has had previous admissions, were all of those admissions also unwarranted? If the client disputes the evidence in the reports, what motive does he ascribe to the reporter for giving that account? Why would the relevant nurse record that he had said or done something if he had not?*

- *Does he consider that he is now functioning at his optimum level? If not, in what respects is he still not entirely back to his normal self?*

Events since admission

Having established the general history and, more particularly, the circumstances preceding and surrounding the use of compulsory powers, the way in which matters have developed since admission should be dealt with. Subsequent events may represent a step backwards from discharge. For example, transfer from an open to a locked ward or to a hospital which has facilities for managing patients whose behaviour is threatening and difficult to control. More often, the patient's situation will have improved so that discharge from hospital or the revocation of compulsory powers are now more realistic options. If the client was admitted to a locked facility, progress typically commences with brief but gradually increasing periods of escorted leave in the hospital grounds; followed by periods of unescorted ground leave and transfer to an open ward; followed by unrestricted ground leave and periods of escorted leave outside hospital; followed by day or weekend leave at home under section 17; followed by unlimited leave at home subject to taking medication, attendance at out-patient clinics, and support from a community psychiatric nurse (CPN); followed by formal discharge from hospital; and, eventually, the discharge or expiration of the application or order authorising his detention. There are, of course, fairly endless variations to this framework but the common theme is a trial period at a lower level of restriction, followed by an indefinite period at that level and, as confidence increases, movement towards the next stage in the discharge and treatment process. Most often, progress is not uniform and, human nature being what it is, some failure to comply fully with leave arrangements is to be expected. A practical approach to minor departures from the regime, such as lateness back from home leave, is normal.

Does the client spend all his time on the ward? If so, is this by choice or because it is a locked ward and part of his management programme? Is he allowed off the ward and, if so, for how long each day? Is this with or without a nursing escort? If without an escort, does he require express permission or does he have a "general pass" to be off the ward? Is he allowed leave only within the confines of the hospital grounds or does he also enjoy town leave? When the client goes into the local town, how does he spend his time? Has the client been granted any day or weekend leave at home? If so, for how long has he had the benefit of this? What, if any, are the conditions imposed on that leave? If the client is currently spending all or most of his time on the ward, what is the more important goal for him? To be at home, even if on section, or to be off section even if in hospital?

910

Matters unhelpful to discharge

As noted, progress is often not uniform and not all developments since admission are helpful. It is crucial that the client is frank with his solicitor about such matters and the importance of this must be emphasised. In section 2 cases the reports are usually only available at the time of the hearing while, in other cases, significant developments may post-date their preparation. The solicitor should therefore stress that he relies on his client to put in context anything which may be construed as adverse, and in sufficient time to enable a response to be prepared. The client needs to be asked whether he has been absent from the hospital without leave, whether he has been restrained or in seclusion, whether it may be said that he has tried to harm himself or others on the ward, whether he has refused medication, and whether there have been any complaints made by other patients or by staff concerning his behaviour. Any allegation of violence or sexual misconduct will inevitably worry the tribunal although, in the former case, it often transpires that the patient was defending himself against attack.

Has the client been restrained or placed in seclusion? Has it been alleged that he has harmed himself or assaulted anyone? Will it be alleged that he has damaged any property on the ward or that he has been physically or verbally threatening? Has anyone complained about his conduct on the ward? Has he refused medication or refused to attend any part of the ward programme? Is it alleged that any untoward incidents have occurred while he has been on leave? Has his leave ever been revoked or cancelled as a result? Has he always returned to the ward from leave at the required time? If not, was he so late returning that he was treated by ward staff as being absent without leave? If so, for how long was he away and did he return of his own volition or was he returned by police or nursing staff? Where was he during his absence? Did he take medication during that period?

MEDICATION AND TREATMENT (12)

In most cases the client will be receiving some form of medication or a physical treatment such as ECT. However, if the reason for his detention is a conduct disorder associated with mental handicap or psychopathic disorder, the role of medication may be limited to dampening down undesired behaviour. Although the sedative effects of antipsychotics are immediate, their antipsychotic effect takes up to three weeks to become evident in cases of schizophrenia and perhaps half of all patients show little or no response. The efficacy of antipsychotic medication in chronic schizophrenia is unclear and some trials have not demonstrated a drug-placebo difference (**1254**). While the opportunities for improvement were considerably less prior to their development, and death was often nature's remedy, none of the drugs has a curative action, and medication probably only postpones rather than prevents relapse. Although the benefits cannot always be demonstrated, and it is sometimes questionable whether the suffering caused by their administration is less than that being alleviated, tribunals invariably see medication in black and white terms. It is simply a question of whether or not the patient can be relied upon to take medication as prescribed, not whether there are reasonable grounds for not taking the medication in the doses prescribed. In other words, it is not a question of whether the patient has the capacity to come to his own decision in a rational manner but whether or not he will comply.

Insight into the need for treatment

By medical custom, insight refers to the patient's awareness of the abnormality of his experiences and the fact that his symptoms are evidence of the presence of a mental illness which requires treatment. Only a patient may lack insight if one chooses to define the word in this artificial way. If one prefers the natural meaning of seeing within and understanding — understanding one's own mental processes or those of another, which is the meaning adopted by psychologists — then a doctor may also lack insight. The main content of any medical report consists of the contents of the patient's mind as elicited and interpreted by the contents of the doctor's mind. If the interviewer is uninterested in the patient's problems and the underlying causes, being interested only in obtaining enough information to sustain a diagnosis and to prescribe a form of medication, such a narrow field of view necessarily leads to a narrow understanding of the overall situation. Nevertheless, although any person's insight into their own or someone else's mind can only ever be partial, the patient's lack of insight may often be gross and involve a failure to distinguish subjective from objective experiences. The patient's view not infrequently tends towards one of two poles. Either the admission was necessitated by malign internal forces (ill-health) or it was the product of malign external forces (a failure to understand his situation by others, parental over-anxiety, malice, a conspiracy, and so forth). Although insight is usually beneficial, because it increases the chances of compliance, it is not essential and, indeed, may sometimes be highly undesirable. Many naturally passive, co-operative or compliant individuals take medication without demur, without ever understanding its role, or feeling that it is necessary. Their complete lack of insight is not considered to be a problem. Ultimately, it often suffices that the patient has insight into the legal if not the medical consequences of non-compliance — he has learnt from experience the "lesson of consequences," the fact that exercising his freedom in a certain way leads to his freedom being taken away. Just as the legal consequence of exercising one's freedom to commit murder is life imprisonment, so the patient sees that the consequence of exercising his "freedom" to stop medication is that other people believe that he is again unwell, and he is then admitted to hospital and forced to take that medication.

Whether compromise is possible

If the patient is not willing to bow to these inevitabilities, the sensible course is to see if some compromise concerning medication can be agreed. While a general advantage of injections over oral medicines is certainty about whether the drug has been received, they are unacceptable for many people. Consequently, this clarity consists only of knowing that the drug has not been received. The real choice may be between compromising on oral medication by consent or compulsory treatment by injection. In the absence of any legal framework for indefinite compulsory out-patient treatment, defaulting on injections becomes an option for all discharged patients. In such cases, a consultant's unwillingness to contemplate what he considers to be the second-line treatment simply leads to no treatment at all and early relapse. Nevertheless, in practice, it is quite surprising how often the same failed strategy is thoughtlessly followed year after year. The alternatives of compromise or guardianship may not work. However, unless the patient has suddenly gained insight after many years without it, the possibility that informal treatment administered by injection will succeed is nil. The following questions may be asked of the client and care taken not to lead him in relation to his answers—

- *If the client considers that he is now functioning normally, does he still need the medication which is being prescribed for him? What would be the likely effects, if any, of now ceasing medication? Would there be any risk of his health deteriorating?*

- *Has the medication been beneficial in any way?*

- *What is the medication given for? Has its purpose been explained to him? What are its likely effects?*

- *Does the medication have any adverse effects? If so, is the client receiving further medication to control the effects of the other medication? If that is the case, does that medication in turn have adverse effects?*

- *Might the client be prepared to consider taking some alternative medication prescribed by his doctor? Has he previously taken any medication which he considers did help and which he was, and would now be, willing to take?*

- *If the client says that he is now well, and that he has not had any kind of mental health problem, then why would he take the medication at all, particular if it has very unpleasant adverse effects?*

- *Has the client attempted to refuse the medication on the ward? If so, was the team called? If he is given the medication orally does he swallow it or sometimes hold it under his tongue?*[49]

- *If the client considers that he has been ill but is now well, what does he think has brought about that improvement? The client may attribute this to rest and a break from problems at home or work — If so, he should be asked if he thinks that the medication prescribed has helped? Is there any significance in the fact that his voices returned (or whatever) when he ceased medication and then went away when the medication was resumed? If he concedes the point, but states that he no longer needs it because he is now cured, he should be asked to consider whether it may be that the medication which has made him well is keeping him well. The prescription of insulin may be used as an example.*

- *If the section was revoked, and he was free to decide for himself whether or not to take that medication, would he take all of it, part of it or none of it? At the current doses or in smaller dosages?*

- *If the client is willing to continue taking medication on an informal basis, then for how much longer? Who will decide that he no longer requires it — the client or the doctor? What if at the end of the period during which he says he will take it, his doctor strongly advises him to continue? Would he heed that advice or not? Does he have any objection to receiving the medication by injection?*

---

[49] Although the patient may tell his solicitor that he is not swallowing the medication, the psychiatric report may nevertheless note the improvement brought about by medication or increasing doses of it.

The ward programme

Details of therapeutic activities can be entered on the case summary form, which includes a table for entering the weekly programme.

Does the client take part in activities such as art therapy, cookery, budgeting, sessions? For how many days or half-days each week? Does he find those activities useful, either as a means of alleviating boredom or as a means of acquiring useful skills? Does he attend a hospital workshop or do gardening, work in the kitchens or hospital stores, or participate in any similar activity? How much is he paid and how does he spend that money? If he was discharged, would he seek similar work outside the hospital? Does the client attend a hospital gymnasium, library, social club, or some such activity?

AFTER-CARE AND SUPERVISION

The representative should establish what kind of after-care the patient has received in the past and what he would be willing to agree to if discharged from hospital. It may be that non-compliance with after-care services was not a factor in the present admission, but there is evidence that the services provided were poorly resourced, poorly planned, or poorly delivered. In restricted cases, it will generally be a condition of discharge that the patient submits to supervision by a social worker and a psychiatrist. This should be explained to him. Chapter 12 summarises the current discharge guidelines and includes an after-care checklist. Chapter 6 explains the statutory duty to provide after-care to patients who have been detained for treatment and the possibility of after-care being provided under statutory supervision. In appropriate cases, where there is little or no evidence of after-care planning, the solicitor may consider commissioning an independent social work report.

What support, if any, would the client be willing to accept when discharged from hospital? Would he be willing to be visited by a community psychiatric nurse, to see a social worker, or to attend out-client appointments at the hospital or a local clinic? Would he be willing to see his General Practitioner periodically if so advised? Does he respect or trust the opinion of any particular professional currently or previously involved in his care? Would he be prepared to accept that person's advice about what medication and other treatment he needs? Would he like an opinion from that professional? Would he be willing to remain in hospital as an informal patient until his doctor is satisfied that appropriate arrangements had been made for his care outside hospital? Has he ever discharged himself against medical advice?

INTERVIEW — 4. MENTAL STATE

When taking the case history, it is sometimes evident that the client has a difficulty remembering events that is more pervasive than the effects of medication or ECT. Alternatively, his answers may lack coherence or demonstrate problems pursuing a chain of thought. More often, the account of the circumstances preceding, surrounding, and following admission is noteworthy because mention is made of beliefs, perceptions or other mental phenomena which merit further consideration. Any evidence of mental disorder needs to be further discussed and carefully recorded.[50] This is rarely awkward. The vast majority of clients are only too happy to discuss their mood, feelings and beliefs and surprisingly often indicate that they have not been previously asked any questions about them.

MEMORY

If a person cannot remember information, or accurately remember it, the problem may lie at any one or more of the different stages of the memory process (**1070**). An inability to give an account of some past experience may be due to failure to register or store the information in the first place (no record was ever made); the loss or degradation of the record (defective retention or an intervening decision to erase it); or an inability to locate the record (the information is available but not accessible, because it was not systematically stored or cannot be systematically searched for). Short-term memory is often tested by giving the patient seven numbers and asking him to repeat them forwards and then backwards; by telling him a name and address and asking him to repeat it verbatim after a single hearing; and by giving him three objects to remember. When the long-term memory is tested, a distinction is usually drawn between "recent" and "remote" memory. Recent memory is tested by asking the patient a question about his activities during the previous 48 hours and then checking the accuracy of his account with a nurse. Remote memory involves remembering events memorised a considerable period ago, such as the client's wedding day or his first day at school. While it is not appropriate to formally test the patient's memory in these ways, the same end can be achieved over the course of an interview by the judicious choice of questions.

MOOD AND AFFECT

A person's affect is how he appears to be emotionally affected by an idea or mental representation. A person whose mood is normal may nevertheless be profoundly affected emotionally by some idea or perception. Affect is often described as being **flat** (absent or very limited emotional range); **blunted** (severe lack of normal emotional sensitivity); **shallow** or **restricted** (reduced); **appropriate, harmonious** or **congruous**; inappropriate or **incongruous**; or **labile** (unstable). Mood is the pervasive and sustained emotion which colours an individual's whole personality and perception of events. Consequently, it is sometimes described as sustained affect and mood disorders said to involve a morbid change of affect. Various words are used to describe the features of heightened mood, many of them essentially interchangeable. **Elation** consists of feelings of euphoria, triumph, immense self-satisfaction or optimism. **Euphoria** is an exaggerated feeling of physical or emotional well-being seen in organic mental states and in toxic and drug-induced states. **Exaltation** is an excessively intensified sense of well-being and is seen in manic states. **Ecstasy** describes a state of elation beyond reason and control or a trance state of overwhelming fervour, for instance religious fervour. **Grandiosity**, although not usually bracketed with affect, describes feelings of tremendous importance, characterised by an inflated appraisal of one's worth, power, knowledge, importance, or identity and commonly expressed as absurd exaggerations. Extreme grandiosity may attain delusional proportions and is seen in mania and schizophrenia.

---

[50]   Paragraph 14 of the case summary can be used to record relevant information.

Depression (depressed mood) describes feelings characterised by sadness, apathy, pessimism and a sense of loneliness. It is characteristic of depressive disorders or bipolar disorders. **Lability of mood** denotes a rapidly changing mood. The person affected may laugh one minute and cry the next without there being any corresponding change in external stimuli to account for this. As to assessing the risk of suicide, see page 734.

Does the client display no real emotion? Is there almost complete lack of interest in surroundings and events and a general lack of initiative? Does it seem that he could not "care less" about things generally? Does he laugh or display no concern when recounting how he is about to be killed or undergo some other type of terrifying ordeal? Is his mood elevated? Is he happy, self-confident, infectiously expansive, jocular? Are his plans for the future wholly unrealistic? Is there evidence of depression and suicidal feelings? Does his mood change rapidly, perhaps laughing one minute and then crying the next?

OTHER EMOTIONAL STATES

Anxiety is characterised by an apprehension, tension, or uneasiness that stems from the anticipation of danger. The associated symptoms include tachycardia, palpitations, breathlessness, and light-headedness. **Phobia** denotes a persistent irrational fear of, and desire to avoid, a particular object or situation. Anxiety may be expressed as **irritability**. The depressed patient may become anxious about his inability to respond positively to the problems surrounding him, which makes him anxious and often increasingly irritable. Conversely, sustained, unremitting anxiety and irritability have a depressive effect over a period of time because the individual's performance is constantly undermined and a measure of dejection sets in. In other cases, uncontrollable anxiety or fear surface in the form of motor restlessness (**agitation**) which, as with tics, both reflects and appears to partially alleviate the underlying tension state. A further way of dealing with anxiety or fear is to attempt to suppress it. Anxiety or fear may surface in discrete periods of sudden onset and be accompanied by physical symptoms — **panic attacks**. Fear may lead to **aggression** and **hostility**. In the case of patients who are irrationally fearful, aggression and hostility perform the same function as where there is an objectively real threat to the individual's safety. The individual attempts to reduce fear by eliminating its cause.

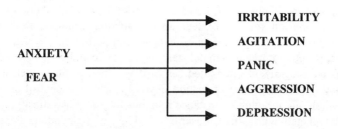

Is the client anxious, fearful, irritable, agitated, aggressive or hostile and, if so, why?

DISORDERED SPEECH OR THOUGHT

If a person's speech is abnormal, this may be because the amount of speech is outside normal bounds; because the production of speech is impaired; because his choice of words is abnormal; because the succession and connection of ideas is illogical; or because its content is abnormal. Having regard to this, abnormalities of speech and thought can be dealt with in the following order: abnormal volume (amount) and rate (tempo) of speech; abnormal delivery of speech (articulation); abnormal choice or use of words (vocabulary); abnormal juxtaposition of words, or the ideas conveyed by them, in phrases and sentences (syntax and the association of ideas); abnormal content of thought (delusions, over-valued ideas, etc.).

The volume (amount) and rate (tempo) of speech

The amount of speech used may be excessive or restricted. Retarded thought (thinking which proceeds slowly towards its goal) is reflected in the individual's speech and, when the amount of speech is very limited, this is sometimes referred to as **poverty of speech.** In extreme cases, the patient is mute, either unable or unwilling to speak. Copious, excessive, production of speech is known as volubility or **logorrhoea**. It may be seen in mania or schizophrenic disorders. Where the amount and rate of a patient's speech is increased so that he is difficult to interrupt, this is referred to as **pressure of speech**. In **flight of ideas**, there is a nearly continuous flow of accelerated speech and the patient jumps from one topic to another, his stream of thought directed by chance associations between each fragment of conversation.

The choice of words and vocabulary

The way certain words or phrases are used may sometimes be distinctive. For example, because they are repeated, clearly have a special significance for the individual, or have been invented by him. **Perseveration** denotes the persistent repetition of words, phrases or ideas. Where the patient instead persistently repeats back a syllable, word or phrase spoken by the interviewer, rather than a word or phrase previously spoken by himself, this is known as **echolalia. Verbigeration** is the stereotyped and superficially meaningless repetition of words or sentences, which is not an echoing of something said to the patient. Where a patient uses a certain *word or phrase* repeatedly throughout a conversation, such that it is clear that it has a special importance or meaning for him, such phrases are known as **stock phrases**. A **neologism** is a new word invented by the patient.

The structure and form of thought

Even though a question is simply expressed and unambiguous, it may be apparent that the client has not understood its meaning or purpose, the information which it was intended to elicit. This may be because the person has interpreted the question too literally and is capable of thinking only in concrete terms — **concrete thinking**. Rational or conceptual thinking involves the use of logic to solve problems. There is sometimes no logical association between the various thoughts expressed in response to a question. The successive thoughts, sentences and topics are not obviously goal-directed or connected in a chain of thought. Marked inability to consciously develop a chain of thought is considered to be indicative of mental disorder and, more particularly, a key feature of schizophrenia. In its mildest form, conversation is vague and answers to questions "woolly." **Tangentiality** means replying to a question in an oblique or even irrelevant manner. In some cases, there is such a loose connection between the successive thoughts expressed by successive sentences that the goal is never attained — **loosening of associations**. Successive thoughts are either unrelated or only obliquely related but the speaker is unaware that the statements which he is juxtaposing lack any meaningful relationship. When loosening of associations is severe, speech may be incoherent. At its most severe, not only is there no logical association between successive thoughts but a lack of association between successive words, which form a meaningless jumble. This is known as **word salad**. By convention, a distinction is drawn between loosening of associations and **circumstantiality of thought**. In the latter case, the clauses or phrases used by the speaker always maintain a meaningful connection and he remains aware throughout of the original point, goal, or topic. However, although relevant to the subject being discussed and eventually answering the question, the response is indirect and delayed in reaching the point because of unnecessary, tedious details and parenthetical remarks. In **derailment of thought**, there is a sudden deviation in the train of thought, as if a train travelling from one station to another (here from question to answer) had been derailed. In **thought blocking**, the patient's stream of thought, and therefore speech, suddenly stops in mid-flow for no obvious reason. He is either unable to account for the stoppage or attributes it to his thoughts being interfered with by a third party.

THE CONTENT OF THOUGHT — BELIEFS AND IDEAS

Even if the structure and form of a person's thought, and therefore speech, appears normal nevertheless the ideas expressed by him (the content of his thought) may be markedly abnormal. A delusion is a belief which is bizarre; not true to fact; cannot be corrected by an appeal to reason; and is out of harmony with the holder's educational or cultural background. Delusional ideas may form part of a logical fixed system of such beliefs — **systematised delusions**. They are usually categorised according to their content: common delusional themes, such as paranoid and grandiose delusions, are summarised in chapter 18 (**1084**). Not infrequently, the individual believes that his thoughts are being controlled, infiltrated, poisoned, stolen or made public. **Thought control** describes a belief that one's thoughts are being controlled by some other person, persons, or outside forces. **Thought insertion** is a delusion that thoughts have been, or are being placed, in one's mind by some other person, persons or outside forces — these are often sexual thoughts and the patient knows that they cannot be his because he is not homosexual or has been brought up not to think in such a filthy way. These intrusive thoughts are experienced by the patient as alien. **Thought withdrawal** is when the individual experiences his own thoughts being withdrawn from his mind or otherwise appropriated by an external agency. **Thought broadcasting** is the belief that one's own thoughts are being broadcast to the outside world or otherwise made public knowledge. Apart from the central idea of interference with thought processes, these beliefs have two other aspects in common. Firstly, their nature is essentially paranoid because they are characterised by a belief that the individual is being harmed by some other person or agency. Consequently, there is a significant potential for violence to any individual thought to be involved in causing this harm. Secondly, like all paranoid delusions, the beliefs are characterised by passivity. External agencies have managed to penetrate the patient's mind and the boundaries between the inner and outer world have been breached. Not only external events but his own inner thoughts are no longer under his own control. Care must be taken to differentiate delusional beliefs from value judgements, over-valued ideas and, more particularly, ideas of reference. An **over-valued idea** is an unreasonable, sustained, idea which is maintained less firmly than a delusional belief. **Ideas of reference** are one kind of over-valued idea. The term denotes an incorrect idea that casual incidents and external events directly refer to oneself which stops short of being a delusion of reference. Apart from delusions, a person's thoughts may be abnormal in a number of other respects. An **obsessional thought** is one which a person cannot prevent himself from repeatedly, insistently, having albeit that the content of the thought is not delusional. A **phobia** is a morbid, persistent and irrational fear of, and desire to avoid, a particular object or situation, associated with extreme anxiety. An **idée fixe** is an unshakeable preconception or conviction.

Persecutory delusions

The client may identify a particular type of person or vehicle as being involved in monitoring or trying to harm him. For instance, grey British Telecom vans, persons of a certain nationality or religion, people who wear spectacles. Alternatively, the conspirators may be identifiable by some sign or gesture they make or an ordinary gesture be interpreted as a hostile, mocking, action. The malign force may be political or religious, *e.g.* the devil interfering with the client's body and making him impotent or sterile. The patient may be asked if anyone has been bothering him or interfering with his day to day life and, if physical violence has occurred, he should be asked if his victim was involved in some plot against him. The following questions should also be asked of the client unless it is absolutely clear that he does not believe that other people may be trying to harm him in any way—

- *Has the client ever had the feeling that other people were talking about him, or referring to him, when he is in public? Do people laugh at him or denigrate him in some way?*

- *Do other people ever listen to his conversations, monitor his telephone calls, or interfere with his post or the contents of his flat?*

- *Has he ever been followed or spied upon? Are any people conspiring against him? If so, did his current admission form part of that conspiracy? Is his family or anyone at the hospital involved in this conspiracy or presently monitoring his activities? Is he safe in hospital?*

- *Has anyone tried to physically harm him? Has his food, drink or medication ever been tampered with?*

- *Do other people spoil plans he makes and hold him back from achieving the success which is due to him?*

- *Does the client believe that his thoughts, body or actions are influenced or controlled by other persons or forces? Has anyone inserted their thoughts into his mind or stolen his thoughts? Does he believe that other people know what he is thinking or that he can read their thoughts?*

919

- *Does he believe that any recent items on the television or radio, or in a newspaper, referred to him or contained a message for him? Has anything else which he has come across included a coded reference to his situation? For example, the message might be in the form of graffiti, a car number-plate, a logo on a chocolate-wrapper, digits displayed on a liquid-crystal display, or certain colours, a yellow shirt meaning "you are a coward."*

- *Is the client frightened? If matters do not improve and the threat remains, how will he deal with the threats to his safety? Would violence ever be necessary or justifiable as a form of self-defence? Would the client ever consider ending his life if the suffering became too intense? Have thoughts of suicide or violence ever been inserted in his mind?*

Grandiose delusions

Paranoid delusional beliefs are commonly associated with grandiose delusions. An obvious question which arises from a paranoid chain of thought is why the identified third party wants to harm the client? The ascribed motive may be jealousy or the fear of some special talent, knowledge or power which the patient possesses. For example, the client has the ability to heal other patients or to bring peace to the world and political or military forces are trying to stop him. Indeed, he may consider that only he can save the world, that he is the son of God or a prophet, or that but for the plotting he would have achieved great success in his life. In other cases, the patient's grandiosity may reveal itself in beliefs that he has great wealth, is a person of national importance, or is related to the royal family.

Does the client possess any particular powers, information, knowledge or abilities which other people on the ward do not also have? If people are trying to harm him, why is that? Can he control what other people think or do and, if so, can he give an example of this? Do they ever pick up his thoughts and act on them? Does the client have a decreased need for sleep? Does he spend money excessively, running up substantial debts which do not concern him because of grandiose delusions about his wealth or the future success of plans which he has made? Is he careless?

Delusions of guilt and sinfulness

By convention, guilt is self-inflicted, in contrast to shame which primarily depends upon the opinions and views of others. Guilt may commence as low self-esteem and devaluation with the individual attributing exaggerated negative qualities to himself. The patient may chastise himself for having material possessions, poor moral standards, or sexually impure thoughts. Delusions of guilt or sinfulness are commonly associated with depression but may also be found in cases diagnosed as schizophrenia and in certain organic conditions. The patient feels immense guilt for things said or done in the past. He may imagine that he is personally responsible for some imaginary disaster or a real misfortune which logically could not be his fault or of his doing. Examples include a patient who believes he is personally responsible for the suicides of other patients in the hospital (they picked up and acted on his own suicidal thoughts); for an aircraft disaster or earthquake; or for the death or illness of a parent. The risk of suicide is extremely high in such cases. The patient may believe that only his death can properly atone for these sins, that he is unworthy to live, or that his suffering and guilt is so intense that death would be a release. Great care must be taken to identify the risk of self-harm and details obtained of any suicide attempts (**734**). It cannot be presumed that because the tablets consumed could not have caused death, or the attempt was discovered shortly after its occurrence, therefore the incident was only a plea for help. The issues of competency and chance need to be considered. A person who intends to kill himself may take too low a dose and learn from that. Likewise, a person who does not intend to kill himself may do so in error if he mistakenly takes too high a dose or he is not discovered, because others tragically depart from their normal timetable. Moreover, some suicide attempts are impulsive so that a lack of planning is not proof of lack of intent. Finally, even if the attempt represented a plea for help it may have been a final desperate plea for a solution and, if help is not given and so the situation then seems totally without hope, the final step before self-destruction.

Does the client feel responsible in any way for the suffering of other people? Has he ever contemplated or planned suicide? Has he ever harmed himself? What does he see as his good points and as being the reasons for wanting to live?

Nihilistic delusions

Nihilistic delusions may accompany delusions of guilt and sinfulness and are seen in cases of very severe depression. However, if the patient says he "feels" dead inside, this may simply be a turn of phrase, descriptive of a general loss of feeling.

Does the client think that his heart or brain no longer exist or that he is dead? Does he believe that his brain, stomach or bowels have rotted or putrefied or are rotting away? Does his skin feel like nothing more than a hollow shell? If his heart has stopped beating or his brain is dead, how is it that he is still able to have this conversation?

Hypochondriacal delusions

If the information previously taken concerning the patient's physical health suggests that his account of being seriously ill may be groundless, the possibility arises that his belief is delusional. It may be that, despite numerous negative investigations and constant medical reassurance that he is in good health, the patient continues to rigidly hold to the idea that he has a fatal disease, claiming that relatives and doctors as not being straight with him.

PERCEPTUAL DISTURBANCES

An hallucination is a sensory perception occurring without external stimulation of the relevant sensory organ. It has the immediate sense of reality of a true perception. Hallucinations are usually categorised according to the sensory modality in which they occur. They may or may not give rise to a delusional interpretation of the hallucinatory experience. The subject of hallucinations is dealt with in greater detail in Chapter 18 (**1086**).

Auditory hallucinations

An auditory hallucination is a hallucination of sound, most commonly of voices. Auditory hallucinations which consist of voices are often described as being in the first-person ("I am wicked"), in the second-person ("you are wicked"), or in the third-person ("he is wicked"). Unless the possibility of auditory hallucinations can be ruled out, the following questions may be raised—

- *Has the client ever heard any other person's voice speaking to him when he has been alone?*

- *Does he ever "hear" voices which seem to emanate from within himself? If so, do these voices seem to be his own thoughts spoken out aloud or someone else's thoughts?*

- *Does he recognise any of the voices? Are they male or female, a single person's voice or several different voices. If several voices, do they speak separately or concurrently and, if separately, as if holding a conversation? Is that conversation about him?*

- *Do the voices comment on things which he is doing or has done? Are they derogatory, perhaps making sexual remarks, or accusatorial? Does he find the voices frightening or has he become accustomed to them? Are the voices a comfort and do they give him helpful advice?*

- *How old was he when he first heard such voices and have they been continuous since then? How often does he hear the voices and do they tend to occur at particular times of the day or in a particular situation? Do the voices always speak at the same volume, or shout, or does the volume vary? Does the medication he receives make any difference to the frequency of the voices, their content or their volume? Does he draw any conclusions from this?*

- *Do the voices give the client instructions? Has he ever done any act because of advice given to him by the voices? Can he resist any commands given to him? Do the voices ever instruct him to do something which he would generally disapprove of?*

- *Have the voices ever told the client to harm himself or someone else or that someone else is trying to harm him?*

Visual hallucinations

A visual hallucination is an hallucination involving sight. Visual hallucinations may be sub-divided into those which are elementary or simple, such as flashes of light, and those which are organised, such as the form of human figures. They must be distinguished from illusions. An illusion is a mental impression of sensory vividness arising out of a misinterpretation of an external stimulus. For example, mistaking a piece of scrunched cotton for a spider or a cat for a rat.

922

Has the client seen anything which strikes him as strange, unusual or frightening or which other people cannot see? If so, do these experiences occur at a particular time of day or night? What does he see? Do objects ever seem larger or smaller than he later knows they really are?

Other hallucinations

A **gustatory hallucination** is an hallucination of taste, such as a metallic taste, often accompanied by chewing, lip smacking or swallowing movements. Most often, unusual tastes are associated with the medication being prescribed. An **olfactory hallucination** is one involving smell and in cases of temporal lobe epilepsy this may typically be described as similar to burning rubber or burning cabbage. A **somatic hallucination** is an hallucination involving the false perception of a physical experience localised within the body. For example, a perception that electricity is running through the body. A **tactile or haptic hallucination** involves the sense of touch, often something on or under the skin.

Has the client ever experienced any strange smells or tastes the source of which he could not locate? Has he ever felt that other people or some outside force was interfering in any way with his body? Has he ever had the sensation that insects or animals were crawling under or on his skin? Has he ever felt that he might have been interfered with while asleep?

The pattern of any perceptual disturbances

It is obviously important to establish any pattern to the hallucinations and whether they may be due to some condition other than schizophrenia or depression. At its most obvious, the content of auditory hallucinations will be highly relevant. However, the possibility that the experiences have an organic basis or, more specifically, are drug-induced must be borne in mind. Some in-patients trade prescribed medication and there may be access on the ward to street drugs brought in by visitors or patients returning from leave.

Is there any pattern to the client's perceptual disturbances? If he is on depot medication does their frequency increase during the day or two immediately prior to the next injection? Has the patient taken any prescribed or non-prescribed drugs which might account for the phenomena? Does the patient believe that any hallucinations he has experienced have a basis in reality or are part of an illness? For instance, a client who hears God's voice commanding him to do some act may insist that he has actually heard God's voice or, if its intensity varies according to whether or not he is on medication, he may say that it is part of an illness (or, indeed, that the medication robs him of his prophetic powers). Similarly, a visual hallucination of a person may be so vivid that the patient is not willing to concede that he did not really see a living person.

Perceptions of time and space

A number of other unusual perceptions are not classified as hallucinations because they relate to the individual's perception of himself in relation to time, space, and place. For instance, it may seem that half an hour has passed in a matter of seconds.

Alternatively, the client may be aware of beginning to cook a meal one moment and the next moment being aware of the food on the table. In other cases, the client's body or the world may seem unreal or he may have experiences of *déjà-vu*.

Has the client ever been aware of time passing more quickly or slowly than at other times? Does he ever feel that he or the world outside him is unreal?

THE FINAL QUESTIONS

Even if there is good evidence of mental disorder, the final questions must always be, "so what?" and "does it matter?" More particularly, is the client or are other people suffering as a result? Furthermore, would alleviating the symptoms and any gain of insight make life more or less bearable for him as matters presently stand?

AFTER THE INITIAL INTERVIEW

The time available for preparation is necessarily limited in section 2 cases by the tribunal's duty to hear the application within seven days of its receipt. Subject to that constraint, taking a comprehensive statement will usually require more than one interview. Furthermore, once the reports are available, it will be necessary to obtain the client's observations on them and he will need to be seen shortly before the scheduled hearing. This is so that final preparations are made on the basis of his contemporaneous mental state. However many times it is necessary to see the client, and he may request additional visits, the steps listed on the following page should be taken following the initial interview.

THE CASE STRATEGY

Based on the diagnosis, history and the client's instructions, it is important to identify the likely hearing issues at an early stage and to plan the case with them in mind. It should be readily apparent what is likely to be the medical diagnosis. This is reached according to a simple system of pattern recognition (**1112**) and in most cases involves no real skill, the pattern of symptoms being as obvious to a lawyer, nurse or social worker as it is to a doctor. Similarly, the prognosis is largely based on the history of response to treatment so that anyone aware of that history can make a shrewd guess as to how matters are likely to progress. It is also important not to be bound by very specific instructions in terms of the preferred outcome. Secondary aims can be pencilled in, and additional evidence gathered with them in mind, in case the declared primary aim is unattainable. For example, if a case for discharge is being prepared, the final submission at the eventual hearing may be that (1) there is a duty to discharge because the statutory criteria are satisfied; (2) in the alternative, the tribunal should exercise its discretion in favour of discharge; (3) in the alternative, if the tribunal decides against discharge, it should recommend that the patient be granted leave of absence. The disappointment at not being discharged will be less if the hearing brings about some improvement in the situation. Furthermore, because an unrestricted patient's liability to detention cannot be renewed if he is on leave, its grant advances the date of discharge.

1. Enter the information from the interview on the case summary form or, if preferred, in the form of a statement.

2. Complete a time record sheet.

3. Notify the tribunal office if this has not already been done, requesting copies of the usual reports when they are available (**662**). Submit the patient's tribunal application where necessary. *In section 2 cases, the reports will only be available from the tribunal clerk about an hour prior to the hearing. It may, however, be possible to obtain copies from the hospital's Mental Health Act Administrator before then.*

4. Submit the completed ABWOR application to the Legal Aid Board, with any request for authority to obtain expert reports (ABWOR 6) and any written confirmation of an extension to the green form limit. *In section 2 cases, it will be necessary to obtain ABWOR and any necessary authority over the telephone.*

5. Write to the client, explaining his legal position and rights, confirming his instructions and the action taken, and setting out how the solicitor expects the proceedings to progress.

6. Make arrangements to obtain any available information and files likely to be relevant to the proceedings

7. Contact relatives and other witnesses, where this has been agreed with the client.

8. Contact the responsible medical officer in writing about inspecting the patient's case notes. *Informal access is preferable to making a statutory application if this can be agreed.*

9. Make inquiries of social services about after-care facilities and discharge planning. *The local community care plan and Longman's Social Services Yearbook will include details.*

10. Lodge any other applications or requests to the tribunal, for directions and so forth.

11. Identify the likely hearing issues and the case strategy.

12. Commission any medical report in a section 2 case.

NOTIFYING THE TRIBUNAL OFFICE

Section 2 cases aside, it is generally unwise to notify the tribunal of having been instructed by the patient until after the first interview has taken place. The fact that the hospital have arranged a solicitor for the client does not invariably mean that he wishes to be represented or that some other person has not made alternative arrangements. Furthermore, the solicitor has not yet been instructed. In section 2 cases, it is worthwhile faxing details of dates to avoid to the tribunal office, although it is rare for the tribunal to be able to accommodate the solicitor.

COMMISSIONING EXPERT REPORTS

In section 2 cases, the grant of ABWOR and of the necessary authority for a medical report can be obtained over the telephone. The psychiatrist should be provided with proper, typed instructions and a copy of all relevant documents and case summaries. Poor instructions devalue the usefulness of an expert's report. Even if the expert is thorough, its value in terms of the tribunal, rather than the patient's future management, depends on the expert being given all the relevant facts and clear instructions about the points which his report should address. An ancillary benefit of a medical report is that it allows the advocate to test in advance the submission which he is formulating in his mind. The expert can be asked to address a number of questions, such as "If I were to argue x, is this an inference which is consistent with a body of psychiatric opinion?" However many sub-headings there are, a good report is in five parts, namely (1) Introduction (patient's name, address, ward, consultant, legal status, admission dates, date of examination, date of report, who was consulted, the reports read, the questions which the expert was asked to address etc.); (2) History, facts and symptoms elicited at interview; (3) Analysis; (4) Opinion/conclusions; (5) Recommendations.[51]

Independent social work reports

In appropriate cases, where there is little or no evidence of proper after-care planning, or no social worker has been allocated, an application for authority to obtain an independent social circumstances report will be worthwhile. This will be particularly relevant in restricted cases if it may help to reduce the possibility of having to defer any subsequent direction for conditional discharge. A social circumstances report may also be more useful than a medical report if the psychiatric issues are clear cut and the issue is whether alternative arrangements to treatment in hospital can be made for a client who requires intensive support.

Independent psychological report

In cases involving mental handicap or psychopathic disorder, a report from a clinical psychologist can be valuable if it may establish that the patient's IQ is above the conventional cut-off point for mental impairment or suggest that key personality traits are within normal bounds.

---

[51] Not uncommonly, it will be found with reports prepared by responsible medical officers that any connection between the opinion and conclusions (4), and the reported facts upon which the opinion is notionally founded (2), is not clearly stated or logically defective. A lengthy report may be evidence of thoroughness and conscientiousness but not of understanding. Summarising a long history at length is no substitute for analysing the facts, and the opinion is often utterly silent as to why the facts justify the inferences drawn.

DISCLOSING REPORTS

Where a medical report is unfavourable, it is sometimes difficult to give the client clear-cut advice about its disclosure to the tribunal and the Secretary of State. It is often said that the tribunal will know that the report has been prepared, because the doctor's visit will be recorded in the notes and may even be referred to at the hearing by the responsible medical officer. The tribunal will therefore infer that the report was unfavourable and perhaps think that it was worse than was the case. The answer to that must simply be that one must rely on the president to ensure that the other members confine themselves to the evidence before the tribunal. Moreover, it is certainly not the case that all reports which conclude by recommending discharge are disclosed. There may be one part of the report which expresses a single reservation not expressed in the other reports. The solicitor may be confident that the tribunal will discharge on the evidence already available, the more so having been reassured that discharge is an acceptable risk, and not wish to open up fresh issues. This may particularly be so in a restricted case where the responsible medical officer favours discharge. The greater difficulty is assessing whether to submit a report which is generally unfavourable but not as damning as the only medical evidence currently before the tribunal. The report may undermine the existing medical evidence in several material respects, and even support a lesser application for leave of absence, but the problem remains that there will then be two reports against the main application for discharge. It helps to know which tribunal members have been appointed and what sort of progress is likely to be made questioning the responsible medical officer's opinion. One must also bear in mind the possibility of the patient making some further improvement by the time of the hearing. If discharge on the existing evidence is a possibility, even if unlikely, then it is generally best not to put the report in evidence. The tribunal require seven copies of any report which is tendered in evidence.

Restricted cases

Where a report commissioned on the patient's behalf relates to a restricted patient, it is important to remember to send a copy to the Secretary of State if it is being disclosed. This avoids any possibility of the hearing being adjourned because the Home Secretary has not had an opportunity to see and comment on the report.

OBTAINING FURTHER INFORMATION

In restricted cases, some of the material originally before the court may be available to the patient's solicitor through alternative sources. For instance, from records held at the Crown Court or deposited in the county archives. These are almost always made available for inspection to the solicitor upon written request, together with a written authority for their disclosure from the patient himself. Other relevant files may be held by the solicitors who acted for the patient at his trial or from a firm which acted for him at a previous tribunal. Again, a written request accompanied by the client's authority for disclosure will normally be required.

Long-stay patients

The relevant local NHS trust will be able to provide details of hostels and other community resources managed by the trust or by bodies with which it has contracted. The local social services authority will have published a community care plan, which includes details of local facilities. They will also have a community care charter, giving the patient a right to a community care assessment within a certain period of time. Details of mental health associations operating in the area may be obtained from the Longman's Social Services Yearbook and from the social services authority itself. Such associations may own or manage suitably staffed hostels or supported housing, or be able to offer some form of day-time support.

CONTACTING FAMILY MEMBERS AND WITNESSES

Initially, there are usually no witnesses who positively support the patient's discharge. However, as his improves, this often changes and the nearest relative may then be willing to make an order for discharge. It is always worthwhile speaking with involved relatives and carers. Firstly, they are likely to attend the tribunal in their own right, so it is important to have advanced warning of what their evidence is likely to be. Secondly, part of the evidence they could give, if asked the relevant question, is likely to be positive. Thirdly, they may have information which contradicts facts in the reports upon which the responsible medical officer's opinion is based. Fourthly, they may disagree with some of the opinions and inferences drawn in the medical report. Fifthly, they may have valuable information concerning the causes of the admission which is important in enlisting the tribunal's sympathy. Sixthly, they may have positive information concerning the prognosis, *e.g.* the patient's condition has always remitted within three weeks, he is then ready to leave hospital and complies with medication. Lastly, the relative may be able to offer support and supervision, which reassures the tribunal.

COMMENTS AND OBSERVATIONS ON THE REPORTS

It is exceptional for reports to be furnished within the statutory period but this does not make it excusable. Enquiries should be made of the hospital and the tribunal if they have not been received by the time the prescribed period expires. Delay in preparing a medical report often means that the consultant does not envisage that a hearing will eventually be necessary because the patient will be discharged by him before then. Hence he has no intention of writing a report which will not be used. Indeed, the patient may be symptom free and compliant so that little can be written in favour of compulsion. That being so, the consultant is often disposed to discharge the patient if he is forced to explain in writing the current justification for the power of detention. For example, because a direction requiring him to furnish a report within seven days is being sought under rule 13. Once the reports have been received, it will obviously be necessary to obtain the client's detailed instructions on them. Relevant factual information can be added to the case summary but the patient's comments should be set out in a separate statement. Every solicitor has their own methods of working but it can also be useful to highlight or underline in red ink those passages to be put to the patient for comment at the hearing, using blue ink for the lines to be put to the writer of the report.

Content of the medical report

The content of any psychiatric report is the product of two things: the content of the patient's mind interpreted by the content of the doctor's mind. The evidence of mental disorder consists of facts (things actually said to or observed by the writer), inferences from these facts, hearsay (facts communicated to the doctor), inferences from hearsay, assumptions about matters not reported or observed, and presumptions about what causes and alleviates severe mental distress. Many matters presented as fact are nothing more tangible than suppositions or inferences based on the assumed content of the patient's mind. There is often scope for hearsay gradually to acquire by virtue of frequent repetition the status of hard fact, or for established facts to become distorted.

Submitting observations to the tribunal

Rule 12 allows the representative to submit written observations on the reports. This enables the issues and any matters in dispute to be clarified and itemised in advance of the hearing. Because the responsible authority's statement is necessarily adverse to discharge, the written observations therefore ensure that the members do not come to the hearing aware only of the reasons for detention and perhaps with an unconscious inclination against discharge. Early observations may also allow the medical member to be aware of the issues likely to be canvassed at the hearing and he can then examine the patient with these in mind before forming his preliminary opinion.

CROSS-REFERENCES

The reader is referred to the following parts of the book in relation to matters which may arise during the preparation of the case.

Legal requirements of reports

Prescribed content	As to the prescribed content of medical and social circumstances reports and their disclosure to the patient, see **662**, **681**, **682**.
Inadequate reports	As to the tribunal's power to direct that a supplementary medical or social circumstances report be furnished where a report is inadequate, see **783**.
Late reports	As to the tribunal's power to direct that a report now due be furnished within a certain period, see **784.**
Discharge powers	As to the statutory criteria for discharge, and a tribunal's other powers, see chapters 7–9.

The medical report

Medical terms	As to the meaning of terms used to describe symptoms of mental disorder, see chapter 18 and the index (*"Words and phrases — Medical"*).
The diagnosis	As to the way in which mental disorders are classified, a diagnosis is made, and the reliability of diagnoses, see chapter 19. As to the legal meaning of "mental disorder" and its four forms, see chapter 2.

Medical tests	As to laboratory tests, EEGs, brain scans and psychometric tests, see Chapter 19.
The treatment	As to a local authority's functions under the National Health Service & Community Care Act 1990, see **154**. As to the provision of accommodation, state benefits and of occupational, medical and community services, see **687**.
Risk assessment & discharge planning	As to the assessment of risks involved in discharge, in particular the risk of suicide or serious violence towards others, and discharge planning, see chapter 12.
Health Service	As to the organisation of the National Health Service, the role of professionals supplementary to medicine, and the functions of the hospital managers, see chapter 3.
Independent reports	As to the patient's statutory right to have an independent medical examination, see **616, 711**.

The social circumstances report

Community care	As to a local authority's functions under the National Health Service & Community Care Act 1990, see **154**. As to the provision of accommodation, state benefits and of occupational, medical and community services, see **687**.
After-care	As to the duty to provide after-care, and the power to provide it under statutory supervision, see chapter 6.
Local authorities	As to the organisation of social services authorities and the statutory functions of approved social workers, see **151, 160**.

The Secretary of State's statement

Home Secretary	As to the Home Secretary's functions, and those of the Aarvold Board, see **162**.
Powers	As to the Home Secretary's powers and approach to cases, see **762, 334 et seq**.

Procedural matters

Procedure	As to the transfer, joinder, and withdrawal of proceedings, see **638 et seq**. As to adjournments, see **817**. As to the giving of notice of the hearing, and the venue, see **794**.

THE HEARING

The hearing is partly inquisitorial and one conducted by an expert body in a manner which is as informal as possible. The role of advocacy is this context is that of adducing oral evidence and conducting a reasoned examination of the arguments advanced in support of compulsory powers. There are several good books on advocacy which contain guidance on questioning medical witnesses, the best of which is John Munkman's *The technique of advocacy* (Butterworths, 1991), on which the text draws. The most helpful advice for a lawyer undertaking his first hearing is not to be embarrassed by any unexpected turn of events: the tribunal will have seen it all before. If the client's behaviour is affected by the stress, or he finds it impossible to give his evidence in a coherent way, support him and be kindly.

THE CLIENT'S EVIDENCE

It is important to get to the hospital in good time for a meeting with the client. Apart from the fact that a doctor or social worker may bring a supplementary report with him to the hearing, the mental state of some clients is quite variable. If so, the way it was envisaged that the case for discharge would be presented may have to be revised, in the light of the client's current mental state. Arriving early also helps the anxious client and enables the representative to remind him of the procedure and to get him in a positive frame of mind. The patient is taken through his case by the representative, the purpose being to draw out the evidence in a complete and orderly way, subject to relevance and selection. This requires a good proof, preferably one that presents the case in an ordered way. The case summary is useful in this respect because it is structured with the hearing in mind and the order of the client's evidence can often follow that set out in the summary. Thus, the client may first be asked about his family circumstances, accommodation, employment opportunities and so forth. This gives him a chance to relax before moving on to the present admission and subsequent developments and, finally, the more difficult areas of insight, medication and after-care. The occasional judicial president likes to move matters on at a greater speed, not seeing the purpose of dealing with non-contentious matters first, but this is precisely the kind of approach calculated to dissuade patients from ever applying again.[52] Where possible, the art is to guide without leading and to raise all those points which tend both towards and against discharge. The client should therefore be warned by his representative that he will be asking questions which the client perhaps prefer were not asked and rather not answer. There is, however, no point in hoping that he will not be asked about matters such as whether he accepts that he is ill and needs medication. He will be and he will also be referred to anything which he has previously said or done which is inconsistent with his evidence to the tribunal. The aim must be to admit and avoid, to tone down the damage and to bring out this evidence without emphasis. If the representative asks those stock questions bound to elicit answers unfavourable to discharge, at least he can set them in a sandwich of favourable points. In restricted cases, a demonstration of remorse is often a prerequisite of discharge, so it is important to deal with the client's attitude to his offending. This is something of a public humiliation for him but tribunals rarely interpret silence for the shame it most often is. Some sample questions, the relevance of which obviously has to be determined according to the particular case, are set out on the following page.

---

[52] See *e.g.* S. Dell and A. Grounds, *The discharge and supervision of restricted clients* (Institute of Criminology, 1996), p.69.

Accommodation

- Where the client proposes to live
- Type of accommodation
- Basis of the client's occupancy
- Who will be living with him
- Community ties and support

Family support

- Details of family members
- Level of family support in hospital
- Family's attitude to the patient returning home
- Divorce/separation issues, if relevant

Employment, education and training

- Employment in the past
- Whether any job is available to the client
- Whether and when he proposes to return to work
- How he will cope with the stress of returning to work
- Any courses or training he proposes to undertake

Financial position

- Debts and savings
- Any pending litigation concerning debts
- How client will cope financially
- Entitlement to state benefits

Physical health

- Any relevant physical health problems

Drugs and alcohol

- Whether client takes illegal drugs
- Attitude to such drugs and their role in his admission
- Whether client accepts that illegal drugs may adversely affect his mental state
- Client's attitude to the risks of combining medication with unprescribed drugs
- Alcohol consumption at the time of admission, if relevant

Forensic history and index offence

Deal with convictions for violence. Take a restricted client through the Secretary of State's account of the index offence, eliciting any mitigating circumstances.

- Does the client regret what he did? If so, why?

- What was the effect on the victim? What does he think the victim's feelings towards him are now? Will the victim have forgotten what happened? If previously an acquaintance, would the victim want to see him again? (psychopathic disorder — issue of empathy)

- Was a restriction order justified? Was it too harsh? If so, what would have been an appropriate punishment?

- Was anyone put at risk by what he did (arson)? What were the possible consequences?

- If he became ill again, might there be a risk that he would do something similar — if not, why not?

- Does he think that he needs supervision on leaving hospital?

Psychiatric history

- Go through the history of admissions, as briefly as possible

- Does the client accept that any of them were necessary?

Present admission and present mental state

- Go through the relevant passages of the medical and social circumstances reports.

- Mood — ask the client about any symptoms of a mood disorder referred to in the reports

- Thought content — ask the client about any delusional beliefs referred to in the reports

- Perception — ask the client about any hallucinations or illusions referred to in the reports

- Compulsive or ritualistic behaviour — ask the client about any compulsive or ritualistic behaviour referred to in the reports

- Does the client accept that such beliefs or behaviour indicate the presence of a mental illness?

- What events or concerns gave rise to the admission? What were the circumstances immediately preceding the decision to invoke compulsory powers which led to that decision being taken?

- Does the client accept that he was mentally unwell at the time of admission and/or that he needed to be in hospital? If he accepts that he required medical help, in what way? How would he describe that illness? What were the symptoms, the exact way in which he was unwell?

- Did the circumstances also justify the conclusion that his admission was justified or necessary for his own health or safety or to protect others?

- Why does he think that he became unwell? Did anything happen before he came to hospital which contributed to his becoming ill?

- Does he consider that his mental state is now different? If so, in what way? Does he consider that he still needs in-patient treatment? If so, for how much longer?

- Does he consider that he is now functioning at his optimum level? If not, in what respects does he feel that he is still not entirely back to his normal self?

933

- If the patient believes that his admission was unnecessary but has had previous admissions, were all of those admissions also unwarranted? If the patient disputes the evidence in the reports, what motive does he ascribe to the reporter for giving that account?

Events since the patient's admission

- *Deal with anything adverse but also emphasise all those things which commonly justify detention but that which haven't happened in this particular case.*

- Does the client spend all his time on the ward. If so, is this by choice or because it is a locked ward and part of his management programme?

- Is he is allowed off the ward and, if so, for how long each day? Is this with or without a nursing escort? If without an escort, does he require express permission or does he have a "general pass" to be off the ward?

- Is he allowed leave only within the confines of the hospital grounds or does he also enjoy town leave? When the client goes into the local town, how does he spend his time?

- Has the client been granted any day or weekend leave at home? If so, for how long has he had the benefit of this? What, if any, are the conditions imposed on that leave?

- Is it alleged that any untoward incidents have occurred while he has been on leave?

- Has his leave ever been revoked or cancelled?

- Has he always returned to the ward from leave at the required time? If not, was he so late returning that he was treated by ward staff as being absent without leave? If so, for how long was he away and did he return of his own volition or was he returned by police or nursing staff? Where was he during his absence? Did he take medication during that period?

- If the client is currently spending all or most of his time on the ward, what is the more important goal for him? To be at home, even if on section, or to be off section even if in hospital?

- Has the client been restrained or placed in seclusion?

- Has it been alleged that he has harmed himself or assaulted anyone?

- Has it been alleged that he has damaged any property on the ward or has been physically or verbally threatening?

- Has anyone formally complained about his conduct on the ward?

Current medication and treatment

- What medication or other treatment is being prescribed?

- Has the client consented to receiving the prescribed treatment?

- Has he refused medication or refused to attend any part of the ward programme?

- Has the medication been beneficial in any way?

- What would be the likely effects, if any, of now ceasing medication? Would there be any risk of his health deteriorating?

- What is the medication given for? Has its purpose been explained to him? What are its likely effects? Does the medication have any adverse effects? If so, is the client receiving further medication to control the effects of the other medication? If so, does that medication in turn have adverse effects?

- Might the patient be prepared to consider taking some alternative medication prescribed by his doctor? Has he previously taken any medication which he considers did help and which he was, and would be, willing to take?

- If he considers that he is now functioning normally, does he still need the medication which is being prescribed for him?

- If he says he is now well, and has not had any kind of mental health problem, then why would he take the medication at all, particular if it has very unpleasant adverse effects?

- If he considers that he has been ill but is now well, what does he think has brought about that improvement? *The client may ascribe this to rest and a break from problems at home or work.* If so, he should be asked if he thinks that the medication has helped? Is there any significance in the fact that his voices returned (or whatever) when he ceased medication and then went away when the medication was resumed? *If he concedes the point but states that he no longer needs it because he is now cured, he should be asked to consider whether it may be that the medication which has made him well is keeping him well. The prescription of insulin may be used as an example.*

- If the section was revoked and he was free to decide for himself whether or not to take that medication, would he take all of it, part of it or none of it? At the current doses or in smaller dosages? If all or some, for how much longer? Who would decide when he no longer required it, he or the doctor? What if at the end of the period he says he will take it for, his doctor strongly advises him to continue? Would he heed that advice or not?

- Does he have any objection to receiving the medication by injection?

The ward programme

- What therapeutic activities does the client participate in — art therapy, occupational therapy, self-care skills (laundry, budgeting, etc.) — whilst in hospital

After-care and supervision

- Previous record of compliance with after-care. Has the client ever discharged himself against medical advice?

- Would he be willing to remain in hospital as an informal patient until his doctor is satisfied that appropriate arrangements had been made for his care outside hospital? How long is he willing to remain for?

- What support, if any, would he be willing to accept when discharged from hospital? Would he be willing to be visited by a community psychiatric nurse, to see a social worker, or to attend out-patient appointments at the hospital or a local clinic? Would he be willing to see his General Practitioner periodically if so advised?

- Restricted patients — does the patient understand the likely consequence of not complying with any conditions of discharge (power of recall)?

Final questions

- Final questions to draw together the main points in favour of discharge — Is it therefore the case that ...

THE RESPONSIBLE AUTHORITY'S EVIDENCE

The aim of questioning the responsible authority's witnesses is to test and probe the accuracy of the evidence, hoping thereby to weaken it, and to elicit further favourable evidence. Thus, Munkman says that the general purpose is like testing the strength of a piece of rope inch-by-inch, strand by strand. Ultimately, however, questioning the facts cannot be expected to shake an account which is substantially true. Questioning is more likely to reveal faulty observation; errors of interpretation; errors of memory; errors of expression, such as exaggeration; and bias in the sense of prejudging some relevant issue. The techniques here are insinuation and probing.

Insinuation and probing

According to Munkman, *Insinuation* involves bringing out new facts and new possibilities, thereby weakening the sting of the version forwarded, and presenting a more favourable view or explanation of the evidence. It may take the form of quietly leading the witness through his evidence, adding facts at one point and modifying details at others. *Probing* involves enquiring thoroughly into the details of the witness's evidence, to discover flaws or to open up a new lead. It may consist of testing whether something stated as a positive fact is in fact that or partly fact and partly the witness's preconceptions or interpretation of the facts. *Bias* is undermined by letting a witness talk and leading him on to show his bias by exaggeration.

RESPONSIBLE MEDICAL OFFICER

The responsible medical officer is questioned first of all by the tribunal's medical member and then by the other tribunal members. It will immediately be apparent whether, based on the reports and the medical member's examination, the tribunal is inclined towards discharge or against discharge. The doctor will either be asked to justify the case for detention or be asked leading questions, along the lines of "do you agree that this is a serious illness?" Consequently, if the responsible medical officer gives his evidence first, before the patient, the extent of the task ahead is made clear. The key is then good preparation and mastering the facts and areas of medical knowledge.

Conclusion must be different if facts different

Any expert's opinion consists of inferences which may or may not be sound, based on facts which may or may not be true. The first approach is to elucidate precisely the facts and inferences upon which the conclusion rests. The facts will often have changed in the patient's favour since the report was written. In general, the first step is to suggest that if the facts are not quite as the expert had been led to believe, or as they had been when his report was written, then the conclusion must be different from that initially given by him. In short, one uses the technique of insinuation to suggest other possibilities. Similarly, if the doctor's conclusion was based on facts which have been disproved then as a matter of logic the inferences to be drawn from the new facts cannot be exactly the same as before.

What conclusion patient's evidence points to if true

Even if the facts remain in dispute, one can put to him the patient's view of events and ask, "if the patient's summary of events were correct, what inferences would you draw; in what way would the view you have forwarded need to be qualified?"

Validity of the inferences given unchanged facts

A further approach is to challenge the validity of the inferences which have been drawn, assuming the facts are as stated by the doctor. This is again by insinuation. The doctor may be referred to authoritative passages from books on medicine or to the patient's own medical opinion, based on the same evidence. The are few universal truths in psychiatry and research can generally throw up alternative evidence favouring treatment in the community and so forth. Complete mastery of the subject is unnecessary because most cases turn on specific, narrow areas. As long as the advocate can identify the relevant areas in advance, he can research those areas in some detail. Most doctors have inadequate time to prepare their case or allot a low priority to tribunals and do not properly prepare their case. The practitioner will not expect the patient's advocate to have a knowledge of his subject. There is then the possibility of drawing out rash statements, not based on the facts or consistent with research. For example, one consultant tried to shore up his case by saying that his diagnosis was based on the guidelines set out in the DSM-III-R classification, thinking that that would put an end to the discussion. In fact, the fourth revision had been in force for eight months, thereby revealing that he did not know the status of one of the two main international classifications of mental disorders.

The silent evidence

It is easy to forget that what does not exist is a fact — it is evidence. A medical report will necessarily record any symptoms of mental disorder, but it will not specify all of the questions asked and the matters raised which, when dealt with, were indicative of normal mental functioning. That being so, it conceals a great deal of normal mental phenomena and the greater truth is sometimes to be found not in what a report says but in what it does not say. The representative must seek out and draw attention to this silent evidence. The question is what may be inferred from the fact that these signs of mental disorder are absent, and the client has not behaved in manner x or y. The burden of proof being on the patient, his task is primarily one of establishing that certain things do not exist and hence the tribunal may be satisfied that he is not mentally disordered or his detention is unnecessary. Unless the case is clear cut, it is fundamental to list all the mental phenomena listed in the diagnostic guidelines for the condition and to ask the consultant whether the symptom or sign has been reported or elicited. Similarly, one must establish that the patient has not absented himself without leave, has complied with the ward programme, has not been violent, has not tried to harm himself, and so forth.

Fall-back positions

Just as lawyers who cannot give a court some authority for a proposition commonly resort to the feeble justifications of "inherent jurisdiction," "first principles," or "the common law," so doctors have a similar range of stock answers when nothing more tangible can be had. They may say that their judgment is based on "clinical experience." Experience can consist of nothing more than making the same misjudgement over a number of years and the question remains, "given your (considerable) clinical experience, what signs of mental disorder have you elicited?" Furthermore, "given your clinical experience, if sign x was present would not a man of your experience usually be able to elicit it." Likewise, if the doctor resorts to the argument that the patient is concealing symptoms, knowing that this cannot be disproved, the obvious and only question is: "How confident are you in your ability as a psychiatrist to elicit any signs of mental disorder when you examine a patient?" If, alternatively, it is asserted that the patient remains mentally disordered but the medication is masking his symptoms, it must be pointed out that the doctor cannot know that. A significant number of patients remit naturally: "how can you know that?" The neat answer, "clinical experience," may be followed with, "But that is clinical experience of other patients: what evidence do you have that *this* patient remains mentally disordered?" Then go through one of the two main international classifications and refer to each symptom one by one, asking the doctor if he has any evidence that it is present. Other common devices include meaningless statements such as "he lacks insight into the fact that he is ill and this demonstrates the fact that he remains ill," "his unwillingness to continue with medication indicates that he is still ill," and "I know the patient." Faced with this kind of reasoning, a third approach is that of undermining the doctor's competence to form an opinion. The aim here is to undermine the very foundations of the evidence by showing that he does not know what he is talking about. Many doctors initially only interview their patients for whatever period they deem necessary to reach a diagnosis and to prescribe a course of medication. The patient may then only see his consultant for five minutes each week and not have been interviewed by him for several months. It is often possible to come up a whole range of previous symptoms and facts unknown to the consultant but which he should know if he had properly assessed the patient. Thus, if the doctor is unaware that a young patient saw a child psychiatrist at school, one may innocently ask, "Do you consider that the treatment which *x* received while at school has any significance in terms of the diagnosis?" or "You must have talked at some length with *x* about his psychiatric difficulties at school?" Alternatively, one may ask whether the client has ever experienced olfactory hallucinations and, having been told not, invite the client to give an account of the fact that he was experiencing them at the time of his admission. Another option is simply to ask the doctor about the support available from the patient's family. Often, he will not know their names or how many siblings there are at home. Unpleasantness being a last resort, the tactic is best reserved as a response to high-handedness. Sample questions which may be asked of the doctor are listed on the next page.

SOCIAL WORK REPORT

By the time the social worker gives evidence, the tribunal has often come to a view. Consequently, the evidence may consist of little more than the professional adopting his report. The most common defect in the social circumstances report is simply that it does not include the information required by Schedule 1, Part B of the Mental Health Review Tribunal Rules 1983. In this case, the social worker should be taken through the schedule and asked to give the evidence orally. Where there are serious omissions in the provision being made by social services, reference should be made to the authority's statutory duties, which are set out in chapters 3, 11 and 12. Where the after-care planning is inadequate, the social worker should be referred to the relevant guidelines concerning the need to have an after-care plan in place when a tribunal sits. If future discharge or deferred conditional discharge may be necessary, how long it will take to make any necessary arrangements must be established. The issue of transfer into guardianship is occasionally an issue, and worth pursuing. In appropriate cases, the representative will now wish to elicit the opinion that a supervision application is unnecessary. He may also venture to obtain an opinion as to whether the patient should remain liable to detention. However, although approved social workers make the vast majority of applications for detention, they are often reluctant to express any opinion as to this.

- Go through relevant passages in medical report.

- Show that the facts have changed since then so the conclusion must also be different.

- Take responsible medical officer through statutory criteria, including (in unrestricted s.3/37 cases) the discretionary discharge matters in s.72(2) and the recommendations referred to in s.72(3) — why would leave of absence be inappropriate?

- What is the diagnosis *(if in doubt or significant to treatment and prognosis)*?

- Expert *y* in his book says, ... Are you aware of his findings ? Has any relevant research been conducted since then tending to show otherwise?

- *Z* has given evidence for the patient that a different approach is appropriate: would you accept that there is no single correct approach? You agree therefore more than one inference can be drawn from these facts?

- What symptoms or signs of mental disorder are currently apparent?

- Is it the case that those symptoms are not sufficient to meet the diagnostic guidelines for .... set out in the ICD-10 classification and the patient is therefore at the very least in remission?

- What is it about the nature or degree of those symptoms which in your view makes them so serious that it is appropriate to deprive this citizen of his liberty?

- What were the circumstances on (date) which dictated that the needs of the situation could not be met except by detaining the patient?

- What progress has been made since then?

- What symptoms present at the time of admission are no longer present?

- Is it the case therefore that not all of the circumstances which in your opinion warranted detention at that time still exist?

- If progress has been made and the patient's mental state is now improved, it must be the case that the risks associated with the patient being at home have also receded?

- Would the patient meet the statutory criteria for being compulsorily admitted to hospital if he was not presently detained?

- Since you have the power to discharge the patient, do you regularly review his case to satisfy yourself that the use of compulsory powers continues to be appropriate? And you weigh up the arguments for and against discharge? *[On the assumption the answer is "yes"]* What are the points for discharge?

- What improvement, and in what areas, would need to be made for you to be satisfied that liability to detention is no longer appropriate?

- Would you accept that the present degree of disorder does not make liability to detention appropriate — your report justifies this on the basis of the history of relapse, that is the nature of the disorder?

- How confident are you in your ability to elicit at examination any symptoms which may be present? (allegation that patient is concealing symptoms)

- Would you agree that the previous admissions have tended to be short-lived; that the patient responds quickly to a resumption of medication?

- Is the patient being treated under the authority of a Form 38 or a Form 39? [If a form 38] So it is the case therefore that you have signed a legal certificate to the effect that x understands the nature, purpose and likely effects of the treatment you are prescribing for him and he consents to that treatment? [Yes] And you would not sign such a certificate, and not call in the Mental Health Act Commission, unless it was true and the client had given a valid and free consent? So, if the client understands the nature, purpose and likely effects of the treatment and consents to it, he has insight, does he not?

- What compulsory powers have been necessary — does the patient presently require actual detention? Has it been necessary to restrain him? Has he absented himself and it been necessary to return him? Has it been necessary to administer medication by force? If none of the powers conferred by the application have recently been necessary, what purpose are the compulsory powers serving? How can they be necessary for his health or safety or to protect others? If they have not been necessary, this is surely because the patient has been compliant and co-operative?

- You would not let a person out of the hospital alone if there was a significant risk that he might harm himself or others? [No] But you let x leave the hospital alone? [Yes] So that must mean that you do not consider there is any such risk to himself or others?

- You have granted x leave to be absent from hospital? [Yes] It is correct that under section 17 you have power to impose any conditions on that leave which you consider necessary in the interests of the patient or for the protection of other persons? And you could even require him to be in custody during his absence? You have not imposed any conditions — so that must mean that x's interests and those of other people do not require that he is escorted or subject to conditions when in the community?

- You have granted x extended leave? You can revoke that under section 17, and recall him to hospital, if that is necessary for his health or safety or to protect others? [Yes] But you have not recalled him? [No] So those grounds for again detaining x have not existed since then? So at present it is not necessary for his health or safety, or to protect others, that he is in hospital?

Chronic patient with very limited insight

- You have been the patient's consultant for x years. During that period have you ever reached agreement about whether he has a mental illness and requires medication? If not, what is the likelihood of a change of attitude now? In the absence of any community treatment order, is this not a case where admission can only ever fulfil the limited practical aim of treating an acute phase of illness and that has been done? What do you realistically hope to achieve through a further prolongation of detention? What foreseeable gain justifies such a continued loss of liberty?

- If the client will always suffer from mental disorder, is he now functioning at his optimum level? If so, and it is not suggested that he needs to remain in hospital for life, what is the discharge plan?

- Lishman has written that, "it is not infrequently noted that patients lack detailed knowledge of key features of their abnormal beliefs and experiences on recovery from schizophrenia or severe affective disorder." (W.A. Lishman, *Organic Psychiatry, The Psychological Consequences of Cerebral Disorder*, 2nd Ed., Blackwell, 1987, p.32.) You would agree that he was a very eminent psychiatrist and that is a leading textbook? It is possible therefore to have recovered but for the rational mind to be unable to comprehend that it had acted so irrationally? (allegation of lack of insight)

- Is it not the case that x has been in hospital for [25 years] and is mentally incapable of arranging his own discharge if informal?

Forensic cases

- Ask questions to highlight the fact that the client has not recently been violent, has not required restraint, has not damaged property, has not absconded.

- Point out that the offence occurred at a time when the illness was undiagnosed and x was not receiving any treatment or supervision. Since he has been receiving proper medication, has he ever been violent?

- If he is on a slow-acting injection, does that not mean that you would have plenty of time to readmit him if he defaulted on medication before his condition deteriorated?

- Would you agree that a ward is in many ways a much more provocative and stressful place than being in the community? There is little privacy and a much higher proportion of disturbed people to contend with? If one can cope with such behaviour without reacting violently, that is a very good sign?

- X was diagnosed as having a psychopathic disorder mainly because of his immaturity. You say he is now much more mature. Would you agree that maturity is not like mental illness, once you have matured — grown up — you cannot later unmature?

- Has any information come to light since the last report which increases understanding of the circumstances surrounding the index offence?

- Is the motivation for behaviour that has put others at risk understood?

- Is there any evidence that the patient has an ongoing preoccupation with a particular type of victim or a particular type of violent/sexual/arsonist activity?

- What are the chances of circumstances similar to those surrounding the offence arising again and similar offences occurring?

- In cases of mental illness, what effects have any prescribed drugs had? Do any symptoms remain? Has stability been maintained in differing circumstances? Does the patient have insight into the need for medication?

- In cases of mental impairment, has the patient benefited from training? Is the patient's behaviour more socially acceptable? Is the patient explosive or impulsive?

- In cases of personality disorder, is the patient now more mature, predictable and concerned about others? Is he more tolerant of frustration and stress? Does he now take into account the consequences of his actions? Does he learn from experience?

- Does the patient now have greater insight into his condition? Is he more realistic and reliable?

- Have alcohol or drugs affected the patient in the past? Did either contribute towards his offences?

- Has the patient responded to stressful situations in the hospital in the past and how does he respond now — with physical aggression or verbal aggression?

- If the patient is a sex offender, has he shown in the hospital an undesirable interest in the type of person he has previously been known to favour as his victim? What form has any sexual activity taken? What have been the results of any psychological tests?

- Emphasise the predictability of the offending behaviour and the specificity of the victim. The circumstances in which the patient might be violent are reasonably well established.

- If the patient is on leave, emphasise that he has already had ample opportunity to cause harm.

SUBMISSIONS

Submissions should be kept brief, so that the determinative points are not lost amongst a welter of secondary considerations. Two to three minutes usually suffices to sum up the points which will be telling, if any are. Where the facts are almost wholly contrary to discharge, the representative has little alternative but to steer well clear of them and to make a technical submission, supported by the odd favourable point of evidence: (1) the patient has told you that he is not mentally ill, and never has been. Accordingly, if you prefer his evidence, you will inevitably discharge and I need not address you further as to that. However, if the tribunal does not accept that evidence, it is nevertheless the case that (2) only ten per cent of in-patients are detained, the threshold for loss of liberty being a high one which few in-patients satisfy; (3) In *Buxton v. Jayne*, Devlin L.J. said that "the unsoundness of mind, whose presence is essential to justify a compulsory order, manifestly means more than mental illness which qualifies a person to be a voluntary patient ... in ordinary language "certifiable" is perhaps more likely to be used to express the same idea." (4) Furthermore, Lord Denning M.R. observed in the case of *Ghani v. Jones* that an Englishman's liberty is not to be denied except on the surest of grounds and that remains the law; (5) taking these points together, it is clear that the circumstances in which liability to detention is appropriate are very few indeed; (6) on the evidence, this is not such an exceptional case that the law can or should sanction deprivation of liberty; (7) in particular, there is no history of violence to others, *x*'s condition has improved since admission, the following symptoms then present are no longer present. etc. [whatever can usefully be said]; (8) there are appropriate facilities available in the community and, if necessary, discharge could be postponed for 21 days for arrangements to be made; (9) the responsible medical officer accepted that progress has been made and this would have the incidental benefit of consolidating that progress prior to discharge; (10) in the alternative, a period of trial leave is appropriate, to establish whether further detention for treatment is necessary and appropriate. As to more hopeful cases, the existence of certain facts is generally favourable to discharge: the absence of any positive symptoms of mental disorder; the fact that the illness was sudden in onset and short-lived; the fact that a patient accepts that he is mentally ill and requires treatment, where that is the case; the fact that a client knows the risks associated with stopping medication against medical advice; the fact that the adverse effects of medication are not debilitating; a willingness to remain in hospital informally; a willingness to attend out-patient appointments and to accept supervision; the fact that in-patient treatment is not presently necessary and the client has extended leave to be absent from hospital; a record of compliance with medication; a history of informal admission; relatives who support the need for treatment and will encourage the patient to take medication; the fact that the client has nowhere else to go and will have to remain in hospital for the time being; an absence of any convictions for violence; treatment on an open ward; such a lack of capacity, or such a predominance of negative symptoms, that the patient is incapable of organising his own discharge; a good therapeutic relationship with nursing staff; that this is a first admission and there is no history of chronicity; the fact that the patient's career or employment prospects will be harmed by a prolonged admission; that the patient has been honest about his symptoms; that this is the first time the patient has been sectioned and he now knows that non-compliance has legal consequences and leads to loss of liberty (one is never free from the legal consequences of one's actions and all discharges are conditional in this sense).

POST-HEARING CONSIDERATIONS

In section 2 cases, the decision is sometimes announced by the tribunal after the members have completed their deliberations. Most often, it is communicated in writing although, if the patient is to be discharged, his written copy of the decision is usually sent down to the ward later that same day. The representative will, of course, remain a while with the client, to discuss with him how the hearing went, and to offer support at the beginning of what is an anxious wait for him. He should also escort him back to the ward (whether or not that has been requested). Once the written decision has been received, the representative should speak with the client if he was not discharged and also write to him concerning the reasons and his further rights of appeal. He may wish to apply to the hospital managers for them to exercise their power of discharge if he has not already done so (**144**).

Provisional decisions

In restriction direction cases, the Secretary of State has 90 days in which to notify the tribunal whether a section 47 patient can be discharged in accordance with its finding (**557**). In restriction order cases, the patient will need to keep the file open if the tribunal deferred a direction for the patient's conditional discharge. The rules do not provide for the tribunal reconvening if satisfactory arrangements complying with the conditions of discharge cannot be made, although tribunals have been known to reconvene in order to receive an explanation of the problems. At any rate, the solicitor will need to periodically liaise with the hospital concerned if there is any prolonged delay. In appropriate cases, it may eventually be necessary to commence High Court proceedings if the local Health Authority and social services authority is not providing services which the tribunal's direction or the appropriate legislation requires them to provide. There is, of course, nothing to prevent the Home Secretary from granting the patient leave or from transferring the patient to a less secure hospital during the intervening period and, given the discharge direction, he should be encouraged to do so.

Statutory recommendations

If the tribunal made a recommendation under section 72 in respect of an unrestricted patient, the decision should specify the date on which the tribunal will further consider the case in the event its recommendation is not complied with. Again, the file will need to be kept open and in this case the tribunal may reconvene if its recommendation is not complied with (**853**). As to whether a tribunal which reconvenes can then discharge the patient, see page 476.

MHRT CASE SUMMARY

1. PRELIMINARY DETAILS

Surname			
First names			
Date of Birth		**Age**	
Ward			
Hospital			
Hospital address			
Hospital number		**Hospital tel.**	
RMO			
Social Worker			
Legal status	Informal (voluntary) / Informal (incapacitated) Section 5(2) / 5(4) / 135 / 136 Section 4 / 2 / 3 / 7 / 25A Section 35 / 36 / 38 / 43 / 48 / 48&49 Hospital Order (s.37) / Guardianship Order (s.37) / Restriction Order (ss.37&41) / Limitation direction (s.45A) / Restriction Order (s.46) / Section 47 / Sections 47&49 / Conditionally discharged		
Nationality	British /	**Language**	

FAMILY

Marital status	Married / cohabiting / divorced / separated / single		
Name of spouse / cohabitee			
Father		**Age**	
Mother		**Age**	
Siblings (give age)			
Level of contact with family/carers			
In care or under supervision now or in the past?			Yes / No
Ward of court now or in the past?			Yes / No
Cared for by a guardian now or in the past?			Yes / No
If the answer to any of the above questions is "yes", give details—			

945

2. STATUTORY NEAREST RELATIVE

Full name		
Relationship		
Address		Tel.
Is the nearest relative likely to be willing to discharge the patient?		Yes / No

DETAILS OF ACTING NEAREST RELATIVE (IF RELEVANT)

Court appointee?	Yes / No	Court & date of order	
Authorised under reg. 14?	Yes / No	Date of written authority	
Name of acting NR			
Address of acting NR			Tel.
Is the acting nearest relative likely to be willing to order discharge?			Yes / No

3. ACCOMMODATION / HOUSING

Client's usual address	(No fixed address)
Type of accommodation	House / flat / maisonette / hostel / group home / hospital ward / residential home / nursing home / other ( )
Number of bedrooms	
Other persons in occupation	
Legal basis of client's occupancy	Privately owned (with mortgage) / private landlord / local authority landlord / housing association
Other relevant information	*(e.g. rent arrears, disrepair, court proceedings concerning the property or the client's occupancy)*

Is the above accommodation likely to be available to the client?	Yes / No
Does the client wish to return there?	Yes / No
Is the client willing to consider other types of accommodation?	Yes / No
If yes—	House / flat / maisonette / hostel / group home / hospital ward / residential home / nursing home / other ( )
Is the client being assessed for specialist accommodation?	Yes / No
If yes, give details—	

4. EDUCATION, TRAINING AND EMPLOYMENT

DETAILS OF EMPLOYMENT OR TRAINING

Current employment status	Paid employment / working in the home / unemployed / student / full-time / part-time / sick leave
Post held / course being taken	
Name and address of present employers, educational or training institution, or relevant benefits office	

EDUCATION AND TRAINING

Date	Place of study / type of institution	Qualifications
Until		
Until		
Until		
Until		
Give brief details of any difficulties with reading, writing or numeracy, whether innate or otherwise		
Brief details of any history of special schooling, truancy etc.		

947

EMPLOYMENT SINCE LEAVING FULL-TIME EDUCATION

Approx. dates	Name of employer	Post, trade, etc.

General nature of previous temporary or part-time work undertaken	
Date when last worked	

EMPLOYMENT OR TRAINING POST-DISCHARGE

Is the above employment likely to be still available to the client?	Yes / No / Not applicable
Employment or training which the client wishes to seek post discharge	
Any statutory help to which the client is or may be entitled	
Details of relevant local employment or training projects	

5. FINANCES AND CAPACITY

SAVINGS

Account	Amount
	£
	£
	£
	£
Total	£

STOCKS, SHARES, SAVINGS CERTIFICATES, etc.

Type	Number	Unit price	Approx value
			£
			£
		Total	£

CURRENT WELFARE BENEFITS

Income support	Yes / No	£ per week
Other current benefits		£ per week
		£ per week
		£ per week
	Total	£

CURRENT EXPENSES

	Mortgage / rent	£ wk/mth
Current expenses		£ wk/mth
		£ wk/mth
	Total	£ wk/mth

DEBTS AND LIABILITIES

Summarise general position.

Accommodation arrears	Mortgage arrears	£
	Rent arrears	£
Accounts owing	Catalogue clubs (a) (b) (c)	£ £ £
	Credit cards (a) (b) (c)	£ £ £
Miscellaneous debts	Other outstanding bills (a) (b) (c) (d)	£ £ £ £
	Total debts=	£

CAPACITY TO MANAGE PROPERTY AND AFFAIRS

Are the client's property or finances subject to—	An appointeeship	Yes / No
	The Court of Protection	Yes / No
	An Enduring Power of Attorney	Yes / No
Is the client at present incapable by reason of mental disorder of managing her/his property and affairs?		Yes / No/ Unclear
Is the client likely to become so incapable in the foreseeable future?		Yes / No/ Unclear

6. PHYSICAL HEALTH

Does the client consider her/himself to be in good physical health?	Yes / No
If no, state why, giving date of onset—	
Has the client suffered from any serious illnesses in the past (ignore the usual childhood illnesses)	Yes / No
If yes, give details—	
Has the client suffered any serious physical injuries in the past (e.g. head injuries, road accidents, periods of unconsciousness)	Yes / No

If yes, give details—	
Has the client or a family member ever suffered from epilepsy?	Yes / No / Unclear
If yes, give details—	
Mobility	
Physical signs (tremor, nystagmus, etc.)	

BIOCHEMISTRY

Give details of any abnormal results

7. DRUGS AND ALCOHOL

Does the client consider that s/he is dependent on alcohol or any type of drug?	Yes / No
Has the client tested positive for any non-prescribed drug since admission?	Yes / No
Did the client take any illegal drugs during the month prior to admission?	Yes / No
If yes, give details—	
Give brief details of illegal drug- taking in the past and of any drug dependency	
Give details of alcohol consumption during the month prior to admission	
Give details of any previous treatment for drug or alcohol dependency	

8. FORENSIC HISTORY

PREVIOUS CONVICTIONS (FORM 609)

Details of previous convictions	
Has the client ever been remanded in custody or sentenced to imprisonment in connection with a criminal matter?	Yes / No
If yes, give details	

THE INDEX OFFENCE (SECTIONS 37, 37/41, 45A, 47)

		Case no.	
Court		**Case no.**	
Offence(s) and brief details	(1) (2) (3) (4)		
Date of offence			
Date of conviction			
Plea tendered	Guilty to Not guilty to Insanity / diminished responsibility /		
Date of sentence			
The sentence imposed			
Section 45A, 47, 49 cases only	EDR=		
Was the conviction or sentence appealed?		No / against conviction / against sentence	

If yes, what was the outcome?	
Does the client believe that s/he was wrongfully convicted?	Yes / No
Name and address of the trial solicitors	

CURRENT CRIMINAL PROCEEDINGS

Court		Case no.	
Charges	(1) (2) (3) (4)		
Date of committal			
(Estimated) trial date			
Date of conviction / finding			
Date of sentence			
Anticipated pleas	Already pleaded guilty to and awaiting sentence Guilty to Not guilty to Not guilty by reason of insanity Diminished responsibility Unfit to plead		
Name and address of solicitors dealing with the case			

RESTRICTED PATIENTS

Home Office case reference number		
Allocated case worker		
Are any proposals for leave, transfer or discharge under consideration?	Yes	No
If yes, give details.		

9. PSYCHIATRIC HISTORY

Approximately how many previous in-patient admissions	

Summarise briefly any history of admissions	

Give dates of the previous period of in-patient treatment	

If a first admission, has the patient received any psychiatric treatment in the past?	Yes / No

If yes—	From General Practitioner Attendance at a mental health community centre As an out-patient As a day-patient From a community psychiatric nurse Other...... **The treatment offered or provided**

Family psychiatric history

Have any blood-relatives ever received hospital treatment for a psychiatric problem?	Yes / No

If yes, give details—	

10. AUTHORITY FOR THE COMPULSORY POWERS

The admission and authority for the detention, guardianship or supervision

Date of informal admission			Not applicable /	
Date on which the current period of detention, guardianship or supervision commenced				
			Section	Date
Give details of the sections under which the patient has been detained or subject to guardianship since he was last an informal patient				

	Form	Details		Date
Details of most recent application	Application	NR / ASW	Consult NR Not consult	
	1st. rec	s.12 / previous acquaintance		Exam Signed
	2nd. rec	s.12 / previous acquaintance		Exam Signed
	Joint med rec	(1) s.12 / previous acquaintance		Exam Signed
		(2) s.12 / previous acquaintance		Exam Signed
	Recorded date of compulsory admission (Form 14)			

Are the court order or the application and any subsequent renewal forms valid on their face?	Yes / No
If no or there are other features of note regarding the statutory documentation, give details here. **Also give date and details of any recall in restricted case.**	

11. CIRCUMSTANCES OF THE PRESENT ADMISSION

Events predating the use of compulsory powers

Give details of stressful events predating the use of compulsory powers
(conjugal, parental, occupational, financial, legal, housing, bereavements, illnesses, etc.)

Give details of any cessation of treatment predating the admission
(discontinuance or reduction of medication, etc.)

In cases of relapse, summarise any other common historical trends or factors
(e.g. cyclical illness, anniversary of some previous distressing event, etc.)

Client's account of the events predating the use of compulsory powers

Client's account of the events leading up to the use of compulsory powers

Include client's own assessment of her/his level of functioning prior to admission; performance at home or work, etc.; attitude of family members to the client's interpretation of events. Give details of any incidents of self-harm, damage to property or violence to others)

Client's statement, continued...

Does the client accept that s/he was mentally unwell when admitted?	Yes / No
Does the client accept that s/he needed to be in hospital at the time of admission?	Yes / No
Does the client consider that being in hospital has had any benefits?	Yes / No

12. CURRENT MEDICATION AND TREATMENT

Medication			
	Name of drug	*Route*	*Dosage*
Prescribed depot (if any)			
Prescribed oral medication (if any)	(1)		
	(2)		
	(3)		
	(4)		
	(5)		

ECT			
When commenced	*Type of ECT*	*Number*	*Ended on*

Is there a Form 38 /39 in existence in relation to the ECT?	Form 38 / Form 39 / Section 62 / Date ...

Side-effects of treatment	
Is the client bothered by any side-effects of the treatment?	Yes / No
If yes, give details—	

Consent and compliance with medication		
Is there a Form 38 /39 in existence?	Form 38/ Form 39/ Form not yet due/ Date ...	
Ground upon which Form 39 issued	Incapacity / patient not consenting	
Is the client taking all the prescribed medication?		Yes / No
If no, give details—		
Are the patient's consultant and the nursing staff aware that the patient is not taking this medication?		Yes / No
If the client was free to decide, would s/he voluntarily take the prescribed medication / treatment?	Yes / No	

If yes, for how long?	
If the client was discharged from section, for how long would s/he be willing to remain in hospital?	
If the client was free to decide, what kinds of treatment or support would s/he be willing to accept upon leaving hospital?	

Events and progress since admission

(seclusion, restraint, self-harm, assaults, absence without leave, leave of absence, transfers)

Non-pharmacological treatment / weekly programme of activities

	am	*pm*	*evening*
Monday			
Tuesday			
Wednesday			
Thursday			
Friday			
Saturday			
Sunday			

13. MENTAL STATE AND PRESENTATION

General appearance	
Description of general appearance	
Facial expression	sad, serious, happy, smiling, masked, grimacing
Hygiene	clean, body odour, unshaven
Posture	erect, slumped, stooped, tense, relaxed
Dress	appropriate, neat, clean, dirty, bizarre, dishevelled
Signs of anxiety	restless, pacing, gesturing, hyperactive, agitated, wringing hands

Ability to function emotionally, mentally, socially	
MENTAL CLARITY (orientation: time/place/person, confused, clear, impaired, intellectual function, stupor)	
AFFECT (euphoric, cheerful, apathetic, sad, hopeless, dejected, angry, labile, incongruous)	
SPEECH (talkative, silent, rapid, slurred, clear)	
THOUGHT PROCESSES (loosening of associations, circumstantiality of thought, etc.)	

THOUGHT CONTENT (delusional, fearful, morose, flight of ideas, appropriate) Delusional (paranoid, grandiose, nihilistic, hypochondriacal, delusions of guilt, etc.) Ideas of reference, over-valued ideas, obsessional thoughts, phobias	
PERCEPTION (evidence of hallucinations, illusions) Hallucinations (auditory, visual, olfactory, gustatory, tactile, visceral, kinaesthetic)	
COMPULSIVE OR RITUALISTIC BEHAVIOUR	
MANNER (accepting, trusting, co-operative, suspicious, hostile, obstructive, resentful)	
SUICIDAL (thoughts, gestures, intent)	
MEMORY (short-term, long-term, confabulation)	

CONCENTRATION (attention span)	
GENERAL BEHAVIOUR (normal, overactive, retarded, verbally aggressive, physically aggressive. Details.	
NEGATIVE SYMPTOMS	
ABNORMAL PERSONALITY TRAITS	
OTHER FEATURES	

Summary of mental state

14. DISCUSSIONS WITH THIRD-PARTIES

Nursing staff

Date	Nurse	Details

RMO and other medical staff

Date	Doctor	Details

Allocated social workers

Date	Name	Details

Family members and other witnesses

Date	Name	Details

15. ACTION SHEET

Details concerning the application or reference	
Application or reference?	
Person making application or reference	
Provision under which made	
Date of the application or reference	
Is the application or reference authorised?	Yes / No

If no, give details—	
Details of MHRT office	
MHRT case reference number	

Representation	
Person referring case to firm	New client direct / existing client / appointed by MHRT /
Terms	Eligible for Green Form advice and assistance ABWOR Fee agreed of £ Pro bono MHRT undertaking to pay costs Court of Protection authorised

Statutory reports			
	Due on	*Received*	*Action?*
Part A, C, E			
Medical			
Social			
Home Office			

Independent reports				
	Necessary	*Commissioned from*	*On (date)*	*Received*
Psychiatric	Yes / No			
Neuropsychiatric	Yes / No			
Forensic psychiatric	Yes / No			
Endocrinological	Yes / No			
Other medical—	Yes / No			
Psychological	Yes / No			
Social circumstances	Yes / No			

Assessment of case	
Points favourable to discharge	*Points not favourable to discharge*

Hearing strategy	
Hearing and outcome	
Date(s)	(1) (2)
MHRT members	
Outcome	Application / reference withdrawn on... Client regraded to informal on.... Discharged forthwith / on *Mandatory discharge / discretionary discharge* Not discharged— no recommendation Not discharged— recommendation as follows Absolute discharge (Deferred) Conditional discharge, conditions as follows— (1) (2) (3) (4) (5) Section 74— entitled to be absolutely discharged Section 74— entitled to be conditionally discharged with a direction that patient not be remitted to prison Reclassification— From.... To........
Client next entitled to apply on—	

APPENDICES TO PART I

Appendix IIA Mental Health Act 1983

Application of Act: "mental disorder"

1.—(1) The provisions of this Act shall have effect with respect to the reception, care and treatment of mentally disordered patients, the management of their property and other related matters.

(2) In this Act—

"mental disorder" means mental illness, arrested or incomplete development of mind, psychopathic disorder and any other disorder or disability of mind and "mentally disordered" shall be construed accordingly;

"severe mental impairment" means a state of arrested or incomplete development of mind which includes severe impairment of intelligence and social functioning and is associated with abnormally aggressive or seriously irresponsible conduct on the part of the person concerned and "severely mentally impaired" shall be construed accordingly;

"mental impairment" means a state of arrested or incomplete development of mind (not amounting to severe mental impairment) which includes significant impairment of intelligence and social functioning and is associated with abnormally aggressive or seriously irresponsible conduct on the part of the person concerned and "mentally impaired" shall be construed accordingly;

"psychopathic disorder" means a persistent disorder or disability of mind (whether or not including significant impairment of intelligence) which results in abnormally aggressive or seriously irresponsible conduct on the part of the person concerned:

and other expressions shall have the meanings assigned to them in section 145 below.

(3) Nothing in subsection (2) above shall be construed as implying that a person may be dealt with under this Act as suffering from mental disorder, or from any form of mental disorder described in this section, by reason only of promiscuity or other immoral conduct, sexual deviancy or dependence on alcohol or drugs.

969

Constitution, etc.

Mental Health Review Tribunals

65.—(1) There shall continue to be tribunals, known as a Mental Health Review Tribunals, for the purpose of dealing with applications and references by and in respect of patients under the provisions of this Act.

(1A) There shall be—

  (a) one tribunal for each region of England, and

  (b) one tribunal for Wales.

(1B) The Secretary of State—

  (a) shall by order determine regions for the purpose of subsection (1A)(a) above; and

  (b) may by order vary a region determined for that purpose;

and the Secretary of State shall act under this subsection so as to secure that the regions together comprise the whole of England.

(1C) Any order made under subsection (1B) above may make such transitional, consequential, incidental or supplemental provision as the Secretary of State considers appropriate.

(2) The provisions of Schedule 2 to this Act shall have effect with respect to the constitution of Mental Health Review Tribunals.

(3) Subject to the provisions of Schedule 2 to this Act, and to rules made by the Lord Chancellor under this Act, the jurisdiction of a Mental Health Review Tribunal may be exercised by any three or more of its members, and references in this Act to a Mental Health Review Tribunal shall be construed accordingly.

(4) The Secretary of State may pay to the members of Mental Health Review Tribunals such remuneration and allowances as he may with the consent of the Treasury determine, and defray the expenses of such tribunals to such amount as he may with the consent of the Treasury determine, and may provide for each such tribunal such officers and servants, and such accommodation, as the tribunal may require.

Applications to tribunals

66.—(1) Where—

(a) a patient is admitted to a hospital in pursuance of an application for admission for assessment; or

(b) a patient is admitted to a hospital in pursuance of an application for admission for treatment; or

(c) a patient is received into guardianship in pursuance of a guardianship application; or

(d) a report is furnished under section 16 above in respect of a patient; or

(e) a patient is transferred from guardianship to a hospital in pursuance of regulations made under section 19 above; or

(f) a report is furnished under section 20 above in respect of a patient and the patient is not discharged; or

(fa) a report is furnished under subsection (2) of section 21B above in respect of a patient and subsection (5) of that section applies (or subsections (5) and (6)(b) of that section apply) in the case of the report; or

(fb) a report is furnished under subsection (2) of section 21B above in respect of a patient and subsection (8) of that section applies in the case of the report; or

(g) a report is furnished under section 25 above in respect of a patient who is detained in pursuance of an application for admission for treatment; or

(ga) a supervision application is accepted in respect of a patient; or

(gb) a report is furnished under section 25F above in respect of a patient; or

(gc) a report is furnished under section 25G above in respect of a patient; or

(h) an order is made under section 29 above in respect of a patient who is or subsequently becomes liable to be detained or subject to guardianship under Part II of this Act,

an application may be made to a Mental Health Review Tribunal within the relevant period—

(i) by the patient (except in the cases mentioned in paragraphs (g) and (h) above) or, in the cases mentioned in paragraphs (d), (ga), (gb) and (gc), by his nearest relative if he has been (or was entitled to be) informed under this Act of the report or acceptance.

(ii) in the cases mentioned in paragraphs (g) and (h) above, by his nearest relative.

(2) In subsection (1) above "the relevant period" means—

(a) in the case mentioned in paragraph (a) of that subsection, 14 days beginning with the day on which the patient is admitted;

(b) in the case mentioned in paragraph (b) of that subsection, six months beginning with the day on which the patient is admitted as so mentioned;

(c) in the cases mentioned in paragraph (c) and (ga) of that subsection, six months beginning with the day on which the application is accepted;

(d) in the cases mentioned in paragraphs (d), (fb), (g) and (gb) of that subsection, 28 days beginning with the day on which the applicant is informed that the report has been furnished;

(e) in the case mentioned in paragraph (e) of that subsection, six months beginning with the day on which the patient is transferred;

(f) in the case mentioned in paragraph (f) or (fa) of that subsection, the period or periods for which authority for the patient's detention or guardianship is renewed by virtue of the report;

(fa) in the case mentioned in paragraph (gc) of that subsection, the further period for which the patient is made subject to after-care under supervision by virtue of the report;

(g) in the case mentioned in paragraph (h) of that subsection, 12 months beginning with the date of the order, and in any subsequent period of 12 months during which the order continues in force.

(3) Section 32 above shall apply for the purposes of this section as it applies for the purposes of Part II of this Act.

Application of section 66 to Part III patients

Section 66 applies to Part III patients subject to the modifications set out in Part I of Schedule 1 to the Act. As modified, the section reads as follows:

66.—(1) Where—

(d) a report is furnished under section 16 above in respect of a patient; or

(e) a patient is transferred from guardianship to a hospital in pursuance of regulations made under section 19 above; or

(f) a report is furnished under section 20 above in respect of a patient and the patient is not discharged; or

(fa) a report is furnished under subsection (2) of section 21B above in respect of a patient and subsection (5) of that section applies (or subsections (5) and (6)(b) of that section apply) in the case of the report; or

(fb) a report is furnished under subsection (2) of section 21B above in respect of a patient and subsection (8) of that section applies in the case of the report; or

(ga) a supervision application is accepted in respect of a patient; or

(gb) a report is furnished under section 25F above in respect of a patient; or (gc) a report is furnished under section 25G above in respect of a patient; or

an application may be made to a Mental Health Review Tribunal within the relevant period—

(i) by the patient... or, in the cases mentioned in paragraphs (d), (ga), (gb) and (gc), by his nearest relative if he has been (or was entitled to be) informed under this Act of the report or acceptance.

(2) In subsection (1) above "the relevant period" means—

(d) in the cases mentioned in paragraphs (d), (fb) and (gb) of that subsection, 28 days beginning with the day on which the applicant is informed that the report has been furnished;

(e) in the case mentioned in paragraph (e) of that subsection, six months beginning with the day on which the patient is transferred;

(f) in the case mentioned in paragraph (f) or (fa) of that subsection, the period or periods for which authority for the patient's detention or guardianship is renewed by virtue of the report;

(fa) in the case mentioned in paragraph (gc) of that subsection, the further period for which the patient is made subject to after-care under supervision by virtue of the report;

(3) Section 32 above shall apply for the purposes of this section as it applies for the purposes of Part II of this Act.

References to tribunals by Secretary of State concerning Part II patients

67.—(1) The Secretary of State may, if he thinks fit, at any time refer to a Mental Health Review Tribunal the case of any patient who is liable to be detained or subject to guardianship or to after-care under supervision under Part II of this Act.

(2) For the purpose of furnishing information for the purposes of a reference under subsection (1) above any registered medical practitioner authorised by or on behalf of the patient may, at any reasonable time, visit the patient and examine him in private and require the production of and inspect any records relating to the detention or treatment of the patient in any hospital or to any after-care services provided for the patient under s.117 below.

(3) Section 32 above shall apply for the purposes of this section as it applies for the purposes of Part II of this Act.

Duty of managers of hospitals to refer cases to tribunal

68.—(1) Where a patient who is admitted to a hospital in pursuance of an application for admission for treatment or a patient who is transferred from guardianship to hospital does not exercise his right to apply to a Mental Health Review Tribunal under section 66(1) above by virtue of his case falling within paragraph (b) or, as the case may be, paragraph (e) of that section, the managers of the hospital shall at the expiration of the period for making such an application refer the patient's case to such a tribunal unless an application or reference in respect of the patient has then been made under section 66(1) above by virtue of his case falling within paragraph (d), (g) or (h) of that section or under section 67(1) above.

(2) If the authority for the detention of a patient in a hospital is renewed under section 20 or 21B above and a period of three years (or, if the patient has not attained the age of sixteen years, one year) has elapsed since his case was last considered by a Mental Health Review Tribunal, whether on his own application or otherwise, the managers of the hospital shall refer his case to such a tribunal.

(3) For the purpose of furnishing information for the purpose of any reference under this section, any registered medical practitioner authorised by or on behalf of the patient may at any reasonable time visit and examine the patient in private and require the production of and inspect any records relating to the detention or treatment of the patient in any hospital or to any after-care services provided for the patient under section 117 above.

(4) The Secretary of State may by order vary the length of the periods mentioned in subsection (2) above.

(5) For the purposes of subsection (1) above a person who applies to a tribunal but subsequently withdraws his application shall be treated as not having exercised his right to apply, and where a person withdraws his application on a date after the expiration of the period mentioned in that subsection, the managers shall refer the patient's case as soon as possible after that date.

Applications and References Concerning Part III Patients

Applications to tribunals concerning patients subject to hospital and guardianship orders

69.—(1) Without prejudice to any provision of section 66(1) above as applied by section 40(4) above, an application to a Mental Health Review Tribunal may also be made—

(a) in respect of a patient admitted to a hospital in pursuance of a hospital order, by the nearest relative of the patient in the period between the expiration of six months and the expiration of 12 months beginning with the date of the order and in any subsequent period of 12 months; and

(b) in respect of a patient placed under guardianship by a guardianship order—

(i) by the patient, within the period of six months beginning with the date of the order;

(ii) by the nearest relative of the patient, within the period of 12 months beginning with the date of the order and in any subsequent period of 12 months.

(2) Where a person detained in a hospital—

(a) is treated as subject to a hospital order or transfer direction by virtue of section 41(5) above, 82(2) or 85(2) below, section 77(2) of the Mental Health (Scotland) Act 1984 or section 5(1) of the Criminal Procedure (Insanity) Act 1964; or

(b) is subject to a direction having the same effect as a hospital order by virtue of section [45B(2),] 46(3), 47(3) or 48(3) above,

then, without prejudice to any provision of Part II of this Act as applied by section 40 above, that person may make an application to a Mental Health Review Tribunal in the period of six months beginning with the date or the order or direction mentioned in paragraph (a) above or, as the case may be, the date of the direction mentioned in paragraph (b) above.

Applications to tribunals concerning restricted patients

70. A patient who is a restricted patient within the meaning of section 79 below and is detained in a hospital may apply to a Mental Health Review Tribunal—

(a) in the period between the expiration of six months and the expiration of 12 months beginning with the date of the relevant hospital order [, hospital direction] or transfer direction; and

(b) in any subsequent period of 12 months.

References by Secretary of State concerning restricted patients

71.—(1) The Secretary of State may at any time refer the case of a restricted patient to a Mental Health Review Tribunal.

(2) The Secretary of State shall refer to a Mental Health Review Tribunal the case of any restricted patient detained in a hospital whose case has not been considered by such a tribunal, whether on his own application or otherwise, within the last three years.

(3) The Secretary of State may by order vary the length of the period mentioned in subsection (2) above.

(4) Any reference under subsection (1) above in respect of a patient who has been conditionally discharged and not recalled to hospital shall be made to the tribunal for the area in which the patient resides.

(5) Where a person who is treated as subject to a hospital order and a restriction order by virtue of an order under section 5(1) of the Criminal Procedure (Insanity) Act 1964 does not exercise his right to apply to a Mental Health Review Tribunal in the period of six months beginning with the date of that order, the Secretary of State shall at the expiration of that period refer his case to a tribunal.

(6) For the purposes of subsection (5) above a person who applies to a tribunal but subsequently withdraws his application shall be treated as not having exercised his right to apply, and where a patient withdraws his application on a date after the expiration of the period there mentioned the Secretary of State shall refer the case as soon as possible after that date.

Powers of tribunals

72.—(1) Where application is made to a Mental Health Review Tribunal by or in respect of a patient who is liable to be detained under this Act, the tribunal may in any case direct that the patient be discharged, and—

(a) the tribunal shall direct the discharge of a patient liable to be detained under section 2 above if they are satisfied—

(i) that he is not then suffering from mental disorder or from mental disorder of a nature or degree which warrants his detention in a hospital for assessment (or for assessment followed by medical treatment) for at least a limited period; or

(ii) that his detention as aforesaid is not justified in the interests of his own health or safety or with a view to the protection of other persons.

(b) the tribunal shall direct the discharge of a patient liable to be detained otherwise than under section 2 above if they are satisfied—

(i) that he is not then suffering from mental illness, psychopathic disorder, severe mental impairment or mental impairment or from any of those forms of disorder of a nature or degree which makes it appropriate for him to be liable to be detained in a hospital for medical treatment; or

(ii) that it is not necessary for the health or safety of the patient or for the protection of other persons that he should receive such treatment; or

(iii) in the case of an application by virtue of paragraph (g) of section 66(1) above, that the patient, if released, would not be likely to act in a manner dangerous to other persons or to himself.

(2) In determining whether to direct the discharge of a patient detained otherwise than under section 2 above in a case not falling within paragraph (b) of subsection (1) above, the tribunal shall have regard—

(a) to the likelihood of medical treatment alleviating or preventing a deterioration of the patient's condition; and

(b) in the case of a patient suffering from mental illness or severe mental impairment, to the likelihood of the patient, if discharged, being able to care for himself, to obtain the care he needs or to guard himself against serious exploitation.

(3) A tribunal may under subsection (1) above direct the discharge of a patient on a future date specified in the direction; and where a tribunal do not direct the discharge of a patient under that subsection the tribunal may—

(a) with a view to facilitating his discharge on a future date, recommend that he be granted leave of absence or transferred to another hospital or into guardianship; and

(b) further consider his case in the event of any such recommendation not being complied with.

(3A) Where, in the case of an application to a tribunal by or in respect of a patient who is liable to be detained in pursuance of an application for admission for treatment or by virtue of an order or direction for his admission or removal to hospital under Part III of this Act, the tribunal do not direct the discharge of the patient under subsection (1) above, the tribunal may—

(a) recommend that the responsible medical officer consider whether to make a supervision application in respect of the patient; and

(b) further consider his case in the event of no such application being made.

(4) Where application is made to a Mental Health Review Tribunal by or in respect of a patient who is subject to guardianship under this Act, the tribunal may in any case direct that the patient be discharged, and shall so direct if they are satisfied—

(a) that he is not then suffering from mental illness, psychopathic disorder, severe mental impairment or mental impairment; or

(b) that it is not necessary in the interests of the welfare of the patient, or for the protection of other persons, that the patient should remain under such guardianship.

(4A) Where application is made to a Mental Health Review Tribunal by or in respect of a patient who is subject to after-care under supervision (or, if he has not yet left hospital, is to be so subject after he leaves hospital), the tribunal may in any case direct that the patient shall cease to be so subject (or not become so subject), and shall so direct if they are satisfied—

(a) in a case where the patient has not yet left hospital, that the conditions set out in section 25A(4) above are not complied with; or

(b) in any other case, that the conditions set out in section 25G(4) above are not complied with.

(5) Where application is made to a Mental Health Review Tribunal under any provision of this Act by or in respect of a patient and the tribunal do not direct that the patient be discharged or, if he is (or is to be) subject to after-care under supervision, that he cease to be so subject (or not become so subject), the tribunal may, if satisfied that the patient is suffering from a form of mental disorder other than the form specified in the application, order or direction relating to him, direct that that application, order or direction be amended by substituting for the form of mental disorder specified in it such other form of mental disorder as appears to the tribunal to be appropriate.

(6) Subsections (1) to (5) above apply in relation to references to a Mental Health Review Tribunal as they apply in relation to applications made to such a tribunal by or in respect of a patient.

(7) Subsection (1) above shall not apply in the case of a restricted patient except as provided in sections 73 and 74 below.

Power to discharge restricted patients

73.—(1) Where an application to a Mental Health Review Tribunal is made by a restricted patient who is subject to a restriction order. or where the case of such a patient is referred to such a tribunal, the tribunal shall direct the absolute discharge of the patient if satisfied—

(a) as to the matters mentioned in paragraph (b) (i) or (ii) of section 72(1) above; and

(b) that it is not appropriate for the patient to remain liable to be recalled to hospital for further treatment.

(2) Where in the case of any such patient as is mentioned in subsection (1) above the tribunal are satisfied as to the matters referred to in paragraph (a) of that subsection but not as to the matter referred to in paragraph (b) of that subsection the tribunal shall direct the conditional discharge of the patient.

(3) Where a patient is absolutely discharged under this section he shall thereupon cease to be liable to be detained by virtue of the relevant hospital order, and the restriction order shall cease to have effect accordingly.

(4) Where a patient is conditionally discharged under this section—

(a) he may be recalled by the Secretary of State under subsection (3) of section 42 above as if he had been conditionally discharged under subsection (2) of that section; and

(b) the patient shall comply with such conditions (if any) as may be imposed at the time of discharge by the tribunal or at any subsequent time by the Secretary of State.

(5) The Secretary of State may from time to time vary any condition imposed (whether by the tribunal or by him) under subsection (4) above.

(6) Where a restriction order in respect of a patient ceases to have effect after he has been conditionally discharged under this section the patient shall, unless previously recalled, be deemed to be absolutely discharged on the date when the order ceases to have effect and shall cease to be liable to be detained by virtue of the relevant hospital order.

(7) A tribunal may defer a direction for the conditional discharge of a patient until such arrangements as appear to the tribunal to be necessary for that purpose have been made to their satisfaction; and where by virtue of any such deferment no direction has been given on an application or reference before the time when the patient's case comes before the tribunal on a subsequent application or reference, the previous application or reference shall be treated as one on which no direction under this section can be given.

(8) This section is without prejudice to section 42 above.

Restricted patients subject to restriction directions

74.—(1) Where an application to a Mental Health Review Tribunal is made by a restricted patient who is subject to [a limitation direction or] a restriction direction, or where the case of such a patient is referred to such a tribunal, the tribunal—

(a) shall notify the Secretary of State whether, in their opinion, the patient would, if subject to a restriction order, be entitled to be absolutely or conditionally discharged under section 73 above; and

(b) if they notify him that the patient would be entitled to be conditionally discharged, may recommend that in the event of his not being discharged under this section he should continue to be detained in hospital.

(2) If in the case of a patient not falling within subsection (4) below—

(a) the tribunal notify the Secretary of State that the patient would be entitled to be absolutely or conditionally discharged; and

(b) within the period of 90 days beginning with the date of that notification the Secretary of State gives notice to the tribunal that the patient may be so discharged,

the tribunal shall direct the absolute or, as the case may be, the conditional discharge of the patient.

(3) Where a patient continues to be liable to be detained in a hospital at the end of the period referred to in subsection (2)(b) above because the Secretary of State has not given the notice there mentioned, the managers of the hospital shall, unless the tribunal have made a recommendation under subsection (1)(b) above, transfer the patient to a prison or other institution in which he might have been detained if he had not been removed to hospital, there to be dealt with as if he had not been so removed.

(4) If, in the case of a patient who is subject to a transfer direction under section 48 above, the tribunal notify the Secretary of State that the patient would be entitled to be absolutely or conditionally discharged, the Secretary of State shall, unless the tribunal have made a recommendation under subsection (1)(b) above, by warrant direct that the patient be remitted to a prison or other institution in which he might have been detained if he had not been removed to hospital, there to be dealt with as if he had not been so removed.

(5) Where a patient is transferred or remitted under subsection (3) or (4) above [the relevant hospital direction and the limitation direction or, as the case may be,] the relevant transfer direction and the restriction direction shall cease to have effect on his arrival in the prison or other institution.

(6) Subsections (3) to (5) of section 73 above shall have effect in relation to this section as they have effect in relation to that section, taking references to the relevant hospital order and the restriction order as references to [the hospital direction and the limitation direction or, as the case may be, to] the transfer direction and the restriction direction.

(7) This section is without prejudice to sections 50 to 53 above in their application to patients who are not discharged under this section.

Applications and references concerning conditionally discharged restricted patients

75.—(1) Where a restricted patient has been conditionally discharged under section 42(2), 73 or 74 above and is subsequently recalled to hospital—

(a) the Secretary of State shall, within one month of the day on which the patient returns or is returned to hospital, refer his case to a Mental Health Review Tribunal; and

(b) section 70 above shall apply to the patient as if the relevant hospital order [, hospital direction] or transfer direction had been made on that day.

(2) Where a restricted patient has been conditionally discharged as aforesaid but has not been recalled to hospital he may apply to a Mental Health Review Tribunal—

(a) in the period between the expiration of 12 months and the expiration of two years beginning with the date on which he was conditionally discharged; and

(b) in any subsequent period of two years.

(3) Sections 73 and 74 above shall not apply to an application under subsection (2) above but on any such application the tribunal may—

(a) vary any condition to which the patient is subject in connection with his discharge or impose any condition which might have been imposed in connection therewith; or

(b) direct that the restriction order or restriction direction to which he is subject shall cease to have effect;

and if the tribunal give a direction under paragraph (b) above the patient shall cease to be liable to be detained by virtue of the relevant hospital order or transfer direction.

General

Visiting and examination of patients

76.—(1) For the purpose of advising whether an application to a Mental Health Review Tribunal should be made by or in respect of a patient who is liable to be detained or subject to guardianship or to after-care under supervision (or, if he has not yet left hospital, is to be subject to after-care under supervision after he leaves hospital) under Part II of this Act or of furnishing information as to the condition of a patient for the purposes of such an application, any registered medical practitioner authorised by or on behalf of the patient or other person who is entitled to make or has made the application—

(a) may at any reasonable time visit the patient and examine him in private, and

(b) may require the production of and inspect any records relating to the detention or treatment of the patient in any hospital or to any after-care services provided for the patient under section 117 below.

(2) Section 32 above shall apply for the purposes of this section as it applies for the purposes of Part II of this Act.

General provisions concerning tribunal applications

77.—(1) No application shall be made to a Mental Health Review Tribunal by or in respect of a patient except in such cases and at such times as are expressly provided by this Act.

(2) Where under this Act any person is authorised to make an application to a Mental Health Review Tribunal within a specified period, not more than one such application shall be made by that person within that period but for that purpose there shall be disregarded any application which is withdrawn in accordance with rules made under section 78 below.

(3) Subject to subsection (4) below an application to a Mental Health Review Tribunal authorised to be made by or in respect of a patient under this Act shall be made by notice in writing addressed to the tribunal for the area in which the hospital in which the patient is detained is situated or in which the patient is residing under guardianship or when subject to after-care under supervision (or in which he is to reside on becoming so subject after leaving hospital) as the case may be.

(4) Any application under section 75(2) above shall be made to the tribunal for the area in which the patient resides.

Procedure of tribunals

78.—(1) The Lord Chancellor may make rules with respect to the making of applications to Mental Health Review Tribunals and with respect to the proceedings of such tribunals and matters incidental to or consequential on such proceedings.

(2) Rules made under this section may in particular make provision—

(a) for enabling a tribunal, or the chairman of a tribunal, to postpone the consideration of any application by or in respect of a patient, or of any such application of any specified class, until the expiration of such period (not exceeding 12 months) as may be specified in the rules from the date on which an application by or in respect of the same patient was last considered and determined by that or any other tribunal under this Act;

(b) for the transfer of proceedings from one tribunal to another in any case where, after the making of the application, the patient is removed out of the area of the tribunal to which it was made;

(c) for restricting the persons qualified to serve as members of a tribunal for the consideration of any application, or of an application of any specified class;

(d) for enabling a tribunal to dispose of an application without a formal hearing where such a hearing is not requested by the applicant or it appears to the tribunal that such a hearing would be detrimental to the health of the patient;

(e) for enabling a tribunal to exclude members of the public, or any specified class of members of the public, from any proceedings of the tribunal, or to prohibit the publication of reports of any such proceedings or the names of any persons concerned in such proceedings;

(f) for regulating the circumstances in which, and the persons by whom, applicants and patients in respect of whom applications are made to a tribunal may, if not desiring to conduct their own case, be represented for the purposes of those applications;

(g) for regulating the methods by which information relevant to an application may be obtained by or furnished to the tribunal, and in particular for authorising the members of a tribunal, or any one or more of them, to visit and interview in private any patient by or in respect of whom an application has been made;

(h) for making available to any applicant, and to any patient in respect of whom an application is made to a tribunal, copies of any documents obtained by or furnished to the tribunal in connection with the application, and a statement of the substance of any oral information so obtained or furnished except where the tribunal considers it undesirable in the interests of the patient or for other special reasons;

(i) for requiring a tribunal, if so requested in accordance with the rules, to furnish such statements of the reasons for any decision given by the tribunal as may be prescribed by the rules, subject to any provision made by the rules for withholding such a statement from a patient or any other person in cases where the tribunal considers that furnishing it would be undesirable in the interests of the patient or for other special reasons;

(j) for conferring on the tribunals such ancillary powers as the Lord Chancellor thinks necessary for the purposes of the exercise of their functions under this Act;

(k) for enabling any functions of a tribunal which relate to matters preliminary or incidental to an application to be performed by the chairman of the tribunal.

(3) Subsections (1) and (2) above apply in relation to references to Mental Health Review Tribunals as they apply in relation to applications to such tribunals by or in respect of patients.

(4) Rules under this section may make provision as to the procedure to be adopted in cases concerning restricted patients and, in particular—

(a) for restricting the persons qualified to serve as president of a tribunal for the consideration of an application or reference relating to a restricted patient;

(b) for the transfer of proceedings from one tribunal to another in any case where, after the making of a reference or application in accordance with section 71(4) or

77(4) above, the patient ceases to reside in the area of the tribunal to which the reference or application was made.

(5) Rules under this section may be so framed as to apply to all applications or references or to applications or references of any specified class and may make different provision in relation to different cases.

(6) Any functions conferred on the chairman of a Mental Health Review Tribunal by rules under this section may, if for any reason he is unable to act, be exercised by another member of that tribunal appointed by him for the purpose.

(7) A Mental Health Review Tribunal may pay allowances in respect of travelling expenses, subsistence and loss of earnings to any person attending the tribunal as an applicant or witness, to the patient who is the subject of the proceedings if he attends otherwise than as the applicant or a witness and to any person (other than counsel or a solicitor) who attends as the representative of an applicant.

(8) A Mental Health Review Tribunal may, and if so required by the High Court shall, state in the form of a special case for determination by the High Court any question of law which may arise before them.

(9) The Arbitration Act 1950 shall not apply to any proceedings before a Mental Health Review Tribunal except so far as any provisions of that Act may be applied, with or without modifications, by rules made under this section.

Interpretation of Part V

79.—(1) In this Part of this Act "restricted patient" means a patient who is subject to a restriction order [, limitation direction] or restriction direction and this Part of this Act shall, subject to the provisions of this section, have effect in relation to any person who—

(a) is subject to a direction which by virtue of section 46(3) above has the same effect as a hospital order and a restriction order; or

(b) is treated as subject to a hospital order and a restriction order by virtue of an order under section 5(1) of the Criminal Procedure (Insanity) Act 1964 or section 6 or 14(1) of the Criminal Appeal Act 1968; or

(c) is treated as subject to a hospital order and a restriction order or to a transfer direction and a restriction direction by virtue of section 82(2) or 85(2) below or section 73(2) of the Mental Health (Scotland) Act 1984,

as it has effect in relation to a restricted patient.

(2) Subject to the following provisions of this section, in this Part of this Act "the relevant hospital order" [,"the relevant hospital direction"] and "the relevant transfer direction, "in relation to a restricted patient, mean the hospital order [the hospital direction] or transfer direction by virtue of which he is liable to be detained in a hospital.

In the case of a person within paragraph (a) of subsection (1) above, references in this Part of this Act to the relevant hospital order or restriction order shall be construed as references to the direction referred to in that paragraph.

(4) In the case of a person within paragraph (b) of subsection (1) above, references in this Part of this Act to the relevant hospital order or restriction order shall be construed as references to the order under the provisions mentioned in that paragraph.

(5) In the case of a person within paragraph (c) of subsection (1) above, references in this Part of this Act to the relevant hospital order, the relevant transfer direction, the restriction order or the restriction direction or to a transfer direction under section 48 above shall be construed as references to the hospital order, transfer direction, restriction order, restriction direction or transfer direction under that section to which that person is treated as subject by virtue of the provisions mentioned in that paragraph.

(6) In this Part of this Act, unless the context otherwise requires, "hospital" means a hospital and the "responsible medical officer" means the responsible medical officer, within the meaning of Part II of this Act.

(7) In this Part of this Act any reference to the area of a tribunal is—

(a) in relation to a tribunal for a region of England, a reference to that region; and

(b) in relation to the tribunal for Wales, a reference to Wales.

PART VI — REMOVAL AND RETURN OF PATIENTS WITHIN UNITED KINGDOM, etc.

Removal of aliens

Removal of alien patients

86.—(1) This section applies to any patient who is neither a British citizen nor a Commonwealth citizen having the right of abode in the United Kingdom by virtue of section 2(1)(b) of the Immigration Act 1971, being a patient who is receiving treatment for mental illness as an in-patient in a hospital in England and Wales or a hospital within the meaning of the Mental Health Act (Northern Ireland) Order 1986 and is detained pursuant to—

(a) an application for admission for treatment or a report under Article 12(1) or 13 of that Order;

(b) a hospital order under section 37 above or Article 44 of that Order; or

(c) an order or direction under this Act (other than under section 35, 36 or 38 above) or under that Order (other than under Article 42, 43 or 45 of that Order) having the same effect as such a hospital order.

(2) If it appears to the Secretary of State that proper arrangements have been made for the removal of a patient to whom this section applies to a country or territory outside the United Kingdom, the Isle of Man and the Channel Islands and for his care or treatment there and that it is in the interests of the patient to remove him, the Secretary of State may, subject to subsection (3) below—

(a) By warrant authorise the removal of the patient from the place where he is receiving treatment as mentioned in subsection (1) above, and

(b) give such directions as the Secretary of State thinks fit for the conveyance of the patient to his destination in that country or territory and for his detention in any place or on board any ship or aircraft until his arrival at any specified port or place in any such country or territory.

(3) The Secretary of State shall not exercise his powers under subsection (2) above in the case of any patient except with the approval of a Mental Health Review Tribunal or, as the case may be, of the Mental Health Review Tribunal for Northern Ireland.

Supplemental

Interpretation

145.—(1) In this Act, unless the context otherwise requires—

"absent without leave" has the meaning given to it by section 18 above and related expressions shall be construed accordingly;

"application for admission for assessment" has the meaning given in section 2 above;

"application for admission for treatment" has the meaning given in section 3 above;

"approved social worker" means an officer of a local social services authority appointed to act as an approved social worker for the purposes of this Act;

"hospital" means—

(a) any health service hospital within the meaning of the National Health Service Act 1977; and

(b) any accommodation provided by a local authority and used as a hospital or on behalf of the Secretary of State under that Act;

and "hospital within the meaning of Part II of this Act" has the meaning given in section 34 above;

["hospital direction" has the meaning given in section 45A(3)(a) above;]

"hospital order" and "guardianship order" have the meanings respectively given in section 37 above;

"interim hospital order" has the meaning given in section 38 above;

["limitation direction" has the meaning given in section 45A(3)(b) above;]

"local social services authority" means a council which is a local authority for the purpose of the Local Authority Social Services Act 1970;

"the managers" means—

(a) in relation to a hospital vested in the Secretary of State for the purposes of his functions under the National Health Service Act 1977, and in relation to any accommodation provided by a local authority and used as a hospital by or on behalf of the Secretary of State under that Act, the Health Authority or Special Health Authority responsible for the administration of the hospital;

(b) in relation to a special hospital, the Secretary of State;

(bb) in relation to a hospital vested in a National Health Service trust, the directors of the trust;

(c) in relation to a mental nursing home registered in pursuance of the Registered Homes Act 1984, the person or persons registered in respect of the home;

and in this definition "hospital" means a hospital within the meaning of Part II of this Act;

"medical treatment" includes nursing, and also includes care, habilitation and rehabilitation under medical supervision;

"mental disorder" "severe mental impairment" "mental impairment" and "psychopathic disorder" have the meanings given in section 1 above;

"mental nursing home" has the same meaning as in the Registered Homes Act 1984;

"nearest relative", in relation to a patient, has the meaning given in Part II of this Act;

"patient" (except in Part VII of this Act) means a person suffering or appearing to be suffering from mental disorder;

the "responsible after-care bodies" has the meaning given in Part II of this Act;

"restriction direction" has the meaning given to it by section 49 above;

"restriction order" has the meaning given to it by section 41 above;

"Special Health Authority" means a Special Health Authority established under section 11 of the National Health Service Act 1977.

"special hospital" has the same meaning as in the National Health Service Act 1977;

"supervision application" has the meaning given in section 25A above.

"transfer direction" has the meaning given to it by section 47 above.

(3) In relation to a person who is liable to be detained or subject to guardianship by virtue of an order or direction under Part III of this Act (other than under section 35, 36, or 38), any reference in this Act to any enactment contained in Part II of this Act or in section 66 or 67 above shall be construed as a reference to that enactment as it applies to that person by virtue of Part III of this Act.

SCHEDULE 2 — MENTAL HEALTH REVIEW TRIBUNALS

1. Each of the Mental Health Review Tribunals shall consist of—

(a) a number of persons (referred to in this Schedule as "the legal members") appointed by the Lord Chancellor and having such legal experience as the Lord Chancellor considers suitable;

(b) a number of persons (referred to in this Schedule as "the medical members") being registered medical practitioners appointed by the Lord Chancellor after consultation with the Secretary of State; and

(c) a number of persons appointed by the Lord Chancellor after consultation with the Secretary of State and having such experience in administration, such knowledge of social services or such other qualifications or experience as the Lord Chancellor considers suitable.

2. The members of Mental Health Review Tribunals shall hold and vacate office under the terms of the instrument under which they are appointed, but may resign office by notice in writing to the Lord Chancellor; and any such member who ceases to hold office shall be eligible for re-appointment.

3. One of the legal members of each Mental Health Review Tribunal shall be appointed by the Lord Chancellor as chairman of the Tribunals.

4. Subject to rules made by the Lord Chancellor under section 78(2)(c) above, the members who are to constitute a Mental Health Review Tribunal for the purposes of any proceedings or class or group of proceedings under this Act shall be appointed by the chairman of the tribunal or, if for any reason he is unable to act, by another member of the tribunal appointed for the purpose by the chairman; and of the members so appointed—

(a) one or more shall be appointed from the legal members;

(b) one or more shall be appointed from the medical members; and

(c) one or more shall be appointed from the members who are neither legal nor medical members.

5. A member of a Mental Health Review Tribunal for any area may be appointed under paragraph 4 above as one of the persons to constitute a Mental Health Review Tribunal for any other area for the purposes of any proceedings or class or group of proceedings; and for the purposes of this Act, a person so appointed shall, in relation to the proceedings for which he was appointed be deemed to be a member of that other tribunal.

6. Subject to any rules made by the Lord Chancellor under section 78(4)(a) above, where the chairman of the tribunal is included among the persons appointed under paragraph 4 above, he shall be president of the tribunal; and in any other case the president of the tribunal shall be such one of the members so appointed (being one of the legal members) as the chairman may nominate.

Appendix IIB The 1983 Rules

THE MENTAL HEALTH REVIEW TRIBUNAL RULES 1983

(Statutory Instrument 1983 No. 942)

Dated June 28 1983 and made by the Lord Chancellor under the Mental Health Act 1983, s. 78.

ARRANGEMENT OF RULES

PART I

INTRODUCTION

PART II

PRELIMINARY MATTERS

PART III

GENERAL PROVISIONS

PART IV

THE HEARING

PART V

DECISIONS, FURTHER CONSIDERATION AND MISCELLANEOUS PROVISIONS

PART VI

REFERENCES AND APPLICATIONS BY PATIENTS DETAINED FOR ASSESSMENT

PART VII

TRANSITIONAL PROVISIONS AND REVOCATIONS

SCHEDULES

PART I — INTRODUCTION

Title and commencement

1. These Rules may be cited as the Mental Health Review Tribunal Rules 1983 and shall come into operation on September 30, 1983.

Interpretation

2.—In these Rules, unless the context otherwise requires—

"the Act" means the Mental Health Act 1983;

"admission papers" means the application for admission under section 2 of the Act and the written recommendations of the two registered medical practitioners on which it is founded;

"assessment application" means an application by a patient who is detained for assessment and entitled to apply under section 66(1)(a) of the Act or who, being so entitled, has applied;

"the authority's statement" means the statement provided by the responsible authority pursuant to rule 6(1);

"chairman" means the legal member appointed by the Lord Chancellor as chairman of the Mental Health Review Tribunal under paragraph 3 of Schedule 2 to that Act or another member of the tribunal appointed to act on his behalf in accordance with paragraph 4 of that Schedule or section 78(6) of the Act as the case may be;

"decision with recommendations" means a decision with recommendations in accordance with section 72(3)(a) or (3A)(a) of the Act;

"health authority" has the same meaning as in the National Health Service Act 1977;

"National Health Service trust" means a body established under section 5(1) of the National Health Service and Community Care Act 1990;

"nearest relative" means a person who has for the time being the functions under the Act of the nearest relative of a patient who is not a restricted patient;

"party" means the applicant, the patient, the responsible authority any other person to whom a notice under rule 1 or rule 31(c) is sent or who is added as a party by direction of the tribunal;

"president" means the president of the tribunal as defined in paragraph 6 of Schedule 2 to the Act;

"private guardian" in relation to a patient means a person, other than a local social services authority, who acts as guardian under the Act;

"proceedings" includes any proceedings of a tribunal following an application or reference in relation to a patient;

"provisional decision" includes a deferred direction for conditional discharge in accordance with section 73(7) of the Act and a notification to the Secretary of State in accordance with section 74(1) of the Act;

"reference" means a reference under section 67(1) or (2), 71(1), (2) or (j) or 75(1) of the Act;

"registration authority" means the authority exercising the functions of the Secretary of State under the Nursing Homes Act 1975;

"responsible authority" means—

(a) in relation to a patient liable to be detained under the Act in a hospital or mental nursing home, the managers of the hospital or home as defined in section 145(1) of the Act; and

(b) in relation to a patient subject to guardianship, the responsible local social services authority as defined in section 34(3) of the Act;

(c) in relation to a patient subject to after-care under supervision, the Health Authority which has the duty under section 117 of the Act to provide after-care services for the patient.

"the Secretary of State's statement" means a statement provided by the Secretary of State pursuant to rule 6(2) or (3);

"tribunal" in relation to an application or a reference means the Mental Health Review Tribunal constituted under section 65 of the Act which has jurisdiction in the area in which the patient, at the time the application or reference is made, is detained or is liable to be detained or is subject to guardianship or is (or is to be) subject to after-care under supervision, or the tribunal to which the proceedings are transferred in accordance with rule 17(2), or in the case of a conditionally discharged patient, the tribunal for the area in which the patient resides.

PART II — PRELIMINARY MATTERS

Making an application

3.—(1) An application shall be made to the tribunal in writing, signed by the applicant or any person authorised by him to do so on his behalf.

(2) The application shall wherever possible include the following information—

(a) the name of the patient;

(b) the patient's address, which shall include—

(i) the address of the hospital or mental nursing home where the patient is detained; or

(ii) the name and address of the patient's private guardian; or

(iii) in the case of a conditionally discharged patient or a patient to whom leave of absence from hospital has been granted, the address of the hospital or mental nursing home where the patient was last detained or is liable to be detained; together with the patient's current address;

(c) where the application is made by the patient's nearest relative, the name and address of the applicant and his relationship to the patient;

(d) the section of the Act under which the patient is detained or is liable to be detained;

(e) the name and address of any representative authorised in accordance with rule 10 or, if none has yet been authorised, whether the applicant intends to authorise a representative or wishes to conduct his own case.

(f) in the case of a patient subject (or to be subject) to after-care under supervision—

(i) the names of the persons who are (or who are to be) the patient's supervisor and community responsible medical officer;

(ii) the name and address of any place at which the patient is (or will be) receiving medical treatment;

(iii) where the patient is subject to after-care under supervision, his current address, or in the case of a patient who is to be subject to after-care under supervision upon leaving hospital, the address of the hospital where he is, or was last, detained or is liable to be detained.

(3) If any of the information specified in paragraph (2) is not included in the application, it shall in so far as is practicable be provided by the responsible authority or, in the case of a restricted patient, the Secretary of State, at the request of the tribunal.

Notice of application

4.—(1) On receipt of an application, the tribunal shall send notice of the application to—

(a) the responsible authority;

(b) the patient (where he is not the applicant); and

(c) if the patient is a restricted patient, the Secretary of State.

(2) Paragraph (1) shall apply whether or not the power to postpone consideration of the application under rule 9 is exercised.

Preliminary and incidental matters

5. As regards matters preliminary or incidental to an application, the chairman may, at any time up to the hearing of an application by the tribunal, exercise the powers of the tribunal under rules, 6, 7, 9, 10, 12, 13, 14(1), 15, 17, 19, 20, 26 and 28

Statements by the responsible authority and the Secretary of State

6.—(1) The responsible authority shall send a statement to the tribunal and, in the case of a restricted patient, the Secretary of State, as soon as practicable and in any case within 3 weeks of its receipt of the notice of application; and such statement shall contain—

(a) the information specified in Part A of Schedule 1 to these Rules, insofar as it is within the knowledge of the responsible authority; and

(b) the report specified in paragraph 1 of Part B of that Schedule; and

(c) the other reports specified in Part B of that Schedule, in so far as it is reasonably practicable to provide them.

(2) Where the patient is a restricted patient, the Secretary of State shall send to the tribunal, as soon as practicable and in any case within 3 weeks of receipt by him of the authority's statement, a statement of such further information relevant to the application as may be available to him.

(3) Where the patient is a conditionally discharged patient, paragraphs (1) and (2) shall not apply and the Secretary of State shall send to the tribunal as soon as practicable, and in any case within 6 weeks of receipt by him of the notice of application, a statement which shall contain—

(a) the information specified in Part C of Schedule 1 to these Rules, insofar as it is within the knowledge of the Secretary of State; and

(b) the reports specified in Part D of that Schedule, in so far as it is reasonably practicable to provide them.

(3A) Where the patient is (or is to be) subject to after-care under supervision paragraph (1) shall not apply and the responsible authority shall send a statement to the tribunal as soon as practicable, and in any case within 3 weeks of the responsible authority's receipt of the notice of application, and this statement shall contain—

(a) the information specified in Part E of Schedule 1 to these Rules, in so far as it is within the knowledge of the responsible authority;

(b) the reports specified in Part F of that Schedule;

(c) the details of the after-care services being (or to be) provided under section 117 of the Act; and

(d) details of any requirements imposed (or to be imposed) on the patient under section 25D of the Act;

and shall be accompanied by copies of the documents specified in paragraph 3 of Part E of that Schedule.

(4) Any part of the authority's statement or the Secretary of State's statement which, in the opinion—

(a) (in the case of the authority's statement) the responsible authority; or

(b) (in the case of the Secretary of State's statement) the Secretary of State,

should be withheld from the applicant or (where he is not the applicant) the patient on the ground that its disclosure would adversely affect the health or welfare of the patient or others, shall be made in a separate document in which shall be set out the reasons for believing that its disclosure would have that effect.

(5) On receipt of any statement provided in accordance with paragraph (1), (2) or (3), the tribunal shall send a copy to the applicant and (where he is not the applicant) the patient, excluding any part of any statement which is contained in a separate document in accordance with paragraph (4).

Notice to other persons interested

7.—(1) On receipt of the authority's statement or, in the case of a restricted patient, the Secretary of State's statement, the tribunal shall give notice of the proceedings—

(a) where the patient is liable to be detained in a mental nursing home, to the registration authority of that home;

(b) where the patient is subject to the guardianship of a private guardian, to the guardian;

(bb) where the patient is, or will upon leaving hospital be, subject to after-care under supervision, to the person who appears to be the patient's nearest relative, and the persons who are, or will be, the patient's supervisor and community responsible medical officer and in the case of a patient who has not yet left hospital, the person who has prepared the medical report referred to in paragraph 1 of Part F of Schedule 1 to these Rules;

(c) where the patient's financial affairs are under the control of the Court of Protection, to the Court of Protection;

(d) where any person other than the applicant is named in the authority's statement as exercising the functions of the nearest relative, to that person;

(e) where a health authority or National Health Service trust has a right to discharge the patient an under the provisions of section 23(3) of the Act, to that authority or trust;

(f) to any other person who, in the opinion of the tribunal, should have an opportunity of being heard.

Appointment of the tribunal

8.—(1) Unless the application belongs to a class or group of proceedings for which members have already been appointed, the members of the tribunal who are to hear the application shall be appointed by the chairman.

(2) A person shall not be qualified to serve as a member of a tribunal for the purpose of any proceedings where—

(a) he is a member or officer of the responsible authority or of the registration authority concerned in the proceedings; or

(b) he is a member or officer of a health authority or National Health Service trust which has the right to discharge the patient under section 23(3) of the Act; or

(c) he has a personal connection with the patient or as recently treated the patient in a professional medical capacity.

(3) The persons qualified to serve as president of the tribunal for the consideration of an application or reference relating to a restricted patient shall be restricted to those legal members who have been approved for that purpose by the Lord Chancellor.

Powers to postpone consideration of an application

9.—(1) Where an application or reference by or in respect of a patient has been considered and determined by a tribunal for the same or any other area, the tribunal may, subject to the provisions of this rule, postpone the consideration of a further application by or in respect of that patient until such date as it may direct, not being later than—

(a) the expiration of the period of six months from the date on which the previous application was determined; or

(b) the expiration of the current period of detention, whichever shall be the earlier.

(2) The power of postponement shall not be exercised unless the tribunal is satisfied, after making appropriate inquiries of the applicant and (where he is not the applicant) the patient, that postponement would be in the interests of the patient.

(3) The power of postponement shall not apply to—

(a) an application under section 66(1)(d) or (gb) of the Act;

(b) an application under section 66(1)(f) of the Act in respect of a renewal of authority for detention of the patient for a period of six months or an application under section 66(1)(gc) of the Act in respect of a report furnished under section 25G(3) concerning renewal of after-care under supervision, unless the previous application or reference was made to the tribunal more than three months after the patient's admission to hospital, reception into guardianship or becoming subject to after-care under supervision;

(c) an application under section 66(1)(g) of the Act;

(d) any application where the previous application or reference was determined before a break or change in the authority for the patient's detention or guardianship or his being (or being about to be) subject to after-care under supervision as defined in paragraph (7).

(4) Where the consideration of an application is postponed, the tribunal shall state in writing the reasons for postponement and the period for which the application is postponed and shall send a copy of the statement to all the parties and, in the case of a restricted patient, the Secretary of State.

(5) Where the consideration of an application is postponed, the tribunal shall send a further notice of the application in accordance with rule 4 not less than 7 days before the end of the period of postponement and consideration of the application shall proceed thereafter, unless before the end of the period of postponement the application has been withdrawn or is deemed to be withdrawn in accordance with the provisions of rule 19 or has been determined in accordance with the next following paragraph.

(6) Where a new application which is not postponed under this rule or a reference is made in respect of a patient, the tribunal may direct that any postponed application in respect of the same patient shall be considered and determined at the same time as the new application or reference.

(7) For the purposes of paragraph (3)(d) a breach or change in the authority for the detention or guardianship or his being (or about to be) subject to after-care under supervision of a patient shall be deemed to have occurred only—

(a) on his admission to hospital in pursuance of an application for treatment or in pursuance of a hospital order without an order restricting his discharge; or

(b) on his reception into guardianship in pursuance of a guardianship application or a guardianship order; or

(c) on the application to him of the provisions of Part II or Part III of the Act as if he had been so admitted or received following—

(i) the making of a transfer direction or

(ii) the ceasing of effect of a transfer direction or an order or direction restricting his discharge; or

(d) on his transfer from guardianship to hospital in pursuance of regulations made under section 19 of the Act.

(e) on his ceasing to be subject to after-care under supervision on his reception into guardianship in accordance with section 25H(5)(b).

997

PART III — GENERAL PROVISIONS

Representation, etc.

10.—(1) Any party may be represented by any person whom he has authorised for that purpose not being a person liable to be detained or subject to guardianship or after-care under supervision under the Act or a person receiving treatment for mental disorder at the same hospital or mental nursing home as the patient.

(2) Any representative authorised in accordance with paragraph (1) shall notify the tribunal of his authorisation and postal address.

(3) As regards the representation of any patient who does not desire to conduct his own case and does not authorise a representative in accordance with paragraph (1) the tribunal may appoint some person to act for him as his authorised representative.

(4) Without prejudice to rule 12(3), the tribunal shall send to an authorised representative copies of all notices and documents which are by these Rules required or authorised to be sent to the person whom he represents and such representative may take all such steps and do all such things relating to the proceedings as the person whom he represents is by these Rules required or authorised to take or do.

(5) Any document required or authorised by these Rules to be sent or given to any person shall, if sent or given to the authorised representative of that person, be deemed to have been sent or given to that person

(6) Unless the tribunal otherwise directs, a patient or any other party appearing before the tribunal may be accompanied by such other person or persons as he wishes, in addition to any representative he may have authorised.

Medical Examination

11. At any time before the hearing of the application, the medical member or, where the tribunal includes more than one, at least one of them shall examine the patient and take such other steps as he considers necessary to form an opinion of the patient's mental condition; and for this purpose the patient may be seen in private and all his medical records may be examined by the medical member, who may take such notes and copies of them as he may require, for use in connection with the application and in the case of a patient subject to after-care under supervision this rule shall also apply to such other records relating to any after-care services provided under section 117 of the Act.

Disclosure of documents

12.—(1) Subject to paragraph (2), the tribunal shall, as soon as practicable, send a copy of every document it receives which is relevant to the application to the applicant, and (where he is not the applicant) the patient, the responsible authority and, in the case of a restricted patient, the Secretary of State and any of those persons may submit comments thereon in writing to the tribunal.

(2) As regards any documents which have been received by the tribunal but which have not been copied to the applicant or the patient, including documents withheld in accordance with rule 6, the tribunal shall consider whether disclosure of such documents would adversely affect the health or welfare of the patient or others and, if satisfied that it would, shall record in writing its decision not to disclose such documents.

(3) Where the tribunal is minded not to disclose any document to which paragraph (1) applies to an applicant or a patient who has an authorised representative it shall nevertheless disclose it as soon as practicable to that representative if he is—

(a) a barrister or solicitor;

(b) a registered medical practitioner;

(c) in the opinion of the tribunal, a suitable person by virtue of his experience or professional qualification;

provided that no information disclosed in accordance with this paragraph shall be disclosed either directly or indirectly to the applicant or (where he is not the applicant) to the patient or to any other person without the authority of the tribunal or used otherwise than in connection with the application.

Directions

13. Subject to the provisions of these Rules, the tribunal may give such directions as it thinks fit to ensure the speedy and just determination of the application.

Evidence

14.—(1) For the purpose of obtaining information, the tribunal may take evidence on oath and subpoena any witness to appear before it or to produce documents, and the president of the tribunal shall have the powers of an arbitrator under section 12(3) of the Arbitration Act 1950 and the powers of a party to a reference under an arbitration agreement under subsection (4) of that section, but no person shall be compelled to give any evidence or produce any document which he could not be compelled to give or produce on the trial of an action.

(2) The tribunal may receive in evidence any document or information notwithstanding that such document or information would be inadmissible in a court of law.

Further information

15.—(1) Before or during any hearing the tribunal may call for such further information or reports as it may think desirable, and may give directions as to the manner in which and the persons by whom such material is to be furnished.

(2) Rule 12 shall apply to any further information or reports obtained by the tribunal.

Adjournment

16.—(1) The tribunal may at any time adjourn a hearing for the purpose of obtaining further information or for such other purposes as it may think appropriate.

(2) Before adjourning any hearing, the tribunal may give such directions as it thinks fit for ensuring the prompt consideration of the application at an adjourned hearing.

(3) Where the applicant or the patient (where he is not the applicant) or the responsible authority requests that a hearing adjourned in accordance with this rule be resumed, the hearing shall be resumed provided that the tribunal is satisfied that resumption would be in the interests of the patient.

(4) Before the tribunal resumes any hearing which has been adjourned without a further hearing date being fixed it shall give to all parties and, in the case of a restricted patient, the Secretary of State, not less than 14 days' notice (or such shorter notice as all parties may consent to) of the date, time and place of the resumed hearing.

Transfer of proceedings

17.—(1) Where any proceedings in relation to a patient have not been disposed of by the members of the tribunal appointed for the purpose, and the chairman is of the opinion that it is not practicable or not possible without undue delay for the consideration of those proceedings to be completed by those members, he shall make arrangements for them to be heard by other members of the tribunal.

(2) Where a patient in respect of whom proceedings are pending moves within the jurisdiction of another tribunal, the proceedings shall, if the chairman of the tribunal originally having jurisdiction over those proceedings so directs, be transferred to the tribunal within the jurisdiction of which the patient has moved and notice of the transfer of proceedings shall be given to the parties and, in the case of a restricted patient, the Secretary of State.

Two or more pending applications

18.—(1) The tribunal may consider more than one application in respect of a patient at the same time and may for this purpose adjourn the proceedings relating to any application.

(2) Where the tribunal considers more than one application in respect of the patient at the same time, each applicant (if more than one) shall have the same rights under these Rules as he would have if he were the only applicant.

Withdrawal of application

19.—(1) An application may be withdrawn at any time at the request of the applicant provided that the request is made in writing and the tribunal agrees.

(2) If a patient ceases to be liable to be detained or subject to guardianship or after-care under supervision in England and Wales, any application relating to that patient shall be deemed to be withdrawn.

(2A) Where a patient subject to after-care under supervision fails without reasonable explanation to undergo a medical examination under rule 11, any application relating to that patient may be deemed by the tribunal to be withdrawn.

(3) Where an application is withdrawn or deemed to he withdrawn, the tribunal shall so inform the parties and, in the case of a restricted patient, the Secretary of State.

PART IV — THE HEARING

Notice of hearing

20. The tribunal shall give at least 14 days' notice of the date, time and place fixed for the hearing (or such shorter notice as all parties may consent to) to all the parties and, in the case of a restricted patient, the Secretary of State.

Privacy of proceedings

21.—(1) The tribunal shall sit in private unless the patient requests a hearing in public and the tribunal is satisfied that a hearing in public would not be contrary to the interests of the patient.

(2) Where the tribunal refuses a request for a public hearing or directs that a hearing which has begun in public shall continue in private the tribunal shall record its reasons in writing and shall inform the patient of those reasons.

(3) When the tribunal sits in private it may admit to the hearing such persons on such terms and conditions as it considers appropriate.

(4) The tribunal may exclude from any hearing or part of a hearing any person or class of persons, other than a representative of the applicant or of the patient to whom documents would be disclosed in accordance with rule 12(3), and in any case where the tribunal decides to exclude the applicant or the patient or their representatives or a representative of the responsible authority, it shall inform the person excluded of its reasons and record those reasons in writing.

(5) Except in so far as the tribunal may direct, information about proceedings before the tribunal and the names of any persons concerned in the proceedings shall not be made public.

(6) Nothing in this rule shall prevent a member of the Council on Tribunals from attending the proceedings of a tribunal in his capacity as such provided that he takes no part in those proceedings or in the deliberations of the tribunal.

Hearing procedure

22.—(1) The tribunal may conduct the hearing in such manner as it considers most suitable bearing in mind the health and interests of the patient and it shall, so far as appears to it appropriate, seek to avoid formality in its proceedings.

(2) At any time before the application is determined, the tribunal or any one or more of its members may interview the patient, and shall interview him if he so requests, and the interview may, and shall if the patient so requests, take place in the absence of any other person.

(3) At the beginning of the hearing the president shall explain the manner of proceeding which the tribunal proposes to adopt.

(4) Subject to rule 21(4), any party and, with the permission of the tribunal, any other person, may appear at the hearing and take such part in the proceedings as the tribunal thinks proper; and the tribunal shall in particular hear and take evidence from the applicant, the patient (where he is not the applicant) and the responsible authority who may hear each other's evidence, put questions to each other, call witnesses and put questions to any witness or other person appearing before the tribunal.

(5) After all the evidence has been given, the applicant and (where he is not the applicant) the patient shall be given a further opportunity to address the tribunal.

PART V — DECISIONS, FURTHER CONSIDERATION AND MISCELLANEOUS PROVISIONS

Decisions

23.—(1) Any decision of the majority of the members of a tribunal shall be the decision of the tribunal and, in the event of an equality of votes, the president of the tribunal shall have a second or casting vote.

(2) The decision by which the tribunal determines an application shall be recorded in writing; the record shall be signed by the president and shall give the reasons for the decision and, in particular, where the tribunal relies upon any of the matters set out in section 72(1), (4) or (4A) or section 73(1) or (2) of the Act, shall state its reasons for being satisfied as to those matters.

(3) Paragraphs (1) and (2) shall apply to provisional decisions and decisions with recommendations as they apply to decisions by which applications are determined.

Communication of decisions

24.—(1) The decision by which the tribunal determines an application may, at the discretion of the tribunal, be announced by the president immediately after the hearing of the case and, subject to paragraph (2), the written decision of the tribunal, including the reasons, shall be communicated in writing within 7 days of the hearing to all the parties and, in the case of a restricted patient, the Secretary of State.

(2) Where the tribunal considers that the full disclosure of the recorded reasons for its decision to the patient in accordance with paragraph (1) would adversely affect the health or welfare of the patient or others, the tribunal may instead communicate its decision to him in such manner as it thinks appropriate and may communicate its decision to the other parties subject to any conditions it may think appropriate as to the disclosure thereof to the patient; provided that, where the applicant or the patient was represented at the hearing by a person to whom documents would be disclosed in accordance with rule 12(3), the tribunal shall disclose the full recorded grounds of its decision to such a person, subject to any conditions it may think appropriate as to disclosure thereof to the patient.

(3) Paragraphs (1) and (2) shall apply to provisional decisions and decisions with recommendations as they apply to decisions by which applications are determined.

(4) Where the tribunal makes a decision with recommendations, the decision shall specify the period at the expiration of which the tribunal will consider the case further in the event of those recommendations not being complied with.

Further consideration

25.—(1) Where the tribunal has made a provisional decision, any further decision in the proceedings may be made without a further hearing.

(2) Where the tribunal has made a decision with recommendations and, at the end of the period referred to in rule 24(4), it appears to the tribunal after making appropriate inquiries of the responsible authority that any such recommendation has not been complied with, the tribunal may reconvene the proceedings after giving to all parties and, in the case of a restricted patient, the Secretary of State not less than 14 days' notice (or such shorter notice as all parties may consent to) of the date, time and place fixed for the hearing.

Time

26.—(1) Where the time prescribed by or under these Rules for doing any act expires on a Saturday, Sunday or public holiday, the act shall be in time if done on the next working week.

(2) The time appointed by these Rules for the doing of any act may, in the Particular circumstances of the case, be extended or, with the exception of the periods of notice specified in rule 16(4), rule 20 and rule 25(2), abridged by the tribunal on such terms (if any) as it may think fit.

Service of Notices, etc.

27. Any document required or authorised by these Rules to be sent or given to any person may be sent by prepaid post or delivered—

(a) in the case of a document directed to the tribunal or the chairman, to the tribunal office;

(b) in any other case, to the last known address of the person to whom the document is directed.

Irregularities

28. Any irregularity resulting from failure to comply with these Rules before the tribunal has determined an application shall not of itself render the proceedings void, but the tribunal may, and shall, if it considers that any person may have been prejudiced, take such steps as it thinks fit before determining the application to cure the irregularity, whether by the amendment of any document, the giving of any notice, the taking of any step or otherwise.

PART VI — REFERENCES AND APPLICATIONS
BY PATIENTS DETAINED FOR ASSESSMENT

References

29. The tribunal shall consider a reference as if there had been an application by the patient and the provisions of these Rules shall apply with the following modifications—

(a) rules 3, 4, 9 and 19 shall not apply;

(b) the tribunal shall, on receipt of the reference, send notice thereof to the patient and the responsible authority; provided that where the reference has been made by the responsible authority, instead of the notice of reference there shall be sent to the responsible authority a request for the authority's statement;

(c) rules 5, 6 and 7 shall apply as if rule 6(1) referred to the notice of reference, or the request for the authority's statement, as the case may be, instead of the notice of application;

(d) a reference made by the Secretary of State in circumstances in which he is not by the terms of the Act obliged to make a reference may be withdrawn by him at any time before it is considered by the tribunal and, where a reference is so withdrawn. the tribunal shall inform the patient and the other parties that the reference has been withdrawn.

Making an assessment application

30.—(1) An assessment application shall be made to the tribunal in writing signed by the patient or any person authorised by him to do so on his behalf.

(2) An assessment application shall indicate that it is made by or on behalf of a patient detained for assessment and shall wherever possible include the following information—

(a) the name of the patient;

(b) the address of the hospital or mental nursing home where the patient is detained;

(c) the name and address of the patient's nearest relative and his relationship to the patient;

(d) the name and address of any representative authorised by the patient in accordance with rule 10 or, if none has yet been authorised, whether the patient intends to authorise a representative or wishes to conduct his own case.

(3) If any of the information specified in paragraph (2) is not included in the assessment application, it shall in so far as is practicable be provided by the responsible authority at the request of the tribunal.

Appointment of a tribunal and hearing date

31. On receipt of an assessment application the tribunal shall—

(a) fix a date for the hearing, being not later than 7 days from the date on which the application was received, and the time and place for the hearing;

(b) give notice of the date, time and place fixed for the hearing to the patient;

(c) give notice of the application and of the date, time and place fixed for the hearing to the responsible authority, the nearest relative (wherever practicable) and any other person who, in the opinion of the tribunal, should have an opportunity of being heard;

and the chairman shall appoint the members of the tribunal to deal with the case in accordance with rule 8.

Provision of admission papers, etc.

32.—(1) On receipt of the notice of an assessment application, or a request from the tribunal, whichever may be the earlier, the responsible authority shall provide for the tribunal copies of the admission papers, together with such of the information specified in Part A of Schedule 1 to these Rules as is within the knowledge of the responsible authority and can reasonably be provided in the time available and such of the reports specified in Part B of that Schedule as can reasonably be provided in the time available.

(2) The responsible authority shall indicate if any part of the admission papers or other document supplied in accordance with paragraph (1) should, in their opinion, be withheld from the patient on the ground that its disclosure would adversely affect the health or welfare of the patient or others and shall state their reasons for believing that its disclosure would have that effect.

(3) The tribunal shall make available to the patient copies of the admission papers and any other document supplied in accordance with paragraph (1), excluding any part indicated by the responsible authority in accordance with paragraph (2).

General procedure, hearing procedure and decisions

33. Rule 5, rule 8 and Parts III, IV and V of these Rules shall apply to assessment applications as they apply to applications in so far as the circumstances of the case permit and subject to the following modifications—

(a) rule 12 shall apply as if any reference to a document being withheld in accordance with rule 6 was a reference to part of the admission papers or other documents supplied in accordance with rule 32 being withheld;

 (b) rule 16 shall apply with the substitution for the reference to 14 days' notice, of a reference to such notice as is reasonably practicable;

(c) rule 20 shall not apply;

(d) rule 24 shall apply as if the period of time specified therein was 3 days instead of 7 days.

PART VII — TRANSITIONAL PROVISIONS AND REVOCATIONS

Transitional Provisions

34. These Rules shall apply, so far as practicable, to any proceedings pending at the date on which they come into operation, and, where their operation is excluded by virtue of the foregoing provision, the rules in force immediately before that date shall continue to apply to such proceedings.

Revocations

35. Subject to rule 34, the rules specified in Schedule 2 to these Rules are hereby revoked.

SCHEDULE 1 (RULES 6 AND 32)

STATEMENTS BY THE RESPONSIBLE AUTHORITY AND THE SECRETARY OF STATE

PART A

INFORMATION RELATING TO PATIENTS (OTHER THAN CONDITIONALLY DISCHARGED PATIENTS AND PATIENTS SUBJECT (OR TO BE SUBJECT) TO AFTER-CARE UNDER SUPERVISION

1. The full name of the patient.

2. The age of the patient.

3. The date of admission of the patient to the hospital or mental nursing home in which the patient is currently detained or liable to be detained, or of the reception of the patient into guardianship.

4. Where the patient is being treated in a mental nursing home under contractual arrangements with a health authority, the name of that authority.

5. Details of the original authority for the detention or guardianship of the patient, including the Act of Parliament and the section of that Act by reference to which detention was authorised and details of any subsequent renewal of or change in the authority for detention.

6. The form of mental disorder from which the patient is recorded as suffering in the authority for detention (including amendments, if any, under section 16 or 72(5) of the Act, but excluding cases within section 5 of the Criminal Procedure (Insanity) Act 1964).

7. The name of the responsible medical officer and the period which the patient has spent under the care of that officer.

8. Where another registered medical practitioner is or has recently been largely concerned in the treatment of the patient, the name of that practitioner and the period which the patient has spent under his care.

9. The dates of all previous tribunal hearings in relation to the patient, the decisions reached at such hearings and the reasons given. (In restricted patient cases this requirement does not relate to decisions before 30th September 1983.)

10. Details of any proceedings in the Court of Protection and of any receivership order made in respect of the patient.

11. The name and address of the patient's nearest relative or of any other person who is exercising that function.

12. The name and address of any other person who takes a close interest in the patient.

13. Details of any leave of absence granted to the patient during the previous 2 years, including the duration of such leave and particulars of the arrangements made for the patient's residence while on leave.

PART B

REPORTS RELATING TO PATIENTS (OTHER THAN CONDITIONALLY DISCHARGED PATIENTS AND PATIENTS SUBJECT (OR TO BE SUBJECT) TO AFTER-CARE UNDER SUPERVISION

1. An up-to-date medical report, prepared for the tribunal, including the relevant medical history and a full report on the patient's mental condition.

2. An up-to-date social circumstances report prepared for the tribunal including reports on the following—

(a) the patient's home and family circumstances, including the attitude of the patient's nearest relative or the person so acting;

(b) the opportunities for employment or occupation and the housing facilities which would be available to the patient if discharged;

(c) the availability of community support and relevant medical facilities;

(d) the financial circumstances of the patient.

3. The views of the authority on the suitability of the patient for discharge.

4. Any other information or observations on the application which the authority wishes to make.

PART C

INFORMATION RELATING TO CONDITIONALLY DISCHARGED PATIENTS

1. The full name of the patient.

2. The age of the patient.

3. The history of the patient's present liability to detention including details of offence(s), and the dates of the original order or direction and of the conditional discharge.

4. The form of mental disorder from which the patient is recorded as suffering in the authority for detention. (Not applicable to cases within section 5 of the Criminal Procedure (Insanity) Act 1964.)

5. The name and address of any medical practitioner responsible for the care and supervision of the patient in the community and the period which the patient has spent under the care of that practitioner.

6. The name and address of any social worker or probation officer responsible for the care and supervision of the patient in the community and the period which the patient has spent under the care of that person.

PART D

REPORTS RELATING TO CONDITIONALLY DISCHARGED PATIENTS

1. Where there is a medical practitioner responsible for the care and supervision of the patient in the community, an up-to-date medical report prepared for the tribunal including the relevant medical history and a full report on the patient's mental condition.

2. Where there is a social worker or probation officer responsible for the patient's care and supervision in the community, an up-to-date report prepared for the tribunal on the patient's progress in the community since discharge from hospital.

3. A report on the patient's home circumstances.

4. The views of the Secretary of State on the suitability of the patient for absolute discharge.

5. Any other observations on the application which the Secretary of State wishes to make.

PART E

INFORMATION AND DOCUMENTS RELATING TO PATIENTS SUBJECT (OR TO BE SUBJECT) TO AFTER-CARE UNDER SUPERVISION

1. The full name, address and age of the patient.

2. The date of the acceptance of the supervision application in respect of the patient.

3. A copy of the original supervision application, details of the after-care services provided (or to be provided) under section 117 of the Act, details of any requirements imposed (or to be imposed) under section 25D(1) of the Act, a copy of any report furnished under section 25G(3)(b) of the Act in relation to renewal of the supervision application and a copy of any record of modification of the after-care services provided.

4. Any reclassification of the form of mental disorder from which the patient is recorded as suffering in the supervision application reported in accordance with section 25F(1) of the Act.

5. The name of the person who is (or is to be) the community responsible medical officer and the period (if any) during which he has been in charge of the patient's medical treatment.

6. The name of the person who is (or is to be) the patient's supervisor.

7. Where a registered medical practitioner other than the community responsible medical officer is or has recently been largely concerned in the treatment of the patient, details of the name and address of the practitioner and the period which the patient has spent under his care.

8. The name and address of any place where the patient (if he has been discharged) is receiving medical treatment.

9. The name and address of the hospital where the patient was detained or liable to be detained when the supervision application was made.

10. The dates of any previous tribunal hearings in relation to the patient since he became subject to after-care under supervision, the decisions reached at such hearings and the reasons given.

11. Details of any proceedings in the Court of Protection and of any receivership order made in respect of the patient.

12. The name and address of the patient's nearest relative or of any other person who is exercising that function.

13. The name and address of any other person who takes a close interest in the patient.

PART F

REPORTS RELATING TO PATIENTS SUBJECT (OR TO BE SUBJECT) TO AFTER-CARE UNDER SUPERVISION

1. An up-to-date medical report, prepared for the tribunal by the patient's community responsible medical officer or, if he has not yet left hospital, his responsible medical officer (or, where there is none, his last responsible medical officer), including the relevant medical history and a full report on the patients mental condition.

2. Where the patient is subject to after-care under supervision an up-to-date report prepared for the tribunal by the patient's supervisor including reports on the following—

(a) the patient's home and family circumstances, including the attitude of the patient's nearest relative or the person so acting and the attitude of any person who plays a substantial part in the care of the patient but is not professionally concerned with any of the after-care services provided to the patient;

(b) his progress in the community whilst subject to after-care under supervision including an assessment of the effectiveness of that supervision.

3. Where the patient has not yet left hospital an up-to-date social circumstances report prepared for the tribunal by a person professionally concerned with the nature of the patient's social circumstances including reports on the following—

(a) the patient's home and family circumstances, including the attitude of the patient's nearest relative or the person so acting;

(b) the opportunities for employment or occupation and the housing facilities which would be available to the patient upon his discharge from hospital;

(c) the availability of community support and relevant medical facilities;

(d) the financial circumstances of the patient.

SCHEDULE 2 — REVOCATIONS (RULE 35)

Titles	References	Extent of Revocation
The Mental Health Review Tribunal Rules 1960	S.I. 1960/1139	The whole Rules
The Mental Health Review Tribunal (Welsh Forms) Rules 1971	S.I. 1971/1772	The whole Rules
The Mental Health Review Tribunal (Amendment) Rules 1976	S.I. 1976/447	The whole Rules

PART II — MEDICAL ISSUES

17. Mental health and mental disorder

INTRODUCTION

It is certainly possible for professionals who have only a bare appreciation of medical terms and ideas to make a useful contribution to tribunal proceedings. For this reason, a legal representative who has only limited time available to acquaint himself with the subject should concentrate on those issues already highlighted in the medical reports which are most obviously critical to the particular case. Chapter 11 deals with the general requirements of such reports while chapter 18 is in effect a glossary of common medical terms. Chapters 21 to 24 examine issues which often arise during proceedings involving patients with relatively common diagnoses such as schizophrenia and depression.

LEGAL SIGNIFICANCE OF MEDICAL CONCEPTS

While the particular situation may dictate a practical approach, an understanding of the concepts upon which the medical evidence is based improves the quality of decision-making and helps to ensure that citizens are not deprived of their liberty except on the surest of grounds. Because tribunal proceedings are a mixture of law and medicine, a purely legal approach to the work is unproductive, even for lawyers: it is not sufficient to understand only the legal part of what is a medico-legal subject. Although nowhere referred to in mental health legislation, various unspoken legal presumptions and conventions underpin the hearing procedures and their relevance and applicability are implicitly understood by all of the lawyers involved — for example, the requirements of natural justice, the duty to give proper and adequate reasons for decisions, the fact that secondary legislation gives way to primary legislation where they conflict, and so forth. The medical evidence similarly conceals a number of fundamental, and therefore unspoken, concepts and presumptions about which the law is silent but which, being accepted by most doctors, have a bearing on the conduct and outcome of the case — for example, the presumption that certain mental disorders are diseases, diagnostic conventions about the classification of disorders, and assumptions about prognosis. These conventions are significant both medically, in determining the treatment given compulsorily, and legally, because of their consequences for the individual's liberty. Consequently, it is important to understand both the legal and medical presumptions involved in any deprivation of liberty. This ability enables tribunal members and advocates to identify medical evidence and opinion which is of questionable validity or reliability, and so minimises the risk of a citizen remaining detained who would have been discharged if the evidence had been rigorously scrutinised. However, while it is impossible to follow the evidence or to identify the salient issues without a knowledge of medical concepts and terms,

the rote-learning of definitions is unhelpful. It is more useful to develop an appreciation of the concepts embraced by the terms; otherwise, what the individual propounds is not always clear even to himself. To summarise, the taking of the evidence
should never deteriorate into purely theoretical debates about legal or medical concepts. At the same time, the ideal situation — in terms of distilling the relevant issues, procedural fairness, and the quality of decision-making — is one where those
present share a common, if usually silent, understanding about what part of the
medical evidence is fact and what opinion, what is expert opinion and what supposi-
tion, which differences of opinion are worth exploring and which are incapable of
resolution.

The role of the legal and lay members of a tribunal

While a positive finding of mental disorder should be founded upon some medical
opinion which accords with an established diagnostic system, the non-medically
qualified tribunal members are not otherwise bound to follow the medical advice.[1]
Whether a citizen is mentally disordered is not an exclusively medical question, nor
is the interpretation of medical evidence solely a matter for the tribunal's medical
member. That this is so is reflected by the presence of two non-medical members on
the tribunal: a lawyer to ensure that, whatever the clinical view, mental illness is not
defined so broadly as to be incompatible with legal principles relating to individual
liberty; a lay member to represent the common-sense view about what constitutes
abnormality of mind — Lord Justice Lawton's ordinary, sensible, person.[2] These
other members cannot derogate from their individual duties to independently assess
the quality of the evidence. There will be times when the medical opinion expressed
at a tribunal is divided and it falls to the non-medical members to exercise a
quasi-clinical judgement about which view is to be preferred. In other cases, where
medical opinion is united, the non-medical members will still have to weigh that
evidence against other relevant considerations, including a civil patient's general
right to liberty. The weight given to the diagnosis, and the value of predictions about
response to treatment, compliance, and outcome, inevitably depend on many factors,
including the validity and reliability of any diagnostic system used.

The role of the patient's authorised representative

The desirability of having an understanding of the medical issues is recognised by
The Law Society, which requires prospective members of its Mental Health Panel to
attend a course which includes a medical component. Because of the tribunal's
obligation to hear certain applications within one week of their receipt, the patient's
representative often has insufficient time to instruct a psychiatrist to provide an
opinion of the evidence. In such cases, the medical report prepared by the patient's
consultant will usually not be available until shortly before the hearing. The
representative will have about half an hour to take further instructions, assess the
evidence, prepare questions, and revise submissions. In other kinds of tribunal
proceedings, the representative may face similar difficulties through being instructed
or appointed late in the day. Whatever the nature of the proceedings, a representative
will often need to consult medical textbooks or journals, examine the patient's case
notes, and discuss medical issues with clients and other mental health professionals.

---

[1]   See *e.g. R. v. Royse* (1981) 3 Cr.App.R.(S.) 58.
[2]   See *W v. L.* [1974] Q.B. 711, C.A.

For all these reasons, the authorised representative requires a basic knowledge of psychiatric terms and classifications in order to present his client's case effectively.

THE PROBLEM OF DEFINITIONS

Professionals who are not legally qualified sometimes conceive of legislation, and legal concepts such as nuisance and the common law, as precise and unambiguous and not susceptible to conflicting interpretations. Many lawyers similarly think of medicine as a science and tend to believe that words like disease and schizophrenia have established meanings which are universally accepted by medical practitioners. This tendency to regard legal and medical terms as having value-free fixed meanings rather than as expressing concepts is, however, misplaced and merely reflects a failure to appreciate the problems which all professions experience in reaching agreement about ideas. Although lawyers have the advantage that certain words and phrases are statutorily defined, this is a limited blessing in practice because the meaning of the words which make up any statutory definition can equally be disputed. Locke observed that it is hardest to know the meaning of words when the ideas they stand for are very complex, or have no certain connection in nature, or when a word's meaning refers to a standard and that standard is not easily known.[3] While acknowledging that some words have no meaning at all, Locke recognised that to require that all men should use words in the same sense and have clear ideas on them would be to expect they should talk of nothing but what they had clear ideas on, which was absurd. Words must be used in order to formulate theories[4] and their precise meaning may only emerge gradually as the ideas in them are submitted to enquiry.[5] While concepts such as disease and illness have "distinct though partly overlapping connotations which can be fairly precisely identified, there is nevertheless an arbitrary element in the labelling."[6] There are also many words which cannot be defined at all. For example, the names of simple ideas such as colours and tastes cannot be defined: "This is clear, for if a thing has no parts you cannot enumerate its parts. Neglect of this simple truth has led to much confusion, persons trying to define everything, and thus giving rise to much wrangling and absurdity."[7]

Definitions and values

"Disease" is a fair example of a word which leaves the impression of being a scientific term capable of precise definition but, as Kendell[8] has noted, is in fact a value-laden concept used in different senses by medical practitioners—

---

[3] J. Locke, *An Essay concerning Human Understanding* (Clarendon Press, 1975), Bk. III, p.477. When a word stands for a very complex idea it is not easy for men to form and retain that idea so exactly that it will not vary now and then. Hence such words have seldom in two men the same significance, and even the meaning changes from day to day. Furthermore, if men have not standards whereby to adjust the signification of these words, then the significance becomes doubtful and, the rule of propriety of language itself being nowhere established, it is often a matter of dispute whether this meaning or that is more correct, according to usage. *Ibid.*, pp.478–479.

[4] K. Popper, "Conversation with Karl Popper" in B. Magee, *Modern British Philosophers* (Paladin, 1973).

[5] M. Roth, "Psychiatric Diagnosis in Clinical and Scientific Settings" in *Psychiatric Diagnosis: Exploration of Biological Predictors* (ed. H.S. Akiskal & W.L. Webb, S.P. Medical & Scientific Books, 1978), p.12.

[6] C. Culver and B. Gert, *Philosophy in Medicine* (Oxford University Press, 1982), p.65.

[7] R.C. Bodkin, *How to Reason* (Browne & Nolan Ltd., 3rd ed., 1906), p.160.

[8] The Chief Medical Officer at the Scottish Office Home and Health Department at the time.

"If ... physicians are asked to explain why they regard some phenomena as diseases, and why they withhold this designation from others, it soon becomes apparent that they use different criteria on different occasions ... Such inconsistencies and contradictions raise the suspicion the 'disease' is not a scientific term ... I am forced to concede that if one studies the way the term is used in practice, by doctors, it is difficult to avoid the conclusion that disease is not a biomedical concept at all, and that doctors do not want to have their freedom of choice restricted by a definition. Whether or not they admit or recognize the fact, 'disease' is used by doctors themselves as a normative, or socio-political, concept. It implies simply that the condition in question is undesirable, and that on balance it is better dealt with by physicians and medical technology than by alternative institutions like the law (which would regard it as crime), or the church (which would regard it as sin) or sociology (which would regard it as deviant behaviour)."[9]

Whether particular kinds of behaviour, or the expression of particular ideas, are defined as a medical or as a legal problem, or both, may therefore be a matter of policy, a question of a society's values. Because this is so, the meaning of medico-legal terms — those medical terms which when applied to individuals have legal consequences — is rarely a matter only of professional judgement or professional interest. Consequently, the people through their Parliament require that tribunals include a lay member, that applications are made by persons other than doctors, and that decisions about whether conduct amounts to mental illness are not determined by medical criteria alone. Although it is fashionable to question the validity of any system which is value-based, the individuals who make up a particular society have different values and these must somehow be reconciled or weighted. In this context, it is simply important to recognise that there are also words the meaning of which people with different sets of values will never be able to agree.[10]

The approach taken in the text

Although the purpose of language is to facilitate communication, many medical terms have over the years become a barrier, rather than an aid, to understanding and progress. Once useful words often no longer carry their original or natural meaning, or have acquired a range of meanings, and the speaker must therefore be asked to clarify what *he* means by the term. The use of euphemisms has led to words being debased and distinctions blurred and authors do not themselves always adhere to the definitions which they give. This laxity is unfortunate because it tends to result in a lack of clarity whereas, as Culver and Gert note, "the logic of terminology should be exploited to reinforce the conceptual framework."[11] In dealing with medical terms and concepts, priority has generally been given in the text to the views of leading British psychiatrists and to definitions contained in internationally recognised medical publications such as the *International Classification of Diseases*, the *Lexicon of Psychiatric and Mental Health Terms*, and the *Diagnostic and Statistical Manual of Mental Disorders*. Occasionally, reference is also made to established American writers, such as Appleton and Kleinman at Harvard, but not to

9   R.E. Kendell, "Schizophrenia: A Medical View of a Medical Concept" in *What is Schizophrenia?* (ed. W.F. Flack, *et. al.*, Springer-Verlag, 1990), pp.61–63. A point also made by Murphy: "too many heroin addicts on the street and a medical problem is redefined as a legal one, of keeping society safe." S. Murphy, *Experiencing and Explaining Disease* (The Open University Press, 1985), p.3.

10 See W.B. Gallie, *Philosophy and the Historical Understanding* (Chatto & Windus, 1964), p.189.

11 *International Classification of Impairments, Disabilities, and Handicaps, A manual of classification relating to the consequences of disease* (World Health Organisation, 1976), pp.32–33.

non-mainstream writers such as Laing and Szasz. This is because a legal textbook is not a proper place for opinions which if put forward before a tribunal would be unlikely to affect the outcome of the hearing. Subject to this restriction, the subject is not one that benefits from rigid lines of demarcation. Although it is customary to study, and therefore think of, the law in terms of theory and practice, the distinction is as artificial as separating out the medical and legal components of the subject, and simply reflects the existence historically of separate career structures for academic lawyers and legal practitioners.[12] Some conceptual framework or fundamental points of reference are a valuable aid to practice.

BIOLOGY AND MEDICINE

By custom, the physical sciences are chemistry and physics while biology is a natural science, the sciences being characterised by their rigorous, systematic, objective, and value-free observation and explanation of factual events. Medicine as a discipline comprises all facets of human biology and, because it is founded on biological knowledge, it is commonly described as medical science. Medical science approaches mental disorders as diseases which can be studied objectively in terms of abnormal cell structures and chemical imbalances. Conventionally, medical scientists are not concerned with "inner meanings" because they cannot be objectively measured. From this, it is sometimes inferred that medical knowledge, and more particularly psychiatric expert evidence, has an objective validity and reliability which sets it apart from most other kinds of evidence.

Medicine and other biological disciplines

Biology involves the scientific study of living organisms, their form, structure, functions, behaviour, origin, and distribution. Morphology, anatomy, physiology, cytology, histology and genetics are all sub-divisions of biology. The terms will be frequently encountered in the medical literature on mental disorder and they are therefore defined below. It should, however, be emphasised that the boundaries between these notionally distinct fields are artificial.

BIOLOGICAL DISCIPLINES

- **Morphology**   The study of the <u>form</u> of animals and plants.

- **Anatomy**   The study of the <u>structure</u> of animals and plants.

- **Physiology**   The study of the <u>function</u> of animals and plants and their parts. Physiology is concerned with life processes, how organs work and function.

- **Cytology**   A cell is the smallest unit of living matter which is capable of independent functioning. Cytology is the study of the structure (anatomy) of cells while cytopathology is the study of changes in cells caused by disease.

---

[12] Problems which can only be surmounted by developing mental health law along medical school lines, with legal practitioners dividing their time between client work and medico-legal academic study. However, the organisation of the legal profession and the legal aid scheme makes this difficult at present.

- **Histology**   Cells are grouped together to form tissues, each of which has a specialised function. Most organs are composed of two or more tissue types which perform one or more common functions. Histology is the study of the structure of tissues while histopathology is the study of changes in tissues caused by disease.

- **Biochemistry**   Chemistry is the study of the properties and interactions of the chemical atoms and molecules from which the world is made. Biochemistry deals with the chemical constitution of living things and involves the study of human structure and functions in terms of their chemistry. The chemical reactions that take place in the body are known collectively as metabolism. Metabolic reactions require a catalyst or enzyme. Enzyme-catalysed reactions result in chemical change, leading to the formation of a new chemical substance.

- **Biophysics**   Physics is the study of the forces that govern the properties of matter in the universe. Biophysics seeks to explain biological phenomena by applying the laws of physics.

- **Genetics**   Genetics is concerned with links between symptoms and inheritance and with the precise nature of inheritance.

The practice of medicine (clinical medicine) and psychiatry

The practice of medicine consists of the application of knowledge concerning human biology to the prevention and treatment of illness.[13] This is often referred to as the biomedical approach to mental disorder. Psychiatry is that branch of medicine concerned with the study, diagnosis, treatment and prevention of mental disorder. A number of related specialist branches of medicine are defined below, although it should again be emphasised that the boundaries between them are artificial.

SPECIALIST BRANCHES OF MEDICINE

- **Psychiatry**   The psyche is the mind, the soul, and the use of the prefixes psych- and psycho- indicate that a discipline deals with the psyche or mind. Although psychiatry literally means the healing of the psyche, in modern usage the word refers to that branch of medicine concerned with the study, diagnosis, treatment and prevention of mental disorder.

- **Neurology**   The use of the prefix neuro- (from the Greek "neuron," nerve) indicates that a discipline is concerned with the nervous system, including therefore the brain. Neurology is the branch of medicine concerned with the organisation and functioning of the brain and the nervous system.

---

[13]   See S.B. Guze, "Validating Criteria for Psychiatric Diagnosis: The Washington University Approach" in *Psychiatric Diagnosis: Exploration of Biological Predictors* (ed. H.S. Akiskal & W.L. Webb, S.P. Medical & Scientific Books, 1978), pp.49–59.

◆ Pathology	The use of the prefix patho- (from the Greek "pathos," suffering) denotes that a discipline is concerned with disease. Pathology is the study of disease and its causes, mechanisms and effects on the body.
◆ Endocrinology	Endocrinology is the branch of medicine which is concerned with the study, diagnosis and treatment of disorders affecting the endocrine (hormonal) system.
◆ Mixed disciplines	Neurophysiology is the study of the physiological basis of the nervous system — that is the relationship between mental events and physical events in the nervous system. Likewise, neuropsychiatry is concerned with the neurological basis of mental disorder and the relationship between the nervous system and mental functioning. Neuroanatomy is principally concerned with the structure of the nervous system.

DISCIPLINES RELATED TO PSYCHIATRY AND MEDICINE

◆ Psychology	Most psychologists have no medical qualification and psychology is not a branch of medicine. Psychology may be defined as the study of the mind and mental processes — behaviour, perception, thought, feeling, emotion, self-awareness and intellectual functioning — and clinical psychology is the application in a clinical setting of the principles derived from such study. Neuropsychology is concerned with the neurological basis of psychological functioning.
◆ Philosophy	Philosophy is literally the study and pursuit of wisdom and principles for the conduct of life. It includes ethics (and therefore medical ethics). Historically, philosophy and biology were the twin pillars of medicine, the practice of medicine requiring a knowledge of philosophy, but the approach is currently out of fashion.

Medical science

By convention, the defining feature of the scientific disciplines is that they share an approach to investigating the natural and physical world known as scientific investigation and scientific reasoning. Sciences deal only in reliable, quantifiable, data capable of being observed in a similar way by everyone. Scientific investigations are systematic, which means that an agreed and rigorous system for performing observations and measurements is followed. The scientific approach stresses the importance of unbiased observation and data collected without any preconceived notions: the observer does not speculate about possible principles before the evidence is collected in order to avoid influencing the data. Similarly, the scientist avoids making value judgements, opinions about whether what is being observed is desirable, because subjectivity of this kind also distorts observation. Only when sufficient facts are collected can principles or laws be sought to explain them. Induction — also referred to as inductive logic, inductive reasoning, or as the empirical approach — is the process of deriving general statements (theories) about the laws of nature from this detailed observation and accurate measurement of phenomena in the physical world. Hypotheses about associations and causal relationships between events are formulated and tested; failure to confirm expectations results in their rejection while success establishes the soundness of the underlying concepts. The value of a hypothesis lies in its predictive power, the purpose of science being to explain why certain events or phenomena occur — to describe the world in an orderly fashion — and so to predict the outcome of events. In contrast to the sciences, the value of the arts and humanities lies in the very fact that they are unsystematic and impressionistic, involving the expression of subjective human experiences through the application of qualities such as sensitivity, intuition, empathy, feeling and creative thought.

Contemporary ideas about science

While the distinction just drawn will be familiar to many people, the classical description of the scientific method represents an ideal and, if used as the yardstick, there is then much that is unscientific about science. It is now generally accepted that the "idea of unbiased observation is a myth ... Sense data are chosen, simplified, and interpreted before being committed to memory."[14] More fundamentally, scientific observation and reasoning have limitations[15] while Popper has emphasised — many would say demonstrated — that observation and logic are not the sole basis for developing scientific theories: the generation of hypotheses may be largely intuitive, although they can be subjected to analytical reason when tested. This ability to intuitively reason, to break free of conventional thought processes and established scientific theory, lies at the root of many scientific breakthroughs and constitutes one of the highest human faculties. In Popper's phrase, "the history of science is everywhere speculative."[16]

Problems applying the scientific method to mental phenomena

Irrespective of whether one prefers the modern or classical viewpoint, there is broad acceptance about the very real problems involved in attempting to apply traditional scientific methods and reasoning to medicine and, in particular, to mental phenomena—

- Bradley has observed that while Newtonian principles of cause and effect leading to a world which is certain and predictable have been successful when applied to a wide spectrum of natural phenomena — including many relevant to medical practice — they fail to deal adequately with complex non-linear systems such as the whole human body, thermodynamics and weather patterns.[17] Such complex systems do not behave predictably and the simple rules of cause and effect do not operate. The awareness that, within certain broad boundaries, it is possible for minor influences to have profound effects because of the amplifying effect of the non-linearity leads to the collapse of predictability.[18]

---

[14] G.W. Bradley, *Disease, Diagnosis and Decisions* (John Wiley & Sons, 1993), p.27.
[15] Hume pointed out that any generalization allowing predictions about an infinite number of possibilities from a finite number of observations is unsound since it involves a leap beyond the observations.
[16] Sir Karl Popper, in J. Horgan, "Profile: Karl R. Popper, the intellectual warrior" *Scientific American* (November 1992), p.21.
[17] G.W. Bradley, *Disease, Diagnosis and Decisions*, supra, pp.x–xi.
[18] This realisation is sometimes referred to by scientists as "chaos theory." However, deprived of its scientific gloss, chaos theory is little more than an acknowledgement of the limits of science, *i.e.* that phenomena as complex as human behaviour cannot be predicted using scientific methods because of the number of variables involved. The importance of the observation in the context of psychiatry and tribunal proceedings mainly relates to assessments of dangerousness. However, it is also possible that certain diseases, such as schizophrenia and some cancers, are the result of "chaos" within the body, *i.e.* small changes in a critical variable but not a particular one.

- Scientific approaches to human conduct are hampered by the fact that the research subjects — human beings — are resistant to the rigid controls demanded by laboratory science.[19] The response of a patient to disease does not allow closely controlled experiments. While, as Bradley notes, the mysteries of life can only be fully understood by examining living organisms, the simplest and most revealing experiments are often unethical.[20]

- Because of this complexity of biological systems when studied in their entirety and the additional restrictions imposed by ethical considerations, it is common to take a reductionist approach and study a relatively small aspect of physiology or biochemistry to allow control of extraneous factors. Unfortunately, real life reintroduces these extraneous factors into the equation.

- The observation of human phenomena is more susceptible to distortion than is the observation of static phenomena. What is observed (that is what is seen and consciously recorded) depends on attentiveness and also personal opinion about what is significant and relevant. Some degree of subjectivity is inevitable and this partly explains why superficially similar research projects, including clinical trials of new drugs, produce different results. As yet there is no way of accurately measuring or compensating for observer distortion.[21]

- The absence of any universally accepted language for describing mental phenomena means that it is impossible to accurately and systematically record or communicate what is observed. Consequently, many controversies about subjects such as schizophrenia are essentially semantic, the by-products of a failure to agree the meaning of abstract nouns.[22] While "all science depends on the ability to measure natural phenomena ... much psychiatric research in the last two decades has been concerned with the first task of science, that of learning how to define and measure the phenomena with which it deals. In psychiatry this is particularly difficult."[23]

- If each person's thoughts and feelings are known only to that individual and cannot be directly observed or measured by others, this recognition that it is only feasible to scientifically observe and study human behaviour — the external manifestations of thoughts and feelings — is also a recognition that traditional scientific methods are limited to explaining surface phenomena. While it may be eminently sensible to restrict scientific inquiry to areas of human life which can be objectively observed and quantified, the scientist who accepts this restriction avoids matters of fundamental significance.

---

[19] See *Studying health and disease* (ed. K. McConway, Open University Press, 1994), pp. 9–20.

[20] G.W. Bradley, *Disease, Diagnosis and Decisions* (John Wiley & Sons, 1993), pp.x–xi.

[21] It would be possible to psychometrically rate the professional, political and social views of researchers and to publish those findings alongside the data concerning the patients' personality and health. Although such an approach has limitations, it might explain some of the variation both in what is observed and the scientific conclusions drawn from those observations (the degree of bias).

[22] Locke's observations are again apposite: "Let us look into books of controversy and we shall see that the effect of obscure terms is only noise about sounds, the controversy is about names not things ... Here I desire it to be considered carefully whether the greater part of the disputes of the world are not about the signification of words and whether if the terms were defined all these disputes would not end of themselves." J. Locke, *An Essay concerning Human Understanding* (Clarendon Press, 1975), Bk. III, pp.510–512.

[23] C. Thompson, *The Instruments of Psychiatric Research* (John Wiley & Sons, 1989), p.2.

- Stated another way, while natural sciences benefit from a traditional scientific approach, establishing causal connections and associations between psychological events requires empathy. Although symptoms and signs — the public manifestation of inner mental processes — may be observed and, arguably, quantified by a neutral unbiased third party, eliciting the underlying causes of such phenomena — the private unobservable conflicts — requires this quality. Without it, there can be no understanding of the individual or the causes of his symptoms. The development and application of sympathy and intuitive understanding becomes a prerequisite for the objective observation of phenomena in others. Thus, Jaspers wrote that "natural science is indeed the groundwork of psychopathology and an essential element in it but the humanities are equally so and, with this, psychopathology does not become any less scientific but scientific in another way."[24]

Summary

An understanding of these obstacles at the outset is important because it places the limitations of professional knowledge about mental disorder in context and explains why so many of the ideas and terms referred to in the text and in psychiatric reports suffer from a lack of clarity. Although science is generally associated with consistency and certainty, the scientific basis of clinical psychiatry is modest. The subject remains essentially impressionistic, lacks clear concepts and a universally agreed use of language, is of modest predictive value, and assessments often rely as much on the views of the examiner as the illness of the patient. In short, we still know less about the structure and functioning of the brain that we do about any other organ in the body and there remains much uncertainty about the diagnosis and management of disease. Given this state of knowledge, the successful practice of psychiatry necessarily relies as much on intuition as objective methodology or enquiry, and is part science and part art — "the artful application of science,"[25] "a personal skill which uses some of the tools of science, but which also goes beyond science,"[26] "the process of making reasonable decisions in uncertain circumstances — a question of judgement involving a combination of knowledge, personal experience, common sense and humanity."[27] Acknowledging that we remain largely ignorant in this area, and will be known as such by future generations, is also a useful reminder of the need to be cautious before interfering with individual liberty and imposing forms of treatment whose mechanisms are not understood. Although one cannot be sure, there seems no reason to believe that our era is the first to escape from the historical trend that some contemporary forms of treatment are with hindsight later shown to have been misconceived. It is important to both seek the truth and to be wary of those who have found it.

---

[24] K. Jaspers, *General psychopathology* (trans. J. Hoening and M.W. Hamilton, Manchester University Press, 1962). The limitations of applying traditional scientific methods to mental phenomena have led some psychiatrists to favour a more humanistic, "phenomenological," approach to mental disorder. Phenomenology is the theory that behaviour is determined by the way in which the subject perceives reality at any moment and not by reality as it can be described in physical, objective terms.

[25] R.S. Greenberg, *Medical Epidemiology* (Appleton & Lange, 1993), p.58.

[26] D. Seedhouse, *Health: The foundations for achievement* (John Wiley & Sons, 1986), p.95.

[27] G.W. Bradley, *Disease, Diagnosis and Decisions* (John Wiley & Sons, 1993), pp.xiii and xvi.

THE CONCEPT OF PERSONALITY

Not all conditions characterised by abnormal mental functioning are conceived of as an illness: certain forms of mental disorder are conceptualised, and therefore categorised, as disorders of the personality. Here, the individual's abnormal mental state is considered to be innate, the manifestation of an abnormal personality rather than the consequence of an illness overlying and distorting that personality. The concept implies a certain cohesion and "consistency of the personality as a backdrop upon which the vicissitudes of illness and other circumstances make transitory patterns, but the underlying features remain constant."[28]

Definitions of personality

The *Lexicon of Psychiatric and Mental Health Terms* defines personality as "the ingrained patterns of thought, feeling, and behaviour characterising an individual's unique lifestyle and mode of adaptation, and resulting from constitutional factors, development, and social experience."[29] Schneider described personality as being the unique quality of the individual, his feelings and personal goals; it is the sum of his traits, habits and experiences; the whole system of relatively permanent tendencies, physical and mental, which are distinctive of a given individual."[30]

Permanence and regularity

Most definitions of personality emphasise the relative permanence and regularity of certain personal characteristics, whether inherited or learnt, which consequently give behaviour an element of predictability. Personality has a genetic component and behaviour genetics is concerned with the pathway from genes to behaviour and the lifelong interactions between the genetic constitution of an individual (the genotype) and his environment. However, certain aspects of each individual's personality are generally considered to be acquired through learning. Learning may be defined as any relatively permanent change in behaviour which is brought about as a result of past experience, that is because of an association of events; the learner is not always aware that learning is taking place.[31] An underlying biological assumption is that "if what is learnt at any one stage did not have some permanence, we would be endlessly open to change in response to events and circumstances ... It is the relative permanence of personality characteristics which fosters the maintenance of individual differences and these are thought to contribute to the preservation of the species within a changing physical and cultural environment."[32]

Personality traits

The study of personality approaches it either by way of surface characteristics (traits) or by underlying tendencies, which may be described in terms of drives, needs and unconscious mechanisms. In genetics, a trait is the characteristic observable expression of a hereditary predisposition, for example red hair. The trait is

---

[28]   A. Sims, *Symptoms in the Mind* (Baillière Tindall, 1988), p.299.
[29]   *Lexicon of Psychiatric and Mental Health Terms* (World Health Organisation, 2nd ed., 1994), p.75.
[30]   K. Schneider, *Clinical Psychopathology* (5th ed., trans. M.W. Hamilton, Grune & Stratton, 1958).
[31]   F.M. McPherson, "Psychology in relation to psychiatry" in *Companion to psychiatric studies* (ed. R.E. Kendell & A.K. Zealley, Churchill Livingstone, 1993), p.24.
[32]   S. Wolff, "Personality development" in *Companion to psychiatric studies, supra,* p.61.

therefore the outward manifestation so that, when the word is used to describe something characteristic about a person's behaviour rather than his physique, a personality trait is "a constant or persistent way of behaving."[33] Although, strictly speaking, the trait is the observed characteristic behaviour rather than the recurrent tendency to it[34] — for example, aggression rather than aggressiveness — the assumption that observable behaviour patterns are the manifestations of unobservable dispositions within the individual's personality has led some authorities to define personality traits in terms of these generalised predispositions. Thus, the *Lexicon of Psychiatric and Mental Health Terms* defines a personality trait as "a constant purposive portion of the personality which is inferred from the totality of an individual's behaviour but never directly observed."[35] The predisposition may be towards some mental state (such as depression) or some mode of conduct (such as aggression or violence).[36] A personality trait is often compared and contrasted with the individual's mental state, which is a momentary or time-limited characteristic. For example, a person's mental state may be characterised by anxiety in a particular setting although he is not an anxious person in general.

Personality and behaviour disorder

What constitutes a disorder of personality depends on how normality and abnormality are defined (**1031**). A personality and behaviour disorder is defined in the *Lexicon of Psychiatric and Mental Health Terms* as one of "a variety of conditions and behaviour patterns of clinical significance that tend to be persistent and appear to be the expression of the individual's lifestyle and mode of relating to self and others. Specific personality disorders, mixed personality disorders, and enduring personality change are deeply ingrained and persisting behaviour patterns, manifested as inflexible responses to a broad range of personal and social situations. They represent extreme or significant deviations from the way in which the average individual in a given culture perceives, thinks, feels, and, particularly, relates to others."[37]

Enduring personality changes

An enduring personality change is defined in the *Lexicon of Psychiatric and Mental Health Terms* as "a disorder of adult personality and behaviour that has developed following catastrophic or excessive prolonged stress, or following severe psychiatric illness, in an individual with no previous personality disorder. There is a definite and enduring change in the individual's pattern of perceiving, relating to, or thinking about the environment and the self. The personality change is associated with inflexible and maladaptive behaviour that was not present before the pathogenic experience and is not a manifestation of another mental disorder or a residual symptom of any antecedent mental disorder."[38]

---

[33] See G.W. Allport, *Personality: a psychological interpretation* (Holt, 1937).

[34] G.L. Klerman and R.M.A. Hirschfield, "Personality as a vulnerability factor: with special attention to clinical depression" in *Handbook of social psychiatry* (ed. A.S. Henderson & G.D. Burrows, Elsevier, 1988), pp.41–53.

[35] *Lexicon of Psychiatric and Mental Health Terms* (World Health Organisation, 2nd ed., 1994).

[36] If this approach is adopted, it must be borne in mind that because the traits are observed from behaviour so the direction of causality cannot be reversed and the trait then used to explain that behaviour.

[37] *Lexicon of Psychiatric and Mental Health Terms, supra, p.75.*

[38] *Ibid.*

Personality and intelligence

Intelligence is sometimes considered to form part of an individual's personality,[39] but it is probably more accurate to say that it is one of the factors which affects the way in which an individual's personality develops. Significant intellectual impairment may be associated with limited personal development and severe behavioural problems[40] although, as the classification of mental disorders set out in the Mental Health Act 1983 recognises, disordered conduct may result from personality problems essentially unrelated to the individual's intelligence — in which case the term "personality disorder" or "psychopathic disorder" is generally used to describe the condition.

Personality and mental illness

The individual's position in a stressful environment is somewhat analogous to that of a boat caught in inclement weather, with the boat representing the individual's brain, its crew his personality, the sea his hostile environment. Some ships are better constructed than others to survive and a well-equipped or well-trained crew is able to respond to the threat with a series of effective emergency measures: battening down the hatches, casting out drogues, pouring oil on troubled waters, and so on. If a ship is well designed and its crew well drilled, it may survive even a tempest largely intact because of its innate seaworthiness and measured responses. By contrast, the fair-weather, poorly-crewed, boats will capsize before the winds ever reach gale-force. Another analogy, used by Freud, is based on the fact that many gemstones split along well-defined cleavage planes which are characteristic for all specimens of that species. These lines of cleavage form along the weakest plane in the structure. Just as when a crystal glass shatters the fragments of glass are not entirely random but reflect the characteristic structure of the original vessel so Freud observed that when an individual becomes mentally ill the way in which he breaks down is determined by his type of personality. More recently, Armstrong has similarly suggested that dispositions are identical with structural causes.[41] For example, the disposition to brittleness of glass is identical to its molecular structure and the habitual dispositions of the brain which we call personality likewise correspond to the structure of the individual's brain and nervous system. Structure and functioning virtually always go hand in hand, the established structure of an organism, or indeed a mechanical device such as a car, limiting and defining the way in which it can function. To summarise, an individual's personality determines and reflects the unique adjustment which he makes to his environment, including the unique way in which he becomes mentally ill. This is not surprising because what we refer to as an individual's personality is simply the tendency of his brain to function in certain characteristic ways — his ingrained patterns of thought, feeling, and behaviour — and these dispositions can only be attributed to the characteristic way in which his brain has developed and adapted to its environment, that is its structure.

---

[39] For example, Wolff describes the components of personality as temperament, intelligence, affect and motivation. See S. Wolff, "Personality development" in *Companion to psychiatric studies* (ed. R.E. Kendell & A.K. Zealley, Churchill Livingstone, 1993), p.60.

[40] As, more rarely, may abnormally high intelligence.

[41] See D.M. Armstrong, *A Materialist Theory of the Mind* (Routledge and Kegan Paul, 1968).

•	*Personality*	The unique quality of the individual, his feelings and personal goals; the sum of his traits, habits and experiences; the whole system of relatively permanent tendencies, physical and mental, which are distinctive of a given individual.
•	*Personality trait*	A constant or persistent way of behaving.
•	*Personality disorder*	A variety of conditions and behaviour patterns that tend to be persistent and appear to be the expression of the individual's lifestyle and mode of relating to self and others; they represent extreme or significant deviations from the way in which the average individual in a given culture perceives, thinks, feels, and, particularly, relates to others.

THE CONCEPT OF MIND

Disorders of the body, including the brain, are commonly referred to as being physical, organic or somatic while those "in the mind" are termed mental, psychological, psychiatric, or functional. The concept of a mind is fundamental to the law, being expressed in legal concepts such as mental illness, mental disorder, disorders and disabilities of mind, mens rea, and abnormality of mind. Descartes believed that the mind or psyche drove the body through the brain and the nerves and was qualitatively different from the body, being non-physical and non-material. It was in possessing a mind or soul that human beings differed from other animals. This distinction between material brain and immaterial mind (Cartesian dualism) encouraged the development of psychiatry and neurology as separate specialist fields. The brain, the sphere of neurology, was the organ through which the mind or psyche, the sphere of psychiatry, expressed itself.[42] Neurology was concerned with organic disease, conditions known to be closely correlated with alterations of brain structure or a disorder of physiological or biochemical function. Psychiatry was the province of functional disturbances which could not be correlated with alterations of brain structure or biological function, the primary cause of which was related to stressful environmental influence. Although neurology dealt directly with the apparatus of the mind by investigating malfunction of the brain, paradoxically it paid scant attention to mental disorder itself. Similarly, psychiatry had relatively little to do with the hardware upon which the mind depended.[43] It is now generally

---

[42] Yellowlees provides a good description of this distinction, "You are a pianist attempting to play Beethoven on a grand piano. The piano is your brain, gross damage to it corresponding to organic disease. You are a mixture of brain and mind, your technique being something little less mechanical than the piano itself, but your other qualities such as your enthusiasm for practice, your power of expression, your critical taste, and so forth, becoming less of the brain and more of the mind till we reach your love of music in general, which can never be learned or acquired but only developed. Your love of music and the quality of the piano on which you are forced to play are two entirely different things. They are, nevertheless, the two extremes of the whole chain of factors which determines the quality of the music you produce." Henry Yellowlees, *To Define True Madness* (Pelican Books, 1955), p.9.

[43] W.A. Lishman, *Organic Psychiatry, The Psychological Consequences of Cerebral Disorder* (Blackwell Scientific Publications, 2nd ed., 1987), p.ix.

considered that this historical distinction between material brain and immaterial mind is artificial and akin to conceiving of the mind as the source of human thought and the heart as the source of human feeling. As Kendell has pointed out, all mental activity has a neurophysiological substrate and all mental events are accompanied by matching somatic events in the brain. In the last analysis "mental" and "biological" are one and the same. A headache may simultaneously be caused by changes in the blood flow through the brain ("biological") and be the effect of pressure of work ("mental"). Which language is used depends on the perceived objective — drugs to change the flow of blood to the brain or altering the conditions of work to lower the pressure.[44] However, while it may be a truism that the mind does not exist apart from the brain, the precise relationship between mind and body — and, more specifically, between mind and brain — remains unsolved, both medically and philosophically.[45] In particular, "the numerous findings that the neurosciences, relying on apparatus of ever-increasing sophistication, have produced about the functioning of the brain have not been accompanied by any significant advance in the understanding of ways in which structures or processes in the brain are translated into mental functioning, or how the brain relates to mind."[46] William James suggested that what we call mental states are functional states resulting from the complex interaction between ourselves and the outside world, a functional outcome of brain-world interaction; by analogy, digestion is the interaction of food with the tissues of the stomach and breathing the interaction of air and the lungs. So mental events refer to interactions between the brain and the environment which cannot be separated.[47] And Sir Gilbert Ryle has suggested that the distinction between mind and body is essentially grammatical whereby brain matter is described using nouns and pronouns, and the mind using verbs, adverbs and adjectives.[48] The two views are not incompatible.

THE BRAIN, MIND AND PERSONALITY

- *Brain*   The organ of the body within which thoughts, feelings, emotions, perceptions, sensations and moods are generated, experienced and memorised in response to stimuli received from the world outside it (the body and the environment).

- *Mind*   The way in which the brain functions, both in the present (an individual's mental state) and its tendency to function and respond to events outside it in certain habitual ways (the individual's personality, his tendency to certain mental states).

- *Mental state*   An individual's contemporaneous thoughts, feelings, emotions, perceptions, sensations, and mood.

- *Personality*   The whole system of relatively permanent abilities and tendencies distinctive of a given individual's brain.

---

[44] S. Murphy, *Experiencing and Explaining Disease* (The Open University Press, 1985), p.2.
[45] J.H. Pincus and G.J. Tucker, *Behavioral Neurology* (Oxford University Press, 1978), p.i.
[46] N Sartorius in *Sources and Traditions of Classification in Psychiatry* (ed. N Sartorius *et al.*, World Health Organisation/ Hogrefe & Huber, 1990), p.2.
[47] W. James, *The principles of psychology* (Dover Press, 1890).
[48] G. Ryle, *The concept of mind* (Hutchinson, 1949).

Categorising mental functioning: cognition, affect and conation

The range of mental experiences being so vast, it is convenient to distinguish different kinds of mental functioning and skills, and mental phenomena have been divided into three great classes: the cognitive, conative and affective[49] —

- Cognition is the quality of knowing and it includes perceiving, recognising, judging, sensing, reasoning and imagining. Cognitive skills represent the ability to take in information, to gain knowledge, to learn and to think; they also involve organising that information and knowledge so that it can be used usefully. Cognition is impaired in mentally impaired persons and organic conditions such as dementia.

- Conation is the faculty of volition, of voluntary action, will, striving, endeavour, desire (the "exertive powers"). Schizophrenia is characterised by passivity, that is impairment of the capacity for goal-directed voluntary action: the individual's well-being and actions are undermined by outside forces and hence outside his own control; in severe cases, these forces manage to penetrate his mind so that even his thoughts are no longer his but controlled, infiltrated, poisoned, stolen or made public by others; in other cases, even the patient's body may be immobile, passively assuming any position in which it is placed; while in enduring cases the passivity may crystallise over time in the form of negative symptoms such as lack of motivation and initiative, loss of interest and withdrawal from social contacts.

- A person's affect is how he appears to be emotionally affected by an idea or mental representation: it is the emotional tone or feeling which accompanies an idea or mental representation, such as happiness or sadness, pleasure or pain. The feelings are intermediate between the cognitions and the conations.[50] For example, an environmental event gives rise to a perception, which gives rise in turn to a feeling (how what is perceived affects the individual), and the way it affects him then determines the voluntary action taken in response to the original perception. Mood is the pervasive and sustained emotion which colours an individual's whole personality and perception of events. Consequently, it is sometimes described as sustained affect and mood disorders to involve a morbid change of affect.

The brain's tendency to distinguish three broad areas or classes of mental functioning gives rise to its corresponding tendency to categorise abnormal mental functioning according to which class of mental functioning and skills is impaired: organic (cognitive) disorders, the schizophrenias (conative disorders), and affective disorders. The three different classes of mental phenomena can be represented graphically. In the diagram below, the area within the dotted triangle represents the individual's mental state (the interaction of his brain with the world outside it) while the development of his personality is represented by the structure of the triangle, which both shapes and is shaped by the way in which his brain now interacts with the environment.

---

[49] See Sir W. Hamilton, *Metaphysics* (1859).
[50] *Ibid.*

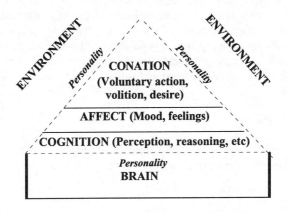

HEALTH

Having considered what is meant by the terms personality and mind, it is necessary to consider what constitutes a healthy or normal personality and mind because a diagnosis of mental disorder implies a departure from a state of health. "Health" is equated with "perfect health" by the World Health Organisation, which describes it as "a state of complete physical, mental and social well-being and not merely the absence of disease or infirmity."[51] In biological terms, health depends on the body maintaining its internal harmony (homeostasis). When that harmony is so disturbed that the body is unable to respond adequately to compensate for that disruption then disease occurs. Not only must the internal environment be maintained in a steady state but of equal importance is the maintenance of harmony with the external environment — with other species, such as bacteria and viruses, with physical factors, such as temperature, and with other people. Health involves such physiological and emotional matters as well as simple relationships with the physical world. The need to maintain both internal and external harmony is a feature of all living organisms and maintenance of this equilibrium requires that the body is able to grow and change over time, *i.e.* to develop normally.[52] In more practical terms, health may be described as the standard of physical and mental functioning necessary for a person to perform the activities which are expected of him, according to the norms of the society in which he lives; all *disabling* disease, illness and handicap must be absent.[53]

NORMALITY AND ABNORMALITY

Although abnormality is generally a key feature of any definition of disease — the identification of which depends on measurements and comparison against normal states — the problem of defining what is abnormal is particularly acute when considering mental phenomena and other medical conditions about which there is considerable debate as to what is normal and abnormal. For example, although risk

---

[51] *Constitution of the World Health Organisation* (Geneva, 1946).
[52] R. Ransom, *The Biology of Health & Disease* (The Open University Press, 1985), p.1.
[53] See Talcott Parsons, "Definitions of Health and Illness in the Light of American Values and Social Structure" in *Concepts of Health and Disease: Interdisciplinary perspectives* (ed. A.L. Caplan *et al.*, Addison-Wesley Publishing Co., 1981), p.69; D. Seedhouse, *Health: The foundations for achievement* (John Wiley & Sons, 1986), p.33.

factors increase in proportion to the blood pressure of persons who are hypotensive and obese, any dividing line between normal and abnormal can only be arbitrary. In order to define a group as normal it is necessary to exclude abnormal people, but to exclude abnormal people it is necessary to know what is normal. In such cases, therefore, distinctions between normal and abnormal states are ultimately arbitrary and prescriptive.[54] The way in which a person defines what is mentally normal and mentally abnormal will necessarily affect his ideas about the causes and treatment of mental disorder.

Types of normality

The word "normal" may be correctly used in at least four senses in the English language,[55] three of which merit consideration in this context.

Value norms

The use of the world "health" by the World Health Organisation to denote a state of complete well-being is often described as a "value norm" since it takes the ideal as its concept of normality and any departure from that ideal constitutes abnormal physical or mental health.[56] What is idealised depends upon our ideas about what is good and healthy which are, in turn, inseparable from our knowledge or thoughts on disease processes.[57] To this extent, illness is a socially defined concept and involves value judgements which are liable to change from time to time and place to place. Thus, Kendell observes that paedophilia is regarded as a psychiatric disorder but not homosexuality, not because of any assumed difference in the underlying causes of the two phenomena, but because our culture strongly disapproves of the former but not of the latter. Similarly, grief after bereavement is both expected and esteemed and we are loathe to label something we esteem as illness. Nevertheless, it is unlikely that the underlying biological mechanisms which we choose to describe as "grief" differ from states of severe depression which have some other cause.[58]

Statistical norms

Since many biological characteristics, such as height, are distributed in a population according to the Gaussian curve, the statistical norm defines abnormality by reference to extreme variations. The statistical norm defines normal health as existing where an individual's level of mental functioning falls within a limited range around the mean or average value. Definitions of intelligence, and therefore mental handicap, are partly based on such statistical norms with an IQ of 100 denoting a person of statistically average intelligence compared with the population at large. Some definitions of disease also use the word "normal" in this way[59] and

---

54 G.W. Bradley, *Disease, Diagnosis and Decisions* (John Wiley & Sons, 1993), pp.17–18. The choice of the population from which normality is defined and environmental factors will be influential in deciding what is normal and abnormal.

55 R.M. Mowbray, R.T. Ferguson and C.S. Mellor, *Psychology in relation to medicine* (Churchill Livingstone, 5th ed., 1979).

56 A. Sims, *Symptoms in Mind* (Baillière Tindall, London, 1988), p.4.

57 G.W. Bradley, *Disease, Diagnosis and Decisions, supra,* p.18.

58 R.E. Kendell, "The nature of psychiatric disorders" in *Companion to psychiatric studies* (ed. R.E. Kendell & A.K. Zealley, Churchill Livingstone, 1993), p.6.

59 For example, Scadding's often-repeated definition of disease as being a statistical variation from the norm carrying "biological disadvantage." Examples of "biological disadvantage" are increased mortality (as in manic-depressive disorders) or decreased fecundity (as in schizophrenia), survival and reproduction being functions typical of our biological species and necessary to achieve the natural goals set by nature. See J.G. Scadding, "Diagnosis: the clinician and the computer" *Lancet* (1967), ii, 877–882.

Culver and Gert have commented on the tendency in medicine to define a normal range for trait x and thereby to have discovered two new diseases — hyper-x and hypo-x.[60] The description of certain behaviour as eccentric — away from a central point — is a geometric expression of what is statistically normal, as are the two-dimensional scales used in psychometric testing.

Individual norms

A further possibility is to apply an "individual norm," that is to define physical and mental health by reference to the level of functioning which a particular individual has consistently maintained over time. Here, abnormality arises if there is a decline in a person's individual overall level of functioning.

Variability and deviation from the norm

However one defines what is normal, most individuals will be found to conform to the norm in relation to some but not all of their mental characteristics so that, when taken in aggregate, most of us fail to escape some departure from the norm.[61] The amount of deviation regarded as being present in any particular case will depend on the definition of the norm in question, whether implicit or explicit. What we regard as illness or disorder appears to shade insensibly into normality and Campbell summarises the situation by stating that abnormality may be the result of disease in some cases and in others the expression of variability.[62] It is, of course, possible to have a tolerant view of what is normal but to be intolerant of abnormality, and vice-versa, and consideration must be given to the feasibility and desirability of intervention to restore the norm.

Legal definitions

In general, definitions of mental impairment rely to a significant extent on a statistical norm, definitions of psychopathic disorder on statistical and value norms, and definitions of mental illness on an individual norm revealed through a full history of the patient's previous, pre-morbid, level of functioning. Another way of making essentially the same point is to say that the difference between normal behaviour on the one hand and mental impairment, neurosis and personality disorder on the other is essentially quantitative, while that between normal behaviour and mental illness is qualitative. In short, the difference between a person who is mentally impaired and a person of statistically average intelligence is one of degree, whereas the difference between sanity and insanity is expressed as absolute and one of kind, that is qualitative.

TERMS USED TO DESCRIBE ABNORMAL HEALTH

Various terms are used to describe abnormal physical and mental states or their consequences — abnormality, affliction, condition, defect, deviation, disability, disfigurement, disorder, disturbance, dysfunction, illness, injury, lesion, reaction, variant, wound.[63] The concepts of disorder (**1034**), illness (**1035**), disease (**1038**),

---

[60]   C. Culver and B. Gert, *Philosophy in Medicine* (Oxford University Press, 1982).

[61]   *International Classification of Impairments, Disabilities, and Handicaps: A manual of classification relating to the consequences of disease* (World Health Organisation, 1976), p.34.

[62]   R.J. Campbell, *Psychiatric Dictionary* (Oxford University Press, 6th ed., 1989), p.4.

[63]   *Ibid.*, p.205.

impairment (**1128**), disability (**1128**) and handicap (**1129**) are of particular medico-legal importance since they are commonly used in both legal and psychiatric classifications of mentally abnormal states.

DISORDER

In their respective classifications, the American Psychiatric Association uses the term "mental disorder" and the World Health Organisation "mental and behavioural disorders" as their main generic terms.[64] "Disorder" is a broad term which denotes any significant departure from a state of normal health and it therefore includes diseases and illnesses. The current edition of the International Classification of Mental and Behavioural Disorders, published by the World Health Organisation, uses "disorder," in preference to disease and illness, to describe abnormal mental phenomena:

> "The term "disorder" is used throughout the classification, so as to avoid even greater problems inherent in the use of terms such as 'disease' and 'illness.' 'Disorder' is not an exact term, but it is used here simply to imply the existence of a clinically recognisable set of symptoms or behaviour associated in most cases with distress and with interference with personal functions. Social deviance or conflict alone, without personal dysfunction, should not be included in mental disorder as defined here."[65]

The term "mental disorder" is therefore relatively neutral and so has the advantage of not prejudicing consideration of the causes or treatment of such states of mind. Mental disorder is simply the opposite of mental health, that is the opposite of an ordered mind.

Mental health  **Mental disorder**

Psychiatry and mental disorder

Kendell notes that although the territory of psychiatry is still formally described as mental disorder, the term now embraces a far broader range of conditions than when first introduced.[66] In practice, the classification of certain disorders as mental or psychiatric is largely determined by the historical fact that these conditions have generally been treated by psychiatrists. Thus, Kendell observes that Alzheimer's disease and anorexia nervosa are classified as mental disorders but if the former were usually treated by neurologists it would be regarded as a neurological condition, and if the latter were usually treated by endocrinologists it would probably be regarded as an endocrine disorder.[67] Likewise, the fact that multi-infarct dementia is regarded and classified as a psychiatric rather than as a vascular disorder ... illustrates the utilitarian basis of such distinctions, and the distinction between neurological disorders and psychiatric disorders may be particularly artificial.[68]

---

[64] P.R. McHugh, "Schizophrenia and the Disease Model" in *What is Schizophrenia?* (ed. W.F. Flack, *et al.*, Springer-Verlag, 1990), p.74.

[65] *Classification of Mental and Behavioural Disorders (Tenth Revision, ICD–10): Clinical Descriptions and Diagnostic Guidelines* (World Health Organisation, 1992), p.5.

[66] R.E. Kendell, "The nature of psychiatric disorders" in *Companion to psychiatric studies* (ed. R.E. Kendell & A.K. Zealley, Churchill Livingstone, 1993), p.2.

[67] R.E. Kendell, "Schizophrenia: A Medical View of a Medical Concept" in *What is Schizophrenia?*, *supra*, pp. 61–62.

[68] R.E. Kendell, "The nature of psychiatric disorders" in *Companion to psychiatric studies*, *supra*, p.4.

ILLNESS

Illness and sickness are essentially synonymous.[69] It has already been observed that there are considerable difficulties applying the concept of illness to mental phenomena because of the problem of deciding what constitutes a deviation from a mentally normal state of health. Illness may, however, be seen as the difference between a person's current state of being and functioning and his state of health immediately prior to the onset of a decline in his health, whether subjectively or objectively apparent.[70] Ill-health represents an interference "with the individual's ability to discharge those functions and obligations that are expected of him. In other words, the sick person is unable to sustain his accustomed social role and cannot maintain his customary relationships with others. This view is sufficiently broad to take account of the vast majority of calls that are likely to be made on a health care system. At one extreme, it embraces life-threatening disease, and, at the other, it includes less medical experiences such as anxiety or the wish for advice and counselling."[71]

Illness and disorder contrasted

In conventional usage, "mental illness" is more specific than "mental disorder" because the latter includes abnormal mental states which are part of an individual's ordinary personality or, more specifically, associated with low intelligence. This division of mentally abnormal states is found in both medical and legal classifications, which reflects the fact that mental health legislation has tended to import the broad classes of mentally abnormal states set out at the time in the World Health Organisation's International Classification of Diseases — the classification having been in official usage in the United Kingdom for half a century. The distinction, although ultimately artificial, is nevertheless useful. Linguistically, there is a need for an inclusive phrase to describe all mental states considered to be abnormal and further terms are then required to describe the different types of abnormal states most frequently encountered. Thus, intelligence is one of the factors affecting the way in which a person's personality develops and the fact that an individual's intelligence is low may give rise to behavioural problems. However, an individual's personality may be abnormal in some respect for reasons essentially unrelated to his intelligence. In other cases, a person's abnormal behaviour may be attributable to a mental illness overlying an distorting his usual personality.

---

[69] Inevitably, some writers distinguish between illness and sickness and would therefore disagree with this statement. For example, Susser describes illness as a subjective state of the person who feels aware of not being well, and "sickness" as a state of social dysfunction, *i.e.* a role that the individual assumes when ill. See M.W. Susser, *Causal Thinking in the Health Sciences* (Oxford University Press, 1973).

[70] Although an illness has been described as a departure from a state of health this is only true insofar as there was no immediately preceding disease or illness. Some writers, for example Kraupl Taylor and Jeremy Bentham, have stressed the self-defining nature of an illness in contrast to a disease which results in identifiable changes to the structure of the body's organs and not merely an alteration or decline in functioning: illness denotes a perception by a person that he or she is not well. The fact of a person perceiving himself to be unwell or attending a surgery with a complaint as to his health defines him as a patient and his complaint may be regarded as an illness since he feels or perceives a decline in his state of health. However, some mentally ill people do not perceive themselves as being in any way unwell and the approach is therefore defective in this respect.

[71] *International Classification of Impairments, Disabilities, and Handicaps: A manual of classification relating to the consequences of disease* (World Health Organisation, 1976), p.10.

MENTAL HEALTH ⸺⸺⸺ MENTAL DISORDER

|

**Mental
Illness**

|

**Personality
disorder**

|

**Mental
Impairment**

Describing the severity of a mental illness

It is common to distinguish between psychotic and neurotic states of mind. In psychosis, there is a disturbance of the patient's judgement of reality and this results in symptoms and disturbances in behaviour and daily living: "Psychosis implies loss of reality judgement, loss of insight and especially such positive symptoms as delusions, hallucinations and thought disorder. In neuroses, the symptoms are out of proportion to the stimulus, they may persist after the stimulus has been removed, and they are disabling; however, the experience of a neurotic patient is on a continuum and therefore within the powers of empathy and identification of a normal person."[72]

Contemporary usage of the term "psychotic"

The term "psychosis" (literally, a diseased or abnormal condition of the mind) was devised by Feuchtersleben in 1845 as a common term for a variety of mental and personality disorders. Since then, the term has acquired a range of meanings, being used to describe severely impaired functioning; a state of mind defined by "impaired reality testing"[73]; the presence of certain symptoms (*e.g.*, hallucinations, delusions or stupor) or symptoms of a certain intensity; or to refer to certain classes of mental disorder such as the schizophrenias ("the psychoses"). The term "neurosis" (literally, a diseased or abnormal condition of the nervous system) underwent a similar change of usage and, by the end of the nineteenth century, had become associated with disorders arising from psychological conflict rather than from any disorder of the nervous system. Because the terms have ceased to have any universal meaning — and, linguistically, may be objected to as reflecting an obsolete dichotomy between disorders of the mind and the nervous system — the traditional division between the neuroses and psychoses (the "neurotic-psychotic dichotomy") has been dropped from the 10th Revision of the International Classification of Diseases. Instead, disorders are "now arranged in groups according to major common themes or

---

[72]   A. Sims and D. Owens, *Psychiatry* (Baillière Tindall, 6th ed., 1993), p.34.
[73]   The capacity to challenge bizarre perceptions — when a person is psychotic, he or she incorrectly evaluates the accuracy of his or her perceptions and thoughts and makes incorrect inferences about external reality, even in the face of contrary evidence. The term when used in this sense does not apply to minor distortions of reality that involve matters of relative judgement.

descriptive likenesses, which makes for increased convenience of use ..."[74] The term "psychotic" is, however, retained as a convenient descriptive term "to indicate the presence of hallucinations, delusions, or a limited number of several abnormalities of behaviour, such as gross excitement and overactivity, marked psychomotor retardation, and catatonic behaviour."[75]

Organic and functional mental illnesses

Apart from differentiating between the psychoses and neuroses, another customary distinction now frequently objected to is the description of different forms of mental illness as either "organic" or "functional." Where the human body is concerned, altered structure and disordered functioning virtually always go together although the severity of the resulting disorder will depend on the locality and extent of the damage, which may be gross or relatively mild.[76] Forms of disordered mental functioning which are attributable to some alteration in the structure of the brain or other organs of the nervous system as a result of disease, infection, or injury are often referred to as organic disorders. However, many individuals suffer from mental disorders which cannot be attributed to any known disease or structural damage to the body. A patient may suffer bizarre delusions for many years and yet, following his death, the post-mortem not reveal any apparent damage to the brain which might account for this. Functional disorders are mental disorders characterised by significant alterations in the functioning, that is in performance or operation, of the brain and the nervous system but without any known cause in terms of organic damage or changes in their structure. The two groups of mental disorders most commonly encountered at tribunals — the schizophrenias and the manic-depressive disorders — are commonly described as functional disorders. Functional disorders may be the result of as yet undiscovered structural defects in the brain or nervous system; have toxic, metabolic or physiological causes; or be "psychogenic" in origin.

Psychogenic disorders

The term "psychogenic disorder" — literally "originating within the mind or psyche" — was introduced into psychiatry by Sommer in 1894 and is used "widely and loosely to indicate attribution of aetiology to mental, psychological or emotional factors rather than to physical causes."[77] The term is sometimes erroneously used as a synonym for "functional disorder." Although psychogenic disorders are functional, in that their symptoms are not based on any detectable alterations in the structure of the brain, it is not true that all functional disorders are of emotional origin. For example, a drug-induced, temporary disturbance may produce many alterations in thinking, affect, and behaviour. Since such a disturbance does not depend upon structural changes in the brain, it is properly termed functional but cannot properly be considered to be of psychogenic origin.[78] As with the terms "neurotic," "organic"

---

[74] *Classification of Mental and Behavioural Disorders (Tenth Revision, ICD–10): Clinical Descriptions and Diagnostic Guidelines* (World Health Organisation, 1992), pp.3–4.

[75] *Ibid.*

[76] It should, however, be noted that structural damage to an organ can also be the *effect* of disordered functioning, rather than its cause, in the same way that faulty posture or functioning of various muscles may lead to curvature of the spine. Similarly, structural alterations in the brain may reflect its functioning in response to environmental stimuli over a sustained period.

[77] *Lexicon of Psychiatric and Mental Health Terms* (World Health Organisation, 1989), Vol. 1, p.64.

[78] Psychogenic disorders should also be distinguished from psychosomatic disorders. The term "psychosomatic" denotes a physical disorder seemingly caused or exacerbated by psychological factors. The ICD-10 classification does not use the term, in part because its use might be taken to imply that psychological factors play no role in the occurrence, course and outcome of other diseases that are not so described.

and "functional," the term "psychogenic" is now falling into disfavour, due to the present ascendancy of the disease model. It is no longer used in the titles of categories of mental disorder in the International Classification of Diseases but still occurs occasionally in the text, where its use indicates that the diagnostician regards obvious life events or difficulties as playing an important role in the genesis of the disorder."[79]

Summary

Many psychiatrists object to the organic–functional distinction because it implies a sort of dualism, "a belief that the world can be divided up into two sorts of causative process, one biological, the other mental."[80] From the biomedical perspective, the presumption that most psychiatric disorders should be assumed to involve a cerebral pathology of some kind implies that the distinction between organic and functional disorders is pointless. If this is true, there are no truly functional disorders although, by definition, intensive research into the brain basis of functional psychoses can never succeed in one sense: when brain disorder is established in particular cases these are no longer considered functional psychoses, precisely because a brain disorder has been established.[81] Nevertheless, because of a lack of alternatives, the terms "organic" and "functional" are convenient epithets to distinguish between affective, schizophrenic and paranoid psychoses from dementias and confusional states. Furthermore, the failure to identify structural changes which account for the functional disorders may indicate that any defects are qualitatively different.[82]

DISEASE

The World Health Organisation notes that "in contemplating illness phenomena it is customary to invoke the concept of disease."[83] However, the term is not defined in the International Classification of Diseases and, as Kendell has written, disease is an imprecise concept and one which is therefore not capable of precise definition.[84] While the function of medicine is to promote and preserve health by seeking out and destroying its enemy disease, in the same way that the law seeks to promote and preserve justice by rooting out injustice, neither can define what it is they are seeking to promote or eliminate. Nevertheless, the use of the term "disease" to describe abnormal mental states is now so widespread that its meaning, and the meaning of associated terms such as morbidity and pathology, must be considered.

Disease processes and the medical model

In general, psychiatrists tend to be "materialists," proponents of the "biomedical model" or "disease model," holding that organic or physiological causes will eventually be found for every kind of mental disorder. In viewing psychiatric disorders

---

[79] *Classification of Mental and Behavioural Disorders (Tenth Revision, ICD–10): Clinical Descriptions and Diagnostic Guidelines* (World Health Organisation, 1992), p5.

[80] S. Murphy, *Experiencing and Explaining Disease* (The Open University Press, 1985), p.57.

[81] D. Rogers, *Motor Disorder in Psychiatry: Towards a Neurological Psychiatry* (John Wiley & Sons, 1992), p.5.

[82] R.E. Kendell, "The nature of psychiatric disorders" in *Companion to psychiatric studies* (ed. R.E. Kendell & A.K. Zealley, Churchill Livingstone, 1993), p.6.

[83] *International Classification of Impairments, Disabilities, and Handicaps: A manual of classification relating to the consequences of disease* (World Health Organisation, 1976), p.23.

[84] R.E. Kendell, "Schizophrenia: A Medical View of a Medical Concept" in *What is Schizophrenia?* (ed. W.F. Flack *et al.*, Springer-Verlag, 1990), p.60. See **1017**.

as disease entities, the medical model attempts to place psychiatry alongside neurology and general medicine. The "medical model of illness is dominated by the concept of disease, which may be depicted symbolically as a sequence,"[85]

$$\textbf{Aetiology} \longrightarrow \textbf{Pathology} \longrightarrow \textbf{Manifestation}$$

(cause)　　　　　**(biological change)**　　　**(symptoms and signs**

Viewing this sequence in reverse, the patient's disease comprises symptoms and signs which are the manifestations of certain pathological changes in the structure or biological functioning of his body, changes initiated by a particular cause or causes (the aetiology[86]). Each type of pathology, or pathological process, produces a particular pattern of symptoms and signs. Although pathological states and processes are most often the product of a genetically determined predisposition within the body to react in a particular way to certain environmental events, more rarely a genetic defect alone is sufficient. The notion of disease and its derivatives, such as the International Classification of Diseases (**1117**), consider pathological phenomena — rather than their causes — as if unrelated to the individuals in whom they occur.[87] Bodies are thought to be complicated biochemical machines and the disease model assumes that medicine has produced a store of knowledge which can be applied to bodies as bodies, rather than bodies as people; disease can be cured by reducing bodies to their smallest constituent parts.[88] According to the disease model therefore, it is the pathology which produces the symptoms and signs, whereas in more psychologically-orientated approaches this middle-stage in the process is either non-existent or largely irrelevant: there is no mediating pathology and the patient's symptoms and signs are the direct consequence of their causes, that is defence mechanisms or other direct but distorted manifestations of the internal conflicts which torment the individual.

Associated terms

Three terms which relate to the disease process are morbidity, pathology and pathogenesis, and these are briefly dealt with below.

Morbidity

The word "morbid" indicates the presence of disease. "Pre-morbid" therefore refers to a patient's state of health prior to the onset of disease. However, the term is often loosely used in psychiatric reports, as a description of the patient's personality and level of functioning prior to some perceived decline in his health, *i.e.* before the onset of mental disorder generally rather than disease specifically.

---

[85]　*International Classification of Impairments, Disabilities, and Handicaps: A manual of classification relating to the consequences of disease* (World Health Organisation, 1976), p.10.

[86]　The American spelling "etiology" is used below in some quotations.

[87]　*International Classification of Impairments, Disabilities, and Handicaps, supra,* p.23.

[88]　D. Seedhouse, *Health: The foundations for achievement* (John Wiley & Sons, 1986), p.45.

Pathology

As a subject, pathology is the study of disease and its causes, mechanisms and effects on the body and it is customary to regard pathology as the basis of medicine and surgery.[89] When the morbid anatomy and altered physiology of a patient are understood, the clinical picture falls into place[90] and so medicine generally aims to make a diagnosis based on pathology, if only by inference.[91] "Pathological" means "relating to disease"[92] while "*the* pathology" is that anatomical or physiological abnormality which is responsible for the decline in the patient's health. Many diseases are named according to the pathological anatomy, for example hepatic cirrhosis, but this is as far as knowledge of the disease has progressed in some cases. Other diseases are not associated with clearly abnormal anatomy. The way organs function is also important; certain diseases are defined in physiological (atrial flutter), biochemical (porphyria) or microbiological (amoebiosis) terms. "True" disease status in general medicine is determined by the most definitive diagnostic method, commonly referred to as a "gold standard." So, for example, the gold standard for breast cancer diagnosis might be histopathologic confirmation of cancer in a surgical specimen.[93]

Pathogenesis

The way in which a particular disease develops, and its precise relationship to the various factors believed to cause the disease process, is often unclear. Pathogenesis refers to "the postulated mechanisms by which the (a)etiologic agent produces disease."[94]

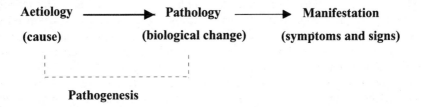

Aetiology ⟶ Pathology ⟶ Manifestation

(cause)   **(biological change)**   **(symptoms and signs)**

Pathogenesis

Psychopathology

Psychopathology literally means the study of mental diseases or mental suffering and, in common usage, the word means nothing more than "the systematic study of abnormal experience, cognition (intellectual processes) and behaviour."[95] The word is therefore often used in psychiatric reports as a collective term for all of the patient's abnormal mental experiences.

---

[89]   J.B. Walter and M.S. Israel, *General Pathology* (Churchill Livingstone, 4th ed., 1974), p.30.

[90]   *Ibid.*

[91]   G.W. Bradley, *Disease, Diagnosis and Decisions* (John Wiley & Sons, 1993), p.19.

[92]   Likewise, a pathogen is an organism capable of causing disease, that is a pathological process, while "pathogenicity refers to "the property of an organism that determines the extent to which overt disease is produced in an infected population, or the power of an organism to produce disease." See *A Dictionary of Epidemiology, supra,* p.122. Although "disease" literally means a state of unease and pathology is the study of suffering, the modern view that most unease and suffering has a physical cause which is best dealt with by doctors has led to this change in the word's usage.

[93]   G.W. Bradley, *Disease, Diagnosis and Decisions, supra,* pp.12 and 15.

[94]   *A Dictionary of Epidemiology* (ed. J.M. Last, 3rd ed., International Epidemiological Association/ Oxford University Press, 1995), p.122.

[95]   A. Sims and D. Owens, *Psychiatry* (Baillière Tindall, 6th ed., 1993), p.8.

A working definition

When people think about disease, the majority of them probably think of it as a process which has the following characteristics. Firstly, disease is a biological process. The process is not consciously desired and is not one within the control of the affected individual. Rather, once set in motion along its natural course, it has a "will of its own." It has a natural course and, without intervention, develops and interferes with the body in a certain characteristic way. Secondly, any changes in the structure of the body are not directly attributable to a recent, time-limited, and externally caused injury. Although mental disorder may result if the brain or nervous system is damaged by some external object penetrating or striking it, the injured organ is not usually thought of as diseased. An organ may therefore be damaged otherwise than through disease. Thirdly, while the recent ingestion of a toxic substance may set a disease process in motion, more often the body's biological harmony is restored following its excretion, in which case the body is not normally considered to have been diseased. Fourthly, the process must be abnormal for a person in that condition of life, because it is possible to be disabled or ill without being diseased. The normal ageing process (though leading to death), morning sickness during pregnancy, and depression following bereavement, are not generally considered to be diseases. Fifthly, as screening programmes demonstrate, a person may have no symptoms of illness and yet be diseased ("sub-clinical disease"). The early recognition of the transition from the healthy to the diseased condition may be difficult, if not impossible, and the individual affected may not be aware that his body is diseased.[96] Insofar as these suppositions are accepted, a "disease" may be defined as a disabling process characterised by involuntary changes in the patient's organs, tissues or cells, or the way in which they function, which is not naturally found in a person with the patient's characteristics in that particular stage of life.

Disease and illness contrasted

Disease is often thought of as the cause of illness, of the symptoms and signs which result in the individual's condition being referred to, or coming to the attention of, a doctor. For example, Field states that disease is somatic while illness relates to the psychological and social level.[97] And Bradley observes that, "in the research field, the research worker aims to discover the cause of disease and in the clinical field the physician seeks the cause of illness."[98] However, it is not true to say that disease is the cause of all illness: symptoms may develop that cannot currently be linked to any underlying disease process. According to the definition given above, a disease may also be described as an illness but not all illnesses are diseases. That is, not all illnesses are attributable to changes in the structure of the body, such as the brain, or to the way in which those structures function.

Disease and disorder contrasted

McHugh notes that disease is "a very loosely employed term in many circles" and "the most obvious laxity has been its drift into an all inclusive concept for

---

[96]   D. Seegal, *Journal of the American Medical Association* (1962) 182: 1031.
[97]   D. Field, "The Social Definition of Illness" in *An Introduction to Medical Sociology* (ed. D. Tuckett, Tavistock, 1976).
[98]   G.W. Bradley, *Disease, Diagnosis and Decisions* (John Wiley & Sons, 1993), p.15.

disorder."[99] To describe all abnormal mental phenomena as diseases is merely a hypothesis. Furthermore, the concept of disease is "much more specific than disorder."[100] The "identification and study of deviance in mental deficiency and personality disorders ... is not, strictly speaking, the study of disease. The study of life burdens and the discouragement they produce in many individuals, and for which counselling is needed, is also not to be viewed as disease reasoning."[101] Indeed, a limitation of the disease model is that it is self-validating and of semantic interest only if it is based upon an all-encompassing definition of what constitutes disease. If disease becomes merely a synonym for disorder then all mental disorders are *per se* diseases. More particularly, if even personality disorders are viewed as diseases, as the Reed Working Group implied,[102] any mental state, gene, or personality trait which is personally or socially undesirable may be conceptualised as a disease and all mental disorders are necessarily diseases. Similarly, the fact that a common set of genes (XYZ) may be common to all persons suffering from schizophrenia might, depending upon one's view, be evidence that it is a disease (its biological pathology has been established) or merely that people with a certain type of personality are predisposed to developing schizophrenia (the XYZ genes determining sensitivity to criticism, low self-esteem, and inflexibility of response to a changing environment). That being so, disease is best viewed as the cause of some but not all kinds of mental illness.

Diseases as concepts

It can be seen from the description of the disease process that diseases are not things in themselves, merely descriptions of entities believed "to have characteristic signs and symptoms with known or discoverable underlying mechanisms and, ultimately, known or discoverable aetiologies."[103] They are simply models,[104] "concepts which make it easier to comprehend the variegated phenomena of ... illness than it would be otherwise."[105] In each case what is described as a disease is a pattern of factors which have occurred in sufficient people for a specific type of deviation from a particular norm to be identified.[106] Typically the process of identifying a "disease" evolves from the description of a few unusual cases, to the description of a general "disease pattern" (called a syndrome) for which the cause is not clear, to the description of a specific condition with a known cause.[107] "Disease reasoning" derives from this assumption that when disease is present,

---

[99]   P.R. McHugh, "Schizophrenia and the Disease Model" in *What is Schizophrenia?* (ed. W.F. Flack, *et al.*, Springer-Verlag, 1990), p.73.

[100]   *Ibid.*

[101]   *Ibid.*, p.75.

[102]   "Despite considerable research ... little is known ... of the cause or causes of diseases in the psychopathic disorder category." *Report of the Department of Health and Home Office Working Group on Psychopathic Disorder* (Department of Health and the Home Office, 1994), para. 9.2. The usage of the term "disease" here is similar to that in T.M. Peery & F.N. Miller, *Pathology* (Little Brown, 1971): "Disease is any disturbance of the structure or function of the body or any of its parts; an imbalance between the individual and his environment; a lack of perfect health."

[103]   C. Culver and B. Gert, *Philosophy in Medicine* (Oxford University Press, 1982).

[104]   P.R. McHugh, "Schizophrenia and the Disease Model," *supra*, p.76.

[105]   R.E. Kendell, "Diagnosis and classification" in *Companion to psychiatric studies* (ed. R.E. Kendell & A.K. Zealley, Churchill Livingstone, 1993), p.278.

[106]   D. Seedhouse, *Health: The foundations for achievement* (John Wiley & Sons, 1986), pp.26–27.

[107]   It is generally at the syndrome stage that the underlying condition acquires the distinction of becoming a 'disease." J.B. Walter and M.S. Israel, *General Pathology* (Churchill Livingstone, 4th ed., 1974), p.30.

"the cluster of features of a disorder that represent the manifestations of the specific disease will — with a complete understanding — turn out to rest upon some structural or functional abnormality of a body part. At some crucial level of organization of the body, patients with a given disease will all be seen to share a distinct anomaly. It will be provoked by several different agencies, but it will, ultimately, help to explain both these patients' qualitative distinction as sufferers of the disease from the broadly construed normal population in which they are sequestered, and their remarkable resemblance to each other in the characteristics marking them as sufferers of the condition."[108]

In psychiatry, the underlying assumption is that psychiatric symptoms coalesce into distinct disorders having different aetiologies, distinguishable clinical presentations and natural courses, and different treatment responses, in the same way as do diseases of other organs. If the disease model is appropriate to a condition such as schizophrenia, knowledge of that condition will eventually "result in an appreciation of some damage to an intrinsic mechanism of the human brain essential to the smooth and proper functioning of mental life."[109] However, until that is established, the ascription of the term 'disease' is ultimately "hypothetical, unvalidated, and challengeable,"[110] and a condition described as a disease "may be the name of a precisely defined disorder identified by a battery of tests, a probability statement based on consideration of what is most likely among several possibilities, or an opinion based on pattern recognition."[111]

Disease as a normal response

The description of certain forms of mental disorder, such as schizophrenia, as diseases sometimes arouses the objection that such a perspective overlooks the fact that the patient's illness and distress represent an understandable and perhaps natural reaction to environmental events, and to that extent has a social or political dimension. In fact, many diseases, for example tuberculosis, are caused by exposure of the individual to environmental influences and social deprivation, and "the characteristics of each individual, and each disease, are the results of the interplay of two basic factors: inherited genetic constitution and environment."[112] Environmental influences may produce permanent changes within the nervous system[113] and only relatively infrequently is the body's response abnormal and the result of innate genetic errors.[114] Disease processes most often involve the body's normal responses to abnormal environmental influences. One example of this is the body's reaction to noxious external influences such as pathogenic organisms and dietary deficiencies.[115] Indeed, "the most characteristic feature of living matter, apart from its reproductive capacity, is its ability to adapt to changing circumstances and to make good any damage that may be sustained. The mechanisms involved in the protective or reparative reactions are of fundamental importance; they are of a structural or

---

[108] P.R. McHugh, "Schizophrenia and the Disease Model" in *What is Schizophrenia?* (ed. W.F. Flack, *et al.*, Springer-Verlag, 1990), p.74.

[109] *Ibid.*, p.75.

[110] *Ibid.*, p.74.

[111] *A Dictionary of Epidemiology* (ed. J.M. Last, 3rd ed., International Epidemiological Association/ Oxford University Press, 1995), p.48.

[112] J.B. Walter and M.S. Israel, *General Pathology* (Churchill Livingstone, 4th ed., 1974), p.30.

[113] J.H. Pincus and G.J. Tucker, *Behavioral Neurology* (Oxford University Press, 1978), intro.

[114] Even here, a few illnesses are advantageous in certain circumstances. For example, to have sickle cell trait in malaria infested countries is advantageous because of the resistance it provides against malaria. G.W. Bradley, *Disease, Diagnosis and Decisions* (John Wiley & Sons, 1993), p.17.

[115] R. Ransom, *The Biology of Health & Disease* (The Open University Press, 1985), p.67.

chemical nature, and may be regarded as the units from which all pathological lesions are built. The fact that certain circumstances are sufficiently common for the body's reaction to them to be regarded as 'diseases' does not detract from this concept."[116] If certain forms of mental disorder are diseases, they are unlikely to be different in this respect.[117] A damaging environmental event results in the registration of a memory and therefore a change within the brain: the "consistency and chronicity of the complex of symptoms developing after overwhelmingly terrifying experiences (post-traumatic stress disorder) strongly suggests that enduring changes in cerebral functioning have occurred, that the revealing phrase 'scarred for life' is more than a metaphor."[118] Quite contrary to the maxim taught to young children, words and perceptions, and not merely "sticks and stones," may break bones.

Disease model and Cartesian dualism

It has already been noted that the historical distinction between material brain and immaterial mind — the world of thoughts, perceptions and feelings which the brain enables us to experience — is essentially artificial. All mental events are accompanied by a corresponding biological event. However, the fact that there is no real difference between the biological and the mental, between the psychological and the neurological, cuts both ways. A distressed body may give rise to abnormal thoughts but, equally, a distressing perception or thought may give rise to bodily disease of the brain, a kind of inflammatory response. As in general medicine, chronic inflammations most commonly arise in response to chronic infection and an inflammatory response may persist for months or years. It is therefore quite possible to conceive of schizophrenia as a disease which constitutes the body's normal pathological reaction to infection, with words and perceptions being the "immaterial" organisms. Because they are received by the body in a biological, that is a material, form, a thought or perception may be a toxic substance or poison in the same way as a "material" thing. The overall effect of these biological inputs (thoughts and perceptions) may be such that compensating for them disrupts the proper functioning of the organ. If so, the pathology comprises the body-brain's normal response to acute or chronic infection by words and perceptions, which constitute the infective organisms or pathogens. Moreover, because psychological approaches are directed towards aetiology and biological approaches towards the resulting pathology, the two approaches are not incompatible. Nevertheless, the fact that the brain's reaction is natural in the sense that it is explicable, and that most people's bodies would have reacted similarly to the environmental inputs, does not mean that the process is not a disease; any more than cancer is not a disease because it is a natural consequence of smoking. Furthermore, addressing and eliminating the cause does not generally suffice once the pathology has commenced its development along a natural course, just as stopping smoking is no cure for a cancer which has developed in response to smoking. The whole controversy about whether mental disorders such as schizophrenia are psychological or biological in origin may therefore be, in more than one sense, simply about the status of words — their reception and committal to memory, and the cancerous effect of many memories, being biological in form.

---

[116]   J.B. Walter and M.S. Israel, *General Pathology* (Churchill Livingstone, 4th ed., 1974), p.30.

[117]   As with external conflict, such internal discord can most readily be understood by applying a dialectical approach, the conflict between the individual/biological organism and his environment (antithesis) producing a "synthesis," a modification of the status quo ante.

[118]   R.E. Kendell, "The nature of psychiatric disorders" in *Companion to psychiatric studies* (ed. R.E. Kendell & A.K. Zealley, Churchill Livingstone, 1993), p.5.

Summary

The disease model has revolutionised general medical practice by revealing the cause of many illnesses[119] and has provided "a very efficient approach to disorders that can be prevented or cured — the impact of illness is relieved secondarily as the underlying condition is brought under control."[120] However, this has also led to "a huge split between the constructed object of biomedical cure — the dehumanised disease process — and the constructed object of most other healing systems — the all-too-humanly narrated pathos and pain and perplexity of the experience of suffering."[121] Providing a meaningful explanation of the illness experience becomes "something physicians undertake with both hands tied behind the back."[122]

Disease model and the organic-functional controversy

The concept of disease is narrower than that of organic disorder, insofar as the latter includes injury to the brain, but broader in that it incorporates the idea of disordered biological functioning not caused by structural damage to an organ such as the brain. Nevertheless, the debate about whether functional disorders such as schizophrenia are diseases is essentially an extension of the debate about whether all functional disorders are merely imperfectly understood organic disorders. The failure to identify structural differences in the brains and bodies of people with schizophrenia and manic-depressive illnesses has led to the revised hypothesis that all seriously disabling mental disorders are attributable to brain damage or disordered biological processes, and never psychogenic in origin.

Validity of the disease model

There is ultimately no agreement about the validity of the disease model as a way of understanding, investigating, and treating schizophrenia and affective disorders. "In the absence of convincing evidence, some continue to consider psychiatric disorders to be similar to ailments in general medicine and thus eventually definable as diseases, with specific causes, symptoms, course and outcome; others — with just as much conviction — preach the view that psychiatric problems are responses that are not specific to causes and therefore not appropriate to a system that classifies disease entities."[123] On the one hand is Kendell's view is that it is valid to assume that there must be something biological, which may one day be measurable, that distinguishes sufferers from non-sufferers: "such differences must exist ... although they are extremely elusive and may be of little help in either explaining or offering treatment for the distress."[124] For example, it may well be that the failure to establish the model's validity for illnesses such as schizophrenia is merely due to the fact that so little is known about how thoughts and perceptions are memorised and how they may later be evoked in ways outside conscious control. Nevertheless, on the other hand, "in spite of its promise, so prominent in the 1960s, research during the past

---

[119] G.W. Bradley, *Disease, Diagnosis and Decisions* (John Wiley & Sons, 1993), p.15.

[120] *International Classification of Impairments, Disabilities, and Handicaps: A manual of classification relating to the consequences of disease* (World Health Organisation, 1976), pp.10–11.

[121] A. Kleinman, "What is Specific to Western Medicine" in *Companion Encyclopaedia of the History of Medicine* (ed. W.F. Bynum & R. Porter, Routledge, 1993), Vol. 1, p.19.

[122] *Ibid.*

[123] N. Sartorius in *Sources and Traditions of Classification in Psychiatry* (ed. N Sartorius *et al.*, World Health Organisation/Hogrefe & Huber, 1990), p.2.

[124] S. Murphy, *Experiencing and Explaining Disease* (The Open University Press, 1985), p.57.

two decades failed to provide evidence that could help to create disease concepts and disease entities in psychiatry."[125] The "most telling reason to reject disease reasoning and this brain-based search for a pathological change in schizophrenia is that it has been the sinkhole of reputations for close to a century ... With proper controls, the claims for the discovery of the pathology of schizophrenia have evaporated. This fact should hold a cautious person back from the disease model."[126] Because legal decisions must be founded on evidence, not hypothesis or conjecture, it is not presently possible to go any further than to say that some mental illnesses may be caused by organic injury, some by disease, and others be functional or psychogenic in origin.

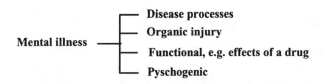

THE CAUSE OF MENTAL DISORDER (AETIOLOGY)

Aetiology is literally the study of causes. It has been noted that, according to the disease model (**1038**), the patient's disease comprises symptoms and signs which are the manifestations of certain pathological changes in the structure or functioning of the body, changes initiated by a particular cause or causes (the aetiology). Because the disease model holds that pathological bodily changes are the direct cause of the patient's symptoms and signs, the aetiology is therefore a step removed from this stage and refers to the causes of the disease process (the pathology). The relationship between the various factors believed to cause a particular disease process, and their connection with the way the disease develops, is usually unclear: the pathogenesis of a disease refers to the postulated mechanisms by which the causal agents produce disease.[127]

NORMALITY AND ABNORMALITY

The World Health Organisation has observed that "the very notion of what will count as a causal agent in disease is connected with a normative view of the normal or healthy organism."[128] In other words, ideas about what causes mental disorder depend on how mental health and, by elimination, mental disorder are defined. A person who has a narrow, perhaps conventional, attitude about what is mentally normal will have a proportionally more inclusive view of what constitutes mental disorder than a person who is more accepting of individual variation. Arising from this, the former will also have a correspondingly broader view of what events may

---

[125] N. Sartorius in *Sources and Traditions of Classification in Psychiatry* (ed. N Sartorius *et al.*, World Health Organisation/Hogrefe & Huber, 1990), p.2.

[126] P.R. McHugh, "Schizophrenia and the Disease Model" in *What is Schizophrenia?* (ed. W.F. Flack *et al.*, Springer-Verlag, 1990), p.76.

[127] *A Dictionary of Epidemiology* (ed. J.M. Last, 3rd ed., International Epidemiological Association/ Oxford University Press, 1995), p.122.

[128] *International Classification of Impairments, Disabilities, and Handicaps: A manual of classification relating to the consequences of disease* (World Health Organisation, 1976), p.33.

"cause" a person to become mentally disordered. Likewise, what is believed to cause severe depression — the aetiology of "major depressive disorders" — depends on whether the diagnostic category is restricted to persons who are suicidal or includes people with less serious disturbances of mood.

WHAT IS MEANT BY CAUSE

Descriptions of the aetiology of different kinds of mental disorder are also affected by ideas of what constitutes a cause. Cause and effect concerns associations in time between events, a point well illustrated by Bradley:

> "If event B follows A it is said to be caused by A. In the simplest form this relationship is invariable; when a billiard ball is hit by a cue, the ball moves, and when a gas is heated in a sealed container the pressure increases. These effects are caused by a transfer of energy and the result of this transfer can be precisely calculated. When the events are closely connected the concept of cause is easily applied; even when there are several steps involved as in A→B→C→D the cause or sequence may be well established and is reliable."[129]

Bradley then makes the following important points—

- While physics and mathematics have traditionally dealt with linear systems of the kind just described — because it is possible to make testable predictions — the situation is usually not so simple because many systems found in nature are non-linear; this is particularly true of biological systems. When a system is non-linear, small differences in the initial conditions can result in vastly different outcomes; although an outcome can be determined accurately if the initial conditions are known precisely, they never are.[130]

- An outcome "often occurs as a result of a whole chain of events which are best regarded together as an effective causal complex. None of the various causes in the sequence may be essential even though, colloquially, they are regarded as the primary cause. A different set of causal factors could have the same end result and the choice of any one particular causal factor in this complex may be arbitrary."[131]

- Very few associations have a simple and invariable causal pathway connecting them; most events are connected by a series of possible causal pathways in parallel. Failure to appreciate this has led to futile arguments about the cause of disease and mental disorder. Although some people may argue that because 70 per cent. of cancers are caused by environmental factors then 50 per cent. cannot be genetically determined, the statements are compatible because, in many cases, both environmental and genetic factors influence disease.[132]

- Notwithstanding these difficulties, "without a belief in cause and effect, without knowing that something will happen predictably, any common sense attempt to understand the world would be frustrated and scientific progress would be in jeopardy."[133]

---

[129] G.W. Bradley, *Disease, Diagnosis and Decisions* (John Wiley & Sons, 1993), p.39.
[130] *Ibid.*, p.45.
[131] *Ibid.*, p.39.
[132] *Ibid.*, p.40.
[133] *Ibid.*, p.47.

Cause and coincidence

Cause is inferred and involves a retrospective interpretation of the likelihood of association between events. It is sometimes difficult to decide whether the occurrence of two or more effects is coincidence or the result of cause and effect. The problem is often seen with regard to a patient's improvement following the prescription of medication. The improvement of a considerable number of patients receiving a placebo during a clinical trial indicates that the improvement of some patients with drug therapy is not due to medication but natural remission and the involvement other factors. Nevertheless, in practice, human vanity means that the coincidental improvement in their conditions is often interpreted by the doctor as having been caused by the treatment which he has prescribed.

Different levels of explanation

Failure to realise that what is regarded as having caused a person to become unwell depends on the perspective of the onlooker has led to many sterile debates about the causes of different kinds of mental disorder. When considering states of ill-health, there are always several levels of explanation and they are sometimes categorised as "bottom up" or "top down." Health and disease can be explained in terms of assumed abnormalities in an individual's biochemical make-up, as being located in the social order to the exclusion of biology, and in terms of the individual's unique personal life history — the level of parts of the person, the level of the individual person, the level of groups of persons. All living creatures, even the simplest, interact dynamically with their environment, constantly changing it, and themselves, in the process. Thus, while reductionist disciplines like biochemistry give up a bottom-up explanation, top-down explanations tend to explore the relationship between the whole animal and its environment. For example, several levels of explanation of why a person has developed tuberculosis are possible — the fact that he has certain bacteria in his body, that he was not immunised, that his mother had it and he has a genetic susceptibility, that he is too poor to heat his flat properly, that lesions formed in his lungs, that he is run down after years of being unemployed.[134] The point is well illustrated by the well known concept of "cause of death" recorded on a death certificate. The death certificate is a medical certificate and hence records all those diseases, morbid conditions, or injuries that resulted in or contributed to death and the circumstances of the accident or violence which produced any such injuries. The certificate does not record other significant circumstances which may have "caused" the death, such as "died of a broken heart," "died from over-work," or "died from poverty." Medical explanations are concerned with parts of the body and therefore termed biomedical explanations. Even here, there are many different levels of interest and what we regard as the causes of events again depends on the level of our interest. Thus, Bradley says that "in the research field, the research worker aims to discover the cause of disease and in the clinical field the physician seeks the cause of illness."[135]

Multifactorial causes the norm

A determinant is any factor, such as a characteristic or an event, that brings about change in a person's health. Mental illness is almost always multifactorial in nature

---

[134]   *Studying health and disease* (ed. K. McConway, Open University Press, 1994), p.5.
[135]   G.W. Bradley, *Disease, Diagnosis and Decisions, supra,* p.39. It will be noted that this statement relates back to an essential difference between the ideas of disease and illness.

so that no single causative agent can be isolated. Biological, psychological and social determinants all need to be taken into account. It may be that many causes acting together have collectively caused the disease to develop: genetic factors (one parent had the illness), constitutional factors (a recent viral infection), psycho-dynamic factors (a recent bereavement), and social factors (the threat of redun-dancy). Some of these causes may be remote in time and the time lag or latent period between exposure to a risk factor and the diagnosis of a disease can be a few hours or decades. Obviously, "the greater the time between an initiating event and recognition of disease, the more difficult it may be to establish the linkage between risk factor and disease occurrence. The task is made even more challenging if the risk factor is a weak determinant ... or if multiple risk factors are involved."[136]

Whether a cause is necessary or sufficient

One way of attempting to make sense of the multiplicity of causes involved in the development of human disease is to search for what are known as necessary and/or sufficient causes. A cause is termed "sufficient" when it inevitably initiates or pro-duces an effect. A cause is "necessary" when it must always precede an effect although the effect need not be the sole result of the one cause. Any given factor may be necessary, sufficient, neither, or both —

RELATIVE IMPORTANCE OF CAUSES

Cause X is necessary and sufficient to cause Y (schizophrenia)	• X and Y are always present together and nothing but X is needed to cause Y (X→Y)
Cause X is necessary but not sufficient to cause Y (schizophrenia)	• X must be present when Y is present but Y is not always present when X is; some addi-tional factor(s) must also be present (X and Z→Y)
Cause X is not sufficient but is necessary to cause Y (schizophrenia)	• X is not necessary but is sufficient to cause Y. Y is present when X is, but X may or may not be present when Y is present, because Y has other causes and can occur without X (X →Y; Z→Y)
Cause X is neither necessary nor sufficient to cause Y (schizophrenia)	• X is neither necessary nor sufficient to cause Y. Again, X may or may not be present when Y is present. However, if X is present with Y, some additional factor must also be present. Here X is a contributory cause of Y in some causal sequences (X and Z →Y; W and Z→Y)

Source: Adapted from A Dictionary of Epidemiology (ed. J.M. Last, Oxford University Press, 3rd Ed., 1995), p.25.

---

[136] R.S. Greenberg, *Medical Epidemiology* (Appleton & Lange, 1993), pp.28–29.

Factors in the causation of disease

Unfortunately, it has not been possible to isolate any necessary or sufficient causes of seriously disabling illnesses such as schizophrenia and manic-depressive states. A further approach, at present largely impressionistic, is to categorise likely causes according to the sort of role they are likely to play in an illness' development. A certain factor may predispose an individual to disease, precipitate (that is trigger) it, or perpetuate it once set in motion. Sims and Owens' summary of some of the most important predisposing, precipitating and reinforcing factors is set out in the table below. Inevitably, different authors use different terms and some epidemiologists also refer to enabling factors (such as housing, nutrition and the availability of medical care) which facilitate the manifestation of disease or ill-health. Although the table below concentrates on factors implicated in the cause of disease, it must be emphasised that it is equally important to identify the factors which predispose or enable an individual to recover, which precipitate recovery, or which reinforce remission or recovery once it has been achieved. Similarly, yet other factors may insure an individual against the development of a particular disease.

FACTORS IN THE CAUSE OF MENTAL ILLNESS

Predisposing factors	Precipitating factors	Perpetuating/reinforcing
• These lie in the background — constitution of the patient, e.g., genetic, early childhood influences, abnormal personality.	• Causes which can be seen to be immediately related in time to the development of the illness, e.g., marital breakdown.	• Disorder is caused to continue, e.g., loss of self-esteem, demoralisation, social withdrawal.
• Predisposing factors are those that prepare, sensitize, or otherwise create a situation such as a level of immunity or state of susceptibility so that the host tends to react in a specific fashion to a disease agent, personal interaction, environmental stimulus, or specific incentive.	• Precipitating factors are those associated with the definitive onset of a disease, illness, accident, behavioural response, or course of action. Usually one factor is more important or more obviously recognisable than others if several are involved and one may often be regarded as "necessary."	• Reinforcing factors are those tending to perpetuate or aggravate the presence of a disease, disability, impairment, attitude, pattern of behaviour, or course of action. They may tend to be repetitive, recurrent, or persistent and may or may not necessarily be the same or similar to those categorised as predisposing, enabling, or precipitating.
• Examples include age, sex, marital status, family size, educational level, previous illness experience, presence of concurrent illness, dependency, working environment, and attitudes towards the use of health services.	• Examples include exposure to specific disease, amount or level of an infectious organism, drug, noxious agent, physical trauma, personal interaction, occupational stimulus, or new awareness or knowledge.	• Examples include repeated exposure to the same noxious stimulus (in the absence of an appropriate immune response) such as an infectious agent, work, household, or interpersonal environment, presence of financial incentive or disincentive, personal satisfaction or deprivation.

Adapted from A. Sims and D. Owens, Psychiatry (Baillière Tindall, 6th ed., 1993), p.28. By permission of the publisher W B Saunders Company Limited, London.

Genetic factors

The genetic study of any individual psychiatric illness "is concerned with whether a link can be found between symptoms and inheritance, and what is the precise nature of inheritance."[137] Establishing familiality (that a condition runs in families) is not sufficient evidence of genetic involvement. The medical literature on the genetic basis of psychiatric disorders has a distinct terminology. There is only space here to deal with the terms most frequently encountered. Diathesis refers to a constitutional or genetic predisposition to disease. The genotype is the genetic constitution of an individual while the phenotype represents the set of observable characteristics of an individual as determined by his genotype and environment. Thus, one can talk of genotypic differences and phenotypic differences. A person's genotype may direct development in various indirect ways. For example, people with genotypic differences create different environments for themselves, so that smiling, "easy" children are less likely to be the target of parental irritability. Thus, the effects of parental behaviour on the psychosocial development of their children partly reflects the child's own genetic make-up.[138] Much of the present understanding of genetic and environmental interaction is derived from two research strategies, the study of twins and of adopted children. Identical or Monozygotic (MZ) twins share exactly the same genes. Non-identical or Dizygotic (DZ) twins have only approximately 50 per cent. of their genes in common. Consequently, they are similar to any pair of siblings except that, by virtue of their similar age, their life experiences should be more similar than those of siblings of different ages.[139] In the case of schizophrenia, twin studies demonstrate a 50 per cent. concordance for monozygotic twins and 17 per cent. for dizygotic. The concordance rates for MZ twins reared together and apart are generally similar, indicating a genetic component. It should be emphasised that genetic control of development does not stop at birth. Genetic factors make a major contribution to personality development throughout adult life. Likewise, throughout life, certain genetically determined physical characteristics and even complex patterns of behaviour are making their first appearance. Thus, the symptoms of Huntington's Chorea, like many other hereditary illnesses, become manifest only in adulthood even though the person has been carrying the gene since conception. In these instances, "environmental stress and learning may have little impact on modifying the expression of genetic endowment. However, in the development of characteristics such as intelligence, personality traits and complex behaviour patterns such as sex role activity, the expression of a genetic predisposition may be radically influenced by the social environment in which the child grows up."[140]

Life events and environmental causes

Genes cannot act independently of their environment and, according to McHugh, "the need for life stresses to bring out what can be construed as an underlying vulnerability, as represented by the multi-hit concept or the diathesis-stress concept,

---

[137]   A. Sims and D. Owens, *Psychiatry* (Baillière Tindall, 6th ed., 1993), p.32.

[138]   M. Rutter, "Family and school influences on cognitive development" *Journal of Child Psychology & Psychiatry* (1985) 26: 683–704; M. Rutter and D. Quinton, "Long-term follow-up of women institutionalised in childhood: factors promoting good functioning in adult life" *British Journal of Developmental Psychology* (1984) 18: 225.

[139]   D.H.R. Blackwood, "The biological determinants of personality" in *Companion to psychiatric studies* (ed. R.E. Kendell & A.K. Zealley, Churchill Livingstone, 1993), p.44.

[140]   *Ibid.*, 1993, p.43.

has much to recommend it."[141] An analogous situation is that of turning on a light. This can generally be done successfully thousands of times over many years in response to impending darkness. However, the switch is merely the trigger which activates an effective response in a particular environmental situation rather than the cause of the light in any meaningful sense. This requires complex wiring, the presence of a current, physical apparatus in correct working order, and so forth. Turning the switch on and off would have no effect at all unless these mechanisms were first in place. If too many lights are added to the circuit in an attempt to respond to increasing levels of darkness, the limitations of the system will become apparent when the switch is next turned and the genetic fuse is blown. The critical role of memory processes in the development of personality and psychiatric illness has been emphasised by Kendell—

> "One of the most important distinguishing characteristics of psychiatric disorders is the contribution which the patient's previous experience and current psychological and social predicaments — his childhood upbringing, recent life events, the fact that he always feels unwanted, or is lonely or demoralised — make to their aetiology. This is hardly surprising, however, if one reflects that it is one of the brain's most important functions to keep a detailed record of past experience ... stressful past experiences and the patient's appraisal regarding his current social environment play a part in the genesis of many illnesses ... To remember what has happened in the past, to appraise current situations in the light of that memory, and to create moods and action plans appropriate to these appraisals are amongst the brain's most important functions. It should not surprise us, therefore, that psychiatric illnesses characteristically involve disorders of perception, memory, cognition, mood and volition. Memory is of central importance because it is involved in most of these activities. Information processing is the brain's most basic function and the means by which meaning, which is derived from the interrelationships between different items of information, is attributed to events and symbols. The brain's memory stores are as crucial to this role as the memory banks of a computer are to its functioning. It is no coincidence, therefore, that memories and meanings play a key role in most psychological theories of the aetiology of psychiatric disorders ... What matters is that memory has a physical substrate in the brain and almost certainly cannot exist in the absence of such a substrate."[142]

EPIDEMIOLOGY

Sims and Owens describe epidemiology and psychopathology as the "twin bases of psychiatric knowledge."[143] Epidemiology is the study of diseases or syndromes (1112) as they affect groups of people, as opposed to individuals. The name of the field reflects the fact that such studies were once often concerned with the outbreak of epidemics. Most of epidemiology concerns causality although it focuses on the determinants of disease development, that is risk factors, rather than with cause *per se*. The major characteristics in descriptive epidemiology can be classified under the headings of persons, place, and time. For example, who develops schizophrenia?; where does schizophrenia occur?; when does schizophrenia occur?[144] To this end,

[141] P.R. McHugh, "Schizophrenia and the Disease Model" in *What is Schizophrenia?* (ed. W.F. Flack *et al.*, Springer-Verlag, 1990), p.79. Diathesis means a predisposition to certain forms of disease.

[142] R.E. Kendell, "The nature of psychiatric disorders" in *Companion to psychiatric studies* (ed. R.E. Kendell & A.K. Zealley, Churchill Livingstone, 1993), pp.3–4.

[143] A. Sims and D. Owens, *Psychiatry* (Baillière Tindall, 6th ed., 1993), p.8.

[144] *A Dictionary of Epidemiology* (ed. J.M. Last, 3rd ed., International Epidemiological Association/ Oxford University Press, 1995), p.56; R.S. Greenberg, *Medical Epidemiology* (Appleton & Lange, 1993), p.25.

general observations are made concerning the relationship of a disease to basic characteristics such as age, sex, race, occupation, social class, and geographical location, and the data is then subjected to analysis. Examining patterns of illness in groups of people may enable epidemiologists to learn why certain individuals develop a particular disease whereas other persons do not, that is to identify persons at "high risk." A basic tenet of epidemiology is therefore that diseases do not develop at random. Not everyone is equally likely to develop a particular disease and certain persons are at comparatively high risk by virtue of their personal characteristics and environment.[145] Any variation of occurrence in relation to personal characteristics "may reflect differences in level of exposure to causal factors, susceptibility to the effects of causal factors, or both exposure and susceptibility.[146]

Risk, prevalence and incidence

Risk is the likelihood that an individual will contract a disease. Prevalence is the amount of a disease already present in a population, *i.e.* the proportion of a population that has the disease of interest at a particular time. Prevalence (P) is measured along a ranges between 0 and 1 so that if P = 0.4 then 40 per cent. of the population being surveyed have the condition in question. The measure of the rapidity of disease occurrence is referred to as an incidence rate (how fast new occurrences of disease arise). This is often measured in terms of new cases per person-year. The usual rate of occurrence for a disease in a population is referred to as the endemic rate. A rapid and dramatic increase over the endemic rate is described as an epidemic rate. In the case of chronic illnesses, an epidemic may emerge over a period of years to decades.[147] Correlation studies seek to determine the extent to which two characteristics —risk factor and disease occurrence are related. Thus, where the coefficient of determination is 0.75 this means that 75 per cent. of the variation in the incidence of the disease under consideration can be accounted by knowing the incidence of some other specified (risk) factor.

---

[145]   R.S. Greenberg, *Medical Epidemiology, supra,* p.2.
[146]   *Ibid.*, p.25.
[147]   R.S. Greenberg, *Medical Epidemiology* (Appleton & Lange, 1993), p.28.

18. Assessing the presence of mental disorder

INTRODUCTION

Assessment is the process of collecting information relevant to the diagnosis, management, and treatment of a patient's clinical condition, including distinguishing or recognising the presence of disease or disorder from its symptoms or manifestations. The mental state examination is equivalent to the detailed physical examination in general medicine.[1] Its purpose is to elicit and observe any signs and symptoms indicative of mental disorder. Various medical terms are used to record and describe what is observed and it is important to have an understanding of their meaning. In addition to recording any symptoms and signs of disorder apparent on examining the patient, the assessment includes conducting any tests necessary to establish a diagnosis, for example biochemical investigations or an EEG. The nature and purpose of these tests are described later (**1089**). Mental illness may be seen as the response of an individual to his life situation so that, as Hamilton has noted, one must always ask the threefold question: "Why did this person break down, in this way, at this time?"[2] More particularly, Sir Denis Hill has emphasised that it is necessary to investigate the patient's psychic reality and experience and the bearing this has on his disorder; it is also necessary to investigate the psycho-social environment and culture within which the patient lives and works; and it is necessary to examined the patient as a biological organism. The psychiatrist's capacity to know, after the initial interview, to which area he should in the main direct his attention is dependant upon his clinical experience and training, his skill in examination, but above all upon his detailed knowledge of the clinical phenomena which mental disorder presents, and their significance.[3]

SYMPTOMS AND SIGNS

A person may be diseased but "symptom-free" which is another way of saying that, following the onset of disease, pathological changes may or may not make themselves evident. When they do, they are described as "manifestations" which, by medical custom, are usually distinguished as "symptoms and signs."[4] A sign is an objective indication of a disease or disorder that is observed or detected by a doctor upon examining and interviewing the patient, in contrast to a symptom which is noticed or reported by the patient. Symptoms are therefore what people complain of and worry about so that the customary distinction is between an objective observation

[1]   A. Sims and D. Owens, *Psychiatry* (Baillière Tindall, 6th ed., 1993), p.8.
[2]   *Fish's Outline of Psychiatry* (rev. Max Hamilton, John Wright & Sons, 4th ed., 1984).
[3]   Sir Denis Hill, in W.A. Lishman, *Organic Psychiatry, The Psychological Consequences of Cerebral Disorder* (Blackwell Scientific Publications, 2nd. ed., 1987), page vii.
[4]   *International Classification of Impairments, Disabilities, and Handicaps: A manual of classification relating to the consequences of disease* (World Health Organisation, 1976), p.25.

and a subjective complaint.[5] In practice, the distinction "often difficult to make where psychological phenomena are concerned,"[6] partly because certain phenomena may be simultaneously experienced and reported by the patient and observed by his doctor. In common usage, and in the text below, the term "symptoms" includes objective signs of pathological conditions.

The purpose of recording the patient's symptoms

"Listen to the patient, he is telling you the diagnosis," the physician William Osler once observed. The recording of a patient's symptoms is undertaken to identify the type of mental disorder from which he suffers — symptoms being pointers towards the underlying pathology — and, following on from this, the most appropriate form of treatment and the patient's likely response to that treatment. As to the diagnostic significance of symptoms, psychiatry often distinguishes between the form and content of mental phenomena such as hallucinations and delusions. The content of an idea may "be meaningful and understandable. But it is even more significant that the idea is a delusion, and not merely an overvalued idea; that the hallucination is occurring in a setting in which other people do not experience false perceptions; and that the patient's difficulty in expressing himself coherently is not explicable in terms of limited vocabulary or education, or emotional arousal."[7] Thus, the form of an experience (*e.g.* the fact that a person is experiencing visual hallucinations) is of diagnostic value. However, the content of the experience (what the person imagines he sees) is determined by the individual's background, has social and cultural determinants, and is less often diagnostically significant.

The relative significance of symptoms

Even if not found in the normal population, and therefore indicative of a pathological process, symptoms may exist as manifestations of several different diseases or disorders and, when viewed in isolation, be incapable of sustaining any single diagnosis.[8] Very few clinical features give unequivocal information.[9] The importance of one finding may depend upon the presence or absence of others, so that a symptom is most often known by the company it keeps. The early, generally non-florid, symptoms of mental disorder are referred to as "prodromal features." A symptom which is characteristic of a particular disease or disorder, and is alone sufficient to establish a diagnosis, is said to be "pathognomonic." In many cases this is simply because the disease is defined in terms of the particular feature. Where a feature has to be present for the diagnosis of a disease, but its presence does not

---

5   Thus, Kleinman writes that "the physician's task is to replace these biased observations with objective data: the only valid sign of pathological processes; they are based on verified or verifiable measurements." A. Kleinman, "What is Specific to Western Medicine" in *Companion Encyclopaedia of the History of Medicine* (ed. W.F. Bynum & R. Porter, Routledge, 1993), Vol. 1, p.18. For the avoidance of doubt, the signs therefore comprise abnormal behaviour observed by the examiner, or described to him by others, and those abnormalities of subjective experience apparent upon questioning the patient. Thus, the statement "I am God" is a sign of mental disorder whereas the statement, "I feel depressed," is a symptom because it represents a subjective complaint by the patient about the way he feels.

6   A. Sims, *Symptoms in the Mind* (Baillière Tindall, London, 1988), p.6.

7   R.E. Kendell, "Schizophrenia: A Medical View of a Medical Concept" in *What is Schizophrenia?* (ed. W.F. Flack *et al.*, Springer-Verlag, 1990), p.69.

8   For example, the persistent repetition of a word ("perseveration") may be a symptom of schizophrenia but it may also be associated with an organic disorder and various other functional disorders.

9   See G.W. Bradley, *Disease, Diagnosis and Decisions* (John Wiley & Sons, 1993), p.56.

guarantee the diagnosis, because the same finding may be present in other diseases, it is sometimes referred to as obligatory. Symptoms which are not pathognomonic or obligatory may nevertheless be commonly present or valuable diagnostically. An exclusionary feature is one which is the opposite of pathognomonic in that its presence excludes a particular diagnosis. A symptom distinctive of an illness may not be considered to have that significance because the classification is erroneous. The severity of a symptom can be rated on a number of different criteria, such as frequency, intensity, duration or degree of incapacitation or tolerability.[10]

ARRANGEMENT OF THE CHAPTER

The arrangement of the chapter, in terms of meaning of words used to describe symptoms and signs commonly referred to in psychiatric reports is shown below.

SYMPTOMS AND SIGNS: ARRANGEMENT OF THE CHAPTER

Consciousness	The client may be unconscious or his consciousness obviously impaired.	1058
Responsiveness	If the client's consciousness is unimpaired, he may nevertheless be unresponsive.	1059
Level of activity	The patient may be markedly over-active or under-active.	1059
Posture, etc.	The client's posture, mannerisms or gestures may be idiosyncratic	1060
Movements	There may be evidence of involuntary movements.	1062
Physical signs	The client's physical state may suggest poor self-care, poor nutrition or an organic disorder.	1067
Memory	The client's answers may indicate problems memorising or recalling information.	1070
Affect, mood	The client's emotional responsiveness (affect) or his underlying mood may be abnormal.	1073
Anxiety, etc.	The client may be anxious or fearful, causing irritability, agitation, panic, hostility or depression.	1075
Speech, thought	Any of the following may be abnormal: the volume or rate of speech; its articulation; the choice of words; the association/juxtaposition of words and phrases; the content of the patient's thoughts.	1076
Perception	The client's statements or behaviour may indicate that he is experiencing hallucinations or other perceptual disturbances.	1086

---

[10] R. Manchanda, *et al.*, "A Review of rating scales for measuring symptom changes in schizophrenia research" in *The Instruments of Psychiatric Research* (ed. C. Thompson, John Wiley & Sons, 1989), p.61.

The reason for dealing with symptoms in this order reflects the order in which they are likely to become apparent to a lay observer. Important information about the patient's mental state may be conveyed before any examination or interview takes place, simply by observing him. It may be apparent that the client is inaccessible, either because his consciousness is impaired or because he is unresponsive. The patient may be markedly over-active or under-active. His posture (the relative position of the different parts of the body at rest or during movement) or certain mannerisms or gestures may be idiosyncratic. In some cases, his general appearance may be suggestive of self-neglect. Involuntary movements may be conspicuous, perhaps affecting the individual's gait (style or manner of walking). Following the interview's commencement, other symptoms and signs of mental disorder may become apparent. It may be noticeable that his memory is impaired or that his mood or emotional state is abnormal. There may be evidence of disordered thought processes or the content of the patient's thought may be abnormal. This may be a consequence of the fact that he is experiencing abnormal perceptions, such as hallucinations.

IMPAIRED CONSCIOUSNESS OR RESPONSIVENESS

Consciousness is the awareness of one's own internal thoughts and feelings together with the ability to recognise one's external environment. It is important to appreciate that a person may be fully conscious and yet profoundly unresponsive to his immediate environment.

Impaired consciousness

To be unconscious is to have no subjective experience. Consciousness is a continuum with full alertness and awareness at one end and brain death at the other.

Full alertness/ awareness	Clouding of Consciousness	Sopor	Coma	Brain death

- **Clouding of consciousness** describes impairment of orientation, perception and attention and it is seen in organic mental disorders. There is difficulty with thinking, attention, perception, memory and usually drowsiness[11] but sometimes excitability. Such clouding is seen in some organic mental disorders.

- **Semi-coma (sopor)** — In cases of semi-coma (sopor), there is a partial response to stimulation which is incomplete and mostly non-purposive; the movements are ineffectual such as scratching the stimulated area.

- **Coma** lies at the opposite end of the spectrum from full alertness and awareness of the environment.[12] The Glasgow coma scale is used to grade the degree or level of coma.

---

[11] Drowsiness is also sometimes used as a general word describing a state of consciousness between full wakefulness and unconsciousness or sleep.

[12] W.A. Lishman, *Organic Psychiatry, The Psychological Consequences of Cerebral Disorder* (Blackwell Scientific Publications, 2nd. ed., 1987), p.5.

Disorientation, attention and concentration

Disorientation is a loss of awareness of oneself in relation to time (the date or time of day), place (where one is) or identity (whether one's own or others), as a result of which speech and behaviour tend to be muddled. Disorientation may be the product of clouding of consciousness, a head injury, a chronic brain disorder such as dementia, or the result of intoxication. To be attentive is to be alert, aware and responsive, while to concentrate is to focus and sustain mental activity on a particular task.[13] Poor attention and concentration are usually the result of tiredness or disinterest. In some cases, the conscious patient's apparent lack of attentiveness simply reflects the fact that his attention is focused elsewhere — **distractibility**. If a patient is distractible, his attention and conversation changes from topic to topic in accordance with stimuli from within or without, for example in response to visual hallucinations. More rarely, impaired attention or concentration is indicative of clouding of consciousness.

Confusion and confusional states

A confusional state is a disorganised mental state in which the abilities to remember, think clearly and reason are impaired. The confusion may be acute or chronic. Delirium is a state of acute mental confusion in which the activity of the brain is affected by fever, drugs, poisons or injury. Chronic confusional states may be the product of long-term use of anxiolytics, dementia or some other organic disorder.

Stupor (awareness accompanied by profound lack of responsiveness)

It is not necessarily the case that a patient who is inaccessible is in a state of coma or sopor. The absence of any obvious signs of activity, movement or response to external stimuli does not of itself mean that consciousness is impaired: a person may be fully conscious and yet profoundly unresponsive to his immediate environment. Consequently, when a person is motionless, and both speech and spontaneous movement are absent or minimal, this lack of response to external stimuli may be misinterpreted as unawareness of it. While terms such as coma and sopor describe a substantial impairment of consciousness, **stupor** describes a profound lack of responsiveness to external stimuli and the environment rather than profound unawareness of it.[14] The two components of stupor are sometimes described as **akinesia** (a voluntary absence of any movement) and **muteness** (a voluntary absence of any speech).[15] Where a state of stupor appears to form part of a catatonic schizophrenic illness, it is usually described as **catatonic stupor**. Catatonic stupor is defined in the DSM Glossary (**1119**) as a marked decrease in reactivity to the environment and reduction in spontaneous movements and activity, sometimes to the point of appearing to be unaware of one's surroundings.

Retardation and psychomotor retardation (a slowing of activity)

Retardation is a general slowing down of the conscious patient's mental and bodily functions — a slowing of his thoughts, speech, actions, reactions and movement. The term **psychomotor retardation** emphasises that this retardation has a psychic

---

13   A. Sims, *Symptoms in the Mind* (Baillière Tindall, London, 1988).
14   W.A. Lishman, *Organic Psychiatry, The Psychological Consequences of Cerebral Disorder* (Blackwell Scientific Publications, 2nd. ed., 1987), p.6.
15   See *e.g.* A. Sims, *Symptoms in the Mind, supra.*

cause, such as depression or catatonic schizophrenia, rather than some neurological cause.

Marked overactivity

Over-activity for substantial periods of time, evidenced by over-talkativeness, restlessness, pacing rapidly up and down, constant talking or loud singing is known as **pressure of activity**. In manic states, such pressure of activity is often accompanied by correspondingly accelerated speech, grandiosity and elation.

Catatonic excitement and catatonic agitation

The phrase **catatonic excitement** is used in the DSM classification (**1119**) to describe excited motor activity which is apparently purposeless and not influenced by external stimuli. The term **catatonic agitation** is preferred in the ICD glossary (**1117**), where it refers to a state in which the psychomotor features of anxiety are associated with catatonic syndromes. In both cases, the patient's restlessness and activity are associated with his abnormal ideas and perceptions rather than with his mood state (the degree of elation or depression present).

Pressure of activity	Normal range of responsiveness	Psychomotor retardation	Stupor
Catatonic excitement			Catatonic stupor

POSTURE, GESTURES AND MANNERISMS

The word **attitude** is most often used in psychiatry to denote a patient's posture or position rather than his personal viewpoint. In cases of catatonic schizophrenia, where a client's preoccupation with overwhelming incapacitating ideas or perceptions has rendered him unresponsive, this unresponsiveness may be accompanied by prolonged, stereotyped, postures.

MANNERISTIC AND STEREOTYPED POSTURES

A patient's posture may sometimes be described as manneristic or stereotyped. Conventionally, manneristic postures differ from stereotyped postures in that the former are not rigidly maintained.

Catatonic posturing

The term **catatonic posturing** describes the voluntary assumption of an inappropriate or bizarre posture which is usually held for a long period of time. For example, a patient standing with arms out-stretched as if he were Jesus on the cross.

Body maintained in a semi-rigid position ("waxy rigidity")

The terms **catalepsy** and **catatonic waxy flexibility** — and, also, the latter's Latin variant, **flexibilitas cerea** — are synonymous. They describe a physical state of sudden onset in which the muscles of the face, body and limbs are maintained by increased muscle tone in a semi-rigid position, possibly for several hours, during which time neither expression or body position changes. Voluntary movement and sensibility are suspended, respiration and pulse are slowed, and body temperature falls. The affected person's limbs can be moulded into any position. When moved in this way, they feel as if made of a pliable wax which enables these externally imposed postures to be maintained. Phenomena of the kind described are observed in catatonic schizophrenia and a number of other conditions.

Body maintained in a rigid position ("iron-pipe rigidity")

Waxlike postures may also appear with rigid rather than flexible musculature. Consequently, a distinction is sometimes drawn between flexible and rigid catalepsy (**catatonic or iron-pipe rigidity**). In the former case, a posture is assumed at the slightest external prompting; in the latter, the patient's self-assumed posture resists external attempts at modification and is maintained by the person against all efforts to be moved.

MANNERISMS, GESTURES OR RITUALS

A person's mannerisms, gestures or rituals may sometimes be highly distinctive and strikingly unusual.

Mannerisms and gestures

A mannerism is a gesture or expression peculiar to a person, such as an odd way of walking or eating. If the mannerism involves taking up an idiosyncratic posture, rather than idiosyncratic movement, it may be referred to as a manneristic posture (*supra*). Mannerisms differ from spontaneous, involuntary, movements (dyskinesias, **1065**) in that they are voluntary, if idiosyncratic, movements. They differ from stereotyped behaviour in that the latter is carried out in an unvarying, repetitive, manner and is not goal-directed.

Repetitive or imitative behaviour

While manneristic behaviour is directed towards some goal (eating in the above example), stereotypy is not. Stereotyped behaviour, or **stereotypy**, is the constant, almost mechanical repetition of an action. For example, pacing the same circle each day, head-banging, rocking or repetitive hand movements, or repeating some phrase over many weeks or months. Stereotyped movements are often rhythmic. **Echopraxia**, which is sometimes a feature of catatonic schizophrenia, refers to the imitative repetitive copying of the movements of another person.

Negativism (contrary behaviour) and catatonic negativism

Negativism is opposition or resistance, whether covert or overt, to outside suggestions or advice. For example, a person drops his arm when asked to raise it. **Catatonic negativism** is a resistance to all instructions or attempts to be moved. The person may do the opposite of what is asked, firmly clenching the jaws in response to being asked to open his mouth.

Automatic obedience (command automatism)

The opposite of negativism is automatic compliance which may be so marked that the individual does more than is required to comply with any instructions. For example, a person who is asked to raise an arm raises both of them in an exaggerated manner. Such undue or automatic compliance is associated with catatonic syndromes and hypnotic states.

Compulsive or ritualistic behaviour

A compulsion is an irresistible impulse to perform an irrational act. The individual experiences a powerful urge to act or behave in a way he recognises is irrational or senseless and which he attributes to subjective necessity rather than to external influences. Performing the particular act may relieve tension. Compulsive behaviour may be attributable to obsessional ideas. For example, a young adult may become obsessed with the idea that his shoelaces must be perfectly tied, continually retying them for twenty minutes, and unable to move on to the next stage of dressing until this objective has been achieved; or he may continually close the refrigerator door until it eventually makes the "right" sound.

Compulsive acts and obsessive thoughts

It can be seen that the terms "obsession" and "compulsion" are not synonymous. The former refers to a thought and the latter to an act. Obsessions are recurrent, persistent ideas, thoughts, images, or impulses that are not experienced as voluntarily produced but as ideas, urges or representations which invade consciousness. A thought may properly be described as obsessional if a person cannot prevent himself from repeatedly, insistently, having that thought albeit that the content of the thought is not delusional in nature. Obsessive thoughts lie behind compulsive acts, and stereotyped or manneristic behaviour, but they may exist without being externally manifested in the form of an observable repetitive action.

ABNORMAL GAIT OR MOVEMENTS

On observing a patient, some uncontrollable movement of the body, affecting the face, head, trunk or limbs, may be apparent. Disordered movement may be the result of damage to the brain or nervous system, damage to the muscles, or the result of a biochemical imbalance, which may be medication related. It should be noted that terms such as tremor, chorea, myoclonus, tics, dystonia, and athetosis are imprecise and descriptive rather than definitive. They are not confined to particular anatomical, physiological, or pathological abnormalities. Nevertheless, their use cannot be avoided and they furnish the clinician with terms that have some practical meaning.[16] The way in which abnormal movements are categorised may be summarised as follows—

---

[16]   J.D. and J.A. Spillane, *An Atlas of Clinical Neurology* (Oxford Medical Publications, 1982), p.263.

- The most prominent functions of muscle tissue are to maintain posture and produce motion.

- The co-ordination of muscular activity involved in maintaining posture and balance mostly takes place below the level of consciousness. By contrast, the movement of joints is mainly under voluntary control of the brain and consciously intended.

- The term "involuntary movement" is used in two different senses. Firstly, movements which occur below the level of consciousness are said to be involuntary movements. Such involuntary movements are, however, entirely normal. Secondly, the execution of voluntary, willed, movements may be disrupted by unwilled and uncontrollable involuntary movements of the body, usually affecting the face, head, trunk or limbs. In this sense, all movement disorders are involuntary even when the disruption involves an interference with voluntary movement.

- **Akinesia** (literally, without movement) denotes an absence or lack of voluntary movement while **dyskinesia** (literally, bad or difficult movement) is a general term used to describe difficult or distorted voluntary movement.[17]

- Information about the state of contraction and stretch of the muscles is transmitted to the brain via nerve fibres contained in each muscle. Nerve impulses transmitted in the other direction, to the muscles, stimulate them, releasing a type of neurotransmitter called acetylcholine. This starts a chain of chemical and electrical events, involving sodium, calcium and potassium ions, which cause the muscle to contract. Potassium depletion causes muscle weakness while a decrease of calcium may cause muscle spasm.

- Contracting a muscle makes it shorter and draws together the bones to which the muscle is attached. Where two or more muscles oppose each other's actions, harmony of posture and movement requires their co-ordinated relaxation and contraction.

- **Apraxia** is an inability to carry out a voluntary ("purposive") movement despite normal muscle power and co-ordination. The defect is caused by damage to the nerve tracts which translate the idea of movement into actual movement. The person knows that he wants to move in a certain way or direction but has lost the ability to recall from memory the sequence of actions necessary to achieve the desired movement.

- **Ataxia** (literally, without order) is an inability to co-ordinate muscles in the execution of voluntary movement. The typical ataxic gait is lurching and unsteady like that of a drunkard, with the feet widely placed and a tendency to reel to one side. This lack of co-ordination and clumsiness may affect balance and gait, limb or eye movements, and cause speech to be slurred.

---

[17] However, while akinesia literally means an absence or lack of voluntary movement, it "has become the term of choice for the state of difficulty in initiating movements or changing from one motor pattern to another that is associated with Parkinson's disease." *Lexicon of Psychiatric and Mental Health Terms* (World Health Organisation, 1989), Vol. 1, p.7 .

- Rapid, rhythmic, alternate contraction and relaxation of a group of muscles produces **tremor (1066)**. This is associated with exertion and emotional arousal, and is commonly experienced by older people, but occasionally has a greater medical significance.

- Skeletal muscle is maintained in a state of partial contraction because this helps to maintain posture, keeps the eyes open, and allows the muscles to contract more efficiently. This natural muscular tension is referred to as **muscle tone**. Tone therefore denotes the natural tension in the fibres of a muscle while **dystonia** literally means bad muscle tone. Abnormally high muscle tone causes spasticity, rigidity and resistance to movement. Abnormally low muscle tone (**hypotonia**) causes floppiness of the body or part of the body affected.

- An individual's muscle tone may reflect his emotional state. Strong emotion may produce a sudden loss of muscle tone, causing the individual to collapse — **cataplexy**. Cataplexy commonly lasts for a number of seconds and, in three-quarters of cases, it is characteristic of narcolepsy. There is no loss of consciousness.

- Abnormally increased muscle tone produces **muscular rigidity** and increased resistance to movement. Muscular rigidity is therefore the result of increased tone in one or more muscles, causing them to feel tight, with the affected part of the body becoming stiff and inflexible. Muscular rigidity may result in unusually fixed postures, strange movement patterns, or painful muscular spasms.

- **Spasms** are powerful, brief, rapid, repetitive contractions of a muscle or group of muscles which are experienced as spasmodic, muscular, jerks. Hiccups, cramp, tics and habit-spasms are all types of muscular spasm. **Tics** and **habit-spasms** may both reflect and help to release emotional tension during periods of stress and so be particularly prominent at times of psychological disturbance.

- Muscles usually respond to being stretched by contracting once and then relaxing. Where stretching sets off a rapid series of muscle contractions, this is referred to as **clonus** (a word meaning "turmoil"). Clonus is therefore an abnormal response of a muscle to stretching and it is suggestive of damage or disease to the nerve fibres carrying impulses to that muscle. Clonic muscle contractions are a feature of seizures in grand mal epilepsy.

- If clonic muscular contractions are rapid and shock-like, they may be referred to as **myoclonus**. Myoclonus (literally, muscular turmoil) is a sudden, brief, shock-like, uncontrollable, jerking or spasm of a muscle or muscles ("myoclonic jerks"), which may occur either at rest or during movement. **Hemifacial spasms** (irregular shock-like contractions of the muscles on one side of the face) are a form of myoclonus.

DYSKINESIA

Dyskinesia (literally, bad or difficult movement) is a general term covering various forms of abnormal movement, including tremor, tics, ballismus, chorea, habit-spasm, torticollis, torsion-spasm, athetosis, chorea, dystonia, and myoclonus.[18] Such conditions typically involve uncontrollable movements of the trunk or limbs which cannot be suppressed and impair the execution of voluntary movements. The whole body may be involved or the problem restricted to a particular group of muscles.

Athetosis (exaggerated, sinuous, writhing movement of muscles)

The term denotes the slow, irregular, and continuous twisting of muscles in the distal (far) portions of the arms and legs. These sinuous movements are bilateral (evident on both sides of the body) and symmetric (both sides are similarly affected). Characteristically, there are exaggerated writhing motions of the fingers, which are spread in a manner reminiscent of a snake-charmer, with alternate flexion and extension of the wrists, and twisting of the muscles in the hands, fingers, feet and toes. The hands and fingers appear to be in continuous motion and the inability to maintain them in a fixed position causes difficulty with writing and tasks such as fastening buttons. When the feet are involved, the ankles and toes intermittently turn inwards, producing an irregular, unbalanced gait. In severe cases, there is grimacing, protrusion of the tongue and abnormal articulation of speech. The patient may be able to regain some control over these movements by way of concentration and they are absent during sleep.

Chorea and choreic movements (irregular, spasmodic, jerky)

Chorea is a Greek word meaning dance (as in choreography). Chorea is characterised by quick, irregular, spasmodic and jerky involuntary movement of muscles, usually affecting the face, limbs and trunk. The movements resemble voluntary movements but are continuously interrupted prior to being completed. They also disappear or are less prominent during sleep. There is a general air of restlessness in chronic patients and an excess of motor activity with impaired ability to maintain a posture. Those parts of the limbs closest to the trunk (the proximal portions) are more affected than those further away (the distal portions) and the trunk itself may be affected. The movements are more rapid and involve more muscle groups than athetotic movements. Unlike tics, they are not predictable and occur at random. Although bilateral, the muscular movements are asynchronous rather than symmetric, that is the chorea frequently affects one side of the body more than the other. **Hemichorea** is chorea affecting one side of the body only.

Choreo-athetoid movements

Choreic and athetotic movements may exist in conjunction, when their combined effect is referred to as choreo-athetosis. The movements may be caused by various pathological processes, including pathological processes initiated as a side-effect of certain drugs.

---

[18]   *Lexicon of Psychiatric and Mental Health Terms* (World Health Organisation, 1989), Vol. 1, p.37.

Tardive dyskinesia (involuntary muscle movements late in treatment)

Tardive means tardy, late. The term tardive dyskinesia refers to a type of movement disorder which appears late in treatment, characteristically after long-term treatment with antipsychotic drugs.[19] The whole body may be involved or the problem restricted to a particular group of muscles. Involuntary, slow, irregular movements of the tongue, lips, mouth, and trunk, and choreo-athetoid movements of the extremities are common. In particular, there may be twisting and protruding movements of the tongue, chewing movements of the jaw, and puckering of the lips. These uncontrollable movements cannot be suppressed.[20]

Tremor

A tremor may be described as a rhythmic, repetitive movement of some part of the body which results from the alternating contractions of opposing muscle groups. There is, however, no single standard description of what movement constitutes tremor.[21] Tremors may be described as fine (6–10 muscle movements per second) or coarse (4–5 muscle movements per second). They may be caused by antipsychotics or antidepressants, withdrawal from drugs or alcohol.

TYPES OF TREMOR

At-rest tremor	At-rest tremors are worse when the affected part of the body is relaxed, supported and at rest, usually improving when the affected limb is used.
Postural tremor	Postural tremor is a fine tremor activated during attempts to sustain a posture (*e.g.*, extending an arm, supporting a leg, holding up the head, turning back the wrists) but absent when the limb is supported and at rest.
Action (intention) tremor	Action tremors occur mainly, or are most marked, when a movement is attempted, with the result that the patient's purpose is frustrated. Hence, they are commonly tested for by asking the patient to touch the tip of his nose with the tip of his finger; as the finger approaches the nose the intention tremor increases.
Essential tremor	A persistent, fine-moderate tremor (6–10 movements per second) not associated with disease. The tremors are fine, mainly affecting the hand and head. They are common in adults, tend to increase with age and to be aggravated by emotional tension, may be temporarily relieved by alcohol, and may affect particular occupations. They may increase when the affected part of the body is moved.

---

[19] In contrast, dystonic reactions to medication usually appear after a few doses.

[20] *Lexicon of Psychiatric and Mental Health Terms* (World Health Organisation, 1989), Vol. 1, pp.37–38. The term **(oro-) facial dyskinesia** is sometimes used to describe repetitive smacking, grimacing, champing, chewing, and swallowing movements involving the lips, tongue, and jaw.

[21] J.D. and J.A. Spillane, *An Atlas of Clinical Neurology* (Oxford Medical Publications, 3rd ed., 1982), p.263.

Tics (habit-spasms)

A tic is a repeated, uncontrolled, purposeless contraction of a muscle or group of muscles. For example, superficially purposeless blinking, mouth twitching, shrugging, or the involuntary contraction of the diaphragm (which results in grunting noises). These habitual, spasmodic, muscular contractions tend to be experienced as irresistible, but they can usually be suppressed for varying periods of time and they disappear during sleep.[22] Tics release emotional tension and are generally a sign of minor psychological disturbance, being made worse at times of stress. Occasionally, they are severe, as in Gilles de la Tourette's syndrome.

AKATHISIA (INABILITY TO SIT STILL)

Akathisia is a restless inability to sit still ("a motor restlessness") associated with a feeling of muscular quivering. It is often seen as a side-effect of neuroleptic medication or as a complication of Parkinson's disease.[23] It may be so intense that the person affected finds it impossible to sit still, day or night.

DYSTONIA (MUSCULAR RIGIDITY CAUSING SPASMS)

Dystonic means relating to abnormal muscular tension and, strictly speaking, the term encompasses both excessive or exaggerated tone and deficient or absent tone. However, in common usage, the term describes an abnormal muscular rigidity causing painful and sustained muscle spasms of some part of the body, unusually fixed postures, or strange movement patterns. Dystonic movements usually take the form of a twisting or turning motion of the neck, the trunk, or the proximal parts of the extremities. They are therefore powerful and deforming, grossly interfering with voluntary movement, and perverting posture.[24] **Acute dystonia** may occur as a transient complication of neuroleptic medication. **Torsion dystonia**[25] — torsion means twisting — is a term sometimes used to describe involuntary movements of a slow, powerful character, which produce tension and torsion spasm of the limbs and spine. The consequential abnormalities of gait may be quite bizarre.[26] **Wry neck** or **torticollis** (Latin for "crooked neck") is a common example of torsion dystonia. It describes a twisting of the neck which causes the head to be rotated and tilted into an abnormal position, in which it remains.[27]

PHYSICAL SYMPTOMS AND SIGNS

Physical health problems may be real or imaginary and also the product of a person's mental state rather than its cause. A **conversion symptom** is a loss or alteration of physical functioning that suggests a physical disorder, but that is actually a direct

---

[22]   *Lexicon of Psychiatric and Mental Health Terms* (World Health Organisation, 1989), p.102.

[23]   R.J. Campbell, *Psychiatric Dictionary* (Oxford University Press, 6th ed., 1989), p. 24.

[24]   J.D. and J.A. Spillane, *An Atlas of Clinical Neurology* (Oxford Medical Publications, 3rd ed., 1982).

[25]   Torsion dystonia is also sometimes referred to as **Dystonia Musculorum Deformans** or as **Generalised Torsion Dystonia**. It is usually familial and particularly common among Jews of Russian descent.

[26]   J.D. and J.A. Spillane, *An Atlas of Clinical Neurology,* supra, p.281 *et seq.*

[27]   Some writers categorise writer's cramp and **blepharospasm** (the involuntary, prolonged contraction of one of the muscles that controls the eyelids, causing the eyes to close) as forms of dystonia.

expression of a psychological conflict or need. The disturbance is not under voluntary control, and is not explained by any physical disorder. **Hypochondriasis** denotes an unrealistic belief or fear that one is suffering from a serious illness despite medical reassurance.

PHYSICAL SIGNS

Eyes
Nystagmus is a condition in which there is involuntary movement of the eyes, usually horizontally and in a manner resembling the action of windscreen wipers. Occasionally, only one eye is affected. Persistent nystagmus appearing in later life usually indicates a disorder of the nervous system such as multiple sclerosis, brain tumour or an alcohol related disorder. An **oculogyric crisis** is a state of fixed gaze lasting minutes or hours in which the eyes are turned in a particular direction, usually upwards, sometimes with accompanying spasms of the head, mouth and neck. This may be drug-induced, the product of emotional stress, a sequela of encephalitis or a sign of Parkinson's Disease. **Exophthalmus** is protrusion of the eye ball and is indicative of a thyroid disorder. **Photophobia** means an uncomfortable sensitivity or intolerance to light. It is most often seen as an adverse effect of antipsychotic medication although it may be a feature of meningitis. **Blepharospasm** is the involuntary, prolonged contraction of one of the muscles that controls the eyelids, causing the eyes to close. This may be the result of photophobia, an inflammation of the eyelids, anxiety or hysteria.

Eyelids
Lid-lag is a momentary delay in the normal downward movement of the upper eyelids that occurs when the eye looks down. In **Lid retraction**, a rim of white sclera is seen above the iris when the patient looks ahead. Both are characteristic of hyperthyroidism . **Ptosis** is the drooping of an upper eyelid when the eyes are open.

Face
Facies is the expression of the face. Hirsuties, mooning and reddening of the face may be features of Cushing's syndrome.

Limbs
As to movement disorders, see **1062**.

Trunk
As to movement disorders, see **1062**. Truncal obesity with relatively thin matchstick legs and a buffalo-hump are classically features of Cushing's syndrome.

Genitalia
Psychotropic medication may cause sexual problems. Antipsychotics may be associated with enlargement of the breasts in men. In other cases, the absence of menstrual periods may be a feature of anorexia nervosa, an endocrinal disorder, Turner's Syndrome, or secondary to emotional stress or depression, or a side-effect of certain drugs.

Skin
Skin problems are most often an adverse effect of medication. The greater the amount of melanin present the darker the colouration. Darkened skin may therefore be caused not only of exposure to the sun but by a hormonal disorder such as Addison's disease or Cushing's Syndrome. It may also be caused by an excess of other types of pigments in the blood, such as the bile pigment bilirubin (in jaundice) or iron.

Weight
Pronounced weight loss is seen in eating disorders, depression, physical illness.

Disturbed sleep

Insomnia is a general term denoting dissatisfaction with the duration or quality of sleep. In depression, the sufferer commonly wakes early in the morning, often between 3am and 5am — **early morning waking**. In contrast, the tendency in anxiety states is to experience difficulty getting to sleep — **initial insomnia**. **Narcolepsy** describes short periods of sleep which occur irresistibly during the day. **Hypersomnia** means an excess of sleep, whether at night or because of periods of day-time somnolence. In manic states, the over-active individual feels a decreased need for sleep and may go several days without sleeping. **Somnambulism** means sleep-walking. More often, what a client describes as sleep-walking is in fact a **night terror**, which occurs early on during sleep. The individual imagines that there is a person at the window or that the ceiling is about to fall in and suffocate him. Feeling that he is in profound danger, he may run from the bedroom in a state of panic. On coming to, he is amnesic for the event and is initially confused about how he came to be in another room or outdoors. Some people suffering from schizophrenia may feel that other people have entered their room and that they have been violated during sleep, either sexually or in some other way. For example, the patient's hair was cut.

General appearance and physical signs

Physical signs may be pointers to the fact that the patient's mental state has an organic cause and the table on the previous page lists some of these features. The patient's physical health may also be a pointer towards his mental health in other, generally obvious, ways. There may be signs of recent physical injury, possibly sustained in the course of the suicide attempt. Superficial, multiple, lacerations of the arms and wrists are most often not indicative of attempted suicide but a way of relieving acute tension. "Track-marks" on the arms may indicate the use of inject-able street drugs. What may cruelly be referred to as physical deformities are sometimes, for that very reason, relevant to the client's mental health since they carry with them a considerable psychological burden.

Self-care and self-neglect

If a patient has not washed, shaved or recently changed his clothes, or is inadequately dressed given the temperature and conditions on the ward, this may be a sign of poor self-care due to an incapacitating mental disorder. Self-neglect of this kind may be a consequence of the negative symptoms of schizophrenia, and part of a general picture of apathy, poor motivation and social withdrawal. In other cases, poor self-care may be attributable to grandiose delusions (the client has let his beard grow and cultivated a Jesus-like appearance); depression with retardation or stupor; dementia; mental impairment; and obsessive-compulsive disorders characterised by incapacitating rituals about dressing and bathing.

Other reasons for dishevelled appearance

There are, of course, many other reasons why a patient's general appearance may be poor, including poverty, the sedative effects of medication, an inefficient hospital laundry service, and the fact that no one has collected any spare clothing or toiletries for him since he was detained.

Memory enables us to give order and meaning to the world (to classify information) and so to predict events and affect their outcomes. Learning depends on memory for its permanency while memory has no content if learning is not taking place. The capacity for new learning is sometimes referred to as "current memorising" and it has the most important clinical implications. Memory failure is a sensitive indicator of cerebral dysfunction. **Amnesia** is a general term which describes loss of memory manifested by a total or partial inability to recall past experiences. Amnesic conditions affect mainly long-term memory. The amnesia may be for events immediately prior to a head injury (**retrograde**) or for events occurring following such a trauma (**anterograde**[28]).

Information which is committed to memory

The following kinds of information are committed to memory —

- internal perceptions or representations of events external to the brain, sometimes in a distorted form (sense data);

- internal perceptions or representations generated internally within the brain (imaginations);

- thoughts (the analysis and interpretation of sense data and imaginations);

- feelings (the emotional connotations associated with stored information).

Data is therefore given a meaning and a feeling and, when recalled, may be reinterpreted: recalled events are reanalysed, rearranged or re-evaluated in light of subsequent information and restored in an amended form. The need to also record any thoughts and feelings associated with each piece of memorised information is essential to survival and learning. Not only must the sequence of events be recalled but also any information associated with it about the quality of the experience and the outcome: whether it was desirable or undesirable, whether a particular response or reaction alleviated or exacerbated the situation, and so forth. Without this, it is impossible to develop judgement and to avoid repeatedly making the same mistake and, consequently, impaired judgement is often a consequence of impaired memory. In rare cases, there may be complete indifference to a situation, as if the emotion associated with a given event has been dissociated from it.

Memorising (registering and storing information)

Memorising is the ability to register and retain what is experienced. Not everything which registers on the sense receptors is stored. About one-hundredth of the sensory information reaches consciousness and of this about one-twentieth may be stored in some form. Sensory input is retained within the immediate memory for about half a second in an essentially unanalysed form. The short-term memory allows the relevance of a limited amount of data to be evaluated, generally by reference to a framework formed by past experience. Material which is considered to be relevant

---

[28] The glossary to the Internal Classification of Diseases uses the term "amnestic."

to the individual's situation is fitted into the long-term memory. Information is therefore memorised at three different levels —

- Immediate memory (sensory storage). Information is held for less than a second in the form in which it was perceived before being replaced by other incoming stimuli. Sensory memory seems to be modality specific: storage occurs within the sensory system that received the information and not at some central location. Additional information entering the same sensory channel immediately disrupts the storage.[29]

- Primary memory (short-term or working memory). Some new material is stored for evaluation in the short-term memory. Approximately six or seven items of information can be stored in the working memory for up to 20 seconds. The method used by the brain to store this information (the "code") appears to be primarily acoustic: information is converted into sound and stored in this form. Because this is so, rehearsal and repetition by mental or verbal speech — for example, repeating a telephone number to oneself or out loud — can increase the memory's duration beyond 20 seconds. Some types of schizophrenia are marked by repetition of this kind and problems emptying the working memory. As new items are added to the short-term memory, previous ones are lost, either disappearing or, where required for future use, being committed to long-term memory.

- Secondary memory (long-term memory). Some new information is fitted into an organized body of knowledge in which case a permanent trace is formed, although this may later be modified by subsequent activity. The capacity of the long-term memory store is large and such memories may endure for the rest of an individual's life. Information is stored in coded form, either semantically (verbal meaning), visually (pictorially), acoustically, or by association with previously stored information. This accounts for the predominance of hallucinations and thought disorder (*e.g.* loosening of associations and idiosyncratic use of vocabulary and language) in schizophrenia; and also the fact that, because little is known about the mechanisms involved in memory, little is known about that illness. Indeed, both schizophrenia and memory are hypothetical constructs.

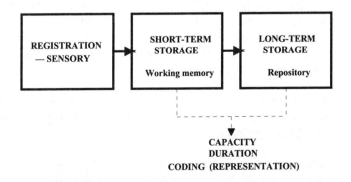

[29]   Richard D. Gross, *Psychology, The Science of Mind and Behaviour* (Hodder & Stoughton, 2nd ed., 1992), p. 311.

Remembering and recognizing things

Remembrance involves the ability to retrieve, recall and reproduce what has been learned or experienced. A new situation requiring the utilization of the information stored in the trace has to be recognized and the required information retrieved, that is isolated from the rest of the stored materials. Recognition is the awareness that something which is now happening is familiar and it involves forming associations between what is now happening and what has previously been memorised. If a person is faced with an unfamiliar fact, place or event, whether because it is new to him or because he fails to recognise that he has previously encountered essentially the same situation, he may feel perplexed or disorientated.

Memory problems

The individual's capacity to record what he is registering and to retain it, that is to store knowledge, may be divided into immediate, recent and remote memory. Immediate or short-term memory is often tested by giving the patient seven numbers and asking him to repeat them forwards and then backwards; by telling him a name and address and asking him to repeat it verbatim after a single hearing; and by giving him three objects to remember. When the long-term memory is tested, a distinction is usually drawn between "recent" and "remote" memory. Recent memory is tested by asking the patient a question about his activities during the previous 48 hours and then checking the accuracy of his account with a nurse. Remote memory involves remembering events which were memorised a considerable period ago, for instance the client's wedding day or first day at school. If a person cannot remember or accurately remember information, the problem may lie at any one or more of the stages which comprise the memory process. The inability may be due to a failure to register or store the information in the first place (no record was ever made); the loss or degradation of the record because of defective retention or an intervening decision to erase it; an inability to locate the record (the information is available but not accessible, because it was not systematically stored or cannot be systematically searched for). More particularly,

- Much information is not selected for storage because its relevance and utility are not considered to warrant this. Other events are so stressful for an individual that they are deliberately not committed to long-term memory. In yet other cases, the individual's capacity to register what is happening, that is to add to his memory store, may be reduced. This incapacity may be temporary, as where fatigue limits the amount of information which can be assimilated, or indicative of a more profound problem.

- The individual's capacity to retain and record what he is registering and to retain it may be defective. Impairment of recent memory may be an early finding in dementias.

- Certain memorised information is later forgotten. This may represent deliberate erasure following a decision that the information is no longer useful or there may be some problem retrieving and recalling stored information. Stored information will be "forgotten" if it is lost (overwritten, degraded, or inaccessible) or cannot be retrieved (squirrel phenomena).

- Information which can be retrieved may be accurately or inaccurately recalled. In other words, it may be a faithful or unfaithful reproduction of what was observed and registered. Information may be distorted or falsified because it was too emotionally charged and distressing in its original form. Whether or not conscious of the fact, the individual prefers not to remember information associated with humiliation.

- The individual may be lying. For example, a person who has committed a serious sexual offence of which he is deeply ashamed may have suppressed certain memories of it or he may be able to recall the whole event but prefer to edit what information he imparts to others.

- Lying (deliberate falsehood) must, however, be distinguished from guessing and **confabulation**. Confabulation involves filling in deficits in memory with false responses or information. It differs from lying in that the person is not consciously attempting to deceive. Confabulation may be a feature of amnesic syndromes such as Korsakoff's syndrome and dementia.

MOOD, AFFECT AND EMOTIONAL STATES

Affect is the way in which a person is emotionally affected by an idea or perception. However, some psychiatrists use the words affect and mood interchangeably while others use "mood" as a term for the prevailing emotional tone (equivalent to affect), referring to the underlying, sustained, mood as the "mood state." Some simply lump together every kind of emotional distress (depression, elation, anger, irritability, panic, fear, anxiety) under the general rubric of "the patient's mood." The approach taken here is to restrict the term mood to states of depression or elation; the term affect to emotional responsiveness; and to deal with other emotions, such as anger, separately. This is because many of these other emotions may or may not be associated with depression or elation and are commonly seen in people whose mood, as defined, is normal.

AFFECT

A person's affect is how he appears to be emotionally affected by an idea or perception. For example, he seems happy, sad, or indifferent. A person whose mood is normal may nevertheless be profoundly affected emotionally by some idea or perception. Psychiatrists are particularly interested in whether a person's emotional responsiveness is impaired. Affect is often described as being **flat** (absent or very limited emotional range); **blunted** (severe lack of normal emotional sensitivity); **shallow or restricted** (reduced); appropriate, harmonious or **congruous**; inappropriate or **incongruous**; or **labile** (unstable). Incongruous affect describes the incongruity between what a person is saying and his affect. For example, a patient laughs or displays no concern when recounting how his imaginary persecutors intend to kill him. **Apathy** is emotional indifference and, as such, it is virtually indistinguishable from flat or blunted affect. It is common in depression and certain forms of schizophrenia although resignation, rather than true indifference, often better describes the patient's lack of responsiveness. Apathy must therefore be distinguished from the hopelessness which is often the final stage of depression and also from **La Belle Indifference** (literally, "beautiful indifference"), a sublime resignation to distressing symptoms which are the product of hysteria.

MOOD

Mood is the pervasive and sustained emotion which colours an individual's whole personality and perception of events. Consequently, it is sometimes described as sustained affect and mood disorders may inaccurately be said to involve a morbid change of affect. The expression **euthymic mood** describes a normal or equable mood. Inferences about mood generally stem from present observations and past events.

Heightened mood

Various words are used to describe the features of heightened mood, many of them essentially interchangeable. **Hyperthymia** is a tendency to be overcheerful and unrealistically optimistic. **Elation** consists of feelings of euphoria, triumph, immense self-satisfaction or optimism. **Euphoria** is an exaggerated feeling of physical or emotional well-being seen in organic mental states and in toxic and drug-induced states. **Exaltation** is an excessively intensified sense of well-being seen in manic states. **Ecstasy** describes a state of elation beyond reason and control or a trance state of overwhelming (often religious) fervour. **Grandiosity**, although not usually bracketed with mood, describes feelings of tremendous importance, characterised by an inflated appraisal of one's worth, power, knowledge, importance, or identity, and commonly expressed as absurd exaggerations. Extreme grandiosity may attain delusional proportions and is seen in mania and schizophrenia.

Depressed mood

Dysthymia is a long-standing tendency to be sad and miserable and a person with this outlook on life is sometimes said to have a **dysthymic personality**. **Depression** describes feelings characterised by sadness, apathy, pessimism and a sense of loneliness. **Melancholia** is simply the Latin word for melancholy and is essentially synonymous with depressión. **Anhedonia** is a feature of depression and refers to an inability to experience pleasure in acts that normally are pleasurable.

Fluctuating Mood

Cyclothymia, a term invented by Kahlbaum, describes a personality characteristic typified by marked changes of mood (cyclothymic personality). **Lability of mood** is emotional instability, a rapidly changing mood. The person affected may laugh one minute and cry the next without there being any corresponding change in external stimuli to account for that.

Inappropriate mood

Mood-congruent psychotic features are delusions or hallucinations the content of which is entirely consistent with the individual's depressed or manic mood. Thus, if the individual's mood is depressed, the content of the delusions or hallucinations involve themes of personal inadequacy, guilt, disease, death, nihilism, or deserved punishment. Likewise, if the mood is manic, their content involves themes of inflated worth, power, knowledge, or identity or special relationship to a deity or a famous person. Conversely, **mood-incongruent psychotic features** are delusions or hallucinations the content of which is inconsistent with either a depressed or a manic mood. If a distinction is drawn between a person's affect and his mood, the patient may instead be described as having an incongruous or inappropriate affect.

OTHER EMOTIONAL STATES

Many other terms are used to describe an individual's emotional state, among them anxiety, fear, agitation, restlessness, panic, and irritability. The customary distinction between the first two of them used to be that fear always had an object (whether a situation or thing) whereas anxiety was fear without an object or dread. Unfortunately, the current definitions of anxiety in the international classifications have eroded this useful distinction.

Anxiety

Anxiety is characterised by an apprehension, tension, or uneasiness that stems from the anticipation of danger. The associated symptoms include tachycardia (abnormal rapidity of heart beat), palpitations, breathlessness, and light-headedness. Both of the main international classifications distinguish between anxiety which is tied to or focused on some particular situation (**specific anxiety**) or object (**phobia**) and generalised anxiety where no such external triggering factor is apparent (**free-floating anxiety**). The ICD classification also distinguishes between **trait anxiety** and **state anxiety**, the former being an enduring aspect of personality and the latter a temporary disorder.

Fear

Phobia denotes a persistent irrational fear of, and desire to avoid, a particular object or situation. In **Agoraphobia**, the fear is one of going into open spaces and of entering public places: the patient is filled with dread at the prospect of venturing out of his home and may experience panic attacks. In some cases, what initially seems to be agoraphobia may transpire to be **claustrophobia** (a fear of enclosed spaces). Thus, a patient may not venture out of his home because of the suffocating, claustrophobic, effects of being in a crowded shopping centre rather than because of a fear of open spaces. If the individual has a chronic abnormal fear that he is ill or diseased, this is termed **hypochondriasis**.

Irritability

Anxiety may be expressed as irritability. The depressed patient may become anxious about his inability to respond positively to the problems surrounding him, which makes him anxious and often increasingly irritable. Conversely, sustained, unremitting anxiety and irritability have a depressive effect over a period of time because the individual's performance is constantly undermined and dejection sets in.

Agitation and restlessness

In other cases, uncontrollable anxiety or fear surface in the form of motor restlessness (agitation) which, as with tics, both reflects and appears to partially alleviate the underlying state of tension. The ICD classification reserves the term "agitation" for cases where anxiety is accompanied by "marked restlessness and excessive motor activity" — states referred to in the DSM classification as **psychomotor agitation**. There is a restless, usually non-productive and repetitious, inability to keep still as a result of the underlying tension. The patient may pace up and down, pick at his clothes or skin, be unable to concentrate or relax and so start but not complete various tasks. In severe cases, there may be shouting or loud complaining. Restlessness caused by certain drugs may mimic agitation (see akathisia, **1067**).

Panic

A further way of dealing with anxiety or fear is to attempt to repress it. Anxiety or fear may surface in discrete periods of sudden onset and be accompanied by physical symptoms — panic attacks. A **panic attack** is a sudden, overwhelming anxiety or fear, sometimes accompanied by an intense fear of dying and associated with particular times, places, thoughts or ideas. Hyperventilation occurs with fast, shallow, breathing and a range of other physical symptoms.

Aggression and hostility

Fear may lead to aggression and hostility. Biologically, aggressiveness is a component of animal behaviour which is released in particular conditions in order to satisfy vital needs or to eliminate an environmental threat. In the case of patients who are irrationally fearful, aggression and hostility perform the same function as in cases where there is an objectively real threat to the individual's safety. The individual attempts to eliminate fear by eliminating its cause.

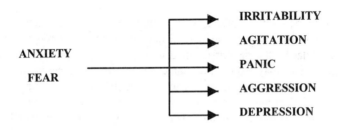

DISORDERED SPEECH OR THOUGHT

Thinking is a form of activity engaged in by a biological organism whenever habitual patterns of action are disrupted and the function of thought is to solve the problems which give rise to it.[30] An individual's thoughts may be kept private or expressed. Expression may be verbal or non-verbal. A thought may be expressed non-verbally by an action, an omission to act, a bodily movement such as a grimace or gesticulation, or a display of emotion such as anger. The movement of muscles to produce speech is an activity, a form of behaviour, just as much as is the movement

---

[30]   See J. Dewey, *Experience and Nature* (Open Court, 1925).

of muscles in the limbs to produce motion or to perform some physical act. Unless thoughts are deliberately concealed, or their articulation is impaired by a poor vocabulary or damage to the mechanics involved in producing speech, its flow and content correspond to the flow of the individual's thoughts, so that disordered speech frequently reflects disordered thought. More particularly, "we are subjectively aware of our thought process being a stream or a flow ... thoughts are capable of acceleration and slowing, of eddies and calms, of precipitous falls, of increased volume of flow, of blockages."[31] The point, though obvious, is nevertheless important because it focuses attention on the fact that many of the terms used to describe abnormal thought processes on the one hand and abnormal speech on the other are for all practical purposes synonymous. Thus, while some textbooks refer to paucity of thought, one can just as well say that the patient's presentation is marked by poverty of speech if the former conclusion is based only on his observed speech output. If a person's speech is abnormal, this may be because the amount of speech is outside normal bounds; because the production of speech is impaired; because his choice of words is abnormal; because the succession and connection of ideas is illogical; or because its content is abnormal. That being so, abnormalities of speech and thought are dealt with in the following order—

- Abnormal volume (amount) and rate (tempo) of speech

- Abnormal delivery of speech (articulation)

- Abnormal choice or use of words (vocabulary)

- Abnormal juxtaposition of words, or the ideas conveyed by them, in phrases and sentences (syntax and the association of ideas)

- Abnormal content of thought (delusions, over-valued ideas, etc.)

THE VOLUME (AMOUNT) AND RATE (TEMPO) OF SPEECH

The amount of speech used may be excessive or restricted. In extreme cases, an individual may be mute or talk incessantly. When seeking to establish the cause of this, it is important to establish whether the amount of speech varies according to the subject under discussion and whether the structure of speech is normal or its rhythm or inflexion disturbed. Due allowance must be made if English is not the patient's usual language and for other factors influencing communication, such as sedating drugs.

No speech or little speech which is slow and laboured

Retarded thought (thinking which proceeds slowly towards its goal) is reflected in the individual's speech and when the amount of speech is very limited this is sometimes referred to as **poverty of speech.** In extreme cases, the patient is mute, being either unable or unwilling to speak. **Mutism** may be seen in cases of catatonic schizophrenia and severe depression. The term **akinetic mutism** describes a state of disturbed consciousness due to a tumour of the third ventricle, as a result of which the patient is mute and almost totally unresponsive. **Aphonia** is a total loss of the

---

[31]   A. Sims, *Symptoms in the Mind* (Baillière Tindall, 1988), p.108.

voice which cannot be accounted for by any disease or injury of the larynx ("voice-box"). It is usually sudden in onset and caused by emotional stress.

Speech is fast, rapid, accelerated

Copious, excessive, production of speech is known as volubility or **logorrhoea**. It may be seen in mania or schizophrenic disorders. Where the amount and rate of a patient's speech is increased so that he is difficult to interrupt, this is referred to as **pressure of speech**. In **flight of ideas**, there is a nearly continuous flow of accelerated speech with no central direction. The patient jumps from one topic to another, his stream of thought directed by chance associations between each fragment of conversation. In some cases, this flitting from subject to subject may be determined not by any logical relationship or progression in terms of subject-matter or meaning but by the way words rhyme or by similarities in sound — **clang associations** or **clanging**.

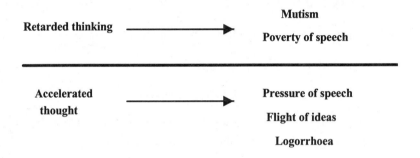

THE DELIVERY OF SPEECH (ARTICULATION)

Whether or not the volume and velocity of thought and therefore speech is normal, its delivery may nevertheless be abnormal. For example, the individual may stammer or stutter, that is show repeated hesitation or delay in uttering words. **Dysarthria** (disturbed articulation) is difficulty in speech production caused by disease or damage to the physical apparatus of speech or to the nerve pathways controlling that apparatus; it is the vocal expression which causes problems. Dysarthria is a common feature of many degenerative conditions such as multiple sclerosis, Parkinson's disease and Huntington's chorea, and it may a side-effect of prescribed medication (*e.g.* tardive dyskinesia). In other cases, the cause may be more mundane, for example alcohol intoxication or ill-fitting dentures.

Dysphonia

Dysphonia has a more restricted meaning than dysarthria and refers only to defects of sound production caused by some disease or damage to the voice-box (larynx) or to the nerve supply to the laryngeal muscles. In cases of depression, the patient may speak with a monotonous voice while manic patients often talk in a particularly animated way.

THE CHOICE OF WORDS AND VOCABULARY

The way certain words or phrases are used may sometimes be distinctive, because they are repeated, or clearly have a special significance for the individual, or represent words which he has invented. More generally, their usage may suggest a limited vocabulary and hence limited education, limited innate intellectual ability, loss of intellectual ability (*e.g.* dementia), or a poor grasp of the language in someone for whom English is not their first language.

Descriptive terms

Echolalia, verbigeration and perseveration describe different kinds of repetition of words and phrases—

- **Perseveration** denotes the persistent repetition of words, phrases or ideas. The initial thought, or train of thought, is maintained despite a change of topic, as in the following example: "Q. What is your name? "A. John Smith. Q. Where do you live? "A. John Smith." Perseveration is most commonly seen in organic mental disorders, schizophrenia, and other psychotic disorders.

- Where the patient instead persistently repeats back a syllable, word or phrase spoken by the interviewer, rather than a word or phrase previously spoken by himself, this is known as **echolalia**. Typical echolalia tends to be repetitive and persistent. The other person's tone and accent may also be echoed, often with a mocking, mumbling, or staccato intonation. Echolalia may occur in cases of schizophrenia, autism, mental impairment, or organic disorder.

- **Verbigeration** is the stereotyped and superficially meaningless repetition of words or sentences, which is not an echoing of something said to the patient.

- Where a patient uses a certain *word or phrase* repeatedly throughout a conversation, such that it is clear that it has a special importance or meaning for him, such phrases are known as **stock phrases**.

- A **neologism** is a new word invented by the patient, often a portmanteau. For example, the word "bancid" may be an amalgam of the words "bad" and "rancid." Neologisms may be observed in schizophrenia and other psychotic disorders.

- Neologisms should be distinguished from the situation where a patient has difficulty finding the correct word or where he uses a known word in an idiosyncratic and not entirely correct way (**metonyms**).

- The term **coprolalia** describes the repeated *involuntary* utterance of socially unacceptable or obscene words and it is sometimes seen in de la Tourette's syndrome. However, most often, the repeated use of swear words and other obscenities is simply voluntary or habitual, a sign of poor social upbringing rather than mental disorder.

Language disorders

A patient's choice of words, or his inability to remember a word, may in rare cases form part of a more pervasive cerebral disorder and be associated with impaired capacity to read or write. **Aphasia** is, strictly speaking, a complete loss of the ability to select the words with which to speak and write caused by damage to the regions of the brain concerned with speech and its comprehension. **Dysphasia** denotes a disturbance rather than a complete absence of these previously acquired language skills. There are several types of aphasia but no agreement as to how to classify them. **Agraphia** is caused by damage to the cerebrum and signifies a loss or impaired ability to write in a person whose hand and arm muscles function normally. Agraphia usually occurs as part of aphasia or, rarely, by itself. **Alexia** (word-blindness) denotes an inability to recognise and name written words in a person who was previously literate, the disorder being caused by damage to the cerebrum. Most often, such alexia occurs as part of aphasia.

THE STRUCTURE AND FORM OF THOUGHT

Minor defects in the form or structure of spoken thoughts may be attributable to inadequate education, fatigue, anxiety, boredom, frustration, or intellectual impairment. Broken or fragmented speech may similarly merely demonstrate a lack of command of English in someone for whom English is not their first language. However, in some cases, the patient's answers suggest that his thought processes are so disturbed that he cannot grasp the point of the question. Alternatively, the way in which words are formed into sentences may be highly idiosyncratic, the successive ideas conveyed by them being conjoined to form phrases or sentences which have little logical connection. They do not appear to form a chain of reasoning.

Failure to grasp the purpose of a question

Even though a question is simply expressed and unambiguous, it may be apparent that the other person has not understood its meaning or purpose, that is the information which it was intended to elicit. This may be because the person has interpreted the question too literally and is capable of thinking only in concrete terms —
concrete thinking. Concrete thinking is seen in schizophrenia and it is characterised by literalness, an inability to abstract or to form the whole from its parts.

Rational or conceptual thinking

Rational or conceptual thinking involves the use of logic to solve problems. It involves recognizing and classifying a problem so that reason can be applied to find a solution.[32] All reasoning represents a logical association of ideas. The thoughts and ideas developed in a patient's answer may flow logically in that there is an obvious connection or "association" between an expressed idea and the thoughts immediately preceding and following it. Conscious thinking therefore has a goal towards which clear and relevant thoughts move. Along the fringe of this main theme (determinative idea) are numerous less clearly defined thoughts or associations running parallel to the main theme.[33]

---

[32]   A. Sims, *Symptoms in the Mind* (Baillière Tindall, 1988), p.107.
[33]   *Ibid.*, Chap. 8.

Associated ideas

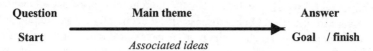

Question	**Main theme**	**Answer**
Start		**Goal** / **finish**

Associated ideas

Loosening of associations

It is sometimes the case that there is no logical association between the various thoughts expressed in response to a question. The successive thoughts, sentences and topics are not obviously goal-directed or connected in a chain of thought. The patient fails to answer the question posed. This lack of association may vary in its severity. Marked inability to consciously develop a chain of thought is considered to be indicative of mental disorder and, more particularly, a key feature of schizophrenia. The terminology used to describe disturbed association of ideas is, however, not firmly established. For example, some psychiatrists use the term loosening of associations or tangentiality of thought to refer to any inability to arrange successive ideas in order, whatever the severity of the disturbance. Subject to this caveat, disturbed associations between ideas may be categorised as follows—

- In its mildest form, conversation is vague and answers to questions "woolly." **Tangentiality** means replying to a question in an oblique or even irrelevant manner.

- In some cases, there is such a loose connection between the successive thoughts expressed by successive sentences that the goal is never attained — **loosening of associations**. Successive thoughts are either unrelated or only obliquely related although the speaker is unaware that the statements which he is juxtaposing lack any meaningful relationship. Loosening of associations therefore represents a disturbance in the association of thoughts which renders speech inexact, vague, diffused or unfocused. The term **knight's move thinking** is also sometimes used to describe such odd, tangential, associations between ideas.

- When loosening of associations is severe, speech may be incoherent. The speech is mostly not understandable owing to a lack of any logical connection between words, phrases, or sentences; the excessive use of incomplete sentences; excessive irrelevancies or abrupt changes in subject matter; idiosyncratic word usage; and distorted grammar. **Incoherence** may be seen in organic mental disorders and schizophrenia but the term is not used if abrupt shifts in topics are associated with a nearly continuous flow of accelerated, manic, speech. This is referred to as **flight of ideas**.

- At its most severe, not only is there no logical association between successive thoughts but a lack of association between successive words, which form a meaningless jumble. This is known as **word salad**.

Circumstantial thought

By convention, a distinction is drawn between loosening of associations and circumstantiality of thought. Circumstantial thought describes speech which, although relevant to the subject being discussed and eventually answering the question is indirect and delayed in reaching the point because of unnecessary, tedious details and parenthetical remarks. Circumstantial replies or statements may be prolonged for many minutes if the speaker is not interrupted and urged to get to the point. Circumstantial thought is also differentiated from **poverty of ideas** in which speech conveys little information because of vagueness, empty repetitions, or use of stereotyped or obscure phrases: the individual speaks at some length but commonly does not give adequate information to answer a question.[34]

Thought blocking and derailment of thoughts

Loosening of associations is further distinguished from thought blocking and derailment of thought although all affect the patient's ability to follow through a chain of ideas. In **derailment of thought**, there is a sudden deviation in the train of thought, as if a train travelling from one station to another (here from question to answer) had been derailed. In **thought blocking**, the patient's stream of thought, and therefore speech, suddenly stops in mid-flow for no obvious reason. He is either unable to account for the stoppage or attributes it to his thoughts being interfered with by a third party. Such blocking aside, the person may be able to pursue a chain of thought. Thought blocking of this kind differs from mere reticence or defensiveness. If a person is simply being defensive, the structure of his speech is normal and some questions are answered promptly. It is only when a sensitive subject is touched upon that any significant hesitancy or pause is apparent in midstream. The patient may at the same time become aroused, anxious, quiet or elevated.

THE CONTENT OF THOUGHT (BELIEFS AND IDEAS)

Even if the structure and form of a person's thought, and therefore speech, appears normal nevertheless the ideas expressed by him (the content of his thought) may be markedly abnormal. When a person has a thought, an idea, he means that he is conscious of having it. Thoughts of which a person is conscious may or may not be verbalised and they may be memorised or forgotten.

Beliefs, ideas and feelings

A belief is a thought which is considered by its holder to have an explanatory value so that the relevance of other thoughts and perceptions is determined by reference to it and the framework which it forms together with the individual's other beliefs. It is therefore an idea which, having been submitted to scrutiny in the light of available evidence, is deemed to account for observed phenomena and so to have an explanatory and predictive quality. An **idée fixe** is an unshakeable preconception or conviction. A "feeling" is a sub-conscious, or barely conscious, thought which is evoked by another thought or perception (something seen, heard, touched, or smelt) but cannot be put into words. A suspicion is a feeling or an idea falling short of a belief that some other person intends to harm the individual or his interests. This commonly leads to reticence, guardedness, defensiveness or secrecy on the individual's part.

---

[34]   A. Sims, *Symptoms in the Mind* (Baillière Tindall, 1988), p.134.

Delusions

In some cases, a belief may be so obviously false and irrational that it constitutes a delusion. A delusion is a belief which is bizarre; not true to fact; cannot be corrected by an appeal to reason; and is out of harmony with the holder's educational or cultural background. The fact that it is manifestly inconsistent with beliefs which the individual is known to have previously held, although not a defining feature, is often the final conclusive evidence that the belief is delusional.

Systematised delusions

Delusional ideas may be fleeting in nature, changeable and unconnected with each other — **unsystematized delusions** — or they may form part of a logical fixed system of such beliefs — **systematized delusions**. An example of the latter is that of a man who, having failed his bar examination, developed the delusion that this occurred because of a conspiracy involving the university and the bar association. He then attributed all other difficulties in his social and occupational life to this continuing conspiracy.

Whether delusions are evidence of disordered thought processes

Opinion varies as to whether the holding of a delusional belief is in itself evidence of disordered thought processes. On the one hand, a delusional belief may represent a logical conclusion given the sensory information which that part of the brain involved in interpreting sensory data believes it has received "in its in-tray" for actioning. In this context, one may take the example of a person who "hears" a neighbour's voice, indistinguishable from that person's real voice, discussing how to poison him. Arguably, the belief that the neighbour is trying to harm him is a logical conclusion to reach on the available "evidence." Against this, many delusional beliefs are clearly based on illogical thinking. Thus, the logic of a patient who writes to the Prime Minister about some political crisis which is then resolved is clearly disturbed if he draws the conclusion that his personal intervention was responsible for the change in Government policy. There are endless variations on the theme but they all involve drawing conclusions from false premises: A writes to B about an event and the event takes a different course. A ascribes the change to his intervention. Alternatively, A writes letter B and learns that C has written to D and forms association between events A and C or between himself and the writer of letter C — **paralogic thinking**. Even here it may be argued that such delusional "ideas" are logical given the prior existence of a primary grandiose delusional "belief" about one's own importance, a belief which then provides the framework for future ideas and reasoning.

Autistic thinking

In many cases, the beliefs which provide such frameworks are the product of what Bleuler called **autistic thinking**: a form of thinking characterised by a turning away from reality, uncommunicativeness, and an excessive indulgence in fantasy. The individual is preoccupied with an inner, private world and, although this gratifies his various unfulfilled fantasies, it results in a total disregard of reality. As a result, his ability to relate to other people and his environment is markedly impaired. The mode of thought which originally compensated for the disappointments of life, by reinventing reality, becomes an established way of life.

Classification of delusions

Delusions are commonly categorised according to their content (*e.g.* grandiose delusions); whether or not they are systematised; whether they are mood-congruent or mood-incongruent (**1074**), and whether they are primary or secondary. With regard to the latter, a hallucination may give rise to a "secondary" delusional belief that the perception is true; it was "so real, it must be true." If the delusion cannot be related to some prior event it is said to be primary or "autochothonous."

COMMON DELUSIONAL THEMES

Delusion of being controlled	A delusion in which feelings, impulses, thoughts, or actions are experienced as not one's own but imposed by an external force.
Delusion of guilt	A delusional belief that one is sinful or wicked or responsible for certain distressing events, *e.g.* that one is responsible for the suicide of another patient. Guilt is self-inflicted, in contrast to shame which primarily depends upon the opinion others are perceived to have of the individual.
Delusion of infestation	A tactile hallucination involving the sensation of something creeping or crawling on or under the skin may give rise to a secondary delusion of being infested by insects or worms.
Delusion of poverty	A delusion that the person is, or will be, bereft of all, or virtually all, material possessions.
Delusion of reference	A delusion that events, objects, or other people in the person's immediate environment have a particular and unusual significance, usually of a negative or pejorative nature. If the delusion of reference involves a persecutory theme, then a delusion of persecution is present as well.
Delusional jealousy	The delusion that one's sexual partner is unfaithful. Also known as "Othello's syndrome."
Grandiose delusion	A delusion the content of which involves an exaggerated sense of one's importance, power, knowledge, or identity. It may have a religious, somatic, or other theme.
Nihilistic delusion	A belief that oneself, others, or the world no longer exist. Often present in very serious depressive disorders.
Persecutory delusion	A delusional belief that the patient himself, or some other person, institution, or group, is being attacked, harassed, cheated, persecuted, or conspired against. In cases of paranoid schizophrenia, such beliefs may be associated with related psychotic phenomena, such as auditory hallucinations or passivity phenomena.
Somatic delusion	A delusion pertaining to the functioning of one's body, *e.g.* a false belief that one is pregnant despite being post-menopausal.

Delusional beliefs about interference with thoughts

The central theme of the following delusional beliefs is the belief that the individual's thought processes are being interfered with by some other person or force —

- **Thought control** describes a belief that one's thoughts are being controlled by some other person, persons, or outside forces.

- **Thought insertion** is a delusion that thoughts have been, or are being placed, in one's mind by some other person, persons or outside forces. These intrusive thoughts are experienced by the patient as alien. One of Schneider's first-rank symptoms of schizophrenia.

- **Thought withdrawal** is when the individual experiences his own thoughts being withdrawn from his mind or otherwise appropriated by an external agency.

- **Thought broadcasting** is the belief that one's own thoughts are being broadcast to the outside world or otherwise made public knowledge.

The individual therefore believes that his thoughts are being controlled, infiltrated, poisoned, stolen or made public. Apart from the central idea of interference with thought processes, it can be seen that these beliefs have two other aspects in common. Firstly, the nature of the delusions are essentially paranoid since they are characterised by a belief that the individual is being harmed by some other person or agency. Consequently, there is a significant potential for violence to any individual thought to be involved in causing this harm. Secondly, and to some extent like all paranoid delusions, the beliefs are characterised by passivity. External agencies have managed to penetrate the individual's mind. The boundaries between the inner and outer world have been breached; not only external events but his own inner thoughts are no longer under his own control. **Thought blocking (1082)** may give rise to the delusional explanatory idea that this blockage is due to interference with the subject's thoughts.

IDEAS FALLING SHORT OF BEING DELUSIONAL BELIEFS

In most cases, it is clear whether or not an idea is delusional in nature. However, care must be taken to differentiate such ideas from value judgements, over-valued ideas and, more particularly, ideas of reference.

Value judgements

According to the DSM glossary, when a false belief involves an extreme value judgement, it is regarded as a delusion only when the judgement is so extreme as to defy credibility. If someone claims he or she is terrible and has disappointed his or her family, this is generally not regarded as a delusion even if an objective assessment of the situation would lead observers to think otherwise; but if someone claims he or she is the worst sinner in the world, this would generally be considered a delusional conviction.

Thoughts disproportionate (over-valued ideas)

An over-valued idea is an unreasonable, sustained, idea which is maintained less firmly than a delusional belief. It differs from an obsessional thought in that the person holding the overvalued idea does not recognise its absurdity and thus does not struggle against it. **Ideas of reference** are one kind of over-valued idea and the term denotes an incorrect idea that casual incidents and external events directly refer to oneself which stops short of being a delusion of reference (**1084**).

OTHER ABNORMAL THOUGHTS

Apart from delusions, a person's thoughts may be abnormal in a number of other ways which have already been considered. An **obsessional thought (1062)** is one which a person cannot prevent himself from repeatedly, insistently, having albeit that the content of the thought is not delusional. A **phobia (1075)** is a morbid, persistent and irrational fear of, and desire to avoid, a particular object or situation, associated with extreme anxiety.

PERCEPTUAL DISTURBANCES

A person may be unable to perceive or recognise something which one would normally expect him to be able to sense. For example, an individual cannot recognise objects despite adequate sensory information about them reaching the brain via the eyes, ears or through touch — **agnosia**. For an object to be recognised, the sensory information about it must be interpreted, which involves the recall of memorised information about similar objects. Agnosia is caused by damage to the areas of the brain involved in these interpretative and recall functions and may occur following head injury or a stroke. It is, however, rare. More commonly, perceptual disturbances involve an individual seemingly perceiving something which is not there.

HALLUCINATIONS

An hallucination is a sensory perception occurring without external stimulation of the relevant sensory organ. A hallucination has the immediate sense of reality of a true perception. Hallucinations are usually categorised according to the sensory modality in which they occur and there may or may not be a delusional interpretation of the hallucinatory experience. For example, a person experiencing auditory hallucinations may, or may not, recognise that the voices are imaginary. If he does not, and he is convinced that the source of his sensory experiences has an independent physical reality, the hallucination has given rise to a secondary delusion. Transient hallucinatory experiences are common in people without mental disorder and many people experience auditory or visual hallucinations while falling asleep (**hypnagogic perceptions**) or awakening from sleep (**hypnopompic perceptions**). Everyone has experiences akin to hallucinations during sleep (dream images).

Auditory hallucination

An auditory hallucination is a hallucination of sound, most commonly of voices. Auditory hallucinations may be organised — commenting or commanding — or elementary, such as a buzzing sound, fragments of music, or the sound of a telephone or door-bell. Auditory hallucinations which consist of hearing voices are often described as being in the first-person ("I am wicked"), in the second-person ("you are wicked"), or in the third-person ("he is wicked"). **Thought echo** is the experience of one's thoughts being repeated or echoed (but not spoken aloud) within one's head: the repeated thought, though identical in content, may be felt as slightly altered in quality. Echoed thoughts of this kind may be harbingers of auditory hallucinations.

Distortions of real perceptions

Auditory phenomena which are not classifiable as hallucinations may nevertheless be significant. For example, a patient with temporal lobe epilepsy may experience a sound as suddenly very remote and distant, or alternatively suddenly very loud, perhaps as loud as thunder.

Gustatory hallucination

A gustatory hallucination is an hallucination of taste, such as a metallic taste, often accompanied by chewing, lip smacking or swallowing movements. Gustatory hallucinations have great significance for the diagnosis of temporal lobe epilepsy. In cases of paranoid schizophrenia, the patient may imagine that his food is being poisoned or tampered and this belief give rise to a vague idea that the food is odd in some way. However, there is rarely an hallucination as such.

Olfactory hallucination

An olfactory hallucination is one involving smell and, again, it has great significance for the diagnosis of temporal lobe epilepsy. In such cases, the smell is typically described as being similar to burning rubber or burning cabbage.

Somatic hallucination

A somatic hallucination is an hallucination involving the false perception of a physical experience localised within the body. For example, a perception that electricity is running through the body. Somatic hallucinations are often distinguished from **tactile hallucinations,** in which the sensation is usually related to the skin, and **kinaesthetic hallucinations**, where the sensation relates to the muscles or joints.

Tactile or haptic hallucination

A tactile or haptic hallucination involves the sense of touch, often something on or under the skin. Almost invariably, the symptom is associated with a delusional interpretation of the sensation. For example, a person may say that the devil is sticking pins into his flesh. **Formication** (formica being the Latin word for an ant) is a particular kind of tactile hallucination, involving the sensation of something creeping or crawling on or under the skin. It may be a feature of schizophrenia or withdrawal from alcohol, cocaine or morphine. There is often a delusional interpretation of the sensation, which may be attributed to insects or worms — **delusion of infestation.**

Paraesthesia

Parietal seizures may produce numbness, tingling, feelings of heat and cold. The seizures may then spread to contiguous areas of the body and even produce pronounced disorders of body image.

Visceral hallucination

A visceral hallucination is literally an hallucination involving one of the organs situated within the chest and the abdomen although the term is commonly used to describe sensations affecting other bodily organs, *e.g.* a person senses that water is dripping in his brain.

Visual hallucination

A visual hallucination is an hallucination involving sight. Visual hallucinations may be sub-divided into those which are elementary or simple, such as flashes of light, and those which are organised, such as the form of human figures. Elementary visual hallucinations may be suggestive of an organic disorder. A scotoma[35] may occur or, more commonly, elementary hallucinations consisting of flashes of light, colours, zig-zag patterns and radiating spectra. Occipital seizures may commence as visual disturbances localised in the half-field of vision opposite to the side affected. One view is that the visual hallucinations of schizophrenia are experienced as often during the day as at night whereas such experiences are more common at night in mood or organic disorders.

Illusions

Visual hallucinations must be distinguished from illusions and also from normal thought processes that are exceptionally vivid. An illusion is a mental impression of sensory vividness arising out of a misinterpretation of an external stimulus. For example, mistaking a piece of scrunched cotton for a spider or a cat for a rat. They are therefore misperceptions or misinterpretations of real stimuli, in contrast to an hallucination when any external stimulus which may account for the perception is absent. Illusions may be caused by anxiety, panic, tiredness, certain drugs or damage to the brain.

Micropsia and macropsia

A Lilliputian hallucination is a visual hallucination in which the hallucinated visual material appears very small. This is different from micropsia in which actual objects appear smaller than normal.[36] Macropsia is a false perception that an actual object is larger than it really is. It may occur following drug intoxication or as a feature of temporal lobe epilepsy.

PERCEPTIONS OF TIME, SPACE, PLACE AND SELF

A number of other sensations not classified as hallucinations relate to the individual's orientation — his perception of himself in relation to time, space, and place — and result in a feeling of disengagement from the world or disorientation. A person

---

[35]   An abnormal blind spot in the visual field.
[36]   W.A. Lishman, *Organic Psychiatry, The Psychological Consequences of Cerebral Disorder* (Blackwell Scientific Publications, 2nd ed., 1987), p.219.

with schizophrenia or temporal lobe epilepsy may describe time passing extremely slowly or rapidly. He may say that half an hour passed in a matter of seconds or that he was aware of beginning to prepare a meal and the next moment the food was cooked and ready on the table. **Depersonalisation** is an alteration in the perception or experience of one's self so that the feeling of one's own reality is temporarily lost. It may include the feeling that one's extremities have changed in size, or a sense of seeming to perceive oneself from a distance (usually from above). Such experiences may be the product of stress, anxiety or tiredness, a side-effect of medication, a symptom of temporal-lobe epilepsy or schizophrenia. Depersonalisation is frequently accompanied by, but should be distinguished from, **derealisation**. Here, the individual concerned does not feel that he himself is unreal, rather the world around him is experienced as unreal. **Déjà-vu** is a false feeling that what one is seeing (a place or person) has been seen previously while **jamais-vu** is a feeling that one has never before seen that which has previously been seen. **Déjà-entendu** is a false feeling that what is being heard has been heard before while **déjà-pensé** is a false feeling that a new thought has been previously experienced or conceived.

SPECIAL ASSESSMENT PROCEDURES

Certain routine tests should ideally "be performed on all psychiatric in-patients, including estimation of haemoglobin, erythrocyte sedimentation rate, serological tests for syphilis, chest X-ray and routine urine examination. The patient's temperature should ... be taken, sometimes with four-hourly recording, if minor rises are suspected. These serve as screening tests for coincidental as well as causally related physical disorders. Other investigations will be indicated on the basis of the history and clinical examination when specific disorders are suspected."[37] Because the vast majority of symptoms found during a mental state examination can be features of a number of mental disorders, the initial diagnosis is often only provisional, or at least should be. A number of possible alternative diagnoses (**differential diagnoses**) may well be noted. The presumption that all seriously disabling forms of mental disorder have underlying structural or biological causes has led to attempts to develop investigative tests which can eliminate some of this uncertainty and provide greater diagnostic accuracy. The mental state examination aside, assessment procedures include physical examination, laboratory tests (**1091**), EEGs and lumbar puncture (**1099**), the use of psychiatric rating scales and psychological tests (**1104**), and behavioural analysis involving the use of behaviour charts. The purpose of a diagnostic test is to move the estimated probability of disease toward either end of the probability scale, thereby providing information that will alter subsequent diagnostic or treatment plans.[38]

THE DIAGNOSTIC VALUE OF SPECIAL INVESTIGATIONS

It is sometimes said that "true" disease status is determined by the most definitive diagnostic method, commonly referred to as a gold standard. For example, the gold standard for breast cancer diagnosis is histopathologic confirmation of cancer in a

---

[37]   W.A. Lishman, *Organic Psychiatry, The Psychological Consequences of Cerebral Disorder* (Blackwell Scientific Publications, 2nd ed., 1987), p.108.
[38]   R.S. Greenberg, *Medical Epidemiology* (Appleton & Lange, 1993), p.58.

surgical specimen.[39] That being so, lawyers and other non-medically qualified professionals sometimes think of laboratory test results, EEG findings, and the results of special investigations such as tissue examination, as constituting infallible scientific evidence of the existence or absence of a particular condition. This is rarely the case. Few special investigations of relevance to psychiatry are capable of proving or disproving a particular diagnosis and, when considering test results, the accuracy, validity and reliability of the particular test, and the possibility of human error and bias, must always be addressed. Although few tests "provide a precise diagnosis ... the result of a test should change the likelihood of a possible diagnosis, otherwise there would be little point in doing it."[40]

The result returned by the test

The result returned by some tests is either positive or negative, present or absent, normal or abnormal. However, test results often occur along a continuum and do not have positive or negative outcomes. The outcome may be suspicious or suggestive of some abnormality but no more than that.

The sensitivity and specificity of the test

Sensitivity and specificity are descriptors of the accuracy of a test. A test with a very low percentage of false-negative results is described as having "high sensitivity." The greater the sensitivity of a test, the more likely it is that the test will detect persons with the disease of interest. Tests with great sensitivity are therefore useful to rule out a disease. A test with a very low percentage of false-positive results is said to have "high specificity." Thus, "the greater the specificity, the more likely that persons without the disease of interest will be excluded by the test ... Very specific tests are often used to confirm the presence of a disease. If the test is highly specific, a positive test result would strongly implicate the disease of interest."[41]

The validity and reliability of the test

The validity and reliability of a particular test must always be considered. Validity is the capacity of a specific test to measure what it purports to measure. In general, a test is neither valid nor invalid but has a variety of validities for different purposes. For example, the selection of a psychological test should be based upon evidence of its validity for the chosen purpose, e.g. measuring the severity of symptoms of depression.[42] Reliability refers to the consistency with which subjects are discriminated from one another. It "is the extent to which scores obtained by testing a patient on one occasion will be the same if that person is re-examined by the same test on a different occasion."[43] If a test is highly reliable (it has a high reliability

---

[39] See A.R. Feinstein, "A bibliography of publications on observer variability" *Journal of Chronic Diseases* (1985) 38: 619–632; G.W. Bradley, *Disease, Diagnosis and Decisions*, supra, p.66; R.S. Greenberg, *Medical Epidemiology* (Appleton & Lange, 1993), p.59.

[40] G.W. Bradley, *Disease, Diagnosis and Decisions* (John Wiley & Sons, 1993), p.xiv.

[41] R.S. Greenberg, *Medical Epidemiology* (Appleton & Lange, 1993), p.60. Care must, however, be taken when speaking of false-positives. For example, EEGs have been said to give a high occurrence of false-positive results in subjects with psychiatric disorders of non-organic aetiology, such as schizophrenia. This is not a false positive result, rather a positive finding of a point of contact which links different disorders at some level (evidence of similarity).

[42] R.A. MacKinnon and S.C. Yudofsky, *Principles of Psychiatric Evaluation* (J.B. Lippincott Co., 1991), p.176.

[43] *Ibid.*, pp.175–176.

coefficient), one can be more confident that any differences in scores are due to actual changes in the responses being measured. To "secure reliable and valid data, it is necessary to control and standardize the fashion in which questions are asked, observations are made, and data are scored and interpreted."[44]

The possibility of error

As Bradley notes, the "interpretation of diagnostic procedures is ... open to error. This must be readily apparent to anyone attending X-ray meetings, and as one might expect, it applies also to interpretation of ECG, EEG and isotope studies as well as endoscopy findings."[45] Histological data is a good example of this problem because most lay people probably believe that the microscopic examination of a human tissue sample provides conclusive evidence of the presence or absence of physical disease. The reality is rather different:

> "Histological data is often taken to be the ultimate gold standard, but the process of making a histological diagnosis is very much one of recognising images and patterns, and may be just as prone to errors as a diagnosis made from clinical findings. When a histological opinion is subjected to the same critical appraisal which has been applied to clinical findings, similar disagreements have been shown ... different pathologists may reach different conclusions when interpreting the same microscopic specimen."[46]

The possibility of bias

There tends to be higher agreement about normality than abnormality when it comes to examining test results. However, normal findings tend to be ignored when judging the effect of a test on the likelihood of disease. Although a negative test should have the effect of making the diagnosis less likely, "the clinician often ignores this evidence."[47] Human vanity may therefore make it difficult for a clinician to accept a finding which contradicts his original, notionally provisional, diagnosis.

LABORATORY INVESTIGATIONS

Most diseases result in chemical changes within the cells of the body so that there is frequently a change in the chemical composition of body fluids, such as blood and urine. These fluids can be chemically analysed to establish whether changes show a particular disease state. The table on page 1094 lists many of laboratory tests which may be undertaken. Depending on the test, the sample type may be blood, urine, or serum (the clear fluid portion of the blood). In theory, tests should only be performed if they will alter the patient's diagnosis, prognosis, treatment, or management.[48] Laboratory tests may be conducted to enable an early diagnosis to be made after the onset of signs or symptoms; to rule out certain differential diagnoses; to determine the stage of a disease; to estimate the activity of a disease; or to monitor the effect of drug and other therapies. According to Rose, the most relevant laboratory investigations are ESR (the erythrocyte sedimentation rate), haemoglobin and blood counts, liver function tests, thyroid function tests and serology for

---

[44] R.A. MacKinnon and S.C. Yudofsky, *Principles of Psychiatric Evaluation* (J.B. Lippincott Co., 1991), p.175.

[45] G.W. Bradley, *Disease, Diagnosis and Decisions* (John Wiley & Sons, 1993), p.65.

[46] R.S. Greenberg, *Medical Epidemiology* (Appleton & Lange, 1993), p.58.

[47] G.A. Gorry, *et al.*, "The diagnostic importance of the normal finding" *New England Journal of Medicine* (1978) 298: 486–489; G.W. Bradley, *Disease, Diagnosis and Decisions, supra*, p.55.

[48] J. Wallach, *Interpretation of Diagnostic Tests* (Little Brown & Co., 5th ed., 1992), p.7.

syphilis. Unfortunately, no laboratory tests in psychiatry can confirm or rule out diagnoses of function disorders such as schizophrenia and manic-depressive disorders. However, they can sometimes rule out organic conditions which may mimic these disorders and so reinforce such a diagnosis.

Format of the laboratory report

Where laboratory tests have been conducted, the laboratory test request form and the print-out of the test results will usually be found filed at the back of the patient's case notes. The request form should include details of any factors which are particularly germane to a test and the interpretation of its results. For example, the time when blood is drawn is important when the test component is subject to marked diurnal variation (cortisol, iron), varies with meals (glucose) or intravenous infusions taken (electrolytes), or depends on the source of specimen (arterial or capillary rather than venous blood). Many tests can be properly interpreted only when such information is known.[49] Laboratory test results generally list the tests conducted, the results of the samples tested, and give a reference range, so that it is easier to see whether any result lies outside the reference range and is abnormal. The format of the print-out is usually similar to that set out below. For an explanation of abbreviations used for units of measurement, see page 1143.

HEATHCLIFFE HOSPITAL		BIOCHEMISTRY	
John Smith	Ward F2	Consultant	Dr. Jones
	Date and time of sample collection		10.09.95
CLINICAL DETAILS : None			
	Test result		*Reference range*
Sodium	141	mmol/L	135–145
Potassium	4.6	mmol/L	3.6–5.0
Urea	2.9	mmol/L	2.5–6.5
Sample type	*Blood*	*Report date*	*10.09.95*

Interpreting laboratory results

According to Wallach, "in the majority of laboratory measurements, the combination of short-term physiologic variation and analytical error is sufficient to render the interpretation of single determinations difficult when concentrations are in the borderline range." That being so, values "are to be used as general guidelines rather than rigid separations of normal from abnormal or diseased from healthy ... A review of the texts, reference books, and current literature in clinical pathology often reveals surprising and considerable discrepancy between well-known sources."[50] More particularly, "considerable variation in test results is due not only to instrumentation, methodology, and other laboratory techniques but also to more subtle preanalytic factors such as position or condition of the patient (*e.g.*, supine or upright, fasting or postprandial), time of day, age, sex, climate, effect of diet or drugs, characteristics of test population. It is therefore essential that the clinician use

[49]   J. Wallach, *Interpretation of Diagnostic Tests* (Little Brown & Co., 5th ed., 1992), p.3.
[50]   *Ibid.*

the reference ranges from the laboratory that is performing those particular tests and which it has determined for its own procedures, patient population, etc. Misinterpretation of laboratory data due to this error, as well as from overemphasising the significance of borderline values, has caused immeasurable emotional pain and economic waste for innumerable patients."[51]

LABORATORY TESTS — WALLACH'S GENERAL PRINCIPLES

---

1. Under the best of circumstances, no test is perfect (*e.g.*, 100% sensitivity, specificity, predictive value). In any specific case, the results may be misleading.

2. Any particular laboratory result may be incorrect for a large variety of reasons regardless of the high quality of the laboratory; all such results should be rechecked. If indicated, a new specimen sample should be submitted, with careful confirmation of patient identification, prompt delivery to the laboratory, and immediate processing; in some circumstances, confirmation of test results at another laboratory may be indicated.

3. The greater the degree of abnormality of the test result, the more likely that a confirmed abnormality is significant or represents a real disorder.

4. Tables of (normal) reference values represent collected statistical data for 95% of the population rather than classification of patients as having disease or being healthy; values outside of these ranges do not necessarily represent disease. The probability of disease if a screening test is abnormal is generally low (0–15%). The frequency of abnormal single tests may be as high as 16.6% (sodium). Based on statistical expectations, when a panel of eight tests is performed in a health programme, 25% of the patients have one or more abnormal results (55% if the panel includes 20 tests).

5. Results may still be within the reference range but be elevated above the patient's baseline, which is why serial testing is important in a number of conditions. An individual's test values, when performed in a good laboratory, tend to remain fairly constant over a period of years when performed with comparable technology; comparison of results with previous values obtained when the patient was not ill (if available) is often a better reference value than "normal" ranges.

6. Multiple test abnormalities are more likely to be significant than single test abnormalities.

7. Characteristic laboratory test profiles represent the full-blown picture of the well-developed or far advanced case, but all abnormal tests may be present simultaneously in only a small fraction (*e.g.*, one-third) of patients with that condition.

8. Clerical errors are far more likely than technical errors to cause incorrect results. Every specimen should always be accompanied by a test requisition form. Busy hospital laboratories receive inordinate numbers of unlabelled, unidentified specimens each day.

9. Users should be aware of variations due to age, sex, race, size, and physiological status (*e.g.* pregnancy) that apply to the particular patient.

10. The effect of drugs on laboratory test values must never be overlooked.

J. Wallach, Interpretation of Diagnostic Tests, 5th Ed., Little Brown & Co., Boston, 1992, pp. 7–8.

---

[51]   J. Wallach, *Interpretation of Diagnostic Tests* (Little Brown & Co., 5th ed., 1992), p.3.

LABORATORY INVESTIGATIONS

Test	Abbrev	Normal Range	Elevated/Raised	Depressed/Lowered	Notes
			BLOOD CELL TESTS		
Red Blood Cell count	RBC	Men: 4.2 – 5.4 million RBC per microlitre of blood; Women: 3.6 – 5.0 million.	Possible polycythaemia	Anaemia or severe bleeding.	Red blood cells are also known as erythrocytes and red corpuscles. Normal RBC counts vary depending on the type of sample, age and gender.
Haemoglobin (Total)	Hb	Men 14-18 gms of Hb per decilitre; women 12-16 gms.	May indicate dehydration.	A low concentration may indicate anaemia.	Haemoglobin is a type of protein in red blood cells, its purpose being to carry oxygen in the blood. Haemoglobin concentration varies, depending on type of sample drawn, age and gender. Red blood cells are also known as erythrocytes.
Erythrocyte sedimentation rate	ESR	0–20 millimetres per hour.	Increased rate : Anaemia, inflammation, TB, rheumatoid arthritis.	Rate slowed : Sickle cell anaemia.	
Platelet count		130,000 – 370,000 platelets per cubic millilitre of whole blood.	Thrombocytosis, high platelet count. Severe bleeding, infections, iron deficiency anaemia, inflammatory disorders.	Thrombocytopaenia, low platelet count. Folic acid or vitamin B_{12} deficiency. Fatal CNS bleeding possible if count below 5,000.	Platelets (thrombocytes) are the smallest formed elements in blood and they promote blood clotting after an injury. CNS = central nervous system.
White blood cell count	WBC	4,000 – 10,000 WBC per cubic millimetre of whole blood.	*Leukocytosis.* May be caused by infection but also associated with lithium and neuroleptic malignant syndrome.	= *Leukopenia* (WBC 2000 – 3500) = *Agranulocytosis* (WBC < 2000). Bone marrow problems caused by *e.g.* viral infections, flu, measles, rubella, toxic reactions to poisons. Reduced resistance to infection.	Leukocytes help the body to fight infection. Also called a leukocyte count. WBC counts may vary by as much as 2,000 on any given day, due to (inter alia) stress and strenuous exercise. Strenuous exercise should therefore be avoided for 24 hours before a test. Certain medications may interfere with the results. Leukopenia and agranulocytosis are associated with certain psychotropic medications, such as phenothiazines and carbamazepine, clozapine.

					There are five major types of white blood cell: neutrophils, eosinophils, basophils, lymphocytes, and monocytes. The white blood cell differential is used to evaluate the distribution of these various leukocytes in the blood.
Differential WBC count		Neutrophils 47.6% – 76.8%; Lymphocytes 16.2% – 43%; Monocytes 0.6% – 9.6%; Eosinophils 0.3% – 7%; Basophils 0.3% – 2%.	Neutrophils — rheumatoid arthritis, thyrotoxicosis, emotional distress; Lymphocytes — thyrotoxicosis, hypoadrenalism; Monocytes — rheumatoid arthritis; Eosinophils — allergies, parasitic infections; Basophils — myxoedema	Neutrophils — hepatitis, folic acid or vitamin B_{12} deficiency; Lymphocytes — high levels of adrenal corticosteroids; Monocytes — immunosuppression; Eosinophils — mental distress, stress response to injury, Cushing's syndrome; Basophils — hyperthyroidism, stress.	

BLOOD ELEMENT TESTS: 1. ELECTROLYTES

Calcium, serum	Ca	8.9–10.1 milligrams per decilitre / 4.5–5.5 millieq. per litre of blood serum.	*Hypocalcaemia.* May be caused by hypoparathyroidism, total parathyroid removal. Associated with depression, irritability, delirium, chronic laxative abuse. May occur with Cushing's syndrome, acute pancreatitis.	*Hypercalcaemia.* May be caused by hyperparathyroidism, multiple fractures, over use of antacids. Associated with delirium, depression, psychosis. Can lead to muscle weakness.	Calcium helps to regulate the body's nerve, muscle, and enzyme activity. Parathyroid hormone plays an important role in helping the intestine to absorb calcium.
Chloride	Cl	100–108 millieq. per litre of blood serum.	*Hypochloraemia.* Underlying causes include prolonged vomiting and Addison's disease.	*Hyperchloraemia.* May cause stupor, even coma.	Low serum chloride levels are usually accompanied by low sodium and potassium levels.
Magnesium	Mg	1.7 – 2.1 milligrams per decilitre / 1.5 – 2.5 millieq. per litre of blood serum.	= *Hypomagnesaemia.* Most commonly caused by chronic alcoholism. Can lead to foot cramps, seizures, tremors.	*Hypermagnesaemia.* May be caused by kidney failure, adrenal insufficiency, Addison's disease. May lead to lethargy, hypotension, muscle weakness, slow and shallow breathing.	Vital to nerve and muscle functioning.
Phosphate	P	2.5 – 4.5 milligrams per decilitre.	*Hypophosphataemia.* Malnutrition, hyperparathyroidism.	*Hyperphosphataemia.* Rarely a medical problem. Skeletal disease, healing fractures, thyroid problems, acromegaly.	Phosphates regulate calcium levels. Serum calcium and phosphate levels have an inverse relationship: if one is elevated, the other is lowered. Phosphate levels are interpreted with calcium results. Levels may be altered by some medications. Phosphate is the dominant anion in the intracellular component.

Potassium	K	3.5 – 5.0 millieq. per litre of blood serum.	*Hyperkalaemia.* Can lead to weakness and nausea. May indicate Addison's disease, kidney failure.	*Hypokalaemia.* Cirrhosis, laxative abuse, decrease common in bulimic patients. Aldosteronism, Cushing's syndrome, loss of body fluids.	Potassium affects kidney function. Potassium is the principal cation in the intracellular component.
Sodium	Na	135 – 145 millieq. per litre of blood serum.	*Hypernatraemia.* Drinking too little water, eating too much salt, diabetes insipidus, severe vomiting, diarrhoea.	*Hyponatraemia.* Diffuse sweating, diarrhoea, vomiting, adrenal insufficiency, chronic poor kidney function.	Sodium helps nerve and muscle functioning and influences chloride and potassium levels.

BLOOD ELEMENT TESTS: 2. ENZYMES

Alkaline phosphatase	Alk. Phos.	Men 90 – 239 int. units per litre; women under 45 = 76 – 196; women over 45 = 87 – 250.	Many causes. Hyperparathyroidism, hepatic disease, phenothiazine use.	Pernicious anaemia	The enzyme is involved in bone calcification.
Amylase		Serum levels range from 30 – 220 int. units per litre.	Acute pancreatitis (peaks at 12-48 hours and returns to normal after 3–4 days).	Chronic pancreatitis, cirrhosis, hepatitis.	More than 20 methods of measuring serum amylase exist and test levels cannot always be converted to a standard measurement.
Aspartate aminotransferase	AST	8–20 int. units per litre.	Hepatic disease, pancreatitis, alcoholism.	Vitamin B6 deficiency.	AST is released into the bloodstream in proportion to the amount of cell damage due to heart or liver problems. AST level fluctuations reflect the extent of cell damage. Increasing levels may indicate increasing disease severity, decreasing disease resolution and tissue repair.
Cholinesterase		Pseudocholinesterase: 8 – 15 int. units per millil. of blood serum.			The cholinesterase test measures the amount of two similar enzymes: acetylcholinesterase and pseudocholinesterase. The first is present in nerve tissue and the grey matter of the brain, the second in the white matter of the brain. Cholinesterase levels may be measured to evaluate response to related substances before ECT.

Test	Abbr.	Normal range			Notes
Creatine kinase	CK	Total CK levels range from 25–130 int. units per litre for men and 10–150 for women. Normal CK levels may be significantly higher in very muscular people.	Increased total CK levels indicate injury to cells. May be due to severe hypokalaemia, carbon monoxide poisoning, following seizures and, occasionally, brain damage.		Lithium may interfere with results. CK$_1$ (CK-BB), a component of CK ("isoenzyme") is found mostly in the brain. It is not usually detectable; if detected, this may indicate brain tissue injury, widespread malignant tumours, severe shock, kidney failure. An increase in CK-MM may be due to skeletal muscle damage following an intramuscular injection.
Creatine phosphokinase	CPK		Neuroleptic malignant syndrome, intramuscular injection, dystonic reactions, use of antipsychotics.		
Gamma glutamyl transferase	GGT	Men 8 – 37 int. units per litre; women 5 – 24.	Any acute liver disorder. Moderately raised levels may indicate acute pancreatitis, kidney disease. Sometimes seen with epilepsy or brain tumours. Levels increase after alcohol ingestion.		The test may be conducted to evaluate liver function and alcohol ingestion.

BLOOD ELEMENT TESTS: 3. PROTEINS

Test	Abbr.	Normal range	Increased	Decreased	Notes
Protein (Total)		6.6 – 7.9 grams per decilitre of serum.	Rheumatoid arthritis	Malnutrition, uncontrolled diabetes mellitus, hyperthyroidism.	The two major proteins in blood are albumin and globulins. Tests determine the protein content of the blood and aid the diagnosis of liver disease and kidney disorders.
Albumin	alb.	(Albumin fraction) 3.3 – 4.5 grams per decilitre of serum.	Dehydration	Malnutrition, nephritis, diarrhoea, hepatic disease, rheumatoid arthritis, hyperthyroidism.	
Globulins			Chronic syphilis, rheumatoid arthritis, diabetes mellitus	Various, including some kidney diseases and blood disorders.	

BLOOD ELEMENT TESTS: 4. PIGMENTS

Bilirubin / Total Bilirubin	Bili.	Indirect serum method: 1.1 millg. per decilitre of blood serum, or less (direct serum method: 0.5).	Hepatic disease (elevated indirect serum bilirubin levels)	Bilirubin is a clear yellow or orange fluid found in bile and produced by the breakdown of red blood cells.
Creatinine		Men = 0.8 – 1.2 millig. per decilitre of blood; women = 0.6 – 0.9.	Kidney disease that has seriously damaged 50% or more of the tissue; may also be associated with acromegaly.	Creatinine occurs in blood in amounts proportional to the body's muscle mass.

BLOOD ELEMENT TESTS: 5. VITAMINS

Folic acid, serum	3–16 nanograms of folic acid per millilitre of blood.	Vitamin B12 deficiencies associated with psychosis, paranoia, fatigue, agitation, dementia, and delirium. Associated with alcoholism, oral contraceptives, and the use of phenytoin.	Often performed together with a test for vitamin B_{12} levels. Influences RBC production.
Vitamin B_2	3–5 micrograms per decilitre of blood.	Stress.	Essential for growth and tissue function.
Vitamin B_{12}	100–700 picograms of B_{12} per millilitre of blood.	Cirrhosis; acute or chronic hepatitis.	Inadequate dietary intake, overactive thyroid, pregnancy, CNS damage. Essential for RBC production.

Sources: *J. Wallach, Interpretation of Diagnostic Tests, 5th Ed., Little Brown & Co., Boston, 1992; W.A. Lishman, Organic Psychiatry, The Psychological Consequences of Cerebral Disorder (Blackwell Scientific Publications, 2nd ed. 1987); S. Breanndan Moore, et al., Medical Tests (Springhouse, 1996).*

LUMBAR PUNCTURE AND CEREBROSPINAL FLUID (CSF)

The cerebrospinal fluid consists of water, mineral salts, glucose, proteins and other similar substances. It supports the brain, maintaining a uniform pressure round the brain and spinal cord, acting as a cushion and shock absorber. Approximately 500 ml. of cerebrospinal fluid (CSF) are produced daily.[52] In psychiatric patients, lumbar puncture "will sometimes be indicated in patients who show disturbance of consciousness or unexplained change of behaviour, even in the absence of definite neurological signs."[53] Examination of the CSF in cases of encephalitis and general paresis may be crucial in alerting the clinician to the diagnosis, although a normal CSF does not mean that a pathological process in the central nervous system can be excluded. Many pathological processes responsible for enduring brain damage and neuropsychiatric disturbance "will have subsided by the time the patient is examined, and will have left a normal fluid in their wake."[54] The information to be obtained from lumbar puncture has been summarised by Walton. The pressure is raised in the presence of tumour, haematoma, abscess, or cerebral oedema, moderately raised in severe arterial hypertension, and may be raised in cases of hypoparathyroidism. An increase in the number of leukocytes (pleocytosis) *inter alia* implies meningitis or encephalitis. In untreated general paresis, 5–50 lymphocytes — a type of white blood cell — are usual. There may be an increase in the protein content in cases of encephalitis, meningitis, neurosyphilis and multiple sclerosis.[55] The form used to record the findings will usually be similar to that for laboratory tests (**1092**), and contain information listed under a number of sub-headings such as the appearance of the fluid (*e.g.* "clear and colourless"), cell counts (red and white blood cells), protein, and culture (*e.g.* "no growth after two days' incubation"). The risk attached to lumbar puncture is generally small.

ELECTROENCEPHALOGRAPHY (EEGs)

The electroencephalogram (EEG), developed in 1929, records the electric potential activity of the brain. It is a safe technique for investigating brain function and causes no discomfort to the patient. An EEG may be performed where epilepsy is suspected and, more particularly, if there is a suggestion of altered levels of consciousness, automatisms, head injury, and hallucinations. Although safe and non-intrusive, there are "certain marked limitations" to its clinical usefulness.[56] In particular, it should immediately be noted that specific "functional" psychiatric disorders (such as schizophrenia, mania and depression) are not associated with pathognomonic EEGs.

EEG procedures

The major determinant in EEG is the electrical activity of the neurones in the uppermost neuronal layers of the cortex.[57] 16 electrodes are placed in standardised positions over the scalp and the graphic recordings from each electrode are drawn by recording pens and placed in montages on the recording paper. Various activating

---

[52]   H. Kaplan and B. Sadock, *Synopsis of Psychiatry* (Williams & Wilkins, 7th ed., 1994), p.92.

[53]   W.A. Lishman, *Organic Psychiatry, The Psychological Consequences of Cerebral Disorder* (Blackwell Scientific Publications, 2nd ed., 1987), p.114.

[54]   *Ibid.*, p.115.

[55]   Sir J. Walton, *Essentials of Neurology* (Pitman, 5th ed., 1982). See Lishman, *supra*, pp. 114–115.

[56]   W.A. Lishman, *Organic Psychiatry, The Psychological Consequences of Cerebral Disorder*, *supra*, p.109.

[57]   H. Kaplan and B. Sadock, *Synopsis of Psychiatry*, *supra*, p.119.

procedures and specialised recording techniques are used to enhance the ability of the EEG to diagnose brain disorders[58]—

1.) **Nasopharyngeal electrodes or sphenoidal electrodes** may be used. Their greater physical proximity to the limbic areas of the brain can enable abnormal electrical activity in the anterior and medial temporal lobe to be picked up in cases where temporal lobe epilepsy is suspected.

2.) **Hyperventilation** for approximately three minutes can cause spikes, sharp waves, or paroxysms of slow-wave activity to emerge more clearly.

3.) Seizure patterns may emerge, and a generalised seizure may even be provoked, following **photic stimulation**.[59] This involves showing the patient a flashing strobe light during the EEG. An abnormal result is the appearance of paroxysmal activity not in phase with the flashing light.

4.) **Sedative-induced sleep** (using a barbitone) or **sleep deprivation**, involving keeping the patient awake at night before the EEG, causes the patient to be drowsy during the EEG procedure. This may elicit EEG changes during sleep, or the transition between wakefulness and sleep, which are indicative of cerebral pathology, including epileptic discharges within the temporal lobes.

5.) **Drug activation** may occasionally be employed because many medications enhance epileptiform activity.

Normal EEG rhythms

Brain electrical activity is evaluated according to the frequency, amplitude, and form (distribution) of brain wave tracings. Evaluation of the EEG also requires inspecting for any paroxysmal bursts, such as spike and wave bursts, which may indicate epileptic activity.

The frequency of EEG rhythms

The frequency of brain waves is measured in cycles per second (c/s), one hertz (Hz) corresponding to one cycle per second (1 c/s). In a normal adult during the awake state, frequencies range from 8 Hz to 13 Hz and such frequencies constitute an alpha rhythm. By convention, the frequency of EEG rhythms are classified according to four classes.[60]

---

[58] See H. Kaplan and B. Sadock, *Synopsis of Psychiatry* (Williams & Wilkins, 7th ed., 1994); W.A. Lishman, *Organic Psychiatry, The Psychological Consequences of Cerebral Disorder* (Blackwell Scientific Publications, 2nd ed., 1987); B.K. Puri and P.J. Tyrer, *Sciences Basic to Psychiatry* (Churchill Livingstone, 1992).

[59] W.A. Lishman, *Organic Psychiatry, The Psychological Consequences of Cerebral Disorder*, supra, p.110.

[60] The terms lambda (λ) and mu (μ) activity will, however, also be encountered. Lambda activity occurs only over the occipital region in subjects with opened eyes. It is related to ocular movements occurring during visual attention. Mu activity occurs over the motor cortex and is related to motor activity, being abolished by movement of the contralateral limb. See B.K. Puri and P.J. Tyrer, *Sciences Basic to Psychiatry* (Churchill Livingstone, 1992), pp.63–64.

THE FREQUENCY OF EEG WAVES

Frequency	Class	Notes
< 4 c/s	Delta (δ) activity	Low-frequency, high-amplitude delta and theta activity do not normally occur in waking adult EEGs but are normal features of sleep.
4–8 c/s	Theta (τ) activity	
8–13 c/s	Alpha (α) activity	Alpha activity represents the resting normal EEG rhythm of an awake adult human with closed eyes.
> 13 c/s	Beta (β) activity	When the awake resting adult opens his or her eyes or is otherwise stimulated out of a state of quiet cerebration, the alpha activity is largely replaced by beta activity. This replacement of alpha activity is known as "alpha blocking," and as the "alerting or arousal response."

Amplitude and paroxysmal activity

The average voltage of the alpha rhythm is 30–50μV with spindle-shaped modulations. "Spikes" are high peaked discharges which rise and fall abruptly, standing out above the general amplitude of the other waves. These transient high peaks, although lasting less than 80 milliseconds, can clearly be differentiated from the general amplitude of the background EEG reading. "Sharp waves" rise steeply and then fall more slowly. These wave formations are conspicuous but, as they fall off more slowly, they last for more than 80 milliseconds. Slow waves may be preceded by several spikes and spikes may also alternate with delta waves.[61]

Interpretation of EEG rhythms and activity

Wave and spike discharges occurring at a rhythm of 3 c/s constitute the classical EEG feature of petit mal epilepsy[62] while absence seizures (petit mal) and Creutzfeldt-Jakob disease are associated with relatively specific EEG features. However, the EEG is not a sensitive test and it has little diagnostic specificity. It is "probably true to say that a normal EEG never excludes any clinical condition, but can serve to diminish the probability of its existence."[63] A certain proportion of healthy patients show abnormal activity and, conversely, the results can be normal in patients with obvious cerebral dysfunction. In particular, approximately 30 per cent. of people with epilepsy have normal EEGs between attacks. Given these limitations, "the most useful help will be obtained ... when the person interpreting the record is fully acquainted with all relevant clinical information about the patient's illness."[64] Further information about the interpretation of EEG results is given in the following table.

---

[61] W.A. Lishman, *Organic Psychiatry, The Psychological Consequences of Cerebral Disorder* (Blackwell Scientific Publications, 2nd ed., 1987), p.109.
[62] *Ibid.*
[63] *Ibid.*, p.110.
[64] *Ibid.*

1. Normal EEG rhythms vary with age. In old age, normal changes include a decrease in the amplitude and average frequency of alpha activity, diffuse slowing, and the presence of brief runs of frontotemporal, mainly left-sided, low-frequency activity (Puri & Tyrer, p.64).

2. The average frequency of normal EEG rhythms varies with the level of alertness and blood sugar level. Such physiological changes in the record "are indistinguishable from those associated with many pathological states, and can readily be misinterpreted as evidence of disease" (Lishman, p.110).

3. The average frequency of alpha rhythm varies in women according to their menstrual cycle. Hyperthermia causes changes in alpha activity and hyperventilation also causes changes in the EEG. The consumption of alcohol can cause changes in the EEG of normal subjects that are usually associated with epilepsy.

4. Scalp muscle activity may be confused with fast beta activity and eye movements may be confused with slow delta activity over the frontal poles (Kaplan and Sadock, p.123). These phenomena are sometimes known as "EEG artifacts."

5. Approximately 15% of "normal" subjects have "abnormal" EEGs and the figure is somewhat higher among patients with neurotic disorders.

6. Patients with epileptic activity are often not detected on a routine EEG (Kaplan and Sadock, p.123). Consequently, a normal EEG cannot be used on its own to exclude a diagnosis, including epilepsy, without investigation

7. Mental disorders "of apparently non-organic origin are known to be associated with an increased incidence of abnormalities in the EEG" (Lishman, p.110). One-half of patients with a psychopathic disorder have abnormal EEGs, rising to 60–70% of patients and prisoners categorised as aggressive psychopaths; up to 20% of patients with manic-depressive disorders show "mildly abnormal" records; and up to 25% of patients with schizophrenia show "more definite" abnormalities, including epileptiform activity, the incidence being particularly high in cases of catatonic schizophrenia; (Lishman, pp.110–111). The percentage of diffusely abnormal EEGs in persons with schizophrenia is two to three times that found in the normal population. There may be increased presence of delta activity.

8. Psychotropic medication may affect EEG results — antidepressants lead to an increase in delta activity, anxiolytics to increased beta activity, and antipsychotics to a decrease in beta activity and an increase in low-frequency delta and/or theta activity. Chlorpromazine and other phenothiazines, antidepressants and lithium potentiate epileptic discharges.

Sources: W.A. Lishman, Organic Psychiatry, The Psychological Consequences of Cerebral Disorder (Blackwell Scientific Publications, 2nd ed., 1987); H. Kaplan and B. Sadock, Synopsis of Psychiatry (Williams & Wilkins, 7th ed., 1994); B.K. Puri and P.J. Tyrer, Sciences Basic to Psychiatry (Churchill Livingstone, 1992).

Format of the EEG report

Some one hundred pages of recording paper may be evaluated. However, a summary of the results of any EEG investigation will usually be found filed at the back of the patient's case notes and these reports are generally in a form similar to that presented immediately below. Abnormal rhythms may be describe as synchronous or asynchronous depending on the coincidence of their appearance in the different electrode leads. The rhythms may be generalised, confined to one side of the brain (unilateral) or focal.

HEATHCLIFFE HOSPITAL		DEPARTMENT OF CLINICAL NEUROPHYSIOLOGY

John Smith	Ward F2	Consultant	Dr. Jones
	Date of EEG		10.09.95

The record is of low amplitude and contains generalised fast activity which is most marked centrally. Generalised, rhythmical theta at 4–5 Hz is also seen, which is at times most marked over the left temporal region. Occasional 3–4 Hz activity is also apparent and minimal amounts of 7 Hz rhythmical components are seen posteriorly. Eye opening and closure has little effect on the record.

Hyperventilation and photic stimulation were not obtained.

Comment/summary

There is a mild asymmetry of the background rhythm. No repetitive complexes are seen. No epilepiform activity is present. The findings are not that of an encephalitis.

Signed	A. Peters	(Consultant Clinical Neurophysiologist)

BRAIN SCANS

There are several different brain imaging techniques, including computed tomography (CT scans), magnetic resonance imaging (MRI scans) and Positron emission tomography (PET scans). Tomography is a method of radiography which can display details in a selected plane within the body.

CT scans

Computed tomography (CT scans, formerly known as CAT scans) enables an X-ray picture of the brain to be obtained. Minute variations in the density of bone, cerebrospinal fluid, blood vessels, and grey and white matter can be assessed by utilising an x-ray source, computer processing, and photographic material. Many brain lesions larger than 1.5cm in cross section can be visualised as, for example, can ventricular size. Although brain changes in patients with schizophrenia have been reported, CT changes in patients with major psychiatric disorders at present have greater research than diagnostic value.[65] However, they may be used to rule out organic brain disorders, such as pituitary tumours, and cerebrovascular diseases.

---

[65] R.A. MacKinnon and S.C. Yudofsky, *Principles of Psychiatric Evaluation* (J.B. Lippincott Co., 1991), p.126. Nasrallah, *et al.*, *Journal of Neuropsychiatry and Clinical Neurosciences* (1989) 1, 1.

Magnetic Resonance Imaging (MRI)

Magnetic resonance imaging (MRI), which involves placing the patient in a long tubular structure containing powerful magnets, produces images of the brain that closely resemble CT scans but are of a superior resolution. The technique reveals highly detailed images of the fine structures of the brain which can resemble anatomical preparations. More particularly, MRI scanning is capable of taking thinner slices through the brain and can distinguish between white and grey matter.[66] Consequently, the presence of lesions can be detected more precisely than with any other brain imaging technique. However, its precision also makes it a highly expensive technique.

Positron Emission Tomography (PET)

Positron emission tomography is an expensive brain imaging technique which involves the introduction of manufactured radioactive compounds. It can produce detailed and specifically coloured images of brain function rather than merely an image of the brain's structure. Again, the procedure's use in cases of major psychiatric disorder currently has greater research than diagnostic value and it is only available at special centres.

PSYCHIATRIC RATING INSTRUMENTS

Psychiatric rating scales, also referred to as rating instruments, attempt to measure (quantify) various aspects of a patient's mental functioning by means of rating the presence, absence or severity of certain symptoms or behaviour. Depending on their design, the scales may be used to measure inner mental phenomena, such as mood or behaviour, or the external manifestations of an individual's mental state. Some instruments are highly specific, concentrating on a single aspect of a person's mental state or behaviour, such as aggression. There are two main types of rating scales. **Likert scales** consist of a number of categories (symptoms), each of which is rated on a scale in terms of its severity (0 = symptom absent, 1 = doubtful, 2 = mild, 3 = moderate, 4 = severe, or as to duration, 0 = never present, 1 = some of the time, 2 = often, 3 = always). **Analogue or graphic scales** consist of a straight line combined with verbal cues, *e.g.* "Not at all sad ____ Extremely sad." The rater places a mark on the line to indicate where the symptom lies on the dimension of severity.[67] Thompson has comprehensively reviewed the problems associated with constructing psychiatric rating scales. He concludes that such ratings "can only be expected to have limited transferability between one situation and another, for example between different groups of patients, between different raters, between different cultures and in the same groups at different times."[68] The most reliable rating scales require a limited amount of judgement or inference on the part of the rater.[69] An excellent overview of the subject may be found in MacKinnon and Yudofsky's *Principles of Psychiatric Evaluation*.[70]

---

[66]   H. Kaplan and B. Sadock, *Synopsis of Psychiatry* (Williams & Wilkins, 7th ed., 1994), p.113.
[67]   C. Thompson *The Instruments of Psychiatric Research* (John Wiley & Sons, 1989), pp.4–5.
[68]   *Ibid.*, p.3.
[69]   H. Kaplan and B. Sadock, *Synopsis of Psychiatry, supra*, p.330.
[70]   R.A. MacKinnon and S.C. Yudofsky, *Principles of Psychiatric Evaluation, supra*.

Intelligence

Wechsler Adult Intelligence Scale (WAIS-R)

An extensively standardised instrument for measuring intelligence. Provides three separate IQ scores: a full scale IQ, a verbal IQ, and a performance IQ. The verbal scales measure the ability of the patient to reason abstractly, his verbal memory capacity, verbal facility, understanding of society's conventions, and a quantitative and qualitative assessment of the patient's educational background. The performance section measures a patient's overall non-verbal, visuo-spatial capabilities, including the ability to integrate perceptual stimuli with motor responses.

Personality and behaviour

Minnesota Multiphasic Personality Inventory (MMPI)

Consists of over 500 statements to which the subject must respond "true," "false," or "cannot say." Scores the patient on ten standard clinical scales (*e.g.* depression, psychopathic deviance). Extensively used. An alternative scale is the Eysenck Personality Questionnaire (EPQ).

Schizophrenia and psychosis

Schedule for Affective Disorders and Schizophrenia (SADs)

Focuses on the one-week period during the current episode when the particular feature was most severe.

Other scales

Scale for the Assessment of Negative Symptoms (SANs); Thought Disorder Index (TDI); Quality of Life Scale (QLS); Chesnut Lodge Prognostic Scale for Chronic Schizophrenia.

Mood disorders

Beck Depression Inventory

Measures depression on Likert-type scale.

Other scales

Hamilton Depression Rating Scale; Standard Assessment of Depressive Disorders (SADD); Zung Self-Rating Scale for Depression; Montgomery-Asberg Scale; Mania Rating Scale.

19. Classifying and diagnosing mental disorder

INTRODUCTION

It was noted in the previous chapter that assessment is the process of collecting information relevant to the diagnosis, management, and treatment of a patient's clinical condition. The recording of a patient's symptoms, and the conduct of any special investigations, is initially undertaken to identify the type of disorder from which he suffers. A diagnosis is a short-hand way of describing what is wrong with a patient and it involves assigning the patient's case to a particular known class, such as schizophrenia, by reference to an accepted classification of mental disorders. Conclusions can then be reached about the causes, probable course, and treatment of the condition in question. Before considering the diagnostic process the way in which mental disorders are classified must therefore first be dealt with.

THE CLASSIFICATION OF MENTAL DISORDERS

Classification is the grouping of things according to a logical scheme for organising and classifying them and assigning them their proper places. More particularly, phenomena are assigned to designated classes on the basis of perceived common characteristics. Both legal and medical classifications of mental disorders exist. Medical classifications indicate which conditions are regarded as being mental or behavioural disorders and therefore suitable for medical treatment. Particular diagnoses are considered to be associated with particular prognoses and outcomes. The precise diagnosis may profoundly affect the clinician's opinion about whether in-patient treatment is necessary for the patient's health or safety or to protect others and, more specifically, the extent to which treatment is likely to alleviate or prevent a deterioration of the patient's condition. Sartorius, until recently the Director of the World Health Organisation's Division of Mental Health, ascribes part of the wide-ranging interest of lawyers in medical classifications to the fact that "the absence of physical signs and laboratory abnormalities in many psychiatric disturbances makes psychiatric disorders much more dependent on the consensus of what in a given society is normal, what is abnormal, what is asocial and what is part of a disease."[1]

LEGAL CLASSIFICATIONS

Section 1 of the Mental Health Act 1983 distinguishes between four legal classes of mental disorder (mental illness, psychopathic disorder, mental impairment, severe

---

[1] N. Sartorius, in *Sources and Traditions of Classification in Psychiatry* (ed. N. Sartorius, *et al.*, World Health Organisation/Hogrefe & Huber, 1990), p.1.

mental impairment) three of which are defined. Various sections of the Act provide for reclassifying the legal form of mental disorder from which a detained patient is recorded as suffering. Legally defining "mental disorder", and sub-dividing mental disorders into different statutory classes, serves the purpose of defining as far as practicable the group of citizens to whom the various compulsory powers conferred by the Act apply and the circumstances in which resort may be made to them. The legal classification of mental disorders set out in section 1 of the Mental Health Act 1983 has already been considered (**051**). Here, it may simply be noted that the classifications set out in mental health legislation have tended to adopt the classification of mentally abnormal states set out at the time in the World Health Organisation's International Classification of Diseases, that classification having been in official usage in the United Kingdom for half a century.

MEDICAL CLASSIFICATIONS

Sartorius has emphasised that classification is a way of seeing the world, a reification of an ideological position and of an accepted standard of theory and knowledge: "Classifying means creating, defining or confirming boundaries of concepts. Through these, in turn, we define ourselves, our future and our past, the territory of our discipline, its importance and its exclusiveness. No other intellectual act is of such importance."[2] These views are shared by Kendell, the foremost authority on the classification of mental disorders, who has variously described the process of classification as one of the most fundamental activities of any branch of learning and necessary if any useful communication is to take place. The whole process of language is based on classification and on assumed associations and relationships between certain objects or phenomena: every common noun, such as a tree, denotes the existence of a category or class of objects. Furthermore, not to attempt to delineate mental disorders is still to classify them, because rejecting the notion of distinct categories of disorder is in essence a statement that there exists only mental health and mental disorder and no distinct sub-types of each.[3] Classification also has important practical benefits. In the first place, until categories can be identified, "one is unable to begin to count, and until counting is possible one cannot know how big the problems are or deploy the resources intelligently in an endeavour to control the problems."[4] The identification of specific syndromes is also an essential first-stage in identifying their aetiology and pathology and "rational treatment can only be based upon a satisfactory system of classification of diagnoses."[5] A distinction between different kinds of mental disorder "is therefore inevitable. The only open issues are whether this classification is going to be public or private, stable or unstable, reliable or unreliable, valid or invalid."[6] Attempting to avoid classification altogether would be "crippling clinically and scientifically."[7]

---

[2] K. Menninger, *The vital balance: the life process in mental health and illness* (Viking Press, 1963).

[3] See *e.g.* R.E. Kendell, "Diagnosis and classification" in *Companion to psychiatric studies* (ed. R.E. Kendell & A.K. Zealley, Churchill Livingstone, 1993), p.277. Psychiatrists are sometimes said to be either "lumpers" or "splitters." The former believe that schizophrenia is a single "disease," with variations in presentation being accounted for by different individual responses to the "disease." The latter consider that there are a number of distinguishable sub-types of schizophrenia, such as hebephrenic schizophrenia, and so forth.

[4] *International Classification of Impairments, Disabilities, and Handicaps: A manual of classification relating to the consequences of disease* (World Health Organisation, 1976), p.35.

[5] A. Sims and D. Owens, *Psychiatry* (Baillière Tindall, 6th ed., 1993), p.34.

[6] R.E. Kendell, "Diagnosis and classification" in *Companion to psychiatric studies* (ed. R.E. Kendell & A.K. Zealley, Churchill Livingstone, 1993), p.277.

[7] J.K. Wing, "Differential diagnosis of schizophrenia" in *Schizophrenia — An overview and practical handbook* (ed. D.J. Kavanagh, Chapman & Hall, 1992), p.19.

ASSOCIATED TERMS

Nomenclature, nosology, ontology, and diagnosis are related and, to some extent, overlapping terms that refer to various aspects of the conceptualisation of disease. The first three of these terms have not yet been dealt with although they are routinely referred to in medical literature. They are therefore briefly mentioned here.

Nomenclature

Nomenclature (literally, "class name") denotes the agreed or approved list of categories or titles of disorders within a classification which are used to communicate the results of the diagnostic process, schizophrenia being one example.

Nosology

Nosology is the study of the classification, grouping and ordering of diseases and their relationship to one another. It includes the formulation of principles for differentiating one disease from another. Ideally, nosology would provide a differentiation of discrete diseases and for each describe a specific cause and specific treatments; a typical clinical picture, natural history and outcome; and objective tests for confirming the diagnosis. The nosology of mental disorders has, however, remained problematic ever since the endeavour was first attempted and the area remains split into rival schools.[8]

Ontology

One definition of classification is that it is "a means of giving order to a group of disconnected facts."[9] Underlying the question of nosology is that of ontology, which is the study of whether things actually exist in the real world or are merely products of our own ways of studying and classifying the world. For example, although we still classify stars by constellations, we now know that their apparent unity is an illusion caused by the perspective of the observer. The different stars within each constellation most often lie not together in space but many light years apart. Akin to this, Allport's view of psychiatric classifications was that "all typologies place boundaries where boundaries do not belong. They are artificial categories ... each theorist slices nature in any way he chooses and finds only his own cuttings worthy of admiration."[10] It is possible therefore that differentiating between different classes

---

[8]   In very general terms, the contemporary biomedical approach reflects the Platonic tradition that the different categories of mental disorder constitute a number of discrete disease entities ("the categorical view"). The Hippocratic or Aristotelian tradition holds instead that mental health and mental disorder form a continuum: differences in presentation relate to the chronicity and severity of mental phenomena, being stages and variants of an indivisible unitary psychosis.

[9]   *A Dictionary of Epidemiology* (ed. J.M. Last, International Epidemiological Association/Oxford University Press, 3rd ed., 1995), p.29.

[10]   A point made by Eliot in the nineteenth century: "Your pier-glass or extensive surface of polished steel made to be rubbed by a housemaid, will be minutely and multitudinously scratched in all directions; but place now against it a lighted candle as a centre of illumination, and lo ! the scratches will seem to arrange themselves in a fine series of concentric circles round that little sun. It is demonstrable that the scratches are going everywhere impartially, and it is only your candle which provides the flattering illusion of a concentric arrangement, its light falling with an exclusive optical selection. These things are a parable. The scratches are events, and the candle is the egoism of any person now absent ..." George Eliot, *Middlemarch* (Penguin English Library, 1965), p.297. First published in 1871–72.

of mental disorder is similar to the division of painters or musicians into different schools, a matter of convenience rather than science. While it may be convenient to classify certain music as jazz or certain art as post-impressionist, these distinctions are essentially artificial and no real, or objectively measurable, unity between the works so classified can be discerned. At any rate, the classification of certain paintings as abstract may, as with mental disorder, be based on a conception that their essential distinguishing feature is a lack of any order. If so, the objects may be placed in the class "disordered" but attempting to then order that class may be contradictory and offend reality. The issue has important practical implications. For example, Schneider was concerned that clinical facts are often ignored in order to prevent the classificatory system breaking down. Consequently, he preferred what he called "unsystematic typologies," within which the different names represented descriptions rather than diagnoses of mental states.

THE STRUCTURE OF A CLASSIFICATION

Ideally, a classification (or "taxonomy") should be characterised by naturalness (the classes correspond to the nature of the thing being classified); *exhaustiveness* and *mutual exclusivity* (every member of the group will fit into one and only one class in the system); *usefulness* (the classification is practical); simplicity (the sub-classes are not excessive); and *constructability* (the set of classes can be constructed by a demonstrably systematic procedure).[11] There may be tiers, sub-classes or sub-divisions. Classes may be dimensional (height 5' 2"–5'4"; IQ 100–120, etc.) or categorical (short, fat, etc.). Traditionally, psychiatry has always used a categorical classification or "typology." That is, "it has divided its subject-matter, psychiatric illness, into a number of separate and mutually exclusive categories like schizophrenia, mania and Alzheimer's disease."[12] The way in which the classification tree is constructed will inevitably affect the results produced so that a person may meet the criteria for a diagnosis of schizophrenia set out in one classification but not another.

The use of hierarchies

Almost every psychiatric symptom of significance is capable of appearing in the presence of nearly every other symptom. Because this is so, Kendell has variously commented upon the problems which then arise in applying to psychiatry one of the fundamental principles of medicine: to try to account for a patient's symptoms by a single diagnosis. The approach usually adopted is to arrange symptoms in an arbitrary hierarchy, with the least common at the top and the most widespread at the bottom, since this represents almost the only way of making a single diagnosis. Thus, if there is clear evidence of brain disease that establishes the diagnosis and, likewise, in the absence of such evidence, clear features of schizophrenia often establish that diagnosis even if affective symptoms are also present. While the approach allows for some sort of ordered classification, the danger is that the classification provides order rather than reflects reality, so that the classification is dictating to the latter rather than accounting for it.

---

[11]   *A Dictionary of Epidemiology* (ed. J.M. Last, International Epidemiological Association/Oxford University Press, 3rd ed., 1995), p.29.

[12]   R.E. Kendell, "Diagnosis and classification" in *Companion to psychiatric studies* (ed. R.E. Kendell & A.K. Zealley, Churchill Livingstone, 1993), p.292.

The classificatory criteria

As a matter of logic, the different methods of classifying mental disorders focus on the different stages of the disease process:

Aetiology ⟶ Pathology ⟶ Manifestation ⟶ Outcome

The classification and diagnosis of physical diseases are mostly based on their aetiology or pathology, that is diseases are classified according to their known causes or biological abnormalities. Most authors take the view that a classification based on aetiology and pathology is most desirable since it is most useful in practice. However, because most psychiatric disorders (including schizophrenia and mood disorders) have no known unifying aetiology or pathology, they must be classified by their outcome, response to treatment, or according to patterns of symptoms observed to frequently occur together (the "syndrome" approach).

Classification by aetiology and pathology

An aetiological classification describes the cause of the disorder and, if it is unique to the specific condition, provides a clear prognosis and treatment plan or focus for research into treatment. Consequently, a classification of infections based on the identity of infecting organisms is more useful than one based on purely clinical phenomena, such as the presence of fever.[13] It is, however, impossible to describe disease purely in terms of an external cause such as an infectious agent because the same agent can produce very different diseases. Many mental disorders are also aetiologically very diverse, that is they have a "multi-factorial aetiology" rather than any simple single cause. For example, "depressive disorder can be regarded as a final common pathway which may have multiple causes, even in a single case."[14] Thus, the same cause may produce very different diseases and the same disease may have many different causes. Consequently, Bradley notes that even if our knowledge of aetiology was complete the classification of disease in terms of cause could never be satisfactory. Abnormalities of structure and function — the pathology which is the basis of symptoms and signs — must be taken into account when diseases are classified. Again, though, pathology cannot provide a satisfactory taxonomy alone because the nature of the infecting organism is often crucially important in the management of the patient. Moreover, in some cases, such as Alzheimer's disease, the precise pathology is not clear until after the patient's death, following post-mortem examination of the brain. In any case, because the aetiology and pathology of the vast majority of severely disabling psychiatric disorders remains unknown — both pre and post mortem — classification by such means is presently impossible.

Classification by outcome or treatment response

Classification by outcome alone is of limited practical value. Such a classification affords no prediction of the outcome since it is the outcome which retrospectively defines the diagnosis, whereas most doctors wish to know the diagnosis and prognosis before commencing treatment. Furthermore, many disorders have a wide range of outcomes. A classification based on response to a particular treatment is similarly unsatisfactory. There are few, if any, specific treatments in psychiatry and

---

[13]   R.E. Kendell, "Diagnosis and classification" in *Companion to psychiatric studies* (ed. R.E. Kendell & A.K. Zealley, Churchill Livingstone, 1993), pp.278–279.

[14]   J.M. Pfeffer and G. Waldron, *Psychiatric Differential Diagnoses* (Churchill Livingstone, 1987).

the different therapies are not mutually exclusive. Response to ECT does not establish that the individual had a depressive disorder, nor does failure to respond to antipsychotics mean that he is not psychotic or does not have schizophrenia.

Classification by symptoms (syndromes)

Although acknowledged not to be particularly satisfactory, the symptomological approach to classification is by default generally used in psychiatry. For a symptom to be used diagnostically, its occurrence must be typical of that condition and it must occur relatively frequently.[15] Clusters of symptoms may be observed to occur in conjunction and to develop or remit according to a broadly identifiable pattern, persisting for a characteristic length of time. These clusters of symptoms therefore occur together as identifiable constellations or syndromes — "syndrome" being a Greek word meaning "running together." The syndrome can be named and classified, *e.g.* schizophrenia. Such a classificatory scheme does not depend upon knowing the cause of the disorder or the abnormal pathology responsible for the patient's symptoms. It is based merely on the identification of a pattern of symptoms sufficiently distinctive to justify an inference that they are the product of some discrete medical condition. A doctor who then examines a patient and observes the characteristic symptom pattern may diagnose that the particular condition and prescribe a certain treatment. Research into the syndrome may later confirm that it is a "disease" with characteristic features in terms of its causes, the people whom it affects, its course and likely outcome. Thus, a person with a certain grouping of symptoms and blood test results has leukaemia, which can be shown to have a certain natural course and to respond better to some treatments than others. Blood tests and other routine examinations may confirm various distinguishable sub-types, the validity of which can be demonstrated by their relatively high predictive power in terms of response to treatment, outcome and test-retest reliability. The problem with many psychiatric disorders is that their existence as distinct illnesses cannot be demonstrated in this way, there being few tests of any diagnostic utility which can distinguish between different types of mental disorder. For example, there is no known organic or physiological abnormality which accounts for hebephrenic schizophrenia and is only found in patients with the disorder. Consequently, the psychiatrist must rely "upon the consensus among his colleagues that a particular constellation of symptoms or phenomena tend to occur together and can be recognised as a syndrome."[16] Whether or not certain recognised syndromes do in reality represent distinct disease processes depends upon the correctness of the observations and inferences made about the way in which symptoms and signs coalesce, as well as the validity of this kind of disease reasoning itself. As matters presently stand, conditions such as schizophrenia are ultimately concepts the validity of which has yet to be demonstrated. Nevertheless, most established diseases were originally defined by their syndromes and "as knowledge about their etiology slowly accumulated they came, one by one, to be defined at some more fundamental level. The clinical syndrome 'phthisis' became pulmonary tuberculosis, defined by the presence of tubercle bacilli in sputum or post-mortem lung ... and Down's syndrome became trisomy 21, defined by the presence of that additional chromosome, as soon as it was apparent that the syndrome was invariably associated with that chromosomal abnormality."[17]

---

15   A. Sims, *Symptoms in the Mind* (Baillière Tindall, 1988), p.6.
16   C. Thompson, *The Instruments of Psychiatric Research* (John Wiley & Sons, 1989), p.3.
17   See R.E. Kendell, "Schizophrenia: A Medical View of a Medical Concept" in *What is Schizophrenia?* (ed. W.F. Flack *et al.*, Springer-Verlag, 1990), p.64.

PROBLEMS CLASSIFYING SYNDROMES

The difficulties involved in constructing any classification of mental disorders by syndrome are formidable and should not be underestimated —

- The approach depends upon pinpointing characteristic and recurring patterns of symptoms and signs. However, while the correct identification of a rump of features distinctive of an illness requires accurate observation, recording and deduction, decisions about even the presence or absence of particular symptoms have been shown to be relatively unreliable.

- This practical limitation is compounded by the absence of any agreed terminology with which to describe what is observed. Although a precise language is necessary to record observed phenomena, psychiatry lacks this. Once language cannot be agreed certainty is impossible. Every research finding must be translated and, as with any form of literature, some distortion and loss of meaning is inevitable. These limitations have led Professor Kathleen Jones to conclude that description and observation must come before the construction of scales and the formulation of hypotheses about associations between symptoms: "it is not only computers which suffer from the problem of 'garbage in, garbage out.'"[18]

- In theory, the construction of syndromes begins with pinpointing characteristic and recurring patterns of symptoms and signs which are not specific to a particular individual and so cannot be explained in terms of his peculiar characteristics but only as the peculiar characteristics of a distinctive illness. However, considerable practical problems arise from the fact that it is not illnesses *per se* which are being classified but people suffering from illness. This distinction is of fundamental importance. Variability "is the law of life. As no faces are the same, so no two bodies are alike, and no two individuals react alike and behave alike under the abnormal conditions which we know as disease."[19] In consequence, widely different symptoms and signs may result from a common cause so that Huntington's chorea, although transmitted by a known single gene, is associated with a wide variety of psychiatric syndromes.[20] The clinical picture is therefore "most often profoundly coloured and sometimes decisively shaped by factors specific to the individual and his environment. Hence the notorious difficulty in identifying separate disease processes in psychiatry."[21] Or, as Yellowlees put it: "As the symptoms of any form of mental disorder vary enormously in different patients, the results ... are analogous to those obtained by arranging

18   K. Jones, "Social science in relation to psychiatry" in *Companion to psychiatric studies* (ed. R.E. Kendell & A.K. Zealley, Churchill Livingstone, 1993), p.12.

19   Sir W. Osler, *Medical education in Counsels and Ideals* (Houghton Mifflin, 2nd ed., 1921).

20   R.E. Kendell, "Schizophrenia: A Medical View of a Medical Concept" in *What is Schizophrenia?* (ed. W.F. Flack *et al.*, Springer-Verlag, 1990), p.67.

21   W.A. Lishman, *Organic Psychiatry, The Psychological Consequences of Cerebral Disorder* (Blackwell Scientific Publications, 2nd ed., 1987), p.3. There is no identifiable single set of symptoms which constitutes normal health and therefore no single syndrome of normal health. The many different syndromes of normal mental health each constitute a norm from which deviation caused by a single pathological process may be observed. Consequently, for each pathological process the number of different types of abnormality precisely equals the number of types of normal health ("no syndrome syndrome").

books in a library, some according to the author, some according to the subject, some according to the size, and some according to the colour of the binding."[22]

- Although marked individual differences can sometimes be explained as atypical presentations, it is often difficult in practice to determine whether a particular constellation of symptoms is an atypical variation of an established syndrome, such as schizophrenia; a discrete sub-type of the disorder, such as hebephrenic schizophrenia; or a mutation of two co-existing but distinct forms of mental disorder, such as schizophrenia and depression ("schizoaffective disorder").[23]

- Certain mental phenomena are found both in people considered to be mentally healthy and those believed to be mentally disordered. For example, a feeling which a person has that he has previously visited a place unknown to him may be a symptom of temporal lobe epilepsy or a manifestation of general anxiety or fatigue. The same symptom observed in two people may therefore be symptomatic of illness in one person but not another and, when considered in isolation, not merely of little diagnostic value but confusing.

- Even when not found in the normal population and so indicative of a pathological process, any given symptom may be symptomatic of several different disorders and, when viewed in isolation, incapable of sustaining a single diagnosis. For example, Schneider's first-rank symptoms of schizophrenia are encountered in temporal lobe epilepsy, brain diseases, and in amphetamine intoxication.[24] The significance of a symptom therefore often depends upon the precise context so that it is known by the company it keeps. Unfortunately, most symptoms are promiscuous and few, if any, are specific to a particular disorder. Symptoms may be commonly present and valuable diagnostically but not universally present or definitive. Some diseases have very few symptoms; others share the same symptoms; and a symptom may sometimes be primary and other times secondary, *e.g.* depression resulting from hypothyroidism.

- It has been noted that some of this variation may be explained as the different effects of the same disease in different bodies. Having regard to this, Kendell has pointed out that each patient has some attributes which he shares with all patients, certain attributes which he shares with some but not all patients, and yet other attributes unique to that individual. Because this is so, the same disorder or disease is likely to affect all people identically in certain respects, different classes of people distinguished by certain key attributes in ways common only to members of the class, and each person within a class in yet other ways peculiar to him. Accordingly, a particular disease or disorder may produce in one person or class of persons symptoms and signs identical to those manifested in another person or group as a result

---

[22] H. Yellowlees, *To Define True Madness* (Pelican Books, Rev. ed., 1955), p.7.

[23] As to this, Crow has noted that schizophrenia and bipolar disorder share many characteristics and several research workers are beginning to wonder whether at least some of their determinants may be common to both. See *e.g.* T. Crow, "Psychosis as a continuum and the virogene concept" *British Medical Bulletin* 43, 754–768.

[24] R.E. Kendell, "Schizophrenia: A Medical View of a Medical Concept" in *What is Schizophrenia?* (ed. W.F. Flack *et al.*, Springer-Verlag, 1990), p.66.

of a quite separate illness, with the result that it is wrongly inferred that the same disorder is responsible for these common symptoms.[25]

- A further complication in defining disease in terms of a specific set of features is that disease patterns change over time for reasons that are poorly understood.[26] This partly reflects the fact that the characteristics of a country's people changes over time — even if there has been no immigration or emigration — so that England, both culturally and medically, is a vastly different country now than a hundred years ago. It is, however, impossible to know whether the people have changed but the disease itself has remained unchanged or whether variations in presentation also reflect an evolution of the disease, in which case even classifications by aetiology or pathology require periodic revision.

- More prosaically, advances in treatment also change the presentation of disease. Few seriously disabling diseases are now allowed to run their natural course and most textbooks describe features which are rarely seen today. Although, as Kendell has noted, this does not necessarily change the spectrum of disease, it influences the type of symptoms and signs commonly observed, upon which syndromes are constructed and classified.

- Some diseases are therefore both anachronistic and anachoristic. If a single disorder is subject to sexual, racial, cultural or temporal fluctuations, the underlying unity may go undetected and it erroneously be construed as a number of separate disorders.

- An imaginative way of addressing these problems is to attempt to identify points of rarity in disease patterns, symptoms which even if not commonly present are nevertheless, when present, evidence of a particular disease. Unfortunately, such attempts have generally been unsuccessful.

- Underlying all these observations is the basic question of the validity of disease reasoning and the syndrome approach. Whether there are genuine boundaries between the clinical syndromes in current classifications, and between those syndromes and normality, is ultimately a conundrum. Although, as Kendell has variously noted, the existence of interforms does not of itself invalidate distinguishing between two different syndromes, most mental disorders do nevertheless appear to lack discrete boundaries and to shade into one another. The traditional research method of comparing people with one diagnosis with control subjects who have another diagnosis or no diagnosis "rests on the assumption that those with the target diagnosis have something in common which is absent in the case of the controls. If this assumption is invalid, the traditional research paradigm cannot hope to yield meaningful findings."[27]

---

[25] Most transparently, people of different genders, races or cultures have some personal characteristics not shared by persons falling outside their particular class. However, it is just as true that a man from one culture may have some characteristics in common with a woman from another culture which he does not also share with other men from his cultural background.

[26] G.W. Bradley, *Disease, Diagnosis and Decisions* (John Wiley & Sons, 1993), p.20.

[27] R.P. Bentall, "The classification of schizophrenia" in *Schizophrenia — An overview and practical handbook* (ed. D.J. Kavanagh, Chapman & Hall, 1992), p.24.

Summary

The picture is therefore kaleidoscopic although it is unclear whether the primary problem is the phenomenal complexity of what is being observed or the perspective from which it is being observed. No single set of observations can ever be precisely replicated. Each individual patient gives the kaleidoscope a turn before the observer looks through the lens at the ever-changing patterns of crystals. Not surprisingly, Osler wrote in 1921 that "the problems of disease are more complicated and more difficult than any others with which the trained mind has to grapple."[28] Some 70 years later, Bradley reached a similar conclusion, writing that the difficulties "cannot easily be overcome making it unlikely that there will ever be a durable classification of disease.[29] It may well be that the symptoms of mental distress are more dictated by personality and environment than by any pathology, the effect of which is simply to imbalance what was previously, if precariously, balanced in the particular individual. Or the answer may be simply that it is logically impossible to classify disorder in an ordered way, to rationally arrange what is deranged. The essential and defining feature of mental disorder is the demolition of structure, disjunction rather than conjunction. Until some underlying and unifying pathology is stumbled upon, the syndrome approach, based as it is on the external manifestations of internal processes, may therefore be contradictory. Having invented the term "mental disorder" to express the idea of behaviour which appears to a rational observer to lack coherence, it is arguably mere vanity to then rigorously scrutinise the idea in the expectation of identifying organised sub-forms of disorder. Whether or not this is so, there may be much to be said for Bentall's suggestion that research should concentrate on particular symptoms before attempting to map their possible constellations—

> "There is a perfectly logical alternative to using diagnostic classifications as independent variables in research into psychopathology: researchers could abandon the attempt to classify psychotic illness (at least for the time being) and make the actual phenomena they encounter in the clinic, that is to say particular types of complaints or behaviours (usually described as 'symptoms') the focus of their efforts. For example, investigators might study hallucinations, delusions, disordered discourse, flat affect, or any other symptom."[30]

CONTEMPORARY CLASSIFICATIONS

Given these considerable problems, it is not surprising that the validity and reliability of both past and contemporary classifications of mental disorder has always been a matter of dispute. In particular, Menninger reviewed and listed many classifications spanning 2500 years and was dismissive of the usefulness and validity of the exercise.[31] Although syndromes such as schizophrenia and depression are still widely used, most attempts to create coherent links between clinical symptoms, causal factors, and prognostic types have failed.[32] Consequently, contemporary classifications vary both with regard to the types of mental disorder considered to be distinct entities and, when this can be agreed, their respective

---

[28]   Sir W. Osler, *Medical education in Counsels and Ideals* (Houghton Mifflin, 2nd ed., 1921).
[29]   G.W. Bradley, *Disease, Diagnosis and Decisions* (John Wiley & Sons, 1993), p.20..
[30]   R.P. Bentall, "The classification of schizophrenia," *supra*, p.34.
[31]   K. Menninger, *The vital balance: the life process in mental health and illness* (Viking Press, 1963).
[32]   N. Sartorius, in *Sources and Traditions of Classification in Psychiatry* (ed. N. Sartorius, *et al.*, World Health Organisation/Hogrefe & Huber, 1990), p.2.

hallmarks. Providing two or more competing classifications are being used appropriately, Kendell has emphasised that one must simply concede that the alternative definitions embrace different populations and examine which of the competing definitions most successfully meets some criterion like homogeneity of outcome or treatment response. This is because, in the last resort, "all diagnostic concepts stand or fall by the strength of the prognostic and therapeutic implications they embody. The ability to predict the outcome of an illness, and to alter this course of events if need be, have always been the main functions of medicine."[33] Unfortunately, although a diagnosis should provide therapeutic and prognostic indicators, these are often relatively weak in psychiatry[34] and "the existing evidence for the validity of most psychiatric disorders is rather meagre, but by no means non-existent."[35]

THE ICD–10 CLASSIFICATION

The classification of mental disorders in official usage in England and Wales is the World Health Organisation's International Classification of Diseases and, more particularly, that part of it dealing with mental and behavioural disorders.[36] The tenth revision (ICD–10), published in 1992, took nine years to prepare and included field trials using the draft text in 194 different countries, after which further revisions were made. The *ICD-10 Classification of Mental and Behavioural Disorders* (the "Blue Book") contains clinical descriptions and diagnostic guidelines for the disorders listed within it.[37] In the tenth revision, the previous distinction between the psychoses and neuroses has been laid aside and all mood disorders are now in a single grouping. Inevitably, the classification reflects "compromises between scientists with the most influential theories and the practice of senior clinicians at national and international level."[38] The classification is not entirely coherent because of the tendency for each class to expand in order to incorporate alternative and sometimes incompatible concepts.[39] Nevertheless, its international status and the need to conduct research according to a common set of guidelines means that there is a mutual obligation to use it.[40]

Format of ICD–10

The classification is divided into major groups ("blocks") of mental disorders. Within these blocks, each type and sub-type of mental disorder is separately listed and coded. Thus, one block is concerned with schizophrenia and similar disorders (Block F20–F29). Schizophrenia is given the code F20 and a further digit is used to record its various sub-types, such as paranoid schizophrenia (F20.0) and catatonic schizophrenia (F20.2).

---

33   R.E. Kendell, "Diagnosis and classification" in *Companion to psychiatric studies* (ed. R.E. Kendell & A.K. Zealley, Churchill Livingstone, 1993), p.290.
34   J.M. Pfeffer and G. Waldron, *Psychiatric Differential Diagnoses* (Churchill Livingstone, 1987), p.4.
35   R.E. Kendell, "Diagnosis and classification," *supra*, p.291.
36   The sixth revision (ICD–6), published in 1948, was the first to include a classification of mental disorders (Section V: "Mental, Psychoneurotic and Personality Disorders"), although it was primarily a classification of psychoses and mental deficiency. The sixth revision and the subsequent (expanded) revisions have all been adopted by the Government.
37   There is also a separate book containing diagnostic criteria for research (The "Green Book").
38   J.K. Wing, "Differential diagnosis of schizophrenia" in *Schizophrenia — An overview and practical handbook* (ed. D.J. Kavanagh, Chapman & Hall, 1992), p.17.
39   R.E. Kendell, "Diagnosis and classification," *supra*, p.287.
40   R.E. Kendell, "Diagnosis and classification," *supra*, p.196.

THE ICD–10 CLASSIFICATION — LIST OF CATEGORIES

Code	Block (major group)	Examples of disorders in block
F00–F09	*Organic mental disorders*	• Alzheimer's disease • Pick's disease • Creutzfeldt-Jakob disease • Parkinson's disease • dementia, delirium.
F10–F19	*Mental and behavioural disorders due to psychoactive substance use*	• due to alcohol • due to opioids, cocaine, etc.
F20–F29	*Schizophrenia, schizotypal and delusional disorders*	• schizophrenia • schizotypal disorder • persistent delusional disorders • schizoaffective disorders.
F30–F39	*Mood (affective) disorders*	• manic episode • bipolar affective disorder • depressive episode
F40–F48	*Neurotic, stress-related and somato-form disorders*	• hypochondriacal disorder • phobic and anxiety disorders • obsessive-compulsive disorder
F50–F59	*Behavioural syndromes associated with physiological disturbances and physical factors*	• Eating disorders • sleep disorders • premature ejaculation
F60–F69	*Disorders of adult personality and behaviour*	• personality disorders • habit and impulse disorders • transsexualism, fetishism
F70–F79	*Mental retardation*	• mental retardation
F80–F89	*Disorders of psychological development*	• childhood autism • specific spelling disorder
F90–F98	*Behavioural and emotional disorders with onset usually occurring in childhood and adolescence*	• hyperkinetic disorders • conduct disorders • tics
F99	*Unspecified mental disorder*	• not applicable

Operational definitions (diagnostic guidelines)

It has previously been noted that almost every symptom in psychiatry is capable of occurring in conjunction with almost any other symptom. Thus, for example, symptoms such as elation, flight of ideas and grandiose ideas are quite common in both schizophrenia and mania. Operational definitions (also known as diagnostic guidelines or criteria) are therefore used to specify which combinations of symptoms are adequate to substantiate a diagnosis. They define what a clinician means when he uses the term "schizophrenia" or "mania" and represent an attempt to standardise clinical practice and understanding. The introduction to the blue book contains the following notes on the diagnostic guidelines set out in the ICD–10 classification—

"When the requirements laid down in the diagnostic guidelines are clearly fulfilled, the diagnosis can be regarded as 'confident'. When the requirements are only partially fulfilled, it is nevertheless useful to record a diagnosis for most purposes. It is then for the diagnostician and other users of the diagnostic statements to decide whether to record the lesser degrees of confidence (such as 'provisional' if more information is yet to come, or 'tentative' if more information is unlikely to become available) that are implied in these circumstances. Statements about the duration of symptoms are also intended as general guidelines rather than strict requirements; clinicians should use their own judgement about the appropriateness of choosing diagnoses when the duration of particular symptoms is slightly longer or shorter than that specified ...

These descriptions and guidelines ... are simply a set of symptoms and comments that have been agreed, by a large number of advisors and consultants in many different countries, to be a reasonable basis for defining the limits of categories in the classification of mental disorders."[41]

THE DSM–IV CLASSIFICATION

The other main international classification of psychiatric disorders is the *Diagnostic and Statistical Manual of Mental Disorders* produced by the American Psychiatric Association, the fourth revision of which (DSM–IV) was published in 1994.[42] This classification is occasionally referred to in the text.

Format of DSM–IV

The classification describes the manifestations of the various mental disorders delineated within it and diagnostic criteria are provided for each of them. Epidemiological data is given for each disorder and differential diagnoses where appropriate. The most distinctive feature of the classification is that it is a "multi-axial" system containing five different axes—

- Axis 1 is used to record clinical conditions which may be the focus of medical attention, such as schizophrenia and mood disorders.

- Axis 2 consists of mental retardation and personality disorders, *e.g.* paranoid personality disorder.

- Axis 3 lists any physical disorder or general medical condition that is present in addition to the mental disorder, *e.g.* an endocrine disorder.

---

[41] *Classification of Mental and Behavioural Disorders, Tenth Revision (ICD-10): Clinical Descriptions and Diagnostic Guidelines* (World Health Organisation, 1992), p.2.

[42] DSM-I was published in 1952, DSM-II in 1968, DSM-III in 1980, and a revised edition of the latter (DSM-III-R) in 1987.

- Axis 4 is used to record psychological, social and environmental problems which have significantly contributed to the development of the current mental disorder or exacerbated it, *e.g.* "housing problems" and "problems with access to health care services."

- Axis 5 comprises the global assessment of functioning scale (GAF Scale), which is used to record the clinician's judgement of the patient's overall functioning during a particular period of time. The patient is rated on a 0–100 scale, with 100 representing superior functioning and 10 "persistent danger of severely hurting self or others" (**222**). Because the GAF scale provides a standard scale for gauging the risks associated with a patient's mental state, it is an extremely useful tool in practice.

Because it is not merely a diagnostic tool, the DSM–IV classification is in many respects superior to the ICD–10 classification. It allows for a more comprehensive recording of the main features of each case: underlying intellectual and personality problems; physical disorders possibly contributing to the mental disorder; contributory social problems; and the effect of the mental disorder on the patient's functioning.

OTHER CLASSIFICATIONS

It must be emphasised that the ICD–10 and DSM–IV classifications, and the diagnostic guidelines which form part of them, are but two of many medical classifications of mental disorder. For conditions such as schizophrenia, none of the competing definitions can be said to be right or wrong since there is as yet no external criterion of validity. It is impossible to decide which is the most valid because this would involve determining which of several different ways of defining the syndrome of schizophrenia most accurately picks out patients possessing an underlying abnormality which has yet to be identified.[43] Although a core of typical patients meet all definitions, there are significant differences in the populations of patients covered by each of them. Each operational definition generates different values for the incidence of a disorder, its heritability, its responsiveness to therapeutic agents, and its prognosis. The concordance between the different sets of operational criteria for conditions such as schizophrenia is "not impressive; in other words the different criteria tend to diagnose different people as schizophrenic."[44] Consequently, it is important to realise that a patient who meets the somewhat inclusive criteria for a diagnosis of schizophrenia in the ICD–10 classification may not satisfy the more tightly-drawn operational criteria of another classification. These observations similarly apply to other kinds of mental disorder.

---

[43] R.E. Kendell, "Schizophrenia: A Medical View of a Medical Concept" in *What is Schizophrenia?* (ed. W.F. Flack *et al.*, Springer-Verlag, 1990), p.63.

[44] R.P. Bentall, "The classification of schizophrenia" in *Schizophrenia — An overview and practical handbook* (ed. D.J. Kavanagh, Chapman & Hall, 1992), p.25.; I.F. Brockington, *et al.*, "Definitions of schizophrenia: Concordance and prediction of outcome" Psychol. Med. (1978) 8, 399–412.

DIAGNOSIS

Diagnosis forms part of the assessment process and, in general usage, the term refers to the process of identifying the specific mental disorder from which the patient suffers.[45] For example, the diagnosis may be that the patient suffers from schizophrenia or, more specifically, from a form of schizophrenia known by the label "hebephrenic schizophrenia." A diagnosis is therefore a "short-hand way of describing what is wrong with the patient"[46] and reaching a diagnosis involves recognising a particular disorder from its signs and symptoms so that, having identified it, conclusions can be reached about its causes, probable course, and treatment. The diagnostic process thus consists of categorising problems in order to solve or ameliorate them using appropriate techniques and skills. The aim of the process is to reduce clinical uncertainty because the diagnosis indicates what the individual patient holds in common with previous patients and so "suggests that a successful treatment plan used for somebody else with the same diagnosis may well lead to benefit."[47] Nevertheless, the diagnostic methods used by different clinicians are not always comparable so that a patient's diagnosis but not his condition may change over time. This is because diagnoses are subject to therapeutic fashions and innovations and depend upon the classification and operational criteria being used.[48] While diagnosing a condition has benefits in terms of communication and research, there is "no very great value in attaching a label to a patient's complaint if exactly the same course of treatment would have been carried out whatever the label,"[49] unless it has a predictive value. The importance of making a diagnosis lies in the fact that it is a recipe for action and a predictor of outcome, rational treatment and prognosis requiring a firm working diagnosis.[50] Inappropriate reassurance, unnecessary treatment and compulsion, and the dissemination of gloom are penalties to be paid for taking too lax an approach to the diagnostic process.[51]

VALIDITY AND RELIABILITY OF THE DIAGNOSIS

The validity of a diagnosis depends on the validity of the classification and operational criteria upon which it is founded and the reliability of the diagnostic process itself. It has already been noted that the validity of diagnoses such as schizophrenia cannot be conclusively demonstrated. Such disorders are hypothetical constructs. While different diagnoses may arise because examiners have different concepts and use different operational definitions, "most psychiatric diagnoses can never be confirmed or refuted, for there is no external criterion to appeal to."[52] Providing a classification is used appropriately, it must ultimately be conceded that it embraces a different population of patients than do other competing operational criteria. Reliability refers to the consistency with which subjects are discriminated from one another; in this context, the extent to which different diagnosticians will agree on a

[45] Some psychiatrists, however, use the term more broadly to refer to a comprehensive evaluation that is not limited to identification of specific disorders.

[46] J.M. Pfeffer and G. Waldron, *Psychiatric Differential Diagnoses* (Churchill Livingstone, 1987).

[47] A. Sims and D. Owens, *Psychiatry* (Baillière Tindall, 6th ed., 1993), p.8.

[48] These operational criteria may be implicit rather than explicit, as where a doctor applies the diagnostic methods imbued in him during his training or makes diagnostic decisions based on personal experience but without ever analysing the basis of the distinctions on which his practice is based.

[49] A. Sims, *Symptoms in the Mind* (Baillière Tindall, 1988).

[50] G.W. Bradley, *Disease, Diagnosis and Decisions* (John Wiley & Sons, 1993), p.50.

[51] *Ibid.*

[52] R.E. Kendell, "Diagnosis and classification" in *Companion to psychiatric studies* (ed. R.E. Kendell & A.K. Zealley, Churchill Livingstone, 1993), p.279.

diagnosis for a given patient. Reliability is therefore a means to an end, rather than an end in itself, and its importance lies in the fact that it establishes a ceiling for validity. The lower it is the lower the validity necessarily becomes.[53] However, the converse is not also true. If the operational criteria applied do not constitute a valid delineation of the disease or disorder in question, reliability can be high while validity remains trivial — in which case, high reliability is of little value.

The reliability of diagnoses

Reliability is usually measured in one of two ways. Either a diagnostic interview is watched by a passive observer who makes his own independent diagnosis at the end (observer method) or a second diagnostician conducts an independent interview with the patient a few hours or days later (reinterview method). The observer method over-estimates reliability because all variation in the conduct of the interview is eliminated. The reinterview method, which in essence is the method used by the tribunal's medical member or a psychiatrist instructed on the patient's behalf, may underestimate reliability because of the time lag and the fact that the patient has practised or thought about his answers. Thus, in one study, there was less than a 50 per cent. chance of a psychiatrist who interviewed a patient some days after a colleague agreeing that a symptom was present.[54] A considerable amount of research has been conducted into the reliability of patients' diagnoses and the findings have generally not been encouraging. Necessarily, a correct diagnosis may not be made when clinical findings are inaccurate. Most studies suggest that agreement about the presence or absence of physical signs is not very good, much of the agreement being due simply to chance. While a study by Beck showed that only 54 per cent. of specialists agreed about diagnosis, Kendell notes that organic and psychotic disorders generally have higher reliability than neuroses and personality disorders. That being so, reliability studies based on in-patients tend to produce higher overall reliability than those based on out-patients. In the latter case, the frequency of neurotic symptoms and maladaptive personality traits in the general population means that quantitative as well as merely qualitative judgements are involved.[55]

Factors affecting the reliability of the diagnosis

There are various reasons for the low reliability of the diagnostic process, some of which reflect the imperfect operation of the assumption that symptoms elicited are present and those not elicited are absent. Bradley and Kendell have summarised the main research findings and the main areas of weakness relate to the collection, interpretation and judging of information[56]:

- Different diagnoses may simply reflect that fact that clinicians have different concepts and use different operational criteria. Because few psychiatric illnesses have pathognomonic symptoms, most conditions have to be defined by the presence of some or most of a group of symptoms rather than by the presence of one key symptom. This "invites ambiguity and lowers reliability still further unless operational definitions are adopted."[57]

[53] R.E. Kendell, "Diagnosis and classification" in *Companion to psychiatric studies* (ed. R.E. Kendell & A.K. Zealley, Churchill Livingstone, 1993), p.290.
[54] N. Kreitman, *et al.*, "The reliability of psychiatric assessment: an analysis" *Journal of Mental Science* (1961) 107: 887–908.
[55] R.E. Kendell, "Diagnosis and classification," *supra*, p.290.
[56] G.W. Bradley, *Disease, Diagnosis and Decisions* (John Wiley & Sons, 1993).
[57] R.E. Kendell, "Diagnosis and classification," *supra*, p.279.

- In other cases, the patient's condition may not conform to the tidy, stereotyped descriptions found in textbooks. When patients possess some but not all of the characteristic features of two or three different diagnostic categories, disagreements and the use of hybrid terms will necessarily be quite common. Although the use of operational definitions increases reliability and makes clear the concepts underpinning the diagnosis, their use varies in practice. The diagnostic criteria applied are often implicit rather than explicit and the clinician may fail to scrutinise or specify the assumed relationship between the symptoms and diagnosis.

- Although structured interviews are generally unsuitable for ordinary clinical purposes, because they do not permit a rapid focusing on the patient's main difficulties, the free-ranging, unstructured, interviews used by clinicians are nevertheless less reliable — and, in consequence, they are no longer used for research purposes.[58] While many of the principles involved in conducting a non-structured interview are "simple enough, even self-evident, ... this does not stop them being flouted even by experienced clinicians who ought to know better."[59]

- Unstructured interviews being relatively subjective, behavioural differences between interviewers account for much of the observed unreliability. A patient may give different accounts to different interviewers, partly because of the way questions are asked. Different interviewers pose different questions, show interest and probe in different places and establish different kinds of relationships with patients. The doctor's perception of the likelihood of a certain diagnosis in his practice (the "prior probability") may affect the information sought so that other information of crucial importance is overlooked. Such preconceptions, in terms of their expectations of finding different symptoms, are reflected both in the wording of questions and the interpretation of ambiguous replies. Fixing on a diagnosis at an early stage may similarly lead to a premature closure of options. Conceptual differences, involving the different usage of words such as anxiety or delusion and the extent to which a graded characteristic had to be evident to be recorded as present, can also affect the symptoms recorded and hence the diagnosis reached.[60]

- The importance attached to information may be inappropriate in several circumstances with a failure to attach correct weights to cues. Cues discovered early on in an interview have been found to be given more emphasis in coming to a diagnosis than the same cues given later on in the examination.

- There is also a natural tendency to overemphasise positive findings when a negative finding may contain just as much information. This reflects a natural human preference for evidence that proves rather than disproves a hypothesis. Similarly, normal findings tend to be ignored when judging the effect of a test on the likelihood of disease. Although a negative test should

---

[58] R.E. Kendell, "Diagnosis and classification" in *Companion to psychiatric studies* (ed. R.E. Kendell & A.K. Zealley, Churchill Livingstone, 1993), p.281.

[59] *Ibid.*, p.280.

[60] *Ibid.*, pp.278–279.

have the effect of making the diagnosis less likely, the clinician often ignores this evidence.[61]

- Even if no inappropriate emphasis is placed on particular clinical findings, a clinician's inexperience may nevertheless result in failure to consider the correct diagnosis in the first place.

- Conversely, clinical experience may occasionally be disadvantageous. While analytical methods are slower but potentially more accurate, particularly for the complicated cases, the doctor who is experienced in the task in hand is more likely to use intuitive methods with a resulting advantage in speed. Nevertheless, "it is as well to remember that whilst experience can be the mainstay of diagnostic skill, overreliance on it can lead to nothing more than making the same mistake with increasing confidence."[62]

DISADVANTAGES OF DIAGNOSIS

Kendell has summarised some of the main disadvantages involved in giving a patient a diagnosis.[63] In the first place, most psychiatric diagnoses have pejorative connotations. A diagnosis of schizophrenia or psychopathic disorder may have a particularly harmful effect on the patient's self-esteem and the attitude and behaviour of others towards him. Secondly, attaching a name to a condition may create a spurious impression of understanding. However, to say that a person has schizophrenia "actually says little more than that he has some puzzling but familiar symptoms which have often been encountered before in other patients."[64] Thirdly, all too often doctors reify the diagnostic concept and treat the "disease" instead of trying to relieve their patient's symptoms, anxieties and disabilities.

DIAGNOSTIC FORMULATIONS

A diagnostic formulation is not the same thing as a diagnosis. For the reasons given, a diagnosis may be an inadequate means of conveying what the clinician regards as the essence of the patient's predicament — why he broke down, in that particular way, at that particular time. A diagnostic formulation involves considering and then specifying these important elements of the case in a short account. Formulation and diagnosis are equally necessary, but for quite different purposes — " ... the idea that a diagnosis can, or should, be replaced by a formulation is based on a fundamental misunderstanding of the nature of both. A formulation which takes account of the unique features of the patient and his environment, and the interaction between them, is often essential for any real understanding of his predicament, and for planning effective treatment, but it is unusable in any situation in which populations or groups of patients need to be considered."[65]

---

[61]   G.A. Gorry, et al., "The diagnostic importance of the normal finding" New England Journal of Medicine (1978) 298: 486–489; G.W. Bradley, Disease, Diagnosis and Decisions (John Wiley & Sons, 1993), p.55. Indeed, it is of fundamental importance in tribunal proceedings to establish and list all of the operational criteria which are not present in the particular case. All too often, a long interview is summarised in two lines stating that features a and b were elicited during examination, while the fact that features c to m were not elicited is implied but goes unrecorded.

[62]   G.W. Bradley, Disease, Diagnosis and Decisions (supra), p.68.

[63]   R.E. Kendell, "Diagnosis and classification" in Companion to psychiatric studies (ed. R.E. Kendell & A.K. Zealley, Churchill Livingstone, 1993), p.278.

[64]   Ibid.

[65]   Ibid., p.277.

20. Treatment and outcome

INTRODUCTION

It has been noted that assessment is the process of collecting information relevant to the diagnosis, management, and treatment of a patient's clinical condition. The recording of a patient's symptoms, and the conduct of any special investigations, is initially undertaken to identify the type of disorder from which the patient suffers. A diagnosis is a short-hand way of describing what is wrong with a patient and it involves assigning the patient's case to a particular known class, such as schizophrenia, by reference to an accepted classification of mental disorders. Conclusions can then be reached about the causes, probable course, and treatment of the condition in question. All diagnostic concepts ultimately stand or fall by the strength of the prognostic and therapeutic implications they embody. However, while a diagnosis should provide therapeutic and prognostic indicators, in psychiatry these are often relatively weak.

Aetiology	Pathology	Symptoms	Diagnosis	Prognosis	Treatment	Outcome

$\longrightarrow$

It is therefore assumed that each disease has a certain natural course although this can sometimes be interfered with by treatment. Consequently, the diagnosis of a particular disease enables the clinician to choose an appropriate form of treatment and to make an assessment of the likely outcome (a prognosis). The actual outcome may differ from that prognosed. Various terms are used to describe the consequences of an illness in terms of the individual's ability to carry out his normal activities (*e.g.* disability and handicap) and the effect which treatment, including the body's own treatments, has on the underlying disease process (*e.g.* remission).

PREDICTING THE COURSE AND OUTCOME

A prognosis is a medical assessment of the probable course and outcome of a patient's condition. Certain disorders have been found to have a natural course and outcome and to respond best to certain treatments. By noting the timing of critical events for each patient with a particular disease — for example, dates of diagnosis, the development of further manifestations, and death — its progression can be subdivided into phases. When summarised over many patients, estimates of the typical sequence of events, the "natural history" of the illness, can be constructed.[1]

---

[1]   R.S. Greenberg, *Medical Epidemiology* (Appleton and Lange, 1993), p7.

1125

For example, 90 per cent. of people with small cell carcinoma of the lung will die within five years of the condition developing. However, even when the ultimate outcome may be predicted with some confidence, the actual sequence of events can vary widely among patients because such predictions are based on the experience of other patients.[2]

DESCRIBING ONSET, COURSE, DURATION AND OUTCOME

The onset, course and duration of a disorder are often described as either acute or chronic. The outcome may be recovery; a complete or partial remission of the symptoms, sometimes followed by relapse; or chronic, with little or no change in the presence or intensity of the patient's symptoms.

Onset and duration

The term "acute" describes a disorder or symptom that comes on suddenly, may or may not be severe, and is usually of short duration. In the context of severe mental illness, the ICD–10 classification defines acute onset as "a change during a period of a fortnight or less from a state without psychotic features to an obviously abnormal psychotic state." When such a change occurs with a period of 48 hours, the onset is said to be "abrupt."[3] "Chronic" describes a disorder or set of symptoms that has persisted for a long time, rather than being of sudden onset and short duration. There is little discernible change in the symptomatology from day to day:

> "The onset is usually insidious; there may be a gradual progression of symptoms, or more permanent problems may develop as the sequel to a number of acute episodes. Confidence and hopes are undermined; the experience is usually difficult to account for, no end is in sight, and self-perception — the sense of identity — is assaulted by changes in the body and its functional performance ... the persistence of problems implicitly reveals limitations in the potency of medical treatment, so that professional advice is often accepted with less assurance ... The prevalence of chronic conditions may be high, but their incidence is relatively low ... the multidimensional quality of problems encountered in people with chronic illness tends to promote needs-based appraisals, which carry with them potentially inflationary consequences for health and welfare services."[4]

The term "sub-acute" is sometimes used to describe a disorder which runs an intermediate course in time, between acute and chronic. Classically, acute onset culminates in a crisis so that acute conditions are severe in terms of their intensity while the severity of chronic conditions lies in their duration and limited response to treatment.[5] It should, however, be emphasised that chronic conditions may have intermittent acute exacerbations.

---

[2] R.S. Greenberg, *Medical Epidemiology* (Appleton and Lange, 1993), p.6.
[3] *Classification of Mental and Behavioural Disorders, Tenth Revision(ICD–10): Clinical descriptions and diagnostic guidelines* (World Health Organisation, 1992), pp.99–100.
[4] *International Classification of Impairments, Disabilities, and Handicaps: A manual of classification relating to the consequences of disease* (World Health Organisation, 1976), p.24.
[5] Thus, "professional usage of the words remains closer to their etymology. Thus 'acute' means 'ending in a sharp point', implying a finite duration, which, classically, culminates in a crisis. On the other hand 'chronic', which is derived from a word meaning 'time', indicates 'long-continued.'" *Ibid.*, p.23.

DESCRIBING THE OUTCOME AND RESPONSE TO TREATMENT

Recovery (or "cure" where recovery follows treatment) describes the elimination of the disease or disorder producing the patient's symptoms. Remission denotes a temporary disappearance or reduction in the severity or symptomatology of a disease or a period during which this occurs. A proportion of patients recover or their symptoms remit naturally, for reasons other than any treatment administered to them. The residual phase of an illness is the phase that occurs after remission of the florid symptoms of the full syndrome. Relapse describes the recurrence of a disorder after an apparent recovery or a return of the symptoms after their remission. Sequelae are the complications of a disorder, *e.g.* the sequelae of a cold may include bronchitis.

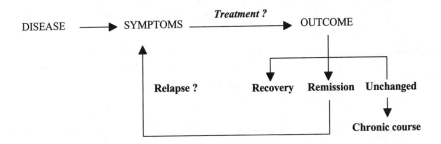

THE CONSEQUENCES FOR THE INDIVIDUAL

According to the World Health Organisation, the disease model of mental disorder (**1038**) is "incomplete because it stops short of the consequences of disease. It is the latter, particularly, that intrude upon everyday life, and some framework is needed against which understanding of these experiences can be developed; this is especially true for chronic and progressive disorders."[6] The *International Classification of Impairments, Disabilities and Handicaps* therefore uses the concepts of impairment, disability and handicap to describe the consequences of disease or injury.[7] All three of these concepts depend on deviations from norms.[8]

IMPAIRMENT, DISABILITY AND HANDICAP

The sequence underlying illness-related phenomena is presented as follows:[9]

6   *International Classification of Impairments, Disabilities, and Handicaps: A manual of classification relating to the consequences of disease* (World Health Organisation, 1976), pp.10–11.

7   *Ibid.* In this section of the text, I have departed from the way in which the International Classification treats the issue of bodily injury, such as the loss of a limb, but the changes are not particularly significant.

8   *Ibid.*, p.33.

9   *Ibid.*, pp.11, 25–27.

The sequence of events presented in this graphic may be interrupted at any stage: an impaired person may never become disabled and, likewise, a disabled person may not become handicapped. Indeed, the value of presenting the concepts in this way is that "a problem-solving sequence is portrayed, intervention at the level of one element having the potential to modify succeeding elements."[10]

IMPAIRMENT, HANDICAP AND DISABILITY

- **Impairment**   An impairment is a permanent or temporary loss or abnormality of bodily structure or function.

- **Disability**   A restriction or lack of ability to perform an activity in the manner or within the range considered normal for a human being

- **Handicap**   Any disadvantage resulting from an impairment or disability which limits or prevents fulfilling a role that is normal for that person. Handicap describes the disadvantages resulting from impairment and disability.

Occurrence of organic injury or the onset of disease

The individual develops some intrinsic abnormality, which may be described as a disease or an injury and have been present at birth or acquired later.

Organic injury or disease resulting in impairment

The damage to the body, whether arising from injury or pathological processes, may or may not be apparent. If the changes make themselves evident they are described as "manifestations," which are usually distinguished as "symptoms and signs." Either the individual himself becomes aware of the manifestations, in the form of clinical disease or organic disorder, or a relative or third party draws attention to them. The individual has become or been made aware that the performance of some part of his body is impaired — he is unhealthy or "ill." An impairment is therefore a permanent or temporary loss or abnormality of bodily structure or function.[11] It represents the occurrence of an anomaly, defect or loss in a limb, organ or tissue or the defective functioning of part of the body, including the systems of mental function."[12] For example, mental impairment is a limitation of intellect or a limitation of the capacity to use that intellect successfully in the world.

Impairment resulting in disabilities

The fact that part of the body is impaired may or may not affect the individual's ability to perform different activities — if so, the impairment has a disabling effect.

---

[10]   *International Classification of Impairments, Disabilities, and Handicaps: A manual of classification relating to the consequences of disease* (World Health Organisation, 1976), p.30.
[11]   *Ibid., p.27.*
[12]   *Ibid.*

A disability is a restriction or lack of ability to perform an activity in the manner or within the range considered normal for a human being as a result of impairment.[13] Disability represents a departure from the norm in terms of performance of an individual, as opposed to the performance of a bodily organ or mechanism. Whereas impairment is concerned with individual functions of the parts of the body, reflecting potential in absolute terms, disability is concerned with compound or integrated activities expected of the person or body as a whole, such as are represented by tasks, skills, and behaviours.[14] Any consequential disabilities may be temporary or permanent, reversible or irreversible, progressive or regressive. By focusing on activities, the idea of disability is concerned with the practical consequences of bodily impairment in a relatively neutral way.

Impairment or disability leading to being handicapped

The fact that a person's body is impaired or his ability to perform certain activities is affected may have adverse social and economic consequences. As in horse racing, the state of being handicapped is relative to others so that a handicap is any disadvantage resulting from an impairment or disability which limits or prevents fulfilling a role that is normal for that person.[15] The degree of handicap experienced will depend on the individual's situation, the support available and the attitudes of other people. A person with severe schizophrenia who has the support of a family or social network may be considerably less disadvantaged than a person whose illness is less severe. Because of the stigma attached to mental illness and compulsory treatment, reflected in a lowering of the individual's status and opportunities within society, a detained patient who has recovered may still be handicapped. For example, a person once diagnosed as having schizophrenia will be at a serious disadvantage when it comes to competing with others for employment, even if the diagnosis ·was erroneous or he has subsequently fully recovered. Although the individual is no longer impaired or disabled, he is handicapped.

Premorbid handicap, primary handicap and secondary handicap

In the context of mental illness, Wing has usefully distinguished between premorbid handicap (disabilities pre-existing the illness), primary handicap (disabilities which arise directly from the illness itself) and secondary handicap (disabilities arising from having been mentally ill, *e.g.*, dependency and loss of skills as the result of institutional care, lethargy and the other effects of drugs, and the effects on employers and relatives).[16]

---

[13] *International Classification of Impairments, Disabilities, and Handicaps: A manual of classification relating to the consequences of disease* (World Health Organisation, 1976), *p.28.*

[14] *Ibid.*

[15] *Ibid.,* p.29.

[16] J.K. Wing, *Schizophrenia: towards a new synthesis* (Academic Press, 1978).

THE TREATMENT OF MENTAL DISORDER

The alleviation of suffering and the cure of the underlying condition causing the patient to suffer are the main goals of medicine. However, the main or immediate professional objective in a particular situation may be management, treatment or cure. The management of seriously disturbed behaviour can involve the use of detention, restraint, seclusion, continuous observation, and sedating drugs. Procedures such as seclusion, restraint and continuous observation are not forms of treatment, merely ways of isolating or protecting a patient who requires treatment. The treatment of mental disorder can be divided into five broad categories: surgical (psychosurgery); physical (ECT); chemical (psychotropic drugs); psychological (nursing, psychotherapy and social therapy); and complementary (various "alternative" remedies). There are few if any specific treatments in psychiatry. For example, depression, schizophrenia and mania may all respond to ECT while schizophrenic and manic illnesses both respond to neuroleptics.[17] Equally, therefore, a seemingly common form of mental disorder may respond to a number of different treatments. Thus, Lader notes that depressive disorders may respond to a range of treatments including ECT, sleep deprivation, antidepressants of a diverse chemical nature, neuroleptics and lithium.[18] To treat a person suffering from disease or disorder is not the same thing as to cure him. Many psychotropic drugs are equivalent to the chemical sprays used by gardeners to control the more extreme, unwanted, external manifestations of diseases which affect plants. They may alleviate the symptoms but are generally ineffective in eradicating the underlying causes. Consequently, the manifestations return if treatment is suspended. Virtually every treatment decision involves, or should involve, a counterbalancing of risks and benefits. Hippocrates cautioned doctors to first do no harm to their patients, observing that "there are some patients we cannot help but no patients we cannot harm."[19]

PSYCHOSURGERY

Psychosurgery is little used and largely reserved for the management of patients with chronic obsessional and depressive disorders which have not responded to prolonged treatment with 'more usual therapies. Section 57 of the 1983 Act (**273**) applies to detained and informal patients alike and it provides that (except in urgent cases) the patient's informed consent is required for any surgical operation which involves destroying brain tissue or the functioning of such tissue. The section contains a number of additional safeguards, including the involvement of the Mental Health Act Commission. In practice, the need for the patient's informed consent means that it is exceptional for a detained patient to receive such surgery.

OPERATING CENTRES

Until its closure in 1995, most psychosurgical operations were performed at the Brook Hospital. Stereotactic techniques — a stereotaxic device being a metal

---

[17] R.E. Kendell, "Diagnosis and classification" in *Companion to psychiatric studies* (ed. R.E. Kendell and A.K. Zealley, Churchill Livingstone, 1993), p.280.

[18] M. Lader and R. Herrington, *Biological treatments in psychiatry* (Oxford Medical Publications, 1990), pp.10–11.

[19] G.W. Bradley, *Disease, Diagnosis and Decisions* (John Wiley and Sons, 1993), p.10.

rectangular frame which fits around the head — allow a precise localisation of the intended lesion, usually by the implantation of radioactive yttrium-90 seeds. In a stereotactic subcaudate tractotomy, the seeds are implanted in the *substantia innominata* below the head of the caudate nucleus. Limbic leucotomy involves disrupting some of the connections between the frontal lobe and the limbic system by placing lesions in lower medial quadrant of the frontal lobe; the cingulum is also lesioned. Diagrams of the different areas of the brain are included in chapter 24.

Operating Centre	Nature of operation
Brook Hospital	Stereotactic subcaudate tractotomy
Pindersfield Hospital	Stereotactic bifrontal tractotomy
Atkinson Morley's Hospital	Limbic leucotomy
University Hospital of Wales	Bilateral anterior capsulotomy

PATIENT CHARACTERISTICS

During the period 1 July 1993 to 30 June 1995, 30 patients (22 female) were referred to the Mental Health Act Commission with a view to psychosurgery. The number of operations subsequently performed was 24, four of the remaining six patients withdrawing their consent to surgery. A recent retrospective survey by the Commission of 34 patients who received surgery revealed that two of them had been diagnosed as having a bipolar affective illness, 18 as suffering from depression, 12 from an obsessional disorder, and two from anxiety states. Some two-thirds of these patients had been aged between 31 and 50 at the time of their operations.[20]

OUTCOME

Information about outcome of psychosurgery, based on reports by the patients' responsible medical officers, is contained in two of the Mental Health Act Commission's biennial reports: the second biennial report (spanning the period 1985–87) and sixth biennial report (1993–95).[21]

Outcome reported by responsible medical officer	Second Biennial	Sixth Biennial
Significant improvement	17 cases (35%)	9 cases (26%)
Some improvement / "modest" improvement	10 cases (20%)	17 cases (50%)
No significant change or deterioration	10 cases (20%)	8 cases (24%)
No information received	12 cases (25%)	—
Total number of cases	49 cases (100%)	34 cases (100%)

---

[20]   Mental Health Act Commission, *Sixth Biennial Report, 1993–95* (H.M.S.O., 1995), p.49 and Appendix 4.1.

[21]   See Mental Health Act Commission, *Second Biennial Report, 1985–87* (H.M.S.O., 1987), p.21; Mental Health Act Commission, *Sixth Biennial Report, 1993–95, supra,* p.49.

The patient groups were necessarily small and the Commission's findings should be interpreted cautiously. As to the outcome of the patients referred to in the second biennial report, the Commission reported that "some" of the patients said to have "significantly improved" did not improve "for some time after the operation," raising the possibility that other factors may by then have influenced the outcome. Furthermore, where a "modest" improvement was reported, this was not always sustained. The fate of the remaining 12 cases is also problematic and might indicate that there was either an unfavourable or an insignificant outcome to report. As to the more recent findings set out in the sixth biennial report, the patients' perception of their outcomes, also surveyed on this occasion, were less favourable. Of the 30 patients who replied, 11 (37 per cent.) reported no change in their mental state, 12 (40 per cent.) some improvement, and only 7 (23 per cent.) a significant improvement. It should lastly be borne in mind that seven of the 34 patients were operated upon at sites other than the Brook Hospital, using different techniques.

STANDARD LEUCOTOMIES

Occasionally, practitioners are involved in a tribunal case involving a patient who received a standard leucotomy during the 1940s or early 1950s and brief details of this procedure are contained in the footnote below.[22]

ELECTRO-CONVULSIVE THERAPY

Electroconvulsive therapy (ECT), also called electroplexy, was introduced in the late 1930s and has subsequently become the subject of some public controversy. Clinically, the treatment is generally considered to be the first line of treatment where a depressive illness is associated with life-threatening complications, such as failure to eat and drink or a high risk of suicide. It tends to be reserved as a second-line treatment for other patients, used where there has been inadequate response to an adequate trial of drugs. Urgent cases aside, the Mental Health Act provides that ECT may not be administered to a patient detained for assessment or treatment unless he understands its nature, purpose and likely effects and consents to receiving it or, where this is not so, its administration has been authorised by an independent doctor appointed by the Mental Health Act Commission (149, 277). There are approximately 138,000 ECT treatments in Britain each year.

---

[22] In 1942, Freeman and Watts described an operation (the standard leucotomy) for dividing the white matter in both frontal lobes of the brain. The editor of *The Journal of Mental Science* suggested in 1944 that any mental illness of long standing duration, apart from chronic mania, epilepsy and general paralysis, could be considered for leucotomy. However, patients were also selected for the operation who had not had previous treatment of any sort. By 1954, leucotomies had been performed on upwards of 12,000 people within the United Kingdom. The procedure carried, on average, a four per cent mortality rate and risked permanent damage to the patient's personality. By 1961, the Ministry of Health review of leucotomies in England and Wales estimated that 3.1 per cent. of all patients were acknowledged to have been harmed by the operation to the point where it prevented subsequent discharge. See David Crossley, "The introduction of leucotomy: a British case history" *History of Psychiatry* (1993) iv, 553–564; W. Freeman and J. Watts, *Psychosurgery: Intelligence, Emotion and Social Behaviour following Prefrontal Lobotomy for Mental Disorders* (Charles C. Thompson, 1942); G.W.T.H. Fleming, "Prefrontal leucotomy" *Journal of Mental Science* (1944) xc, 491; G.C. Tooth and M.P. Newton, *Leucotomy in England and Wales 1942–1954* (Ministry of Health Reports on Public Health and Medical Subjects, No. 104, H.M.S.O., 1961).

THE ADMINISTRATION OF ECT

There is historical evidence that seizures caused by the administration of drugs or photic stimulation were effective therapeutically.[23] However, electricity is now preferred as the seizure-inducing agent because of its relative safety and ease of administration. ECT was originally given unmodified but it is nowadays preceded by the injection of a general anaesthetic and a muscle relaxant which minimises the actual convulsions produced. The technique consists of giving a general anaesthetic, followed by an intravenously administered muscle relaxant injected through the same needle as the anaesthetic, the needle being left in the vein between injections. Once the muscle relaxant has caused complete relaxation, and the patient has been adequately oxygenated — by means of a face mask and bag connected to a cylinder of oxygen — a brief electric pulse is passed between padded electrodes. These are moistened with a saline solution and placed either over both temples (bilateral ECT) or over one temple and a point on the scalp on the same side of the head (unilateral ECT). The amount of electricity necessary to induce a generalised seizure (the "seizure threshold") depends on many factors. ECT is generally administered twice weekly and the usual number of treatments is between six and eight, depending upon the clinical response of the patient.

UNILATERAL AND BILATERAL ECT

It is usual practice in the United Kingdom to administer ECT unilaterally to the non-dominant hemisphere, usually the right side of the head. This position of the electrodes is thought to reduce to a minimum post-ECT confusion and the slight retrograde amnesia (**1070**) which accompanies any seizure.[24] Although some clinicians also consider unilateral ECT to the non-dominant hemisphere to be as effective as bilateral ECT for depression,[25] a number of studies have found it to be slower acting and less successful. Consequently, the recent APA Task Force on ECT recommended bilateral ECT where rate of response was most important and unilateral ECT where minimising the risk of cognitive side-effects was the overriding factor.[26] There is, however, no consensus. Because of post-treatment confusion and amnesia, some clinicians take the view that bilateral ECT is best reserved for patients who do not show the expected improvement with unilateral treatment.[27]

HOW ECT WORKS

How or why ECT is effective remains unclear and it is therefore an empirical treatment. Because simulated ECT can be an effective treatment for depression,[28] this suggests that repeated general anaesthesia may be efficacious and the benefits of ECT only partly derive from the induced seizure.

---

23 The use of convulsive therapy to treat mental disorder is ancient. A Roman treatment for headaches involved placing a Mediterranean torpedo fish (which produces 100–150 volts) across the patient's brows and camphor-induced convulsions for melancholia were used by Oliver in 1785.

24 *Essential Psychiatry* (ed. N. Rose, Blackwell Scientific Publications, 1988), p.184.

25 G.L. Ahern, *et. al.*, "Selected Topics in Behavioural Neurology" in *Manual of Clinical Problems in Psychiatry* (ed. S.E. Hyman and M.A. Jenike, Little, Brown and Co., 1990), p.115.

26 *American Psychiatric Association Task Force on Electroconvulsive therapy, The Practice of Electroconvulsive therapy: Recommendations for Treatment, Training and Privileging* (APA, 1990).

27 *Essential Psychiatry, supra*, p.184.

28 See P.G. Janicak, *et. al.*, "Efficacy of ECT: a meta-analysis" *American Journal of Psychiatry* (1985) 142, 297–302.

INDICATIONS

ECT may be used to treat patients with depression marked by psychotic symptoms, stupor, failure to eat or drink or a risk of suicide, and those whose conditions have not responded to antidepressants. It is also used in cases of catatonia, schizo-affective depression, manic states unresponsive to drug treatment, post-partum affective psychosis, and following serious adverse reactions to medication (*e.g.* neuroleptic malignant syndrome and drug-induced extrapyramidal disorders).

As a first-line or second-line treatment

The treatment is generally considered to be the first-line treatment if a fast response to treatment is necessary to relieve intense suffering or to save the patient's life (depressed patients who are suicidal or not eating or drinking; patients with manic frenzy leading to exhaustion). It tends to be reserved as a second-line treatment in other situations, used where there has been inadequate response to an adequate trial of drugs; in particular antidepressants for the treatment of a depressive disorder.[29]

COMBINING ECT WITH OTHER TREATMENTS

Electroconvulsive therapy is often given to patients who are receiving drug treatments, often because a drug regime has been established before a decision to employ ECT is made. Many drugs alter seizure thresholds or alter the duration of a generalised seizure so that the efficacy of electroconvulsive therapy may be affected.[30] If ECT is ineffective and, especially, if convulsions do not occur or are very brief, any drug regime should be reviewed.[31] More deliberately, ECT may be combined with lithium for treating manic states, with antidepressants for depressive illness, and with antipsychotics in treating schizophrenia. Although tricyclic antidepressants and phenothiazines enhance seizure activity, their concurrent use with ECT does not improve its efficacy or reduce the number of applications which are needed to treat depressive illnesses. There is, however, "fairly good evidence" that ECT combined with antipsychotic drugs is more effective in relieving acute schizophrenic episodes than ECT or drugs alone.[32]

EFFICACY

There is indisputable evidence that ECT is a highly effective treatment for severe depressive illnesses (particularly those associated with psychotic delusions) and for the other conditions for which it is a first-line treatment.[33] In particular, patients

---

[29]   T. Lock, "Advances in the practice of electroconvulsive therapy" *Advances in Psychiatric Treatment* (1994) vol. 1, 47–56 at p.47.

[30]   M. Lader and R. Herrington, *Biological treatments in psychiatry* (Oxford Medical Publications, 1990), p.27.

[31]   *Ibid.*

[32]   *Ibid.*

[33]   Assuming, of course, that the ECT is properly administered. The first ECT audit to the Royal College of Psychiatrists in 1981 stated that about one in three ECT clinics was ill-equipped, the staff poorly trained, and the treatment ineffective. Approximately one in four treatment applications was unlikely to result in therapeutically effective seizures. See J. Pippard and L. Ellam, "Electroconvulsive treatment in Great Britain" *British Journal of Psychiatry* (1981) 139, 563–568, summarised in T. Lock, "Advances in the practice of electroconvulsive therapy" *Advances in Psychiatric Treatment* (1994) vol. 1, 47–56 at pp. 48–49.

treated with ECT, or a combination of ECT and medication, have shown a more rapid and complete response in the short term (the initial 4–6 weeks of treatment) than patients treated only with drugs or without medication. However, whether ECT is more effective than vigorous, higher dose, drug treatment remains uncertain; as is the issue of whether ECT has any longer-term advantages over alternative drug treatments after the initial 4–6 week treatment period.[34] Recovery after six to nine treatments administered over two to three weeks is often followed by relapse. Although relapse is not a specific disadvantage of ECT, being a feature of all treatments of depression, Klerman has estimated that 65 per cent. of depressed in-patients and out-patients relapse to some extent within the first year.[35] For this reason, maintenance drug treatment following ECT is generally considered to be as necessary as it is when antidepressants are continued for three months or more following improvement on medication alone.[36] As with drug treatment, a sudden onset and short duration of illness is an indicator of good outcome.[37] ECT tends to be an ineffective treatment for patients who suffer from reactive depression; or from mild, long-term depression with hypochondriasis; or for whom anxiety is a primary problem; or who have an underlying personality disorder.[38]

SAFETY

The major risk involved in ECT is not the application of the current or the resulting seizure but the accompanying anaesthetic procedure. The contraindications are therefore those of high anaesthetic risk. The morbidity rate of one death per 50,000 treatments is similar to that of general anaesthesia in minor surgical procedures.[39] There is no evidence that ECT causes structural brain damage or that it is associated with the development of spontaneous seizures.[40]

SIDE-EFFECTS

ECT produces confusion, amnesia, and recent memory loss. More specifically, ECT produces an anterograde amnesia (an inability to recall newly learned material) that may last for a few hours after the treatment as well as a retrograde amnesia in the form of an inability to recall events occurring just prior to the treatment. Mild anterograde deficits may persist for a number of weeks following a full course of ECT therapy but long-term deficits are unusual. Unilateral ECT causes fewer side

---

[34] T. Lock, "Advances in the practice of electroconvulsive therapy" (*supra*), p.48. For reviews of research data in relation to specific syndromes, see Royal College of Psychiatrists' Special Committee on ECT, *The Practical Administration of Electroconvulsive Therapy* (Gaskell, 2nd ed., 1994).

[35] G.L. Klerman, "Long-term treatment of affective disorders" in *Psychopharmacology: A Generation of Progress, 1967-1977* (ed. M.A. Lipton, *et al.*, Raven Press, 1978), pp.1303–1311.

[36] W. Appleton, *Practical Clinical Psychopharmacology* (Williams and Wilkins, 3rd ed., 1988), p.117.

[37] T. Lock, Advances in the practice of electroconvulsive therapy, Advances in Psychiatric Treatment (1994), vol. 1, pp. 47–56 at p.48.

[38] Practical Clinical Psychopharmacology, Third Ed., William Appleton (Clinical Professor of Psychiatry, Harvard Medical School). Williams and Wilkins, Baltimore, 1988., p. 117-118.

[39] B.A. Kramer, "Use of ECT in California 1977–1983" *American Journal of Psychiatry* 142, 1190–1192. See T. Lock, "Advances in the practice of electroconvulsive therapy" (*supra*), p.47.

[40] See *e.g.* R. Abrams, *Electroconvulsive Therapy* (Oxford University Press, 2nd ed., 1992). Nevertheless, despite the fact that magnetic resonance imaging of the brain has found no evidence of structural brain damage, it, of course, remains possible that ECT causes some subtle damage — just as psychiatrists argue that subtle brain changes may be responsible for schizophrenia although they are not apparent from scanning.

effects and, in consequence, some clinicians recommend beginning with the unilateral ECT, but switching to bilateral, if four to six or more unilateral treatments prove ineffective.

MEDICATION

The administration of medication for mental disorder to patients detained for assessment or treatment is regulated by Part IV of the Mental Health Act 1983 (**273**). Medicines used in the treatment of mental disorder are variously referred to as psychotropic drugs, psychoactive drugs, or as psychotherapeutic drugs and these general terms are synonymous. Psychotropic drugs are traditionally divided into six classes according to their actions: (1) antipsychotics, (2) antidepressants, (3) antimanics, (4) antiepileptics, (5) anxiolytics, and (6) hypnotics. The drugs used to treat schizophrenia and other psychotic states, referred to here as antipsychotics, may sometimes be called major tranquillisers or neuroleptics. However, the term "major tranquilliser" is misleading because it suggests that these drugs are similar to "minor tranquillisers" such as diazepam. Furthermore, for conditions such as schizophrenia, the tranquillising effect is of secondary importance and whether a particular drug has a major tranquillising effect depends on the dose administered. The word "neuroleptic" refers to the effect of antipsychotic drugs on motor activity rather than their clinical effects and so, according to some authorities, is less appropriate than the term antipsychotic.

PSYCHOTROPIC DRUGS

---

* Anti-psychotics   Drugs, such as chlorpromazine, used to treat schizophrenia and other psychotic states

* Anti-depressants   Drugs, such as amitriptyline, used to treat depression.

* Anti-manics   Drugs, such as lithium, used to treat mania.

* Anti-epileptics   Drugs, such as carbamazepine, used in the treatment of epilepsy.

* Anxiolytics   Drugs, such as diazepam, used to treat anxiety states.

* Hypnotics   Drugs, such as temazepam, used to treat insomnia.

THE REGULATION OF MEDICINES

The availability of medicines is controlled on the basis of their safety, quality and efficacy, in accordance with the Medicines Act 1968 and EEC directives. The Secretary of State for Health, acting on behalf of the various Ministers who together constitute "The Licensing Authority," is responsible for the control of medicines for human use. The UK Medicines Control Agency (MCA), which reports to the Secretary of State, is the executive body which regulates the pharmaceutical sector and implements policy. A statutory advisory body called The Medicines Commission advises the Licensing Authority through the Secretary of State on all matters relating to the implementation of the Medicines Act, and on medicines in general. Applications from the pharmaceutical industry for product licences for medicines are made to the UK Medicines Control Agency, which assesses the drug's likely benefits and risks. A product licence authorises the holder to manufacture or import, and to sell or supply, the stated medicinal product. Different arrangements apply where authority for the clinical trial of a new product is sought. The Committee on Safety of Medicines (CSM) is responsible for encouraging the collection and investigation of reports on suspected adverse reactions to medicines already on the market. Under a new scheme administered by the Association of the British Pharmaceutical Industry, which came into force in 1996, patients are able to get information both about a medicine's safety and adverse effects and the scientific studies used to obtain approval for it.

Clinical trials

All new active substances are subjected to clinical trials designed to determine their safety and efficacy, as are some established medicines if a new clinical use is claimed for the product. The "development of the clinical trial is a product of the application of modern scientific method to clinical medicine. The purpose of the clinical trial is to provide clinicians with information that will help them prescribe appropriate, timely treatment for their patients."[41] The Licensing Authority may grant a clinical trial certificate (CTC) authorising a trial, which certificate then remains valid for a period of two years. However, over 90 per cent. of all clinical trials are now conducted under a clinical trial exemption scheme (CTX) introduced in 1981.[42] Where an exemption from the need to hold a clinical trial certificate is granted, this exemption generally remains valid for three years. Details of the proposed drug trial ("the protocol") are then considered by the Medical Research Ethics Committee at each hospital where it is proposed to conduct the research. The efficacy of the new drug is determined by giving it to a group of patients with the target condition (*e.g.* major depressive illness) and a placebo or well-established drug treatment to a second control group of similar patients. The trial may include a wash-out period, the duration of which depends on the previous treatment and the tolerance to withdrawal of medication. A randomised, controlled clinical trial of one therapy versus another is the accepted standard by which the usefulness of a treatment is judged. In a single-blinded study, the treatment assignment — trial drug or placebo — is not known to the patients. In a doubled-blinded study, the treatment assignment is not known either to the patients or to their doctors. It is only revealed if there are serious or unexpected side-effects or when the study is completed.

Clinical trials involving detained patients

Tribunals periodically consider the cases of detained patients who are, or have recently been, involved in the clinical trial of a new drug. Difficult legal and ethical considerations arise when detained patients are included in clinical drug trials. Half of the patients in the trial will normally be receiving a placebo or a trial drug the efficacy of which is unproven and essentially theoretical. Necessarily, this often

---

[41]   R.S. Greenberg, *Medical Epidemiology* (Appleton and Lange, 1993), pp.68–69.
[42]   See The Medicines (Exemption from Licences) (Clinical Trials) Order 1981. As to trials using products for which product licences have been granted, see The Medicines (Exemption from Licences) (Clinical Trials) Order 1974.

entails first withdrawing an established drug previously prescribed for the patient. This drug may be known to suit him and, in some cases, have improved his condition so that discharge is anticipated in the near future. Not surprisingly, patients who change from an antipsychotic to a placebo relapse significantly more frequently.[43] In terms of the legalities, patients entitled to a tribunal hearing will be detained under section 2 or for treatment. A patient detained under section 2 has no right to refuse treatment given under the direction of his responsible medical officer but does have a right to refuse a placebo and treatment which is directed by some other person, such as a researcher. After an initial three month medication period, a patient who is detained for treatment may generally only be given psychotropic medication if he is capable of consenting to it and gives consent or, if he is incapable of giving consent, or refuses consent, its administration has been authorised by a doctor appointed by the Mental Health Act Commission (**149, 277**). A certificate authorising treatment may only be given by such a doctor if he is of the opinion that, having regard to the likelihood of the particular treatment alleviating or preventing a deterioration of the patient's condition, it should be given. The fact that the new drug's likely benefits and adverse effects are not firmly established, and the patient may not receive the drug at all if he is in the placebo group, is therefore problematic. As far as a tribunal is concerned, these issues are matters to be taken into account when considering whether or not to exercise its discretionary power of discharge. A tribunal must consider whether the patient's continued detention for treatment is justified if the power to give compulsory treatment is being used in a way which undermines the purpose of his detention, which is to treat him so as to be able to end his detention.

A DRUG'S ACTION

Pharmacodynamics is the study of the effects of drugs on the body whereas pharmacokinetics is the study of the body's effect on drugs.

Pharmacodynamics (potency, tolerance, etc.)

Pharmacodynamics is the study of the effects of drugs on the body and the mechanism of drug action.[44] The major pharmacodynamic considerations include receptor mechanisms, the dose-response curve, the therapeutic index, and the development of tolerance, dependence, and withdrawal phenomena.[45] The potency of a drug refers to the relative dose required to achieve a certain effect. Thus, only 5mg of haloperidol are generally required to achieve the same therapeutic effect as 100mg of chlorpromazine. Both drugs are, however, equal in their maximum efficacies, that is the maximum clinical response achievable by their administration. As a rule, the lower potency drugs produce more sedation, orthostatic hypotension, and anticholinergic effects than the high potency drugs, which cause more frequent and severe extrapyramidal symptoms. The therapeutic index is a relative measure of a drug's toxicity. For example, lithium has a low therapeutic index in the order of 3–4, being

[43] S.R. Hirsch, *et al.*, "Outpatient maintenance of chronic schizophrenic patients with long-acting fluphenazine: double-blind placebo trial" *British Medical Journal* (1973) i, 633; G.E. Hogarty, *et al.*, "Drugs and sociotherapy in the aftercare of schizophrenic patients" *Archives of General Psychiatry* (1974) 31, 603.

[44] *Melloni's Illustrated Medical Dictionary* (Pathenon Publishing, 3rd ed., 1993), p.369.

[45] H.I. Kaplan and B.J. Sadock, *Synopsis of Psychiatry* (Williams and Wilkins, 7th ed., 1994), p.867.

the ratio of toxic to therapeutic doses. A person may become less responsive to a particular drug as it is administered over time, which is referred to as tolerance. The development of tolerance is associated with the appearance of physical dependence, that is the necessity to continue administering the drug in order to prevent the appearance of withdrawal symptoms.

Pharmacokinetics (absorption, distribution, metabolism, excretion)

Pharmacokinetics is the study of the body's effects on drugs, which determines whether the drug gets to its site of action and in what concentrations.[46] It involves studying the passage of a drug through the body; the extent and rate of absorption; its distribution, localisation in tissues, metabolism, and elimination.

Absorption and distribution

The principal divisions of pharmacokinetics are drug absorption, distribution, metabolism and excretion. Orally administered drugs must dissolve in the fluid of the gastrointestinal tract before the body can absorb them. Some antipsychotic drugs are available in injectable depot forms that allow the drug to be administered only once every 1–4 weeks. The distribution of a drug to the brain is determined inter alia by the blood-brain barrier. The volume of distribution can vary with the patient's age, sex and disease state.

Metabolism and excretion

The liver is the principal site of metabolism and the most important organ for the excretion of drugs and drug metabolites is the kidney. Clearance is a measure of the amount of drug excreted per unit of time; if some disease process or other drug interferes with the clearance of a psychoactive drug, it may reach toxic levels. A drug's half-life is defined as the amount of time it takes for one-half of a drug's peak plasma level to be metabolised and excreted from the body.

ROUTE OF ADMINISTRATION

Medicines come in a variety of forms depending upon the condition to be treated and the way in which this may be done. The purpose of these various forms of medication is to carry the active constituent (the drug) to the area where it is most needed and to avoid or minimise unwanted effects on other areas of the body. Enteral administration (literally, through the intestine) includes oral, buccal, sublingual and rectal administration. Prescribing tablets or capsules has obvious disadvantages if it is unclear whether the patient is able or willing to take them as prescribed. Parenteral routes — by which the drug is taken into the body otherwise than through the alimentary canal — include intramuscular, intravenous and subcutaneous injections and topical administration. Injections introduce medication through the skin into blood vessels or subcutaneous tissues, muscles and other tissues in the body. A general advantage over oral medicines is certainty about whether or not the drug has been received as prescribed. Against this, injections are unacceptable for many patients. Consequently, in practice, this clarity may be

---

[46]   M. Lader and R. Herrington, *Biological treatments in psychiatry* (Oxford Medical Publications, 2nd ed., 1990), p.109.

limited to knowing that the patient has not attended for an injection and again defaulted on the treatment. The real choice is often between compromising on oral medication by consent or compulsory treatment by injection. In the absence of any legal or practical framework allowing indefinite compulsory out-patient treatment, defaulting on injections in due course becomes an option for all discharged patients. In such cases, a consultant's unwillingness to contemplate what he considers to be the second-line treatment may lead to no treatment and early relapse.

Oral (PO) administration

Drugs may be taken orally in tablet, liquid or capsule form. Liquid administration may be preferred for detained patients if it is suspected that the patient has not been swallowing prescribed tablets and disposing of them later. The abbreviation SL stands for sublingual.

Intravenous (IV) injection

Intravenous administration is the quickest route to achieve therapeutic blood levels, but it also carries the highest risk of sudden and life-threatening adverse effects. The drug enters the systemic circulation quickly so that it has a rapid effect, making the route useful in emergencies. Adverse effects may, however, occur equally rapidly. Once administered "it is difficult to recall the drug; in comparison stomach washouts and emetics can be used following oral overdosage."[47] Other disadvantages include the risk of sepsis, thrombosis and air embolism. The drug may be accidentally injected into the tissues surrounding the vein, or into the artery, leading to necrosis and spasm respectively.[48]

Intramuscular (IM) injection

Intramuscular administration is often used for the relief of acute symptoms in disturbed patients and for administering long-acting depot injections of anti-psychotic drugs for maintenance therapy. Depot injections are administered by deep intramuscular injection at intervals of one to four weeks. The disadvantages of intramuscular administration include its painfulness, leading to non-compliance, and a risk of damaging structures such as nerves.

PRESCRIPTION AND ADMINISTRATION OF DRUGS

Kaplan summarises the clinical principles underlying drug prescription as involving applying the five Ds: diagnosis, dialogue, drug selection, dose, and duration.[49] The World Health Organisation has published a book setting out the factors to be considered by medical practitioners when prescribing psychoactive drugs.[50]

---

[47] B.K. Puri and P.J. Tyrer, *Sciences Basic to Psychiatry* (Churchill Livingstone, 1992), p.108.
[48] *Ibid.*
[49] H.I. Kaplan and B.J. Sadock, Synopsis of Psychiatry (Williams and Wilkins, 7th ed., 1994), chap. 33.
[50] *Psychoactive Drugs: Improving Prescribing Practices* (ed. H. Ghobe and I. Khan, World Health Organisation, 1988).

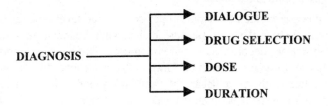

DIAGNOSIS
- DIALOGUE
- DRUG SELECTION
- DOSE
- DURATION

DRUG SELECTION

The patient's diagnosis, his history of responding to particular drugs, the psychiatrist's familiarity with different drugs, their side-effects and routes of administration will all be factors taken into account when it comes to selecting a drug from those available to treat the target condition. Many of the drugs available within a particular class are equivalent in overall efficacy but differ immensely in how well they are tolerated and how lethal they are in overdose. Where this is the case, the most important reasons to choose a drug will be its relative side-effect profile and safety.[51]

Polypharmacy

Multiple prescriptions, commonly known as polypharmacy, are to be avoided unless clearly indicated. This is because "changes in clinical state are difficult to judge if medication is constantly altered and side-effects and drug interactions are likely to be more common than if a single drug is used."[52] It "is generally recognised that the use of several drugs simultaneously is undesirable because it is not easy to decide which constituents of such combinations should be altered when a change in clinical state occurs, the incidence of unwanted effects and drug interactions increases, and patient compliance with treatment declines as it becomes more complex. Yet it is common for such cocktails to develop, often unwittingly, and a constant effort has to be made to prevent this happening."[53]

Therapeutic uses of antipsychotics

Antipsychotic drugs have a range of uses, including the management of severe anxiety, so that in this respect the term is somewhat misleading.

Use as an antipsychotic

The major therapeutic effects are seen when used to treat acute psychoses. The effects include a reduction of positive symptoms such as hallucinations, delusions and thought disorder. There is also a normalisation of psychomotor activity (excitement or retardation) and information processing. Although the sedative effects are immediate, the antipsychotic effects take up to three weeks to become evident in the case of schizophrenia.

[51] *Psychoactive Drugs: Improving Prescribing Practices* (ed. H. Ghobe and I. Khan, World Health Organisation, 1988).
[52] M. Lader and R. Herrington, *Biological treatments in psychiatry* (Oxford Medical Publications, 2nd ed., 1990), p.19.
[53] *Ibid.*, p.26.

Use as a form of maintenance therapy

Maintenance doses are generally about 60 per cent. of the level required to resolve the symptoms in the initial phase. Because maintenance treatment may need to be long-term, slow-release depot injections are often used. Their only real purpose is to ensure compliance. In its most common form, the antipsychotic drug is prepared as an ester, most frequently as a decanoate, although pipothiazine is given as the palmitate salt and fluspirilene is given in aqueous injection at weekly intervals.[54]

Use as a short-term treatment or form of management

As a short-term measure, they may be used to alleviate severe anxiety and to quieten, *i.e.* manage, disturbed patients whatever the underlying psychopathology.

Use in the treatment of agitation and anxiety

Because of their sedative effect and the fact that they do not produce pharmacological dependence, the drugs are often used in low doses as hypnotics or to treat mild agitation and anxiety.

DOSE AND DOSAGE

Different patients require different amounts of a drug for optimal therapeutic effect. Consequently, no standard dose exists and the correct dose must be determined empirically. Usually, increasing the dose of a drug increases the effect although below and above a certain range there is little change with dose and "paradoxical" effects may even appear. Some tricyclic antidepressants, notably nortriptyline, show antidepressant action over a restricted dose range: either side of this therapeutic window the therapeutic action weakens and disappears.[55]

Micro-dose maintenance treatment

Patients relapse significantly more frequently if antipsychotic drug dosage is cut below the level necessary to produce dopamine receptor blockade — an approach sometimes known as micro-dose maintenance treatment.[56]

British National Formulary (BNF) guideline doses

The British National Formulary is published twice a year by the British Medical Association and the Royal Pharmaceutical Society of Great Britain. It contains recommended guideline maximum doses for most drugs, with separate guidance for special categories of patients such as the elderly, children and pregnant women.[57] The Royal College of Psychiatrists has given the following advice about prescribing doses above BNF upper limits.

---

[54]   B.K. Puri and P.J. Tyrer, *Sciences Basic to Psychiatry* (Churchill Livingstone, 1992), p.126.

[55]   M. Lader and R. Herrington, *Biological treatments in psychiatry* (Oxford Medical Publications, 2nd ed., 1990), p.75.

[56]   J.M. Kane, *et al.*, "Low-dose neuroleptic treatment of chronic schizophrenia" *Archives of General Psychiatry* (1983) 40, 893.

[57]   The British National Formulary (B.N.F.) is very reasonably priced and readily available. American guidelines should be treated with caution because of a tendency to give drugs in "heroic" dosages.

British National Formulary (March 1997) 33, 159

"Unless otherwise stated, doses in the BNF are licensed doses — any higher dose is therefore unlicensed ....

1. Consider alternative approaches including adjuvant therapy and newer or atypical neuroleptics such as clozapine.

2. Bear in mind risk factors, including obesity — particular caution is indicated in older patients especially those over 70.

3. Consider potential for drug interactions ...

4. Carry out ECG to exclude untoward abnormalities ... repeat ECG periodically ....

5. Increase dose slowly and not more than once weekly.

6. Carry out regular pulse, blood pressure, and temperature checks; ensure that patient maintains adequate fluid intake.

7. Consider high-dose therapy to be for limited period and review regularly; abandon if no improvement after 3 months (return to standard dosage)."

RECORDING THE PRESCRIPTION

Various standard abbreviations are used to record a patient's prescription, the most common of which are listed in the table below.

PRESCRIBING MEDICATION — ABBREVIATIONS

Rx	Recipe, treat with	b.d.	bis die (twice daily)
t.d.s.	ter die sumendus (3x daily)	q.d.s.	quater die sumendus (4x daily)
o.m.	omni mane (in the morning)	o.n.	omni nocte (every night)
PO	Per orum (by mouth)	nocte	at night
PRN	pro re nata (as/if required)	sd/stat	single dose
bu	buccal	iv	intravenous injection
mp	implant	pr	per rectum
im	intramuscular injection	sl	sublingual
tabs	tablets	caps	capsules
mg	milligram	µg	microgram
g	gram	ml	millilitre
mmol/L	milli-mole-litre	mg/L	milligrams per litre

INPATIENT PRESCRIPTION AND ADMINISTRATION CARD

Surname	Hospital No.	Consultant	Date of admission
First Names	Date of Birth	GP	Special Diet

Drug idiosyncrasies	
Drug	*Reaction*

ONCE ONLY MEDICATION

Pharmacy	Date	Drug	Dose	Time	Route	Signature	Given by

TTO's Sent to Pharmacy		TTO's Received on Ward	
DATE		DATE	

REGULAR PRESCRIPTIONS

Drug (Approved Name)					Date and Month		
				Time			
Dose 1	Dose 2	Start Date 1	Start Date 2	6			
Doctor's signature		Review Date 1	Review Date 2	10			
Additional instructions			Pharmacy	13			
				18			
				22			

AS REQUIRED DRUGS

Drug (Approved Name)				Date			
Dose	Max Freq	Route	Start date	Time			
Signature		Review / Stop	Pharmacy	Dose / Route			
Additional Instructions				Given by			

1144

INPATIENT PRESCRIPTION CARDS

The medication prescribed for each patient, and the medication actually administered, will be recorded on a prescription and administration card kept on the ward. This card will be found either in the patient's notes or in a separate ward file containing all such cards. The format varies from hospital to hospital but is normally similar to the example set out on the previous page. Some cards include separate sections for recording depot injections and medication given during periods of leave. Discontinued drugs are shown by drawing a line through the prescription box and a similar line through the adjacent recording panels. As a matter of good practice, if a statutory certificate has been issued under Part IV of the Act, authorising a drug's administration to a detained patient, it should be attached to the card (277). This enables nursing staff to verify that the treatment may lawfully be given.

Recording the medicine's administration

The nurse who administers the prescription inserts his initials in the relevant box on the prescription and administration card to show that the dose has been given. Where the medication was refused, there will normally be an entry in the clinical or nursing notes explaining the precise circumstances. The list of approved abbreviations should be set out on the first page of the card. The following table lists a number of common abbreviations in case this is not so.

Administration of medication — Abbreviations

A	Absent	O	Out of stock
D	Drowsy	S	Sleeping
L	Leave medication given	DOC	Doctor consulted / advised
R	Refused	ECT	Electroconvulsive therapy

ADVERSE EFFECTS OF PRESCRIBED DRUGS

Paracelsus once observed that everything is poisonous and it is only in the dose that a poison differs from a remedy. Most drugs have effects in addition to the main therapeutic action and these usually detract from any benefit derived from the treatment.[58]

Adverse events associated with a drug

Adverse events known to be generally associated with a particular drug may be categorised, in descending order of adversity, as representing a hazard, a contra-indication, a side-effect, or a precaution. Adverse events may occur as a single episode or be ongoing or recurrent and the eventual outcome for the patient may be recovery, persistent residual effects, or death. In any particular case, it may

---

[58] M. Lader and R. Herrington, *Biological treatments in psychiatry* (Oxford Medical Publications, 2nd ed., 1990), p.22.

be difficult or impossible to establish whether an adverse event is a consequence of medication administered to the patient. The relationship between an adverse event and a prescribed drug may be categorised as definite, probable, possible, unlikely, or unrelated, depending on the temporal relationship between the therapy and the reaction and other relevant factors, such as the nature of the patient's illness, any concomitant remedies, and the patient's history (whether similar adverse effects followed the prescription of the same or similar drugs in the past). A known response pattern to the suspected drug or reasonable temporal association with drug administration, which disappears or decreases following a cessation or reduction in dose, would indicate a definite or probable relationship.

Adverse effects for the particular patient

Adverse effects following the prescription of medication include the emergence of new symptoms or complaints during treatment, an increase in the severity or frequency of pre-existing symptoms or complaints, abnormal laboratory results, physical abnormalities, and the occurrence of accidents related to medication. The maximum severity of any adverse effect or effects experienced by the patient may be described as mild (slight discomfort but no limitation of usual activities); moderate (significant discomfort and/or some limitation of usual activities); severe (intolerable discomfort or pain and/or inability to carry out usual activities); or catastrophic (fatal, life threatening or permanently or severely disabling). Likewise, a particular patient's tolerability for the drug may be described as excellent (absence of any reported or noted adverse event); good (very few insignificant events); moderate (some adverse events of mild to moderate severity); poor (the patient feels uncomfortable); or very poor (moderate to serious adverse events).

CLASSIFYING ADVERSE REACTIONS

The adverse effects of medication are often categorised according to the physiological system affected by the drug.

Extrapyramidal system effects

The term "extrapyramidal system" describes a system of neural pathways that control and integrate motor functions and also some cognitive functions. Drug-related movement disorders such as parkinsonism, akathisia, dystonia, tardive dyskinesia, and tremor are all extrapyramidal symptoms. They can be measured using rating scales such as the Simpson extrapyramidal Scale. Extrapyramidal effects are dose related, with an onset usually within two or three weeks.

Akathisia
Akathisia is described by Lader and Herrington as "the most distressing neurological effect" of antipsychotic medication. It is a common extrapyramidal side-effect, particularly in response to piperazine phenothiazines. There is uncontrollable agitation and restlessness, an inability to sit still, sometimes with shuffling and rocking. Although commonest after a week or two of treatment, it can appear later and it is not greatly relieved by antiparkinson medication.[59] The severity of the symptoms can be measured using rating scales such as the Akathisia (Barnes) Scale.

---

[59]   M. Lader and R. Herrington, *Biological treatments in psychiatry* (Oxford Medical Publications, 2nd ed., 1990), p.235.

It has been documented that untreated akathisia can lead to combativeness, assaults, suicide by violent means, and homicidal attacks on others.

Dystonia

Dystonia denotes abnormal muscular rigidity causing painful muscle spasms, unusually fixed postures or strange movement patterns (1067). Such movements usually take the form of a twisting or turning motion of the neck, the trunk, or the proximal parts of the extremities. They are powerful and deforming, grossly interfering with voluntary movement, and perverting posture. The "earliest neurological effect during a course of (antipsychotic) treatment is acute dystonia which may even be seen after a single dose of a high-potency compound such as fluphenazine or haloperidol. It occurs in about 2.5 per cent of patients treated with antipsychotic drugs and it is commoner in men and children than in women. The features are diverse and often bizarre and include torticollis,[60] retrocollis, facial grimaces and distortion, tongue protrusion, dysarthria ... and oculogyric crises ... The antipsychotic medication must be discontinued or its dosage reduced."[61]

Parkinsonian symptoms

Parkinson's disease is caused by depletion of dopamine in the basal ganglia and a drug-induced reduction of dopamine causes the same symptoms: stiffness of limbs, paucity of movement and facial expression (hypokinesis), coarse tremor of the hands and the head at rest, and dribbling. Parkinsonism (sometimes called "pseudo-parkinsonism") usually occurs after the first week and in older patients.[62]

Tardive dyskinesia

Dyskinesia (literally, bad or difficult movement) is a general term covering various forms of abnormal movement which typically involve uncontrollable movements of the trunk or limbs, cannot be suppressed, and impair the execution of voluntary movements. Tardive dyskinesia — tardive meaning late, tardy — generally occurs some 2–5 years after commencing treatment with antipsychotics, although onset may occur upon withdrawing the drug. It is characterised by continuous writhing movements of the head and tongue and postural changes. These effects are not dose related and anticholinergic drugs merely exacerbate the problem. The antipsychotic drug should be slowly withdrawn. Unfortunately, in most cases, this does not lead to any improvement in the patient's condition and, indeed, the syndrome is sometimes made worse. Because it has a different cause and treatment to the other extrapyramidal symptoms, some writers do not classify tardive dyskinesia as an extrapyramidal system effect.

Autonomic nervous system effects

The internal environment of the body is controlled and regulated in part by the autonomic nervous system and in part by hormones. The autonomic nervous system (literally, self-regulating) is involved in involuntary, automatic, reflex activities carried out and co-ordinated in the brain below the level of consciousness. It is divided into two parts, the sympathetic and parasympathetic—

---

[60] Torticollis, also known as wry neck, is twisting of the neck, causing the head to be rotated and tilted into an abnormal position.

[61] M. Lader and R. Herrington, *Biological treatments in psychiatry* (Oxford Medical Publications, 2nd ed., 1990), p.234.

[62] *Ibid.*, p.22.

- Drugs which inhibit the action of parasympathetic nerves, by the blockade of muscarinic acetylcholine receptors, are said to have **anticholinergic or antimuscarinic effects**. The resulting symptoms include dry mouth, increased salivation, nasal congestion, constipation, blurred near vision, glaucoma, urinary hesitancy or retention, sexual dysfunction, sweating, flushing, vomiting, and diarrhoea. These effects tend to be prominent early in treatment and are a major source of non-compliance.

- The effects of antipsychotic drugs on the sympathetic nervous system are due to their **alpha-adrenergic blocking effect**. These effects may be manifested as postural (orthostatic) hypotension, hypothermia, tachycardia, dizziness, and sexual dysfunction.

Postural hypotension

Postural hypotension is seen most often with aliphatic phenothiazines, mainly chlorpromazine, at high doses or when given intramuscularly. Antidepressants and phenothiazines "frequently induce postural hypotension usually after about three weeks of treatment. This is particularly troublesome in the elderly whose ability to regain balance is impaired, with consequent falls, injury and occasional stroke."[63]

Endocrine and metabolic effects

The endocrine system consists of a collection of glands that produce hormones. A hormone is a chemical messenger which, having been formed in one organ or gland, is carried in the blood to a target organ or tissue where it influences activity. The effects of antipsychotic drugs on the endocrine system may include impotence, the absence of menstruation (amenorrhoea), the growth of breasts in men (gynaecomastia), and the discharge of milk from breasts (galactorrhoea).

Behavioural toxicity

A psychotropic drug may cause behavioural changes, which are sometimes quite subtle, and this phenomenon is loosely referred to as "behavioural toxicity." Examples include confusional reaction, excitement or agitation, increased motor activity, insomnia, drowsiness and lassitude.

Cardiovascular effects

The effects of drugs on the cardiovascular system include tachycardia (an attempt by the body to compensate for postural hypotension), dizziness and circulatory collapse.

Other effects

Other effects include skin-rash, urticaria, decreased appetite, headache, photophobia (an abnormal or uncomfortable sensitivity or intolerance of the eyes to light which may be a reaction to antipsychotics), "bronzing" of the skin, jaundice, ocular disorders, lowering of the seizure threshold.

---

[63]   M. Lader and R. Herrington, *Biological treatments in psychiatry* (Oxford Medical Publications, 2nd ed., 1990), p.23.

Sedation

The blockade of central histamine (H_1) receptors has a sedative effect. Antipsychotic drugs have antihistaminic properties and this contributes significantly to their sedative action, which may or may not be desired. The degree to which a patient is sedated may be rated on the following scale: falls into sleep and/or remains sleeping most of the time; dozing most of the time or falls back in a dozing state after being approached; slightly slowed down; fully awake and able to perform daily activities.

Neuroleptic malignant syndrome

Neuroleptic malignant syndrome (NMS) is a rare but sometimes fatal reaction to antipsychotic medication, characterised by fever, severe muscular rigidity, autonomic instability and altered consciousness. The drugs most often implicated are haloperidol, chlorpromazine and fluphenazine.[64]

THE CONTROL OF ADVERSE EFFECTS

When a distressed tribunal patient quite reasonably complains about the adverse effects of a prescribed drug the symptoms he describes are usually anticholinergic or extrapyramidal effects. In other words, the complaint relates to the autonomic nervous system or some kind of movement disorder. In some cases, the extrapyramidal effects would, if not a side-effect of medication, be features of a neurological condition so that it is not unreasonable for the patient to question whether the cost of alleviating his "psychiatric" symptoms — the emergence of "neurological" symptoms — represents an overall alleviation of his distress. If it is necessary to override a detained patient's legitimate concerns about the possible effects of antipsychotic medication, and it is not always necessary or beneficial to do so, the safe option is to prescribe as cautiously as the particular situation allows. Although it is impossible to know precisely how a particular patient will respond to a particular medication, both with regard to its efficacy and its adverse effects, "many unwanted effects derive from their recognised psychopharmacology and they are therefore predictable and dose-dependant."[65] The ways of retrospectively dealing with adverse effects include withdrawing the medication causing the undesired effects and (if necessary) substituting an alternative drug for the target condition; reducing the dosage; and treating the unwanted symptoms (symptomatic therapy). Because many unwanted effects derive from their recognised psychopharmacology and are dose-dependant, they "should be managed initially by dosage reduction so long as this is compatible with continued efficacy. Should this not be possible, a different psychotropic drug should be substituted ... If a solution cannot be found in this way an antidote to the unwanted reactions might be added but is less desirable because all drugs have unwanted effects (for example, antiparkinson agents are anticholinergic) and the problems of polypharmacy develop."[66] For example, while procyclidine, orphenadrine, benztropine and benzhexol are anticholinergic drugs which improve tremor and stiffness, they can produce antimuscarinic effects of their own in higher dosage.

---

[64]   G. Addonizio, *et al.*, "Neuroleptic malignant syndrome: review and analysis of 115 cases" *Biological Psychiatry* (1987) 22, 1004–1020.

[65]   M. Lader and R. Herrington, *Biological treatments in psychiatry* (Oxford Medical Publications, 2nd ed., 1990), p.23.

[66]   *Ibid.*

Drug	Proprietary	BNF guideline doses
Benzhexol Hydrochloride	▪ Artane (tablets) ▪ Broflex (syrup)	1mg daily gradually increased; usual maintenance dose 5–15mg daily.
Benztropine Mesylate	▪ Cogentin (tablets, injection)	*By mouth* 0.5–1mg daily, maximum 6mg daily, usual maintenance dose 1–4mg daily. *By IM or IV injection* 1–2mg, repeated if symptoms reappear.
Biperiden	▪ Akineton (tablets, injection)	*By mouth* 1mg b.d., gradually increased to 2mg t.d.s. with usual maintenance dose of 3–12mg daily. *By IM or slow IV injection*, 2.5–5mg up to four times daily.
Orphenadrine Hydrochloride	▪ Biorphen (elixir) ▪ Disipal (tablets)	150mg daily gradually increased, maximum 400mg daily.
Procyclidine Hydrochloride	▪ Procyclidine (tablets) ▪ Arpicolin (syrup) ▪ Kemadrin (tablets, injection)	*By mouth* 2.5mg t.d.s., usual maximum 30mg (60mg exceptionally). Acute dystonia: *IM injection*, 5–10mg, maximum 20mg daily; *IV injection*, 5mg and the occasional patient may need 10mg or more and require 30 minutes to obtain relief.

Source: British National Formulary (British Medical Association and Royal Pharmaceutical Society of Great Britain, September 1997), 34, 222.

CAUSES OF TREATMENT SUCCESS AND FAILURE

In general terms, a prescribed drug may bring about a satisfactory response, have an inadequate effect, exacerbate the patient's condition, or have intolerable side effects. What constitutes treatment failure is determined by the treatment aims and expectations: eliminating hallucinations, improving socialisation, decreasing hyperactivity, improving self-care, eliminating assaultativeness, etc. It also depends on the perspective of the individual making the judgement. Not infrequently what the doctor considers to be a "good" outcome the patient does not.

Underdosing and inadequate therapeutic trial

From a clinical viewpoint, the two most important causes of treatment failure involving psychotropic drugs are underdosing and an inadequate therapeutic trial of the drug. For most psychotropic drugs, three weeks is the minimum period of treatment needed to determine whether it will prove effective. Although some patients may show some immediate improvement in agitation or anxiety when started on an antipsychotic drug, these effects are mainly the result of non-specific sedation. The actual impact of the drugs on psychotic symptoms develops with regular administration over a period of several weeks. Although failure to respond to a particular drug, or a worsening of the patient's condition, may indicate that the dosage is too low, it may also reflect a mistaken diagnosis. The effect on mood of antidepressant medication similarly increases over time and it may take a number of weeks before maximum benefit is achieved.

- **Semantic**

  What constitutes success or failure depends on the aims and expectations of the individual making the judgement. If a patient expects or hopes that a particular drug will cure him of his illness, rather than alleviate the worst symptoms, he but not his doctor may later consider that the treatment was a failure. What constitutes failure therefore depends upon how failure is to be measured, *e.g.* failure to restore normal health or failure to improve patient's function in certain key areas.

- **Misdiagnosis**

  The treatment prescribed is not an effective treatment of the misdiagnosed underlying condition. Unless a patient's condition naturally remits, or the same treatment is conventionally used both for the real illness and the misdiagnosed condition, failure to alleviate the symptoms is a likely consequence of misdiagnosis. Any natural or fortuitous recovery may be misinterpreted by the clinician as confirmation of his erroneous diagnosis so that, if relapse later occurs, the same diagnosis is made and the same treatment prescribed.

- **Non-compliance**

  Treatment may be ineffective if the prescribed drug has not been administered or taken as prescribed, *e.g.* patient has defaulted on the treatment by holding some or all of his oral medication under the tongue, later disposing of it. In drug trials, insufficient compliance with treatment is sometimes taken to constitute missing more than 50 per cent. of the prescribed dose in two consecutive weeks. Lack of co-operation is not invariably related to therapeutic or adverse experiences.

- **Biological variability**

  The degree of response to a drug is highly variable. There are many possible reasons for this, including pharmacokinetic differences and differences in biological sensitivity. For example, a study of the plasma concentrations of the antidepressant nortriptyline in 25 patients receiving a standard oral dose found a thirty-fold range.

- **Drug interactions**

  If the patient is taking more than one prescription or also taking unprescribed drugs, the resulting drug interactions may reduce (or, indeed, potentiate) the effect of one or more of the substances. Common drug interactions are listed in the BNF (**1142**).

- **Inadequate dosage**

  The dosage may be too high or too low or the patient have developed a tolerance for the drug in question.

• **The milieu**	The milieu within which the drug is taken may undermine its effect, *e.g.* the ward atmosphere, a family home with high expressed emotion, or a poor doctor-patient relationship. Research conducted at the John Hopkins University indicated that registrars possessing the qualities of empathy, genuineness and warmth had a higher success rate in treating depressed people than colleagues who did not possess these skills.
• **Inadequate period of treatment**	The lack of response may be due to the fact that there has been insufficient time since the drug's prescription for it to have a therapeutic effect. The antipsychotic action of neuroleptics takes about six weeks to develop. The mood-elevating effect of tricyclic antidepressants is not evident for about a fortnight and then takes four to six weeks to develop fully.
• **Early withdrawal of treatment**	A treatment will fail if it has to be discontinued because of intolerable adverse effects, unacceptable laboratory results, or the emergence of an intercurrent illness or condition (such as pregnancy) which requires treatment incompatible with that prescribed.
• **Other clinical reasons**	Maximum therapeutic effect may often be clinically undesirable.
• **Treatment ineffective**	The treatment may have been mistakenly licensed or approved as an effective treatment for the target condition.
• **Condition untreatable**	The condition may be untreatable at present, *i.e.* no effective treatment is currently available.

Insight and reasons for non-compliance

Relapse rates amongst discharged in-patients have been estimated to be more than 50 per cent. in the first year and 70 per cent. in the second year after hospitalisation.[67] It has also been estimated that 25–50 per cent. of out-patients omit sufficient of their medication to impair therapeutic efficacy.[68] A "medication-therapeutic alliance" is essential because only if the clinician wins the patient's co-operation will he take medication following discharge.[69] Lader has summarised a number of factors or situations which contribute to poor co-operation: complicated drug regimes, unpleasant side-effects, lack of insight into the nature of the illness and its treatment, opposition to the use of medication to treat mental illness, the need to continue with medication for some time after symptoms have been suppressed, and delay in the

---

[67] N. Sulliger, "Relapse" *Journal of Psychosocial Nursing Mental Health Services* (1988) 26(6): 20–23.

[68] M. Lader and R. Herrington, *Biological treatments in psychiatry* (Oxford Medical Publications, 2nd ed., 1990), p.21.

[69] W.S. Appleton, *Practical Clinical Psychopharmacology* (Williams and Wilkins, 3rd ed., 1988), p.21.

onset of relapse after stopping medication, so that the patient thinks he is well without drugs.[70] The reasons given by patients for medication non-compliance in one recent survey included the following factors: do not see the need for medication; side-effects; forgot to take medication; felt better and stopped taking it; medication not effective; do not want to be on medication; got tired of taking it; like the high feeling; Lord told me not to take it; do not want poison in my body; my spouse does not like me on medication; no transportation to pharmacy; do not want to take medication every day. The nurses' perceptions of the reasons for these patients' non-compliance were considerably less varied. Some of the reasons given by patients were interpreted by them as mere camouflage for a belief that the medication was unnecessary. Half of the defaulting patients were considered to hold this belief.[71]

Causes of treatment success

The factors affecting treatment success are to some extent the reverse of those applicable in relation to treatment failure. However, with regard to psychotropic drugs, it is important to realise that "inevitably, guesswork is a major element in this activity, and any good which comes from it is at least partly attributable to spontaneous drifts in the severity of illness and to non-specific processes in the treatment situation."[72] It is important therefore that the contribution of natural processes, both biological and social, is not overlooked[73] and drug responses are undoubtedly influenced by placebo effects.[74] Spontaneous remission may partly account for the fact that a patient does not respond to a particular drug when he seemed to have responded to in the past.

PSYCHOLOGICAL TREATMENTS

There are many different kinds of psychological treatments available, including behaviour therapy, cognitive therapy, psychoanalysis, family therapy, psychotherapy, counselling, group therapy, self-help groups, and social skills training. The first three of these are particularly important in relation to the treatment of severe psychiatric disorders. Other kinds of assistance, such as general social work support, are not treatments as such although important prophylactically. Similarly, marital therapy may be beneficial in terms of improving a patient's social situation but does not have any significant effects on symptoms.

BEHAVIOUR THERAPY

Behaviour therapy seeks to modify learned maladaptive behaviour patterns and it may be used to treat conditions such as compulsive disorders, eating disorders, and phobias. The approach is based on the principles of learning theory, in particular operant conditioning and classical conditioning, which are sometimes collectively

---

[70]   M. Lader and R. Herrington, *Biological treatments in psychiatry (supra)*, p.21.
[71]   V.E. Lund, *et al.*, "Helping the Medicine Go Down: Nurses' and Patients' Perceptions About Medication Compliance" *Journal of Psychosocial Nursing* (1991) Vol. 29, No. 7, 6–9.
[72]   M. Lader and R. Herrington, *Biological treatments in psychiatry* (Oxford Medical Publications, 2nd ed., 1990), p.12.
[73]   *Ibid.*
[74]   *Ibid.*, p.27.

referred to as associative learning.[75] Classical conditioning is that first famously demonstrated by Pavlov. If event A (the sounding of a bell) is habitually followed by event B (the bringing of food), which event initiates the behavioural response C (salivation), it will commonly be found that the occurrence of event A itself eventually initiates the behavioural response C. Operant conditioning is a form of learning in which a voluntary behaviour is engaged in because its occurrence is reinforced by being rewarded. Such behaviour is independent of stimuli and was termed operant behaviour by Skinner.[76] Behaviour may be reinforced positively, by way of reward, or negatively, by eliminating or withdrawing an unpleasant consequence previously associated with a particular form of behaviour.

Token economy programmes

The treatment of chronic schizophrenia may include the use of token economy programmes, in which tokens are awarded for desirable behaviour which can then be used to buy ward privileges. This is normally portrayed as an example of positive reinforcement because a desired behavioural response is followed by a rewarding event, with the aim of strengthening and making more frequent that behaviour. However, the fact that the "privileges" — being allowed out of bed, being allowed notepaper and stamps, being allowed cigarettes, etc. — must first be withdrawn before they can be offered as prizes means that the benefits of compliance are usually viewed by the patient as a restoration of rights rather than as rewards, which undermines the proposition. In other words, the association of events formed in the patient's mind is that certain behaviour leads to compulsory hospitalisation and a withdrawal of rights rather than that a cessation of the behaviour leads to reward. Not surprisingly, resentment is common and the legality of withdrawing what many people would regard as basic rights by designating them as privileges has yet to be challenged in the courts. Although section 63 of the Mental Health Act 1983 provides that a detained patient's consent is not required for treatment given under the direction of his responsible medical officer, it must be doubtful whether the more draconian regimes could survive an application to the European Court of Human Rights.

COGNITIVE THERAPY *

Cognitive therapy is based on the assumption that an individual's affect and behaviour are largely determined by the way in which he structures the world. The focus is therefore on maladaptive patterns of thinking. The cognitive approach includes four processes: (1) eliciting automatic thoughts; (2) testing automatic thoughts; (3) identifying maladaptive underlying assumptions; and (4) testing the validity of maladaptive assumptions.[77] It is often found that a patient's automatic thoughts form patterns which represent maladaptive general assumptions that guide the patient's life, as in the following abbreviated example of a flowchart compiled by Beck[78]—

---

[75]   Cognitive learning, which forms the basis of cognitive therapy, is a more complicated process and refers to the process by which information perceived by the brain is interpreted in the context of previous information in order to solve problems.

[76]   B.K. Puri and P.J. Tyrer, *Sciences Basic to Psychiatry* (Churchill Livingstone, 1992), p.280.

[77]   H.I. Kaplan and B.J. Sadock, *Synopsis of Psychiatry* (Williams and Wilkins, 7th ed., 1994), p.861.

[78]   See A.T. Beck, *et al.*, *Cognitive therapy of depression* (Guilford, 1979), p.33.

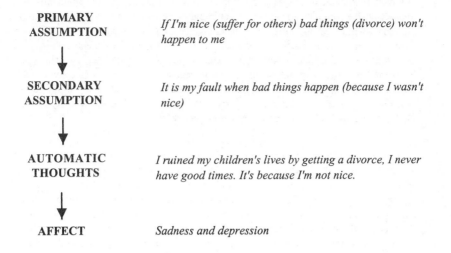

| PRIMARY ASSUMPTION | *If I'm nice (suffer for others) bad things (divorce) won't happen to me* |

↓

| SECONDARY ASSUMPTION | *It is my fault when bad things happen (because I wasn't nice)* |

↓

| AUTOMATIC THOUGHTS | *I ruined my children's lives by getting a divorce, I never have good times. It's because I'm not nice.* |

↓

| AFFECT | *Sadness and depression* |

The behavioural techniques used to modify cognitive dysfunction include schedules of activities, assignments, cognitive rehearsal, role playing and diversion techniques. Cognitive therapy has been applied mainly to depressive disorders, in relation to which studies have clearly shown that it is effective and, in some cases, superior or equal to medication alone. It can be used in conjunction with medication to treat major depressive disorders. Medication appears to be ineffective in changing depressive attitudes and there is increasing evidence that the mere alleviation of symptoms is less effective in preventing relapse than combining drugs with other forms of treatment. Cognitive therapy has also been used to treat other conditions, such as obsessive-compulsive disorders and paranoid personality disorders, and it has an important role to play in improving compliance with prescribed medication. For example, where the patient's limited adherence reflects difficulty acknowledging either that he is mentally unwell or that he may have to rely on medication for much of his life.[79]

PSYCHOANALYSIS

The brain does not have unlimited or unconditional access to the material stored by it and, according to Freud, a purely biomedical approach to mental disorder can never be satisfactory. Psychoanalysis aims to provide psychiatry with the missing psychological foundation; to lay open the origin, mechanism, and interrelation of the symptoms which make up the clinical pictures; and to discover the common ground upon which a correlation of bodily and mental disorder becomes comprehensible:

> "The second difficulty you will find in connection with psycho-analysis is not, on the other hand, inherent in it, but is one for which I must hold you yourselves responsible, at least in so far as your medical studies have influenced you. Your training will have induced in you an attitude of mind very far removed from the psycho-analytical one. You have been trained to establish the functions and disturbances of the organism on an anatomical basis, to explain them in terms of chemistry and physics, and to regard them from a biological point of view; but no part of your interest has ever been

---

[79]   See A.T. Beck, *et al.*, *Cognitive therapy of depression* (Guilford, 1979), p.72.

directed to the mental aspects of life, in which, after all, the development of the marvellously complicated organism culminates. For this reason a psychological attitude of mind is still foreign to you, and you are accustomed to regard it with suspicion, to deny it a scientific status, and to leave it to the general public, poets, mystics, and philosophers. Now this limitation in you is undoubtedly detrimental to your medical efficiency; for on meeting a patient it is the mental aspects with which one first comes into contact, as in most human relationships, and I am afraid you will pay the penalty of having to yield a part of the curative influence at which you aim to the quacks, mystics, and faith-healers whom you despise.

... It is true that the psychiatric branch of medicine occupies itself with describing the different forms of recognisable mental disturbances and grouping them in clinical pictures but in their best moments psychiatrists themselves are doubtful whether their purely descriptive formulations deserve to be called science. The origin, mechanism, and interrelation of the symptoms which make up these clinical pictures are undiscovered: either they cannot be correlated with any demonstrable changes in the brain, or only with such changes as in no way explain them. These mental disturbances are open to therapeutic influence only when they can be identified as secondary effects of some organic disease.

This is the lacuna which psycho-analysis is striving to fill. It hopes to provide psychiatry with the missing psychological foundation, to discover the common ground on which a correlation of bodily and mental disorder becomes comprehensible. To this end it must dissociate itself from every foreign preconception, whether anatomical, chemical, or physiological, and must work throughout with conceptions of a purely psychological order, and for this very reason I fear that it will appear strange to you at first."[80]

Abreaction and free association

Psychoanalysis attempts to integrate previously repressed ideas or experiences with conscious material so as to relieve the underlying causes of the patient's symptoms. The patient gradually becomes aware of previously unacknowledged significant connexions between thoughts and behaviour. Before this happens, resistance to dealing with noxious psychic material is almost inevitably encountered and the transference to other people of certain emotions and fantasies is also common. Abreaction is a process by which repressed material is brought back into consciousness. Free association is a method which involves relaxing the patient and getting him to express the thoughts and emotions which then spontaneously flow through his brain. Psychoanalysis is not available under the National Health Service but it may be used in private clinics and hospitals to treat anxiety disorders, phobias, obsessive-compulsive disorders and some forms of depression.

FAMILY THERAPY

Familial factors are involved in the development of schizophrenia. Family-orientated treatments may include a brief educational programme, a relatives' group, and family sessions including the patient and key relatives (**1264**).

---

[80]   S. Freud, *Introductory Lectures on Psychoanalysis* (trans. J. Riviere, George Allen and Unwin, Rev. ed., 1929), pp.15–16.

PSYCHOLOGICAL THERAPIES

- **Behavioural therapy** — Based on the principles of learning theory, in particular operant conditioning and classical conditioning. Seeks to modify learned maladaptive behaviour.

- **Cognitive therapy** — Focuses on maladaptive patterns of thinking patterns behind the individual's affect and behaviour. Available on the NHS.

  British Association for Behavioural and Cognitive Psychotherapies, Dept. of Clinical Psychology, Northwick Park Hospital, Watford Road, Harrow HA1 3UJ. Tel. 0181 869 2325.

- **Cognitive analytical therapy** — Combines cognitive therapy with psychotherapy. Average of 16 sessions. Available on the NHS.

  British Association of Cognitive Analytic Therapists, Munro Clinic, Guy's Hospital, London SE1 9RT. Tel. 0171 955 4822.

- **Counselling** — A form of psychotherapy in which a person who faces a specific challenge is helped to clarify and find solutions to the problem.

  British Association for Counselling, 1 Regent Place, Rugby, Warwicks CV21 2PJ. Tel. 01788 550899.

- **Family therapy** — Regards the family as the patient. Behavioural methods are commonly used.

  The Institute of Family Therapy, 43 New Cavendish Street, London W1M 7RG.

- **Gestalt therapy** — Involves acting out conflicts and feelings, often in a very physical way.

  Gestalt Centre, 64 Warwick Road, St. Albans AL1 4DL. Tel. 01727 864606.

- **Hypnotherapy** — A form of psychotherapy in which the patient goes into a voluntary state of deep relaxation. Repressed feelings are brought to conscious level and explored.

  The National Register of Hypnotherapists and Psychotherapists, 12 Cross Street, Nelson, Lancs BB9 7EN. Tel. 01282 699378.

- **Primal therapy** — Based on the idea that certain behaviours result from suppressed primal frustrations. Not available on the NHS.

  London Association of Primal Psychotherapists, 18a Laurier Road, London NW1 1SH. Tel. 0171 267 9616.

- **Psychoanalysis** — Aims to bring repressed conflicts into consciousness. Not available on the NHS. 3–5 sessions per week for up to 5 years. Cost £50 per hour.

  Institute of Psychoanalysis, 63 New Cavendish Street, London W1M 7RD. Tel. 0171 580 4952.

- **Psychotherapy** — A general term. Variants include personal construct therapy, analytic psychotherapy and hypnotherapy.

  British Association of Psychotherapists, 37 Mapesbury Road, London NW2 4HJ. Tel. 0181 452 9823.

Sources: A. Neustatter, Independent on Sunday, 17 March 1996, pp. 11–12; Essential Psychiatry, Ed. N. Rose, Blackwell Scientific Publications, Oxford, 1988. The qualification of practitioners in the various fields varies and many private practitioners are unregulated.

COMPLEMENTARY AND ALTERNATIVE REMEDIES

Complementary or alternative remedies for mental disorder include homeopathy, acupuncture, hypnotherapy, dietary regimes, aromatherapy, movement and exercise therapies, such as dance therapy. Apart possibly from acupuncture, there is no evidence that these approaches are, properly speaking, remedies when it comes to major psychiatric disorders, although some of them have a role to play as one part of an overall treatment programme. In a tribunal context, their relevance is mainly limited to the fact that seriously ill young patients not uncommonly voice a preference for such alternative "natural" remedies. While this is understandable, given the range of adverse effects associated with psychotropic medication, it is almost invariably unrealistic. Furthermore, nature's answer to major psychiatric disorder during the period before modern drug therapy was all too often death. Thus, while the safe approach to prescribing toxic drugs is a cautious one, it must also be acknowledged that the movement from institutional to community care since the 1950s was largely made possible by the development of antipsychotic drugs.

SECLUSION

Seclusion (solitary confinement) is defined in the Code of Practice as the supervised confinement of a patient alone in a room which may be locked for the protection of others from significant harm.[81] The practice first became commonplace in the early 1840s as mechanical restraint fell into disrepute.[82] It is not a procedure that is specifically regulated by the 1983 Act although it may sometimes constitute medical treatment as defined by section 145. Many hospitals have nevertheless discontinued the practice, including some regional secure units which are able to manage disturbed patients by the use of intensive care areas. In 1995, the Mental Health Act Commission noted that the overall use of seclusion on open wards had declined to relatively low levels. It was, however, more frequently employed in high dependency units and Special Hospitals but to a decreasing extent.[83] Seclusion is unused in general psychiatry hospitals in Scotland and the Mental Welfare Commission for Scotland is against the practice.

THE CASES FOR AND AGAINST SECLUSION

Some of the respective arguments for and against seclusion were examined in the *Report of the Committee of Inquiry into Complaints about Ashworth Hospital* (the "Ashworth Report").[84]

---

[81] *Mental Health Act 1983: Code of Practice* (Department of Health and Welsh Office, 2nd. ed., 1993), para. 18.15.

[82] See P. Fennell, *Treatment without consent* (Routledge, 1996), pp. 20–21. According to the Report of the Metropolitan Commissioners in Lunacy for 1843, at pp.145–146: "Seclusion or solitary confinement is now getting into general use in the treatment of the insane, and great numbers of the proprietors of public and private asylums throughout the country are fitting up and bringing into use solitary cells, and padded rooms for violent and unmanageable lunatics."

[83] Mental Health Act Commission, *Sixth Biennial Report, 1993–95* (H.M.S.O., 1995), p.31.

[84] *Report of the Committee of Inquiry into Complaints about Ashworth Hospital*, Cmnd. 2028 (1992). See chapter xxii.

The case for seclusion

" ... seclusion retains its supporters among those committed to the highest standards of psychiatric care and treatment, although these supporters would wish to see its use reduced to an irreducible minimum. They argue, with force, that seclusion effectively controls disturbed behaviour, and prevents disturbance from escalating and spreading, by isolating the person or persons involved. It offers a safe and non-stimulatory environment in which the person or persons may 'cool off'."[85]

Other arguments for continuing to permit the practice include that its prohibition would lead to more locking of wards, to the development of more secure facilities, to the prescription of higher levels of medication (particularly on acute intensive care units), and to greater use being made of control and restraint.[86] Furthermore, hospitals might be reluctant to accept from the prison service, or from high or medium secure units, patients who require a high degree of security or who are thought to be potentially violent.

The case against seclusion

"Critics of seclusion have consistently argued that it is an inhuman and degrading way to respond to a crisis; that it is too often used for minor disturbances or transgression of rules; that people are kept in seclusion longer than is necessary to control the initial unmanageability; that it is used as a sanction by staff seeking to impose control over patients; and that little or no attention is paid to psychological and physical effects of isolation on those who are mentally fragile."[87]

Patient surveys have confirmed that seclusion is widely disliked by patients, being perceived by them as a punishment and causing feelings of depression and of being trapped and abandoned. Its use may also increase persecutory delusions and hallucinations.[88] The Ashworth Committee concluded that the evidence pointed strongly to the fact that seclusion lacks any therapeutic value. It recommended that legislation should provide that, during the patient's waking hours on the ward, a patient shall not be denied human contact and be kept in isolation in a room, the door of which is fastened or held so that he or she is unable, contrary to expressed desire, to leave the room at will. The report recommended the phasing out and ultimate ending of seclusion over a two to three year period—

"We adhere ... to the principle that seclusion is unnecessary, ought not to be used in the care of mentally disordered people, and should be prohibited by statute."[89]

---

[85]   *Report of the Committee of Inquiry into Complaints about Ashworth Hospital*, Cmnd. 2028 (1992), at p.204.

[86]   According to the Ashworth Report, "certainly, staffing would have to be stepped up on those, not very frequent, occasions when the behaviour called for three or four nurses staying with the patient, exercising restraint techniques, for some little time. We take the view that such moments provide a good opportunity for nursing staff to understand the springs of aggressive human behaviour and to learn to predict when the patient is likely to become assaultative, given certain environmental and personal factors. Human contact in the shape of skilled nursing is, perhaps, more essential at times of crisis intervention than in periods of patient calm." *Ibid.*, p.205.

[87]   *Ibid.*, p.204.

[88]   R. Cope, Royal College of Psychiatrists' Forensic Section Meeting, 12 February 1993.

[89]   *Report of the Committee of Inquiry into Complaints about Ashworth Hospital*, *supra*, pp.205–206.

Nursing attitudes

Some nursing approaches to the ethical problems involved in using seclusion have summarised by Morris[90]:

> "McCoy (1983)[91] argues that an ethical dilemma arises when a nurse contemplates the use of seclusion. It is where to draw the line between the infringement of personal liberty for a difficult or potentially dangerous patient and the probable benefits of the other patients on the ward from that infringement. Pilette (1978)[92] strongly objects to decisions on seclusion being made on this basis. She rather harshly comments that in such a utilitarian approach essentially anything that disturbs the tranquillity of the mental ward is punishable by seclusion. Morrison (1987)[93] considered seclusion to be associated more with the traditional custodian mode of psychiatric nursing than with current nursing ideologies ... Gibson (1989)[94] remarks that if one accepts that the use of seclusion is largely determined by staff levels, then one must accept that this is a misuse of seclusion as the client would not need the intervention of seclusion if staffing levels were satisfactory."

Seclusion and restraint

It is noticeable that the current debate about seclusion mirrors in many respects that in the 1840s about the use of mechanical restraint. Some of the observations in the Report of the Metropolitan Commissioners in Lunacy for 1844 are particularly pertinent:

> "Those who profess the entire disuse of restraint, employ manual force and seclusion as parts of their method of management, maintaining that such measures are consistent with a system of non-restraint ... But in cases where he is held by the hands of attendants, or when he is for any excitement or violence forced by manual strength into a small chamber or cell, it is said that restraint is not employed, and the method adopted in these cases, is called the 'non-restraint system.' ... it is difficult to understand how this also can be reconciled with the profession of abstaining from all restraint whatsoever, so as to be correctly termed 'Non-restraint.' It seems to us that these measures are only particular modes of restraint, the relative advantages of which must depend altogether on the results."[95]

Those who advocated never using any mechanical restraint contended *that* their practice was the most humane and the most beneficial to the patient, soothing instead of coercing him during irritation, and encouraging him when tranquil to exert his faculties, in order to acquire complete self-control; *that* a recovery thus obtained was likely to be more permanent; *that* mechanical restraint had a bad moral effect in that it degraded the patient in his own opinion; *that* mechanical restraint was liable to great abuse from keepers and nurses, who would often resort to it for the sake of

90 B.E. Morris, "Seclusion: Does the previous literature reflect the same message as the recently published Code of Practice?" *Forensic Psychiatric Nursing Journal* (1990) 3, 6–7.
91 S.N. McCoy & S. Garritson, "Seclusion — The process of intervening" *Journal of Psychosocial Nursing and Mental Health Services* (1983) 21, 8–15.
92 P.C. Pilette, "The Tyranny of Seclusion: A Brief Essay" *Journal of Psychosocial Nursing and Mental Health Services* (1978) 16(10), 19–21.
93 P. Morrison, "The Practice of Seclusion" *Nursing Times* (1987) 83(19), 62–66.
94 B. Gibson, "The Use of Seclusion" *Nursing* (1989) 3(43).
95 *Report of the Metropolitan Commissioners in Lunacy for 1844* (Bradbury & Evans, 1844), pp.137–138.

avoiding trouble to themselves; and *that* patients could be controlled as effectually without mechanical restraint, as with it. Those who adopted non-restraint as the general rule, but made exceptions in certain extreme cases, affirmed *that* it was necessary to possess a certain degree of authority or influence over the patient; *that* the occasional use of slight mechanical restraint had in many cases promoted tranquillity; *that* it prevented the patient from injuring himself or others; *that* the patient's safety and tranquillity were not the only considerations; *that* the expense of recruiting more attendants was impracticable; and *that* minor mechanical restraint was preferable to the act of "forcing him into a place of seclusion, and leaving him at liberty to throw himself violently about for hours altogether." Furthermore, "when a Patient is forced into and secluded in a small room or cell, it is essentially coercion, in another form and under another name; and ... it is attended with quite as bad a moral effect, as any that can arise from mechanical restraint."[96]

THE CASES FOR AND AGAINST ALLOWING SECLUSION

Arguments for allowing seclusion	*Arguments against allowing seclusion*
• It effectively controls disturbed behaviour.	• Seclusion is unnecessary given reasonable staffing levels and the use of intensive care areas.
• It prevents disturbance from escalating and spreading.	• Seclusion is inhuman and degrading and little or no attention is paid to the psychological and physical effects of isolation on those who are mentally fragile.
• It offers a safe and non-stimulating environment within which the secluded person may "cool off."	• The evidence strongly suggests that seclusion lacks any therapeutic value. Human contact in the shape of skilled nursing is more essential at times of crisis intervention than in periods of patient calm.
• Other patients have a right to be protected from disturbed behaviour, including not being distressed by witnessing disturbed behaviour.	• Seclusion may, moreover, be counter-therapeutic, being perceived as punishment, causing depression and feelings of being trapped and abandoned, and an increase of persecutory delusions and hallucinations.
• Nursing staff have a right to be protected from assault and physical confrontation.	• There is an inevitable tendency to abuse the practice so that it is used for minor disturbances or transgression of rules and allowed to continue after the immediate crisis has passed.

---

[96] *Report of the Metropolitan Commissioners in Lunacy for 1844* (Bradbury & Evans, 1844), pp.157–159.

- Prohibiting the use of seclusion may have the effect of increasing reliance on high doses of medication.

- Prohibiting the use of seclusion may lead to more locking of wards and to more locked wards being developed, and thus an overall decline in the liberty enjoyed by patients.

- Prohibiting the use of seclusion may lead to greater use of control and restraint techniques.

- Prohibiting the use of seclusion may have the effect that open/low secure wards are more reluctant to accept potentially violent patients from prisons and from high or medium secure units.

- The argument that prohibiting seclusion would simply lead to an increase in other equally undesirable practices (more locking of wards, more locked wards, high levels of medication, greater use of restraint) is spurious. Adequate nursing levels will ensure against this and the hospital budget should make provision for this.

THE CODE OF PRACTICE

The Mental Health Act 1983 and the regulations made under that Act are both silent about the practice of seclusion but it is a practice which is subject to guidance in Chapter 18 of the Code of Practice. This chapter, which deals with issues concerning patients who present particular management problems, emphasises the importance of distinguishing between the need to control patients who pose an immediate threat to themselves or those around them and the need to keep some detained patients in a secure environment.[97] In most cases, the Commission has found that any use made of seclusion is consistent with its guidance although the frequency of use in some units specialising in learning disability or acquired brain injury has caused the Commission some concern.[98] The Commission has also had reservations about practice in secure private hospitals which lack residential 24 hour medical cover and justify seclusion as a beneficial form of treatment.[99]

The definition of seclusion

Seclusion is defined in the Code as the supervised confinement of a patient alone in a room which may be locked for the protection of others from significant harm. Previously, the Mental Deficiency Regulations 1948 and the Mental Treatment Rules 1948 provided that a patient "shall be deemed to be kept in seclusion if at any time between the period commencing at 8am and ending at 7pm he is isolated in a room the door of which is fastened or held so that he is unable to leave the room at will, but not if he is isolated in a room in which the lower half of the door is so fastened or held but the upper half left open."[100] Seclusion has elsewhere been

---

97   *Mental Health Act 1983: Code of Practice* (Department of Health and Welsh Office, 2nd. ed., 1993), para. 18.1.
98   Mental Health Act Commission, *Sixth Biennial Report, 1993–95* (H.M.S.O., 1995), pp.31–32.
99   *Ibid.*, p.110.
100   Mental Deficiency Regulations 1948, reg. 24(2); Mental Treatment Rules 1948, r.57(2).

defined as "the supervised confinement of a patient specifically placed alone in a locked room for a period at any time of the day or night for the protection of self or others from serious harm"[101] and as the act of temporarily locking a disturbed patient in a locked room.[102]

Inadequacy of definitions

The definition in the Code is inadequate. According to it, if a patient is not being supervised then he is not being secluded and, similarly, he is not being secluded if he is in solitary confinement as part of a behaviour modification programme. Likewise, the definition in the 1948 Regulations is not entirely satisfactory. The issue is whether the patient is being confined to a particular room, not the time of day, or whether the room within which he is being isolated is also his bedroom. Nor is it helpful to distinguish between seclusion and "time-out" for these purposes.[103] Seclusion is solitary confinement. Confinement means that the person is not free to leave the cell or room in which he is confined and a definition of solitary confinement would be as follows: "'solitary confinement' means the confinement of a patient alone in a room at any time of the day or night and a patient is confined to a room if he may not leave that room at will."

When seclusion may be permissible

The sole aim of seclusion is to contain severely disturbed behaviour which is likely to cause harm to others.[104] Even then, it should not be used if there is a risk that the patient may take his own life or otherwise harm himself[105] or if increased staffing would deal with the problem. It is an emergency measure, a last resort, to be invoked only after all reasonable steps have been taken to avoid its use, and only then as little as possible and for the shortest possible time.

When seclusion should not be used

Seclusion should never be used where there is a risk that the patient may take his own life or otherwise harm himself.[106] It is not a treatment technique. It should not

---

101   *Review of Special Hospitals Seclusion Procedures* DHSS, 1985, para. 3.6.
102   W. Campbell, *et al.*, "The Use of Seclusion" *Nursing Times* (1982) 1821–1825.
103   The element of deprivation of liberty is the same and both can involve the detention and restraint of an individual which is justified as a form of behaviour therapy. Thus, Gostin commences a sentence in his textbook with the words, "Short term seclusion, sometimes referred to as 'time out' or 'cooling down'" (L. Gostin, *Mental Health Services — Law and Practice* (Shaw & Sons Ltd.), para. 20.08A.
104   *Mental Health Act 1983: Code of Practice* (supra), para. 18.15. The Ashworth Report refers to the use of seclusion to protect the patient from serious self-harm: "If seclusion is to continue as a permissible instrument of patient-care, we are of the view that it should be definably restricted to those cases where there is a clear and present danger to the life and limb of the patient, or others on the ward." *Report of the Committee of Inquiry into Complaints about Ashworth Hospital*, Cmnd. 2028 (1992), p.204.
105   As to this, see also the observations in the Ashworth Report: "seclusion should never be used for suicidal patients or patients who threaten to harm themselves. If a patient is thought to have a potential for self-injurious behaviour the proper management response is to remain in contact with the patient and not thrust the patient out of sight or out of immediate care." *Ibid.*, p.203.
106   Almost all policies now state that seclusion should only be used if there is no other way of dealing safely with a patient who is posing a serious physical risk to himself or others. However, there is ultimately no agreement about whether seclusion can ever be justified as a way of dealing with the risk of self-harm. The Commission's view is that the patient's despair indicates a need for intensive therapeutic contact, not isolation.

feature as part of any treatment programme, be used as a punitive measure or to enforce good behaviour,[107] as a response to staff shortages, or because property is being damaged.[108] Notwithstanding these injunctions, the reasons for seclusion are sometimes recorded in terms such as, "Placed in seclusion after making several attempts to leave the ward. Secluded due to this reason and insufficient staff."

Policies and procedures

Hospitals should have clear written guidelines on the use of seclusion. The policy should aim to promote alternative approaches to the care and treatment of disturbed behaviour and to limit the use of seclusion to exceptional circumstances.[109] These guidelines should distinguish between seclusion and time-out;[110] ensure the safety and well-being of the patient in a dignified and humane environment; contain instructions on environmental standards; define the roles and responsibilities of all staff members; set down procedures for monitoring, recording, reviewing and following up decisions to seclude; and make provision for any care and support to a patient rendered necessary by their seclusion.[111] In general terms, every clinical team should assess whether or not the ward can cease to use the practice and, if continuing to use it, they should promote alternative responses to disturbed be-

---

[107] As to this, see p.203 of the Ashworth Report: "We believe that seclusion is seen by staff as a way of correcting or managing deviant behaviour. This deviant behaviour may be interpreted as anything that interferes with the smooth running of the ward or challenges the authority of staff. Thus, patients may be secluded for failing to obey instructions, or failing to carry out ward tasks, or for venting anger or abuse on another. We believe this to be unacceptable. We believe that seclusion has become so familiar a management technique that staff have ceased to question its use ... We believe that corrective isolation has no place in modern psychiatric services ... [Although] it is accepted that there is no place for seclusion as a punitive or disciplinary measure, ... there is suspicion from time to time that patients are secluded as a disguised punishment for violent behaviour."

[108] *Mental Health Act 1983: Code of Practice* (Department of Health and Welsh Office, 2nd. ed., 1993), para. 18.15. The Ashworth Committee emphasised that "seclusion must never be used to deal with patients' self-harm, as a response by nursing staff to verbal abuse or a single-blow assault by a patient, nor for non-compliance with a task of ward routine, and never for failing to obey instructions from nursing staff. We mention these seemingly obvious 'don'ts', because in the course of our Inquiry we have come across instances when seclusion was employed for these reasons." *Report of the Committee of Inquiry into Complaints about Ashworth Hospital*, Cmnd. 2028 (1992), p.206.

[109] See *e.g. The Use of Seclusion and the Alternative Management of Disturbed Behaviour within the Special Hospitals: A Policy Statement* (The Special Hospitals Service Authority, 1993).

[110] According to the Code of Practice, hospital guidelines should include a clear definition of time out and procedures for noting and monitoring its use on individual patients (para. 19.10). The important principles of time out are: (a) to enable the patient, if his behaviour is changed, to lead a less restricted life within his usual surroundings or any other setting to which he is likely to go; (b) to form part of a programme where the achievement of positive goals is as much a part of the treatment plan as reducing unwanted behaviour (para. 19.11). It is "a behaviour modification technique which denies a patient for a period (lasting from a few seconds to no more than 15 minutes) opportunities to participate in an activity or to obtain positive reinforcers following (normally immediately) an incident of unacceptable or unwanted behaviour, and which then returns the patient to his original environment. Time out should never include the use of a locked room. Time out should be clearly distinguished from seclusion, which is for use in an emergency only and should never form part of a behavioural programme. All staff working in units which use behaviour modification techniques must be familiar with the principles of time out and the distinction between time out and seclusion. Time out should not normally take place in a room which is used for seclusion on other occasions. It should be seen as one of a range of planned methods of managing a difficult or disturbed patient, and not as a spontaneous reaction to such behaviour" (para. 19.9). To the legal mind, time-out is a variant of seclusion and appears to be merely the adult equivalent of sending a poorly-behaved child to his room.

[111] *Mental Health Act 1983: Code of Practice, supra*, para. 18.16.

haviour, share responsibility for its reduction or future eradication, audit the reasons for its use, and participate in reviews of incidents leading to seclusion.

The decision to seclude

The decision to use seclusion can be made in the first instance by a doctor, the nurse in charge of the ward, a nursing officer or senior nursing officer. Where the decision is taken by someone other than a doctor then arrangements must be made for a doctor to attend immediately.[112] A lack of 24 hour medical cover means that secluded patients within the hospital "can be considered to be at 'high risk'."[113]

Living conditions of secluded patients

Seclusion should be in a safe, secure and properly identified room, where the patient cannot accidentally or intentionally harm himself. The room should have adequate heating, lighting, ventilation and seating, and any bed should be fixed. It is a matter for local judgment what the patient is allowed to take into the room but he should always be clothed.[114] The room should offer complete observation from the outside while also affording the patient privacy from other patients.[115] This is generally achieved by placing a curtain on the outside of the seclusion room door.

Observation of the patient during seclusion

The aim of observation is to ascertain the state of the patient and whether seclusion can be terminated. A nurse should be readily available within sight and sound of the seclusion room at all times and present at all times with a patient who has been sedated.[116] If the patient has not been sedated, the level of observation should be decided on an individual basis but a report must be made every 15 minutes.[117]

Reviewing the need to continue seclusion

Time spent in seclusion should be as short as is necessary to control the patient. If seclusion needs to continue, a review should be carried out in the seclusion room by two nurses every two hours, with a review every four hours by a doctor. If seclusion continues for more than eight hours consecutively, or for more than 12 hours intermittently over a period of 48 hours, an independent review must take place with a consultant and a team of nurses and other health care professionals not directly involved with the patient's care. Where there is no agreement on how to proceed, the matter should be referred to the unit general manager.[118]

Seclusion records

Detailed records should be kept in the patient's case notes of any periods of seclusion, the reasons for secluding the patient, and any subsequent activity.[119] These

---

[112]   *Mental Health Act 1983: Code of Practice* (Department of Health and Welsh Office, 2nd. ed., 1993), para. 18.17.
[113]   Mental Health Act Commission, *Sixth Biennial Report, 1993–95* (H.M.S.O., 1995), p.111.
[114]   *Mental Health Act 1983: Code of Practice, supra,* para. 18.21.
[115]   *Ibid.*, para. 18.22.
[116]   *Ibid.*, para. 18.18.
[117]   *Ibid.*, para. 18.19.
[118]   *Ibid.*, para. 18.20.
[119]   The keeping of a seclusion register was first recommended by the Metropolitan Commissioners in Lunacy in 1843 and was a legal requirement during the period 1845–1960.

records should cross-refer to a special seclusion book, or seclusion forms, which contain a step-by-step account of the seclusion procedure. The principal entries should be made by the nurse in charge of the ward and the record should be countersigned by a doctor and a unit nursing manager.

Monitoring seclusion

The managers should monitor and regularly review the use of seclusion.[120] This is only possible if the seclusion records are sufficiently specific to enable the monitors to ascertain the reasons for its use and if they specify times of commencement and cessation. It is patently insufficient to record "hostility to staff" as the reason for a patient being placed in seclusion for three consecutive days. Staff incident reviews should seek to establish the sequence of internal and external events which led to the incident and how can these events can be controlled in future. Being able to explain and understand the patient's behaviour, and the indicators and precursors to violence, may help the patient and staff to develop strategies for controlling that behaviour in other ways.

THE LAW CONCERNING SECLUSION

The law concerning seclusion may be considered under the following heads: (1) the Mental Health Act 1983; (2) the common law and related powers; (3) the European Convention on Human Rights.

Mental Health Act 1983

In the Commission's second biennial report, it was said that the practice of seclusion not being directly addressed by the Mental Health Act 1983 the justification for it must be sought at common law.[121] However, various sections of the Act authorise a person's detention for medical treatment. The first question must be whether, as a matter of law, confining a patient in a particular room constitutes part of his detention, part of his treatment, or is part detention and part treatment. This is not an easy question. Fennell describes seclusion as continuing "to occupy a 'twilight zone' between medical treatment and coercion."[122] Hoggett similarly observes that—

> "In a hospital such as Broadmoor, where the secure and highly disciplined environment is itself regarded as a therapy for the patients, the dividing line between what is permitted in the name of treatment and what can only be justified in the name of detention is particularly difficult to draw. But neither concept could be used to justify any and every regime, however harsh, arbitrary or excessive."[123]

Seclusion as an authorised form of detention

The word "detention" is not defined by the statute. However, in the Australian case of *Paul v. Paul*, it was said that the word "refers to the case of a person lawfully held

---

120   *Mental Health Act 1983: Code of Practice, supra,* para. 18.23. Experience shows that the use of seclusion diminishes sharply as soon as it is monitored and this has also been the case with the use of solitary confinement in prisons.
121   Mental Health Act Commission, *Second Biennial Report, 1985–87* (H.M.S.O., 1987), p.55.
122   P. Fennell, *Treatment without consent* (Routledge, 1996), p.225.
123   B. Hoggett, *Mental Health Law* (Sweet & Maxwell, 4th ed., 1996), p.142.

against his will, one who is not free to depart when he pleases."[124] The House of Lords has held that the power to detain a patient embraces the use of reasonable force on occasion in order to ensure that control is exercised over patients:

> "Although the Act deals comprehensively with the circumstances in which and the method by which an effective detention order can be made, and deals in some detail with the management and control of the patient's property, it does not, perhaps understandably, deal specifically with the powers of nurses in the hospital, or the detailed control of the patients who are inmates for the time being. There can however in my judgment be no doubt that the conception of detention and treatment necessarily implies that the staff at the hospital, including the male nurses, can and on occasion must use reasonable force in order to ensure that control is exercised over the patients."[125]

> "[Hospital] orders are made where the mental disorder of the named person 'warrants the detention of the patient in a hospital for medical treatment' ... and that necessarily involves the exercise of control and discipline."[126]

A person may only be detained in hospital under Part II of the Act if that is necessary or justified for his own health or safety or to protect others. Detention implies restraint (otherwise the patient could leave when he wished) and protecting others, including other patients, implies a power to segregate the patient from them. The better view therefore is that, if the occasion requires it, using reasonable force to remove a patient to a separate room, and detaining him there, represents a lawful exercise of the *statutory* power of detention.

The limits of the detainer's powers

Any power given to one person over another is capable of being abused, the more so if the latter is not free to escape his detainer and if his word is not given the same weight as that of other people. An unqualified power to control, restrain or discipline a person receiving treatment in hospital would be unacceptable and the law does not allow power to be used arbitrarily. It is noteworthy that it is not a condition of admission under section 3 that it is necessary for the patient's health or safety, or to protect others, that he is detained. The condition is that it is necessary for these reasons that he receives in-patient treatment, which treatment cannot be provided *unless* he is detained. The purpose of the statutory powers is that they enable necessary treatment to be given to a patient whose behaviour is putting himself or others at risk, the aim being to eliminate the risk of harm, or further harm, being done. This is the statutory objective, not the imposition of discipline, control and force for their own sake. A hospital is not a boot camp and the use of restraint is not a statutory objective. Both it, and the power of detention, are means, not ends. It is simply the case that detention and restraint may sometimes be necessary to the successful completion of a programme of hospital treatment. The patient's recovery, like that of any other patient, depends on the maintenance of a safe, calm, therapeutic environment, and this is only possible if medical and nursing staff can control violent behaviour. However, there must be no malice, no ill-treatment or

---

[124] *Paul v. Paul* (1954) V.L.R. 331.
[125] Dicta of Widgery C.J. adopted by the House of Lords in *R. v. Bracknell JJ., ex p. Griffiths* [1976] A.C. 314 at 318.
[126] *Ibid.*, per Lord Edmund-Davies, at 335G, H.L.

wilful neglect,[127] and any force used must be reasonable in the circumstances. Restraint greater in degree, more severe in character, or longer in duration than necessary for the security and care of the patient is an offence.[128] Furthermore, if the conditions of detention are so poor as to amount to a breach of the hospital's duty of care to the patient, damages for any injury resulting from that negligence will be recoverable. There will not, however, be an action for false imprisonment. In *R. v. Deputy Governor of Parkhurst ex p. Hague* [1992] 1 A.C. 58, the House of Lords rejected the submission that a person whose detention has been properly authorised will be unlawfully detained if the conditions in which he is detained become intolerable.

Seclusion as a form of treatment

In practice, the reason for a patient's seclusion may sometimes not be a need to manage disturbed behaviour which is putting other people at immediate and significant risk. Rather, its use is justified as a form of medical treatment. It may be said that the decision to seclude reflects the fact that patient's mental state settles in a non-stimulating environment or that its use forms part of a behaviour modification programme. For example, the Commission's Sixth Biennial Report observed that the use of seclusion in certain secure private hospitals "is viewed as a beneficial form of treatment for their particularly difficult group of patients."[129]

Historical note

The justification of seclusion as a form of treatment was particularly prevalent in the nineteenth century. Indeed, it was initially championed by non-restrainers not as a more humane alternative to mechanical restraint but as one of a range of more enlightened treatments. In 1843, the Commissioners wrote that:

> "Seclusion is found to have a very powerful effect in tranquillising and subduing those who are under temporary excitement or paroxysms of violent insanity .... As a temporary remedy, for very short periods, in case of paroxysms and of high excitement, we believe seclusion to be a valuable remedy. We are convinced, however, that it should only be permitted for short periods, and that it should not be permitted as a means of managing and treating those persons who are permanently violent or dangerous."[130]

That any seclusion should be for a short period only was emphasised in 1854 when the Commissioners made the disuse of prolonged solitary confinement a priority, the achievement of which would be "an important improvement in the treatment of the insane."

Sections 63 and 145

The admission criteria permit a person's detention where medical treatment in a hospital is justified or necessary for that person's own health or safety. The

---

[127] Under section 127(1) of the 1983 Act, it is an offence for any hospital manager or employee to ill-treat or wilfully to neglect an in-patient receiving treatment for mental disorder.

[128] *R. v. Roberts,* Commissioners 8th Report, p.37. Such excessive restraint was held in that case to be an offence at common law punishable on indictment. There is no reason to think that such conduct would not amount to ill-treatment within section 127.

[129] Mental Health Act Commission, *Sixth Biennial Report, 1993–95* (H.M.S.O., 1995), p.110.

[130] *Report of the Metropolitan Commissioners in Lunacy for 1843*, pp.145–146, referred to P. Fennell, Treatment without consent (Routledge, 1996).

definition of medical treatment in section 145 provides that the term "medical treatment" includes nursing and also care under medical supervision, but it does not exclude anything. Section 63 provides that a patient's consent is not required for any form of medical treatment for mental disorder which is not specified in that Part of the Act, provided it is given by or under the direction of the responsible medical officer.

Nurses isolating the patient in an emergency

The emergency seclusion of a patient by nursing staff in order to protect others cannot constitute a section 63 treatment. It is not an action undertaken as a form of medical treatment given under the direction of the responsible medical officer. The aim here is the immediate protection of the patient or others by means of the patient's isolation, not medical treatment for that person's mental disorder.

Behaviour modification programmes

The use of seclusion as part of a behaviour modification programme has a greater claim to being a medical treatment provided under the direction of the responsible medical officer. Indeed, it has been contended that the practice of seclusion (from 2–40 minutes) is integral to certain behavioural modification programmes.[131] Such programmes may combine the use of seclusion with other similar forms of "treatment." In two cases reported by the Commission in its Third Biennial Report, the medical notes indicated that if the patients displayed certain forms of behaviour they were to be placed in seclusion for a period, followed by a further period of detention on the secure ward. One of the patients had been secluded for three hours followed by 45 hours on the secure ward and the other for 30 minutes followed by 47 hours 30 minutes on the secure ward. The plans were written up in the form of a behavioural programme and endorsed by the responsible medical officer.[132] As to the legal status of these programmes, Hoggett's opinion is that:

> "Expecting patients to conform to very high or artificial norms of behaviour, to fit into the system for the system's sake rather than their own, or to be punished for their misdeeds prior to their admission to hospital ... can scarcely qualify as medical treatment under the widest definition. But a carefully designed programme of behaviour modification ... which will meet the needs of the particular group of patients for whom it is designed obviously can qualify."[133]

If there is a legal distinction between placing a patient in solitary confinement in order to protect himself or others and secluding him in order to discourage the repetition of unwanted behaviour, it is that the former has as its end the protection of the patient or others from harm, and this end is achieved through and legally justified as an exercise of the power of detention, whilst the latter has as its end the therapeutic purpose of alleviating the patient's mental disorder, which is achieved by giving him compulsory "treatment" without his consent under section 63. When it comes to some psychopathic disorders, the distinction between discipline and therapy is not entirely clear, the therapy appearing to consist of nothing more than

---

[131] See *e.g.* Mental Health Act Commission, *Sixth Biennial Report, 1993–95* (H.M.S.O., 1995), p.111.
[132] Mental Health Act Commission, *Third Biennial Report, 1987–89* (H.M.S.O., 1989), p.53.
[133] B. Hoggett, *Mental Health Law* (Sweet & Maxwell, 4th ed., 1996), p.144.

instilling discipline in a previously undisciplined adult.[134] Nevertheless, the first kind of seclusion is justified in terms of protection whereas the second kind is justified on the ground that (like medication) it will improve the patient's mental state. The justification claimed for the latter being the patient's benefit, "..all unnecessary severity, all confinement other than that for the purpose of the unhappy person's recovery" will be subject to censure," *per* Lord Mansfield in *R. v. Coate* (1772) Lofft. 73.

Seclusion to prevent self-harm

Secluding a patient in order to prevent self-harm is a procedure which has a recognisable medical objective, being the preservation of the patient's physical health and safety. If the seclusion is directed by the responsible medical officer then whether it is a section 63 treatment depends on whether it constitutes a medical treatment "for the mental disorder from which he is suffering." In *B. v. Croydon Health Authority* [1995] 1 All E.R. 683, the Court of Appeal held that the definition of medical treatment in section 145 included a range of acts ancillary to the core treatment. Treatment, in the form of tube feeding, to alleviate the symptoms of mental disorder, in the form of a refusal to eat in order to inflict self-harm, was just as much a part of treatment for the disorder as that directed to remedying its underlying cause. It therefore fell within the ambit of the power conferred by section 63 and could be administered to the patient without her consent. The court dismissed the argument that, whilst force-feeding may be a prerequisite to a treatment for mental disorder, or it may be treatment for a consequence of the mental disorder, it cannot be said to be treatment for that disorder. Furthermore, in the court's opinion, it would be strange if a hospital could, without a suicidal patient's consent, give him treatment for the underlying mental illness but not without such consent be able to treat the consequences of a suicide attempt. In the court's judgment, the term "medical treatment ... for mental disorder" in section 63 included such ancillary acts. With this judgment in mind, it may be that the courts would hold that a responsible medical officer's decision to seclude a suicidal patient, in order to prevent self-harm, and the treatment of injuries following an episode of self-harm, are both "just as much a part of treatment for the disorder as that directed to remedying its underlying cause" and they fall within the ambit of section 63.

Seclusion as a tranquil environment

Applying the judgment in B. to the situation of profoundly agitated patients who are secluded because their confinement in a non-stimulating environment is considered to be clinically appropriate, it may again be the case that this constitutes a section 63 treatment if given under the direction of the responsible medical officer. The more so because the immediate and primary aim is to alleviate the patient's mental state. As with all other kinds of medical treatment, the responsible medical officer prescribing this "treatment" owes the patient a duty of care (in his capacity as his consultant) and this must include taking reasonable care to ensure that the regime is not in fact harmful to the patient's health.

---

[134] Indeed, the two terms may be synonymous, the preference for one term over the other being determined only by the patient's location (prison–discipline, hospital–treatment).

The common law and related powers

Seclusion involves the detention of an individual, time-out at best a restraint, and treatment without consent is *prima facie* an assault. These three actions potentially involve committing the torts of false imprisonment, trespass to the person and battery. If there is no statutory authority for such acts, the question becomes when, if ever, the common law or some other statutory power provides a legal justification:

- It is lawful at common law to restrain, and if need be detain, a "furious" or "dangerous" lunatic whose state of mind is such that he is a danger to himself and others;[135]

- It is lawful to administer to a patient who "lacks the capacity to give or to communicate consent to that treatment" whatever treatment is judged in the best interests of the patient as being "necessary to preserve the life, health or well-being of the patient" or "to ensure improvement or prevent deterioration in her[/his] physical or mental health."[136]

- It is lawful to use reasonable force in self-defence or to defend other persons or property and a person "may use such force as is reasonable in the circumstances in the prevention of crime, or in effecting the lawful arrest of offenders or suspected offenders or persons unlawfully at large."[137]

- It is justified to detain a person if that is immediately necessary to prevent a breach of the peace. Such a breach occurs where "harm is actually done or is likely to be done to a person or in his presence to his property or a person is in fear of being so harmed through an assault, an affray, an unlawful assembly or other disturbance."[138] "Every citizen in whose presence a breach of the peace is being, or reasonably appears to be about to be, committed has the right to take reasonable steps to make the person who is breaking or threatening to break the peace refrain from doing so; and those reasonable steps in appropriate cases will include detaining him against his will."[139]

The common law should not be used to justify protracted periods of seclusion and these powers of detention and restraint are subject to a reasonableness test. For the use of force to be reasonable, the force used must be no more than is in fact necessary to accomplish the object for which it is allowed and the reaction must be in proportion to the harm threatened. Acts which involve unreasonable force include gross over-reaction to a situation, the continuation of force once the need for it is over, retaliation, punishment. Thus, Hoggett says that[140]:

---

135   *Brookshaw v. Hopkins* (1772) Lofft. 240 at 243; *Anderton v. Burrows* (1830) 4 Car. & P. 210 at 213; *Re Greenwood* (1855) 24 L.J.Q.B. 148; *Fletcher v. Fletcher* (1859) 1 El. & El. 420; *Scott v. Wakem* (1862) 3 F. & F. 328 at 333; *Symm v. Fraser* (1863) 3 F. & F. 859 at 882–883; *Re Shuttleworth* (1846) 9 Q.B. 651; *Re Gregory* (1901) A.C. 128; *Black v. Forsey*, 1987 S.L.T. 681.

136   *Re F* [1989] 2 W.L.R. 1025 at 1064, 1067, 1078, 1080, 1085, 1088.

137   Criminal Law Act 1967, s.3(1). As Hoggett notes, this power applies only to the prevention of crime which is actually in progress or about to be committed. B. Hoggett, *Mental Health Law* (Sweet & Maxwell, 4th ed., 1996), p.140.

138   *R. v. Howell* [1982] Q.B. 416. A breach of the peace can occur on private property: *McConnell v. Chief Constable of Greater Manchester Police* [1990] 1 W.L.R. 364.

139   *Albert v. Lavin* [1982] A.C. 546.

140   B. Hoggett, *Mental Health Law* (Sweet & Maxwell, 4th ed., 1996), p.141.

"A prolonged period of confinement or sedation would not be permitted under these principles, even if it was in fact necessary to prevent the patient doing harm. This is because of the second element in 'reasonableness', which is that the reaction must be in proportion to the harm threatened ... these common law principles should not be used as a substitute for the procedures laid down in the Mental Health Act, which have replaced the hospitals' common law powers to detain the insane (*Black v. Forsey, 1988 S.L.T. 572*)."

The European Convention

Article 3 of The European Convention on Human Rights and Fundamental Freedoms provides that "no one shall be subjected to torture or to inhuman or degrading treatment or punishment." The suffering occasioned or the humiliation or debasement involved must attain a particular level before it can be classified as inhuman or degrading punishment contrary to Article 3. The "assessment of this minimum is, in the nature of things, relative; it depends on all the circumstances of the case, such as the duration of the treatment, its physical or mental effects and, in some cases, the sex, age and state of health of the victim, etc."[141]

The conditions of seclusion

The case of *A. v. United Kingdom (1980) 3 E.H.R.R. 131* concerned a complaint that the conditions and circumstances of a patient's seclusion in Broadmoor Hospital in 1974 amounted to inhuman and degrading treatment, contrary to Article 3. The patient alleged that he had been deprived of adequate furnishing and clothing, that the conditions in the room had been insanitary, and it had been inadequately lit and ventilated. A friendly settlement was reached with an ex gratia payment to the patient of £500 being made by the Government.

Seclusion not usually violation of Art. 3

In *Dhoest v. Belgium 12 E.H.R.R. 135,* the Commission noted that it would not normally consider the segregation for security, disciplinary or protective reasons, of persons committed to hospital in the course of criminal proceedings as constituting inhuman treatment or punishment. In "making an assessment in a given case, regard must be had to the surrounding circumstances including the particular conditions, the stringency of the measure, its duration, the objective pursued and its effects on the person concerned."[142]

Need continuously to review detention arrangements

In *McFeely v. United Kingdom 3 E.H.R.R. 161,* the Commission had previously held that prison authorities, when faced with what is regarded as an unlawful challenge to their authority, must nevertheless maintain a continuous review of the detention arrangements employed with a view to ensuring the health and well-being of all prisoners with due regard to the ordinary and reasonable requirements of imprisonment. In *Dhoest*, it held that the same reasoning applied *mutatis mutandis* to mental health patients detained in a custodial mental institution under provisions similar to restriction orders under the 1983 Act.[143]

---

[141] *Ireland v. United Kingdom* 2 E.H.R.R. 25, at para. 162. See also *Tyrer v. United Kingdom* 2 E.H.R.R. 1; *B. v. United Kingdom* 6 E.H.R.R. 204, at para. 172.

[142] *Dhoest v. Belgium* 12 E.H.R.R. 135, at 142 (para. 117), Committee of Ministers.

[143] Ibid., at 143 (para. 121).

CONCLUSIONS AND SUMMARY

Having regard to the above and the disagreements concerning this difficult and contentious subject, it is submitted that—

1. Where a serious incident cannot be managed by talking with, and calming, the patient and some restraint is unavoidable, the relative advantages of solitary confinement, control and restraint, emergency medication, and transfer to a locked facility depend altogether on the results; the aim must be to choose that method of dealing with the immediate threat to others which is likely to be least distressing for the particular patient, and so least damages his therapeutic relationship with those using force;

2. Further research into the possible advantages and disadvantages of these different kinds of restraint should be a priority[144];

3. Because, in certain undesirable situations, solitary confinement may conceivably be the least undesirable way of managing dangerous behaviour, it is premature to advocate its prohibition by legislation or setting a target for phasing out the practice[145];

4. Solitary confinement should be regulated within very narrow margins by a gradual yielding to a growing consensus of opinion, and by statutory rules[146];

---

[144] If seclusion has a therapeutic value, the question then becomes how the use of the practice can be properly regulated so that it is only used as a form of treatment in situations where it is known to have some therapeutic benefit. Otherwise, acknowledging its therapeutic value might provide a cloak for its use as a way of managing disturbed behaviour. If the answer is that seclusion has no therapeutic value then one is left with the problem that the law appears to regard it as a form of medical treatment which does not require a detained patient's consent, provided his consultant has authorised it. If the answer is uncertain, the first aim will be to obtain more reliable information through research, *e.g.* as to the therapeutic outcome following the use of seclusion and medication levels on wards not practising seclusion.

[145] There are four possible approaches: (1) to enact primary legislation prohibiting the seclusion of patients; (2) to enact primary legislation limiting its use to certain clearly defined situations; (3) to regulate the practice more effectively by means of secondary legislation made under the present statute; (4) to do nothing.

[146] This approach, which aims to limit the use of seclusion within very narrow margins, is essentially that successfully adopted in the nineteenth century in relation to the use of mechanical restraint. In 1927, the Board of Control asserted that although restraint had never been abolished "by a gradual yielding to a growing consensus of opinion, and by statutory rules, it has been regulated within very narrow margins." *Fourteenth Annual Report of the Board of Control for the Year 1927*, HMSO, London, 1928, pp.73—77. Apart from defining in any future statute the circumstances in which a patient may be secluded, defining seclusion, renaming it solitary confinement, and the use of a prescribed register and forms, are possible ways of ensuring that the practice is very much a last resort. There are weighty arguments in favour of making regulations which once more define what constitutes seclusion and which prescribe that a common form of seclusion record be kept. Firstly, if all hospitals are required to adhere to a common method of recording its use, it will be easier to see whether a particular hospital, ward, nurse or medical practitioner may be relying too heavily on the practice. Secondly, the use of a common register will enable the Commission to obtain accurate data across England and Wales about the use of seclusion, which will be useful in later deciding whether legislation is necessary. Thirdly, experience in the prison system shows that less use is made of solitary confinement when the practice is properly regulated. The need to keep records at all, the need to record reasons, and the existence of a system for scrutinising its use, all discourage its use.

5.   More particularly, the 1983 Regulations should be amended so as to require a prescribed seclusion register and forms to be kept[147];

6.   Furthermore, any use of solitary confinement as a form of medical treatment for mental disorder should be regulated under Part IV;

7.   The Code of Practice should abandon the term "seclusion" for "solitary confinement," defined as "the confinement of a patient alone in a room at any time of the day or night and a patient is confined to a room if he may not leave that room at will";

8.   The circumstances in which a patient may be isolated in a room on the ground that his behaviour is putting the safety of others at immediate risk should in due course be defined and regulated by statute[148];

9.   Nurses' and other professionals' powers of restraint, including the use of solitary confinement, should be put on a clearer statutory basis at that time.

---

[147]   The maintenance of a seclusion register was a legal requirement between 1845 and 1960. Article 94 of the Mental Treatment Rules 1930 required all institutions for mental patients to keep a "register of mechanical restraint and seclusion", the precise form of which was set out as Form 9 in the schedule to those rules. These provisions also applied to poor law establishments by Article 48(1) of the Public Assistance Order 1930, which was in the following terms: "Every case in which a person of unsound mind or a person alleged to be of unsound mind is placed in a padded room or is otherwise compulsorily secluded, shall be recorded in a book in the form 6 in the First Schedule, which may be included in the register of mechanical restraint, and the book shall be produced to every commissioner or inspector of the Board of Control visiting the institution." It is worth noting that section 32(2)(c) now provides that the regulations made under the Act may in particular make provision for requiring such bodies as may be prescribed to keep such registers or other records as may be prescribed in respect of patients who are liable to be detained or subject to guardianship or after-care under supervision.

[148]   For example, by enacting a section along the following lines: *Solitary confinement.* **134A.—(1)** A patient shall not be placed or kept in solitary confinement unless either— (a) his solitary confinement is immediately necessary and represents the minimum interference necessary to prevent the patient from behaving violently or being a danger to himself or others; *or* (b) his being placed or kept in solitary confinement is a medical treatment which has been authorised by a certificate in writing given under section 58(3) above. **(2)** A member of the Mental Health Act Commission may at any time direct that a person who is being kept in solitary confinement otherwise than under subsection 1(b) above shall immediately cease to be so confined and, where he does so, he shall record his reasons for doing so in writing. **(3)** A full record in the form prescribed by regulations of every case of solitary confinement shall be kept from day to day and a copy of the records and certificates made under this section shall be sent to the Mental Health Act Commission at the end of every quarter. **(4)** In this section— "solitary confinement" means the confinement of a patient alone in a room at any time of the day or night and a patient is confined to a room if he may not leave that room at will; "patient" means a person suffering or appearing to be suffering from mental disorder. **(5)** This section applies to all hospitals and residential care homes in England and Wales. **(6)** Any person who wilfully acts in contravention of this section shall be guilty of an offence. **145(1)** In this Act, unless the context otherwise requires— ... "medical treatment" includes .... the solitary confinement of a patient whose solitary confinement has been authorised by a certificate in writing given under section 58(3) above and excludes all other instances of solitary confinement; "solitary confinement" has the meaning given in section 134A and the term includes seclusion and other cognate expressions.

21. Personality disorders

INTRODUCTION

Not all conditions characterised by abnormal mental functioning are conceived of as an illness. Certain forms of mental disorder are conceptualised and therefore categorised as disorders of the personality. The individual's mental state is here considered to represent his normal, although compared with other people abnormal, personality rather than the consequence of any disease or illness overlying and distorting that personality. The concept of personality implies a certain cohesion and "consistency of the personality as a backdrop upon which the vicissitudes of illness and other circumstances make transitory patterns, but the underlying features remain constant."[1] Whether or not an abnormality of personality actually manifests itself in the form of disordered behaviour, and is defined as a personality disorder, depends to a considerable extent on social circumstances.[2] Although this is so in practice, a particular kind of disturbed behaviour can be exhibited by more than one personality group with different mechanisms pertaining to each.[3]

PERSONALITY

Personality is what makes one individual different from another.[4] It is the unique quality of the individual, his feelings and personal goals; the sum of his traits, habits and experiences and the whole system of relatively permanent tendencies, physical and mental, which are distinctive of a given individual.[5] Alternatively, the ingrained patterns of thought, feeling, and behaviour which characterise an individual's unique lifestyle and mode of adaptation, and which result from constitutional factors, development, and social experience.[6] These personal characteristics are present since adolescence; stable over time despite fluctuations in mood; manifest in different environments; and recognisable to friends and acquaintances.[7] Personality has a genetic component and behaviour genetics is concerned with the pathway from genes to behaviour and the lifelong interactions between the genetic constitution of an individual and his environment. However, certain aspects of each individual's personality are generally considered to have been acquired through learning. An underlying biological assumption is that "if what is learnt at any one stage did not have some permanence, we would be endlessly open to change in response to events and circumstances."[8]

---

[1]   A. Sims, *Symptoms in the Mind* (Baillière Tindall, 1988), p.299.
[2]   *Ibid.*, p.285.
[3]   C.P.L. Freeman, "Personality disorders" in *Companion to psychiatric studies* (ed. R.E. Kendell & A.K. Zealley, Churchill Livingstone, 1993), p.592.
[4]   *Ibid.*, p.588.
[5]   K. Schneider, *Clinical Psychopathology* (5th ed., trans. M.W. Hamilton, Grune & Stratton, 1958).
[6]   *Lexicon of Psychiatric and Mental Health Terms* (World Health Organisation, 2nd ed., 1994), p.75.
[7]   C.P.L. Freeman, "Personality disorders," *supra*, p.588.
[8]   S. Wolff, "Personality development" in *Companion to psychiatric studies*, *supra*, p.61.

Personality types and personality traits

The observed behaviour of individuals is sufficiently similar in certain respects to suggest that it may be possible to formulate personality traits and personality types. In genetics, a trait is the characteristic observable expression of a hereditary predisposition, for example red hair. The trait is the outward manifestation so that, when the word is used to describe something characteristic about a person's behaviour, a personality trait is "a constant or persistent way of behaving,"[9] rather than the recurrent tendency towards such behaviour.[10] Nevertheless, the belief that observable behaviour patterns are the manifestations of unobservable dispositions within the individual's personality means that personality traits are most often defined in terms of these generalised predispositions. The underlying assumption is that "there are universal traits (such as hostility) present to different degrees in all people and which influence behaviour in the same ways in different situations and at different times, so that trait measures can be used predictively."[11] These traits vary in intensity and are usually regarded as abnormal when they pass beyond what is socially tolerable. Personality types considered to be abnormal are classified according to personality traits in various international classifications of mental disorders. The practical usefulness of these classifications can be tested by, and largely depends upon, their predictive accuracy. The trait and type approaches are therefore closely related to psychometrics, which uses standardised tests of personality to compare large numbers of individuals and groups or classes of individuals.[12] Unfortunately:

"research has failed to show as much personality consistency as theorists would lead us to believe ... Studies which have looked at general traits such as anxiety or hostility have found that individual differences in the strength of a trait account for little of the variability of behaviour. What appears to matter most is the interaction of the differences in individuals with the differences in situations. In other words, it is not very useful to talk about general traits such as anxiety or hostility without considering the situation in which they may be exhibited. The importance of this in helping people with personality disorders is that one's efforts may be much more fruitfully directed towards finding situations in which the individual behaves less deviantly than in trying to change personality with psychotherapy."[13]

That being so, Powell has emphasised the importance of considering the underlying traits, stating clearly the specific behaviour causing concern, and describing the social context in which the personality problems exhibit themselves.[14] The underlying personality trait causing most difficulty, for example aggressiveness, can be rated by a single score on an appropriate psychometric test.

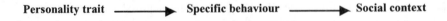

Personality trait ⟶ Specific behaviour ⟶ Social context

9   See G.W. Allport, *Personality: a psychological interpretation* (Holt, 1937).
10   G.L. Klerman and R.M.A. Hirschfield, "Personality as a vulnerability factor: with special attention to clinical depression" in *Handbook of social psychiatry* (ed. A.S. Henderson & G.D. Burrows, Elsevier, 1988), pp.41–53.
11   C.P.L. Freeman, "Personality disorders" in *Companion to psychiatric studies* (ed. R.E. Kendell & A.K. Zealley, Churchill Livingstone, 1993), p.588.
12   See R. Gross, *Psychology: The Science of Mind and Behaviour* (Hodder & Stoughton, 2nd ed., 1992), p.11.
13   C.P.L. Freeman, "Personality disorders," *supra*, p.591.
14   G.E. Powell, "Personality" in *Scientific principles of psychopathology* (ed. P. McGuffin *et al.*, Grune & Stratton).

Personality disorders

While acknowledging that the concept of personality disorder is an untidy concept and "an abstraction built upon several tenuous theories," Sims recently concluded that it is clinically useful.[15] What constitutes a disordered personality ultimately depends on how normality and abnormality are defined and so is partly determined by the social context (**1031**). Definitions of personality disorder are usually value-based. A person is considered to have an abnormal personality if he has to an excessive extent a personality trait which is considered to be undesirable (*e.g.* hostility) or possesses insufficiently a trait considered necessary for a person to be normal (*e.g.* empathy). More particularly:

- Schneider defined an abnormal personality as being a variation upon an accepted yet broadly conceived range of average personalities. It was immaterial whether the distinctive excess or deficiency of some personal quality which thereby rendered the individual markedly different from others was conceived of as good or bad, desirable or undesirable. The saint and the criminal both had abnormal personalities. A personality disorder was an abnormality of personality which caused the patient or other people, "the community," to suffer.[16]

- A personality and behaviour disorder is defined in the *Lexicon of Psychia-*
  ~~tric and Mental Health T~~
  iour patterns of clinical significance that tend to be persistent
  be the expression of the individual's lifestyle and mode of relating to self and others. Specific personality disorders, mixed personality disorders, and enduring personality change are deeply ingrained and persisting behaviour patterns, manifested as inflexible responses to a broad range of personal and social situations. They represent extreme or significant deviations from the way in which the average individual in a given culture perceives, thinks, feels, and, particularly, relates to others."[17]

- The American DSM–IV classification defines a personality disorder as "an enduring pattern of inner experience and behavior that deviates markedly from the expectations of the individual's culture, is pervasive and inflexible, has an onset in adolescence or early adulthood, is stable over time, and leads to distress or impairment."[18]

Enduring personality changes

Conventionally, an individual's personality may undergo enduring change during adulthood. This may be for the better, in terms of late maturation and the development of emotional sensitivity, or represent a deterioration in the individual's capacity to cope with his environment. An enduring personality change is defined in the *Lexicon of Psychiatric and Mental Health Terms* as "a disorder of adult personality and behaviour that has developed following catastrophic or excessive prolonged

---

[15]   A. Sims, *Symptoms in the Mind* (Baillière Tindall, 1988), p.284.
[16]   K. Schneider, *Psychopathic personalities, 9th ed.* (trans. M.W. Hamilton, Cassel, 1950).
[17]   *Lexicon of Psychiatric and Mental Health Terms* (World Health Organisation, 2nd ed., 1994), p.75.
[18]   *Diagnostic and Statistical Manual of Mental Disorders, Fourth Revision (DSM–IV)* (American Psychiatric Association, 1994), p.629.

stress, or following severe psychiatric illness, in an individual with no previous personality disorder. There is a definite and enduring change in the individual's pattern of perceiving, relating to, or thinking about the environment and the self. The personality change is associated with inflexible and maladaptive behaviour that was not present before the pathogenic experience and is not a manifestation of another mental disorder or a residual symptom of any antecedent mental disorder."[19]

PERSONALITY

- *Personality*
  The unique quality of the individual, his feelings and personal goals; the sum of his traits, habits and experiences; the whole system of relatively permanent tendencies, physical and mental, which are distinctive of a given individual.

- *Personality trait*
  A constant or persistent way of behaving.

- *Personality disorder*
  A variety of conditions and behaviour patterns that tend to be persistent and appear to be the expression of the individual's lifestyle and mode of relating to self and others; they represent extreme or significant deviations from the way in which the average individual in a given culture perceives, thinks, feels, and, particularly, relates to others.

PERSONALITY AND MENTAL ILLNESS

The way in which a human's genetic potential expresses itself is largely determined by his environment and the state of any biological organism is the result of the interplay of genes with their environment. When the environment is less than perfect, as it always is, the way in which the brain develops represents a response to the environmental stimuli which it receives. Certain potentials and responses are stimulated while others are discouraged. By analogy, the soil within which an acorn is planted, and amount and distribution of light in the immediate environment, affect the way in which it develops into an oak — the extent of the root system, the height of the tree, the shape of its bole, the distribution of its leaves and the direction in which they incline. Planted in a different place, the same acorn would develop differently and only rarely is the appearance of an oak so markedly different from its neighbours that its profile represents the expression of innate defects in the acorn's structure. Likewise, although limited development of the personality in a human being may occasionally be caused by an innate structural defect, such as mental retardation, this is relatively rare. The manner in which an organism such as a brain or tree develops from its seed in order to survive is therefore characterised by a high degree of adaptability which includes a capacity to compensate for some degree of environmental deprivation. However, once the growth of an organic structure such as a tree or brain is complete, and their roots and branches have been developed and shaped according to the stimuli received during the formative period, the capacity for further change is usually limited. This reflects the fact that structure and

---

[19]   *Lexicon of Psychiatric and Mental Health Terms* (World Health Organisation, 2nd ed., 1994), p.75.

functioning virtually always go hand in hand, the established structure of an organism limiting and defining the way in which it can function. Certain kinds of environment, whether soil types or domestic and social conditions, are particularly common in any particular country, as therefore are particular structural patterns of human and plant adaptation. As concerns human development, the ingrained patterns of thought, feeling, and behaviour which characterise these different modes of adaptation are often referred to as personality types. Because the capacity for further structural change is limited once the formative period is over, the form taken by the structure may be such that it is poorly-equipped to function adequately in certain kinds of environment encountered by members of the species. The way in which the structure has evolved may then be viewed as abnormal if these situations are relatively common — notwithstanding that, in the brain's case, it refers by habit to its habitual responses to environmental stimuli as constituting its mind or personality. Thinking is a form of activity engaged in by a biological organism whenever habitual patterns of action are disrupted and the function of thought is to solve the problems that give rise to it. Various outcomes are possible when an environmental event requires a thoughtful response. If a person's environment produces no food because of a drought, he will starve unless the environment fortuitously changes and produces food, or he can modify his environment (by introducing an irrigation system), or he can change himself biologically (so that he requires little or no food). However, there are strict limits as to how far an individual's biological system can adapt to survive devastating environmental change. Sometimes the response is only partially effective, limiting rather than eliminating the threat. Thus, the bacteria causing leprosy often provoke such a severe inflammation that the blood supply around infected areas is cut off and large areas of tissue are damaged or destroyed. The position is similar with "mental" events since these are received and stored by the brain in biological form, the brain being a biological instrument. If an individual's brain is challenged by environmental events, resolving the disturbance requires modifying one of the two factors at variance, the environment or the brain's habitual ways of dealing with and making sense of its surroundings — what we call the individual's personality. However, it is often not possible to change the environment at an objective level and, after events such as bereavement, such modification is impossible. Likewise, because the habitual dispositions of the brain and nervous system correspond to their established structures, the brain's capacity to add to or modify its established range of "natural" responses is limited. Consequently, its natural responses, which comprise its various established habitual responses, become increasingly pronounced and exaggerated when the necessary equilibrium is still not restored. Under severe conditions, the brain which is disposed to interpret events in a paranoid manner no longer merely has that disposition but actually engages in paranoid misinterpretations of environmental events. The resulting mental state is then regarded as a form of mental illness (specifically, a "delusional disorder"). The individual's personality therefore shapes his mental state during everyday life and determines the unique adjustment which he makes to the environment, including therefore the way he becomes mentally ill. As with a crystal, the structure gives way along the well-defined lines of cleavage which constitute its weakest plane so that it is artificial to draw an absolute distinction between personality and mental illness or to view the onset of mental illness as unrelated to any pre-existing personality disorder. The clinical picture is profoundly coloured by the individual's personality in the same way that a gem's structure determines how it shatters and the impurities within it give it its colour.

EPIDEMIOLOGY

The number of persons in any given population who have a disordered personality depends upon how normality and abnormality are defined and, more specifically, the precise criteria used to determine what constitutes abnormal behaviour. Historically, definitions within a given society have been based on that society's values. Necessarily, this requires periodically revising what is considered to be abnormal or deviant as the values and conduct of people change over time. The tendency has been to restrict the designation to a small proportion of the population whose behaviour grossly deviates from accepted norms. The alternative approach, to base the criteria on standards of mental functioning and behaviour which contravene certain relatively fixed value-norms ("ideals") without taking account of how many people violate those norms, has not been acceptable. To categorise behaviour indulged in by the majority of the population as a manifestation of their abnormal personalities would be unacceptable to that majority. Nevertheless, basing notions of normal and abnormal conduct on patterns of behaviour which are normal in the sense of being commonplace also has its problems. Given that some 30–40 per cent. of young men now have at least one criminal conviction, so that criminal behaviour is statistically approaching the norm, the tendency is to revise ideas about what constitutes an abnormal personality and abnormal behaviour in order to avoid vast numbers of people, perhaps even the majority eventually, being categorised as "abnormal." If enough people infringe the law by engaging in anti-social behaviour, the effect of this may be only that such behaviour is no longer considered to be abnormal or the expression of an abnormal personality — even though the undesirability of that behaviour, and the personality traits giving rise to it, remain the same and no less damaging to society.[20] Estimates of how many people have an abnormal personality or behave abnormally must therefore always be carefully scrutinised and often have fairly limited usefulness. All that can be said is that a lifetime prevalence of personality disorder of between 2.1 and 18 per cent. has been found depending on the population and the criteria used and that about 7–8 per cent. of the in-patient hospital population has a diagnosed personality disorder.[21]

CLASSIFYING PERSONALITY DISORDERS

The classification of mental disorders in official usage in England and Wales is the World Health Organisation's International Classification of Diseases, now in its tenth revision (ICD–10); and, more particularly, that part of it dealing with mental and behavioural disorders. One section or "block" of the classification is concerned with "disorders of adult personality and behaviour" (block F60–F69) and, within this block, each type and sub-type of disorder is separately listed and coded. For example, specific personality disorders are given the code F60.0 and a further digit is used to record its various sub-types such as paranoid personality disorder (F60.0) and schizoid personality disorder (F60.1). Operational definitions (diagnostic guidelines or criteria) are used to specify which combinations of symptoms are adequate to substantiate a diagnosis. They define what a clinician means when he uses the term "paranoid personality disorder" and represent an attempt to standardise

---

[20]   It is, of course, true that as more criminal law is passed so there is more law for people to infringe. Consequently, even if a people's behaviour remains unchanged over a generation, more of them will today be "convicted criminals" and fewer remain of good character. The quickest way to reduce the crime rate is to reduce the number of crimes.

[21]   P. Casey, "The epidemiology of personality disorder" in *Personality Disorders: Diagnosis, Management and Course* (ed. P. Tyrer, Wright, 1988), pp.77, 79.

clinical practice and understanding. Inevitably, the classification represents "compromises between scientists with the most influential theories and the practice of senior clinicians at national and international level."[22]

Other classifications

The ICD–10 classification, and the diagnostic guidelines which form part of it, comprise one of many medical classifications of mental disorder. Although a core of typical patients meet all definitions, there are significant differences in the populations of patients covered by each of them. Each operational definition generates different values for the incidence of a disorder, its heritability, its responsiveness to therapeutic agents, and its prognosis. Because defining what constitutes a disordered personality is profoundly difficult, and has significant consequences for any individual so categorised, the operational criteria used in the other main international classification (DSM–IV) are set out below, before considering the ICD–10 scheme is in greater detail.

DSM–IV General diagnostic criteria for a personality disorder

---

A. An enduring pattern of inner experience and behavior that deviates markedly from the expectations of the individual's culture. This pattern is manifested in one (or more) of the following areas:

(1) cognition (*i.e.* ways of perceiving and interpreting self, other people, and events)

(2) affectivity (*i.e.* the range, intensity, lability, and appropriateness of emotional response)

(3) interpersonal functioning

(4) impulse control

B. The enduring pattern is inflexible and pervasive across a broad range of personal and social situations.

C. The enduring pattern leads to clinically significant distress or impairment in social, occupational, or other important areas of functioning.

D. The pattern is stable and of long duration and its onset can be traced back at least to adolescence or early childhood.

E. The enduring pattern is not better accounted for as a manifestation or consequence of another mental disorder.

F. The enduring pattern is not due to the direct physiological effects of a substance (*e.g.*, a drug of abuse, a medication) or a general medical condition (*e.g.*, head trauma).

---

[22]   J.K. Wing, "Differential diagnosis of schizophrenia" in *Schizophrenia — An overview and practical handbook* (ed. D.J. Kavanagh, Chapman & Hall, 1992), p.17.

THE ICD–10 CLASSIFICATION

The section of the International Classification of Mental and Behavioural Disorders (ICD–10) which deals with "disorders of adult personality and behaviour" (Block F60–F69) sub-divides them into various types —

- specific personality disorders (F60)

- other personality disorders (F61)

- enduring personality changes (F62)

- habit and impulse disorders, such as pyromania (F63)

- sexual behaviour, orientation and development (F64–66).

PERSONALITY DISORDERS AND PERSONALITY CHANGE

The "specific" personality disorders differ from enduring personality changes in two major respects—

- in their timing and the mode of their emergence — personality disorders are developmental conditions, which appear in late childhood or adolescence and continue into adulthood; it is therefore unlikely that the diagnosis of personality disorder will be appropriate before the age of 16 or 17 years.[23]

- in that they are not secondary to another mental disorder or brain disease, although they may precede and coexist with other disorders. In contrast, personality change is acquired, usually during adult life, following severe or prolonged stress, extreme environmental deprivation, serious psychiatric disorder, or brain disease or injury.[24]

SPECIFIC PERSONALITY DISORDERS (F60)

A specific personality disorder is described as "a severe disturbance in the characterological constitution and behavioural tendencies of the individual, usually involving several areas of the personality, and nearly always associated with considerable personal and social disruption."[25] Such conditions comprise deeply ingrained and enduring behaviour patterns, manifesting themselves as inflexible responses to a broad range of personal and social situations, and they represent either extreme or significant deviations from the way the average individual in a given culture perceives, thinks, feels, and, in particular, relates to others. These behaviour patterns tend to be stable and to encompass multiple domains of behaviour and psychosocial functioning. They are frequently, but not always, associated with various degrees of subjective distress and problems in social functioning and performance.

---

[23] *Classification of Mental and Behavioural Disorders, Tenth Revision (ICD–10): Clinical descriptions and diagnostic guidelines* (World Health Organisation, 1992), pp.200, 202.

[24] *Ibid.*, p.200.

[25] *Ibid.*, p.202.

Specific personality disorders — diagnostic guidelines

The ICD–10 diagnostic guidelines for specific personality disorders are set out in table below.

Specific personality disorders — Diagnostic guidelines (ICD–10)

Conditions not directly attributable to gross brain damage or disease, or to another psychiatric disorder, meeting the following criteria—

- *a.* markedly dysharmonious attitudes and behaviour, involving usually several areas of functioning, *e.g.* affectivity, arousal, impulse control, ways of perceiving and thinking, and style of relating to others;

- *b.* the abnormal behaviour pattern is enduring, long standing, and not limited to episodes of mental illness;

- *c.* the abnormal behaviour pattern is pervasive and clearly maladaptive to a broad range of personal and social conditions;

- *d.* the above manifestations always appear during childhood or adolescence and continue into adulthood;

- *e.* the disorder leads to considerable personal distress but this may only become apparent late in its course;

- *f.* the disorder is usually, but not invariably, associated with significant problems in occupational and social performance.

In making a diagnosis of personality disorder, the clinician should consider all aspects of personal functioning, although the diagnostic formulation, to be simple and efficient, will refer to only those dimensions or traits for which the suggested thresholds for severity are reached ... If a personality condition precedes or follows a time-limited or chronic psychiatric disorder, both should be diagnosed.

Source: The ICD–10 Classification of Mental and Behavioural Disorders: Clinical descriptions and diagnostic guidelines, World Health Organisation, Geneva, 1992, p.202.

SPECIFIC PERSONALITY DISORDERS — SUB-TYPES

Specific personality disorders are sub-divided in the ICD–10 classification according to clusters of traits that correspond to the most frequent or conspicuous behavioural manifestations. These sub-types are considered by the World Health Organisation to be "widely recognised" as major forms of personality deviation.[26] For the diagnosis of "most of the subtypes listed, clear evidence is usually required of the presence of *at least three* of the traits or behaviours given in the clinical description."[27] The different sub-types are listed in the following table.

---

[26]   *Classification of Mental and Behavioural Disorders, Tenth Revision (ICD–10): Clinical descriptions and diagnostic guidelines* (World Health Organisation, 1992), pp.200–201.

[27]   *Ibid.*

SPECIFIC PERSONALITY DISORDERS : MAIN SUB-TYPES (ICD-10)

F60.0	*Paranoid*	A personality disorder characterised by excessive sensitivity to setbacks and rebuffs; a tendency to bear grudges; suspiciousness; a pervasive tendency to misconstrue the neutral or friendly actions of others as hostile or contemptuous; and preoccupation with unsubstantiated "conspiratorial" explanations of events.
F60.1	*Schizoid*	A personality disorder characterised by emotional coldness and detachment; limited capacity to express warmth; preference for solitary activities; excessive preoccupation with fantasy and introspection; lack of confiding relationships; marked insensitivity to prevailing social norms and conventions.
F60.2	*Dissocial (psychopathic)*	A personality disorder characterised by callousness; gross and persistent irresponsibility and disregard for social norms, rules and obligations; incapacity to maintain enduring relationships; very low tolerance to frustration and a low threshold for discharge of aggression; incapacity to experience guilt and to profit from experience; marked proneness to blame others.
F60.3	*Emotionally unstable*	A personality disorder characterised by a marked tendency to act impulsively without consideration of the consequences, together with affective instability. Outbursts of intense anger may often lead to violence or behavioural explosions, which are easily precipitated when impulsive acts are criticised or thwarted by others.
F60.4	*Histrionic*	A personality disorder characterised by theatricality and exaggerated displays of emotions; suggestibility; shallow, liable affect; continual seeking for excitement and being the centre of attention; inappropriate seductiveness and concern with physical attractiveness.
F60.5	*Anankastic*	A personality disorder characterised by excessive doubt and caution; preoccupation with rules, lists, order, organisation; perfectionism that interferes with task completion; excessive conscientiousness and undue preoccupation with productivity to the exclusion of pleasure and relationships; excessive pedantry and rigidity; intrusion of insistent and unwelcome thoughts or impulses.
F60.6	*Anxious (avoidant)*	A personality disorder characterised by persistent and pervasive feelings of tension and apprehension; belief that one is socially inept, unappealing or inferior; excessive preoccupation with being criticised or rejected; avoidance of situations that involve significant personal contact because of fear of criticism, disapproval, or rejection.
F60.7	*Dependent*	A personality disorder characterised by encouraging or allowing others to make most of one's important life decisions; subordination of one's own needs to those of others on whom one is dependent and undue compliance with their wishes; preoccupations with fears of being abandoned; limited capacity to make everyday decisions without excessive advice and assurance.

PARANOID PERSONALITY DISORDER (F60.0)

A paranoid personality disorder is characterised by excessive sensitivity to setbacks and rebuffs; a tendency to bear grudges; suspiciousness and a pervasive tendency to misconstrue the neutral or friendly actions of others as hostile or contemptuous; a combative and tenacious sense of personal rights; recurrent unjustified suspicion regarding sexual fidelity; a tendency to experience excessive self-importance, manifest in a persistent self-referential attitude; preoccupation with unsubstantiated "conspiratorial" explanations of events.[28] Fixed delusions are absent. The prevalence of paranoid personality disorder is variously estimated as being between 0.5 and 2.5 per cent and more common in men than women.

Management and treatment

The prognosis is unclear but the very concept of personality implies that the particular traits will be resistant to change. In some cases, the paranoid traits may be a harbinger of a paranoid delusional disorder or of paranoid schizophrenia. Psychotherapy may be offered although the patient's suspicious attitude and tendency to misinterpret the actions of others may make progress difficult. Antipsychotics may be employed if there is evidence of quasi-delusional thinking.

SCHIZOID PERSONALITY DISORDER (F60.1)

Schizoid personality disorders have usually been linked to the presence of schizophrenia and, for this reason, they are considered in the chapter dealing with that form of illness (**1243**).

DISSOCIAL ("PSYCHOPATHIC") PERSONALITY DISORDER (F60.2)

Dissocial personality disorder includes conditions previously or elsewhere described as amoral, antisocial, psychopathic, or sociopathic personality disorders. A dissocial personality disorder is a personality disorder which usually comes to attention because of a gross disparity between behaviour and the prevailing social norms and is characterised by callous unconcern for the feelings of others; gross and persistent irresponsibility and disregard for social norms, rules and obligations; incapacity to maintain enduring relationships, though having no difficulty in establishing them; very low tolerance to frustration and a low threshold for discharge of aggression, including violence; incapacity to experience guilt and to profit from experience, particularly punishment; marked proneness to blame others, or to offer plausible rationalisations, for the behaviour that has brought the patient into conflict with society. A conduct disorder during childhood and adolescence may further support the diagnosis.[29]

Psychopathic disorder

The term "dissocial personality disorder" is synonymous with psychopathic disorder. There has never been any consensus about whether "psychopathic disorder is an illness with social consequences which can be treated medically or a social condition

---

[28]   *Classification of Mental and Behavioural Disorders, Tenth Revision (ICD–10): Clinical descriptions and diagnostic guidelines* (World Health Organisation, 1992), pp.202–203.

[29]   *Ibid.*, p.204.

which needs to be managed or addressed in a non-medical environment."[30] These differences of opinion are linked to different ideas about responsibility and free will and the extent to which the personalities of some people do not enable them to resist or to refrain from anti-social conduct.

Historical development of the concept

In 1801, Phillippe Pinel described a condition which he called "manie sans délire", the specific features of which were a pronounced disorder of the affective functions and a blind impulse to acts of violence in the absence of any specific alteration in the intellectual functions, perception, judgment, imagination and memory.[31] In 1812, Rush described a condition of "moral derangement" which was characterised by innate, constitutional, moral depravities and was suitable for medical treatment.[32] In 1818, Gröhmann wrote of "moral diseases of the mind", including "moral dullness", "congenital brutality" and "moral imbecility." In 1835, James Pritchard referred to moral insanity as a "morbid perversion of the natural feelings, affections, inclinations, temper, habits, moral dispositions and natural impulses, without any remarkable disorder or defect of the intellect or knowing or reasoning faculties and particularly without any insane illusion or hallucination."[33] In 1839, Morel then distinguished four types of degeneratives: idiots, imbeciles, the feeble-minded and "degeneres superieurs," persons who were of average or superior intellects but morally defective. In 1885, Maudsley wrote that "as there are persons who cannot distinguish certain colours ... so there are some who are congenitally deprived of moral sense."[34] The term "psychopathic inferiorities" was introduced by Koch in 1891, to denote all those mental irregularities which influence a man and cause him to seem not fully in possession of normal mental capacity but which do not amount to psychoses. These variations in personality from the norm constituted an abnormal deviation from normal mental life.[35] Kraepelin, describing psychopathic personalities in 1915, believed that they represented a form of degenerative disorder quite separate from neuroses and psychoses.[36] In 1927, Schneider defined psychopathic personalities as abnormal personalities, that is persons deviating from the norm of a variety of traits, who either suffer themselves or cause society to suffer.[37] Partridge introduced the concept of the "sociopath" in 1930, his use of the term emphasising the effects of life-long anti-social behaviour on society, behaviour which was difficult to influence by social, penal or medical means. The notion of "sociopathy" therefore denotes a propensity for behaviour which is regarded as criminal or anti-social. In 1939, Henderson and Gillespie described psychopaths as "individualistic, rebellious, emotionally immature, lacking foresight and behaving like dangerous children; they fail to learn from their mistakes and the stupidity of their actions is appalling."[38] This inadequacy, or deviation, or failure to adjust to ordinary social life was not mere wilfulness or badness which could be threatened or "thrashed out" of the individual but

[30] Report of the Department of Health and Home Office Working Group on Psychopathic Disorder (Department of Health/Home Office, 1994), p.9.
[31] P. Pinel, A Treatise on Insanity in Which Are Contained the Principles of a New and More Practical Nosology of Mental Disorders, 1801.
[32] B. Rush, Medical Inquiries and Observations upon the Diseases of the Mind, 1812.
[33] J. Pritchard, A Treatise on Insanity and other Disorders affecting the mind (London, 1835).
[34] H. Maudsley, Responsibility in Mental Disease (Kegan Paul, Trench & Co., 1885).
[35] J.L.A. Koch, Die Psychopathischen Minderwertigkeiten (Ravensburg, 1891).
[36] E. Kraepelin, Der Verfolgungswahn der Schwerhorigen Psychiatrie, Vol. 8 Part IV, (Barth, 1915).
[37] K. Schneider, Psychopathic personalities (9th ed., trans. M.W. Hamilton, Cassel, 1950).
[38] D.K. Henderson, Psychopathic States (Norson, 1939).

a true illness for which there was no specific explanation. Such psychopaths were of three types — aggressive, inadequate and creative. In 1941, Cleckley conceived of psychopathic disorder as a "moral psychosis; such persons were chameleons, suiting their conversation and behaviour to what they considered others wished it to be, rather than by reference to any internalised values.[39] The Percy Commission of 1954–57, which reviewed the existing mental health legislation, described "mentally abnormal patients whose daily behaviour shows a want of social responsibility and of consideration for others, of prudence and foresight, and of ability to act in their own best interests and whose persistent anti-social mode of conduct may include inefficiency and lack of interest in any form of occupation, pathological lying, swindling, slandering, alcoholism, drug addiction, sexual offences, violent acts with little motivation and an entire absence of self-restraint which may go as far as homicide ... Punishment or the threat of punishment influences their behaviour only momentarily and its more lasting effect is to intensify their vindictiveness and anti-social attitude."[40] Reviewing the literature in 1960, Scott considered that the major definitions of psychopathic disorder shared four common elements: an absence of any psychiatric disease or defect; anti-social behaviour, whether aggressive or inadequate; persistence of the behaviour from an early age; and the need for a specialised form of handling by society.[41] In 1966, Robins demonstrated the persistence of the disorder from childhood to adulthood, showing that it ran in families and carried a poor prognosis with death commonly resulting from self-neglect, suicide, fighting, careless accidents, and the effects of too much alcohol or other drugs.[42] More recently, in 1975, Whiteley defined a "psychopath" as an individual who persistently behaves in a way which is not in accordance with the accepted social norms of the culture or times in which he lives; who appears to be unaware that his behaviour is seriously at fault; and whose abnormality cannot be readily explained as resulting from "madness" or "badness" alone.[43] During the previous year, Sir Aubrey Lewis had summarised the historical development of the concept in the following terms:

"Psychopathic personality is one of a cluster of terms which have been used, interchangeably or successively, in the last 150 years to denote a life-long propensity to behaviour which falls midway between normality and psychosis. Mania sine delirio, moral insanity, moral imbecility, psychopathy, degenerate constitution, congenital delinquency, constitutional inferiority — these and other semantic variations on a dubious theme have been bandied about by psychiatrists and lawyers in a prodigious output of repetitious articles."[44]

Management and treatment

Various treatment strategies have been suggested although none of them has been shown to be effective in a controlled evaluation.[45] The options include individual

---

39   H. Cleckley, *The Mask of Sanity* (Henry Kimpton, 1941).

40   *Report of the Royal Commission on the Law Relating to Mental Illness and Mental Deficiency*, Cmnd. 169 (1957).

41   P.D. Scott, "The treatment of psychopaths" *British Medical Journal* (1960) i, 1641–1646.

42   L. Robins, *Deviant Children Grow Up* (Livingstone Press, 1966). See E. Fottrell, "Violent behaviour by psychiatric patients" in *Contemporary Psychiatry* (ed. S. Crown, Butterworths, 1984), p.21.

43   J.S. Whiteley, "The psychopath and his treatment" in *Contemporary Psychiatry* (ed. T. Silverstone and B. Barraclough, Headley Brothers, 1975).

44   Sir A. Lewis, "Psychopathic disorder: A most elusive category" *Psychological Medicine* 4, 133.

45   M. Gelder, *et al.*, *Oxford Textbook of Psychiatry* (Oxford University Press, 3rd ed., 1996), p.130; Quality Assurance Project, "Treatment outlines for borderline, narcissistic and histrionic personal-

psychotherapy, small-group therapy and treatment in a therapeutic community, such as that provided at the Henderson Hospital in Surrey. Seriously disturbed behaviour which is the manifestation of a psychopathic disorder may be managed by legal or medical means, or by a combination of the two in the case of detention under the Mental Health Act 1983. Whether detention in a psychiatric hospital has any therapeutic advantage over imprisonment in more than a small minority of cases has still to be established. Most often, the greatest hope lies in the possibility of late maturation, perhaps after forming an understanding relationship with someone, and the fact that anti-social behaviour tends to become less frequent as individuals get older. The main motivation for dealing with dangerous anti-social offenders by committal to hospital under a restriction order may lie in the fact that it provides a mechanism for indefinite preventative detention in cases where a discretionary life sentence is inappropriate, rather than any hope that treatment received there will be efficacious.

EMOTIONALLY UNSTABLE PERSONALITY DISORDER (F60.3)

Emotionally unstable personality disorders are those in which there is a marked tendency to act impulsively without consideration of the consequences, together with affective instability. The ability to plan ahead may be minimal, and outbursts of intense anger may often lead to violence or behavioural explosions, which are easily precipitated when impulsive acts are criticised or thwarted by others. The classification specifies two variants —

- *Emotionally unstable personality disorder, impulsive type* is characterised by emotional instability and lack of impulse control; outbursts of violence or threatening behaviour are common, particularly in response to criticism by others.

- *Emotionally unstable personality disorder, borderline type* is characterised by emotional instability, disturbed self-image, chronic feelings of emptiness, and a liability to become involved in intense and unstable relationships, which may cause repeated emotional crises and be associated with excessive efforts to avoid abandonment and a series of suicidal threats or acts of self-harm.

HABIT AND IMPULSE DISORDERS (F63)

The legal definition of what constitutes a psychopathic disorder (082) is not confined to specific personality disorders, such as dissocial personality disorders. Certain other psychiatric conditions are not uncommonly legally classified as psychopathic disorders. In particular, habit and impulse disorders and certain kinds of sexual behaviour (089) may in practice be so classified. The habit and impulse disorders are characterised by repeated acts that have no clear rational motivation and generally harm the patient's own interests and those of other people.[46]

---

[46]   *Classification of Mental and Behavioural Disorders, Tenth Revision (ICD–10): Clinical descriptions and diagnostic guidelines* (World Health Organisation, 1992), p.212.

PATHOLOGICAL FIRE-SETTING (PYROMANIA) (F63.1)

Pyromania is characterised by "multiple acts of, or attempts at, setting fire to property or other objects, without apparent motive, and by a persistent preoccupation with subjects related to fire and burning. There may also be an abnormal interest in fire-engines, in other associations of fire, and in calling out the fire service."[47] The essential features incorporated in the diagnostic guidelines are (a) repeated fire-setting without any obvious motive such as monetary gain, revenge, or political extremism; (b) an intense interest in watching fires burn; and (c) reported feelings of increasing tension before the act, and intense excitement immediately after it has been carried out.[48]

DSM–IV Classification

According to the DSM–IV classification, the essential feature of pyromania is "the presence of multiple episodes of deliberate and purposeful fire setting (Criterion A). Individuals with this disorder experience tension or affective arousal before setting a fire (Criterion B). There is a fascination with, interest in, curiosity about, or attraction to fire and its situational contexts (e.g., paraphernalia, uses, consequences) (Criterion C). Individuals with this disorder are often regular 'watchers' at fires in their neighbourhoods, may set off false alarms, and derive pleasure from institutions, equipment, and personnel associated with fire ... (They) experience pleasure, gratification, or a relief of tension when setting the fire, witnessing its effects, or participating in its aftermath (Criterion D). The fire setting is not done for monetary gain, as an expression of socio-political ideology, to conceal criminal activity, to express anger of vengeance, to improve one's living circumstances, or in response to a delusion or a hallucination (Criterion E). The fire setting does not result from impaired judgment (e.g., in dementia, mental retardation, or substance intoxication). The diagnosis is not made if the fire setting is better accounted for by a conduct disorder, a manic episode, or an antisocial personality disorder (Criterion F)."[49]

Alternative explanations

Pyromania should be distinguished from criminal conduct where there is an obvious motive; fire-setting as part of a general conduct disorder or personality disorder including theft, aggression, truancy, and a lack of concern for others; schizophrenia, when fires are started in response to delusional ideas or auditory hallucinations; organic mental disorder, when fires are started accidentally as a result of confusion, poor memory, or a lack of awareness of the consequences of the act.

INTERMITTENT EXPLOSIVE DISORDER

The category "Other habit and impulse disorders (F63.8)" is used in the ICD–10 classification for persistently maladaptive behaviour which is not attributable to a recognised psychiatric syndrome but in which there is repeated failure to resist impulses to carry out the behaviour. This includes conditions classified in the DSM–IV classification under the rubric of "intermittent explosive disorder," the essential features of which are—

---

[47]   *Classification of Mental and Behavioural Disorders, Tenth Revision (ICD–10): Clinical descriptions and diagnostic guidelines* (World Health Organisation, 1992), p.212.

[48]   *Ibid.*, p.213.

[49]   *Diagnostic and Statistical Manual of Mental Disorders, Fourth Revision (DSM–IV)* (American Psychiatric Association, 1994), p.614.

- the occurrence of discrete episodes of failure to resist aggressive impulses that result in serious assaultative acts or destruction of property (criterion A)

- the degree of aggressiveness expressed during an episode is grossly out of proportion to any provocation or precipitating psychosocial stressor (Criterion B)

- other mental disorders or general medical conditions that might account for the episodes of aggressive behaviour have been ruled out and the aggressive episodes are not drug-induced (Criterion C).

DISORDERS OF SEXUAL BEHAVIOUR (F64–F66)

These disorders are divided into three types, only two of which have any relevance to legal proceedings—

- Gender identity disorders, *e.g.*, transsexualism (F64)

- Disorders of sexual preference, *e.g.* fetishism, exhibitionism, voyeurism, paedophilia, sadomasochism (F65)

The most important of these "disorders" are described below. It should, however, be noted that section 1(3) of the Mental Health Act 1983 provides that no person shall be dealt with under the Act by reason only of "promiscuity, other immoral conduct (or) sexual deviancy." Nevertheless, the limits of this prohibition have not been firmly established, and tribunals and courts have tended to deal with paedophilia on the basis that it is the expression of a psychopathic disorder. The problem is considered in greater detail in chapter 2 (**089**).

Transsexualism (F64.0)

Transsexualism is a desire to live and be accepted as a member of the opposite sex, usually accompanied by a sense of discomfort with, or the inappropriateness of, one's anatomic sex and a wish to have hormonal treatment and surgery to make one's body as congruent as possible with the preferred sex.[50]

Fetishism (F65.0)

Fetishism is a "reliance on some non-living object as a stimulus for sexual arousal and sexual gratification. Many fetishes are extensions of the human body, such as articles of clothing or footware."[51]

---

[50]   *Classification of Mental and Behavioural Disorders, Tenth Revision (ICD–10): Clinical descriptions and diagnostic guidelines* (World Health Organisation, 1992), p.215.
[51]   *Ibid.*, p.218.

Exhibitionism (F65.2)

Exhibitionism is "a recurrent or persistent tendency to expose the genitalia to strangers (usually of the opposite sex) or to people in public places, without inviting or intending closer contact."[52] So defined, men who expose themselves on a single occasion do not come within the operational criteria. Exhibitionists make up about one-third of sexual offenders referred for psychiatric treatment and about a quarter of sexual offenders dealt with in the courts.[53] The reconviction rate is low after a first conviction but high after a second conviction. It is not correct that all exhibitionists are inadequate and passive. In terms of risk assessment, the circumstances of the index offence are paramount, in particular the age of the victim, the degree of aggression, and any pleasure taken in causing distress. As "a broad generalization, two groups of exhibitionists can be described. The first group includes men of inhibited temperament who struggle against their urges and feel much guilt after the act; they sometimes expose a flaccid penis. The second group includes men who have aggressive traits, sometimes accompanied by features of antisocial personality disorder. They usually expose an erect penis, often while masturbating. They gain pleasure from any distress they cause and often feel little guilt."[54] Apart from treating any underlying mental illness, such as depression, various psychological treatments may be employed — including psychoanalysis, individual and group psychotherapy, and aversion therapy — but their effectiveness has yet to be established.[55] According to Gelder, a practical approach combines counselling and behavioural techniques.[56]

Voyeurism (F65.3)

Voyeurism is a recurrent or persistent tendency to look at people engaging in sexual or intimate behaviour such as undressing.[57] Again, there is no reliable information about prognosis or the benefits of particular psychological treatments.

Paedophilia (F65.4)

Paedophilia is defined as "a sexual preference for children, usually of prepubertal or early pubertal age. Some paedophiles are attracted only to girls, others only to boys, and others again are interested in both sexes."[58] The prognosis has been summarised by Gelder: "In the absence of reliable information from follow-up studies, prognosis has to be judged in individual patients by the length of the history, the frequency of the behaviour, the absence of other social and sexual relationships, and the strengths and weaknesses of the personality. Behaviour that has been frequently repeated is

52 *Classification of Mental and Behavioural Disorders, Tenth Revision (ICD–10): Clinical descriptions and diagnostic guidelines* (World Health Organisation, 1992), p.219.
53 I. Rosen, "Exhibitionism, scotophilia and voyeurism" in *Sexual deviations* (ed. I. Rosen, Oxford University Press, 2nd ed., 1979); M. Gelder, *et al.*, *Oxford Textbook of Psychiatry* (Oxford University Press, 3rd ed., 1996), p.501.
54 M. Gelder, *et al.*, *Oxford Textbook of Psychiatry, supra*, p.501.
55 *Ibid.*, p.502; J.S. Witzig, "The group treatment of male exhibitionists" *American Journal of Psychiatry* (1968) 125, 179–185; F.G. Rooth & I.M. Marks, "Persistent exhibitionism: short-term response to aversion self-regulation and relaxation treatment" *Archives of Sexual Behaviour* (1974) 3, 227–243.
56 M. Gelder, *et al.*, *Oxford Textbook of Psychiatry, supra*, p.501.
57 *Classification of Mental and Behavioural Disorders, Tenth Revision (ICD–10): Clinical descriptions and diagnostic guidelines* (World Health Organisation, 1992), p.219.
58 *Ibid.*

likely to persist despite efforts at treatment."[59] There is no convincing evidence that group treatment or behaviour therapy leads to good results in the majority of cases.[60]

Sadomasochism (F65.5)

The term "sadomasochism" denotes "a preference for sexual activity that involves bondage or the infliction of pain or humiliation ... Sexual sadism is sometimes difficult to distinguish from cruelty in sexual situations or anger unrelated to eroticism. Where violence is necessary for erotic arousal, the diagnosis can be clearly established."[61] There is no reliable information about prognosis and no evidence that any particular form of treatment is effective.

---

[59]   M. Gelder, *et al.*, *Oxford Textbook of Psychiatry* (Oxford University Press, 3rd ed., 1996), p.500.

[60]   *Ibid.*; V. Hartmann, "Notes on group therapy with paedophiles" *Canadian Psychiatric Association Journal* (1965) 10, 283–288; H.R. Beech, *et al.*, "Classical conditioning of a sexual deviation: a preliminary note" *Behaviour Therapy* (1971) 2, 400–402.

[61]   *Classification of Mental and Behavioural Disorders, Tenth Revision (ICD–10): Clinical descriptions and diagnostic guidelines* (World Health Organisation, 1992), p.220.

22. Mood disorders

INTRODUCTION

In mood disorders, the fundamental disturbance is a change of mood to depression (with or without associated anxiety) or elation. This mood change is normally accompanied by a change in the overall level of activity and most other symptoms are either secondary to, or easily understood in the context of, such changes. Most of these disorders tend to be recurrent and the onset of individual episodes is often related to stressful events or situations.[1] Mood disorders tend to be cyclic in nature, with stable seasonal fluctuations in the incidence of suicide, and many depressed people experience diurnal variation of mood.

ASSESSMENT, DIAGNOSIS AND CLASSIFICATION

When a patient is examined prior to admission, or immediately following admission, the first task is to assess the kind of disorder (if any) which is troubling him so that, having identified it, conclusions can be reached about its causes, probable course, and treatment. Assessment is the process of collecting information relevant to the diagnosis, management, and treatment of a patient's clinical condition, including therefore this art of distinguishing the presence of a particular disorder, for example mania or depression, from the existence of a characteristic pattern of symptoms or manifestations. A diagnosis is a "short-hand way of describing what is wrong with the patient"[2] and involves assigning the patient's case to a predesignated diagnostic class according to some reliable medical classification of mental disorders.

Classifying mood disorders and using operational criteria

Because some symptoms are commonly features of a number of different conditions — for example, they may occur as symptoms of both schizophrenia and mood disorders — operational definitions specify which combinations of symptoms are adequate to substantiate a diagnosis. They define what a clinician or researcher means when he uses the term "depression" and hence represent a pragmatic approach to the problems of syndromes and an attempt to standardise clinical practice and understanding. Over the past two decades there has been a multiplication of classifications and diagnostic criteria to cope with the different conceptions of mood disorders.[3] Although a core of typical patients meet all of the definitions, there are significant differences in the populations of patients covered by each of them, and each generates

---

[1]   *Classification of Mental and Behavioural Disorders, Tenth Revision (ICD–10): Clinical descriptions and diagnostic guidelines* (World Health Organisation, 1992), p.112.
[2]   J.M. Pfeffer and G. Waldron, *Psychiatric Differential Diagnoses* (Churchill Livingstone, 1987), p.4.
[3]   C. Thompson, *The Instruments of Psychiatric Research* (John Wiley & Sons, 1989), p.4.

different values for the incidence of the disorder, its heritability, its responsiveness to therapeutic agents, and its prognosis. The classification of mental disorders in official usage in England and Wales is the International Classification of Diseases, now in its tenth revision (ICD–10), and, more particularly, that part of it dealing with mental and behavioural disorders.

Mood and affect

A distinction is often drawn between an individual's mood and his affect (**1073**). A person's affect is how he appears to be emotionally affected by a particular idea or mental representation; for example, he is happy, sad or indifferent upon being given certain news. Mood is the pervasive and sustained emotion which colours an individual's whole personality and perception of events. Consequently, it is sometimes described as sustained affect and mood disorders are said to involve a morbid change of affect. It should, however, be emphasised that this distinction is not universally made. Some authorities use the words "affect" and "mood" interchangeably, in which case the terms affective disorder and mood disorder are synonymous.

Unipolar and bipolar disorders

Depression and mania may be viewed as lying at two opposite poles and classifications of mental disorder generally distinguish between unipolar and bipolar mood disorders. According to the classical model, the disturbed mood of some people will be confined to either depression or mania — unipolar disorder. The mood of other individuals is more variable, sometimes located at one pole (depression), sometimes at the other (mania). Mood disorders characterised by fluctuations of this kind are referred to as bipolar disorders and the patient's history characteristically includes one or more episodes of both depression and mania. In reality, of course, the mood of most people is rarely either equable — at the equator, to use the same analogy — or polar but located at some point in either hemisphere. When a person first experiences disordered mood, it is impossible to predict with certainty what course the illness will take and whether there will be subsequent episodes. In particular, it is not known whether his mood may later change from depression to mania, or vice-versa, and within what time scale. What is generally known is that a substantial proportion of patients have only one episode of illness and, consequently, single episodes are usually distinguished from bipolar and other multiple episode disorders. A serious initial depressive episode will be classified simply as a "depressive episode." Despite the multiplicity of classifications, a patient with a history of at least three separate episodes of psychotic depression, with complete remission in between and no history of mania, would satisfy the operational criteria for unipolar disorder in most classifications.

COURSE, TREATMENT AND OUTCOME

The risk of suicide is high in both unipolar and bipolar illness. The consensus of several studies suggests that the lifetime risk in manic-depressive illness is at least 15 per cent. and that it is greatest in the early years of illness.[4] Nevertheless, on average, mood disorders carry a considerably better prognosis than schizophrenia. Kendell summarises the position by writing that it "has been shown many times that

---

[4]   S.B. Guze and E. Robins, "Suicide and primary affective disorders" *British Journal of Psychiatry* (1970) 117, 437–438.

patients with affective illnesses are more likely to make a full recovery from their original illness, spend less time in hospital both in the short and the long run, and experience less social deterioration than those with schizophrenia."[5] While there is some evidence that the interval between episodes gets progressively shorter as time goes on, in both unipolar and bipolar disorders,[6] these averages obscure considerable individual variation in terms of the risk of recurrence and the duration and spacing of successive episodes. Consequently, "the best estimate of the future is provided by [the patient's] own past history."[7] As to the effectiveness of available in-patient treatments, there is "little firm evidence that the long-term outlook of mood disorders has been improved by any of the therapeutic measures at our disposal. Despite the undoubted efficacy of ECT and tricyclic antidepressants in the acute treatment of depression there is little evidence that either treatment has reduced the suicide rate. And despite the proven ability of maintenance treatment with lithium or tricyclic antidepressants to reduce the risk of further episodes no one has yet demonstrated a reduction in the incidence of non-first episodes of either depression or mania in any geographically defined population."[8]

THE ICD–10 CLASSIFICATION OF MOOD DISORDERS

The classification of mental disorders in official usage in England and Wales is the International Classification of Diseases, now in its tenth revision (ICD–10), and, more particularly, that part of it dealing with mental and behavioural disorders. One section or "block" of the classification is concerned with "mood (affective) disorders" (Block F30–F39), within which each type and sub-type of disorder is separately coded. For example, a first manic episode is diagnosed as a "manic episode (code F30)" and a first depressive episode as a "depressive episode (F32)." In many instances, the particular diagnostic category includes different grades of severity, and depressive episodes are distinguished as mild, moderate or severe. These distinctions provide a useful general framework for tribunals because they help to gauge a disorder's severity and have implications for treatment. Inevitably, the ICD–10 classification involves "compromises between scientists with the most influential theories and the practice of senior clinicians at national and international level."[9]

MANIC EPISODES AND BIPOLAR DISORDERS

The ICD–10 classification notes that "bipolar affective disorder" is "characterised by repeated (*i.e.* at least two) episodes in which the patient's mood and activity levels are significantly disturbed, this disturbance consisting on some occasions of an elevation of mood and increased energy and activity (mania or hypomania), and on

5   R.E. Kendell, "Diagnosis and classification" in *Companion to psychiatric studies* (ed. R.E. Kendell & A.K. Zealley, Churchill Livingstone, 1993), p.447.

6   J. Angst, *et al.*, "The course of monopolar depression and bipolar psychosis" *Psychiatria Neurologia Neurochirurgia* (1973) 76, 489–500.

7   R.E. Kendell, "Diagnosis and classification," *supra*, p.447.

8   *Ibid.*, p.448.

9   J.K. Wing, "Differential diagnosis of schizophrenia" in *Schizophrenia — An overview and practical handbook* (ed. D.J. Kavanagh, Chapman & Hall, 1992), p.17.

others of a lowering of mood and decreased energy and activity (depression)."[10] While this is the characteristic pattern, it has been found that some 80–90 per cent of manic patients will eventually experience a full depressive episode, although the converse is not also true — only 10 per cent of patients suffering from depression will later have a manic episode. It is therefore relatively rare for patients to suffer only from repeated episodes of mania and even these patients resemble those who have at least occasional episodes of depression in terms of their family history, pre-morbid personality, age of onset, and long-term prognosis. Because this is so, patients who experience a second manic episode are, according to the ICD–10 classification, reclassified as suffering from a "bipolar affective disorder" rather than from recurrent manic episodes, despite the absence of any history of intervening depression.[11]

PERSONALITY DISORDERS AND BORDERLINE STATES

Some people are constitutionally inclined to feeling depressed or "high," seemingly either naturally low-spirited or high-spirited, so that a further problem when attempting to classify mood disorders is the precise relationship between an individual's personality and his mood. Legal and medical classifications of mental disorder generally distinguish between personality disorders and mental illnesses. In the former case, the individual's abnormal mental state is considered to be an expression of his normal — albeit, compared to other people, abnormal — personality, rather than the consequence of a depressive illness overlying and distorting that personality. Some people who are prone to depression may therefore be described as having a depressive personality disorder and treatment with antidepressants may have only a limited beneficial effect in such cases.

Borderline states and persistent mood disorders (F34)

It may nevertheless often be unclear whether a person's depression or unstable mood is a long-standing depressive illness distorting a previously well-adjusted, equable, personality or a manifestation of his ordinary personality. Various terms are used to describe such borderline states, *e.g.* affective personality disorder, cyclothymic personality, depressive neurosis, depressive personality disorder, neurotic depression, persistent anxiety depression. Contemporary descriptions of such states most often reflect the current diagnostic fashion rather than any advance in knowledge or understanding. At present, the idea of neurotic depression is out of vogue. The view enshrined in the latest revision of the International Classification of Mental Disorders (ICD–10) is that persistent mood disorders of this kind are genetically related to commonly accepted forms of mood disorder and sometimes amenable to the same treatments. At present, they are therefore grouped with mood disorders in the classification rather than as forms of personality disorder. For these reasons, persistent and usually fluctuating mood disorders which last for years at a time but in which individual episodes are rarely (if ever) so severe as to warrant being described as mild manic or depressive episodes are now categorised as "persistent mood (affective) disorders." Two kinds of persistent mood disorders are distinguished: cyclothymia and dysthymia.

---

[10]   *Classification of Mental and Behavioural Disorders, Tenth Revision (ICD–10): Clinical descriptions and diagnostic guidelines* (World Health Organisation, 1992), p.116.
[11]   *Ibid.*

CYCLOTHYMIA AND DYSTHYMIA (ICD–10)

Synonyms	*Main features*

F34.0 Cyclothymia

- affective personality disorder
- cyclothymic personality
- cycloid personality

A persistent instability of mood, involving numerous periods of mild depression and mild elation, which frequently fails to come to medical attention. The mood swings are usually perceived by the individual as being unrelated to life events. It may persist throughout adult life, cease temporarily or permanently, or develop into more severe mood swings meeting the criteria for bipolar affective disorder or recurrent depressive disorder.

F34.1 Dysthymia

- depressive neurosis
- depressive personality disorder
- neurotic depression
- persistent anxiety depression

Dysthymia has much in common with the concept of neurotic depression. The essential feature is a very long-standing depression of mood which is never, or only very rarely, severe enough to fulfil the criteria for recurrent depressive disorder of mild or moderate severity, although the criteria for mild depressive episode may have been fulfilled in the past, particularly at the onset of the disorder. Sufferers usually have periods of days or weeks when they describe themselves as well, but most of the time they feel tired and depressed; everything is an effort and nothing is enjoyed. They brood and complain, sleep badly and feel inadequate, but are usually able to cope with the basic demands of everyday life.

THE DIAGNOSTIC CATEGORIES

These observations or assumptions having been made, the classificatory scheme may be summarised as follows—

- Long-standing borderline mood disorders characterised by fluctuations of mood or depression are classified as cyclothymia and dysthymia respectively. However, if a person's mood is sufficiently disordered that he meets the criteria for a depressive or manic episode, this will be the appropriate diagnosis.

- Depressive episodes are distinguished according to their severity as mild, moderate or severe and, in the latter case, psychotic symptoms may or may not be evident. The severity of manic episodes are hypomania or mania and again, in the latter case, psychotic symptoms may or may not be present.

- If a person who has experienced a single depressive episode has a subsequent depressive episode the diagnosis is changed to that of a recurrent depressive disorder. However, if a person who has had a manic episode subsequently experiences either a depressive episode or a further manic episode, the diagnosis is changed to that of bipolar affective disorder. This diagnosis will also be appropriate in cases where a person who has had a depressive episode subsequently experiences a manic episode.

- Where a patient's mental state during a single episode is highly variable — being characterised by either a mixture or a rapid alternation (usually within a few hours) of hypomanic, manic, and depressive symptoms — this is classified as a mixed affective episode.

- In certain cases, some features of the patient's illness may be characteristic of a mood disorder and other symptoms characteristic of schizophrenia, in which case a diagnosis of schizoaffective disorder (**1247**) may be made. In yet other cases, the patient's disturbed mood may be attributable to a physical disorder, such as a thyroid disorder, or to substance abuse, so that a different diagnosis is also appropriate.

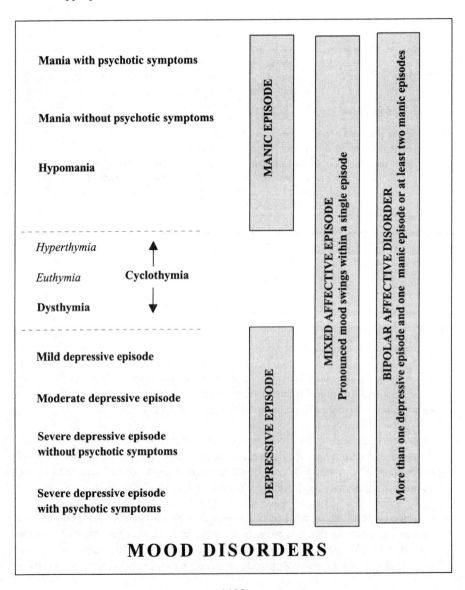

MOOD DISORDERS

CLASSIFICATION OF MOOD DISORDERS (ICD–10)

Type and Code	Brief diagnostic guidelines	Sub-types and grades of severity
· **Persistent mood (affective) disorders (F34)**	Persistent, usually fluctuating, mood disorders lasting for years at a time, in which individual episodes are rarely (if ever) severe enough to warrant being described as hypomania or mild depressive episodes.	1. Cyclothymia (F34.0) 2. Dysthymia (F34.1)
· **Depressive episode (F32)**	The category is only used for a single (first) depressive episode. Further depressive episodes are classified as recurrent depressive disorder.	1. Mild (F32.0) 2. Moderate (F32.1) 3. Severe without psychotic symptoms (F32.2) 4. Severe with psychotic symptoms (F32.3)
· **Recurrent depressive disorder (F33)**	If a manic episode occurs, the diagnosis is changed to bipolar affective disorder.	The severity of the current depressive episode is graded using the scale set out in F32, *e.g.* "recurrent depressive disorder, current episode moderate."
· **Manic episode (F30)**	The category is only used for a single manic episode.	1. Hypomania (F30.0) 2. Mania without psychotic symptoms (F30.1) 3. Mania with psychotic symptoms (F30.2)
· **Bipolar affective disorder (F31)**	If there is a history of both manic and depressive episodes, or of more than one manic episode, the diagnosis is revised to bipolar affective disorder.	The severity of the current episode is graded using the scales set out in F30 and F32, *e.g.* "bipolar affective disorder, current episode hypomanic" or "bipolar affective disorder, current episode moderate depression."

1199

DEPRESSION

Major depression is a serious life-threatening illness which is only partially understood. It is often particularly difficult for tribunals to deal with because of the co-existence in some cases of a wish to die together with little medical prospect of any cure. The nature of the illness in its severest form is vividly expressed by an anonymous patient at the Gartnavel Asylum in the 1850s,

> "In the acute form of the disease, the impulse may be as sudden and irresistible as if the victim was blown from a canon's mouth; in the more subdued, but more miserable form, it may be deliberate and slow — no haste, no hurry, but equally certain if left to itself; and no ray of hope pierces that deep sense darkness which weighs upon the soul like lead. Both of these states are the direct offspring of disease, whatever may have been the cause that produced it, and through one or other of these states the suicide must pass."[12]

EPIDEMIOLOGY

Depression affects some 10 per cent. of men and 20 per cent. of women at some stage during their lives and in any one year 2–3 per cent. of men and 5–10 per cent. of women will suffer from it. For about 3 persons in 1000 it is so severe as to result in a hospital admission and of those suffering from a major depressive illness some 15 per cent. will eventually commit suicide. The mean age of onset is 40 with 10 per cent. of new cases occurring in the over–60s and 50 per cent. prior to the age of 40. Depression is approximately twice as common in women as men. It is not clear whether this difference is biologically or socially determined although women in lower socio-economic groups are particularly likely to be affected. Approximately 15–20 per cent. of women suffer depression during the first six weeks after giving birth and between one-fifth and two-fifths of women admitted to a psychiatric unit during the postpartum period have a major depressive disorder. Unemployment is associated with an increased prevalence of depressive symptoms and depression is more common in urban than rural areas. There is no reliable evidence of significant differences in the incidence, prevalence or symptomatology of depression among people of different race or culture. There is, however, some evidence to suggest that the incidence of depression may be increasing rapidly in industrial countries, with a reduction in the age of the first episode.

AETIOLOGY AND PATHOLOGY

No known structural damage to the brain or other clear-cut aetiological factors account for depression and it can be regarded as a final common pathway which may have multiple causes, even in a single case. It should not be expected that so complex a phenomenon would have a single treatment or even that its treatment would be limited to one modality such as drugs.[13] Factors implicated in depression include genetic causes, biochemical imbalance, endocrine abnormalities, upbringing, and life events, such as divorce, separation and desertion.

---

[12]   Anon., *The Philosophy of Insanity* (1860). The nature of the illness is also captured in Tennyson's poem, "The two voices," in which he described his struggle to resist an inner voice urging him to suicide, and in poems by Hopkins ("O the mind, mind has mountains; cliffs of fall/ Frightful, sheer, no-man-fathomed") and Cowper ("Him the vindictive rod of angry Justice/ Sent quick and howling to the centre headlong;/ I, fed with judgement, in a fleshy tomb, am/ Buried above ground.")

[13]   E.S. Paykel, *Handbook of affective disorders* (ed. E.S. Paykel, Churchill Livingstone, 1992).

TERMINOLOGY

Depressive states are sometimes categorised as primary or secondary, retarded or agitated, psychotic or neurotic, endogenous or reactive, typical or atypical. Although some of these terms are now falling into disfavour, they will all be encountered in practice and their meaning is therefore considered here.

Primary and secondary depression

It remains common to distinguish between primary and secondary depression. Primary depressive disorders are those which are not the product of any other pre-existing physical or mental disorder. By contrast, the defining feature of secondary depressive disorders is that the individual's depression has developed as a consequence of some other pre-existing disorder. Depressive symptoms may be attributable to drug abuse, prescribed medication (*e.g.* corticosteroids or phenobarbitone) or any one of a vast array of "organic" mental disorders, including hypothyroidism (**1300**), Cushing's syndrome (**1297**), Addison's disease (**1297**), Simmond's disease (**1295**), hypoparathyroidism (**1302**), hypercalcaemia (**1095**), Huntington's chorea (**1286**), cerebral tumours and metabolic disorders such as potassium depletion (**1096**). It is noteworthy that some eight per cent of all patients with depression have a thyroid illness.[14] The importance of the distinction in a tribunal context is that any underlying physical problem may often be easily remedied, leading to a relatively rapid resolution of symptoms.

Retarded and agitated depression

A further distinction sometimes drawn is that between retarded and agitated depression. Motor retardation "implies slowness of the initiation, execution and completion of physical activity."[15] It is frequently associated with retardation of thought, characterised by delayed response to questions, indecision, poor concentration, loss of clarity and poor registration of events. This combined slowing of thought and physical activity is known as "psychomotor retardation." Agitation "implies mental disturbance causing physical restlessness and increased arousal."[16] It occurs with or without retardation in depressive disorders and the two may alternate although retardation is more common. In a tribunal context, the importance of the distinction may be two-fold. Suicidal impulses may be prevented from expression by retardation whereas agitation may render expression more likely. Arising from this, the risk of suicide may increase as the patient's condition begins to respond to treatment and the degree of retardation reduces. However, while severe retardation and stupor may temporarily stifle the expression of suicidal intent, they can lead to a life-threatening deficiency in food and water intake and an inability to voluntarily consent to treatment.

---

[14] H.I. Kaplan and B.J. Sadock, *Synopsis of Psychiatry* (Williams & Wilkins, 7th ed., 1994), p.206. Related to this , the Dexamethasone-Suppression Test (DST), which is occasionally used to help confirm a diagnosis of major depression, is associated with a large number of false-positive results. False-positive results are, *inter alia*, associated with phenytoin, barbiturates, carbamazepine, hypertension, dehydration, temporal lobe disease, pregnancy, Cushing's disease, unstable diabetes mellitus, extreme weight loss, acute psychosis, old age. False-negative results are associated with hypopituitarism and Addison's disease.

[15] A. Sims, *Symptoms in the Mind* (Baillière Tindall, 1988), p.272.

[16] *Ibid.*

Psychotic and neurotic depression

It was until recently commonplace to distinguish between psychotic and neurotic depression. Most often, the distinction being drawn was between psychotic patients, with florid symptoms such as nihilistic delusions, and "neurotic people" who retained a normal level of insight into their condition and whose perception of reality was not significantly impaired. However, both terms eventually acquired multiple meanings and the distinction became increasingly blurred. For example, the label neurotic depression might, depending on the author, mean that the condition was non-incapacitating, non-psychotic, non-remitting, non-situational, that the patient had a depressive personality, or any combination of these and similar features. Consequently, the use of the term "neurotic", and the traditional division between the neuroses and psychoses was abandoned in the tenth revision of the International Classification of Diseases. The term "psychotic" is nevertheless retained as a convenient descriptive term "to indicate the presence of hallucinations, delusions, or a limited number of several abnormalities of behaviour, such as gross excitement and overactivity (or) marked psychomotor retardation."[17]

Endogenous and reactive (exogenous) depression

The term "endogenous" literally means originating or growing from within and it was invented by Moebius in 1895 to describe a condition which was associated with heredity and had a strong genetic component. For many years, it was customary to distinguish between endogenous and reactive, or exogenous, depression and the distinction is still sometimes made. Endogenous depression, having a strong genetic component, often occurred without any obvious external cause or trigger while, in contrast, reactive depressive disorders appeared to be a response to an obviously stressful situation, such as a bereavement, separation or redundancy. Again, the term "endogenous" acquired a range of other meanings over the years as claims were made that this form of depression was associated with characteristic symptom patterns. The word was, for example, used as a short-hand term for a constellation of vegetative signs such as weight loss, early morning waking and fatigability; to describe persistent depressed mood qualitatively different from the normal depressions of every-day life and associated with unremitting hopelessness; and as a synonym for "psychotic depression," indicating the presence of stupor, hallucinations or delusions (the endogenous–reactive, psychotic–neurotic divide). The resulting ambiguity eventually led to the term being dropped from the third revision of the main American classification (DSM–III) and also from the ICD–10 classification, being replaced by the concepts of melancholic and somatic depression respectively — or, more specifically, "major depression with melancholia" and "depressive episode with somatic symptoms."

Atypical depression

Inevitably, tribunals periodically deal with cases involving patients diagnosed as suffering from "atypical depression." Recent research suggests that this may be a distinct type of depressive disorder associated with weight gain and increased appetite, oversleeping and hypersomnia, chronic fatigue and significant elements of anxiety intermixed with the depression, sometimes expressed in the form of

---

[17] *Classification of Mental and Behavioural Disorders, Tenth Revision (ICD–10): Clinical descriptions and diagnostic guidelines* (World Health Organisation, 1992), pp.3–4. The meaning of these terms is also considered on page 1036.

agoraphobia or panic attacks.[18] According to the ICD classification, atypical presentations are particularly common in adolescence. In some cases, anxiety, distress, and motor agitation may be more prominent at times than the depression, and the mood change may also be masked by added features such as irritability, excessive consumption of alcohol, histrionic behaviour, hypochondriacal preoccupations and exacerbation of pre-existing phobic or obsessional symptoms.[19]

SOMATIC SYMPTOMS

According to the ICD–10 classification, these symptoms have special clinical significance. In particular, this somatic syndrome will almost always be present in a severe depressive episode. The most typical somatic symptoms are specified in the classification and given in the table below. It should be noted that the classification states that the somatic syndrome is not usually regarded as present unless "about four of these symptoms are definitely present."[20] There is a caveat to this. If two or three are present but they are unusually severe, a diagnosis of a mild depressive disorder with somatic symptoms may be justified.[21]

TYPICAL SOMATIC SYMPTOMS

- loss of interest or pleasure in activities that are normally enjoyable

- lack of emotional reactivity to normally pleasurable surroundings and events

- waking in the morning 2 hours or more before the usual time

- depression worse in the morning

- objective evidence of definite psychomotor retardation or agitation (remarked on or reported by other people)

- marked loss of appetite

- weight loss (often defined as 5 per cent. or more of body weight in the past month)

- marked loss of libido

Source: ICD–10 Classification of Mental and Behavioural Disorders: Clinical descriptions and diagnostic guidelines. WHO, Geneva. 1992, p.120.

DEPRESSIVE EPISODES (F32)

The description of a typical depressive episode given in the ICD–10 classification is based upon three "typical" symptoms and a number of "other common symptoms." These are set out in the table below and some of them may be sufficiently marked that a syndrome of somatic symptoms is apparent (see above).

---

[18] F.M. Quitkin, *et al.*, "Phenelzine and imipramine in mood reactive depressives" (1989) *Archives of General Psychiatry* 46, 787–793.

[19] *Classification of Mental and Behavioural Disorders, Tenth Revision (ICD–10): Clinical descriptions and diagnostic guidelines* (World Health Organisation, 1992), p.120.

[20] *Ibid.*

[21] *Ibid.*, p.122.

THE TYPICAL SYMPTOMS	OTHER COMMON SYMPTOMS
A. depressed mood	A. reduced concentration and attention
B. loss of interest and enjoyment	B. reduced self-esteem and self-confidence
C. reduced energy leading to increased fatigability and diminished activity	C. ideas of guilt and unworthiness (even in a mild type of episode)
Typically, the lowered mood varies little from day to day, and is often unresponsive to circumstances, yet may show a characteristic diurnal variation as the day goes on. Marked tiredness after only slight effort is common.	D. bleak and pessimistic views of the future
	E. ideas or acts of self-harm or suicide
	F. disturbed sleep
	G. diminished appetite

Source: ICD–10 Classification of Mental and Behavioural Disorders: Clinical descriptions and diagnostic guidelines. WHO, Geneva. 1992, p.119.

The number of symptoms and their duration

As to the number of symptoms which must be present and for how long before a depressive episode is diagnosed, the general position may be summarised as follows—

- A definite diagnosis of a mild depressive disorder "usually" requires that at least two of the three typical symptoms, plus at least two of the other common symptoms listed above, are present for at least a fortnight, although none should be of an intense degree.[22]

- A diagnosis of a moderate depressive disorder requires that at least two of the three typical symptoms, plus at least three (and preferably four) of the other common symptoms, are present for at least a fortnight. Several symptoms are likely to be present to a marked degree but this is not essential if a particularly wide variety of symptoms is present overall.[23]

- A diagnosis of a severe depressive episode usually requires that all three of the typical symptoms and at least four of the other common symptoms are present for at least a fortnight, some of which should be of severe intensity, although the diagnosis may be reasonable and justified if the symptoms are unusually severe and of rapid onset.[24]

---

[22] *Classification of Mental and Behavioural Disorders, Tenth Revision (ICD–10): Clinical descriptions and diagnostic guidelines* (World Health Organisation, 1992), p.121.

[23] *Ibid.*, p.122.

[24] *Ibid.*, pp.120 and 123.

The severity of depressive episodes

The classification of depressive episodes specifies three levels of severity — mild (F32.0), moderate (F32.1), and severe (F32.2). Severe depressive episodes are of two kinds — severe depressive episode without psychotic symptoms (F32.2) and severe depressive episode with psychotic symptoms (F32.3). For each grade of depression, the classification describes the usual consequences for the individual in terms of how disabling the illness is and the likely care setting.

THE SEVERITY OF A DEPRESSIVE EPISODE

Severity	For a definite diagnosis	Interference	Care setting
• Mild	At least <u>two</u> typical symptoms are present plus at least <u>two</u> of the other common symptoms for a minimum duration of about 2 weeks, but none to an intense degree.	• The individual is usually distressed by the symptoms and has some difficulty in continuing with ordinary work and social activities, but will probably not cease to function completely.	Individuals with mild depressive episodes are common in primary care and general medical settings
• Moderate	At least <u>two</u> typical symptoms are present plus at least <u>three</u> of the of the other common symptoms for a minimum duration of about 2 weeks. Several symptoms are likely to be marked but this is not essential if a particularly wide variety of symptoms is present overall.	• The individual will usually have considerable difficulty in continuing with social, work or domestic activities.	Variable. May be able to continue to work.
• Severe without psychotic symptoms	<u>All three</u> of the typical symptoms are present plus at least <u>four</u> of the other common symptoms, some of which should be of severe intensity. Although the depressive episode should usually last at least 2 weeks, the diagnosis may be justified after less than 2 weeks if the symptoms are particularly severe and of very rapid onset. Loss of self-esteem or feelings of uselessness or guilt are likely to be prominent.	• It is very unlikely that the sufferer will be able to continue with social, work, or domestic activities, except to a very limited extent. He usually shows considerable distress or agitation, unless retardation is a marked feature. Suicide is a distinct danger in particularly severe cases.	Psychiatric in-patient units deal largely with patients suffering from the more severe grades.
• Severe with psychotic symptoms	A severe depressive episode meeting the criteria given in which delusions, hallucinations, or depressive stupor are also present. The delusions usually involve ideas of sin, poverty, or imminent disasters, responsibility for which may be assumed by the patient. Auditory or olfactory hallucinations are usually of defamatory or accusatory voices or of rotting filth or decomposing flesh. Severe psychomotor retardation may progress to stupor.		

Source: ICD–10 Classification of Mental and Behavioural Disorders: Clinical descriptions and diagnostic guidelines. WHO, Geneva. 1992, p.119–124.

Using psychiatric rating scales to assess severity

The severity of a depressive episode may be measured using psychiatric rating scales. Where a depression measure yields a global score, it is important to realise that the same numerical score may have very different clinical meanings. Thompson has summarised the main rating scales used in cases of depression in a tabular form, from which it can be seen that the scales differently weight the different features of depression.

DEPRESSION RATING SCALES

	HDRS	Bech	MADRS	BDI	Zung	Wake	Carroll
Mood	8	18	30	9.5	15	25	8
Vegetative	28	18	30	29	35	33	35
Motor	12	18	0	0	5	8	15
Social	8	9	0	5	0	8	0
Cognitive	28	27	30	52	35	0	27
Anxiety	16	9	10	0	5	17	15
Irritability	0	0	0	5	5	8	0

- *Mood* includes sadness, loss of enjoyment, distinct quality to mood, weeping and diurnal variation.

- *Vegetative* includes sleep disturbance, appetite change, weight change, loss of libido, constipation and fatigue.

- *Motor* includes retardation, agitation and restlessness.

- *Social* includes withdrawal, isolation and inability to function at work or other tasks.

- *Cognitive* includes thoughts of hopelessness and helplessness, suicide, illness and guilt, as well as loss of insight and indecision.

- *Anxiety* includes psychic and somatic and phobic anxiety.

- *Irritability* includes both inwardly and outwardly directed hostility.

Abbreviations: HDRS = Hamilton Rating Scale; Bech = Bech-Rafaelson Melancholia Rating Scale; MADRS = Montgomery Asberg Depression Rating Scale; BDI = Beck Depression Inventory; Zung = ; Wake = Wakefield Depression Inventory.

Source: Professor C. Thompson, The Instruments of Psychiatric Research (John Wiley & Sons, 1989), p.5.

Hamilton Rating Scale (HRS)

The Hamilton Rating Scale (HRS) is the most widely user observer scale for rating depressed patients and it is a measure of severity and not a diagnostic instrument. Over 20 items (*e.g.*, mood, guilt, suicidal tendencies, diurnal variation) are rated on a 0–2 or a 0–4 scale. The scale is generally considered to have high reliability, validity and international acceptance but has been criticised for failing to differentiate adequately between moderate and severe depression.

Beck Depression Inventory

There are two forms of the Beck Depression Inventory. The short form is for use by general practitioners in screening patients for depression. The long form is designed to provide a quantitative assessment of the severity of depression. It is not designed for diagnostic purposes, that is as a way of determining whether a person is or is not clinically depressed. As with the Hamilton Rating Scale, the inventory has generally been found to be reliable but has been criticised for failing to differentiate adequately between moderate and severe depression, and for being open to observer bias when the interviewer rates the patient.

Zung Self-Rating Depression Scale (SDS)

The scale has been criticised for insensitivity to clinical differences at the lower end of the severity range and awkward wording of items. Severity is measured almost exclusively by reference to the frequency of a symptom rather than its tolerability.

RECURRENT DEPRESSIVE DISORDER (F33)

Recurrent depressive disorders are characterised by repeated episodes of mild, moderate or severe depressive episodes without any history of independent episodes of mood elevation and overactivity fulfilling the criteria of mania. The diagnosis requires at least two depressive episodes each lasting for a minimum of two weeks and separated by several months without significant mood disturbance. According to the ICD classification, individual episodes generally last between three and twelve months, with a median duration of about six months, and they are often precipitated by stressful life events. Recovery is usually complete between episodes. In cases of recurrent depressive episode, the severity of the present episode may be graded in the same way as a single episode.

MANAGEMENT AND TREATMENT OF DEPRESSION

The management of severe depressive episodes may necessitate hospital admission and, if there is a significant risk of suicide, continuous observation. In-patient treatment almost invariably includes medication (**1208**) or ECT (**1132**). Cognitive therapy (**1154**) or some other kind of psychological treatment may be indicated. Several trials suggest that the relapse rate following cognitive therapy is lower than after drug treatment alone. In rare, intractable cases psychosurgery is occasionally offered (**1130**). The outcome for mood disorders is generally more favourable than for schizophrenia. However, cases requiring in-patient treatment tend to be severe, chronic, recurrent, or accompanied by a high risk of suicide. As to these patients, there is "little firm evidence that the long-term outlook of mood disorders has been improved by any of the therapeutic measures" available.[25] In particular, there is "little evidence" that ECT and tricyclic antidepressants have reduced the suicide rate

---

[25]   R.E. Kendell, "Diagnosis and classification" in *Companion to psychiatric studies* (ed. R.E. Kendell & A.K. Zealley, Churchill Livingstone, 1993), p.447.

or that maintenance treatment with tricyclic antidepressants reduces the risk of further episodes, and no one has demonstrated a reduction in the incidence of non-first episodes of either depression or mania in any geographically defined popula-tion.[26] After an interval of eighteen years, Lee and Murray reinterviewed 94 per cent. of 89 individuals who had originally received in-patient treatment for depression in 1965–66. Although 61 per cent. had been first admissions the overall outcome was poor despite the frequent use of tricyclic antidepressants and lithium throughout the follow-up period. Only 11 of 89 patients had a good outcome (*i.e.* no further admissions, no suicide attempts and good social functioning at follow-up) and 25 had a very poor outcome (suicide or other unnatural death, repeated episodes of illness and poor social functioning at follow-up). There was a striking relationship between the symptomatology of the index illness and outcome, those with the most psychotic or endogenous symptoms having the worst outcome.[27] Alcohol abuse is a high-risk factor in most suicide indicators and a disproportionate percentage of depressed persons drink excessively. Where the alcoholism is primary and the depressive disorder consequent upon it, medication and treatment is of little benefit without abstinence. In Desmond Kelly's famous phrase, it is like painting over rust.

THE NEED FOR HOSPITAL ADMISSION

According to Kendell, "the decision whether or not to admit the patient to hospital, or to try to persuade them to come into hospital, is largely governed by three considerations — the risk of suicide, the need for ECT, and whether or not the patient is still at work. The most important of these is the risk of suicide, and the patient should always be questioned about this. Merely having had thoughts about suicide, or having wished not to have to wake up in the morning, are not necessarily cause for alarm, for they are almost invariable in severe depressions. But if the patient is preoccupied with thoughts of suicide, planning how he might kill himself, or frightened that he might do so, he probably needs to be under observation in hospital. So too does anyone who is seriously depressed and living alone. Age, sex, previous suicidal attempts and alcohol intake are other important determinants of risk. Whether the patient is still at work is important partly as an indication of the severity of the illness and partly because anyone who is already unable to work has much less to lose by coming into hospital. And in the writer's view anyone who is ill enough to need ECT needs to be either an in-patient or a day patient."[28]

ANTIDEPRESSANT MEDICATION

Anti-depressants may be divided into four broad categories: (1) tricyclic and related antidepressants; (2) MAOIs; (3) SSRIs and related antidepressants; and (4) other medication with antidepressant properties, such as flupenthixol and tryptophan. The choice of anti-depressant is governed by various considerations including their effectiveness, safety and comparative cost; the tolerance of side-effects; the age of

[26]   R.E. Kendell, "Diagnosis and classification" in *Companion to psychiatric studies* (ed. R.E. Kendell & A.K. Zealley, Churchill Livingstone, 1993), p.447.

[27]   *Ibid.*; A.S. Lee and R.M. Murray "The long-term outcome of Maudsley depressives" *British Journal of Psychiatry* (1988) 153, 741–751. A 15 year follow-up of 145 Australian patients ... produced rather similar findings. Although "the overall prognosis was rather less gloomy, only 20 per cent. had no further episodes of depression and 9 per cent. committed suicide. See L.G. Kiloh, *et al.*, The long-term outcome of depressive illness *British Journal of Psychiatry* (1988) 153, 752–757.

[28]   R.E. Kendell, "Diagnosis and classification" in *Companion to psychiatric studies, supra*, p.451.

patient; the existence of a concurrent illness or the administration of concurrent drug therapy; the psychiatrist's familiarity with the available drugs; and the type of depression from which the patient suffers. An extensive review of the literature by Appleton showed that some 70 per cent. of patients responded to tricyclics compared to 40 per cent. for placebos and, in general terms, it appears that approximately 20–30 per cent. of additional recoveries occur with the assistance of medication when compared with no treatment or treatment with placebo.[29] Medication also has a short-term prophylactic role in terms of reducing the risk of relapse. While the results of research studies vary, the risk of relapse is approximately halved if tricyclics are continued for a period of six to eight months following remission whereas cessation within two months of remission leads to a relapse rate variously described as between 20 and 50 per cent. Assuming that medication is effective, and some 30 per cent. of patients fail to respond to tricyclic medication, Appleton's view is that tricyclic medicines should be continued for between three and twelve months at a dosage of 100–150mg of imipramine or equivalent.[30] There is some evidence that a "maintenance dose" of 75–100 mg per day is less effective[31] although higher doses may encourage non-compliance because of their side-effects.

TRICYCLIC AND RELATED ANTIDEPRESSANTS

These antidepressants, which inhibit the re-uptake of the monoamines serotonin and noradrenaline, are called tricyclics because of their three-ringed chemical structure. The first of them, imipramine, was introduced in 1959. Some of the newer related drugs have four rings and may be referred to as tetracyclics.

Efficacy

In 62 of the 93 trials reviewed by Morris, patients receiving tricyclic antidepressants showed greater improvement than those receiving a placebo.[32] The actual response relative to placebo may be greater than this because the initial dosage advice is now generally considered to have been too low.[33]

The choice of tricyclic

There is little evidence that tricyclics differ from one another in clinical efficacy but they do differ in their side-effects. The pronounced sedative action of amitriptyline may be useful if there is some immediate gain through a reduction of anxiety and tension. However, some patients complain of over-sedation in which case a less sedative preparation such as imipramine may be preferred. Clomipramine may be effective when a depressive illness has obsessive-compulsive features and imipramine where there is retardation. Safer drugs like mianserin are valuable for patients who are likely to attempt to kill themselves or who develop intolerable anticholinergic side-effects on amitriptyline or imipramine.

---

[29] W. Appleton, *Practical Clinical Psychopharmacology* (Williams & Wilkins, 3rd ed., 1988).

[30] *Ibid.* Prien and Kupfer found that treatment needed to be continued for four months after full recovery but no longer. R.F. Prien and D.J. Kupfer "Continuation drug therapy for major depressive episodes: how long should it be maintained?" *American Journal of Psychiatry* (1986) 143, 18–23.

[31] E. Frank, *et al.*, "Three year outcomes of maintenance therapies in recurrent depression" *Archives of General Psychiatry* (1990) 47, 1093–1099.

[32] J.B. Morris and A.T. Beck, "The efficacy of antidepressant drugs, A review of research (1958–1972)" *Archives of General Psychiatry* (1974) 30, 667–674.

[33] W. Appleton, *Practical Clinical Psychopharmacology* (Williams & Wilkins, 3rd ed., 1988).

TRICYCLIC AND RELATED ANTIDEPRESSANTS (B.N.F. 4.3.1)

Drug	Proprietary	Indications	BNF guideline doses	Notes
Amitriptyline Hydrochloride	• Amitriptyline (tablets) • Lentizol (capsules) • Tryptizol (tablets, mixture, injection)	Depressive illness, particularly where sedation is required	By mouth initially 75mg daily, increasing to maximum 150mg daily. Usual maintenance dose 50–100mg daily. IM or IV injection 10–20mg q.d.s.	More sedative than imipramine and has more pronounced anticholinergic effects. Often used where anxiety or agitation are apparent. Some 70 per cent. of depressed in-patients respond.
Amoxapine	• Asendis (tablets)	Depressive illness	Initially 100–150mg daily. Maximum dose 300mg daily. Usual maintenance dose of 150–250mg daily.	Chemically related to the antipsychotic loxapine. Tardive dyskinesia reported and endocrine disorders in women.
Clomipramine Hydrochloride	• Clomipramine (capsules) • Anafranil (capsules, syrup, injection, tablets)	Depressive illness, phobic and obsessional states	By mouth initially 10mg daily, maximum 250mg daily, usual maintenance 30–50mg daily. IM injection initially 25–50mg daily, maximum 100–150mg daily. IV infusion initially 25–50mg increasing to usual dose of 100mg daily for 7–10 days.	Strongly sedative.
Desipramine Hydrochloride	• Pertofran (tablets)	Depressive illness	75mg daily initially, usual maximum dose of 200mg daily (in resistant depression max. 300mg daily with plasma concentration monitoring). Usual maintenance 75–100mg daily.	Slight stimulant effect. Discontinued in 1997.
Dothiepin Hydrochloride	• Dothiepin (tablets, capsules) • Prothiaden (tablets, capsules)	As for amitriptyline	Initially 75mg daily, increasing as necessary to 150mg daily or in some circumstances (e.g., hospital use) 225mg.	Similar to amitriptyline.
Doxepin	• Sinequan (capsules)	As for amitriptyline	Initially 75mg daily, increased as necessary to 300mg daily. Range 30–300mg daily.	May have fewer unwanted effects than amitriptyline.
Imipramine Hydrochloride	• Imipramine (tablets) • Tofranil (tablets, syrup)	Depressive illness	Initially up to 75mg daily, increased gradually to 150–200mg (up to 300mg in hospital patients). Usual maintenance 50–100mg daily.	Less sedating than Amitriptyline.

Drug	Preparation	Indication	Dose	Comments
Lofepramine	▪ Lofepramine (tablets, syrup) ▪ Gamanil (tablets)	*Depressive illness*	Range 140–210mg daily.	Less sedating than Amitriptyline. Safe in overdose. May cause agitation in the elderly. Hepatic disorders reported.
Nortriptyline	▪ Allegron (tablets)	*Depressive illness*	Low dose initially increased as necessary to 75–100mg daily. Maximum 150mg. daily in hospital patients (plasma concentration monitoring above 100mg).	Less sedating than Amitriptyline.
Protriptyline Hydrochloride	▪ Concordin (tablets)	*Depressive illness, particularly with apathy and withdrawal*	Initially 10mg 3–4 times daily. Usual range 15–60mg daily.	Strongly stimulant. Anxiety, agitation, restlessness more common.
Trimipramine	▪ Surmontil (tablets, capsules)	*As for amitriptyline*	50–75mg daily, increased as necessary to maximum 300mg daily for 4–6 weeks, then reduced to usual maintenance dose 75–150mg daily.	Sometimes advocated for MAOI combination therapy. Strongly sedative.

Related antidepressants

Drug	Preparation	Indication	Dose	Comments
Maprotiline Hydrochloride	▪ Ludiomil (tablets)	*As for amitriptyline*	Initially 25–75mg, maximum 150mg daily.	Antimuscarinic effects may be less frequent than with Amitriptyline but rashes common. Increased risk of convulsions at higher doses.
Mianserin Hydrochloride	▪ Mianserin (tablets)	*As for amitriptyline*	Initially 30–40mg daily, increased gradually as necessary. Usual dose range 30–90mg.	Tetracyclic. Safe in overdose. Leukopenia, agranulocytosis, jaundice reported.
Trazodone Hydrochloride	▪ Molipaxin (tablet, capsules, liquid)	*As for amitriptyline*	Initially 150mg daily, maximum 300 mg daily or (in hospital patients) 600mg daily.	Chemically unrelated to other antidepressants. Mechanism of action unclear. Fewer antimuscarinic and cardiovascular effects compared to Amitriptyline.
Viloxazine Hydrochloride	▪ Vivalan	*Depressive illness*	300 mg daily, maximum 400mg daily.	Less sedating than Amitriptyline. Fewer and milder antimuscarinic and cardiovascular effects.

Dosage and response

The normal adult dose of most tricyclic antidepressants is 150mg per day. The elderly will usually only be able to tolerate half this amount. According to Kendell, and the guidelines in the British National Formulary, it is important to start with a maximum dose of 75mg per day in everyone so as to minimise the impact of sedative and anticholinergic side-effects.[34] Initial response to tricyclic medication generally takes ten to fourteen days and six weeks may be required for maximum therapeutic effect; improvement in somatic symptoms is often the first feature to be noted.[35] This means that little or no improvement in a section 2 patient's condition may be apparent by the time his case is heard but, providing the dose is adequate, maximum response should have been achieved by the date of any section 3 hearing. After a year, the therapeutic effect of tricyclics wanes and after two years of continuous treatment they are probably of little or no benefit.[36] Because of their delayed action "no patient under the age of 60 years should be deemed to have failed to respond to a tricyclic drug until they have taken 150mg/day for at least three weeks. If there is no improvement within this time it is usually better to increase the dose still further (*i.e.* to 200 or 250mg/day of amitriptyline) than to change to a different drug, unless side-effects have prevented an adequate dose being taken or poor compliance is suspected. This probably applies to the newer tetracyclic drugs as well, though at present there is little evidence either way."[37]

Predicting who will respond

Some 30 per cent. of depressed patients fail to respond to tricyclics. The general reasons for treatment failure have already been summarised (**1150**). In relation to depressive disorders, there is some evidence that "endogenous depression" tends to respond better than do "neurotic" depressive disorders,[38] and unipolar psychotic epi-sodes respond fairly poorly, ECT being likely to achieve a better response.[39] Symptoms commonly found to be susceptible to improvement are depressed mood (sadness), guilt and worthlessness, and decreased involvement in work and interests (lassitude).[40] According to Kendell, the "most appropriate treatment for patients with severe depressions which have failed to respond both to a tricyclic drug in full dosage and to ECT is very uncertain. Possible strategies include an MAOI in high dosage, combining a tricyclic and an MAOI in moderate doses, combining lithium with a tricyclic or an MAOI, prescribing an MAOI and tryptophan. For non-responders whose illnesses are "reactive" or "neurotic" in character the best alter-native treatment is usually either an MAOI or cognitive therapy.[41]

---

[34]   R.E. Kendell, "Diagnosis and classification" in *Companion to psychiatric studies* (ed. R.E. Kendell & A.K. Zealley, Churchill Livingstone, 1993), p.449.

[35]   M. Lader and R. Herrington, *Biological treatments in psychiatry* (Oxford Medical Publications, 2nd ed., 1990), p.141.

[36]   R.E. Kendell, "Diagnosis and classification" in *Companion to psychiatric studies, supra*, p.449.

[37]   *Ibid.*

[38]   E.C. Johnstone, *et al.*, "Neurotic illness and its response to anxiolytic and antidepressant treatment" *Psychological Medicine* (1980) 10, 321–328.

[39]   W. Appleton, *Practical Clinical Psychopharmacology* (Williams & Wilkins, 3rd ed., 1988).

[40]   See J.C. Nelson, *et al.*, "Drug-responsive symptoms in melancholia" (1984) *Archives of General Psychiatry* 41, 663–668; S.A. Montgomery & M. Asberg, "A new depression scale designed to be sensitive to change" (1979) *British Journal of Psychiatry* 134, 382–389; P. Bech, *et al.*, "The Hamilton Rating Scale: Evaluation of objectivity using logistic models" (1981) *Acta Psychiatrica Scandinavica* 63, 290–299; M. Lader and R. Herrington, *Biological treatments in psychiatry* (Oxford Medical Publications, 2nd ed., 1990), p.141.

[41]   R.E. Kendell, "Diagnosis and classification" in *Companion to psychiatric studies, supra*, p.451.

Adverse effects

Approximately 400 deaths due to tricyclic overdoses are reported annually and they are considerably more dangerous than phenothiazines in overdose. Even a week's supply of an antidepressant at full dosage can be lethal and a dose of imipramine or amitriptyline above 600mg is likely to produce serious effects. Symptoms usually appear within four hours.[42]

Prescribed medication

The side-effects of medication taken according to prescription include drowsiness, torpor, a feeling of detachment, tremor and confusional reactions in the elderly, postural hypotension, constipation, urinary retention, delayed ejaculation, weight gain, headache and nausea.

SELECTIVE SEROTONIN RE-UPTAKE INHIBITORS (SSRIs)

Serotonin is stored in synaptic vesicles and, following its release into the synaptic cleft, the main method of inactivation is via re-uptake by presynaptic neurones (1270).[43] The SSRIs are a structurally diverse group but they all selectively inhibit this re-uptake, having no significant effect on noradrenaline or dopamine reuptake.

Efficacy

The evidence suggests that the drugs are as effective as amitriptyline, have fewer side-effects and comparatively safe in overdose. The latter is necessarily an important consideration if there is a significant risk of suicide. Opinion varies as to whether SSRIs or tricyclics should be used as the initial treatment in cases of major depression because it is not yet firmly established that they are as effective in treating severely depressed patients.[44] They may, however, be particularly effective where a depressive disorder is associated with obsessional or phobic thoughts.

Adverse effects

SSRIs are less cardiotoxic than tricyclic antidepressants, much safer in overdose, non-sedating and lack antimuscarinic (anticholinergic) effects. They are also not associated with weight gain. The fact that SSRIs have fewer debilitating adverse effects may mean that patient compliance with prescriptions is higher than when a tricyclic antidepressant is prescribed.[45] The most common adverse effects include nausea, loss of appetite, dry mouth, diarrhoea, constipation, insomnia, headache, dizziness, tremor, sweating, and sexual problems such as retarded ejaculation. Gastro-intestinal side-effects (diarrhoea, nausea and vomiting) are dose-related.[46] Akathisia and extrapyramidal effects have been reported with fluoxetine.[47] It is hazardous to combine an SSRI with an MAOI or to prescribe the latter drug within several weeks of stopping the former.

---

[42]   M. Lader and R. Herrington, *Biological treatments in psychiatry (supra)*, p.151.

[43]   B.K. Puri and P.J. Tyrer, *Sciences Basic to Psychiatry* (Churchill Livingstone, 1992), p.103.

[44]   M.V. Rudorfer and W.Z. Potter, "Antidepressants: a comparative view of the clinical pharmacology and therapeutic use of the 'newer' versus the older drugs" (1989) *Drugs* 37, 713–738.

[45]   F. Song, *et al.*, "Selective serotonin reuptake inhibitors: a meta-analysis of efficacy and acceptability" (1993) *British Medical Journal* 306, 683–687.

[46]   *British National Formulary* (March 1996) 31, 176.

[47]   J.F. Lipinski, *et al.*, "Fluoxetine-induced akathisia: clinical and theoretical implications" (1989) *Journal of Clinical Psychiatry* 50, 339.

Drug	Proprietary	Guideline doses
Fluoxetine	Prozac (capsules, liquid)	*Depressive illness* 20mg daily. *Bulimia nervosa* 60mg daily. *Obsessive-compulsive disorder* initially 20mg, maximum 60mg daily (if no response after several weeks).
Citalopram	▪ Cipramil	20 mg daily increased to maximum 60mg daily.
Fluvoxamine Maleate	▪ Faverin (tablets)	100mg daily, maximum 300mg daily.
Paroxetine	▪ Seroxat (tablets, liquid)	Usually 20mg mane, maximum 50mg daily
Sertraline	▪ Lustral (tablets)	Initially 50mg daily, maximum 200mg daily, usual maintenance dose of 50mg daily. Doses of 150mg or greater should not be used for more than 8 weeks.

Related antidepressants

Drug	Proprietary	Guideline doses
Nefazone Hydrochloride	▪ Dutonin (tablets)	Initially 100mg twice daily, increased after 5–7 days to 200mg twice daily. May be gradually increased to maximum 300mg twice daily.
Venlafaxine	▪ Efexor (tablets)	Initially 75mg daily increased if necessary after several weeks to 150mg. *Severely depressed or hospitalised patients* — Initially 150mg daily, increasing in steps every 2/3 days to maximum 375mg daily then gradually reduced.

MONOAMINE OXIDASE INHIBITORS (MAOIs)

The enzyme monoamine oxidase is responsible for the metabolic degradation of the neurotransmitters noradrenaline, serotonin and dopamine. MAOIs inhibit the enzyme, thereby causing an accumulation of amine neurotransmitters (**1270**) and this has an antidepressant effect. Unfortunately, the enzyme is also responsible for inactivating other amines such as tyramine which is present in food, drink and drugs. When monoamine oxidase is inhibited, tyramine is not broken down and this results in dangerously elevated blood pressure. Such a hypertensive crisis may occasionally be fatal. Consequently, patients taking MAOIs must avoid tyramine-rich foods, such as cheese (which is responsible for 80 per cent. of all reported fatalities) and yeast products, alcohol and certain drugs.

Efficacy

Early studies showed that MAOIs had only a very limited effect over and above placebo but it is now clear that the initial dosage guidelines were only half the therapeutic level.[48] As with tricyclics, the drugs must be given for several weeks and in adequate dosage and "in the case of phenelzine this usually means 60–90 mg/day,

---

[48]   W. Appleton, *Practical Clinical Psychopharmacology* (Williams & Wilkins, 3rd ed., 1988).

or whatever dose is needed to provide 80–90 per cent. inhibition of platelet MAO activity if the assay is available."[49] There is a long tradition that MAOIs are particularly effective forms of treatment for patients with atypical or "neurotic" depression characterised by anxiety, panic attacks, hypochondria, hysterical features or agoraphobia. Five recent studies have confirmed this by demonstrating a vastly superior patient response to MAOIs compared with imipramine in persons suffering from atypical depression.[50] Because of the dietary restrictions, MAOIs tend to be reserved as a second-line treatment for major depressive disorders, being used only for conditions which are refractory to treatment. Nevertheless, recent studies indicate that MAOIs are generally equivalent to tricyclic antidepressants in their efficacy, including as a treatment for "endogenous depression."[51]

MONOAMINE-OXIDASE INHIBITORS (B.N.F. 4.3.2)

Drug	Proprietary	BNF guideline doses
Phenelzine	▪ Nardil (tablets)	Initially 15mg t.d.s., increased if necessary after 2 weeks to 15mg q.d.s. (hospital patients maximum 30mg t.d.s.). Then reduced to lowest possible maintenance dose – 15mg on alternate days may be adequate.
Isocarboxazid	▪ Isocarboxazid (tablets)	Initially up to 30mg daily, increased after 4 weeks if necessary to max. 60mg daily for up to 6 weeks under close supervision only; then reduced to usual maintenance dose 10–20mg daily (but up to 40mg daily may be required).
Tranylcypromine	▪ Parnate (tablets)	Initially 10mg b.d. Doses above 30mg daily under close supervision only.
Reversible MAOIs		
Moclobemide	▪ Manerix (tablets)	Initially 300mg daily, adjusted according to response. Usual range 150–600mg daily.

Adverse effects

Because the effects of non-compliance with dietary restrictions are severe, prescriptions are restricted to patients who can be relied upon to adhere to the necessary regime. However, selectively prescribed, there is no evidence that MAOIs are less safe than tricyclic anti-depressants and, indeed, the number of recorded deaths per million MAOI prescriptions is generally considerably less. There is no proven advantage in prescribing tricyclic anti-depressants and MAOIs together and it may be hazardous to do so.

---

[49] R.E. Kendell, "Diagnosis and classification" in *Companion to psychiatric studies* (ed. R.E. Kendell & A.K. Zealley, Churchill Livingstone, 1993), p.450.

[50] F.M. Quitkin, *et al.*, "Phenelzine and imipramine in mood reactive depressives" (1989) *Archives of General Psychiatry* 46, 787–793.

[51] E.S. Paykel, "Monoamine oxidase inhibitors: when should they be used" in *Dilemmas and difficulties in the management of psychiatric patients* (ed. K. Hawton & P.J. Cowen, Oxford University Press, 1990), pp.17–30; P.J. Cowen, "Depression resistant to tricyclic antidepressants" (1988) *British Medical Journal* 297, 435–436.

Reversible MAOIs (Moclobemide)

Many of the dangerous interactions associated with MAOIs do not apply to the newer drug moclobemide, which is known as a reversible MAOI. However, there is little evidence that it is as effective as the older MAOIs as a treatment for atypical depression.

MANIC EPISODES AND BIPOLAR DISORDERS

In the ICD–10 classification, the terms mania and severe depression are used to denote the opposite ends of the spectrum of mood disorders.[52] Three degrees of severity of manic episode are specified in the ICD classification, all of which share the common underlying characteristics of elevated mood and an increase in the quantity and speed of physical and mental activity: hypomania; mania without psychotic symptoms; and mania with psychotic symptoms. If a patient who has had a manic episode (F30) has a subsequent manic episode, the diagnosis is revised to bipolar affective disorder (F31). This reflects the fact that the vast majority of such patients will eventually experience an episode of depression. The frequency of episodes and the pattern of remissions and relapses are very variable.

AETIOLOGY, PATHOLOGY AND EPIDEMIOLOGY

While many hypotheses have been advanced, the underlying aetiology and pathology are not known. Most studies have found a raised incidence of life events preceding the onset of manic illnesses. Bipolar disorder is less common than unipolar disorder. The first episode may occur at any age from childhood to old age but the mean age of onset of bipolar illness is 21 years. The initial episode occurs before the age of 30 in over 60 per cent of cases and before the age of 50 in almost 90 per cent. of cases.[53] The lifetime risk of bipolar disorder is about 1 per cent. While the risk is the same for men and women it may be somewhat greater for people in higher socio-economic classes.

MANIC EPISODES (F30)

Manic episodes are characterised by elevated mood and an increase in the quantity and speed of physical and mental activity. They usually begin abruptly and last for between two weeks and four of five months, with a median duration about four months.[54] The length of subsequent episodes appears to be similar[55] although the interval between episodes decreases as their number increases.[56]

---

[52] *Classification of Mental and Behavioural Disorders, Tenth Revision (ICD–10): Clinical descriptions and diagnostic guidelines* (World Health Organisation, 1992), p.112.

[53] J Angst, *et al.*, "The course of monopolar depression and bipolar psychosis" (1973) *Psychiatrica, Neurologica, Neurochirurgia* 76, 486–500.

[54] *Classification of Mental and Behavioural Disorders, Tenth Revision (ICD–10): Clinical descriptions and diagnostic guidelines* (World Health Organisation, 1992), p.116.

[55] J Angst, *et al.*, "The course of monopolar depression and bipolar psychosis," *supra.*

[56] P. Roy-Byrne, *et al.*, "The longitudinal course of recurrent affective illness: life chart data from research patients at the NIMH" *Acta Psychiatrica Scandinavica* 71, 1–34.

Differential diagnosis

Mania with psychotic symptoms may sometimes be difficult to distinguish from schizophrenia in cases where the psychotic state obscures the basic mood disorder. The manifestations of some other medical conditions may also include symptoms most commonly seen in manic episodes, including thyrotoxicosis and hypoparathyroidism. The possibility that the condition has been induced by prescribed or non-prescribed drugs must always be borne in mind. Drugs associated with manic symptoms include amphetamines, cocaine, corticosteroids, MAOIs and anticholinergics (procyclidine and benzhexol).

The severity of manic episodes

Three degrees of severity of manic episode are specified in the ICD classification, namely hypomania (F30.0); mania without psychotic symptoms (F30.1); and mania with psychotic symptoms (F30.2).

HYPOMANIA (F30.0)

Hypomania is a lesser degree of mania, an intermediate state without delusions, hallucinations, or complete disruption of normal activities, which is often but not exclusively seen as patients develop or recover from mania.[57] Thus, it covers the range of mood disorders and activity levels which lie between cyclothymia (1197) and mania; the abnormalities of mood are too persistent and marked to be included under cyclothymia but are not accompanied by hallucinations or delusions.[58]

SYMPTOMS OF HYPOMANIA

- Persistent mild elevation of mood for at least several days on end.

- Increased energy and activity.

- Usually marked feelings of well-being and both mental and physical efficiency.

- Increased sociability, talkativeness, overfamiliarity and sexual energy and a decreased need for sleep are often present but not to the extent that they lead to severe disruption of work or result in social rejection.

- Irritability, conceit, and boorish behaviour may take the place of the more usual euphoric sociability.

- Concentration and attention may be impaired, thus diminishing the ability to settle down to work, but this may not prevent the appearance of interests in quite new ventures and activities, or mild over-spending.

Source: ICD–10 Classification of Mental and Behavioural Disorders: Clinical descriptions and diagnostic guidelines. WHO, Geneva. 1992, p.113.

---

[57] *Classification of Mental and Behavioural Disorders, Tenth Revision (ICD–10): Clinical descriptions and diagnostic guidelines* (World Health Organisation, 1992), p.113.

[58] *Ibid.*, p.112.

Diagnostic guidelines

The diagnostic guidelines provide that several of the features listed in the above table, consistent with elevated or changed mood and increased activity, should have been present for at least several days on end, to a degree and with a persistence greater than that described for cyclothymia (1197). Hallucinations and delusions should be absent. While "considerable" interference with work or social activity is consistent with a diagnosis of hypomania, if disruption of these is "severe or complete" then mania should be diagnosed.[59]

MANIA WITHOUT PSYCHOTIC SYMPTOMS (F30.1)

The diagnostic guidelines for mania state that the episode should last for at least one week and be severe enough to disrupt ordinary work and social activities more or less completely. The mood change should be accompanied by increased energy and several of the symptoms referred to in the table below. Pressure of speech (1078), decreased need for sleep, grandiosity, and excessive optimism, should be evident.

SYMPTOMS OF MANIA WITHOUT PSYCHOTIC SYMPTOMS

- The individual's mood is elevated out of keeping with his circumstances and may vary from carefree joviality to almost uncontrollable excitement.

- Elation is accompanied by increased energy, resulting in overactivity, pressure of speech, and a decreased need for sleep. However, in some manic episodes the mood is irritable and suspicious rather than elated.

- Normal social inhibitions are lost, attention cannot be sustained, and there is often marked distractibility.

- Self-esteem is inflated, and grandiose or over-optimistic ideas are freely expressed.

- Perceptual disorders may occur, such as the appreciation of colours as especially vivid and beautiful and subjective hyperacusis.

- The individual may embark on extravagant and impractical schemes, spend money recklessly, or become aggressive, amorous, or facetious in inappropriate circumstances.

Source: ICD–10 Classification of Mental and Behavioural Disorders: Clinical descriptions and diagnostic guidelines. WHO, Geneva. 1992, p.114.

---

[59] *Classification of Mental and Behavioural Disorders, Tenth Revision (ICD–10): Clinical descriptions and diagnostic guidelines* (World Health Organisation, 1992), p.113. Similarly, the American DSM–IV classification states that by definition the disturbance in hypomania is not severe enough to cause marked impairment in social or occupational functioning or to require hospitalisation, which is required for the diagnosis of a manic episode.

MANIA WITH PSYCHOTIC SYMPTOMS (F30.2)

The term "psychotic" is used in the ICD–10 classification as a convenient descriptive term to indicate the presence of hallucinations, delusions, or a limited number of several abnormalities of behaviour, such as *gross* excitement and overactivity. The clinical picture is that of a more severe form of mania than mania without psychotic symptoms (F30.1).[60] While the diagnostic guidelines for mania set out in the table above should be satisfied, psychotic symptoms of the kind described below should also be evident.

SYMPTOMS OF MANIA WITH PSYCHOTIC SYMPTOMS

- Inflated self-esteem and grandiose ideas may develop into delusions, and irritability and suspiciousness into delusions of persecution. In severe cases, grandiose or religious delusions of identity or role may be prominent, and flight of ideas and pressure of speech may result in the individual becoming incomprehensible.

- Severe and sustained physical activity and excitement may result in aggression or violence, and neglect of eating, drinking, and personal hygiene may result in dangerous states of dehydration and self-neglect.

- If required, delusions or hallucinations can be specified as congruent or incongruent with the mood. "Incongruent" should be taken as including affectively neutral delusions and hallucinations; for example, delusions of reference with no guilty or accusatory content, or voices speaking to the individual about events that have no special emotional significance.

Source: ICD–10 Classification of Mental and Behavioural Disorders: Clinical descriptions and diagnostic guidelines. WHO, Geneva. 1992, p.115.

BIPOLAR AFFECTIVE DISORDERS (F31)

It has been noted that the diagnosis of a manic episode (F30) is only used for a first manic episode and also that a significant proportion of manic patients subsequently experience further periods of mania or depression. Bipolar affective disorder is characterised by two or more episodes in which the patient's mood and activity levels are significantly disturbed, this disturbance consisting on some occasions of an elevation of mood and increased energy and activity (mania or hypomania), and on others of a lowering of mood and decreased energy and activity (depression).[61] However, as patients who suffer only from repeated episodes of mania are comparatively rare, and resemble those who also have at least occasional episodes of depression in terms of their family history, premorbid personality, age of onset, and long-term prognosis, patients who experience a second manic episode are reclassified as having a bipolar affective disorder even if there is no history of depression.

---

[60] *Classification of Mental and Behavioural Disorders, Tenth Revision (ICD–10): Clinical descriptions and diagnostic guidelines* (World Health Organisation, 1992), p.115.
[61] *Ibid.*, p.116.

Sub-types and diagnostic guidelines

The main sub-types of bipolar affective disorder are listed below, from which it can be seen that the sub-types are distinguished according to the type of disordered mood which defines the current episode. The diagnostic guidelines are two-fold—

- The first is that the current episode meets the usual criteria for the particular kind of mood disorder. So, for example, a definite diagnosis of "bipolar disorder, current episode hypomania" requires that the patient's present condition meets the diagnostic guidelines for hypomania already given.

- The second diagnostic guideline relates to the nature of the previous episode, or episodes, and rests on the distinction to which reference has been made. Namely, that while a person who experiences a second manic episode is reclassified as having a bipolar disorder, a person who has an episode of depression is only reclassified as having a bipolar disorder if and when he subsequently has a manic episode.

- Accordingly, if the present illness meets the criteria for a manic episode the second diagnostic guideline is simply that there has been at least one previous episode of any type of mood disorder.[62] However, if the current episode is depressive, a diagnosis of a bipolar affective disorder requires that there has been a manic episode or a mixed affective episode (alternating mania and depression) at some time in the past.

SUB-TYPES OF BIPOLAR AFFECTIVE DISORDER (F31)

Patient's current condition fulfils the criteria for a manic episode

- Bipolar disorder, current episode hypomanic (F31.0)

- Bipolar affective disorder, current episode manic without psychotic symptoms (F31.1)

- Bipolar affective disorder, current episode manic with psychotic symptoms (F31.2)

Patient's current condition fulfils the criteria for a depressive episode

- Bipolar affective disorder, current episode mild or moderate depression (F31.3)

- Bipolar affective disorder, current episode severe depression without psychotic symptoms (F31.4)

- Bipolar affective disorder, current episode severe depression with psychotic symptoms (F31.5)

- Bipolar affective disorder, current episode mixed (F31.6)

- Bipolar affective disorder, currently in remission (F31.7)

Source: ICD–10 Classification of Mental and Behavioural Disorders: Clinical descriptions and diagnostic guidelines. WHO, Geneva. 1992, pp.116–119.

---

[62]   Excluding, of course, cyclothymia and dysthymia.

COURSE AND PROGNOSIS

Prior to the introduction of modern drug therapies the mortality rate of in-patients with mania was approximately 20 per cent., with two-fifths of the deceased dying from exhaustion.[63] Manic episodes usually begin abruptly and last for between two weeks and four to five months with a median duration of about four months.[64] The "risk of recurrence is high, particularly if the first episode occurs before the age of 30 years ... once someone has had a manic illness in adolescence or early adult life they are almost certain to have further illnesses, and in the long run some of these further illnesses are almost certain to be depressions."[65] Indeed, the manic episodes tend to become less frequent and the depressive episodes more frequent with the passage of time. Characteristically, recovery is usually complete between episodes.

MANAGEMENT

The treatment of manic episodes may require hospitalisation. According to Kendell, it is usually advisable to admit the patient to hospital, "for the risks of attempting to treat even hypomania on an out-patient basis are considerable. Because he feels fine, and cannot be convinced that he is ill, the patient rarely takes medication regularly. He may also squander money he can ill afford, get himself into all manner of embarrassing situations which may jeopardise his job or his position in the community, and endanger himself and other people by reckless behaviour.[66] Considerable nursing skill is required. The "patient's boisterous overactivity, sudden whims and capacity for causing mayhem have to be restrained. An experienced nurse can often do this by distracting his energies into other and less dangerous channels, or by winning his co-operation by entering his mood of playful good humour. A less skilful nurse tries to forbid or physically restrain, which annoys the patient and easily provokes him to violence."[67] As mood returns to normal, observation is important because of the considerable risks of relapse or a sudden swing into depression.

ANTIPSYCHOTIC DRUGS USED TO CONTROL MANIA

Following admission, the initial treatment normally includes the use of an antipsychotic (**1141**). Haloperidol and droperidol are widely believed to control motor overactivity more effectively than chlorpromazine but they can also cause severe extrapyramidal side-effects. In severe illnesses, chlorpromazine in doses of up to 1000mg daily or haloperidol in doses of up to 40mg per day are used because of their more immediate effect on over-activity. The sedative effects of antipsychotics are immediate and this may partly explain why manic symptoms generally begin to respond after a few days. Sedation can be hastened by intravenous administration. In one large-scale trial, chlorpromazine was found to control disturbed behaviour in highly active patients within a few days while the effects of lithium were delayed until the tenth day. However, the two were equally effective for mildly ill patients and lithium produced fewer side effects, leaving the patient feeling less sluggish and fatigued.

---

[63]   I.M. Derby, "Manic-depressive exhaustion deaths" (1933) *Psychiatric Quarterly* 7, 435–439.

[64]   *Classification of Mental and Behavioural Disorders, Tenth Revision (ICD–10): Clinical descriptions and diagnostic guidelines* (World Health Organisation, 1992), p.116.

[65]   R.E. Kendell, "Diagnosis and classification" in *Companion to psychiatric studies* (ed. R.E. Kendell & A.K. Zealley, Churchill Livingstone, 1993), p.446. However, the proportion of patients having a single manic episode has been variously estimated at between one and 50 per cent.

[66]   *Ibid.*

[67]   *Ibid.*, p.448.

ANTIPSYCHOTIC DRUGS USED TO CONTROL MANIA (NOT DEPOTS)

Introductory note: Many of the drugs are not recommended for children, and reduced doses are recommended for children or the "elderly."

Drug	Proprietary	Indications	BNF guideline doses
Chlorpromazine Hydrochloride (CPZ)	▪ Chlorpromazine (tablets, elixir, injection, suppositories) ▪ Largactil (tablets, syrup, suspension, injection)	*Mania, short-term adjunctive management of severe anxiety, psychomotor agitation, excitement, and violent or dangerous impulsive behaviour.*	*Mania — by mouth* initially 75mg daily, usual maintenance dose of 75–300mg daily but up to 1g daily may be required in psychoses. *By deep IM injection* for relief of acute symptoms, 25–50mg every 6–8 hours.
Droperidol	▪ Droleptan (tablets, oral liquid, injection)	*Tranquillisation and emergency control in mania*	*Tranquillisation and emergency control in mania — by mouth* 5–20mg repeated every 4–8 hours if necessary. *By IM injection,* up to 10mg repeated every 4–6 hours if necessary. *By IV injection,* 5–15mg repeated every 4–6 hours if necessary.
Fluphenazine Hydrochloride	▪ Moditen (tablets, depot injection see **1263**)	*As for Chlorpromazine*	*Mania — by mouth* initially 2.5–10mg daily, adjusted according to response to 20mg daily. Daily doses above 20mg "only with special caution."
Haloperidol	▪ Haloperidol (tablets) ▪ Dozic (oral liquid) ▪ Haldol (tablets, oral liquid, injection, depot injection) ▪ Serenace (tablets, capsules, oral liquid, injection)	*As for Chlorpromazine*	*Mania — by mouth* initially 1.5–3mg twice or thrice daily; 3–5mg twice or thrice daily in severely affected or resistant patients. *By IM injection,* 2–10mg with subsequent doses every 4–8 hours according to response (up to hourly if necessary) — severely disturbed patients may require initial dose of up to 30mg.
Oxypertine	▪ Oxypertine (tablets, capsules)	*As for Chlorpromazine*	*Mania —* Initially 80–120mg daily, adjusted according to response. Maximum 300 mg daily.

Drug	Proprietary	Indications	BNF guideline doses
Perphenazine	Fentazin (tablets)	As for Chlorpromazine	*Mania* — Initially 4mg t.d.s., thereafter adjusted according to response. Maximum dose 24 mg. daily.
Pimozide	Orap (tablets)	Mania, hypomania, short-term adjunctive treatment of excitement and psychomotor agitation.	*Mania, hypomania* — Initially 10mg daily in acute conditions, thereafter adjusted according to response to maximum of 20mg daily.
Prochlorperazine	Prochlorperazine (tablets) Stemetil (tablets, syrups, sachets, injection, suppositories)	Mania	*By mouth*, 12.5mg b.d. for 7 days, thereafter adjusted according to response to usual daily dose of 75–100mg. *By deep IM injection*, 12.5–25mg twice or thrice daily.
Thioridazine	Thioridazine (tablets, oral solution) Melleril (tablets, suspension, syrup)	As for Chlorpromazine	*Mania* — 150–600mg daily; maximum 800 mg. daily for up to 4 weeks (hospital patients only).
Trifluoperazine	Trifluoperazine (tablets, oral solution) Stelazine (tablets, spansules, syrup)	As for Chlorpromazine	*Mania — by mouth*, initially 10mg daily, increased by 5mg after 1 week, then at intervals of 3 days according to response. *By deep IM injection*, 1–3mg daily to maximum of 6mg daily.
Zuclopenthixol Acetate	Clopixol Acuphase (injection, oily)	Mania	*By deep IM injection into the gluteal muscle or lateral thigh*, 50–150 mg, if necessary repeated after 2–3 days (1 additional dose may be needed 1–2 days after the first injection). Treatment should not exceed 2 weeks — maximum of 4 injections and maximum cumulative dose of 400mg per course.

1223

LITHIUM

The mainstay of treatment is Lithium although several anticonvulsants and calcium channel blockers may serve as alternatives. Lithium is a natural substance which occurs in food and water and small amounts can therefore be found in the body. It acts in a quite different way from neuroleptics. Its side-effects are much less unpleasant and, if it works, it controls all the symptoms of the illness, including the racing thoughts, instead of simply sedating the patient and slowing him down. However, it takes several days to act, which is a serious disadvantage if the patient is aggressive and disruptive so that immediate control of disturbed behaviour is necessary.[68]

Indications

Lithium helps to control acute episodes of mania and reduces the risk of relapse. Its primary use is in the prophylaxis of bipolar affective disorder. It has the advantage of minimising the risk of a swing into depression.

Contra-indications

Lithium is excreted mainly by the kidneys. Any impairment of renal function virtually excludes treatment and it is usually necessary to determine renal function before deciding on the treatment. However, according to Kendell, if lithium is to be used to treat an acute manic episode in a young adult with no history of renal disease it is not necessary to wait for the results of detailed tests of renal function. Indeed, those which involve collecting an accurate 12 or 24 hour urine sample are usually impracticable until the patient has become more co-operative.[69] Cardiac and thyroid function must also be normal before starting lithium. Lithium impairs the uptake of iodine by the thyroid gland and can induce hypothyroidism.

Efficacy

The precise mechanism of action is unknown but lithium has been shown to be effective in preventing attacks of recurrent depression and mania and, to a lesser extent, in treating them. Inevitably, some people taking lithium do not respond to the treatment or respond only partially. More specifically, lithium treatment of manic patients is unsuccessful in about a quarter of cases, and between a third and one half of patients maintained on lithium relapse in a two year period.[70] In terms of predicting who will respond, Lader and Herrington have summarised the relevant research findings:[71] the more typical the patient the more likely he is to respond; a family history of manic-depressive illness predicts a good response[72]; pyknic body build is twice as common among responders as non-responders; response is associated with cyclothymic traits and non-response with withdrawn, anxious and obsessive personalities; a history of schizophrenia, schizo-affective disorder, or of four or more affective episodes per annum during the two to three year period preceding treatment, is associated with a poor prognosis.

---

[68] See R.E. Kendell, "Diagnosis and classification" in *Companion to psychiatric studies* (ed. R.E. Kendell & A.K. Zealley, Churchill Livingstone, 1993).

[69] *Ibid.*, p.448.

[70] M. Lader and R. Herrington, *Biological treatments in psychiatry* (Oxford Medical Publications, 2nd ed., 1990), p.206.

[71] *Ibid.*, p.210. A pyknic build is characterised by a short, stocky, well-rounded body.

[72] J. Ananth and J.C. Pecknold, "Prediction of lithium response in affective disorders" *Journal of Clinical Psychiatry* (1978) 39, 95–100.

Dose and plasma concentrations

Lithium has a low therapeutic index — toxic concentrations are not much greater than therapeutic concentrations — and it is therefore necessary to keep a regular check on serum lithium levels. Serum levels are estimated between eight and 12 hours after the last dose and guideline lithium levels are given in the table below. Lower levels apply to older patients. Serum estimations are initially frequent, up to twice weekly, but may be reduced to every three months once the treatment has been established. When lithium is used as a treatment for mania, rather than prophylactically, higher serum levels may be necessary. The serum level usually needs to be at least 1.0 mmol Li$^+$/l to control manic behaviour[73] but should not exceed 1.5 mmol Li$^+$/litre.[74] Toxicity generally occurs at levels over 2.0 mmol Li$^+$/l.[75] The dose needed to sustain a level of 1.0 mmol Li$^+$/l "may produce some toxic effects but there is little risk involved when the patient is under constant observation and the serum level can be checked at any time."[76] Lithium estimations should complement clinical observation and not form a "blind substitute"; some patients are helped despite lithium concentrations below 0.5 mmol and others show signs of incipient toxicity with concentrations hardly exceeding 1.0 mmol.[77]

LITHIUM (B.N.F. 4.2.3)

Drug	Proprietary	BNF guideline doses	BNF plasma concentrations
Lithium Carbonate	▪ Camcolit (tablets)	*Treatment* initially 1.5–2g. daily. *Prophylaxis* initially 0.5–1.2g. daily.	"Doses are adjusted to achieve a plasma concentration of 0.4–1.0 mmol Li$^+$/litre (lower end of the range for maintenance therapy and elderly patients) on samples taken 12 hours after the preceding dose. It is important to determine the optimum range for each individual patient." (B.N.F., 34, p.172).
	▪ Liskonum (tablets)	*Treatment* initially 450–675mg. twice daily. *Prophylaxis* initially 450mg twice daily.	
	▪ Priadel (tablets, liquid)	*Treatment and prophylaxis* initially 0.4–1.2g. daily.	
Lithium Citrate	▪ Li-Liquid (oral solution)	*Treatment and prophylaxis* initially 1018–3054mg daily.	
	▪ Litarex (tablets)	*Treatment and prophylaxis* initially 564mg twice daily.	
	▪ Priadel (tablets, liquid)	*Treatment and prophylaxis* initially 1.04–3.12g. daily.	

Adverse effects

Side-effects early on during treatment include dry mouth, increased thirst, nausea, mild stomach cramps, tremulousness, and decreased libido. Certain side-effects sometimes persist after the body has adjusted to lithium, including excessive weight gain, skin rash and thyroid changes. Hypothyroidism and kidney damage may

73   R.E. Kendell, "Diagnosis and classification" in *Companion to psychiatric studies* (ed. R.E. Kendell & A.K. Zealley, Churchill Livingstone, 1993), p.448.
74   *Drugs in psychiatric practice* (ed. P.J. Tyrer, Butterworths, 1982).
75   M. Lader and R. Herrington, *Biological treatments in psychiatry* (Oxford Medical Publications, 2nd ed., 1990), p.200.
76   R.E. Kendell, "Diagnosis and classification" in *Companion to psychiatric studies*, *supra*, p.448.
77   M. Lader and R. Herrington, *Biological treatments in psychiatry, supra*, p.201.

occasionally be long-term effects. Toxic interactions have been reported between lithium and antipsychotic drugs such as haloperidol and thioridazine. Lithium toxicity is characterised by diarrhoea, vomiting, increased tremor, dysarthria (**1078**), drowsiness, and ataxia (**1063**) and in the most severe cases by restlessness, confusion, nystagmus, fits, delirium and eventually death.[78]

Combining lithium with other drugs

Haloperidol is commonly combined with lithium, the former providing immediate control of symptoms while the effects of lithium build up to the point where the antipsychotic medication can be withdrawn.[79] However, according to Kendell, there is no evidence that lithium and haloperidol are more effective in the control of severe mania than haloperidol alone. Furthermore, "there are reports of patients developing an acute brain syndrome, followed in some cases by lasting extrapyramidal and cognitive deficits, on large doses of the two drugs together."[80]

CARBAMAZEPINE

In cases of resistant mania or bipolar affective disorder, carbamazepine (CBZ) is sometimes used instead of, or in conjunction with, lithium. It may also be used as a prophylactic although one study showed that while lithium doubled the mean time in remission, carbamazepine only increased it by 50 per cent.[81] Because it may depress the white cell count, regular checks on this are necessary, particularly early on during treatment. The drug is available as Carbamazepine (tablets), Tegretol (tablets, liquid, suppositories), and Tegretol Retard (tablets). The BNF guideline dose is 400mg initially, increased until the symptoms are controlled, with a usual range of 400–600mg daily and a maximum of 1600mg. Common adverse effects include mild leukopenia, nausea and vomiting. Carbamazepine decreases blood levels of haloperidol and tricyclic antidepressants and suppresses circulating levels of T_3 and T_4 (**1298**).

CALCIUM CHANNEL BLOCKERS

Calcium channel blockers such as verapamil and nifedipine, which are usually prescribed for heart conditions such as angina, have also been used to treat mania and they may act by blocking serotonin receptors.

ELECTROCONVULSIVE THERAPY (ECT)

ECT has a role for patients with severe manic illnesses which do not respond to medication (**1132**). One recent trial demonstrated that bilateral ECT given three times a week was more effective than lithium.[82]

---

[78] M. Lader and R. Herrington, *Biological treatments in psychiatry* (Oxford Medical Publications, 2nd ed., 1990), p.208.

[79] J. Biederman, *et al.*, "Combination of lithium carbonate and haloperidol in schizo-affective disorder" *Archives of General Psychiatry* (1979) 36, 327–333; M. Lader and R. Herrington, *Biological treatments in psychiatry, supra*, p.203.

[80] R.E. Kendell, "Diagnosis and classification" in *Companion to psychiatric studies* (ed. R.E. Kendell & A.K. Zealley, Churchill Livingstone, 1993), pp.448–449.

[81] S.E. Watkins, *et al.*, "The effect of carbamazepine and lithium on remission from affective illness" *British Journal of Psychiatry* (1987) 150, 180–182; M. Lader and R. Herrington, *Biological treatments in psychiatry* (Oxford Medical Publications, 2nd ed., 1990), p.210.

[82] J.G. Small, *et al.*," Electroconvulsive treatment compared with lithium in the management of manic states" *Archives of General Psychiatry* (1988) 45, 727–732.

23. Schizophrenia and related psychoses

INTRODUCTION

The majority of people detained under the Mental Health Act 1983 are diagnosed as suffering from a form of mental illness known as schizophrenia. Schizophrenia is commonly thought of as a psychiatric term for a range of experiences which the majority of the population describe as "madness." For this reason, to be diagnosed as having schizophrenia carries a stigma which other diagnoses do not. Beyond the public perception, what schizophrenia is is difficult to define. Innumerable definitions and models have been suggested but it is impossible to point to any single defining pathology, symptom or cluster of symptoms, common to all people so diagnosed. It is therefore important to realise at the outset that schizophrenia is a model, an organisational concept the purpose of which is to make it easier to comprehend the variegated phenomena of illness than it would otherwise be.[1] Whether the various presentations collectively classified as forms of schizophrenia do indeed share a particular unifying pathology, and are homogenous at some fundamental level, or instead represent several different kinds of illness or disease process, has still to be established. For the moment, the description of schizophrenia given in the International Classification of Diseases gives an idea of the broad range of experiences associated with the diagnosis[2] —

> "The schizophrenic disorders are characterised in general by fundamental and characteristic distortions of thinking and perception, and by inappropriate or blunted affect ... The most intimate thoughts, feelings, and acts are often felt to be known to or shared by others, and explanatory delusions may develop, to the effect that natural or supernatural forces are at work to influence the afflicted individual's thoughts and actions in ways that are often bizarre. The individual may see himself or herself as the pivot of all that happens. Hallucinations, especially auditory, are common and may comment on the individual's behaviour or thoughts ... Perplexity is also common early on and frequently leads to a belief that everyday situations possess a special, usually sinister, meaning intended uniquely for the individual. In the characteristic schizophrenic disturbance of thinking ... thinking becomes vague, elliptical, and obscure, and its expression in speech sometimes incomprehensible. Breaks and interpolations in the train of thought are frequent, and thoughts may seem to be withdrawn by some outside agency. Mood is characteristically shallow, capricious, or incongruous. Ambivalence and disturbance of volition may appear as inertia, negativism, or stupor. Catatonia may be present."

---

[1] R.E. Kendell, "Diagnosis and classification" in *Companion to psychiatric studies* (ed. R.E. Kendell & A.K. Zealley, Churchill Livingstone, 1993), p.278. Janzarik once described the history of schizophrenia as a history not of medical discoveries but of intellectual models on which the orientation of psychiatry is based.

[2] *Classification of Mental and Behavioural Disorders, Tenth Revision (ICD–10): Clinical descriptions and diagnostic guidelines* (World Health Organisation, 1992), pp.86–87.

ASSESSMENT, DIAGNOSIS AND CLASSIFICATION

When a patient is examined prior to admission, or immediately following admission, the first task is to establish the kind of disorder (if any) which is troubling him or others so that, having identified it, conclusions can be reached about its causes, probable course and treatment. Assessment is the process of collecting information relevant to the diagnosis, management, and treatment of a patient's clinical condition; including, therefore, this process of distinguishing the presence of a particular syndrome, such as schizophrenia, from the existence of a characteristic pattern of symptoms. A diagnosis is a "short-hand way of describing what is wrong with the patient"[3] and it involves assigning the patient's case to a predesignated diagnostic class according to a reliable medical classification of abnormal mental phenomena.

International Classification of Mental Disorders (ICD–10)

The classification of mental disorders in official usage in England and Wales is the World Health Organisation's International Classification of Diseases, now in its tenth revision (ICD–10); and, more particularly, that part of it dealing with mental and behavioural disorders. One section or "block" of the classification is concerned with schizophrenia and similar disorders (Block F20–F29). Within this block, each type and sub-type of mental disorder is separately listed and coded. Schizophrenia is given the code F20, and a further digit is used to record various sub-types such as paranoid schizophrenia (F20.0) and catatonic schizophrenia (F20.2). Inevitably, the classification involves "compromises between scientists with the most influential theories and the practice of senior clinicians at national and international level."[4]

Operational definitions (diagnostic guidelines)

Every symptom seen in cases of schizophrenia may also be present in some other type of mental disorder. For example, symptoms such as elation, flight of ideas and grandiose ideas are quite common in both schizophrenia and mania. Operational definitions (diagnostic guidelines or criteria) are used to specify which combinations of symptoms are adequate to substantiate a diagnosis. They define what a clinician means when he uses the term "schizophrenia" and represent an attempt to standardise clinical practice and understanding.

Other classifications

The ICD–10 classification, and the diagnostic guidelines which form part of it, are but one of many medical classifications of mental disorder. Over the past quarter of a century there has been a multiplication of diagnostic criteria, reflecting the many different ideas held by psychiatrists about schizophrenia. At least 20 have been published since 1972.[5] Kendell notes that the co-existence of alternative definitions at least serves the purpose of being a reminder that all definitions are arbitrary. None of the competing definitions can be said to be right or wrong since there is as yet no external criterion of validity. It is impossible to decide which is the most valid because this would involve determining which of several different ways of defining the syndrome of schizophrenia most accurately picks out patients possessing an

---

[3] J.M. Pfeffer and G. Waldron, *Psychiatric Differential Diagnoses* (Churchill Livingstone, 1987), p.4.

[4] J.K. Wing, "Differential diagnosis of schizophrenia" in *Schizophrenia — An overview and practical handbook* (ed. D.J. Kavanagh, Chapman & Hall, 1992), p.17.

[5] C. Thompson, *The Instruments of Psychiatric Research* (John Wiley & Sons, 1989), p.4.

underlying abnormality which has yet to be identified.[6] Although a core of typical patients meet all definitions, there are significant differences in the populations of patients covered by each of them. Each operational definition generates different values for the incidence of a disorder, its heritability, its responsiveness to therapeutic agents, and its prognosis. Various studies have demonstrated poor agreement between clinicians about who merited the diagnosis[7] and the concordance between the different sets of operational criteria for schizophrenia is "not impressive; in other words the different criteria tend to diagnose different people as schizophrenic."[8] Similarly, statistical techniques have not yielded convincing evidence either of a naturally occurring group of correlated psychotic traits or of discrete groups of individuals who share a common set of schizophrenic symptoms.[9] It is therefore important to realise that a patient who meets the very inclusive criteria for a diagnosis of schizophrenia in the ICD–10 classification may not satisfy the more tightly-drawn operational criteria of another classification. It is also the case that a considerable minority of apparently well-adjusted people have reported schizophrenic-like experiences and behaviour.[10]

SYMPTOMS AND SIGNS

The idea that schizophrenia is a distinct type of disease carries with it an expectation that certain characteristic symptoms or symptom-patterns will be found in the vast majority of patients diagnosed as having the condition. These symptoms will fit together in some fashion because of the common underlying disease process. However, the symptoms of people diagnosed as having the condition do not conjoin in this fashion whatever operational definition is used: "disjunction is its essence and any one symptom is capable of replacing another in the descriptive term 'schizophrenia.'"[11] No symptom has been found to be "pathognomonic"; that is, there is no symptom the existence of which establishes the diagnosis.

[6]   R.E. Kendell, "Schizophrenia: A Medical View of a Medical Concept" in *What is Schizophrenia?* (ed. W.F. Flack, *et al.*, Springer-Verlag, 1990), p.63.

[7]   R.P. Bentall, "The classification of schizophrenia" in *Schizophrenia — An overview and practical handbook* (ed. D.J. Kavanagh, Chapman & Hall, 1992), p.24; K. Blashfield, *The Classification of Psychopathology: Neo-Kraepelinian and Quantitative Approaches* (Plenum, 1984).

[8]   R.P. Bentall, "The classification of schizophrenia," *supra*, p.25; I.F. Brockington, *et al.*, "Definitions of schizophrenia: Concordance and prediction of outcome" *Psychological Medicine* (1978) 8, 399–412.

[9]   R.P. Bentall, "The classification of schizophrenia," *supra*, p.25; K. Blashfield, *The Classification of Psychopathology: Neo-Kraepelinian and Quantitative Approaches, supra*; P.D. Slade and R. Cooper, "Some conceptual difficulties with the term 'schizophrenia': an alternative model" Brit. J. Soc. Clin. Psychol. (1979) 18, 309–317; B.S. Everitt, *et al.*, "An attempt at validation of traditional psychiatric symptoms by cluster analysis" *British Journal of Psychiatry* (1971) 119, 399–342; R.E. Kendell and J.A. Gourlay, "The clinical distinction between the affective psychoses and schizophrenia" *British Journal of Psychiatry* (1970) 117, 261–266; I.F. Brockington and R.S. Wainwright, "Depressed patients with schizophrenic or paranoid symptoms" *Psychological Medicine* (1980) 10, 665–675; R.E. Kendell and I.F. Brockington, "The identification of disease entities and the relationship between schizophrenic and affective psychoses" *British Journal of Psychiatry* (1980) 137, 324–331. Bentall summarises the position by stating that, taken together, the studies cast doubt on the existence of a unique schizophrenia syndrome.

[10]   The relevant studies are referred to by Bentall in R.P. Bentall, "The classification of schizophrenia," *supra*, p.32.

[11]   "... One is left with the hope that a lesion in the brain will either be discerned or excluded. It seems that only if disease is validated by such discernment can we hope to appreciate the linkages within the variety of symptoms, and the distinctions between those symptoms, that are pathognomonic of the disorder and those that are pathoplastic to the individual and his situation." P.R. McHugh, "Schizophrenia and the Disease Model" in *What is Schizophrenia?* (ed. W.F. Flack, *et al.*, Springer-Verlag, 1990), p.77.

The form and content of the experience

Jung once noted that "in our dreams we are all schizophrenic" by which he meant that just as the symbolism of dreams is not random and meaningless so the perceptions and ideas of persons with that diagnosis are pointers to the root conflict which the mental illness addresses. A carefully taken history often reveals the nature of this conflict between the individual and his environment and why it became so intense that the impasse could seemingly only be resolved by acquiescence and self-destruction or by some reconstruction of beliefs and perceptions capable of bridging the chasm between objective reality and subjective need. Listening to a client's views offers the professional a window through which he can perceive, if at times only dimly, the individual's predicament and the constellation of internal conflicts which have given rise to the symptoms. However, while such an approach is essential if progress is to be made, it is nevertheless only part of the picture, and psychiatry traditionally distinguishes between the content of a person's subjective experiences and their form. Thus, Kendell writes that the content of an idea may "be meaningful and understandable. But it is even more significant that the idea is a delusion, and not merely an overvalued idea; that the hallucination is occurring in a setting in which other people do not experience false perceptions; and that the patient's difficulty in expressing himself coherently is not explicable in terms of limited vocabulary or education, or emotional arousal."[12]

Front-rank symptoms

Certain symptoms are sometimes referred to as "front-rank" symptoms because of the diagnostic significance attributed to them by Schneider.

SCHNEIDER'S FRONT-RANK SYMPTOMS

Front-rank symptoms	*Second-rank symptoms*
• Audible thoughts	• Other disorders of perception
• Voices arguing or discussing or both	• Sudden delusional ideas
• Voices commenting	• Perplexity
• Somatic passivity experiences	• Depressive and euphoric mood changes
• Thought withdrawal and other experiences of influenced thought	• Feelings of emotional impoverishment
• Thought broadcasting	• Various others
• Delusional perceptions	
• All other experiences involving volition, made affects, and made impulses	

---

[12]   R.E. Kendell, "Schizophrenia: A Medical View of a Medical Concept" in *What is Schizophrenia?* (ed. W.F. Flack, *et al.*, Springer-Verlag, 1990), p.69.

Positive and negative symptoms

A further distinction which is often made is to describe certain symptoms of schizophrenia as being positive or negative. Positive symptoms are those which appear to reflect an excess or distortion of normal functions, whereas negative symptoms reflect a diminution or loss of normal functions and are mainly behavioural.[13] Positive symptoms include distortions or exaggerations of inferential thinking (delusions), perception (hallucinations), language and communication (disorganised speech).[14] They are most clearly recognised when an articulate patient is describing his inner experiences.[15] Negative symptoms consist of restrictions in the range and intensity of emotional expression (emotional blunting/affective flattening), in the fluency and productivity of thought and speech, and in the initiation of goal-directed behaviour. Conversation is restricted, speech and movement are slow. There is a lack of motivation and initiative, a loss of interest in the patient's immediate environment and the wider world, and a withdrawal from social contacts.[16] Social withdrawal may lead to a worsening of positive as well as negative symptoms. Patients commonly report that their auditory hallucinations recede when they are engaged in workshop activities[17] and they occur less frequently when the person is in the presence of an interviewer than when alone.[18] The picture is seen in a wide range of psychiatric conditions, including dementia and mood disorders, and is well-known to neurologists.[19] Patients who are discharged from hospital free of positive symptoms often retain negative symptoms for between one and two years after discharge.[20]

Negative symptoms and institutionalism

It is unclear to what extent negative symptoms are induced by a deprived social environment, as opposed to being an integral part of the schizophrenic process.[21] Wing and Brown demonstrated wide variations between three psychiatric hospitals in the amount of activity provided for patients and commensurate differences in the prevalence of negative symptoms.[22]

Negative symptoms the natural consequence of positive symptoms

Care must be taken to distinguish between true emotional indifference about one's situation and mere indifference about communicating one's ideas and feelings to

[13] *Diagnostic and Statistical Manual of Mental Disorders, Fourth Revision (DSM–IV)* (American Psychiatric Association, 1994), p.274.

[14] *Ibid.*, pp.274–275.

[15] J.K. Wing, "Differential diagnosis of schizophrenia" in *Schizophrenia — An overview and practical handbook* (ed. D.J. Kavanagh, Chapman & Hall, 1992), p.9.

[16] *Diagnostic and Statistical Manual of Mental Disorders, Fourth Revision (DSM–IV), supra*, p.275; J. Leff, "Schizophrenia: social influences on onset and relapse" in *Community Psychiatry: The Principles* (ed. D.H. Bennett and H.L. Freeman, Churchill Livingstone, 1991), p.208.

[17] *Ibid.*, p.210.

[18] 9 per cent. of the time, compared with 55 per cent., according to Cooklin. See R. Cooklin, *et al.*, "The relationship between auditory hallucinations and spontaneous fluctuations of skin conductance in schizophrenia" *British Journal of Psychiatry* (1983) 142, 47–52. The observation is important in the context of tribunal hearings because some patients may appear to be free of such phenomena when their attention is engaged at the hearing or when interviewed prior to the hearing.

[19] J.K. Wing, "Differential diagnosis of schizophrenia" in *Schizophrenia — An overview and practical handbook* (ed. D.J. Kavanagh, Chapman & Hall, 1992), p.6.

[20] J. Leff, "Schizophrenia: social influences on onset and relapse" in *Community Psychiatry: The Principles* (ed. D.H. Bennett & H.L. Freeman, Churchill Livingstone, 1991), p.209.

[21] *Ibid.*

[22] J.K. Wing and G.W. Brown, *Institutionalism and schizophrenia* (Cambridge University Press, 1970).

others. Prolonged failure to establish any rapport with others about experiences which dominate a person's life inevitably leads eventually to a withdrawal from further social contact with them. Communication becomes futile and emotionally unrewarding, so that the patient's withdrawal is the natural final consequence of his long-standing positive symptoms, such as hallucinations and delusions.

Measuring the severity of symptoms

The severity of a symptom can be rated on a number of different criteria, such as frequency, intensity, duration or degree of incapacitation or tolerability.[23] Various rating scales, such as the Present State Examination (PSE), are commonly used to assess schizophrenic phenomena.

ICD–10 DIAGNOSTIC GUIDELINES FOR SCHIZOPHRENIA

The ICD–10 classification divides symptoms of special diagnostic importance into nine groups of symptoms which often occur together. The table on page 1234 lists these symptom groups with an explanation of the meaning of medical terms.[24] It will be seen that where one "very clear" symptom from a certain number of first-rank symptoms has endured for a period of one month or more then its presence alone establishes the diagnosis. Thus, while acknowledging that "no strictly pathognomonic symptoms can be identified," the classification nevertheless comes close to establishing them.

SYMPTOMS OF LESS THAN ONE MONTH'S DURATION

One of the diagnostic guidelines for schizophrenia is that the symptoms listed in the table have been present for a minimum period of one month. However, some people become acutely psychotic without any obvious organic cause for this, such as dementia, delirium, or intoxication by drugs or alcohol. Acute onset is defined as a change during a period of a fortnight or less from a state without psychotic features to an obviously abnormal psychotic state. Such psychotic states may prove transient or persist for a month or longer and the presentation may include schizophrenia-type symptoms. If the psychotic symptoms are comparatively stable and fulfil the criteria for schizophrenia but have lasted for less than one month, the diagnosis made is that of an "acute schizophrenia-like psychotic disorder (F23.2)." If the schizophrenic symptoms then persist for more than one month, the diagnosis is changed to schizophrenia.[25]

Highly variable and changeable mental state

Acute polymorphic psychotic disorders are a further type of acute psychotic episode. "Polymorphic" means "having many forms", and these disorders are characterised

---

23 See R. Manchanda, *et al.*, "A Review of rating scales for measuring symptom changes in schizophrenia research" in *The Instruments of Psychiatric Research* (ed. C. Thompson, John Wiley & Sons., 1989), p.61.

24 More detailed explanations of some of the terms will be found in chapter 18.

25 *Classification of Mental and Behavioural Disorders, Tenth Revision (ICD–10): Clinical descriptions and diagnostic guidelines* (World Health Organisation, 1992), p.103.

by their rapidly changing and variable state. Several types of hallucinations, delusions, and perceptual disturbances are obvious but markedly variable, changing from day to day or from hour to hour. The patient's emotional state is similarly changeable, and perplexity, preoccupation, and inattention are often present. There is usually an abrupt onset (within 48 hours) followed by a rapid resolution of symptoms. If symptoms fulfilling the criteria for schizophrenia have been present for the majority of the time since an obviously psychotic state developed, and these then persist for more than one month, the diagnosis is changed to schizophrenia.[26]

Outcome of acute psychotic episodes

There is some evidence that acute onset is associated with a good outcome, and it may be that the more abrupt the onset, the better the outcome. Abrupt onset is defined as within 48 hours or less. Complete recovery usually occurs within two to three months, often within a few weeks or even days, and only a small proportion of patients with these disorders develop persistent and disabling states.[27]

BORDERLINE AND MIXED MENTAL STATES

In practice, many patients do not conform to stereotypes and the diagnosis is not always clear cut. Some borderline states may be suggestive of a schizophrenic-type process but no more than that. Other patients may have some features indicative of a personality or mood disorder but also some symptoms commonly found in schizophrenia. Following an explanation of the diagnostic guidelines for schizophrenia and its three historical sub-types (**1239**), the following topics are therefore briefly considered —

- schizophrenia and personality disorders (**1243**)

- schizophrenia and borderline states (**1244**)

- schizophrenia and mood disorders (**1247**)

Summary

- A diagnosis of schizophrenia may be appropriate if a certain symptom or symptoms have been present for one month or more.

- In acute cases where the symptoms have not endured for that period, a diagnosis of acute schizophrenia-like psychotic disorder is made or, if the patient's mental state is highly variable and changeable, one of acute polymorphic psychotic disorder.

- In borderline cases, consideration must be given to whether the patient's disorder represents a disorder of the personality and or an amalgam of schizophrenia and a mood disorder.

---

[26] *Classification of Mental and Behavioural Disorders, Tenth Revision (ICD–10): Clinical descriptions and diagnostic guidelines* (World Health Organisation, 1992), pp.101–102.

[27] *Ibid.*, pp.99–100.

SCHIZOPHRENIA (ICD–10 DIAGNOSTIC GUIDELINES)

- The normal requirement is that a minimum of one very clear symptom (and usually two or more if less clear-cut) belonging to any of the groups (a) to (d) below, or symptoms from at least two of the groups referred to as (e) to (h), should have been clearly present for most of the time during a period of one month or more.

- Conditions meeting these symptomatic requirements but of a duration less than one month (whether treated or not) should initially be diagnosed as acute schizophrenic-like psychotic disorder (**1232**) and reclassified as schizophrenia if the symptoms persist for longer periods. The one-month duration criterion applies only to the specified symptoms and not to any prodromal non-psychotic phase.

- Schizophrenia should not be diagnosed in the presence of overt brain disease or during states of drug intoxication or withdrawal.

- The diagnosis of schizophrenia should not be made in the presence of extensive depressive or manic symptoms unless it is clear that schizophrenic symptoms antedated the affective disturbance.

SYMPTOMS WHICH IF CLEAR-CUT MAY ALONE ESTABLISH THE DIAGNOSIS

(a) *thought echo, thought insertion or withdrawal, and thought broadcasting;*

The individual's thoughts are being repeated or echoed, but not spoken aloud, within his head (*thought echo*) or they are being broadcast to the outside world (*thought broadcasting*). Some other person, persons or outside forces are placing thoughts in his mind (*thought insertion*) or withdrawing his thoughts from his mind (*thought withdrawal*).

(b) *delusions of control, influence or passivity, clearly referred to body or limb movements or specific thoughts, actions, or sensations; delusional perception;*

The individual believes that his feelings, impulses, thoughts, sensations, actions or bodily movements are being controlled or influenced by some other person, persons or outside forces (*delusions of influence or control*). He is the passive object of these active outside influences (*passivity phenomena*).

(c) *hallucinatory voices giving a running commentary on the patient's behaviour, or discussing the patient among themselves, or other types of hallucinatory voices coming from some part of the body;*

The individual hears imaginary voices commenting on his behaviour or discussing him or hears voices which seem to emanate from somewhere within his body.

The individual holds some belief which is bizarre, not true to fact, cannot be corrected by an appeal to reason, and is out of harmony with his educational or cultural background (a delusion). The central theme may, *inter alia*, be some absurd exaggeration of his own importance, power, knowledge, or identity (*grandiose delusion*); a belief that events and the actions of others refer to him in some special way, *e.g.* a belief that programmes on the radio are being broadcast to him especially (*delusion of reference*); a belief that he or someone else is being attacked, harassed, cheated, persecuted, or conspired against (*persecutory/paranoid delusion*); or relate to the way his body functions, *e.g.* a false belief that one is pregnant despite being post-menopausal (*somatic delusion*). Delusional beliefs may be fleeting, changeable and unconnected with each other (*unsystematised*) or form part of a logical fixed system of such beliefs (*systematised*).

(d) *persistent delusions of other kinds that are culturally inappropriate and completely impossible, such as religious or political identity, or superhuman powers and abilities (e.g. being able to control the weather, or being in communication with aliens from another world)*

OTHER SYMPTOMS

The individual experiences a sensory perception in the absence of any external stimulation of the relevant sensory organ (hallucination). The hallucination may relate to sounds or voices (*auditory hallucination*); sight (*visual hallucination*); taste (*gustatory hallucination*); smell (*olfactory hallucination*); touch (*tactile/haptic hallucination*), or to the perception of a physical experience within the body (*somatic hallucination*), such as the muscles or joints (*kinaesthetic hallucination*) or an internal organ (*visceral hallucination*). An overvalued idea is an irrational belief or idea which is not as firmly held as a delusion.

(e) *persistent hallucinations in any modality, when accompanied either by fleeting or half-formed delusions without clear affective content, or by persistent over-valued ideas, or when occurring every day for weeks or months on end*

The patient's stream of thought, and therefore speech, suddenly stops and he is unable to account for this stoppage (thought blocking). He may invent new words (neologisms), which have a known meaning for him and are often an amalgam of real words, *e.g.* "bancid" = "bad" and "rancid." Where the association between successive thoughts is disturbed and successive sentences or topics are only obliquely related (*loosening of associations*), speech becomes inexact, vague, diffused or unfocused. In severe cases, there may be a lack of logical or meaningful connection between words, phrases, or sentences (*incoherence*).

(f) *breaks or interpolations in the train of thought, resulting in incoherence or irrelevant speech, or neologisms*

(g) *catatonic behaviour, such as excitement, posturing, or waxy flexibility, negativism, mutism, and stupor*

The patient may voluntarily assume some inappropriate or bizarre posture, often held for a long period of time, during which neither expression nor bodily position changes (*catatonic posturing*). The muscles of the limbs may be maintained in a semi-rigid position and can be moulded into any position by an examiner, as if made of pliable wax (*catatonic waxy flexibility*). Although conscious, the individual may not respond to external stimuli (*catatonic stupor*) or resist all instructions or attempts to be moved, perhaps doing the opposite of what is asked (*catatonic negativism*). He may be mute. In other cases, there is excited and apparently purposeless motor activity not influenced by external stimuli (*catatonic excitement*).

(h) *"negative" symptoms such as marked apathy, paucity of speech, and blunting or incongruity of emotional responses, usually resulting in social withdrawal and lowering of social performance; it must be clear that these are not due to depression or to neuroleptic medication*

Certain symptoms of schizophrenia are sometimes distinguished as being positive or negative. Positive symptoms (such as delusions, hallucinations and disorganised speech) are said to reflect an excess or distortion of normal functions. In contrast, negative symptoms (such as low motivation, lack of initiative, loss of interest, social withdrawal, restricted fluency and productivity of thought and speech, and blunting of affect) appear to reflect a diminution or loss of normal functions. There may be a lack of feeling, emotion, interest or concern (*apathy*) and limited use of speech (*paucity of speech*). Emotional responses may be incongruous.

(i) *a significant and consistent change in the overall quality of some aspects of personal behaviour, manifest as loss of interest, aimlessness, idleness, a self-absorbed attitude, and social withdrawal.*

This category overlaps considerably with that immediately above. A preoccupation with one's own, often overbearing, internal experiences or fantasies will generally lead to a corresponding lack of engagement with the outside world.

Source: Classification of Mental and Behavioural Disorders, Tenth Revision (ICD-10): Clinical descriptions and diagnostic guidelines (World Health Organisation, 1992), pp. 87–88.

THE SUB-TYPES OF SCHIZOPHRENIA

Kraepelin recognised three main sub-types of schizophrenia: catatonic, hebephrenic and paranoid.[28] Paranoid schizophrenia aside, the sub-types have been found to be unstable and heterogeneous over time both with respect to symptom content and outcome. In other words, the persons assigned to each of the three categories show a marked variability both in terms of their symptoms and outcomes.[29] The sub-types of schizophrenia recognised in the ICD–10 classification are listed and described below. Brief notes then follow on the three main sub-types: paranoid, hebephrenic and catatonic schizophrenia. Residual schizophrenia is referred to later in the section on the course and outcome of schizophrenic disorders (**1252**); simple schizophrenia, schizoid personality disorder, and schizotypal disorder in the section on personality and schizophrenia (**1244**); and post-schizophrenic depression in the section on mood and schizophrenia (**1248**).

Schizophrenia : Main sub-types (ICD-10)

F20.6	*Simple Schizophrenia*	A disorder in which there is an insidious but progressive development of oddities of conduct, inability to meet the demands of society, and decline in total performance. The characteristic negative features of residual schizophrenia develop without being preceded by overt psychotic symptoms.
F20.0	*Paranoid Schizophrenia*	Paranoid schizophrenia is dominated by relatively stable, often paranoid delusions, usually accompanied by hallucinations, particularly of the auditory variety, and perceptual disturbances. Disturbances of affect, volition and speech, and catatonic symptoms, are absent or relatively inconspicuous.
F20.1	*Hebephrenic Schizophrenia*	A form of schizophrenia in which affective changes are prominent, delusions and hallucinations fleeting and fragmentary, behaviour irresponsible and unpredictable, and mannerisms common. The mood is shallow and inappropriate, thought is disorganised, and speech is incoherent. There is a tendency to social isolation. Hebephrenia should normally be diagnosed only in adolescents or young adults.

---

28   E. Kraepelin, *Textbook of Psychiatry* (MacMillan, 1907).
29   K.S. Kendler, *et al.*, "Sub-type stability in schizophrenia" *American Journal of Psychiatry* (1985) 142, 827–832; R.E. Kendell, *et al.*, *Prognostic implications of six different definitions of schizophrenia* Arch. Gen. Psych. (1979) 36, 25–31.

F20.2	*Catatonic Schizophrenia*	Catatonic schizophrenia is dominated by prominent psychomotor disturbances that may alternate between extremes such as hyperkinesis and stupor, or automatic obedience and negativism. Constrained attitudes and postures may be maintained for long periods. Episodes of violent excitement may be a striking feature.
F20.5	*Residual Schizophrenia*	A chronic stage in the development of a schizophrenic illness in which there has been a clear progression from an early stage to a later stage characterised by long-term, though not necessarily irreversible, "negative" symptoms, *e.g.* psychomotor slowing; underactivity; blunting of affect; passivity and lack of initiative; poverty of quantity or content of speech; poor non-verbal communication by facial expression, eye contact, and posture; poor self-care and social performance.
F20.4	*Post-Schizophrenic Depression*	A depressive episode, which may be prolonged, arising in the aftermath of a schizophrenic illness. Some schizophrenic symptoms, either "positive" or "negative," must still be present but no longer dominate the clinical picture. These depressive states are associated with an increased risk of suicide.

Disorders resembling or possibly associated with schizophrenia

F21	*Schizotypal disorder*	A disorder characterised by eccentric behaviour and anomalies of thinking and affect which resemble those seen in schizophrenia, though no definite and characteristic schizophrenic anomalies occur at any stage.
F60.1	*Schizoid personality disorder*	A personality disorder characterised by emotional coldness and detachment; limited capacity to express warmth; preference for solitary activities; excessive preoccupation with fantasy and introspection; lack of confiding relationships; marked insensitivity to prevailing social norms and conventions.

PARANOID SCHIZOPHRENIA (F20.0)

Paranoid schizophrenia is the sub-type of schizophrenia most commonly encountered in tribunal proceedings. According to Kraepelin, paranoid schizophrenia is characterised by suspiciousness and well-organised delusions, usually of persecutory or grandiose content.[30]

Clinical picture

The ICD–10 classification describes the clinical picture as dominated by relatively stable, often paranoid, delusions, usually accompanied by hallucinations, particularly of the auditory variety, and perceptual disturbances. Disturbances of affect, volition, and speech, and catatonic symptoms, are not prominent. Thought disorder may be obvious in acute states but does not prevent the typical delusions or hallucinations from being described clearly. Mood disturbances such as irritability, sudden anger, fearfulness, and suspicion are common.[31] Examples of the most common paranoid symptoms are:

- delusions of persecution, reference, exalted birth, special mission, bodily change, or jealousy;

- hallucinatory voices that threaten the patient or give commands, or auditory hallucinations without verbal form, such as whistling, humming, or laughing;

- hallucinations of smell or taste, or of sexual or other bodily sensations; visual hallucinations may occur but are rarely predominant.[32]

Onset and course

The onset tends to be later than in the hebephrenic and catatonic forms.[33] The course of paranoid schizophrenia may be episodic, with partial or complete remissions, or chronic. In chronic cases, the florid symptoms persist over years and it is difficult to distinguish discrete episodes.

Diagnostic guidelines

The diagnostic guidelines are as follows —

- The general criteria for a diagnosis of schizophrenia must be satisfied (1234).

- In addition, hallucinations and/or delusions must be prominent, and disturbances of affect, volition and speech, and catatonic symptoms must be relatively inconspicuous.

---

[30] R.P. Bentall, The classification of schizophrenia" in *Schizophrenia — An overview and practical handbook* (ed. D.J. Kavanagh, Chapman & Hall, 1992), p.29.

[31] *Classification of Mental and Behavioural Disorders, Tenth Revision (ICD–10): Clinical descriptions and diagnostic guidelines* (World Health Organisation, 1992), pp.89–90.

[32] *Ibid.*, p.89.

[33] *Ibid.*, pp.89–90.

- The hallucinations will usually be delusions of control, influence or passivity, clearly referred to body or limb movements or specific thoughts, actions, or sensations; delusional perception; hallucinatory voices giving a running commentary on the patient's behaviour, or discussing the patient among themselves, or other types of hallucinatory voices coming from some part of the body.

- Delusions can be of almost any kind but delusions of control, influence, or passivity, and persecutory beliefs of various kinds are the most characteristic.[34]

- It is important to exclude epileptic and drug-induced psychoses, and to remember that persecutory delusions might carry little diagnostic weight in people from certain countries or cultures.[35]

Delusional disorders (F22.0)

Paranoid schizophrenia is distinguished from paranoid personality disorder (**1185**) and also from paranoid delusional disorders. Delusional disorders are characterised by the development of a single delusion or set of related delusions which are usually persistent and sometimes lifelong. The delusions are often persecutory, hypochondriacal, or grandiose. They may be concerned with litigation or jealousy or a belief that other people think the individual smells or is homosexual. The content of the delusion, and the timing of its emergence, can often be related to the individual's life situation. Onset is commonly in middle age. Depressive symptoms may be present intermittently, and olfactory and tactile hallucinations may develop in some cases. Clear and persistent auditory hallucinations, schizophrenic symptoms such as delusions of control and marked blunting of affect, and definite evidence of brain disease, are all incompatible with the diagnosis. The diagnostic guidelines specify that the delusions must constitute the only or most conspicuous clinical characteristic, have been present for at least three months, and clearly be personal rather than sub-cultural.[36] When the central delusion has a persecutory theme, the disorder is sometimes referred to as paranoia, paranoid psychosis, or a paranoid state. If a paranoid delusional disorder develops in old age, sometimes following loss or deterioration of hearing or eyesight, the term paraphrenia may be used. If paranoid delusions are accompanied by symptoms satisfying the criteria for a diagnosis of schizophrenia, the diagnosis will be one of paranoid schizophrenia (**1239**).

HEBEPHRENIC SCHIZOPHRENIA (F20.1)

According to Kraepelin, hebephrenic schizophrenia was characterised by over-scrupulousness about trivial matters, emotional indifference, laughing and immature speech. Although Schneider did not consider that the condition represented a distinct sub-type, recent research indicates a move backwards to regarding hebephrenia with its preponderantly negative symptoms as a separate disorder.[37]

---

[34] *Classification of Mental and Behavioural Disorders, Tenth Revision (ICD–10): Clinical descriptions and diagnostic guidelines* (World Health Organisation, 1992), p.90.

[35] *Ibid.*

[36] *Ibid.*, pp.97–98.

[37] See R.P. Bentall, The classification of schizophrenia" in *Schizophrenia — An overview and practical handbook* (ed. D.J. Kavanagh, Chapman & Hall, 1992), p.29.

Clinical picture

The ICD–10 classification describes hebephrenic schizophrenia as "a form of schizophrenia in which affective changes are prominent, delusions and hallucinations fleeting and fragmentary, behaviour irresponsible and unpredictable, and mannerisms common. The disturbances of affect, volition, and thought disorder are usually prominent but, when present, not hallucinations and delusions. The mood is shallow and inappropriate and often accompanied by giggling or self-satisfied, self-absorbed smiling, or by a lofty manner, grimaces, mannerisms, pranks, hypochondriacal complaints, and reiterated phrases. Thought is disorganised and speech rambling and incoherent. A superficial and manneristic preoccupation with religion, philosophy, and other abstract themes may add to the listener's difficulty in following the train of thought. There is a tendency to remain solitary and behaviour seems empty of purpose and feeling.[38]

Onset and course

The form of schizophrenia usually starts between the ages of 15 and 25 years. Hebephrenic schizophrenia tends to have a poor prognosis because of the rapid development of negative symptoms, particularly flattening of affect and loss of volition. Drive and determination are lost and goals abandoned, so that the patient's behaviour becomes characteristically aimless and empty of purpose.[39]

Diagnostic guidelines

The diagnostic guidelines are as follows—

- The general criteria for a diagnosis of schizophrenia (**1234**) must be satisfied.

- Hebephrenia should normally be diagnosed for the first time only in adolescents or young adults.

- The premorbid personality is characteristically, but not necessarily, rather shy and solitary.

- For a confident diagnosis of hebephrenia, a period of two or three months of continuous observation is usually necessary, in order to ensure that the characteristic behaviour is sustained.[40]

CATATONIC SCHIZOPHRENIA (F20.2)

In 1874, Kahlbaum described catatonia as a severe motor disorder consisting of strange attitudes, odd movements and postures, together with stupor and mental deterioration. According to Kraepelin, who believed that some cases of catatonia represented a distinct sub-type of the condition now known as schizophrenia, catatonic schizophrenia is characterised by pronounced motor symptoms and swings from stupor to extreme excitement.

---

[38]   *Classification of Mental and Behavioural Disorders, Tenth Revision (ICD–10): Clinical descriptions and diagnostic guidelines* (World Health Organisation, 1992), pp.90–91.
[39]   *Ibid.*
[40]   *Ibid.*, p.91.

Clinical picture

According to the ICD–10 classification, prominent psychomotor disturbances are essential and dominant features and may alternate between extremes such as hyperkinesis and stupor, or automatic obedience and negativism. Constrained attitudes and postures may be maintained for long periods. Episodes of violent excitement may be a striking feature of the condition. These catatonic phenomena may be combined with a dream-like (oneiroid) state with vivid scenic hallucinations.[41]

Onset and course

There is some evidence that catatonic symptoms may be more common in developing countries and also that the condition has become much less common in Europe during the course of this century.[42]

Diagnostic guidelines

- The general criteria for a diagnosis of schizophrenia must be satisfied (1234).

- Transitory and isolated catatonic symptoms may occur in the context of any other subtype of schizophrenia but for a diagnosis of catatonic schizophrenia one or more of the following behaviours should dominate the clinical picture:

    a. stupor (marked decrease in reactivity to the environment and in spontaneous movements and activity) or mutism;

    b. excitement (apparently purposeless motor activity, not influenced by external stimuli);

    c. posturing (voluntary assumption and maintenance of inappropriate or bizarre postures);

    d. negativism (an apparently motiveless resistance to all instructions or attempts to be moved, or movement in the opposite direction);

    e. rigidity (maintenance of a rigid posture against efforts to be moved);

    f. waxy flexibility (maintenance of limbs and body in externally imposed positions); and

    g. other symptoms such as command automatism (automatic compliance with instructions), and perseveration of words and phrases.[43]

---

[41] *Classification of Mental and Behavioural Disorders, Tenth Revision (ICD–10): Clinical descriptions and diagnostic guidelines* (World Health Organisation, 1992), p.91.

[42] In one survey of 172 long-term attenders at psychiatric day care units serving a district in South East London, only one person had signs of catatonia, notwithstanding that the patients had an average of 15 years in contact with services. See T.S. Brugha, *et al.*, "The problems of people in long-term psychiatric day care" *Psychological Medicine* (1988) 18, 443–456.

[43] *Classification of Mental and Behavioural Disorders, Tenth Revision (ICD–10), supra, pp.91–92.*

Differential diagnoses

Catatonic phenomena are not limited to schizophrenic psychoses but may be associated with organic cerebral disease (*e.g.* encephalitis), other physical disease, metabolic disturbances, alcohol or drugs, and affective illness. Indeed, Wing states that "nowadays, in psychiatric practice, catatonic symptoms are more often observed in people with disorders in the autistic spectrum than in people with schizophrenia."[44] In uncommunicative patients with behavioural manifestations of catatonic disorder, the diagnosis of schizophrenia may have to be provisional until adequate evidence of the presence of other symptoms is obtained.

SCHIZOPHRENIA, PERSONALITY AND MOOD

Many patients to not conform to stereotypes and their conditions do not neatly correspond to the descriptions found in medical textbooks. In some cases, the onset of schizophrenia-type symptoms may be acute or even abrupt and they may then resolve with similar rapidity. Because schizophrenia was originally formulated as an insidious and progressive disease, it is uncertain whether these short-lived conditions represent a form of acute schizophrenia — the onset of schizophrenia in a person whose body is able to deal with it rapidly and effectively — or represent a process which is fundamentally different at some level. Similarly, it is not yet established whether a person can have schizophrenia and yet be symptom-free ("sub-clinical disease"). In other cases, experiences associated with, or suggestive of, schizophrenia may be present but it be unclear whether they are the early "prodromal features" of a developing illness or indicative of a personality disorder. Finally, in the case of people who are obviously psychotic there may exist both symptoms commonly found in schizophrenia and others typical of a mood disorder. Thus, the presentation is often highly complex and many different ideas have been formulated, and terms invented, to describe these borderline and mixed states.

PERSONALITY AND SCHIZOPHRENIA

What constitutes personality and a disorder of the personality has already been considered (**1025, 1175**). Briefly, and by way of recap, personality represents the sum of a person's traits, habits and experiences; the whole system of relatively permanent tendencies, physical and mental, which are distinctive of a given individual.[45] Certain forms of mental disorder are conceived of as disorders of the personality and both legal and medical classifications generally distinguish between personality disorders and mental illnesses. In the International Classification of Diseases, the different types of personality disorder are grouped together in one block (F60-69). However, the dividing line between personality disorders and mental illness may well be arbitrary. The notion of personality describes the tendency of the brain to function in certain habitual ways so that, in many cases, a particular type of personality predisposes the individual to becoming mentally ill in a particular way. For example, a person with a paranoid personality will be more prone to developing the paranoid form of schizophrenia.

---

[44]   J.K. Wing, "Differential diagnosis of schizophrenia" in *Schizophrenia — An overview and practical handbook* (ed. D.J. Kavanagh, Chapman & Hall, 1992), p.13.
[45]   K. Schneider, *Clinical Psychopathology* (5th ed., trans. M.W. Hamilton, Grune & Stratton, 1958).

Schizoid personality disorders (F60.1)

Kretschmer described the "schizoid personality,"[46] by which he meant people with a rich inner life and, consequently, difficulties in making emotional contact with others. A preoccupation with internal fantasies, and a corresponding lack of engagement with the external world, may give rise to unconventional behaviour not far removed from that sometimes seen in cases of schizophrenia. Nevertheless, that behaviour is sometimes interpreted as an expression of the individual's normal — albeit, compared with other people, abnormal — personality, rather than as the consequence of a schizophrenic illness overlying and distorting that personality. The person is often described as having a schizoid personality, and diagnosed as suffering from a schizoid personality disorder. The diagnostic guidelines for schizoid personality disorder are summarised in the table on page 1246.[47]

BORDERLINE STATES (SCHIZOTYPAL DISORDER)

It may sometimes seem improbable that the bizarre beliefs and conduct of an individual who does not meet the criteria for schizophrenia can be accounted for solely in terms of his personality. There is a suspicion that some kind of illness or disease process is contributing to the presentation. When viewed retrospectively, "it may be clear that a prodromal phase in which symptoms and behaviour, such as loss of interest in work, social activities, and personal appearance and hygiene, together with generalised anxiety and mild degrees of depression and preoccupation, preceded the onset of psychotic symptoms by weeks or even months."[48] Many diagnostic terms have been used to describe such borderline states: borderline schizophrenia, latent schizophrenia, latent schizophrenic reaction, pre-psychotic schizophrenia, prodromal schizophrenia, pseudoneurotic schizophrenia, and schizotypal disorder. If no definite and characteristic schizophrenic anomalies have occurred, the latter is the diagnostic term currently used in ICD–10 to describe a disorder characterised by eccentric behaviour and anomalies of thinking and affect which resemble those seen in schizophrenia. There is "no dominant or typical disturbance"[49] but the picture is more common in individuals related to sufferers of schizophrenia and so is believed to be part of the genetic "spectrum"' of schizophrenia. Schizotypal disorders are thought to run a chronic course with fluctuations of intensity — much like a personality disorder in this respect — although occasionally evolving into overt schizophrenia. The diagnostic guidelines for schizotypal disorder are summarised in the table on page 1246.[50] It should, how- ever, be noted that although the diagnostic category is used in the ICD–10 classification, its general use is not recommended because it is not clearly demarcated from simple schizophrenia or from schizoid or paranoid personality disorders.

SIMPLE SCHIZOPHRENIA (F20.6)

Another diagnosis used to describe conditions which do not fit into any of the established sub-types of schizophrenia (paranoid, catatonic and hebephrenic) is that

---

[46] E. Kretschmer, *Medizinische psychologie* (G. Thieme, 1956).
[47] *Classification of Mental and Behavioural Disorders, Tenth Revision (ICD–10): Clinical descriptions and diagnostic guidelines* (World Health Organisation, 1992), p.203.
[48] *Ibid.*, p.88.
[49] *Ibid., p.95.*
[50] *Ibid.*, p.203.

of "simple schizophrenia" (*schizophrenia simplex*).[51] This is described in the ICD–10 classification as "an uncommon disorder in which there is an insidious but progressive development of oddities of conduct, inability to meet the demands of society, and decline in total performance. Delusions and hallucinations are not evident, and the disorder is less obviously psychotic than the hebephrenic, paranoid, and catatonic subtypes. The characteristic "negative" features of residual schizophrenia (*e.g.* blunting of affect, loss of volition) develop without being preceded by any overt psychotic symptoms. With increasing social impoverishment, vagrancy may ensue and the individual may then become self-absorbed, idle, and aimless."[52] The ICD–10 classification states that simple schizophrenia is a difficult diagnosis to make with any confidence. This is because it depends on establishing the slowly progressive development of the characteristic "negative" symptoms of residual schizophrenia[53] manifest as a marked loss of interest, idleness, and social withdrawal but without any history of hallucinations, delusions, or other manifestations of an earlier psychotic episode.[54]

SUMMARY

It can be seen from the table on the following page that there is a considerable overlap in the phenomena described in the ICD–10 classification guidelines as constituting the features of schizoid personality disorder, schizotypal disorder, and simple schizophrenia. Indeed, as drafted, the guidelines for diagnosing a schizotypal disorder are arguably more stringent than those set down for simple schizophrenia. Part of the difficulty arises from the very loose criteria adopted for schizophrenia itself, which allow simple schizophrenia to be diagnosed if there is marked social withdrawal but an absence of the positive symptoms associated with the paranoid and catatonic sub-types. In particular, the diagnostic guidelines for schizophrenia are satisfied if there is evidence of the existence for more than one month of symptoms referred to in paragraphs (h) and (i) —

- (h) "negative" symptoms such as marked apathy, paucity of speech, and blunting or incongruity of emotional responses, usually resulting in social withdrawal and lowering of social performance; it must be clear that these are not due to depression or to neuroleptic medication

- (i) a significant and consistent change in the overall quality of some aspects of personal behaviour, manifest as loss of interest, aimlessness, idleness, a self-absorbed attitude, and social withdrawal.

As can be seen, social withdrawal and loss of interest are referred to in both paragraphs and their lack of mutual exclusivity means that if a person's behaviour is marked by persistent social withdrawal and emotional introspection it is somewhat arbitrary which diagnosis is used. Perhaps all that can honestly be said is that the diagnostic categories are not mutually exclusive, the product of drafting by committee, and a somewhat unsatisfactory basis for depriving a citizen of his liberty.

---

[51] The category of simple schizophrenia was added by Bleuler to describe mixed psychotic symptoms which did not fit into any of the three sub-types propounded by Kraepelin: paranoid, catatonic and hebephrenic schizophrenia.

[52] *Classification of Mental and Behavioural Disorders, Tenth Revision (ICD–10): Clinical descriptions and diagnostic guidelines, supra,* p.95.

[53] See page 1252.

[54] *Classification of Mental and Behavioural Disorders, Tenth Revision (ICD–10): Clinical descriptions and diagnostic guidelines, supra,* p.95.

	Schizoid personality disorder	Schizotypal disorder	Simple Schizophrenia
General behaviour	Marked insensitivity to prevailing social norms and conventions.	Behaviour or appearance that is odd, eccentric, or peculiar.	Insidious but progressive development of oddities of conduct, inability to meet the demands of society, and decline in total performance. There are significant changes in personal behaviour.
Affect	Emotional coldness, detachment or flattened affectivity; few, if any, activities provide pleasure.	Inappropriate or constricted affect. The individual appears cold and aloof.	Blunting of affect, marked loss of interest, idleness.
Rapport	Almost invariable preference for solitary activities. Lack of close friends or confiding relationships and of desire for such relationships.	Poor rapport with others. Tendency to social withdrawal.	Social withdrawal.
Form of thought	No disorder in the form of thought	Vague, circumstantial, metaphorical, overelaborate, or stereotyped thinking, manifested by odd speech or in other ways, without gross incoherence.	No obvious psychotic thought processes.
Content of thought	Excessive preoccupation with fantasy and introspection.	Odd beliefs or magical thinking; suspiciousness or paranoid ideas; obsessive ruminations, often with dysmorphophobic, sexual or aggressive contents; occasional transient quasi-psychotic episodes with delusion-like ideas.	No history of delusions.
Perception	No perceptual disturbances	Unusual perceptual experiences including somatosensory (bodily) or other illusions, depersonalisation or derealisation. Occasional transient quasi-psychotic episodes with intense illusions, auditory or other hallucinations	Hallucinations are not evident.
Notes	A personality disorder.	No definite, characteristic, schizophrenic anomalies have occurred at any stage. 3 or 4 of the above features should have been present, even if only episodically, for at least 2 years. Use of the diagnosis not recommended.	Meets the criteria for schizophrenia set out in the table on pages, *i.e.* symptoms in paras. ((h) and (i) — negative symptoms and social withdrawal.

SCHIZOPHRENIA AND MOOD

Some of the patient's symptoms may commonly be present in a schizophrenic illness and others characteristically present in persons suffering from a mood (affective) disorder. Because most psychiatric syndromes shade into one another, psychiatrists are forced to resort to employing terms such as schizoaffective disorder to describe mental states in which are found symptoms characteristic of more than one type of disorder.

Schizoaffective disorders (F25)

According to the ICD–10 classification, schizoaffective disorders are "episodic disorders in which both affective and schizophrenic symptoms are prominent within the same episode of illness." The diagnostic guidelines are that the diagnosis should be made only when both definite schizophrenic and definite affective symptoms are prominent simultaneously, or within a few days of each other, within the same episode of illness and when, as a consequence of this, the episode of illness does not meet criteria for either schizophrenia or a depressive or manic episode. The diagnostic category should not be applied to (a) conditions in which affective symptoms are superimposed upon or form part of a pre-existing schizophrenic illness or (b) to patients who exhibit schizophrenic symptoms and affective symptoms only in different episodes of illness; for example persons suffering from post-schizophrenic depression (**1248**). Three sub-types are recognised, depending upon whether the affective symptoms are those of mania ("schizoaffective disorder, manic type"), or of depression ("schizoaffective disorder, depressive type"), or of both ("schizoaffective disorder, mixed type).[55]

Schizo-affective disorder, manic type (F25.0)

There must be a prominent elevation of mood, or a less obvious elevation of mood combined with increased irritability or excitement. Within the same episode, at least one and preferably two of typically schizophrenic symptoms set out in paragraphs (a)-(d) on page 1234 should be clearly present. Such disorders are usually florid psychoses with an acute onset. Although behaviour is often grossly disturbed, full recovery generally occurs within a few weeks.[56]

Schizoaffective disorder, depressive type (F25.1)

There must be prominent depression, accompanied by at least two of the characteristic depressive symptoms or associated behavioural abnormalities listed for depressive episode (**1204**). In addition, at least one and preferably two of the symptoms typical of schizophrenia (**1234**, paras. (a)-(d)) should be clearly present within the same episode. Schizoaffective episodes of the depressive type are usually less florid and alarming than schizo-affective episodes of the manic type, but tend to last longer and the prognosis is less favourable. Although the majority of patients recover completely, some eventually develop a schizophrenic defect.[57]

---

[55]   *Classification of Mental and Behavioural Disorders, Tenth Revision (ICD–10): Clinical descriptions and diagnostic guidelines* (World Health Organisation, 1992), pp.105–106.
[56]   *Ibid.*, pp.106–107.
[57]   *Ibid.*, pp.107–108.

Post-schizophrenic depression (F20.4)

A depressive episode, sometimes prolonged, may arise in the aftermath of a schizo-phrenic illness and such episodes are associated with an increased risk of suicide.[58] Some schizophrenic symptoms must still be present but no longer dominate the clinical picture. It is uncertain to what extent the depressive symptoms have merely been uncovered by the resolution of earlier psychotic symptoms (rather than being a new development) or are an intrinsic part of schizophrenia (rather than a psycho-logical reaction to it). They are rarely sufficiently severe or extensive to meet criteria for a severe depressive episode and it is often difficult to decide which of the patient's symptoms are due to depression, which to neuroleptic medication, and which to the schizophrenia itself.

EPIDEMIOLOGY, AETIOLOGY AND PATHOLOGY

Once a discrete psychiatric disorder has been identified, evidence may be acquired about its prevalence and distribution (epidemiology), causes (aetiology) and pathology.

EPIDEMIOLOGY

How many people suffer from schizophrenia depends upon how the disorder is defined. The epidemiological findings have been summarised by Kendell.[59] The lifetime risk of developing the disorder is in the region of 0.85–1.00 per cent. The incidence of the disorder (the annual rate of new cases) is approximately 10–15 new cases per 100,000 population. The age of onset of is characteristically between the ages of 15 and 45. Although the disorder is as common in males and females, males are on average first admitted to hospital some four to five years earlier.[60] The disorder is more prevalent among persons in the lower socio-economic groups, a phenomenon which has, not wholly convincingly, been explained in terms of a downward drift in the social scale because of the disabling nature of the disorder.[61] Similarly, it is more common in urban than rural areas, particularly in the centres of large cities. This may again be a result of downward drift and migration to bedsits and hostels rather than a cause of the disorder. There is some evidence to support the propositions that (1) schizophrenia became much commoner towards the end of the eighteenth century and its prevalence increased during the next hundred years;[62] and (2) during the present century, the hebephrenic and catatonic forms have become much less common and paranoid schizophrenia considerably more common. The

---

[58]   *Classification of Mental and Behavioural Disorders, Tenth Revision (ICD–10): Clinical descrip-tions and diagnostic guidelines* (World Health Organisation, 1992), pp.93–94.

[59]   R.E. Kendell, "Schizophrenia" in *Companion to psychiatric studies* (ed. R.E. Kendell & A.K. Zealley, Churchill Livingstone, 5th ed., 1993), pp. 406–409.

[60]   H. Hafner, *et al.*, "How does gender influence age at first hospitalisation for Schizophrenia?" *Psychological Medicine* 19: 903–918.

[61]   E.M. Goldberg and S.L. Morrison, "Schizophrenia and social class" *British Journal of Psychiatry* (1963) 109: 785–802.

[62]   See R.E. Kendell, "Schizophrenia" in *Companion to psychiatric studies, supra*, p.407; E.H. Hare, "Schizophrenia as a recent disease" *British Journal of Psychiatry* (1988) 153: 521–531; J.M. Eagles and L.J. Whalley, "Decline in the diagnosis of schizophrenia among first admissions to Scottish mental hospitals from 1969–78" *British Journal of Psychiatry* (1985) 146: 151–154. As to possible explanations, see J.K. Wing, "Differential diagnosis of schizophrenia" in *Schizophrenia — An overview and practical handbook* (ed. D.J. Kavanagh, Chapman & Hall, 1992), p.19.

incidence is significantly higher in unmarried persons and sufferers have reduced fertility prior to admission. Research has tended to show that migrants are more likely to suffer from schizophrenia but, within the context of immigration to the United Kingdom, political considerations have made objective discussion of the studies difficult.[63] Persons suffering from schizophrenia are more likely to have been born during the winter months (January to March) and correspondingly less likely to have been born during the summer (July to September). It appears that outcome is more favourable in economically developing countries: "despite the much more extensive follow-up treatment in the industrial countries, a high proportion of their patients had further psychotic episodes, whereas Columbian, Nigerian and Indian patients did not."[64]

AETIOLOGY AND PATHOLOGY

The aetiology of a disease consists of the postulated causes that initiate the disease process, control of which may lead to its prevention. In the case of schizophrenia, the considerable research during the past century "has not produced the discovery of a specific cause. It seems probable that such a cause does not exist."[65] Virtually every variable known to influence human conduct has at one time been implicated as a potential cause of schizophrenia; aetiological hypotheses have included genetic endowment, abnormalities of brain structure and neurochemistry, diet, viral agents, birth complications, the socio-economic environment, unpleasant life events, and family structure.[66]

Neuropathology

The majority of controlled studies have shown some pathological changes in the medial temporal lobe, probably as a result of damage before birth, with abnormalities usually more prominent on the left side of the brain. This may indicate damage before birth and reflect an increased incidence of obstetric complications. It is usually the lower birth weight twin who becomes psychotic, raising the possibility that schizophrenia is a neurodevelopmental disorder. Where one identical twin has developed schizophrenia but not the other, in the vast majority of cases both lateral ventricles were larger, and both hippocampi smaller, in the affected twin. Three-quarters of CT studies have shown modest ventricular enlargement in persons diagnosed as having schizophrenia although this does not then increase, suggesting that any enlargement precedes onset rather than developing as the disorder progresses. There is some evidence that the brains of persons with schizophrenia are shorter and lighter, weighing about six per cent less. There is also some evidence of a reduction in the number of cells in certain parts of the brain and of abnormalities of cerebral blood flow and eye-tracking movements. However, no neurological peculiarities are present in all cases of schizophrenia, either before or after the onset of the illness, and they can also be found in some non-sufferers. None of the abnormalities are therefore universally present, some of them are not specific to schizophrenia, and all of them may be contradicted by later research or susceptible to alternative interpretations.

---

63   For an analysis of the reliability of the studies, see R.E. Kendell, "Schizophrenia," *supra*, pp. 407–408.

64   *Ibid.*, p.416.

65   M. Bleuler, "The Concept of Schizophrenia in Europe During the Past One Hundred Years" in *What is Schizophrenia?* (ed. W.F. Flack, *et al.*, Springer-Verlag, 1990), p.7.

66   R.P. Bentall, "The classification of schizophrenia" in *Schizophrenia — An overview and practical handbook* (ed. D.J. Kavanagh, Chapman & Hall, 1992), p.24.

Genetics and constitutional factors

While the current evidence indicates a genetically transmitted component in schizophrenia, the concordance rate in identical twins is less than 50 per cent. and this therefore only partially accounts for the disorder's development.[67] The 20–30 year delay before the onset of the psychosis is explained in maturational terms, by the fact that certain key developments in the brain and nervous system are incomplete until or after puberty.[68]

Biochemical factors

It is well established that the ingestion of certain drugs which increase dopaminergic activity, for example amphetamines, can produce a psychotic state which is virtually indistinguishable from that seen in schizophrenia. Conversely, antipsychotic drugs effective in the treatment of schizophrenia block dopamine receptors and reduce dopamine levels. It is therefore likely that there is a biochemical component to the disorder.

Social and environmental factors

Whatever the biological basis of the disorder, "careful investigations over several decades have revealed an important role for social factors, both in the onset and in the relapse of schizophrenia. Hence, there is ample opportunity for appropriate social management to improve the outlook for patients, although preventative measures so far remain elusive."[69] It appears that the role played by life events is as important for the first episode of schizophrenia as it is for subsequent attacks and the crucial period is the three weeks immediately prior to onset.[70] Schizophrenia tends to recur in families and familial factors are therefore involved in its development. There is evidence that prolonged over-dependence on the mother is common as are homes in which the parents live under the same roof but in a state of mutual withdrawal. It is also possible that factors implicit in low socio-economic status, such as poor living conditions, contribute to the aetiology of schizophrenia.[71]

---

[67] Twin studies demonstrate a 50 per cent. concordance for identical (monozygotic) twins and a 17 per cent. concordance for non-identical (dizygotic) twins. The concordance rates for identical twins reared apart is generally similar. This suggests a genetic component, a neurodevelopmental problem specific to identical twins, or the development of particular personality traits and ways of interacting with others within the womb. The principal methods for identifying mode of transmission are known as segregation analysis and genetic linkage analysis. No precise mode of inheritance has been established. A major series of genetic investigations, referred to by Bentall, *supra*, p.32, failed to find evidence that schizophrenia is inherited when only breakdowns leading to hospitalisation are considered. This led to the concept of schizotypal personality disorder being developed, and the suggestion that what is inherited is a polygenically determined vulnerability to schizophrenia which a person may have to a greater or lesser degree.

[68] R.E. Kendell, "Schizophrenia" in *Companion to psychiatric studies* (ed. R.E. Kendell & A.K. Zealley, Churchill Livingstone, 5th ed., 1993), p.414.

[69] J. Leff, "Schizophrenia: social influences on onset and relapse" in Community Psychiatry: The Principles (ed. D.H. Bennett & H.L. Freeman, Churchill Livingstone, 1991), p.189.

[70] *Ibid.*, p.194.

[71] *Ibid.*, p.192.

COURSE AND OUTCOME

Historically, schizophrenia was believed to run a progressive downhill course while affective disorders relapsed repeatedly but recovered fully each time. However, "it is now clear that this is not so, or perhaps no longer so. Not only is the long-term prognosis much better than we used to believe, the course of the illness is very variable."[72] Although it remains true that patients with affective illnesses are more likely to make a full recovery from their original illness, there is this considerable individual variation.[73] The outcome varies between prolonged recovery, intermittent course, and prolonged psychosis of severe or mild degrees.[74]

DESCRIBING THE LONGITUDINAL COURSE AND OUTCOME

Recovery aside, schizophrenic disorders may be continuous (prominent symptoms are present throughout the observation period) or episodic (the episodes being defined by the re-emergence of prominent psychotic symptoms). The degree of deficit apparent during successive episodes may be stable or progressively worsen. Remission may be natural or a response to treatment. Where the illness is continuous, only partially remits, or there are residual symptoms, it is important to assess whether there are prominent negative symptoms.

PATTERNS OF OUTCOME

Approximately one-third of patients diagnosed as suffering from schizophrenia completely recover from their illnesses, one-third show an intermediate outcome, and in one-third of cases the illness takes the traditional deteriorating course.[75] More specifically, four patterns of outcome can be identified —

- Some resolve completely, with or without treatment, and never recur (Pattern A)

- Some recur repeatedly with full recovery every time (Pattern B)

- Others recur repeatedly but recovery is incomplete; there is a lasting damage to the personality ("persistent defect state") that characteristically becomes more pronounced after each successive relapse (Pattern C)

- Some illnesses pursue a downhill progressive course from the beginning (Pattern D).

The relative frequency of these different outcomes depends a great deal on how schizophrenia is defined. Thus, Kendell observes that if it is defined to exclude patients with prominent affective symptoms, or restricted to patients with a six-month history of schizophrenia, the proportion of patients making a full recovery is

---

[72]   R.E. Kendell, "Schizophrenia" in *Companion to psychiatric studies* (ed. R.E. Kendell & A.K. Zealley, Churchill Livingstone, 5th ed., 1993), p.416.

[73]   *Ibid.*, p.449.

[74]   M. Bleuler, "The Concept of Schizophrenia in Europe During the Past One Hundred Years" in *What is Schizophrenia?* (ed. W.F. Flack, *et al.*, Springer-Verlag, 1990), p.5.

[75]   M. Bleuler, "The long-term course of schizophrenic psychoses" in *The Nature of Schizophrenia* (ed. L.C. Wynne *et al.*, Wiley, 1978), pp.631–640; L. Ciompi, "Is there really a schizophrenia?; the long-term course of psychotic phenomena" *British Journal of Psychiatry* 145, 636–640.

reduced. The prognosis is relatively good in about 50 per cent. of cases (Patterns A and B). In patterns C and D, a defect state develops characterised by emotional blunting and apathy, and often accompanied by the faded remnants of previous delusions and hallucinations. On the whole, patients do not deteriorate further after the first 5–10 years.

Residual schizophrenia (F20.5)

The negative symptoms of schizophrenia, which are features of Patterns C and D, include underactivity; blunting of affect; passivity and lack of initiative; poverty of quantity or content of speech; poor non-verbal communication by facial expression, eye contact, voice modulation, and posture; poor self-care and social performance; and psychomotor slowing (1231). They are not necessarily irreversible. When a chronic schizophrenic process develops characterised by such long-term negative symptoms, this may be categorised as residual schizophrenia. The diagnostic guidelines are essentially threefold. There must be historical evidence of at least one clear-cut psychotic episode meeting the diagnostic criteria for schizophrenia; prominent "negative" symptoms present for a period of a year or more, during which the intensity and frequency of florid symptoms, such as delusions and hallucinations, have been minimal or substantially reduced; the negative symptoms cannot be accounted for in terms of chronic depression, institutionalism, or an organic brain disease such as dementia.[76]

PREDICTING THE OUTCOME

Experience shows that no matter how the diagnosis is formulated it never ensures a predictable course and outcome. Nevertheless, Vaillant demonstrated that a simple rating scale based on the presence or absence of seven items predicted outcome with 80 per cent. accuracy.[77] The circumstances of the illness and the patient's premorbid personality tend to determine outcome more than the symptomatology. Illnesses that develop acutely in response to stress have a much better prognosis. Being married and a normal premorbid personality are associated with a good outcome while low intelligence, early age of onset, insidious development, a poor work record, prominent schizoid personality traits, and emotional blunting with a bad outcome.[78] The prognosis for men is worse than for women and patients with enlarged ventricles tend to be male, to have poor premorbid adjustment, early age of onset, poor cognitive performance and poor prognosis.[79] Gelder has very usefully summarised the factors associated with a good and poor prognosis according to research studies.

---

[76]   *Classification of Mental and Behavioural Disorders, Tenth Revision (ICD–10): Clinical descriptions and diagnostic guidelines* (World Health Organisation, 1992), p.94.

[77]   See Manfred Bleuler, "The Concept of Schizophrenia in Europe During the Past One Hundred Years" in *What is Schizophrenia?* (ed. W.F. Flack, *et al.*, Springer-Verlag, 1990), p.5; R.E. Kendell, "Schizophrenia" in *Companion to psychiatric studies* (ed. R.E. Kendell & A.K. Zealley, Churchill Livingstone, 5th ed., 1993), pp.414–15.

[78]   J.H. Stephens, *et al.*, "Long term prognosis and follow up in schizophrenia" *Schizophrenia Bulletin* (1978) 4, 25–47; J.A. Lieberman and S.N. Sobel, "Predictors of treatment response in course of schizophrenia" *Current Opinion in Psychiatry* (1993) 6, 63–69; R.E. Kendell, "Schizophrenia," *supra*, p.415.

[79]   These items are acute onset (in this context within the previous six months); a stressful event or situation at the time of onset; a family history of depressive illness; no family history of schizophrenia; no schizoid traits in the premorbid personality; confusion or perplexity; prominent affective symptoms. See R.E. Kendell, "Schizophrenia," *supra*, p.410.

Good prognosis	*Poor prognosis*
▪ Sudden onset	▪ Insidious onset
▪ Short episode	▪ Long episode
▪ No previous psychiatric history	▪ Previous psychiatric history
▪ Prominent affective symptoms	▪ Negative symptoms
▪ Paranoid type of illness	▪ Enlarged lateral ventricles, male gender
▪ Older age at onset	▪ Younger age at onset
▪ Married	▪ Single, separated, widowed, divorced
▪ Good psychosexual adjustment	▪ Poor psychosexual development
▪ Good previous personality	▪ Abnormal previous personality
▪ Good work record	▪ Poor work record
▪ Good social relationships	▪ Social isolation
▪ Good compliance	▪ Poor compliance

Source: M. Gelder, et al, Oxford Textbook of Psychiatry (Oxford University Press, 3rd ed., 1996), p.283.

MANAGEMENT AND TREATMENT

Outcome is affected, for better and worse, by treatment and by social and environmental influences. It is not possible to predict which patients will respond to antipsychotic medication nor to distinguish those patients who will make a natural recovery from those who will require medication in order to improve.[80] It appears that the number of patients receiving medication who relapse within a given period is about half that of patients taking a placebo.[81] Nevertheless, medication probably only postpones rather than prevents relapse.[82] Medication and social intervention appear to produce the best outcome and psychotherapy adds little.[83]

---

[80]   J.M. Davis, *et al.*, "Important issues in the drug treatment of schizophrenia" *Schizophrenia Bulletin* (1980) 6, 70–87.

[81]   G.E. Hogarty and R. Ulrich, "Temporal effects of drug and placebo in delaying relapse in schizophrenic out-patients" *Archives of General Psychiatry* (1977) 34, 297–301; M. Gelder, *et al.*, *Oxford Textbook of Psychiatry* (Oxford University Press, 3rd ed., 1996), p.287.

[82]   M. Lader and R. Herrington, *Biological treatments in psychiatry* (Oxford Medical Publications, 2nd ed., 1990), p.230.

[83]   Quality Assurance Project, "Treatment outlines for the management of schizophrenia" *Australian and New Zealand Journal of Psychiatry* (1984) 18, 19–38. See M. Lader and R. Herrington, *Biological treatments in psychiatry, supra*, p.228.

ANTIPSYCHOTICS

The major therapeutic effects of these drugs are seen when they are used to treat acute psychoses. Their effects include a reduction of positive symptoms such as hallucinations, delusions and thought disorder. There is also a normalisation of psychomotor disturbance (excitement or retardation) and information processing. Although the sedative effects are immediate, the antipsychotic effects take up to three weeks to become evident in the case of schizophrenia.[84] Antipsychotics are also used in the long-term treatment of patients in remission (maintenance therapy).

Efficacy

There is no doubt that antipsychotics have a major effect on the symptoms of acute schizophrenic illnesses but patients with chronic symptoms generally respond less well. In acute cases, the condition is kept in check so that the acute, initial attack is cut short and subsequent relapses minimised.[85] However, none of the drugs has a curative action and perhaps half of all patients with a diagnosis of schizophrenia show little or no response to "typical" antipsychotic drugs.[86]

Long-term benefits

While the long-term course of chronic disorders may be altered, in terms of the time spent in hospital, there is little doubt that the effects on the long-term prognosis are less impressive than the short-term effects. A "disturbingly high proportion still remain chronically handicapped by defect states or recurring hallucinations and delusions and still require repeated admissions to hospital despite long-term drug therapy."[87] The efficacy of antipsychotic medication in chronic schizophrenia is therefore less clear and some trials have failed to demonstrate any drug-placebo difference. Negative, or deficit, symptoms. such as apathy, poverty of speech and social withdrawal, persist over time, even during remissions, and are difficult to treat. It is these symptoms which usually predominate in the chronic stage.[88]

Maintenance therapy

Because some 20–30 per cent. of patients recover from a first attack of a schizophrenic-type illness without any recurrence, the benefits of long-term maintenance medication are less clear-cut in such cases. Thus, 46 per cent. of patients receiving medication and 62 per cent. of patients on placebo in a large Northwick Park study of first episodes of schizophrenia relapsed during the two year period following discharge.[89]

---

[84] B.K. Puri and P.J. Tyrer, *Sciences Basic to Psychiatry* (Churchill Livingstone, 1992), p.126.

[85] M. Lader and R. Herrington, *Biological treatments in psychiatry* (Oxford Medical Publications, 2nd ed., 1990), p.227.

[86] See R.P. Bentall, "The classification of schizophrenia" in *Schizophrenia — An overview and practical handbook* (ed. D.J. Kavanagh, Chapman & Hall, 1992), p.26. As to the efficacy of more recently introduced "atypical" antipsychotics (clozapine, olanzapine, risperidone and sertindole) in cases refractory to treatment with the older, "typical," antipsychotics, see **1256**.

[87] R.E. Kendell, "Schizophrenia" in *Companion to psychiatric studies* (ed. R.E. Kendell & A.K. Zealley, Churchill Livingstone, 5th ed., 1993), p.416.

[88] *Ibid.*, p.417.

[89] E.C. Johnstone, *et al.*, "The Northwick Park study of first episodes of schizophrenia. I. Presentation of the illness and problems relating to admission" *British Journal of Psychiatry* (1986) 148, 115–120.

ANTIPSYCHOTICS — CHEMICAL GROUPS

Chemical group	Drug	General characteristics

Phenothiazines

▪ Group 1 — aliphatic phenothiazines	• Chlorpromazine (Largactil) • Methotrimeprazine • Promazine (Sparine)	Pronounced sedative effects, moderate anti-muscarinic and extrapyramidal side-effects.
▪ Group 2 — piperidines	• Pericyazine • Pipothiazine • Thioridazine (Melleril)	Moderate sedative effects, marked antimuscarinic effects but fewer extrapyramidal effects than groups 1 and 3.
▪ Group 3 — piperazines	• Fluphenazine (Modecate) • Perphenazine • Prochlorperazine • Trifluoperazine (Stelazine)	Fewer sedative effects, fewer antimuscarinic effects but more pronounced extrapyramidal effects than groups 1 and 2.

Other chemical groups

▪ Butryophenones	• Benperidol • Droperidol • Haloperidol (Haldol, Serenace)	These three groups are similar to Group 3 (the piperazines) in having relatively few sedative and autonomic (antimuscarinic) effects but pronounced extrapyramidal effects.
▪ Diphenylbutyl-piperidines	• Fluspirilene • Pimozide (Orap)	
▪ Thioxanthenes	• Flupenthixol (Depixol) • Zuclopenthixol (Clopixol)	
▪ Substituted benzamides	• Sulpiride	These drugs specifically block D_2 dopamine receptors whereas other antipsychotic drugs block both D_1 and D_2 receptors. It is possible that there may be a reduced risk of tardive dyskinesia and of other adverse effects.
▪ Dibenzoxazepine	• Loxapine	Chemically similar to the other antipsychotics but may have a lower incidence of extrapyramidal effects. Also has no endocrine effects.
▪ Miscellaneous	• Oxypertine	Oxypertine may be used to treat anxiety.

Miscellaneous "atypical" antipsychotics

▪ Miscellaneous	• Clozapine	Clozapine is different from other antipsychotic. It blocks serotonin, alpha-adrenergic and histamine receptors with much less dopamine receptor-blocking activity. It may be effective in patients resistant to other compounds.
	• Olanzapine	Olanzapine is a novel antipsychotic which affects dopaminergic, serotonergic, muscarinic and adrenergic activities.
	• Risperidone	Studies suggest that it is less likely than haloperidol to induce extrapyramidal movement disorders.
	• Sertindole	Activity appears to be specific to D_2, 5-HT2 and alpha-1 adrenergic receptors and largely confined to the limbic dopamine system.

Choice of antipsychotic

Which drug is prescribed will depend upon the degree of psychosis, whether sedation is desirable, whether side-effects are tolerable, the degree of compliance, the patient's drug history, the clinician's familiarity with the different drugs, and the age of the patient. Antipsychotics vary significantly both in terms of their pharmacokinetics and pharmacodynamics but there is little evidence of consistent superiority of one compound over another, with the exception of clozapine and possibly risperidone.[90] A patient may respond well to one but badly to another similar drug.

Clozapine

Clozapine is the only drug which has been demonstrated to significantly improve the condition of patients who fail to respond to conventional antipsychotics. About half of the people within this treatment-resistant group respond to the drug. Improvement has been noted in both negative and positive symptoms although patients with paranoid ideation and thought disorder may benefit the most. It is also the case that most of the side-effects associated with the conventional drugs do not occur with clozapine. In particular, it is not known to cause tardive dyskinesia or akathisia. Against this, the drug has a damaging effect on the white blood cells of a small minority of patients.[91] Consequently, all patients taking clozapine must have regular blood tests, initially weekly and then fortnightly. If laboratory results are sufficiently adverse, this leads to the treatment's cessation. Bearing these factors in mind, Cutting has suggested that the general guidelines for prescribing the drug should be as follows: (1) it should only be given to people with schizophrenia if they have not done well with at least three conventional anti-schizophrenic drugs at proper doses; (2) the diagnosis must be quite definite; (3) after an initial period of weaning off the other conventional drugs (about three months), no other anti-schizophrenic drugs are needed; (4) the dose of clozapine can be reduced with time; whether or not a person responds to clozapine is obvious within two months.[92]

Olanzapine

The evidence suggests that olanzapine is superior to haloperidol and is relatively well tolerated.[93] It appears to be significantly more likely to improve negative symptoms, such as affective blunting and apathy.[94] It is reported to be effective in maintaining clinical improvement in patients who have responded to initial treatment.[95] The most common side effects are somnolence and weight gain, but sexual dysfunction may be less likely.

---

[90]   M. Gelder, *et al.*, *Oxford Textbook of Psychiatry* (Oxford University Press, 3rd ed., 1996), p.286. The therapeutic advantage of "atypical antipsychotics" has been attributed to alpha-2 adrenergic antagonist effects. D.J. Nutt, "Putting the 'A' in atypical: does alpha-2 adrenoceptor antagonism account for the therapeutic advantage of new antipsychotics?" *Journal of Psychopharmacology* (1994) 8, 193–5.

[91]   Clozapine was developed in the late 1950s but withdrawn from clinical studies in the 1970s because of a two per cent. incidence of agranulocytosis.

[92]   J. Cutting, *Open Mind* (December 1993) 66, 28.

[93]   G.D. Tollefson, *et al.*, "Olanzapine versus haloperidol in the treatment of schizophrenia and schizoaffective and schizophreniform disorders; results of an international collaborative trial" *American Journal of Psychiatry* (1997) 154(4) 457–465; G.D. Tollefson, *et al.*, "Olanzapine versus haloperidol in the treatment of first episode psychosis" *Schizophrenia Research* (1997) 24, Issues 1 and 2).

[94]   G.D. Tollefson and T.M. Sanger, "Negative Symptoms: a path-analytic approach to a double-blind, placebo and haloperidol-controlled clinical trial with olanzapine" *American Journal of Psychiatry* (1997) 154(4) 466–473

[95]   *British National Formulary* (British Medical Association and the Royal Pharmaceutical Society of Great Britain, March 1997) 33, 161.

Risperidone

Risperidone is an antipsychotic for patients who have not responded satisfactorily to at least two conventional antipsychotics.[96] It may have an antidyskinetic effect. Although risperidone-induced extrapyramidal reactions have been reported,[97] the drug is less likely to cause extrapyramidal effects than conventional antipsychotics.[98] Efficacy in the treatment of negative symptoms, and the drug's long-term efficacy, have yet to be firmly established.[99] Side effects include sedation, headache, insomnia, anxiety, agitation and extrapyramidal symptoms (approximately 20 per cent. of patients).

Sertindole

Sertindole is licensed for the treatment of acute and chronic schizophrenia and schizoaffective psychoses, including positive and negative symptoms. Its advantages are said to include efficacy in respect of negative as well as positive symptoms, a lack of sedation, and the fact that extrapyramidal symptoms do not exceed those of placebo (thereby improving long-term compliance).[100] Postural hypotension can occur if treatment is initiated too quickly. However, the drug "is associated with QT interval prolongation which may lead to serious ventricular arrhythmias (abnormal heart rhythm)."[101]

Dosage

Individual responses to antipsychotic drugs are very variable and to achieve optimum effect, dosage and dose interval must be titrated according to the patient's response.[102] The correct dosage is that which adequately controls the patient's psychopathological state and behaviour with minimal side-effects.[103] In general terms, a whole series of controlled trials have failed to demonstrate any general advantage in prescribing very high doses — what the Americans call "heroic doses" — and many patients respond to quite low doses.[104] After stabilisation, the long half-life of antipsychotics allows the total daily dose to be given as a single dose in most cases.

---

[96]   Chouinard, *et al.*, "A Canadian Multicenter placebo–controlled study of fixed doses of risperidone and haloperidol in the treatment of chronic schizophrenia patients" *Journal of Clinical Psychopharmacology* (1993) 13(1), 25–40; Guy Edwards J., "Risperidone for schizophrenia" *British Medical Journal* (1994) 308,1311–12.

[97]   T. Mahmood, "Risperidone–induced extrapyramidal reactions" *Lancet* (1995) 346, 1226.

[98]   *British National Formulary* (British Medical Association and the Royal Pharmaceutical Society of Great Britain, March 1997) 33, 161.

[99]   G. Robert, *Risperidone for the treatment of refractory schizophrenia* (Research and Development Directorate, 1995)

[100]   B. Green, *Focus on Sertindole* (Priory Lodge Education, 1997); D.P. Van Kammen, *et. al.*, "A randomised, controlled, dose-ranging trial of sertindole in patients with schizophrenia" *Psychopharmacology* (1996)124, 168–175.

[101]   *British National Formulary (British Medical Association and the Royal Pharmaceutical Society of Great Britain, March 1997) 33, 161.* European restrictions include ECG monitoring before and during sertindole therapy i.e. at 1–2 weeks, after 4–6 weeks, after six months, and yearly thereafter. The purpose of the pre-treatment ECG being to exclude patients whose QT interval is already prolonged and to avoid prescribing other drugs concurrently which also have this effect, e.g. tricyclic and tetracyclic antidepressants. The drug is contraindicated in patients who have significant cardiac disease.

[102]   *British National Formulary* (British Medical Association and Royal Pharmaceutical Society of Great Britain , March 1996) 31, 161.

[103]   M. Lader and R. Herrington, *Biological treatments in psychiatry, supra*, p.244.

[104]   For a summary of these studies, see *ibid.*, pp.244–245.

ANTIPSYCHOTIC DRUGS – NON-DEPOT PREPARATIONS (BNF 4.2.1)

Drug	Proprietary	B.N.F. Indications	BNF guideline doses	Notes
Chlorpromazine Hydrochloride (CPZ)	· Chlorpromazine (tablets, oral sol., injection, suppositories) · Largactil (tablets, syrup, suspension, injection)	Schizophrenia and other psychoses, mania, short-term adjunctive management of severe anxiety, psychomotor agitation, excitement, and violent or dangerously impulsive behaviour.	By mouth initially 75mg daily, usual maintenance dose of 75–300mg daily but up to 1g daily may be required in psychoses. By deep IM injection for relief of acute symptoms, 25–50mg every 6–8 hours.	Marked sedative properties with tranquillisation, indifference to surroundings and injuries, lack of temperature control, coupled with retention of mental facilities (orig., "lobotomie pharmacologique"): See Lader and Herrington, 2nd ed., p.217. Extrapyramidal symptoms (**1146**), reversed by dose reduction or antimuscarinic drugs (**1149**).
Benperidol	· Anquil (tablets)	Control of deviant antisocial sexual behaviour.	0.25-1.5 mg. daily adjusted according to response.	Contra-indications and side-effects, see haloperidol.
Clozapine	· Clozaril (tablets)	Schizophrenia in patients unresponsive to, or intolerant of, conventional antipsychotic drugs.	Initial dose of 12.5mg once or twice on first day. If tolerated, slowly increased. Maximum dose 900 mg daily. Usual antipsychotic dose 200–450mg daily. Usual maintenance dose 150–300mg daily.	See **1256**. More sedating than chlorpromazine. Extrapyramidal symptoms may occur less frequently and less likely to cause tardive dyskinesia. High incidence of antimuscarinic symptoms. Other side-effects include neutropenia and agranulocytosis. Only initiated in hospital setting. Special patient registration and monitoring required. Risk of rebound psychosis if abruptly withdrawn.
Droperidol	· Droleptan (tablets, oral liquid, injection)	Tranquillisation and emergency control in mania.	By mouth 5–20mg repeated every 4–8 hours if necessary. By IM injection, up to 10mg repeated every 4–6 hours if necessary. By IV injection, 5–15mg repeated every 4–6 hours if necessary.	Contra-indications and side-effects, see haloperidol.
Flupenthixol	· Depixol (tablets; depot injection see **1263**) · Fluanxol	Schizophrenia and other psychoses, particularly with apathy and withdrawal but not mania or psychomotor hyperactivity.	Initially 3–9mg twice daily adjusted according to response; maximum 18 mg. daily.	Less sedating than chlorpromazine but higher incidence of extrapyramidal symptoms (**1146**) — 25 per cent. of patients. To be avoided in senile confusional states, excitable and overactive patients.

Drug	Preparations	Indications	Dose	Notes
Fluphenazine Hydrochloride	· Moditen (tablets, depot injection see **1263**)	*As for chlorpromazine*	Schizophrenia and other psychoses, mania — by mouth initially 2.5–10mg daily, adjusted according to response to 20mg daily. Daily doses above 20mg "only with special caution."	Less sedating than chlorpromazine and fewer antimuscarinic or hypotensive symptoms. However, high incidence of extrapyramidal symptoms, particularly akathisia and dystonic reactions. To be avoided in depression.
Haloperidol	· Haloperidol (tablets) · Dozic (oral liquid) · Haldol (tablets, oral liquid, injection, depot injection) · Serenace (tablets, capsules, oral liquid, injection)	*As for chlorpromazine*	By mouth initially 1.5–3mg twice or thrice daily; 3–5mg twice or thrice daily in severely affected or resistant patients. In resistant schizophrenia up to 100mg (rarely 200mg) may be needed; adjusted according to response to lowest effective maintenance dose (as low as 5–10mg daily). By IM injection, 2–10mg with subsequent doses every 4–8 hours according to response (up to hourly if necessary) — severely disturbed patients may require initial dose of up to 30mg.	Less sedating than chlorpromazine and fewer antimuscarinic or hypotensive symptoms. However, high incidence of extrapyramidal symptoms, particularly akathisia and dystonic reactions.
Loxapine	· Loxapac (capsules)	Acute and chronic psychoses	Initially 20–50mg daily, increased as necessary over 7–10 days to 60–100mg daily. Maximum 250mg daily, usual maintenance dose of 20–100mg daily.	Side-effects similar to chlorpromazine but no endocrine effects yet reported. Nausea and vomiting, ptosis, hyperpyrexia, paraesthesia have been reported.
Methotrimeprazine	· Nozinan (tablets)	Schizophrenia; as an adjunctive treatment in terminal care.	By mouth, initially 25–50mg (bedpatients 100–200mg) daily, increased as necessary to 1g daily.	More sedating than chlorpromazine. Risk of postural hypotension particularly in patients over 50 years of age.
Olanzapine	· Zyprexa (tablets)	Schizophrenia	See **1256**.	See **1256**. Limited experience of its use. May be fewer extrapyramidal side-effects than with CPZ. Said to be effective in maintaining clinical improvement.
Oxypertine	· Oxypertine (tablets, capsules)	*As for chlorpromazine*	Initially 80–120mg daily, adjusted according to response. Maximum 300 mg daily.	Extrapyramidal symptoms may be less frequent than with chlorpromazine. With low doses agitation and hyperactivity may occur and with high doses sedation.
Pericyazine	· Neulactil (tablets, syrup)	*As for chlorpromazine*	*Schizophrenia and other psychoses* — Initially 75mg daily, increased as necessary at weekly intervals. Usual maximum 300 mg daily.	More sedating than chlorpromazine. Hypotension common when treatment initiated.

Perphenazine	• Fentazin (tablets)	*As for chlorpromazine*	Initially 4mg t.d.s., thereafter adjusted according to response. Maximum dose 24mg daily.	Less sedating than CPZ but extrapyramidal symptoms (esp. dystonia) more frequent, particularly at high dosage. Not indicated for agitation and restlessness in the elderly.
Pimozide	• Orap (tablets)	Schizophrenia; monosymptomatic hypochondriacal psychosis; paranoid psychoses; mania, hypomania, short-term adjunctive treatment of excitement and psychomotor agitation.	*Schizophrenia* — Initially 10mg daily in acute conditions, thereafter adjusted according to response to maximum of 20mg daily. Prevention of relapse — initially 2mg daily, range 2–20mg daily. *Paranoid psychoses* — Initially 4mg daily, thereafter adjusted according to response to maximum of 16mg daily.	Highly antipsychotic, long acting, minimal extrapyramidal side-effects; less sedating than CPZ. However, "serious arrhythmias reported ... following reports of sudden unexplained death, Committee on Safety of Medicines recommends ECG before treatment in all patients, periodic ECGs at doses over 16mg daily." CSM further warns that it should not be given with other antipsychotics, tricyclic antidepressants. *BNF*, 34, 167.
Prochlorperazine	• Prochlorperazine (tablets) • Stemetil (tablets, syrups, sachets, injection, suppositories)	Schizophrenia and other psychoses, mania.	By mouth, 12.5mg b.d. for 7 days, thereafter adjusted according to response to usual daily dose of 75–100mg. By deep IM injection, 12.5–25mg twice or thrice daily.	Less sedating than chlorpromazine but extrapyramidal symptoms, particularly dystonia, more frequent.
Promazine Hydrochloride	• Promazine (tablets, injection) • Sparine (suspension)	Short-term adjunctive management of psychomotor agitation; agitation and restlessness in the "elderly."	By mouth, 100–200mg q.d.s. By IM injection, 50mg repeated if necessary after 6–8 hours.	Contra-indications and side-effects, see chlorpromazine.
Risperidone	• Risperdal (tablets)	Acute and chronic psychoses.	Initially 2mg daily increased to 6mg by third day. Usual range 4–8mg daily (maximum 16mg). Doses above 10mg daily only if benefit considered to outweigh risk.	See **1257**. Agitation may occur more frequently than with CPZ. Nausea, anxiety, concentration difficulties, fatigue reported.
Sertindole	• Serdolect (tablets)	Schizophrenia	Initially 4mg daily, increased at intervals of 4/5 days to usual maintenance of 12–20mg as single daily dose. Maximum 24mg daily.	See **1257**. Limited experience of its use. Less sedating than CPZ and extrapyramidal symptoms appear not to exceed placebo. Associated with QT interval prolongation, which may lead to serious ventricular arrhythmias.

Drug	Formulation	Indication	Dose	Notes
Sulpiride	· Dolmatil (tablets) · Sulparax (tablets) · Sulpitil (tablets)	Schizophrenia	200–400mg b.d. Maximum 800 mg daily in patients with predominately negative symptoms; 2400 mg in patients with mainly positive symptoms.	Structurally distinct from, and less sedating than, CPZ. Not associated with jaundice or skin reactions. In high doses controls florid, positive symptoms and in low doses has an alerting effect in apathetic, withdrawn states.
Thioridazine	· Thioridazine (tablets, oral sol.) · Melleril (tablets, suspension, syrup)	As for chlorpromazine	Schizophrenia and other psychoses, mania — 150–600mg daily; maximum 800 mg. daily for up to 4 weeks (hospital patients only). Short-term adjunctive management of psychomotor agitation, excitement, violent or dangerously impulsive behaviour — 75–200mg daily.	Less sedating than chlorpromazine. Extrapyramidal symptoms and hypothermia are rare and it is therefore popular for treating the elderly. Sexual dysfunction may occur as may, rarely, pigmentary retinopathy (brownish colouring of vision, impaired night vision).
Trifluoperazine	· Trifluoperazine (tablets, oral sol.) · Stelazine (tablets, spansules, syrup)	As for chlorpromazine	By mouth, initially 10mg daily, increased by 5mg after 1 week, then at intervals of 3 days according to response.	Less sedating than chlorpromazine and hypotension, hypothermia, and antimuscarinic symptoms are less frequent. However, high incidence of extrapyramidal symptoms, particularly akathisia and dystonic reactions.
Zuclopenthixol Acetate	· Clopixol Acuphase (injection, oily)	Short-term management of acute psychosis, mania, or exacerbations of chronic psychosis.	By deep IM injection into the gluteal muscle or lateral thigh, 50–150 mg, if necessary repeated after 2–3 days (1 additional dose may be needed 1–2 days after the first injection). Treatment should not exceed 2 weeks — maximum of 4 injections and maximum cumulative dose of 400mg per course.	Contra-indications and side-effects, see chlorpromazine.
Zuclopenthixol Dihydrochloride	· Clopixol (tablets, depot injection see **1263**)	Schizophrenia and other psychoses, particularly when associated with agitated, aggressive, or hostile behaviour.	Initially 20–30mg daily, increasing to a maximum of 150mg daily if necessary. Usual maintenance dose 20–50mg daily.	Contra-indications and side-effects, see chlorpromazine. Should not be used in apathetic or withdrawn states.

Adverse effects

Antipsychotics affect cholinergic, alpha-adrenergic, histaminergic, and serotinergic receptors, while dopamine blockade in the extrapyramidal system causes extrapyramidal side-effects and hypoprolactinaemia. The subsidiary effects may therefore be categorised as sedative, extrapyramidal and autonomic. The meaning of these terms and the most common types of adverse effect have already been summarised (1146). However, it is useful to list some of the well-documented adverse effects of chlorpromazine (CPZ) because the side-effect profiles of other drugs are often stated by reference to this commonly prescribed drug. The adverse effects in any particular case may include extrapyramidal symptoms (1146), which may sometimes be reversed by dose reduction or antimuscarinic drugs (1150); anti-muscarinic symptoms (1148), such as a dry mouth, nasal congestion, constipation, difficulty micturating, and blurred vision; occasionally, following prolonged administration, tardive dyskinesia (1147); hypothermia (occasionally pyrexia); apathy, depression and, more rarely, agitation; endocrine effects; damage to the eye following prolonged high dosage; skin reactions (photosensitisation is more common than with other antipsychotics).

LONG-ACTING DEPOT PREPARATIONS AND MAINTENANCE

Depot antipsychotics are slow-release long-acting oily preparations administered by way of deep intramuscular injection into the gluteal muscle. The intervals between injections varies between one and four weeks. Pain may occur at the injection site and occasionally erythema, swelling, and nodules. In general, no more than 2–3 mL of oily injection should be administered at any one site.[105] Depot medications may have advantages in terms of convenience and compliance compared with oral preparations but are associated with a higher incidence of extrapyramidal reactions, and also with hypotension and tachycardia. Because the drugs may have undesirable and long-lasting side-effects — it may take a month or more following discontinuance for side-effects to subside — a test dose is generally recommended. Treatment requires careful monitoring both to achieve optimum effect and to control side-effects.

Choice of depot

According to the British National Formulary, all of the drugs are indicated for use in the maintenance of schizophrenia and other psychoses, while an additional indication for clopixol is evidence of aggression and agitation. Depots are contra-indicated in confusional states, parkinsonism, and where there is intolerance to antipsychotics. Brief notes on the drugs given in the table below.

Efficacy

Although maintenance therapy reduces the risk of relapse (1254), studies have not established that depot injections have any significant advantages over oral preparations.[106] This may be because patients with poor histories of compliance are

---

[105]   *British National Formulary* (British Medical Association and Royal Pharmaceutical Society of Great Britain, March 1996) 31, 165.

[106]   N.R. Schooler, *et al.*, "Prevention of relapse in schizophrenia" *Archives of General Psychiatry* (1980) 37, 16–24; G.E. Hogarty, *et al.*, "Fluphenazine and social therapy in the aftercare of schizophrenic patients: relapse analysis of two year controlled study of fluphenazine decanoate and fluphenazine hydrochloride" *Archives of General Psychiatry* (1979) 36, 1283–1294.

left out of such studies, although voluntary compliance with depot medication may not be greater than compliance with oral medication. A general advantage of injections over oral medicines is certainty about whether or not a the drug has been received as prescribed. Against this, injections are unacceptable for many patients. Consequently, in practice, this clarity may be limited to knowing that the medicine has not been received as prescribed. The real choice is therefore often between compromising on oral medication by consent or compulsory treatment by injection. In the absence of any legal or practical framework allowing indefinite compulsory out-patient treatment, defaulting on injections in due course becomes an option for all discharged patients. In such cases, a consultant's unwillingness to contemplate what he considers to be the second-line treatment may simply lead to no treatment and early relapse.

ANTIPSYCHOTIC DEPOT PREPARATIONS (BNF 4.2.2)

Drug	Proprietary	Notes and BNF guideline doses
Flupenthixol Decanoate	▪ Depixol ▪ Depixol Conc. ▪ Depixol low volume	Test dose 20mg. Usual maintenance dose range of 50mg every 4 weeks – 300mg every 2 weeks. Maximum 400mg weekly. May have a mood elevating effect but can cause over-excitement in agitated or aggressive patients. Aggression or agitation may necessitate using an alternative antipsychotic. Extrapyramidal symptoms usually appear 1–3 days after administration and continue for about five days but may be delayed.
Fluphenazine Decanoate	▪ Modecate ▪ Modecate Concentrate	Test dose 12.5mg. Thereafter, 12.5–100mg at intervals of 2–5 weeks, adjusted according to response. Contra-indicated in severely depressed states. Extrapyramidal symptoms usually appear a few hours after the dose has been administered and continue for about two days but may be delayed.
Fluspirilene	▪ Redeptin	This drug has been withdrawn.
Haloperidol Decanoate	▪ Haldol Decanoate	Initially 50mg every 4 weeks. Increasing in 50mg steps to 300mg every 4 weeks if necessary, and "higher doses may be needed in some patients." The side-effects are similar to those for chlorpromazine.
Pipothiazine Palmitate	▪ Piportil Depot	Test dose 25mg. Usual maintenance range 50–100mg (maximum 200mg) every 4 weeks. Side-effects similar to chlorpromazine.
Zuclopenthixol Decanoate	▪ Clopixol ▪ Clopixol Conc.	Test dose 100mg. Thereafter increasing to 200–400mg every 2–4 weeks, maximum 600mg weekly. Less sedating that chlorpromazine and may be particularly suitable in cases of aggression and agitation, but it can cause porphyria.

Note: All of the available preparations listed above are oily injections administered by deep intramuscular injection into gluteal muscle (i.e. the buttocks). In each case, the B.N.F. indicator for the drug is the "maintenance in schizophrenia and other psychoses."

ELECTROCONVULSIVE THERAPY (ECT)

Catatonia is generally considered to be a definite indication for ECT. However, following a review of the research studies, Lader and Herrington concluded that the view that ECT is valuable in some cases of schizophrenia is not supported by firm evidence; that it was consistently less effective than either drugs or drugs plus psychotherapy; that any benefits were short-lived; but that it will undoubtedly continue to be used by some psychiatrists in patients with catatonia, affective symptoms, or drug-resistant states.[107] For further information about ECT, see page 1132.

FAMILY THERAPY

During the past quarter of a century, much emphasis has been placed on the significance of the patient's relationship with relatives, in terms both of the occurrence of the disorder and relapse. Schizophrenia tends to recur in families and familial factors are involved in its development. There is considerable evidence that the parents of people with schizophrenia are more often psychiatrically disturbed than are the parents of other children. The fact that a parent has psychiatric problems suggests that the child's subsequent illness has a genetic cause, or that it is attributable to the family environment, or both. It also appears that mothers are more protective towards their children even before the onset of illness.[108] This may lead to the so-called double bind, a term coined by Bateson to refer to the contradictory emotional attitudes which sufferers have to their parents. Children who develop schizophrenia have been found to more often come from homes in which parents live under the same roof but in a state of mutual withdrawal or conflict ("emotional divorce").[109] It should, however, been emphasised that none of these well-substantiated parental and family problems are invariably present.[110]

Relatives and the domestic environment

The literature concerning the family environment has been extensively reviewed by Leff[111] and much of it centres around the concept of "expressed emotion" (EE). The Camberwell Family Interview (CFI) has five principal scales for rating the expression of emotion: critical comments, hostility, over-involvement, warmth and positive remarks. In an early study, Brown "found that in a nine-month period following discharge, a high level of criticism, the presence of hostility, and high over-involvement were each related to relapse of schizophrenia. Conversely, high warmth was related to a good outcome over the same period, and this latter finding is of great importance, since it indicates that relatives can influence the course of schizophrenia

---

[107] M. Lader and R. Herrington, *Biological treatments in psychiatry* (Oxford Medical Publications, 2nd ed., 1990), p.230.

[108] P. O'Neal and L.N. Robins, "Childhood patterns predictive of adult schizophrenia: a 30 year follow-up study" *American Journal of Psychiatry* (1958) 115: 385-391; D.F. Ricks and C. Nameche, "Symbiosis, sacrifice and schizophrenia" *Mental Hygiene* (1966) 50: 541-551. This finding is, of course, liable to more than one interpretation because, if a child is vulnerable, a mothers' protectiveness may be well founded rather than overly intrusive.

[109] M. Waring and D. Ricks, "Family patterns of children who become adult schizophrenics" *Journal of Nervous & Mental Diseases* (1965) 140: 351-364. See J. Leff, "Schizophrenia: social influences on onset and relapse" in *Community Psychiatry: The Principles* (ed. D.H. Bennett & H.L. Freeman, Churchill Livingstone, 1991), p.190.

[110] R.E. Kendell, "Schizophrenia" in *Companion to psychiatric studies* (ed. R.E. Kendell & A.K. Zealley, Churchill Livingstone, 5th ed., 1993), pp.412–413.

[111] See J. Leff, "Schizophrenia: social influences on onset and relapse," *supra*.

in a beneficial way."[112] Patients returning to live with high-EE relatives were found by Brown to have a relapse rate of over 50 per cent. over nine months, compared with only 16 per cent. for those in low-EE homes. These findings were almost exactly replicated by Vaughn and Leff.[113] During the two years following discharge, Leff and Vaughn found that the high-EE patients relapsed at almost twice the rate of low-EE patients: after two years, the overall relapse rates were 62 per cent. and 20 per cent. respectively.[114] This association between relatives' expressed emotion and the course of schizophrenia has been found to hold true for a variety of cultural settings and is strongly related to relapse even when there is no disturbed behaviour on the patient's part to mediate the relationship.[115]

Management strategies

In cases where a high level of expressed emotion is problematic, studies by Leff and Vaughn have identified two protective factors: regular maintenance treatment with neuroleptic drugs and low social contact between the relative and patient.[116] Patients who spent less than 35 hours per week in the same room with high-EE relatives were found to have a significantly lower relapse rate than those in high contact. The two protective factors appeared to have an additional effect, with the result that if patients were in low contact and took regular neuroleptic drugs, their relapse rate was lower than if only one protective factor was present. Family-orientated treatments may include a brief educational programme, a relatives' group, and family sessions in which the patient and key relatives in the household are included. Face-to-face contact is reduced by making use of day centres, day hospitals, hostels and classes run by local authority social services.

[112] G.W. Brown, J.L.T. Birley, J.K. Wing, "Influence of family life on the course of schizophrenic disorders: a replication" *British Journal of Psychiatry* (1972) 121: 241–258. See J. Leff, "Schizophrenia: social influences on onset and relapse," *supra*, p.195.

[113] C.E. Vaughn and J.P. Leff, "The influence of family and social factors on the course of psychiatric illness: a comparison of schizophrenic and depressed neurotic patients" *British Journal of Psychiatry* (1976) 129: 125–137.

[114] J.P. Leff and C. Vaughn, "The role of maintenance therapy and relatives' expressed emotion in relapse of schizophrenia: a two year follow-up" *British Journal of Psychiatry* (1981) 139: 102-104.

[115] J. Leff, "Schizophrenia: social influences on onset and relapse" in *Community Psychiatry: The Principles* (ed. D.H. Bennett & H.L. Freeman, Churchill Livingstone, 1991), p.196.

[116] *Ibid.*

24. Organic disorders

INTRODUCTION

The organic disorders (**1037**) considered in this chapter are those commonly arising in old age, such as dementia; epilepsy; endocrine disorders; and toxic disorders. It has already been noted that the classification of mental disorders in official usage in England and Wales is the World Health Organisation's International Classification of Diseases, now in its tenth revision (ICD–10); and, more particularly, that part of it dealing with mental and behavioural disorders.[1] Diagnostic guidelines set out in the classification are used to specify which combinations of symptoms are adequate to substantiate a diagnosis. Before considering the different disorders, it is useful to briefly outline the way in which the brain functions and the meaning of terms commonly used to describe injury to it (**1277**).

THE BRAIN AND THE NERVOUS SYSTEM

The nervous system comprises the central nervous system, the peripheral nervous system and the autonomic (self-regulating) nervous system —

- The central nervous system (CNS) consists of the brain and the spinal cord. Its overall role is to receive sensory information from organs such as the eyes, ears and receptors within the body, to analyse this information, and to initiate an appropriate motor response, for example the contraction of a muscle.

- Nerves fan out from the central nervous system to the peripheries of the body — the muscles, skin, internal organs and glands. The peripheral nervous system (PNS) consists of all the nerves which carry signals between the CNS and the rest of the body.

- The autonomic nervous system is involved in involuntary, automatic, reflex activities; bodily functions such as heart rate carried out and co-ordinated in the brain below the level of consciousness. The effects of autonomic control are mainly the stimulation or depression of glandular secretion and the contraction of cardiac and smooth muscle tissue.

---

[1] *Classification of Mental and Behavioural Disorders, Tenth Revision (ICD–10): Clinical descriptions and diagnostic guidelines* (World Health Organisation, 1992).

- For descriptive purposes, the autonomic nervous system is divided into two parts: the sympathetic and parasympathetic. Sympathetic stimulation prepares the body to deal with exciting and stressful situations ("fight or flight") while parasympathetic stimulation has a tendency to slow down body processes. Normally the two systems function simultaneously producing a regular heart beat, normal temperature and an internal environment compatible with the immediate surroundings.[2]

Nerve cells and nerve impulses

Cells are the basic structural unit of the body. The nucleus is the control centre of a cell, governing its activities and functions —

- The physiological units of the nervous system are nerve impulses, akin to tiny electrical charges. Nerve tissue is "irritable" which means that it has the capacity to initiate nerve impulses in response to thought and external stimuli. Thus, a particular thought may give rise to a voluntary, that is willed, movement of the muscles of an eye or limb.

- The nervous system consists of a vast number of neurones. Each neurone consists of a nerve cell (the "grey matter"), in the centre of which is the nucleus, and extensions of the nerve cell located deep in the brain (the "white matter").

- The nerve cells of some neurones initiate nerve impulses while others act as relay stations at which impulses are passed on or redirected.

- Each neurone has two types of extension, an axon and dendrites. Axons carry nerve impulses away from the nerve cell while dendrites carry nerve impulses to the nerve cell. Axons and dendrites which are located in the peripheral nervous system (outside the brain and spinal cord) are commonly referred to as "nerves."

- Sensory nerves transmit information to do with the senses to the brain where the sensation is perceived. Motor nerves transmit impulses away from the centre towards the periphery, to bring about some action or movement in response to a sensory input.

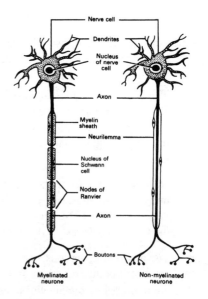

Source: K.J.W. Wilson, Ross and Wilson, Anatomy and Physiology in Health and Illness (Churchill Livingstone, 7th ed., 1990), fig. 12.2. With permission.

---

2   K.J.W. Wilson, *Ross and Wilson, Anatomy and Physiology in Health and Illness* (Churchill Livingstone, 7th ed., 1990), p.270.

Sensory nerves

Sensory nerves divide into fine branching filaments, the sensory nerve endings. A **receptor** is the small structure in which a sensory nerve fibre terminates. Sensory nerves originate in the peripheries of the body — the limbs, eyes, skin, muscles, internal organs — and transmit information to do with the senses to the brain where the sensation is perceived. Taking the brain as the central point of the process, sensory nerves therefore convey nerve impulses from the peripheral nervous system in to the central nervous system (the brain and spinal cord). Because sensory nerves transmit nerve impulses from the sensory organs in towards the central nervous system, where they can be analysed and acted upon, they are often referred to as ascending or afferent nerves; afferent meaning to convey inwards. There are several kinds of sensory nerve —

- special senses are concerned with the higher senses of sight, hearing, smell and taste;

- cutaneous senses originate in the skin and are stimulated by touch, pain, heat and cold;

- proprioceptor senses, which are stimulated by stretch, originate in the muscles and joints and they control balance and posture;

- autonomic afferent nerves originate in internal organs and tissues and are associated with reflex regulation of activity and visceral pain.

Motor nerves

In contrast to sensory nerves, motor nerves transmit impulses *away* from the centre towards the periphery, to bring about some action or movement in response to a sensory input. Consequently, they are often referred to as descending or efferent nerves, efferent meaning to convey outwards. Motor neurone stimulation results in the contraction of skeletal (voluntary) and smooth (involuntary) muscle. The motor nerves divide into fine filaments terminating in minute pads called **motor end-plates**. One motor nerve has many end-plates and each stimulates a muscle fibre. The nerve impulse is transmitted across the gap between the end-plate and the muscle fibre by chemical means, the substance involved being called a neurotransmitter.

Voluntary and involuntary movements

The contraction of the muscles which move the joints is mainly under the control of the will, which means that the stimulus to contract originates at the level of consciousness in the cerebrum. However, some nerve impulses which affect skeletal muscle contraction are initiated in the midbrain, brainstem and cerebellum. The activity here occurs below the level of consciousness and is associated with the *co-ordination* of muscle activity. For example, very fine balancing movements and the maintenance of posture and balance.[3]

---

[3]   K.J.W. Wilson, *Ross and Wilson, Anatomy and Physiology in Health and Illness* (Churchill Livingstone, 7th ed., 1990), p.255.

Mixed nerves

In the spinal cord, sensory and motor nerves are arranged in separate cables or tracts. Outside the spinal cord, sensory and motor nerves are enclosed within the same sheath of connective tissue and called "mixed nerves." Most of the nerves of the peripheral nervous system are composed of sensory nerve fibres conveying impulses from sensory end organs to the brain, and motor nerve fibres conveying impulses from the brain through the spinal cord to the effector organs, *e.g.*, skeletal muscles, smooth muscle and glands.

Synapses

The transmission of all sensory and motor nerve impulses involves more than one nerve cell (neurone) so at some stage a change-over has to be effected. The process is often likened to an athletics relay, with the nerve impulse being a baton passed on at the conclusion of each stage to the next runner. The point at which a nerve impulse passes from one neurone to another is the **synapse**. As has been noted, axons carry nerve impulses away from a nerve cell while dendrites carry nerve impulses towards the nerve cell. At its free end, the axon of one neurone breaks up into minute branches which terminate in small swellings called **boutons**. These boutons are in close proximity to the dendrites of the next neurone in the chain but not touching them. The space between them is known as the **synaptic cleft** and the nerve impulse is transmitted across that space chemically — by substances known as **neurotransmitters**. These chemical transmitters are secreted by the nerve cells and stored at the end of the boutons in spherical **synaptic vesicles**. The action of chemical transmitters is short-lived and immediately they have stimulated the next neurone they are neutralised by enzymes.

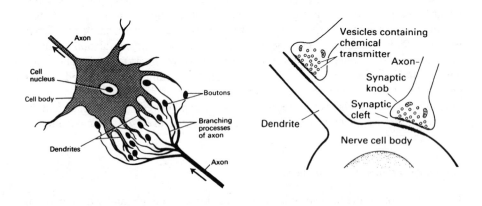

Source: K.J.W. Wilson, Ross and Wilson, Anatomy and Physiology in Health and Illness (Churchill Livingstone, 7th ed., 1990), figs. 12.4A and 12.4B. With permission.

THE BRAIN

The brain comprises—

- the cerebrum

- the diencephalon

- the brain stem, which includes the midbrain

- the cerebellum or hindbrain

THE CEREBRUM

The cerebrum is the largest and most developed part of the brain and the site of most conscious and intelligent activities. This is the structure which most people think of as "the brain" and it is concerned with conscious thought, perception and motor activity. It can override most other components in the nervous system. It consists of both nerve cells ("grey matter") and nerve fibres which connect the cells and transmit nerve impulses from one cell to another along a chain ("white matter").

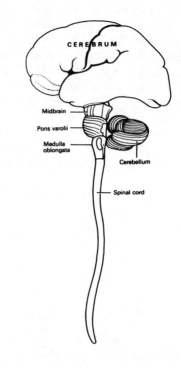

Source: K.J.W. Wilson, Ross and Wilson, Anatomy and Physiology in Health and Illness (Churchill Livingstone, 7th ed., 1990), fig. 12.12. With permission.

The hemispheres

The cerebrum is divided by a deep ravine or cleft ("**the longitudinal fissure**") into two hemispheres, consisting of two large out-growths from the main part of the brain-stem which together form an almost continuous mass which envelops most of the rest of the brain.

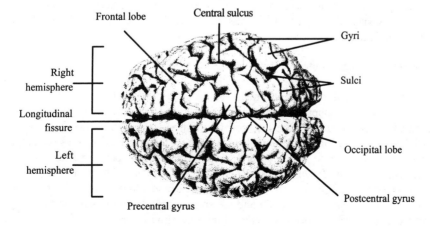

Source: Rod R. Seeley, et al., Anatomy & Physiology (Mosby Year Book, 2nd ed., 1992), fig. 13–8A. With permission.

1271

The cerebral cortex and the lobes

The surface of each cerebral hemisphere (known as the "cerebral cortex") is about one centimetre deep and made up of "grey matter." It can also be seen from the diagram above that the surface of the cerebrum ("the cerebral cortex") is not smooth and flat but undulating, its many irregular hills or folds (**"the gyri"**) being separated by ravines or fissures (**"sulci"**). If one looks at the overall impression formed by these undulations, the most pronounced fissures seem to be like boundaries which divide the landscape into distinct regions. That being so, the surface areas of the cerebrum are named, partly for descriptive purposes, after the four bones of the skull under which they lie — the **frontal, occipital, parietal and temporal lobes**, a lobe being simply a "projection" (as in "ear-lobe"). The diagram shows the boundaries of the lobes, which are connected by masses of nerve fibres.

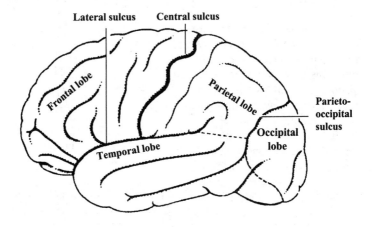

Source: K.J.W. Wilson, Ross and Wilson, Anatomy and Physiology in Health and Illness (Churchill Livingstone, 7th ed., 1990), fig. 12.13. With permission.

The ventricles

Each of the hemispheres contains within it a space called a "ventricle" ("the lateral ventricles") which is filled with cerebro-spinal fluid. An inner layer adjacent to the ventricles consists of important clusters of nerve cells, in particular the basal ganglia, thalamus and hypothalamus.

Connecting the hemispheres

The corpus callosum consists of tracts of nerve fibres ("white matter") which connect the two hemispheres deep within the cerebrum, so as to allow for the transmission of nerve impulses from one cell to another across the divide. Just as the nerve fibres known as the **corpus callosum** connect the two hemispheres so arrays of interconnecting nerve fibres (called **association fibres**) connect areas of the cerebral cortex within the same hemisphere. Yet other tracts of nerve fibres (called **projection fibres**) allow signals to be transmitted and relayed from the cerebral cortex to the other parts of the brain and the spinal cord. All nerve impulses passing to and from the cerebral cortex are carried by projection fibres, which form what is known as the **internal capsule**.

THE DIENCEPHALON

The diencephalon is the part of the brain between the brainstem and the cerebrum, the main components of which are —

- the thalamus;

- subthalamus;

- hypothalamus; and

- epithalamus.

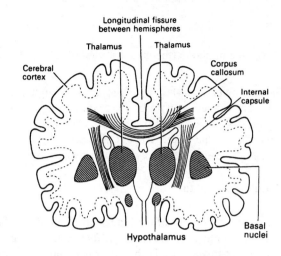

Source: K.J.W. Wilson, Ross and Wilson, Anatomy and Physiology in Health and Illness (Churchill Livingstone, 7th ed., 1990), fig. 12.14. With permission.

Thalamus

The thalamus constitutes four-fifths of the total weight of the diencephalon. Within the thalamus is the third ventricle. Most sensory input projects to the thalamus where afferent neurones synapse with thalamic neurones and send projections to the cerebral cortex. These impulses include auditory and visual nerve impulses. The thalamus also plays an important role in bodily movement associated with strong emotions such as rage and fear.

Sub-thalamus

A small portion of the red nucleus and the substantia nigra (**1275**) extend to the subthalamic region, which is also associated with basal ganglia. The sub-thalamus is involved in controlling motor functions.

Epithalamus

The epithalamus is involved in emotional and visceral responses to smell and may possibly also be concerned in the sleep-wake cycle. It includes the **pineal gland**.

Hypothalamus

The hypothalamus plays a number of important functions, generally associated with mood and the emotions. Efferent fibres originating in the hypothalamus pass to the brain stem and the cerebral cortex where they synapse with neurones of the autonomic nervous system. The hypothalamus is involved in olfactory reflexes and emotional responses to smells. It is also important in controlling the secretion of hormones from the pituitary gland and with control of the autonomic nervous system, *e.g.* defensive reactions associated with fear and rage.

BRAINSTEM (INCLUDING THE MIDBRAIN)

The brain stem comprises —

- the medulla oblongata;

- pons; and

- the midbrain (the **mesencephalon**).

These structures are less involved in the complicated task of integrating the senses and more concerned with basic, primitive physiological functions such as controlling an individual's level of arousal. The brainstem connects the spinal cord to the remainder of the brain. All but two of the cranial nerves enter or exit the brain through the brainstem and even small areas of damage to the brain stem can be fatal.

Medulla oblongata

The most inferior part of the brainstem. From the surface, the spinal cord appears to blend into it although the spinal tracts within each are in fact different. The medulla acts as a pathway for both ascending and descending nerve tracts and is also involved in regulating various reflex actions such as a person's heart-rate. Several cranial nerves are located within the medulla.

The pyramids and the olives

On the anterior surface of the medulla are two prominent enlargements called the **pyramids**. They consist of descending nerve tracts involved in the conscious movement of skeletal muscles. Near their inferior ends the descending nerve tracts cross over to the opposite sides, in the manner of a crossroads or a figure "X." This accounts in part for the fact that each half of the brain controls the opposite side of the body. The technical term for this is that the tracts "decussate." The **olives** are two rounded structure, shaped like olives, which protrude from the anterior surface of the medulla. The olives consist of nuclei (clusters of grey matter deep inside the brain) involved in the functions of balance, co-ordination, and the modulation of sound impulses from the inner ear structures.

Pons Varolii

The Pons, located above the medulla oblongata, contains several ascending and descending nuclei ("the **pontine nuclei**"). The pontine nuclei relay information from the cerebrum ("the brain") to the cerebellum ("the little brain"). It consists mainly of nerve fibres which form a bridge between the two hemispheres of the cerebellum and of fibres passing between the higher levels of the brain and the spinal cord.

Mid-brain

The midbrain, or mesencephalon, is the smallest region of the brainstem and consists of groups of nerve cells and nerve fibres which connect the cerebrum with lower parts of the brain and with the spinal cord.

The tectum

The tectum (literally "the roof") of the midbrain consists of four nuclei which form mounds on the dorsal surface. Each mound is called a colliculus (Latin for a hill), there being two superior colliculi and two **inferior colliculi**. The inferior colliculi are an integral part of the auditory pathways within the central nervous system and are involved in hearing. Neurones transmitting impulses from the structures of the inner ear all synapse in the inferior colliculi. The **superior colliculi** are involved in visual reflexes, such as sudden flashes of light, and receive input from the eyes, the skin and the inferior colliculi. They play an important function in tracking moving objects, and the turning of the eyes and head.

The tegmentum

The tegmentum (literally "floor") of the midbrain consists of ascending tracts from the spinal cord to the brain and contains the **red nuclei** — so named because they have a pinkish colour in fresh brain specimens due to an abundant blood supply. The red nuclei aid in the unconscious regulation and co-ordination of motor activities. The **substantia nigra** (literally "black substance"), a mass of nuclei situated close to the tegmentum, is involved in co-ordinating movement and muscle tone.

The reticular formation

A reticle is a network of fine threads and the reticular formation is a collection of neurones scattered dust-like through most of the brainstem. When considered to-gether with its various connections, the system is known as the reticular activating system, which is concerned with the sleep-wake cycle and thus with phenomena such as alertness and attention and, conversely, drowsiness, sleep and coma.

THE CEREBELLUM

The cerebellum is a region of the brain concerned primarily with the maintenance of posture and balance and with the co-ordination of movement. Disease or damage to it (due, for example, to a stroke, multiple sclerosis or a brain tumour) may cause **cerebellar ataxia**. The gait is jerky and staggering, and other movements uncoord-inated, accompanied in some cases by slurred speech (dysarthria), hand tremor, and nystagmus. Because alcohol impairs cerebellar functions, it may produce similar symptoms.

THE SPINAL CORD

The spinal cord is the elongated, almost cylindrical part of the central nervous system, continuous above the medulla oblongata and about the thickness of the little finger. The white matter of the spinal cord is arranged in three columns or tracts; anterior, posterior and lateral. Except for the cranial nerves, the spinal cord is the nervous tissue link between the brain and the rest of the body. Nerves conveying impulses from the brain to the various organs and tissues descend through the spinal cord. At the appropriate level they leave the cord and pass to the structure they supply. Similarly, sensory nerves from organs and tissues enter and pass upwards in the spinal cord to the brain.

THE CRANIAL NERVES

There are 12 pairs of cranial nerves originating from nuclei in the brain, some sensory, some motor and some mixed. By way of example, the olfactory nerves make their central connection in the temporal lobe of the cerebrum and their peripheral connection in the mucous membrane in the roof of the nose and the optic nerves arise in the occipital lobe and the cerebellum and connect to the retina in the eye.

PROTECTING THE BRAIN AND SPINAL CORD

The brain and spinal cord are protected in the following ways.

The meninges

The brain and the spinal cord are completely surrounded by three membranes which lie between the brain and the skull. These membranes are collectively known as the meninges, an infection of the meninges being called meningitis. Furthest from the brain, on the skull side, is the **dura mater,** dura meaning literally "hard" or "durable." The middle membrane is the **arachnoid mater**, named because of its shape after the Greek word for a spider ('arachnoid'). The inner membrane which adheres to the cerebrum is the **pia mater**, pia being an Arabic word meaning "thin." The meninges descend down the spinal cord, enveloping and protecting it in a similar fashion, and acting as a protective layer between the spinal cord extending from the brain and the skeletal surround (the backbone or vertebrae). There are spaces in between each of the meningeal layers, known as **potential spaces**, and also between the inner layer, the pia mater.

Central spinal fluid

The central spinal fluid consists of water, mineral salts, glucose, proteins and other similar substances and supports the brain, maintaining a uniform pressure round the brain and spinal cord, acting as a cushion and shock absorber.

Neuroglia (the blood-brain barrier)

The central nervous system consists of nerve cells ("neurones") and supporting tissue ("neuroglia"). The neuroglia play an important role in forming a barrier between the blood and the brain (the blood-brain barrier).

DESCRIBING INJURY TO THE BODY

Various words are used to describe injury or damage to the body. **Encephalopathy** denotes any disease or disorder affecting the brain, especially one of a chronic or degenerative nature. Disease, inflammation, or damage affecting the peripheral nerves is referred to as **neuropathy**. Neuropathy may produce symptoms which include numbness, tingling, pain, or muscular weakness depending upon which nerves are attacked. The term **idiopathic** (literally "one's own disease"), as in idiopathic epilepsy, denotes a disorder the cause of which is unknown but presumed to be organic.

1276

WORDS DESCRIBING INJURY OR DAMAGE TO THE BODY

Anoxia A complete absence of oxygen within a body tissue, *e.g.* the brain. Hypoxia denotes a reduction rather than an absence in oxygen supply.

Atrophy The shrinking or wasting away of a tissue or organ due to a reduction in the size or number of its cells.

Lesion An all-encompassing term for any abnormality of structure or function in any part of the body. The term may refer to a wound, infection, tumour, abscess, or chemical abnormality.

Neoplasm Neoplasm is a medical term for a tumour and therefore denotes any abnormal new growth.

Seizure A sudden episode of uncontrolled electrical activity in the brain, also known as a fit. Recurrent seizures are called epilepsy and may be partial or generalised.

Toxin A poisonous protein produced by pathogenic bacteria.

Trauma A physical injury or a severe emotional shock. It may result in a disorder known as post-traumatic stress disorder.

Tumour Strictly, any swelling and usually synonymous with neoplasm. It refers to an abnormal mass of tissue which forms in a specific area when cells there reproduce at an abnormal rate.

DISORDERS AFFECTING OLDER PEOPLE

Compulsory admission is used for about five per cent of people aged 65 or over who come into psychiatric wards, usually when paranoid, manic, or dangerously depressed, and less often when confused.[4] The use of the term "older people" in the text refers to people aged 65 or over. A general principle of psychogeriatric care is that older people fare best in familiar environments and removal from home should be avoided where possible. About five per cent of them live in institutions, the same proportion as at the beginning of the century.[5]

FUNCTIONAL MENTAL DISORDERS

Dementia is the most characteristic disorder affecting older people because it is rarely seen in the young. However, older people experience the same range of mental disorders and mood disorders contribute up to half the workload of a comprehensive psychogeriatric service. Because their presentation can sometimes mean that they are difficult to differentiate from organic disorders it is important to briefly consider them first. It is worth noting that some hospitals maintain separate

---

[4] B. Pitt, "Management problems in psychogeriatrics" in *Contemporary Psychiatry* (ed. S. Crown, Butterworths, 1984), p.97.

[5] C. Oppenheimer, "The Elderly" in *Essential Psychiatry* (ed. N. Rose, Blackwell Scientific Publications, 1992), p.131.

wards for patients with organic and functional mental disorders although opinion differs as to whether this is advantageous.

Mood disorders

Major mood disorders are present in some two to three per cent of older people. Recurrent mood disorders sometimes become more disabling as periods between illnesses shorten and the duration of illnesses lengthen.[6] Suicide is more common in old age than in youth while attempted suicide is less common. Men are at greater risk than women. It is sometimes difficult to distinguish depression from dementia and mania from delirium. Although a manic episode can start by resembling delirium (an acute confusional state), the confusion passes while the euphoric irritable hyperactivity remains.[7]

Depression

Approximately 22 per cent of people over 60 suffer depression and some 10 per cent of depressive disorders develop in the over–60s. The Mental Health Act Commission biennial reports suggest that most second opinions authorising ECT involve older detained patients suffering from depression with life-threatening problems of nutritional intake. Continued physical ill-health is an important factor in maintaining depressive symptoms[8] but it is also easy to dismiss depression as understandable, even inevitable, and to thereby commit the patient to unnecessary suffering.[9] The prognosis is worse than in cases with a younger age of onset. It is quite common for the patient to be left with a residue of mild symptoms which interfere with the routine tasks of daily life. If tricyclic medication (1209) is prescribed, this will normally consist of a second generation tricyclic because these drugs are associated with fewer adverse effects for older people. Most older patients require full adult dosages.[10] Depressive states may sometimes be misdiagnosed as dementia (1280).

Paranoid states

Failure of the special senses of hearing and vision is widely recognised to predispose to paranoid states, while failing health in general, and consequent reduced mobility and restricted contact with the outside world, also seem to possess the potential.[11] Paranoia may arise from confusion, paraphrenia, or personality. Confusional paranoia results from the patient blaming others for difficulties arising from his forgetfulness which he fails to recognise. The paranoia takes the form of outbursts that pass quite quickly. Medication is of little value.[12] The sustained delusions, hallucinations, and hostility of paraphrenia may erupt into violence towards neighbours (although this is rarely dangerous) or result in withdrawal into a state of siege with a serious risk of self-neglect and malnutrition.[13]

---

[6]   A.T. Beck, *Depression: clinical, experimental and theoretical aspects* (Staples Press, 1967).

[7]   B. Pitt, "Management problems in psychogeriatrics" in *Contemporary Psychiatry* (ed. S. Crown, Butterworths, 1984), pp.92 and 96.

[8]   F. Post, *The Significance of affective symptoms in old age* (Oxford University Press, Maudsley Monograph No. 10, 1962); R.C. Baldwin and D.J. Jolley "The prognosis of depression in old age" *British Journal of Psychiatry* (1986) 149, 574–583.

[9]   S. Jolley and D. Jolley, "Psychiatric disorders in old age" in *Community Psychiatry: The Principles* (ed. D.H. Bennett and H.L. Freeman, Churchill Livingstone, 1991), p.269.

[10]   B. Pitt, "Management problems in psychogeriatrics," *supra*, p.94.

[11]   S. Jolley and D. Jolley, "Psychiatric disorders in old age," *supra*, p.269.

[12]   B. Pitt, "Management problems in psychogeriatrics" in *Contemporary Psychiatry* (ed. S. Crown, Butterworths, 1984), p.97.

[13]   B. Pitt, "Management problems in psychogeriatrics," *supra*, p.97.

Personality disorder

Personality clashes between spouses, parent and child, neighbours or helpers are as common among older people as younger people but more likely to lead to labelling as mentally ill. Long-established personality traits that cause difficulty "such as cantankerousness, obstinacy, parsimony, hoarding, and reclusiveness are sometimes hopefully attributed to mental illness with the vague expectation that the psychiatrist will be able to remove the symptoms."[14] Similarly, suicidal threats may wrongly be thought to indicate illness when in fact they may be an expression of disturbed relationships.

Prescribing medication

The principles concerning prescribing medication for older people have been enumerated by Pitt and his advice merits detailed consideration. According to him, a fundamental principle of treatment is not to overtreat or undertreat. "Drastic drugging is rarely justified and talking to the patient until he has settled, nursing in a side room, or the use of a mild hypnotic ... often suffices."[15] Overtreatment is apparent when a confused patient has been rendered drowsy, dehydrated, hypotensive, and ataxic. Incontinence, bed sores, fractures, and hypostatic pneumonia are other hazards of such overtreatment. The dilemma "is that the cure may be as bad as the disease. The best course is to treat only when the disorder is truly troublesome, to use the lowest effective dose possible and oral medication where compliance seems at all likely, to be especially cautious in the presence of confusion or physical infirmity, to use antiparkinsonian drugs at the first sign of side effects, to try occasional drug holidays, and to maintain close supervision during follow up."[16] As to the risks of undertreatment, examples are the overcautious prescription of antidepressants, not giving ECT when it is needed, and denying the older patient psychological treatments that take time and skill such as psychotherapy and behaviour therapy.[17]

Anxiety, agitation and restlessness

Anxiety, agitation, restlessness, and difficulty in getting off to sleep "may all respond to major tranquillisers used in low/moderate doses: perphenazine 2mg, haloperidol 1–2mg, promazine syrup 50–100mg nocte, and chlorpromazine syrup 50–100mg nocte ... Higher doses of major tranquillisers and/or the use of more potent compounds ..., are required when persecutory ideas, delusions, and hallucinations are prominent. Care must be taken by clinicians to avoid becoming so determined to eradicate these phenomena that the patient's drive, sparkle, and ability to cope and survive are steam-rollered out of existence. There are quite a number of paranoid old people who are better off when left medication-free, for they do not suffer much and cause little bother, as long as they are known and understood."[18]

---

14 B. Pitt, "Management problems in psychogeriatrics" in *Contemporary Psychiatry* (ed. S. Crown, Butterworths, 1984), p.92.
15 *Ibid.*, p.93.
16 *Ibid.*, pp. 93–94.
17 *Ibid.*, p.94.
18 S. Jolley and D. Jolley, "Psychiatric disorders in old age" in *Community Psychiatry: The Principles* (ed. D.H. Bennett and H.L. Freeman, Churchill Livingstone, 1991), p.284.

DELIRIUM

Delirium is a state of acute mental confusion characterised by impairment of consciousness which manifests itself as reduced clarity of awareness of the environment. It is quite common among older people, particularly those with concurrent physical illness, and surveys indicate that up to one-fifth of older people admitted to medical and geriatric wards suffer from it. Physical illnesses such as pneumonia and strokes may precipitate a crisis by adding an acute delirium to a pre-existing mild dementia or by imposing hospital care on a person just maintaining his grasp of reality at home.[19] There may be accompanying incontinence, ataxia (**1063**) and falls leading to fractures.[20] Delirium may be drug related and common offending drugs include digoxin, hypnotics, phenothiazines, anti-parkinsonian agents, hypotensive drugs, and diuretics.[21] The basic requirement in management is to search for and treat the underlying cause. While this treatment is taking effect, psychotropic drugs can provide symptomatic relief. Small doses of haloperidol or a phenothiazine are usually effective without increasing confusion. Since many of the causes of delirium threaten life, the mortality of delirium is high.[22] The features which distinguish delirium from dementia are considered below (**1287**).

DEMENTIA

Dementia is not a single disease but a generic term covering numerous conditions that have certain clinical features in common. More particularly, it is a syndrome associated with a variety of diseases in which there is degeneration and atrophy of the brain. The characteristics of a dementing illness are global intellectual impairment (impairment of several aspects of cognition at the same time) and preservation of clear consciousness.[23] Memory impairment and loss of intellectual capacities are severe enough to interfere with social or occupational functioning.

DEMENTIA

"Dementia is a syndrome due to disease of the brain, usually of a chronic or progressive nature, in which there is disturbance of multiple higher cortical functions, including memory, thinking, orientation, comprehension, calculation, learning capacity, language and judgement. Consciousness is not clouded. Impairments of cognitive function are commonly accompanied, and occasionally preceded, by deterioration in emotional control, social behaviour, or motivation ... Dementia produces an appreciable decline in intellectual functioning, and usually some interference with personal activities of daily living, such as washing, dressing, eating, personal hygiene, excretory and toilet activities. How such a decline manifests itself will depend largely on the social and cultural setting in which the patient lives."

ICD–10 Classification of Mental and Behavioural Disorders: Clinical descriptions and diagnostic guidelines, World Health Organisation, Geneva, 1992, p.45.

---

[19]   C. Oppenheimer, "The Elderly" in *Essential Psychiatry* (ed. N. Rose, Blackwell Scientific Publications, 1992), p.132.
[20]   J.B. Macdonald and E.T. Macdonald *British Medical Journal* (1977) ii, 483.
[21]   E.H. Jarvis, *Adverse Drug Reaction Bulletin* (1981) 86, 312.
[22]   M. Gelder, *et al.*, *Oxford Textbook of Psychiatry* (Oxford University Press, 3rd ed., 1996), p.520.
[23]   C. Oppenheimer, "The Elderly," *supra*, p.134.

ICD–10 diagnostic guidelines

The ICD–10 diagnostic guidelines are as follows[24]—

- The primary diagnostic requirement is evidence of a decline in both memory and thinking which is sufficient to impair personal activities of daily living, such as washing, dressing, eating, personal hygiene, excretory and toilet activities.

- The impairment of memory typically affects the registration, storage, and retrieval of new information, but previously learned and familiar material may also be lost, particularly in the later stages.

- There is impairment of thinking and of reasoning capacity and a reduction in the flow of ideas.

- The processing of incoming information is impaired, in that the individual finds it increasingly difficult to attend to more than one stimulus at a time, such as taking part in a conversation with several persons, and to shift the focus of attention from one topic to another. If dementia is the sole diagnosis, evidence of clear consciousness is required. However, a double diagnosis of delirium superimposed upon dementia is common.

- The above symptoms and impairments should have been evident for at least six months for a confident clinical diagnosis of dementia to be made.

The prevalence of dementia

The prevalence of moderate to severe dementia rises markedly with age, from about two per cent in persons aged 65–70 to approximately 20 per cent in those over 80. The prevalence of dementia continues to rise as a consequence of increasing longevity in the population.

Types of dementia and diagnosis

Traditionally, dementing illnesses were divided into presenile (under 65 years of age at onset) and senile (over 65 years of age at onset). Some researchers have also categorised dementias as either reversible or irreversible, treatable or untreatable. Conclusive diagnosis of the precise type of dementing illness in any particular case must usually await the post-mortem. In the majority of cases, the type of dementia is established as Alzheimer's disease (**1282**), which is found at post-mortem in 60 per cent of deceased hospitalised patients previously diagnosed as having dementia. Cerebrovascular disease (**1283**), including strokes, is established as the cause in a further 20 per cent of cases and a combination of the two in another 10 per cent. In life, both diagnoses are made presumptively, that is the diagnosis must await confirmation after death. Rarer causes of dementia include Pick's disease (**1285**) and Huntington's chorea (**1286**). A whole range of other conditions may also cause dementia but they account for very few cases each year.

---

[24]   *Classification of Mental and Behavioural Disorders, Tenth Revision (ICD–10): Clinical descriptions and diagnostic guidelines* (World Health Organisation, 1992), p.46.

ALZHEIMER'S DISEASE (F00)

Dementia in Alzheimer's disease is a degenerative cerebral disease of unknown cause which has characteristic neuropathological and neurochemical features, such as a marked reduction in the number of brain cells and in some neurotransmitters. The research and literature concerning the disease have recently been examined by Terry.[25]

Diagnostic guidelines

According to the ICD–10 diagnostic guidelines, the features set out in the following table below are essential for a definite diagnosis.[26]

ALZHEIMER'S DISEASE — ICD–10 DIAGNOSTIC GUIDELINES

- presence of a dementia as described (**1281**)

- insidious onset with slow deterioration

- absence of clinical evidence, or findings from special investigations, to suggest that the mental state may be due to other systemic or brain disease which can induce a dementia (*e.g.*, hypothyroidism, hypercalcaemia, vitamin B_{12} deficiency, niacin deficiency, neurosyphilis, normal pressure hydrocephalus, or subdural haematoma)

- absence of a sudden, apoplectic onset, or of neurological signs of focal damage such as hemiparesis, sensory loss, visual field defects, and incoordination occurring early in the illness.

Prevalence of the disorder

It has been noted that Alzheimer's disease is the most common cause of dementia in older people. Autopsy information, based largely on hospitalised patients, has consistently shown that an Alzheimer pathology is the most common variety of dementia encountered and occurs in some half to two-thirds of patients.[27] The disease is slightly more common in women, and patients with Down's syndrome are at high risk of developing it.[28]

Onset and development

The disease is usually insidious and develops slowly but steadily over a period of years. The progress is usually gradual for the first two to four years, with increasing memory disturbance and lack of spontaneity. Disorientation in unfamiliar

---

[25]   R.D. Terry, *et al.*, *Alzheimer's disease* (Raven Press, 1994).

[26]   *Classification of Mental and Behavioural Disorders, Tenth Revision (ICD–10): Clinical descriptions and diagnostic guidelines* (World Health Organisation, 1992), p.48.

[27]   W.A. Lishman, *Organic Psychiatry, The Psychological Consequences of Cerebral Disorder* (Blackwell Scientific Publications, 2nd ed., 1987), p.372.

[28]   *Classification of Mental and Behavioural Disorders, Tenth Revision (ICD–10): Clinical descriptions and diagnostic guidelines, supra*, p.47.

surroundings is normally an early sign.[29] It usually begins after the age of 70 although the onset can be in middle adult life or even earlier. In cases with onset before the age of 65, there is the likelihood of a family history of a similar dementia, a more rapid course, and prominent features of temporal and parietal lobe damage. In cases with a later onset, the course tends to be slower and to be characterised by more general impairment of higher cortical functions. The disease is as yet untreatable. The erosion of the patient's intellectual and emotional reserves leaves him progressively more dependent on the work of others to provide an appropriate environment for him.[30] Death usually occurs within five to eight years of the appearances of the first signs of the disease.[31]

Management and treatment

The management and treatment of dementia is considered below (1287). Four kinds of drugs may be prescribed in cases of Alzheimer's disease, namely cholinergic drugs, vasodilators, neuropeptides and enhancers of brain metabolism. However, clinical trials have shown little or no benefit and Gelder concludes that their administration is not recommended.[32]

VASCULAR DEMENTIA (F01)

This form of dementia, formerly known as arteriosclerotic dementia, is caused by cerebrovascular disease: the term cerebrovascular denotes the blood supply of the brain. The meaning of other terms will be less familiar to many professionals and some of the more common of them are briefly defined below.

The terminology of vascular dementia

- *Arteriosclerosis*   Disease of the arteries resulting in the thickening and loss of elasticity of the arterial walls

- *Cerebrovascular accident*   The medical term for a stroke, the rupture of a blood vessel in the brain causing loss of consciousness.

- *Embolism*   An embolus is a fragment of material that travels in the blood circulation and causes obstruction of an artery. An embolism is more serious and the fragment (a blood clot, a bubble of air, a piece of tissue or tumour) causes actual blockage of the artery. A cerebral embolism may cause a stroke.

- *Infarction*   An infarct is an area of dead tissue caused by a lack of blood supply (ischaemia), often due to obstruction in the artery supplying the area. Infarction is the formation of an infarct and multi-infarct dementia (F01.1) is a form of vascular dementia brought about by a number of minor ischaemic episodes.

---

29   M. Gelder, *et al.*, *Oxford Textbook of Psychiatry* (Oxford University Press, 3rd ed., 1996), p.522.
30   C. Oppenheimer, "The Elderly" in *Essential Psychiatry* (ed. N. Rose, Blackwell Scientific Publications, 1992), p.134.
31   M. Gelder, *et al.*, *Oxford Textbook of Psychiatry*, *supra*, p.522.
32   *Ibid.*, p.526.

- *Ischaemia*   An insufficient supply of blood to a specific organ or tissue. Ischaemia is usually caused by a disease of the blood vessels such as artherosclerosis.

- *Thrombosis*   A thrombus is a blood clot that has formed inside an intact blood vessel and which may obstruct supply to the brain or, if it grows large enough, block the artery. The condition is known as thrombosis. If a fragment of the thrombus breaks off, this may then obstruct or block the blood circulation elsewhere : see *embolism.*

Onset and development

The onset of vascular dementia is usually in the late sixties or the seventies. It is slightly more common in men than in women and the prevalence increases with age, approximately doubling every five years.[33] Arteriosclerosis will often be obvious. The onset may be acute, often following a succession of strokes from cerebro-vascular thrombosis, embolism of haemorrhage — **vascular dementia of acute onset** (F01.0). In other cases the onset may be more gradual, following a number of minor ischaemic episodes which produce an accumulation of infarcts in the cerebral tissue — **multi-infarct dementia** (F01.1). When the onset is gradual, "emotional or personality changes may antedate definite evidence of memory and intellectual impairment. Other common early features include somatic symptoms such as headache, dizziness, tinnitus and syncope (fainting) which may be the main complaints for some considerable time. Once established the cognitive impairments characteristically fluctuate in severity, varying from day to day and sometimes even from hour to hour. In large measure this may be due to episodes of clouding of consciousness which are a feature from the early stages."[34] The disease often follows a "stepwise progression," with periods of deterioration being followed by partial recovery for a few months. From the time of diagnosis the life-span varies widely but averages about four to five years. Death is attributable to ischaemic heart disease in about half the cases.

Diagnostic guidelines

The ICD–10 diagnostic guidelines for vascular dementia are firstly that dementia is evident, as described above. In addition, "impairment of cognitive function is commonly uneven, so there may be memory loss, intellectual impairment, and focal neurological signs. Insight and judgement may be relatively well preserved. An abrupt onset or a stepwise deterioration, as well as the presence of focal neurological signs and symptoms, increases the probability of the diagnosis."[35] Associated features include hypertension, emotional lability with transient depressive mood, weeping or explosive laughter and transient episodes of delirium. Personality is believed to be relatively well preserved but changes may be evident in a proportion of cases with apathy, disinhibition, or accentuation of previous traits such as egocentricity, paranoid attitudes, or irritability.[36]

---

[33]   M. Gelder, *et al.*, *Oxford Textbook of Psychiatry* (Oxford University Press, 3rd ed., 1996), p.525.

[34]   See W.A. Lishman, *Organic Psychiatry, The Psychological Consequences of Cerebral Disorder* (Blackwell Scientific Publications, 2nd ed., 1987), pp.385–391.

[35]   *Classification of Mental and Behavioural Disorders, Tenth Revision (ICD–10): Clinical descriptions and diagnostic guidelines* (World Health Organisation, 1992), p.48.

[36]   *Ibid.*

Management and treatment

The management and treatment of dementia is considered below (**1287**). According to Gelder, there "is no specific treatment for vascular dementia apart from the control of blood pressure, low-dose aspirin, and if indicated, surgical treatment of carotid artery stenosis."[37]

PICK'S DISEASE (F02.0)

Pick's disease (Dementia in Pick's disease) constitutes about five per cent of all irreversible dementias. Women are affected twice as often as men. The features of the disease have been reviewed by Brown.[38] The area of the brain most affected is distinctive. In contrast to the parietal-temporal distribution of pathology in Alzheimer's disease, Pick's disease is characterised by a preponderance of atrophy in the frontotemporal regions.[39]

Onset and development

Pick's disease is a progressive dementia of unknown cause which usually commences in middle life between the ages of 50 and 60 years. Characteristically, it is marked by slowly progressing changes of character and social deterioration, followed by impairment of intellect, memory, and language functions, with apathy, euphoria, and occasionally extrapyramidal phenomena. The early stages of the disease are thought to be more often characterised by personality and behavioural changes than in cases of Alzheimer's disease[40] although the distinction is generally made at autopsy rather than in life.[41] These behavioural changes may include disinhibition, sometimes affecting sexual conduct, a deterioration of conventional manners, tactless and grossly insensitive behaviour, foolish jokes and pranks, and sometimes marked loss of drive and apparent indolence. As the disease progresses, impairment of intellect and memory become more obvious and slowly increase in severity.[42] Death occurs after between two and ten years.

Diagnostic guidelines

The ICD–10 diagnostic guidelines for Dementia in Pick's disease (F02.0) are three-fold. The following features are required for a definite diagnosis: (a) a progressive dementia; (b) a predominance of frontal lobe features with euphoria, emotional blunting, and coarsening of social behaviour, disinhibition, and either apathy or restlessness; (c) behavioural manifestations, which commonly precede frank memory impairment.[43]

Management and treatment

The management and treatment of dementia is considered below (**1287**).

---

[37]   M. Gelder, *et al.*, *Oxford Textbook of Psychiatry* (Oxford University Press, 3rd ed., 1996), p.526.
[38]   J. Brown, "Pick's disease" in *Baillière's clinical neurology* (Baillière Tindall, 1992), pp.535–553.
[39]   H.I. Kaplan and B.J. Sadock, *Synopsis of Psychiatry* (Williams and Wilkins, 7th ed., 1995), p.347.
[40]   *Ibid.*
[41]   M. Gelder, *et al.*, *Oxford Textbook of Psychiatry*, *supra*, p.323.
[42]   See W.A. Lishman, *Organic Psychiatry, The Psychological Consequences of Cerebral Disorder* (Blackwell Scientific Publications, 2nd ed., 1987), pp.391–393.
[43]   *Classification of Mental and Behavioural Disorders, Tenth Revision (ICD–10): Clinical descriptions and diagnostic guidelines* (World Health Organisation, 1992), p.52.

HUNTINGTON'S CHOREA (F02.2)

Huntington's chorea is normally inherited as an autosomal dominant gene and each child of an affected parent therefore has a 50 per cent chance of developing the disease. It is associated with progressive degeneration of the basal ganglia (**1273**) and the cerebral cortex (**1272**). The prevalence of the disorder is approximately 5–6 cases per 100,000 persons.

Terminology

Chorea (**1065**) is a type of movement characterised by quick, irregular, spasmodic and jerky involuntary movement of muscles, usually affecting the face, limbs and trunk. Those parts of the limbs closest to the trunk (the proximal portions) are more affected than those further away (the distal portions) and the trunk itself may be affected. The word choreiform means resembling chorea.

Onset and development

Huntington's chorea usually begins between the ages of 35 and 50 years. Psychiatric changes are often present for some considerable time before chorea or intellectual impairment develops. In consequence, between one-third and two-thirds of cases are initially misdiagnosed, with schizophrenia and paranoid psychosis being the most common errors. Personality change "may be marked, the patient becoming morose and quarrelsome, or slowed, apathetic, and neglectful of home and person ... Paranoid developments may be the earliest change, with marked sensitivity and ideas of reference (**1086**). Sometimes a florid schizophrenic illness may be present for several years before the true diagnosis becomes apparent. Depression and anxiety may be marked from the onset, perhaps appearing abruptly and being ascribed to some stressful event."[44] Psychotic features become obtrusive in many cases, most commonly a depressive psychosis. The early neurological signs are choreiform movements of the face, hands, and shoulders. These movements are sudden, unexpected, aimless, and forceful.[45] At first the patient is usually thought to be clumsy or fidgety. Dementia develops insidiously and is usual in the later stages but its severity and progress vary widely. Death usually occurs 15 to 20 years after onset.

Diagnostic guidelines

The diagnostic guidelines for "Dementia in Huntington's disease" (F02.2) are the association of choreiform movement disorder, dementia, and a family history of the disease. Involuntary choreiform movements, "typically of the face, hands, and shoulders, or in the gait, are early manifestations. They usually precede the dementia and only rarely remain absent until the dementia is very advanced."[46]

---

[44] W.A. Lishman, *Organic Psychiatry, The Psychological Consequences of Cerebral Disorder* (Blackwell Scientific Publications, 2nd ed., 1987), p.396.

[45] M. Gelder, *et al.*, *Oxford Textbook of Psychiatry* (Oxford University Press, 3rd ed., 1996), p.324.

[46] *Classification of Mental and Behavioural Disorders, Tenth Revision (ICD–10): Clinical descriptions and diagnostic guidelines* (World Health Organisation, 1992), pp.53–54.

Treatment and management

The condition cannot presently be cured. In general, the treatment is similar to that of other dementing disorders (*infra*). Phenothiazines (**1255**) and butyrophenones (**1255**) have been reported as effective for the specific control of choreiform movements. Antidepressants are useful for major depressive symptoms.[47]

DEMENTIA AND DIFFERENTIAL DIAGNOSES

The main differential diagnoses in apparent cases of dementia are mental handicap, delirium, depression and other neurological conditions. Motivational or emotional factors, particularly depression, in addition to motor slowness and general physical frailty, rather than loss of intellectual capacity, may account for failure to perform.[48]

Distinguishing between dementia and delirium

In contrast to the onset of delirium, the onset of dementia is usually insidious and it is distinguished from delirium by the absence of any clouding of consciousness (**1058**); the patient with dementia is usually alert.

Dementia and depression (pseudodementia)

The term pseudodementia describes a condition in which the patient's cognitive deficits are secondary to depression. Depression may be misdiagnosed as dementia "when the patient is slow and vague. A previous or family history of depression, the onset of depressive symptoms before apparent memory impairment, the presence of malaise and querulousness if not frank nihilism and despair, early waking, diurnal variation in mood, weight loss, a failure to confabulate, and ultimately the response to antidepressant therapy of electroplexy are all helpful in reaching the correct conclusion."[49]

THE MANAGEMENT AND TREATMENT OF DEMENTIA

Older people are the group most discriminated against in society. Oppenheimer has drawn attention to the fact that there has often seemed to be a philosophy of second best when it comes to providing medical services for older people and that in many cases very difficult choices have to be made—

> " ... for too many old people the reality is still one of harsh choices within a narrow range of options. A widow struggling against loneliness as her friends die one by one may have no choice but to give up the flat in which all her married life was spent, to move into an old people's home, sharing a bedroom and sitting at table with companions she would not freely have chosen. For a proudly independent man, disabled by a stroke, to be bathed and dressed by a cheery Care Assistant who calls him Dad may be a heavy price to pay for remaining in his own home."[50]

---

[47] M. Gelder, *et al.*, *Oxford Textbook of Psychiatry* (Oxford University Press, 3rd ed., 1996), p.325.
[48] *Classification of Mental and Behavioural Disorders, Tenth Revision (ICD–10): Clinical descriptions and diagnostic guidelines* (World Health Organisation, 1992), p.45.
[49] B. Pitt, "Management problems in psychogeriatrics" in *Contemporary Psychiatry* (ed. S. Crown, Butterworths, London, 1984), p.92.
[50] C. Oppenheimer, "The Elderly" in *Essential Psychiatry* (ed. N. Rose, Blackwell Scientific Publications, 1992), p.131.

Assessment

Management and treatment should, as always, be based on a thorough assessment of the patient's mental state and circumstances. Assessment at home enables the problem to be seen where it presents, family and neighbours to be met, the local assets and liabilities to be noted, and the correct social diagnosis as well as the medical one to be made.[51]

Clinical pictuire

The clinical picture is made up of the patient's premorbid personality and intellect (the kind of person the patient is), the distribution and severity of the pathological process in the brain and the specific handicaps arising from that; the response of the patient to the illness (emotional response and coping strategies); the effect on the patient of other people's reactions. Within such a framework it becomes easier to understand the origins of problems for which help is being sought and to determine what kinds of intervention might help with them.[52] Physical examination should look for causes, complications such as dehydration, and additional disabilities such as arthritis. Mental functioning should be tested.

Testing cognitive functioning

The examination of cognitive function "should at a minimum include tests of orientation, remote memory, and registration and recall of new (simple) information; and should make some estimation of the use of language, abstract thought and visuo-spatial skills. Several short tests of mental function are available."[53] The use of rating scales in old age psychiatry has been reviewed by Copeland and Wilson.[54] The *Blessed Dementia Rating Scale* (BDRS),[55] which concentrates on memory and orientation, remains widely used. Where a single score is required as an indication of the severity of already recognised dementia, the scale can be recommended with confidence.[56] The *Mini Mental State Examination* (MMSE) takes between five and ten minutes to administer and consists of two parts, verbal and performance. Four verbal subtests with a maximum score of 21 points evaluate orientation in time, memory and attention. Two performance subtests with a maximum score of 9 points involve the naming of objects, execution of written or spoken orders, writing, and copying a complex polygon. Anthony found that 87 per cent of a sample of patients with clinical dementia scored below 23 points and similar findings have been reported by Roth.[57] The *Global Deterioration Scale* (GDS) grades dementia, mainly by disabilities of memory, according to seven levels of clinical descriptions ranging from normality to severe Alzheimer's disease.

---

[51]   B. Pitt, "Management problems in psychogeriatrics" in *Contemporary Psychiatry* (ed. S. Crown, Butterworths, London, 1984), p.90.

[52]   C. Oppenheimer, "The Elderly" in *Essential Psychiatry* (ed. N. Rose, Blackwell Scientific Public-ations, 1992), p.134.

[53]   *Ibid.*

[54]   J.R.M. Copeland and K.C.M. Wilson, "Rating scales in old age psychiatry" in *The Instruments of Psychiatric Research* (ed. C. Thompson, John Wiley and Sons, 1989).

[55]   G. Blessed, *et al.*, "The association between qualitative measures of dementia and senile change in the cerebral grey matter of older subjects" *British Journal of Psychiatry* (1968) 114, 797–811.

[56]   J.R.M. Copeland and K.C.M. Wilson, "Rating scales in old age psychiatry," *supra*, p.313.

[57]   J.C. Anthony, *et al.*, "Limits of the Mini-Mental State as a screening test for dementia and delirium among hospital patients" Psychological Medicine (1982) 12, 397–408; M. Roth, "Differential diagnoses of psychiatric disorders in old age" *Hospital Practice* (1986) 15, 111–125; J.R.M. Copeland and K.C.M. Wilson, Rating scales in old age psychiatry, *supra*, p.314.

Psychiatric services for older people

The general principles underlying the development of a psychiatric service for older people have been described by Arie, Bergmann, Oppenheimer and Pitt. The expertise of the psychogeriatrician is as much administrative as clinical.[58] He "must develop a multi-disciplinary team that undertakes responsibility for the problems of old people needing psychiatric help in a defined area. Ready availability, prompt appraisal, swift action where necessary, and deft liaison with the primary health care team, the geriatric and social services, and families and caring neighbours are of the first importance."[59] These agencies must work together to provide a pattern of care at the level of intensity suited to the patient's needs at each stage of the illness until death.

Hospital admission

Pitt has written that "after early and correct diagnosis the next principle of psychogeriatric treatment is to keep the patient at home as long as possible provided neither he nor those caring for him suffer unduly. Not only are institutional resources scarce but also old people fare best in familiar surroundings."[60] Following admission, the individual may be "disorientated by strange people and surroundings, bewildered by bizarre procedures, puzzled by the incongruous familiarity of very young nurses and their meaningless endearments, drugged into immobility and somnolence, and deprived of personal clothing, possessions, occupation, and choice."[61] Removal from familiar surroundings is therefore upsetting, and hospitalisation may simply avoid rather than solve problems.[62] Admission will, however, be indicated in cases where there will otherwise be a significant risk of severe self-neglect. The advantages of in-patient care have been summarised by Oppenheimer: skilled observation over long periods of time; access to specialist input; freedom of action for the patient in an environment tolerant of odd behaviour, with a stable and predictable timetable, and a variety of activities and levels of sociability. Good in-patient services should concentrate on maintaining the individual's personality and self-respect and improving his quality of life. This includes addressing him by his proper name and title; consulting his wishes; ensuring that he has the use of glasses, hearing aids, and other essential devices[63]; providing a locker for personal possessions, keeping medication to a minimum; providing cheerful, clean surroundings and a full programme of activities, including exercise; allowing unrestricted visiting; and the use of reality orientation therapy (teaching simple and useful facts by the frequent reiteration of information about time, place and person and the use of commonly encountered objects). The need for consultation applies no less to citizens who have been detained. While it may not always be possible to observe their wishes, they should as a matter of common decency be adhered to wherever possible. The purpose of invoking compulsory powers is not to dictate every aspect of the patient's life, merely to protect him and others from his worst follies.

---

[58] T. Arie, *British Medical Journal* (1971) iii, 166.
[59] B. Pitt, "Management problems in psychogeriatrics" in *Contemporary Psychiatry* (ed. S. Crown, Butterworths, London, 1984), p.90.
[60] *Ibid.*, p.92.
[61] *Ibid.*, p.95.
[62] C. Oppenheimer, "The Elderly" in *Essential Psychiatry* (ed. N. Rose, Blackwell Scientific Publications, 1992), p.133.
[63] Some 30–40 per cent. of persons over 65 living at home have hearing difficulties.

Professional support in the community

Many social problems which may affect mental health or its treatment are particularly prevalent amongst older people so that illnesses are often triggered or compounded by problems such as financial hardship, poor housing or loneliness. Professional support includes increasing personal social services where appropriate; visits by the patient's General practitioner, a health visitor, a district nurse, and a home-help; the prescription of medication to be taken at home; the allocation of a community psychogeriatric nurse, who can provide counselling and support, supervision, follow-up, and administer drugs; out-patient consultations; day hospital attendance; psychotherapy and marital therapy for personality and relationship problems; and short-term admissions and respite care to help carers, although the patient's confusion may temporarily be increased and the carer's tolerance reduced.[64] Practical measures taken by social workers include arranging state benefits, arranging laundry services for the incontinent[65]; paying neighbours to oversee the patient; explaining the patient's situation to neighbours and local shopkeepers; liaising with street and estate wardens; providing sheltered housing and arranging nursing home care if necessary.

Family and social support in the community

Approximately four per cent of persons aged over 65, and 20 per cent of persons aged over 85, are bedfast or housebound. Family and social support is, however, often sadly lacking. Most older people live alone or with another person of similar age and half of all women aged over 65 are widows. One-third of older people have no surviving children or never had any. This is particularly unfortunate because Bergmann concluded from a study of day hospital patients with dementia that family support was the most important factor determining their continuing life in the community.[66] The chances of providing a pattern of care suited to the patient's needs at each stage until death is greatest where there are family members who have the will and strength to act as the backbone of the care. The professional input can then "be concentrated on helping the family members, by offering a shared understanding of the illness, emotional support, time and space away from the task of caring in a reliable routine, immediate response in crises, and partnership in planning each step into the future."[67]

Modifying the patient's home

Practical modifications may improve the home environment and make it safer. For example, low-level light to guide the way to the bathroom, door catches to prevent the individual wandering onto a busy road, and the use of storage heaters.

Ways of relieving stress

Oppenheimer has suggested various ways of helping to relieve stress on the patient. These include treating any additional illnesses and disabilities; making the patient's

---

64   B. Pitt, "Management problems in psychogeriatrics" in *Contemporary Psychiatry* (ed. S. Crown, Butterworths, London, 1984), p.93.

65   In those over 75 years of age, 16 per cent. of women and eight per cent. of men have regular episodes of urinary incontinence.

66   K. Bergmann, *et al.*, *British Journal of Psychiatry* (1978) 132, 441.

67   C. Oppenheimer, "The Elderly" in *Essential Psychiatry* (ed. N. Rose, Blackwell Scientific Publications, 1992), p.134.

environment as consistent and predictable as possible, with clear cues to place and time; reinforcing the environment's comprehensibility at every natural opportunity, by introducing yourself by name, addressing the patient by name, explaining where you are; adapting communication strategies to the abilities of the patient (reinforcing words with gestures, avoiding ambiguity and distraction, keeping sentences simple); giving the patient access to enjoyable activities tailored to his competence; returning to areas of expertise, such as recollecting the past, as a break from demands of present difficulties; utilising memory impairment and the fact that the memory of upsetting experiences fades after a minute or two.[68]

EPILEPSY

Approximately five per cent of the population have a fit at some stage during their lives and about 4–6 persons per thousand suffer from epilepsy. About 40 per cent of cases arise after the age of 20. A disproportionate number of people with epilepsy experience psychiatric problems, possibly half of those suffering from temporal lobe epilepsy (**1293**). However, these problems most commonly fall within the "neurotic spectrum." Assessment usually includes an EEG (**1099**).

Terminology

Seizures are characterised by abnormal electrical activity in the brain. More specifically, a seizure is a transient paroxysmal disturbance of cerebral function that is caused by a spontaneous, excessive discharge of neurones. Patients are said to have epilepsy if they have a chronic condition characterised by recurrent seizures.[69]

The terminology of epilepsy

Generalised seizure	Generalised epileptic seizures involve the entire brain and do not clearly originate in one part of it. There are two main kinds, grand mal and petit mal. These are nowadays referred to by doctors as "generalised tonic-clonic seizures" and as "absences" respectively.
Partial seizure	Partial seizures start in one locality of the brain and the seizure activity may or may not then spread through the brain. Partial seizures which do not involve any impairment of consciousness are commonly described as simple partial seizures while those that result in altered consciousness are known as complex partial seizures.
Focal seizure	In general usage, synonymous with partial seizure, the word focal simply meaning localised.

---

[68] C. Oppenheimer, "The Elderly" in *Essential Psychiatry* (ed. N. Rose, Blackwell Scientific Publications, 1992), p.135.

[69] H.I. Kaplan and B.J. Sadock, *Synopsis of Psychiatry* (Williams and Wilkins, 7th ed.), p.364.

Prodromata	Prodromata are symptoms, such as mounting irritability, which precede a seizure.
Aura	The symptoms which usher in a partial seizure, their content being determined by the area of the brain within which the seizure is originating. Some attacks may proceed no further.
Ictus	The seizure itself. The ictal phase lasts up to one or two minutes. The post-ictal phase following the seizure usually includes confusion.
Temporal lobe epilepsy	A form of complex partial seizure arising in the temporal lobe. The majority of complex partial seizures originate here.

Generalised seizures (petit mal and grand mal)

Petit mal is seen most commonly in children. Three varieties are distinguished but by far the most common is the petit mal absence or "simple absence." Here, the individual without warning "loses contact with his environment, usually for four or five seconds but occasionally for as long as half a minute. To the onlooker he appears momentarily dazed, stops speaking and becomes immobile. The face is pale, the eyes assume a fixed glazed appearance, and the pupils may be observed to be fixed and dilated. Posture and balance are usually well maintained ... There are usually no after-effects whatever ... The frequency of episodes is commonly five to ten per day."[70] Generalised tonic-clonic seizures are what most people think of as constituting an epileptic attack. An aura is lacking and there is no evidence of a local onset. The fit is usually followed by a deep sleep which may then be succeeded by nausea, vomiting and headache. If sleep does not occur a period of confusion is usually seen during which the patient is disorientated, often restless, rambling and incoherent, and sometimes unaware of his personal identity.[71]

Focal or partial epilepsy

Focal symptoms in the form of an aura usher in the seizure, the precise symptomatology depending on the area of the brain in which the discharge originates and the direction of its subsequent spread. The auras which precede focal epileptic attacks "are of great clinical importance ... the symptoms appear abruptly, and in the majority of cases are experienced passively as foreign intrusions on the stream of awareness. They probably rarely occupy more than a few seconds or perhaps a minute, though subjectively the time course may appear much longer."[72] Auras are distinguished from prodromata, which do not appear abruptly but build up slowly for hours or days before the attacks occur. Typically, they consist of "psychological manifestations — mounting irritability, apprehension, sullenness, apathy or periods of mental dullness."[73] Such prodromata lack the clinical significance of the well-defined aura.

• **Parietal seizures**	Paraesthesiae, numbness, tingling, feelings of heat and cold, which spread to contiguous areas of the body; pronounced disorders of body image.
• **Occipital seizures**	Visual disturbances, well localised within the opposite half-field of vision; simple visual hallucinations consisting of flashes of light, colours, zig-zags, or radiating spectra.
• **Temporal lobe seizures**	Varied and complex auras. Churning fear or pain in the stomach rising towards the throat; salivation, flushing, pallor, subjective dizziness. Altered perceptual experiences: complex hallucinations of scenes, faces or visions of past events; objects seem larger or smaller, nearer or further away; auditory hallucinations in the form of ringing and buzzing, organised experiences of music or voices; sounds seem suddenly remote or intensely loud; feelings of derealisation or depersonalisation; déjà vu and jamais vu; gustatory and olfactory hallucinations (*e.g.* smell of burning rubber or burning cabbage); chewing, swallowing or smacking movements; speech automatisms; time appearing to rush by or standstill; strong affective experiences such as fear, anxiety, depression, guilt, anger.

Source: *W.A. Lishman, Organic Psychiatry, The Psychological Consequences of Cerebral Disorder, 2nd Ed., Blackwell Scientific Publications, Oxford, pp.217–220.*

Temporal lobe epilepsy

In a tribunal context, the importance of identifying temporal lobe epilepsy lies mainly in the fact that it is sometimes misdiagnosed for another condition which cannot be so readily brought under control. Schizophrenia-type episodes may be transient. In other cases, a schizophrenic illness may occur in someone known to have epilepsy, either coincidentally or by association, although even here the prognosis may be more favourable than is usual. Thus, Perez found that most patients with a dual diagnosis seemed to avoid institutionalisation and to live reasonably well in the community.[74] It should, however, be added that adult patients with temporal lobe epilepsy may be more prone to personality disturbance including, rarely, explosive aggression.

---

[74] M.M. Perez, *et al.*, "Epileptic psychosis: an evaluation of PSE profiles" *British Journal of Psychiatry* (1985) 146, 155–163.

ANTICONVULSIVE DRUGS

Anticonvulsive drugs form the mainstay of treatment. There are many effective drugs available, some of the most important of which are noted in the table below.

ANTIEPILEPTIC DRUGS (B.N.F. 4.8)

Drug	Proprietary	BNF guideline doses
Carbamazepine	• Carbamazepine (tablets) • Tegretol (tablets, liquid, suppositories) • Tegretol Retard (tablets)	*By mouth* initially 100–200mg once or twice daily, increased to usual daily dose of 0.8–1.2g (some cases 1.6–2g). *By rectum* maximum 7 days use, 125mg approximately equivalent to 100mg tablet, maximum 1g daily. Plasma concentration for optimum response 4–12mg/litre (20–50 micromol/litre).
Ethosuximide	• Emeside (capsules, syrup) • Zarontin capsules, syrup)	Initially 500mg daily, increased to usual daily dose of 1–1.5g. Occasionally up to 2g may be needed. Plasma concentration for optimum response 40–100mg/ litre (300–700 micromol/litre).
Phenytoin	• Phenytoin (tablets, capsules) • Epanutin (tablets, suspension)	*By mouth* initially 3–4mg/kg daily or 150–300mg daily, increased gradually as necessary. Usual dose 300–400mg daily, maximum 600mg daily. Plasma concentration for optimum response 10–20mg/litre (40–80 micromol/litre).
Sodium Valproate	• Sodium Valproate (tablets, oral solution) • Epilim (tablets, liquid, syrup) • Epilim Chrono (tablets) • Epilim Intravenous (injection) • Convulex (valproic acid capsules)	By mouth, initially 600mg daily increasing by 200mg/day at 3-day intervals to a maximum of 2g daily (20–30 mg/kg daily). By IV injection or infusion, same as current dose by oral route.

ENDOCRINE DISORDERS

The internal environment of the body is controlled and regulated partly by the autonomic nervous system (**1267**) and partly by hormones. The endocrine system consists of a collection of glands[75] that produce hormones, secreting them directly into the bloodstream. A hormone is a chemical messenger which, having been formed in one organ or gland, is carried in the blood to a target organ or tissue where it influences activity.[76] Endocrine disorder can be accompanied by prominent mental abnormalities and epochs of life marked by endocrine change, such as pregnancy and the menopause, appear to be associated with special liability to mental disturbance.

---

[75] A gland is a group of specialised cells that manufacture and release chemical substances such as hormones and enzymes for use in the body.

[76] K.J.W. Wilson, *Ross and Wilson, Anatomy and Physiology in Health and Illness* (Churchill Livingstone, 7th ed., 1990), p.311.

1294

With some endocrine disorders, such as myxoedema and Addison's disease, the psychiatric abnormalities are regularly intrusive to such a degree that there is a constant risk of mistaken diagnosis.[77]

TROPHIC HORMONES

Many glands are regulated by trophic (gland-stimulating) hormones secreted by the pituitary, which is itself influenced by hormones secreted by the hypothalamus in the brain. Production of too much or too little hormone by a gland is prevented by feed-back mechanisms: variations in the blood level of the hormones are detected by the hypothalamus, which prompts the pituitary to modify its production of trophic (gland-stimulating) hormone accordingly.

PITUITARY GLAND

The pituitary gland and the hypothalamus (1273) function as a unit and are attached by a short stalk of nerve fibres. The pituitary is a pea-sized structure that hangs from the base of the brain and lies in a cavity in the skull. It consists of three lobes known, because of their relative positions, as the anterior, intermediate and posterior lobes. The different lobes produce a range of hormones. The anterior pituitary produces ACTH (adrenocorticotrophic hormone), which stimulates hormone production by the adrenal glands, and TSH (thyroid-stimulating hormone), which stimulates hormone production by the thyroid gland.

Disorders of the pituitary

Any abnormality of the pituitary gland usually means that it produces either too much or too little of one or more hormones and this causes changes elsewhere in the body. Pituitary tumours are rare and usually benign but they often cause visual field defects and may result in either overproduction of pituitary hormones (hyperpituitarism) or underproduction (hypopituitarism). The tumour may also cause the gland to produce too much thyroid-stimulating hormone (TSH), causing hyperthyroidism (1298), or too much adrenocorticotrophic hormone (ACTH), causing Cushing's Syndrome (1297). The diagnosis is made from measurements of the levels of different hormones in the blood and urine, from CT scanning (1103) or MRI of the brain (1104), and from visual field testing. Treatment for a pituitary tumour may be by surgery, radiotherapy, or hormone replacement. Radiotherapy may cause general underactivity of the gland.

Simmond's disease (hypopituitarism)

The condition is commonly of long duration. Symptoms and signs include weakness, ready fatigue, marked sensitivity to cold, amenorrhoea in females and impotence in males, loss of weight, a thin dry skin which fails to tan normally, dull expressionless face, loss of pubic and axillary hair (hair in the armpit), low body temperature, blood pressure and pulse.

---

[77] W.A. Lishman, *Organic Psychiatry, The Psychological Consequences of Cerebral Disorder* (Blackwell Scientific Publications, 2nd ed., 1987), p.428.

Psychiatric symptoms

In one survey of patients with Simmond's disease, 90 per cent of patients showed psychiatric symptoms and in half these were severe. Alterations of mood form an integral part of the clinical picture and take the form of apathy, anergia and indifference. Depression may be marked, sometimes with bursts of irritability, self-neglect, and occasionally impairment of memory. Impairment of memory may give the impression of a dementing process and episodes of delirium may be seen. Chronic paranoid hallucinatory states are very occasionally seen but it is exceptional for hypopituitarism to give rise to a functional psychosis.

Anorexia nervosa

The "principal differential diagnosis is from anorexia nervosa. Many of the early reported cases of hypopituitarism seem in retrospect to have been anorexia nervosa."[78] The differentiating features are that in cases of Simmond's disease severe weight loss is rare, except terminally; there are no distinctive attitudes to food and no distorted body image; appetite may be well preserved; and patients are dull or apathetic, rather than restless and active. Conversely, loss of pubic and axillary hair is rare in anorexia.

ADRENAL GLANDS

The adrenal glands are a pair of small, triangular, glands located above the kidney. Each gland comprises two distinct parts, the outer adrenal cortex and the smaller inner adrenal medulla.

The adrenal cortex

The adrenal cortex secretes hydrocortisone (cortisol), corticosterone, and small amounts of androgen hormones, the production of which is governed by other hormones made in the hypothalamus and pituitary gland. Hydrocortisone is the most important human corticosteroid, controlling the body's use of fats, proteins, and carbohydrates. The rate of hydrocortisone secretion is controlled by the release of ACTH (adrenocorticotrophic hormone) by the pituitary gland (**1295**).

The adrenal medulla

The adrenal medulla is part of the sympathetic division of the autonomic nervous system and secretes the hormones adrenaline and noradrenaline in response to stimulation by sympathetic nerves.

Disorders of the adrenal glands

Adrenal tumours are rare and usually cause excess secretion of hormones. Tumours of the adrenal cortex may secrete hydrocortisone, causing Cushing's Syndrome (**1297**). Similarly, because hydrocortisone production is regulated by the pituitary gland, a pituitary disorder can cause excess ACTH secretion, too much hydrocortisone and, hence, Cushing's Syndrome. Deficient production of hormones by the adrenal cortex due to disease of the adrenal glands is called Addison's Disease.

---

[78]   W.A. Lishman, *Organic Psychiatry, The Psychological Consequences of Cerebral Disorder* (Blackwell Scientific Publications, 2nd ed., 1987), p.444.

Cushing's Syndrome

In some 80 per cent of cases, Cushing's Syndrome is due to pituitary overproduction of ACTH (**1295**). The disorder is more common in women, usually starting in young middle-age. A tendency has been noted for it to start during puberty, pregnancy or the menopause, or while the subject is undergoing a prolonged period of psychological stress.[79] Almost half of the patients in Cohen's study had a family history of depression or suicide or a past history of early bereavement or separation; over 20 per cent had had an emotional disturbance shortly prior to onset, generally a loss of some kind such as separation or bereavement; and 86 per cent showed a significant degree of depression.[80] The physical changes are summarised by Lishman and they include moon face, buffalo hump, truncal obesity, insidious weight gain, plethoric complexion and hirsuties, excessive bruising, skin pigmentation, muscular weakness, hypertension, amenorrhoea in females and impotence, testicular atrophy or gynaecomastia in males.

Psychiatric symptoms

The chief diagnostic hazard lies with those patients who develop psychotic features early in the illness before the physical changes are marked. Psychiatric features are "strikingly frequent and can be severe."[81] Depression is the most frequent psychiatric symptom and paranoid features are also very common. A wide range of other mental abnormalities is seen: emotional lability with gross over-reaction to emotional stimuli, uncooperative behaviour, or sudden outbursts of restless hyperactivity, acute anxiety, states of apathy verging on stupor. A successful psychiatric outcome can be expected when the endocrine disorder is effectively treated: the physical and psychiatric symptoms usually improve in parallel and the resolution of psychotic features is sometimes dramatic.[82]

In-patients and psychoses

The "severe psychoses accompanying Cushing's syndrome are again mostly depressive in nature. Typically they are florid illnesses with delusions and auditory hallucinations and often with paranoid symptoms. Retardation tends to be severe, sometimes bordering on stupor ... Marked fluctuations in the severity of the condition appear to be characteristic."[83] Classic schizophrenic-type psychoses are rare.

Addison's Disease

Addison's disease is more common in males and usually presents in early adult or middle life. The onset of symptoms is gradual. The usual presentation is of chronic physical exhaustion, with tiredness and general weakness, loss of appetite and loss of weight, sensitivity to infections, amenorrhoea in females and impotence in males, hypotension, fainting, and pigmentation on exposed skin surfaces. Adequate replacement therapy is usually highly successful in alleviating both physical and mental disturbances.

---

[79]   W.A. Lishman, *Organic Psychiatry, The Psychological Consequences of Cerebral Disorder* (Blackwell Scientific Publications, 2nd ed., 1987), p.436.

[80]   S.I. Cohen, "Cushing's syndrome: a psychiatric study of 29 patients" *British Journal of Psychiatry* (1980) 136, 120–124.

[81]   W.A. Lishman, *Organic Psychiatry, The Psychological Consequences of Cerebral Disorder*, *supra*, p.436.

[82]   *Ibid.*, pp.438–439.

[83]   *Ibid.*, p.437.

Psychiatric symptoms

Psychiatric symptoms are present almost without exception, the commonest of them being depressive withdrawal and irritability (50 per cent of cases), apathy and negativism (80 per cent of cases), and loss of drive. There may be sudden fluctuations of mood, and difficulties with memory form a major feature in up to three-quarters of cases.[84]

In-patients and psychoses

Psychotic pictures of a depressive or schizophrenic nature "are rare in contrast to the situation in Cushing's disease ... From the psychiatric point of view an erroneous diagnosis of neurosis or early dementia may easily be made."[85]

THYROID GLAND

The thyroid gland is situated in the front of the neck, just below the larynx (voice-box). It consists of two lobes, one on each side of the trachea (windpipe), joined by a narrower portion of tissue called the isthmus. Thyroid tissue is composed of two types of secretory cells: *follicular cells*, which make up most of the gland and which secrete the iodine-containing hormones thyroxine (T_4) and triiodothyronine (T_3), and *parafollicular cells*, which produce the hormone calcitonin. T_4 (the hormone produced in greatest amounts by the thyroid gland) and T_3 regulate metabolism.[86] Their secretion by the thyroid is controlled by a hormonal feedback system involving the pituitary gland and the hypothalamus. Calcitonin acts in conjunction with the parathyroid hormone (**1301**) to regulate the level of calcium in the body.

Thyroid disorders

The function of the thyroid gland is controlled by both the pituitary gland and the hypothalamus, so thyroid disorders may be due not only to defects in the gland itself but also to disruption of the hypothalamic-pituitary hormonal control system. Insufficient thyroid hormone production is known as hypothyroidism and overproduction as hyperthyroidism. Thyroid tumours may be benign or malignant. Thyrotoxicosis is a general term for any condition that results from hyperthyroidism.

Hyperthyroidism (thyrotoxicosis)

Hyperthyroidism affects females more commonly than males, in a ratio of 6 to 1. It is commonest in the second and third decades of life. The onset is often abrupt and may follow directly some stressful event or emotional crisis. Tachycardia, fine finger tremor, palpitations and loss of weight are often features. In descending order of discriminating value, the symptoms of most importance in indicating the disorder

---

[84] W.A. Lishman, *Organic Psychiatry, The Psychological Consequences of Cerebral Disorder* (Blackwell Scientific Publications, 2nd ed., 1987), p.439; R.A. Cleghorn, "Hormones and tumours" in *Hormonal Steroids. Biochemistry, Pharmacology, and Therapeutics* (ed. L. Martini and A. Pecile, Academic Press, 1965), Vol. 2; R.P. Michael and J.L. Gibbons, "Interrelationships between the endocrine system and neuropsychiatry" *International Review of Neurobiology* (1963) 5, 243–302.

[85] W.A. Lishman, *Organic Psychiatry, The Psychological Consequences of Cerebral Disorder*, *supra*, p.440.

[86] Metabolism is the chemical activity in cells that releases energy from nutrients or uses energy to create other substances such as proteins.

have been found to be sensitivity to heat and preference for cold, increased appetite, loss of weight, sweating, palpitations, tiredness.[87] In the majority of cases, laboratory investigations give unequivocal results with raised serum thyroxine (T_4) and triiodothyronine (T_3).

Psychiatric symptoms

Lishman, the leading expert on organic disorders, has summarised the psychiatric manifestations of the endocrine disorder.[88] Psychological disturbance in some degree is universal with thyroid overactivity and probably the result of increased thyroxine levels: "The patient becomes restless, overactive and irritable, sometimes with hyperacuity of perception and over-reaction to noise. Heightened tension leads to impatience and intolerance of frustration, and there may be emotional lability with unreasonable or histrionic behaviour. Fluctuating depression is occasionally a prominent feature, though unaccompanied by retardation ... The over-arousal leads to distractibility so that concentration is impaired and effort cannot be sustained ... The emotional disturbance can reach a degree which leads to difficulty in clinical management ... States of extreme anxiety or hostile irritation may emerge as a direct extension of the heightened emotional tension."[89] It seems that some emotional instability characterises a significant proportion of subjects and this may explain why some patients remain emotionally unstable after resolution of the endocrine disorder.[90] However, the result of treatment is generally satisfactory.

In-patients and psychoses

Psychotic developments have been reported in up to 20 per cent of cases.[91] McLarty, *et al.*, found eight patients with thyrotoxicosis in two psychiatric hospitals with a combined population of 1200 patients. The existence of hyperthyroidism had not been suspected in six of these patients prior to the survey and in five cases it seemed to be contributing to the mental illness.[92] Affective and schizophrenia-type psychoses are sometimes indistinguishable from the naturally occurring disorders, with mania said to be more frequent than depression. It is generally agreed that a distinctive colouring may be lent by the hyperthyroidism: agitation is often profound in the presence of depression and most observers agree that paranoid features are especially common whatever form the psychosis may take. "Apathetic hyperthyroidism" is rare but may be easily overlooked and the typical picture is of a middle-aged or older patient with considerable weight loss and apathy or depression.[93]

---

[87]   E.J. Wayne, "Clinical and metabolic studies in thyroid disease" *British Medical Journal* (1960) 1, 1–11, 78–90.

[88]   See W.A. Lishman, *Organic Psychiatry, The Psychological Consequences of Cerebral Disorder* (Blackwell Scientific Publications, 2nd ed., 1987), pp.429–432.

[89]   *Ibid.*, p.429.

[90]   W.A. Lishman, *Organic Psychiatry, The Psychological Consequences of Cerebral Disorder, supra*, p.429; referring to C. Gurney, *et al.*, "A study of the physical and psychiatric characteristics of women attending an out-patient clinic for investigation for thyrotoxicosis" *(Communication to the Scottish Society for Experimental Medicine, 1967).*

[91]   W.A. Lishman, *Organic Psychiatry, The Psychological Consequences of Cerebral Disorder, supra*, p.430.

[92]   D.G. McLarty, *et al.*, A study of thyroid function in psychiatric in-patients. British Journal of Psychiatry (1978) 133, 211–218.

[93]   F.B. Thomas, *et al.*, "Apathetic thyrotoxicosis: in a distinctive clinical and laboratory entity" *Annals of Internal Medicine* (1970) 72, 679–685.

Myxoedema (hypothyroidism)

Lishman has written that "myxoedema is of great importance in psychiatric practice and notorious for leading to mistakes in diagnosis. It is liable to be overlooked on account of its insidious development."[94] Hypothyroidism affects females more commonly than males, in a ratio of 8 to 1, and presents most frequently in middle age. Patients on long-term lithium therapy are at increased risk of developing the disorder. Lishman summarises the main physical features. The skin is dry and rough with swelling of face and limbs due to oedema. The appearance "is characteristic, with a pale puffy complexion and baggy eyelids ... The patient may have noticed increased loss of hair, which has become lank and dry in texture. Speech is slow, and the voice often coarse, thick and toneless. The whole disposition of the patient is sluggish and inert ... Appetite is diminished, the patient is constipated ... Menorrhagia is common in females, and impotence in males."[95] Neurological abnormalities may include the occurrence of fits, fainting, strokes and cerebellar disturbance, e.g., nystagmus, dysarthria or ataxia. Laboratory investigations confirm the diagnosis with low thyroxine (T_4) and triiodothyronine (T_3) levels. The protein in the cerebrospinal fluid may be moderately raised. Elevated plasma TRH indicates primary thyroid failure in distinction to hypopituitarism.

Psychiatric symptoms

The typical picture is of mental lethargy, general dulling of the personality, and slowing of all cognitive functions. Ready fatigue may be a conspicuous feature, with a marked inability to sustain mental exertion. Memory is often affected from an early stage, with failure to register events and forgetfulness for day-to-day happenings. The typical mood change is towards apathy rather than depression, and irritability is a frequent feature, with some patients becoming markedly agitated and aggressive.[96] Treatment is "highly rewarding" and the "great majority of patients" with serious psychiatric developments can be expected to respond.[97] However, in the case of affective or schizophrenic-type illnesses, a duration of mental illness exceeding two years indicates a need for other forms of treatment in addition to thyroid replacement therapy, reflecting the fact that the psychiatric abnormalities are probably linked to constitutional factors.

In-patients and psychoses

The "only unifying feature, upheld by many observers, is the frequency of a paranoid colouring whatever form the psychosis may take."[98] The commonest form of severe psychiatric illness is an organic psychosis but a picture of dementia or, more rarely, a severe depressive psychosis or schizophrenic-type illness may develop—

- the common organic psychosis usually shows the features of delirium, with florid delusions and hallucinations, mental confusion, and impairment of consciousness. Delusions of persecution may be gross and bizarre. Auditory hallucinations appear to be particularly common.

---

[94] W.A. Lishman, *Organic Psychiatry, The Psychological Consequences of Cerebral Disorder* (Blackwell Scientific Publications, 2nd ed., 1987), p.433.
[95] *Ibid.*
[96] *Ibid.*, p.433.
[97] *Ibid.*, p.436.
[98] *Ibid.*

- depressive psychosis and schizophrenic-type psychoses may be accompanied by organic features and paranoid symptoms figure prominently. The depressive features are often severe, with agitation or bizarre hypochondriasis, and may prove particularly resistant to treatment until the myxoedema is discovered. Schizophrenic-type psychoses are usually coloured by mental slowing, often with features indicative of organic cerebral impairment.

PARATHYROID GLANDS

The parathyroid glands are two pairs of oval, pea-sized, glands which lie behind the lobes of the thyroid gland in the neck. The glands secrete parathyroid hormone, which maintains the calcium level in the blood. This requires constant regulation because even small variations from normal levels can impair muscle and nerve function.

Disorders of the parathyroid glands

In rare cases, the parathyroid glands may become overactive (hyperparathyroidism) or underactive (hypoparathyroidism). A parathyroid tumour may cause excess secretion of the parathyroid hormone into the bloodstream. In most cases, surgery provides a complete cure although occasionally hypoparathyroidism may result.

Hyperparathyroidism

Hyperparathyroidism is a rare but important cause of psychiatric morbidity and is important because the diagnosis may be missed, resulting in many years of chronic mental ill-health.[99] Women are affected more often than men and cases usually present in middle age. Physical symptoms and signs include pain, fracture or deformity of bones; muscular weakness; increased thirst, polyuria, anorexia and nausea. There is renal calcification in two-thirds of cases. Serum phosphate may be low and the serum alkaline phosphatase is raised when the bones are involved.

Psychiatric symptoms

The diagnosis should be borne in mind in patients who show chronic affective disorder in association with suspicious physical symptoms such as thirst.[100] Psychiatric symptoms are common, severe in approximately one-third of cases, and may dominate the picture. The commonest mental change is depression with anergia. There is tiredness and listlessness, the patient unable to work, sometimes accompanied by tension and irritability. Organic mental symptoms (chiefly impairment of memory and general mental slowing) are sometimes present. The cause of the psychiatric disturbance lies chiefly with the elevation of serum calcium and confirmation of the disease is by way of a raised serum calcium: affective disorders corresponding to a serum calcium of 12–16 mg/100 ml, acute organic reactions with florid delirium appearing at 16–19 mg/100 ml, and somnolence and coma with levels exceeding 19 mg/100 ml.[101] The mental disorder is commonly found to be wholly reversible and parallels the fall in serum calcium.

---

[99]   W.A. Lishman, *Organic Psychiatry, The Psychological Consequences of Cerebral Disorder* (Blackwell Scientific Publications, 2nd ed., 1987), p.447.
[100]   *Ibid.*, p.449.
[101]   P. Peterson, "Psychiatric disorders in primary hyperparathyroidism" *Journal of Clinical Endocrinology and Metabolism* (1968) 28, 1491–1495.

In-patients and psychoses

Acute organic psychoses are occasionally seen, with spells of mental confusion, or acute delirious episodes with hallucinations, paranoia and aggressive behaviour. A mistaken diagnosis of pre-senile dementia may result.

Hypoparathyroidism

The literature on hypoparathyroidism is replete with examples of failure to diagnose the condition, sometimes over very many years.[102] The commonest cause is removal of the parathyroid glands at thyroidectomy or interference with their blood supply in the course of other operations on the neck. Calcium deposits may occur in the skin and the brain. A history of operation on the neck should bring the possibility of the condition to mind. Hypoparathyroidism should also be suspected in patients with symptoms of chronic tetany or when ocular cataracts develop at an unusually young age. Tetany occurs in the form of numbness and tingling in the hands and feet or around the mouth and, if more severe, the patient experiences muscular cramps and stiffness in the limbs. Epilepsy can be the first and sometimes the only manifestation. In addition to cataracts, patients may have a dry, coarse skin, scanty hair, trophic changes in the nails and poor dental development.[103] The deficiency of parathormone leads to low serum calcium and a raised serum phosphate. The response to correction of the serum biochemistry is usually excellent.

Psychiatric symptoms

A wide variety and high incidence of psychiatric disturbances are seen. Acute organic reactions with features typical of delirium may develop. In more insidious cases, there may be difficulty with concentration, emotional lability, impairment of intellectual functions, "pseudo-neurosis" (depression, nervousness, irritability with frequent crying spells and marked social withdrawal). Hypoparathyroidism may be mistaken as mental impairment, presenile dementia or, where mood-swings are apparent, manic-depressive disorder.

In-patients and psychoses

Psychotic illnesses of manic-depressive or schizophrenic type may more rarely be seen, particularly in cases due to surgery. Spontaneous remission or response to other forms of treatment may delay diagnosis.

TOXIC PSYCHOSES

The taking of certain drugs and the abuse of alcohol may adversely affect the user's mental state. It may initially be unclear whether the ingestion of illegal drugs has triggered an episode of mental illness, which may then be prolonged, or whether the symptoms will begin to subside once the drug exits the body. The subject of toxic psychoses has been succinctly reviewed by Davidson.[104] Although section 1(3) of

---

[102]   W.A. Lishman, *Organic Psychiatry, The Psychological Consequences of Cerebral Disorder* (Blackwell Scientific Publications, 2nd ed., 1987), p.450.

[103]   *Ibid.*, p.451.

[104]   K. Davidson, "Toxic psychosis" in *Contemporary Psychiatry* (ed. S. Crown, Butterworths, 1984), p.93.

the Mental Health Act 1983 precludes the detention of a person on the sole ground that he is dependant on alcohol or drugs, it should be emphasised that this does not preclude the detention of individuals who become psychotic as a result of alcohol or drug abuse (063).

AMPHETAMINES

Prolonged high doses of amphetamines may lead to a mental state indistinguishable from paranoid schizophrenia. The condition usually subsides in about a week but occasionally persists for several months. Severe withdrawal effects include serious depression, anxiety, fatigue, and narcolepsy type symptoms (1069).[105]

CANNABIS

Some studies suggest that excessive use of cannabis over long periods of time can cause psychiatric disturbance but the evidence is inconclusive. It is probable that individuals are affected by cannabis on a continuum, "ranging from the relatively benign effects of intoxication ... to episodes of severe psychiatric disturbance ... in only a small percentage of users. The more florid disturbances are seen usually in markedly unstable individuals."[106] The following points emerge from the literature:

1. It is generally agreed that there is no specific cannabis psychosis, the content of the episode being determined *inter alia* by individual predisposition and the circumstances in which the drug is taken;

2. Acute paranoid or schizophrenic reactions probably occur mainly in subjects who are specially predisposed and such disturbances tend to gradually subside as the drug is cleared from the body;

3. In longer lasting psychotic episodes it can be hard to decide how far the drug is responsible, especially if use has been habitual over a lengthy period;

4. Longer lasting psychotic illnesses precipitated by the toxic effects of cannabis which then follow an independent course usually take the form of manic-depressive or schizophrenia-like psychoses.[107]

To summarise, while cannabis use may have insignificant adverse effects for many users in terms of their mental health, detained patients generally have obvious and often gross psychiatric problems. The issue therefore becomes to what extent cannabis use contributes to their abnormal mental state. It is certainly striking how many detained patients take cannabis, although this may be because persons predisposed to mental disorder are also predisposed to taking psychoactive drugs which seem to them to alleviate their distress. However, the safe option must be to refrain from further use and to see if the mental state improves. There is an illogicality in any bald assertion that psychoactive drugs available from a doctor can have adverse effects but not those supplied by a street vendor and this may also be

---

[105] M. Gelder, *et al.*, *Oxford Textbook of Psychiatry* (Oxford University Press, 3rd ed., 1996), p.475.

[106] W.A. Lishman, *Organic Psychiatry, The Psychological Consequences of Cerebral Disorder* (Blackwell Scientific Publications, 2nd ed., 1987), p.525.

[107] *Ibid.*, pp.523–525.

pointed out. Furthermore, there is little personal or social benefit in taking one psychoactive drug, cannabis, if the practical effect is that the user will thereby be compelled to take another psychoactive drug, such as haloperidol.

COCAINE

The effects of cocaine are similar to those of amphetamines and it blocks the re-uptake of dopamine. Chemically pure cocaine may be extracted to produce "crack" which has a very rapid onset of action. The psychological effects of ingesting cocaine include excitement, increased energy, and euphoria. Higher doses can result in visual and auditory hallucinations, prolonged heavy use to a paranoid psychosis. Formication (**1087**) may be a feature of cocaine abuse.[108]

LYSERGIC ACID DIETHYLAMIDE (LSD)

The acute effects of ingestion include dilation of the pupils, some rise in body temperature and, in severe reactions, muscular tremors and twitching. A heightened state of awareness is maintained, and thought processes characteristically remain clear. Euphoria is usually the predominant change of mood but this may be followed by sudden swings to depression, panic or a profound state of desolation. Some subjects become paranoid and hostile to their surroundings. Perceptual distortions, illusions and hallucinations are usually in the visual sphere but can affect all modalities. Distortions of body image usually figure prominently and can take bizarre forms. The use of LSD as an adjunct to psychotherapy was known to very occasionally lead to long lasting psychiatric complications, the more serious psychotic developments being attributed to the release of overwhelming conflict-laden material. The "psychoses which follow are usually of schizophrenic type. Catatonic and paranoid forms have been reported, often with elements similar to those seen during acute LSD intoxication. Visual hallucinations may be prominent, highly coloured and mobile, and euphoria and grandiosity are often much in evidence."[109] The vast majority of reported cases have concerned persons with markedly unstable personalities or long-standing schizophrenic illnesses, where the ingestion has acted as a trigger, and whether LSD can provoke a prolonged psychosis in a person without any special predisposition remains unresolved.[110]

LABORATORY TESTS

Following admission, a urine sample may be taken from a detained patient and screened from the presence of illegal drugs. It is important to know the length of time following ingestion during which the substance remains detectable. For example, amphetamines are no longer detectable after two days and, if tested for, a negative result generally has little significance. As to cannabis use, plasma levels of up to 1ng/ml may be found up to six days after smoking one marijuana cigarette and cannabinoid metabolites may still be detectable in the urine of chronic users for 46 days after last use.[111]

---

[108] M. Gelder, et al., Oxford Textbook of Psychiatry (Oxford University Press, 3rd ed., 1996), p.476.
[109] W.A. Lishman, Organic Psychiatry, The Psychological Consequences of Cerebral Disorder (Blackwell Scientific Publications, 2nd ed., 1987), p.532.
[110] Ibid.
[111] J. Wallach, Interpretation of Diagnostic Tests (Little Brown and Co., 5th ed., 1992), pp.765–766.

Drug	Length of time detected in urine
Amphetamine	48 hours
Barbiturates	24 hours (short-acting); 3 weeks (long-acting)
Benzodiazepines	3 days
Cannabis	3 days–6.5 weeks depending on use.
Cocaine	6–8 hours (metabolites 2–4 days)
Heroin	36–72 hours
Methadone	3 days

ALCOHOL–RELATED DISORDERS

Alcohol-related disabilities fall into four groups: intoxication phenomena, withdrawal phenomena, chronic nutritional disorders, and associated psychiatric disorders.[112] Because of the prohibition in section 1 of the Mental Health Act 1983 **(063)**, the conditions most frequently encountered by tribunals are alcohol withdrawal states and the Wernicke-Korsakoff syndrome.

ALCOHOL AND MENTAL HEALTH PROBLEMS

• **Alcohol withdrawal syndromes**	Alcoholic tremor, irritability, nausea, hallucinosis, fits, delirium tremens (vivid hallucinations, delusions, profound confusion, tremor, agitation, sleeplessness in the full syndrome).
• **Wernicke's Encephalopathy**	An *acute* organic reaction to severe thiamine deficiency, often resulting from alcoholism combined with an inadequate food intake. Mental confusion (90 per cent.), staggering gait, *i.e.* ataxia (87 per cent. cases), ocular abnormalities such as nystagmus (96 per cent.). Sometimes nausea, vomiting, lethargy. Completely reversible with treatment.
• **Korsakoff's psychosis**	Wernicke's Encephalopathy may progress to the chronic condition known as Korsakoff's psychosis. Only about 20 per cent. of patients recover. Profound impairment of recent memory. New learning is grossly impaired and there is often confabulation **(1023)**.

Sources: W.A. Lishman, Organic Psychiatry, The Psychological Consequences of Cerebral Disorder (Blackwell Scientific Publications, 2nd ed., 1987), pp.491–521; H.I. Kaplan and B.J. Sadock, Synopsis of Psychiatry (Williams and Wilkins, 7th ed.), p.407.

---

[112]   M. Gelder, *et al.*, *Oxford Textbook of Psychiatry* (Oxford University Press, 3rd ed., 1996), p.448.

INDEX

1328

1333